LYALL ON LAND LAW

Andrew Lyall
LLD (LOND) FLS
of Gray's Inn, Barrister

FOURTH EDITION BY

Niamh Howlin
BCL, PhD, PGCHET

AND

Noel McGrath
BCL, PhD, *Barrister-at-Law (King's Inns)*

ROUND HALL

THOMSON REUTERS

Published in 2018 by
Thomson Reuters Ireland Limited
(Registered in Ireland, Company No. 416940.
Registered Office and address for service:
12/13 Exchange Place, IFSC, Dublin 1, Ireland)
trading as Round Hall

Typeset by
Deanta Global, Dublin

Printed by
CPI Group (UK) Ltd, Croydon, CR0 4YY

ISBN   978-0-41406-634-2

A catalogue record for this book
is available from the British Library

Preface to the Fourth Edition

The eight years since the publication of the third edition of this book have witnessed the bedding down of the revolutionary reform of Irish land law brought about by the Land and Conveyancing Law Reform Act 2009. This process has not been an entirely smooth one with amending legislation proving necessary in 2011 and 2013 to correct difficulties created by the LCLRA 2009 in respect of the acquisition of easements by prescription and the enforcement of mortgages respectively. Both the Oireachtas and the Central Bank of Ireland (acting in its regulatory capacity) have been active during this period in adjusting the law of mortgages in the interests both of protecting consumers and of attempting to prevent the financial catastrophe suffered by the State in the aftermath of the global financial crisis of 2008 from recurring in the future. In other areas, the law of real property has continued to experience neglect at the legislature's hands—it is now some seven years since the publication of the Draft General Scheme of the Landlord and Tenant Law Reform Bill in 2011. According to the Government's legislative programme, work on the Bill is still continuing at the time of writing. Reform of the law of landlord and tenant is long overdue in this jurisdiction and it is to be hoped that the promised work on this Bill will come to fruition in time for the fifth edition.

The great strength of the previous editions of *Land Law in Ireland* has been the emphasis on placing the rules and principles of land law in their historical context. While the LCLRA 2009 excised most (though by no means all) of the remnants of the feudal period from Irish land law, an historical approach remains relevant, not only as the key to understanding the content of the contemporary law, but also so that the rules of modern Irish land law can be understood and judged against the social and political context from which they emerged and developed. In preparing the fourth edition of what will now become known as *Lyall on Land Law*, we have sought to build on the strengths of previous editions.

We would like to record our gratitude to Dr Andrew Lyall, the author of the first three editions, for entrusting us with the task of writing a new edition of his work. *Lyall on Land Law* is a testament to Andrew's scholarship and erudition, as well as to his passion for the subject matter. Both of us had the benefit of Andrew's teaching whilst undergraduates at what was then the UCD Faculty of Law. His writing and teaching sparked in us an interest in property law which has proved enduring and we are honoured to share in the continuation of Andrew's work. We hope that this edition goes some way towards emulating the high standard of what has gone before.

We would like to thank our friends and colleagues at the UCD Sutherland School of Law for their help and support in writing this book; a special mention must go to Professor Oonagh Breen and Dr Karen Lynch-Shally, both of whom were kind enough to read and comment on draft chapters of the text, as well as to Dr Liam Thornton who co-taught property law with us while we were preparing this work, and Mr Paul Ward who fielded queries about family law. We would also like to thank Professor Joe McMahon and Professor Imelda Maher, successively Deans of the Law School during this project, for their encouragement. In common with all teachers, we have learnt much from our students; we are grateful to them for sharing their insights and ideas over the time we have taught property law at UCD and for sharpening our own understanding of many issues along the way. Frieda Donohue, Alana Gerring, Jo Slinn and Donough Cassidy of Round Hall provided invaluable support and encouragement in bringing the text to completion.

We have endeavoured to state the law as it appears from the materials known and available to us as of 1 March 2018. The inevitable errors and omissions are entirely our own.

Niamh Howlin
Noel McGrath
UCD Sutherland School of Law
March 2018

Table of Contents

CHAPTER 7   REGISTRATION OF DEEDS AND TITLE

CHAPTER 8   FEE SIMPLE

CHAPTER 9   FEE FARM GRANTS

CHAPTER 10 FEE TAIL

CHAPTER 11 LIFE ESTATES

CHAPTER 12 FUTURE INTERESTS

CHAPTER 13 CLASS GIFTS AND RULES AGAINST REMOTENESS

CHAPTER 14 POWERS

CHAPTER 15 TRUSTS OF LAND

CHAPTER 16 THE IRISH LAND PURCHASE ACTS

CHAPTER 17 CO-OWNERSHIP

CHAPTER 18 FAMILY PROPERTY

CHAPTER 19 LICENCES, ESTOPPEL AND CONSTRUCTIVE TRUSTS

CHAPTER 20 LANDLORD AND TENANT

CHAPTER 21 STATUTORY CONTROL AND ENLARGEMENT OF TENANCIES

CHAPTER 22 COVENANTS

CHAPTER 23 EASEMENTS AND PROFITS

CHAPTER 24 MORTGAGES

CHAPTER 25 ADVERSE POSSESSION

CHAPTER 26 SUCCESSION

CHAPTER 26 SUCCESSION

Table of Cases

Table of Articles of the Constitution

Table of Statutes

Statutes of the Parliaments of England and Great Britain (Pre-Union)

Statutes of the Parliament of the United Kingdom of Great Britain and Ireland (During the Union)

Statutes of the Oireachtas of Saorstát Éireann (Irish Free State) and the Oireachtas (Post-1922 Acts)

Northern Ireland Legislation

[**Note:** The list includes statutes of the Parliament of Northern Ireland and Orders in Council made under the UK Northern Ireland (Temporary Provisions) Act 1972, numbered as Statutory Instruments, which have effect as statutes of the Parliament of Northern Ireland. Northern Ireland subsidiary legislation made under Orders in Council, known as Statutory Rules, are included in the Table of Subsidiary Legislation.]

Statutes of the Parliament of the United Kingdom of Great Britain and Northern Ireland (Post-1922 Statutes)

European Treaties and Legislation

European Union

Council of Europe

Other Foreign Legislation and International Treaties

Australia

Canada

Germany

Guernsey

India

New Zealand

Norway

Singapore

Switzerland

United States of America

International

Table of Subsidiary Legislation

Northern Ireland Statutory Rules

Abbreviations

Ab. Ca.	Abridged Cases
Abr. Cas.	Abridged Cases
Ad. & E.	Adolphus and Ellis's Reports
AG	Attorney General
Al. & N.	Alcock & Napier's Reports
Alc. & Nap.	See Al & N.
All E.R.	All England Reports
An. Hib.	Analecta Hibernica
App.	Appendix
Ar. L.Q.	Arab Law Quarterly
Arm. M. & O.	Armstrong Macartney & Ogle, Irish *Nisi Prius*
Art.	Article
Atk.	Atkyn's Law Reports
Aust. Prop. L.J.	Australian Property Law Journal
B. & B.	Ball & Beatty's Reports [also Ba & B; Call & B]
Barn. Ch.	Barnardiston's Chancery Reports
Bat.	Batty's Reports
Beatty	Beatty's Reports
Beav.	Beavan's Rolls Court Reports
Bing.	Bingham's Reports
Bl. Comm.	Blackstone, *Commentaries on the Laws of England*
Bl. D. & Osb.	Blackham, Dundas & Osborne
Bligh NS	Bligh's Reports, New Series
B. Rev.	Bar Review
Cro. C.C.	Brown's Chancery Cases
Bro. P.C.	Brown's Cases in Parliament
Burr.	Burrow's Reports
CA	Court of Appeal
Camb. L.J.	Cambridge Law Journal
Cambrian L.R.	Cambrian Law Review
Camp.	Campbell's *Nisi Prius* Reports
C.B.	Common Bench/Chief Baron
CCMA	Code of Conduct on Mortgage Arrears
Ch.	Chancery
Chan. Cas.	Cases in Chancery
Cir.	Circuit
Civ.	Civil
C.J.	Chief Justice
C.L.	Common Law
C.L.P.	Commercial Law Practitioner
Co Inst	Coke's Institutes of the Lawes of England
Co Litt	Coke on Littleton (Coke's *Commentaries on Littleton*)
Colum. L.R.	Columbia Law Review
Conv.	Conveyancer and Property Lawyer
Co. Rep.	Coke's Reports
Cowp.	Cowper's Reports
C.o.A.	Coat of Arms

C.P.D.	Common Pleas Division
C.P.L.J.	Conveyancing and Property Law Journal
Cr. & Dix	Crawford & Dix Reports
Cr. M. & R.	Crompton, Meeson and Roscoe's Reports
Cro. Car.	Croke's King's Bench Reports *tempore* Charles
Cro. Eliz.	Croke's King's Bench Reports *tempore* Elizabeth
Curt.	Curteis' Ecclesiastical Reports
D.	Division
d.	demise
Davies	Davies Reports
De G. & J.	De Gex & Jones' Reports
De G. M. & G.	De Gex, Macnaughten and Gordon's Reports
Dick.	Dicken's Chancery Reports
D.L.R.	Dominion Law Reports
DPP	Director of Public Prosecution
Drew	Drewry's Vice Chancellors' Reports
Dru. & Wal.	Drury & Walsh's Reports
Dru. & War.	Drury & Warren's Reports
Dru. t Nap.	Drury *tempore* Napier
Dru. t P.	Drury *tempore* Plunket: See Dru & Wal.
Dru. t Sug.	Drury *tempore* Sugden
D.U.L.J.	Dublin University Law Journal
E & W	England and Wales
ECHR	European Convention for the Protection of Human Rights and Fundamental Freedoms
ECtHR	European Court of Human Rights
ECHR Act	European Convention on Human Rights Act 2003
Ec. Hist. Rev.	Economic History Review
Eden	Eden's Chancery Reports
E.H.R.L.R.	European Human Rights Law Review
E.H.R.R.	European Human Right Reports
EIAR	Environmental Impact Assessment Regulations
EIS	Environmental Impact Statement
Eng. Hist. Rev.	English Historical Review
Eq.	Equity
Esp.	Espinasse's Reports
EWCA	Court of Appeal of England and Wales
EWHC	High Court of England and Wales
F. & S.	Fox & Smith's Reports, Irish King's Bench, 1822–24
FHPA	Family Home Protection Act 1976
FL	FirstLaw number (unreported judgments) (followed by number).
Fl. & K.	Flanagan & Kelly's Reports
Frewen	Frewen's Reports
Glas.	Glascock's Reports
Gaz. L. Soc. Ir.	Gazette of the Law Society of Ireland
H. & B.	See Hud & Br.
H. & J.	Hayes & Jones' Reports
H. & N.	Hurlstone and Norman's Reports
Hayes	Hayes' Reports
Hare	Hare's Reports

Harv. L.R.	Harvard Law Review
HC	High Court
H. & C.	Hurlstone & Coltman's Exchequer Reports
HL	House of Lords
H.L.C.	Clark's House of Lords Cases
HMSO	Her Majesty's Stationery Office
Hud. & Br.	Hudson & Brooke's Reports
ICCPR	International Covenant and Civil and Political Rights
I.C.L.M.D.	Irish Current Law Monthly Digest
IECA	Court of Appeal of Ireland
IEHC	High Court of Ireland
IESC	Supreme Court of Ireland
I.H.S.	Irish Historical Studies
I.J.E.C.L.	International Journal of Estuarine and Coastal Law
I.J.F.L.	Irish Journal of Family Law
I.L.R.M.	Irish Law Reports Monthly
I.L.T.	Irish Law Times
I.L.T.R.	Irish Law Times Reports
I.L.T.S.J.	Irish Law Times and Solicitor's Journal
Ind. L.J.	Indiana Law Journal
Insolv. Int.	Insolvency Intelligence
Inst	Justinian's *Institutes*
I.P.E.L.J.	Irish Planning and Environmental Law Journal
I.P.L.J.	Irish Probate Law Journal
I.R.	Irish Reports
Ir.	Irish
Ir. Ec. Soc. Hist.	Irish Economic and Social History
Ir. Jur.	Irish Jurist
J.	Justice; Judge
J. & B.	Jebb & Bourke's Reports
J. & S.	Jebb & Symes's Reports
J. Eur. R.E.R.	Journal of European Real Estate Research
J. & H.	Johnson & Hemming's Reports
J.H. Ec.	Journal of Housing Economics
J. Leg. Hist.	Journal of Legal History
J. Soc. Arch.	Journal of the Society of Archivists
Jebb & B.	See J. & B.
Jebb & S.	See J. & S.
Jo.	Jones's Reports
Jo. & Ca.	Jones & Carey's Reports
Jo. & La T.	Jones & La Touche's Reports
K.B.	King's Bench
L. & T.	Longfield & Townsend's Reports
L. & T.R.	Landlord and Tenant Reports
Law Rec	Irish Law Recorder
LCLRA	Land and Conveyancing Law Reform Act
Ld. Raym.	Lord Raymond's Reports
Lev.	Levinze's Reports
L.G.R.	Local Government Reports/Review
Litt	Littleton, *Tenures*
Ll. & G.	Lloyd & Goold

L.M.C.L.Q.	Lloyd's Maritime and Commercial Law Quarterly
Longf. & T.	See L. & T.
L.C.	Lord Chancellor
L.J.	Lord Justice
LPA	Law of Property Act 1925 (E & W)
L.Q.R.	Law Quarterly Review
LRC	Law Reform Commission
L.R.	Law Reports
L.S.	Legal Studies
L.T.	Law Times
LTLRB	Landlord and Tenant Law Reform Bill 2011
M. & W.	Meeson & Welsby's Reports
Mac. & G.	Macnaughten & Gordon's Reports
Macq.	Macqueen's Scotch Appeal Cases
Madd.	Maddock's Chancery Reports
Miami L.Q.	Miami Law Quarterly
Miami L. Rev.	Miami Law Review
Mich.	Michaelmas
Mich. L.R.	Michigan Law Review
M.L.R.	Modern Law Review
Moll.	Molloy's Reports
Moo. K.B.	Moore's King's Bench Reports
M.R.	Master of the Rolls
My. & K.	Mylne & Keen's Chancery Reports
NI	Northern Ireland
N.I.L.Q.	Northern Ireland Legal Quarterly
N.I.J.B.	Northern Ireland Judicial Bulletin
ns	new series
NSW	New South Wales
NZ	New Zealand
os	old series
ord.	Order
P.	Probate
P. & C.R.	Property, Planning and Compensation Reports
P. & P.	Past & Present
PD	Probate Division
P. Wms.	Peere-Williams' Cases
Q.B.	Queen's Bench
QSC	Queensland Supreme Court
R.	Reports
r.	Rule
RDTA	Registration of Deeds and Title Act 2006
RdTA	Residential Tenancies Act 2004
Rep.	Reports
Rest. L. Rev.	Restitution Law Review
Ridg. L. & S.	Ridgway, Lapp and Schoales
Ridg. P.C.	Ridgway's Parliamentary Cases
Rob. Ecc.	Robertson's Ecclesiastic Reports
Rowe	Rowe's Interesting Cases
RSC	Rules of the Superior Courts
RTA	Registration of Title Act 1964

Russ.	Russell's Chancery Reports
Sausse & Sc.	Sausse & Scully' Reports
SC	Supreme Court
Sch. & Lef.	Schoales & Lefroy's Reports
Sel. Cas. Ch.	Select Cases in Chancery
S.I.	Statutory Instrument
Sim. & St.	Simons & Stuart's Reports
Sixteenth Cent. J.	The Sixteenth Century Journal
S.J.	Solicitors' Journal
SLRA	Statute Law Revision Act
Sm. & Bat.	Smith & Batty's Reports
SO	Stationary Office
Stanford L.R.	Stanford Law Review
Stark.	Starkie's *Nisi Prius* Reports
St. Tr.	State Trials
Swans.	Swanston's Reports
Taun.	Taunton's Reports
TLATA	Trusts of Land and Appointment of Trustees Act 1996 (E & W)
T.L.R.	Times Law Reports
U.C.D.L.R.	University College Dublin Law Review
UCTD	Unfair Contract Terms Directive
Vaugh.	Vaughan's Reports
Ves. Jun.	Vesey Junior's Reports
Ves. Sen.	Vesey Senior's Reports
Ver. & Scr.	Vernon and Scriven's Reports
Vern.	Vernon's Reports
W.L.R.	Weekly Law Reports
Wash. & Lee L. Rev.	Washington and Lee Law Review
Yale J.L. & Human.	Yale Journal of Law & the Humanities
YB	Yearbook

CHAPTER 1

Introduction

It is one of the maxims of the civil law that definitions are hazardous.

— Dr Samuel Johnson, *Rambler,* No. 125, 1

Whilst there is much appeal in the philosophy - "From each according to his ability, to each according to his need," (Karl Marx - Criticism of the Gotha Programme) it is not an aid to statutory construction.

— McCarthy J. in *Quirke v Folio Homes Ltd* [1988] I.L.R.M. 496 at 500

INTRODUCTION

1–01 Land law is the branch of law governing rights and interests in land and things attached to land. Land law is a subset of the law of property. In this introductory chapter, therefore, it is necessary to consider the nature and meaning of property and introduce the common law scheme of property rights more generally. One of the key difficulties in the law of property is to distinguish between the social and legal understandings of the term "property". Indeed Ackerman has suggested that the primary function of a property law course is to root out students' "primitive lay notions of ownership".[1]

1–02 The lay notion of property usually considers property to be a relationship between a person (the owner) and the thing which is owned. Thus, it is common to speak of "my book" or "his chair". When speaking in this way, property appears to be a characteristic of a thing. The book is "mine" in the same way as it has a certain colour or size. People speak of interests in land in a similar way. One might say that "X has a lease of that house". Whilst statements of this sort are acceptable and meaningful in ordinary conversation, closer examination reveals a more complex picture. Property is not an attribute of physical objects which exist in the real world. A book cannot be "mine" in the same way that it can have a red cover, or be printed on A5 paper. Instead, property is a set of rights and duties which are legally created.

---

[1] B. Ackerman, *Private Property and the Constitution* (New Haven: Yale University Press, 1987), pp.26–27.

1–03 In declaring that a book is "the property of X", what is being advanced is in fact a complicated set of claims that X is entitled to certain rights in respect of the book as against other members of the community. The content of those rights (and obligations) will be considered below but for now it suffices to point out that the meaning of property is legally and socially constructed. Thus, the law determines what "things" may be the subject of property rights. The category of things which may be the subject of property is not stable. Under existing law it is not possible, for example, to make a human being the subject of ownership, though as even a cursory examination of the legal history of slavery reveals, this has not always been the case. An opposing example can be found in *Victoria Park Racing v Taylor*[2] where the High Court of Australia held that there could be no property rights in a public spectacle such as a horse race. The law also controls the substantive content of property rights. As will be seen in a later chapter, a lease of land must, as a matter of law, endure for an ascertainable time period. It is not possible, for example, to create a lease which will endure for as long as the present Taoiseach remains in office.[3]

1–04 Once it is clearly understood that the law shapes the nature and content of property rights, it is possible to recast the lay notion of ownership. A book is not "mine" in the same way that its cover might be red in colour because the meaning of the term "mine" is constructed by the law and is subject to change over time. Property, in truth, is a socially and legally approved power relationship between people with respect to things. The tendency to treat property as though it were a thing in itself, rather than a relationship between people, is sometimes referred to as "reification". Reification is a tendency which should be resisted. Rules about property rights, whether private or communal, are inescapably political in a broad sense. They represent a particular distribution of power over aspects of the external world. They therefore require to be justified on the basis of wider political, moral or economic theory. An examination of such theory is outside the scope of this book; however, students of property law must be able to see through the illusion of reifying vocabulary so that they can be aware of the issues of justice and theories of distribution that lie beyond the rules themselves. It is then for the reader to decide whether the rules are persuasive or morally defensible.

1–05 It has to be admitted that much of this book is taken up with an exposition of the rules of land law and that in the course of that exposition there is a focus on the logical implications of various rules. This is unavoidable if the content of the rules themselves is to be understood. The book nevertheless aims to move from explanation to exposition, from explaining the rules in a technical sense, to an exposition of the real issues that lie beneath them. The tendency to reify interests in land also makes property law more difficult, and less interesting, for students to learn, because it induces them to believe

---

[2]   (1937) 58 C.L.R. 479.
[3]   *Prudential Assurance Co Ltd v London Residuary Body* [1996] 2 A.C. 386.

that they are trying to grasp by some intuitive process the inherent qualities of property concepts. In fact, these "qualities" are no more than *choices* made by judges or legislators about how rights and duties *should* be distributed. Such choices necessarily involve social values. The tendency to reify disguises as facts what are in reality normative statements about how society *ought to be* organised. By disguising these choices, reification has another effect: it serves to inculcate in students the political or moral values on which these choices are based when they may not be fully aware that this is being done. It disarms a critical approach to the rules.

THE LEGAL CONCEPT OF PROPERTY

1–06 The legal nature of property has been the subject of much debate amongst political philosophers and legal theorists.[4] There is little agreement on precisely what constitutes property. In *Nokes v Doncaster Amalgamated Colliers Ltd*,[5] Lord Porter suggested that the term "property" has no fixed legal meaning and that its meaning in any particular context must be derived from the document or statute in which it appears. An attempt at a definition was made by Lord Wilberforce in *National Provincial Bank Ltd v Ainsworth*:

"Before a right or an interest can be admitted into the category of property ... it must be definable, identifiable by third parties, capable in its nature of assumption by third parties, and have some degree of permanence or stability."[6]

1–07 This definition in *Ainsworth* has been criticised by Gray and Gray who point to its circular nature: rights are not proprietary because they are enforced against third parties but are enforceable against third parties because of their proprietary nature.[7]

1–08 Australian courts have also attempted to define "property". In *Yanner v Eaton*, the High Court of Australia suggested that the term denotes "a degree of power that is recognised in law as power permissibly exercised over the thing",[8] though significantly the court did not consider what degree of power must be exercised before property can be said to have arisen. Whilst this description of

---

[4] For important contributions to the legal literature, see: A.M. Honoré, "Ownership" in A.G. Guest (ed.), *Oxford Essays in Jurisprudence* (London: Oxford University Press, 1961), pp.107–147; J.E. Penner, *The Idea of Property in Law* (Oxford: Oxford University Press, 1997); C.M. Rose, "Property as Storytelling: Perspectives from Game Theory, Narrative Theory, Feminist Theory" (1990) 2 Yale J.L. & Human. 37; R. Posner, *The Economic Analysis of Law*, 5th edn (New York: Aspen, 1998), pp.36–45.

[5] [1940] 1 A.C. 1014 at 1051.

[6] [1965] A.C. 1175 at 1247–1248.

[7] K.J. Gray and S.F. Gray, *Elements of Land Law*, 5th edn (Oxford: Oxford University Press, 2009), pp.97–98.

[8] (1999) 201 C.L.R. 351 at 389.

property has an obvious attraction, it is suggested that it is of limited assistance in classifying claims into proprietary and non-proprietary categories. A better approach to understanding property might be to entirely eschew attempts at definition and instead focus on the characteristics of property rights.

1–09 Legal theorists have produced more complex approaches. Penner suggests that property in common law systems should be understood as involving a right of exclusive use:

"… the right to determine the use of disposition of a separable thing (i.e. a thing whose contingent association with any particular person is essentially impersonal and so imports nothing of normative consequence), in so far as that can be achieved or aided by others excluding themselves from it and includes the rights to abandon it, to share it, to license it to others (either exclusively or not) and to give it to others in its entirety."[9]

1–10 Penner's thesis rests on two basic ideas. First there is a relationship between the thing which is owned as property and the person who owns the property. For Penner, there must be a separation between the owner and thing which is owned. Thus, the nature of the thing which is owned must not meaningfully change with the identity of its owner and individual human characteristics are not property—"we do not trade our talents, give away our personalities, licence our friendships … or pay tax with our eyesight".[10] The second aspect of Penner's theory is the exclusion thesis. This is the idea that "the right to property is a right to exclude others from things".[11] The right of exclusion, as Penner points out, is easily misunderstood. It does not necessarily mean that the property holder has an immediate right to physically exclude others from enjoyment of the property. Instead, the right of exclusion is a correlative of the duty imposed on others not to interfere with the owner's rights in the property concerned.

PROPERTY INTERESTS AND THE CONCEPT OF OWNERSHIP

1–11 The differences between the social and legal understandings of property concepts are nowhere more clearly demonstrated than in discussions of ownership. For the layperson, the concept of ownership is an obvious one. Ownership is at the heart of property; it is, in Blackstone's oft-quoted phrase, "that sole and despotic dominion which one man claims and exercises over the external things of the world, in total exclusion of the right of any other individual in the universe".[12] Just as with the notion of property itself, a close analysis of claims to ownership reveals a more complicated picture. Nowhere does the

---

[9] Penner, *The Idea of Property in Law* (1997), p.152.
[10] Penner, *The Idea of Property in Law* (1997), p.112.
[11] Penner, *The Idea of Property in Law* (1997), p.71.
[12] 2 Bl Comm 2.

law permit one person a "sole and despotic dominion" to control the external world. The ownership of a book does not carry with it the right to use the book as a weapon with which to bludgeon another person. Nor is it obvious how the law can be said to allow a "total exclusion" of the rights of persons. Property which is "owned outright" is capable of being seized or garnished in the execution of a judgment and can be taken by a liquidator or the official assignee in bankruptcy in the event of insolvency. Ownership can also be viewed as being largely irrelevant in Irish legal practice. In a common law adversarial system, courts are usually faced with deciding disputes about possession. The plaintiff's claim will be that he or she has a better claim to the thing in question than the defendant. The court's function is to resolve the dispute before it. An abstract inquiry into the true "ownership" of the property in question is neither necessary nor desirable to achieve that objective.

1–12 In the introduction to this chapter, it was suggested that property is a socially and legally approved relationship between persons in respect of things. If this is correct, then strictly speaking it is meaningless to say that a person is the owner of a thing. To do so suggests that the property relationship is one between the person who owns and the thing which is the subject of his or her ownership. In fact what is happening is that the law recognises certain persons as having certain *rights* in respect of the thing which are enforceable against others. The term "ownership" is really shorthand for the rights which the "owner" of property has. Take the following example:

> *A Ltd purchased an aircraft with the assistance of a bank loan from B Ltd. Repayment of this loan is secured on the aircraft by way of a mortgage. A Ltd then leased the aircraft for a 10-year period to C Ltd.*

1–13 Who can be said to own this aircraft? In one sense the answer is not clear; all three companies have a form of right with respect to the aircraft which the law recognises as being of a proprietary character. The matter becomes clearer if the question is reframed to enquire about the property interests which affect the aircraft. Each of the three companies mentioned has a different *interest* in the aircraft, and each interest carries with it different legal rights and obligations. Put very crudely, C Ltd has a present right to possess the aircraft which will continue until the end of its lease. B Ltd has a right to seize and sell the aircraft in the event that A Ltd defaults in its obligation to repay the loan. A Ltd has the largest interest in the aircraft in the sense that A Ltd has the prospect of enjoying the sole proprietary interest in the aircraft at a future date, after it has repaid the loan from B Ltd and after the lease to C Ltd has come to an end. This residuary interest, the largest which is recognised by the law, is the closest thing which can be identified as ownership in Irish law.

1–14 The statement that ownership is the largest interest in property which is recognised by law explains little about the actual rights and obligations which

make up ownership. In an essay published in 1961,[13] Honoré set out to describe
the most common incidents which, when taken collectively, make up the concept of ownership. For Honoré, the incidents need not be united in one person
before that person can be called an owner. Honoré was interested in describing
the features which a legal system must recognise and must allow to be united
in one person before it can be said to have a concept of private ownership.
The incidents are as follows:

1. The Right to Possess

This is a right to exclusive control of a thing, described by Honoré as
the "foundation on which the whole superstructure of ownership rests."
Protection of the right to possess requires rules that enable the owner to
obtain, retain and if necessary regain possession of the property from
others.

2. The Right to Use

The right to use is a right of the owner to use the thing at his or her
discretion. This right is clearly not absolute in that it may be controlled
by the general law, but as Honoré points out, restrictions on the right to
use property tend to be closely defined exceptions—the general principle
being that the owner has a right to use.

3. The Right to Manage

The right to manage amounts to a right to license others to use one's
things, the right to control such use and the right to contract effectively
with others in relation to such use.

4. The Right to the Income

The right to the income is a right to the output or produce of things,
whether that output is in the form of fruits, profits or rents. There is a
significant overlap between the right to the income and the rights to use
and manage, and Honoré identifies it as a surrogate of the right to use.

5. The Right to the Capital

The right to the capital encompasses the right of an owner to consume,
waste and destroy his or her things as well as the right to alienate property
by transferring it to others, whether by way of sale, gift or otherwise.

6. The Right to Security

The right to security protects an owner's entitlement to maintain his or
her position as owner into the future if he or she so chooses. Honoré
acknowledges that the State, or other individuals, may possess powers of interference with, and expropriation of, an owner's property, but

---

[13] Honoré, "Ownership" in *Oxford Essays in Jurisprudence* (1961), pp.107–147.

contends that the right to security still exists, provided that these powers are only available exceptionally.

7. The Incident of Transmissibility

The incident of transmissibility refers to the owner's ability to pass his or her property to others, either before or after his or her death. The possibility of transfer is present whether or not the owner wishes to exercise it.

8. The Incident of Absence of Term

The incident of absence of term encapsulates the idea that the owner's rights are not limited by the happening of some particular event and that they will not determine at a particular time.

9. The Duty to Prevent Harm

The duty to prevent harm embraces not only a prohibition on the use of one's own property to cause harm to others, but also a duty not to permit one's property to be used by others to cause harm to third parties.

10. Liability to Execution

A feature of ownership is that property may be taken away through a judgment debt or on insolvency. Honoré acknowledges that it might be possible to think of liabilities to tax or liability to expropriation as incidents of ownership in a similar way, but suggests that the limited range of circumstances in which this is possible militates against their inclusion among the standard incidents.

11. The Residuary Character of Ownership

Honoré does not deny that there are property interests other than ownership and gives a number of examples of these, including leases and bailment. What is distinctive about ownership is that when lesser rights terminate, the residuary reverts to the owner.

Types of Property Regime

1–15 So far, this chapter has discussed the most common type of property regime which is encountered in law and society—that of private property in which property rights are held by individual natural or legal persons. Whilst private property regimes predominate both legal and social thought about property, it is worth noting that there are other types of property regimes.

1–16 Some resources have no property regime attached to them. The atmosphere itself is one important example. Another might be the right to download freely available information from the internet. No one person can assert a legal right to exclude others from its enjoyment but, by contrast, there is no positive legal right guaranteeing access to such resources. The latter point was illustrated by the decision of the House of Lords in *Hunter v Canary Wharf Ltd*.[14] In that case, residents of housing in East London objected to the erection of a tower block, in part on the basis that it would interfere with their ability to receive free-to-air terrestrial television signals. The action failed because the law does not recognise a positive *right* to receive television signals. In other situations, forms of communal property can be identified, such as a public right of way over land in which the community at large enjoys a positive right of access to the property in question. Clarke and Kohler classify such rights as a form of "open access communal property".[15]

1–17 The vesting of ownership of a resource in the State or in a local authority is surprisingly commonplace. State ownership may look very similar to private ownership of property, with the State or local authority in question excluding others from enjoyment of State assets. In other cases, a State ownership regime may play an important role in ensuring public access to resources. A particular example of the latter can be found in Ireland in respect of archaeological objects. In *Webb v Ireland*, Finlay C.J. spoke of heritage and knowledge of its origins as ranking among the "most important national assets".[16] The recognition of the cultural value of archaeological objects led the court to expressly prefer a State ownership regime over the common law's traditional private property regime for such items upon their discovery.

<h2 style="text-align:center">PERSONAL RIGHTS VS PROPERTY INTERESTS</h2>

1–18 Any introduction to property rights would be incomplete without a discussion of the distinction between personal and property rights. The classic illustration of this distinction is to be found in the decision of the Court of Exchequer in *Hill v Tupper*.[17] The plaintiff had acquired the exclusive right to operate pleasure boats for reward on a canal from the canal company. The canal company had the exclusive power to license such activities on the canal under the legislation which had authorised its construction. The plaintiff sought to enforce this right against the defendant, an inn-keeper who, according to the plaintiff, had hired out pleasure boats for use on the canal from his premises on the opposite bank of the canal. The court held that the plaintiff could not succeed. The agreement by which the plaintiff had an exclusive right to operate pleasure boats was binding on the plaintiff and the canal company only. The doctrine of privity prevented the enforcement of such a private contract against a third party. The plaintiff sought to argue that the effect of the agreement was to vest in him the canal company's rights to control access to the canal, drawing an analogy with the law of easements and *profits à prendre*.

[14] [1997] A.C. 655.
[15] A. Clarke and P. Kohler, *Property Law* (Cambridge: Cambridge University Press, 2004), p.37.
[16] [1988] 1 I.R. 353 at 383.
[17] (1863) 2 H.& C. 121.

The court rejected this argument, holding that the law does not permit the creation of new forms of property right by private agreement.[18]

1–19 *Hill v Tupper* illustrates two fundamental features of property interests. First, in contrast to contractual rights, they are enforceable against third parties. This feature of property rights is vitally important since it allows the holder of such rights to stake a claim to control of resources which will survive a change in the identity of other interested parties and which will survive the insolvency of other parties. Secondly, the types and content of property rights are determined by the law itself rather than the intentions or desires of those who deal with property rights. As Pollock C.B. put it in *Hill v Tupper*:

> "[T]he law will not permit the owner of an estate to grant it alternately to his heirs male and heirs female. A new species of incorporeal hereditament cannot be created at the will and pleasure of the owner of property; but he must be content to accept the estate and the right to dispose of it subject to the law as settled by decisions or controlled by act of parliament. A grantor may bind himself by covenant to allow any right he pleases over his property, but he cannot annex to it a new incident, so as to enable the grantee to sue in his own name for an infringement of such a limited right as that now claimed."[19]

1–20 The idea that only a limited number of property interests are recognised by the law is known as the *numerus clausus* principle. The rationale for this principle is to be found in the need to achieve a reasonable degree of certainty in the form of property rights which affect land and the need to prevent land-ownership from being cluttered with socially disadvantageous restrictions which might prove unsuitable in the long term. As will be seen in later chapters, the *numerus clausus* principle is not always strictly applied. Irish courts have, for example, been prepared to recognise some highly idiosyncratic rights of residence. Gray and Gray suggest that the principle may be in decline, pointing to recent developments in the law of contractual licences and the emergence of new forms of property in carbon sequestration rights and greenhouse gas emission permits.[20]

CLASSIFICATION OF PROPERTY RIGHTS IN THE COMMON LAW SYSTEM

Real Property

1–21 For historical reasons, freehold interests in land have attracted their own special rules. During the early development of the common law, the royal

---

[18] See also *Keppell v Bailey* (1834) 2 My. & K. 517; *Ackroyd v Smith* (1850) 10 C.B. 164.

[19] (1863) 2 H. & C. 121 at 126–127.

[20] See Gray and Gray, *Elements of Land Law* (2009), pp.138–139. See also, *Re Celtic Extraction* (No.3) [2001] Ch. 475 and *Armstrong DLW GmbH v Winnington Networks Ltd* [2010] EWHC 10 (Ch).

courts developed a number of forms of legal procedure which allowed freehold tenants who had been dispossessed of their land to recover possession.[21] These actions became known as the "real actions" because the remedy available to the successful plaintiff was the actual recovery of the land itself. In other forms of legal procedure, the appropriate remedy was the award of damages. Interests in land thus became known as real property, while other forms of property became known as personal property. These procedural distinctions were largely abolished by the late 19th century, though traces of them can still be found in the law today. For example, specific performance is generally available to enforce a contract for the sale of an interest in land—a remedy which is not usually granted in respect of contracts for the sale of other kinds of property.

1–22 Historically, real property also attracted special rules in the law of succession. Real property descended to the *heir-at-law* of a deceased person on intestacy, whereas personal property passed to the *next-of-kin*. In contemporary Irish law, this distinction has been abandoned by the Succession Act 1965 which provides a uniform scheme for both real and personal property.

1–23 It is important to realise from the outset that in the law of real property, what is owned is not the land itself. Instead, what is owned is an *estate* or an *interest* in the land. An estate in land refers to a time period during which the owner has rights and obligations in respect of the land. A life estate in land gives its holder rights over the land for a limited period, i.e. the life of some person. A *fee simple* estate, by contrast, is potentially perpetual since it passes by will or to the owner's successors on intestacy. *Interests* in land are also held for estates. Thus, an easement or a right of way over another's land can be held in fee simple or for life.

1–24 The system of estates is responsible for much of the complexity in land law. As with the concept of property itself, there is a tendency to reify the estates and interests in land and to treat them as though they were "things" in themselves with inherent qualities of their own. This obscures the fact that land law is really about power relationships between people and is focused on who has the best right to possess, sell and develop land either against private persons or the State. As will be seen in later chapters, the law of estates never applied to forms of property other than land. An attempt to pass an estate in personal property from one person to another is treated as a transfer of outright ownership.[22]

---

[21] See A.W.B. Simpson, *A History of the Land Law*, 2nd edn (Oxford: Clarendon, 1986), pp.25–46.

[22] *Portman v Viscount Portman* [1922] 2 A.C. 473.

Personal Property

1–25 Although this book focuses on the law of real property, it is helpful at the outset to have a clear overview of personal property. Personal property consists of all things which are capable of being the subject of property rights other than real property. Historically, the loss of such property could result only in an award of damages.

1–26 Personal property can be subdivided into a number of categories. The first of these are chattels, a word derived from the word "cattle". Chattels comprise all tangible objects which are not land and which are not affixed to land. Personal property also includes *choses in action*. These are intangible rights which may be traded and treated as property. Examples include debts,[23] shares and debentures in companies,[24] and the various categories of intellectual property rights. There are significant differences in how the law treats chattels and *choses in action*. In particular, the tort of conversion is not generally available to protect the ownership of a *chose in action*[25] and some remedies, such as the lien granted to repairers and improvers of chattels, are not available in respect of intangibles.[26]

1–27 Strictly speaking, leases of land are included within the category of personal property. As ever, the reasons for this are to be found in legal history. Initially, the common law regarded a lease as a simple contract between the holder of a freehold estate in land and the leasehold tenant. In the late Middle Ages, the law developed a special action known as *ejectment* which permitted the leaseholder to recover possession of the land if he had been ejected from it during the continuance of the lease. This gave the leaseholder an equivalent, and in many respects superior, remedy to that available to freeholders.[27] By the time the action of ejectment had developed, the distinction between real and personal property was well established and so leases of land were accommodated in a separate category of their own, known as "chattels real". This distinction survives today; even though ejectment and the other old forms of action have long been abolished, an agreement for the creation or assignment of a lease can be enforced by specific performance.[28]

---

[23] See the Supreme Court of Judicature (Ireland) Act 1877 s.28(6).

[24] *Société Générale de Paris v Walker* (1885) 11 App. Cas. 20; *Borland's Trustee v Steel Brothers & Co* [1901] 1 Ch. 279.

[25] See *OBG v Allan* [2007] 1 A.C. 1. See S. Douglas, "The Scope of Conversion: Property and Contract" (2011) 74 M.L.R. 329.

[26] *Your Response Ltd v Datastream Business Media Ltd* [2015] 1 Q.B. 41.

[27] See Simpson, *A History of the Land Law* (1986), Ch.7.

[28] *Walsh v Londsdale* (1882) 21 Ch. D. 9; *Kelly v Enright* (1883) 11 L.R. Ir. 379; *Ó Siodhachain v O'Mahony* [2002] 4 I.R. 147 at 157.

Property Rights in Public Law

1–28 The protection of property rights, and of private property in particular, is often spoken of as a mainstay of democratic principles and personal liberty. As set out earlier, the right to security and freedom from public or private expropriation is often thought of as a fundamental aspect of the concept of ownership itself. It is not perhaps surprising to find that the right to private property features prominently in human rights instruments. Thus, Art.17 of the Charter of Fundamental Rights of the European Union contains reference to the right of every person to "own, use, dispose of and bequeath" their possessions. Article 1 of the First Optional Protocol to the European Convention on Human Rights (ECHR) protects the right of both natural and legal persons to the peaceful enjoyment of their possessions. At the domestic level, the Constitution contains not one, but two provisions which protect property.

1–29 Yet for all of this, the status of the right to private property as a fundamental right is not without its detractors.[29] The inclusion of property in fundamental rights documents is not universal. The 1922 Constitution contained no general protection of private property rights.[30] In the ECHR, the property provision does not appear in the main text of the ECHR but is relegated to a protocol. Although the right to property appears in Art.17 of the (non-binding) Universal Declaration of Human Rights, it does not appear in the binding instruments intended to implement the Declaration in international law.[31] The property aspects of the 1937 Constitution of Ireland have played a relatively minor role in the development of Irish constitutional jurisprudence, with O'Donnell J., writing before his elevation to the Supreme Court, referring to property as "the Cinderella of the fundamental rights provisions of the Irish Constitution".[32]

1–30 The circumstances under, and the terms upon which, the State may expropriate private property is perhaps the tension which features most prominently in public law discussions of the right to private property. Many Irish statutes empower local authorities, State bodies or Government ministers to acquire land by compulsory purchase.[33] Generally, the exercise of such powers

---

[29] See J. Kingston, "Rich People Have Rights Too? The Status of Property as a Fundamental Human Right" in L. Heffernan (ed.), *Human Rights: A European Perspective* (Dublin: Round Hall Press, 1994), pp.284–297.

[30] Article 8 of the Constitution of Saorstát Éireann did provide a specific protection for the property of religious denominations and educational institutions, but there was no general protection equivalent to that found in Art.40.2 or 43 of the 1937 Constitution of Ireland.

[31] The International Covenant on Civil and Political Rights and the International Covenant on Economic, Social and Cultural Rights respectively.

[32] D. O'Donnell, "Property Rights in the Irish Constitution: Rights for Rich People, or a Pillar of Free Society?" in E. Carolan and O. Doyle (eds), *The Irish Constitution: Governance and Values* (Dublin: Round Hall, 2008), p.412.

[33] For a useful list, see Law Reform Commission, *Issues Paper on Compulsory Acquisition of Land* (LRC IP 13-2017), Appendix A.

requires the payment of compensation in the amount of the market value of the land concerned.[34] The State's power to take land for public purposes, such as building roads and other public infrastructure, is not controversial. In recent years, however, compulsory powers have been used to acquire land with the express intention of conveying it to other private citizens who will develop it in a manner thought to be socially useful.

1–31 In a series of cases beginning with *Central Dublin Development Association v Attorney General*,[35] the courts have rejected challenges to the compulsory acquisition of land for development purposes in circumstances where the land was to be acquired by a public body and then transferred to private companies for redevelopment. In *Clinton v An Bord Pleanála*,[36] the applicant was the owner of a plot of land on O'Connell St in Dublin. The applicant had, together with the owners of adjoining plots, obtained planning permission for a development scheme for the land in question; however, the planned development had never been carried to fruition. After some years, the local authority formed the view that the applicant lacked both the expertise and the financial resources needed to complete the proposed development. The authority sought to compulsorily acquire the land with a view to either carrying out the development itself or in conjunction with another private developer, though at the time that notice of the acquisition was served, no decision had been taken as to how the scheme of development would proceed.

1–32 Having failed in the High Court, the applicant appealed to the Supreme Court. Geoghegan J., giving the judgment of the Supreme Court, held that the Planning and Development Act 2000 gave the local authority a power to acquire land for development purposes and that the site had been acquired for this purpose. The legislation in question required that the local authority demonstrate that the compulsory purchase was desirable in the public interest in order to achieve its development objective. It was not necessary for the authority to set out exactly how its scheme of development would be carried out.

1–33 Walsh has criticised this decision, and others like it, saying that they have the effect of "undermining security of possession of property and [reducing] the right to private property to a right to compensation".[37] The cases certainly raise an important question as to whether the protection of property rights under the Constitution provides protection of rights in the thing which

---

[34] For details of the method of calculation of compensation, see E. Galligan and M. McGrath, *Compulsory Purchase and Compensation in Ireland: Law and Practice*, 2nd edn (Haywards Heath: Bloomsbury Professional, 2013), Part III.

[35] (1975) 109 I.L.T.R. 69. The cases are reviewed in detail in R. Walsh, "'The Principles of Social Justice' and the Compulsory Acquisition of Private Property for Redevelopment in the United States and Ireland" (2010) 32 D.U.L.J. 1.

[36] [2007] 4 I.R. 701.

[37] R. Walsh, "'The Principles of Social Justice' and the Compulsory Acquisition of Private Property for Redevelopment in the United States and Ireland" (2010) 32 D.U.L.J. 1 at 14.

is owned, or whether it is merely a protection of the economic value associated with property. The answer to this question is not easy and, in large extent, depends on one's views about the role of the State and the market place in the development of land.

1–34 The potential injustices associated with broad powers of compulsory acquisition are amply demonstrated by a review of analogous American cases. In *Poletown Neighbourhood Council v City of Detroit*,[38] a large area of land was compulsorily acquired in order to provide a site for a car-manufacturing plant. The development scheme provided a clear economic benefit to the local area but required the compulsory acquisition and subsequent demolition of a large number of homes and businesses. Most of the residents involved were elderly and were drawn from immigrant communities, many having spent much of their lives living in the area.[39] The plaintiff challenged the use of compulsory purchase powers, claiming that the defendant's power of compulsory purchase for a public purpose did not extend to acquiring land in order to re-convey it to another private person. By majority, the Michigan Supreme Court held that a sufficient public benefit, in the form of economic development, had been demonstrated in order to justify the scheme.

1–35 In *Kelo v City of New London*,[40] the United States Supreme Court considered a similar scheme to compulsorily acquire a large number of properties in order to facilitate the building of a research facility, shopping centre and ancillary development. By a 5:4 majority, the US Supreme Court upheld the proposed acquisition. Stevens J., giving the judgment of the court, held that the compulsory acquisition was a part of a carefully planned scheme of development and that the interests of the plaintiffs had to be viewed in light of the benefits of the plan as a whole. In dissent, O'Connor J. suggested that the effect of the decision was that,

> "[u]nder the banner of economic development, all private property is now vulnerable to being taken and transferred to another private owner, so long as it might be upgraded – i.e. given to an owner who will use it in a way that the legislature deems more beneficial to the public."[41]

1–36 Although the decision in *Kelo* permitted the compulsory acquisition of the land in question, it is perhaps worth pointing out that the redevelopment

---

[38] 304 NW 2d 455 (Mich., 1981), doubted in *City of Novi v Robert Adell's Children's Funded Trust* 659 NW 2d 615 (Mich., 2002) and overruled by *Wayne County v Hathcock* 684 NW 2d 765 (Mich., 2004).
[39] For the background to the case, see J.J. Bukowzyk, "The Decline and Fall of a Detroit Neighbourhood: *Poletown vs GM and the City of Detroit*" (1984) 41 Wash. & Lee L. Rev. 49 at 62.
[40] 545 US 469 (2005).
[41] 545 US 469 (2005) at 494.

scheme was not successful and the research centre at its core was closed after only eight years in operation.[42]

1–37 In assessing the Irish and US redevelopment cases, Walsh has argued that the courts may have gone too far in deferring to the legislature in their assessment of the purposes put forward to justify compulsory purchase and the means selected to carry out such schemes. She notes that the Irish courts have yet to decide on a *Poletown* or *Kelo*-type case in which compulsory purchase of a private dwelling house is sought for redevelopment purposes. She argues that the courts should adopt a cautious approach in such cases, to take greater account of the value of community and the peculiar emotional impact which compulsory acquisition of a home may have on individuals.[43]

1–38 Legislation providing for the protection of the natural and cultural environment, as for example the protection of areas of natural beauty, areas of special scientific interest and archaeological sites, may raise jurisprudential issues as to whether they constitute a deprivation of the landowner's property, or whether on the other hand they are a legitimate regulation of use. In *O'Callaghan v Commissioners of Public Works*,[44] the plaintiff purchased land in Dublin which included the site of an historic promontory fort. At the time of the sale, the fort had been listed under s.8 of the National Monuments (Amendment) Act 1954, which had the effect of prohibiting its demolition or alteration without the consent of the defendant. The purchaser had learned of the listing from his predecessor in title but, upon completion of the sale, he nevertheless employed contractors to plough part of the area occupied by the fort. The defendant Commissioners then made a preservation order under s.8 of the National Monuments Act 1930. This order was made without consultation with the plaintiff, who could not be contacted at the time the order was made. The effect of this order was to prevent the plaintiff or any other person (including the contractors) from interfering with the monument on pain of criminal sanction. The plaintiff claimed that s.8 of the National Monuments Act 1930 was an unconstitutional attack on his property rights in the land. He argued that the section made no provision for the payment of compensation to a landowner whose land was made subject to the order, and that the order in question was not limited in respect of time. He further noted that he had had no opportunity to make representations to the Commissioners prior to the making of the order and that the statute provided no mechanism by which the Commissioners' decision could be appealed.

---

[42] P. McGeehan, "Pfizer to Leave City that Won Land-Use Case", *New York Times*, 12 November 2009.

[43] R. Walsh, "'The Principles of Social Justice' and the Compulsory Acquisition of Private Property for Redevelopment in the United States and Ireland" (2010) 32 D.U.L.J. 1. The decision in *Irish Life & Permanent plc v Duff* [2013] 4 I.R. 96, in which Hogan J. emphasised the need to consider the constitutional protection afforded to the dwelling house in the context of mortgage possession cases, may add some weight to this argument.

[44] [1985] I.L.R.M. 364.

1–39 The Supreme Court held that the Commissioners' powers to preserve national monuments were a legitimate restriction on the plaintiff's right to use his property and were not an unjust attack on his property rights. The court identified the preservation of "the prized relics of the past" as a legitimate aspect of the common good and noted that the legislation operated only in the limited circumstances where a national monument was in danger of destruction, or was actually being destroyed. Dealing with the absence of compensation, the court noted that the plaintiff was on notice of the limitations imposed by the national monuments legislation in respect of the land at the time when he acquired title to it. On this basis, the court held that the plaintiff was not entitled to compensation for playing his part in the preservation of the monument. In doing so, the court held, he was simply discharging "the common duty of all citizens".

1–40 In *O'Callaghan*, the Supreme Court approved of a significant and uncompensated interference in the rights of landowners to deal with their land. Whilst the Supreme Court suggested that all citizens have a common obligation to assist in preserving culturally important historic sites, the plaintiff landowner could be forgiven for taking the view that he was being asked to shoulder a very particular burden in respect of the site concerned. One might argue that if the preservation of historic sites is the common duty of all citizens, then all citizens should contribute to the costs of preservation through the tax system. On the other hand, the plaintiff in *O'Callaghan* had clearly acquired the land in the full knowledge of the presence of the national monument on the site. It could be argued that in doing so, he implicitly consented to the limitations on user which the law imposes on the landowners of such sites. Would a landowner who finds his user of land subject to a new restriction as a result of a new preservation order be in a stronger position to demand compensation or to argue that his property rights have been infringed? The existing case law appears not to provide a definitive answer to such questions.

THE IMPACT OF HUMAN RIGHTS LAW

1–41 The ECHR was incorporated into Irish law by the European Convention on Human Rights Act 2003. Section 3 of the ECHR Act 2003 requires that courts consider the State's obligations under the ECHR when interpreting and applying rules of law and statutory provisions. The effect of incorporation on Irish land law has been, as yet, quite limited.

1–42 In the United Kingdom, the incorporation of the ECHR under the Human Rights Act 1998 has had some impact on private property rights as between private owners. Although the Human Rights Act 1998 imposes a significantly stronger interpretive obligation on the UK courts than is the case with their Irish counterparts, the UK cases show the potential for human rights claims to impact on property law in general, and land law in particular, and thus are worthy of examination.

1–43 In *Harrow LBC v Qazi*,[45] a housing authority had rented a house to Qazi and his then wife in 1992. The marriage broke down and in 1999, Qazi's wife wrote to the council terminating the tenancy. It was common case that this notice had the effect of terminating the tenancy. Qazi applied for a new tenancy of the house in his sole name but was refused by the council on the basis that the house was unsuitable for a single person. Qazi did not vacate the house but continued to live there with another partner whom he married in 2000. When the council sought an order for possession of the premises, Qazi argued that the court should consider his right to respect for his home and family life under Art.8 of the ECHR. In particular, he argued that the council's application for possession amounted to a disproportionate interference with his Art.8 rights.

1–44 By a bare majority, the House of Lords decided that the local authority was entitled to an order for possession and that Art.8 of the ECHR could not provide a defence to a claim for possession.[46] Lord Steyn, dissenting, suggested that the majority's decision had ignored the new landscape created by the Human Rights Act 1998, and in particular that they had allowed "domestic notions of title, legal and equitable rights, and interests, to colour the interpretation of Article 8(1)"[47] of the ECHR.

1–45 The compatibility with the ECHR of the majority approach in *Qazi* was subsequently questioned in the aftermath of the decision of the European Court of Human Rights (ECtHR) in *Connors v United Kingdom*.[48] In that case, the ECtHR held that there had been a violation of Art.8 of the ECHR in circumstances where members of the Travelling Community had been evicted from local authority land upon which they had made their home for 13 years. The ECtHR held that respect for Art.8 required that the council should establish a substantive justification for the eviction of the applicants beyond legal title itself.

1–46 In the aftermath of *Connors* the House of Lords reconsidered *Qazi* in a series of conjoined appeals under the title of *Kay v Lambeth LBC*.[49] A bare majority upheld *Qazi*, holding that a defence which was based on the personal circumstances and Art.8 rights of the applicant alone should be struck out. Doubts about the *Kay* decision were immediately raised by the decision of the ECtHR in *McCann v United Kingdom*.[50] In that case, the ECtHR described the loss of one's home as "the most extreme form of interference with the right to respect for the home", and held that an applicant "should in principle be able to have the proportionality of the measure determined by an independent tribunal

---

[45] [2004] 1 A.C. 983.
[46] [2004] 1 A.C. 983 at 1014–1015 (Lord Hope); 1020 and 1024–1025 (Lord Millet); and 1030–1032 (Lord Scott).
[47] [2004] 1 A.C. 983 at 997.
[48] (2005) 40 E.H.R.R. 9.
[49] [2006] 2 A.C. 465.
[50] (2008) 47 E.H.R.R. 40.

... notwithstanding that, under domestic law, his right of occupation has come to an end".[51] The House of Lords considered the issues yet again in *Doherty v Birmingham County Council*[52] when Lord Hope sought to clarify *Kay v Lambeth LBC* and to identify exceptional circumstances in which a human rights challenge might be mounted to an order for possession.

1–47 In *Manchester City Council v Pinnock*,[53] the UK Supreme Court overruled *Qazi*, *Kay* and *Doherty* and recognised that Art.8 of the ECHR provides a free-standing defence to an action for possession and that courts should consider in all cases the proportionality of making a possession order where one is sought.

1–48 In *Pinnock* and the other cases discussed above, the courts were considering claims by local authority landlords. Such bodies are, of course, creations of the State itself, and the control of such bodies falls within well-understood public law principles. The extent to which similar human rights arguments might be made against a private landlord is unclear. The UK Supreme Court expressly stated that the principles identified in *Pinnock* would not apply to private landlords.[54] The ECHR Act 2003 imposes a less stringent interpretive obligation on Irish courts than is the case in the UK. Nonetheless, Irish courts have had to grapple with the ECHR in the context of actions for possession of local authority housing, a point which will be returned to in later chapters.

---

[51] (2008) 47 E.H.R.R. 40 at paras 50–51.

[52] [2009] 1 A.C. 367.

[53] [2011] 2 A.C. 104.

[54] [2011] 2 A.C. 104 at para.50. For a general review of these cases and the current UK position, see I. Loveland, "Twenty Years Later – Assessing the Significance of the Human Rights Act 1998 to Residential Possession Proceedings" [2017] 3 Conv. 174.

CHAPTER 2

Land

A human being needs only a small plot of ground on which to be happy, and even less to lie beneath.

— Johann Wolfgang Von Goethe, *The Sorrows of Young Werther and Selected Writings* (1774)

GENERAL PRINCIPLES

2–01 The common law has long recognised not only the obvious fact that land is three-dimensional, but that rights in it are also three-dimensional.[1] It is sometimes said that the physical extent of landownership is expressed in the Latin maxim, *cuius est solum, ejus est usque ad coelum et usque ad inferos*[2] ("the owner of the soil also owns as far as the heavens above and below to the centre of the earth"). This is not accurate as far as airspace above the surface is concerned and has many qualifications as to the earth below the surface. Two other Latin maxims are not only closely related, but more accurate in their application. *Superficies solo cedit*[3] ("a building becomes part of the ground") means that a building which cannot be removed without demolition or damage becomes part of the land.[4] *Quiquid plantatur solo, solo cedit*[5] ("whatever is attached to the ground becomes part of it") means that fixtures attached to the land, or to buildings which are part of the land, become part of the realty also. As to fixtures, there are tests as to the degree and purpose of annexation which are considered later.

STATUTORY DEFINITION

2–02 Blackstone, in his *Commentaries on the Laws of England*, remarked in the 18th century that land is "a word of very extensive signification".[6] The Land

---

[1] K.J. Gray and S.F. Gray, *Elements of Land Law*, 5th edn (Oxford: Oxford University Press, 2009), paras 1.002–1.009.

[2] Co Litt 4. See *Butler v Dublin Corporation* [1999] 1 I.R. 565 at 586.

[3] Or *aedificatum solo, solo cedit* ("that which is built upon the land goes with the land"): Co Litt 4a.

[4] *Elitestone Ltd v Morris* [1997] 1 W.L.R. 687; *Holland v Hodgson* (1872) L.R. 7 C.P. 328.

[5] *Vandeleur v Malcolmson* (1865) 17 Ir. C.L.R. 569 (weir attached to bed of river). See also Justinian I, *The Institutes of Justinian*, 2.1.29: *omne quod solo inaedificatur solo cedit* ("everything which is built upon the soil passes with the soil").

[6] 2 Bl Comm 16.

and Conveyancing Law Reform Act 2009 ("LCLRA 2009") recognises the three dimensions of land by providing in s.3 that "land" includes, inter alia:

"(b) mines, minerals and other substances in the substratum below the surface, whether or not owned in horizontal, vertical or other layers apart from the surface of the land,

(c) land covered by water,

(d) buildings or structures of any kind on land and any part of them, whether the division is made horizontally, vertically or in any other way,

(e) the airspace above the surface of land or above any building or structure on land which is capable of being or was previously occupied by a building or structure and any part of such airspace, whether the division is made horizontally, vertically or in any other way …".

2–03 Section 71 of the LCLRA 2009 further provides that a conveyance of land includes, and conveys with the land, all buildings, drains, fences, fixtures, hedges, water, watercourses and other features forming part of the land, and if the land has houses or other buildings on it, the conveyance includes, and conveys with the land, all cellars, drains, fixtures, gardens, lights, outhouses, passages, sewers, watercourses and other features forming part of the land, houses or other buildings.[7]

BUILDINGS

2–04 The ancient principles of *superficies solo cedit* and *quiquid plantatur solo, solo cedit* are confirmed by s.3 of the LCLRA 2009, so that, for example, the top flat in a block of flats is "land".

2–05 There are two tests as to whether a structure has become annexed to the freehold:

1. The degree of annexation to the land, the test being whether the structure is attached to the land by more than the force of gravity—this is sometimes known as the "Newton plus" test.
2. The purpose of annexation. The latter test is not that of subjective intention, but the purpose judged from an objective point of view.

2–06 In the past, the main test was the degree of physical attachment, but the law now adopts a more sophisticated approach and emphasises the purpose or intention of attachment. In *Elitestone Ltd v Morris*,[8] a wooden chalet resting on concrete pillars attached to E's land was constructed by M's predecessor in title. The structure could not be removed without being demolished. The House

---

[7] Re-enacting s.6 of the Conveyancing Act 1881.
[8] [1997] 1 W.L.R. 687.

of Lords held unanimously that the structure was not attached by more than gravity, and so did not satisfy the Newton plus test. However, the chalet had clearly been intended to become part and parcel of the freehold. A mobile home or house boat with plug-in or temporary attachments for electricity, etc. does not become a part of the land.[9]

Fixtures

The Principle

2–07 In *Holland v Hodgson*,[10] Blackburn J. said:

"There is no doubt that the general maxim of the law is, that what is annexed to the land becomes part of the land; but it is very difficult, if not impossible, to say with precision what constitutes an annexation sufficient for this purpose. It is a question which must depend on the circumstances of each case, and mainly on two circumstances, as indicating the intention, viz., the degree of annexation and the object of the annexation. ... Perhaps the true rule is, that articles not otherwise attached to the land than by their own weight are not to be considered as part of the land, unless the circumstances are such as to shew that they were intended to be part of the land, the onus of shewing that they were so intended lying on those who assert that they have ceased to be chattels, and that, on the contrary, an article which is affixed to the land even slightly is to be considered as part of the land unless the circumstances are such as to shew that it was intended all along to continue a chattel, the onus lying on those who contend that it is a chattel."[11]

2–08 The trend in modern authorities is to place greater emphasis on the purpose for which the object was placed on the land.[12] In *Re Moormac Developments Ltd*,[13] Laffoy J. considered the status of crushed limestone which had been spread on land as the preliminary stage of road building within a housing development project. The court found that the rubble was not affixed by anything other than its own weight but nonetheless had no difficulty in finding that the limestone had become affixed to the land, since it was clear that it was placed on the land with the intention that it would form a part of a road. A television aerial has been held to be a fixture both because of the substantial way in which it is fixed to the building and also because its obvious purpose is to enhance the use of the building as a dwelling house; however, a television set is not a fixture.[14] If a house is sold, fixtures pass automatically unless excluded

---

[9] *Chelsea Yacht and Boat Club Ltd v Pope* [2000] 1 W.L.R. 1941.
[10] (1872) L.R. 7 C.P. 328.
[11] (1872) L.R. 7 C.P. 328 at 334–335.
[12] *Re the Companies (Consolidation) Act 1908 and Ross and Boal Ltd* [1924] 1 I.R. 129.
[13] [2013] IEHC 572.
[14] *Maye v Revenue Commissioners* [1986] I.L.R.M. 377.

by contract.[15] *Botham v TSB Bank plc*[16] applied the test to residential houses. Kitchen cabinets were held to be fixtures, but "white goods" such as washing machines and cookers were not, even though such appliances are typically physically connected to the land by electricity and gas cables.

THE SUBSOIL

2–09 The ownership of the subsoil itself was extensively reviewed by the UK Supreme Court in *Bocardo SA v Star Energy UK Onshore Ltd*.[17] The defendants had a statutory licence to extract oil from a naturally occurring reservoir which was partially located beneath the plaintiff's land. The plaintiff made no claim to ownership of the oil, title to which was vested in the Crown. For technical reasons in order to enable the oil to be extracted, the defendants had drilled a series of tunnels into the reservoir, three of which passed under land owned by the plaintiff at depths of between 900 and 2,900 feet. The plaintiff claimed that this drilling, along with the installation of casing and tubing in the tunnels, amounted to a trespass.

2–10 Lord Hope of Craighead DPSC held that the maxim *cuius est solum, ejus est usque ad coelum et usque ad inferos* still has some relevance as regards the ownership of land below the surface.[18] The true rule is that the surface owner is also the owner of the strata beneath the surface. His Lordship declined to identify a physical limit of such ownership but noted that, at some depth, one would reach a point at which physical features of the Earth, including temperature and pressure, would render the concept of ownership absurd.

2–11 Although the UK Supreme Court was unanimous in holding that the plaintiff had rights in the subsoil, the court was divided on the calculation of damages. The majority held that damages should be calculated on the basis of the cost of compulsorily acquiring a wayleave under the land in question, and rejected the suggestion that the plaintiff was entitled to any portion of the oil extracted through its land.

2–12 The common law principle that the landowner owns soil beneath the surface was indirectly recognised in Ireland in connection with the Dublin Port Tunnel scheme. The Roads (Amendment) Act 1998[19] gave power to acquire the subsoil under land, but not the surface, for the three-dimensional space

---

[15] *Irish Civil Service Building Society v Mahony* (1876) 10 I.L.T.R. 153.

[16] (1996) 73 P. & C.R. D1.

[17] [2011] 1 A.C. 380.

[18] [2011] 1 A.C. 380 at 393–396.

[19] Amending the Roads Act 1993. The 1998 Act amends the definition of substratum, which the Minister could acquire, by s.2: "'substratum of land' means any subsoil or anything beneath the surface of land required—(a) for the purposes of a tunnel or tunnelling or anything connected therewith, or (b) for any other purpose connected with a scheme".

to be occupied by the tunnel. Later, s.48 of the Planning and Development (Strategic Infrastructure) Act 2006 amended s.2 of the Acquisition of Land (Assessment of Compensation) Act 1919 by providing that the value of any land lying 10 metres or more below the surface "shall be taken to be nil, unless it is shown to be of a greater value by the claimant". The extent to which this approach, which effectively authorises an expropriation of subsurface property rights without compensation, is compatible with the Constitution remains to be seen. Future technological developments may increase the value of the subsoil, in particular as carbon capture and storage technology develops.[20]

AIRSPACE

2–13 The maxim *cuius est solum, ejus est usque ad coelum et usque ad inferos* is heavily qualified when it comes to the airspace above land. In *Bernstein v Skyviews Ltd*,[21] the defendant flew over the plaintiff's land to take an aerial photograph of his country house. It then offered it for sale to the plaintiff, who sued for trespass. Griffiths J. noted the existence of the maxim but pointed out that there was no reported case in which it had been applied to give an owner unrestricted rights to the airspace above land. The court cited *Pickering v Rudd*[22] to the effect that it would not be a trespass to pass over someone's land in a balloon, nor to fire a bullet across it, unless the bullet fell on the ground. Griffiths J. adopted a statement by Lord Wilberforce in *Commissioner for Railways v The Valuer-General*,[23] namely that the maxim was so sweeping, unscientific and unpractical a doctrine, it was unlikely to appeal to the common law mind. He held that an owner's right extended to such a height as was necessary for the ordinary use and enjoyment of the land and the structures on it. Above that height, the owner had no more right than anyone else. The US Supreme Court considered a similar issue in *United States v Causby*,[24] in which the owners of a chicken farm complained of damage to their business and stock by reason of overflights by military aircraft taking off and landing at a nearby airfield. The US Supreme Court held that the maxim has no application to modern circumstances and that private rights in land do not reach above the surface beyond the immediate reaches of the atmosphere.

2–14 Section 55 of the Air Navigation and Transport Act 1936[25] provides that no action shall lie for trespass or nuisance by reason only of the flight of aircraft over any property at a height above the ground which is reasonable having

---

[20] J. Morgan, "Digging Deep: Property Rights in Subterranean Space and the Challenge of Carbon Capture and Storage" (2013) 62 I.C.L.Q. 587.

[21] [1977] 3 W.L.R. 136.

[22] (1815) 4 Camp. 219.

[23] [1974] A.C. 328 at 351.

[24] 328 US 256 (1946).

[25] As amended by the Air Navigation and Transport Act 1988 s.47.

regard to wind, weather and all the circumstances.[26] In *Bernstein* the court said
that a person could not be held liable in tort if he or she was at a reasonable
height and complying with air safety regulations,[27] but flying below a reasonable level could give rise to an action in trespass, and repeated flying causing
noise is an actionable nuisance.[28] Recent technological developments, particularly the increase in the number of unmanned aerial vehicles being flown
in Irish airspace, have led to calls for legislative clarification of the rights of
property owners in this field.[29] The extent to which the law of property provides
a suitable mechanism for regulating the use of such aircraft is less than clear.

2–15 Outside the aviation context, rights to the airspace above land have given
rise to a small body of case law. In *Woollerton & Wilson Ltd v Richard Costain
Ltd*,[30] the English High Court granted an injunction to restrain an aerial trespass
arising from the operation of a crane which was being used by the defendant
for construction work on an adjoining premises. The court suspended the
injunction for one year in order to allow the work to be completed.[31] In *Keating
& Co Ltd v Jervis Street Shopping Centre Ltd*,[32] the Irish High Court declined
to grant an interlocutory injunction restraining the operation of a crane in similar circumstances because the plaintiff failed to establish that damages were an
inadequate remedy.

OBJECTS FOUND ON OR BELOW THE SURFACE OF LAND

2–16 The finding of lost objects on or below the surface of land has been the
cause of much case law. Where the true owner of such goods can be located,
then that person's ownership of the goods will usually continue unabated.[33]
Where the true owner does not come forward to claim the goods, the law faces
a more difficult choice between the claims of the landowner and those of the
finder of the goods.

---

[26] There was no claim for nuisance in *Bernstein* because it could not be maintained that a single
flight fell within that tort.

[27] Rule 3 of the Schedule to the Irish Aviation Authority (Rules of the Air) Order 2004 (S.I. No.
72 of 2004) establishes minimum operating altitudes for aircraft in Irish airspace.

[28] See *Roedean School Ltd v Cornwall Aviation Co Ltd*, *The Times*, 3 July 1926.

[29] K. O'Sullivan, "Low Flying Drones and the Ownership of Airspace in Ireland" (2016) 21
C.P.L.J. 7.

[30] [1970] 1 W.L.R. 411.

[31] This aspect of the decision was described as insupportable by Bingham M.R. in *Jaggard v
Sawyer* [1995] 1 W.L.R. 269 at 279.

[32] [1997] 1 I.R. 512.

[33] *Webb v Ireland* [1988] I.R. 353 at 389–390. Walsh J. rejected the suggestion that the owner of
the land would have a better claim than the original owner, holding that such a rule would be
incompatible with the constitutional protection of property rights.

Objects below the Surface

2–17 In their famous essay on possession, Pollock and Wright set down the general rule:

"The possession of land carries with it in general, by our law, possession of everything which is attached to or under that land, and, in the absence of a better title elsewhere, the right to possess it also. And it makes no difference that the possessor is not aware of the thing's existence."[34]

2–18 Thus, in *City of London Corporation v Appleyard*,[35] it was held that a box of banknotes which was found concealed within the walls of a building was the property of the lessees of the building. In *Elwes v Brigg*,[36] land had been leased to a gas company which was excavating on the land in order to erect a gasholder. A prehistoric boat discovered six feet below the surface was held to be the property of the lessor, although the lessor was ignorant of the existence of the boat at the time the lease was granted. The court held that the lease had not passed possession of the boat to the lessee.[37] There are many qualifications on the principle that the freeholder has a superior title to things below the surface. Some of these, such as minerals and treasure trove, are dealt with below.

Things Found above the Surface

2–19 When things are found above the surface of the land, it is less likely that the owner of the land will be able to show both possession and an intention to possess such as to give him or her a better title than the finder of the objects.

2–20 In the famous case of *Armory v Delamirie*[38] in 1722, a boy chimney sweep found a jewel in a chimney. He took it to a jeweller and offered it for sale. The jeweller took the jewel and then refused to pay for it. The boy, through an adult friend, sued the jeweller. The jeweller pleaded in the action that he was not under an obligation to return it because some third party evidently was the true owner and not the boy. In other words, the jeweller pleaded *jus tertii*, i.e. that a third party had a better title than the boy. The court held that he could not do so. As between the jeweller and the boy, the boy had the better title, and that was sufficient for him to succeed.

2–21 In *Hanna v Peel*,[39] the defendant was the owner of a house which he had never occupied. The house was requisitioned during the war to billet soldiers. The plaintiff, a soldier, found a brooch in a crevice on top of a window frame.

---

[34] F. Pollock and R.S.W. Wright, *An Essay on Possession in the Common Law* (Oxford: Clarendon, 1888).

[35] [1963] 1 W.L.R. 982.

[36] (1886) 33 Ch. D. 562.

[37] See also, *Waverley Borough Council v Fletcher* [1996] Q.B. 334.

[38] (1722) 1 Str. 505; *Quinn v Coleman* (1898) 33 I.L.T.R. 79.

[39] [1945] K.B. 509.

The true owner was not known. There was no evidence that the owner of the house knew it was there. The police handed it over to the owner of the house. The plaintiff claimed that he was entitled to it. The court held that the soldier was entitled to it as against everyone except the true owner. The court distinguished *Elwes v Brigg* on the ground, apparently, that as to things above the surface of the land, the title of an owner depends on the concept of possession which applies in relation to personal property. The owner has a superior title to a finder only if he has the requisite intention to possess the item. Such an intention could be of a general kind, as where there was evidence that he had intended to exercise control over everything on the land. The court found that there was no such evidence here, as the owner had never occupied the land.[40]

2–22 In *Parker v British Airways*,[41] the plaintiff found a gold bracelet lying on the floor in a passenger lounge at Heathrow Airport. He handed it to a British Airways official with his name and address, saying that if it was not claimed by the true owner, they should return it to him. The owner never came forward and the defendant sold the bracelet. The plaintiff sued. The English Court of Appeal held that he was entitled to the money. Donaldson M.R. held, following *Hanna*, that a finder of an article who is lawfully on land and who finds the article on the land which is not attached to it or buried under it and who takes it into his care and control, has a title to it good against all except the true owner. He also held that where property is found in a building, the owner of the building has a superior right to the finder only if the owner of the building has manifested an intention, before the finding, to exercise control over the building and articles found in it. Where the article is found under the surface, then in order to obtain possession of it, the finder would have to dig it up. In doing so, the finder would either be a trespasser—in which case the owner of the land would have a better title—or would do so under a licence from the owner—in which case whether the finder had a better title would depend on the terms of the licence.

---

[40] See also *Re Cohen* [1953] Ch. 88. A husband, who owned a business in London, had lived with his wife in a house owned by the wife. After both had died, money was found hidden in the house. The issue was whether the money belonged to the husband's estate, or that of the wife. The court held that in the absence of evidence as to whom it belonged, the wife's executors had to rely on the principle that the owner owns chattels found on land, and that the money belonged to the wife's estate. In *Grigsby v Melville* [1973] 3 All E.R. 455, the English Court of Appeal held that in the absence of anything to the contrary, a conveyance of land included not only the whole surface but the whole substratum. A basement to which there was no access from within the building was held to be included. In *Mustafa v Baptists Union Corp Ltd* (1983) 266 E.G. 812, a similar situation arose in the case of a room above the surface but which was inaccessible from within the building. It was held that a person reading the particulars of sale would not have concluded that the room was excluded.

[41] [1982] 1 All E.R. 834.

ARCHAEOLOGICAL OBJECTS

The Pre-1994 Law: Treasure Trove

2–23 Treasure trove was a royal prerogative and was the Crown's right to the ownership of objects made substantially of gold or silver[42] which had been buried with the intention of recovering them[43] and which had no known owner.[44] The claim of the Crown did not prejudice the claim of a person who could show original ownership of the objects or a title derived from the original owner.[45] At common law, there had to be an inquest by a coroner to establish the title to the treasure. It was also an offence on the part of the finder to conceal treasure trove.[46] It had also become the practice to give a reward to the finder, but it was *ex gratia* and was not the subject of a right.

Limits on Treasure Trove at Common Law

2–24 *Bracton* only mentions the title of the finder and did not confine the doctrine to objects made of gold or silver, although he did confine it to metal objects.[47] By the time of Sir Edward Coke, Chief Justice of the King's Bench until 1616, the royal prerogative had been established and the doctrine had also been confined to gold and silver.[48] The reason for the restriction was that the Crown regarded treasure trove as a useful source of metal for the Royal Mint. This indicates that the origin of the doctrine had nothing to do with preserving objects of archaeological interest: on the contrary, it resulted in their destruction. In *Attorney General of Lancaster v Overton Farms*,[49] the English Court of Appeal reaffirmed that the English doctrine was confined to objects containing a substantial amount of gold and silver, although Denning M.R. suggested that it would be desirable for Parliament to amend the law so as to increase the scope of the doctrine.[50]

2–25 The prerogative also applied only to objects buried with thought of recovery. Grave goods were not treasure trove even if they were of gold or

---

[42] *Attorney General of Lancaster v Overton Farms* [1982] 1 All E.R. 524.

[43] *Attorney General v Trustees of the British Museum* [1903] Ch. D. 598.

[44] On the English doctrine, see C.S. Emden, "The Law of Treasure Trove, Past and Present" (1926) 167 L.Q.R. 368; N.E. Palmer, "Treasure Trove and the Protection of Antiquities" (1981) 44 M.L.R. 178; Treasure Act 1996.

[45] 3 Co Inst 132, approved in *Attorney General of Lancaster v Overton Farms* [1982] 1 All E.R. 524. See also, *Webb v Ireland* [1988] I.R. 353 at 381.

[46] *R. v O'Toole* (1867) 11 Cox C.C. 75. The case concerned coins of the reigns of Elizabeth I, Charles I and the Commonwealth found at Booterstown, near Dublin. The judge directed the jury that if the accused did not know the coins were silver, he should be acquitted. See also, "Treasure Trove" (1894) I.L.T.S.J. 127 (10 March 1894).

[47] The legal treatise, *De Legibus et Consuetudinibus Angliae* ("On the Laws and Customs of England") is universally known as *Bracton*.

[48] 3 Co Inst 132.

[49] [1982] 1 All E.R. 524.

[50] This has now been done in England, Wales and Northern Ireland by the Treasure Act 1996 s.1.

silver. The leading case on the question of burial with intention of recovery is *Attorney-General v Trustees of the British Museum*,[51] which concerned the "Broighter Hoard" consisting of a collection of objects, including a gold model boat and a gold torque, now in the National Museum of Ireland. The objects were turned up by a farmer when ploughing his field near Lough Foyle. The objects made their way into the hands of an antiquary who sold them to the British Museum. The Royal Irish Academy, to whom the prerogative of treasure trove found in Ireland had been transferred, claimed the hoard as treasure trove. It was argued on behalf of the British Museum that the objects had been placed at the edge of an ancient lake which in the past had extended to the area where they were found, and that they were a votive offering to the Irish god of the sea and lakes, Manannán mac Lir. If this were so, they were not treasure trove since there had been no intention of recovery. A great deal of archaeological evidence was adduced[52] to prove the existence of an ancient beach at the site. However, it did not convince the judge. He also seems to have been impressed by the fact that all the objects were found together in the same place, whereas if they had been placed at the edge of a lake, it would be more likely that the action of the water would have dispersed them. The judge also held that once it was proved that the objects had been found buried and were of gold or silver, there was a presumption that they were treasure trove and it was for those who denied this to prove from the circumstances of their burial that they were not. The British Museum had not rebutted the presumption.

Webb v Ireland

2–26 The case of *Webb v Ireland*[53] concerned the finding of the Derrynaflan hoard of early Irish communion silver and is of great cultural interest. It led to the enactment of the National Monuments (Amendment) Act 1994 and so is worth considering in some detail.

The High Court

2–27 *Webb v Ireland* concerned the application of the treasure trove prerogative to the finding of the Derrynaflan hoard. This was a collection of five liturgical objects, including a chalice, paten and strainer, all of remarkable workmanship and beauty. The plaintiffs had approached the owners of land in County Tipperary upon which the ruined Derrynaflan church stands. The church is the subject of a preservation order under the National Monuments Acts. Permission was granted to the plaintiffs to visit the church, though no permission was given to dig on the site. Indeed, having regard to the restrictions on interference with national monuments provided for under s.14 of the National Monuments Act 1935, the landowners could not have authorised the plaintiffs to dig in the protected area. The plaintiffs nevertheless used a metal

---

[51] [1903] 2 Ch. 598.
[52] See (1904) XXV Sec C *Proceedings of the Royal Irish Academy* Nos 5, 6, 144 and following.
[53] [1988] I.R. 353.

detector which gave a positive return in an area close to the church. Upon digging, they discovered the group of ecclesiastical objects. Without informing the authorities, they proceeded to remove the objects from the ground and took them to their home. The plaintiffs delivered the objects to the National Museum together with a solicitor's letter which stated that the objects were supplied to the Museum pending the determination of their legal ownership and subject to any rights of payment or reward which might accrue to the plaintiffs. The Director of the National Museum told the plaintiffs that they would be "honourably treated" by the State in respect of the find.

2–28 After an exchange of correspondence, the Chief State Solicitor offered the plaintiffs the sum of £10,000. This was rejected by the finders who then sought the return of the objects. In order to buttress its position, the State paid the landowners the sum of £25,000 each for any interest which they might have in the objects. In March 1982, the plaintiffs issued proceedings seeking the return of the objects. They argued that the National Museum was holding the objects as a bailee for the plaintiffs, who, as finders and bailors, had a superior title to the objects and were entitled to their return.

2–29 The State argued that the landowners had a better title to the objects and that the State had acquired that title by purchase. The State also argued that it had a superior title to that of the plaintiffs by virtue of the treasure trove prerogative. In the High Court, Blayney J. held that the State had accepted possession of the objects as a bailee of the plaintiffs. As such, the State was bound by the well-established rule that a bailee is estopped from denying the title of the bailor. The court held that the law of bailment does not allow a bailee to rely on a superior title to the goods which was acquired by the bailee after the date of the bailment. Because the court took the view that the action was solely one between bailor and bailee, Blayney J. held that it was not necessary for him to consider whether the plaintiffs had title to the objects as finders.

2–30 Blayney J. also held against the State on the treasure trove argument. Citing the decision of the Supreme Court in *Byrne v Ireland*,[54] the court held that the royal prerogative of treasure trove had not survived the enactment of the 1922 Constitution of Saorstát Éireann and, as such, had not been carried forward by the 1937 Constitution of Ireland. Accordingly, Blayney J. ordered the delivery of the objects to the plaintiffs subject to the payment of an allowance to the State by the plaintiffs in respect of the work done by the National Museum in the preservation of the objects.

The Supreme Court

2–31 The Supreme Court reversed the High Court's decision. Finlay C.J. gave the lead judgment with which Henchy and Griffin JJ. both concurred. Walsh and McCarthy JJ. both delivered separate concurring judgments. Finlay

---

[54] [1972] I.R. 241.

C.J. held that the express terms upon which the objects had been transferred to the National Museum rebutted any suggestion that the State had impliedly acknowledged the plaintiffs' title to the goods. Walsh J. declined to follow this line of reasoning. However, both Walsh J. and Finlay C.J. held that where a bailee has subsequently established a superior title in himself to bailed goods, this terminates the bailment and any accompanying estoppel. The question therefore arose as to whether the State, either by purchase from the landowners or by some other means, had acquired such a superior title.

2–32 Applying *Elwes v Briggs & Co*,[55] *South Staffordshire Water Co v Sharman*[56] and *Parker v British Airwards Board*,[57] Finlay C.J. held that at the time of the finding, the landowner had a superior title to that obtained by the plaintiffs when they initially took possession of the objects. Finlay C.J. noted that the plaintiffs were trespassers at the time of the finding; as such, public policy leaned against allowing them to acquire rights of ownership in things found in the land, but Finlay C.J. did not consider this necessary to reach the conclusion that the landowners, in any event, enjoyed a prior title to the objects prior to their discovery. The effect of purchasing the landowners' rights to the objects was therefore to give the State good title to them as against all but their true owners. Walsh J. expressed agreement with the Chief Justice on the finding points, though he was at pains to point out that the rights of a finder or even those of a landowner to possession of lost chattels upon their rediscovery would not avail against a claim from the true owner of the goods and that such a landowner obtains a mere possessory title only. On this view, Walsh J. concluded that the State acquired no title to the objects from the landowners—the landowners never had possession of the objects in the first place, so they had none to transfer. McCarthy J. delivered perhaps the most intriguing judgment on this point. Having considered *Parker* and *Armory v Delamarie*,[58] McCarthy J. appeared to reject the notion that a landowner has a better right to possession than a finder of chattels, even where those chattels are found under the surface of the land itself.

2–33 On the question of whether the State had a separate title to the objects as a result of the prerogative of treasure trove, all members of the Supreme Court held that treasure trove, as a royal prerogative, had not survived the enactment of the Constitution. However, this was not the end of the judgment. A reading of Art.5 of the Constitution, which declares Ireland to be a sovereign, independent and democratic state, and Art.10, by which the State claims ownership of natural resources, royalties and franchises, led Finlay C.J. to conclude that the State possesses a right to "treasure trove", not as an inheritance of the royal prerogative of the pre-independence era but as an inherent aspect of its own sovereignty. Finlay C.J. further expressly stated that the State's prerogative

---

[55] (1886) 33 Ch. D. 562.
[56] [1896] 2 Q.B. 44.
[57] [1982] Q.B. 1004.
[58] (1722) 1 Str. 505.

power in this area could be extended by statute. Finlay C.J. suggested that the boundaries of this State prerogative were similar to those of the former royal power, and he noted in particular that though the finders of treasure trove had been traditionally rewarded with *ex gratia* payments, this was a matter of custom which created no liability that might attach to the exercise of the State's constitutional prerogatives. For Walsh and McCarthy JJ., a similar prerogative existed (possibly, in the case of Walsh J., not confined to gold and silver objects only), though for them, the constitutional basis of the power rested in Art.5 alone.

2–34 Finally, all members of the court held that although the plaintiffs were not entitled to a reward as of legal right, the assurance of honourable treatment given to them by the Director of the National Museum had created a legitimate expectation of reward from which the State could not resile. The court ordered the payment of £50,000 to the finders in satisfaction of this expectation.

2–35 The wisdom, or indeed propriety, of judges identifying novel constitutional principles which have, at best, a tenuous basis in the text of the Constitution itself is beyond the scope of this work. It suffices to note that the prerogative power identified in *Webb* itself seems to have initially mirrored the traditional prerogative power. This might strike a cynical mind as a remarkable coincidence, especially in the context of the constitutional revolution brought about by the enactment of the rest of the 1937 Constitution. At a practical level, the majority judgment meant that State ownership of archaeological objects would still be limited to items of gold and silver buried with thought or intention of recovery, and that grave goods, for example, would still be outside the prerogative's scope. Finlay C.J. nevertheless indicated that it was open to the legislature to expand the doctrine to the extent defined by the constitutional principle.[59]

2–36 One aspect of the judgment that has attracted criticism was the introduction of a test of nationality into a doctrine concerned with the preservation of cultural heritage from which it was previously absent. Kelly argued that the term "national" can too readily be given a narrow or even bigoted meaning. Referring to the removal of statues of William III and George II from Dublin and to stripping of the crowns from Kingsbridge, Kelly continued:

"This bridge, erected to commemorate the visit of George IV in 1821, recalled, like all the other monuments I mentioned, a national history which, if I could, I would turn back and reshape in a sense happier for the ancient Irish race, dispossessed in the 16th and 17th centuries of land, power, influence and self-respect; but I cannot do it, and it certainly cannot be done by such mean and spiteful acts of rage against inanimate objects. These objects, of course, did not belong to the category of things which *Webb* was about;

---

[59] [1988] I.R. 353 at 386.

but the sort of mentality which could violently or officially exclude objects of similar provenance from our 'national heritage' is still with us, and I would be apprehensive, therefore, about anchoring in our constitutional law a concept so readily abused by the official or the unofficial bigot."[60]

The National Monuments (Amendment) Act 1994

2–37 The Supreme Court in *Webb* indicated that the specific doctrine of treasure trove applicable in this jurisdiction could be enlarged by the legislature to fill out the boundaries of the constitutional principle laid down in that case, and indeed invited the legislature to do so. The legislature could remove the limits of gold and silver, burial with intent to recover, etc. The doctrine could be expanded to include all "objects which constitute antiquities of importance which are discovered and which have no known owner".[61] The statutory expansion of the doctrine was carried out by the National Monuments (Amendment) Act 1994 (the "1994 Act").[62]

Archaeological Objects

2–38 Section 2 of the 1994 Act implements the suggestion in *Webb* by the following provision:

"2.—(1) Without prejudice to any other rights howsoever arising in relation to any archaeological object[63] found before the coming into operation of this section, there shall stand vested in the State the ownership of any archaeological object found in the State after the coming into operation of this section where such object has no known owner at the time when it was found. (2) In this section 'owner' means the person for the time being having such estate or interest in the archaeological object as entitles him to the actual possession thereof."

2–39 The phrase "no known owner at the time when it was found" presumably does not exclude the right of an owner who subsequently makes a claim in view of the protection of property by the Constitution and the remarks of Walsh J. in *Webb v Ireland*.[64] Subsection (2) seems designed to exclude the finder from the term "owner". Section 3 provides that the Director of the National Museum may waive the rights of the State. Section 5 creates offences

---

[60] J. Kelly, "Hidden Treasure and the Constitution" (1988) 10 D.U.L.J. 5 at 18.

[61] [1988] I.R. 353 at 383 per Finlay C.J.

[62] See also the National Monuments (Amendment) Act 2004, and the Architectural Heritage (National Inventory) and Historic Monuments (Miscellaneous Provisions) Act 1999.

[63] "Archaeological object" is defined for the purpose of the Act (by s.2 of the National Monuments (Amendment) Act 1987, as amended by s.14 of the 1994 Act) as "any chattel whether in a manufactured or partly manufactured or an unmanufactured state which by reason of the archaeological interest attached thereto or of its association with any Irish historical event or person has a value substantially greater than its intrinsic (including artistic) value, and the said expression includes ancient human, animal or plant remains."

[64] [1988] I.R. 353 at 390.

of failing to report the possession of archaeological objects and failing to give information about them. The 1994 Act also established a record of monuments and places where there are believed to be monuments.[65]

Reward

2–40 Section 10 of the 1994 Act now provides that the State "may" pay a reward to the person who finds an archaeological object, the owner of the land and the occupier of the land on or under which the object was found, where the object is retained by the State. In assessing the amount of the award, the Director of the National Museum must take into account "any or all" of the following criteria: the intrinsic value of the object and its general historical and archaeological importance; the circumstances of the finding; and the amount of rewards paid by the State in the case of comparable archaeological objects. In *Re La Lavia*,[66] the Supreme Court held that the payment of rewards is voluntary and that the general practice in the past that rewards were paid does not, of itself, create a legitimate expectation of future payments.

Operation of Metal Detectors

2–41 The National Monuments (Amendment) Act 1987 introduced new criminal offences in respect of the operation of metal-detecting equipment. Under s.2 of that Act, it is a criminal offence to be in possession of a metal detector in or at the site of a national monument or to use such equipment for the purposes of searching for archaeological objects in any other place without a licence granted by the Commissioners of Public Works. Section 7 of the 1994 Act confers power on the Gardaí to seize metal detectors found at or near a national monument without warrant and also permits the court to order the forfeiture or destruction of such equipment where a person is convicted of an offence involving the use of a metal detector under the National Monuments legislation.

HISTORIC AND NATIONAL MONUMENTS

2–42 The National Monuments Acts 1930–2014 give varying forms of protection to historic[67] and national[68] monuments,[69] including restrictions on altering them or damaging them. National monuments may be compulsorily

---

[65] See now the Architectural Heritage (National Inventory) and Historic Monuments (Miscellaneous Provisions) Act 1999.
[66] [1996] I.L.R.M. 194.
[67] National Monuments (Amendment) Act 1987 s.2.
[68] National Monuments Act 1930 s.2. The definition includes every monument in Saorstát Éireann to which the Ancient Monuments Protection Act 1882 applied immediately before the passing of the 1930 Act. Newgrange, Knowth and Dowth are scheduled in the 1882 Act together with several other sites in Ireland.
[69] "Monument" is defined by s.2 of the 1930 Act, as amended by s.11 of the 1987 Act.

acquired,[70] but historic monuments and national monuments which have not
been so acquired are protected, although the fee simple or other interest in
the land on or in which they are located remains vested in a private owner.
There is some doubt about who decides what counts as a national monument.
The term "monument" is extensively defined in s.2 of the National Monuments
Act 1930.[71] Section 2 declares that a national monument is one "the preservation of which is a matter of national importance by reason of the historical,
architectural, traditional, artistic, or archaeological interest attaching thereto",
but does not clarify who is to make a judgement as to who should decide that
a particular monument's preservation is of national importance. The operation
of the legislation was extensively considered by Barrett J. in *Moore v Minister
for Arts, Heritage and the Gaeltacht*,[72] in which the court held that a number
of streets in the Moore Street area of Dublin were a national monument on
the basis of their being the site of the surrender of the GPO garrison during
the 1916 Rising. The Court of Appeal reversed this decision and held that the
courts have no power to declare an area to be a national monument.[73] Hogan
J. held that the designation of a national monument is "at its heart a symbolic
choice amounting, in effect, to a statement by the State as to the versions of
history, architecture and the arts we choose to venerate as part of our official
narrative".[74] He went on to hold that the courts have no "freestanding" power
to make a declaration as to the existence of a national monument, although
there is a power to review the actions of the executive in this sphere against the
ordinary standards of judicial review, such as rationality, vires, etc.[75]

2–43 One way of viewing such provisions is to see them as qualifications or
reductions of private property rights which otherwise rightfully belong to the
owners of the land and which therefore require compensation for their loss.
Another view is that historic and national monuments are a more general form
of property, of a national, communal and cultural character, and the detailed
provisions of the law in this sphere serve to reconcile the two forms of property.
On this basis, there is no reduction from an assumed prior and all-pervasive
private property right and therefore no necessary right to compensation. As set
out in the previous chapter, the Supreme Court in *O'Callaghan v Commissioners of Public Works*[76] seems to have adopted the latter view.

---

[70] National Monuments Act 1930 s.11, as amended by s.6 of the 1987 Act.
[71] As inserted by s.11 of the National Monuments (Amendment) Act 1987 Act.
[72] [2016] IEHC 150 at paras 110–143, 163–167, and 395.
[73] [2018] IECA 28.
[74] [2018] IECA 28 at para.54.
[75] [2018] IECA 28 at paras 59–61.
[76] [1985] I.L.R.M. 364.

HORIZONTAL LAYERS

2–44 Freehold land can be held in separate horizontal layers, each one being a separate fee simple estate.[77] These are known to lawyers as "flying freeholds". The definition of land in s.3 of the LCLRA 2009 makes clear that Irish law will recognise a flying freehold by expressly including vertical and horizontal divisions of the airspace above land within the definition. Even prior to the LCLRA 2009, the Irish courts had recognised the possibility of such an arrangement.[78] An obvious case where one might expect to find such freeholds in practice would be apartment blocks.[79]

2–45 Historically there have been some difficulties with the concept of a flying freehold, though as Gray and Gray put it, the difficulties have "always been practical rather than conceptual".[80] Flying freeholds require rights of support, maintenance and repair which need to be imposed on the layers below. There is a common law right of support, though this is confined to support for land in its natural state.[81] Legal *easements* of support could be granted, but they would be ineffective without positive covenants of maintenance and support, the burden of which would have to bind the owner for the time being of the flat below and be enforceable by the owner for the time being of the flat above. Historically it was difficult to ensure that such a freehold covenant was binding on future purchasers of the land. The LCLRA 2009 has attempted to resolve some of these problems by making it easier to enforce such covenants.

2–46 In other jurisdictions, special statutory regimes have been introduced to deal with the problems associated with freehold title in different strata. In England and Wales, the Commonhold and Leasehold Reform Act 2002 permits each unit-holder within an apartment block to take freehold ownership of his or her own unit. Each unit is also subject to a commonhold community statement which sets out standard rights and obligations which are binding on each unit-holder and his or her successors in title. Similar schemes have been

---

[77] *Iredale v Loudon* (1908) 40 S.C.R. 313; *Doe d Freeland v Burt* (1787) 1 Term 701; *Evans and Finch's Case* (1637) Cro. Car. 473, 79 E.R. 1009.

[78] *O'Gorman v JES Holdings Ltd* [2005] IEHC 168.

[79] See *Metropolitan Properties Ltd v O'Brien* [1995] 2 I.L.R.M. 383; E.H. Bodkin, "Rights of Support for Buildings and Flats" [1962] 26 Conv. (NS) 210; J. Leyser, "Ownership of Flats: Comparative Study" (1958) 7 I.C.L.Q. 31; S.M. Tolson, "Land Without Earth: Freehold Flats in English Law" [1950] 14 Conv. (NS) 350; E.H. Scamell, "Legal Aspects of Flat Schemes" (1961) 14 Curr. L.P. 161; *Sturge v Hackett* [1962] 3 All E.R. 166; *Gatehouse v Vise* [1957] 2 All E.R. 183; *Penn v Gatenex* [1958] 1 All E.R. 712; *Re Wonderland Cleethorpes* [1963] 2 All E.R. 775; *Reilly v Booth* (1890) 44 Ch. D. 12; *Harris v Ryding* (1839) 5 M. & W. 60; *Yorkshire Insurance v Clayton* (1881) 8 Q.B.D. 421.

[80] Gray and Gray, *Elements of Land Law* (2009), para.1.2.19.

[81] *State (McGuinness) v Maguire* [1967] I.R. 348; *Latimer v Official Co-operative Society* (1885) 16 L.R. Ir. 305. Note that a similar rule laid down in *Dalton v Angus & Co* (1881) 6 App. Cas. 740 and upon which *Latimer* is based has been abandoned in Singapore: *Xpress Print Pte Ltd v Monocrafts Pte Ltd* [2000] 3 S.L.R. 545.

introduced in other common law jurisdictions,[82] and some have argued for the introduction of such a scheme in Ireland.[83]

2–47 Because of the perceived difficulties in creating layers of freehold, the practice in Ireland has been to utilise very long leases to arrange landholding in multi-unit residential developments. Under this approach, the freehold in the apartment building together with its common areas, lifts, roof, etc. is vested in a management company. Individual units are then leased on a long term (500 or 999 years). The leaseholders then become members of the management company. A long lease of this nature is, for all practical purposes, very similar to freehold ownership. In 2008, the Law Reform Commission considered the introduction of commonhold-type legislation into Ireland.[84] It rejected its introduction, arguing that there was little demand from the market place for such legislation; instead, it recommended the introduction of a more limited range of reforms which have been partially implemented by the Multi-Unit Developments Act 2011.[85]

MULTI-UNIT DEVELOPMENTS

2–48 The Multi-Unit Developments Act 2011 applies to land upon which there stands erected a building or series of buildings divided into units of which at least five are intended for residential use. The Act also provides for a less onerous scheme which applies to developments consisting of between two and five residential units. The Act was designed to overcome practical difficulties which had emerged in the completion and conveyancing of multi-unit development projects, especially apartment blocks. In a 2008 report, the Law Reform Commission noted that there had been difficulties with developers maintaining control over property management companies well after completion, and with delays in transferring title to common areas to the management company. At the same time, the Commission noted, there were practical difficulties with the calculation and collection of service charges.[86]

2–49 Section 3 of the Act prevents the sale of units in a multi-unit development before:

---

82 Strata Title Act 1973 (New South Wales); Unit Titles Act 2010 (New Zealand); Land Titles (Strata) Act (Singapore).

83 U. Woods, "Commonhold: An Option for Ireland?" (2003) 38 Ir. Jur. 285.

84 Law Reform Commission, *Consultation Paper on Multi-Unit Developments* (LRC CP 42-2006), para.10.14; *Report on Multi-Unit Developments* (LRC 90-2008), para.6.13.

85 For a critical assessment of the Multi-Unit Developments Act 2011's implementation of the Law Reform Commission's Report, see J. McCarthy, "The Multi-Unit Developments Act 2011: Are We Still Stuck in the MUD?" (2011) 16 C.P.L.J. 8.

86 Law Reform Commission, *Report on Multi-Unit Developments* (LRC 90-2008), para.2.03.

(a)   an owner's management company (OMC) has been established at the developer's expense;

(b)   legal ownership of the common areas has been transferred to the OMC;

(c)   a certificate has been obtained from a qualified person that the development has been constructed in compliance with the fire safety certificate issued under the Building Control Acts 1990 and 2007; and

(d)   a written contract has been entered into between the OMC and the developer providing for the completion of the development.

2–50 Section 3(7) provides that the transfer of ownership "reserves the beneficial interest" to the transferee and that this includes the interest of any mortgagee or charge holder over the land concerned. Upon completion of the development, s.11 requires the holders of such beneficial interests to make a statutory declaration "for the benefit of the owners' management company that the beneficial interest concerned stands transferred to the owners' management company concerned". The effect of the statutory declaration is stated to be that "the beneficial interest and legal interest stand merged."[87] Section 11 is oddly drafted. Interests in land are normally conveyed by deed rather than by sworn documents, and it is not readily apparent why a statutory declaration is used in this context. Even more strangely, the Act makes no provision for the registration of such a declaration with the Registry of Deeds in the case of unregistered land.[88] Section 7 makes it clear that the transfer of ownership of the common areas of the OMC does not relieve the developer of its obligations to complete the development in compliance with planning permission or the Building Control Acts 1990 and 2007.

2–51 The Act makes provision for the governance of OMCs, including a prohibition on life directorships and a requirement that voting rights within the company be structured such that one vote attaches to each unit within the multi-unit development.[89] It also requires OMCs to establish a scheme of annual service charges to defray costs of maintenance, insurance and repair of the common areas and a sinking fund to fund refurbishment, improvement and other non-recurring costs related to the development as a whole.[90] Section 23 permits an OMC to develop (with the approval of its members) a scheme of "house rules" which are aimed at advancing the peaceful enjoyment of the development by its owners and occupiers and which make equitable provision for balancing the rights of occupiers and unit owners. Under s.23, the house rules are binding on unit owners and their tenants, as well as employees, servants and licensees of owners and tenants, and the OMC may recover the reasonable cost of remedying a breach of the house rules from any such person in breach of them.

---

[87]   Multi-Unit Developments Act 2011 s.11(1). The making of the declaration requires the consent of any mortgagee or charge holder but such consent may not be unreasonably withheld.

[88]   In the context of registered land, these "beneficial" interests are presumably protectable as cautions or inhibitions.

[89]   Multi-Unit Developments Act 2011 ss.14–17.

[90]   Multi-Unit Developments Act 2011 ss.18–22.

FORESHORE

2–52 The foreshore is land between the high and low water marks which is intermittently covered by the tide. Under Art.10 of the Constitution and the Foreshore Act 1933,[91] ownership of the foreshore, i.e. land lying between the ordinary or neap tides,[92] is vested in the State.[93] The State may grant leases or licences to individuals to use the foreshore.[94] It may also serve on any person a notice prohibiting the removal of beach material.[95] Individuals may acquire rights over the foreshore against the State by adverse possession for 60 years.[96]

2–53 Seaweed between the high and low water mark drifting and ungathered is not the property of the owner of the foreshore. As such, the gathering of such seaweed is not theft.[97] It seems that the seaweed must be drifting in the sea and that the right is part of a more general public right to fish and gather other things from the sea.[98] The right to all minerals under the foreshore is vested in the State.[99]

WATER RIGHTS

2–54 An owner of land through which water flows is known as a riparian owner. Water itself is generally regarded as being incapable of direct ownership,[100] and Gray and Gray have described water as "a matter of some doctrinal embarrassment".[101] Where an owner of land owns one bank of a river, the owner's riparian rights are presumed to extend to the centre of the

---

[91] See also the Foreshore (Amendment) Act 1992, and S. Dodd, "Development on the Foreshore" (2006) 13 I.P.E.L.J. 63.

[92] *O'Sullivan v Aquaculture Licences Appeal Board* [2001] 1 I.R. 646 (land covered by the spring tides and high spring tides did not belong to the State).

[93] At common law, it was normally vested in the Crown: *Blundell v Catterall* (1821) 5 B. & Ald. 268.

[94] See Foreshore Act 1933 s.3 and Fisheries (Consolidation) Act 1959. Applicants for a foreshore licence must furnish an environmental impact statement—see Foreshore Act 1933 s.19 and Foreshore Act 1933 s.19A; *Cobh Fishermen's Association Ltd v Minister for the Marine and Natural Resources*, unreported, High Court, O'Sullivan J., 29 August 1997. In respect of aquaculture licences see Fisheries (Amendment) Act 1997 and Fisheries and Foreshore (Amendment) Act 1998. Foreshore leases are subject to forfeiture: *Minister for Communications, Marine and Natural Resources v Figary Water Sports Development Co Ltd* [2015] IESC 74; though the Minister must exercise constitutional justice in exercising the right of forfeiture: see *Madden v Minister for the Marine* [1993] I.L.R.M. 436 (HC), [1997] 1 I.L.R.M. 136 (SC).

[95] Foreshore Act 1933 s.7, as amended by Foreshore (Amendment) Act 1992 s.4.

[96] Statute of Limitations 1957 s.13(1)(b); *Attorney General v McIlwaine* (1939) 73 I.L.T.R. 104.

[97] *The Queen v Clinton* (1869) I.R. 4 C.L. 6. But see *Brew v Haren* (1878) I.R. 11 C.L. 198, affirming (1875) I.R. 9 C.L. 29, in which the court held it was bound by *Clinton* but held that a person taking seaweed away is liable in tort. This seems doubtful.

[98] *Brew v Haren* (1877) I.R. 11 C.L. 198 at 201–202 per Lawson J.

[99] Foreshore Act 1933 s.2(1), as amended by Minerals Development Act 1940 s.55(d). See also the Foreshore (Amendment) Act 1992.

[100] *Thames Heliport v Tower Hamlets LBC* (1997) 74 P. & C.R. 164 at 177.

[101] Gray and Gray, *Elements of Land Law* (2009), para.1.2.86.

river.[102] A riparian owner has no absolute right to the water flowing in a defined channel,[103] but has rights of user set out below. There is no common law right to water percolating through the ground and not in a defined channel,[104] and there is no right in A to prevent an adjoining owner, B, drawing-off percolating water in such a way as to reduce that available for A.[105]

Fishing

2–55 A riparian owner has the right to fish in the water, subject to private fishing rights which may exist as *profits à prendre* or in conjunction with ownership of the river bed.[106] The public has no right to fish except in tidal waters.[107]

Flow

2–56 The riparian owner may sue if the stream or river is diverted or dammed-up,[108] but at common law does not have an unrestricted right to draw-off water.[109] A riparian owner has a right to the flow of water through the land unaltered in quality and quantity, subject to the rights of user of riparian owners upstream, and is bound by a corresponding obligation to riparian owners downstream. Obstruction of the flow of water is actionable *per se* by a riparian owner.[110] The rights of user are as follows[111]:

Ordinary Use

2–57 The riparian owner has the right to use water necessary for ordinary purposes connected with the riparian tenement, even though this exhausts the stream. Ordinary purposes include watering cattle, or domestic water supply. Whether they include water for manufacturing purposes is unclear. One important limitation is that the use must be connected with the tenement and not to the advantage of other land nearby. In *McCartney v Londonderry & Lough Swilly Railway Co*,[112] a railway company sought to extract water to be stored in tanks beside the line from which locomotives could refill their boilers. It was held that this was an illegal use to the extent that the water would be used to fill tanks not on the riparian tenement itself.

---

[102] *Tennent v Clancy* [1987] I.R. 15.

[103] *Thompson v Horner* [1927] N.I. 191.

[104] *Black v Ballymena Township Commissioners* (1886) 17 L.R. Ir. 459.

[105] *Chasemore v Richards* (1859) 7 H.L.C. 349.

[106] *Gannon v Walsh* [1998] 3 I.R. 245.

[107] *Pery v Thornton* (1889) 23 L.R. Ir. 402.

[108] *Massereene v Murphy* [1931] N.I. 192.

[109] *McCartney v Londonderry & Lough Swilly Railway Co* [1904] A.C. 503. For an extensive discussion of common law riparian rights, see W. Howarth and S. Jackson, *Wisdom's Law of Watercourses*, 6th edn (London: Sweet & Maxwell, 2011), Ch.3 and J. Getzler, *A History of Water Rights at Common Law* (Oxford: Oxford University Press, 2006).

[110] *Palmer v Persse* (1877) I.R. 11 Eq. 616.

[111] *Palmer v Persse* (1877) I.R. 11 Eq. 616.

[112] [1904] A.C. 503.

Extraordinary Use

2–58 The riparian owner has the right to use water necessary for extraordinary purposes connected with the riparian tenement provided the use is reasonable and the water is restored substantially undiminished in quality and quantity. Extraordinary purposes include irrigation and, in all areas, manufacturing purposes. Use in excess of the above limits can only be authorised by statute or acquired as easements.[113]

ACCRETION

2–59 Where a river adds soil to an adjoining bank, the additions of soil belong to the owner of the bank provided the process is imperceptible in its progress, i.e. as it occurs.[114] The doctrine derives from the Roman law doctrine of *alluvion*.[115] An increase is imperceptible as it occurs; it will become perceptible after a lapse of time, but this does not prevent the application of the doctrine, as Abbot C.J. pointed out in *Gifford v Yarborough*[116]:

"An accretion extremely minute, so minute as to be imperceptible even by known antecedent marks or limits at the end of four or five years, may become, by gradual increase, perceptible by such marks or limits at the end of a century, or even after forty or fifty years. ... And considering the word 'imperceptible' in this issue, as connected with the words 'slow and gradual,' we think it must be understood as expressive only of the manner of the accretion, as the other words undoubtedly are, and as meaning imperceptible in progress, not imperceptible after a long lapse of time."

2–60 This is also clearly the meaning of the Roman doctrine:

"Alluvion means latent increment, because what is added by alluvion is added so slowly that you cannot tell how much is added at any moment of time."[117]

---

[113] *Pullan v Roughfort Bleaching and Dyeing Co Ltd* (1888) 21 L.R. Ir. 73; *Hanna v Pollock* [1900] 2 I.R. 664.

[114] Sir Matthew Hale, *De Jure Maris* (London, 1746); R. Callis, *On the Statute of Sewers*, 4th edn (London: W Clarke, 1810), p.51; *Gifford v Yarborough (Lord)* (1824) 2 B. & C. 91, sub nom. *R. v Yarborough (Lord)*, affirmed by the House of Lords at (1828) 5 Bing. 163; *Attorney General v McCarthy* [1911] 2 I.R. 260; *Southern Centre of Theosophy Inc v South Australia* [1982] 1 All E.R. 283 (Privy Council); A. Lyall, "The Case of the Moveable Land" (1968) 1 E. Afr. L. Rev. 95.

[115] 2 Co Inst 1, 20–24, via *Bracton* ii. 44–45. See Callis, *On the Statute of Sewers* (1810), p.51, quoted by Blackstone, 2 Bl Comm 262.

[116] (1824) 2 B. & C. 91, sub nom. *R. v Yarborough (Lord)*, affirmed by the House of Lords: (1828) 5 Bing. 163.

[117] 2 Co Inst 1, 20.

2–61 Doubt was cast on this position in the 19th century by *Attorney General v Chambers*[118] and *Hindson v Ashby*,[119] in which the idea gained ground that if land were laid out with precise boundary marks, the doctrine would not apply, but this fallacy was based upon a misunderstanding of the Roman doctrine of *ager limitatus*, and was exposed by Maitland.[120] In *Hazlett v Prensel* the High Court of Australia acknowledged that a boundary can change by alluvion even if it were still possible to discern the old boundaries.[121]

DILUVION AND AVULSION

2–62 Diluvion is in a sense the opposite of accretion, and based on the same principle. If part of a landowner's land is gradually eroded away, and the erosion is imperceptible in its progress, the eroded land is lost to the landowner.[122]

2–63 However, if the erosion is rapid and perceptible, as where a river changes course, or a piece of land is torn off by a seasonal torrent and deposited elsewhere, there is no loss of ownership.[123] Land in these circumstances can be "moveable" property. The landowner can follow the land to its new site.[124] Similarly where a sudden addition is made to land by a natural or an artificial process, the land does not accrete to the former littoral owner.[125]

TREES

2–64 Land as property includes all trees, shrubs, bushes, hedges and flowering plants, whether cultivated or wild.[126] Such plants are part of the realty and presumptively pass on a conveyance of it.[127]

2–65 The occupier of land has the right to cut branches of trees encroaching on his or her land from that of a neighbour.[128] They can be cut without notice, if

---

[118] (1859) 4 De G. & J. 55.

[119] [1896] 2 Ch. 1 at 13.

[120] Professor Maitland explained the doctrine and exposed the fallacy: F.W. Maitland (ed.), *Select Passages from the Works of Bracton and Azo*, Publications of the Selden Society, Vol.8 (London: B. Quaritch, 1895), p.iii.

[121] (1982) 149 C.L.R. 107 at 116.

[122] *Southern Centre of Theosophy Inc v South Australia* [1982] A.C. 706 at 716.

[123] *Nebraska v Iowa* 143 US 359 (1892); A. Lyall, "The Case of the Moveable Land" (1968) 1 E. Afr. L. Rev. 95 (dry river bed became raging torrent in the wet season in Tanzania).

[124] 2 Co Inst 1, 21. Callis, *On the Statute of Sewers* (1810), p.51, quoted by Blackstone, 2 Bl Comm 262.

[125] See *Hume v Tennyson* [1987] N.I. 139 in which the court accepted that a small strip of land on the former shore line of Lough Neagh which had become uncovered as a result of public works on the lake remained the property of Shaftsbury Estate which owns the bed of the lake.

[126] *Monsanto plc v Tilly* [2000] Env. L.R. 313 (genetically modified crops).

[127] 2 Bl Comm ii. 18; *Alexander v Godley* (1857) 6 I.C.L.R. 445.

[128] *Norris v Baker* (1616) 1 Roll. 393.

they are projecting onto the occupier's side.[129] The occupier may also bring an action for an injunction and damages if the overhanging trees damage crops.[130] But there is no right of entry onto a neighbour's land to cut trees there. If roots encroach, the occupier may cut them, and there is an action in nuisance if they cause damage.[131]

2–66 The owner whose trees encroach onto a neighbour's land does not acquire title to the airspace occupied by branches after the limitation period of adverse possession (12 years). The reason is that it would be impractical. The relevant airspace would be the space the branches occupied 12 years ago, and it would be impossible to establish exactly what space was occupied by the branches at that time.[132] For the same reason, an encroaching owner does not acquire an easement by prescription after 20 years. A neighbour does not acquire property in the encroaching branches themselves or the fruit, and is liable for conversion if he or she retains them against the will of the adjoining owner.[133]

2–67 If trees overhang a road and collapse into it causing damage, then the owner of the land may be liable in negligence if he or she has failed to carry out regular inspections.[134] Trees may be the subject of a tree preservation order[135] under the Planning and Development Act 2000.

Wild Animals and Birds

2–68 Animals *ferae naturae* (of a wild nature) do not belong to anyone so long as they remain free.[136] Once they are tamed and confined,[137] captured or killed, they become personal property, and the same is true of birds, fish and even reptiles and insects, although the meaning of "confinement" seems to vary subtly in the case of birds or bees. A beekeeper has qualified property in

---

[129] *Lemmon v Webb* [1895] A.C. 1.

[130] *Smith v Giddy* [1904] 2 K.B. 448; *Crowhurst v Amersham Burial Board* (1878) 4 Ex. D. 5 (overhanging yew trees poisoned a horse).

[131] *Delaware Mansions Ltd v Westminster City Council* [2001] UKHL 55; [2002] 1 A.C. 321.

[132] *Mills v Brooker* [1919] 1 K.B. 555.

[133] *Mills v Brooker* [1919] 1 K.B. 555.

[134] *Lynch v Hetherton* [1991] I.R. 405; *Lynch v Dawson* [1946] 1 I.R. 504; *Noble v Harrison* [1926] 2 K.B. 332.

[135] Planning and Development Act 2000 s.205(1).

[136] 3 Bl Comm 391; *The Case of Swans* (1592) 7 Co. Rep. 15b at 17b; *Blades v Higgs* (1865) 11 H.L.C. 621. But as to the US, see *McKee v Gratz* 260 US 127 (1922) per Holmes J.: "The strict rule of the English common law as to entry upon a close must be taken to be mitigated by common understanding with regard to the large expanses of unenclosed and uncultivated land in many parts at least of this country. Over these it is customary to wander, shoot and fish at will until the owner sees fit to prohibit it."

[137] 2 Bl Comm 392.

bees in the hive, although they are not effectively prevented from flying-off.[138] If they swarm, the beekeeper retains property in them as long as they are in sight, and can pursue them, subject to the law of trespass.[139] If the swarm settles on the land of another, they revert to being *ferae naturae*.[140] The ownership of a hawk is based on proof of its habit of returning.[141] An owner of land has a qualified property in swans on his or her land, even if not marked, although it would be prudent to do so.[142] The owner may pursue them if they stray onto a public river.[143]

2–69 What is the position if P goes onto A's land and kills rabbits or game there? P is a trespasser, but it is P who has reduced them into possession. One might expect on the above principle, however, that they would belong to P, since he reduced them into possession. But surely a person cannot establish a title by a wrongful act? In *Blades v Higgs*,[144] an armed gang of professional poachers from London went by train to a country estate and captured a large number of rabbits, which they intended to take back to the city and sell. Game-keepers, also armed, caught up with them at a nearby railway station. They demanded the gang hand over the rabbits. The gang refused to hand them over. They said they had not stolen them because they had never been in the possession of the owner of the estate. The British House of Lords held that the "qualified property"[145] of a landowner in wild animals on his or her land means that he or she has an exclusive right to reduce them into possession.[146] Once they were reduced into possession, even by trespassers, they became the property of the landowner.[147]

2–70 A chases a rabbit from his own land on to B's land and kills it there. Who owns it? It would seem to be B. A had not reduced it into possession on his own land and it remained wild until captured on B's land. Suppose P,

---

[138] 2 Bl Comm 393. *O'Gorman v O'Gorman* [1903] 2 I.R. 573 demonstrates that the beekeeper may be liable for damage caused by swarming bees.

[139] 2 Bl Comm 393; *Kearry v Pattinson* [1939] 1 K.B. 471; G.W. Paton, "Bees and the Law" (1939–41) 2 Res Jud. 22; Gray and Gray, *Elements of Land Law* (2009), para.1.2.84.

[140] *Kearry v Pattinson* [1939] 1 K.B. 471.

[141] 2 Bl Comm 392.

[142] *The Case of Swans* (1592) 7 Co. Rep. 15b. In the UK a royal prerogative survives, which is still exercised, to mark otherwise unmarked swans on public rivers, in which case they become the property of the Crown. Presumably the State or a local authority in Ireland has the right, as any private owner, to mark swans on lakes in parks vested in a State or local authority.

[143] Proof of ownership might be difficult if they are not marked. Again, the right to pursue and recover them is subject to the law of trespass. The owner has a right of action to recover them if they stray onto private land: *The Case of Swans* (1592) 7 Co. Rep. 15b at 16a.

[144] (1865) 11 H.L.C. 621.

[145] 2 Bl Comm 391.

[146] *Hanson v Fergus Falls National Bank & Trust Co* 242 Minn. 498 (1954).

[147] *State v Mallory* 73 Ark. 236 (1904) ("special property" in fish).

a trespasser, enters A's land, and chases rabbits from A's land onto B's land and kills them there. Who owns the rabbits? Again, it would appear to be B.[148]

MINERALS

2–71 Before 1922, minerals became vested in the State primarily through the operation of the Land Purchase Acts.[149] When the Irish Land Commission acquired the fee simple from a landowner it then vested it in the tenant but reserved minerals to the State.[150] Article 11 of the 1922 Constitution provided that

"... all the lands and waters, mines and minerals, within the territory of Saorstát Éireann hitherto vested in the State, or any department thereof, or held for the public use or benefit, and also the natural resources of the same territory (including the air and all forms of potential energy), and also all royalties and franchises ... shall, from and after the date of coming into operation of this Constitution, belong to Saorstát Éireann, subject to any trusts, grants, leases or concessions then existing in respect thereof, or any valid private interest therein ...".

2–72 Article 43 of the 1937 Constitution vests in the State mines and minerals vested in the State in 1922.[151] The Minerals Development Act 1979 vests in the Minister the exclusive right to work minerals.[152] This is apparently intended to be so even where minerals are privately owned, although the statute may be vulnerable to constitutional challenge on that ground. The right to explore and exploit minerals beneath the territorial seas of the State is vested in the Minister.[153] All rights to petroleum in the State and in designated areas of the continental shelf vest in the Minister.[154] All mines of gold and silver vest in the State.[155] The extent of State ownership of minerals is unknown, but it is estimated that approximately 60–65 per cent of potential mineral resources in

---

[148] However, Holt C.J. in *Sutton v Moody* (1706) 8 Salk. 290 held that it was P, but this was explained in *Blades*, in that the property was always in the owner of a royal forest in that case.

[149] Especially the Irish Land Act 1903, the Irish Land Act 1907, the Irish Land Act 1909, the Land Act 1923 and the Minerals Development Act 1940. See also *Webb v Ireland* [1988] I.R. 353; E. Donelan, *Energy and Mineral Resources Law in Ireland* (Dublin: Round Hall, 1985), p.36.

[150] Land Act 1903 s.13(3), as amended by s.45(5) of the Land Act 1923. See Irish Land Commission (Dissolution) Act 1992 s.4 (in force from 31 March 1999 (S.I. No. 75 of 1999)); Minerals Development Act 1999 s.2 (minerals vested in Land Commission vested in State).

[151] Constitution of Ireland Art.10; Minerals Development Act 1940.

[152] Minerals Development Act 1979 s.12. The section is subject to s.14 which creates an exception where some other person was lawfully operating a mine before 15 December 1978.

[153] Constitution of Ireland Art.2.

[154] Petroleum and Other Minerals Development Act 1960 s.5(1); Continental Shelf Act 1968 s.2(1).

[155] Minerals Development Act 1940 s.5(e).

Ireland are State-owned.[156] When minerals become vested in the State or some-body else, for example by an exception or reservation in a conveyance, the subterranean area becomes severed from the rest of the land and is in separate ownership, but that does not automatically carry with it the right to access the minerals in order to remove them.[157]

---

[156] Donelan, *Energy and Mineral Resources Law in Ireland* (1985), p.36, fn.32. See also, Oireach-tas Library & Research Service, *Ireland's Mineral Exploration and Mining Policy* (25 July 2015).

[157] *Re Markham Main Colliery Ltd* (1925) 134 L.T. 253; *Bocardo SA v Star Energy UK Onshore Ltd* [2011] 1 A.C. 380.

CHAPTER 3

Possession

Possession, prima facie, is a title good against everyone who cannot prove a better title ...

— Palles C.B. in *Kennan v Murphy* (1880) 8 L.R. Ir. 285 at 293

INTRODUCTION

3–01 Possession is often spoken of as the central concept of the law of real property. Possession, rather than ownership, has been the main focus of the common law throughout its history. In part, this is a consequence of the adversarial system. Many, if not most, of the land-related cases which are heard before the courts stem from disputes over the possession of land or some part of land. A law of possession is obviously needed in order to resolve such disputes. Yet, surprisingly, the idea of possession is fraught with difficulties—the law "never worked out a completely logical and exhaustive definition of possession".[1]

THE MEANING OF POSSESSION

3–02 As with much else in real property law, the major difficulty with possession is that the term is used with different meanings in different contexts.[2] As a matter of ordinary English, to be in possession of land denotes a factual, physical condition. Possession is a state of control, of physical occupation. But mere physical control does not capture the legal concept of possession. A person may be in occupation without being in possession. In *JA Pye (Oxford) Ltd v Graham*,[3] Lord Browne-Wilkinson imagines the case of a person who is in a locked house for an evening. If he is on the premises with the permission of the owner in order to act as a caretaker, then he is in occupation though not in possession.[4] It is also possible for a person to be in possession without necessarily being in occupation of the land itself. Wonnacott gives the example of the holder of the fee simple in land which is the subject of a short-term lease.

---

[1] *United States of America v Dollfus Mieg et Cie SA and Bank of England* [1952] A.C. 582 at 605.

[2] M. Wonnacott, *Possession of Land* (Cambridge: Cambridge University Press, 2006), pp.2–14.

[3] [2003] 1 A.C. 419.

[4] [2003] 1 A.C. 419 at 435–436.

In this case the freeholder will not normally be in occupation of the premises until after the lease comes to an end. Nevertheless, such a freehold owner has a reversionary interest in the land and receives the rent and thus can be said to be in possession of some interest in the land.[5]

3–03 Wonnacott's example highlights a second point: possession is also used to denote the status of holding an interest in the land itself. In the example above, the land is physically in the possession of the tenant. This is not the end of the matter, however, for the landlord is also, in a slightly different sense, in possession of the land in that he or she is entitled to the economic profits arising from it.

FACTUAL POSSESSION

3–04 In order to be in possession of land, a person must satisfy two tests: first, he or she must acquire the requisite physical control of the land; secondly, he or she must evince an intention to possess the land. The two tests are conceptually distinct though interrelated in the sense that the intention to possess is frequently demonstrated by reference to acts of control.

Control

3–05 The degree of physical control is dependent, inter alia, on "the nature of the land and the manner in which land of that nature is commonly used or enjoyed".[6] The nature of the required possession may differ significantly according to whether the land is a dwelling or uncultivated land.[7] One common indicator of possession is control over entry to the premises,[8] and extensive fencing will usually be sufficient to demonstrate the necessary control.[9]

3–06 *Hume v Tennyson*[10] provides a good example of the control test. The plaintiff (P) was the registered owner of land on a lakeshore. The defendant (D) lived in a nearby house which he rented from P. For many years D had fished for eels in the lake using boats which were moored on P's shoreline without objection. In 1959, the lake's level was lowered by several feet as a result of flood control works carried out by public authorities. This exposed a new strip of ground which was in the ownership of a third party, T, who was the owner of the lake-bed itself. An offer was made by the public authority to both P and D to build a new quay so that both could have access to the

---

[5] Section 3(1) of the Land and Conveyancing Law Reform Act 2009 provides that possession "includes the receipt of, or the right to receive, rent and profits, if any".

[6] *Powell v McFarlane* (1977) 38 P. & C.R. 452 at 471; *McDonnell v Giblin* (1904) 23 N.Z.L.R. 660 at 662; *Newington v Windeyer* (1985) 3 N.S.W.L.R. 555 at 564A.

[7] *Mabo v Queensland (No.2)* (1992) 175 C.L.R. 1 at 213.

[8] *Dooley v Flaherty* [2014] IEHC 528.

[9] *Tower Hamlets LBC v Barrett* [2006] 1 P. & C.R. 132.

[10] [1987] N.I. 139; [1987] 2 N.I.J.B. 12.

lakeshore. P objected on the basis that the riparian rights were his alone and an amended offer was subsequently made to P only. P permitted D to erect fencing around the new quay for safety reasons and to prevent P's cattle from interfering with fishing equipment. Relations between P and D subsequently deteriorated when D attempted to carry out additional dredging work. P sought an injunction to restrain further trespass by D. D argued that P did not have the necessary possession to found such a remedy. The basis of this argument was that D had erected fencing around the relevant portion of the land. The Court of Appeal rejected the argument that D had possession of the land, holding that since P had authorised the erection of the fencing, P had retained control over access to the land.

Intention

3–07 The necessary intention is one to exclude the world at large, including the paper title owner so far as is reasonably practicable.[11] *JA Pye (Oxford) Ltd v Graham* raised a novel point on intention. In that case, a squatter claimed title to the land by means of adverse possession. The squatter conceded in evidence that he would have been prepared to pay for access to the land during the adverse possession period had he been asked to do so. The court held that this was not material to the question of whether he had the necessary intention to possess the land.[12] What is required for possession is an intention to exclude others from the enjoyment of the land, not an intention to acquire title.

3–08 The intention to possess must be an intention to possess on behalf of the person who is in physical control. In *Bula Ltd v Crowley (No.3)*,[13] the court confirmed that a person who takes physical possession with the intention that some third party be in possession of the land lacks the necessary intention.

POSSESSION AS TITLE

3–09 The notion of a single "owner" is absent from the common law system of land law. The historical reasons for this may be found in the feudal origins of the law. As will be seen, the feudal system was one in which hierarchical social relations coincided with economic relationships to land. The legal expression of these relationships was found in the doctrine of tenure and estates. Although the feudal relations have gone, land law is still marked by these basic concepts.

3–10 Although possession is a singular concept, in the sense that only one person may be in possession of an estate or interest in land at a time, the concept

---

[11] *JA Pye (Oxford) Ltd v Graham* [2003] 1 A.C. 419; *Keelgrove Properties Ltd v Shelbourne Development Ltd* [2005] IEHC 238.

[12] [2003] 1 A.C. 419 at paras 46, 60 and 78.

[13] [2003] 1 I.R. 397 (SC), approving Barr J. in *Bula Ltd v Crowley (No.3)* [2003] 1 I.L.R.M. 55 (HC) at 66–67: "There is no possession without right or authority which is the essence of 'adverse possession' within the meaning of the [Statute of Limitations 1957]."

of title is relative. Title is the proof of one's right to a particular piece of land. If ownership was an absolute concept, then there would only be one title—the true title to the land. Legal disputes over title would simply be contests as to who could prove they had the true title. But the common law does not work in this way. It knows only relative titles to land.[14]

3–11 If A sues B, claiming that B is occupying land that belongs to him, all that A needs to prove is that he has a better title to the land than B. He does not have to show that he has the best or only title to it. Equally, B cannot resist A's claim merely by showing that C has the "true title". B cannot, in general, plead *jus tertii* (the right of a third party). The second point is that, at common law, titles are based ultimately upon the proof of prior possession. This has been consistently asserted by judges in Ireland. In *Keenan v Murphy*, Palles C.B. held that "[p]ossession, prima facie, is a title good against everyone who cannot prove a better title".[15] In a famous essay on possession, Pollock and Wright took a similar approach, saying:

> "The possession of land carries with it in general, by our law ... in the absence of a better title elsewhere, the right to possess it also ... [T]he legal possession rests on a real *de facto* possession constituted by the occupier's general power and intent to exclude unauthorised interference."[16]

3–12 Title at common law is derived from possession. O is in possession of Blackacre. O is dispossessed of the land by D (for example, D fences off a portion of the land and takes possession of the fenced-off portion). The law will allow O to recover possession from D simply on the basis that O had prior possession of the land and did not voluntarily transfer it to D.[17] As with most other civil actions, O is not allowed to delay enforcing his rights indefinitely and must commence his action within the relevant limitation period. In the case of land, this will normally be 12 years from the date that D dispossesses O.[18] On the expiration of the limitation period, O's title to the land is extinguished.[19]

Before the Limitation Period Has Expired

3–13 In the example given above, O can succeed in an action against D prior to the expiration of the limitation period. But before O commences his action,

---

[14] *Perry v Clissold* [1907] A.C. 73 at 79; *Ocean Estates v Pinder* [1969] 2 A.C. 19, [1969] 2 W.L.R. 1359 (Privy Council); K. McNeil, *Common Law Aboriginal Title* (Oxford: Clarendon, 1989), Ch.2.

[15] (1880) 8 L.R. Ir. 285 at 293.

[16] F. Pollock and S. Wright, *An Essay on Possession in the Common Law* (Oxford: Clarendon Press, 1888), p.41. Endorsed by the Supreme Court in *Webb v Ireland* [1988] IR 353 at 378.

[17] *Hamilton v Marquess of Donegal* (1795) 3 Ridg. P.C. 291 at 323 (possession alone allows a person to bring an action on the case); *Hume v Tennyson* [1987] N.I. 139 (possession alone sufficient to bring trespass action).

[18] Statute of Limitations 1957 s.13(2)(a).

[19] Statute of Limitations 1957 s.24.

what right does D have in the land? The answer to this question depends to
some extent on the circumstances in which it is asked. D has no right to the
land as against O. But suppose that D is subsequently dispossessed by another
person, Z. In these circumstances, D can successfully recover the land from
Z on the basis that D has a better title to the land than Z.[20] All that D must prove
is prior possession of the land.[21] As Lefroy C.J. said in *Williams v Williams*[22]:

> "It would be sufficient to sustain the action [of trespass] if the plaintiff was
> actually in possession, or had a legal right to the possession; and that is a
> totally different thing to having a right of property."

3–14 The same is true of interests in land such as easements: mere possession
is enough to found an action against someone interfering with their exercise.[23]
Possession *is* title as against someone with a lesser title.[24] D also has an interest
in land which he can dispose of,[25] either by will or conveyance by deed if he
can find someone willing to buy it, or which will pass on D's intestacy to his
intestate successors, and D can make any other disposition which an owner can
make.[26] If D transfers his rights to Z, Z can add the period of D's possession to
his own to make up 12 years' adverse possession, and bar O's title.[27] At common law, D's possession gives him a *fee simple estate* relative to everyone
except O or a person with an even better claim to possession than O.[28]

3–15 The converse is also true. Suppose that, prior to commencing an action
in trespass against D but within the limitation period, O transfers his rights in
the land to a third party, Y. Y will now be able to recover possession against
D as O's successor in title so long as the limitation period has not expired.[29]

3–16 It also follows that neither D nor D's successor in title can defend an
action by O or O's successor in title, on the basis that a third party, X, has

---

[20] *Matson v Cook* (1838) 4 Bing. N.C. 392.

[21] *Hamilton v Marquess of Donegal* (1795) 3 Ridg. P.C. 291 at 323.

[22] (1861) 10 Ir. C.L.R. 37.

[23] *Pullan v Roughfort Bleaching & Dyeing Co Ltd* (1888) 21 L.R. Ir. 73.

[24] *Catteris v Cowper* (1812) 4 Taun. 547.

[25] *Irish Land Commission v Davies* (1891) 27 L.R. Ir. 334 at 346, citing *Asher v Whitlock* (1865)
L.R. 1 Q.B. 1.

[26] Co Litt [472], [474], [476], [477]. The principle may not operate in the criminal law of theft
and related offences: see *R. v Edwards* [1978] Crim. L.R. 49.

[27] *Clarke v Clarke* (1868) I.R. 2 C.L. 395; *Mount Carmel Investments Ltd v Peter Thurlow Ltd*
[1988] 3 All E.R. 129.

[28] *Asher v Whitlock* (1865) L.R. 1 Q.B. 1; *Allen v Roughly* (1955) 94 C.L.R. 98. Holdsworth
maintained that judges in the 19th century had begun to allow the plea of *jus tertii*: W. Holdsworth, *History of English Law* (London: Methuen, 1925), Vol.7, pp.62–69. For an alternative
view, see A.D. Hargreaves, "Terminology and Title in Ejectment" (1940) 56 L.Q.R. 376. See
also Holdsworth's reply: (1940) 56 L.Q.R. 479.

[29] This is the position at common law. But even before the limitation period has expired, equitable principles, such as proprietary estoppel, may prevent O or a person claiming through O
from recovering possession. See *McMahon v Kerry County Council* [1981] I.L.R.M. 419.

a better title than O. This is known as the rule against *jus tertii* claims.[30] The rights of a third party are irrelevant to a dispute between O and D or their successors in title.

3–17 These principles are illustrated in *Asher v Whitlock*.[31] L was dispossessed by H. H died and left his interest in the land by his will to his widow for life, or on her remarriage, to his daughter. The widow remarried. After her death, her second husband remained in possession of the land. Subsequently, the heir of H's daughter brought an action against the husband to recover the land. The action was successful. The heir had succeeded to the daughter's title, which was better than that of the second husband. L was not a party to the proceedings, and although it was not proven that L's title had been extinguished by the Statute of Limitations, this was no barrier to the heir's success. L's rights were simply irrelevant to the proceedings.

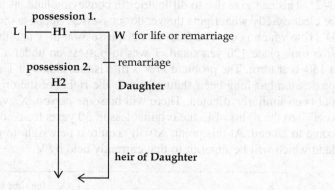

3–18 Another example can be found in *Lysaght v Royse*.[32] In that case, a lease of the land for 500 years was granted in 1703. Between 1725 and 1840, representatives of the lessee dealt with the land as though it was held in fee simple, even though the rights of the lessor were never in fact released to them. A dispute arose between two parties, both of whom claimed to be entitled to possession under a deed executed in 1770. It was held that *as between those parties* there was a presumption that a release of the freehold reversion had been executed. Such a presumption would not, however, affect a person claiming to be entitled to lessors' rights under the original lease. The case is a good example of relativity of title. Even though there was evidence that the title to the land was leasehold, rather than the freehold which the deed of 1770 purported to convey, the court could ignore this fact. All that the court was concerned with was which of the parties before it had a better right relative to the other. The absolute ownership of the land itself was irrelevant.

---

[30] *Rhatigan v Gill* [1999] 2 I.L.R.M. 427.
[31] (1865) L.R. 1 Q.B. 1.
[32] (1862) 12 Ir. Ch. R. 444.

After the Limitation Period Has Run

3–19 If O is dispossessed by D, O's title will be extinguished by the Statute of Limitations 1957 on the expiry of the relevant limitation period (usually 12 years). After the expiry of the limitation period, it might be assumed that D would have an absolute title to the land; however, this is not necessarily the case.

3–20 Suppose that T is in possession of land under a long lease from L, e.g. a lease for 150 years. D dispossesses T by taking possession and remaining in possession for a period of 12 years. The law takes the view that D has extinguished T's rights to the land but not the rights of L. Time will not begin to run against L until the original lease to T has expired and L is once again entitled to possession of the land.[33]

3–21 This can give rise to difficulties in conveying land, as it may not always be clear exactly what rights the vendor possesses. Suppose that V has inherited D's title which is derived from D's dispossession of T and that the dispossession took place 120 years ago. T was in possession under a lease from L for a 150-year term. The problem in V's title is that although T's right to recover possession has long been statute barred, the rights of the original lessor have not been similarly affected. There will be some person, X, who will have succeeded to the rights of L, the original lessor. 30 years from now, this lease will come to an end. At this point, X will acquire a new right to possession of the land which will be superior to that currently held by V.

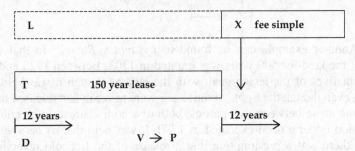

3–22 The relativity of title causes practical problems in conveyancing. While in principle it should be possible to prove a root of title dating back to a grant of land from the Crown at some date (depending on the part of the country), in practice this is very unlikely to be possible. It would be unfair on the vendor to require the production of historical records which are unlikely to be available. A requirement to produce such documentation would also pose problems for the purchaser who would require specialist historical assistance in examining documentation executed centuries ago. Section 56 of the Land and Conveyancing Law Reform Act 2009 establishes that the vendor must prove title for

---

[33] *Battelle v Pinemeadow Ltd* [2002] IEHC 120; *Perry v Woodfarm Homes Ltd* [1975] I.R. 104 at 117, 119 and 124.

a period of 15 years commencing with a good root of title. It is worth noting that this period must be shown only where the contract of sale is a so-called "open contract"; s.56(3) allows the contract to specify an alternative period, whether shorter or longer. The normal practice in Ireland has been to seek a good root of title of at least 20 years, though in recent years this has reduced to 15 years unless there is a good reason to seek an older root.[34] There is no statutory definition of a good root of title, though what is needed is typically a document which deals with the whole legal or equitable interest which is to be sold and which is not dependent for its validity on any other document and which contains nothing which would cast a doubt on the title of the disponing parties.[35] A conveyance from the Landed Estates Court will always operate as a good root of title.[36]

THE END OF RELATIVE TITLE?

3–23 In England and Wales, the Land Registration Act 2002 has effected a shift in the philosophical basis of English land law away "from empirically defined fact to officially defined entitlement, from property as a reflection of social actuality to property as a product of state-ordered or political fact."[37] In England, the orthodox view is that title to registered land, at least, is now determined by entry into the Land Registry alone. Section 58 of the Land Registration Act 2002 provides that the entry of a person's name as proprietor of a legal estate has the effect of vesting the legal estate in that person even where this result would not otherwise follow—a provision frequently referred to as resulting in the acquisition of the legal estate by "statutory magic".[38]

3–24 This represents a fundamental change in social attitudes towards land ownership and titles. Under the old, unregistered system, title was based on the objective fact of possession. Under the new system, it is divorced from the factual possession and based on a State-maintained database. Under the old system, the law was concerned with contests between private litigants and the disputes between them. Under the new universal registration system in England and Wales, the State has taken a major role in providing an authoritative

---

[34] G. Brennan and N. Casey (eds), *Conveyancing* (Oxford: Oxford University Press, 2016), para.4.7.4.1.

[35] Brennan and Casey (eds), *Conveyancing* (2016), para.4.7.4.2.

[36] *Earl of Antrim v Grey* (1875) I.R. 9 Eq. 513, which is based on the wording of s.85 of the Landed Estates Court (Ireland) Act 1858. A similar suggestion has been made in respect of vesting certificates issued under s.22 of the Landlord and Tenant (Ground Rents) (No. 2) Act 1978, but this seems unlikely and appears not to be relied upon in practice: see G. Brennan, "Vesting Certificates as Good Roots of Title: Fact or Fiction?" (1998) 3 C.P.L.J. 75.

[37] K.J. Gray and S.F. Gray, *Land Law*, 7th edn (Oxford: Oxford University Press, 2011), para.2.036.

[38] *Patel v Freddy's Ltd* [2017] EWHC 73 (Ch) at para.20; *Swift 1st Ltd v Chief Land Registrar* [2015] Ch. 602 at 623; *MacLeod v Gold Harp Properties Ltd* [2015] 1 W.L.R. 1249 at 1261.

database of titles and has established itself as the guarantor of the title of registered owners. This is justified on the ground of simplifying and reducing the cost of land transactions, which in itself is no doubt a desirable aim. But it is at a certain cost. Rather than the individual having the responsibility of protecting his or her own interests, the State has stepped in on one side of a dispute, to protect those who have shown little interest, arguably, in protecting their own interests, or have abandoned them. It is legitimate to question whether this is a proper role for the State and whether it weakens individual responsibility. Recent scholarship on the English system has questioned the extent to which the Land Registration Act 2002 has succeeded in practice in convincing judges to give full effect to title by registration in all circumstances. Goymour has documented a large number of cases in which English courts and tribunals have taken an expansive view of concepts of fraud and mistake in order to defeat the "statutory magic" of s.58.[39]

3–25 Irish law has yet to reach the stage at which it could be said that title is determined by registration, with no regard to be paid to possession. Although compulsory registration has now been extended to the whole of the country, the Registration of Title Act 1964 recognises a far broader range of qualifications on registered title than is the case with its English counterparts.

THE HISTORY OF ACTIONS TO RECOVER LAND

The forms of action we have buried, but they still rule us from their graves

— FW Maitland, *The Forms of Action at Common Law* (1910)

3–26 The early common law was not created by careful and rational thought about the policy and subject matter of its rules. Instead, the content of the law was shaped by the disputes which came before the courts which, in their turn, were deeply conditioned by the rules and procedures by which those courts organised their business.

3–27 The common law originally made a fundamental distinction between the procedures and remedies available for disputes regarding land and those regarding moveable objects. If one sued to recover moveable objects, then, even if one succeeded, the defendant was left with a choice: he or she could return the object or its equivalent in money. The law regarded money as the equivalent of the thing. It took no regard of sentimental value. It was economic value which it took to be real. When it came to land, the common law recognised that land was different in that every plot of land occupies a unique space. The common law therefore developed a distinct set of actions in which one

---

[39] A. Goymour, "Mistaken Registrations of Land: Exploding the Myth of 'Title by Registration'" (2013) 72 Camb. L.J. 617.

sued to recover land, or rather interests in land, in which the right to possess the land could be recovered.

3–28 The first and most ancient of the real actions was the writ of right. It became increasingly encrusted with procedural complications over the centuries, which increased its cost, and although this made it more attractive to lawyers, it made it less so for litigants. It also had some archaic, indeed primitive, features. Most serious of all, the defendant in the action could offer trial by battle as a means of resolving the dispute—a primitive rule which was not formally abolished until 1819.[40] In the reign of Henry II, a more rational alternative to trial by battle was introduced. This was the grand assize in which the case was tried by 12 knights of the shire and was the origin of the jury.

3–29 The writ of right had one characteristic that is still relevant to the question of possession and title. The result of the action only bound the parties to it. This is fundamental because when the procedure becomes abstracted into a concept, it can be seen that title to land is relative. A decision in a dispute between A and B, to the effect that A has title and B does not, is only binding between A and B. It does not prejudice C who may at a later time be able to prove he or she has a title superior to that of A. In other words, a decision between A and B in favour of A is only a decision that, *as between A and B*, A has a *better* title. It does not decide that A is "the owner" of the land in an absolute sense.

3–30 In order to avoid the complications of the writ of right, new forms of *possessory assizes (or actions)* were introduced in the reign of Henry II in the last quarter of the 12th century. The earliest of these was called *novel disseisin*.[41] It was based upon an allegation that the *demandant*, as the plaintiff in a real action was called, had recently been dispossessed of his or her land. All the demandant had to do was to allege a possession prior to that of the tenant and an act of dispossession, or *disseisin*, on the part of the tenant. It made no difference that the tenant was the true owner and had resorted to self-help to recover the land. Self-help was to be discouraged. It can be seen that the action had a "public law" function as well as a private law one, in that it preserved the peace. This is also seen in the rule that the possessory assizes had to be brought in the royal courts.

3–31 In novel disseisin, the plaintiff was essentially asserting that he or she had a *better right to possession* than the present tenant. The general replacement

---

[40] The Appeal of Murder Act 1819 (59 Geo III c 46) s.2, passed in response to *Ashford v Thornton* (1818) 1 B. & Ald. 423. The last reported case in which trial by battle was offered to settle a land dispute (writ of right) was *Claxton v Lilbourn* (1638) Cro. Car. 522. See A.W.B. Simpson, *A History of the Land Law*, 2nd edn (Oxford: Clarendon, 1986), p.27.

[41] The assize was provided for in Ireland in 1310 by 3 Edw II c 5 (Ir): "that there shall be certain justices assigned to take the assizes of mortdauncestor, and of novel disseisin, in all the counties of Ireland".

of the writ of right by novel disseisin as a means of vindicating rights to land therefore had as a consequence the establishment of the notion that right, or title, to land was not some absolute concept detached from factual possession, but consisted simply of a better right to possession.

3–32 Other possessory assizes were developed to protect possession in other situations and these also had effects upon the concept of title. *Mort d'ancestor* could be brought where the plaintiff had never possessed the land personally, but alleged that an ancestor had died and had been dispossessed by the defendant, the plaintiff claiming that he or she was rightfully entitled to possession having become entitled by inheritance to the title of his or her ancestor.[42] Thus, *mort d'ancestor* is the starting point of the notion that *a title*, as a right to possession, can be completely detached from any factual possession on the part of the claimant. In novel disseisin, the plaintiff was claiming that he or she ought to be put back into possession because he or she had *in fact* possessed the land before the defendant. In *mort d'ancestor*, the plaintiff claimed that he or she ought to be put into possession because he or she ought to have been in possession before the defendant. Possession as a fact and possession as title became truly distinct for the first time.

Seisin
3–33 The real actions were essentially actions to recover *seisin*. Seisin was the feudal concept of the right to possession. Only freeholders had seisin, even if the land was factually in the possession of an unfree tenant, such as a villein, or a tenant holding by an unfree tenure. It followed that only freeholders could bring the real actions.[43] Those other than freeholders, who probably constituted the bulk of the population, were left to the lord's court. Since their claim might well be against the lord, this system effectively denied them access to an impartial tribunal. Freeholders suffered from the same disability in actions over land before the assize of novel disseisin put them in the king's courts. Secondly, and this is of fundamental importance in the substantive law, the actions were tests of competing claims to seisin, and so only decided who, as between the parties to the dispute, had a better title. Seisin still remains part of the law in theory but to say today that someone is seised of land means little more than saying that no other person is in adverse possession.

Ejectment and Freeholders
3–34 The Tudor period had seen the development of the action of ejectment by which leaseholders could recover possession and without the technicalities of the freehold writs.[44]

---

[42] *Calendar of State Papers (Ireland) 1171–1251*, 344 (No. 2314); *Calendar of State Papers (Ireland) 1253*, 42, (No. 282).

[43] See *Tamworth BC v Fazeley* (1978) 77 L.G.R. 238; *Re Sirett (deceased)* [1968] 3 All E.R. 186.

[44] J.H. Baker, *An Introduction to English Legal History*, 4th edn (Oxford: Oxford University Press, 2007), p.301.

3–35 The inconvenience of the real actions led freeholders to find ways in which they might avail of the more informal procedure by which to settle the claim of title. At first it seems that freeholders would actually grant leases in order to make use of the new procedure, but the court soon allowed an action by a fictitious leaseholder against a fictitious defendant. The creation of this fictitious action has been attributed to Chief Justice Rolle during the Commonwealth.[45] The fiction was that the freehold plaintiff had granted a lease to one John Doe, "the feigned lessee", who had then been evicted by Richard Roe, the "casual ejector". In Ireland, the fictional plaintiff was sometimes referred to as the "Lessee of …", and in one case, the fictional Barnaby Rudge.[46] The "casual ejector" in Ireland sometimes went under the name of John Thrustout.

3–36 The plaintiff's solicitor began the action by sending a "declaration in ejectment" to the defendant's solicitor purporting to be an action by Doe against Thrustout, alleging that Thrustout had ejected him from the land. To this declaration was attached a letter, purporting to be from Thrustout, to the defendant, advising him that he should defend the action in Thrustout's place, otherwise both Thrustout and he would be "thrust out".[47] The freehold plaintiff was then permitted to defend the action in place of Thrustout but only if he admitted the lease, the entry of Doe and the ouster by Thrustout. The only issue at the trial was therefore whether Doe had a good title to the land and that resolved itself into whether the plaintiff, Doe's supposed landlord, had a better title than the defendant. The title of the action would be in the form *Doe [fictitious lessee] on the demise of A [the true plaintiff] v B [the true defendant]*, suing in place of Thrustout, the fictitious ejector. This was abbreviated to *Doe d A v B*. But different styles existed. It was common in Ireland to refer to the plaintiff simply as the "Lessee of A" and the defendant as the "Casual Ejector". It seems that in Ireland the fictitious action could be defended by a wider class of claimants than in England, i.e. by anyone who had a legal or equitable estate, including an equity of redemption, in the land claimed,[48] probably for the reason that they could grant a lease. One of the drawbacks of the action was that it was not available to holders of a freehold interest, such as annuitants, who had less than an estate in the land.[49] The fictitious action was abolished in 1850.[50]

---

[45] W. Holdsworth, *History of English Law*, 3rd edn (London), Vol.7, p.10; T. De Moleyns, *The Landowner's and Agent's Practical Guide*, 8th edn (Dublin: E. Ponsonby, 1899), p.432.

[46] *Barnaby Rudge, Lessee of Hull v McCarthy* (1841) 4 Ir. L.R. 157. Dickens' novel of that name was published in the same year.

[47] Forms of the documents are printed in 3 Bl Comm, App.2.

[48] *Boardman v Greer* (1824) F. & S. (Ir.) 55; *Doe d Greene v Casual Ejector* (1824) F. & S. (Ir.) 56.

[49] *Lessee of Balfour v Casual Ejector* (1786) Ver. & Scr. 98.

[50] Supreme Court (Ireland) Act 1850 (13 & 14 Vict c 18) s.1, and Supreme Court (Ireland) Act 1850 (13 & 14 Vict c 19) s.1.

Abolition of the Forms of Action

3–37 The real actions, with the exception of the writ of dower and related writs, were abolished in Ireland by the Real Property Limitation Act 1833, which also abolished the mixed actions. The Act applied to Ireland except in relation to advowsons.[51] The writ of dower and related writs were abolished by the Common Law Procedure Amendment Act Ireland 1870.[52]

3–38 The next major step was that the personal actions themselves were abolished by the Common Law Procedure Amendment Act (Ireland) 1853. Section 5 abolished the old actions, while s.6 provided that there should be two forms of personal action in future: a general form and the action of ejectment.[53] The Act provided for the actions to be begun and tried in the manner set out in the Act.[54] Thus, there remained in theory two separate forms of personal action in Ireland, but they were practically indistinguishable. One consequence of the reforms is that from 1853 onwards, a plaintiff has not had to allege any fiction or engage in technical pleadings. All he or she has to do is to show a cause of action good in substance,[55] and the courts would not strike down pleadings because they failed to state which of the two personal actions was being brought.[56] The Rules of the Superior Courts now provide that proceedings are instituted by the single form of summons.[57] Although the old forms have been abolished, the substantive law has not fundamentally been affected, so that ejectment on title, or an action to establish title to land as it might now be called, still depends on trespass and prior possession. Prior possession is itself enough to sustain an action against a wrongful dispossessor:

"In ejectment against a person who has entered forcibly without any title, evidence of possession is sufficient to entitle [the] Plaintiff to recover; and the plaintiff does not have to lose his right to recover possession by setting up a title which he fails to establish in proof."[58]

---

[51] Real Property Limitation Act (3 & 4 Will IV, c 27) s.44. For comments on the writ of assize, see *Corporation of Dublin v Herbert* (1863) 12 Ir. C.L.R. 502 at 512.
[52] *Nolan v Morgan* (1869) I.R. 4 C.L. 603; *Cranston v Scott* (1869) I.R. 4 C.L. 481.
[53] In England, the Common Law Procedure Act 1852 abolished the forms of action and replaced them with a single form of civil action. This Act did not apply to Ireland: s.236.
[54] Common Law Procedure Amendment Act (Ireland) 1853 s.6.
[55] *Leslie v Johnstone* (1861) 10 Ir. C.L.R. 83.
[56] *Leslie v Johnstone* (1861) 10 Ir. C.L.R. 83.
[57] Rules of the Superior Courts 1986 Ord.1 r.1.
[58] *Davison v Gent* (1857) 1 H. & N. 744 per Bramwell B, cited by Whiteside C.J. in *Nagle v Shea* (1875) I.R. 9 C.L. 389. "Forcibly" should be taken to mean "without consent". There is no authority in the cases for a distinction between forcible entry and non-forcible but non-consensual entry: *Doe d Harding v Cooke* (1831) 5 Moo. & Pay. 181; *Doe d Pitcher v Anderson* (1816) 1 Stark. 262. But see *Nagle v Shea* (1874) I.R. 8 C.L. 224.

3–39 Prior possession is good against all who cannot show a better title.[59] Relativity of title still prevails in the action to recover land, at least in unregistered land.

---

[59] *Doe d Hughes v Dyeball* (1829) Moo. & Mal. 346; *Catteris v Cowper* (1812) 4 Taun. 547; *Roe d Haldane v Harvey* (1769) 4 Burr. 2484; *Doe d Johnson v Baytup* (1835) 3 Ad. & E. 188.

CHAPTER 4

Estates

"For a while" is a phrase whose length can't be measured. At least by the person who's waiting.

— Haruki Murakami, *South of the Border, West of the Sun* (1999, Eng. Tr.)

4–01 Tenure concerns the terms and conditions under which someone holds land, while the doctrine of estates concerns the length or duration of the interest which a person has in land. Land in common law systems has a fourth dimension. As Lord Hoffmann put it[1]:

"[I]t is important to bear in mind that, in English law, rights of property in land are four-dimensional. They are defined not only by reference to the physical boundaries of the property but also by reference to the time for which the interest will endure."

This four-dimensional characteristic has been expressly recognised by common law judges since at least the 16th century. In *Walsingham's Case*,[2] the court expressed it as follows:

"[T]he land itself is one thing, and the estate in the land is another thing, for an estate in the land is a time in the land, or land for a time, and there are diversities of estates, which are no more than diversities of time."

4–02 Section 10 of the Land and Conveyancing Law Reform Act 2009 ("LCLRA 2009") expressly retains the doctrine of estates:

"10.—(1) The concept of an estate in land is retained and, subject to this Act, continues with the interests specified in this Part to denote the nature and extent of land ownership."

The concept of "estate", as the Explanatory Memorandum says, "remains a central feature of the modern system of land ownership. The notion of dividing ownership according to different periods of time is what makes land ownership

---

[1] *Newlon Housing Trust v Alsulaimen* [1999] 1 A.C. 313 at 317.
[2] (1573) 2 Plowd. 547.

under a common law system flexible".[3] It also points out that Art.10.1 of the Constitution refers expressly to "estates and interests" in the context of natural resources.

4–03 Time is only one aspect of estates. The length of time for which an estate endures is also related to the substantive rights an owner of an estate enjoys during that time. Thus, an estate is both a package of certain rights and the time for which one has them. The content of the package depends upon how long the estate is. For example, the holder of a life estate has more limited rights to do what he or she likes with the land than a fee simple owner. The owner of a life estate cannot generally commit *waste*, i.e. use that land in a way which will reduce its value to the person entitled to it on his or her death. But the holder of a fee simple, an estate which will pass to intestate or testate successors, is not affected by any such restrictions. A fee simple estate confers "the widest powers of enjoyment in respect of all the advantages to be derived from the land itself and from anything found upon it".[4]

4–04 Estates are also related to the concept of tenure. In most common law jurisdictions, tenure has ceased to have significant practical effects, although it remains of importance in understanding the subject. The LCLRA 2009 abolished the concept of freehold tenure, with the exception of rights relating to some fee farm grants.[5] This exception is one reason for continuing to treat freehold tenure in books such as this. Another is that leasehold tenure, which developed by analogy to freehold, retains a significant practical importance. The relationship of landlord and tenant may exist where there is a lease, i.e. a written document, but it may also exist where there is merely an oral agreement and then it is usual to speak of a tenancy.

Fee Simple

4–05 Since estates concern the duration of an interest, the different estates can be ranked according to how long they are likely to last. The largest estate known to the common law, because it is the one which can last the longest time, is the fee simple. In *Walsingham's Case*,[6] the court expressed this idea of time in relation to the fee simple:

> "[H]e who has a fee-simple in land has a time in the land without end, or the land for time without end."

---

[3] LCLRA 2009 Explanatory Memorandum, p.3.
[4] *Wik Peoples v Queensland* (1996) 187 C.L.R. 1 per Gummow J.
[5] i.e fee farm grant *non obstante* the Statute *Quia Emptores* 1290.
[6] (1573) 2 Plowd. 547.

Owners of the fee simple may come and go, but the estate is potentially infinite in duration.[7]

4–06 If A has a fee simple then when A dies (without making a will) it will pass to her intestate successors, i.e. the people designated by the Succession Act 1965 to take the property on that event. When A's intestate successor dies, the fee simple passes to that person's intestate successor, and so on, so long as the person holding the fee simple for the time being does not leave it by will or sell it.

4–07 On the other hand, A may leave her estate by will to X, in which case when X dies it will pass to X's intestate successors and so on. A may also *alienate* her estate, i.e. sell it, create leases out of it, etc. This freedom of alienation of the fee simple estate has its origin in the Statute *Quia Emptores* 1290, discussed in more detail in the chapter on tenure. At common law, the owner of a fee simple could grant lesser estates and more than one estate, or a combination of them, out of the fee simple. Where the fee simple was divided up into successive estates the situation was known as a *settlement*, and the land said to be *settled land*. The major change that the LCLRA 2009 made is that fees tail may no longer be created at all, and although life estates may still be created, they can only take effect in equity under a trust, and therefore as equitable estates. Settlements have become *trusts of land*. This change is further discussed below.

Fee Tail

4–08 The fee tail (from Law French *taillé*, or "cut down") was a lesser estate than the fee simple in a number of respects. If T was granted a fee tail it would pass on his death only to his children or, if they had died, to their children, i.e. to descendants only. These were known to the common law as *heirs of the body* and the old rules were retained by the Succession Act 1965 for the fee tail. A fee tail did not pass to cousins or aunts or other collateral relatives. Thus, a fee tail was a lesser estate because fees tail were, in general, of lesser duration than fees simple. Of course, a fee tail over plot A would not necessarily, as matters turned out, end before a fee simple over plot B, but it was, from the beginning, less likely to last as long. The purpose was to enable landowning families to keep land within their family over generations and played a central part in family settlements from the 17th to the 19th century and even beyond. For that reason, so long as the fee tail remained unchanged it was inalienable. If T had a fee tail he could not sell it, nor could he dispose of it by will. Methods were adopted by which a fee tail could be changed into a fee simple, i.e. "barred", and so enable the holder of the land to alienate it again. However, it was increasingly obvious that the old rules of descent were unacceptable as

---

[7] K.J. Gray and S.F. Gray, *Elements of Land Law*, 5th edn (Oxford: Oxford University Press, 2009), para.1.046.

discriminatory, both on age and gender grounds. In addition, fees tail were normally part of family settlements and there was little point in creating such settlements any more since the Settled Land Acts, passed in the 19th century to free the land of such restrictions, had long given statutory powers to sell the fee simple. The LCLRA 2009 therefore converts existing fee tail estates into fees simple and prohibits their creation in future.[8]

LIFE ESTATE

4–09 Even lower in the scale of estates is the life estate. Normally this exists, for example, when A holds for her own life. A modified form of life estate exists when A holds for the life of some other person, such as B. This can occur either by A conveying her life estate to B, or, rarely, by a grantor granting an estate to A for the life of B. The law regards this as a lesser form of life estate, known as an estate *pur autre vie*. In such a case, B has no interest in the land. It is just that B's life is simply used as a measure of the duration of the estate. B is known as the *cestui que vie* (Law French for "the one who lives").

4–10 Since, under the LCLRA 2009, the only *legal* (common law) estate that may now exist is "a fee simple in possession",[9] life estates must take effect in equity under a trust of land.

LEASEHOLDS

4–11 In addition to freehold estates, there are leasehold estates. At common law these were really only of two kinds: a definite period of time of any length in weeks, months or years, and periodic tenancies which are successive definite periods, such as a tenancy from week to week or from year to year, which will end when one party gives notice to the other. Lawyers often say that the difference between leasehold and freehold estates is that leasehold estates are for definite periods of time while freehold estates are for indefinite periods, i.e. human lives. But this neat distinction is not really true of periodic tenancies. Definitions are hazardous.

4–12 Section 11 of the LCLRA 2009 introduced a further complication by permitting leaseholds to be created for "a term which is uncertain".[10] Section 11 also permits leasehold estates to exist as legal estates irrespective of whether they take effect "immediately in possession or in future".[11]

---

[8] LCLRA 2009 s.13.
[9] LCLRA 2009 s.11.
[10] LCLRA 2009 s.11(3)(c).
[11] LCLRA 2009 s.11(3)(a).

HYBRID ESTATES

4–13 In most common law jurisdictions, a freehold estate implies freehold tenure. Equally, in most common law jurisdictions a leasehold estate implies leasehold tenure, or a landlord and tenant relationship. The problem in Ireland is that it is possible to have "hybrid" interests in which a person has a freehold estate but there exists a relationship of landlord and tenant (known as "lease-hold tenure" in other jurisdictions).[12] An example is a leasehold fee farm grant in which the "tenant" has the fee simple estate but must still pay a rent to a person who in theory is a "landlord". The relationship is in fact modified in such cases so that the "landlord" may not have all the remedies of an ordinary landlord, but the existence of such hybrid interests makes it difficult to define clearly the distinction between freehold and leasehold.

4–14 One of the policies behind the LCLRA 2009 was to get rid of these hybrid interests, since they do not accord with the popular view of land law—that there should be a clear distinction between freehold "ownership" and the rented sector. Section 12 prohibits their creation in future, but existing ones were left intact out of concern that an attempt to convert them wholesale might attract constitutional challenge.

THE NEW LAW OF ESTATES

4–15 The LCLRA 2009 made fundamental changes to the doctrine of estates. The changes can be seen in broad terms as adopting, in one giant leap, the radical pattern of both the English Law of Property Act 1925 and the Trusts of Land and Appointment of Trustees Act 1996, with necessary qualifications for Ireland and some unique features. The effect of the LCLRA 2009 on leaseholds will be considered later. The changes, so far as freehold estates are concerned, are as follows.

Before the LCLRA 2009
4–16 Before the LCLRA 2009 there were three freehold estates at common law: the fee simple, the fee tail and the life estate. Each had variants, and could exist as estates at common law or in equity under a trust. They could also take effect in succession, either at common law or in equity. The typical case of successive estates was under a family deed of settlement and this usually created a succession of legal estates. Successive estates, whether at common law or equity, were governed by the Settled Land Acts 1882–1890. This gave powers of management to the tenant for life and protected those entitled to estates in remainder by the appointment of trustees of the settlement (even though there were no trustees of the land).

---

[12] Or even freehold tenure, in the case of the rare survival of a *non obstante* grant.

After the LCLRA 2009

4–17 There is now only one freehold estate that can exist at common law: a "fee simple in possession".[13] The fee simple may be absolute, but "fee simple" nevertheless includes fees simple conditional subject to a right of entry or re-entry,[14] or determinable fees simple,[15] which are liable to come to an end on certain events, and fees simple subject to certain other rights.[16] This is explained further in the chapter on the fee simple. A fee tail cannot be created in future and an attempt to do so will result in a fee simple.[17] Existing fees tail are converted to fees simple.[18] All other estates, i.e. a life estate and any future estates (life estates or fees simple) take effect in equity under a new statutory form, the "trust of land".[19] The definition of trust of land includes those cases previously coming within the definition of a "settlement" for the purposes of the Settled Land Acts, but includes an additional case which previously fell outside them, namely, a *bare trust*[20] where the beneficial interest under a trust is a fee simple held by one person or several persons as co-owners.

4–18 These changes have consequences in terms of the relationship between jurisdictions. Before 2009, the land law of Ireland and that of Northern Ireland had strong similarities, in contrast to that of England and Wales, where land law had been radically reformed in 1925 and again in 1996. After 2009, land law in Ireland most closely resembles that in England and Wales.

REVERSIONS AND REMAINDERS

At Common Law

4–19 One basic principle of estates is that there is always a fee simple in relation to any land. If, therefore, someone created a fee tail, or a life estate, it is because he or she had a fee simple out of which the lesser estates were created. Since a life estate, or a fee tail, was a lesser estate than a fee simple, there remained a part of the fee simple vested in the grantor. This is known as a *reversion*.[21]

---

[13] LCLRA 2009 s.11.

[14] LCLRA 2009 s.3 defines "right of entry" as "a right to take possession of land or of its income and to retain that possession or income until some obligation is performed", and "right of re-entry" as "a right to forfeit the legal owner's estate in the land".

[15] LCLRA 2009 s.11(2). To compare English law, see Gray and Gray, *Elements of Land Law* (2009), para.3.1.35.

[16] LCLRA 2009 s.11(2). It includes fees simple subject to a power of revocation, an annuity and a right of residence in Irish law which is not an exclusive right over the whole land.

[17] LCLRA 2009 s.13(2).

[18] LCLRA 2009 s.13(3) and (4).

[19] LCLRA 2009 Pt 4.

[20] LCLRA 2009 s.18(2)(b).

[21] Co Litt 22b.

4–20 Again, the theory of estates is that a grantor can grant away *any number of estates less than a fee simple* and there still remains a part of the fee simple left over: the reversion. So in the past the grantor might grant a life estate followed by a fee tail, or a series of such legal estates to different people.

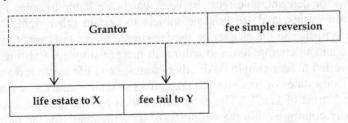

4–21 In fact, the holder of a fee simple could grant any number of lesser estates, either retaining the fee simple reversion or ending with the grant of the fee simple in remainder. In this example, when X dies, the land goes to Y. When Y dies, the land reverts to the grantor, or, since he or she may be dead, to the grantor's intestate successors, since the grantor's interest is a fee simple. In this example there is both a fee tail in remainder and a fee simple reversion.

4–22 A reversion is a single interest in land, viewed in its reified form, but is in fact a number of different rights vested in the grantor. Thus, even in its reified form, it may be useful to represent it as having two different "parts".[22]

4–23 The point can best be made using the example of a lease:

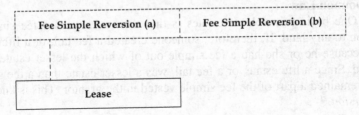

4–24 "Reversion" is sometimes used in sense (a) to mean the rights which the lessor has in relation to the lessee while the lease is running and the lessee is entitled to possession. This includes the right to rent and the benefit of whatever covenants are in the lease. In this sense, however, "reversion" is really the same thing as what, in the case of freehold, used to be called tenure, or in this example, the landlord and tenant relationship. Rent was once a service of tenure and today of the landlord/tenant relationship. The "reversion" in the correct sense (b) includes the right to possess the land after the end of the lease,[23] or to sell the reversion, in the sense of selling the right to possess the land after the lease comes to an end, and the right to create leases to take effect after the first lease.

---

[22] *Burton v Barclay* (1831) 7 Bing. 745 at 751; *Matures v Westwood* (1598) Cro. Eliz. 599.
[23] Plowden 160a; *Burton v Barclay* (1831) 7 Bing. 745.

4–25 The grantor in the past might, on the other hand, grant away the fee simple in the same grant that created a series of lesser estates. If he did, then he had parted with all his estate. This was also a consequence of *Quia Emptores* 1290. There would then have been a remainder in fee simple to take effect after the prior estates had come to an end.

Grantor $\longrightarrow$	life estate to X	fee tail to Y	fee simple to Z

4–26 In this example there is a life estate to take effect at once, known as an estate "in possession" (or in old books and reports, the "particular estate"), a fee tail to take effect in future, known as a *remainder*, and an ultimate remainder in fee simple.[24] The grantor is left with nothing. If there was a fee simple remainder, there could be no reversion. There can be no reversion after a fee simple.[25]

Under the LCLRA 2009

4–27 Legal life estates can no longer be created and fees tail cannot be created at all, but a grantor can grant one or more life estates, followed or not by a fee simple remainder, under a trust of land. In the case of a trust, the legal fee simple is held by the trustees and, so long as the grantor does not end the series of equitable estates by a grant of the fee simple, then, since the grantor has not disposed of the whole beneficial interest, there will be a *resulting trust* in fee simple for the grantor.

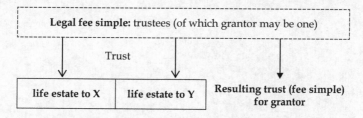

4–28 It follows that freehold remainders now exist only in equity and a freehold reversion can no longer be created.[26] The grant of a lesser estate than a fee simple will result in a trust of land, and, if the grantor does not part with the whole beneficial interest, a resulting trust. Reversions on legal *leases*, on the other hand, still occur as before.

---

[24] Co Litt 49a.

[25] Either before or after *Quia Emptores* 1290.

[26] Section 14 of the LCLRA 2009 did not convert existing leases for lives, so in the rare case where any exist, there would be a reversion in fee simple. A possibility of reverter can exist after a determinable fee simple, but that is not regarded as having the status of an estate.

4–29 A grantor can also create a trust of land with one or more life estates followed by the equitable fee simple, in which case the grantor does not retain any beneficial interest in the land.[27]

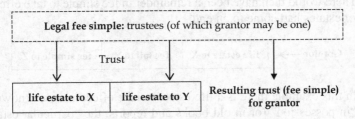

4–30 There is no resulting trust after the fee simple remainder.[28] The grantor has parted with the whole of his beneficial interest.

---

[27] Although the settler may be one of the trustees: LCLRA 2009 s.19(1)(b)(iv).
[28] In the example, after X and Y die, Z holds the beneficial fee simple giving rise to a *bare trust*, which will be discussed later in the book.

CHAPTER 5

Tenure

WHY STUDY TENURE?

5–01 One of the major theoretical changes introduced by the Land and Conveyancing Law Reform Act 2009 ("LCLRA 2009") was to abolish feudal tenure, with exceptions. Section 9(2) provides that "in so far as it survives, feudal tenure is abolished". Nevertheless, subs.(3) provides that this does not affect the alienability of the fee simple or:

"(a) the position of the State under—
  (i) the State Property Act 1954,
  (ii) section 73 of the Act of 1965,[1]
(b) the concept of an estate under section 10,[2]
(c) any fee farm grant made in derogation of the Statute Quia Emptores 1290,
(d) any surviving customary right or franchise."

5–02 It is therefore necessary to justify an extensive discussion of tenure in a book of this kind. These justifications are:

1. A full understanding of Irish land law requires a knowledge of tenure.
2. Many of the consequences of abolition as a general rule have not been considered by the courts.
3. A well-educated lawyer should know not only the law as it is, but how it came to be.
4. Land law is influenced by its history, to a greater extent than other subjects in the common law.
5. Some common law jurisdictions have retained the concept of tenure to a greater or lesser extent and increasing globalisation means that lawyers in the modern world are more likely than before to have contact with other jurisdictions.
6. The practice of land law and conveyancing will continue to require the study of old deeds and titles.
7. The study of land law, more than any other legal subject, provides insights into how a body or doctrine based on one form of society has

---

[1] Succession Act 1965 s.73 (the right of the State as ultimate intestate successor).
[2] See also LCLRA 2009 s.10(2), which retains the concept of estate and also provides that it "retains its pre-existing characteristics, but without any tenurial incidents".

been adapted incrementally to a society based on different economic and
social relationships, and this process will continue in future.

8. Knowledge is precious, regardless of whether or not it serves any immediate practical need.

The implications and the exceptions of the reform are considered in this
chapter.

INTRODUCTION TO TENURE

5–03 At common law, the concept of estate defined the duration of a person's
interest in land, while tenure (from Latin *tenere*, to hold) defined the terms
upon which land was held. The system of land law in Ireland today is based
upon the system of land tenure introduced into Ireland by the Anglo-Normans
in the 12th century. It has been transformed into a system appropriate to a
capitalist or market economy. To understand the modern law, it is therefore
necessary to appreciate the nature of this underlying change. To do that, it is
necessary to have some appreciation of the feudal economy and how it differed
from a capitalist one.

5–04 The system which was the economic basis of feudal land law was introduced in England with the Norman Conquest in 1066 and, with some modifications, in Ireland with the establishment and spread of Anglo-Norman rule—a
process of conquest which was initiated in Ireland about 100 years later by
Henry II in 1171–1172.[3] The process of conquest was far more protracted in
Ireland than in England and was not completed until the 17th century. The initial imposition in the 12th century onwards took the form of Anglo-Norman
lords being granted land already held by the indigenous population, and the
superimposition of a ruling class on top of existing communities. It was complicated by the fact that Anglo-Normans tended to become Gaelicised and to
adopt indigenous ways of life, language and loyalties. By the 17th century,
after the Protestant Reformation, a second form of the imposition of land law
and of conquest was underway. This was "plantation", a word which in Irish
history imports not so much the planting of land with crops, but the planting of
land with people. It entailed the replacement of the indigenous population of
cultivators with English and Scots peasant farmers.

THE MANOR

5–05 The manor was the basic unit of the Anglo-Norman economic system.
Typically, it would comprise the lord's fortified stockade or castle surrounded

---

[3] See W.J. Johnson, "The First Adventure of the Common Law" (1920) 36 L.Q.R. 9; F.H. Newark, "Notes on Irish Legal History" (1946–48) 7 N.I.L.Q. 121.

by the lord's own fields, or *demesne*,[4] which in turn would be surrounded by three great unenclosed fields. The serfs, or *villeins*,[5] produced their own means of subsistence on these fields. Thus, they were unlike modern wage workers who work in return for wages with which they purchase items of subsistence through the mechanism of the market.

5–06 The technology of the time did not permit putting fields under permanent cultivation. Crop rotation was practised on two of the three fields while the third lay fallow. In the next year, the fallow field would be brought under cultivation again and one of the others would lie fallow. On the fields that were cultivated in one year, the villeins cultivated strips which they distributed among themselves, often by means of *field juries* chosen from among them. Each villein would have several strips in different parts of the cultivated fields so that fertile and infertile land was to some extent equitably distributed. The system of crop rotation meant that each villein only had temporary rights over the strips and these rights would be lost when the field was left fallow.

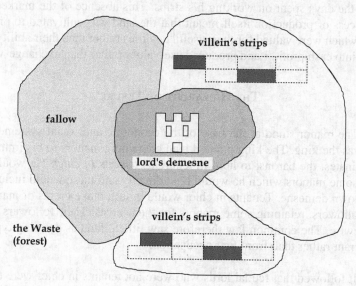

5–07 During the early period of feudalism, villeins were personally unfree and could not leave the manor to move to another one. In addition to producing their own food on the strips of the three-field system, the villeins produced food for the lord and his household by working a number of days each year

---

[4] Pronounced as "demain", having the same root as "domain", in medieval Latin, *dominium*.
[5] Oxford English Dictionary: Anglo-French, from "vill", hence, an inhabitant of a village.

on the demesne. In Ireland, unfree tenants were called *betaghs*,[6] from the Irish word *biatach*, meaning "food-provider" or "food-rent provider".[7]

5–08 The working year was thus divided into distinct periods of subsistence production and periods in which the villeins produced a surplus product which was appropriated by the lord. Within the manor, in addition to the villeins there were free tenants of the lord holding their land in one of the free tenures. Tenants who were personally free could hold land in villeinage tenure, but villeins could not hold in free tenure.

5–09 The villeins might exchange surplus products produced on their own strips in a local market, but the economic mechanism of the market did not distribute their labour-time or the product of the demesne. It was law, not the market, which distributed these, through the mechanism of the custom of the manor and the degree of respect which the lord paid to it. Custom determined the ratio of days in the year spent by the villein on working the demesne in relation to the days spent on working his strips. This absence of the market from the process of production itself meant that the land was cultivated to produce things which were valued for their useful qualities rather than their ability to be turned into cash profit. Land produced use-values rather than exchange-values.

THE HIERARCHY OF TENURE

5–10 The manor stood at the base of the economic and social system. At its apex was the king. The king granted land containing manors to his immediate subordinates, the barons, to hold in tenure as *tenants in chief*. He would also retain some manors which he would hold directly and these would include the king's own demesne. Tenants in chief would in turn make grants of manors to their followers, retaining some manors for themselves. Their followers would do likewise. The common law therefore saw title to land as deriving typically from grant rather than from first occupation.[8]

5–11 It followed that feudal lords who were not tenants in chief were tenants of some other lord higher up the system. These intermediate holders of land were called *mesne*[9] lords. The entire system was a pyramid with the king at the top, layers of tenure below him, and the manor and its free and unfree tenants

---

[6] A.J. Otway-Ruthven, *A History of Medieval Ireland* (London: Benn, 1968), pp.110–111, and A.J Otway-Ruthven, "The Native Irish and English Law in Medieval Ireland" (1950) 7 I.H.S. 1, especially 7–12.

[7] Probably from *bíathad* (food-rent), also used to mean the food provided by a *briugu* (hospitaller). See D.A. Binchy, *Críth Gablach*, Mediaeval and Modern Irish Series Vol.11 (Dublin: Stationery Office, 1941), p.76.

[8] J.E. Hogg, "The Effect of Tenure on Real Property Law" (1909) 98 L.Q.R. 178.

[9] Pronounced "mean": a variant of "mean", as in mean temperature, etc.

at the bottom. It was a maxim that there was no land which was *allodial*, i.e. without a lord.

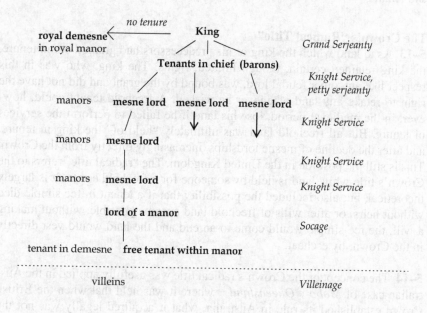

Royal Demesne

5–12 There was, however, some land that was not held in tenure, namely, land that the king held directly.[10] Neither the doctrine of estates nor the doctrine of tenure[11] applied to it. An example was *royal demesne*. The king held some manors directly, i.e. he was lord of the manor himself. The lord's demesne in such manors was therefore the king's demesne, held directly and not granted out in tenure for estates. The same might be true of royal forests, which medieval kings used for hunting deer, or any unallocated land. Land held directly by the Crown was the only case of absolute ownership in medieval land law. This form of ownership survives in the United Kingdom.[12] All other land was

---

[10] Sir Edward Coke said: "All lands owned by subjects in England are holden of some lord, the King's lands are not holden of any superior, but he is lord paramount"; cited in J.E. Hogg, "The Effect of Tenure on Real Property Law" (1909) 98 L.Q.R. 178 at 182. As Hogg points out, this is not quite the same as saying, as Blackstone did, that the king owned land allodially. See also, K. McNeil, *Common Law Aboriginal Title* (Oxford: Clarendon, 1989), Ch.3.

[11] *Stroud's Case* (1572) 3 Dyer 313a. Blackstone stated: "The king, therefore, only hath *absolutum et directum dominium*, but all subjects' land are in the nature of *feudum* or fee" (2 Bl Comm 105).

[12] The Land Registration Act 1925 (England and Wales) only provided for the registration of estates in land, freehold or leasehold. Land held directly by the Crown, the "royal demesne", not being held for an estate, could not be registered. This was commented upon by the Law Commission of England and Wales. As a result, the Land Registration Act 2002 (England and Wales) s.79(1) now provides: "Her Majesty may grant an estate in fee simple absolute in possession out of demesne land to Herself."

held in some kind of tenure with its mutual rights and obligations between lord and tenant.

The Crown's "Radical Title"

5–13 As to land which the king or his predecessors had granted out in tenure, the king retained certain, though limited, rights. The king, who was in this respect like any other feudal lord, was bound by the grant and did not have the right to retake any land whenever he wished. A freehold tenant could, however, in the medieval period, lose his land if he failed to perform the services of tenure. But all freehold land was ultimately "held of" the king in tenure, and after the decline of mesne lordships, increasingly directly from the Crown. This is still the position in the United Kingdom. The "radical title" refers to the Crown's title while land is held by someone for a freehold estate. It is largely theoretical, but also included the possibility that if a tenant in fee simple died without heirs, or after wills of freehold land became possible, without making a will, the fee simple would come to an end and the land would vest directly in the Crown, by escheat.

5–14 The concept of the Crown's radical title was usefully applied in the Australian case of *Mabo v Queensland*,[13] where it was held that when the British Crown established its rule in Australia, what it acquired legally was not the immediate beneficial ownership but only the radical title to the land, so that the pre-existing rights of the Aboriginal peoples continued until specifically extinguished.[14]

Tenure as Political Ideology

5–15 The concept of tenure was important in one other respect: it performed an ideological function. It brought some concept of unity to a society sharply and brutally divided by status and wealth. The tenants holding in free and unfree agricultural tenures actually provided the food and other necessities of life for the lords who provided none of these for themselves. But since the lords were also under obligations under their tenure to provide valuable services to their superior lords, it appeared that everyone shared a common experience of being under obligations to those higher up the system in return for their land, and this obscured the reality that the wealth of society was produced only by those at the bottom of the tenurial system.

5–16 The tenurial system had implications for the concept of property in feudal society. The king's legal position as lord in relation to his immediate tenants did not differ from other lords in relation to their tenants except for a few special privileges. The main difference, which was political and economic

---

[13] (1992) 66 A.L.J.R. 408; *Mabo v Queensland (No.2)* (1992) 175 C.L.R. 1.

[14] For analysis of *Mabo* in a broader context, see U. Secher, *Aboriginal Customary Law: A Source of Common Law Title to Land* (Oxford: Hart Publishing, 2014).

rather than legal, was that the king was the only lord in the system who was not also a tenant of someone else.

SUMMARY OF TENURES

5–17 Tenures were classified according to their legal characteristics. These classifications changed over time, but it is as well to set out a simple classification before describing each of them in detail.

1. Free Tenures:
   a) Military Tenures or Tenures in Chivalry
      i) Knight Service
      ii) Grand Serjeanty
   b) Tenures in Socage
      i) Common Socage
      ii) Petty Serjeanty
      iii) Burgage
   c) Spiritual Tenures
      i) Frankalmoin
      ii) Divine Service
2. Unfree Tenures:
   a) Villeinage
   b) Copyhold
3. Irish Laws Assimilated to Tenure:
   a) Irish Gavelkind
   b) Rundale
   c) Commonage

FREE TENURES

5–18 Tenures had two main aspects: services and incidents. Services were the obligations which the tenant was to perform, the amount of which was the subject of agreement between the original parties to the charter creating the tenure. In the case of knight service, for example, the services involved military duties. In the case of socage, the services were agricultural labour or the supply of agricultural products. Incidents were obligations attached to the tenure by the general law and whose nature depended on the type of tenure. Having chosen a particular tenure, the parties were powerless to alter the incidents. The existence of these obligations meant that voluntary agreement or contract was not the dominant legal idea in the feudal period.

Knight Service

5–19 Originally the service of this tenure was military.[15] The king made grants to tenants in chief and they in turn made grants in knight service. The tenant had to go himself and bring a number of other knights with him. If the tenant held the land for the service of going himself and taking five knights with him, then he was said to hold the land for six *knights' fees*.[16] A knight's fee was not really a measure of land since services were a matter for agreement when the tenure was created and so could vary depending on the bargain struck.[17] Raising an army in this way had disadvantages as well as advantages for the king. Ambitious lords, particularly tenants in chief, might be tempted to turn their own knights into a private army and use it against the king. The feudal state based on military tenure was an inherently unstable political form. It became the practice, therefore, to commute the service to money and the king used the money to hire mercenaries—an early example of wage labour in feudal society. The commuted payments were called *scutage*,[18] "shield money", or in Ireland, *royal service*.[19] Since the payments were fixed, inflation reduced them over time to insignificant amounts. This was one of the factors in the decline of tenure itself.

Tenant's Obligations to the Lord

5–20 The incidents of tenure varied according to the type of tenure. Those described below refer to knight service, but some were found in other tenures. *Primogeniture* was a characteristic shared by knight service, socage and the serjeanties. It was a peculiarity of Norman rule both in Ireland and England and meant that when the tenant died, the land passed to the eldest son. In knight service and socage, if there was no son but there were daughters, all the daughters inherited in a form of co-ownership called *coparcenary*.[20] *Fealty* was the personal oath to perform the services of the tenure and applied even to unfree tenure.[21] *Homage* applied only to military tenures and was the oath of loyalty

---

[15] A.W.B. Simpson, *A History of the Land Law*, 2nd edn (Oxford: Clarendon Press, 1986), pp.7–9; J.H. Baker, *An Introduction to English Legal History*, 4th edn (Oxford: Oxford University Press, 2011), Ch.13; F. Pollock and F.W. Maitland, *The History of English Law before the Time of Edward I*, 2nd edn (Cambridge: University Press, 1898), Vol.i, pp.252–282; T.F.T. Plucknett, *A Concise History of the Common Law*, 5th edn (Boston: Little Brown, 1956), pp.531–533; J.C.W. Wylie, *Irish Land Law*, 5th edn (Dublin: Bloomsbury, 2013), para.1.19.

[16] E. St J. Brooks, *Knights' Fees in Counties Wexford, Carlow and Kilkenny*, Irish Manuscripts Commission Vol.41 (Dublin: Stationery Office, 1950); A.J. Otway-Ruthven, "Knight's Fees in Kildare, Leix and Offaly" (1965) 91 J.R.S.A.I. 163; S. Harvey, "The Knight and the Knight's Fee in England" (1970) 49 P. & P. 3.

[17] Otway-Ruthven, *A History of Medieval Ireland* (1968), pp.104 and 107–108.

[18] From Latin *scutum*, shield.

[19] A. Cosgrove (ed.), *A New History of Ireland. Vol.II, Medieval Ireland, 1169–1534* (Oxford: Oxford University Press, 2008), p.442.

[20] Coparcenary was restated for Ireland in 1236 (Otway-Ruthven, *A History of Medieval Ireland* (1968), p.6) but abolished by the Succession Act 1965.

[21] Co Litt 67b.

or allegiance to the lord to follow him in time of war.[22] *Suit of court* was the obligation to attend the lord's court and take part in its proceedings.[23]

5–21 *Wardship of the tenement* was a peculiar incident of knight service,[24] and in Ireland also of socage. If a tenant died and the heir was under-age, which was 21 for males and 14 for females, the tenure was suspended and the feudal lord "dropped down" into the position of the former tenant until the heir came of age.

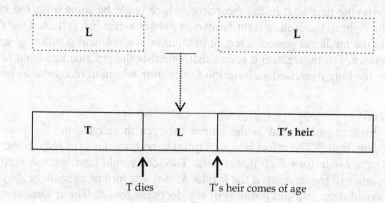

5–22 If T had *subinfeudated*, i.e. created a layer of tenure, in favour of a subtenant, L became entitled to whatever services had been reserved on the sub-tenure. When the tenant attained majority, he or she had a legal action to recover the land from the lord, known as *ousterlemain* (i.e. "to oust the hand" of the lord).

5–23 *Wardship of the body* was the lord's right to custody of the body of the person of the heir who was under-age. With it went the profitable right of marriage, i.e. the right to arrange the marriage of the minor tenant and receive payment from the other partner or their family.

5–24 *Aid* at first was a form of private taxation levied by lords when they had particular need for cash, but tenants secured a limitation on the occasions which justified aids. Magna Carta of 1215 limited them to raising a ransom if the lord was captured in war or for the expenses incurred when the lord's son became a knight or his daughter married.

---

[22] Co Litt 64b, 65a.

[23] F.W. Maitland, "Introduction" to *Select Pleas in Manorial and Other Seignorial Courts*, Publications of the Selden Society, Vol.1 (London: B. Quaritch, 1889); Pollock and Maitland, *The History of English Law* (1898), Vol.i, p.558 and following.

[24] Pollock and Maitland, *The History of English Law* (1898), Vol.i, pp.318–329; Simpson, *A History of the Land Law* (1986), pp.16–19; Plucknett, *A Concise History of the Common Law* (1956), pp.534–535.

5–25 *Relief* was payable if the heir was of full age when the former tenant died so there was no wardship. Instead, the heir had to pay a *relief*[25] before taking over the tenement. This shows that at first the heir of the deceased tenant was not entitled to the land purely by inheritance. Reliefs were often equal to one year's value of the land.[26]

5–26 *Primer seisin* applied if the land was held directly of the king. The heir was not entitled to seisin by paying a relief. An inquest had to be held to determine who the heir was. In the meantime, which could be some time, the king had the right to the land, a right known as *primer seisin*.[27] It reflected the fact that, in the medieval period, a tenant in chief held a political position of great importance. For this reason it seems that, whether the practice had legal force or not, the king exercised a discretion in deciding whom to recognise as heir.

Escheat

5–27 Escheat put an end to the tenure between the tenant and the tenant's immediate lord.[28] The effect was to terminate both the layer of tenure and the fee simple estate for which it was held. The lord would then become entitled to the seisin of the land, or, if the former tenant was lord of a tenure below, the lord would drop into the position of the deceased tenant. There were several forms of escheat of which the more important were *propter defectum sanguinis* and *propter delictum tenentis*.

Propter Defectum Sanguinis

5–28 This was escheat "due to a defect in the blood". This form of escheat occurred when a tenant died without heirs. In such a case the fee simple estate came to an end. It also meant that the layer of tenure came to an end.

---

[25] Pollock and Maitland, *The History of English Law* (1898), Vol.i, pp.307–318; Simpson, *A History of the Land Law* (1986), pp.16–17; Plucknett, *A Concise History of the Common Law* (1956), p.536.

[26] W.A. Holdsworth, *A History of English Law* (London: Methuen, 1903–1966), Vol.iii, p.60.

[27] Pollock and Maitland, *The History of English Law* (1898), Vol.i, pp.307–318; Simpson, *A History of the Land Law* (1986), pp.16–17.

[28] Simpson, *A History of the Land Law* (1986), pp.19–20; Pollock and Maitland, *The History of English Law* (1898), Vol.i, pp.351–356; Plucknett, *A Concise History of the Common Law* (1956), p.536.

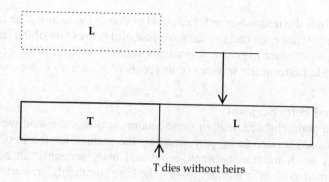

T dies without heirs

5–29 There was no *reversion* on a fee simple; there was an escheat. L would "drop down" into the position of T permanently and if T had subinfeudated, L would become entitled to whatever services had been reserved on the sub-tenure. This was to be a significant factor in the decline of tenure.

Propter Delictum Tenentis

5–30 This was escheat "due to the tenant's wrong". If the tenant committed a felony and had either been convicted and executed for it, or had fled and been outlawed, the tenant's real property escheated.[29] A felony was an offence against the king as representing public order and this was recognised in the king's entitlement to *year, day and waste*, i.e. the right to seisin and the right to commit waste for a year and a day before the tenure escheated to the lord.[30]

Forfeiture

5–31 Forfeiture was distinct from escheat and occurred if the tenant commit-ted treason. In this case the king was entitled to the land indefinitely. Treason destroyed all tenures between the tenant and the king. The king could therefore make a new grant of the land.

Lord's Obligations to the Tenant

5–32 The lord owed his tenant the duty of *warranty*. If someone brought an action against the tenant claiming a better title to the land, the tenant could *vouch* his lord *to warranty* and the lord would have to take over the defence.[31] If the claimant succeeded, i.e. he established a better title to the land than the lord, the tenant would also lose his right to the land. In such a case the tenant could enforce the warranty and his remedy was to claim land of equal value from the lord. This was the lord's duty of *exchange*. The lord could not claim

---

[29] There is one example of escheat for felony in the Irish reports: *Anonymous* (1842) 4 Ir. Eq. R. 701. The convict was transported for felony and the land vested in the Crown.

[30] Personal property could not be held in tenure and so escheated to the Crown permanently: *McDowell v Bergen* (1861) 12 Ir. C.L.R. 391.

[31] J. Williams, *Principles of the Law of Real Property*, 13th edn (London: H. Sweet, 1880), p.9.

the land from the tenant himself, i.e. could not deny the tenure. The lord had a duty of *acquittance*: he had to guarantee peaceful possession of the land by the tenant. A disturbance to possession was most likely to occur if the lord himself had failed to perform the services or incidents of his tenure to his own lord.

Grand and Petty Serjeanty

5–33 The main characteristic of these tenures was that the land was held for some personal service to be performed by the grantee for the lord.[32] At first there was no distinction between grand and petty serjeanty. In addition to lands granted to them in military tenure, the king commonly granted some land to tenants in chief for some honorary service as a reward or political bribe. The service might be to present him with a lance or a sword once a year, or to lead his army into war, which could be a dubious honour, or to act as constable of one of his castles.[33] Land was also granted to those of lower status in return for more lowly services, such as to be the king's butler or cook.

5–34 Tenants in chief and mesne lords also granted land in serjeanty, examples of service being to act as bodyguard or to preside over the manorial court.[34] In fact, serjeanty tenure was a method of providing services which came to be provided under capitalism by wage labour or salaried employment. This kind of service became known as petty serjeanty. With the development of this economic form, the petty form of serjeanty tenure tended to decline. The fact that grand serjeanty was an honorary form of tenure and that petty serjeanty tended to be replaced by wage labour meant that neither form was likely to develop into the main form of tenure in the future. In the 13th century serjeanty came to be confined to tenants in chief, in which case it was always grand serjeanty.

5–35 The legal characteristics of the tenure came to reflect this. For example, since grand serjeanty was a tenure in chief the incident of primer seisin necessarily applied to it.

5–36 Relief did not apply to grand serjeanty; after the king's primer seisin the heir entered without payment as a privilege of the tenure. Serjeanties involved a personal relationship and, in the case of grand serjeanty, a political one also. For this reason they were held to be inalienable. Probably for the same reason they were also held to be *impartible*, i.e. they could not be held

---

[32] Simpson, *A History of the Land Law* (1986), pp.9–10 and 13–14; Pollock and Maitland, *The History of English Law* (1898), Vol.i, pp.282–290.

[33] *Duke of Buckingham's Case* (1569) Dyer 285b.

[34] Manorial courts were local courts of limited jurisdiction presided over by the local lord. They dealt with minor civil and criminal matters, and were generally less formal and more accessible than the royal courts. See R. Gillespie, "A Manor Court in Seventeenth Century Ireland" (1998) 25 Ir. Ec. Soc. Hist. 81 and R. McMahon, "Manor Courts in the West of Ireland Before the Famine" in D.S. Greer and N.M. Dawson (eds), *Mysteries and Solutions in Irish Legal History* (Dublin: Four Courts Press, 2001). They were abolished by the Manor Courts Abolition (Ireland) Act 1859 (22 & 23 Vict c 14).

in co-ownership. If the tenant died leaving no sons but a number of daughters, there was no coparcenary. The eldest daughter inherited alone.

5–37 Petty serjeanty became increasingly assimilated to socage, except that one privilege of the tenure was that there was no incident of wardship of the tenement. In petty serjeanty the lord was only the personal guardian of an under-age heir. The absence of wardship of the tenement in petty serjeanty meant that the tenure would decline in the long term.

Socage

5–38 After the Norman invasion of England the Normans recognised some Anglo-Saxon peasantry as free men, as they had been before the conquest, and recognised therefore a free form of agricultural tenure.[35] This tenure was called *socage* which according to *Bracton* comes from the Norman French *soc*, meaning plough.[36]

5–39 One characteristic which was supposed to indicate the free nature of the tenure was that the services consisted of a definite amount of agricultural labour. At first socage was free tenure within a manor, but in the course of time the tendency was for the service to be commuted to money payment and as this happened the tendency also was for the tenure to spread up the feudal ladder. It was to become the residual tenure of real property law.

Relief

5–40 Reliefs were payable in socage, but they may not have been legally enforceable.

Fee Farm

5–41 Where the rent was substantial, i.e. enough to provide an income for the lord, it was known as *fee farm*. A grant of land in fee farm in Ireland is recorded in 1253.[37] Originally fee farm may have been a distinct form of tenure, but it had become assimilated to socage during the reign of Edward I. In Ireland the term is still used to denote a fee simple estate held at a rent.

Wardship of the Tenement

5–42 In England wardship in socage did not go to the lord, but to the nearest relative of the heir as guardian. He could not keep the profits.[38] In Ireland socage was militarised and lords in Ireland insisted on wardship even in socage

---

[35] Simpson, *A History of the Land Law* (1986), pp.11–14; Plucknett, *A Concise History of the Common Law* (1956), p.537.

[36] Oxford English Dictionary: *socage*. It may also refer to the duty to attend the lord's court.

[37] *Calendar of Documents, Ireland* (HMSO), p.43, item 291.

[38] At least after the Statute of Marlbridge [Marlborough] 1267, which gave an action for account when the heir became 14.

tenure. In *Comyn's Case*,[39] which was before the courts from 1277–1294 and again in 1331, the Irish practice was upheld.

Frankalmoin

5–43 Frankalmoin, meaning "free alms", was the tenure by which religious bodies held land.[40] Again, it was an extension of the concept of tenure to a situation which had little in common with the military and agricultural relationships on which the feudal system had been established. Nevertheless, the medieval church was a powerful economic institution, and frankalmoin tenure gave it something approaching absolute ownership in the land it held. Only ecclesiastic bodies could hold land in frankalmoin (monasteries, priories and convents), and individual clerics in right of their office (bishops, abbots and parish priests). The motive for making a grant in frankalmoin was charitable or religious and often the grant was made nominally to God or a saint, the idea being that the religious body merely held it on behalf of the spiritual donee. The economic purpose was to provide an income to support the poor, or the religious body itself. The service of the tenure was an obligation to pray for the soul of the grantor, but it was indefinite and not legally enforceable. If the grantor's lord did not confirm the grant, the lord retained the right to levy distress[41] on the land if the grantor failed to render his own service to the lord.

5–44 If the land was wrongfully occupied by some person, religious bodies enjoyed the privilege of a remedy in the king's court, similar to the writ of right, to recover land held in frankalmoin, called the assize of utrum.

5–45 In a variant of frankalmoin, known as *divine service*, the service was fixed as a certain number of masses a week or a year, and the obligation was enforceable in both the king's courts and the ecclesiastical courts. The existence of this variant may suggest that there was some abuse of the moral trust imposed by frankalmoin and that sometimes the services of that tenure were forgotten or neglected.

5–46 Because the service was nominal, frankalmoin tenure became a way by which religious institutions came to undermine the feudal system. What in form was a donation for charitable purposes sometimes became, in substance, a purchase of land by the religious body, the monastery or abbey, paying the "donee" a lump sum and so acquiring a virtually absolute right to the land. Frankalmoin was also free of some of the incidents of tenure which attached to other tenures.

---

[39] G.J. Hand, *English Law in Ireland 1290–1324* (Cambridge: Cambridge University Press, 1967), pp.178–185.

[40] Simpson, *A History of the Land Law* (1986), p.10.

[41] i.e. a power to enter the tenement and seize chattels and impound them until the service was rendered.

No Wardship

5–47 There was no wardship in frankalmoin, since there was no heir to inherit.

No Escheat

5–48 There was no escheat for lack of heirs for the same reason. If land was held by a corporation sole, such as the abbot of a monastery or the priest of a particular parish, and the individual cleric committed a felony, the land passed to his successor in office.

No Relief

5–49 Relief was not payable, again, because the religious body never died.

Burgage

5–50 This was the tenure by which free persons in towns or boroughs held their land.[42] As with socage, tenants held for the service of a money rent. Social relationships in the towns and cities in the Middle Ages differed considerably from that in the countryside. Work was governed less by the seasons or by the need for organised periodic activities, such as at harvest or during the division of strips in the common fields. Petty commodity production in the form of craft industry developed. Craftsmen, owning their own means of production, i.e. the tools of their trade, and often employing wage labourers, called journeymen, produced commodities for sale. The craftsmen did not provide their own subsistence as villeins did, directly in articles of consumption, but indirectly by selling the commodities they produced and then spending the money on the purchase of food. Although this was quite an "un-feudal" situation, medieval lawyers applied to it the dominant feudal legal concept of tenure by analogy. They still thought of this new economic relation in terms of the old legal concepts. Nevertheless, the concept had to be adapted to fit the greater freedom of people in the towns. Burgage tenants, for example, had a freedom not achieved by tenants in socage or knight service until the 16th century: the freedom to leave their tenement by will.

UNFREE TENURES

Villeinage

5–51 Villeinage was not only a tenure by which land was held, but also a status.[43] Villeins were bondsmen, bound to the manor in which they lived. Villeins necessarily held by unfree tenure, but freemen could hold land by villeinage tenure. Villeins did not have seisin of the land. The main service was labour in the direct form; the villein had to work two or three days a week on

---

[42] Simpson, *A History of the Land Law* (1986), pp.14–15 and 21.

[43] Simpson, *A History of the Land Law* (1986), pp.145–150; Pollock and Maitland, *The History of English Law* (1898), Vol.i, pp.356 and 383.

the lord's demesne and at times of the year such as at harvest when the needs of agriculture required a lot of work to be done, often by larger work teams, four or even six days in the week. In the time that was left, he had to produce his own subsistence on the strips on the open fields. Villeins sometimes also had to pay rent in kind to the lord as well. The essential point is that the services were uncertain. The only restriction on the lord's power to set the number of days to be worked on his demesne was the custom of the manor. If any dispute arose it could only be litigated in the lord's court. Villeins had no right to bring an action in the king's courts. The villein's unfree status meant that he had no rights against the lord; the relationship was one of power—the power of the lord over the tenant—rather than a relationship of law in which the parties had rights and duties in relation to each other.

5–52 Villein tenure changed over time and so did villeinage status. The change was accelerated in England by the epidemic of bubonic plague known as the Black Death of 1349. It has been estimated that the epidemic killed about one-third of the population but one consequence was that it strengthened the bargaining position of those who survived. The development of wage labour in new forms of employment also played a part. By the mid-15th century, the services of villeinage had been commuted to money rent and villeins had become personally free.[44]

5–53 In England there was another form of unfree tenure known as *ancient demesne*.[45] This occurred in manors held by the Crown, before the Norman conquest of England, by the Anglo-Saxon kings. The Normans recognised that tenants within these manors enjoyed certain privileges under the previous Anglo-Saxon law.[46]

5–54 No similar tenure, relating to land held from one of the kings of the four Irish traditional kingdoms, was recognised in Ireland. For one thing, large parts of the country remained unconquered until the 17th century and within those areas the indigenous law in Ireland remained untouched. The military suppression of those remaining areas in the 17th century was accompanied by an ideology which was extremely hostile to indigenous Irish culture and had as its object the extirpation of the elements of it which remained.

Copyhold
5–55 Villeinage became known as *copyhold*, indicating that the tenant held by copy of the manorial roll. A copyhold tenant could not sell the land directly,

---

[44] C. Harpum, S. Bridge and M. Dixon, *Megarry & Wade: The Law of Real Property*, 7th edn (London: Sweet & Maxwell, 2008), p.26.

[45] See, for example, *Stafford's Case* (1554) 2 Dyer 111b and *Merttens v Hill* [1901] 1 Ch. 842. Ancient demesne may have survived the 1922–25 legislation in England.

[46] One of these was access to the royal courts. While the manor was held by the king, this was logical, since the royal court was also the court of the lord of the manor, but the privilege was that access to royal courts still applied even if the king granted the manor to another lord.

but instead conveyed it by "surrender and admittance". This involved surrendering the tenure to the lord who then admitted the person nominated by the former tenant as the new tenant of the land. Once the transformation from villeinage to copyhold had taken place, the lord no longer had any power to refuse such a transfer. Nevertheless, since the transfer was recorded in the court roll, the incidents of the tenure were often preserved. One of these was *heriot*, the right of the lord to take the tenant's "best beast" at his death.[47] A few examples of copyhold occurred in Ireland at the time of the Tudor settlements[48] but the tenure became obsolete.[49]

IRISH LAWS ASSIMILATED TO TENURE

Irish Gavelkind

5–56 Under the Brehon laws, which survived in Ireland until the 17th century, there was no relationship which corresponded precisely to the Anglo-Norman concept of tenure. There were relationships involving the loan or grant of cattle which created patron/client relationships which had many similarities with tenure and similar[50] relationships in relation to land, but, since in the Gaelic communities the patrons and the clients, or lord and vassals, generally belonged to the same kinship group and claimed descent from a common ancestor, the purely "economic" relationship involving the land or cattle was mitigated and permeated by kinship ties.

5–57 The indigenous Irish laws of succession varied in a number of respects from that of the Anglo-Normans. The Anglo-Normans followed the practice of primogeniture, the land passing to the eldest son. The Irish divided land among all the sons equally. Originally the division was probably made by the father before his death. An interesting variant occurred, which ensured an equal division. The youngest son divided the land into equal parts. Then the eldest chose a piece for himself, then the second son, and so on until the youngest son took the last piece. It was thus in the youngest son's own interest to divide the land equally, for he would be left with the last piece.

---

[47] *Inchquin v Burnell* (1795) 3 Ridg. P.C. 425 (Ir. HL).

[48] R. Dunlop, "The Plantation of Munster 1584–1589" (1888) 3 Eng. Hist. Rev. 250 at 255; R. Dunlop, "The Plantation of Leix and Offaly" (1891) 6 Eng. Hist. Rev. 61.

[49] R. Dunlop, "The Plantation of Munster 1584–1589" (1888) 3 Eng. Hist. Rev. 250 at 255–256. Manorial courts did exist, although they may have dated only from the pseudo-feudal tenures of the plantation period. See *Boyd v Magee* (1849) 13 Ir. L.R. 435 (appointment of coroner and seneschals); *Costelloe v Hooks* (1848) 11 Ir. C.L.R. 294 (manor of Newry); but see *Herbert v Maclean* (1862) 12 Ir. Ch. R. 84 (covenant to attend manorial court in Merrion Square, Dublin).

[50] *Case of Gavelkind* (1605) Dav. 49; H. Pawlisch, *Sir John Davies and the Conquest of Ireland* (Cambridge: Cambridge University Press, 1985), Ch.4; *Fauconberg (Earl) v Kingsland (Viscount)* (1790) 2 Ridg. P.C. 147.

5–58 The relationship of the variant rule to the rule of division by the father is not clear. The variant form may have been a local variation, or it may have taken place if the father died without being able to make a division. It may also have tended to replace the division by the father and become the general rule since it ensured greater equity among the sons (a father might show favouritism). At any rate, it is mentioned in surviving Chancery pleadings from Westmeath-Offaly in the 1590s.[51]

5–59 "Gavelkind" was the name given by the Anglo-Normans to this Irish inheritance law which, since the Normans thought in terms of tenures, they saw as a separate tenure. It reminded them of English gavelkind—a form of landholding found in Kent and which they had recognised. The English form, like the Irish form, was probably not really a tenure in the Norman sense, but a local Anglo-Saxon form of inheritance.[52]

5–60 The Irish law differed in two other respects from the Anglo-Norman law of succession: the Irish did not permit females to inherit in the absence of males, and did not exclude the sons resulting from informal sexual relationships. In fact, the Gaelic Irish did not have a concept of illegitimacy as the Normans did. While the Gaelic system still survived, the Irish Chancery recognised "gavelkind", but by the 1590s had refused in a number of cases to recognise the exclusion of females from inheritance.[53] With the end of the Gaelic order at the end of the 16th century, the process of physical colonisation was accompanied, as it invariably was, by attacks on the culture of the indigenous population. In the *Case of Gavelkind*,[54] both the exclusion of females[55] and the inclusion of children considered illegitimate under the imposed law were used to denounce the Irish custom as barbaric and it was declared illegal.[56]

5–61 The concept of an Irish form of gavelkind was revived during the period of the Penal Laws. The "Gavelkind Act", in fact a section of a statute of Queen Anne,[57] was used to force Catholic Irish landowners to divide their land among their sons on their death. The evident purpose of this was to

---

[51] K. Nicholls, *Gaelic and Gaelicised Ireland in the Middle Ages* (Dublin: Gill and Macmillan, 1972), p.61. See also, K. Nicholls, "Some Documents on Irish Law and Custom in the Sixteenth Century" (1970) 26 An. Hib. 105 at 106.

[52] Pollock and Maitland, *The History of English Law* (1898), Vol.ii, p.269; W. Blackstone, *Blackstone's Commentaries*, 2nd edn (London: W. Maxwell, 1856), p.436.

[53] Nicholls, *Gaelic and Gaelicised Ireland in the Middle Ages* (1972), p.60.

[54] (1605) Dav. 49; Pawlisch, *Sir John Davies* (1985), Ch.4.

[55] K. Nicholls, "Some Documents on Irish Law and Custom in the Sixteenth Century" (1970) 26 An. Hib. 105 at 107; K. Nicholls, "Irishwomen and Property in the Sixteenth Century" in M. MacCurtain and M. O'Dowd (eds), *Women in Early Modern Ireland* (Edinburgh: Edinburgh University Press, 1991), p.17.

[56] As Pawlisch, *Sir John Davies* (1985), points out, the case report is a fake and was invented for propaganda purposes. The land had already been recovered by an order in equity.

[57] 2 Anne c. 6, s.10 (Ir.).

weaken the Catholic landowning class by reducing the size of holdings over a period.

Rundale

5–62 Again, this is not a tenure in the Anglo-Norman sense, but probably the survival of native Irish, i.e. Brehon law.[58] Within the areas where rundale survives, which are the Western counties of Ireland, rights of pasture are held in common by local landowners, while arable plots are held individually but periodically redistributed among them.[59]

Commonage

5–63 These are common rights to pasture only vested in local landowners. There are no arable plots associated with the tenure and this distinguishes it from rundale. Rights of commonage exist on hill or mountain pasture.[60] These commonage rights are also, somewhat confusingly, referred to as "rundale". Commonage survives today in parts of Ireland. There is provision for compulsory partition under s.24 of the Land Act 1939.[61]

INTRODUCTION OF TENURE INTO IRELAND

The Establishment of Anglo-Norman Rule

5–64 The system of tenure was introduced into Ireland in the wake of the advent of Anglo-Norman rule in Ireland in the 12th century and the expansion of Anglo-Norman control in the 13th century. The process was slower than in England due to the continued resistance by the indigenous Irish. Some of the grants made were over territory that had not in fact been conquered and such grants were in substance a licence to subdue the land granted. Grants were in knight service except where churches or monasteries had held in the land before the conquest, in which case they were recognised as holding in frankalmoin. The first grant was the entire Irish kingdom of Leinster by Henry II in 1171–1172 to Richard de Clare, known as Strongbow, who had

---

[58] See T. Yager, "What Was Rundale and Where Did it Come From?" (2002) 70 *Béaloideas* 153.
[59] There is a similar form of landholding in Scotland called *runrig*: Oxford English Dictionary, "rundale".
[60] *Re Commonage at Glennamaddoo* [1992] 1 I.R. 297; Wylie, *Irish Land Law* (2013), para.1.15.
[61] *Re Commonage at Glennamaddoo* [1992] 1 I.R. 297.

led the army which conquered it. The grant was for a service of 100 knights' fees.[62]

5–65 A special feature of the early grants in Ireland was that they were not, as had been the case in England, grants of territory which had already been conquered, but rather were authorisations to conquer and feudalise the areas concerned. Military service was nevertheless commuted to scutage at an earlier date than that in England. The labour service of betaghs was commonly commuted to money payments by the end of the 13th century.[63]

The Tudor and Stuart Period

5–66 The expansion of "feudal" tenure during this period can be attributed to a distinct historical cause: the development of capitalism in England. Money, made in commerce or money rent itself, came to be invested in agricultural production and at the same time landlords, whose income was formed from rent rather than capital, sought capitalist farmers as tenants. The picture is further complicated by the fact that the income of the "lords" appears not to have come so frequently from the services of tenure as from the incidents. By the Tudor period in England the services of tenure had declined in importance while the incidents of tenure, especially wardship in knight service, remained of value. Indeed, it was often the case that lordships were now bought more for the incidents that went with them than for the services. It was probably the case that those who had made money in commerce or finance were buying lordships as a form of speculation in the hope or expectation that a wardship would occur and thus the lordship would come to have a substantial value. The different methods by which tenure came to be introduced in this period will be set out below.

Surrender and Regrant

5–67 In the 1540s officials of Henry VIII negotiated with previously independent lords, of both Irish and Anglo-Norman descent, to surrender their lands in return for regrants in knight service at a rent. This was part of a process which led to the decline of the Gaelic order of society and the replacement of Brehon law with Anglo-Norman law.[64]

---

[62] The next large grant was of the kingdom of Meath in 1172 by Henry II to Hugh de Lacy for 50 knights' fees. In 1177 King John made grants of the kingdoms of Cork to Robert FitzStephen, and Limerick to Philip de Braose. In the 1190s the whole of Connaught was granted to William de Burgo although it had not been conquered at the time. In 1185 King John made smaller grants of land to tenants in chief in knight service in Counties Clare, Offaly, Tipperary, Limerick, Louth, Armagh, Monaghan and also the Irish kingdom of Uriel. In 1205 Hugh de Lacy was granted the entire kingdom of Ulster, which had been partly conquered and ruled as an independent lordship by John de Courcy.

[63] A.J Otway-Ruthven, "The Native Irish and English Law in Medieval Ireland" (1950) 7 I.H.S. 1 at 9.

[64] See C. Maginn, "'Surrender and Regrant' in the Historiography of Sixteenth-Century Ireland" (2007) 38(4) Sixteenth Cent. J. 955.

Plantations

5–68 The plantation process began in the reign of Phillip and Mary in the 1550s and continued until the reign of William III. It differed from the other methods in that the primary producers on the land were replaced with immigrants. In legal terms, it involved a two-stage process. First, the previous lords or occupants of the land lost their rights by forfeiture for what the English Crown and the courts considered to be treason in resisting English rule. This act of forfeiture left the title in the Crown. A royal title might also be established by escheat or through special statutes providing that landowners who were absent from Ireland for a period forfeited their rights. In the latter case this meant that those who were ineffectual in conquering an area could be replaced by those who would be more effective. Secondly, new grants were made to settlers as quasi-feudal tenants of the Crown.

5–69 The first plantation took place in Leix and Offaly. In 1557 the Irish Parliament was induced to declare lands including Leix and Offaly as belonging to Philip and Mary through forfeiture for treason. Grants were made in knight service at a money rent. The tenants were of Irish as well as English descent who had participated in the conquest of the area.

5–70 The second area was Munster. The pretext was the rebellion of the Earl of Desmond, the lands being those of the Earl and his followers. Grants were made in socage (or "fee farm") at a money rent. Each tenant was to retain some land himself as demesne and grant the rest out in freehold socage, or in leasehold tenure or on copyhold. In fact more land was leased than was granted out in other types of tenure, showing the growing importance of leasehold as expressing the increasingly commercial nature of landholding.

5–71 The largest area of plantation was, of course, Ulster.[65] The area was forfeited and regranted after the "Flight of the Earls" in 1607. Most of the land in Armagh, Cavan, Donegal, Fermanagh, Tyrone and in Coleraine was held to have been forfeited to the Crown. Most of the land was granted to English and Scottish settlers in socage at a money rent, with further sub-grants by these tenants.

Composition

5–72 This was the method used in Connaught. A commission, established in 1585, inquired into the ownership of land in the area. The commission entered into agreements with persons successfully claiming land whereby they could have their titles confirmed and the Crown relinquished its right to "cess"—a type of tax used to pay for the military government of the area. Landowners usually agreed to hold their land in knight service from the Crown. Lesser landowners were acknowledged as holding in the same tenure from higher "lords".

---

[65] See J. Bardon, *The Plantation of Ulster: British Colonisation in the North of Ireland in the Seventeenth Century* (Dublin: Gill & Macmillan, 2011).

5–73 By 1640 most land in Ireland was subject to one kind of tenure or another. The few gaps that remained were filled during the Commonwealth and in the reign of William III, through confiscations and regrants. The Williamite regrants were in socage at a money or "quit" rent.

THE CREATION OF A LAYER OF TENURE

5–74 A new tenure would come into existence when a landholder granted land to another person who would thereby become a tenant and the grantor would become a lord in relation to the new tenure. This process of creating a new layer of tenure was known as *subinfeudation*. In the 11th and 12th centuries, most people, including feudal lords, were illiterate. An agreement creating tenure was not drawn up in the form of a document but took the form of a ceremony before witnesses. This was the *feoffment* (pronounced "feffment") and it consisted of a ceremony whereby the grantor of the land presented the grantee with a clod of earth or turf cut from the plot as a symbolic gesture. It was symbolic of the transfer of seisin. Seisin was the legal concept incorporating the notion of possession, but misrepresenting it at the same time. Since land produced use-values for its lord, physical possession of the land in some sense was a necessary part of "owning property" in land. To be sure of receiving tribute payments, the lord, through subordinates, would have to have means of enforcement at hand.

5–75 The tenants themselves would have possession in an even more real sense in that they cultivated the soil. At this point, however, the law misrepresented reality because the king's courts did not recognise the possession of cultivators, i.e. the villeins, as seisin. Only freeholders had seisin and access to the king's courts. This was ensured by the system of forms of action.

5–76 In order to succeed in court a claimant had to prove that the facts of his case came within one of the recognised forms, and these generally specified that the claimant should be a freeholder. By the 13th century the feoffment was reduced to writing in a charter of feoffment. This would contain a statement of the services of the tenure which were, in amount, a matter for agreement between the grantor and the grantee. The incidents of tenure on the other hand were rights and duties which applied automatically and which depended on what type of tenure was created. The ceremony of feoffment was still performed and comprised of three acts: an act of homage, in the case of military tenures, by which the grantee swore allegiance to the lord to be loyal in time of war; an act of fealty, which was a personal oath to perform the services and applied even in unfree tenures; and an act of seisin whereby it was transferred. The ceremony, and the later evidence of it in the form of the deed,[66] was

---

[66] Such a deed, dated 1628/9, in Dublin, is reproduced in M.J. McEnery and R. Refaussé, *Christ Church Deeds* (Dublin: Four Courts Press, 2001), p.309, item 1498. It is a mortgage and the mortgagor is to "deliver seisin ... by giving a clid of earth ...".

collectively called a feoffment with livery of seisin.[67] It was the oldest conveyance known to the common law.

FORMS OF ALIENATION AND THEIR EFFECTS

Subinfeudation

5–77 The usual method of alienating, i.e. transferring an interest in land, until about 1200 was by subinfeudation. Suppose L, who held land in fee simple, granted land to T1 by knight service for an estate in fee simple. L constituted himself a lord and T1 as his freehold tenant. It can be said that while T1 held the "land" in fee simple, L held a *seignory*[68] or *lordship* in fee simple.

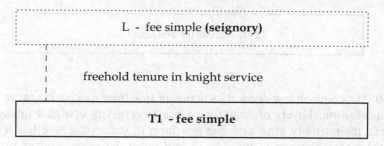

5–78 L had created a new layer of freehold tenure. L's seignory, his rights as lord of the tenure, entitled him to the services and the incidents of the tenure.

5–79 T1 in turn may have wished to grant land out to tenants in order to obtain services from them himself. Suppose T1 granted, i.e. subinfeudated, to T2 in knight service, for an estate in fee simple. A new layer of tenure was created. T1 made himself into a lord. He had created a seignory or lordship in himself. There were now three people to consider. L was still T1's lord, and he was the *lord paramount* of T2. T2 was T1's tenant, and in relation to L was a *tenant paravail*. T1 was a tenant in relation to L, but a lord in relation to T2.

---

[67] "Livery" meaning delivery.

[68] *Delacherois v Delacherois* (1859) 8 Ir. C.L.R. 1 per Pigot B. "On the other hand, a right remained in the lord (after a grant made) called a seignory consisting of services to be performed by the tenant and a right to have the land returned on the expiration of the grant ... a right afterwards called an escheat." *Burgess v Wheate* (1757–9) 1 Eden 128 at 176.

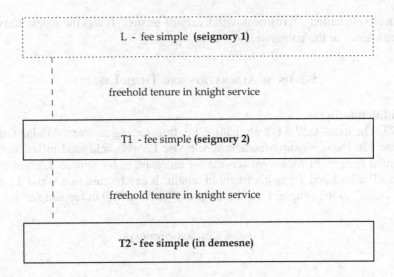

5–80 The common law derived its notion of title from relative claims regarding possession. Layers of tenure gave rise to relativity of rights in another aspect: the relativity of tenure. The new layer of tenure had no effect legally on the tenure between L and T1. T1 still owed the same services to L as before. He could not force L to accept some of the services directly from T2. Moreover, L still had his right of *distress* against the *whole* tenement which he granted to T1. L's right of distress entitled him to go onto the land and seize chattels on the land and hold them until T1 performed his service. L was entitled to seize chattels, even if the chattels in fact belonged to T2. T2 could not legally resist the lord paramount.[69] But he did have a remedy against his own lord who had failed in his obligation of acquittance owed to his tenant through the tenure between them. T2 could bring a *writ of mesne* against T1, the *mesne*, or intermediate lord.

5–81 Thus, the obligations of the superior tenure were not merely personal rights as between the parties to the tenure; they were "burdens on the land".[70] The two private individuals, T1 and T2, had made an agreement between themselves, but could not do so without involving legal relations with L who was not a party to the agreement. The relationship was quite different, therefore, from a modern contract. T2 could not enter into an agreement with T1 without being subjected to burdens already determined between T1 and L and which were enforceable against his, T2's, own property, his cattle and personal belongings. Whatever immediate lord T2 chose, there would be similar burdens created by superior tenures. In the technical language of the period, the services which a tenant owed to his own lord were *intrinsec*, i.e. inside the

---

[69] The same rule was applied to leasehold tenure by analogy: *Heawood v Bone* (1884) 13 Q.B.D. 179, until reformed by the Law of Distress Amendment Act 1908.

[70] This involves a form of reification even under feudal relations. Reification has a long history.

bargain between them and voluntarily agreed. The obligations of the superior tenure were *forinsec*, i.e. applied by "law". They appeared to be law of a general kind, like public law today, even though their origin was simply the agreement between L and T1. The relativity of tenure meant that the distinction found today between public and private law did not really exist in the medieval period.

5–82 Of equal importance, historically, was the fact that the lord paramount was incapable of determining the content of the obligations between his own tenant and any sub-tenant to whom his tenant subinfeudated. L had no power to determine the content of the bargain between T1 and T2 even though this bargain could adversely affect L, by, for example, reducing T1's ability to perform his services to L. These obligations constituted a powerful limitation on the freedom of feudal lords themselves to control the economic relations of society.

Substitution

5–83 This form became possible in the early 13th century. The grantee replaced the grantor as tenant of the grantor's lord. He would owe the same services to the lord as the grantor had done, since the layer of tenure was the same. Until the Statute *Quia Emptores* 1290, one disadvantage was that the consent of the grantor's lord was needed to the substitution.

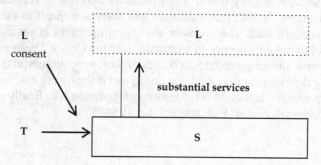

Mortmain

5–84 Mortmain was not really a single type of alienation or conveyance, but simply meant a grant in favour of a perpetual body such as a monastery or other ecclesiastical institution. The name "mortmain" was from the Norman French *morte main*, meaning "dead hand". Let us say that L has granted land to T by subinfeudation. T then decides to grant part of the land to an abbey in frankalmoin tenure by further subinfeudation. The services of frankalmoin are of no economic value. If an escheat occurred of T's tenure, then L would lose whatever valuable services could have been obtained from the part subinfeudated to the abbey. Furthermore, since the abbey was a perpetual body, feudal incidents such as relief or aid did not arise. Mortmain tended to deprive the lords and the king of revenue. It undermined feudal economic relations. Moreover, the medieval church acquired a great deal of land. As it grew in economic wealth, so it grew in political importance and came to be seen as a threat to the king's political dominance.

5–85 Mortmain was a threat to feudal political relations. However, it was open to another objection of a different kind. If land passed into the "dead hand" of a perpetual body, particularly an ecclesiastical one, it was unlikely ever to come on the market again. The land was withdrawn from the economic sphere of the market altogether. Mortmain was thus also objectionable from a market or capitalist point of view. Strong action was taken by the Statute of Mortmain 1279.[71] Under the Statute, if a tenant attempted to grant his or her tenement or part of it to a perpetual body or person, the tenure came to an end.

5–86 At this time, the king still asserted the power to grant exemptions from the operation of statutes to individuals: the "dispensing power". Hence the king began to grant licences to bodies to acquire land in mortmain despite the statute.[72] Granting licences in mortmain not only extended his patronage; it provided an additional source of income as well. It became accepted by the courts that the king had such a power.

5–87 Statutes regulating mortmain were passed from time to time and it was only in the 20th century that it was eventually abolished. This can probably be explained by the fact that mortmain was seen as a threat to the expansion of the market in land. There was in any case little point in requiring limited companies to obtain a licence in mortmain from the Crown[73] before purchasing land, because, unlike ecclesiastical bodies, if they were successful then the land was being developed, or producing a profit, and if they were not, they could be wound up and the land sold off. Mortmain legislation was finally repealed by the Mortmain (Repeal of Enactments) Act 1954.[74]

---

[71] It was made by the king on the advice of the council and transmitted to Ireland for observance here, and a version was copied into the Irish Red Book of the Exchequer: A.G. Donaldson, *The Application in Ireland of English and British Legislation made before 1801* (PhD, 2 vols (Queen's University, Belfast, 1952)); H.F. Berry (ed.), *Statutes, Ordinances and Acts of the Parliament of Ireland: King John to Henry V* (Dublin: HMSO, 1907).

[72] There are examples of the Statute being enforced in Ireland. In 1300 and again in 1349 the Prior of Louth was summoned to answer for procuring land contrary to the Statute and without a licence: M. Archdall, *Monasticon Hibernicum* (Dublin: L White, 1786), p.482.

[73] The dispensing power having been abolished by the Bill of Rights 1689, the power to grant licences in mortmain was subsequently given by statute, latterly under s.2 of the Mortmain and Charitable Uses Act 1888.

[74] Similarly, in Northern Ireland by the Mortmain (Repeals) Act 1960.

ENDING OF THE BOND OF TENURE

5–88 A layer of tenure could be destroyed or come to an end in a number of ways, some of which have already been noted.

Escheat
5–89 This has already been dealt with above.

Forfeiture for Treason
5–90 This has already been dealt with above.

Disavowal
5–91 If a tenant denied the title of his lord in legal proceedings, the tenure was destroyed.

Surrender
5–92 The tenant could surrender the land to his lord if, for example, the services were too onerous.

Mortmain
5–93 If a tenant made a grant in favour of a perpetual body without a licence from the Crown, the tenure came to an end by virtue of the Statute of Mortmain 1279.

Gift of Frankalmoin
5–94 If land granted in frankalmoin was granted away by the donee, that would defeat the purpose of the gift and be something like a fraud on the donor. It was a gift to charity and if the church did not want the land, then it was thought that it should go back to the donor or his family. The Statute of Westminster II 1285 gave the donor's heirs a right of action to recover it.

Failure to Perform Services
5–95 Originally the only remedy of the lord if the tenant failed to perform services was to levy a distress on the land. However, the tenant could render the remedy valueless by arranging in advance that there would be no distrainable goods, or none of any value, on the land. The Statute of Gloucester 1278 and the Statute of Westminster II 1285, Chapters 21 and 41, provided that if the tenant ceased to do services for two years and arranged that there should be no distrainable chattels on the land, or prevented the lord having access to them, the lord had action to recover possession. Apart from the statutory provision, the lord had no right to terminate the tenure unless there was an express forfeiture clause in the grant.

Eminent Domain?

5–96 In the United States the courts developed the doctrine of *eminent domain* which allows public, and in some cases even private, bodies to acquire land compulsorily for public purposes on payment of compensation. The supposed origin of this doctrine in Anglo-Norman feudal law is, however, without any foundation. The doctrine found its way into the law of the United States from the law of New Spain.[75] The doctrine gave more extensive or despotic power to the monarchy in New Spain than was accorded to the Crown by the common law.

THE DECLINE OF TENURE

The Effect of Subinfeudation on the Incidents

5–97 Some of the lord's incidents were unaffected by subinfeudation: suit of court, aids, relief, homage, fealty and wardship of the body. But others were affected. The incident of marriage, for example, was made less valuable since its value was related to the value of the land still held in demesne by the tenant. The effect on other incidents is considered below. The decline in the value of incidents eventually led to the decline of the feudal system.[76]

Wardship of the Tenement

5–98 If the tenant had subinfeudated some or all of his land, then when a wardship occurred, the lord would step into the shoes of the tenant and would be entitled only to such services as the tenant had reserved on the grant of the tenure with the tenant paravail.

Escheat

5–99 In the case of escheat, the same was true, except that the lord stepped permanently into the shoes of the former tenant.

Sale of Land

5–100 During the feudal period a new economic relationship developed. Land was used to produce products primarily for sale on the market. One of the earliest such products was wool. Tracts of land came to be valued for the amount of money they produced from the sale of wool and other commodities. Land came to have a money value itself. Freehold tenants wanted to sell land and realise this money value. How could they do it? Substitution was the obvious method, but it had disadvantages.

---

[75] See *United States v Castillero* 67 US 17 (1862); *Doe d Clark v Braden* 57 US 635 (1850).

[76] J.M.W. Bean, *The Decline of English Feudalism, 1215–1540* (Manchester: Manchester University Press, 1968).

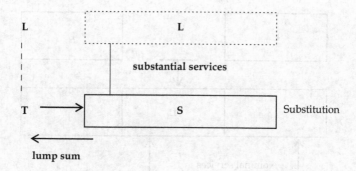

substantial services

T ——→   S   Substitution

←——

lump sum

5–101 If S paid T a lump sum for the land, he would have to take over the services due under the tenure to L. In addition, L's consent was required to the transaction between T and S. T and S were not free to contract between themselves. Further, if T sold part of the land to S, T remained liable for all the services due on the tenure unless he could get L to agree to apportion them between T and S.

5–102 Subinfeudation, the typically feudal form, was paradoxically more attractive as a vehicle for sale. By the 13th century lords had lost control over subinfeudations. The buyer and seller were free to make their own bargain.

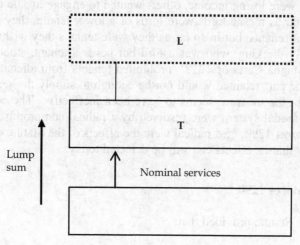

Lump
sum   Nominal services

5–103 S would agree to pay T a nominal rent such as a peppercorn each year or a rose at midsummer. Nominal services caused problems for L. Legally he was still entitled to the same services from T as before, but T might be less able to pay them. More serious was the effect on incidents. If a wardship occurred, L "dropped down" into the position of T but only became entitled legally to nominal services from S. S could keep all the profits of the land and give L merely a peppercorn.

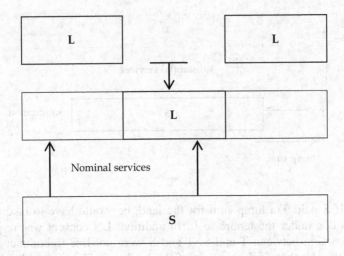

Nominal services

5–104 Even more serious was the effect on escheat. If T died without heirs, L became entitled only to nominal services from S, but in this case, permanently.

5–105 Sale of land was undermining the feudal system, depriving lords of their feudal income. Yet the situation was complicated by the fact that while some lords were losing income, others wanted to engage in sale to raise lump sums. Insofar as mesne lords were lords of a lower tenure, they were against sale by their tenants, but in so far as they were tenants they wished to be able to sell. Only the king, who was a lord but never a tenant, stood to lose but not gain. Magna Carta of 1217[77] prohibited tenants from alienating so much land that the part retained would not be enough to supply the services due to the lord, but the measure seems to have been ineffective. The contradictions within the feudal system were resolved by a radical compromise, the Statute *Quia Emptores* 1290.[78] So radical were the effects of the Statute on the theory of land law that its effects can still be detected today.

Quia Emptores 1290
The Statute
5–106 The Statute provided that:

---

[77] 18 John c 39. An Irish version of the Great Charter, *Magna Carta Hiberniae*, was promulgated in Ireland: see H.G. Richardson, "Magna Carta Hiberniae" (1942) 3 I.H.S. 31; *Hamilton v The Marquess of Donegall* (1795) 3 Ridg. P.C. 267; *Moore v Attorney-General* [1934] I.R. 44; *Little v Cooper* [1937] I.R. 1; *Foyle and Bann Fisheries Ltd v Attorney-General* (1949) 83 I.L.T.R. 29; R. Dudley-Edwards, "Magna Carta Hiberniae" in J. Ryan (ed.), *Féil-Sgríbhinn Eóin Mhic Néill: Essays and Studies Presented to Professor Eóin MacNeill on the Occasion of his Seventieth Birthday* (Dublin: Three Candles 1940), pp.307–318; and P. Crooks and T. Mohr, *Law and the Idea of Liberty in Ireland from Magna Carta to the Present* (Dublin: Four Courts Press, 2018) (forthcoming).

[78] Called after the first words of the Statute: "Whereas purchasers of lands …". See T.F.T. Plucknett, *Legislation of Edward I* (Oxford: Oxford University Press, 1949), pp.102–109; D.W. Sutherland, *The Assize of Novel Disseisin* (Oxford: Clarendon, 1973), pp.95–96.

1. Subinfeudation for a fee simple estate was prohibited in future.[79]
2. Substitution was to be the only method of granting land in fee simple and would no longer require the lord's consent. The statute established the important principle of the free alienability of fee simple estates, which has been specifically preserved by the LCLRA 2009.[80]
3. If a tenant sold part of the tenement then the feudal services were to be apportioned between the two parts. Each party would be liable to distress by L only to the extent of the proportion of the services due from that part.
4. The Statute did not bind the Crown.[81] The Crown could and did create new tenures. It did so in the settlement of Ireland in the Tudor and Stuart periods.

5–107 There are references to the Statute in Ireland in pleadings during the period 1295–1303.[82] The Statute had been applied by the courts in Ireland in modern times.[83] The LCLRA 2009 finally repealed *Quia Emptores*,[84] but the preservation of the principle of free alienability of the fee simple and the exception of *non obstante* grants, considered in the section below, means that its influence has not entirely disappeared.

The Effect of the Statute on Tenure

5–108 The Statute meant that every time an escheat occurred, a layer of tenure was destroyed and could not be replaced.[85] Mesne lordships became rarer in course of time.[86] The feudal pyramid shrank. Eventually, almost everyone would become a tenant in chief.[87]

---

[79] *Re Holliday* [1922] 2 Ch. 698.

[80] LCLRA 2009 s.9(4).

[81] Co Litt 43b; C. Sweet (ed.), *Challis's Law of Real Property*, 3rd edn (London: Butterworth, 1911), p.20; *Abbot of Barking's Case* YB 10 Hen VII f 23a; *Verschoyle v Perkins* (1847) 13 Ir. Eq. R. 72.

[82] In a case before the justiciar in 1302, the king's serjeant pleaded successfully "the statute by which it is enacted that no one may alien a tenement in fee, to hold of the feoffor, or of any others, than the chief lords of the fee." A.G. Donaldson, *The Application in Ireland of English and British Legislation made before 1801* (PhD, 2 vols (Queen's University, Belfast, 1952)); Hand, *English Law in Ireland 1290–1324* (1967), p.162.

[83] *Verschoyle v Perkins* (1847) 13 Ir. Eq. R. 72; *Corporation of Dublin v Herbert* (1862) 12 Ir. C.L.R. 502; *Delacherois v Delacherois* (1864) 11 H.L.C. 62; *Chute v Busteed* (1864) 14 Ir. C.L.R. 115 at 127 per Pigot C.B.

[84] LCLRA 2009 Sch.2, Pt 2.

[85] Sweet (ed.), *Challis's Law of Real Property* (1911), p.22.

[86] Thus, when escheats occurred, they usually did so for the benefit of the Crown: see *Lysaght v McGrath* (1882) 11 L.R. Ir. 142.

[87] *Quia Emptores* 1290 allowed alienation by substitution without the consent of the lord of the tenure, but the Statute did not bind the Crown and implied that, as most freeholders came to hold directly of the Crown, they would require consent to a substitution. However, a statute of 1327 gave tenants in chief the right of free alienation (1 Edw III st 2 cc 12, 13 (Eng) (1327)).

5–109 Some historians have seen evidence of a free market in land in England at a much earlier period than in most European countries.[88] It might be easy to draw the further conclusion that the English possessed at an early stage a sense of individualism conducive to entrepreneurship and capitalism. It may well be true that considerable buying and selling was going on in the Middle Ages, but lawyers may ask what it was that was being sold. The common law never took the view that what was sold was *land*, as opposed to rights or interests in land. Freeholders owed services of tenure and suffered from disabilities unthinkable in a truly market economy, such as the inability to prevent lords paramount levying a distress on their land to recover debts which they did not owe. In the long-term, *Quia Emptores* led to the decline of tenure and assisted in the decline of feudalism. Its immediate purpose, and probably its short-term effect, may well have been to discourage sale of land since, by requiring compliance with the legal form of substitution, it also required that the "purchaser" continue to pay the services of tenure owed by the former tenant. So long as these remained substantial, purchasers of land remained in a worse position than if they had taken by subinfeudation before the Statute.

Quia Emptores in Ireland
The Statute of 1293
5–110 The statute 21 Edw. I, c. 2 of 1293,[89] transmitted to Ireland by Edward I, modified *Quia Emptores* as to Ireland.

1. The statute recognised that tenants in chief of the king in Ireland had alienated without licence from the king up to that time and indeed asserted the right to do so.
2. The statute validated subinfeudations in breach of *Quia Emptores* up to that time.
3. It declared that in future if tenants in chief alienated without licence from the king, their lands were to escheat and that in future no one was to have the right to grant land held in chief of the king "save to hold of the King in chief", i.e. they could not subinfeudate.
4. But it went on to say that "in land of war or in the marches", i.e. on the border beyond the Pale, the tenants in chief of the king continued to have full power to enfeoff[90] others to hold of them "for the defence of the land …",[91] i.e. they could continue to subinfeudate in fee simple.
5. The king had power to recall the right.

---

[88] See A. Macfarlane, *The Origins of English Individualism: The Family, Property and Social Transition* (Oxford: Blackwell, 1978).

[89] *Early Statutes of Ireland* (Dublin: HMSO, 1907–1910), p.192; Hand, *English Law in Ireland 1290–1324* (1967), p.162.

[90] i.e. grant in fee.

[91] "… if it be not in land of war or in the marches and that there the lords that hold of the King have full power to enfeoff [i.e. grant at common law] others to hold of them for the defence of the land …". *Early Statutes of Ireland* (Dublin: HMSO, 1907–1910), p.192.

5–111 The statute was thus an adaptation of *Quia Emptores* for Ireland.[92] The reference to defence implies that tenants in chief found it necessary to grant lands to be held of them in freehold in order to acquire military tenants who would owe homage to them and fight with them if attacked. It is an early example of exceptions to *Quia Emptores* being allowed in Ireland and does much to explain certain characteristic institutions and unique features of Irish land law as a common law system. It explains the tendency or preference in Ireland for forms of subinfeudation after *Quia Emptores*, or the substitute for it, the lease for lives renewable forever, and even the rule in leaseholds in Ireland that, unlike England, a tenant can sublet for the whole term of his own lease, that is it does not take effect as an automatic assignment, but can create leasehold tenure.

5–112 As to the statute of 1293, there is no evidence that the king ever recalled the power. The exemption could have been used until the end of military resistance to English rule at the beginning of the 17th century.

Non Obstante Grants in Ireland

5–113 Over time, with the ending of indigenous military resistance, the exception in the statute of 1293 would have become obsolete. Nevertheless, it seems there remained a demand in Ireland on the part of lords to be able to grant land for a fee simple estate and still retain tenure. This may have been a matter of social prestige as much as for the economic benefits of being a freehold lord. In Ireland, mostly dating from the Plantation period, the Crown granted land in fee simple to freehold tenants purporting at the same time to give them a power to subinfeudate further *non obstante* (notwithstanding) *Quia Emptores*, i.e. to grant a fee simple to a subtenant, creating a new layer of tenure. In other words, the Crown granted them an exemption from the statute—an exercise by the Crown of the "dispensing power" exercised by medieval kings. These *non obstante* grants, as they are known, reserved a rent to the Crown, the Crown rent being known in Ireland as a "quit rent".[93] These grants continued to be made until the end of James II's reign. The Bill of Rights 1689 abolished the dispensing power of the Crown, as part of the newly-dominant Parliament's restrictions on the royal prerogative, and specifically prohibited *non obstante*

---

[92] A.G. Donaldson, *The Application in Ireland of English and British Legislation made before 1801* (PhD, 2 vols (Queen's University, Belfast, 1952)), p.80; Hand, *English Law in Ireland 1290–1324* (1967), p.162. See further, A. Lyall, "Quia Emptores in Ireland" in O. Breen, J. Casey and A. Kerr (eds), *Liber Memorialis: Professor James C. Brady* (Dublin: Round Hall Sweet & Maxwell, 2001), pp.275–294.

[93] *Esdaile v Stephenson* (1835) 1 Ll. & G.t.P. 122; *Tuthill v Rogers* (1844) 6 Ir. Eq. R. 439; *Allen v Linehan* (1860) 9 Ir. C.L.R. 291. By the 19th century the courts tended to regard quit rents as a type of tax or charge rather than as a rent service. The Landed Estates Court had power to redeem quit rents: R.C. Macnevin, *The Practice of the Landed Estates Court in Ireland* (Dublin: Hodges Smith & Co., 1859), p.12.

grants.[94] However, in so far as any still exist, they are preserved by s.9 of the LCLRA 2009. These grants are considered in more detail in the chapter on fee farm grants.

Leases for Lives Renewable Forever

5–114 Leases for lives renewable forever were known in Ireland from the mid-17th century. They were essentially the grant of an estate *pur autre vie* for a number of lives, which could be renewed. Although the estate was freehold, they were known as "leases" because they were commercial interests and a rent was reserved. Since *Quia Emptores* only prohibited subinfeudation in fee simple, an estate *pur autre vie*, as a form of life estate, could create freehold tenure and the rent was therefore the service of freehold tenure. They were thus a device to avoid *Quia Emptores*. After *non obstante* grants were prohibited they became the only device to avoid *Quia Emptores*, while not contravening the literal provisions of the Statute. They became common in Ireland and by the end of the 18th century much land was held, at some level, in such leases. The creation in future of leases for lives is now prohibited by the LCLRA 2009.[95] Existing ones are now rare and it was not thought necessary to convert them.[96]

Other Effects of Quia Emptores on Real Property
Lesser Estates

5–115 Since the Statute only applied to subinfeudations in fee simple, a grant of an estate less than a fee simple, such as a life estate or fee tail, could still create tenure,[97] and so (i) could reserve a rent to the grantor without creating a separate rentcharge, and (ii) could impose freehold covenants binding between successors to the grantor and those who inherit the estate. The point had, however, little practical significance in modern times, since life estates and fees tail were part of family settlements and members of the same family do not normally charge each other rent. Freehold tenure was created in the grant of leases for lives, but they were commercial interests and not family

---

[94] Bill of Rights 1689 ss.1 and 2 (1 W & M sess. 2, c. 2 (Eng)). See Lyall, "Quia Emptores in Ireland" in *Liber Memorialis* (2001), pp.275–294.

[95] LCLRA 2009 s.14.

[96] LCLRA 2009 Explanatory Memorandum, p.11. Had it been, they would presumably have been converted to fees simple.

[97] Sweet (ed.), *Challis's Law of Real Property* (1911), p.22. In *Delacherois v Delacherois* (1864) 11 H.L.C. 62, it was held that, where a grant could take effect as a substitution or as a subinfeudation, an intention had to be shown that it was to take effect as a subinfeudation.

arrangements.[98] The abolition of freehold tenure by the LCLRA 2009[99] means that freehold tenure can no longer be created on the grant of a life estate. Life estates can now only exist in equity under a trust of land.[100]

Fees Simple

5–116 Since the Statute still applied to fee simple estates, a grant of a fee simple in modern times could not create freehold tenure between grantor and grantee and so could not, for example, reserve a rent to the grantor without creating a separate rentcharge. Such a rent (i.e. not being a separate rentcharge) could only exist as a *rent service*, i.e. a service of tenure, and no such service could be created after 1290. Land subject to *non obstante* grants was the exception. In Ireland, hybrid grants under Deasy's Act 1860 created *leasehold* tenure in respect of a fee simple estate and a *leasehold* rent. They were a form of fee farm grant, i.e. a fee simple at a rent. The LCLRA 2009 has now prohibited the creation of fee farm grants in future. Existing fee farm grants are retained.[101]

Reversion and Tenure after 1290

5–117 After the Statute, the fallacy gained ground in England[102] that reversion and tenure were in some way connected, so that tenure could not exist without a reversion. No similar view developed in Ireland because exceptions to *Quia Emptores* 1290 existed. The English view was a purely reifying concept—it was not the solution to a practical problem. It was thought to "follow" from the rules. It was true, of course, that *after* the Statute in England one could not create tenure without at the same time creating a reversion. The Statute did not prevent subinfeudation for grants of estates less than a fee simple and on the grant of such an estate, one necessarily also created a reversion. But *before* the Statute one could certainly create tenure without a reversion; that is exactly what happened when a subinfeudation in fee simple occurred. There was no reversion on a fee simple, before or after the Statute, only an escheat.

5–118 The fallacy had little significance in relation to freehold itself, but when leaseholds were developed by the courts similar ideas found their way into concepts of leasehold estates in England. It gave rise to the idea that a sublease

---

[98] It had little practical importance in modern times, (a) because grants of freehold estates less than a fee simple intended to create tenure were rare, and (b) because where such estates were created, as in family settlements, they were usually granted to members of the grantor's own family and the grantor did not retain a rent, which would be one of the indications of tenure. The indication of tenure would be that the rent was a rent service, i.e. a service of the tenure, and not a rentcharge, which is a separate property interest.

[99] LCLRA 2009 ss.9 and 10.

[100] LCLRA 2009 s.11.

[101] LCLRA 2009 s.12(5). Where dwellings are held under a fee farm grant (or a lease) at a ground rent, ground rents legislation provides that the holder may buy out the rent and thus acquire the fee simple free of leasehold tenure.

[102] See, e.g., Williams, *Principles of the Law of Real Property* (1880), p.252, who apparently uses tenure and reversion interchangeably.

could not be created for the entire term of the head lease: no reversion, so no tenure. The Statute was applied by analogy, as it were, to leaseholds.[103] However, the Irish courts did not adopt this position, no doubt because examples of tenure without reversion still occurred in Ireland, either under the statute of 1293 or later under *non obstante* grants. Irish courts allowed a sublease for the full term of the head lease. This difference of doctrine caused a controversy between the English and Irish courts in the 18th and early 19th centuries. The Irish practice was re-enacted by Deasy's Act 1860,[104] which remains in force.[105]

Tenure and Reversion in Irish and English Land Law	
Ireland	**England**
Freehold	**Freehold**
1. *Before Quia Emptores*	1. *Before Quia Emptores*
Tenure without reversion, on subinfeudation in fee simple.	Same.
2. *After Quia Emptores*	2. *After Quia Emptores*
1293 statutory exception.	No subinfeudation in fee simple.
Non obstante grants.	Subinfeudation for life estate, estate tail
Device to avoid: leases for lives renewable forever.	possible, but then reversion also. Therefore, no tenure without reversion.
Still examples of tenure without reversion.	
Leasehold	**Leasehold**
1. *Before the Union of 1801*	No tenure without reversion: grant for full term
Irish cases: tenure without reversion; may sublet for whole term of lease.	is an assignment, not a subletting.
2. *Between Union and Deasy's Act 1860*	
British appeals: no tenure without reversion.	
3. *After Deasy's Act 1860*	
Section 3 restores pre-Union position: tenure without reversion.	

The Abolition of Military Tenures

5–119 The decline of the economic power of the feudal lords meant also that the political power was increasingly concentrated at the apex of the political system. It led to the emergence of an absolutist monarchy under the Tudors and the early Stuarts.[106]

5–120 On the other hand, the rising economic power of non-feudal classes—the bankers, financiers and small landowners who invested their rent as capital—was not reflected in political power. The absolutist monarchy acted in

---

[103] *Quia Emptores* 1290 did not apply literally to leaseholds, and the analogy was unnecessary.
[104] Deasy's Act 1860 s.3.
[105] LCLRA 2009 Explanatory Memorandum, pp.5–7.
[106] See P. Anderson, *Lineages of the Absolutist State* (New York: Verso, 2013), pp.113–142; B. Moore, *Social Origins of Dictatorship and Democracy: Lord and Peasant in the Making of the Modern World* (Boston: Beacon Press, 1993), Ch.1.

ways that were not conducive to free trade and investment. It claimed the right to grant monopolies over trade in certain goods or services and its arbitrary exercise of power increased the risks faced by those contemplating investment in trade.[107]

5–121 One of the functions of the 17th century revolution in England was to destroy this arbitrary power, the remnant of feudalism, and replace it by a form of government more conducive to the development of capitalism. It was antagonistic to the remnants of feudal relationships that remained. Cromwell is said to have called the law of real property "a tortuous and ungodly jumble".[108] The opportunity was taken to abolish many of the features of feudal tenure.[109]

5–122 The first step was taken in Ireland in 1641 by a resolution of the Irish Parliament, to be followed five years later in England by an ordinance of the Long Parliament in 1646.[110] This was later enacted as a statute of the Commonwealth in 1656.[111] The Restoration Parliament of Charles II did not recognise the statutes of the Commonwealth and so re-enacted the legislation in Ireland[112] as the Tenures Abolition Act 1662[113] (the "1662 Act").

5–123 By s.3 of the 1662 Act all existing tenure in knight service was converted to "free and common socage".[114] "Free" does not mean free of rent. The lawyers of the time were under the mistaken impression that at some time in the past there had been an unfree version of socage tenure. The Crown was prohibited from creating new tenures except in "free and common socage". Here again, "free" did not imply "free of rent" and so the statute did not prevent the Crown from reserving a rent on the grant of a freehold tenure.[115]

5–124 The 1662 Act did not abolish serjeanty; in fact the honorary services were expressly preserved by s.11.[116] The 1662 Act did, however, abolish most of the incidents. Nor did the 1662 Act abolish frankalmoin; examples of it may still have existed in modern times as to some land held by the Church of

---

[107] D.O. Wagner, "Coke and the Rise of Economic Liberalism" (1935) 6 Ec. Hist. Rev. 30.

[108] R.E. Megarry and H.W.R. Wade, *The Law of Real Property*, 3rd edn (London: Stevens, 1966), p.1.

[109] D. Veall, *The Popular Movement for Law Reform, 1640–1660* (Oxford: Clarendon Press, 1970).

[110] Ordinance for removing the Court of Wards, 24 February 1645–1646; C.H. Firth and R.S. Rait, *Acts and Ordinances of the Interregnum 1642–1660* (London: HMSO, 1911), Vol.1, p.833.

[111] An Act for taking away the Court of Wards and Liveries, 27 November 1656; Firth and Rait, *Acts and Ordinances of the Interregnum 1642–1660* (1911), Vol.2, p.1043.

[112] In England as the Tenures Abolition Act 1660.

[113] See Short Titles Act 1962.

[114] *Inchquin v Burnell* (1795) 3 Ridg. P.C. 425; *Verschoyle v Perkins* (1847) 13 Ir. Eq. R. 72 at 77.

[115] See *Stuart v Easton* 170 US 383 (1898).

[116] There are still examples of serjeanties held in chief in England.

Ireland.[117] The 1662 Act did not abolish the services of socage, which was a money rent by this time. Nor did it prevent the Crown reserving a rent when creating a new tenure in socage. Statutes in Ireland at the time of the Stuart settlements provided for the granting of freehold at rents.[118]

The Decline of Incidents

5–125 Homage was abolished by the 1662 Act as to all tenures. The military incident had ceased to be appropriate. Fealty was expressly saved by the 1662 Act but has become obsolete in practice. Suit of Court tended to be commuted to money payments from the 13th century onwards. It was preserved by the 1662 Act but had become obsolete. Manorial courts were abolished in 1859.[119] They had become defunct before that in most cases.[120] Aids were abolished for all tenures by the 1662 Act. They had come to be of little value, having been fixed in amount in 1275 for mesne lords,[121] and in 1350 for tenants in chief.[122] Reliefs in most cases had been fixed and inflation had reduced them to worthless amounts. The effect of the Statute of Wills (Ireland) 1634 was that no relief was payable if the land was left by will but continued to be payable on intestate succession. The 1662 Act preserved reliefs.

5–126 Wardship in England was an incident of the military tenures and so the effect of the 1662 Act was to abolish it there since the statute converted knight service to socage and abolished the incidents of serjeanty.

Escheat

5–127 Escheat was not abolished by the 1662 Act.

---

[117] Frankalmoin may not have been abolished in England: the Administration of Estates Act 1925 repealed s.7 of the English Act of 1660, which had merely declared that nothing in s.1 should affect frankalmoin.

[118] Settlement of Ireland Act 1634 (10 Car I sess. 3 cc 2, 3, Ir.); Settlement of Ireland Act 1639 (15 Car I sess. 2 c 6, Ir.); Settlement of Ireland Act 1665 (17 & 18 Car II c 2, Ir.), repealed in Northern Ireland by the Property (Northern Ireland) Order 1978 (1978 No. 459 (N.I. 4) and in Ireland by the Statute Law Revision (Pre-Union Irish Statutes) Act 1962.

[119] Manor Courts Abolition (Ireland) Act 1859 (22 Vict c 14). Their jurisdiction transferred to petty sessions, but some manorial incidents were preserved. Manorial courts in England only lost their legal jurisdiction by the Administration of Justice Act 1977 s.23 and Sch.4. Copyhold tenure does not appear to have been abolished in Ireland. In England most of the incidents of copyhold were abolished by s.128 of the Law of Property Act 1922, although some, such as rights of the lord to markets and fairs, were preserved indefinitely, and so the tenure itself was not abolished: R. Megarry and H.W.R. Wade, *The Law of Real Property*, 4th edn (London: Stevens, 1975), p.37.

[120] *Boyd v Magee* (1849) 13 Ir. L.R. 435; *Costelloe v Hooks* (1848) 11 Ir. C.L.R. 294; *Herbert v Maclean* (1862) 12 Ir. Ch. R. 84.

[121] 3 Edw I st 1 c 36.

[122] 25 Edw III st 5 c 11.

5–128 The Corruption of Blood Act 1814[123] reduced the scope of escheat for felony to murder and petit treason. Escheat for felony was abolished by s.1 of the Forfeiture Act 1870.

5–129 The 1870 Act did not abolish escheat for outlawry.[124] The 1870 Act was repealed by the Criminal Law Act 1997, and the law of felony assimilated to that of misdemeanour.[125]

5–130 Escheat for want of heirs was not abolished until the Succession Act 1965, s.11(3) of which reads:

"Escheat to the State and escheat to a mesne lord for want of heirs are hereby abolished."

5–131 Under s.73(1) of the 1965 Act, if any person dies intestate and without other intestate successors, possessed of land held for an estate in fee simple,[126] the property passes to the State as "ultimate intestate successor". Where a person dies in similar circumstances possessed of an absolute interest in personal property, the same provision takes effect.

5–132 What happens in theory to a fee simple in such circumstances is open to question. It could be argued that it remains a fee simple, in which case after 1 January 1967, a fee simple never comes to an end. Under the State Property Act 1954, the Minister for Public Expenditure and Reform can waive the right of the State in favour of any person as he thinks fit.[127]

Residual Forms of Escheat
Land Registered under Local Registration of Title Act 1891
5–133 As regards agricultural land bought out under the Land Purchase Acts and compulsorily registered under the Local Registration of Title Act 1891, *all* escheats were abolished in that year, since such land was to devolve as personal property.

5–134 Personal property, including leaseholds,[128] passed to the State as *bona vacantia* if no one else was entitled. As regards personal property owned by real persons, the doctrine of *bona vacantia* was replaced by the principle of the State taking as "ultimate intestate successor" under s.73(1) of the Succession Act 1965. *Bona vacantia*, i.e. "ownerless goods" belonged to the Crown

---

[123] 54 Geo III c 145, repealed by the Statute Law Revision Act 1983.
[124] Forfeiture Act 1870 s.1. It was abolished in Northern Ireland by the Criminal Procedure (Northern Ireland) Act 1951 s.2.
[125] Criminal Law Act 1997 ss.3 and 16 and Schedule.
[126] *Fawcett v Hall* (1833) Alc. & Nap. 248 at 253 (escheat an incident [*sic*] of the fee simple estate and not of other estates).
[127] State Property Act 1954 s.26.
[128] *Re Sir Thomas Spencer Wells* [1933] Ch. 29.

at common law as a royal prerogative. The right, where it survives, is assumed to adhere to the State, probably under some constitutional principle similar to that announced in *Webb v Ireland*.[129] This could be challenged by the same argument as was used in *Webb*, that the prerogative did not survive into the 1937 Constitution. However, it would probably be dealt with in the same way by the Supreme Court, i.e. that the common law doctrine survives, not as stemming from a prerogative of the Crown, but as part of the sovereign rights of the People vested in the State.

Companies

5–135 In the past, an escheat occurred where land was vested in fee simple in a limited company and the company was wound up before the fee simple became vested in any other party.[130] As regards land registered under the Local Registration of Title Act 1891, that principle was replaced by *bona vacantia*. Other land continued to be governed by escheat.

5–136 Section 28(2)(a) of the State Property Act 1954 now provides that all land vested in or held in trust for a body corporate "immediately before its dissolution", other than land held by the body corporate on trust for another person, vests in the State. "Body corporate", however, would not include unincorporated bodies such as clubs, friendly societies or voluntary associations.[131]

5–137 The exception, where property was held by the dissolved body corporate at the date of its dissolution upon trust for another person, has occurred in some cases.[132]

5–138 In *Re Heidelstone Co Ltd*,[133] the applicants were the majority of the owners of apartments and townhouses in a residential development. A management company had been set up and the scheme contemplated that it would hold the freehold title, would grant long leases to the individual apartment and townhouse purchasers, and retain the freehold title to the common areas in the scheme, i.e. the internal stairways in the case of the flats, surrounding lawns, car parks, etc. Control of the management company was then to be vested in the purchasers. The completion of the scheme of disposal became impossible because the vendor and the management company were struck off the register of companies for failing to make returns and were dissolved without the scheme of disposal having been fully implemented. Laffoy J. made an order pursuant to s.26 of the Trustee Act 1893 vesting the interest of the vendor

---

[129] [1988] I.R. 353.

[130] *Re Strathblaine Estates Ltd* [1948] Ch. 228.

[131] The property may revert to the grantor: *Hastings Corp v Letton* [1908] 1 K.B. 378 at 384; Co Litt 13b. But this may have been a characteristic of frankalmoin tenure: see Sweet (ed.), *Challis's Law of Real Property* (1911), p.467.

[132] See *Re Kavanagh and Cantwell*, unreported, High Court, Costello J., 23 November 1984. There, the company was a trustee before it was dissolved.

[133] [2007] 4 I.R. 175.

company and/or the management company in a new management company which had been incorporated by the applicants.

Forfeiture

5–139 Forfeiture for treason was abolished by the Forfeiture Act 1870.[134]

THE ABOLITION OF FEUDAL TENURE

The State's Radical Title?

5–140 Prior to the LCLRA 2009 it was probably correct to speak of the State's "radical title". It gave the State few if any rights, since (a) there was no theory of eminent domain, and (b) if the State wished to acquire land it had to do so by using the legislation on compulsory purchase, as is still the case. Furthermore, escheat to the State had been replaced with the concept of the State as ultimate intestate successor. It could have been argued that the 1937 Constitution had replaced the radical title based on tenure and that it was inconsistent with a Republic in which individuals are citizens, rather than subjects of a monarch, but the point had not been argued in this jurisdiction.

5–141 The LCLRA 2009 has produced the same effect in Ireland, with the rare exception of *non obstante* grants, which are the only surviving example of freehold tenure existing between an individual and the State. Fees simple are no longer "held of" the State in any feudal sense. An individual holds a fee simple allodially, protected by the Constitution, and subject to rights and duties as determined by law. The relationship between an individual owner of a fee simple and the State is no longer a matter of land law but of constitutional law.

State Land

5–142 It is questionable whether the traditional view, that the doctrine of estates did not apply to the State as landowner, and that if the State held land directly it held it as absolute owner, ever applied after 1937. Moreover, s.5(1) of the State Property Act 1954 provides:

> "5.—(1) ... all land, which immediately before the operative date is State land and is not then vested in a State authority, shall, by virtue of this subsection, stand vested in the Minister [for Finance]."

5–143 Under the Registration of Title Act 1964, the Minister would be registered, as any other proprietor, as "full owner"[135] of "freehold land", which, as amended by the LCLRA 2009, means "land the ownership of which is an estate in fee simple in possession".[136]

---

[134] Forfeiture Act 1870 ss.1 and 3.
[135] Registration of Title Act 1964 s.27.
[136] Registration of Title Act 1964 s.3(1), as amended by LCLRA 2009 s.127.

Grants by the State

5–144 The traditional doctrine held that where the State grants land it does so by subinfeudation, which is clearly no longer the case. The State could no doubt create a new fee simple over land vested in it, if required, but the prohibition by the LCLRA 2009 on the creation in future of fee farm grants would seem to preclude the reservation of a rent in such a case. Section 9 of the LCLRA 2009 exempts the position of the State under the State Property Act 1954, but s.10(1) of the 1954 Act, providing for the sale or lease of State land, seems to contemplate only an outright sale, i.e. in fee simple, for a lump sum, or the creation of a leasehold interest at a rent.

State Rents

5–145 Existing State rents (quit rents) may still survive on freehold land. The Crown was not bound by *Quia Emptores* 1290, and the Tenures Abolition Act 1662 allowed the Crown to create new layers of tenure in free and common socage. They could have arisen either by grants made on the settlement of Ireland or by *non obstante* grants, i.e. the fee simple granted in tenure to a tenant in chief.[137] The present State would have succeeded to them in 1922, or 1937, and so State rents may have survived until the LCLRA 2009.[138]

5–146 Existing fee farm grants are specifically preserved by s.12(5) of the LCLRA 2009. Thus, in so far as they exist or survive, s.9 of the LCLRA 2009 exempts the position of the State under the State Property Act 1954. Section 13 of the 1954 Act provides that a State authority may waive the payment of any rent otherwise due to the State, and "rent" includes "a former crown rent, a rent charge, a rent service and a rent sec".

---

[137] It seems that many grants on the settlement of Ireland in the Stuart period also contained *non obstante* clauses.

[138] They could therefore exist in any land, not merely that subject to *non obstante* fee farm grants.

CHAPTER 6

Equity

A Chancery Judge once had the kindness to inform me that the Court of Chancery was almost immaculate.

— Dickens, *Bleak House* (Preface, 1853)

INTRODUCTION

6–01 The common law had many rigidities of procedure which, in a sense, had been necessary in their time but over the course of centuries and with societal changes came to be seen as deficiencies. The forms of action were not only defined legal rights but also excluded from the king's courts those who were not freeholders. Originally this exclusion extended to the mass of the population, who were villeins. Their only recourse was to the court of their own lord and since their dispute might well be against their lord, their chance of obtaining justice was limited. Legal notions based on equality of status were foreign to a society in which the law enforced unequal status. There was no concept of equality before the law, nor of the notion that a person should not be a judge in his or her own cause. Even for freeholders, the common law had many shortcomings. The forms of action were highly technical and one could easily fail for lack of some formality. Wills of real property were not recognised. The only recourse was to appeal to the king as the "fountain of justice". In the reigns of Edward II and Edward III, many petitions were presented to the king. After the time of Edward III, they were regularly referred to the Chancellor, one of the king's ministers. The Chancellor was often a cleric. For this reason, the jurisdiction of his department, the Chancery, was often exercised on moral grounds, taking into account the conscience of the plaintiff or defendant. In the time of Elizabeth I, the post was secularised and the Chancellor became "the Keeper of the Queen's conscience". At this time, there were no reports of cases decided by the Chancellor, probably because they wished to retain a wide discretion and precedent would tend eventually to confine it, which is indeed what happened to equity when reports of equity decisions came to be published. No reports of the decisions of Cardinal Wolsey (c.1475–1530) or Sir Thomas More (1478–1535) survive.

6–02 Wolsey was the last of the English medieval ecclesiastical chancellors[1] and More the first of the modern lawyers. Under Lord Ellesmere (1596–1617), and particularly Lord Nottingham (1673–1682), equity developed into a distinct body of principles, aided by the recording of equity decisions.[2]

6–03 If the courts of law gave a judgment which equity thought inequitable, it issued its own special remedy, the "common injunction", to prevent the person who had succeeded at common law from enforcing the judgment he or she had obtained. This of course created a conflict between the common law courts and the Chancellor. Matters came to a head in 1615 in several cases,[3] principally the case of *Glanvill v Courtney*.[4]

6–04 The Irish Chancery began in 1232 when Henry III granted the English Chancellor, Ralph Neville, Bishop of Chichester, the Chancery of Ireland for life.[5] Neville nominated a deputy to execute the office in his place and it is likely therefore that the Irish Chancery was in fact established by Neville's deputy, Geoffrey de Turville. From Neville's death in 1244, his deputy, Robert Luttrell, continued as Chancellor of Ireland and thenceforth the office had a continuous independent existence until 1922.[6] The Irish Chancery seems to have been largely administrative at first and did not emerge as a court until the 1470s.

6–05 In Ireland, the equity jurisdiction of the Court of Exchequer ("the equity side of Exchequer") may have been somewhat more important than in England.[7] The jurisdiction was abolished by the Exchequer Equitable Jurisdiction (Ireland) Act 1850.[8] But the expertise in equity of the Exchequer barons was not entirely lost because in the previous year the Incumbered Estates Court had been established and one of the three Commissioners of Incumbered Estates had to be a baron of the Exchequer.[9]

---

[1] In Ireland, ecclesiastics held the office later than in England. Archbishop Adam Loftus held the office in 1581, and Michael Boyle, Archbishop of Armagh, was Chancellor after the Restoration: F.E. Ball, *The Judges in Ireland, 1221–1921* (Dublin: Round Hall Press, 1993), Vol.i, pp.137, 138, 156 and 295.

[2] L.A. Knafla, *Law and Politics in Jacobean England: the Tracts of Lord Chancellor Ellesmere* (Cambridge: Cambridge University Press, 1977); D.E.C. Yale (ed.), *Lord Nottingham's Manual of Chancery Practice and Prolegomena of Chancery and Equity* (Cambridge: Cambridge University Press, 1965).

[3] J.H. Baker, "The Common Lawyers and the Chancery" (1969) Ir. Jur. (n.s.) 368–392.

[4] (1615) Cro. Jac. 343. The report is of the proceedings at common law before Sir Edward Coke.

[5] Ball, *The Judges in Ireland, 1221–1921* (1993), Vol.i, pp.6–10; A.J. Otway-Ruthven, *A History of Medieval Ireland* (London: Benn, 1968), p.154 and following.

[6] Otway-Ruthven, *A History of Medieval Ireland* (1968), p.154.

[7] Otway-Ruthven, *A History of Medieval Ireland* (1968), pp.154–155; G.J. Hand, *English Law in Ireland, 1290–1324* (Cambridge: The University Press, 1967), pp.99–103.

[8] The last case in equity to come before the court was *Massy v O'Dell* (1860) 9 Ir. Ch. R. 441. It was later transferred to the Court of Chancery.

[9] The Incumbered Estates (Ireland) Act 1849.

6–06 The role of equity was frequently, but not exclusively, to make the legal system more attuned to a society based on the market as a mechanism for the production and distribution of wealth. The common law still suffered from having procedures developed for a feudal society.

NEW PROCEDURE

6–07 A feature of the Chancery was that it acted against persons. An action in Chancery was begun by *subpoena*, a summons to the defendant to appear on pain (*sub poena*) of forfeiture of a sum of money if the defendant failed to appear.

NEW REMEDIES

6–08 At common law if A was dispossessed by B then A could recover possession of the land by one of the forms of action. But in the case of personal property, the common law generally only provided the remedy of damages. Equity granted *specific performance* of contracts. It ordered the promissor to carry out his promise, not just pay damages for breach of contract as the common law courts did. It issued *injunctions* to order a person to desist from a course of action or to do something. At common law, if a person proved his case he was entitled to a remedy even if he had not acted entirely honourably. Equitable remedies were and still are discretionary.[10] In modern times, new equitable remedies have been developed, such as *Mareva* injunctions[11] and *Anton Piller* orders[12] Such remedies are granted in advance of full proof of the facts, and their use is sometimes controversial.

NEW RIGHTS

6–09 Equity developed *uses* and later *trusts*: equitable estates in the beneficial interest of property corresponding to legal estates. It also developed the *equity of redemption* in mortgages to protect mortgagors of property. The equitable courts in Ireland before the 18th century invented the *equity to renew leases for lives renewable forever* which made such interests practically equivalent to fee simple estates. Irish courts also devised the doctrine of *graft*. A person who was acting in a fiduciary capacity and not for his own benefit, and who acquires more property because of his position, may not take the benefit for himself. Equity today is often used to intervene in situations in which it would

---

[10] *Doran v Carroll* (1861) 11 Ir. Ch. R. 379.

[11] *Mareva Compania Naviera SA v International Bulk Carriers SA* [1975] 2 Ll. Rep. 509; *Nippon Yusen Kaisha v Karageorgis* [1975] 1 W.L.R. 1093; *Re John Horgan Livestock Ltd*; *O'Mahony v Horgan* [1996] 1 I.L.R.M. 161.

[12] *Anton Piller KG v Manufacturing Processes Ltd* [1976] Ch. 55.

be unjust for the holder of a common law title to take the benefits, or all the benefits, of ownership. Proprietary and promissory estoppel are examples of new principles developing out of this intervention, as are the principles relating to the acquisition by a spouse of an equity in the matrimonial home when the legal estate is vested in the other spouse. The constructive trust is a doctrine which has developed, and continues to develop, in this context.

USES

The Rise of the Use
The General Form
6–10 When a grantor conveyed a legal estate to a feoffee to hold it for uses which the grantor declared, the Chancellor did not refuse to recognise that there had been a change in the legal title. Equity, as the maxim states, "follows the law" (i.e. the common law). Equity recognised that the feoffee was now the person who could, if required, make a conveyance of the legal title. The Chancellor nevertheless forced the feoffee as holder of the legal title to use the land for the benefit of the *cestui que use*, the person whom equity considered to be so entitled. Equity would not permit the feoffee to accept the grant and then take advantage of the failure of the common law courts to recognise the uses. The following diagram shows the general form of the use:

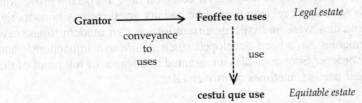

Wills
6–11 At common law it was not possible to leave land by will. On the tenant's death the land went to the heir or heirs as determined by the rules of descent. At the beginning of the 16th century uses began to be developed as a device to avoid the common law rules of descent and such devices were recognised by the Chancellor.[13] The *grantor* or *settlor*, a person who creates successive interests in property, conveyed the land to the feoffee to the use, (a) that the feoffee should hold it to the use of the grantor until the grantor's death,[14] and then (b) that on the grantor's death to the use that the feoffee should convey the legal estate to X, the person to whom the grantor wished to leave the land.

---

[13] J.L. Barton, "The Medieval Use" (1965) 81 L.Q.R. 562 at 570.
[14] Hence, the grantor gave himself or herself an equitable life estate.

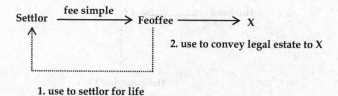

1. use to settlor for life

6–12 The conveyance to feoffees might also be made first, instructing them to hold the land to the uses of the will, which would be declared later by a separate document.[15] The use had another effect: when the settlor died, he or she did not die seized of the legal estate, and so no relief was payable, nor would wardships occur. By the 16th century, mesne lordships were becoming less common and so reliefs were often payable directly to the Crown as lord of the tenure. It was thus the Crown which stood to lose the reliefs and wardships.[16] Since the device had the effect of avoiding reliefs, this early form of will still had a purpose even if X was the eldest son of the settlor, i.e. the person who would inherit the land under the rules of descent by primogeniture.

6–13 One more development was needed to perfect the use as a device for succession. What if X died before the settlor, or the settlor changed his or her mind as to who should inherit the land? The second use needed to be revocable by the settlor during his or her life. This final refinement was achieved in *Duke of Buckingham's Case*[17] which held that the uses were revocable.

Conveyance to Self, or Self and Another

6–14 At common law, A could not convey seisin to himself. This was a strict, technical rule. But why should anyone wish to convey seisin to themselves in any case? Suppose H was getting married and wanted to put the land in the joint names of himself and his wife.[18] The common law rule prevented H from making a feoffment in favour of himself and his wife, W, as joint tenants. If you could not convey the common law estate to yourself, it followed, so the common law courts held, that you could not convey to yourself and someone else jointly. Again, the use provided a way of avoiding this awkward rule which the common law courts felt unable to change. H conveyed the fee simple to feoffees to the use of himself and his wife.

---

[15] See the Irish will of the lawyer Richard Netterville, in M.C. Griffith, *Calendar of Exchequer Inquisitions, Formerly in the Office of the Chief Remembrancer of the Exchequer Prepared from the MSS of the Irish Record Commission* (Dublin: Stationery Office for the Irish Manuscripts Commission, 1991), Vol.i, p.353. The will, i.e. the declaration of uses, is dated 11 April 1607.

[16] *Re Lord Dacre of the South* (1535) YB Pasch 27 Hen VIII f 7b pl 22; J. Baker, *Baker and Milsom: Sources of English Legal History*, 2nd edn (Oxford: Oxford University Press, 2010), p.105.

[17] (1504) YB Mich 20 Hen VII f 10 pl 20.

[18] J.L. Barton, "The Medieval Use" (1965) 81 L.Q.R. 562 at 566.

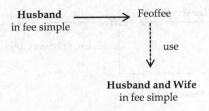

Settlements

6–15 The common law rule against conveying seisin to yourself also interfered with another transaction involving landowners: the settlement. From about the 16th to the 19th centuries, landowners were constantly devising ways of keeping land within their families and preventing some future improvident heir from selling the estate. Settlements depended on creating successive interests in land. If landowner X was to give himself a life estate, then a fee tail to his eldest son, how was he to do this? The common law courts would not recognise a deed in which X, who had a fee simple and therefore seisin, purported to convey a life estate to himself.[19] Again, uses could be used to achieve a settlement. X could convey the fee simple to a feoffee to the use that the feoffee should hold it for X for life, X's son in tail, and so on.

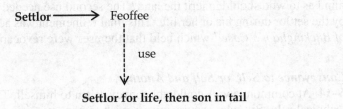

6–16 If the uses were *to convey* corresponding legal estates to X and his son, a legal settlement could be created.

Implied and Resulting Uses

6–17 Apart from recognising these devices, equity developed its own rules about the effect of conveyances in order to prevent anyone taking the benefit of land where this might not have been the intention of the conveyor. Equity nevertheless made assumptions about the intention of those who entered into transactions and these assumptions often reflected the ideas of the rising age of capitalism. Equity in general assumed that individuals acted in their own self-interest in the absence of proof to the contrary. A leading example was the "feoffment without consideration".

---

[19] See now s.50 of the Conveyancing Act 1881.

Conveyance without Consideration

6–18 If a person executed a feoffment in favour of another and no mention was made in the document of any consideration (payment), or if none was actually paid,[20] then equity presumed that the grantee held the legal estate in the land to the use of the grantor.[21]

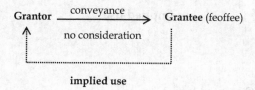

Grantor ———conveyance———> **Grantee** (feoffee)

no consideration

implied use

6–19 Equity had its own definition of consideration, distinct from the common law. In this context, equity recognised "natural love and affection" between near relatives as good consideration.

6–20 There are two interconnected explanations of equity's attitude to a feoffment without consideration. First, grantors who made feoffments as devices to avoid feudal incidents would normally convey to feoffees without consideration, although they would normally declare the uses expressly. By implying a use where none was declared, equity assumed that the deed was a device rather than a genuine conveyance of the beneficial interest, and it made the device effective by enforcing the use. It assisted in the avoidance of feudal incidents, helping to hasten the decline of feudal legal relations. Although this was the feudal origin of the rule, equity in later centuries was probably content to retain it because the result also accorded with the values of a capitalist or market economy in which individuals appear as sellers of commodities and part with their own only if they obtain its price. In other words, equity presumed that grantors acted out of their own self-interest and not altruistically in making conveyances.

Vendor and Purchaser (Bargain and Sale)

6–21 Equity also intervened to regulate the position between a vendor of land and a purchaser after a contract of sale had been entered into, and before the conveyance was executed—in other words, where A had "bargained and sold" the land to B. The vendor, who still held the legal estate, was considered in equity to hold it, for some purposes at least, to the use of the purchaser.

---

[20] F.W. Sanders, *An Essay on the Nature and Laws of Uses and Trusts* (London, 1791), p.68.

[21] *Lord Camoy's Case* (1410). J.H. Baker, *An Introduction to English Legal History*, 4th edn (Oxford: Oxford University Press, 2011) puts the development "as early" as 1465. T.F.T. Plucknett, *A Concise History of the Common Law*, 5th edn (Boston: Little Brown, 1956), p.97, estimates that it was during the time of Edward IV.

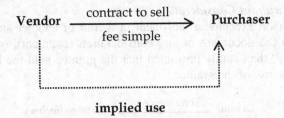

implied use

Resulting Uses
6–22 Suppose G granted land

> *to F in fee simple to the use of A for life.*

What happens when A dies? F still has the legal fee simple estate. It will last as long as his heirs survive. But the grantor has not said what is to happen to the beneficial interest after A's death. Equity assumes, unless there is some contrary intent, that F is not to take any benefit. There is a *resulting use* in favour of G. Equity assumes that G did not intend to make a gift of the remainder of the fee simple to F but intended to retain the benefit himself.

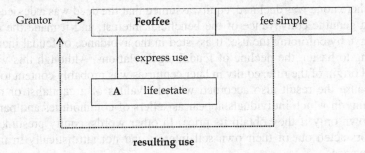

resulting use

Cestui Could Not Have a Greater Estate than the Feoffee
6–23 A situation that in a way was the opposite of the resulting use was as follows:

> *to F for life to the use of A and his heirs.*

In this instance the estate given to F is "shorter" than that which, supposed under the grant, is to go to the *cestui*. The Chancellor solved the problem by holding that the *cestui* could not have a greater interest than that given to the feoffee.[22] In the example, despite the words of the grant, A had only an estate

---

[22] *Re Ottley's Estate* [1910] 1 I.R. 1 at 11; Sanders, *An Essay on the Nature and Laws of Uses and Trusts* (1791), p.113; Cro. Car. 231.

for the life of F, i.e. an estate *pur autre vie*. A reversion in fee simple remained in the grantor following on F's life estate.

Development of Recognition of the Use

6–24 At first the Chancellor enforced the use against the feoffee named in the deed.[23] That would not, however, be enough to protect the interest of the *cestui*. Suppose the feoffee died. His or her heir inherited the legal estate. In 1482 the Chancellor enforced a use against an heir.[24] The heir had paid nothing for it, and so did not lose anything. In 1466 a purchaser from the feoffee was held bound by the use if he had express notice.[25] In such a case the Chancellor held that the conscience of the purchaser was affected. This was the beginning of the equitable doctrine of notice, which is discussed in more detail below.

The Problem of Uses

6–25 Uses were a problem for the king. The decline of mesne lordships meant that by the time of the Tudors most landowners held their land directly from the Crown. Reliefs and other feudal incidents were paid to the king as lord of the tenure. Uses, by avoiding feudal incidents, reduced the royal revenue. Moreover, Henry VIII wanted to increase his income by making new grants in tenure with incidents of real value attached to them. This policy has been called "fiscal feudalism" because it was an attempt to re-establish some of the feudal forms of landholding but only for the purpose of raising money.

6–26 Henry VIII wanted to solve the "problem" of uses. The difficulty was that many large landowners had conveyed the legal fee simple in their land to nominees, often lawyers, to hold to the landowners' use. If Henry VIII had induced Parliament to pass a statute which said that uses were ineffective or void, the result would have been a social revolution: the lawyers would have been left with the legal estate for their own benefit and the landowners would no longer be landowners. Clearly, this was not a solution. Henry VIII's lawyers therefore proposed an alternative solution. If a legal estate was conveyed to A to hold to the use of X, the new statute would give X the legal estate and A would have nothing. Uses would not be abolished but "executed". Thus, if Z conveyed the legal estate to A in fee simple to the use of X in fee simple, the words "to the use of X in fee simple" were not ineffective: on the contrary, X was to have an estate at law equivalent to the estate which he would previously have had in equity. This was the basis of the Statute of Uses 1535. A slightly adapted version was introduced in Ireland in 1634.

---

[23] A.W.B. Simpson, *A History of the Land Law*, 2nd edn (Oxford: Clarendon Press, 1986), p.176. An early recorded case was *Myrfyn v Fallan* (1446): *Calendars of the Proceedings in Chancery in the Reign of Queen Elizabeth* (3 vols, Record Commission, London, 1827–1832), Vol.ii, p.xxi.

[24] YB Pasch 22 Edw IV f 4 pl 18; Simpson, *A History of the Land Law* (1986), p.180.

[25] YB Mich 5 Edw IV f 7 pl 16; J. Baker and S.F.C. Milsom, *Sources of English Legal History* (London: Butterworths, 1986), p.97; Simpson, *A History of the Land Law* (1986), p.180.

Statute of Uses 1634

6–27 Section 1 of the Statute reads:

"Where any person or persons stand to be seized, or at any time hereafter shall happen to be seized, of any honours, castles, mannors, lands, tenements, rents, services, reversions, remainders, or other hereditaments, to the use, confidence, or trust of any other person or persons, or any body politique, by reason of any bargaine, sale, feoffment, fine, recovery, covenant, contract, agreement, will or otherwise, by any manner or means whatsoever it be, that in every such case, all and every such person and persons, and bodies politique, that have, or hereafter shall have any such use, confidence or trust, in fee simple, fee tayle, for terme of life or years, or otherwise; or any use, confidence or trust, in remainder or reverter, shall from henceforth stand and be seized, deemed, and adjudged in lawfull seizin, estate, and possession, of and in the same honours ... [etc.] to all intents, constructions and purposes in the law, of and in such like estate, as they had or shall have, in use, trust or confidence ...".

6–28 The Statute therefore applied where a person or persons were seized to the use, confidence or trust of another person or persons or body politic. The effect of the Statute was that the person or persons or body politic that had the benefit of the use should have legal estates in the property for the same estates as they had under the use. In other words, instead of estates which were only recognised in equity, they were to have estates at law.

Uses Executed, Not Abolished

6–29 The Statute did not "abolish" uses. It did not render meaningless words in a deed which referred to uses, but rather gave them a new meaning. The Statute did not simply apply to deeds existing at the date the Statute was passed, but continued to affect the operation of deeds until the Statute was repealed by the Land and Conveyancing Law Reform Act 2009 ("LCLRA 2009"). Where such limitations were contained in deeds, one had to consider what effect the deed would have had before the Statute, and then consider whether the Statute executed the uses or not.

No Transfer of the Estate from the Feoffee

6–30 The Statute did not transfer the estate of the feoffee to the *cestui que use*. Rather, it converted the estate of the *cestui que use* from an equitable estate to a corresponding legal estate. This difference can be seen in the following limitation:

to X and his heirs to the use of B for life.

The Statute executed the use giving B a legal *life estate*; it did not transfer X's legal fee simple to B. In the limitation *to A for life to the use of B and her heirs*

an attempt had been made to give the *cestui que use* a greater estate than the feoffee. Before the Statute of Uses, equity did not recognise that this could be done. Despite the words of the deed, B only had an equitable estate for the life of A. The Statute converted this into a legal estate for the life of A.

"Seized"

6–31 The Statute applied only if a person was "seized" to the use, confidence or trust of another person. It therefore applied only if the feoffee had a freehold estate. If, before the Statute, a grantor granted land

to A and her heirs to the use of B for 10 years

A was seized of a freehold estate to the use of B. B had an equitable leasehold interest. Since A was seized to the use of B, the Statute executed the use and B had a *legal* lease for 10 years. A had nothing. At the end of 10 years the resulting use arose. A was now seized of the freehold estate for the benefit of the grantor. The Statute executed this use, giving the legal freehold to the grantor. The entire legal interest was disposed of. A had nothing, B had a legal lease from the grantor for 10 years (the grantor being his landlord for this time), and then the grantor had the remainder of the legal interest. One should notice that the effect of the Statute was that A, the feoffee, was left with nothing at all. After the Statute a feoffee was a mere name on the face of the deed if the use was executed.

6–32 Consider the following limitation

to A for 10 years to the use of B for 10 years.

The Statute did not apply to the limitation at all because A was not seized to the use of B. A had only a leasehold estate.[26] The use was not executed, and A held the legal leasehold interest to the use of B who had an equitable leasehold estate.

6–33 It was further held that the grantor had to first be seised of the property before the grant to uses could take effect, i.e. the property had to be in existence before the grant was made.[27] It was thought that otherwise there would be no seisin to vest in the feoffee. The problem did not arise in relation to land itself but affected incorporeal hereditaments such as easements. A new

---

[26] *Opinion of the judges* (1580) Dyer 369a; Simpson, *A History of the Land Law* (1986), p.194.
[27] *Yelverton v Yelverton* (1595) Cro. Eliz. 401; Sanders, *An Essay on the Nature and Laws of Uses and Trusts* (1791), pp.111–112.

easement could therefore not be granted in a feoffment to uses.[28] This pedantic rule was not reformed until the Conveyancing Act 1881 provided, by s.62, that a conveyance to the use that a person should have an "easement, right, liberty or privilege" operated to vest the right in the grantee.

6–34 The Statute of Uses also dealt with another kind of incorporeal hereditament, the rentcharge. Section 4 provided that a rentcharge could be created by a grant to uses and the *cestui que use* of the rentcharge was deemed to be seised of it on execution of the conveyance. The section also conferred a statutory right of distress which otherwise would have to be expressly reserved.

"Use, Confidence or Trust"
6–35 The operation of the Statute did not depend on what words were used to describe the use. The question was whether in substance a use had been created to which the Statute applied, regardless of the words used.

"... of any other person ..."
6–36 The Statute did not apply if a person was seized to his or her *own* use, so in the limitation

> *to A and his heirs to the use of A for life, remainder to the use of B and his heirs*

the use in favour of A for life was not executed and A had an equitable life estate, whereas the use of the remainder to B was executed and B took a legal fee simple.

Bargain and Sale: Section 17
6–37 Under the law of uses, when X entered into a contract to convey an estate to Y supported by consideration, equity regarded X as holding the land for some purposes to the use of Y. X had "bargained and sold" the land to Y. At common law X had bargained it, i.e. entered into a contract to sell it, but had not "sold" it, i.e. had not executed a common law conveyance. Equity, however, treated X as if he had "sold" it and treated Y for some purposes as already the owner in equity.

6–38 The effect of the Statute of Uses would have been to execute the use, giving Y the legal estate without anything more needing to be done. It would have created a new kind of conveyance and without a public ceremony. At this time, secret conveyances were regarded with suspicion, since, at least as far as large landowners were concerned, the king wanted to know that he could trust them. This effect was realised at the last moment by the draughtsmen of

---

[28] *Yelverton v Yelverton* (1595) Cro. Eliz. 401; Sanders, *An Essay on the Nature and Laws of Uses and Trusts* (1791), pp.111–112.

the Statute, and in the same session of Parliament, the Statute of Enrolments 1535 was passed. When the Irish Statute was enacted in 1634, the provision was incorporated into the Statute as s.17. It provided that no bargain and sale of freeholds would be effective unless it was indented[29] in writing, sealed and enrolled in the "King's Court" (later taken to be the High Court in Dublin) within six months. Thus, a bargain and sale of freehold still required a public act.[30] In theory this form of conveyance could still have been done until 2009, but few solicitors would have wanted to do so because, at the time of entering into a contract for the sale of land, the title had yet to be investigated.

6–39 The bargain and sale, if enrolled, provided a new form of conveyance, although one that was a public act. A later development—the "lease and release, bargain and sale combined"—provided a private form of conveyance using s.17 as part of the device.[31] Section 2 of the Real Property Act 1845 finally did away with the need for the bargain and sale and the release, by providing that "all corporeal hereditaments lie in grant", i.e. that a simple deed of conveyance is sufficient to grant freehold estates in land. But it did not abolish the old forms. It did, however, provide that after 1845 the feoffment with livery of seisin was void unless evidenced by deed. The old ceremony was no longer enough by itself.

Implied and Resulting Uses

6–40 The Statute applied to implied and resulting uses as well as to express ones. Thus, if land was granted

> *to F in fee simple to the use of A for life*

a resulting use arose on A's death in favour of the grantor. After the Statute, the use to A was executed, giving A a legal life estate, and on A's death the resulting use would be executed giving the fee simple back to the grantor.

Corporations

6–41 Before the Statute of Uses, equity had not developed remedies which could be used against a corporation, or "body politic" as it was then called. Its main remedy, if its orders were not complied with, was imprisonment for contempt, and corporations could not be imprisoned. The words of the Statute were therefore carefully chosen. The Statute does not apply where a corporation is seized to the use of another person.[32] In the following limitation the use was not executed:

---

[29] i.e. by a deed indenture. An indenture was a deed between two or more persons.

[30] But it does not require entry: *Dwyer v Rich* (1869) I.R. 4 C.L. 424 at 436, affirmed on appeal (1872) I.R. 6 C.L. 144.

[31] See earlier editions of this work for a description of these conveyances.

[32] Plucknett, *Concise History of the Common Law* (1956), p.581.

to Acme Ltd to the use of B and his heirs.

6–42 At the time the Statute was enacted the use would not have been enforced either, but today remedies have been developed by which a modern trust may be enforced against a corporation. There was no problem, even then, however, in a corporation being a *cestui que use*, and if so, the Statute applied, so that the following gave Acme Ltd the legal fee simple:

to A and her heirs to the use of Acme Ltd.

Active Uses

6–43 The Statute was held not to apply to "active uses", i.e. where the feoffee had active duties to perform.[33] The main purpose of the Statute was to deal with uses as devices to avoid effects that would otherwise apply at common law. The lawyers at the time argued that the Statute should only be applied to such uses and not to uses similar to what today would be called trusts, i.e. uses where the feoffees had active duties to perform and were not just passive holders of the legal estate. The judges upheld this view.[34]

Statute of Wills (Ireland) 1634

6–44 Uses were employed to make what amounted to a will in equity and this device caused a loss to the royal revenue. It was therefore the declared purpose of the English Statute of Uses 1535 to abolish the power to make a will by this method and therefore to abolish the power to make wills generally. This effect of the Statute caused a popular outcry and contributed to demonstrations known as the Pilgrimage of Grace of 1539. Henry VIII compromised. The Statute of Wills 1540 granted the power to make wills of all land held in fee simple by socage tenure and two-thirds of all land held in fee simple by knight service. But it also provided that the devisee was to be liable for feudal incidents as if he or she were the heir. The king was to get his revenue. The Tenures Abolition Act had the effect of completing the freedom of testation by converting land held in knight service to socage.

6–45 The Statute of Wills (Ireland) 1634 was passed in the same year as the Irish Statute of Uses which therefore never had any effect in relation to wills in Ireland, although it curiously contained the same preamble as the English Statute. The Irish Statute of Wills contained the same provision as the English Statute imposing reliefs on devisees and these were not abolished by the Tenures Abolition Act 1662, but they became obsolete through inflation.

---

[33] This was confirmed in modern times by the Northern Ireland Court of Appeal in *Re Sergie* [1954] N.I. 1. See the second edition of this book.

[34] R. Brooke, *La Graunde Abridgement* (London, 1573); "Feffements al Uses", pl. 50 (1545), cited in S.F.C. Milsom, *Historical Foundations of the Common Law* (London: Butterworths, 1969), p.403.

The Rise of the Trust
Express Trusts

6–46 Before the Statute, uses were used by landowners to avoid feudal incidents payable to the lord. Since mesne lordships had tended to disappear after *Quia Emptores*, that lord was often the king, who procured the Statute to recover his revenue. The Statute, by executing most uses, would effectively have prevented the creation of equitable interests in land. These were much too useful to landowners for a variety of purposes for them to accept this readily and they set their lawyers the task of finding ways of avoiding the Statute. The first method attempted was to convey land to a feoffee to the use of someone else and then to create a second use, often referred to as a "trust", to distinguish it from the first one, to take effect in favour of the intended beneficiary. So the limitation would be in the form:

> *to A [the feoffee] and his heirs to the use of B and his heirs in trust for C and his heirs [or for life, etc.]*

6–47 The use of the word "trust" instead of "use" would not in itself have the effect of avoiding the Statute, because the Statute expressly applied to a "use, confidence or trust", but the hope was that the courts might hold the second use to be effective. The first response of the courts, in *Jane Tyrrel's Case* in 1557,[35] was to hold that a use upon a use was void.[36] The court held that the Statute executed the first use, giving B the legal estate, but it also held that it was still the case, as it had been before the Statute, that a "use upon a use" was void, and so C got nothing.

6–48 However, it was not long before the attitude of the courts underwent a change. One of the principal benefits of uses—the ability to create wills—had already been conceded by the Statute of Wills. The first case which changed the position was long thought to be *Sambach v Daston* (or Dalston) in 1635[37] but Baker demonstrated in 1977 that the first enforcement of a trust in the form of a use upon a use can be traced to *Bertie v Herenden* in 1560, if not before.[38] The result of the recognition was: (a) that a "use upon a use" was valid, reversing *Tyrell's Case*, and (b) that it was not executed by the Statute. There was little logic in this position, but it suited the purpose of avoiding the Statute. After this recognition, therefore, all that had to be done to avoid the effect of

---

[35] (1557) 2 Dy. 155a; N.G. Jones, "Tyrrel's Case (1557) and the Use upon a Use" (1993) 14 J. Leg. Hist. 75.

[36] Strictly, it only did so in the case of a bargain and sale: J.H. Baker, *Oxford History of the Laws of England* (Oxford: Oxford University Press, 2003), Vol.vi, pp.685–686; N.G. Jones, "Tyrrel's Case (1557) and the Use upon a Use" (1993) 14 J. Leg. Hist. 75 at 79.

[37] (1635) 163 Toth. 188; sub nom. *Morris v Darston* (1635) Nels 30, per Lord Keeper Coventry.

[38] *Bertie v Herenden* (1560) British Library Mss Lansdowne 1067, f.2, cited in H. Baker, "The Use upon a Use in Equity 1558–1625" (1977) 93 L.Q.R. 33 at 36; N.G. Jones, "The Use upon a Use in Equity Revisited" (2002) 33 Cambrian L.R. 67; W.H. Bryson (ed.), *Cases Concerning Equity and the Courts of Equity 1550–1660* (London: Selden Society, 2001), Vol.i, p.93.

the Statute was to insert a use to exhaust the effect of the Statute and then insert the second use upon a use or trust:

to A... to the use of B... in trust for C...

The first use was executed, giving B the legal estate as trustee, while the second use took effect, giving C the equitable estate.

6–49 One technical disadvantage of this form was that B, the trustee, obtained the legal estate by virtue of the Statute, i.e. by operation of law, and not by the deed. A more refined method overcame this disadvantage:

to B ... to the use of B ... in trust for C ...

The Statute did not execute the first use as B was seised to his own use, so that B obtained the legal estate by the initial words of the limitation.[39] The courts were prepared to treat the words "to the use of B" as superfluous, in the sense that it did not give B anything more, and held the "use upon a use" valid as before, giving C the equitable estate. Later the formula was shortened to:

unto and to the use of B ... in trust for C ...

6–50 Before the LCLRA 2009, this was the formula used to create a trust in this jurisdiction. If the trust was an active one, then it would not be necessary to use it and one could use the formula:

to B ... in trust for C.

6–51 However, lawyers preferred to be on the safe side and normally employed the use upon a use.

Implied, Resulting, and Constructive Trusts
6–52 In the following example:

unto and to the use of T and U in fee simple to the use of A for life

T and U were trustees and there was an express trust in favour of A. A trust was, broadly, a use which was not executed by the Statute. The remainder of the beneficial interest was not disposed of and equity raised a resulting, or implied, trust in favour of the grantor. However, since there was no express use-upon-a-use it could have been argued that this resulting "trust" was therefore a single use and should have been executed by the Statute. Section 5 of the Statute of Frauds 1695[40] resolved the doubt by providing that such trusts were

---

[39] *Doe d Lloyd v Passingham* (1827) 6 B. & C. 305.
[40] 7 Will III c 12 (Ir), 1695.

not executed by the Statute.[41] There were therefore still distinct situations in which *uses* were implied or resulted, and which were executed, and in which *trusts* were implied or resulted or were constructed, and were not executed.

The Abolition of the Statute of Uses 1634

6–53 Before the LCLRA 2009 the Statute of Uses 1634 still applied and its effects had to be taken into account by conveyances. The LCLRA 2009 has now repealed the Statute,[42] and the repeal has the following principal effects:

(a) Words necessary to create a trust.
(b) Voluntary conveyances.
(c) Vendor and purchaser (bargain and sale).
(d) Covenant to stand seized.
(e) Conveyance to self or self and another.
(f) Express reservation of an easement.
(g) Future interests.
(h) Powers of appointment and sale.

Words Necessary to Create a Trust

6–54 The formula "unto and to the use of A in fee simple in trust for B for life", etc. need no longer be used in order to vest the legal fee simple in A as trustee and the equitable life estate in B. It would be sufficient to say "to A in fee simple in trust,[43] for B for life", etc.

Conveyance without Consideration

6–55 In the conveyance of an estate in which there was no mention of consideration, known as a "voluntary" conveyance, equity generally presumed that the conveyance was not intended to be a gift and implied a use back to the grantor. The presumption can be rebutted by evidence that the beneficial interest is to be conferred on the grantee. Thus, if the deed states that it was executed in favour of X in consideration of "natural love and affection", such consideration is for this purpose sufficient, since it rebuts the presumption that X is not to take the benefit. If the donor and donee are closely related by blood or marriage, equity presumed natural love and affection is the consideration.[44]

---

[41] Sanders, *An Essay on the Nature and Laws of Uses and Trusts* (1791), p.211; *Lamplugh v Lamplugh* (1709) 1 P. Wms. 112.

[42] LCLRA 2009 Sch.2, Pt 1.

[43] The word "trust" need not be used, since "use, confidence or trust" were sufficient under the old law to refer to a use, provided it is clear that B is to take the beneficial, i.e. equitable, interest.

[44] *Ellis v Nimmo* (1835) Ll. & G.t.S. 333; *Re Luby's Estate* (1909) 43 I.L.T.R. 141.

6–56 The presumption of advancement also arose in some relationships. If X was the son of the grantor, the father and son relationship raises the presumption of advancement.[45]

6–57 Where the presumption of resulting use was raised but not rebutted, a use was implied back to the grantor. The Statute executed implied uses as well as express ones, and the result was that the grantor got the legal estate back again.[46] The whole conveyance was ineffective.

6–58 In order to make a conveyance without consideration effective in Ireland before the abolition of the Statute of Uses, words had to be inserted to indicate that the grantee was indeed to have the beneficial interest. The usual form in such a case was, "unto and to the use of X and his [or her] heirs".[47] The words "to the use of" indicated that X was to take *both* the legal estate *and* the beneficial interest in the land. Since there was an express use in favour of the grantee, there was no implied use back to the grantor for the Statute to execute. The express use was not executed because X was seised of the legal estate to his own use.

6–59 Section 62(3) of the LCLRA 2009 provides that in a voluntary deed executed after 1 December 2009, "a resulting use to the grantor is not implied merely because the land is not expressed to be conveyed for the use or benefit of the grantee".[48] This had previously been enacted in relation to registered land.[49] The presumption is reversed: it is presumed that the grantee is to take the benefit unless the contrary is shown.

Vendor and Purchaser
6–60 The repeal of the Statute of Uses, including s.17, has done away with bargain and sale and enrolment. Section 62(1) of the LCLRA 2009 provides that an estate or interest in land may only be conveyed by deed, and s.62(4) expressly provides that a bargain and sale is "no longer effective to create or to convey a legal estate or legal interest in land".[50] The word "legal" is significant.

---

[45] See *Redington v Redington* (1794) 3 Ridg. P.C. 106.

[46] Sanders, *An Essay on the Nature and Laws of Uses and Trusts* (1791), p.106; *Armstrong v Wolsey* (1755) 2 Wils. K.B. 19; *Beckwith's Case* (1589) 2 Co. Rep. 56 at 58; *Read v Errington* (1591) Cro. Eliz. 321.

[47] *Savill v Bethell* [1902] 2 Ch. 523. See also, *Doe d Lloyd v Passingham* (1827) 6 B. & C. 305; *Orme's Case* (1872) L.R. 8 C.P. 281; C. Sweet (ed.), *Challis's Law of Real Property*, 3rd edn (London: Butterworth, 1911), p.389.

[48] LCLRA 2009 s.62(3). See also, LCLRA 2009 Explanatory Memorandum, p.30.

[49] Registration of Title Act 1964 s.123(3).

[50] Section 62(4) also applies to a "covenant to stand seised, feoffment with livery of seisin or any combination of these".

Contracts for the sale of land today therefore give rise to a kind of trust, the "purchaser's equity", which is the equivalent of the old implied use.[51]

Covenant to Stand Seised

6–61 Before the Statute of Uses an owner of land might enter into a covenant (a contract under seal) to "stand seised" of the land in favour of someone else. In other words, instead of conveying the legal estate to a feoffee to hold to the use of X, the grantor simply declared that he held the legal estate himself to the use of X. The common law did not recognise the use, but equity recognised "natural love and affection" as consideration sufficient to enforce a covenant to stand seised, provided the parties were in fact near relations: a child, sibling, nephew, niece, or cousin.[52] Equity developed the doctrine further by recognising certain transactions as implied covenants to stand seised. For example, if X covenanted with his son, Y, to grant land to Y on his forthcoming marriage, but never did so, equity would treat the covenant as one by which X stood seised of the land to the use of Y.[53] Furthermore, a feoffment without livery of seisin, ineffective at common law, might be treated in equity as a covenant to stand seised if the parties were near relations.[54]

6–62 The effect of the Statute of Uses was to execute the use, conveying the legal estate to the relation. This was another example of the Statute giving rise to a new form of conveyance, but one of limited use, because it was only effective if the parties were near relatives.

6–63 The repeal of the Statute of Uses 1634 means that the use is no longer executed and a covenant to stand seised, if made after the LCLRA 2009, would no longer convey the legal estate to the *cestui que use*. This is confirmed by s.62(4) of the LCLRA 2009, which includes the covenant to stand seised in the list of old conveyances which are no longer effective "to create or to convey a legal estate or legal interest in land". The use nevertheless remains. So a covenant to stand seised, if one were made after the LCLRA 2009, would operate as a declaration of trust, if the court was of the view that this would be in accordance with the intention of the covenantor, since equity looks to the intent and not the form.[55]

---

[51] Irish cases suggested that this trust only arose if part of the purchase money is paid: *Tempany v Hynes* [1976] I.R. 101. Appendix A in the first and second editions of this work criticised the case. Section 52 of the LCLRA 2009 restores the previously accepted view that the entire beneficial interest in land passes to the purchaser upon entering into the contract for sale, regardless of how much of the purchase price is paid at that time (LCLRA 2009 Explanatory Memorandum, p.28).

[52] *Sharrington v Strotton* (1565) 1 Plow. 298; K.E. Digby, *Introduction to the History of the Law of Real Property* (Oxford: Clarendon Press, 1875), p.252.

[53] *Maguire v Scully* (1862) 12 Ir. Ch. R. 153.

[54] *Shove v Pincke* (1793) 5 T.R. 124, (1793) 5 T.R. 310; *Habergham v Vincent* (1790) 2 Ves. Jun. 204 at 226.

[55] See also, LCLRA 2009 s.1(7): "Nothing in this Act affects judicial recognition of equitable interests."

Conveyance to Self, or to Self and Another

6–64 At common law freehold could not be conveyed to oneself or to oneself and another party, because the feoffment involved a transfer of seisin. The common law adopted the strict rule that if a person was already seised, he could not transfer it to himself. After the Statute of Uses, lawyers used a feoffment to uses, the use then being executed by the Statute, to achieve this.[56] Transfer to oneself was necessary in two instances: (1) in the process of disentailing a fee tail, and (2) if a man wanted to transfer property to himself and his wife, or vice versa.

6–65 Since fees tail are abolished by the LCLRA 2009, (1) is no longer necessary, and as to (2), the LCLRA 2009 now provides that "any property may be conveyed by a person to that person jointly with another person in the same way in which it might be conveyed by that person to another person",[57] and "a person may convey, but not lease, property to that same person in a different capacity".[58]

FORMALITIES

Creation

6–66 Section 4 of the Statute of Frauds 1695 requires any "declarations or creations" of "trusts or confidences" of lands or hereditaments to be in writing and signed by the party able to make them. The word "confidence" recalls the words of the Statute of Uses 1634 and appears to mean that the section applies regardless of what word is used to refer to the trust. Section 5 exempts implied and constructive trusts.

6–67 The phrase "trusts or confidences" probably does not include the declaration or creation of other equitable interests. A purchaser's equity is created by implication of equity, and so need not itself be in writing, although in this instance it will necessarily arise only if there is an enforceable contract. Section 2 of the Statute of Frauds 1695, which required a note or memorandum in writing for the contract to be enforceable, with part performance as an alternative, has been re-enacted by s.51 of the LCLRA 2009:

> "51.—(1) Subject to subsection (2), no action shall be brought to enforce any contract for the sale or other disposition of land unless the agreement on which such action is brought, or some memorandum or note of it, is in writing and signed by the person against whom the action is brought or that person's authorised agent.
> (2) Subsection (1) does not affect the law relating to part performance or other equitable doctrines."

---

[56] These methods were considered in more detail in the second edition of this book.
[57] LCLRA 2009 s.66(1).
[58] LCLRA 2009 s.66(2)(a).

Assignment

6–68 Section 6 of the Statute of Frauds 1695 (which is not repealed by the LCLRA 2009) requires "grants and assignments" of "any trust or confidence" to be in writing. Thus, any subsequent assignment of the beneficial interest under a trust requires writing. There is, however, no requirement of writing for the assignment of equities not falling within the phrase "trust or confidence", such as a purchaser's equity.

MERGER OF LAW AND EQUITY

The Problems of Separate Jurisdictions

6–69 By the 17th century, law and equity were still separate systems of justice. Litigants who wanted damages or the recovery of their land had to go to one of the common law courts. Litigants who wanted an injunction, or specific performance of a contract, had to go to the Court of Chancery, or the equity side of the Court of Exchequer. Equity regarded itself as supplementary to the common law and so if a remedy existed at common law, the courts of equity refused to intervene and merely referred the party to the common law courts.[59]

6–70 In Ireland, the Court of Chancery began to modify this rule and to allow actions to be brought where a common law remedy existed but was useless or difficult to obtain.[60] Differences in jurisdiction still caused problems. Courts of equity still had sometimes to consider granting injunctions to prevent actions at law.[61] Courts of equity had no jurisdiction to award damages[62] until the Chancery Amendment Act 1858 (Lord Cairns' Act), which is still in force in Ireland, conferred jurisdiction to award damages "in addition to or in substitution for" specific performance or an injunction.[63]

6–71 Following the Industrial Revolution, business in the courts of common law and equity increased, worsening the delays experienced by litigants. The courts of equity were under-funded and under-staffed. In addition to the delays in Chancery, there was also an element of uncertainty for litigants in having to choose between three courts of common law (King's Bench, Common Pleas and Exchequer).

Supreme Court of Judicature (Ireland) Act 1877

6–72 The Supreme Court of Judicature (Ireland) Act 1877 (the "1877 Act"), like its English counterpart, created a single High Court in which both law

---

[59] For example, *McCarthy v Barry* (1860) 9 Ir. Ch. R. 377.

[60] *Brady v Fitzgerald* (1850) 12 Ir. Eq. R. 273.

[61] For example, *Mountcashell (Earl) v O'Neill (Viscount)* (1855) 3 Ir. Ch. R. 455; *Johnson v Young* (1876) I.R. 10 Eq. 403.

[62] *Clinan v Cooke* (1802) 1 Sch. & Lef. 22 at 25 (no power to grant damages for non-performance of an agreement).

[63] The Act was repealed in England by the Statute Law Revision and Civil Procedure Act 1883.

and equity would be administered. For convenience, the court sat in divisions corresponding to the types of disputes dealt with by the old courts, but all divisions had identical jurisdiction.[64] On some points, law and equity had adopted different rules, leading to awkward and absurd conflicts within what was supposed to be a single legal system.[65] Section 28(11) of the 1877 Act provides for the resolution of conflicts between law and equity on some specific points.[66]

> "In all matters not hereinbefore mentioned in which there is any conflict or variance between the rules of equity and the rules of common law with reference to the same subject matter, the rules of equity shall prevail."[67]

6–73 The first major case on this subsection was *Walsh v Lonsdale*.[68] Lonsdale (L) agreed in writing not under seal to grant a seven-year lease of a mill to Walsh (W). One of the terms of the written lease was that one year's rent was to be paid in advance. After 18 months L demanded the rent in advance. W refused. He said he would pay quarterly. L then distrained for the rent. W sued him for wrongful distress.

6–74 It was clear that the written document was not a valid lease because it was at that time required to be by deed: if not, it was "void at law".[69] Before the 1877 Act there were two different approaches where a document was not valid as a lease. At common law if a person went into possession of land and paid rent on a basis referable to a year (e.g. quarterly), he or she held the land on a common law tenancy from year to year. He or she held on the terms of the written document not inconsistent with such a tenancy.[70] Equity, on the other hand, held that a written document not valid as a lease could be treated as an agreement to grant a lease (i.e. a contract) and equity "would regard as done that which ought to be done" and would treat the parties as if there already was a lease in equity.[71]

6–75 W's argument, based on the common law, was that he was a tenant from year to year at common law, that the provision for one year's rent in advance was inconsistent with such a tenancy and so must be struck out. Therefore, L's distress was unlawful. L's argument, based on equity, was that the agreement

---

[64] *Barber v Houston* (1886) 18 L.R. Ir. 475 (equity prevailed even in the common law divisions of the court).

[65] For example, *Johnson v Midland Great Western Railway* (1857) 5 Ir. Ch. R. 264.

[66] For example, *Feehan v Mandeville* (1891) 28 L.R. Ir. 90. See s.25 of the English Supreme Court of Judicature Act 1873.

[67] See *Barber v Houston* (1886) 18 L.R. Ir. 475.

[68] (1882) 21 Ch. D. 9.

[69] The applicable provisions were the English Statute of Frauds 1677 and the Real Property Act 1845. In *Parker v Taswell* (1858) 2 De. G. & J. 559, it was held that "void at law" did not mean void for all purposes.

[70] *Fahy v O'Donnell* (1869) I.R. 4 C.L. 332; *McCreesh v McGeogh* (1872) I.R. 7 C.L. 236 (tenant under agreement could maintain trespass against landlord).

[71] *Parker v Taswell* (1858) 2 De. G. & J. 559 at 573.

created a lease in equity and so all the terms in the written document were binding on the parties, including the provision for one year's rent in advance. Therefore the distress was lawful.

6–76 The court held in favour of L. There was a conflict between the rules of law and the rules of equity on the same issue and the rules of equity now prevailed. In the words of Jessel M.R.:

> "There are not two estates as there were formerly, one estate at common law by reason of the payment of rent from year to year, and an estate in equity under the agreement. There is only one court and the equity rules prevail in it."[72]

6–77 It should be noticed that there is a shift in ideas here. The common law rule expressed the concepts of a pre-market society. It applied tests to determine what type of interest the parties had created and then supplied the contents of each available "type" of interest. The parties could not change these terms by agreement. By the late 19th century the common law had begun to recognise the importance of the agreement between the parties. It recognised such of the terms of the written agreement as were not inconsistent with the tenancy imposed by the common law. In equity, on the other hand, agreement was fundamental. Equity in this respect expresses in a clear and uncompromising way the concepts of a market or capitalist society. Equity left the parties to make their own bargain and confined itself to examining what had been agreed and then to giving effect to it.

The "Merger" of Law and Equity?

6–78 For many purposes, legal and equitable rights remain distinct after the 1877 Act. There are still distinct legal and equitable estates: the 1877 Act did not abolish trusts. There are still distinctions between legal and equitable remedies, principally that equitable remedies are discretionary.[73] This discretion has been somewhat reduced to recognisable rules, but that does not affect the point that a claimant may be disentitled from obtaining an equitable remedy on grounds which would not have a similar effect on a legal remedy.

6–79 However, it is clear that law and equity are no longer as distinct as they were before the 1877 Act. For example, an injunction may now be granted to give effect to a legal right.[74] There are some rules which cannot be classified

---

[72] (1882) 21 Ch. D. 9 at 14f.

[73] There is even still some distinction in jurisdiction, since it appears that the District Court, although it has civil jurisdiction, has only a limited jurisdiction to grant equitable remedies. See Courts of Justice Act 1924 s.77, as amended by Courts of Justice Act 1936 ss.52 and 94, Local Government Act 1946 s.48 and Courts Act 1971 Sch.3.

[74] *Corporation of Cork v Rooney* (1881) 7 L.R. Ir. 191.

as legal or equitable, such as the law relating to rent review clauses in leases.[75] Actions for breach of confidence or to protect privacy[76] developed after the merger of the jurisdictions, and so cannot be characterised either as equitable or legal actions.

THE NATURE OF EQUITABLE INTERESTS

Definite Property

6–80 In general, if a trustee (T) holds property in trust for a beneficiary (B), then B cannot direct T how to go about her duties. T can use her own discretion and need not even consult B, who may only sue T if she acts in breach of trust; in other words, if T acts contrary to the terms of the trust or to the standards of conduct laid down by the courts of equity.

6–81 But is B the real owner of the property? Let us say that income from the trust, such as dividends or rent, is received by T. Is each sum of money the property of B, subject only to T's right to deduct expenses, or has B only an action of account against the trustee to account for the balance? The courts have held that for this purpose the beneficiary "owns" each sum of money[77] and so is liable to pay income tax on the gross amount, before the trustee deducts expenses.[78] On the other hand, where a trustee has granted a lease of trust property, it has been held that the trustee, and not the beneficiary, is entitled to distrain for the rent.[79] For this purpose the trustee was held to be the "owner" of the trust property.

6–82 Someone entitled as a potential beneficiary under a discretionary trust, who therefore only has a contingent interest in the property, has nevertheless been held to be entitled to bring an action to prevent dissipation of the fund[80] or to remedies appropriate to monitor the administration of the fund and its investments.[81] Even though he might never receive any of the property, if the trust fund is dissipated, he will lose even the possibility of receiving any, and that possibility is his property interest.

---

[75] *United Scientific Holdings v Burnley BC* [1978] A.C. 904; *Hynes v Independent Newspapers* [1980] I.R. 204 at 218; *Ely Ltd v ICR Ltd*, unreported, High Court, McWilliam J., 3 April 1979.

[76] For example, *Cream Holdings Ltd v Banerjee* [2005] 1 A.C. 253.

[77] *Baker v Archer-Shee* [1927] A.C. 844; *Forbes (Inspector of Taxes) v GHD* [1964] T.I.T.R. 491.

[78] If the beneficiary is entitled under a settlement executed in Ireland to securities held abroad, the test of the "proper law" is applied to the foreign securities and liability to tax is not determined by the fact that the settlement was made in Ireland: *Re Knox* [1963] I.R. 263.

[79] *Schalit v Joseph Nadler Ltd* [1933] 2 K.B. 79. One explanation of this is that distress was a common law remedy before the 1877 Act and this may be another example of the survival of the distinction between common law and equitable remedies.

[80] *Jacob v Revenue Commissioners*, unreported, High Court, McWilliam J., 6 July 1983.

[81] *Chaine-Nickson v Bank of Ireland* [1976] I.R. 393.

Definite Right

6–83 In the case of common law rights, a plaintiff who establishes an infringement of his or her rights is entitled to a remedy, even if it is only nominal damages. In equity there is no such entitlement because all equitable remedies are discretionary. So even if X proves he or she is entitled to an equitable interest, he or she will not get a remedy if he or she has acted inequitably, e.g. dishonestly in some way. The maxim is: "he who comes to equity must come with clean hands".[82]

Enforceability

6–84 It has been said that legal rights are rights *in rem* (rights to a thing), whereas equitable rights are rights *in personam* (rights against persons). Legal rights are available against everybody, but equitable rights are available only against a limited class of people. However, this is misleading. All rights to property are really rights against persons. Even in the case of common law rights there is relativity of title in land rights, so that the holder of a legal title to land may be able to defend it against most people, but not all. Like most misleading statements, there is some truth in it. Equitable rights are enforceable against a more limited class of people than legal rights.

Common Law Rights

6–85 L, the owner of land in fee simple, grants a legal lease of it to T for 50 years. Later, L assigns his freehold reversion in fee simple to L2. Let us suppose that for some reason L2 thought she was buying the fee simple in possession—the immediate fee simple in the land—and was not aware of the lease in favour of T. L2 is nevertheless bound by T's lease. It is a legal interest and, as such, binds everyone, regardless of notice. L2's remedy is against L, if L has misled L2 as to the state of the title. But T has the right to remain in possession, provided T pays L2 the rent and complies with the other terms of the lease.

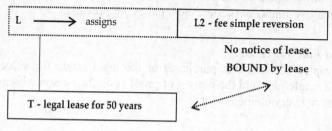

6–86 The assignee is bound. It matters not whether the assignee has notice of the prior legal right or not.[83] As between two legal interests, the first in time prevails.

---

[82] See *Re French's Estate* (1887) 21 L.R. Ir. 283.
[83] *Corry v Cremorne* (1862) 12 Ir. Ch. R. 136; *Finch v Shaw* (1854) 19 Beav. 500.

Equitable Rights

6–87 When courts began to recognise equitable interests, they at first gave only a personal action against the trustee if he or she misused the property. But suppose the trustee sold the legal title to someone else? Courts of equity decided that they would not interfere with the alienability of legal estates. To do so would certainly have placed a restriction on the operation of the market and it may be that in developing this principle equity was again showing its preference for market relations.

6–88 Equity "follows the law". It does not deny that the trustee as owner of the legal estate has the right to transfer it. Instead, it says that the person who takes the legal estate from the trustee is, under some circumstances, bound by the equity. But when was such a person to be bound? Equity produced a compromise. It would enforce the equitable interests against everyone except a bona fide purchaser of the legal estate without notice of the equity, or anyone taking from such a person. This has been called the "Polar Star Rule"[84] of equity, the guiding principle of all equitable interests.

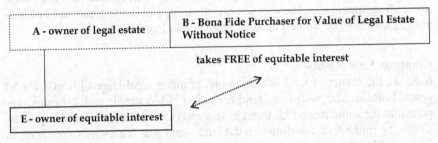

6–89 The courts expressed the rule as to the priority of the two interests in the maxim, "where the equities are equal the law prevails". "Equity" is not used here in the sense of equitable interests but in the sense of moral claims. As between two innocent parties, the legal estate prevails.

The Bona Fide Purchaser

6–90 The plea of bona fide purchaser of the legal estate for value without notice is a single plea and the burden of proof is on the person who asserts the plea to prove every element of it.[85]

Bona Fide

6–91 This requirement means that the purchaser must act in good faith according to equitable principles.[86]

---

[84] *Stanhope v Earl Verney* (1761) 2 Eden 81 at 85.

[85] *Heneghan v Davitt* [1933] I.R. 325; *Allied Irish Banks plc v Finnegan* [1996] 1 I.L.R.M. 401.

[86] *Re O'Neill, a Bankrupt* [1989] I.R. 544.

Purchaser

6–92 "Purchaser" traditionally has had a special meaning in the law of real property. It denotes a person who takes other than by operation of law, i.e. by some act of a party or parties. Thus, someone who takes under a will is a purchaser, but a person who takes on intestacy is not. The word in this technical sense does not imply that value has been paid.[87]

For Value

6–93 The purchaser also has to give value for the legal estate. Thus, someone who takes under a will is a *purchaser* in the technical sense of real property, i.e. takes the interest otherwise than by operation of law, but does not pay value and so will not take free of equitable interests. Here again equity shows that it favours the operation of a free market. As between two innocent parties, equity favours the one who pays money for the property as a commodity and not the owner of an equitable interest who may have come by it gratuitously under a trust.

6–94 The fact that this rule expresses a fundamental compromise favouring the market is also shown by the definition of "value" in this context. It includes money or money's worth, i.e. land, services, etc., and also includes the satisfaction of an existing debt,[88] but it does not include "natural love and affection" which equity recognises as consideration in other contexts.[89]

Of the Legal Estate

6–95 In order to take the property free of an equitable estate or interest, the purchaser must have the legal estate. The only qualification on this is if the interest which is first in time is a lesser type of equity, known as "mere equity".

Without Notice

6–96 There are three kinds of notice: actual, imputed and constructive.[90] Actual notice is actual knowledge of facts, however acquired, although one need not listen to mere rumours.[91] Imputed notice means that the notice of a legal representative, actual or constructive, is imputed to the client. Constructive notice occurs if the person has actual notice that the property is affected in some way by another interest and fails to make inquiries as to the nature of the other interest, when such inquiries would have revealed what it was. Alternatively, constructive notice arises where a person deliberately abstains from making inquiries in order to avoid actual notice, or omits by carelessness or

---

[87] See, for example, *Re Nisbett and Pott's Contract* [1906] 1 Ch. 386 (a "squatter" was not a purchaser because he had acquired his interest by operation of law).

[88] The satisfaction of an existing debt is not consideration at common law: *Foakes v Beer* (1884) 9 App. Cas. 605.

[89] Such as consideration sufficient to support a covenant to stand seized.

[90] *Bank of Ireland Finance Ltd v Rockfield Ltd* [1979] I.R. 21 at 29.

[91] *Waldron v Jacob & Millie* (1870) I.R. 5 Eq. 131; *Aldritt v Maconchy* [1906] 1 Ch. 333.

any other reason to make an inquiry which a purchaser acting on proper legal advice ought to make and which would have revealed the interest.

6–97 Section 86 of the LCLRA 2009 re-enacts s.3 of the Conveyancing Act 1882 by placing some restrictions on the doctrine of constructive notice[92]:

> "86.—(1) A purchaser is not affected prejudicially by notice of any fact, instrument, matter or thing unless—
>   (a) it is within the purchaser's own knowledge or would have come to the purchaser's knowledge if such inquiries and inspections had been made as ought reasonably to have been made by the purchaser, or
>   (b) in the same transaction with respect to which a question of notice to the purchaser arises, it has come to the knowledge of the purchaser's counsel … or solicitor or other agent … or would have come to the knowledge of the solicitor or other agent if such inquiries and inspections had been made as ought reasonably to have been made by the solicitor or agent.
> (2) [A purchaser is still liable under covenants and restrictions in any instrument under which the purchaser's title is derived.]
> (3) A purchaser is not, by reason of anything in this section, affected by notice in any case where the purchaser would not have been so affected if this section had not been enacted."

6–98 The effect of constructive notice is also mitigated by s.21 of the LCLRA 2009 which provides for equitable interests under a trust of land to be overreached on sale by the fee simple owner.

6–99 In *Northern Bank v Henry*,[93] Henchy J. expressed the view that s.3 of the Conveyancing Act 1882 "gave statutory stress to the existing judicial insistence that constructive notice could be found only when the lack of knowledge was due to such careless inactivity as would not be expected in the circumstances from a reasonable man." He went on to draw a distinction between the conduct of a prudent person in business and that of a reasonable person who is the subject of the legal test[94]:

> "The default of a reasonable man is to be distinguished from the default of a prudent man. The prudence of the worldly wise may justifiably persuade a purchaser that it would be unbusinesslike to stop and look more deeply into certain aspects of the title. But the reasonable man, in the eyes of the law, will be expected to look beyond the impact of his decisions on his own affairs, and to consider whether they may unfairly and prejudicially affect

---

his 'neighbour,' in the sense in which that word has been given juristic currency by Lord Atkin in *Donoghue v. Stevenson.*"

6–100 Thus the judge refused to reduce the test of notice to the morality of a person acting in pursuit of his or her own economic self-interest.[95] Although the "reasonableness test" enlarges the scope of inquiries a purchaser should make, Blayney J. has pointed out that there are difficulties in regarding it as a *duty* owed to the owner of the equity.[96] If the purchaser fails to make the necessary inquiries it is the purchaser who loses, because he or she is then bound by the equity.

6–101 In *Bank of Ireland Finance Ltd v Rockfield Ltd,*[97] the Supreme Court approved of a line of authority to the effect that constructive notice should not be applied to purely commercial transactions, i.e. where both parties are engaged in a commercial undertaking, other than buying land.

Length of Title
6–102 At common law, if the contract did not specify the length of title to be shown by the vendor (i.e. if it was an "open" contract), the title was to be investigated back for 60 years. If a "good root of title" was not encountered at that point, then the investigation continued until one was found. Section 1 of the Vendor and Purchaser Act 1874 provided that in unregistered conveyancing a purchaser had to accept a good root of title at least 40 years old.[98] Section 56(1) of the LCLRA 2009 now provides that in an open contract "after the commencement of this Chapter, a period of at least 15 years commencing with a good root of title is the period for proof of title which the purchaser may require".[99] The purchaser may agree in the contract to investigate the title for a shorter period than 15 years, although given the shortness of the period, this would seem unlikely in practice.[100] Can the purchaser, by doing this, avoid notice of interests she would have discovered if she had investigated title back for the full period? Whatever the position was before the Conveyancing Act 1882, the courts made it clear that under s.1(2) of the 1882 Act she cannot

---

[95] Where a third party, such as a bank, seeks consent of a spouse to a mortgage or charge of a family home under s.3 of the Family Home Protection Act 1976, there is an analogous doctrine of notice, but in *Bank of Ireland v Smyth* [1996] 1 I.L.R.M. 24, the Supreme Court held that the third party does not owe a duty to the non-conveying spouse.

[96] *Bank of Ireland v Smyth* [1996] 1 I.L.R.M. 24. The case involved the Family Home Protection Act 1976.

[97] [1979] I.R. 21 at 29.

[98] See J.C.W. Wylie and U. Woods, *Irish Conveyancing Law*, 3rd edn (Dublin: Butterworths, 2005), paras 13.54 and 14.56.

[99] LCLRA 2009 s.56(2) provides: "Where the title originates with a fee farm grant or lease, subsection (1) does not prevent the purchaser from requiring production of the fee farm grant or lease." The section is intended to replace s.1 of the Vendor and Purchaser Act 1874: LCLRA 2009 Explanatory Memorandum, pp.28–29.

[100] LCLRA 2009 s.56(3) provides: "Subsection (1) takes effect subject to the terms of the contract for the sale or other disposition of the land."

do so.[101] It would be unfair for a vendor and purchaser, by agreeing between themselves to accept a shorter period, to prejudice the rights of a third party entitled to an equity.

6–103 In *Re Nisbett and Pott's Contract*,[102] the vendor, who claimed through the squatter, would also be bound by the restrictive covenant unless he could prove the plea of bona fide purchaser. He failed to do so because he had not investigated the title back for the full statutory period. Had he done so he would have discovered the restrictive covenant. He therefore had constructive notice of the covenant.

Rights of Persons in Occupation
6–104 Normally a purchaser should inquire as to whether anyone is in occupation of the premises for he will have constructive notice of their rights if he does not.[103]

Priority between Equitable Interests
6–105 If the bona fide purchaser only has an equitable estate, then prima facie the "equities are equal", i.e. there are two estates of equal status and the first in time prevails, just as is the case with two legal estates. However, in equity, time of creation is not the only factor to be considered. Since equitable remedies are discretionary, the holder of the equitable interest which is first in time may lose priority over a later equity of equal "rank" because he has not acted equitably himself.[104] Thus, even though equity A and equity B both rank as equitable estates, and equity A is prior in time, the holder of equity A may lose priority over equity B if he has acted fraudulently or otherwise inequitably in the circumstances of the case.

6–106 There is one exception to the principle that in general priority between equitable interests is determined by the rule that the first in time prevails. There is an inferior type of equity known as a "mere equity". A mere equity can be defeated by the later bona fide purchaser of an equitable estate or interest, taken for value and without notice of the mere equity.

Or a Person Taking from Such a Purchaser
6–107 Successors in title to a bona fide purchaser for value of the legal estate without notice will also take free of the equity, even if they have notice of

---

[101] *Somers v Weir* [1979] I.R. 94 at 108; *Northern Bank v Henry* [1981] I.R. 1; *Re Cox and Neve* [1891] 2 Ch. 109; *Re Nisbet and Pott's Contract* [1905] 1 Ch. 391, [1906] 1 Ch. 386.

[102] [1906] 1 Ch. 386.

[103] *Delap v Richardson*, in A. Lyall (ed.), *Irish Exchequer Reports: Reports of Cases in the Courts of Exchequer and Chancery in Ireland 1716–1734* (London: Selden Society, 2008), p.127, per Lord Midleton L.C.; *Hamilton v Lyster* (1844) 7 Ir. Eq. R. 560; *Hunt v Luck* [1902] 1 Ch. 428; *Northern Bank v Henry* [1987] I.R. 7.

[104] *Re Ffrench's Estate* (1887) 21 L.R. Ir. 283.

it themselves, provided they are bona fide.[105] An exception is the case of a fraudulent purchaser. In *Re Stewart's Estate*, Monroe J. held as follows[106]:

> "A purchaser with notice from a purchaser without notice is protected if the transaction be *bona fide*, the only exception being the case of a trustee buying back trust property which he has sold[107]; or that of a fraudulent person, who has acquired property by fraud, saying he has sold it to a *bona fide* purchaser without notice, and has got it back again."

6–108 This aspect of the bona fide purchaser doctrine does not seem particularly equitable. On the contrary, it seems that equity is acquiescing in conduct which falls short of the high standards it expects elsewhere. A possible explanation is that equity's concern with the conscience of individuals is superficial, and that it is more concerned with the efficient working of a market economy.[108]

Mere Equities

6–109 Mere equities are usually rights to equitable relief, such as the right to have a document rectified for mistake[109] or to have a transaction set aside for fraud[110] or undue influence.[111] They are a lesser kind of equitable interest in that they are more easily defeated than equitable estates. A mere equity can be defeated by a bona fide purchaser for value of a legal *or equitable* estate without notice of the equity.

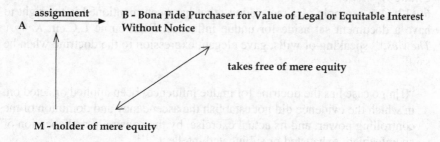

6–110 In *Allied Irish Banks v Glynn*,[112] a father was the registered owner of a piece of land. He executed a transfer of the land in favour of his son.

---

[105] *Salsbury v Bagott* (1677) 2 Sw. 603; *Mertins v Jolliffe* (1756) Amb. 311 at 312.
[106] (1893) 31 L.R. Ir. 405 at 415. See also, *Wilkes v Spooner* [1911] 2 K.B. 473; *Re Stapleford Colliery Co (Barrow's Case)* (1880) 14 Ch. D. 432 at 455.
[107] See also *Kennedy v Daly* (1803) 1 Sch. & Lef. 355 at 379.
[108] For example, see *Wilkes v Spooner* [1911] 2 K.B. 473 and *Re Stewart's Estate* (1893) 31 L.R. Ir. 405.
[109] *Re Ottley's Estate* [1910] 1 I.R. 1; *Maguire v Conway* [1950] I.R. 44; *Smith v Jones* [1954] 1 W.L.R. 1089.
[110] *Allied Irish Banks v Glynn* [1973] I.R. 188; *Ernest v Vivian* (1863) 33 L.J. Ch. 513.
[111] *Kelly v Thewles* (1854) 2 Ir. Ch. R. 510 at 541; *Allied Irish Banks v Glynn* [1973] I.R. 188.
[112] [1973] I.R. 188.

The son later mortgaged the land by an equitable mortgage in favour of the bank. An equitable mortgage ranks as an equitable estate. The High Court held that the father's right to set aside the transfer was a mere equity which must yield to the equitable mortgage, even though the mortgage was later in time. The bank was a bona fide purchaser of an equitable estate without notice of the mere equity.

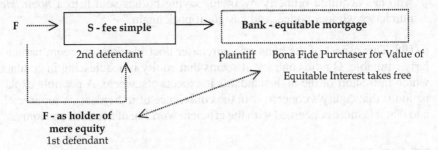

6–111 The father would still have a remedy against the son to recover the fee simple, but would hold it subject to the bank's mortgage. He would also have a remedy against the son for money paid to the bank in respect of the mortgage.

Undue Influence

6–112 One example of a mere equity that has been mentioned is the right to have a document set aside for undue influence. Blackburne L.C. in *Kelly v Thewles*,[113] speaking of wills, gave elegant expression to the doctrine when he said:

> "[I]n no case has the doctrine [of undue influence] been applied or acted on, in which the evidence did not establish the ascendancy and dominion of the controlling power, and its actual exercise, by the constraint and coercion of an enfeebled, exhausted or subjugated intellect."[114]

6–113 In *inter vivos* dispositions, certain relationships—such as parent and child,[115] uncle and nephew,[116] guardian and ward,[117] doctor and patient,[118] solicitor and client,[119] trustee and beneficiary,[120] and religious adviser and lay

[113] (1854) 2 Ir. Ch. R. 510.

[114] (1854) 2 Ir. Ch. R. 510 at 541.

[115] *Carroll v Carroll* [1998] 2 I.L.R.M. 218 at 229; *Gregg v Kidd* [1956] I.R. 183; *Wallace v Wallace* (1842) 2 Dru. & War. 452.

[116] *Carroll v Carroll* [1998] 2 I.L.R.M. 218 at 229; *Gregg v Kidd* [1956] I.R. 183.

[117] *Mulhallen v Marum* (1843) 3 Dru. & War. 317; *O'Connor v Foley* [1906] 1 I.R. 20.

[118] *Gregg v Kidd* [1956] I.R. 183; *Ahearne v Hogan* (1844) Dru. t. Sug. 310.

[119] *Gregg v Kidd* [1956] I.R. 183; *Taafe v Merrick* (1931) 65 I.L.T.R. 36.

[120] *Provincial Bank of Ireland v McKeever* [1941] I.R. 471.

person[121]—give rise to a *presumption* of undue influence.[122] Other relationships may give rise to the presumption.[123] The burden of proof is upon the benefited party to prove that there was no such influence brought to bear on the donor. Where no such relationship exists, the onus is on the party alleging undue influence to prove it.[124]

Escheat

6–114 Equity did not generally follow purely feudal aspects of the common law; it was a modernising influence. Equity did not apply the common law of escheat to equitable estates, even if it would have been possible to do so.

6–115 In *Burgess v Wheate*,[125] it was held that if A and B held the legal estate as trustees for C in fee simple and C died intestate and without heirs, the beneficial interest did not escheat to the Crown. The trustees were held to be entitled beneficially to the land. The case was correct as to legal history: the courts of equity did not apply feudal concepts like escheat to the new, post-feudal equitable interests. But the case had undesirable practical consequences. If a beneficiary died intestate with no obvious heirs, the trustees might be less than enthusiastic about tracing possible claimants since it was they who stood to gain if none were found.

6–116 Section 4 of the Intestates Estates Act 1884 provided that in future equitable estates should escheat as if they were legal estates. Hence, in such a case, the trustees would have held the legal estate on trust for the Crown.[126] The Act applied to Ireland[127] but was repealed by the Succession Act 1965. Section 11(3) of the Succession Act 1965 abolished escheat to the State and s.73(1) of the same Act provides that in default of any person taking the estate of an intestate, the State takes as "ultimate intestate successor". The position would therefore seem to be that in such a case the trustees hold on trust for the State.

---

[121] *Gregg v Kidd* [1956] I.R. 183; *Whyte v Meade* (1840) 2 Ir. Eq. R. 420.

[122] There is no presumption in wills, as between testator and beneficiary.

[123] *Carroll v Carroll* [1998] 2 I.L.R.M. 218; *Gregg v Kidd* [1956] I.R. 183; *R. (Proctor) v Hutton (No.2)* [1978] N.I. 139.

[124] *Carroll v Carroll* [1998] 2 I.L.R.M. 218. In *Bank of Nova Scotia v Hogan* [1997] 1 I.L.R.M. 407, the Supreme Court held that a spouse is not entitled to the same amount of protection from the doctrine of undue influence in relation to placing a burden on his or her own property, as a spouse giving consent under the Family Home Protection Act 1976 to a dealing by the other spouse with a family home vested in that spouse. Contrast *Bank of Ireland v Smyth* [1996] 1 I.L.R.M. 24.

[125] (1757–9) 1 Eden 128, 176; *Cox v Parker* (1856) 22 Beav. 168; *Taylor v Haygarth* (1844) 14 Sim. 8; *Beale v Symonds* (1853) 16 Beav. 406.

[126] *Re Lowe's Will Trusts* [1973] 2 All E.R. 1136.

[127] Intestates Estates Act 1884 s.9.

The Personal and Proprietary Remedies
General
6–117 It is sometimes said that equity acts *in personam* whereas the common law acts *in rem*.[128] This is true in some senses but untrue in others. It is true that if a person disobeys an equitable order of court he or she may be imprisoned for contempt, which does not automatically follow in the case of common law orders. Common law orders usually meant an award of damages and so the person's property could be sold before he or she need be punished or coerced by imprisonment. Although common law rights in property are available against all persons, equitable rights are available only against a restricted class. However, both are more accurately seen as rights against people. Property is essentially a relationship between people, and therefore mediated by moral and political values, rather than a thing or a relationship to a thing. In this sense there are, accurately, no rights *in rem* at all.

6–118 A further important proof that equity is just as "proprietary" as the common law lies in the fact that there are both proprietary and personal remedies in equity. The doctrine of the bona fide purchaser for value of the legal estate without notice, and his or her successors, i.e. the Polar Star Rule, defines the scope of the *proprietary* remedy. Such a bona fide purchaser is beyond the reach of the proprietary remedy, but this does not mean that everyone within the scope of the Polar Star Rule is personally liable to make good any loss even if they no longer have the property. Someone who takes the property with notice of the equity certainly is so liable: his notice makes him a constructive trustee. However, someone who is liable under the rule but who is "wholly innocent", for example, someone who takes without notice but without value, is only liable to restore the property if he still has it.[129] He is not personally liable to make good deficiencies in the trust property or other losses to the beneficiaries.

6–119 On the other hand, the proprietary remedy may not be available because the property has been dissipated, or has been mixed with other property. In this case the person may be within the scope of the Polar Star Rule in that he received the property at some stage, with notice, but he no longer has it. In other cases, a person may never have received the property or an interest in it, but was a party to or assisted in a "fraudulent design". In either case the *personal* remedy is available and the person will be personally liable as constructive trustee.[130]

---

[128] For example, see F.W. Maitland, *Equity: A Course of Lectures* (Cambridge: University Press, 1936).

[129] *Re Diplock* [1948] Ch. 465 at 477–479.

[130] *Adair v Shaw* (1803) 1 Sch. & Lef. 243, 262; *Alleyne v Darcy* (1856) 4 Ir. Ch. R. 199; *Barnes v Addy* (1874) L.R. 9 Ch. App. 244; *Belmont Finance Corp Ltd v Williams Furniture Ltd* [1979] Ch. 250; *Selangor United Rubber Estates Ltd v Cradock (No.3)* [1968] 1 W.L.R. 1555 at 1582; *Karak Rubber Co Ltd v Burden* [1972] 1 All E.R. 1210.

Tracing

6–120 Finally, equity developed the concept of *tracing* property in a more effective way than the common law concept of "following". Equity would allow the proprietary remedy even if the trust property had been changed into another form, e.g. from money into land or *vice versa*. Equity in this sense is more "proprietorial" than the common law. The common law tended to regard property as a thing, or things, in the feudal sense, as objects with different and incomparable physical attributes. Equity, by contrast, tends to view property as commodities, as things in movement in a market, as exchange values. In relation to tracing, equity approaches this concept, but does not fully realise it, because it has to maintain some distinction between trust property and other property of individuals. So the remedy is lost if the trust property becomes mixed inextricably with other property.

6–121 In *Re Ffrench's Estate*,[131] the Irish Court of Appeal started a line of cases which suggested that in some circumstances the beneficiaries' interest under a trust is reduced to little more than a mere equity.[132] In that case a tenant for life under a money fund had induced the trustees to advance the whole of the fund to him in breach of trust. He then used the money to buy land and then used the land as security for an equitable mortgage from a third party, telling the third party that there were no prior equitable interests affecting the land. The contest was between the other, innocent, beneficiaries under the trust and the later equitable mortgagee. The equities being equal, the first in time (i.e. the beneficiaries) should have prevailed, but the court decided that the later equitable mortgage took priority. The judges gave a number of different reasons for their decision, but two of them were controversial. Porter M.R. held that because the trust property had been changed from money into land, so that the beneficiaries had to rely on the remedy of tracing, their right was defeated by the later bona fide purchaser for value of an equitable interest (the equitable mortgage) without notice of the trust.[133] In other words, a beneficiary's interest under a trust in Ireland would amount to a mere equity if the beneficiary had to rely on the remedy of tracing. Since this reason is put forward by only one judge, it cannot strictly be the *ratio decidendi* of the case. The other two judges, Fitzgibbon L.J.[134] and Barry L.J.,[135] among other reasons, held that beneficiaries under a trust lost priority to the later equitable interest whenever a third party was put at risk due to misconduct by the trustees, even if the beneficiaries under the trust were themselves innocent, although Fitzgibbon

---

[131] (1887) 21 L.R. Ir. 283. The case is discussed in more detail in the first edition of this work.

[132] See V.K. Delaney, "Equitable Interests and Mere Equities" [1957] 21 Conv. 195; A.P. Bell, *Modern Law of Personal Property in England and Ireland* (Dublin: Butterworths, 1989), pp.155, 468–469 and 520; R. Keane, *Equity and the Law of Trusts in the Republic of Ireland*, 2nd edn (Haywards Heath: Bloomsbury Professional, 2011), para.5.07; J.C.W. Wylie, *Irish Land Law*, 5th edn (Haywards Heath: Bloomsbury Professional, 2013), para.3.92.

[133] (1887) 21 L.R. Ir. 283 at 312.

[134] (1887) 21 L.R. Ir. 283 at 319.

[135] (1887) 21 L.R. Ir. 283 at 336–337.

L.J. suggested it was otherwise if the trustees' conduct amounted to fraud, which was not the case there.[136] This second proposition would virtually reduce the beneficiaries' interest under a trust in Ireland to a mere equity in almost all cases, because, if the beneficiaries were innocent, an innocent third party would usually be put at risk precisely because of a breach of trust by the trustees. It has been pointed out[137] that the decision in *Re Ffrench* was inconsistent with the decision of the British House of Lords in *Shropshire Union Railways & Canal Co v The Queen*,[138] which was not cited to the court and which at the time was binding upon it.

6–122 *Re Ffrench* was followed in a number of cases[139] before 1922 by Irish courts which considered themselves bound by it, and in *Scott v Scott*,[140] a decision of the Court of Appeal of the Irish Free State. In *Allied Irish Banks Ltd v Glynn*,[141] Kenny J. described the issue of tracing as a "difficult and controversial problem".[142] Neither *Re Ffrench* nor the *Shropshire Union* case would be binding on the Supreme Court today. It would therefore have to address the issue of principle. It certainly seems wrong to suggest, as Porter M.R. did, that the misconduct of the trustees must be held to bind even innocent beneficiaries "whose remedy, if any, would be against the trustees and their estates",[143] as if their principal remedy were *in personam*. Even apart from tracing, the Polar Star Rule lays down the scope of the main proprietary remedy. There were narrower grounds for holding that the equities were not equal in *Re Ffrench*, namely that even the beneficiaries who were innocent of fraud were guilty of laches,[144] whereas the equitable mortgagee had done everything possible to secure his title.[145]

Bare Trusts

6–123 There are instances where a trust exists but the beneficial interest is a fee simple vested in a single adult beneficiary, or in a number of adult co-owners who are in agreement about how to dispose of the property. For example, a deed grants land

> *to F and G in fee simple in trust for A in fee simple (A is of full age)*

---

[136] (1887) 21 L.R. Ir. 283 at 319.
[137] *Scott v Scott* [1924] 1 I.R. 141; Keane, *Equity and the Law of Trusts in the Republic of Ireland* (2011), para.5.08.
[138] (1875) L.R. 7 H.L. 496. See also, *Cave v Cave* (1880) 15 Ch. D. 639.
[139] *Bank of Ireland v Cogry Flax* [1900] 1 I.R. 219; *Bourke v Lee* [1904] 1 I.R. 280; *Re Bobbett's Estate* [1904] 1 I.R. 461.
[140] [1924] 1 I.R. 141.
[141] [1973] I.R. 188.
[142] [1973] I.R. 188 at 193.
[143] *Re Ffrench's Estate* (1887) 21 L.R. Ir. 283 at 311.
[144] LF, idleness, slackness, delay. Pronounced "laychiz" or "lay-cheez". See the French *lâcheté*.
[145] *Re Ffrench's Estate* (1887) 21 L.R. Ir. 283 at 311.

or a testator grants land in her will

> *to F and G in fee simple in trust for A for life, remainder to the children of A alive at her death in fee simple.*

A has died and the land is now vested in a number of children of A, all of whom are of full age. The following diagram illustrates the basic position:

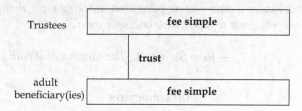

6–124 In these circumstances an English court in *Saunders v Vautier*[146] took the view that equity would not intervene to enforce the terms of the trust if the beneficiaries did not wish it to continue, even if the intention of the grantor was that it should continue. Equity, in the court's view, intervenes to protect beneficiaries. If they do not require its protection, equity would not insist on enforcing the grantor's wishes. The beneficiaries can require the trustees to convey the legal fee simple to them and can sue the trustees for an order if they refuse. The same situation has been held to occur if A, an adult, has a life estate plus a general power of appointment by will.[147] In a general power, A can appoint to herself, and so such a limitation gives her the whole interest.

6–125 Again, it is possible to detect in this rule a market-oriented value. The notion is that the law will not intervene to enforce the grantor's wishes if they conflict with those of adult individuals. An adult human being is assumed to be autonomous and the best judge of his or her own interests.

---

[146] [1835–42] All E.R. 58. See *Wharton v Masterman* [1895] A.C. 186; *Napier v Light* (1974) 236 E.G. 273; *Re Holt's Settlement* [1969] 1 Ch. 100; *Re Clore, decd* [1982] Fam. 113; *Re Myers Will Trusts*, unreported, English Court of Appeal, 12 April 1983.

[147] *Re Johnston* (1964) 48 D.L.R. (2d) 573.

Chapter 7

Registration of Deeds and Title

That's what makes it ours - being born on it, working on it, dying on it. That makes ownership, not a paper with numbers on it.

— John Steinbeck, *The Grapes of Wrath* (1939), Ch.5

INTRODUCTION

7–01 Most jurisdictions maintain a public register of rights in land in one form or another. The maintenance of such records serves a number of functions. First, the records enable landowners to prove their title and thereby increase the security of property rights. Secondly, records of rights in land enable those parties to deal in those rights with reasonable certainty about what is being traded. This provides enhanced security to those seeking to purchase interests in land and is of particular importance in jurisdictions such as Ireland where the law recognises a complex array of rights in land.

7–02 Transfers of land have long been carried out using formal procedures. In the early period of the common law, freehold estates were transferred using the feoffement with livery of seisin. This involved a public ceremony which Holdsworth argues was specifically intended to provide evidence that a transaction had occurred and to avoid the transfer of land by secret means.[1] Over time the livery of seisin was gradually superseded by written deeds. The existence of deeds meant that a claim of title to land could be proven using a written document rather than by the oral testimony of those who had witnessed the ceremonial livery of seisin.

7–03 Whilst written deeds have significant advantages as evidence of title, deeds can, and do, become unavailable due to loss over time. In addition to accidental losses, deeds are also vulnerable to forgery. One solution to such problems is the establishment of a centralised system of deeds recording, under which the parties to a deed can record the essential terms of their transaction in a publicly maintained office. Such a system has existed in Ireland since the establishment of the Registry of Deeds by the Registration of Deeds (Ireland) Act 1707 (the "1707 Act").

---

[1] W.E. Holdsworth, *A History of English Law* (London: Methuen, 1964), Vol.iii, pp.221–225.

7–04 An alternative, and more radical, model of land registration was first introduced in Ireland by the Record of Title (Ireland) Act 1865, though the system did not become widespread until the passage of the Local Registration of Title (Ireland) Act 1891. It is presently governed by the Registration of Title Act 1964 ("RTA 1964"), as amended. Registration of title has its origins in a Royal Commission on the Registration of Title which reported in 1857.[2] The aim of title registration is to simplify the process of transferring interests in land from one person to another. Where this is done in the traditional way, conveyancing solicitors instructed by each party to a transaction must examine the available collection of deeds which record prior transactions in respect of the land concerned, to determine the nature of the interest which the seller is proposing to transfer to the buyer. Depending on the underlying facts, this process may be of considerable complexity and it needs to be repeated each time the land is sold or transferred. In order to avoid this duplication of effort, title registration systems establish a public register of the ownership of title to land. In Ireland the register is maintained by the Land Registry under the authority of the Property Registration Authority (PRA).

7–05 There are two essential differences between the two systems. First, the Land Registry contains a conclusive record of the person(s) who hold title to the land. It is a register of ownership. The Registry of Deeds, by contrast, contains summaries of documents from which this information can be derived. It is a register of documents. Secondly, when dealing with registered land it is mandatory that transactions be registered in the Land Registry as a condition of their validity. This is not the case with unregistered land. Most (though not all) deeds may be legally effective without registration; however, an omission to register may have significant consequences.

7–06 It is common to speak of land, the title to which has been registered in the Land Registry as "registered land". Other land, records of transfers of which will be found in the Registry of Deeds, is usually referred to as "unregistered land". Strictly speaking, the registration of deeds system and registration of title are not mutually exclusive in relation to the same *land* as is sometimes supposed. If the title to an estate or interest in land is registered under the RTA 1964, the registry of documents system ceases to apply to that *estate or interest*,[3] but it does not cease to apply to estates or interests in the same land which are not registered under the RTA 1964.[4]

---

[2] Walpole Commission, *Report of the Royal Commission to Consider Registration of Title, with Reference to Sale and Transfer of Land* (C-2215, 1857).

[3] RTA 1964 s.116(2), as amended by RDTA 2006 s.67.

[4] RTA 1964 s.116; see Local Registration of Title Act 1891 s.19. The first Act in Ireland providing for the registration of titles, the Record of Title (Ireland) Act 1865, by s.16, provided for the removal of all *land* the title to which was registered from the registration of documents system, but this was unnecessary and inconvenient.

The Property Registration Authority

7–07 The Registration of Deeds and Title Act 2006 ("RDTA 2006") established the PRA as a single body to manage and control both the Registry of Deeds and the Land Registry. The PRA has a statutory mandate under s.10(1)(b) of the RDTA 2006 to promote the registration of title to land. Public policy, therefore, is to complete the Land Registry as soon as possible, at which time the Registry of Deeds will cease to have any practical importance, though its records will continue to be an important source for historians and genealogists. According to the PRA's 2015 Annual Report, approximately 88 per cent of all land titles in Ireland are now registered, representing approximately 93 per cent of the total land mass in the State.[5]

REGISTRATION OF DEEDS

7–08 The Registry of Deeds is the oldest public register of property interests in operation in Ireland today, having opened for business in March 1708. For three centuries, successive Registrars have recorded, catalogued and indexed a wide variety of documents pertaining to land transactions in Ireland and in doing so have provided historians with a rich archive of social and economic history.[6] The Registry was established by the 1707 Act.[7] This Act, as amended, was still in force in Ireland[8] until the passage of the RDTA 2006. The 1707 Act was primarily motivated by a desire to suppress frauds associated with secret conveyances, though its preamble makes clear that the measure also formed a part of the wider system of anti-Catholic penal laws which were being passed at the time. The 1707 Act is closely modelled on a system of deeds registration introduced in West Yorkshire in 1703.[9] Deeds registers are also common in other parts of world.[10] A number of the Canadian provinces retain deeds registries, though title registration systems are gradually becoming

---

[5] Property Registration Authority, *Annual Report 2015* (Dublin, 2016).

[6] For an assessment of the Registry of Deeds as an historical archive, see P. Roebuck, "The Irish Registry of Deeds: A Comparative Study" (1973) 18 I.H.S. 61.

[7] 6 Anne c 2 (Ir), as amended. The amendments are listed in Pt 1 of the Schedule to the RDTA 2006. See also, D.H. Madden, *A Practical Treatise on the Registration of Deeds, Conveyances, and Judgment-Mortgages*, 2nd edn (Dublin: W. McGee, 1901); J.A. Maguire, *A Compendium of the Law and Practice Relating to the Registration of Deeds, Wills, Judgment Mortgages, and Other Facts Affecting Title to Land in Ireland* (Dublin: Hodges, Figgis, 1900).

[8] In Northern Ireland the Acts were replaced by the Registration of Deeds Act (Northern Ireland) 1970.

[9] 2 & 3 Anne, c.4 (Eng.). The system was extended to the whole of Yorkshire in stages between 1708 and 1735. A second deeds registry was introduced in England for Middlesex in 1708 (8 Anne, c.20 (Eng)) but the system was never extended throughout England. Both deeds registries were closed in the 1970s. For a historical survey of the operation of the English legislation, see F. Sheppard and V. Belcher, "The Deeds Registries of Yorkshire and Middlesex" (1980) 6 J. Soc. Arch. 275.

[10] The Registration Act 1908 established a system of deeds registration in what was then British India; the legislation is still in force in India, Pakistan Bangladesh and Burma.

dominant.[11] In the United States, deeds registration continues to be the dominant system in most states.[12]

Deeds and Documents

7–09 Section 32 of the RDTA 2006 provides a non-exhaustive definition of a deed for the purposes of the Registry of Deeds. The essence of the definition is that any "document by which an estate or interest in land is created, transferred, charged or otherwise affected" is capable of registration as a deed. Section 32 then provides a lengthy list of documents which are expressly included as registrable, including conveyances and documents which are not attested. The list then re-enacts (with some amendments) a list of documents which were made registrable in the Registry of Deeds by various statutes passed prior to the RDTA 2006. These include vesting certificates under the Landlord and Tenant (Ground Rents) (No. 2) Act 1978, the Bankruptcy Act 1988, receipts issued on the discharge of mortgages by building societies, housing authorities and industrial and provident societies, as well as judgment mortgages, court orders and assents under the Succession Act 1965. It is important to note that the list in s.32 is not exhaustive. A memorandum accompanying the deposit of title deeds by way of security, which creates an equitable mortgage, has been held to be a registrable document.[13]

Wills

7–10 Wills were registrable under the 1707 Act but were excluded from the provisions as to priority between registered and unregistered documents. The reason for this exclusion is unclear—it may have been to prevent the principle of registration interfering in the existing mechanisms for revoking wills. Whatever the reason, there was nothing to be gained by registering wills and it was rarely done in practice. The provisions for registration were repealed by s.8 of, and the Second Schedule to, the Succession Act 1965.[14]

Leases Not Exceeding 21 Years

7–11 Leases for a term not exceeding 21 years, where actual possession is in accordance with the lease, are not registrable.[15]

---

[11] Registration of Deeds Act 2009 (Newfoundland and Labrador); Registry Act (Prince Edward Island).

[12] R. Cunningham, W. Stoebuck and D. Whitman, *The Law of Property* (St Paul, Minn.: West Pub. Co, 1984), p.773.

[13] *Rennick v Armstrong* (1829) 1 Hud. & Br. 727.

[14] They have also been repealed in Northern Ireland: Registration of Deeds (Amendment) Act (NI) 1967 s.2.

[15] RDTA 2006 s.5(1). This was also the case under s.14 of the 1707 Act: *Fury v Smith* (1829) 1 Hud. & Br. 735; *Fleming v Neville* (1830) Hayes 23.

Registration Process

7–12 The Registry of Deeds does not contain original deeds themselves or even copies thereof. Prior to the RDTA 2006, what was registered was a memorial of the deeds. This was a short document which summarised the principal provisions of the underlying deed. The contents of the memorial were specified in s.7 of the 1707 Act. The memorial had to be signed by one of the parties to the original deed and witnessed by two witnesses, at least one of which had to be a witness to the original deed. In *Rennick v Armstrong*,[16] the Irish Court of King's Bench held that, under s.6 of the 1707 Act, the witness attesting the execution of the deed or conveyance had to attest the execution of the deed by the grantor and that attestation of execution by the grantee alone made the registration void. Section 39(1) of the RDTA 2006 has retrospectively cured this defect for memorials prior to its commencement. The section does not affect any judgment given prior to the commencement of the RDTA 2006 and does not apply to any proceedings which were in being at that date.

7–13 The modern application process uses a set of prescribed forms set out in the Registration of Deeds Rules 2008[17] ("RODR 2008"). Rule 6(1) of the RODR 2008 requires that the appropriate form be used. In the case of court orders, vesting certificates and judgment mortgages, a certified copy of the relevant instrument is registered. The RODR 2008 state that the register, in respect of each registration, should contain a record of the name of the deed, the date of the deed, the name of each grantor, the name of one grantee, the description of the property, the serial number, the date of registration and the general nature of the deed.

7–14 Section 37 of the RDTA 2006 provides that a serial number is to be assigned to each application on its receipt by the Registry. Under the RODR 2008 the serial numbers are to be numbered annually and sequentially. In the event that two applications are received simultaneously, serial numbers are to be allotted randomly unless both applications are lodged by the same party. In this scenario the registering party may give written direction as to the order in which the applications are to be registered.[18] This system of random allocation is a necessary consequence of the paper-based system of registration. The rule is required in order to deal with the possibility of registrations arriving simultaneously by post. An electronic registration system, similar to that utilised in the company charge registration system, would obviate the need for random allocations and would thus be preferable in future.[19]

---

[16] (1819) 1 Hud. & Br. 727 at 730–731

[17] S.I. No. 52 of 2008.

[18] RODR 2008 r.7(2).

[19] Mandatory electronic registration of company charges was introduced by the Companies Act 2014 (Section 897) Order 2015 (S.I. No. 203 of 2015). For details, see N. McGrath, "Reforming the Company Charge Register in Ireland" in L. Gullifer and O. Akseli (eds), *Secured Transactions Law Reform: Principles, Policies and Practice* (Oxford: Hart, 2016), Ch.10.

The Deeds Registry

7–15 The register can be maintained in paper form or electronic form, or partly in one form and partly in the other,[20] and in the Irish or English language.[21] It may be noticed that the register does not contain an index of individual plots of lands. An Index of Lands was established by s.17 of the Registry of Deeds (Ireland) Act 1832 but ceased to be maintained after 31 December 1946.[22] Under s.46 of the RDTA 2006 it is now "deemed to have been closed" on that date. The failure to maintain it and its absence from the new scheme is regrettable both from the perspective of practitioners and historians. The records of the Registry established by the 1707 Act are to be kept by the PRA.[23] That register, having been maintained since 1708, is of great historic and cultural interest and contains memorials of documents by nearly every significant figure in Irish history since then, including Jonathan Swift, Wolfe Tone, Charles Stewart Parnell, Éamon de Valera, and others.

Failure to Register

7–16 Registration of documents is not compulsory in the sense that there is no criminal penalty for failure to register. There are, however, two legal consequences for failure to register: some documents are ineffective without registration, while others remain effective in themselves but will lose priority as against a registered document.

Documents Ineffective without Registration

7–17 The RDTA 2006 provides that a judgment mortgage shall be registered[24] and that a *lis pendens* (pending land action) shall be registered in the High Court[25] but it does not contain a complete list of documents ineffective without registration. As to other documents, the position is less clear. The RODR 2008[26] refer to provisions in other Acts in a manner which appears to require the registration of certain documents, including: a property adjustment order on judicial separation under the Family Law Act 1995 or on divorce under the Family Law (Divorce) Act 1996; a vesting certificate issued under the Landlord and Tenant (Ground Rents) (No. 2) Act 1978; a certificate of

---

[20] RDTA 2006 s.35(2)(c); RODR 2008 r.4(2).

[21] RODR 2008 r.4(4).

[22] D. Brady, "Abolish Memorials and Bring Back the Lands Index in the Registry of Deeds" (1990) 8 I.L.T. 173. Brady says its maintenance was only abandoned after 1949, and also points out that the State was acting illegally in not maintaining it.

[23] RODR 2008 r.4(6).

[24] LCLRA 2009 s.116(2): "A judgment mortgage shall be registered in the Registry of Deeds or Land Registry, as appropriate"; Judgment Mortgage (Ireland) Act 1850 ss.6–8; Registration of Deeds (No. 2) Rules 2009 (S.I. No. 457 of 2009).

[25] LCLRA 2009 s.121. A *lis pendens* registered under s.10 of the Judgments (Ireland) Act 1844 which has not been vacated before the repeal of that section continues to have effect: LCLRA 2009 s.121(4).

[26] See ROTR 2008 rr.10, 11 and 14.

vesting of property in the Official Assignee under the Bankruptcy Act 1988[27]; and a notification under the Land Reclamation Act 1949. Some, but not all, of these are registered as a matter of course by court officials.

Documents Losing Priority without Registration

7–18 Section 38(1) of the RDTA 2006 provides that registered deeds are "deemed and taken as good and effectual both in law and equity according to the priority[28] determined by the serial numbers allocated to them ...", and "as regards any right, title, interest or liability arising from their execution, rank in priority among themselves according to the priority determined by the serial numbers so allocated." Unregistered deeds are "void against a registered deed affecting the land concerned".[29] As between a document which is capable of being registered but is unregistered and a later registered document, the normal rule as to legal interests—that the first in time prevails—is replaced by the principle that the first to be registered prevails.

7–19 Section 38(3) then provides that "this section is without prejudice to the application of any rule of law or equity in cases where a person claiming under a registered deed had knowledge, or is deemed to have had knowledge, of a prior unregistered deed". This appears to be intended to give statutory force to the long line of case law under the 1707 Act by which the owner of a registered deed is affected by *actual* notice of a prior unregistered deed if the actual notice was acquired at the time the owner of the registered deed entered into the transaction.

Searches

7–20 Under the RDTA 2006 and the RODR 2008,[30] any person may apply to search the register personally[31] or may request an official search.[32]

7–21 Under the 1707 Act, searches of the register took the form of (a) "hand searches", undertaken by the applicant personally, (b) "common searches" conducted by one official of the Registry, the accuracy of which was not warranted, and (c) "negative searches" conducted by two officials of the Registry, as to which a certificate was issued warranting that no memorials were registered other than those mentioned in the applicant's application and other than those abstracted in the certificate. The Registrar was liable, whether or

---

[27] Bankruptcy Act 1988 s.46(1) (only where "according to law, any conveyance of land is required to be registered", then the certificate is required to be registered).

[28] The wording up to this point is identical with that in s.4 of the 1707 Act, which continued "... the time of registering the memorial ...".

[29] RDTA 2006 s.38(2).

[30] RODR 2008 rr.9 and 19.

[31] RODR 2008 r.9. An applicant may "make extracts from or take short notes of the register and records".

[32] RDTA 2006 s.43; RODR 2008 r.19.

not he or she had signed the certificate, and an assistant registrar was liable if he or she had signed it, to a party aggrieved or injured by "fraud, collusion or neglect".[33] Negative searches were instituted by the Registration of Deeds (Amendment) Act (Ireland) 1721,[34] and before the RDTA 2006 came into force, were governed by the Registry of Deeds (Ireland) Act 1832.[35] The RDTA 2006 replaced common and negative searches with the concept of an official search.[36] The liability of the Registrar for errors is not clear, though it should be noticed that the courts have been cautious in recognising a duty of care on the part of public bodies to individuals who make use of or depend upon their services.[37]

The Effect on Priority between Deeds
Registered vs Registered
7–22 The main principle of deed registration is that priority between registered deeds is governed by order of their registration.[38] A deed that is registered earlier takes priority over a deed that is registered later. There is no difference in such a case between legal and equitable estates.[39] For example, a deed creating an equitable interest is registered. Later, a deed conveying the legal estate is registered. The person taking the conveyance of the legal estate takes it subject to the equity, whether he or she had notice of the equity or not. The later purchaser could have examined the register. The principle of notice is replaced by the principle of registration.

Unregistered vs Unregistered
7–23 Here the registration system has no application. Unregistered principles apply.[40] If the first deed is a legal lease of land, and the second is a conveyance of the landlord's reversion, the lease binds the purchaser of the reversion regardless of notice as a legal interest. If the earlier transaction is an equitable mortgage and the later transaction is a sale of the legal fee simple, the later purchaser is bound unless he or she can prove the plea of *bona fide* purchaser for value without notice.

---

[33] Registry of Deeds (Ireland) Act 1832 s.26.
[34] 8 Geo I c 15, s.2, repealed in part by 25 Geo III c 47, itself repealed by the Statute Law Revision (Ireland) Act 1879. See Madden, *Registration of Deeds* (1901), p.241.
[35] Registry of Deeds (Ireland) Act 1832 ss.22–27.
[36] RDTA 2006 s.43; RODR 2008 r.19, Form 12.
[37] *Yeun Kun Yeu v Attorney General of Hong Kong* [1988] A.C. 175.
[38] RDTA 2006 s.38(1).
[39] *Eyre v Dolphin* (1813) 2 Ball & B. 290 at 300.
[40] *Tench v Molyneux* (1914) 48 I.L.T.R. 48 concerned the Local Registration of Title (Ireland) Act 1891, but the point is the same.

Unregistrable vs Registered

7-24 If a transaction is not reduced to writing there is nothing that can be registered, and the registration system has no effect.[41] An example is an equitable mortgage created by deposit of the title deeds without any memorandum in writing. If there is a memorandum, then the mortgage is registrable.[42] It would be unfair to give priority to a later registered deed when the other party could not have protected his or her interest by registration. In the words of Pigot C.B. in *O'Connor v Stephens*[43]:

> "It is but imputing common sense to the Legislature to hold that, when they framed the Registry Act, they could not have intended so far to repeal the Statute of Frauds as to enact that a registered deed should, by reason of its registry, acquire priority over another deed, which it was impossible by any diligence to register under the Act ...".

7-25 Thus, priority between the equitable mortgage and a later registered instrument is not governed by the RDTA 2006, but by general equitable principles. Such a mortgage would be defeated therefore only by a later purchaser for value of a legal estate without notice, actual or constructive, of the earlier equity.[44]

7-26 A more modern (and commercially potentially more significant) example is to be found in s.11 of the Multi-Unit Development Act 2011. Section 3 of that Act requires "ownership" (presumably meaning legal title) of the common areas in multi-unit developments, such as apartment blocks, to be transferred to an owner's management company prior to the sale of individual units in the development. Section 3(7) states that such a transfer "shall reserve the beneficial interest therein to the person transferring the ownership of those parts (including any mortgagee or the owner of a charge affecting any such beneficial interest)." The Act envisages the "determination" of these "beneficial interests" upon the completion of the development by the making of a statutory declaration "for the benefit of the owner's management company". Such a declaration (which requires the consent of any mortgagee or charge

---

[41] *Re Stephens* (1876) I.R. 10 Eq. 282; *Cleary v Fitzgerald* (1880) 5 L.R. Ir. 351, (1881) 7 L.R. Ir. 229 (CA); *Re Burke's Estate* (1882) 9 L.R. Ir. 24 (CA); *Re Ffrench's Estate* (1887) 21 L.R. Ir. 283 at 305; *Re Stevenson's Estate* [1902] 1 I.R. 23.

[42] *Re Stephens* (1876) I.R. 10 Eq. 282; *Rennick v Armstrong* (1829) 1 Hud. & Br. 727.

[43] (1862) 13 Ir. C.L.R. 63 at 68, cited in *Reilly v Garnett* (1872) I.R. 7 Eq. 1.

[44] *Re Stephens* (1876) I.R. 10 Eq. 282 suggested that the owner of a registered mortgage would take subject to an earlier *unregistrable* equitable mortgage only if he or she had "express" notice of it. Since registration principles do not apply, the correct position should be that any form of notice would bind the owner of a legal estate acquired for value. *Re Burke's Estate* (1882) 9 L.R. Ir. 24 suggested that an unregistrable equitable mortgage took priority over a later registered deed—apparently regardless of whether it dealt with a legal or equitable right—even if the owner of the registered deed had no notice at all of the unregistered right. Again, the owner of the later legal right obtained for value and without any form of notice should take free.

holder) is stated to have the effect that "the beneficial interest and legal interest stand merged."[45] The statutory declaration required by s.11 is clearly intended to affect title to the common areas of multi-unit developments, yet a statutory declaration is not a deed within the meaning of s.32 of the RDTA 2006. The consequences for priorities are as yet untested.

Registrable but Unregistered vs Registered
7–27 Unregistered deeds are "void against a registered deed affecting the land concerned".[46] The registered document takes priority even if it was executed later than the unregistered one. The holder of a deed, who can register it, but fails to do so, runs the risk of losing priority to a deed which has been registered.[47] There is no distinction in this between legal and equitable interests.[48] Thus, if a person obtains a document conferring an equitable interest and registers it, a later purchaser of a legal interest in the same land cannot make the plea of *bona fide* purchaser for value without notice. There are nevertheless two qualifications to this general rule: actual notice and volunteers.

Actual Notice
7–28 A rule which permits a person to obtain priority over an unregistered interest of which he or she was aware would, if unqualified, express a robust if extreme form of individualism favoured by those who believe that the market should be the sole mechanism for distributing property rights. On this view, each person must look out for his or her own interests, and need have no regard to the interests of others if those others are capable of looking after themselves and fail to do so. Nevertheless, the courts found it difficult to accept such a self-centred view of morality. Two situations were distinguished on moral grounds:

(a) A knows that B is entitled to some interest in land under a registrable but unregistered deed. A obtains a similar or conflicting interest in the same land by deed and then registers it, with the intention of gaining priority over B.

(b) A acquires an interest in land under a deed without knowledge at the time of its execution that B, under a prior deed, had obtained a similar or conflicting interest. Having become aware of B's deed, A registers his own with the intention of gaining priority over B.

---

[45] Multi-Unit Developments Act 2011 s.11(1).
[46] RDTA 2006 s.38(2).
[47] *Re McDonagh's Estate* (1879) 3 L.R. Ir. 408; *Cleary v Fitzgerald* (1880) 5 L.R. Ir. 351, (1881) 7 L.R. Ir. 229 at 250–255.
[48] *Drew v Norbury (Lord)* (1846) 9 Ir. Eq. R. 171.

7–29 The courts held that in the first situation, A was guilty of fraud,[49] but that in the second A was acting legitimately in his own self-interest. In the second case, A was not bound by B's right after he had registered his own:

> "I hold it to be undoubted law that a vendee whose equitable title has become complete before notice of a prior unregistered equity, but who afterwards obtains such notice, is perfectly free to protect himself by registration, as it is familiar learning that he may do by getting in the legal estate. To purchase *and* register after notice of a prior title is fraud. But if the purchase has been completed (though only equitably so) before notice, it is no fraud at all for that purchaser, when he afterwards hears of the impending danger, to grasp at the *tabula in naufragio* [plank in the shipwreck] which is afforded him by the Registry Act."[50]

7–30 The cases on this point go back to *Forbes v Deniston*[51] in 1722 when the British House of Lords upheld a decision of Viscount Midleton L.C. in the Irish Court of Chancery,[52] to the effect that A's conscience was affected if he had *actual notice* of the prior unregistered right at the time of the conveyance. The result was contrary to the literal words of the 1707 Act, but the courts took the view that the statute, which had been passed to prevent fraud, should not be used as an engine of it.

7–31 *Forbes* was followed in England in *Le Neve v Le Neve*,[53] in which Lord Hardwicke L.C. in the English Court of Chancery said[54]:

> "The ground of it plainly is this, that the taking of a legal estate after notice of a prior right, makes a person a *mala fide* purchaser ... this is a species of fraud and *dolus malus* itself; for he knew the first purchaser had the clear right of the estate, and after knowing that, he takes away the right of another person by getting the legal estate."

---

[49] *Bushell v Bushell* (1806) 1 Sch. & Lef. 92 at 100; *Blades v Blades* (1727) 1 Eq. Cas. Abr. 358 (English Yorkshire Registry).

[50] *Reilly v Garnett* (1872) I.R. 7 Eq. 1 at 25.

[51] (1722) 4 Bro. P.C. 189; A. Lyall, *Irish Exchequer Reports: Reports of Cases in the Courts of Exchequer and Chancery in Ireland 1716–1734*, Publications of the Selden Society, Vol.125 (London: Selden Society, 2008), cxxxii–cxxxiii.

[52] Lord Hardwicke L.C. in *Le Neve v Le Neve* (1748) 3 Atk. 646 at 653: "The decree [in *Forbes v Deniston*] was reversed, not because Lord *Middleton* [sic] had proceeded on a wrong principle, but had drawn a wrong inference from it, for Lord Forbes did not insist merely on the register, but that the lease was made contrary to the power ...".

[53] (1748) 3 Atk. 646.

[54] (1748) 3 Atk. 646 at 654.

7–32 In *Duchess of Chandos v Brownlow*,[55] Lord Fitzgibbon L.C. restated the point in the Irish House of Lords[56]:

> "The principle is admitted, that if a man acquires a legal title under the registry act, with notice of a prior unregistered title in another to the same land, that a court of equity may control him in the exercise and assertion of his legal title, notwithstanding the words of the registry act."

7–33 Similar authority can be found in a series of other cases.[57] Imputed notice through a solicitor achieves the same outcome.[58] Constructive notice, however, is not sufficient.[59] There is some evidence of a shift in judicial attitudes towards the meaning of actual notice in this context. The earlier approach can be seen in *Workingmen's Benefit Society v Higgins*,[60] decided in 1947, in which it was suggested that gross negligence by a purchaser in not discovering the existence of an earlier unregistered instrument would fix the purchaser with notice and defeat the registered instrument.

7–34 In *Re Fuller and Co Ltd*,[61] the High Court held that it was irrelevant that the holder of a registered deed had knowledge of facts from which knowledge of an unregistered instrument could be inferred. The court characterised this as constructive notice, though this is questionable. If a person possesses knowledge of facts which are sufficient to make an ordinary person suspect that there might be some unregistered document and the existence of the document would be discovered by making further inquiries, that is clearly constructive notice and would not affect the result. If, on the other hand, a person has knowledge of facts from which the existence of an unregistered deed can be inferred with logical certainty, then knowledge of the deed is not a matter of making further enquiries, but of mental deduction. This would seem to be more accurately characterised as actual notice.

7–35 It may be that the court in *Fuller*, a case decided in the 1980s, leant more to the individualistic, and less altruistic, view that a person should look after

---

[55] (1791) 2 Ridg. P.C. 345.
[56] (1791) 2 Ridg. P.C. 345 at 429. See A. Lyall, *The Irish House of Lords as a Court of Law 1782–1800* (Dublin: Clarus Press, 2013).
[57] *Delacour v Freeman* (1854) 2 Ir. Ch. R. 633; *Montgomery v McEvoy* (1857) 5 Ir. Ch. R. 126; *Clarke v Armstrong* (1861) 10 Ir. Ch. R. 263; *Re Flood's Estate* (1863) Ir. Ch. R. 312; *Agra Bank v Barry* (1874) L.R. 7 H.L. 135; *Re Fuller* [1982] I.R. 161.
[58] If a solicitor actually knows of an unregistered deed, then that actual notice is imputed to the client. The client is bound even if an independent solicitor, exercising reasonable diligence, might not have discovered the unregistered deed: *Re Rorke's Estate* (1864) 14 Ir. Ch. R. 442 at 446 (Ch. App.); *Marjoribanks v Hovenden* (1843) 6 Ir. Eq. R. 238; *Espin v Pemberton* (1859) 3 De G. & J. 547 at 554.
[59] *Reilly v Garnett* (1872) I.R. 7 Eq. 1 at 24: "This, however, is but *constructive* notice, and, therefore, though it takes away the protection of the legal estate, it is of no avail against the Registry Act, for which nothing but *actual* notice will do."
[60] [1945] Ir. Jur. Rep. 38.
[61] [1982] I.R. 161.

his own interests and that if he fails to do so, the party who has done so by registering her deed does not owe a moral duty towards him. *Forbes v Deniston*[62] and the cases that follow it can be thought of as denying that it is legitimate for persons to consciously take advantage of the failings of others to protect their own interests. *Forbes* in this regard is perhaps reflective of the moral expectations about the conduct of the 18th century landed gentry. The extent to which such expectations hold true today is debatable.[63]

7–36 *Forbes* may also be defended based on an argument about the distribution of risk. A prospective transferee or grantee who has actual notice of an earlier unregistered transaction can avoid the risk of loss by not entering into his or her own proposed transaction. Therefore, he or she does not require the protection of the Registry of Deeds, or the court. The role of the law, on this view, is to set a framework in which the market can operate efficiently by reducing only those risks which operators in the market cannot rationally avoid by themselves. It reduces risks that cannot be calculated or avoided, not those that can. The weakness of this argument is that it equally applies to the other party, since the law has provided a means of avoiding the risk of loss by registration.

7–37 The distribution of risk argument is not one that would appeal to an aggressive speculator, keen to make a profit wherever it can be found. Such a speculator might argue that the market operates most efficiently if those who see where a profit is to be made are allowed to pursue it, exclusive of all other considerations, and should not be deterred from entering into transactions by having to take into account the interests of others who have shown themselves inefficient at protecting their own interests. This argument is still based on an ethical choice and has not found acceptance in the context of registration of deeds, although it has been favoured in registration of title.[64]

Volunteers
7–38 If the owner of the registered document has not given consideration in the transaction to which the document relates, then he or she is bound by an earlier unregistered deed, regardless of notice. In the words of Christian L.J. in *Reilly v Garnett*[65]:

> "An unregistered title or right is binding upon the grantor himself, and upon all who claim under him as volunteers. His heir or devisee is bound by everything which bound the ancestor or testator, registered or unregistered, known or unknown."

---

[62] (1722) 4 Bro. P.C. 189.
[63] See the remarks of Lord Diplock to this effect (albeit in a different context) in *Pettitt v Pettitt* [1970] 2 A.C. 777 at 824.
[64] See *Midland Bank Trust Co Ltd v Green* [1981] A.C. 513.
[65] (1872) I.R. 7 Eq. 1 at 27; *Eyre v McDowell* (1861) 9 H.L.C. 619 at 620.

7–39 This reproduces the result in the equitable doctrine of notice in which a donee or intestate successor, since they were not purchasers for value, took subject to equities affecting the donor etc., regardless of notice. Here again equity intervened to protect the purchaser in a market who had advanced and risked money.

REGISTRATION OF TITLE

Historical Background

7–40 Registration of title is an entirely different method of recording information about land ownership. It does not involve the registration of documents about land transactions; instead, ownership of interests in the land is established and recorded by a State agency—in the Irish context, the Land Registry—and thereafter the register is updated to reflect subsequent changes to the ownership of the registered interests. Title registration has been described as being founded on three principles: the mirror principle, the curtain principle and the indemnity principle.[66] The mirror principle is the idea that the register should give a complete account of the interests which bind the land. The curtain principle states that trusts and other equitable interests are to be kept off the register and are to be overreached by any sale of the land, while the indemnity principle requires that any person who suffers loss as a result of an error in the Registry be compensated from a State fund.

7–41 Registration of title to land in Ireland started with the Record of Title (Ireland) Act 1865 which established a voluntary system of title registration for conveyances registered by the Landed Estates Court. The 1865 Act was based on the work of Sir Robert Torrens. Torrens, who was born in Cork in 1814, served as the first Premier of South Australia and whilst there had developed a comparable system of land registration.[67] Torrens lectured in Dublin, Belfast and Derry in 1863 and 1864 and prepared a bill for the registration of title in Ireland which was presented to the Government by the Lord Lieutenant. An amended version of this bill eventually became law in 1865.

7–42 The 1865 Act permitted any person who had obtained a conveyance from the Landed Estates Court to have his or her conveyance entered on a record of title to be kept by the court. The Act provided that the record was to

---

[66] T. Rouff, *An Englishman Looks at the Torrens System* (Sydney: Law Book Co, 1957), cited by K.J. Gray and S.F. Gray, *Elements of Land Law*, 5th edn (Oxford: Oxford University Press, 2009), para.2.217.

[67] There is some question as to the originality of Torrens's scheme. He was accused at the time of some degree of plagiarism. The basic ideas behind the scheme may have been developed by Dr Ulrich Hübbe, a German lawyer living in South Australia in the 1850s who modelled it on the Hanseatic system of title registration: Gray and Gray, *Elements of Land Law* (2009), para.2.2.16, fn.2; B. Edgeworth, C.J. Rossiter and M.A. Stone, *Sackville and Neave, Property Law: Cases and Materials*, 7th edn (Chatswood, N.S.W.: LexisNexis Butterworths, 2004), para.5.14; S. Robinson, *Transfer of Land in Victoria* (Sydney: Law Book Co, 1979), pp.11–20.

be conclusive evidence of the owner's title and permitted the use of simplified forms for subsequent conveyances of recorded land. The Act did not, however, make it compulsory to register conveyances obtained from the Landed Estates Court, nor was it compulsory to utilise the new forms when subsequently conveying recorded land. Section 32 of the Act permitted the owner of recorded land to require the folio to be closed and to return the land to the unregistered system. The Act also made no provision for an insurance fund to protect from fraud or error in the operation of its provision. The 1865 Act was a failure and comparatively few titles were ever recorded using it. Dowling ascribes this failure to the omission of an insurance fund, professional opposition from solicitors in Ireland and the expense involved in the recording process.[68]

7–43 The modern system of title registration dates to the Local Registration of Title (Ireland) Act 1891. This Act was largely the work of D.H. Madden, who became Attorney General for Ireland in 1889 and was subsequently elevated to the bench in 1892. The 1891 Act was seen as "a necessary corollary"[69] of the State-aided land purchase schemes and the purpose of title registration was to ensure that the new peasant landholders would not have to bear the expense of registering deeds when dealing with their land. The 1891 Act established local title registries in each county of Ireland. Registration was compulsory for land acquired under the land purchase schemes. Provision was made for the voluntary registration of other titles in the Act, but in practice this was not frequently utilised; however, such was the extent of the Land Purchase schemes that by the early 1960s approximately 80 per cent of the land in the State had been registered.[70] The 1891 Act continued in force until the enactment of the RTA 1964 which provides the legal basis for the present system.

Compulsory Registration

7–44 The principal innovation of the RTA 1964 was to expand the circumstances in which it would become compulsory to register title. Section 23 of the RTA 1964, as amended by the RDTA 2006, requires the registration of title to land in the following circumstances:

(a) where land was conveyed under the Land Purchase Acts, the Labourers Acts 1883–1962 and land sold, conveyed or vested under the Irish Church Act 1869[71];

(b) where freehold or leasehold land has been acquired by any statutory authority;

(c) where s.24 applies.

---

[68] A. Dowling, "Of Ships and Sealing Wax: The Introduction of Land Registration in Ireland" (1993) 44 N.I.L.Q. 360 at 374–377.

[69] F. Browning, *Registration of Title in Ireland*, 2nd edn (Dublin: E. Ponsonby, 1912), p.2.

[70] See 208 *Dáil Debates* Col.1134 (7 November 1963).

[71] RTA 1964 s.23(1A), inserted by RDTA 2006 s.52(c).

7–45 Section 24 creates a power for the Minister for Justice to specify areas of the country in which registration of title shall be compulsory. Where an area has been designated as a compulsory area under s.24, the registration of ownership of the land concerned, if not already compulsory, becomes compulsory:

(a) in the case of freehold land, upon its conveyance on sale; and
(b) in the case of a "leasehold interest", i.e. a lease for a term of over 21 years,[72] or "such other number as may be prescribed",[73] on the grant or assignment on sale of the interest.[74]

Other dispositions may be specified by order.[75]

7–46 Orders under s.24 have now been made covering all of the land in the State with the result that all unregistered land must be registered on the occurrence of the next conveyance or assignment. The dates from which compulsory registration entered force were as follows:

- Meath, Carlow and Laois with effect from 1 January 1970[76];
- Longford, Roscommon and Westmeath (from 1 April 2006)[77];
- Clare, Kilkenny, Louth, Sligo, Wexford and Wicklow (after, but not on, 30 September 2008)[78];
- Cavan, Donegal, Galway, Kerry, Kildare, Leitrim, Limerick, Mayo, Monaghan, North Tipperary, Offaly, South Tipperary and Waterford (after, but not on, 31 December 2009)[79];

---

[72] RTA 1964 s.3.

[73] RTA 1964 s.3, as amended by RDTA 2006 s.50(d). The definition of "leasehold interest" in s.3 of the RTA 1964, as amended by RDTA 2006 s.50 and LCLRA 2009 s.127, now "means an estate in land under a lease for a term of years of which more than twenty-one (or such other number as may be prescribed) are unexpired at the date of registration, not being a term for securing money, with or without a covenant for renewal, and includes an interest held at a rent under a lease for a life or lives, or determinable on a life or lives, and the right or interest of a person who has barred, under the Statute of Limitations 1957, the right of action of a person entitled to such leasehold interest, and where a lease in possession and a reversionary lease to take effect in possession upon the expiry of the first-mentioned lease are so held that the interest under both leases belongs to the same person under the same right, such leases, so far as they relate to land comprised in both leases, shall be deemed to create one continuous term in possession."

[74] RTA 1964 s.24(2).

[75] RTA 1964 s.24(2A), inserted by RDTA 2006 s.53.

[76] Compulsory Registration of Ownership (Carlow, Laoighis and Meath) Order 1969 (S.I. No. 87 of 1969).

[77] Registration of Title Act 1964 (Compulsory Registration of Ownership) (Longford, Roscommon and Westmeath) Order 2005 (S.I. No. 605 of 2005).

[78] Registration of Title Act 1964 (Compulsory Registration of Ownership) (Clare, Kilkenny, Louth, Sligo, Wexford and Wicklow) Order 2008 (S.I. No. 81 of 2008).

[79] Registration of Title Act 1964 (Compulsory Registration of Ownership) (Cavan, Donegal, Galway, Kerry, Kildare, Leitrim, Limerick, Mayo, Monaghan, North Tipperary, Offaly, South Tipperary and Waterford) Order 2009 (S.I. No. 176 of 2009).

- Cork, Dún Laoghaire-Rathdown, Fingal, South Dublin and the cities of Cork and Dublin from 1 June 2011.[80]

Therefore, from 1 June 2011, compulsory registration now applies to all land in the State.[81]

7–47 Section 25 deals with the effect of a failure to register title where it is compulsory to do so. It provides:

"A person shall not acquire an estate or interest in land in any case in which registration of ownership of the land is or becomes compulsory under section 23 or 24 unless the person is registered as owner of the estate or interest within 6 months after the purported acquisition or at such later time as the Authority (or, in case of refusal, the court) may sanction in any particular case, but on any such registration the person's title shall relate back to the date of the purported acquisition, and any dealings with the land before the registration shall have effect accordingly."

7–48 Thus, after an area is designated as a compulsory area under s.24, registration of the title to particular land becomes compulsory on the next conveyance on sale, and the estate or interest will not vest in the purchaser unless the title is registered within six months of the date of the purported conveyance.

7–49 It is possible to register a title where the existing owner is not obliged to do so. Voluntary registration is rare since it involves expense for the party undertaking registration and there are few practical advantages to justify this expenditure.

The Register
7–50 Under s.8 of the RTA 1964, the Land Register consists of three separate registers:

1. the register of freehold interests;
2. the register of leasehold interests; and
3. the register of incorporeal hereditaments in gross and other rights.[82]

7–51 Other interests in land may appear on the register in the form of burdens on the title of other interests.

---

[80] Registration of Title Act 1964 (Compulsory Registration of Ownership) (Cork and Dublin) Order 2010 (S.I. No. 516 of 2010).

[81] Under s.107(7) of the National Asset Management Agency Act 2009, ss.23 and 25 of the RTA 1964 do not apply to the National Asset Management Agency (NAMA) or to a NAMA group entity.

[82] RTA 1964 s.8.

7–52 The register is now kept almost exclusively in electronic form.[83] The form and contents of the registers are set out in detail in r.3 of the Land Registration Rules 2012 ("LRR 2012").[84] The registers are kept in folios; each folio has a unique number within its county division. Folios are kept in three parts as follows.

- The first part of the folio contains:
  - (a) a description of the property together with reference to the registry maps of the affected land;
  - (b) a description of any part of the land which is transferred to another folio;
  - (c) information relating to—
    - i. easements and rights for the benefit of the property,
    - ii. the inclusion/exclusion of mines and minerals from the property,
    - iii. the boundaries of the property.[85]
- The second part of the folio contains:
  - (a) the name of the owner of the property and an address within the State for the service of notices;
  - (b) such information as is necessary relative to—
    - i. the classes of title held by the owner,
    - ii. the devolution of the property,
    - iii. information relating to co-ownership of an interest or a charge on the land under s.91 of the RTA 1964;
  - (c) cautions and inhibitions affecting the registration of dispositions of the property;
  - (d) a note as to the death of the registered owner and the names of his or her personal representatives.[86]
- The third part contains:
  - (a) details of burdens registered under s.69 of the RTA 1964;
  - (b) the ownership of a registered charge, where it is not registered in the register of incorporeal hereditaments in gross and other rights;
  - (c) notice of the exemption from, or existence of, s.72 burdens;
  - (d) cautions or inhibitions against dealing with a registered burden which is not registered in the register of incorporeal hereditaments in gross and other rights.

Conclusiveness of the Register

7–53 The basic principle behind title registration is the "mirror" principle. This is the idea that the register should be a mirror of the title to the land itself

---

[83] A small number of folios concerning State bodies are still kept in electronic form. See J. Deeney, *Registration of Deeds and Title in Ireland* (Haywards Heath: Bloomsbury Professional, 2014), p.30.

[84] Land Registration Rules 2012 (S.I. No. 483 of 2012).

[85] LRR 2012 r.3(6).

[86] LRR 2012 r.3(7).

reflecting all interests which affect the land so that a purchaser need not make any further inquiries in order to discover interests which will bind him or her.

7–54 Section 31(1) of the RTA 1964 establishes the mirror principle by declaring that the register is "conclusive evidence of the title of the owner to the land as appearing on the register and of any right, privilege, appurtenance or burden as appearing thereon". This broad statement of principle is qualified in a number of respects:

   (a) s.31 of the RTA 1964 provides a jurisdiction for the court to rectify the register on grounds of "actual fraud or mistake";

   (b) s.85(2) of the RTA 1964 provides that neither the register nor its accompanying maps are conclusive as to the boundaries of registered land;

   (c) s.72 provides a list of burdens which affect the land without registration. These will be considered below.

7–55 In *Miscampbell v McAlister*,[87] the Court of Appeal in Northern Ireland held that the conclusive effect of the register did not extend to the existence or otherwise of incorporeal rights such as easements or covenants. The governing law at the time was s.34 of the Local Registration of Title (Ireland) Act 1891, which did not include reference to rights, privileges or appurtenances. It would appear, in fact, that s.31 of the RTA 1964 is specifically drafted to avoid a similar conclusion being reached today.

7–56 Section 32 provides for the rectification of errors in the register and/ or the registry maps. Under s.32(1)(a), the PRA may rectify an error in the register provided it obtains the consent of the registered owner and any other interested parties. Rectification by the PRA must be based on a written agreement between the parties. Section 32(1)(b) provides the PRA with an alternative jurisdiction to rectify errors of its own motion where rectification can be achieved without loss to any person.

7–57 Section 32(1)(c) provides the court with an equitable jurisdiction to rectify errors in the register provided that rectification can be achieved "without injustice" to any party. The court has a broad discretion to set the terms of rectification, including making orders as to costs. Where rectification has taken place and a party has suffered a financial loss in consequence, an application for compensation from the Central Fund may be brought under s.120 of the RTA 1964.

7–58 The jurisdiction to rectify under s.32 of the RTA 1964 was considered in *Boyle v Connaughton*,[88] in which a small triangular portion of land which the plaintiff believed to be his was shown on the land registry maps as forming a

---

[87] [1930] N.I. 74.
[88] Unreported, High Court, Laffoy J., 21 March 2000.

portion of the neighbouring portfolio. The difficulty for the plaintiff was that a small part of an extension to his dwelling house had been built on the contested portion of land. The defendant was also in a similar difficulty in that a parcel of land he considered his (and upon which a piece of his dwelling had been constructed) was listed on the registry map as forming a part of the plaintiff's folio. The two pieces of contested land were not of identical size, with the portion sought by the plaintiff being around 100m² smaller than that sought by the defendant. Relations broke down between the neighbours and the plaintiff commenced proceedings seeking an order that the defendant vacate the contested land and an injunction restraining further trespass. The defendant, by way of counterclaim, sought an order for the rectification of the Registry map. Laffoy J. held that since the plaintiff had been aware of the defendant's encroachment onto his part of the folio at the time that he purchased the house, he had no basis for resisting the rectification of the Land Registry map.

Boundaries and Maps

7–59 Mapping is an important feature of registered land, indeed the completion of the Ordnance Survey's 6-inch map of Ireland in 1846 was a part of the impetus for the establishment of the Registry in the 19th century.[89] Section 85 of the RTA 1964 requires that registered land be described by reference to the Land Registry's mapping system. Today, the Land Registry uses a digital mapping system based on work by Ordnance Survey Ireland. The maps are accessible online through *landdirect.ie*.

7–60 Section 85 of the RTA 1964 provides that neither the Land Registry nor its maps are conclusive as to boundaries.[90] This has been a feature of the Irish system since its modern inception in 1891. In *Boyle v Connaughton*,[91] Laffoy J. held that this provision was intended to account for minor errors in calculation and mapping and to protect the State's compensation fund from resulting claims. However, s.85 will not prevent compensation being payable where a boundaries error is more than marginal. In *Lagan Bitumen Ltd v Tullagower Quarries Ltd*,[92] the court held that an error affecting approximately one-third of the area of a parcel of land could not be described as minor.

Classification of Interests

7–61 Although the registration system introduces a new classification of interests, the various categories are not mutually exclusive, as will be seen.

---

[89] A. Dowling, "Of Ships and Sealing Wax: The Introduction of Land Registration in Ireland" (1993) 44 N.I.L.Q. 360 at 374.
[90] RTA 1964 s.85(2), re-enacting Local Registration of Title (Ireland) Act 1891 s.55.
[91] Unreported, High Court, Laffoy J., 21 March 2000.
[92] [2017] IEHC 258.

Registered Interests: Section 8
Types of Interests
7–62 These are principally legal estates. They include:

1. Freehold land.
   "Freehold land" means "land the ownership of which is an estate in fee simple in possession".[93]
2. Leaseholds for more than 21 years unexpired.
   Section 8 of the RTA 1964 only refers to "leasehold interests", but s.3 defines "leasehold interest" as an interest in land under a lease for a term of years of which more than 21 are unexpired at the date of registration. Tenancies created for any term not exceeding 21 years or for any lesser estate or interest fall within s.72(1)(i) of the RTA 1964 where there is occupation under the tenancy and are binding without registration.
3. Incorporeal hereditaments in gross.
   These exclude easements and restrictive covenants since both such interests are always held for the benefit of dominant land. Such interests appear on the register as burdens registered against the servient land and as beneficial rights on the folio for the benefit of the dominant land. They include:
   (a) legal *profits à prendre*;
   (b) legal rentcharges, including a fee farm rent created by rentcharge; and
   (c) other, now rare, legal interests such as franchises (e.g. right to hold markets, fish in tidal waters) and fee farm rents created by feudal tenure.

Special Cases
Co-Ownership: Section 91
7–63 Two or more persons can be registered as the owners of a single estate or interest. Under s.91(2) of the RTA 1964, two or more such persons are deemed to be joint tenants unless there is an entry on the register to the contrary. Where persons are registered as tenants in common, the register will also show the size of the share they each own.[94]

Trusts: Section 92
7–64 Where there is a trust, it is the trustees, as owners of the legal estate, who are registered as owners.[95] "Trust" includes express, implied or constructive trusts.[96] The interests of the beneficiaries are not automatically entered on the register. They are classified as minor interests. The normal practice is for the trustees to protect the interests of the beneficiaries by entering or applying

---

[93] RTA 1964 s.3, as amended by LCLRA 2009 s.127.
[94] RTA 1964 s.91(1); LRR 2012 r.63.
[95] *Re O'Doherty* [1894] 1 I.R. 58 (on the 1891 Act).
[96] RTA 1964 s.92(3).

for the entry of an inhibition or a caution. The Registrar may advise trustees to do so even if they do not apply themselves. Trustees who fail to do so may be liable to beneficiaries for any loss occurring through failure to do so. The effect of such an entry depends on whether the equitable interest is a minor interest of the type which is overreached on sale or not.[97] Such an entry will prevent or restrict dealing with the registered legal title. Trustees remain liable personally to beneficiaries.[98]

7–65 Beneficial interests under trusts of land arising from (i) a strict settlement, or (ii) a trust, including a trust for sale, of land held for persons by way of succession, or (iii) land vested in or held on trust for a minor, are overreached on sale[99] and therefore cannot be protected by registration, because they do not affect purchasers. Other trusts of land, i.e. arising under resulting or constructive trusts, not overreached may be protected by registration or, where the beneficiaries are in actual occupation of the land, under s.72. Such beneficiaries may be unaware that they are entitled to such interests.

7–66 Beneficial interests provide an example of the overlapping nature of the provisions of the RTA 1964, since a person entitled to such an interest who is in possession may be protected under s.72 without registration and also be able to enter an inhibition or caution.[100] There is nothing to prevent a person creating equitable estates and interests in the land or in a registered charge just as an unregistered owner may do.[101] Thus, not only may express equitable interests be created, but other equitable interests, such as constructive trusts or interests arising under the doctrine of proprietary estoppel, may also be created. If the estate of a registered owner becomes subject to a trust after first registration, then s.92(2) provides that none of the following persons shall be affected by notice of the trust merely by the receipt by the Registrar of an instrument, e.g. the trust deed, for registration:

(a) the Registrar;
(b) a registered transferee for valuable consideration;
(c) a registered owner of a charge created for valuable consideration;
(d) a person claiming an interest created for valuable consideration in a registered burden.

7–67 One should notice the qualification of "for valuable consideration" in (b), (c) and (d). Persons who take registered land otherwise than for valuable

---

[97] RTA 1964 ss.96–98.
[98] RTA 1964 s.37(4).
[99] LCLRA 2009 s.21(2)(a).
[100] RTA 1964 s.105(5).
[101] RTA 1964 s.68(2). Note that the section does not restrict the power to create interests to the registered owner.

consideration are bound by more interests than those who pay valuable consideration for it, as will be seen below.

Burdens

7–68 These will be dealt with below.

Classes of Title

7–69 Section 33 of the RTA 1964, as amended, provides a number of classes of freehold and leasehold title which may be registered.

7–70 Freehold interests may be registered in three classes:

(a) absolute freehold title;
(b) qualified freehold title;
(c) possessory freehold title.[102]

Absolute Freehold Title

7–71 Section 37 of the RTA 1964 states the effect of a registration of absolute title to freehold land:

> "On registration of a person as full owner of freehold land with an absolute title, an estate in fee simple in the land, together with all implied or express rights, privileges and appurtenances belonging or appurtenant thereto, shall vest in the person so registered."

7–72 Absolute freehold title is the strongest form of title protected by the RTA 1964. As McGovern J. put it in *ACC Bank v Barry*, "the folio is the title so far as these lands are concerned."[103] Although the use of the term "absolute" implies that there are no qualifications to the owner's title, this is not in fact the case, and even the statement of McGovern J. requires qualification. Section 37(3) provides that absolute title is subject to any registered burdens and to burdens which affect land without registration under s.72 of the RTA 1964. Section 37(4) confirms that where the registered owner holds as trustee, the estate is also subject to the duties and liabilities of a trustee.

Qualified Freehold Title

7–73 A qualified freehold title will usually arise where an applicant is unable to establish a good root of title to the land which is more than 15 years old at the date of first registration. Qualified freehold title is provided for in s.33(5), which permits the registration of qualified title where:

---

[102] RTA 1964 s.33(1), as inserted by RDTA 2006 s.55.
[103] [2014] IEHC 322 at para.15.

"(a) it appears to the Authority that title can be established for a limited time period only or subject to certain reservations, and

(b) the Authority, by an entry in the register, excepts from the effect of registration any right—

(i) arising before a specified date,

(ii) arising under a specified instrument, or

(iii) otherwise particularly described in the register."

Possessory Freehold Title

7–74 Possessory freehold title arises where an application is made for first registration based on a possessory rather than a documentary title. Section 38(1) provides that possessory freehold title has the same basic effect as the registration of absolute freehold title, but that the registered owner's rights are subject to the additional qualification that registration does not impact on any right adverse to, or in derogation of, the registered owner's rights which subsisted or was capable of arising at the date of first registration. The effect is that the folio is not conclusive nor guaranteed by the State as far as pre-registration title is concerned.

Absolute Leasehold Title

7–75 Absolute leasehold title is granted where the PRA has approved title to the leasehold itself, to the freehold interest in the land and to any intermediate lease.[104]

Good Leasehold Title

7–76 Good leasehold title is the most common form of registration for a leasehold interest and is granted where the PRA has approved title to the leasehold itself. Good leasehold title does not affect any claim which might arise from a dispute about the lessor's right to grant the lease but is otherwise the same as absolute leasehold title.

Qualified Leasehold Title

7–77 As with qualified freehold title, qualified leasehold title can be granted where the PRA is of the view that leasehold title can only be established for a limited period, or where there is some instrument which qualifies the title in some way.

Possessory Leasehold Title

7–78 Section 40(7) of the RTA 1964 provides for the registration of possessory leasehold titles. The effect is the same as for possessory freehold titles, i.e. the title is not conclusive as far as the pre-registration title is concerned.

---

[104] See RTA 1964 s.40(4), as inserted by RDTA 2006 s.57.

Incorporeal Hereditaments Held in Gross

7–79 Rule 187(1) of the LRR 2012 provides for the registration of absolute and possessory titles to incorporeal hereditaments in gross. Where such interests are created by the holders of registered interests, r.187(3) provides that title to such an interest follows that of the grantor.

Conversion of Title
Compulsory Conversion

7–80 Where land was vested in a person by the Irish Land Commission and registered with possessory title and has been so registered for 15 years, the Registrar shall, provided he is satisfied that the registered owner is in possession, register the title as absolute in the case of freehold land and good leasehold in the case of leasehold land.

Voluntary Conversion

7–81 Where land was vested in a person by the Irish Land Commission and the title is deemed to be possessory and has been registered for 30 years, the Registrar may convert it to absolute title on the registration of a disposition or on transmission on death. Where the title registered is deemed possessory and has been so registered for at least 12 years and the person entitled wishes to transfer for value, it may be converted to absolute or good leasehold title. The latter provision shows that a person who wishes to enter the market is placed in a more favourable position than is the case with non-market transactions.

Applications for First Registration

7–82 An application for first registration must be made where it is compulsory to register land under ss.23 and 24 of the RTA 1964. The purpose of the first registration procedure is to enable the Land Registry to investigate title to land as it is registered and to ensure that the registered owner is registered as holding the correct class of title. Sections 92 and 94 of the RTA 1964 give the Land Registry powers of discovery where necessary to aid it in investigating titles. Rule 19 of the LRR 2012 has introduced a modified investigation regime where first registration is sought for a property with a market value below €1,000,000.

7–83 An application for first registration can be made on the basis of an existing documentary title or on the basis of adverse possession. The application must normally be made by a person who is in possession or in receipt of the rents and profits of the property concerned.[105]

7–84 Where an application for first registration for the ownership of freehold is made based on an existing documentary title, the LRR 2012 require that the applicant provide a statement of the title to the property which he or she relies

---

[105] *Re Vandeleur* (1915) 49 I.L.T.R. 206.

upon. This will ordinarily be a title of at least 15 years' duration commencing with a good root of title.[106] Where such a title cannot be shown, an application will result in registration of a qualified title.[107] The application should provide a statement of the title relied upon which should provide the Examiner of Titles in the Land Registry with a clear picture of the title to the property. Rule 15(1)(b) requires that the applicant supply all original deeds and documents in his or her possession or under his or her control relating to the title. The applicant must also provide any searches relating to the title and must supply an application map showing the physical bounds of the property on a Land Registry compliant map.

7–85 Rule 17 of the LRR 2012 allows for the making of an application for first registration based on a possessory title. This procedure is used where an applicant desires to register a title which he or she has acquired by adverse possession and which he or she now wishes (or is obliged) to register. The application is made using a standard form (Form 5) which requires the applicant to establish the title (freehold or leasehold) which he or she claims to have extinguished and proof of possession for the relevant statutory period.

7–86 Similar principles apply when making an application for first registration of a leaseholder title. Rule 16 of the LRR 2012 requires that such applications be accompanied by the original lease or a certified copy thereof.

7–87 Once the application has been made, the Land Registry will register title in the appropriate classification. The normal practice is to register with absolute title where it is possible to do so. Where this is not possible, a qualified or possessory title may be registered. Rule 18 of the LRR 2012 permits the PRA to accept titles about which there are doubts subject to the applicant agreeing to indemnify the PRA and the State from any loss or damages arising from the registration of the title.

Transfers of Registered Land

7–88 Once title to land has been registered, subsequent transfers are carried out by registered transfer.[108] A transfer includes a lease. The LRR 2012 provide statutory forms which are used to effect transfers.[109] Registered title differs from unregistered title in that the estate or interest in land does not pass to the transferee until the transfer is registered.[110] An executed transfer

---

[106] See LCLRA 2009 s.56. There is no fixed definition of a good root of title. For further details, see Deeney, *Registration of Deeds and Title in Ireland* (2014), Ch.28.

[107] RTA 1964 s.33, as substituted by RDTA 2006 s.55.

[108] RTA 1964 s.51.

[109] LRR 2012 r.67.

[110] RTA 1964 s.51(2). Priorities are determined in accordance with LRR 2012 r.58; *Crumlish v Registrar of Deeds and Titles* [1991] I.L.R.M. 37.

for consideration[111] which has been delivered but not registered is nevertheless valid against the registered owner and his or her devisee, as an "unregistered right".[112] In principle it would extend to any transferee not for valuable consideration from the registered owner.

Burdens

7–89 The RTA 1964 makes provision for two separate kinds of burden which may affect title to registered land. Section 69 creates a list of registrable burdens, i.e. those which must be disclosed on the register if they are to affect a purchaser or a chargee of the land concerned. Section 72, on the other hand, sets out a list of burdens which affect the land without registration. In *Tynan v County Registrar for Kilkenny*,[113] Laffoy J. held that ss.69 and 72 are mutually exclusive and that an interest which is capable of affecting the land by registration under s.69, cannot simultaneously be capable of affecting the land without registration under s.72.

Section 69 Burdens
Burdens Affecting Land by Registration
7–90 These are interests under s.69 and, when registered, bind the title of registered interests. They are typically, but not exclusively, legal interests of minor importance:

    (a) Incumbrances existing at the time of first registration.
    (b) A charge on land created after first registration. This is the equivalent in registered title of a legal mortgage. Under s.62 a charge confers the same remedies as a mortgage by conveyance with proviso for redemption or by way of demise, but does not transfer such an estate to the mortgagee.[114]
    (c) A rentcharge or fee farm or other perpetual rent. The fee simple of a fee farm grant is registered as a registered interest and the rent reserved to the grantor is registered as a burden on the fee simple under this section.
    (d) A power to charge land with the payment of money.

---

[111] It is otherwise if the transfer is voluntary: *Pim v Coyle* [1907] 1 I.R. 330.

[112] *Re Strong* [1940] I.R. 382; *Devoy v Hanlon* [1929] I.R. 246, on the Local Registration of Title (Ireland) Act 1891 ss.35 and 44. Unregistered rights only bind a transferee without consideration, apart from s.72.

[113] [2011] IEHC 250.

[114] In *Gale v First National Building Society* [1985] I.R. 609, the registered charge contained a term whereby the chargor agreed that if he defaulted in the repayments of a loan, the chargee had the right to enter the land. After a default the chargee entered the land. Costello J. refused an injunction to prevent the chargee continuing in possession, holding that the charge created a contractual licence, and that it was not necessary to register the right of entry other than in the charges register. It is unclear, however, if the judge intended to imply that the right would be effective against a transferee of the contracting party. If so, then contractual licences, at least ones of this type, would have achieved the status of property interests which they have yet to do in unregistered land.

(e) A trust for securing money.

(f) A lien of a vendor on land for unpaid purchase money. (If the vendor is in actual possession then it is a s.72 interest and binding without registration).[115]

(g) A lease for a life or lives or determinable on life or lives,[116] or over 21 years (or such other period as may be prescribed)[117] or where it is for a lesser term but occupation is not in accordance with the lease. If the lease is for a term not exceeding 21 years or less and the tenant is in occupation, then the lease is a s.72 interest and is binding without registration under s.72(1)(i). No matter how long the original term, if more than 21 years are unexpired, the title to the lease is itself registrable under ss.8 and 3.

In *An Application of O'Sullivan, Folio 27742 Co Cork*,[118] D'Arcy J. held that a lease granting "week No 25 in each year" for a total term of 1,100 years did not fall within this section, since the term referred to had to be continuous. This leaves time-share leases on an insecure footing. A note under s.72(3) could then be entered; however, it does not seem desirable to increase the scope of that section as doing so would further undermine the mirror principle.

(h) A judgment or order of a court which includes orders under the Family Law Act 1995 (judicial separation) and the Family Law (Divorce) Act 1996 (orders on divorce).

(i) A judgment mortgage, recognizance, State bond, inquisition or *lis pendens*.

(j) Easements, *profits à prendre* or mining rights created by express grant or reservation after first registration.

(jj) Easements and *profits à prendre* acquired by prescription under the terms of ss.33–38 of the Land and Conveyancing Law Reform Act 2009 ("LCLRA 2009") in which the acquisition of the easement is not contested.[119]

(k) Restrictive covenants or conditions as to the use of land. Under s.69(3) any covenant or condition registered under the section can be modified or discharged by an order of the court on proof that the covenant does not run with the land or is not capable of being enforced against the owner of the land.

(kk) a freehold covenant within the meaning of s.48 of the LCLRA 2009.[120]

---

[115] *London & Cheshire Insurance v Laplagrene* [1971] Ch. 499.

[116] If purported to be granted after the LCLRA 2009, such purported grants are void both at law and in equity: s.14. If perpetually renewable they take effect as a fee simple: s.12(2)(b).

[117] As amended by RDTA 2006 s.59.

[118] Unreported, High Court, D'Arcy J., 24 March 1983.

[119] See RTA 1964 s.49A, as inserted by Civil Law (Miscellaneous Provisions) Act 2011 s.41. The registration procedure is detailed in r.46 of the LRR 2012, as substituted by Land Registration Rules 2013 r.2 (S.I. No. 389 of 2013). For details of the scheme and its background, see Deeney, *Registration of Deeds and Title in Ireland* (2014), pp.311–314.

[120] As amended by LCLRA 2009 s.129.

(l)   Any estate in dower.[121]

(m)   Licences and other conditions under s.54 of the Forestry Act 1946.

(n)   Rights of the Irish Land Commission[122] to lay pipes.

(o)   Power of appointment.

(p)   Power of distress or entry.

(q)   Rights of residence or a lien for money's worth in or over the land, such as a right of support.[123]

(r)   Burdens created by statute or under a statutory power and which is not a s.72 burden.

(rr)   An order opening proceedings under the Insolvency Regulation.[124]

(rr)   An agreement regarding the use or management of land for wildlife and conservation purposes which expressly provides that the agreement shall bind the successors in title to the land.[125]

(rrr)   A natural heritage area order made under s.18 of the Wildlife (Amendment) Act 2000.[126]

Burdens Affecting Land without Registration: Section 72
Introduction

7–91 Section 72 introduces a list of interests which may affect the land but which are *not* disclosed on the register. Such interests, sometimes known as "overriding interests", are the single most significant qualification of the mirror principle in that a prospective transferee is bound by these interests whether or not they appear on the register. Section 72(3) allows the PRA to note such interests in the register where their existence is demonstrated to its satisfaction and where the registered owner consents to such a note.

7–92 Section 72 burdens which are not on the register are binding regardless of whether a transferee has notice of them or not. This is not such a departure from unregistered conveyancing as it might first appear since most of them will be found to be interests of persons in actual occupation of the land which would give rise to notice in equity under the unregistered system, or to be legal interests which would be binding regardless of notice in the unregistered system.

---

[121] Dower was abolished by s.11(2) of the Succession Act 1965.

[122] Now the Minister for Agriculture, Food and the Marine: Irish Land Commission (Dissolution) Act 1992 s.4.

[123] In *Tynan v Country Registrar for County Kilkenny* [2011] IEHC 250, the High Court held that a right of residence which has not been registered under s.62(1)(q) could not be protected as a burden under s.72(1)(j) even though the plaintiff there had been in actual occupation.

[124] Article 3(1) of Regulation (EU) 2015/848 of 20 May 2015 on insolvency proceedings (recast) [2015] OJ L141/19. Regulation 3(1) of the European Communities (Personal Insolvency) Regulations 2002 (S.I. No. 334 of 2002) inserts this item as subpara.(rr) of s.69(1) of the RTA 1964. This seems to have been a drafting error as subpara.(rr) had in fact already been created by s.66 of the Wildlife Act 1976.

[125] See Wildlife Act 1976 s.18 and Wildlife Act 1976 s.66, inserting subpara.(rr) into s.64(1) of the RTA 1964.

[126] Inserted by Wildlife (Amendment) Act 2000 s.77.

Section 72 Burdens

7–93 Section 72(1) sets out the following overriding interests:

(a) Succession duty, estate duty, gift tax and inheritance tax,[127] farm tax,[128] State rents arising under fee farm grants and payments in lieu of tithe rentcharges.[129]

(b) Land improvement charges and drainage charges.

(c) Annuities or rentcharges for the repayment of advances made under the Land Purchase Acts to enable agricultural tenants to buy the fee simple of a farm.

(d) Rights of the Irish Land Commission[130] or of any person under a vesting order made by the Commission under the Land Purchase Acts.

(e) Rights of the Irish Land Commission on execution of an order for possession under s.37 of the Land Act 1927.

(f) Public rights, e.g. public rights of way.

(g) Customary rights arising from tenure. It is doubtful if any still exist.

(h) Easements and *profits à prendre* unless created by express grant or reservation after first registration. If they are so created, they are registrable as a burden against the land under s.69.

(hh) Rights such as wayleaves, such as under the Gas Act 1976,[131] etc.

(i) Tenancies for a term not exceeding 21 years "or such other period as may be prescribed"[132] or for any lesser estate or interest, in cases where there is occupation under the tenancy. If the unexpired term exceeds 21 years, the lease itself is a registrable interest under ss.3 and 8, and is also registrable as a burden on the fee simple under s.69.

(j) Rights of every person in actual occupation of the land or in receipt of the rents or profits unless inquiry is made of such persons and they do not disclose their rights. This is the most important "overriding interest" since it is so general and is further discussed below. It was intended to be the equivalent in registered land of the rule in *Hamilton v Lyster*[133] and *Hunt v Luck*.[134]

(k) Where the title is possessory, qualified or good leasehold title, all rights excepted from the effect of registration.

---

[127] Capital Acquisitions Tax Consolidation Act 2003 s.113.

[128] Farm Tax Act 1985 s.21(6)—repealed by the Local Government Act 1994.

[129] Note that tithe rentcharges and other payments into the Church Temporalities Fund were abolished by s.7 of the Land Act 1984.

[130] Now the Minister for Agriculture, Food and the Marine: Irish Land Commission (Dissolution) Act 1992 s.4.

[131] Gas Act 1976 s.43. Under s.22 of the Gas (Amendment) Act 2000, this includes rights under written agreements granted to or by the Irish Gas Board, etc.

[132] RDTA 2006 s.60.

[133] (1844) 7 Ir. Eq. R. 560; the earliest reported example of the rule in Ireland is *Delap v Richardson*, in Lyall, *Irish Exchequer Reports: Reports of Cases in the Courts of Exchequer and Chancery in Ireland 1716–1734* (2008), clxi, p.127.

[134] [1902] 1 Ch. 428.

(l)   A perpetual yearly rent superior to a rent registered as a burden on
       registered land.

       This occurs when there are successive grants in fee farm, as under
       Deasy's Act. This facilitates first registration of the fee simple. The
       tenant in fee simple may register it with the rent reserved to the
       grantor registered as a burden, and even if the fee farm grantor held
       subject to a rent, that need not be proved, but will still be protected
       under this section. Thus, if X made a grant in fee farm to A and later
       A made a further grant under Deasy's Act in fee farm to B, A retains
       only a rent, having parted with the fee simple. B's fee simple may be
       registered, with the rent B pays to A registered as a burden, but no
       investigation is made of the title further back to reveal the rent paid
       by A to X. This "superior rent" is nevertheless binding on B under
       this section.

(m)   Covenants and conditions contained in a deed or document creating
       a superior rent. This applies to the same situation in (l) above. Where
       the grantor of a fee farm grant himself held under a grant in fee farm,
       the grant to him may contain covenants and they are preserved by
       this section.

(n)   A purchase annuity payable in respect of a cottage which is the sub-
       ject of a vesting order under the Labourers Act 1936.

(o)   Restrictions imposed by s.21 of the Labourers Act 1936 on the mort-
       gaging or charging of cottages purchased under that Act.

(p)   Rights acquired or in the course of being acquired under the Statute
       of Limitations 1957. When a person has acquired the land by adverse
       possession, then before the register is amended his or her interest
       binds the land under this section. Even before the limitation period
       has expired, his or her possessory title is preserved.

(q)   Statutory restrictions on assignment, subletting[135] or subdivision[136]
       which are specifically preserved by s.59, and, where the registered
       owner does not have the right to mines and minerals, the rights of
       persons who do.[137]

       Section 59 provides that "nothing in this Act shall affect the provi-
       sions of any enactment by which the alienation, assignment, subdivi-
       sion or subletting of any land is prohibited or in any way restricted".
       This would include not only such restrictions in leases, but also
       special conditions imposed on a sale of a dwelling by a housing
       authority.[138]

---

[135] Now under Landlord and Tenant (Amendment) Act 1980 ss.65 and 67.

[136] Formerly agricultural land could not be subdivided without the consent, formerly, of the Irish
Land Commission (Land Act 1965 s.12), later, the Minister for Agriculture, Food and the
Marine: Irish Land Commission (Dissolution) Act 1992 s.4. Under s.45 of the Land Act 1965,
certain restrictions applied, such as citizenship, to certain land. The Land Act 1965 ss.12 and
45 were repealed by Land Act 2005 s.12.

[137] RTA 1964 s.73.

[138] Housing Act 1966 s.89, as amended by Housing (Miscellaneous Provisions) Act 1992 s.25.

(r) Covenants continued in force by s.28 of the Landlord and Tenant (Ground Rents) (No. 2) Act 1978. Where a person enlarges a lease into a fee simple, some of the covenants under the lease are preserved.[139]

Section 72(1)(j)

7–94 Section 72(1)(j) is perhaps the most significant of the s.72 burdens, in that it provides protection to the holders of equitable interests who are in occupation of the land.

7–95 In Ireland there is less authority on these than in England. In England, the courts have found many types of interests to fall within the equivalent section.[140] This may indicate a judicial aversion to the registration principle. Among the interests found to be overriding have been the following:

1. A purchaser's equity.[141] It would be highly unusual for a purchaser to be in occupation before completion.
2. An option to purchase the freehold.[142]
3. An unpaid vendor's lien.[143]
4. A purchaser's lien for the deposit.[144]
5. A tenancy under the doctrine of "feeding the estoppel".[145]
6. Interests under constructive trusts.[146]
7. A wife's equity acquired by contributions to the purchase of the matrimonial home.[147] A spouse who is in occupation with an equity is therefore protected from his or her equity being overreached on sale. Such an equity would fall within s.21(3)(b)(iii) of the LCLRA 2009.
   Where a spouse has only an equitable interest, the courts have held that consent is required under the Family Home Protection Act 1976,[148] so that "other spouse" includes such a spouse, and his or her consent is required to a conveyance by a spouse. Section 21 of the LCLRA 2009 also preserves a spouse's rights under the 1976 Act,[149] so even a spouse not in occupation retains those.
8. An occupational licence, perhaps.[150]
9. The right to rectify the register.[151]

---

[139] Landlord and Tenant (Ground Rents) (No. 2) Act 1978 s.28.
[140] Land Registration Act 1925 s.70; Land Registration Act 2002 Schs 1 and 3.
[141] *Bridges v Mees* [1957] Ch. 475.
[142] *Webb v Pollmount* [1966] Ch. 584.
[143] *London & Cheshire Insurance Co v Laplagrene Property Co Ltd* [1971] Ch. 499.
[144] *Lee Parker v Izzett* [1971] 1 W.L.R. 1.
[145] *City Permanent Building Society v Miller* [1952] 1 Ch. 840.
[146] *Hodgson v Marks* [1971] 1 Ch. 892.
[147] *Friends Provident Life Office v Doherty* [1992] I.L.R.M. 372.
[148] *AL v JL*, unreported, High Court, Finlay P., 27 February 1984.
[149] LCLRA 2009 s.21(6).
[150] *Re Sharpe* [1980] 1 W.L.R. 219.
[151] *Blacklocks v JB Developments Ltd* [1981] 3 All E.R. 392.

(10) An equitable interest in land the subject of a conveyance by the National Asset Management Agency Act 2009.[152]

Excluded Interests

7–96 Judges have expressed the view that s.72 does not create new types of property interest, it only classifies existing ones.[153]

- ● **Spouse's Veto over Conveyance of Family Home**

7–97 A spouse's power to refuse consent to a conveyance under the Family Home Protection Act 1976 has been held not to be a s.72 interest. It is not a property interest.[154]

- ● **Planning Permission**

7–98 It seems unlikely that planning permission is a "right" within s.72(1)(j). Carroll J. in the High Court in *Electricity Supply Board v Gormley*[155] held that planning permission was not a "right" within s.52(1) of the RTA 1964. That section provides that on the registration of a transferee of freehold land as full owner with an absolute title, the instrument of transfer vests in the registered transferee an estate in fee simple in the land transferred, subject to registered burdens under s.69 and unregistered burdens under s.72, but "free from all other rights, including rights of the State". Planning permission was, the judge said, just that: a permission and not a right. This probably means that it is not a right within s.72(1)(j) either.

7–99 Section 39(1) of the Planning and Development Act 2000 provides that the grant of planning permission "shall enure for the benefit of the land" and enforcement procedures also attach to the land.[156] In *Readymix Eire Ltd v Dublin County Council*,[157] Henchy J. described planning permission as "an appendage to the title to the property". Nevertheless, although the person having the benefit of a planning permission has a right to develop land accordingly, this does not extend to taking actions which interfere with the rights of third parties. It is thus doubtful that planning permission is a form of *property* right.

---

[152] National Asset Management Agency Act 2009 s.143.
[153] In *Esso Petroleum v Epps* [1973] 1 W.L.R. 1071, it was held that intermittent parking of a car is not an overriding interest because it is not an easement, but see now *London & Blenheim Estates Ltd v Ladbroke Retail Parks Ltd* [1993] 1 All E.R. 307, where it was held inter alia that a right to park cars could be an easement if it did not deprive the servient owner of effective use of the land.
[154] *Guckian v Brennan* [1981] I.R. 478; *Murray v Diamond* [1982] I.L.R.M. 113.
[155] [1985] I.R. 129 at 144 (appeal allowed on other issues).
[156] Planning and Development Act 2000 Pt VIII.
[157] Unreported, Supreme Court, 30 July 1974, cited with approval in *Dublin County Council v Jack Barrett Ltd*, unreported, Supreme Court, 28 July 1983.

"Actual Occupation"

7–100 In unregistered title a purchaser will be held to have constructive notice of the rights of persons in occupation of the land unless it would be inequitable to fix him or her with such notice.[158] Section 76(1)(j) enacts a similar principle in registered land. The meaning of actual occupation has been explored in a number of English cases.[159] In *Thompson v Foy*,[160] the English High Court provided a useful summary of the applicable principles:

1. The words "actual occupation" are ordinary words of plain English and should be interpreted as such. The word "actual" emphasises that physical presence is required.
2. It does not necessarily involve the personal presence of the person claiming to occupy. A caretaker or the representative of a company can occupy on behalf of his or her employer.
3. However, actual occupation by a licensee (who is not a representative occupier) does not count as actual occupation by the licensor.
4. The mere presence of some of the claimant's furniture will not usually count as actual occupation.
5. If the person said to be in actual occupation at any particular time is not physically present on the land at that time, it will usually be necessary to show that his or her occupation was manifested and accompanied by a continuing intention to occupy.

7–101 A sense of the application of these principles can be gleaned from the recent decision of the English Court of Appeal in *Link Lending v Bustard*.[161] The respondent was the registered owner of her home. In 2004, whilst suffering from a serious mental illness she executed a transfer of the property to a third party, H. The court held that in executing this transfer, the respondent had been taken advantage of. The respondent continued to live in the property. In 2007, she was admitted to hospital involuntarily and was later transferred to a residential care home where she underwent treatment. She was not permitted to return to her home except for occasional supervised visits to check the property and pick up post. In 2008, the appellant was granted a charge over the property by H in consideration of advances made to H. H defaulted and in June 2008, the appellant began possession proceedings. At first instance the court held that the respondent had been in actual occupation at the time when the appellant secured its charge. In reaching this conclusion, the court relied on the fact that the respondent wished to return to the property, which she regarded as her home, and was only prevented from doing so under the terms of the mental health legislation; regular bills in connection with the property, such

---

[158] *Hamilton v Lyster* (1844) 7 Ir. Eq. R. 560; *Hunt v Luck* [1902] 1 Ch. 428.

[159] See *Williams & Glyn's Bank v Boland* [1981] A.C. 487; *Abbey National Building Society v Cann* [1991] 1 A.C. 56; *Strand Securities Ltd v Caswell* [1965] Ch. 958; *Hoggett v Hoggett* (1980) 39 P. & C.R. 121.

[160] [2009] EWHC 1076 at para.127.

[161] [2010] EWCA Civ 424.

as community charges, were being discharged from the respondent's funds; and she was still visiting the property, albeit under supervision. The Court of Appeal upheld this conclusion.

7–102 It is questionable whether time-share leases would fall within the section. Is occupation for one or two weeks in the year sufficient to constitute "actual occupation" within the subsection? If a prospective purchaser inspects the land during the week leased to X and finds X in residence, is X then within the subsection, but not the others who were not in occupation during that week? If the purchaser inspects it when X is not in residence and finds Y in occupation, and Y says that he has a time-share, is that not enough to give notice to the purchaser that X has a time-share, or put the purchaser on inquiry? On the face of it, an inspection which revealed a time-share should not then distinguish between the time-sharers merely on the basis of who happened to be present at the time, although whether the ones who were not could be described as "in actual occupation" must be open to doubt.

Enquiries
7–103 The words "save where, upon enquiry made of such person, the rights are not disclosed" incorporate a test analogous in some respects to the doctrine of notice in equity. It is clear that if a purchaser or other party is to take free of an unregistered interest falling within the section, then the enquiries must be made of the person entitled to the unregistered interest who does not then disclose it. Enquiries directed to a husband or wife will have no effect even if the husband or wife owns the legal estate in the land.

7–104 In *Friends Provident Life Office v Doherty*,[162] Mr D bought some land as the site of the matrimonial home. He was duly registered as proprietor of the land. Mrs D paid for the construction of the house. Some years later Mr D applied for a substantial loan from the plaintiff on security of a mortgage of the house. Mr D made the usual statutory declaration to the effect that none of the burdens under s.72 of the RTA 1964 affected the folio. Mr and Mrs D together then made a statutory declaration to the effect that they were lawfully husband and wife, that the house was a family home, that the land was in the sole name of Mr D, and that Mrs D consented to the mortgage. The mortgage was executed, and Mrs D endorsed a consent for the purposes of the Family Home Protection Act 1976 on the mortgage. Mr D fell behind in repayments and Friends Provident sued for and obtained an order for possession. Mr D appealed, but in the meantime Mrs D applied to the Circuit Court applying under s.12 of the Married Women's Status Act 1957 for a declaration that she had an interest in excess of 50 per cent in the house.

7–105 The Circuit Court held against her and she then appealed. Blayney J. in the High Court held that she did have an equity in the house within s.72, which

---

[162] [1992] I.L.R.M. 372.

existed before the mortgage was executed. The company had argued that her interest fell outside s.72 because it had made enquiries of her in its requisitions on title and she had not revealed the interest. The judge rejected this as the requisitions were addressed to Mr D alone. He held that she therefore did have an interest within s.72. He nevertheless held that on the facts of the case she was estopped from pleading it because by her statements and conduct she had represented to Friends Provident that she had no interest in the house. The judge was led to this conclusion because Mrs D had stated that she consented to the mortgage and also that she had stated that the premises were in the sole name of her husband. The effect of the estoppel was not that she had no interest in the property, but was to postpone it to the interest of Friends Provident.

7–106 It was further argued by Mrs D that the company had not in fact made enquiries of her and so, in the terms of s.72, should be bound by her interest. The judge held that in the circumstances the company had no reason to do so as she had volunteered the information which gave it the impression that she had no interest. Moreover, Mrs D was advised by a solicitor and there was no reason to suppose that Mrs D did not understand the effect of the mortgage. The case thus adds a gloss to s.72 in that a party who does not make enquiries of the person in actual occupation will *not* be bound by an interest if the person in occupation took the initiative in leading him or her to believe that no interest was being claimed, or that there was no interest having priority to the one which he or she sought to register. Nevertheless, these situations can give rise to subtleties of interpretation and the danger is that the court may go to the extent of shifting the initiative fully to the occupier which the section does not appear to require. It may also have been the case that Mrs D was not aware that she had an equity in the house or that a court would have found such an interest if the issue had arisen. Ignorance of the law may not on its own be an excuse, but when the issue is whether a person deliberately misled another as to his or her interests in property, then the ignorance of law is relevant to his or her factual state of mind and must be considered.

7–107 In *Ulster Bank v Shanks*,[163] the Northern Ireland High Court arguably went too far in placing the onus on the occupier. In that case a house had been mortgaged by demise and the husband and wife later went to a bank to arrange a second mortgage, also by demise. The wife in the meantime had acquired an equity in the house through her contributions to the deposit and to paying off the first mortgage. The bank did not ask the wife if she had an equity and the wife did not volunteer the information. Murray J. in the Northern Ireland High Court held that the wife's equity did not take priority over the second mortgage. It was, he thought, inequitable for a party to stand by and not mention an equity and then seek to rely on it later.[164]

---

[163] [1982] N.I. 143.
[164] See also, *Paddington Building Society v Mendelsohn* (1985) 50 P. & C.R. 244.

7–108 Essentially the same point was also decided in *Northern Bank Ltd v McNeill*.[165] Nevertheless, the corresponding provision to s.72(1)(j) in Northern Ireland, which was in almost identical terms, did not place the onus on the person in actual occupation to reveal his or her right and neither does s.72(1)(j). The right of such persons are to be binding "*save* where, upon enquiry made of such person, the rights are not disclosed". The onus is clearly on the purchaser to inquire of the person in occupation what rights he or she has, and only if he or she does not reveal them is the purchaser then free of the rights. This is essentially also the case with unregistered land where the decision in *Hunt v Luck* and such cases was that constructive notice is normally to be imputed to the purchaser where a person is in occupation. There may be cases where the fact of occupation is difficult to discover and it may be unfair in those circumstances to hold the purchaser bound by constructive notice, but in both the Northern Ireland cases the occupation by the wife was known to the bank. In the *Ulster Bank* case, the judge quoted s.3 of the Conveyancing Act 1882, which dealt with constructive notice at the time, and evidently believed it supported his view:

> "3.—(1) A purchase shall not be prejudicially affected by notice of any instrument, fact, or thing unless—
> It is within his own knowledge, or would have come to his knowledge if such inquiries and inspections had been made as ought reasonably to have been made by him ...".

7–109 It is difficult to agree with the result in the case. The bank knew the wife was in occupation and once it had that knowledge there were obvious questions which should then have been asked. If the bank had asked her about her rights, there is no reason to suppose they would not have been revealed. There seems to be no need for the courts to go out of their way to assist a bank which was so negligent as not to ask about the wife's contributions when she was in the manager's office and she and her husband were applying for a mortgage. One would expect, given the state of the law, that the bank would have included such a question on the application form itself. The *Friends Provident* case is distinguishable on the ground that, there, the wife volunteered information which clearly represented that she claimed no interest in priority to the company.

Section 72(1)(j) and Equitable Interests

7–110 The LCLRA 2009 preserved this category of interest from the general extension of overreaching in the Act, although this was the subject of debate.[166]

---

[165] Unreported, NI Chancery Division, Murray J., 14 February 1986.

[166] See Law Reform Commission, *Report on Reform and Modernisation of Land Law and Conveyancing Law* (LRC 74-2005). The draft Bill dispensed with the exception for rights in actual occupation, thereby favouring purchasers at the expense of those entitled to equities. See also the LCLRA 2009 Explanatory Memorandum on s.21.

7–111 Section 21(2)(a) of the LCLRA 2009 extended overreaching specifically to equitable interests under trusts of land where the trust comprises:

"(i) a strict settlement, or
(ii) a trust, including a trust for sale, of land held for persons by way of succession, or
(iii) land vested in or held on trust for a minor [i.e. in cases where a conveyance must be made by at least two trustees or a trust corporation]."[167]

7–112 Equitable interests are not overreached in the following cases[168]:

"(a) any conveyance made for fraudulent purposes of which the purchaser has actual knowledge at the date of the conveyance or to which the purchaser is a party, or
(b) any equitable interest—
   (i) to which the conveyance is expressly made subject, or
   (ii) protected by deposit of documents of title relating to the legal estate or legal interest, or
   (iii) in the case of a trust coming within subsection (2)(b), [i.e. trusts other than those within s.21(2)(a), above, mainly constructive trusts] protected by registration prior to the date of the conveyance or taking effect as a burden coming within section 72(1)(j) of the 1964 Act [i.e. rights of persons in actual occupation] (or, in the case of unregistered land, which would take effect as such a burden if the land were registered land)."

7–113 In other words, interests under "s.21(2)(b) trusts" are not overreached on sale of the legal estate, but the beneficial interests are protected under s.72(1)(j) where the person entitled is in actual occupation, or he or she is protected by registration.

7–114 The LCLRA 2009 preserves the former position whereby a purchaser takes subject to the interests of persons in actual occupation. Here again, there was a policy issue as to the balance between on the one hand, (a) reducing the uncertainties of title in the interests of purchasers, i.e. the "efficient" working of a market from the point of view of purchasers, and on the other hand, (b) the interests of doing justice to persons who may be entitled on grounds of equity to a beneficial interest in the land. The LCLRA 2009 therefore preserves the latter rights where they are registered or the person is in occupation, at some expense to a ruthless application of a market principle. The risk to purchasers is reduced by the fact that they may discover those interests by inspecting the register and the land and make inquiries as to occupation.

---

[167] LCLRA 2009 s.21(2)(a).
[168] LCLRA 2009 s.21(3).

7–115 Thus, the effect appears to be that where an equitable interest arises by resulting or constructive trust (where a conveyance may be made by a single trustee) and the beneficiary is in actual occupation, the equity is protected from being overreached by the RTA 1964, either by registration or, even if not registered, by s.72(1)(j).

Cautions and Inhibitions

7–116 Section 69 does not exhaust all the interests which may be protected by an entry on the register. Other interests may be protected by a caution under s.97 or an inhibition under s.98.[169] Cautions and inhibitions are used to protect the holders of equitable interests. Section 92(2) of the RTA 1964 prohibits the direct entry of such interests on the register.

Cautions

7–117 Section 97 of the RTA 1964 deals with cautions. The purpose of a caution is to ensure that the holder of an unregistered interest receives prior notice of a dealing with registered land. Where a caution has been registered, the PRA will not register any dealing with the land without giving prior notice to the cautioner. This gives the cautioner an opportunity to take any steps (such as court action) which he or she considers necessary to protect his or her interest.

7–118 Cautions are registered using a standard form supported by an affidavit of the cautioner which must show prima facie evidence that the cautioner has a right (defined in s.3 of the RTA 1964 as including "any estate, interests, equity or power") which is capable of protection by caution. Once a caution is registered, the PRA will notify the registered owner of the land of the existence of the caution.

7–119 Where the PRA receives a transfer of land for value which is subject to a caution, it will inform the cautioner that the caution will lapse within 21 days. If no action is taken by the cautioner, the dealing will be registered and the caution will be allowed to lapse.

Inhibitions

7–120 An inhibition enables a person entitled to unregistered or unregisterable interests in land to protect his or her interest. An inhibition will normally prevent the registration of any dispositions that would prejudice the rights of the inhibitor.[170] Inhibitions are therefore a more significant interference in the rights of the registered owners than are cautions.

7–121 An inhibition may be ordered by a court or inserted onto the register following an application to the PRA. The applicant must satisfy the PRA that

---

[169] RTA 1964 s.98(4)(a) was repealed by LCLRA 2009 ss.2 and 8(3) and Sch.2, Pt 5.
[170] Other forms of inhibition are possible: see Form 77, r.128(1) of the LRR 2012.

he or she is entitled to an interest which would justify the insertion of an inhibition. Where there are conflicts between interested parties as to the facts, the PRA will decline to proceed with an application and will leave it to the courts to resolve any disputes between interested parties.

7–122 Inhibitions are commonly used to protect interests under trusts, options to purchase and pre-emption rights. Under s.35 of the Criminal Justice Act 1994 and s.10 of the Proceeds of Crime Act 1996, inhibitions may be used to further orders made for the confiscation of criminal assets. Section 103 of the RTA 1964 provides for the entry of an inhibition in respect of any land affected by the presentation of a bankruptcy petition. Section 80 of the RTA 1964 provides that a charge created by a company shall not affect registered land unless it is registered as a s.69 burden, or protected by a caution or inhibition. Deeney suggests that this is because such charges are ordinarily floating in nature[171] but since a floating charge does not (and indeed by definition cannot[172]) affect the company's entitlement to dispose of the charged property in the course of business, this explanation seems improbable.

7–123 Section 121 of the RTA 1964 permits the PRA to enter an inhibition for the purposes of protecting the Central Fund from compensation where an error capable of rectification is discovered. This procedure was judicially considered in *State (Philpott) v Registrar of Titles*,[173] in which the High Court held that this power must be exercised in a judicial manner and only in circumstances where there is a real probability of a claim on the Central Fund. Ordinarily the PRA is required to give prior notice to the registered owner of a proposal to enter an inhibition under this section, though in urgent cases that notice may be dispensed with.

Land Certificates

7–124 Prior to the passage of the RDTA 2006, the Land Registry issued certificates which showed title to registered land, including particulars such as the registered ownership, cautions, inhibitions and burdens affecting the land. Certificates of registered charges were also issued. Section 105(5) of the RTA 1964 provides that the deposit of such a certificate has the effect of creating an equitable mortgage by deposit.

7–125 Land certificates were abolished by s.73 of the RDTA 2006 over a three-year period following its commencement on 1 January 2007. During this transitional period, mortgages created by deposit of the land certificate were registered by the PRA as a lien on the land which was deemed to be a

---

[171] Deeney, *Registration of Deeds and Title in Ireland* (2014) p.287.

[172] *Re Keenan Brothers Ltd* [1985] I.R. 401; *Re Brumark Investments Ltd* [2001] 2 A.C. 710, as approved by *Re JD Brian Ltd* [2015] 2 I.L.R.M. 441.

[173] [1986] I.L.R.M. 499.

s.69 burden on the land. The transitional period ended on 31 December 2009 and any outstanding land certificates ceased to have any legal effect as of that date.[174]

Transfers and Priority Questions

7–126 This section considers the extent to which the transferee of registered land may rely on the information contain in the Land Registry as evidence of title to land. The answer will depend on whether the transfer concerned is voluntary or for value.

Transferee for Value

7–127 A transferee of registered land who takes for valuable consideration takes the title subject to[175]:

1. registered burdens under s.69;
2. cautions and inhibitions;
3. s.72 interests which are binding despite not being registered and regardless of notice. This may include interests acquired by adverse possession[176];
4. Actual fraud or mistake.[177] The court may order the register to be rectified in such a case.

Transferees Not for Valuable Consideration

7–128 Such a transferee takes subject to:

1. all the interests mentioned in the preceding section; and, in addition,
2. under s.52(2) of the RTA 1964, any *unregistered* rights which bound the transferor. The same applies in the case of a *charge* obtained otherwise than for valuable consideration under s.68(3).[178]

Judgment Mortgages

7–129 A judgment mortgage is not a charge for valuable consideration and so the judgment mortgagee takes subject to unregistered rights affecting the judgment debtor. A judgment mortgage is merely a form of remedy. It would not be equitable to give to an unsecured debtor priority over earlier equities merely because the debtor chose a judgment mortgage as a remedy.

---

[174] RDTA 2006 s.73(2). Section 73(5) provides for a limited compensation regime for lien holders who failed to register liens by deposit of the land certificate prior to the end of the transitional period.

[175] See RDTA 2006 s.31 (conclusiveness of register), s.37 (effect of absolute title) and s.52(1) (transferees).

[176] If *Chowood v Lyall (No.2)* [1930] 2 Ch. 156 is accepted in this jurisdiction.

[177] RDTA 2006 s.31(1).

[178] RDTA 2006 s.71(4)(c).

7–130 In *Curran v Curran*,[179] a husband was registered as full owner of a house. The wife claimed the whole or an undivided share of the beneficial interest. The wife had paid off part of the mortgage debt. The husband had got into debt and had agreed to the debt being secured by a legal charge over the house. None was ever executed. The creditor company sued on the debt and subsequently registered a judgment mortgage against the house. The judge held that the wife had a 50 per cent share of the beneficial interest in the house.[180] The judge held that the wife's equity acquired by contributions was an "unregistered right" within s.52(2) and that it therefore had priority over the judgment mortgage.

Lis Pendens

7–131 A *lis pendens* (pending court action) is now governed by Pt 12 of the LCLRA 2009. Section 121 defines it as any action in the Circuit Court or the High Court in which a claim is made to an estate or interest in land whether by way of claim or counterclaim or any proceedings to have a conveyance of an estate or interest in land declared void.[181]

7–132 In *Coffey v Brunel Construction Ltd*,[182] the plaintiff entered into a contract to buy land from B and paid the purchase money. A transfer was executed but not registered. The defendant then started an action in the High Court claiming that B held the land in trust for it. The suit was registered as a *lis pendens* against B's title. The Supreme Court held that the *lis pendens* was not a charge obtained for valuable consideration. Thus the purchaser's earlier unregistered equity prevailed over the registered *lis pendens*. The court held that the equity would not have prevailed against a transferee for valuable consideration nor against a chargee for valuable consideration but the holder of a *lis pendens* was not such. Priority between registered, or registrable, burdens was governed by s.69 which ranks them in the order in which they are registered, but the court held that a purchaser's equity was not capable of registration under s.69, since it did not feature in the list of interests in the section, and so it was unaffected by the section.

7–133 One should note that the purchaser was not in actual occupation. If he had been, the right would probably have bound a transferee or chargee for valuable consideration under s.72(1)(j).

---

[179] Unreported, High Court, McWilliam J., 10 March 1981.
[180] The judge further held that the beneficial interest in the house was held by the wife and the company in equal shares, but this appears to have ignored s.71(4) which provides that the registration of a judgment mortgage over registered land does not transfer the debtor's interest in the house.
[181] LCLRA 2009 s.121(2).
[182] [1983] I.R. 36.

Is Notice Relevant?

Transferee Not for Value

7–134 Under s.52(2) a transferee not for valuable consideration is bound by unregistered interests which bound the transferor or chargor regardless of notice.[183] The principle in s.52(2) is intended to reproduce in registered land the result that would occur in unregistered title. In order to take free of equitable interests, a purchaser or mortgagee of a legal interest would have to prove that he was a *bona fide* purchaser for value of a legal interest in the land without notice. If he fails as to any element of the plea, he takes subject to the interest.[184] Hence, if he can prove he is a purchaser of a legal interest, but cannot prove consideration, he takes subject to the equitable interest. The law assists the buyer of commodities in the market, but not those who take, even innocently, outside the market.

7–135 In the English case of *Peffer v Rigg*,[185] it was suggested that a transferee not for valuable consideration was bound by an unregistered express trust, inter alia, because she knew of it. Mr Rigg, the first defendant, and the plaintiff, his brother-in-law, bought a house mainly as a residence for their mother-in-law. The first defendant and the plaintiff were married to sisters. The house was transferred into the name of Mr Rigg alone to be held by him on trust for them both as tenants in common in equal shares. The mother-in-law lived in the ground floor flat until her death. The top flat was rented. Later Mr Rigg obtained a divorce from his wife, the second defendant, and as part of the arrangements then made, he agreed to transfer the legal estate in the house to her. He executed a transfer to her "as beneficial owner" in consideration of £1. The second defendant was registered as proprietor. There was no note on the register as to the plaintiff's interest, nor was the plaintiff in actual occupation.

7–136 Graham J. in the English High Court held that the second defendant held the registered title subject to the plaintiff's share as equitable tenant in common. First, he held that since the second defendant had given only nominal consideration, she should be treated as a transferee without valuable consideration.[186] Secondly, the second defendant actually knew of the plaintiff's interest. Referring to the equitable doctrine of "knowing reception" of trust property, the judge concluded that since the wife "knew … that the property was trust property when the transfer was made to her", she took the title "on a constructive trust in accordance with general equitable principles".[187]

---

[183] There is one respect in which registered title may differ in this context from unregistered title. Section 52(2) is not expressly limited to equitable interests. A transferee not for valuable consideration of registered land may in principle, therefore, take subject to unregistered legal rights affecting the transferor, if indeed there are any such things.

[184] *Heneghan v Davitt* [1933] I.R. 325.

[185] [1977] 1 W.L.R. 285.

[186] [1977] 1 W.L.R. 285 at 293.

[187] [1977] 1 W.L.R. 285 at 294.

7–137 Since the judge had already found that the wife was not a purchaser for valuable consideration, the second reason was, it is suggested, erroneous, and in Ireland would be a result contrary to s.52. The wife would have been bound whether she had notice or not. On general equitable principles she could not establish the full plea of bona fide purchaser for value without notice, because she did not take for value. There is no reason why the position should be different under registered title. *Peffer v Rigg* was criticised in England and seems increasingly to have been an aberrant decision.[188]

Transferee for Value

7–138 It would be quite a different matter to assert that a transferee *for valuable consideration* takes subject to unregistered rights affecting the transferor if the transferee has actual notice of them, apart from actual fraud. As Cross J. observed in *Strand Securities v Caswell*,[189] it is "vital to the working of the land registration system that notice of something which is not on the register should not affect a transferee unless it is an overriding interest." One might add, "transferee for value".

7–139 Brightman J. in *De Lusignan v Johnson*[190] held that to register in the knowledge that unprotected rights existed was not "bad faith" and that it "would be stretching the language" to say that it was. He sought to draw a distinction between "fraud" and "notice of the existence or possible existence" of unprotected rights. Only the former, he said, was a relevant ground of complaint against a purchaser of registered land. This position has now been reinforced in England by the decision in *Midland Bank Trust Co Ltd v Green*.[191]

7–140 The issue of when notice may amount to fraud in the registration of deeds system has already been dealt with. In the context of that system, the judges in the 18th and 19th centuries[192] made a distinction between two situations. If A entered into a transaction in ignorance of unregistered rights and then, having discovered them, registered her interest to protect herself, this was not held to be fraud. On the other hand, if A, the prospective transferee, already had knowledge of the unprotected right before she entered into the transaction and then, after completing the transaction, registered in order to gain priority, that was regarded as fraud.

7–141 The Supreme Court has not departed from this view in the context of the registration of deeds system, although it seems to have narrowed the

---

[188] Gray and Gray, *Elements of Land Law* (2009), para.8.2.24, fn.11.
[189] [1965] Ch. 373 at 390A–B; Gray and Gray, *Elements of Land Law* (2009), para.8.2.24.
[190] (1973) 230 E.G. 499.
[191] [1981] A.C. 513 at 530A–B.
[192] *Forbes v Deniston* (1722) 4 Bro. P.C. 189; *Delacour v Freeman* (1854) 2 Ir. Ch. R. 633; *Montgomery v McEvoy* (1857) 5 Ir. Ch. R. 126; *Clarke v Armstrong* (1861) 10 Ir. Ch. R. 263; *Agra Bank v Barry* (1874) L.R. 7 H.L. 135.

definition of actual notice.[193] Even if a person, before he or she takes the benefit of a transfer of registered land, has knowledge that a third party claims some interest in it, this has been held not to oblige the intending transferee to withdraw from the sale. In *Persian Properties Ltd v Registrar of Titles*,[194] the plaintiff purchased a site which was registered as freehold land. The map lodged with the original application for registration had been inaccurate but, apart from this error, the Land Registry in preparing its map also accidentally overstated the width of the laneway at its entrance. As soon as the sale was complete, the plaintiff demolished a gate and wall on its neighbour's property. Proceedings in the High Court resulted in the court upholding the neighbour's title to the disputed ground.[195] The plaintiff subsequently claimed compensation under s.120 of the RTA 1964. The Registrar refused the application and the plaintiff then appealed to the High Court. Carroll J. held in favour of the plaintiff. The defendants appealed to the Supreme Court in the course of which they submitted that the plaintiff's loss had been partially or substantially caused or contributed to by its own fault, in that it had proceeded with completion of the purchase of the site in the knowledge that a third party claimed the disputed strip. The Supreme Court allowed the appeal, in part, and substituted for the order of the High Court an order awarding the plaintiff the value of the strip of land. The court held: (a) that the plaintiff had been entitled to rely on the register as conclusive evidence of title and complete the sale when it did; and (b) that the mere indication by a third party that it was asserting its title to the disputed strip did not oblige the plaintiff to withdraw from the sale or enter into negotiations with the vendor for a reduction in the price. The case is, of course, no guide as to what would have been the position if the plaintiff had been aware of an unregistered right of a definite nature.

7–142 It is true that registration of title, if it is to achieve its object, may require a harsher view. It may require that those who claim interests should be under the obligation to register them unless they fall within the category of overriding interests. On the other hand, it can be argued that if the above distinction is maintained, an intending purchaser who has actual notice of unregistered rights before he or she enters into a transaction does not require the protection of the registration system in order to avoid a loss. However, it is also true that a speculator who sees that a profit can be made from a piece of land would not be satisfied by being told not to enter into the transaction in the first place. It may be that the harsh view is not motivated simply by a concern to maintain the integrity of the registration system, but by a concern that the registration system should accommodate speculators or entrepreneurs. In the past the religiously-inspired injunction that one should be one's "brother's keeper" no doubt influenced the attitude of judges, and their sense of a moral attitude shared by the wider society. In a more secular age it may no longer

---

[193] *Re Fuller* [1982] I.R. 161.
[194] [2003] 1 I.R. 450.
[195] See *Tomkin Estates Ltd v O'Callaghan and Persian Properties Ltd*, unreported, High Court, McCracken J., 16 March 1995.

be regarded as a moral requirement to avoid taking advantage of the failure of others to protect their own interests where they are able to do so.

Adverse Possession
General
7–143 The Statute of Limitations 1957 applies to registered land just as it applies to unregistered land.[196] While time is running against the registered owner, the adverse possessor has an overriding interest under s.72(1)(p) of the RTA 1964. This would not seem to give any protection to the adverse possessor against the registered owner or an assignee, just as in unregistered land an adverse possessor cannot resist a better title, and may only be intended to indicate that an adverse possessor has the right to evict those who attempt to set up a later possession.

7–144 Where a person has acquired title to registered land by adverse possession, he or she can apply to the Registrar to have his or her title registered.[197] Section 49(3) of the RTA 1964 states that "upon such registration the title of the person whose right of action to recover the land has expired shall be extinguished."[198]

7–145 An adverse possessor is not a transferee for valuable consideration, and so s.52 applies and so would hold the land subject to all unregistered rights subject to which the transferor held.

Leasehold
7–146 If an adverse possessor remains in possession of leasehold land for 12 years and then obtains registration as proprietor of the lease under s.49(3), the title of the ousted lessee to the lease is then extinguished.[199] There can be no question of the ousted lessee retaining any interest which can be merged with or forfeited in favour of the lessor so as to affect the squatter in any way. Only the registered proprietor of an interest can transfer it or otherwise deal with it.[200] This suggests that in relation to the registration of title by adverse possession, there may be something in the nature of a "parliamentary conveyance".[201]

---

[196] RTA 1964 s.49(1).

[197] RTA 1964 s.49(2).

[198] Under the 1891 Act, an adverse possessor could only be registered by an order of court. But an owner registered "subject to the equities"—who might be an adverse possessor against another, unregistered, title—could have the note as to equities cancelled without an order of the court on showing that he had acquired the title under the Limitation Act: see *Dwyer v Whitelegge* (1899) 33 I.L.T.R. 179.

[199] See *Perry v Woodfarm Homes* [1975] I.R. 104 at 119–120.

[200] RTA 1964 s.51(2). "Transfer" includes lease: RTA 1964 s.51(2A), as inserted by RDTA 2006 s.58.

[201] See *Perry v Woodfarm Homes* [1975] I.R. 104 at 120, and *Spectrum Investments v Holmes* [1981] 1 All E.R. 6.

CHAPTER 8

Fee Simple

Here's the lord of the soil come to seize me for a stray, for entering his fee-simple without leave.

— Shakespeare, *King Henry the Sixth, Part 2,* Act IV, Scene X

INTRODUCTION

8–01 The fee simple is the only legal freehold estate which can exist in land since the commencement of the Land and Conveyancing Law Reform Act 2009 ("LCLRA 2009").[1] The fee simple may exist in a number of modified forms, principally the determinable fee[2] and the conditional fee.[3] A fee farm grant is a fee simple which is held under a form of rent. The LCLRA 2009 prohibits their creation in future,[4] but does not affect fee farm grants existing at 1 December 2009.

HERITABILITY

8–02 The life estate was probably the earliest estate in land developed by the common law. Until late in the 12th century, no one had the *right* to inherit the land on the death of the freehold tenant. Inheritance posed a dilemma for the law. On the one hand, a feudal lord wanted to choose the person who would become the next tenant; on the other, the tenants wanted to pass the land on to their children. The conflict was resolved by a compromise: *primogeniture*, i.e. the eldest son would inherit.[5] Tenants won the right to pass the land on to the next generation of their family, while the lord at least knew the identity of the next tenant. The right to inherit the fee simple was tacitly acknowledged in the coronation charter of Henry I in 1100, which provided that only reasonable reliefs were to be levied on inheritance. Inheritance was recognised as a right by Henry II in the Assize of Northampton, 1176. This was, in effect, the origin of the fee simple estate. After 1176 the heir had a *right* to succeed, not merely a customary expectation.

---

[1] LCLRA 2009 s.11.

[2] LCLRA 2009 s.11(2)(a) (i.e. fee simple subject to a possibility of reverter: s.11(4)(e)).

[3] LCLRA 2009 s.11(2)(b) (i.e. a fee simple subject to a right of entry or of re-entry).

[4] LCLRA 2009 s.12.

[5] Or daughters in a form of co-ownership called coparcenary.

8–03 The common law also developed a principle of alienation at an early date. The tenant in fee simple could convey his estate to another, although at first the consent of the lord of the tenure was required. By the early 13th century it was held that if A held land in fee simple and then conveyed to B in fee simple, the land would pass to B's heirs on B's death.[6] This was necessary, of course, if the conveyance of the fee simple was to be effective at all. By conveying the land, A had disinherited his own heirs.

8–04 Later, the Statute *Quia Emptores* 1290 permitted freehold tenants to convey their estate by substitution without the lord's consent. This established the principle of free alienability of the fee simple which remains in force today. By the mid-17th century the fee simple owner had acquired the freedom to devise land by will. If A held land in fee simple and left it by will to B, who was not his heir, the land would pass to B's heir on B's death, unless, of course, B left it to someone else or sold it during his lifetime. The heirs of a tenant in fee simple are thus said to have a mere *spes successionis*, i.e. a hope of inheriting (which is not a property interest at all) and this is still the case today.[7]

8–05 "Heirs" at common law meant those persons determined by the old rules of descent, i.e. primogeniture. These discriminated both on grounds of age and gender and were not consistent with modern concepts of human rights. They were abolished by s.11(1) of the Succession Act 1965[8] and replaced by new rules which apply to personal property as well. Section 111 of the Succession Act 1965 provides that if a testator leaves a spouse and no children, the spouse has a right to half the estate (i.e. the property the testator left when he or she died). If the testator leaves a spouse and children, the right of the spouse is to one-third. This legal right overrides any devise in the will and so reintroduces a limitation on the freedom of testation. It may be seen as an expression of social policy, i.e. that persons who can be provided for by their families should not be a burden on the welfare state.

THE RIGHT TO ALIENATE

8–06 Grantors of interests in land occasionally wish to impose conditions on the persons to whom the grantee may alienate the land. In the case of the fee simple, the courts have closely controlled the degree to which such restrictions can be imposed.

---

[6] *Arundel's Case* (1225) in F.W. Maitland (ed.), *Bracton's Note Book* (London: C.J. Clay & Sons, 1887) (tenant in fee simple who conveyed in his lifetime with a warranty for quiet enjoyment barred his own son); R.R.B. Powell, *Law of Real Property* (New York: Matthew Bender, 1968), para.193.

[7] *Re Butler* [1918] 1 I.R. 394 at 400; *Re the goods of Black* [1971] N.I. 68.

[8] As to the fee simple. They remained applicable to fees tail until the LCLRA 2009 prohibited the creation in future of fees tail and also converted existing ones to fee simple estates: s.13.

Ordinary Fees Simple

8–07 Ever since *Quia Emptores* 1290 it has been the policy of the law that restrictions cannot be imposed on the freedom of the holder of a fee simple estate to alienate it, whether those restrictions arise by custom, or by the grantor attempting to impose them in the grant.[9]

Custom

8–08 In *Merttens v Hill*,[10] it was argued that restrictions arose by custom. The defendant bought a fee simple in the Manor of Rothley, Leicestershire in which freehold tenants held in the tenure of ancient demesne, i.e. it had belonged to the Saxon Crown before 1066. The lord of the manor claimed as a custom of the tenure that he was entitled to levy a fine on any purchaser who bought land within the manor and who was a "foreigner", i.e. came from outside the manor. It was held that even if the custom existed, it was void as contrary to *Quia Emptores* 1290.

Grants
General

8–09 An example of the general rule applied in Ireland is *Re Lunham*.[11] The grant contained a proviso that the grantee was not to subdivide the land into more than four lots without the consent in writing of the grantor, his heirs and assigns. Flanagan J. in the Landed Estates Court held the proviso void as "repugnant" to the fee simple estate.[12]

8–10 Twentieth century cases reiterated the general rule. In *Byrne v Byrne*,[13] a testator left land in his will to his nephew subject to the condition that,

> "in the event of my nephew … attempting to sell the said farms … or in any way parting with the possession of them I revoke the bequest of the said farms to him and in that event I leave them to the next heir on the same condition … as it was my intention that my said nephew, should work and keep my said farms and that they should remain the property of one of my kin."

Budd J. held the condition void as repugnant to the power of alienation.

---

[9] *Troy v Kirk* (1832) Al. & Nap. 326; *Penny v Gardner* (1833) Al. & Nap. 345; *Re Quin* (1858) 8 Ir. Ch. R. 578; *Re McNaul's Estate* [1902] 1 I.R. 114.

[10] [1901] 1 Ch. 842.

[11] (1871) I.R. 5 Eq. 170. The grant was in fee farm but by rentcharge, and so the fee simple was an ordinary one.

[12] See also *Re Cockerill* [1929] 2 Ch. 131 (condition that if the land was to be sold the holder of the fee simple should give an option to the governors of a school to buy at a price which proved to be half the market value. The condition was held void).

[13] (1953) 87 I.L.T.R. 183.

8–11 On the other hand, in *Fitzsimons v Fitzsimons*,[14] the testator had gifted land to his son in fee simple. By his will, he made a further devise of land to his son, on the condition that the son was still the owner in fee simple of the first parcel of land which had been gifted to him during the testator's lifetime. The son argued that the effect of his father's will was to prevent him from alienating the first parcel of land without losing his rights to the second parcel. Keane J. disagreed, noting that the terms of the bequest were not uncertain and pertained only to conditions under which the son would become entitled to the second parcel of land.

8–12 In the case of "ordinary" fees simple the law is less clear when an attempt is made to restrict the alienation of the land to a particular class. An attempt to restrict alienation to one named person only is certainly void.[15] On the other hand, a condition which restricts alienation to everyone *except* a named person may well be valid.[16] Between these two extremes the issue is whether a condition which restricts alienation to a particular group such as a family, or which permits alienation to all except a particular group, is valid or not.

8–13 Whatever the position in other jurisdictions, in Ireland conditions which restrict alienation to a particular group are invalid in principle.[17] The Irish case of *Billing v Welsh*[18] held, inter alia, that a covenant prohibiting alienation except to a certain specified and limited class was repugnant to the nature of an estate in fee simple. O'Brien J. said[19]:

> "The general principles upon which covenants against alienation contained in a deed granting lands in fee simple are held to be void as being repugnant to the estate granted by that deed, ... no condition or limitation, whether by act executed, limitation or use, or devise, that contains in it matter repugnant to the estate is good. It is true ... that if a feoffment or other conveyance be made of land, upon condition that the feoffee or grantee should not alien to certain persons, such condition would be good; but the author adds that if the condition be that the feoffee or grantee should not alien the thing granted to any person whatsoever ... such a condition is void ... as repugnant to the nature of the estate."

---

[14] [1993] I.L.R.M. 478.

[15] *Re McDonnell's Will* [1965] I.R. 354; *Attwater v Attwater* (1853) 18 Beav. 330.

[16] Co Litt 361.

[17] The main authority in favour of upholding such conditions is the English case of *Re Macleay* (1875) L.R. 20 Eq. 186 which upheld a restriction to sell only to members of the holder's family, on the ground that it was a large and increasing class. But this case has been criticised in England and has not been followed in Ireland: *Doe d Gill v Pearson* (1805) 6 East 173; *Attwater v Attwater* (1853) 18 Beav. 330. See also, *Re Rosher* (1884) 26 Ch. D. 801.

[18] (1871) I.R. 6 C.L. 88.

[19] (1871) I.R. 6 C.L. 88 at 101.

8–14 In *Crofts v Beamish*,[20] land was granted to brothers with the provision that if any of the brothers died under the age of 30 his portion was to go to the other brothers. The Irish Court of Appeal did not think that it was a condition subsequent but held that, if it had been, it would have been repugnant to the power of alienation and void.[21] In *Re McDonnell's Will*,[22] the testator directed that his freehold should not be sold or assigned to any person "who is not a member or a descendant of a member of my family". Budd J. held that the restriction was repugnant to the fee simple and void.

8–15 Conditions which seek to permit alienation *to all except* a selected group restrict alienation to a lesser extent and may not be objectionable on that ground. In *Re Dunne*,[23] the High Court considered a will which left freehold land subject to a condition that it was not to be transferred to "any member of the Meredith families of O'Moore's Forest, Mountmellick". O'Hanlon J. held that the condition was void both for uncertainty and as against public policy in that it tended to perpetuate old family resentments and antagonisms. Referring to O'Brien J. in *Billing v Welsh*[24] quoted above, he went on[25]:

"That statement of the law would appear to support the validity of what was done by the testator in the present case. I would have reservations, however, about the consistency with public policy of incorporating conditions in the grant or devise of freehold property, the obvious purpose of which is to per- petuate old resentments and antagonisms and bind the grantee or devisee to bear them in mind and give effect to them when contemplating any further disposition of the property. This is particularly so when, as in the present case, the grantor or testator seeks to bind by the condition imposed, not merely the grantee or devisee but his or her successors and assigns as well apparently for all time in the future."

8–16 Kinship or family solidarity is a detectable policy in land law, but it is only given expression where it does not conflict with the efficient working of a market economy. In this case the two policies coincide. Both family solidarity and freedom of alienation point to striking down such conditions.

8–17 Conditions in fees simple which attempt to exclude sale to a particu- lar racial group have been held void in the United States as an unacceptable restriction on the power of alienation.[26] They may also violate the constitu- tional right to equality before the law or to equal treatment.

---

[20] [1905] 2 I.R. 349.
[21] The court in *Re Brown* [1954] Ch. 39 arrived at a similar result, on the ground that "brothers" was a limited and diminishing class.
[22] [1965] I.R. 354.
[23] [1988] I.R. 155.
[24] (1871) I.R. 6 C.L. 88.
[25] [1988] I.R. 155 at 156–157.
[26] *Wayt v Patee* 205 Cal. 46 (1928).

Gifts to Charity

8–18 It is said that the general rule against restrictions on alienation does not apply to gifts to charities, so that the grant of a fee simple to a charity may contain a condition preventing the charity alienating the land.[27] This was held in two New Zealand cases, *Caldwell v Fleming*[28] and *Re Clark*,[29] which cited English authorities. Those cases were followed by the High Court in Northern Ireland in *Re Richardson*,[30] although without close analysis.[31] While it is settled that the rule against inalienability does not apply to charities, the exception is generally considered in the context of grants of personal property.[32] For these reasons, the issue as to whether restrictions can be applied in the grant of a fee simple to a charity cannot be regarded as settled in this jurisdiction.

Statutory Schemes
Land Purchase Acts

8–19 The Land Purchase Acts were a legislative response to agricultural distress in Ireland and to the reaction on the part of the rural population to the intolerable conditions under which they led their lives. The Land Law (Ireland) Act 1881 established the Irish Land Commission to finance the purchase by tenants of the fee simple in their farms.

8–20 Under s.2 of the Land Act 1946, the Irish Land Commission[33] was empowered to issue a notice to a freeholder to whom the fee simple had been conveyed under the Acts, to reside continuously on the land to the satisfaction of the Commission. The constitutionality of such restrictions was confirmed by the Supreme Court in *Foley v Irish Land Commission*,[34] holding that the imposition of a condition as to residence in s.2 of the Land Act 1946 amounted to a restriction on property rights "with a view to reconciling their exercise with the exigencies of the common good" and in accordance with the principles of social justice. The court noted that the Land Purchase Acts, of which the Land Act 1946 forms part, constituted an important branch of Irish social legislation,[35] the object of which was not only to give secure residence to those who cultivated the land, but also to prevent a re-emergence of rural landlordism. The conditions as to residence gave legal effect to these policies.

---

[27] P. Coughlan, "Restraint on the Alienation of Fee Simples – A Repugnant Policy?" (1990) 12 D.U.L.J. 147 at 152–153.

[28] [1927] N.Z.L.R. 145.

[29] [1961] N.Z.L.R. 635.

[30] [1988] 3 N.I.J.B. 35.

[31] P. Coughlan, "Restraint on the Alienation of Fee Simples – A Repugnant Policy?" (1990) 12 D.U.L.J. 147.

[32] *Chamberlayne v Brockett* (1872) 8 Ch. App. 206 at 211; C. Harpum, S. Bridge and M. Dixon, *Megarry & Wade: The Law of Real Property*, 8th edn (London: Sweet & Maxwell, 2012), para.9-161.

[33] See now, Irish Land Commission (Dissolution) Act 1992 s.4.

[34] [1952] I.R. 118.

[35] [1952] I.R. 118 at 153; cited in *Dreher v Irish Land Commission* [1984] I.L.R.M. 94 and in *Re Soden* [1985] I.L.R.M. 685.

8–21 Section 6 of the Land Act 1946 prohibited imposed restrictions on later subdivision of certain lands which had been granted by the Irish Land Commission. These restrictions were repealed by the Land Act 2005.[36] The Land Act 2005 further provides that the Minister for Agriculture, Food and the Marine can make new vesting orders of certain lands subject to a purchase annuity and any terms laid down in the order.[37]

Labourers Acts 1883–1965

8–22 The Labourers Acts 1883–1965 created a further restriction on certain fees simple in Ireland.[38] The purpose of these Acts was to provide an equivalent to the land purchase scheme for houses occupied by agricultural labourers. The houses were purchased in fee simple under a scheme providing for repayment of the purchase price by an annuity. During the period of repayment, a statutory covenant restricted alienation "otherwise than by operation of law or by sale with consent of" the local authority.[39] Breach of the covenant caused a forfeiture. Thus, the fee simple could pass on intestacy but a devise in a will contravened the covenant,[40] although legislation made an exception for certain persons in possession at the death of the labourer, such as a widow or children.[41] Subletting was held to be an "alienation" and therefore if made without consent contravenes the covenant.[42] The Labourers Act 1965[43] did not abolish these restrictions wholesale, but provided instead for county councils to redeem annuities and to remove restrictions imposed under the Acts. Restrictions were removed from "cottage plots" which were declared to be, and to always have been capable of being, mortgaged, subdivided or alienated otherwise than by devise or by operation of law, with the county council's consent.[44]

Housing Act 1966

8–23 Dwellings sold by a housing authority[45] could be made subject to "special conditions",[46] which include a condition not to mortgage, charge or alienate the dwelling otherwise than by devise or operation of law (which would not

---

[36] Land Act 2005 s.12(c), repealing Land Act 1946 s.6.

[37] Land Act 2005 s.8, replacing Land Act 1931 s.28.

[38] Some provisions of the Labourers Act 1936 remain in force. See the First Schedule to the Housing Act 1966; *Westmeath County Council v Claffey* [1952] I.R. 1; *Rogers v Louth County Council* [1981] I.R. 265; *Attorney General (Annaly) v Guardians of Ballymallon Union* (1888) 21 L.R. Ir. 534.

[39] Labourers Act 1936 s.17(2).

[40] *Cork County Council v O'Shea* [1947] I.R. 369.

[41] See Labourers Act 1936 s.19(4), applying Local Registration of Title (Ireland) Act 1891 Pt IV to land purchased under the Labourers Act scheme.

[42] *Westmeath County Council v Claffey* [1952] I.R. 1.

[43] Labourers Act 1965 ss.3 and 4.

[44] Labourers Act 1965 s.2.

[45] Housing Act 1966 s.90, as replaced by Housing (Miscellaneous Provisions) Act 1992 s.26.

[46] Housing Act 1966 s.89.

require consent) without the consent of the housing authority,[47] and subject to conditions as to residence.

Fee Farm Grants

8–24 The question of restrictions on the alienability of fee farm grants is dealt with in Ch.9.

Conclusions

8–25 In the previous edition of this work, it was suggested that restrictions on the alienation of the fee simple imposed under the statutory schemes above may no longer apply in light of the principle of alienability set out in s.9(4) of the LCRLA 2009.[48] In the view of the present authors, it seems unlikely that s.9(4) has the effect of implicitly repealing any restrictions on the alienability of a fee simple which are imposed by earlier statutes. First, s.9(4) states that "a fee simple *remains* freely alienable" (emphasis added). The use of the word "remains" might be read as indicating that the section is intended to codify the existing principle of alienability and not to create new law in this area. Secondly, had the legislature intended to repeal prior statutory provisions, it would surely have made express provision for such repeal. Thirdly, while Irish law does recognise a doctrine of implied appeal,[49] the Supreme Court has held that the courts will "lean against the repeal or exclusion of statutory provisions by implication".[50] Fourthly, s.9(4) establishes a general principle that the fee simple should be freely alienable. Application of the principle *generalia specialibus non derogant* would appear to indicate that such a provision should not affect particular rules applied to discrete situations by specialist legislation.[51]

8–26 It is questionable today whether, as a matter of policy, any of the above restrictions on alienability should continue to apply to fee simple estates. They have led to the creation of second-class fee simple estates whose owners have fewer rights than the owners of "first class" fees simple. In so far as it may be desirable to ensure that land ownership by local communities should be protected, other more appropriate means should be explored. It might also be argued that restrictions on the alienability of a fee simple conflict with the guarantee under Art.43.1.2° of the Constitution of the general right to transfer property.

---

[47] Housing Act 1966 s.89(c).
[48] A. Lyall, *Land Law in Ireland*, 3rd edn (Dublin: Round Hall, 2010), p.182.
[49] *McLoughlin v Minister for Public Service* [1986] I.L.R.M. 28.
[50] *DPP v Grey* [1986] I.R. 317 at 326.
[51] See *Baker v Edger* [1897] A.C. 748 at 754, endorsed in *McGonagle v McGonalge* [1951] I.R. 123.

Words of Limitation

8–27 The following discussion refers to the words used to convey "ordinary" fees simple. The position as to fee farm grants in Ireland is dealt with in Ch.9.

History
8–28 At common law in order to pass or create a fee simple estate in land the correct words of limitation had to be used. To pass the fee simple a grant had to be made to the grantee "and his/her heirs". Nothing else would do. Sir Thomas Littleton stated the rule in the 15th century in his *Tenures*:

> "For if a man would purchase lands or tenements in fee simple, it behoveth him to have these words in his purchase, To have and to hold to him and to his heirs: for these words, his heirs, make the estate of inheritance. For if a man purchase lands by these words, To have and to hold to him for ever, or by these words, To have and to hold to him and his assigns for ever; in these two cases he hath but an estate for term of life, for that there lack these words, his heirs, which words only make an estate of inheritance in all feoffments and grants."[52]

8–29 No account was taken of the intention of the maker of the document. It was a ritualistic formula characteristic of early legal systems. In the late 18th century and early 19th century, which saw the rise of industrial capitalism, it became apparent that there existed a conflict within the legal system between two competing views, both of which were derived from the needs of the new economic system itself and which were concerned about the nature of changes it made necessary in legal rules as to property.

8–30 On the one hand, if individual capitalists were to be able to buy land as a means of production, land had to be freely available to be bought and sold. On this view, the need to use a strict formula to pass a fee simple estate constituted a restriction on this desired free alienability. In addition, industrial capitalism favoured the view that individual capitalists should be left to themselves to develop the economy by entering contracts together as freely as possible from the interference of State institutions. The Enlightenment of the 18th century gave rise to the notion that people were capable of arranging their affairs in a rational way and were entitled to expect that the law would give effect to their intentions.[53] The role of law was then simply to give effect to the

---

[52] E. Wambaugh (ed.), *Littleton's Tenures in English* (Washington, DC: J. Byrne, 1903), Bk I, Ch.1, section 1. The first edition was published in Law French about 1481. As *Coke on Littleton*, published with the commentary of Sir Edward Coke, the 19th edition was published in 1832 (Wambaugh, Bibliography).

[53] P.S. Atiyah, *The Rise and Fall of Freedom of Contract* (Oxford: Clarendon Press, 1979), pp.122–123.

intentions of the parties to such transactions rather than, in interpreting them, to impose rules which had other functions.

8–31 On the other hand, if purchasers of land were to be sure of the titles which they acquired, it was necessary for them to be sure that the vendors themselves had a good title to convey to them. In unregistered conveyancing, which then prevailed, a rule that no title would pass unless a strict formula was adhered to would favour this certainty required by purchasers. If no special formula was required, it might not be possible to know whether a title had passed under a deed unless one went through the expense of court proceedings.

8–32 The chief proponent of the "liberal" view—that courts should seek the parties' intentions and that therefore no special words should be required—was Lord Mansfield.[54] Opposed to this view and in favour of strict words was Fearne, author of a famous work on contingent remainders.[55]

8–33 The rules that operate in Ireland since the LCLRA 2009 have opted decisively for the liberal view. This has, however, complicated matters by attempting to make the change retrospective, an issue which is discussed further below.

Conveyances Inter Vivos
At Common Law
Natural Persons

8–34 Until the end of the 12th century, a person who held a fee simple could not alienate it without the consent of his or her heirs. In other words, the heirs had a real interest in the property. The relationship of kinship was treated as more important than the relationship of the market, but this changed over the course of time and it came to be accepted that the tenant in fee simple could sell the land without the consent of the heirs. This meant that after this change had taken place, if a grant were made

> *to A and his heirs*

the words "to A" were "words of purchase" giving A an interest in the property, but the words "and his heirs" were only "words of limitation" which did not give the heirs an interest in the property but served merely to indicate the duration of the estate given to A.

8–35 It was held that if A, during his lifetime, made a grant of his fee simple to B, then B held the land for himself and *his* heirs. A can make a grant "to B and

---

[54] *Loveacres d Mudge v Blight* (1775) 1 Cowp. 352; *Hogan d Wallis v Jackson* (1775) 1 Cowp. 299.

[55] C. Fearne, *An Essay on the Learning of Contingent Remainders and Executory Devises* (London, 1772).

his heirs" and again, only the words "to B" are words of purchase. The words "and his heirs" are again words of limitation. This further change meant that the fee simple became likely to endure for a long period. Even if A had no heirs, so that the fee simple would otherwise come to an end, he could, in his lifetime, make a grant to B in fee simple and it could pass to B's heirs.

8–36 Over time the common law formula became rigid, so that only that form of words and no other would pass the fee simple. The person to take the estate had to be named, followed by the phrase "and his [or her] heirs". Nothing else would do. Thus, even if the intention was clearly to grant a fee simple, if the words used were "to A for ever" or "to A and her relatives" or "to A and his issue" or even, until altered by statute, "to A in fee simple", A only acquired a life estate.

8–37 Thus, in *Re Adam's Estate*[56] where a settlement granted land "to the use and behoof of the second third fourth fifth sixth and of every other the son and sons of [A]", with a gift over if they died without issue, the court held that although the intention was to grant a fee simple to the sons of A, they only took life estates. In *Re Coleman's Estate*,[57] C, who owned a house in fee simple, agreed with H to allow H to occupy the house, C covenanting for "herself, her heirs, executors and assigns" and H covenanting for his "executors, administrators and assigns." It was held that H took only a life estate despite the fact that the court accepted that the intention was to grant H an indefinite right. The word "heirs" had not been used in relation to H.

Corporations

8–38 A *corporation aggregate* is a corporate body on whose behalf a number of persons act together, e.g. a limited company. A *corporation sole* is an office occupied by a single person and recognised as such by common law or statute, as for example, in the past, a bishop or priest of an established church. Church of Ireland clergy ceased to be corporations sole on the disestablishment of that church in 1869.[58] Roman Catholic clergy were corporations sole at common law, since that was the universal church when the common law was formed, but that status did not survive the Reformation and the Penal Laws. It seems unlikely that the status has revived since 1937. Corporations sole today would include ministers of the government, and other constitutional office holders such as the President of the High Court.

8–39 At common law a conveyance to a corporation aggregate in its corporate name, e.g.

>   *to Acme Ltd*

---

[56] [1965] I.R. 57.
[57] [1907] 1 I.R. 488.
[58] Irish Church Act 1869 s.13, repealed by the Statute Law Revision (No. 2) Act 1893.

gave it a fee simple without the need for words of limitation, for the reason that such a body cannot hold land for a fee tail estate since it does not have heirs of the body nor may it hold land for a life estate. This is not entirely logical as it could be argued on that basis that since it does not have "heirs" it could not hold land in fee simple, but this would mean that it could not hold land at all and so logic gives way to practical necessity. It does, however, mean that the fee simple has a different meaning when held by a corporation aggregate. It is then an estate which will endure so long as the corporation or its successors endure and will only come to an end if a corporation is wound up without the fee simple becoming vested in a successor before that happens. This at least was the position in the past when an escheat would then occur or the land would become *bona vacantia.*[59]

8–40 A conveyance to a corporation sole at common law, if it was to convey the fee simple to the office, had to use words of limitation in the form:

to the Minister of X and his [or her] successors.

A conveyance to the Minister "and his [or her] heirs" would have given him or her a fee simple in the Minister's private capacity.[60]

In Equity
8–41 The question here was whether the same words of limitation were needed in the grant of a trust as they were in the conveyance of a fee simple at common law. If the limitation created a trust

for A for ever …

the legal fee simple was clearly vested in the trustees, but did the equitable fee simple vest in the beneficiary, A, by the informal words "for ever"?

8–42 In *Meyler v Meyler,*[61] it was suggested that the same words of limitation were required in equity as at common law.[62] However, in *Re Houston,*[63] land

---

[59] Nevertheless, courts tried to avoid this result if possible: *Re Strathblaine Estates* [1948] Ch. 228.

[60] In *Gibson v Representative Church Body* (1882) 9 L.R. Ir. 1, there was a bequest to the R chapel on trust to pay the income to the person who was the chaplain at the testator's death for life and then to his successors. It was held that the intention was to benefit chaplains for the time being and not the person who filled the office at her death personally, so that when that person retired the income ceased to be payable to him and became payable to his successor. A gift to a person "and his [or her] successors", if not a corporation sole, gave only a life estate: *White v Baylor* (1846) 10 Ir. Eq. R. 53.

[61] (1883) 11 L.R. Ir. 522; *Re Courtney* [1981] N.I. 58.

[62] Also *Barron v Barron* (1859) 8 Ir. Ch. R. 366, although in that case the interest was a lease for lives. A grant of it in a marriage settlement to trustees on trust "for ever" to the issue male of the marriage passed only life estates, and not a quasi fee, to the sons of the marriage.

[63] [1909] 1 I.R. 319.

was conveyed to trustees on trust for a number of persons as tenants in common without words specifying what estate they were to take. The court held that they took fees simple, and indicated that in such a case the court looked at the intention of the settlor. In *Jameson v McGovern*,[64] the court approved of the distinction in *Re Bostock's Settlement*[65] between formal words, which were construed formally, and informal words which were given the effect intended. In the case itself a fee simple was held to pass without words on limitation.[66]

Conveyancing Act 1881

8–43 The position as to conveyances *inter vivos* was modified by s.51 of the Conveyancing Act 1881,[67] which provided that "in fee simple" could be used as an alternative to "and his/her heirs". The alternative was construed just as strictly as the older one. Thus, "to A in fee" would only give a life estate.[68] The equitable doctrine of rectification, which permits a court to order the alteration of a document so as to reflect the intentions of the parties, has been used to pass the fee simple in some such cases.[69]

Wills

8–44 The principle in wills has long been to give effect to the wishes of the testator as far as possible. This is particularly important when it is remembered that if a mistake has been made, it is too late by the time the will takes effect, i.e. at the testator's death, for the testator to remedy it. Before 1838 it was only necessary to show an intention to pass a fee simple for it to pass under the will, so that "to A for ever"[70] or "to A absolutely"[71] would be enough to pass the fee simple, but "to A" would not pass more than a life estate unless there was something else in the will to show that a fee simple was intended.

8–45 The Wills Act 1837 created a presumption that fee simple would pass unless the contrary intention was shown.[72] This made it even easier for a fee

---

[64] [1934] I.R. 758.

[65] [1921] 2 Ch. 469. But see *Re Harte's Settlement* (1947) 81 I.L.T.R. 78.

[66] *Savage v Nolan*, unreported, High Court, Costello J., 20 July 1978.

[67] Repealed by LCLRA 2009 s.8, Sch.2, Pt 4.

[68] *Re Ethel & Mitchell & Butler's Contract* [1901] 1 Ch. 945 at 949.

[69] *Re Ottley's Estate* [1910] 1 I.R. 1 (a disentailing assurance under the Fines and Recoveries (Ireland) Act 1834); *Re Ford & Ferguson's Contract* [1906] 1 I.R. 607 (an interpretation clause in the deed stated that "grantee" should include the "grantee, his heirs and assigns"); *Annesley v Annesley* (1893) 31 L.R. Ir. 457.

[70] *Doe d Dacre v Roper* (1809) 11 East 518.

[71] *Hogan d Wallis v Jackson* (1775) 1 Cowp. 299 ("all my worldly substance" to X). The fee simple passed to X. But "to A and his heirs" might only pass a fee tail, if such was the intention: *Idle v Cook* (1699) 2 Ld Raym. 1144; 2 Salk. 620; 11 Mod. 57.

[72] Wills Act 1837 s.28. The section applied to existing fees simple, not to estates created *de novo* such as on the creation of a new rentcharge: *Nichols v Hawkes* (1853) 10 Hare 342, M. & W. 795; *Re Hutchin's Estate* (1887) 19 L.R. Ir. 215. Thus a new rentcharge created in a will "for ever" did not grant it for a fee simple estate.

simple to pass.[73] This was consistent with a policy in favour of a market economy in that it meant that it was more likely than before that the land would be held for a fee simple in the hands of the person entitled under the will. This presumption was retained by s.94 of the Succession Act 1965. Thus, the words "to A" have long been sufficient to pass the fee simple or the whole of whatever interest the testator has in the property, unless a contrary intention is shown.[74]

Registered Land

8–46 Section 123 of the Registration of Title Act 1964 ("RTA 1964") provides that no words of limitation are necessary in a transfer of registered land. A transfer of registered land without words of limitation passes the fee simple "or the other entire estate or interest" which the grantor had power to create or convey, unless a contrary intention appears in the transfer. This is consistent with the position that the estate in registered land is transferred when the entry is made on the register and not when the transfer is executed. Registration of a person as "full owner" will vest the fee simple in that person and, if this is done, the fact that the transfer itself said merely "to A" will not affect the vesting of the fee simple.

8–47 The RTA 1964[75] also provided that a conveyance of registered land to a corporation sole by that person's corporate designation passes to the corporation the fee simple or other entire estate or interest which the grantor had power to create or convey unless a contrary intention appears in the conveyance, and the use of the word "successors" is no longer necessary.

Unregistered Land: LCLRA 2009

8–48 Section 67 of the LCLRA 2009 significantly simplifies words of limitation in unregistered land. Section 67(1) provides that a conveyance conveys the fee simple or other entire estate which the grantor had power to convey unless a contrary intention appears in the conveyance itself. This principle applies whether words of limitation are used or not; thus, the use of the words "and his heirs" or "in fee simple" are no longer required in order to pass the fee simple estate after the commencement of the LCLRA 2009. Section 67(2) provides that a conveyance to a corporation sole passes the property to the corporation rather than to the existing office holder in a personal capacity unless a contrary intention appears. The use of the word "successors" is no longer required.

8–49 The changes brought about by s.67 appear to be made partially retrospective by a combination of ss.67(4) and 68 of the LCLRA 2009. Under s.67(4), the new rules created by s.67 are declared to apply to conveyances executed

---

[73] *Fowler v Lightburne* (1861) 11 Ir. Ch. R. 495.
[74] See *Re Ball* [1933] N.I. 173 (a gift to "my brother JB or his heir" held to confer a fee simple. The word "heirs" had been originally written, but the final "s" crossed through.)
[75] RTA 1964 s.123(2).

before the coming into force of the LCLRA 2009, but "without prejudice to any act or thing done or any interest disposed of or acquired ... in consequence of failure to use words of limitation". The effect of this language is unclear. If subs.(4) is to have retrospective effect, then it is difficult to see how it can avoid prejudicing estates and interests acquired as a result of previous failures to use words of limitation.

8–50 Section 67(4) must be read along with s.68, to which it is expressly subject. Section 68 purports to extinguish estates and interests created in the past as a result of a failure to use words of limitation. The holders of such estates are permitted to apply to court to retain their interest for a period of 12 years after the commencement of the LCLRA 2009. The court may declare that the applicant has an interest in the land in question, may refuse to do so (provided that this does not result in any injustice), or may order a third party to pay compensation to the applicant in lieu of a declaration that the applicant has an interest in the land concerned. Orders made under s.68 must be registered in the Land Registry/Registry of Deeds as a condition of their effectiveness.

8–51 Section 68 may cause difficulties from a constitutional perspective. Imagine a situation in which land has been conveyed by the holder of a fee simple "to A". Under the previous law, A would take a life estate with the fee simple in reversion remaining with the grantor. Section 68 would appear to extinguish the reversionary interest of the grantor after the expiration of a 12-year period without any compensation at all if no application is made to court by the holders of the reversionary interest. Even where an application is made, the court has the option to order the extinction of the reversionary rights without any compensation.[76] Whether this approach is consistent with the State's obligation to protect property rights from "unjust attack" is unclear but it is certainly arguable that the section is vulnerable to challenge on constitutional grounds.

THE RULE IN SHELLEY'S CASE

8–52 The LCLRA 2009 also reformed a complex rule known as the rule in *Shelley's Case*.[77] The rule dates at least to the 16th century and is probably significantly older than *Shelley's Case* itself. The rule is covered in detail in the first and second editions of this book. The rule in *Shelley's Case*, as it applied to *inter vivos* dispositions, states that

---

[76] LCLRA 2009 s.68(b).
[77] (1581) 1 Co. Rep. 88b, 3 Dy. 373b. Recent historical scholarship has suggested that the rule in *Shelley's Case* is not derived from the judgment itself but from a "sleight of hand" by Sir Edward Coke in his report of the cases. See D.A. Smith, "Was There a Rule in *Shelley's Case?*" (2009) 30 J. Leg. Hist. 53.

when an estate of freehold[78] is given to a person and under the same disposition an estate is limited in remainder either mediately or immediately to his or her heirs or to the heirs of his or her body, then the words 'heirs' or 'heirs of his/her body' are words of limitation and not words of purchase.[79]

8–53 The rule in *Shelley's Case* was a rule of law which applied to conveyances of the legal estate regardless of the intention of the parties. There is some evidence that the position was less strict in respect of dispositions of equitable interests.[80] The rule did not apply to dispositions by will.

Legal Estates Inter Vivos
8–54 In the limitation

> *to A for life, remainder to A's heirs*

it would seem that A obtains a life estate and then the remainder gives some interest to A's heirs, but, under the rule, the words "A's heirs" are not words of *purchase* giving an interest to the heirs, but words of *limitation* describing what interest is given *to A*. A therefore takes a life estate and a fee simple by the remainder. These merge to give A a fee simple in possession.

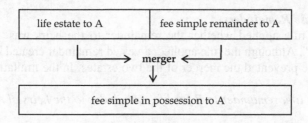

The result is the same as if the limitation had been "to A and his/her heirs".

Same Person
8–55 For the rule to apply, the estate in the remainder clause had to be in favour of the heirs of the person to whom the previous freehold estate was given. If the limitation had been instead

> *to A for life, remainder to B's heirs*

then *Shelley's Case* would not apply. The word "heirs" in the remainder clause was therefore a word of purchase.

---

[78] The rule had no application to personal property: *Atkinson v L'Estrange* (1885) 15 L.R. Ir. 340.

[79] (1581) 1 Co. Rep. 104a; *Van Grutten v Foxwell* [1897] A.C. 658; *Mandeville v Lord Carrick* (1795) 3 Ridg. P.C. 352 at 368–369.

[80] See *Whitelaw v Whitelaw* (1880) 5 L.R. Ir. 120.

Informal Words

8–56 It should be noticed that in order for the rule to apply, the words in the remainder clause had to be capable of functioning as words of limitation in relation to A, so that in an *inter vivos* deed the word "heirs" had to be used. If the limitation was

> *to A for life, remainder to A's issue*

informal words had been used in the remainder clause. "Issue" could not give a fee simple in an *inter vivos* conveyance. The rule in *Shelley's Case* did not apply and therefore the words were words of purchase, giving interests to A's "issue". Since no words of limitation had been used in relation to them, they took joint life estates.

8–57 If the word "heir" was used in the singular, as in the limitation

> *to G for life, remainder to G's heir*

the position was the same. "Heir" did not comply with the strict rule as a word of limitation and so had to function as a word of purchase.

Intermediate Remainders

8–58 The rule applied whether the remainder to the heirs was "mediate or immediate". Although the rule applied, a vested remainder created by the same conveyance prevented the merger of the two estates. In the limitation

> *to A for life, remainder to B for life, remainder to the heirs of A [or to A's heirs]*[81]

the vested life estate to B prevented A's two estates merging to give a fee simple to A in possession. When the life estate ended, merger then took place, so that when B died, A would have the fee simple on possession. Where the remainder was contingent, merger took place initially, but if the remainder vested, the two estates opened up again, letting in the remainder. In the limitation

> *to A for life, remainder to A's eldest son in tail, remainder to the heirs of A [A had no son at the date of the conveyance]*

A had a fee simple in possession at once, while A's son remained unborn, but as soon as the son was born the fee simple divided into the two estates, and A then had a life estate in possession and a fee simple in remainder, allowing the son's vested remainder to fall into place.[82]

---

[81] *Shannon v Good* (1885) 15 L.R. Ir. 300 (CA) (remainder to the "issue").

[82] *Lewis Bowle's Case* (1615) 11 Co. Rep. 79b; *Archer's Case* (1698) 1 Co. Rep. 66b. As to trustees to preserve contingent remainders, see *Rochford v Fitzmaurice* (1842) 4 Ir. Eq. R. 348.

Wills

8–59 The rule was modified as to wills since the Wills Act 1837,[83] and s.94 of the Succession Act 1965 no longer required words of limitation to confer a fee simple by will. The whole interest of the testator in the property passed unless there was a contrary intention in the will. Thus, the rule in *Shelley's Case* could have applied even if the word "heirs" was not used. The effect of the reform was therefore to extend the scope of *Shelley's Case*, although it is unclear whether this was intended or not.

8–60 If the testator intended[84] the words to refer to the whole succession of heirs as a class, then the rule applied and the words in the remainder clause are treated as words of limitation.[85]

8–61 If, on the other hand, the words were intended to refer to a specific person or persons (*personae designatae*), then the rule did not apply and the persons took by purchase.[86] So, for example, if the words in the will were

to A for life, remainder to his issue

the question to be decided by the court, taking the will as a whole, was whether the testator intended only the first generation, as individuals, to take interests, or whether the testator intended the word "issue" to refer to future generations; in other words, to mean the same thing as "heirs". In the former case they took by purchase and since no words of limitation had then been used in relation to them, they took a fee simple jointly. If the latter was the case, then A took a fee simple.[87]

8–62 Even if the word "heirs" was used, this was not necessarily decisive. It was still open to the court to find that the testator intended to refer only to the first generation as individuals, so that the children took by purchase.[88]

8–63 There had therefore been a shift from a rule of law applied irrespective of the testator's intention, towards a rule of interpretation based on intention, but the transition was not completely made. The courts generally treated the question of intention as relating solely to the issue of whether specific persons, or the heirs collectively, however described, were referred to, although they may not always have observed this fine distinction. If the heirs collectively were intended to benefit by the remainder, *Shelley's Case* applied regardless

---

[83] For a case on a will before the Wills Act 1837, see *Rotheram v Rotheram* (1884) 13 L.R. Ir. 442.

[84] *Mandeville v Lord Carrick* (1795) 3 Ridg. P.C. 352 at 365.

[85] *Re Keane's Estate* [1903] 1 I.R. 215.

[86] *Whitelaw v Whitelaw* (1880) 5 L.R. Ir. 120; *Van Grutten v Foxwell* [1897] A.C. 658.

[87] *Shannon v Good* (1885) 15 L.R. Ir. 300 (intermediate estates tail prevented merger); *Kavanagh v Morland* (1853) Kay 16; *Montgomery v Montgomery* (1845) 3 Jo. & La T. 47.

[88] *Crozier v Crozier* (1843) 5 Ir. Eq. R. 419; *Phillips v Phillips* (1847) 10 Ir. Eq. R. 519.

of whether the result was intended by the testator.[89] For example, if the limitation was "to A for life, remainder to A's issue", it might well have been the intention that A should take a life estate and that A's children should take a fee simple at his death, the next generations benefiting by inheritance, but once it was shown that the intention was to benefit collectively all those who would in the course of devolution inherit his property, the rule applied and A took a fee simple.

8–64 If the word "heir" was used in the singular, i.e.

> *to A for life, remainder to his heir ...*

then the conclusion was more readily drawn that a specific person was intended and *Shelley's Case* did not apply.[90]

Equitable Estates Inter Vivos

8–65 Although there was some conflict in the authorities, it seems that equity did not require the same strict words of limitation as were required in a deed at common law. Equity looked to the intent and not the form in limitations of this kind and would seek to discover what estate was intended to be granted. Thus, if the limitation created a trust

> *for A for life, remainder in trust for A's heirs*

equity would apply a similar rule to that applicable to wills. If the intention was to refer to specific persons, they took by purchase.[91] If, on the other hand, the intention was to refer to the whole class of intestate successors, the rule would apply, and A took the fee simple.

The Policy of the Rule

8–66 Part of the fascination of the rule in *Shelley's Case* is the mystery that surrounds its origin and purpose. There are at least two possible policy explanations of the rule. One is a feudal explanation and the other is an explanation in terms of the effect on the operation of a market economy.

---

[89] In *Gilbourne v Gilbourne*, unreported, High Court, Kenny J., 9 July 1975, the testator left freehold land of which he was the registered owner to his nephews P and W "as joint tenants so that the same shall pass to the heir at law of the survivor of them". Kenny J. held that *Shelley's Case* did not apply. "Heir at law" was intended to refer to a specific person, namely, the person who should turn out to be the heir at law of the survivor. That, as it turned out, was the plaintiff, the heir of P. The judge found that this was indicated both by the use of "heir" in the singular and by the phrase "so that the same shall pass", which implied words of purchase.

[90] *Gilbourne v Gilbourne*, unreported, High Court, Kenny J., 9 July 1975.

[91] *Brennan v Fitzmaurice* (1840) 2 Ir. Eq. R. 113 at 122.

8–67 There are strong grounds for believing that the rule was of feudal origin and had as its object the preservation of the lord's feudal incident of relief. If a grant was made "to A and his heirs" or "to A and the heirs of her body", then when A died the heirs or heirs of the body would have taken the land under the rules of descent. The incident of relief would have become payable before they could succeed to the tenancy. On this view, the typical limitation which attracted the rule was therefore an attempt to avoid the feudal incident by giving the estate to A's heir or the heir of the body by purchase and not by descent. The rule prevented this result and so protected the income of feudal lords.[92] On this view the rule is clearly an anachronism.

8–68 Simpson[93] suggests that the rule may have evolved before contingent remainders were recognised in the 14th century. A living person had no heir (only an heir apparent or an heir presumptive); thus, if an interest had been given to the heir of A, and A was living, the remainder would be contingent, which the courts found a difficult concept. The rule avoided recognising such remainders. Judges at the time also adhered to the view that an heir should take by descent. The idea of an heir taking by purchase was a strange and unfamiliar concept.

8–69 From a different point of view, the rule has the effect of making land more freely alienable and so promotes a market economy. The result of the rule is that A gets a fee simple, which can freely be bought and sold, or a fee tail which could be barred and so he or she could obtain a fee simple. The whole interest in the land was thus immediately alienable. If the rule did not apply, and the heirs took by purchase, then A would only have had a life estate and the land would cease to be marketable for a considerable period. As a justification for the rule, this reason was greatly diminished in significance by the provisions of the Settled Land Acts 1882–1890 which gave power to a life tenant to convey a fee simple, but it may explain why the rule survived for so long in so many jurisdictions.

8–70 The fact that originally the rule was a rule of law, applied regardless of intention, showed that the rule was intended to impose a general policy which might not coincide with the intention of the grantor, or, if the feudal explanation is correct, would always defeat it. The modern tendency, realised in wills and perhaps even as it was applied to *inter vivos* deeds, was paradoxically to treat the rule as an aid to discovering the intention of the grantor. In some cases

---

[92] *John Abel's Case* (1324) YB Mich 18 Edw. II pl 56 fol 577–578, Seipp No. 1324.177, cited in *Harrison v Harrison* (1844) 7 Man. & Gr. 938 at 941. The case did not make a decision on the rule, although it suggested its existence, because the creditor who sought payment of a life tenant's debt after the death of the life tenant had released the debt. If he had not done so, the court would have had to decide whether the apparent life tenant had instead a fee simple, under the rule. See also, *Mandeville v Lord-Carrick* (1795) 3 Ridg. P.C. 366 at 369.

[93] A.W.B. Simpson, *A History of the Land Law*, 2nd edn (Oxford: Clarendon Press, 1986), pp.96–99.

that might be so, in deeds drafted without technical knowledge, but since the rule was never designed for this purpose, this may also have been merely a way of rendering the rule partially inoperative without breaking the convention of legal discourse that judges do not abolish rules, or make law.

The Abolition of the Rule
8–71 Section 67(3) of the LCLRA 2009 provides as follows:

"Where an interest in land is expressed to be given to—

(a)   the heir or heirs, or
(b)   any particular heir, or
(c)   any class of heirs, or
(d)   issue,

of any person in words which, under the rule known as the rule in *Shelley's Case*, would have operated to give that person a fee simple, those words operate as words of purchase and not of limitation and take effect in equity accordingly."

Thus, in the typical limitation "to A for life, remainder to his heirs", A will now take only a life interest. The word "heirs" in the remainder are words of purchase giving an interest to the heirs, which will be a fee simple or other entire estate or interest which the grantor had power to convey.

8–72 Unfortunately, the effect of s.68(3) appears to be partly retrospective. Sections 67(4) and 68, which have been discussed above in the context of words of limitation generally, are also framed to apply to *Shelley's Case*. Again, the problem here is that if in the limitation "to A for life, remainder to the heirs of A", A had acquired a fee simple under the rule in *Shelley's Case*, then s.68 would confiscate it unless A successfully applies to court within 12 years of the commencement of the LCLRA 2009. In addition to the constitutional concerns raised above, this aspect of ss.67–68 fails to achieve one of the main purposes of the LCLRA 2009, which was to simplify the law, since it would require judges to apply *Shelley's Case* when, but for the section, it would not be required to do so. The contrast with s.131 of the English Law of Property Act 1925, which abolished the rule in *Shelley's Case* with prospective effect only, seems quite striking.

"HEIRS" AS A WORD OF PURCHASE

8–73 The abolition of the rule in *Shelley's Case* means that in the typical limitation to which it used to apply, s.67(3) of the LCLRA 2009 now requires that the words in the remainder clause are words of purchase. There were, and are, also other limitations, to which *Shelley* never applied, in which "heirs" are used as words of purchase. In the examples

> *to A's heir and her [or his] heirs*
> *to the heir of A and her [or his] heirs*

it is clear that the words "and her heirs" are words of limitation, but the words "A's heir" and "the heir of A" are intended to be words of purchase. There is no rule that prevents them being so. But the problem was, and is, to identify the person who is referred to as A's heir.

At Common Law

8–74 At common law the position was, both as to wills and *inter vivos* deeds, that, in the above examples, if A were dead at the time the limitation took effect, then the heir, determined according to the old rules of descent, took the interest. The words of purchase "to A's heir" took effect and the words of limitation "and her [or his] heirs" indicated that the heir took a fee simple.

8–75 On the other hand, if A were alive when the limitation took effect, then the gift to the "heir" was void. At common law a living person had no heir: *nemo est heres viventis*.[94] He or she might have an *heir apparent*, i.e. someone who would be A's heir if he or she survived A, such as (under the old rules of descent) A's eldest son, or an *heir presumptive*, i.e. someone who would be A's heir if he or she (a) outlived A and also (b) was not displaced by someone with a better claim. For example, if A were alive and had a daughter, but no son, the daughter was the heir presumptive, but, under the rule of descent favouring males over females, would be displaced if A later had a son (who would then become the heir apparent). But A had no determined heir while he was alive. If A had an eldest son he would be the heir apparent, but he might die before his father and never become the heir. It was not a mere matter of semantics. If A was alive it could not be known who, as matters turned out, would be entitled to A's property when he died.

8–76 Even at common law there was at least one apparent exception to the general rule. If a gift were in the form

> *to A for life, remainder to A's heir and his heirs [or for life, etc.]*

---

[94] Co Litt 8.

then, even if A were alive, the remainder was held valid.[95] By the time the remainder took effect in possession, A would be dead and the identity of the heir would then be known.[96]

Registered land: Local Registration of Title (Ireland) Act 1891 and RTA 1964

8–77 Section 89 of the Local Registration of Title (Ireland) Act 1891 reformed words of limitation in respect of registered land. This provision was re-enacted as s.114(a) of the RTA 1964 which provides that as to registered freehold land, "heir" or "heirs" used as a word of *limitation* in "any enactment, deed or instrument passed or executed either before or after the passing of this Act shall have the same effect as if this Act had not been passed". Section 114 therefore does not affect the rules as to "heir" or "heirs" used as words of limitation under the provisions already discussed. As to "heir" or "heirs" as a word of purchase, the section continues:

"(b) 'heir' or 'heirs' used as a word of purchase in any enactment, deed or instrument passed or executed before the commencement of this Act shall bear the same meaning as if this Act had not passed".

8–78 The reform was therefore not to be retrospective. However, as to instruments executed after the RTA 1964, the section continues:

"(c) 'heir' or 'heirs' used as a word of purchase in any enactment, deed or instrument passed or executed after the commencement of this Act shall, unless a contrary intention appears, be construed to mean the person or persons, other than a creditor, who would be beneficially entitled to the personal estate of the ancestor if the ancestor had died intestate".

8–79 The effect is that in the typical limitation

to A's heir and her [or his] heirs

---

[95] *Re Beaupré's Trusts* (1888) 21 L.R. Ir. 397. If the gift is "to A for life, remainder to B's heir in fee simple", the remainder should be valid if at A's death B is also dead: *Gilbourne v Gilbourne*, unreported, High Court, Kenny J., 9 July 1975. In the latter case the person whose heir was referred to was dead by the time the case got to court, which the court evidently thought sufficient.

[96] *Shelley's Case* would not apply in the above example in an *inter vivos* deed because "heir" was used in the singular. In *Re Midleton's Will Trusts* [1969] 1 Ch. 600, the English High Court refused to recognise that a gift to the person who should become A's heir on A's death gave a contingent interest, making the distinction that a gift to "B, who shall be A's heir" would give such an interest if B did in fact become A's heir. But it is suggested that this is incorrect, since an interest can be contingent because the person to take it is unascertained. See also *Gilbourne v Gilbourne*, unreported, High Court, Kenny J., 9 July 1975.

even if A were alive at the date the instrument took effect, the gift is not void, and "A's heir" is taken to mean the person who would inherit A's property if A had died intestate immediately before the instrument took effect. "A's heir" takes the whole estate or interest which the grantor had power to convey, since "and her [or his] heirs" is not a contrary intention.

Unregistered Land: Succession Act 1965

8–80 Section 15 of the Succession Act 1965 repeats the wording of s.114 of the RTA 1964 in the context of succession law, but appears wide enough to apply to all conveyances of unregistered land, since it repeats the phrase "any enactment, deed or instrument":

> "(3) The word 'heir' or 'heirs', used as a word of purchase in any enactment, deed or instrument passed or executed after the commencement of this Act [i.e. 1 January 1967] shall, unless the contrary intention appears, be construed to mean the person or persons, other than a creditor, who would be beneficially entitled under Part VI to the estate of the ancestor if the ancestor had died intestate."

8–81 The repetition of the exact wording of the RTA 1964 is curious, since the section is in an Act dealing primarily with wills and succession, because the section does not then expressly refer to wills. More oddly, "passed or executed" suggests that s.15 retains the dichotomy between deeds executed before or after the Act came into force, whereas the general rule as to wills, contained in s.89 of the Succession Act 1965, is that a will takes effect on the death of the testator.

8–82 Therefore, if T leaves property in a will "to A's heir and her heirs", and A is alive, *quaere* at the date of the will, the person who would be entitled if A had died intestate takes the property.

MODIFIED FEES

8–83 Estates can be made subject to "conditions" which may bring them to an end before they would normally do so, or which have to be satisfied before they can arise. The word "conditions" is used in inverted commas because the law makes a technical distinction between conditional interests and determinable interests, and so "conditions" should be reserved for the former type of interest. The word "modified" is used to cover both types and "determining event" as the equivalent of "condition" when discussing determinable interests. At common law any legal estate could theoretically be made the subject of conditions or determining events. In practice, the fee simple was the estate which was most commonly modified in this way.[97]

8–84 It might have been thought that the LCLRA 2009 would have swept away the modified forms of fee simple in line with its broader objective to simplify and clarify the law of real property. This point has even more force when it is recalled that Porter M.R. once described the distinction between conditional and determinable fees as "little short of disgraceful".[98] The Explanatory Memorandum published alongside the Land and Conveyancing Law Reform Bill 2006 states that the modified forms of fee simple had been retained to facilitate situations in which it would not be appropriate to impose the trusts of land regime set out in Pt 4 of the Bill. The Explanatory Memorandum took the view that the restrictions imposed by conditional and determinable fees simple were "relatively minor qualifications on the ownership of the fee simple". The extent to which this is true is debatable, though the courts have historically exercised a degree of supervision and control over conditions which might be regarded as objectionable from a public policy perspective.

Conditions Precedent and Subsequent

8–85 A condition may be a condition precedent or a condition subsequent. If it is a condition precedent, the estate will not vest until the condition is fulfilled. Such estates are therefore future interests and are dealt with in a later chapter. If the condition is a condition subsequent, the estate vests at once but will be divested later if the condition occurs. The law was neatly summarised by Lowry L.C.J. in the Northern Ireland case of *Re Porter*[99]:

"Whether the condition is precedent or subsequent to the vesting of the interest given depends on the intention of the testator as gathered from the words used. It has been stated that there are no technical words to distinguish a condition precedent from a condition subsequent and that, where it is doubtful whether a condition is precedent or subsequent, the court leans towards a construction which will hold it to be a condition subsequent, for that construction will lead to the early vesting of the gift and there is a presumption in favour of early vesting. A void condition precedent will prevent the gift from vesting, but a void condition subsequent will cause the donee to take free from the condition. The setting of a time limit for performance may show a condition to be precedent: *In re Doherty* [1950] NI 83; but, where a specific time is mentioned for the performance of the condition but not for the vesting of the estate or interest, the condition, it is said, will in general be subsequent: *Walker* v *Walker* (1860) 2 De GF & J 255; 45

---

[97] See R. Powell, "Determinable Fees" (1923) 23 Colum. L.R. 207; A. Lyall, "Human Rights and Conditional and Determinable Interests in Freeholds" (1987) Ir. Jur. 250.
[98] *Re King's Trusts* (1892) 29 L.R. Ir. 401 at 410.
[99] [1975] N.I. 157 at 160, cited with approval in *Morgan v McCaughey*, unreported, NI Chancery Division, 8 September 1986.

ER 619. It has further been suggested that, if the condition is capable of being performed *instanter*, it will probably be precedent, whereas, if time is requisite for its performance, it is more likely to be subsequent. If the nature of the interest is such as to allow time for the performance of the act before the interest can be enjoyed, it is generally precedent, whereas, if it is reasonable to suppose that the interest must vest in possession before the donee can be expected to comply with the condition, it will be subsequent."

8–86 Whether a condition is precedent or subsequent may depend on the situation of the person referred to and the knowledge of the grantor of that situation. Take, for example, a condition specifying that X should reside at a certain house. If X does not at the time of the disposition reside there, the condition is precedent, at least if that fact is known to the grantor, for then that must be the grantor's intention. If X resides there already, then it is a condition subsequent. As the judge points out, the general principle is to hold the condition a condition subsequent so that the property vests at once: the presumption favours the early vesting of property.[100] This can be seen as a market-specific principle. A market or capitalist economy is likely to work more efficiently if property interests are vested sooner rather than later, rather than being suspended until some event or condition occurs, for in the meantime they will be effectively inalienable. Thus, the rule is not perhaps so much a rule of interpretation as a rule of social policy to be imposed unless deliberately excluded by the testator.

8–87 Conditions subsequent which would operate to defeat a vested estate are construed strictly,[101] and so the Supreme Court has held that a condition as to marriage which it held unobjectionable in itself was not severable from a condition as to residence with which it was combined and which the court held void for uncertainty, so that the composite condition failed as a whole.[102]

Modified Fees at Common Law

8–88 Section 11 of the LCLRA 2009 provides that the only freehold estate that can exist as a legal estate is a fee simple in possession, but that includes modified fees, i.e. both conditional and determinable fees.[103] Rights of entry, which follow conditional fees, and possibilities of reverter, which follow determinable fees, were never classified as estates, being "mere possibilities", but existed as legal interests. It would appear that they still do so under s.11(4) and (5) of the LCLRA 2009 which provide for their existence as legal interests with the same attributes as at common law.

---

[100] The point is applied in *Re McDonnell's Will* [1965] I.R. 354 (High Court, Budd J.), citing *Re Greenwood* [1903] 1 Ch. 749.

[101] *In the Estate of Coghlan, deceased* [1963] I.R. 246 at 249; *Clavering v Ellison* (1859) 7 H.L. Cas. 707.

[102] *In the Estate of Coghlan, deceased* [1963] I.R. 246.

[103] LCLRA 2009 s.11(2)(a) and (b).

8–89 In the past a distinction was drawn by judges between a condition and a determining event. The reason for this can be traced to the old common law remainder rules. These rules have received extensive consideration in earlier editions of this book and were mainly feudal in character. The distinction between conditional and determinable interests arose out of a judicial attempt to avoid the effect of the rule which prevented a remainder cutting short a prior estate.[104]

8–90 It is a matter of construction whether a deed gives rise to a determinable or a conditional interest. The effect of many decisions on many deeds is that words suggesting a natural continuation up to a point—such as[105] "while", "during", "as long as"[106] or "until"—indicate a determinable fee, whereas words suggesting an artificial interruption or cutting short of an interest that would otherwise continue—such as[107] "provided that", "on condition that", "but if" or "if it happen that", create a conditional interest:

Determinable	Conditional
while	provided that
during	on condition that
as long as	but if
until	if it happen that

The distinction, according to the textbooks, is purely linguistic, although it cannot be stated with complete confidence that judges always attach the same meaning to those expressions.

Conditional Fees
Effects
8–91 A conditional fee, unlike a determinable interest, does not end automatically if the event occurs. When the event specified in the condition occurs, the grantor can exercise a *right of entry for condition broken*.[108] The limitation

> *to D in fee simple, on condition he does not become an accountant*

creates a legal conditional fee in favour of D and a legal right of entry for condition broken in the grantor if the event occurs. Other examples are or might be:

---

[104] Under the common law remainder rules there could be no remainder after a fee simple, even a conditional and determinable one, and a remainder could not cut short a prior estate, but a determinable *life estate* followed by a remainder offended against neither of these rules.

[105] C. Sweet (ed.), *Challis's Law of Real Property*, 3rd edn (London: Butterworth, 1911), p.252.

[106] *Attorney General v Cummins* [1906] I.R. 406.

[107] *Mary Portington's Case* (1613) 10 Co. Rep. 35b; *Re Rosher* (1884) 26 Ch. D. 801.

[108] M.I. Goldstein, "Rights of Entry and Possibilities of Reverter as Devices to Restrict the Use of Land" (1940) 54 Harvard L.R. 248.

> to B in fee simple, provided the land is used for the extraction of turf[109]
>
> to P in fee simple provided he marries within a year[110]
>
> in trust for F in fee simple conditional upon him being the beneficial owner
> of the estate which the testator had transferred to F during his lifetime.[111]

8–92 "Right of entry" is used rather loosely to mean both the possibility and the right that becomes immediate if the event occurs.[112] If the event occurs the grantor may recover the fee simple.

8–93 At common law a right of entry in the grantor was the only interest it was possible to have after a conditional fee. The grantor could not, in the same document, create a conditional fee simple and then provide that, if the event occurred, the land was to pass to some third party by a remainder.[113] This was due to one of the old common law remainder rules. These have been abolished by the LCLRA 2009,[114] but that Act provides as to conditional fees that only a conditional fee in possession, followed by a right of entry, can exist as a legal estate.[115] Thus, in the limitation

> to D in fee simple, but if he becomes an accountant, [then over to E in fee simple]

the gift to E cannot exist as a legal estate, and is void, but there is presumably nothing now to prevent it existing under a trust of land, if so limited, e.g. [then over to T & U in trust for E in fee simple].

8–94 The courts have treated the condition as separable from the estate it qualifies. If the *condition itself* is objectionable on grounds of public policy or as infringing constitutional or human rights, then it will be struck out, leaving the grantee with a fee simple absolute. Thus in the limitation

> to A in fee simple provided she remains unmarried

---

[109] See *O'Brien v Bord na Móna* [1983] I.L.R.M. 314. Bord na Móna had statutory powers to acquire land compulsorily for turf extraction. The landowner requested that the land be returned to him when it was no longer so used, but Bord na Móna replied that it was its policy to "acquire the fee simple". They did not appear to consider acquiring a conditional fee only.

[110] Such a condition was upheld in *In the Estate of Coghlan, deceased* [1963] I.R. 246, although it was combined with a condition as to residence which was held void for uncertainty and not to be severable.

[111] *Fitzsimons v Fitzsimons* [1993] I.L.R.M. 478.

[112] See Lord Brougham in *Cole v Sewell* (1848) 2 H.L.C. 185 at 231.

[113] Co Litt 143a; C. Saint Germain, *Doctor and Student, or Dialogues between a Doctor of Divinity and a Student of the Laws of England: Containing the Grounds of Those Laws* (Dublin, 1792), Chs 20 and 21; F.W. Sanders, *An Essay on the Nature and Laws of Uses and Trusts* (London, 1791), p.144. The reason was that it would be a remainder after a fee simple.

[114] LCLRA 2009 s.16(a).

[115] LCLRA 2009 s.11(2)(b), 11(4)(i) and 15(2)(b).

the condition is void as infringing the right to marry, but it can be severed from the rest of the limitation so that A obtains the fee simple free of the condition. This contrasts with determinable interests in which the determining event is regarded as part of the estate it qualifies.

Right of Entry

8–95 The limitation

> *to M in fee simple on condition the land be used as a school*

creates a valid legal conditional fee with a legal right of entry in the grantor, which would pass like a fee simple to the grantor's successors, if the land ceases to be used as a school, at any time in the future.[116] The person then entitled to the right of entry would have 12 years under the Statute of Limitations 1957 to assert his or her right.

8–96 At common law rights of entry for condition broken were heritable, i.e. they passed to the heirs on intestacy, but could not be assigned or released.[117] The Wills Act 1837 first made them devisable by will, and this Act was replaced by the Succession Act 1965 (ss.10 and 76).[118] Section 11(9) of the LCLRA 2009 provides that all estates and interests in land, whether legal or equitable, may be disposed of.

Determinable Fees
Effects
8–97 The determinable fee[119] is a fee simple which will end *automatically* on the happening of a contingency, i.e. a specified event which may never happen, "for it is an essential characteristic of all fees, that they may by possibility

---

[116] The rule against perpetuities was abolished by LCLRA 2009 s.16, but rights of entry for condition broken at common law were never subject to the perpetuity rule in Ireland: *Walsh v Wightman* [1927] N.I. 1. Section 13(1) of the Perpetuities Act (Northern Ireland) 1966 provides that a right of entry in respect of a fee simple for condition broken shall not be exercisable after the perpetuity period. Section 13(3) provides that a possibility of reverter under a determinable fee or a possibility of resulting trust shall cease to exist at the end of the perpetuity period and that the fee or interest in question shall cease to be determinable.

[117] *Orr v Stevenson* (1843) 5 Ir. L.R. 2. They were a "mere possibility": *Denham v Dormer* 2 And. 84.

[118] Section 6 of the Real Property Act 1845 made rights of entry alienable *inter vivos*, but specifically referred to rights of entry "in England". It read: "… a contingent, an executory, and a future interest, and a possibility coupled with an interest, in any tenements or hereditaments of any tenure … also a right of entry, whether immediate or future, and whether vested or contingent, into or upon any tenements or hereditaments in England, of any tenure, may be disposed of by deed …". Also, in *Hunt v Remnant* (1854) 9 Exch. 635 at 640, Pollock C.B. said that the phrase did not refer to rights of entry *for condition broken*. Section 6 was amended by s.19 of the Married Women's Status Act 1957, but the amendment did not affect the words referred to.

[119] R. Powell, "Determinable Fees" (1923) 23 Colum. L.R. 207.

endure for ever".[120] If the event is one which, by its nature, *must* happen, then the interest is not a determinable (or a conditional) fee, but something else. For example,

> *to A in fee simple until B dies*

gives A an estate *pur autre vie*, while

> *to C and his heirs for 25 years*

gives C a lease for 25 years.[121] An example of a determinable fee would be:

> *to B and his heirs until he qualifies as an accountant.*

8–98 The grantor has a *possibility of reverter*. At common law, if the determining event occurs, the land reverts automatically to the grantor or if he or she is dead, to whoever has become entitled to his or her interest. The grantor has the possibility of a reverter. Indeed, this is the only interest that can exist after the determinable fee simple at common law. At common law the grantor cannot, in the same deed create a determinable fee and then provide that if the event occurs, the land is to pass to someone else.[122] The grantor cannot create, as a common law interest, a gift over to a third party after a determinable fee. So in the limitation *inter vivos*

> *to X in fee simple until he becomes an accountant, [then to Y in fee simple]*

the gift to Y is void. In the past the reason was that the old common law remainder rules did not allow a remainder after a fee simple, even a determinable one,[123] and the reason now is that the LCLRA 2009 does not allow a future interest[124] to exist at law.[125]

---

[120] Sweet (ed.), *Challis's Law of Real Property* (1911), p.251.

[121] In the 15th century, Littleton says that a fee simple granted by A to B in fee simple, on condition that if A should pay B a sum of money then A should have a right of re-entry, did not create a conditional fee, but a mortgage: Wambaugh (ed.), *Littleton's Tenures in English* (1903), Bk III, section 332.

[122] *Corrigan v Corrigan* [2007] IEHC 367 (McGovern J., citing this passage from the second edition of this book).

[123] *City of Klamath Falls v Bell* 490 P 2d 515 (1972).

[124] LCLRA 2009 s.11(4)(e) and (i).

[125] However, there appears to be nothing to prevent a gift over after a determinable fee being created as an equitable interest taking effect under a trust of land, e.g. *to T and U in fee simple in trust for X in fee simple until he becomes an accountant, then to T and U in fee simple in trust for Y in fee simple*. The same seems to be true of interests in wills, since they take effect initially as equitable interests, the legal title being vested in the personal representatives.

8–99 If X dies without becoming an accountant then the event can no longer occur and the fee simple becomes absolute. This will be the case whatever the event.

8–100 By contrast with a conditional fee, the determining event is regarded at common law as an integral part of the estate which it qualifies, so that if it fails, the whole limitation fails.[126] If the determining event is contrary to public policy, or infringes constitutional rights or human rights, the whole determinable interest is void. So the limitation

to A in fee simple until she marries

is prima facie void as a total restraint on marriage and A gets nothing. This is the most unsatisfactory aspect of determinable fees.

Possibility of Reverter
8–101 The limitation

to X and his heirs so long as the land shall be used for agriculture

creates a determinable fee followed by a valid possibility of reverter in the grantor. If the land ceases to be used for agriculture at any time in the future,[127] the fee simple to X comes to an end and the land reverts to the grantor or those who have by then become entitled to the grantor's right of reverter. Again, they have 12 years in which to assert it.

8–102 At common law a possibility of reverter could not be transferred by the grantor: it could only descend as on intestacy to the heir-at-law. Section 3 of the Wills Act 1837[128] made such interests devisable. Section 10 of the Succession Act 1965 provides that all the real and personal property of a person shall, on his or her death, devolve on his or her personal representatives and s.76 provides that a person by his or her will may dispose of all property to which he or she is beneficially entitled to at his or her death and which on his or her death devolves on his or her personal representatives.[129] Formerly, it was not clear whether possibilities of reverter could be alienated *inter vivos*

---

[126] This common law position is now modified by s.51(2) of the Settled Land Act 1882. A determining event which would or might prevent a tenant for life under the Act from exercising the powers under the Act is severed from the estate and the tenant for life continues to enjoy the estate free of the restriction: *Re Ames* [1893] 2 Ch. 479.

[127] In Ireland the perpetuity rule never applied to possibilities of reverter: *Attorney General v Cummins* [1906] I.R. 406; *Walsh v Wightman* [1927] N.I. 1.

[128] *Pemberton v Barnes* [1899] 1 Ch. 544.

[129] Note that the case of *Pemberton v Barnes* [1899] 1 Ch. 544 held that a possibility of reverter on a determinable fee in copyholds was within the Wills Act 1837.

in Ireland,[130] but s.11(9) of the LCLRA 2009 now provides that all estates and interests in land, whether legal or equitable, may be disposed of and thus it would seem that the possibility of a reverter is now freely transferable, whether *inter vivos* or by will.

Summary

8–103 The main differences between conditional and determinable fees may be summarised as follows:

Conditional	Determinable
1. Words suggesting premature cutting short.	1. Words suggesting natural continuation.
2. Followed by right of entry.	2. Followed by possibility of reverter.
3. Does not terminate automatically.	3. Terminates automatically.
4. Condition separable from estate.	4. Event part of limitation.

Future Trusts

Gifts Over

8–104 "Gifts over" after determinable or conditional equitable estates can be created as equitable interests.[131] So a gift

> *to T and U in fee simple in trust for A in fee simple until she qualifies as a accountant, then in trust for B in fee simple*

gives a valid equitable determinable fee to A followed by a gift over in fee simple to B. Since the perpetuity rule has been abolished by the LCLRA 2009,[132] the limitation

> *to F and G in fee simple in trust for O in fee simple so long as the land is used for agriculture, then in trust for P in fee simple*

would also give a valid gift over to P in fee simple, despite the fact that, if the event occurs, it might do so at a remote time in the future. The gift

> *to T and U and their heirs in trust for P and his heirs, but if he becomes a accountant, then in trust for Q and his heirs*

gives a valid equitable conditional fee to P followed by a gift over to Q.

---

[130] Section 6 of the Real Property Act 1845 provided that "… a possibility coupled with an interest, in any tenements or hereditaments of any tenure … may be disposed of by deed …". A possibility of reverter might have come within the phrase "possibility coupled with an interest", the interest being the determinable fee simple.

[131] Sanders, *An Essay on the Nature and Laws of Uses and Trusts* (1791), Vol.i, p.144 (executory interest under Statute of Uses); *Tisdall v Tisdall* (1840) 2 Ir. C.L. 41.

[132] LCLRA 2009 s.16.

Possibilities of Resulting Trust
8–105 In the example

> *to T and U and their heirs in trust for R and his heirs, on condition the land is used for agriculture*

there remains a possibility of a resulting trust in the grantor which was never subject to the perpetuity rule.[133] The same would no doubt apply if the event were phrased as a determining event:

> *to T and U in fee simple in trust for R and his heirs, so long as the land is used for agriculture.*

R gets a determinable fee in equity which comes to an end if the land ceases to be used for agriculture. The trustees then hold the land on trust for the grantor, or whoever is by then entitled to the grantor's property.

Invalidity of Determining Events or Conditions
Introduction
8–106 Determining events or conditions (referred to as "restrictions") may be held void as contrary to public policy or constitutional rights. Where a restriction on a common law estate is avoided in this way, the distinction between determinable and conditional interests is significant. At common law, if a determinable event is held to be void, then the whole interest which was intended to be conveyed is void. This result was the consequence of a device to avoid an old common law rule which prevented a remainder cutting short a prior estate. Courts have been reluctant to hold determining events void because to do so would deprive the intended victim of unlawful discrimination of the intended gift in its entirety. A different principle applied to conditional interests: where the condition was held to be void for public policy, the condition was severed from the rest of the grant leaving the donee to take the estate free from the unlawful condition.[134]

Relief against Forfeiture
8–107 There is a general jurisdiction in equity to grant relief against forfeiture arising by reason of a condition subsequent. However, the normal rule is that no relief will be granted if there is a gift over in the event of the condition

---

[133] *Walsh v Wightman* [1927] N.I. 1. The court upheld Palles C.B.'s view in *Attorney General v Cummins* [1906] I.R. 406 that a right of entry at common law was not void for perpetuity and went on to decide that the same applied even if a similar interest occurred under a trust. In *Re Cooper's Conveyance Trusts* [1956] 1 W.L.R. 1096, a conveyance was made to trustees in fee simple on trust for an orphan girls' home, and on failure of that trust, then in trust for persons mentioned elsewhere in the deed. It was held that the gift over was void for perpetuity, but there was a valid resulting trust in favour of the grantor's estate.

[134] See *McConnell v Beattie* (1904) 38 I.L.T.R. 133.

occurring.[135] To relieve the holder of the conditional interest in such a case would at the same time be to deprive the person entitled to the gift over. Since one is divested of, and the other invested with, the property on the event occurring, the only question in such a case is whether the event has occurred or not.

Restrictions on Alienability

8–108 Conditions which seek to prevent or restrict alienation by a fee simple owner are likely to be held void as contrary to the policy of the law, stemming from the Statute *Quia Emptores* 1290.

Restrictions on Occupation or Ownership

8–109 Attempts to restrict *occupation* or *ownership* by particular racial, religious or other social groups may be void as restraints on the power of alienation but are also challengeable on constitutional or human rights grounds. In jurisdictions such as the United States, they have often taken the form of restrictive covenants. In Ireland, discrimination involving property rights has often been carried out using conditional or determinable estates and has tended to focus on religious belief or marriage to a person holding a particular faith. Discrimination in Ireland generally is now dealt with by the Equal Status Acts 2000–2015 . This legislation will be discussed below, but as it does not cover dispositions of land by will or gift,[136] the older cases still require examination.

Restrictions on Residence

8–110 Conditions which seek to make residence a condition precedent or subsequent may be impugned on a number of grounds.

8–111 In *Re Johnston; Morgan v McCaughey*,[137] such a condition was struck down on the ground that, in the case at hand, it would cause a child to live separately from his parents. The testator left property on trust for his sister for life with remainder after her death to his grandnephew Nathaniel, "provided he comes to live in the said property after my death and continues to reside therein with my said sister … until the death of my said sister". Nathaniel was to have no legal or equitable right to reside on the property during the life of the sister "otherwise than as licensee of [my sister]". Nathaniel was 15 years old at the time of the testator's death. He offered to go and live with the testator's sister but she declined the offer. Nathaniel occasionally stayed at the house with his mother at weekends. In 1972 the sister engaged a paid companion, on medical advice, and this arrangement lasted until her death. There was no ill will between the parties and Nathaniel continued to visit the sister until her death, but the effect was that, while Nathaniel had done everything he could

---

[135] *Morgan v McCaughey* [1986] N.I. 229.
[136] Equal Status Act 2000 s.5(2)(k).
[137] [1986] N.I. 229.

to comply with the condition, the sister's preference to arrange her own affairs prevented him from living in the house.

8–112 The judge first held that the condition was a single one and was subsequent. The remainder would vest in interest in Nathaniel immediately, and under the will would be divested if he ceased to continue to reside, although the judge noted that it had not been argued that he should necessarily continue to reside until the sister's death. The judge then held that the condition, whether valid or not, had not been performed. Nathaniel had done his best to perform it, but the testator had given his sister the power to frustrate the performance of the condition and she had done so. The judge further held that a condition which tended to lead to the separation of a child from his parents was void as contrary to public policy.[138] Nathaniel therefore took the estate free of the condition.[139] In Ireland, the protection afforded to the family by the Constitution would probably be sufficient reason to hold such a condition void.[140]

8–113 In *Re Fitzgibbon, deceased*,[141] the testator left a farm to his grand-nephew "provided he lives and works on the land" with a gift over to his niece on breach of the condition. Carroll J. held that where there was a doubt as to whether a condition in a will was a condition precedent or subsequent, the court would apply the presumption in favour of early vesting and treat it prima facie as subsequent. The judge further held, however, that the condition was void for uncertainty, citing *Re Hennessy, deceased*,[142] in which Budd J. had held a condition "to farm it and carry on same as he thinks best" as subsequent and as void for uncertainty. On the other hand, Gavan Duffy J. in *Re Callaghan*[143] held that although a condition precedent that a devisee "arranges within ... three months of my death to take over possession and permanently reside" on a farm was void for uncertainty, the further condition precedent that he "actually takes up his residence within six months" was valid as sufficiently definite.

8–114 In the past, conditions as to residence might also fall foul of s.51 of the Settled Land Act 1882 which prohibited any attempt to prevent the exercise of the powers of the tenant for life.[144]

---

[138] *Re Boulter* [1922] 1 Ch. 75. See also, *Re Sandbrook* [1912] 2 Ch. 471; *Re Piper* [1946] 2 All E.R. 503 (condition causing forfeiture if children went to live with their father held void).

[139] *Re Elliott* [1952] Ch. 217; *Re Piper* [1946] 2 All E.R. 503.

[140] Article 41.

[141] [1993] I.R. 520.

[142] (1963) 98 I.L.T.R. 39.

[143] [1937] I.R. 84.

[144] *Re Fitzgerald* [1902] 1 I.R .162; *Atkins v Atkins* [1976–77] I.L.R.M. 62 (Kenny J.); *Re Thompson* (1888) 21 L.R. Ir. 109. It is a difficult question as to what effect s.51 would have on limitations framed as determinable interests.

Name and Arms Clauses

8–115 Property is sometimes given in family settlements subject to the condition that the person entitled shall use the name and coat of arms of some particular individual, usually the testator or settlor. Such conditions may be precedent or subsequent, or both. In theory they could also create determinable interests. It is a matter of interpretation for the court to decide which type of interest has been created.

8–116 Name and arms clauses have not been treated sympathetically by the judiciary in Ireland since 1922. In *Re Montgomery*,[145] the clause in issue was a condition subsequent, and so the court was concerned with a condition which was to apply when a person *ceased* to use the name and arms specified. The High Court held such a clause void for uncertainty, not on the ground that the acts or omissions were in themselves uncertain, which the court declined to hold, but on the ground that it was uncertain as to when the acts or omissions might occur.

8–117 In *Re de Vere's Will Trusts*,[146] the court was concerned with that part of the disposition which created a condition subsequent terminating the property interest. Budd J. held the condition void for uncertainty. The English Court of Appeal in *Re Neeld*[147] had used the *de minimis* principle to overlook mistakes or forgetfulness or temporary lapses in use. In *Kearns v Manresa Estates Ltd*,[148] Kenny J. held a clause in defeasance to be void for uncertainty. The judge was critical of *Re Neeld*. How many lapses would bring the principle into operation? How many would mean that it no longer applied? Must they be intentional or unintentional? He went on:

> "None of the judgments in *Re Neeld* deal with the question as to how the Court is to decide that at any given moment of time … a person has disused or discontinued to use the surname which he is obliged to assume."

8–118 Conditions requiring the use of a name as a condition precedent may cause less difficulty. One can adopt a name by deed poll, and although one can also adopt a name by repute, the condition in *de Vere* was limited to the use of the name in documents. In such a case it could be argued that a single instance of the person using the name in a document would satisfy the condition precedent.

8–119 Arms to individuals and corporations may be obtained by grant from the Chief Herald of Ireland and possibly can only be used for authentication in this way, although there is some doubt as to the exact status of coats of arms in

---

[145] (1955) 89 I.L.T.R. 62.
[146] [1961] I.R. 224.
[147] [1962] Ch. 643.
[148] Unreported, High Court, Kenny J., 25 July 1975.

Ireland.[149] The children of a person entitled to bear arms may adopt a version of them with a suitable difference.[150] In England, it was held by the Court of Chivalry[151] in *Manchester Corporation v Manchester Palace of Varieties Ltd*[152] that arms could be freely used as ornament, but their use by a person or body other than the bearer for the purpose of authenticating documents, etc., or as claiming a right to them, could be restrained by law.

8–120 In *Bevan v Mahon-Hagan*,[153] it was held that a surname may be adopted voluntarily,[154] but the Court of Appeal did not agree as to whether or in what circumstances a person had the right to bear arms other than, at that time, under a royal licence issued by the Ulster King of Arms.[155] Porter M.R. held that it was possible to assume arms, Fitzgibbon L.J. held that one could not bear arms without a grant, and Barry L.J. found that the right of a person to bear arms otherwise than under a grant from the Crown was so obscure that he could not express an opinion on it. The court held that the Crown could grant a coat of arms to a minor, and so a condition to adopt the name and arms of X before attaining the age of majority was capable of being performed.[156]

Restrictions on Marriage
Total Restraints
8–121 It has long been held that a condition or determining event involving a *total* restriction on marriage would be void on grounds of public policy, so that a limitation

---

[149] On heraldry in Ireland, see M.C. O'Laughlin, *The Irish Book of Arms: Genealogy and Heraldry from the Earliest Times to the 20th Century* (Kansas City: Irish Genealogical Foundation, 2000); N. Williams, *Armas: Sracfhéachaint ar Araltas na hÉireann* (Baile Átha Cliath: Coiscéim, 2001); C. Lynch-Robinson and A. Lynch-Robinson, *Intelligible Heraldry* (London: Macdonald, 1953); A. Lyall, "Irish Heraldic Jurisdiction" (1993) 10 C.o.A. (ns) 134–142; (1994) 10 C.o.A. (ns) 179–187, 238–244 and 266–275; National Cultural Institutions Act 1997 ss.12–13.

[150] Where arms exist and are borne by the head of a family, junior or collateral members of the family may bear a version of the arms altered in some way to distinguish them from the head of the family. Arms may be associated with a name, but there are no "family" arms, nor is a person with the same surname entitled to use the undifferentiated arms. Arms pertain to individuals and were used to distinguish one individual from another when wearing armour, particularly in jousts. Thus, the "arms of de Vere" are properly those of the head of the main branch of the de Vere family.

[151] The court had not sat since 1737 but had never been abolished and was reconvened for the *Manchester Case*: G.D. Squibb, *The High Court of Chivalry: A Study of the Civil law in England* (Oxford: Clarendon Press, 1959).

[152] [1955] P. 133.

[153] (1891) 27 L.R. Ir. 399, V-C.

[154] See also, *Doe d Luscombe v Yates* (1822) 5 B. & Ald. 544.

[155] Ulster King of Arms' heraldic authority, despite the title, extended throughout Ireland: A. Lyall, "Irish Heraldic Jurisdiction" (1993) 10 C.o.A. (ns) 134 (Pt 1), (1994) 10 C.o.A. 179 (Pt 2).

[156] See *Bevan v Mahon-Hagan* (1891) 27 L.R. Ir. 399.

to A in fee simple until she marries

is prima facie void and would only be upheld if the court were convinced that the intention was not to induce A not to marry, but to provide for her until marriage. Courts appear more likely to come to this conclusion in the case of a determinable interest, in order to save the gift. If they held the determining event invalid, the intended donee would get nothing. This is a clear example of the way in which the conditional/determinable distinction distorts the treatment of human rights issues. Thus, in *Re Robson*[157] the High Court of Northern Ireland held a gift of property to A "whilst remaining unmarried" to be a valid determinable interest in spite of the suggestion of the words that a restraint was intended.

8–122 In *Re King's Trusts*,[158] an annuity was given to each of five children of the testator's brother for their lives "or until any of them shall marry", the annuity to cease on their death or marriage. There was no gift over on the event occurring. The court held the proviso was a valid determinable interest and that the plaintiff had forfeited the annuity on marriage.

Partial Restraints on Marriage

8–123 Historically, the courts took the view that a partial restraint was not necessarily void on that account, but would be so only if it restrained marriage to an extent which conflicted with public policy. In *Keily v Monck*,[159] real property was devised to the testator's daughters subject to the proviso that should any of them marry someone who was not, at the time of the marriage, seized of a freehold estate of the clear yearly value of Stg£500 over and above every charge and incumbrance, then the legacy to such a daughter was to be forfeited. The proviso would only have been satisfied by a very wealthy man indeed. In the Irish House of Lords, Clare L.C. held that it would amount virtually to a total restraint on marriage, and was void. The judge's indignation was aroused by the thought that it would have excluded all members of the legal profession at the time, and the growing mercantile classes. The judge's remarks are interesting in that they provide some evidence that the judiciary was more sympathetic to these professional and capitalist classes at the time than to the landed aristocracy. He said that in *Jarvis v Duke*,[160] the case was

"that a condition in restraint of marriage excluding a particular profession is void. How many particular professions are naturally excluded by that condition? What man of the profession of the law has set out with a clear unincumbered real estate of £500 a year, or has acquired such an estate for years after entering the profession? … It will in effect exclude ninety-nine

---

[157] [1940] Ir. Jur. Rep. 72.
[158] (1892) 29 L.R. Ir. 401.
[159] (1795) 3 Ridg. P.C. 205.
[160] (1681) 1 Vern. 20.

men in one hundred of every profession, whether civil, military, or ecclesiastical. It in effect excludes nearly every mercantile man in the kingdom
… In a word, the condition which this weak old man would impose upon
his daughters … does, to my judgment, clearly and unquestionably lead to
a total prohibition of their marriage, and as such ought to be condemned in
every Court of Justice."[161]

8–124 In *Greene v Kirkwood*,[162] at the end of the 19th century the court upheld
a condition that gave rise to a forfeiture in the event of a daughter marrying a
man "beneath her in life, that is to say, below her in social position". The court
upheld the validity of the condition. Distinctions of social rank may still have
been widely accepted in 1895, or at least by the judges, but today such a condition would fail for lack of certainty.

8–125 In *Duggan v Kelly*,[163] the testator left bequests to his children, including
sums to two of his daughters to be paid to them at the age of 21, provided they
married with the consent of the executors of the will. The will also provided
that if any of his children "at any time hereafter intermarry with a Papist, or
person professing the Roman Catholic religion or Popish religion, or a reputed
Papist", the gift to that child was to be revoked, the child concerned was to
receive the sum of one shilling, and their share was to be distributed equally
among the "survivors". The question was whether one of the daughters had
forfeited her interest by marrying a Catholic. The Master of the Rolls held the
condition against marrying a Catholic to be legal and to extend to the whole life
of the legatees, because it specified "at any time". On appeal the validity of the
condition was upheld, but the restrictions as to consent and as to not marrying
a Catholic were held to apply only during a minority, so that if a child attained
21 she would be paid her legacy and could then marry as she chose. Richards
B. felt constrained to this interpretation because if it were otherwise, it would
be possible for a daughter to marry a Protestant, with consent, while under
age, have children who were Protestants and then for her husband to die and
for her to then marry, after coming of age, a Catholic. This would then cause
a forfeiture of her interest which would not then pass by the normal course of
devolution to her children, who were Protestants. The judge took the view that
such a result could not have been intended by the testator.

The Constitutional Right to Marry
8–126 The Constitution accords to marriage a particularly important place
as an institution. Article 41.3.1° states that "the State pledges itself to guard
with special care the institution of Marriage, on which the Family is founded
and to protect it against attack." The Constitution does not expressly provide
for a right to marry, as opposed to rights flowing from the protection of the

---

[161] (1795) 3 Ridg. P.C. 205 at 263.
[162] [1895] 1 I.R. 130.
[163] (1847) 10 Ir. Eq. R. 295, 473.

institution of marriage itself, but such a right has been established in a line of decisions beginning with that of Kenny J. in *Ryan v Attorney General*,[164] who held that Art.40.3.1° created an unenumerated right to marry. Kenny J. repeated this view in *MacAuley v Minister for Posts and Telegraphs*.[165] This dictum was also cited in *McGee v Attorney General* by Budd J.[166] and by Griffin J. in the Supreme Court.[167] In the same case, Fitzgerald C.J. said:

> "The right to marry and the intimate relations between husband and wife are fundamental rights which have existed in most, if not all, civilised countries for many centuries. These rights were not conferred by the Constitution in this country in 1937. The Constitution goes no further than to guarantee to defend and vindicate and protect those rights from attack."[168]

8–127 The implication is that the fact that the right to marry is not expressly stated in the Constitution does not detract from its existence, but on the contrary it was taken to be so fundamental as not to require statement at all.[169] In addition to domestic law, international law, most notably Art.12 of the European Convention on Human Rights, recognises the right to marry. It is clear, therefore, that the right to marry exists and is worthy of extensive protection.

8–128 It is arguable that the enforcement of restrictions which are intended to influence the exercise of the right to marry would be constitutionally unsound. This might be argued either on the basis that such rights are themselves unconstitutional interferences with the right to marry, or that courts could not give legal force to such conditions without infringing constitutionally protected rights. The extent to which the Constitution can be relied upon in litigation against a non-State party has not been conclusively determined by the Irish courts. In *Educational Company of Ireland v Fitzpatrick (No.2)*,[170] Budd J. suggested that constitutional rights create correlative duties for other members of the community to refrain from interference with them. This was endorsed by the Supreme Court in *Meskell v Coras Impair Éireann*[171] with Walsh J. adding the further suggestion that "to infringe another's constitutional rights, or to coerce him into abandoning or waiving them is unlawful as constituting a violation of the fundamental law of the State."[172] The courts have refused to

---

[164] [1965] I.R. 294 at 313.
[165] [1966] I.R. 345 at 357.
[166] [1974] I.R. 284 at 322.
[167] [1974] I.R. 284 at 333.
[168] [1974] I.R. 284 at 301.
[169] Kenny J.'s statement has also been cited with approval, or without dissent, in *Murray v Attorney General* [1985] I.R. 532; *Norris v Attorney General* [1984] I.R. 36 at 97; *RSJ v JSJ* [1982] I.L.R.M. 263 at 264; *State (KM and RD) v Minister for Foreign Affairs* [1979] I.R. 73 at 80; *State (C) v Frawley* [1976] I.R. 365 at 374. The High Court in *Somjee v Minister for Justice* [1981] I.L.R.M. 324 assumed such a right to exist.
[170] [1961] I.R. 354 at 388.
[171] [1971] I.R. 121 at 133.
[172] [1971] I.R. 121 at 143.

enforce a restriction on constitutional grounds which would have interfered with parents' Article 42 rights to make decisions for children's welfare.

8–129 In the first post-1937 case, constitutional rights were not argued. In *Re McKenna*,[173] trustees were to apply the income of a fund for the testator's daughter until she became 21 or married before that time, and afterwards to her for life, provided that if she should marry a Roman Catholic, she should forfeit the interest and the property should go instead to her issue. Gavan Duffy P. declined to hold that the test was void for uncertainty, which was the main issue argued in the case.[174] He held that whether an individual was a Catholic or not did not involve any theological test, but was a matter of applying the words as understood by ordinary people, and that the best evidence of whether a person was of a particular faith was his own testimony in court.[175] This may indicate that the courts, although they may not have articulated it in that way, have produced a test which adopts a principle that the individual's freedom to choose a religion is to be respected, and have rejected the notion that a person could be found to be a "Catholic" or "Protestant" if he himself denies the epithet. Where the test itself involves the assessment of the degree of adherence to a faith, however, it may fail for uncertainty. In *Re Burke's Estate*,[176] Gavan Duffy P. himself held a condition void for uncertainty in that it purported to give rise to a forfeiture if the recipient of the property ceased to "practise the Roman Catholic religion".

Ethnic or Sectarian Restrictions

8–130 Some forfeiture clauses which may at first sight appear to fall into one or other or both of the previous categories may, when analysed, involve a form of discrimination which goes beyond an attempt to impose a particular form of ideology on another person. *Re Knox*,[177] a pre-1937 decision, provides an example. The condition was that if the testator's son should marry, he should "marry a Protestant wife, the daughter of Protestant parents, and who have always been Protestants." The issue of uncertainty was not argued before the court. The judgment of the Irish Court of Appeal was delivered by Naish J. who said:

> "Conditions of this kind, requiring a legatee or devisee to marry persons of a particular religious denomination, and forfeiting their interest if they did not, have been repeatedly held valid, and it is now too late to question their validity."[178]

---

[173] [1947] I.R. 277.
[174] Citing *Re Sandbrook* [1912] 2 Ch. 474.
[175] Citing *Re Samuel* [1942] Ch. 1 at 13.
[176] [1951] I.R. 216. See also, *Re Waring's Will Trusts* [1985] N.I. 105.
[177] (1889) 23 L.R. Ir. 542.
[178] (1889) 23 L.R. Ir. 542 at 544.

8–131 The problem is that the clause did not in fact require a person to marry a person of a particular religious denomination. It went beyond that to require that her *parents* should also have been of that religious denomination and even that they should have been so from birth. This involves a fundamentally different form of test. The test is not concerned with the beliefs or faith of the intended spouse at all but with factors which can only be described as sectarian in character. The court in *Knox* failed to perceive this distinction and this failure means that the reason given by the court does not logically support the conclusion. Even if it were the case that clauses requiring a devisee to marry "persons of a particular denomination" were valid, it would not follow that a clause in the form before the court in *Knox* would be valid. The intended spouse in this example cannot satisfy the test by changing her religion or by any other means, even supposing that to be a tolerable imposition on a person. It is as if someone had given property to another, subject to being forfeited if he married a person of a certain race or ethnic group.

8–132 A similar issue would arise if a grant of land were made subject to a proviso that it should not be sold to or occupied by persons belonging to a particular ethnic group. These issues bring into play the guarantee of equality before the law contained in Art.40.1 of the Constitution. The main authority on the issue is the statement of Walsh J. in *Quinn's Supermarket Ltd v Attorney General*[179]:

> "[T]his provision is not a guarantee of absolute equality for all citizens in all circumstances but it is a guarantee of equality as human persons and (as the Irish text of the Constitution makes quite clear) is a guarantee related to their dignity as human beings and a guarantee against any inequalities grounded upon an assumption, or indeed a belief, that some individual or individuals or classes of individuals, by reason of their human attributes or their ethnic or racial, social or religious background, are to be treated as the inferior or superior of other individuals in the community. This list does not pretend to be complete; but it is merely intended to illustrate the view that this guarantee refers to human persons for what they are in themselves rather than to any lawful activities, trades or pursuits which they may engage in or follow."

8–133 This dictum has been applied in a number of subsequent decisions.[180] But they have all been concerned with challenges to legislation or to subsidiary legislation. Would it be true to say that Art.40.1 is confined only to State action, and if so, what form of State action? Since it is a guarantee of equality

---

[179] [1972] I.R. 1 at 11.

[180] *East Donegal Cooperative v Attorney General* [1970] I.R. 317; *Madigan v Attorney General* [1986] I.L.R.M. 136; *McHugh v Commissioner of the Garda Síochana* [1985] I.L.R.M. 606; *Tormey v Attorney General* [1984] I.L.R.M. 657; *Brennan v Attorney General* [1984] I.L.R.M. 355.

before the law and law is enforced only by State action, the qualification is in a sense self-evident. The real issue is as to what is meant by State action.

8-134 In the United States, the Fourteenth Amendment to the Constitution, which guarantees equal treatment before the law, is confined expressly to "state action", which refers to actions by the individual states which make up the Union. Even so, such action has been held to include judicial action as well as legislative measures, so that the courts of a state were held, in *Barrows v Jackson*,[181] to be precluded from enforcing racially discriminatory covenants at law and, in *Shelley v Kraemer*,[182] in equity. The court in *Shelley* rejected the so-called "neutral principles" approach to constitutional interpretation promoted by conservatives in the United States[183] under which the enforcement by the courts of private agreements, regardless of their content—whether it be racist, sectarian or otherwise—and regardless of the effect on the human rights of third parties, is seen as "neutral". Both *Barrows* and *Shelley* concerned restrictive covenants rather than conditional or determinable interests.

8-135 In *Evans v Newton*,[184] land was left to a municipal authority to be used for a park for white persons only. The city operated it for some time as a segregated park but later opened it for use by all citizens. The managers of the park sought to have the city removed as trustee, since it, as a public body, could not legally operate a segregated park. The managers claimed that if the title were to be vested in them, they could then operate it as a segregated park. The Supreme Court held in *Evans v Newton* that the public character of the park rendered it subject to the Fourteenth Amendment, whoever held the title. The Supreme Court of Georgia then held, the trust having been held to be unenforceable, that the land should revert to the testator's heirs. A majority in the United States Supreme Court[185] upheld this view, with dissenting judgments by Douglas and Brennan JJ. The majority held that the Supreme Court of Georgia was empowered to construe the will only so as to give effect to the testator's intent and that, the trust having been held unenforceable, the only jurisdiction under the Georgia cy-pres statutes to vary the terms of the trust was to conform as closely to this intent as possible and that therefore the land reverted to the heirs. Douglas J., dissenting, expressed the view, inter alia, that as there was no express provision for reverter to the heirs, the construction adopted by the Supreme Court of Georgia did as much violence to the testator's intent as returning the land to the heirs. He also pointed out that the testator had left "all remainders and reversions" arising under his will to the city.

---

[181] 346 US 249 (1953)

[182] 334 US 1 (1948)

[183] See R.H. Bork, *The Tempting of America: Political Seduction of the Law* (New York: Free Press, 1997), pp.78, 147–148, and on *Shelley*, 151; and R.H. Bork, "Neutral Principles and Some First Amendment Problems" (1971) 47 Ind. L.J. 1.

[184] 382 US 296 (1966).

[185] *Evans v Abney* 396 US 435 (1970).

8–136 The majority did not accept that their ruling involved the courts lending their power to enforce an unconstitutional discrimination, apparently on the ground that it had not been proved that the Georgia judges had been motivated by racial prejudice in coming to their decision. This indicates that the majority were adopting the "neutral principles" approach and also shows up the weak point in that theory. Once it is conceded that a private choice ceases to be simply a matter of private choice once the State lends its power to the transaction by enforcing it by law, the "neutral principles" thesis collapses. Again, once that point is conceded, then it is irrelevant what the motives of the judges were. The question is as to whether the law can then be said to be acting consistently with the commitment to equality and to be vindicating the rights of all citizens, not merely those confined within the bounds of a property transaction.

8–137 In Ireland, O'Hanlon J.'s decision in *Re Dunne*[186] rejected the basis of the "neutral principles" approach in that it recognised that social consequences could result from a restriction entered into between individuals. O'Hanlon J. indeed went further than the United States cases in declaring such a restriction to be illegal in itself, not merely unenforceable.

Religious Restrictions

8–138 Restrictions on freedom of religion may occur independently of marriage. Such tests may sometimes be held void for uncertainty. Since a definite interest in property is to pass to someone or to remain vested in the present owner on the happening of an event, or the presence or absence of some quality, the courts will refuse to uphold the validity of such a test if it cannot definitely be stated when the event has occurred or when the quality is present or absent. On the other hand, one suspects that the test of certainty has been used, particularly in jurisdictions without a constitutional bill of rights, to dispose of cases in which the substantive issue is one of discrimination on religious or racial grounds.

8–139 The Northern Ireland Court of Appeal in *McCausland v Young*[187] held that the term "Roman Catholic" was not void for uncertainty,[188] but Gavan Duffy P. in *Re Burke's Estate*[189] held that the phrase "cease to practise the Roman Catholic religion" was void on this ground. The law itself is to some degree uncertain here, for the extent to which a person practises or does not practise a religion would seem to have some bearing on whether he can be described, or would describe himself, as adhering to it. Furthermore, religion and national or cultural identity are not always distinct attributes, so that a person who does not practise the Jewish religion may nevertheless still regard himself as being having a Jewish identity.

---

[186] [1988] I.R. 155.
[187] [1949] N.I. 49, consisting of only two judges.
[188] See also, *Blathwayt v Cawley (Lord)* [1976] A.C. 397.
[189] [1951] I.R. 216.

8–140 Irish courts have not yet had to decide whether an interest given to a person on condition that it is to be forfeited if he or she becomes a Catholic (or a Protestant or a Jew, etc.) is void as discriminating on religious grounds.[190] The court in the first case after the 1937 Constitution did examine the question of constitutional rights, but only on the issue of the freedom of parents to educate their children. In *Re Burke's Estate*,[191] a testator by her will left the residue of her property upon trust to pay and use the income for the purpose of maintaining, educating in Ireland and bringing up an infant as a Roman Catholic. The will directed the trustees should have the power to determine which school the infant would attend and that upon his leaving school, the income should be paid to him until the age of 25 years whereupon the residue should be paid to him absolutely. The testator further provided that if at any time the infant should leave Ireland without the consent of the trustees for any period exceeding six months or should cease to practise the Roman Catholic religion, he should forfeit all benefit under the will. The child in question had lived in England for about three years prior to the testator's death and had continued to live there. Gavan Duffy P. held that the direction that the selection of a school should be in the absolute discretion of the trustees conflicted with the parental authority to determine the education of children as set out in Art.42 of the Constitution. He further held that since the child had resided outside of Ireland before the testator's death, the condition as to residence was void. The religious test was held void for uncertainty, with the outcome that the child was entitled to have the fund transferred to him on attaining his majority.

8–141 The same issue arose in the case of *Re Blake*.[192] A legacy was given to trustees to apply the income to maintain the children of the grantor's daughter "provided they should be brought up in the Roman Catholic faith". The High Court held that the condition was unconstitutional as it infringed the right of parents to provide for the education of their children.

8–142 In *McCausland v Young*,[193] a deed of resettlement, executed by father and son, conferred a life estate on a father and a life estate on his son with further remainders to his son's children. The deed provided that if a tenant for life or a person entitled in remainder became, or professed to be, a Roman Catholic, then the interest was to be forfeited. The Court of Appeal

---

[190] In *Re Vaughan* [1925] I.R. 67, a testator who died in 1923 devised and bequeathed all his freehold and leasehold estate to trustees in trust for his wife for life and after her death for such persons as she should by deed or will appoint. By a codicil he provided that in the case that any person who might come into possession of the property should "profess to be, or become a Roman Catholic, or marry a Roman Catholic", the bequest to him or her was to be "absolutely void". It was held that the gift in the will of a life estate followed by a general power of appointment gave the wife an absolute interest which had already vested before the codicil and therefore the attempt to impose a condition subsequent in the codicil was ineffective. The decision did not deal with the issue of public policy or human rights.

[191] [1951] I.R. 216.

[192] [1955] I.R. 89.

[193] [1949] N.I. 49.

for Northern Ireland, consisting of only two judges, held: (1) that the term "Roman Catholic" was not void for uncertainty; and (2) that where the choice of religion may involve a forfeiture, the court will not hold the beneficiary to have made a binding choice until he or she is of age, so such a condition did not interfere with the parent's right to determine the religious education of the child. The court went on to hold that since the deed had been executed without the benefit of legal advice, the son was in principle entitled to have it set aside for undue influence; however, the court divided on the question of whether the son had abandoned his right by delaying in commencing the proceedings. Since the Court of Appeal was split on this point, the High Court judgment refusing rectification was allowed to stand.

8–143 The House of Lords in *Blathwayt v Cawley (Lord)*[194] held there was no public policy prohibiting religious discrimination by a testator in framing the provisions of a will. In that case a testator had made a gift by will to a person on the condition that the property was to be forfeited if the donee of the gift became a Roman Catholic.[195] Lord Wilberforce, while conceding that conditions which discriminated on religious grounds "are, or at least are becoming, inconsistent with standards now widely accepted", did not feel able to introduce a rule against them, both on the narrow ground that the particular will before him had been before the courts on previous occasions and had not been impugned on that ground, but also because such a rule would interfere with testamentary freedom, which he therefore impliedly treated as having a superior value.[196]

8–144 Lord Cross recognised that "it is true that it is widely thought nowadays that it is wrong for a government to treat some of its citizens less favourably than others because of differences in their religious beliefs", but went on to say that "it does not follow from that that it is against public policy for an adherent of one religion to distinguish in disposing of his property between adherents of his faith and those of another". If it were, he thought that it would amount to saying that, although it is in order for a person to have a mild preference for one religion as opposed to another, it would be "disreputable for him to be convinced of the importance of holding true religious beliefs and of the fact that his religious beliefs are the true ones".

8–145 However, the issue was not one of the strength or weakness of the testator's adherence to his or her own religious beliefs. A court could, with consistency, uphold the right of religious freedom and yet at the same time deny that a person is justified in using his or her property as a means of inducing another person to give up his or her faith, or to gain a convert to the property owner's preferred religion. Had either of these two cases occurred in Ireland,

---

[194] [1976] A.C. 397.
[195] [1976] A.C. 397.
[196] [1976] A.C. 397 at 426.

the court would have been bound to consider the issue as a conflict between competing freedoms: the freedom of the property owner to make such disposi- tions as he or she may choose, and the freedom of the donee to practise his or her religion free of interference. The religious freedom of the donor was not in issue, because the freedom of the donor to practise his or her religion would be unaffected. Moreover, a condition which attempts to induce the donee to put his or her own financial interest before moral or religious belief is arguably in itself an invasion of the donee's freedom of religious belief and should be held void for that reason.

Equal Status Acts 2000–2015

8–146 Section 6 of the Equal Status Act 2000, as amended,[197] provides that a person shall not discriminate, on the grounds specified in the Act, on "dis- posing of any estate or interest in premises". Prohibited grounds are gender, marital status, family status, sexual orientation, religion, age (except where a person is under the age of 18[198]), disability, race, colour, nationality or ethnic or national origins, membership of the traveller community, and victimisation, i.e. where a person has applied for redress on any of the above grounds.[199] The grounds apply where the condition exists, or did in the past or may possi- bly in future. Family status includes being pregnant, being a parent or a person in *loco parentis* and being a resident primary carer.[200]

8–147 Section 6, however, exempts disposal by will or gift,[201] and any dis- posal of an estate or interest which is not available to the public generally or a section of the public,[202] the provision of accommodation by a person in a part (other than a separate and self-contained part) of the person's home, or where it affects the person's private or family life or that of any other person residing in the home.[203]

8–148 As de Londras[204] points out, these exemptions are so far-reaching as to appear to remove determinable and conditional dispositions of fees simple from the general principle of non-discrimination embodied in the Equal Status

---

[197] Equality Act 2004 s.49; Equality (Miscellaneous Provisions) Act 2015 s.14.

[198] Equal Status Act 2000 s.3(3)(a), as amended by Equality Act 2004 s.48(b).

[199] Equal Status Act 2000 ss.2, 3 and 4, as amended.

[200] Equal Status Act 2000 s.2.

[201] Equal Status Act 2000 s.6(2)(a).

[202] Equal Status Act 2000 s.6(2)(e).

[203] Equal Status Act 2000 s.6(2)(d).

[204] F. de Londras, *Principles of Irish Property Law*, 2nd edn (Dublin: Clarus Press, 2011), para.4–35.

Act 2000. Indeed, the Act seems careful, perhaps too careful,[205] to exclude an area defined in terms of private accommodation from the Act, including tenancies. However, what the Act does not prohibit is not thereby legitimised. The extent to which it is, or is not, permissible to discriminate in determinable and conditional fees continues to be governed by the courts in applying the tests already discussed, and in addition, the human rights obligations of the State under the European Convention on Human Rights (ECHR) and the ECHR Act 2003.

European Convention on Human Rights

8–149 Article 14 of the ECHR provides that the rights and freedoms in the ECHR should be enjoyed without discrimination on grounds of sex, race, religion, national or social origin, etc. or other status. Article 14 therefore only becomes operative once the breach of a substantive right or freedom has been established. As to property, Art.1 of the First Optional Protocol of the ECHR protects the peaceful enjoyment of "possessions" and requires that no one shall be deprived of them, except in the public interest, etc., but, as de Londras argues,[206] this does not seem language appropriate to control restrictions imposed on the acquisition of a limited interest in property. It would be difficult for such a person to argue, having accepted a determinable or conditional fee simple, that a subsequent forfeiture would amount to a deprivation of property, since it had always been subject to such a restriction. De Londras further argues, with cogency, that the only immediate prospect of increased control over discrimination in this area would be a principled extension of the decision in *Re Dunne*[207] to include all grounds of discrimination as being contrary to public policy. It could also be argued that for the State to lend its support in any way to the enforcement of such restrictions would be a breach of its obligations under the ECHR.

---

[205] Section 8 of the Equal Status Act 2000 bans discrimination in "private" clubs, i.e. clubs to which membership is restricted. See *Equality Authority v Cuddy* [2010] 1 I.R. 671. Section 12 prohibits advertising which indicates an intention to engage in prohibited conduct, but that would appear to allow advertising of accommodation in the "private area" defined by the Act, in which discrimination is allowed, i.e. it would allow discriminatory terms to appear in such advertising, even though the advertising is, by its nature, public and could therefore be seen by groups discriminated against. See also, *Equality Authority v Portmarnock Golf Club* [2009] IESC 73.

[206] de Londras, *Principles of Irish Property Law* (2011), para.4–32.

[207] [1988] I.R. 155.

CHAPTER 9

Fee Farm Grants

How now! A kiss in fee farm!

— Shakespeare, *Troilus and Cressida*, Act III, Scene 2

INTRODUCTION

9–01 A fee farm grant is a fee simple held subject to a rent payable by the grantee and his or her successors in title to the grantor and his or her successors in title.[1] Fee farm grants are a peculiar, but not unique, feature of the Irish law of real property.[2] The surviving feudal fee farm grants, however, do appear to be unique to Ireland.

9–02 The Land and Conveyancing Law Reform Act 2009[3] ("LCLRA 2009") prohibits the creation of fee farm grants in future, and provides that an attempt to do so vests in the purported grantee a fee simple "freed and discharged from any covenant or other provision relating to rent, but all other covenants or provisions continue in force so far as consistent with the nature of a fee simple."[4] However, the LCLRA 2009 does not convert existing fee farm grants or abolish such rents[5] existing at law when the LCLRA 2009 came into force. They continue as legal estates and may be disposed of.[6] There are three major types of fee farm grant in Ireland:

---

[1] *Browning v Beston* (1553) Plowd. 131 at 132a. Section 3 of the LCLRA 2009 defines "fee farm grant" as any "(a) grant of a fee simple, or (b) lease for ever or in perpetuity, reserving or charging a perpetual rent, whether or not the relationship of landlord and tenant is created between the grantor and grantee, and includes a sub-fee farm grant". It is unclear why a lease "for ever or in perpetuity" is included. Leases for lives renewable forever were never classified as fee farm grants.

[2] In some parts of England rentcharges are commonly reserved on a grant in fee simple, which is one kind of fee farm rent, and the only kind in England: C. Harpum, S. Bridge and M. Dixon, *Megarry & Wade: The Law of Real Property*, 8th edn (London: Sweet & Maxwell, 2012), para.6–013. The Rentcharges Act 1977 (England and Wales) prevents the creation of rentcharges in future, with some exceptions, e.g. under family trusts of land: *Megarry & Wade* (2012), paras 31–018 to 31–019.

[3] LCLRA 2009 s.12(1).

[4] LCLRA 2009 s.12(3).

[5] It was thought that this would be contrary to the protection of property rights in Art.40.2 of the Constitution.

[6] LCLRA 2009 s.12(4)–(6)

1. Feudal tenure;
2. Leasehold tenure (hybrid)
   (a) Conversion grants
       (i) from Bishop's Leases
       (ii) from College Leases
       (iii) under the Renewable Leasehold Conversion Act 1849
       (iv) under s.74 of the Landlord and Tenant Act 1980
   (b) Deasy's Act grants; and
3. No tenure at all—rentcharge fee farm grants.

FEUDAL TENURE

9–03 It has already been noted that the LCLRA 2009[7] specifically exempts from the abolition of feudal tenure "any fee farm grant made in derogation of the Statute *Quia Emptores* 1290".

Origins

9–04 Before *Quia Emptores* 1290 a private person who had a fee simple could make a grant by subinfeudation in fee simple. If this was done at an economic rent, it was called a fee farm grant. After 1290 *Quia Emptores* forbade such grants by all parties other than the Crown. This type of fee farm grant is more common in Northern Ireland, having been frequently created during the Ulster Plantation. Land was granted by the Crown to a grantee in fee simple, often in return for a *chief rent*, or *quit rent*.[8] After 1662 the Crown could still create fee farm grants provided the tenure was "free and common socage".

9–05 Some grants by the Crown in Ireland contained a licence giving the *grantees* themselves the power to subinfeudate further *non obstante Quia Emptores*, i.e. notwithstanding *Quia Emptores* 1290. These grants seem to have been part of the plantation policy of creating a landowning class dependent on the Crown, and examples can be found in both parts of Ireland.[9] Since *Quia Emptores* expressly prohibited subinfeudation in fee simple by private persons, the *non obstante* clause was an exercise of the "dispensing power", i.e. the prerogative power of the king to exempt individuals from the operation of statutes. There was little doubt as to the validity of the power before

---

[7] LCLRA 2009 s.9(3)(c).

[8] Not to be confused with quit rents in England, where the term was used to refer to rent payable by a copyhold tenant to the lord of the manor: J.C.W. Wylie, *Irish Land Law*, 5th edn (Haywards Heath: Bloomsbury Professional, 2013), para.6.09. Copyhold, to the extent that it existed, has long disappeared in Ireland.

[9] *Calendar of State Papers Relating to Ireland 1633–1647*, i, 4 (12 March 1633, Brittas); ii, 353 (17 January 1664, manor of Roscommon); ii, 438 (28 September 1664, manor of Mount Kennedy, Wicklow); A. Lyall, "Quia Emptores in Ireland" in O. Breen, J. Casey and A. Kerr (eds), *Liber Memorialis: Professor James Brady* (Dublin: Round Hall Sweet & Maxwell, 2001), pp.275–294.

the English Bill of Rights,[10] but by the 17th century it had come to be seen as despotic and inconsistent with the supremacy of Parliament, established by the Civil War between King and Parliament. In England King James II asserted the dispensing power, seemingly as a means of exempting Catholics from the Penal Laws, and this contributed to him being deposed in 1688. The dispensing power was abolished in England by the Bill of Rights 1689.[11] In Ireland no Bill of Rights was enacted[12] but seemingly the dispensing power was not used after 1689. At any rate, James II's Stuart predecessors had purported to exercise the power in Ireland in the preceding decades and a compliant Irish Parliament had confirmed the *non obstante* grants.[13] Some feudal fee farm grants survive today, although they are few in number. The validity of such titles was recognised in the 19th century.[14]

9–06 The following diagram shows the situation that obtained after such a grant and further subinfeudation by the grantee:

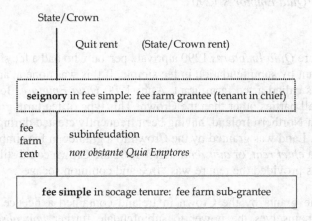

9–07 Hence there are two types of feudal fee farm grant. The first is the original grant from the Crown to the grantee in fee simple at a quit rent. The second is the subinfeudation by the grantee in exercise of the *non obstante* power,

---

[10] *Case of Non Obstante or Dispensing Power* (1581) 12 Co. Rep. 18; *Godden v Hales* (1686) 2 Show. K.B .475. Licences in mortmain, i.e. exemptions granted by the king from the Statute of Mortmain, had been an example, but after the Bill of Rights such licences were granted under statute.

[11] 1Wm & Mar sess 2, c. 2.

[12] W.N. Osborough, "The Failure to Enact an Irish Bill of Rights: A Gap in Irish Constitutional History" (1998) 33 Ir. Jur. 392.

[13] Settlement of Ireland Acts 1634 (10 Car I c 3; 10 Car I sess 3 cc 2, 3); 1639 (15 Car I sess 2 c 6); 1665 (17 & 18 Car II c 2); 1695 (7 Wm III c 3). Section 1 of the 1634 statute (10 Car I sess 3 c 2) includes among defects, "lack or omission of sufficient and special non obstantes of particular statutes", not conceding any doubt as to the *non obstante* clauses themselves. *Non obstante* grants continued to be made after 1634. The Settlement of Ireland Acts were repealed in Ireland by the Statute Law Revision (Pre-Union Irish Statutes) Act 1962.

[14] *Verschoyle v Perkins* (1847) 13 Ir. Eq. R. 72; *Delacherois v Delacherois* (1864) 11 H.L.C. 62.

which is a sub-grant in fee simple reserving a rent payable to the grantee by the sub-grantee.

9–08 The interest of the grantor is not a reversion. There could be no reversion on a fee simple.[15] The grantor has a seignory in fee simple. Freehold tenure exists between the grantor and the grantee and the service of the tenure is a rent. Previously the grantor, as lord of the tenure, had the incident of escheat. Since the Wills (Ireland) Act 1634 that incident could be defeated by a will made by the tenant.

9–09 Section 11 of the Succession Act 1965 abolished escheat to the State and to a mesne lord for want of heirs. Therefore, if the heirs of the sub-grantee die out, the estate will pass to the State as "ultimate intestate successor". The State would then become liable to pay the fee farm rent to the grantee, i.e. the "tenant in chief". This would create the odd situation where the State would hold land of the grantor (a private person) as its feudal superior. The State Property Act 1954[16] provides that in such a case the Minister for Public Expenditure and Reform may disclaim the interest and vest it in the grantor or his or her successors. It also provides that the rent shall thereupon cease.

9–10 Even where the grantor holds by such a title, courts have leaned against construing the grant as a subinfeudation where another interpretation is possible. *Delacherois v Delacherois*[17] concerned a grant by Charles I of estates in free and common socage with a licence to grant in fee simple, notwithstanding *Quia Emptores*. In 1721 the holders of the grant granted a part of the estate in fee simple subject to a rent and reserved an express power of distress. A successor to the holder of the original grant made a will devising the entire estate. The gift was only valid as to the part if the grantor had retained some interest having made the grant in fee simple. It was held as follows:

(a) The grant of a part of the estates, if it were to take effect by subinfeudation, would have to show an express intention to do so.

(b) The reservation of an express power of distress ousted the intention to subinfeudate and the grant was an outright sale of the part of the estates, reserving only a rentcharge.

(c) Hence, at the time of the will the successor of the holder of the whole estate had no interest left in the part granted and so no right in such land passed under the will.

---

[15] *Delacherois v Delacherois* (1864) 11 H.L. Cas. 62.
[16] State Property Act 1954 s.32.
[17] (1864) 11 H.L. Cas. 62.

Characteristics
Words of Limitation
9–11 Words of limitation would have been necessary unless one of the old forms of conveyance had been used. Early English and Irish statutes may apply to the power. One statute which did so expressly was the Fee Farm Rents (Ireland) Act 1851, which extended the remedies for recovery of the rent, but the Act was repealed by LCLRA 2009.[18]

Rent
9–12 The fee farm rent is a rent service, carrying with it the ancient common law self-help remedy of distress, but that remedy conflicts with the European Convention on Human Rights (ECHR) and the ECHR Act 2003, at least as to dwelling houses, and has been abolished in relation to them.[19] Since it did not require resort to a court, it may be vulnerable to constitutional challenge and its abolition has been recommended by the Law Reform Commission.[20]

Forfeiture
9–13 Under the principle of feudal tenure, the tenant's denial of the lord's title forfeits the tenant's interest. There will be forfeiture for non-payment of rent either if the agreement to pay rent is a condition of the grant or if there is an express clause for forfeiture. The grantee has a right of relief against forfeiture in equity.

Covenants
9–14 As to covenants in the grant, the law as to their enforcement is obscure, since it depends on the extent to which covenants run in feudal freehold tenure. In *Chandos (Duchess) v Brownlow*,[21] Lord Fitzgibbon L.C.[22] had to consider the running of covenants in freehold tenure in the context of a lease for lives. He held that the Irish Grantees of Reversions Act 1634[23] applied and that,[24]

> "[f]irst, the covenant must relate to the land or other thing demised; or to use a term of art, it must be a covenant running with the land. And secondly, there must be a privity of estate between the assignee and the covenantee".

---

[18] It provides that a person entitled to the rent has all the remedies provided for by the Renewable Leasehold Conversion Act 1849 except ejectment.

[19] By s.19 of the Housing (Miscellaneous Provisions) Act 1992.

[20] Law Reform Commission, *Consultation Paper on the General Law of Landlord and Tenant* (LRC CP 28-2003), pp.121–122.

[21] (1791) 2 Ridg. P.C. 345.

[22] (1791) 2 Ridg. P.C. 345 at 406–407.

[23] (1634) 10 Car. I, sess. 2, c 4 (Ir.). In the same terms as the English Act, 32 Hen. VIII, c 34 (Eng.), 1540.

[24] (1791) 2 Ridg. P.C. 345 at 407–408.

He continued[25]:

"The covenant runs, not with the land, but with the estate of the lessor in the land—a covenant, which runs with the land, attends the estate which the lessor had in the lands when he made the lease ... but the moment that estate is spent, the covenant is at an end, as against the possessor of the land."

9–15 In theory, it would seem that all covenants which are not purely personal will run at law both as to the benefit and burden, i.e. both parties as between whom tenure exists can both sue and be sued on the covenant.

Redemption

9–16 The Chief Rents Redemption (Ireland) Act 1864 provided a mechanism whereby the tenant could redeem the quit rent by agreement, but this Act has been repealed.[26] There would not appear to be any objection to redemption by agreement in any case. There is a controversy as to whether the Redemption of Rent (Ireland) Act 1891[27] applies to a feudal fee farm grant. The Act only applies to agricultural land and gives an occupying tenant the right to redeem the rent. Most fee farm grants over such land would not have survived the land purchase schemes which provided for redemption, and so the issue is probably of little importance.

9–17 The definition of a "lease" under the Landlord and Tenant (Ground Rents) (No. 2) Act 1978 includes a fee farm grant. Where the conditions in the Act in ss.9 and 10 are satisfied (restricting the operation of the Act to occupational, building and proprietary leases), it would seem that the holder of an existing fee farm grant has the "right to a fee simple" under the Act. It could be argued against this that the holder already has a fee simple. However, it must be assumed that the phrase refers to an "ordinary" fee simple, since the legislation is intended to recognise the holder of an interest coming within the Act as the substantial owner of the premises and to allow him or her to acquire a fee simple free of rent. Since, however, the Landlord and Tenant (Ground Rents) Act 1967, which the No. 2 Act of 1978 modifies, defines "fee simple" as not including a fee farm grant, the grantee can only exercise the power if he or she is willing to redeem any other rents affecting the fee simple. That is, where superior fee farm interests exist, by earlier subinfeudations, the fee farm grantee "in demesne" will have to redeem those also in order to acquire the fee simple free of rent under the Act.

---

[25] (1791) 2 Ridg. P.C. 345 at 410.
[26] LCLRA 2009 s.8, Sch.2, Pt 4.
[27] This statute was expressly retained by Statute Law Revision Act 2007 s.2, Sch.1, Pt 3.

9–18 Another kind of fee farm grant occurs when the grant of a fee simple estate also creates the modern relationship of landlord and tenant. Such has been held to occur in Ireland under various statutes.

Conversion Grants
Origins
9–19 All these arose from the statutory conversion of perpetual or virtually perpetual leases. There are four types.

Church Temporalities Act 1833
9–20 These arise by conversion of "Bishop's Leases". Irish statutes limited the power of bishops to grant leases of land belonging to the Church of Ireland. Bishops thereafter took to granting leases with a covenant to renew, subject to payment of a fine.[28] Hence, they were virtually perpetual interests. This Act gave the tenants power to buy the fee simple subject to the fee farm rent. The Irish Church Act 1869, which disestablished the Church of Ireland, prohibited any more conversion grants after 1 January 1873. They were therefore all created between 1833 and 1874. Most would have been redeemed under the Land Purchase Acts and the Redemption of Rent (Ireland) Act 1891.[29]

Trinity College Dublin Leasing and Perpetuity Act 1851
9–21 These are converted "College Leases". Various statutes limited the power of Trinity College Dublin to grant leases. The College avoided these provisions by granting renewable leases that were virtually perpetual interests. Section 3 of the Act allowed tenants to demand a grant of a fee simple at a rent, providing the tenant applied within four years of the passing of the Act.

Renewable Leasehold Conversion Act 1849
9–22 This statute and the Renewable Leasehold Conversion (Ireland) Act 1868 were, together, the main source of conversion fee farm grants. Both Acts were repealed by the LCLRA 2009.[30] In the 18th and 19th centuries landowners granted "leases for lives", i.e. estates *pur autre vie*, at a rent with covenants for renewal of the lives upon payment of a sum of money called a fine. Again, these were virtually perpetual interests, especially as the courts in Ireland recognised that the tenant had an equity to renew, known as "the old equity of the country", even after all the lives had died and the common law interest had therefore come to an end. The right was confirmed by s.1 of the Tenantry Act 1779.

---

[28] For example, *Haig v Homan* (1841) 8 Cl. & F. 8; *Lanauze v Malone* (1855) 3 Ir. Ch. R. 354.
[29] This statute was expressly retained by Statute Law Revision Act 2007 s.2, Sch.1, Pt 3.
[30] LCLRA 2009 s.8, Sch.2, Pt 4.

9–23 As to such leases existing on 1 August 1849, the Renewable Leasehold Conversion Act 1849 (the "1849 Act") gave lessees the right to a fee farm grant[31] from the lessor. The rent was to be recoverable by *leasehold* remedies, including ejectment.[32] Where the power was exercised, it has been assumed that the effect of the 1849 Act was to convert the pre-existing freehold tenure into leasehold tenure. Although the tenure of leases for lives had always been freehold, Irish judges had nevertheless treated the tenure as identical to leasehold tenure.

9–24 Section 37 provided that leases for lives made *after* 1 August 1849 operated automatically as fee farm grants under the provisions of the 1849 Act.[33] The 1849 Act also applied to leases for years with a covenant for renewal.[34] Under the LCLRA 2009 any grant of, or contract to grant, a lease for lives after 1 December 2009 is void both at law and in equity.[35]

Landlord and Tenant (Amendment) Act 1980 s.74

9–25 Leases existing on 1 August 1849 and not converted under the power contained in the 1849 Act and still subsisting in 1980, were converted on 8 September 1980[36] into a fee simple by this section. The fee simple was a "graft" on the previous interest. The "rights and equities" affecting the lease for lives continue to affect the fee simple. The section therefore seems to have created a new category of fee farm grants. Wylie argues that the rent no longer applies because the definition of "fee simple" incorporated in the Act excludes a fee farm rent.[37] However, what follows the words "fee simple", i.e. the "graft" provision, appears inconsistent with that interpretation. It would also be anomalous if a person were to be in a better position as a result of *not* exercising the power under the 1849 Act than he or she would be in if it had been exercised. Also, abolition of the rent without compensation is open to constitutional challenge and an interpretation that is constitutional is to be preferred to one that is not.[38]

9–26 It is open to question whether the effect of s.74 was to convert the freehold tenure of such "leases" into leasehold tenure. Judges in Ireland treated the tenure in leases for lives as leasehold in all but name, but it could be argued that the tenure has not been converted to leasehold and that Deasy's Act, for example, does not apply. The provisions of the 1849 Act would not seem to

---

[31] Provided the lessor had a fee simple. If the lessor had only a life estate, a grant in fee farm did not bind the remaindermen or reversioners: *Brereton v Twohey* (1859) 8 Ir. C.L.R. 190.

[32] Renewable Leasehold Conversion Act 1849 s.20.

[33] See *Gun-Cunningham v Byrne* (1892) 30 L.R. Ir. 384 (Land Commission).

[34] *Re Gore* (1859) 8 Ir. Ch. R. 589.

[35] LCLRA 2009 s.14.

[36] The commencement date of the Act: S.I. No. 271 of 1980.

[37] Wylie, *Irish Land Law* (2013), para.4.82.

[38] It was the intention of the Government in introducing the Bill to preserve the rent: see *Dáil Debates*, 24 February 1980, col.514.

apply to grants within s.74 of the Landlord and Tenant (Amendment) Act 1980, since they are not converted by the Act. These points should be borne in mind in considering the following characteristics.

Characteristics
Words of Limitation

9–27 *Re Johnston's Estate*[39] held that in the case of a purported grant of a lease for lives after 1 August 1849, the grant took effect under the 1849 Act as a fee farm grant and no words of limitation were therefore required to create the fee simple. On the face of it, the deed created a lease for lives, but under the 1849 Act, took effect as a fee farm grant.

Rent

9–28 Sections 20 and 21 of the 1849 Act provided that the rent was recoverable by the same remedies as for a leasehold rent and in addition included a special statutory remedy of ejectment for non-payment, but as already noted, the 1849 Act has been repealed by the LCLRA 2009. The sections never applied to a conversion grant under s.74 of the Landlord and Tenant (Amendment) Act 1980.

Forfeiture

9–29 Where a statutory remedy of ejectment applied, it made an express clause for forfeiture unnecessary. The 1849 Act conferred a statutory remedy of ejectment on fee farm grants converted under the Act, but the 1849 Act was repealed by the LCLRA 2009.

9–30 On the other hand, s.52 of Deasy's Act provides for a statutory remedy of ejectment for non-payment of rent not only in the case of Deasy's Act grants but also other landlord and tenant relationships. It is arguable that this remedy is no longer available as to grants in respect of dwelling houses where the fee farm grant comes within the definition of a "ground rent" under the Landlord and Tenant (Ground Rents) (No. 2) Act 1978, so that the tenant has the right to acquire the unincumbered fee simple. The argument is as follows. Section 27 of the No. 2 Act of 1978 provides that s.52 of Deasy's Act shall not apply where a person has a right to acquire the fee simple in a "dwellinghouse" within the meaning of the No. 2 Act of 1978. The reason for s.27 is clear: it would be inappropriate to give such a radical remedy to the person entitled to the rent where the tenant is in a position to acquire the fee simple free of the rent. The No. 2 Act of 1978 does not specifically take account of the similar situation of conversion fee farm grants where the owner of the rent had a similar remedy under ss.20 and 21 of the 1849 Act. However, it would be equally inappropriate for such a remedy to be given where the fee farm grantee had the right to acquire the fee simple in a dwelling house free of the rent.

---

[39] [1911] 1 I.R. 215.

9–31 Section 14 of the Conveyancing Act 1881,[40] which contains restrictions on and relief against forfeiture clauses in leases, does not apply to covenants to pay rent.

Covenants

9–32 What effect do covenants in the original lease have after the conversion of the estate into a fee farm grant and therefore a fee simple? A particular problem here relates to covenants which purport to restrict the alienation by the tenant, either by sale, assignment, or subletting. These are not uncommon in a lease, but in a fee simple they were inconsistent with the Statute *Quia Emptores* 1290 and the policy of the law, of which it was an early expression, that a fee simple be a freely marketable commodity, sometimes reified into the notion that such a condition is "repugnant" to the "nature" of the fee simple estate. Such conditions are now inconsistent also with the restatement of the principle of free alienability of the fee simple by s.9(4) of the LCLRA 2009.

9–33 In *Re McNaul's Estate*,[41] a covenant in the original lease for lives provided that the tenant was to pay an increased rent if he alienated without the lessor's consent to someone other than the child or grandchild of the lessor. The Irish Court of Appeal held (1) that it was doubtful if such a condition would be valid in an ordinary conveyance in fee simple, but (2) that it was valid in a fee farm grant by conversion under the 1849 Act. The court expressly overruled the earlier case of *Billing v Welch*.[42] In that case it had been held that if a covenant would be void in a grant of an ordinary fee simple, it should also be void in a grant under the 1849 Act. The court in *Re McNaul's Estate*[43] took the view that a fee simple by conversion was a special statutory fee simple and that the common law rules did not apply.

9–34 This was always an unsatisfactory result. The real issue was whether fees simple should be subjected to a leasehold regime, in the sense of rent and covenants restricting alienability. If such restrictions do apply, then in principle so should the statutory controls over such conditions which are now contained in s.66 of the Landlord and Tenant (Amendment) Act 1980. These apply to "tenements" as defined by s.5 of the 1980 Act, i.e. land mostly covered in buildings where there is a lease and it had not been granted for temporary convenience only. "Lease" in the 1980 Act includes a fee farm grant. Section 66 provides that a covenant seeking absolutely to prohibit alienation takes effect as a covenant not to alienate without the landlord's consent. Where there is a covenant

---

[40] Conveyancing Act 1881 s.14(8), as amended by Conveyancing Act 1892 ss.2 and 5 (not repealed by the LCLRA 2009).
[41] [1902] 1 I.R. 114.
[42] (1871) I.R. 6 C.L. 88, and impliedly *Re Quin* (1859) 8 Ir. Ch. R. 578.
[43] [1902] 1 I.R. 114.

not to alienate without the landlord's consent, the section provides that consent shall not be unreasonably withheld.[44]

9–35 However, the argument in favour of free alienability has been strengthened in this context by the re-assertion of the principle of alienability of the fee simple by s.9(4) of the LCLRA 2009, which is categorical in terms and contains no express exceptions for "special" kinds of fee simple, especially in relation to fees simple converted from perpetual or virtually perpetual interests. One major theme of the LCLRA 2009 is to draw a clear distinction between freely alienable, full fee simple ownership and private landlord and tenant relationships which are regulated by statute, and to remove the half-way house of hybrid interest that have for so long dogged Irish property law.

Redemption

9–36 There was no authority as to the application of the Chief Rents Redemption (Ireland) Act 1864, but the Act has now in any case been repealed by the LCLRA 2009.[45] The Redemption of Rent (Ireland) Act 1891[46] applies to conversion fee farm grants over agricultural land. The 1891 Act was part of the land purchase legislation and aimed to remove incumbrances on the fee simple.

9–37 In the Landlord and Tenant (Ground Rents) (No. 2) Act 1978, "lease" includes a fee farm grant and so the Act applies if the grant qualifies as a "ground rent" under ss.9 and 10.

Deasy's Act Grants
Origin

9–38 This is the largest group of surviving fee farm grants existing in Ireland today. Section 3 of the Landlord and Tenant (Amendment) Act 1860 (Deasy's Act) provides that the relationship of landlord and tenant is founded on contract, express or implied, and not upon tenure or service, and "shall be deemed to subsist in all cases in which there shall be an agreement by one party to hold land from or under another in consideration of any rent". Section 4 speaks of leases or contracts "whereby the relation of landlord and tenant is intended to be created for any freehold estate or interest …" . Irish courts held this to mean that the relationship could be created under Deasy's Act even where the *estate* granted was freehold.[47] In *Chute v Busteed*,[48] it was held that ss.3 and 4 allowed

---

[44] Landlord and Tenant (Amendment) Act 1980 s.3.

[45] LCLRA 2009 s.8, Sch.2, Pt 4.

[46] This statute was expressly retained by Statute Law Revision Act 2007 s.2, Sch.1, Pt 3. See *Hamilton v Casey* [1894] 2 I.R. 224 (grants under the Church Temporalities Act 1833); *Gormill v Lyne* (1894) 28 I.L.T.R. 44 (Trinity College Dublin Act 1851); *Langtry v Sheridan* (1896) 30 I.L.T.R. 64; *Gun-Cunningham v Byrne* (1892) 30 L.R. Ir. 384 (Land Commission (grant under the Renewable Leasehold Conversion Act 1849)).

[47] *Stevelly v Murphy* (1840) 2 Ir. Eq. R. 448 (grant of fee simple at a rent before Deasy's Act could not create landlord and tenant relationship).

[48] (1865) 16 Ir. C.L.R. 222.

fee farm grants to be created in this way.[49] In Ireland, a person could therefore in the past grant a fee simple reserving a rent without creating a separate rent-charge. Hence, in a Deasy's Act grant the *estate* is freehold but the *tenure* (if one should still use the term in view of s.3), is leasehold. Such a grant must indicate an express intention to create the relationship of landlord and tenant. Like other fee farm grants, an attempt to create one now results in the grant of a fee simple "freed and discharged from any covenant or other provision relating to rent, but all other covenants or provisions continue in force so far as consistent with the nature of a fee simple".[50]

9–39 In *Irish Land Commission v Holmes*,[51] it was held that in such a grant the grantor did not retain any reversion: there can be no reversion after a fee simple. There is simply a statutory right to recover the fee simple if the covenants are broken. The fee simple is a conditional one, the sanction being the statutory right rather than a right of entry.

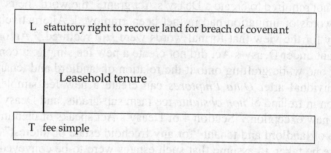

9–40 In view of ss.3 and 4 of Deasy's Act, there seems no reason why a Deasy's Act grantee should not make a Deasy's Act sub-grant, creating a further "layer" of leasehold tenure and retaining a statutory right to recover the fee simple.

Characteristics
Words of Limitation
9–41 One view[52] is that s.3 of Deasy's Act 1860 abolished the requirement of words of limitation in the creation of a grant taking effect under the statute. On this view, the creation of landlord and tenant relations is, under s.3, founded upon contract and so one must look to the agreement of the parties to see how

---

[49] It was also held that Deasy's Act was not retrospective, and so such grants could only be created from 1 January 1861 onwards.

[50] LCLRA 2009 s.12.

[51] (1898) 32 I.L.T.R. 85.

[52] R. Cherry, *The Irish Land Law and Land Purchase Acts 1860 to 1901*, 3rd edn (Dublin: J. Falconer, 1903), p.5, note (c), citing *Twaddle v Murphy* (1881) 8 L.R. Ir. 123 and the following dictum of Palles C.B. in *Hodges v Clarke* (1883) 17 I.L.T.R. 82 at 84: "When we are obliged to determine for what period a tenant holds, we are bound to look to the agreement of the parties."

long the relationship is to subsist. If this is so, then "to A for ever" would have granted a fee simple and therefore a Deasy's Act grant. "To A" would not, as there must be a contractual intention to create a fee simple within the Act. Even if this view is correct, it would only have referred to the creation of a new Deasy's Act grant, not to the assignment of an existing one, since an assignment did not fall within s.3.[53] In *Twaddle v Murphy*,[54] a deed, which was confused to say the least, "granted and demised" land

> *to A and B, their heirs and assigns, for the lives of C, D and E, or for 999 years, or for ever, which ever should last the longest.*

It was held that this created a fee farm grant. The fee simple "absorbed" the lesser estates.

9–42 Although Cherry cites the case in favour of the view that words of limitation are not required to create a Deasy's Act grant,[55] the word "heirs" was used and so words of limitation had in fact been employed. Alternatively, there is authority for the view that formal words were still required.[56] An original fee farm grant under Deasy's Act did not create a new fee simple: it conveyed the existing one while grafting onto it the relation of landlord and tenant. No private individual after *Quia Emptores* can create a new fee simple, with the exception in Ireland of *non obstante* fee farm sub-grants, and Deasy's Act created no new exception.[57] Section 4 of Deasy's Act speaks of creating the relationship of landlord and tenant "for any freehold estate or interest" and might therefore be taken to assume that such estates were to be conveyed as before the Act. Section 51 of the Conveyancing Act 1881, now repealed,[58] passed after Deasy's Act, introduced "in fee simple" as an alternative to the common law formula, and in so doing assumed that the common law words were still required before the Act. The 1881 Act did not contain any special exceptions for Deasy's Act grants. The standard words used by practitioners to create a Deasy's Act grant were:

> *to A, his [or her] heirs and assigns for ever.*

Rent
9–43 The landlord has the usual remedies: an action for debt and distress, which did not have to be expressly reserved since it applied automatically from

---

[53] *Re Courtney* [1981] N.I. 58.

[54] (1881) 8 L.R. Ir. 123.

[55] Cherry, *Irish Land Law and Land Purchase Acts* (1903), p.5.

[56] *Re Ford & Ferguson's Contract* [1906] 1 I.R. 607 ("unto and to the use of the grantee for ever" held insufficient to pass the fee simple on a new grant under Deasy's Act).

[57] *Irish Land Commission v Holmes* (1898) 32 I.L.T.R. 85. There can be no reversion on a fee simple and the grantor does not retain a seignory under Deasy's Act: the grantor's fee simple passes to the grantee subject to conditions which may lead to its return.

[58] LCLRA 2009 s.8, Sch.2, Pt 4.

the creation of leasehold tenure, just as it did in the case of freehold tenure. Distress is essentially the ancient common law self-help remedy which was available to the lord of a feudal tenure and then applied by analogy to lease-hold relationships.[59] Since it does not require resort to a court, it is probably contrary to the Constitution,[60] the ECHR Act 2003 and ECHR provisions,[61] at least as to dwelling houses, and has been abolished in Ireland in relation to them.[62] Its general abolition has been recommended by the Law Reform Commission.[63] It has been abolished in Northern Ireland.[64]

9–44 Section 52 of Deasy's Act provides a statutory action for ejectment, thus dispensing with the requirement at common law that there should be a forfeiture clause in the lease to confer such a right. This position is now modified where the rent reserved on a Deasy's Act grant qualifies as a "ground rent" within the Landlord and Tenant (Ground Rents) (No. 2) Act 1978. Section 27 of the No. 2 Act of 1978 provides that s.52 of Deasy's Act no longer applies to dwelling houses where a person "is entitled to acquire the fee simple". Section 3 of the No. 2 Act of 1978 defines "lease" to include a fee farm grant, so that a person with such an interest can enlarge it into a fee simple free of the covenants except for those preserved by s.28. A person with a Deasy's Act grant already has a fee simple vested in him or her, but the policy of the No. 2 Act of 1978 is that the tenant under the grant is the substantial owner of the property and so should not only be entitled to the fee simple free of rent, but also that a mere holder of a ground rent should not be able to disturb the possession of such an owner.

Forfeiture

9–45 There may be an express clause for forfeiture in the lease, in which case the landlord need not rely on the statutory remedy in s.52 of Deasy's Act. As to forfeiture for breach of covenants other than rent, they are governed by s.14 of the Conveyancing Act 1881, which places restrictions on their enforcement.[65]

Covenants

9–46 Deasy's Act implies certain covenants into leases and the provisions apply to grants in fee farm coming within the Act. Section 41 implies a

---

[59] *Juson v Dixon* (1813) 1 M. & S. 601 held that even an innocent stranger's goods could be seized, which was a direct analogy to the feudal law as to freehold. This would almost certainly be unconstitutional under Arts 40 and 43.

[60] Article 40.5 states: "The dwelling of every citizen is inviolable and shall not be forcibly entered save in accordance with law." The last phrase implies a proper legal process.

[61] Article 8 (respect for private and family life and the home).

[62] By s.19 of the Housing (Miscellaneous Provisions) Act 1992.

[63] Law Reform Commission, *Consultation Paper on the General Law of Landlord and Tenant* (LRC CP 28-2003), pp.121–122.

[64] Judgments (Enforcement) Act (NI) 1969 s.132, Sch.6, consolidated in Judgments Enforcement (NI) Order 1981.

[65] Retained by LCLRA 2009 s.8, Sch.2, Pt 4.

covenant by the landlord for good title and quiet enjoyment. Section 42 implies a covenant by the tenant to pay the rent, taxes and do repairs. By ss.12 and 13, successors in title to the landlord and tenant are bound by the covenants.

9–47 Does s.66 of the Landlord and Tenant (Amendment) Act 1980 apply to such grants? If so, it would seem impliedly to recognise restraints on the alienability of a fee simple estate, subject to the provisions of the section as to consent to alienation not being unreasonably withheld.

9–48 The "freehold" argument is that such restraints are contrary to *Quia Emptores* 1290 unless the restraint has a minimal effect on alienability. On this view, one should first look to see whether the restraint would have been valid if it had been contained in a grant of an ordinary fee simple. If so, it is valid in a grant in Deasy's Act, but is subject to the control of s.66.

9–49 The "leasehold" argument is that the fee simple under a Deasy's Act grant should be regarded as a special statutory fee simple to which can be appended restraints which are valid in an ordinary lease. To this it could be objected that Deasy's Act does not create the fee simple, which passes under the deed, but merely allows leasehold tenure to be created at the same time. One advantage of the Deasy's Act grant, and the reason it was used in practice, was to provide a technical means of ensuring that the benefit and burden of either restrictive or positive covenants affecting the use of the land could be made to pass to successors in title of the original grantor and grantee. Sections 40 and 48 of the LCLRA 2009 have now rendered this unnecessary by providing for the running of the benefit and burden of freehold covenants generally.

9–50 The argument seems now to be tilted in favour of the "freehold" argument by the restatement of the principle of free alienability of the fee simple by s.9(4) of the LCLRA 2009.

Redemption

9–51 The Chief Rents Redemption (Ireland) Act 1864 seems to have applied to Deasy's Act grants, but this has been repealed by the LCLRA 2009.[66] The Redemption of Rent (Ireland) Act 1891 was applied to Deasy's Act grants of agricultural land by s.14(b) of the Land Law (Ireland) Act 1896, although the latter Act was repealed by the Statute Law Revision Act 2007 which nevertheless expressly retained the 1891 Act.[67] The 1891 Act was part of the land purchase legislation and, as such, aimed to remove incumbrances on the fee simple.

---

[66] LCLRA 2009 s.8, Sch.2, Pt 4.
[67] Statute Law Revision Act 2007 s.2, Sch.1, Pt 3.

9–52 The Landlord and Tenant (Ground Rents) (No. 2) Act 1978 would seem to apply, provided the grant qualifies as a "ground rent" within the conditions laid down in ss.9 and 10 of the Act.

RENTCHARGE FEE FARM GRANTS

Introduction
9–53 An interest in the nature of a fee farm grant was created if a grantor granted a fee simple estate and at the same time created a rentcharge in his or her own favour burdening the land of the grantee. No tenure was created, either freehold or leasehold. The grantor could just as easily have created a rentcharge in favour of a third party, and could have done so in addition to the rentcharge in his or her own favour.

Characteristics
Words of Limitation
9–54 Words of limitation were the same as for a grant *inter vivos* of an ordinary fee simple, since that is what the fee simple was. Words of limitation were not required in a will, under s.94 of the Succession Act 1965. For the rentcharge, words of limitation had to be used even in a will if the grantor of the land, or any third party, was to have a rentcharge in fee simple. Section 94 of the Succession Act 1965 did not apply to a newly created rentcharge.

Rent
9–55 There is an action for debt at common law by the *pernor of the profits*, i.e. the person entitled to the profits of the rentcharge, against the *terre tenant*, i.e. the freeholder for the time being entitled in possession to the land the subject of the rentcharge.[68] As there is no tenure, the rent was a *rent seck*[69] at common law, i.e. without right of distress, unless a right of distress was expressly reserved in the grant, until a statute of Queen Anne gave an automatic right to distress to rents seck.[70] The LCLRA 2009 abolished distress for the recovery of rentcharges, which may now be recovered as simple contract debts only.[71]

Forfeiture
9–56 There is only a right to re-entry for non-payment of the rent if such a right was expressly inserted in the deed.

---

[68] *Swift v Kelly* (1889) 24 L.R. Ir. 107.
[69] Anglo-French, *rente secque*, literally "dry rent".
[70] Distress for Rent Act 1712, 11 Anne c 2 (Ir.). It also gave the remedy to chief rents. The short title was given by the Statute Law Revision (Pre-Union Irish Statutes) Act 1962, which largely retained the 18th century Irish statutes on distress.
[71] LCLRA 2009 s.42. Under the Fee Farm Rents (Ireland) Act 1851 the owner of the rentcharge had all the remedies of a landlord under a lease except ejectment, but that Act was repealed by the LCLRA 2009.

9–57 Since there is no tenure, statutory provisions applying to forfeiture of a tenancy do not apply. Thus, unlike conversion grants under the Renewable Leasehold Conversion Act 1849 and Deasy's Act, there is no special statutory remedy of ejectment in this type of fee farm grant (subject to the ground rents legislation already mentioned earlier), which makes it especially important for practitioners to establish which kind of grant they are dealing with.

Covenants

9–58 Any restraints in the deed granting the fee simple will be judged on the same basis as any other ordinary fee simple and so will be void if they restrict alienation to any substantial extent. In *Re Lunham's Estate*,[72] a grant of a fee simple reserving a rentcharge to the grantor provided that the land was not to be subdivided into more than four lots without the consent of the grantor. The restriction was held void as "repugnant" to the fee simple estate.

Redemption

9–59 The Chief Rents Redemption (Ireland) Act 1864 seemed to apply to rentcharge fee farm grants, but the Act has now been repealed by the LCLRA 2009.[73] The Redemption of Rent (Ireland) Act 1891 does not apply because there is no landlord and tenant relationship.[74] Under s.5 of the Conveyancing Act 1881 the owner of land subject to an incumbrance, which included a rentcharge, could sell the land free of it by obtaining the permission of the court to lodging a sum of money in court, the sum being sufficient to provide an income, after investment in government securities, to pay the annual amount.[75] Section 5 has, however, now been repealed by the LCLRA 2009.[76]

9–60 The Landlord and Tenant (Ground Rents) Act 1967 and the No. 2 Act of 1978 seem to apply since they do not distinguish between different kinds of fee farm grant.

---

[72] (1871) I.R. 5 Eq. 170.
[73] LCLRA 2009 s.8, Sch.2, Pt 4.
[74] *Christie v Peacocke* (1892) 30 L.R. Ir. 646.
[75] *Re McGuiness's Contract* (1901) 35 I.L.T.R. 65.
[76] LCLRA 2009 s.8, Sch.2, Pt 4.

CHAPTER 10

Fee Tail

"Oh! my dear," cried his wife, "I cannot bear to hear that mentioned. Pray do not talk of that odious man. I do think it is the hardest thing in the world, that your estate should be entailed away from your own children; and I am sure that if I had been you, I should have tried long ago to do something or other about it."

Jane and Elizabeth attempted to explain to her the nature of an entail. They had often attempted it before, but it was a subject on which Mrs Bennett was beyond the reach of reason; and she continued to rail bitterly against the cruelty of settling an estate away from a family of five daughters, in favour of a man whom nobody cared anything about.

— Jane Austen, *Pride and Prejudice*[1]

INTRODUCTION

10–01 Section 13 of the Land and Conveyancing Law Reform Act 2009 ("LCLRA 2009") took the major step of prohibiting in future the creation of a fee tail estate at law or in equity. Any attempt to do so results in a fee simple instead. Section 13(3) provides that if any person was entitled to a fee tail at law or in equity before the LCLRA 2009 came into force, or becomes entitled to it afterwards, a fee simple at law or in equity, as the case may be, vests in that person. Section 13(4) then continues:

"(4) In subsection (3) 'fee tail' includes—
  (a) a base fee provided the protectorship has ended,
  (b) a base fee created by failure to enrol the disentailing deed, but does not include the estate of a tenant in tail after possibility of issue extinct."

10–02 Knowledge of the fee tail is still clearly necessary to understand these provisions. Furthermore, such knowledge is also necessary for educated property lawyers and, from a more practical point of view, in order to identify when a fee tail was created in the past.

---

[1] See G.H. Treitel, "Jane Austen and the Law" (1984) 100 L.Q.R. 549.

ORIGINS

10–03 In the feudal period many freehold tenants wanted to ensure that their land remained within their own immediate family: they wanted an estate which their descendants could not sell or otherwise alienate. In a sense this demand contradicted another demand: the right to alienate freely. But both were aspects of a more general demand by tenants: to control land free of the lord's interference. Tenants wanted the flexibility to buy or sell land or to retain land in the family at their own discretion. After *Quia Emptores* 1290 the fee simple no longer satisfied the demand to have an inalienable estate, since it then became fully alienable by substitution by any tenant of the land for the time being.

10–04 The fee tail derived from a form of marriage gift, common in the 13th century, the *maritagium*.[2] This was a gift of land on marriage, usually by a father on the marriage of his daughter. Land would be conveyed to the daughter or her husband, or to both, "and the heirs of their bodies". In the 13th century the courts took the view that the phrase "heirs of their bodies" imposed a condition that issue should be born. Before issue were born, the donee merely had a life estate. Once issue were born, the donee took a fee simple, subject to a condition that issue should continue, so that if the issue died out the estate would revert to the donor. In the meantime, however, the donee was free to alienate the land, just as in the case of an ordinary fee simple.[3] This interpretation was not popular with landowners because it frustrated their intention that the land should remain within the new family. The Statute *De Donis* 1285 solved this problem by creating the fee tail.

DE DONIS 1285

10–05 The Statute *De Donis Conditionalibus* 1285[4] (Of Conditional Gifts), or as it is often called, *De Donis*, provided that a grant by someone who had a fee simple

> *to X and the heirs of his [or her] body*

---

[2]　J.H. Baker, *Introduction to English Legal History*, 4th edn (Oxford: Oxford University Press, 2011), p.271.

[3]　*Nevill's Case* (1605) 7 Co. Rep. 33a at 35. The estate resembled what would now be termed a base fee.

[4]　Statute of Westminster II, 13 Edw I c 1, extended to Ireland by writ. H.F. Berry (ed.), *Statutes and Ordnances, and Acts of Parliament of Ireland. John to Henry V* (Dublin: HMSO, 1907), pp.47 and 105–177. Confirmed 13 Edw II c 2 (Ir), 1319, Berry, *Statutes and Ordnances* (1907), p.281.

or a similarly-phrased grant should take effect according to the intention of the donor expressed in the form of the gift (*forma do ni*).[5] The estate had several distinctive features. First, it passed only to the *descendants* of the *original grantee*. Secondly, a fee tail was not alienable by the person who held it, either *inter vivos* or by will. So long as a fee tail remained unbarred, the heirs of the body had the right to inherit it.[6]

TYPES OF FEE TAIL

10–06 The descent of a fee tail could be limited to a particular kind of descendants. A grant

> *to T and the heirs male of his [or her] body*

created a *fee tail male*.[7] It passed only to male descendants of T. A grant

> *to K and the heirs female of her [or his] body*

gave a *fee tail female*.[8] A fee tail could also be limited to the descendants of a person by a particular spouse:

> *to Q and the heirs of her body by her husband R*

created a *fee tail special*. Other varieties of fee tail special were also possible.[9]

10–07 A fee tail special could give rise to a peculiar interest in property. In the above example, if R predeceased Q leaving no children, there was no possibility that the fee tail would continue after Q's death. Q was known as a *tenant in tail after possibility of issue extinct*. Such a tenant was more like a life tenant. For this reason tenants in tail after possibility could not bar the entail.[10] Section 13(4)(b) of the LCLRA 2009 does not convert such an interest to a fee simple.

---

[5] Baker, *Introduction to English Legal History* (2011), p.273. Co Litt ss.14 and 15, i.e. according to primogeniture, the eldest son to survive him, or if no sons, all the daughters.

[6] Decided after the Statute by *Helton v Brampton* (1344) YB Mich 18 Edw III fo 195 pl 52.

[7] *Helton v Brampton* (1344) YB Mich 18 Edw III fo 195 pl 52. Co Litt s.21.

[8] Co Litt s.22.

[9] In *Re Elliot* [1916] 1 I.R. 30, "[t]o TE and the heirs of his body, excluding his eldest son", created a valid fee tail special which excluded the eldest son.

[10] Fines and Recoveries (Ireland) Act 1834 s.15. They could not even bar it partially to produce a base fee.

Descent

10–08 The descent of an entail was always traced from the original donee.[11] This again followed from the wording of the Statute *De Donis*, to the effect that the issue of the donee took according to the words of the grant. Section 11(1) of the Succession Act 1965 specifically preserved the old rules of descent as to entails, so that primogeniture still applied. These rules were modified, as to dispositions made after the Status of Children Act 1987, to include non-marital and adoptive children unless there was a contrary intent.[12]

Human Rights

10–09 Although the issue was never litigated, the validity of fees tail male and female was open to challenge on the ground that it breached the guarantee in Art.40.1 of the Constitution of equality between citizens as human persons.

10–10 Whatever the constitutional concerns, it appears that the decision to prohibit the creation of new fees tail and to convert existing ones into fees simple in the LCLRA 2009 was dominated by pragmatic considerations. The fee tail was regarded as overly complicated in the new structure and it must be conceded that since the Settled Land Acts 1882–1890 it could play little if any role in the practice of estate planning.[13] Whilst prohibition on the creation of new fees tail in the future would find few opponents, it is not self-evident that the State should interfere with existing private property arrangements without some overriding public policy considerations. The mere fact that law reformers regard those arrangements as pointlessly complex does not seem sufficient justification.[14]

10–11 The conversion of existing entails might itself raise constitutional issues. Those entitled in remainder or reversion on an entail might object that their property rights had been abolished without compensation. However, the fact that it has been the case for centuries that entails could be barred, either by fines and recoveries at common law or under the Fines and Recoveries (Ireland) Act 1834, destroying such interests without compensation, and that therefore remainders or reversions after fees tail were always regarded as slight

---

[11] *Doe d Gregory v Wichelo* (1799) 8 T.R. 211.

[12] Sections 3 and 27 of the Status of Children Act 1987 provide that references to relationships between persons in dispositions of property made after 14 December 1987, "including a disposition creating an entailed estate", included non-marital as well as marital children unless a contrary intention was shown.

[13] J. Mee, "The Fee Tail: Putting Us Out of its Misery" (2005) 10(1) C.P.L.J. 4.

[14] The Trusts of Land and Appointment of Trustees Act 1996 in England and Wales prevented their creation after 1997, but did not affect existing fees tail, although, oddly, that is not explicitly stated in the statute: C. Harpum, S. Bridge and M. Dixon, *Megarry & Wade: The Law of Real Property*, 8th edn (London: Sweet & Maxwell, 2012), para.3–031.

interests, always subject to such a possibility, would probably defeat such a challenge.

WORDS OF LIMITATION

Inter Vivos

10–12 The consequence of the LCLRA 2009 and its conversion of fees tail into fees simple is that words used in a deed which in the past would have created a fee tail will, if used, in future create a fee simple instead.[15] At common law a limitation intended to create a fee tail had to use the word "heirs" and "words of procreation". The most common phrase used was "to A and the heirs of his body" but other formulations such as "to A and the heirs from her proceeding" would also be accepted. The Conveyancing Act 1881 provided an alternative formula as words of limitation: "to A in tail" or "in tail male" or "in tail female", etc. The rule in *Shelley's Case*, discussed in Ch.8 in respect of the fee simple, also applied to the fee tail.

By Will

10–13 Prior to the commencement of the Succession Act 1965, any words showing an intention to create an entail were sufficient to do so in a will. In one Irish case the court construed "to the sons of A" as giving them successive fees tail where earlier in the will other property had been so given to them.[16] If the words were "to A and his children" a special rule applied, called the rule in *Wild's Case* which is discussed below.

10–14 The Succession Act 1965 made it more difficult to create a fee tail. Section 95(1) provided that an estate tail, of whatever kind, could only be created[17] in a will by the use of the same words of limitation as were required *inter vivos*. If those words were not used then s.95(2) provided that words of limitation in a will in respect of real estate which did not create a fee simple or an estate tail were to have the same effect as words used in a deed in respect of personal property. If a phrase such as "to A and his issue" was used in a will after the Succession Act 1965, then it would not create an entail under s.95(1), and under s.94 any expression would pass a fee simple unless there was a contrary intention. The limitation would probably therefore have given a fee simple to A, or jointly to A and any issue alive at the testator's death.

---

[15] LCLRA 2009 s.13(2).

[16] *Studdart v Von Steiglitz* (1889) 23 L.R. Ir. 564.

[17] Note the use of the word "created". An existing fee tail could not be disposed of by will.

The Rule in Wild's Case
Wills
10–15 Formerly the rule in *Wild's Case*[18] applied when a testator made a gift of realty[19] in his or her will:

> *to A and his [or her] children.*

Most rules of construction as to wills are applied when the will takes effect, i.e. at the testator's death, but *Wild's Case* was an exception. The effect depended on the facts existing at the time the will was *made*. If at that time A had no children, then, since there were no children to take by purchase,[20] the words "and his children" were treated as words of limitation and A took an estate tail, even if by the time the testator died, children had been born to A.[21] If at the time the will was made A had children, the rule was that A took jointly with all his or her children living at the testator's death, i.e. "and his children" were then treated as words of purchase.[22] Children born between the date when the will was made and the testator's death were allowed to participate in the gift. The rule in *Wild's Case* did not apply to *inter vivos* deeds.

Equitable Estates Inter Vivos
10–16 In the case of equitable estates *inter vivos* there was no similar provision to that contained in s.95 of the Succession Act 1965 as to wills. Since the general approach of equity was to look at the intention, it was probably the case that a similar rule applied to that applied in wills before the Succession Act 1965.[23]

POWERS OF A TENANT IN TAIL

10–17 Apart from the restrictions on alienation, tenants in tail had all the powers of a fee simple owner. They were not liable for waste of any kind.[24]

---

[18] (1599) 6 Co. Rep. 16b. For a more detailed explanation of the rule and its application see previous editions of this book.

[19] It did not apply to personalty: *Heron v Stokes* (1842) 4 Ir. Eq. R. 286.

[20] *Clifford v Koe* (1881) 5 App. Cas. 447. The House of Lords reaffirmed the rule and held (1) that "children" in its primary meaning referred to the first generation only, (2) that this meaning was displaced by *Wild's Case*, which was a rule of construction, but (3) it should not be departed from in cases where it applied.

[21] See *Clifford v Brooke* (1877) I.R. 10 C.L. 179 at 185–186, affirmed at (1880) 6 L.R. Ir. 439, sub nom *Clifford v Koe* (1881) 5 App. Cas. 447. See also, *Re Moyle's Estate* (1878) 1 L.R. Ir. 155; *Seale v Barter* (1801) 2 B. & P. 485; *Doe d Davy v Burnsall* (1794) 6 T.R. 30; *Phillips v Phillips* (1847) 10 Ir. Eq. R. 520.

[22] *Hayes v Ward* (1788) 2 Ridg. P.C. 85.

[23] *Brennan v Fitzmaurice* (1840) 2 Ir. Eq. R. 113 at 122.

[24] *Megarry & Wade: The Law of Real Property* (2012), para.3–077; *Lord Glenorchy v Bosville* (1733) Cas. t. Talb. 3 at 16 (not liable for equitable waste).

10–18 Tenants in tail, having only an interest in the premises for their own life, at common law were in the same position as regards creating leases as were tenants for life. Any lease they granted would come to an end at their death.[25] They could not create leases which would bind either the issue in tail after their death or those entitled in remainder or reversion after the end of the fee tail. A statute from 1634 gave a general power to create leases for three lives or 41 years binding on the issue in tail.[26] The leases were not binding on those entitled in remainder or reversion.[27] Leases in excess of the statutory power were not void: the issue in tail could confirm them.[28] This seems to have been the origin of leases for lives and years in Ireland. The Settled Land Acts 1882–1890 gave a tenant in tail the same leasing powers as a tenant for life.[29]

BARRING THE ENTAIL

10–19 With the development of the market in land the courts began to look favourably on attempts by tenants in tail to change the estate into a fee simple. There were two principal methods. The effectiveness of a collusive action known as a common recovery was confirmed by *Taltarum's Case*, decided in 1472.[30] A second form of action, called a *fine*, could be brought instead which barred the issue in tail but not remaindermen or reversioners.[31] This created a peculiar type of estate called a *base fee*.

Fines and Recoveries (Ireland) Act 1834
10–20 The 1834 Act abolished fines and recoveries and replaced them by a single deed, called a "disentailing assurance".[32] Since it was an *inter vivos* conveyance, entails could not be barred by will.[33] This remained the case in Ireland until the abolition of the fee tail. The deed had to be enrolled in the High Court within six months of execution.[34] The Act also provided for a person called the "protector of the settlement". The protector was the person entitled to the first freehold estate, or lease determinable on life, created by the *settlement*, i.e.

---

25 *Homan v Skelton* (1861) 11 Ir. Ch. R. 75 (quasi-tail).
26 10 Chas I sess 3, c. 6 (Ir), 1634.
27 Co Litt 44a.
28 *Earl of Bedford's Case* (1587) 7 Co. Rep. 7b (on the English statute 32 Hen VIII, c. 28, 1540).
29 Settled Land Act 1882 s.58(1)(i).
30 YB Mich 12 Edw IV, fo 14b pl 16, fo 19a, pl 25.
31 *Hume v Burton* (1785) 1 Ridg. P.C. 204 at 207.
32 See *Re Ottley's Estate* [1910] 1 I.R. 1.
33 *Campbell v Sandys* (1806) 1 Sch. & Lef. 281 at 295. Entails could not be barred by will before the Act, since a common recovery could only be brought, necessarily, by a living person.
34 Fines and Recoveries (Ireland) Act 1834 s.39. The section also provided that a disentailment by bargain and sale was valid despite not being enrolled under s.17 of the Statute of Uses 1634, if it was enrolled under the 1834 Act.

the deed or will creating successive interests in land.[35] The Act also allowed the grantor to appoint not more than three persons who together would act as "special protector" and they could be anyone.[36] The consent of the protector was necessary if a fee simple was to result.

10–21 Suppose G, the father of A, who had a fee simple, created a settlement. B was the son of A.

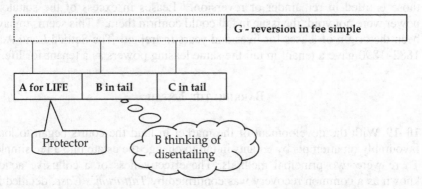

A was the protector. If B wanted to disentail in his father's lifetime so as to produce a fee simple, he had to get A's consent. If he executed a disentailing assurance without A's consent, only a *base fee* was produced, which only barred the right of B's issue in tail (descendants) to inherit the entail, but not C or C's issue in tail or the grantor or his successors.[37] If A consented, B obtained a fee simple but still subject to A's life estate unless A also released the life estate. Usually in such a situation, A would do so, because it would usually be part of a *resettlement* of the land in which A, who would normally have been the father of B, would join with B to produce a complete fee simple which they would then re-settle, i.e. split up again into successive estates. Take the above example, but assume that A had died. When A died the protectorship came to an end. B was now a tenant in tail in possession. If B wanted to disentail, all he had to do was to execute a disentailing assurance and a fee simple would result.

10–22 If the grant had only created a fee tail then a protectorship never existed and again, B could disentail so as to produce a fee simple without anyone's consent. The invention of the protector cleverly reproduced the results of the

---

[35] Fines and Recoveries (Ireland) Act 1834 s.19; *Re Dudson's Settlement* (1878) 8 Ch. D. 628; *Re Blandy Jenkins' Estate* [1917] 1 Ch. 46. He remains the protector even if he parts with his estate.

[36] Fines and Recoveries (Ireland) Act 1834 s.30.

[37] For an explanation of the base fee estate, see below. This result reproduced the effect of a fine: *Megarry & Wade: The Law of Real Property* (2012), para.3–075; An Act for the Exposition of the Statute of Fines 1634 (10 Car I sess 2 c 8 (Ir)).

old actions.[38] In the old actions it was necessary, if a fee simple was to be produced, to obtain the consent of the person seised of the land.[39]

10–23 Whether a protectorship existed or not, the tenant in tail *did not require the consent of the remaindermen or the reversioner*. The effect of the Fines and Recoveries (Ireland) Act 1834, as was the case with the old actions it replaced, was simply to destroy the remainders and reversion without any compensation. Disentailing cost the tenant in tail nothing, except the cost of the deed.

10–24 Under s.58(1) of the Settled Land Act 1882 a tenant in tail in possession was given the extensive powers of a tenant for life under the Act. This included a statutory power to sell the fee simple. However, if he or she were to exercise that power, the proceeds of sale would be invested and the tenant in tail was only entitled to the income for life. The interests of the remaindermen and reversioners were not destroyed by the exercise of the statutory power of sale, but only *overreached*, i.e. turned into interests in the money from the sale. A tenant in tail in possession would therefore almost always be better off by disentailing under the 1834 Act instead.

Unbarrable Entails

10–25 It became a rule that it was impossible to create an unbarrable entail and that any attempt to restrain a tenant in tail from barring was ineffective.[40] As exceptions to the general rule, tenants in tail after possibility were incapable, and certain persons may have been unable to bar, such as those lacking mental capacity[41] or bankrupts.[42]

CONVERSION: LCLRA 2009

10–26 Section 13 of the LCLRA 2009 abolishes the fee tail, including base fees, and provides that future attempts to create a fee tail are deemed to pass the fee simple. Remainders and reversions due to take effect after the end of a fee tail are destroyed by conversion, as they would have been in the past by a

---

[38] A disentailing assurance did differ in at least one respect from the fine or recovery which it replaced. If T, a life tenant with power to lease, joined with U who was entitled in tail in remainder, and they disentailed in favour of T for life with remainder to U in fee simple, T's power of leasing was not destroyed by the disentailing deed: *O'Fay v Burke* (1859) 8 Ir. Ch. R. 225.

[39] It was only they who could create the warranty on which the actions depended. The Act replaced seisin with the protector. It was brilliantly imaginative in its technical means and utterly conservative in its effect.

[40] *Megarry & Wade: The Law of Real Property* (2012), para.3–082. In England, certain entails were made unbarrable by statute, but there do not appear to have been any such estates in Ireland.

[41] *Hume v Burton* (1785) 1 Ridg. P.C. 204 (Irish House of Lords).

[42] Bankruptcy Act 1988 s.44.

successful bar. In the past a fee tail, like a fee simple, could be made subject to a condition subsequent or a determining event. Section 13(5)(b) makes it clear that the fee simple is subject to any such conditions subsequent or determining events which affected the fee tail. In effect it transfers such conditions subsequent or determining events to the fee simple.

10–27 As to a tenancy in tail after possibility of issue extinct, existing at the date of the LCLRA 2009, the effect of the Act is to convert it into an equitable interest under a trust of land. As to base fees, we shall first consider the nature of a base fee and then the effect of the Act.

BASE FEE

Characteristics
10–28 As the Fines and Recoveries (Ireland) Act 1834 defined it,[43] a base fee was, and to the extent that some may still exist (i.e. where a protectorship still exists) is, "that estate in fee simple into which an estate tail is converted where the issue in tail are barred, but persons claiming estates by way of remainder or otherwise [i.e. in reversion] are not." A base fee was, or is, a type of *fee simple* in that it is alienable and it passed on intestacy to the heirs of the holder. It is different from an ordinary fee simple in that it only continues to exist as long as the heirs of the body of the original tenant in tail continue to exist.

10–29 For example, land is initially held by A for life, remainder to B in tail, remainder to C in fee simple. A is the protector. Assume B barred the entail without A's consent and therefore received only a base fee. On A's death the situation is as follows:

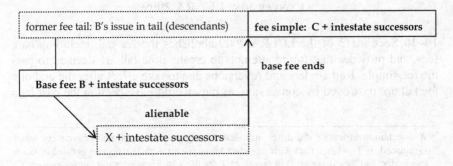

B barred the right of the heirs in tail to inherit, the heirs in tail being the descendants of B. But he did not bar the estate in remainder: the fee simple vested in C. Thus, the estate now held by B will come to an end when B's descendants die out. Before the entail was barred the heirs in tail had the right to inherit

---

[43] Fines and Recoveries (Ireland) Act 1834 s.1.

the estate, but now their lives are merely measures of the duration of the estate vested in B, or whoever then holds it. If that happens then C or C's successors in title, or the person to whom C has conveyed his future interest, will become entitled to the land in fee simple.

10–30 In the meantime, B can sell his base fee *inter vivos* to X or leave it by will to Y: a base fee is an alienable estate. If B sells it to X, X will have an estate which will come to an end when B's heirs in tail die out. Meanwhile X's estate will pass to X's intestate successors, unless X leaves it by will. If B leaves it by will to Y, it will also end when B's heirs in tail die out. When B's heirs in tail die out, C, etc. will then become entitled in fee simple.

Voidable Base Fee

10–31 A technical defect in disentailing, such as failure to enrol the deed, gave rise to a base fee voidable by the heirs in tail.[44] The heirs in tail could put an end to the base fee by entering the land, or by action. Entering the land, which presupposes a right to possession, would no longer be applicable, since voidable base in possession would now be converted to a fee simple by the LCLRA 2009. If the protectorship still existed, the heirs in tail might still put an end to a voidable base fee by action, but there would be little point in doing so since the result would be that the fee tail would again take effect. Furthermore, it is interesting to note that s.13(4)(b) of the LCLRA 2009 is not limited to where the protectorship has ended, so it may be that a voidable base fee would be converted even though in remainder. The qualification in subs.(4)(a) might be read as applying also to subs.(4)(b), but then it is difficult to see why subs.(4)(b) was necessary at all.

Enlargement of a Base Fee

10–32 The examples we have just considered did not take into account the power to enlarge a base fee into a fee simple. The power to enlarge arose in various ways including the execution of a new disentailing assurance with the protector's consent under the Fines and Recoveries (Ireland) Act 1834. Under the LCLRA 2009 once the protectorship ends the LCLRA 2009 converts the base fee into a fee simple in any case.[45] If the protectorship still exists, that does not apply and the holder of the base fee could only enlarge it into a fee simple by buying out the remaindermen and reversioner.[46] The protector's consent is

---

[44] *Re St George's Estate* (1879) 3 L.R. Ir. 277; *Witham v Notley* [1913] 2 I.R. 281.

[45] LCLRA 2009 s.13(4)(a).

[46] Formerly a base fee in possession could be barred under s.19 of the Statute of Limitations 1957 by the person entitled to possession "by virtue of the disentailing assurance" remaining in possession for 12 years after the tenant in tail would have been able to effect a complete bar: *Re Domvile* (1879) 3 L.R. Ir. 282. Clearly s.19 is no longer applicable since if the base fee were in possession, it would be converted to a fee simple by s.13(4)(a) of the LCLRA 2009.

not required.[47] Also, the holder of the base fee would not obtain a fee simple in possession unless he or she also bought out the prior life estate, and therefore it would probably be preferable, to put it bluntly, to wait for the life tenant to die.

LCLRA 2009

10–33 If land was held at the time the LCLRA 2009 came into force by A for life, followed by a base fee vested in B, then the base fee is not converted into a fee simple, but the interests are converted into equitable interests under a trust of land. When A dies, B's base fee is converted by the LCLRA 2009. Presumably B would then hold a fee simple under a trust of land on a bare trust.

---

[47] Because it does not involve a disentailing assurance. The 1834 Act required the consent of the protector to a disposition "as aforesaid", i.e. a disentailing assurance. The 1834 Act actually provided, by s.37, that if the holder of the base fee bought out the reversioner and/or remaindermen the base fee was thereby enlarged into a fee simple absolute, and not merely merged with them. Merger might have left a doubt as to whether a fee simple absolute had been produced.

CHAPTER 11

Life Estates

*I think he'd become your tenant, for the whole of your share, at a rent of
five-hundred a year; and maybe he'd give you three hundred pounds for the
furniture and stock, and things about the place. If so you should give him a
laise of three lives.*

— Anthony Trollope, *The Kellys and the O'Kellys*, Ch.20

INTRODUCTION

11–01 The life estate seems to have been the earliest estate recognised at common law.[1] Grants of land were originally grants for the life of the recipient.
In time, estates of inheritance in the form of the fee tail and fee simple evolved
which enabled the tenant to pass his interest to his heirs on his death. The life
estate then took on a new role. By the 13th and 14th centuries, many life estates
were not created by grant but arose by operation of law: they were imposed
on the parties in the form of inheritance principles of dower and curtsey. Life
estates which arose in this way (or which were expressly created as part of
a family settlement), served to provide land and an income for the grantee.
At a time when the most important form of wealth was land, it made sense to
provide an income to family members in this way. In modern times, wealth is
increasingly held in the form of financial instruments and other investments,
with the result that provision out of land is encountered less frequently.

11–02 Life estates exist in two basic forms. First, the life estate can endure
for the life of the tenant himself. Alternatively, in an estate *pur autre vie*, the
duration of the estate is measured by the life of another person, known as the
cestui que vie.[2] Estates *pur autre vie* normally arise by grant. This can occur
in two ways:

1. If A has an estate for her own life, or is a tenant in tail after possibility[3]
   and makes a grant of it to B, B obtains an estate *pur autre vie*, namely,
   for the life of A. A is the *cestui que vie*.
2. P has a fee simple and makes a grant "to Q for the life of X".

---

[1] 2 Bl Comm 120.

[2] Pronounced "settee kuh vee". The plural is correctly "ceux que vie" but is often rendered as
"cestuis que vie".

[3] C. Sweet (ed.), *Challis's Law of Real Property*, 3rd edn (London: Butterworth, 1911), p.357.

Words of Limitation

11–03 Prior to the Land and Conveyancing Law Reform Act 2009 ("LCLRA 2009"), no words of limitation were required to transfer a life estate either *inter vivos* or by will.[4] Courts tended to construe expressions such as "to A" or "to A for ever" as creating life estates.[5] Section 67(2) of the LCLRA 2009 now provides a presumption that a conveyance is intended to pass the fee simple estate or the entire estate that the grantor had the power to convey. Section 67(2) does not specify any particular words of limitation by which the presumption that the fee simple is to pass can be rebutted.

Characteristics of Life Estates: Alienability and the Power to Lease

11–04 An estate *pur autre vie*, like any life estate, can now exist only as an equitable interest under a trust of land.[6] The primary characteristic of the life estate, however created, is that the only interest the tenant can convey is an estate *pur autre vie*, i.e. an estate for the life of another, the other being the original life of the tenant. If A holds an estate for his land which he conveys to B, B gets an estate for the life of A. A does not retain any interest in the land. A is called the *cestui que vie*, Law French for "the one who lives". A is a kind of human egg-timer. His life is used to measure the length of B's estate. Grants of lesser interests by A are not void, but voidable, like grants by a tenant in tail.[7]

11–05 A tenant *pur autre vie* can dispose of his interest *inter vivos*. Like a life tenant, a tenant *pur autre vie* can only grant an estate *pur autre vie* with the same *cestui que vie* as determined the length of his own estate. If A grants his life estate to B, B holds the land for the life of A. If B subsequently grants her estate to C, C also holds it for the life of A. It will be easily appreciated that such an interest in land is of little if any economic value since there is no way of knowing when the life of the *cestui que vie* will come to an end. As will be seen in a later chapter, the position of the tenant *pur autre vie* was radically altered by the Settled Land Acts 1882–1890.

11–06 At common law the life tenant was able to grant leases, but any lease granted came to an end when the tenant died, regardless of the length of the term granted by the lease. This limitation hindered the development of landed estates. Power to grant mining leases that would bind the remaindermen or reversioners was conferred by a series of statutes in the 18th and 19th

---

[4]   2 Bl Comm 121; *Re Murray; Murray v Condon* [1916] 1 I.R. 302 at 304.

[5]   *Jameson v McGovern* [1934] I.R. 758.

[6]   LCLRA 2009 s.11(6)

[7]   The Statute of Gloucester, 1278 c. 7, laid this down as to dower. Courts subsequently extended the rule to all life estates.

centuries.[8] A power to lease could also be conferred by private act of parliament.[9] Escheat and forfeiture for treason brought a life estate to an end.

Rules of Occupancy

11–07 Where A holds land for his own life and makes a grant of it to B, B then holds the land for the life of A. The question arises as to what happens if B dies before A. There is still something left of the estate, but who gets it? In the past, this question was resolved by what were known as the rules of occupancy.[10] The last of these were abolished by s.11(2) of the Succession Act 1965. The interest of the deceased tenant will now devolve like any other property, by will or on intestacy.

Dower and Curtesy

11–08 Two forms of life estate arose historically by operation of succession law. Dower was a life estate given to the widow in *one third* of her husband's land which he held for estates of inheritance (i.e. fee simple, fee tail), provided her children could inherit them.[11] Originally the widow had the right of dower over the husband's land, including land sold or granted away during the marriage. The widow had the right to occupy and retain rents of dower land for her life. This gave rise to the practice of building dower houses on land for the occupation of widows. This may have protected widows but it was a severe restriction on the marketability of land. The Dower Act 1833 abolished this aspect of dower. Dower itself was abolished by s.11(2) of the Succession Act 1965. It was replaced by the surviving spouse's legal right to a share of the deceased's estate.

11–09 Curtesy was the life estate which the widower had in *all* the land of his deceased wife which she held for an estate of inheritance, and provided his children could inherit. The estate also only arose if his wife had borne him living children. Curtesy was abolished by s.11(2) of the Succession Act 1965. The Succession Act 1965 entitles the spouse of a deceased person to a legal share of his or her estate and does not discriminate, as the old law did, between male and female spouses.

---

[8] Mines Act 1723 (10 Geo I c 5 (Ir)); Mines Act 1741 (15 Geo II c 10 (Ir)); Mining Leases (Ireland) Act 1749 (23 Geo II c 9 (Ir)); Mines (Ireland) Act 1806; Mining Leases (Ireland) Act 1848. See J.C.W. Wylie, *Irish Land Law*, 5th edn (Haywards Heath: Bloomsbury Professional, 2013), para.4.158.

[9] For private acts, see *Herbert v Madden* (1858) 6 Ir. C.L.R. 28. The leasing power was later governed by the Settled Land Acts 1882–1890.

[10] For a full account, see previous editions of this work.

[11] *Re Duignan* [1894] 1 I.R. 138 at 140.

WASTE

11–10 A person holding property for a limited period of time has no incentive to consider the long term in his or her exploitation of the land. The law developed the doctrine of waste as a means of discouraging life tenants from causing damage to the property or exploiting it without regard to the interests of those who will take possession of the land after his or her death. The LCLRA 2009's conversion of the life estate into an equitable interest does not affect liability for waste.[12] A tenant *pur autre vie* is generally liable for waste in the same way as an "ordinary" life tenant.[13]

Voluntary Waste

11–11 Voluntary waste is a positive act which reduces the value of the property for the reversion or the remainders, i.e. it will still be apparent when the interest of the person next entitled falls into possession. Examples include opening and working mines, and felling timber. At common law "timber" comprises oak, ash and elm at least 20 years old. Other trees may rank as timber by local custom.[14] A tenant for life is liable for voluntary waste unless the settlement exempts him or her expressly. If it does so, then the tenant for life is said to be "unimpeachable of waste".

Estovers

11–12 At common law *estovers*,[15] the Norman French name for a number of rights originally recognised by Anglo-Saxon law, are an exception to the restrictions on voluntary waste. Tenants have the right to cut suitable wood for the purpose of repairing the house occupied by the tenant or burning as fuel in it ("housebote" and "firebote"), or fences and ditches ("haybote"), or making and repairing farm implements ("ploughbote" and "cartbote").[16] The doctrine is restricted to suitable wood and a tenant who cuts live wood where dead wood is suitable would be liable for waste.[17] In Irish common law it includes the right to cut turf for fuel (but not for sale) in the house where the land includes turf bog.[18]

---

[12] LCLRA 2009 s.18(4).

[13] For differences regarding the operation of the Irish Timber Acts, see below.

[14] *Countess of Cumberland's Case* (1610) Moo. K.B. 812; *Aubrey v Fisher* (1809) 10 East 446; C. Harpum, S. Bridge and M. Dixon, *Megarry & Wade: The Law of Real Property*, 8th edn (London: Sweet & Maxwell, 2012), para.3–094.

[15] From Latin *stuffare*, to furnish. J.H. Baker, *Manual of Law French* (Amersham: Avebury, 1979), "estover".

[16] Co Litt 41b.

[17] E.H. Burn and J. Cartwright, *Cheshire and Burn's Modern Law of Real Property*, 18th edn (Oxford: Oxford University Press, 2011), p.237.

[18] *Howley v Jebb* (1859) 8 Ir. C.L.R. 435; *Jones v Meany* [1941] Ir. Jur. Rep. 50.

Irish Timber Acts

11–13 The doctrine of waste in relation to timber was altered by the Irish Timber Acts,[19] a series of statutes aimed at encouraging the growing of timber and replanting of forests in Ireland.[20] Under this legislation tenants for life or lives could register trees planted by them. The life tenants then became entitled to cut and sell the same trees.[21] Until cut down, the trees remained part of the land and passed with it.[22] The right was withdrawn as to tenants under leases in 1791[23] but the Acts exempted tenants under leases for lives renewable forever. The Forestry Act 1946 now imposes general restrictions on the cutting of timber outside of urban areas.[24]

Equitable Waste

11–14 Equitable waste is an act "which a prudent man would not do in the management of his own property",[25] e.g. acts of wanton destruction such as cutting down ornamental timber,[26] or stripping lead from a roof and selling it. A tenant for life is liable for equitable waste unless the settlement or other document expressly exempts him or her from equitable waste. If it merely says he or she is to be "unimpeachable of waste" or some such phrase, that will not be enough to render the tenant for life unimpeachable for equitable waste. Equity intervenes here to restrain a person who was expressly made not liable for voluntary waste from abusing that privilege. It does not interfere with acts which will develop the estate economically in a rational way.

Ameliorating Waste

11–15 Ameliorating waste improves the property and therefore at first sight there seems to be no problem about such "waste". But operations which improve the value of property may be destructive to the environment, such as ploughing up old meadows or pastures. In *Murphy v Daly*,[27] it was held that pasture which has been in grass for 20 years or more is "ancient pasture" and

---

[19] Timber Acts (Ireland) 1698 (10 Will III c 12 (Ir)); 1705 (4 Anne c 9 (Ir)); 1710 (9 Anne c 5 (Ir)); 1721 (8 Geo I c 8 (Ir)). Land Improvement Acts (Ireland) 1735 (9 Geo II c 7 (Ir)); 1765 (5 Geo III c 17 (Ir)); 1767 (7 Geo III c 20 (Ir)); 1775 (15 & 16 Geo III c 26 (Ir)); 1784 (23 & 24 Geo III c 39 (Ir)); (9 Geo IV c 53 (Ir)) s.1; Statute Law Revision (Ireland) Act 1879. This legislation was repealed by the LCLRA 2009. See *Kirkpatrick v Naper* (1945) 79 I.L.T.R. 49; *Standish v Murphy* (1854) 2 Ir. Ch. R. 264. The 1775 Act did not enlarge the common law definition of "timber" which comprises oak, ash and elm: *Kirkpatrick and Maunsell v Naper* (1945) 79 I.L.T.R. 49.

[20] See generally, W.D. Ferguson, *Tenure and Improvement of Land in Ireland* (Dublin: E.J. Milliken, 1851), pp.130–132.

[21] *Mountcashel v O'Neill* (1857) 5 H.L.C. 937; *Pentland v Somerville* (1851) 2 Ir. Ch. R. 289.

[22] *Re Pigott (Deceased)* [1919] 1 I.R. 23; *Alexander v Godley* (1857) 6 Ir. C.L.R. 445; *Galway v Baker* (1840) 7 Cl. & F. 379.

[23] 31 Geo III c 40 (Ir).

[24] See Forestry Act 1946 s.37.

[25] *Turner v Wright* (1860) 2 De G.F. & J. 234 at 243.

[26] *De la Bedoyere v Nugent* (1890) 25 L.R. Ir. 143.

[27] (1860) 13 Ir. C.L.R. 239.

it is waste to plough it up. This may be regarded as an example of the common law protecting the environment at the expense of the short-term interest of the tenant for life.

11–16 *Doherty v Allman*[28] establishes that the courts will not restrain a tenant for life from causing ameliorating waste. This indicates a shift of judicial opinion at the end of the 19th century in favour of industrial development at the expense of the environment.

Permissive Waste

11–17 This a failure to do what ought to be done to preserve the value of the property, such as a failure to repair. The common law does not impose liability for permissive waste and a tenant for life is only liable if the settlement itself expressly imposes liability.

Emblements

11–18 Where a tenant has a term which is uncertain as to its duration, such as a life estate or a term of years determinable on an uncertain event during the period, a particular problem arises: the tenancy may come to an end unexpectedly and, in the case of agricultural land, while crops are still standing on the land. In the case of a tenancy for life, the personal representatives, or, in the case of an estate *pur autre vie*, the tenant, have a right to *emblements*, i.e. the right to enter the land after the tenancy has come to an end in order to remove the crops sown during the tenancy.[29] It only applies to cultivated crops.[30]

LEASES FOR LIVES RENEWABLE FOREVER

11–19 Leases for lives renewable forever (or perpetually renewable)[31] were common in Ireland by the 18th century. A lease for lives perpetually renewable was a species of estate *pur autre vie*, the difference being that there were commonly three *cestuis que vie* and the grant contained a clause providing that when any of the *cestuis* died they could be replaced with another life on payment of a "fine", i.e. a lump sum to the grantor. The typical form of grant was: "to X for the lives of A, B and C", with a covenant[32] to renew the lives of the *cestuis que vie*, A, B and C. As with other estates *pur autre vie*, A, B and C had no property interest in the land and their lives served simply to measure the duration of the estate.

---

[28] (1878) 3 App. Cas. 709.

[29] *Short v Atkinson* (1834) H. & J. 682; *O'Connell v O'Callaghan* (1841) L. & T. 157; T. de Moleyns, *The Landowner's and Agent's Practical Guide* (Dublin: E. Ponsonby, 1899), Ch.26.

[30] *Flanagan v Seaver* (1858) 9 Ir. Ch. R. 230.

[31] It was a matter of construction whether the right to renew was perpetual. In *Sheppard v Doolan* (1842) 3 Dru. & War. 1, "renewable forever" in the habendum of the deed was held enough.

[32] A separate covenant was not necessary: *Chambers v Gaussen* (1844) 2 Jo. & Lat. 99.

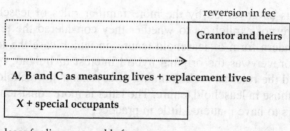

A, B and C as measuring lives + replacement lives

X + special occupants

lease for lives renewable forever

11–20 The origin of leases for lives renewable forever is obscure.[33] Sugden[34] was of the view that the tenure was introduced as a means of conveying land to Catholics at a time when the Penal Laws were in force, but, as Smythe[35] and Finlay point out,[36] the earliest examples of such leases pre-date the first Penal Law affecting landed property,[37] and so do not explain the origin. Leases for lives were certainly useful in evading some of the Penal Laws. In particular, the Gavelkind Act,[38] under which land held by Catholics was to be divided among the sons of the landowner (unless the eldest son was, or thereupon became, a Protestant), did not apply to leases for lives renewable forever.[39]

11–21 Leases for lives created a form of hybrid tenure. The interest was called a *lease* because the tenant paid a rent and it was a commercial relationship, rather than a family one. But the estate was freehold and not leasehold. At common law this meant that the *tenure* was freehold. Freehold tenure could still be created by such a grant after *Quia Emptores* 1290 because the Statute only prohibited subinfeudation for a fee simple estate.[40] Since there was freehold tenure, a rent and other covenants could be attached. The law as to the running of the benefit and burden of covenants in the grant would be governed by the law of freehold tenure. By the 18th century this law had become extremely obscure. Thus, even before Deasy's Act allowed the modern landlord and tenant relationship to be grafted onto virtually any estate, Irish courts treated

---

[33] For a fuller discussion of the historical development of leases for lives, see the earlier editions of this work.

[34] *Attorney General v Hungerford* (1834) 2 Cl. & Fin. 371.

[35] H. Smythe, *The Law of Landlord and Tenant in Ireland* (Dublin: A. Milliken, 1842), pp.229–232.

[36] J.T. Finlay, *A Treatise on the Law of Renewals* (Dublin: J. Cumming, 1829), pp.262–263.

[37] The first Penal Law affecting landed property was 2 Anne c 6 (Ir), 1703. The lease in *Boyle v Lysaght* (1787) 1 Ridg. P.C. 384 dated from 1660; in *Nangle v Smith* 1 West 184, 1 Law Rec. 3rd ser, Eq. 119, from 1672; in *Brown v Tighe* (1834) 8 Bligh N.S. 272 from 1663; in *Inchquin v Burnell* (1795) 3 Ridg. P.C. 376 from 1668; and in *Ross (Earl) v Worsop* (1740) 1 Bro. P.C. 281 from 1682.

[38] Actually, 2 Anne c 6 (Ir), s.10.

[39] 2 Anne c 6 (Ir), s.12. See *Redington v Redington* (1794) 3 Ridg. P.C. 201.

[40] One of the reasons for the use of leases for lives renewable forever may have been that it effectively avoided *Quia Emptores* 1290.

the covenants as governed by the more familiar rules of leasehold tenure.[41]
The cases are not explicit as to whether they considered the tenure *actually
to be* the modern form of leasehold tenure, in which case the lease for lives
renewable forever was the original hybrid interest in Ireland, or merely that
they assumed the rules as to the running of covenants in freehold tenure to be
identical to those in leasehold tenure. The latter is more consistent in principle,
but it appears to have mattered little in practice.

Presumption of Death

11–22 One problem with leases for lives was that it might be uncertain
whether one or more of the *cestuis que vie* were still alive. The normal legal
presumption is in favour of life.[42] The Life Estates Act 1695[43] reversed this
presumption where it was shown, by the lessor or a reversioner, that a *cestui
que vie* of a lease for lives or other life estate had been "absent or beyond the
seas" for seven years or more with no proof that he was still alive. He was then
presumed to be dead. Section 18(5) of the LCLRA 2009 re-enacts the presumption of death after seven years where doubt arises "by reason of absence from
the State or otherwise" about whether a person is alive or not.

11–23 When the presumption of death under the Life Estates Act was applied
to leases for lives renewable forever, the effect was to entitle the tenant to
renew on payment of a fine or to bring the estate to an end and entitle the
grantor to recover the land. If the tenant was ejected from the land under
the Act and then the absentee *cestui que vie* later turned up alive, s.3 of the
Act provided that the tenant could re-enter the land and had an action for loss
of profits against the lessor or reversioner who brought ejectment.[44]

11–24 Section 18(6) of the LCLRA 2009 was intended to replace that provision but has been poorly drafted. The section states: "If such presumption is
applied to a person but subsequently rebutted by proof to the contrary, *that
person* may bring an action for damages or another remedy for any loss suffered." "[T]hat person" appears to refer to the *cestui que vie*, but the person
who might suffer damage in such a case is not the *cestui que vie*, but the tenant
for lives. This appears to be an error in the drafting. Section 18(7) provides
that in such an action the court "may make such order as it appears to it to be
just and equitable in the circumstances of the case". A re-appeared *cestui que
vie* might be prevailed upon by the tenant for lives to bring an action and the

---

[41] *Peacock v O'Grady* (1849) 13 Ir. C.L.R. 292.

[42] *Chard v Chard* [1955] P. 259.

[43] 7 Wm III c 8 (Ir). It was based on the English Cestui que Vie Act 1665 (18 & 19 Chas II c 11).
    The English Act was followed by c. 1, the Cestui que Vie Act 1707 (6 Anne c 72), (6 Anne c
    18) in Ruffhead, but no equivalent Irish statute was passed. See Smythe, *The Law of Landlord
    and Tenant in Ireland* (1842), pp.576–581.

[44] *Hurly v Hanrahan* (1867) I.R. 1 C.L. 700; *Caruth v Northland* (1831) Hayes 233 (otherwise if
    the tenant voluntarily surrendered under belief that the *cestui que vie* was dead).

court might then make an order in favour of the tenant, but it does not appear that the *cestui* could be forced to do so.

The Equity to Renew

11–25 From the early 18th century, Irish courts held that tenants holding under leases for lives had equitable entitlement to a renewal of the lives on their expiry. This equitable right was in addition to any contractual rights derived from the grant itself. The existence of this equity is usually dated to the decision of Gilbert C.B. in *Sweet v Anderson*.[45]

11–26 In *Sweet v Anderson* land was leased to Arthur Anderson for his own life and that of his nephew, "Black John" Anderson, with a covenant to renew the lives on payment of a fine within 12 months of the death of the life concerned. Black John vanished from Ireland in 1697. Arthur died in 1714 leaving his interest to the respondent. The respondent's application for a renewal of the lives was refused on the basis that no application had been made after the presumed death of Black John. In 1718 the case came before the Irish Court of Exchequer. Gilbert C.B. noted that Black John had been absent for 21 years. He came up with a novel solution. Since Black John would have been presumed dead after seven years, the respondent could have his renewal if he paid three fines, i.e. one fine for every seven years. These became known as *septennial fines*. The decision, which temporarily[46] made Gilbert C.B. the most popular Englishman in Ireland, at least among tenants, was upheld on appeal to the British House of Lords in 1722.[47]

11–27 Thereafter it became common for the courts in Ireland to renew the lives in almost all cases.[48] Purchasers, relying on these authorities, bought land in Ireland under titles which were only an equity to renew and treated them as in the nature of fees simple, by settling and mortgaging them.

11–28 In a series of appeals before the British House of Lords in the late 18th century, doubt was cast upon the status of the equity to renew.[49] These doubts

---

[45] (1772) 2 Bro. P.C. 256, affirmed 430. Lord Lifford L.C. in *Bateman v Murray* (1779) 1 Ridg. P.C. 187 suggested that the equity to renew pre-dates the decision in *Sweet*, saying (at 196): "Lord Chief Baron Gilbert only invented the mode of making satisfaction for lapse of time by the rule he adopted respecting septennial fines."

[46] He became unpopular again by following the British House of Lords in preference to the Irish House in *Annesley v Sherlock* (1718) 21 *Journals of the House of Lords [Great Britain]* 55, reversing *Sherlock v Annesley* (1716) 2 *Journals of the House of Lords [Ireland]* 541. See also, M. Sinnott, "The Appellate Jurisdiction of the Houses of Lords of Great Britain and Ireland: Chief Barron Gilbert's Role in the *Annesley v Sherlock* Affair" (2016) 16 U.C.D.L.R. 90.

[47] (1772) 2 Bro. P.C. 256.

[48] *Murray v Bateman* (1776) Wal. Lyn. 181; *Boyle v Lysaght* (1787) 1 Ridg. P.C. 384 at 405–406.

[49] *Bateman v Murray* (1779) 1 Ridg. P.C. 187 at 201; *Kane v Hamilton* (1776) 1 Ridg. P.C. 180 at 185.

were removed by the Tenantry Act 1779[50] which recognised the Irish equity and gave it statutory form. The Tenantry Act came into force in September 1780 and *Freeman v Boyle*[51] reached the Irish House of Lords, to whom jurisdiction had been restored,[52] in 1782. The Irish House promptly reaffirmed the Irish equity to renew on payment of septennial fines.[53] Subsequent Irish cases confirmed that renewal would be granted even after all the lives had died out.[54] By the early 19th century it was held that the equity overrode any express term in the leases seeking to restrict the right to renew.[55] In that respect it had become comparable to the equity to redeem a mortgage.

11–29 The result of these decisions was that leases for lives came to be treated as something akin to a fee simple. Tenants had mortgaged them and "settled"[56] them, creating jointures in favour of family members.[57] Mortgagees and those entitled to jointures would lose their interests if the lease was held to have terminated.

Waste
11–30 Tenants for life or lives were liable for waste from an early period.[58] In Ireland before the Union it seems that tenants under leases for lives renewable forever were not held liable for waste by Irish courts, or only in

---

[50] Tenantry Act 1779 (19 & 20 Geo III c 30 (Ir)). The bill was before the Irish House of Lords in August 1780 and received the royal assent on 7 September 1780. For a detailed consideration of its terms and effect, see the third edition of this work.

[51] (1780) 2 Ridg. P.C. 69.

[52] There had been confusion as to the court of ultimate resort in Ireland. See A. Lyall, *The Irish House of Lords as a Court of Law 1782–1800* (Dublin: Clarus Press, 2013); M.S. Flaherty, "The Empire Strikes Back: *Annesley v Sherlock* and the Triumph of Imperial Parliamentary Supremacy" (1987) 87 Colum. L.R. 593; and M. Sinnott, "The Appellate Jurisdiction of the Houses of Lords of Great Britain and Ireland: Chief Barron Gilbert's Role in the *Annesley v Sherlock* Affair" (2016) 16 U.C.D.L.R. 90.

[53] (1787) 1 Ridg. P.C. 384 at 405.

[54] (1787) 1 Ridg. P.C. 501.

[55] In *Kirkwood v Lord Tyrone*, unreported, cited by counsel in *Bateman v Murray* (1779) 1 Ridg. P.C. 187 at 192, a renewal was decreed in equity after a recovery in ejectment at common law. This point was upheld by the British House of Lords after the Union in *Mountmorris (Earl) v White* (1814) 2 Dow. 459.

[56] See "Quasi-settlements" below, and for an example see *Keating v Sparrow* (1810) 1 Ball. & B. 367.

[57] Carleton as counsel in *Boyle v Lysaght* argued in his pleadings that the lands were "security for creditors and a fund for family settlements – circumstances in the contemplation of the legislature at the enacting of that salutary law [i.e. the Tenantry Act 1779]." "House of Lords Appeals" (Pleadings) 1787–90, Vol.47, King's Inns.

[58] Statute of Gloucester 1278, 6 Edw 1 c 5, extended to Ireland by writ, 1285 (H.F. Berry (ed.), *Statutes and Ordinances, and Acts of the Parliament of Ireland: King John to Henry V* (Dublin: HMSO, 1907), pp.47 and 87–101). Confirmed: 13 Edw. II, c 2 (Ir) (Berry, *Statutes and Ordinances* (1907), p.281); A.G. Donaldson, *The Application in Ireland of English and British Legislation Made before 1801*, PhD, 2 vols (Queen's University, Belfast, 1952).

exceptional circumstances.[59] This was consistent with the view in Ireland that they were perpetual interests. After the Act of Union the English view, that such tenants were liable for waste, prevailed until Deasy's Act 1860. Section 25 of Deasy's Act made lessees of perpetually renewable leases unimpeachable of waste other than "fraudulent or malicious" waste.[60]

11–31 It has been seen that the Irish Timber Acts permitted tenants for life to register trees which they had planted themselves and allowed them to fell these registered trees. A statute of 1765,[61] one of the Irish Timber Acts, made tenants for lives renewable forever unimpeachable of waste as to any trees planted by them after the Act, any covenant in a grant notwithstanding.[62] They were also exempted when the general right under the Irish Timber Acts to fell registered trees was abolished in 1791.[63]

Assignment and Subletting

11–32 There was some controversy in the 19th century and probably before, as to what constituted a "subletting", i.e. a subinfeudation, of a lease for lives renewable forever, as opposed to an outright assignment. Judicial opinion seemed settled that if A held for the lives of X, Y and Z, renewable, and made a grant in favour of B for *different* lives, also renewable, there was a subletting. A could thus reserve a rent service on the grant.[64] This was probably also the case if *some* of the lives were the same and some were different.[65] The position was less clear if A made a grant for the same, renewable, lives.[66] In *Pluck v Digges*,[67] the British House of Lords after the Union, but before Deasy's Act 1860, had held, overruling the Irish Court of Exchequer Chamber, that such a grant was necessarily an assignment, but that was because they held that in such a case the grantor retained no reversion and that, according to the English doctrine, a reversion was necessary for tenure, which had never been the position in Ireland before the Union.[68] Also, *Quia Emptores* 1290

---

[59] Smythe, *The Law of Landlord and Tenant in Ireland* (1842), pp.243 and 728; *Hunt v Browne* (1827) 1 Sausse & Sc. 178.

[60] The phrase is not defined by the Act.

[61] 5 Geo III c 17 (Ir), s.1. *Pentland v Somerville* (1852) 2 Ir. Ch. R. 289; *Ex p. Armstrong* (1857) 8 Ir. Ch. R. 30; *Moore's Estate* (1902) 36 I.L.T.R. 14.

[62] *Pentland v Somerville* (1852) 2 Ir. Ch. R. 280. Such a covenant would not be carried over in a fee farm grant under the Renewable Leasehold Conversion Act 1849 since a fee simple owner is not liable for waste: *Ex p. Armstrong* (1859) 8 Ir. Ch. R. 30; *Re Moore's Estate* (1902) 36 I.L.T.R. 14.

[63] By 31 Geo III c 40 (Ir).

[64] *Church v Dalton* (1847) 9 Ir. C.L.R. 355; *Kent v Stoney* (1859) 8 Ir. Ch. R. 249, (1860) 9 Ir. Ch. R. 249.

[65] *Lord Clanmorris v Bourke* (1849) 13 Ir. C.L.R. 305.

[66] *Roberts v Mayne* (1859) 8 Ir. Ch. R. 523; *Tobin v Redmond* (1861) 11 Ir. Ch. R. 445.

[67] (1828) 2 Hud. & Br. 1.

[68] Before *Quia Emptores* 1290 a subinfeudation in fee simple produced tenure without a reversion and in Ireland the existence of *non obstante* grants meant that in those cases the same could still occur after 1290.

did not prohibit subinfeudation on a grant of an estate less than a fee simple. As to leases for lives perpetually renewable which survived the Renewable Leasehold Conversion Act 1849, the Irish doctrine was restored by Deasy's Act 1860.

The LCLRA 2009

11–33 The LCLRA 2009[69] provides that after its commencement, "a grant of a lease for life or lives renewable for ever or for any period which is perpetually renewable, vests in the purported grantee or lessee a legal fee simple or, as the case may be, an equitable fee simple", and any contract after the commencement of the LCLRA 2009 for such a grant operates to create such a fee simple. The fee simple is discharged from the payment of rent, but "all other covenants or provisions continue in force so far as consistent with the nature of a fee simple".

THE CONVERSION OF LEASES FOR LIVES

11–34 This section shows how existing renewable leases for lives, or attempts to grant them, were dealt with before the LCLRA 2009.

Grants after 1 August 1849, until the LCLRA 2009

11–35 Section 37 of the Renewable Leasehold Conversion Act 1849 (the "1849 Act")[70] provided that "every lease of lands in Ireland for one or more life or lives, with or without a term of years determinable upon one or more life or lives, or for years absolute, with a covenant or agreement for perpetual renewal'" granted after 1 August 1849, operated automatically to create a fee farm grant.[71] The estate was a fee simple and the old rent was preserved. This was provided, of course, the grantor was capable of granting a fee simple.

Grants Subsisting on 1 August 1849
Power Exercisable by Tenant

11–36 Where land in Ireland was held on 1 August 1849, under a "lease in perpetuity", s.1 of the 1849 Act gave a power to the tenant[72] to demand the grant in fee farm from the grantor of the lease whether or not the date for renewal had arrived.[73] The tenant thus acquired a fee simple estate subject to the rent. The power applied where the lease for lives was originally granted before the operative date but was renewed after 1849 under the covenant for

---

[69] LCLRA 2009 s.12(2)(b).

[70] Repealed by LCLRA 2009 s.8(3) and Sch.2, Pt 1.

[71] See also the Renewable Leaseholds Conversion (Ireland) Act 1868.

[72] Where there were co-owners they all had to concur: *Betty v Humphreys* (1872) I.R. 9 Eq. 332.

[73] In *Morris v Morris* (1872) I.R. 7 C.L. 73, it was held that the grant destroyed any quasi-entail. See also *Betty v Humphreys* (1872) I.R. 9 Eq. 332.

renewal.[74] If the power was exercised, the tenant obtained a fee farm grant. The holder of the reversion in fee simple was not entitled to compensation unless a special loss was incurred.[75] This was open to constitutional challenge on the ground that it amounted to an unjust attack on property rights.

11–37 One question is whether the section applied to land held on 1 August 1849, under an equity to renew, i.e. where the lives had died before that date. There would seem no reason why the maxim that "equity regards as done that which ought to be done" would not apply, in which case the tenant entitled to an equity to renew held under an equitable lease.[76] As there was a "lease in perpetuity", the section applied and the person entitled, in addition to the right to demand a renewal of the contractual lease, had a right under the 1849 Act to demand a fee farm grant, which would normally be preferable to a renewal.[77]

Landlord and Tenant (Amendment) Act 1980 s.74
11–38 As to leases for lives renewable forever subsisting on 1 August 1849, there remained in theory, and probably in practice also, a category of interests which had not been converted to fee farm grants. Either the person would have a lease as to which lives had been renewed since 1849, or it might be that all the lives had expired, in which case the tenant would be holding under an equity to renew under s.1 of the Tenantry Act 1779.

11–39 Section 74 of the Landlord and Tenant (Amendment) Act 1980 (the "1980 Act") provides that a person entitled to "an interest in land the title to which interest originated under a lease for lives renewable forever which was created prior to[78] the 1st day of August 1849 and was not converted into a fee farm grant" under the 1849 Act, "shall from the commencement of this Act hold the land for an estate in fee simple". The fee simple "shall be deemed to be a graft upon the previous interest and shall be subject to any rights or equities arising from its being such graft". This appears to mean that the covenants in the original lease still have effect, including the covenant to pay rent and, if included, covenants restricting alienation or parting with possession.[79] It seems unfortunate that another category of fee simple with "leasehold"

---

[74] *Ex p. Barlow* (1854) 2 Ir. Ch. R. 272.

[75] Renewable Leasehold Conversion Act 1849 s.5, and see *Re Lawless* (1856) 4 Ir. Ch. R. 230; *Thackwell v Jenkins* (1856) 4 Ir. Ch. R. 243.

[76] Section 35 of the Renewable Leaseholds Conversion Act 1849 also defined the "owner of the lease" for the purposes of the Act as including a "person entitled at law or in equity to a lease … in perpetuity".

[77] If, as seems unlikely, "lease in perpetuity" referred only to the contractual lease, then the person entitled to the equity had no immediate power to demand a fee farm grant under the 1849 Act, although he would still have had his right to renew under the Tenantry Act 1779. If he renewed after 1849, and before 1980 in Ireland, then it would seem that the renewal itself would operate automatically as a fee farm grant under the 1849 Act. If he did not, and the equity still existed in 1980, it would have been converted by the 1980 Act.

[78] This would appear to exclude inadvertently leases created on 1 August 1849.

[79] Such would be subject to statutory control under s.66 of the 1980 Act.

characteristics has been created in Ireland, but the drafters of the 1980 Act may have felt constrained by constitutional concerns.

11–40 In effect, s.74 created a new kind of fee farm grant by conversion. The 1980 Act did not expressly convert the tenure from freehold to leasehold. If it did, then there continues to be leasehold tenure. If not, then any freehold tenure which existed from the date of the 1980 Act between the holder of the fee simple and the owner of the rent would be destroyed by the LCLRA 2009,[80] which would also have the effect, presumably, of destroying any covenants surviving the 1980 Act. A constitutionally sensitive interpretation would point towards a court holding that the 1980 Act converted the tenure to leasehold.

11–41 Wylie, in the second edition of his book,[81] pointed out that the 1980 Act incorporates definitions in earlier statutes under which "fee simple" does not include a fee farm grant and so argues that the rent was abolished. If this is correct, then a person who had exercised the power under the 1849 Act would be in a worse position than someone who had not done so, because the former would still have to pay a rent while the latter would not. Furthermore, the abolition of the rent without compensation is open to constitutional challenge as an unjust attack on property rights, and one would expect a court, where there is doubt, to favour the interpretation which is consistent with the Constitution. More technically, even if "fee simple" *on its own* does not include a fee farm grant, the "fee simple" referred to in the section is said be a graft, and subject to existing "rights or equities", one of which is surely the rent.

11–42 The expression "interest in land the title to which originated under a lease for lives renewable forever ..." seems to have been intended to apply not only to leases for lives where the contractual or common law lease was still running in 1980,[82] i.e. a lease as to which lives had been renewed, but also equitable leases arising from the equity to renew. Such equities were still governed at the time by the Tenantry Act 1779.[83] The further issue might arise as to whether the landlord had made a demand for renewal under the Tenantry Act 1779 prior to 1980 or not. If he or she had made a demand, then if a reasonable time had elapsed before 1980 without renewal, the interest had ceased to exist before 1980. If a demand had not been made, or it had been made, but a reasonable time had not elapsed before 1980, the equity to renew still existed in 1980 and s.74 converted it to a fee farm grant.

---

[80] LCLRA 2009 s.9(2).

[81] J.C.W. Wylie, *Irish Land Law*, 2nd edn (Abingdon: Professional Books, 1986), para.4.082.

[82] For example, the lease in *Re Supatone (Eire) Ltd* (1973) 107 I.L.T.R. 105 concerning Rathfarnham Golf Club had originally been granted in 1738 but the current lease was dated 1938. See also, *Clancy v Whelan and Considine* (1958) 92 I.L.T.R. 39 which concerned a lease dating from 1793.

[83] Even if it was not, the tenant holding under such an interest could renew, if the Tenantry Act 1779 was satisfied, and then, since it would be a lease first made before 1 August 1849, exercise the power to acquire a fee farm grant.

QUASI-ENTAILS

11–43 A lease for lives renewable forever was a virtually perpetual interest and the courts recognised that it could be entailed just like a fee simple estate. Such an entail was not a "real" entail because it was not created out of a "real" fee simple. It was known as an estate "in quasi-tail", or a "quasi-entail". Suppose G had a fee simple and granted land "to X and his heirs for the lives of A, B, and C" with a covenant for perpetual renewal. G retained the reversion in fee. X made a grant, *inter vivos* or by will, in favour of "Y (his son) and the heirs of his body". Y had a quasi-entail in the lease for lives. X now held a "reversion for lives". After Y's death the land passed to his descendants, unless he barred the quasi-entail or the lease for lives came to an end.

Barring
Method
11–44 Quasi-entails could be barred by any *inter vivos* disposition.[84] The Fines and Recoveries (Ireland) Act 1834 did not apply.[85] Nevertheless, the courts did hold, by analogy to the statute, that if the quasi-entail was preceded by a quasi-life estate, the tenant in quasi-tail required the consent of the quasi-life tenant to bar successfully.[86] If the tenant in quasi-tail did not obtain the consent of this "quasi-protector", the result was a quasi-base fee. Apart from this, quasi-entails could be barred by any act which vested a new interest in a person, e.g. a sale of the lease for lives,[87] or a renewal of the lives, by the tenant in quasi-tail[88] or, after 1849, a deed vesting a fee farm grant in the tenant in quasi-tail under the 1849 Act.[89]

---

[84] *Allen v Allen* (1842) 4 Ir. Eq. R. 472.

[85] *Allen v Allen* (1842) 4 Ir. Eq. R. 472; *Walsh v Studdart* (1872) I.R. 7 C.L. 482, affirming (1870) I.R. 5 C.L. 478; *Lynch v Nelson* (1870) I.R. 5 Eq. 192; *Morris v Morris* (1872) I.R. 7 C.L. 295, affirming (1872) I.R. 7 C.L. 73; *Blackhall v Gibson* (1878) 2 L.R. Ir. 49; *Batteste v Maunsell* (1876) I.R. 10 Eq. 314 at 337; *Re Carew's Estate* (1887) 19 L.R. Ir. 483. Any heirs depending on such an estate tail are entirely in the power of the first taker in tail, and may be destroyed by any conveyance, or even by articles, in equity: *Norton v Frecker* (1737) 1 Atk. 524.

[86] *Allen v Allen* (1842) 4 Ir. Eq. R. 472; *Edwards v Champion* (1853) 3 De G.M. & G. 202.

[87] It seems that after the Renewable Leasehold Conversion Act 1849, a contract of sale of the fee simple by a tenant in quasi-tail would show a good title, on the ground that it would bar the quasi-entail: *McClenaghan v Bankhead* (1874) I.R. 8 C.L. 195. This, however, assumes that the tenant in quasi-tail would obtain, and was bound to obtain, a fee farm grant from the reversion in fee before the conveyance.

[88] *Re McNeale* (1858) 7 Ir. Ch. R. 388; *Baker v Bayley* (1691) 2 Vern. 225 (quasi-entails not within *De Donis*); *Betty v Humphreys* (1872) I.R. 9 Eq. 332. See also, *Leake v Leake* (1843) 5 Ir. Eq. R. 361; *Steele v Mitchell* (1841) 3 Ir. Eq. R. 1; *Crozier v Crozier* (1843) 5 Ir. Eq. R. 415.

[89] *Morris v Morris* (1872) I.R. 7 C.L. 295, affirming (1872) I.R. 7 C.L. 73.

11–45 Quasi-entails could not be barred by will.[90] They were treated as true entails in this respect.[91]

Effect

11–46 In the example taken above, if Y barred the quasi-entail he became the tenant under the lease for lives, i.e. he barred his descendants and X, the holder of the reversion for lives. The reversion in fee was not barred. The reason for this is explained in the next section.

Quasi-settlements

11–47 The following diagram illustrates the complicated situation that could arise:

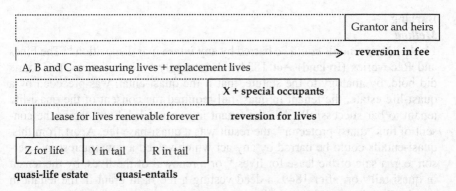

G, the owner in fee simple, made a grant to X for the lives of A, B and C renewable forever. X made a grant of the lease for lives "to Z for life, remainder to Y and the heirs of his body, remainder to R and the heirs of her body". Z had a quasi-life estate and Y had a quasi-entail in remainder. R had a further quasi-entail in remainder.

11–48 After Z's death, if Y barred the quasi-entail this resulted in Y becoming the tenant for lives. The ultimate reversion in fee remained unaffected. If Y, by barring the quasi-entail, could bar the reversion in fee then he could destroy G's entitlement to the rent and fines. In the case of a true fee tail the holder of the reversion in fee would have no such valuable interest. A lease for lives renewable forever, on the other hand, was a commercial interest and the reversion in fee upon it gave the grantor economically valuable rights to rent and fines. Furthermore, if barring a quasi-entail were to bar the reversion in fee, then all a tenant for lives renewable would have had to do to get the

[90] *Campbell v Sandys* (1802) 1 Sch. & Lef. 281 at 294; *Lessee of Hopkins v Ramage* (1826) Bat. 365; *Dillon v Dillon* (1808) 1 B. & B. 77; *Allen v Allen* (1842) 4 Ir. Eq. R. 472.

[91] *McClenaghan v Bankhead* (1874) I.R. 8 C.L. 195 (Ex. Ch.); *Morris v Morris* (1872) I.R. 7 C.L. 295, affirming (1872) I.R. 7 C.L. 73.

whole fee simple would have been to entail the lease in his or her own favour and then bar it.[92]

11–49 The courts did not appear to distinguish between the tenant in quasi-tail and the person entitled to the lease for lives in reversion (i.e. X or X's special occupant). This was probably because they would usually be the same person. It was quite usual for the tenant for lives to create a quasi-entail in favour of his own son in his will. Let us assume that X had left the lease for lives in his will to his son, Y "and the heirs of his body" and then died. Y was then the donee in quasi-tail, but also X's heir general. Thus, while the quasi-entail existed, if one of the *cestuis que vie* of the lease for lives died, Y could apply for a renewal. Strictly this was because Y was entitled to the reversion for lives, rather than as quasi-tenant in tail, but the distinction is not always made clear. It was also Y who could demand a fee farm grant under the 1849 Act, due to the definition of "owner of the lease" in the 1849 Act.[93]

QUASI-FEE

11–50 A *quasi-fee*, i.e. a quasi-fee simple, arose if a person who held a lease for lives renewable forever granted it to someone else "and his [or her] heirs".[94] Words of limitation were not necessary to create a quasi-fee and it would arise if some other expression were used which indicated an intention that the entire interest of the tenant for lives should pass.[95] It would seem that the only effect of the expression "quasi-fee" was to indicate that the interest was subject to special occupancy at a time when special occupancy still existed.

LEASES FOR LIVES NOT PERPETUALLY RENEWABLE

The LCLRA 2009
11–51 Section 14 of the LCLRA 2009 now provides that "[t]he grant of a lease for—

---

[92] Moreover, if a tenant for lives had been able to do this then the Renewable Leasehold Conversion Act 1849 would have been unnecessary.

[93] Renewable Leaseholds Conversion Act 1849 s.35 defined the "owner of the lease" for the purposes of the Act as including a "person entitled at law or in equity to a lease ... in perpetuity for the whole estate ... or for any derivative estate in tail, or quasi in tail, for life or lives or for a term of years absolute ...".

[94] See *Wall v Byrne* (1845) 2 Jo. & La T. 118; *Doe d Lewis v Lewis* (1842) 9 M. & W. 662; *Re English* (1854) 2 Ir. C.L.R. 284; *Keefe v Kirby* (1858) 6 Ir. C.L.R. 591; *Fetherstone v Mitchell* (1848) 11 Ir. Eq. R. 35; *Barron v Barron* (1859) 8 Ir. Ch. R. 366 at 372: "an estate quasi in fee or an estate quasi in tail male ..."; *Courtney v Parker* (1866) 16 Ir. Ch. R. 320; *Croker v Brady* (1879) 4 L.R. Ir. 653 at 660; *Chism v Lipsett* (1904) 38 I.L.T.R. 259.

[95] In *McClintock v Irvine* (1861) 10 Ir. Ch. R. 480, a lease for lives renewable was conveyed "for all the estate" of the tenant to trustees as trustees for JWB "for his use and benefit and no other", and this was held to vest an equitable quasi-fee in JWB.

(a) a life or lives,

(b) a life or lives combined with a concurrent or reversionary term of any
     period,

(c) any term coming to an end on the death of a person or persons,

and any contract for such a grant [after the section came into force] is void both
at law and in equity."[96]

Existing Leases for Lives and Years

11–52 Existing leases for lives, or leases for lives and years, which are not
renewable are not affected by the LCLRA 2009. As the LCLRA 2009 Explanatory Memorandum explains: "The Law Reform Commission took the view
that they are so rare in modern times that there was no need for conversion
provisions relating to any existing ones. What few ones exist can be left to run
their course."

11–53 A lease for lives and years was an estate *pur autre vie* but there was
annexed to it a leasehold term of years, usually between 30 and 99 years.[97] This
rather curious type of hybrid interest may have had its origin in a statute of
Charles I which allowed tenants in tail to create leases for a maximum of three
lives or 41 years which would bind the issue in tail after their death.[98] To the
extent they still exist, there are two kinds.

Concurrent

11–54 A lease for lives and years is said to be concurrent where the term of
years begins at the date of the grant and runs concurrently with the lives. While
the freehold estate continues the term of years is suspended and the estate is
freehold.[99] When the last of the lives die, the estate becomes a leasehold for
the remainder of the term. In the past while the lives survive the tenure was
freehold, but that is abolished by the LCLRA 2009. Whether that means there
is no tenure, or a leasehold relationship governed by Deasy's Act 1860, is open
to question. When the last of the lives die the tenure is leasehold and would
be governed by Deasy's Act. If the term expires while at least one of the lives
survives, then the estate continues to be freehold.

---

[96] In Northern Ireland, leases for lives at a rent or in consideration of a fine cannot be created at
    law or in equity after 10 January 2000: Property (Northern Ireland) Order 1997 (SI 1179, NI
    8), art.37(1)(a) and (2). Subsisting leases are converted to a term of 90 years determinable after
    the dropping of the last or only life.

[97] *Maultby v Maultby* (1854) Ir. Ch. R. 32.

[98] 10 Chas I sess 3 c 6 (Ir), 1634. It was held on earlier statutes that the leases would not bind
    remaindermen or reversioners: Co Litt 44a; *Keen v Cope* (1597) Cro. Eliz. 602; Smythe, *The
    Law of Landlord and Tenant in Ireland* (1842), pp.5–6.

[99] *Jones v Duggan* (1841) 4 Ir. L.R. 91; *Midland Railway v Craig* (1852) 13 Ir. C.L.R. 1. This
    was apparently the opinion of lawyers at the beginning of the 19th century.

Consecutive

11–55 In this case the term of years is to start on the death of the survivor of the lives.[100] The estate is freehold while the lives survive and then becomes leasehold. In theory, the tenure would have been freehold while the lives survive, and then become leasehold when they die, but again, freehold tenure was abolished by the LCLRA 2009 and again, the effect of that is not clear.

11–56 If granted after Deasy's Act, the Act itself allowed the creation of the modern landlord and tenant relationship even while the estate was freehold.

EXISTING LEASES DETERMINABLE ON LIFE

11–57 In the past a grant to A "for 50 years [or any other number of years] so long as X shall live" created a purely leasehold estate determinable on the event specified. The event did not have to be the ending of a life and the mention of X's life did not create an estate *pur autre vie*, in addition to the leasehold term. Since they do not involve a freehold life estate, they are dealt with in Ch.21 on landlord and tenant.

---

[100] *Long v Rankin*, reported by E.B. Sugden, *A Treatise of the Law of Property as Administered by the House of Lords* (London: S. Sweet, 1849), App. Case No. 2, p.481; *Fitzgerald v Vicars* (1839) 2 Dru. & War. 298.

CHAPTER 12

Future Interests

For who shall interest us in contingent remainders while Chinese metaphysics remain unexplored?

— F.W. Maitland, *The Law of Real Property* (1879)

VESTED OR CONTINGENT

12–01 Interests in land may be (a) vested in possession, (b) vested in interest, or (c) contingent. If they fall within either (b) or (c) then they are future interests. "Vested in possession" means the present right to present enjoyment, not a future interest. "In possession" does not imply physical possession necessarily, but rather the immediate freehold interest. The land may be let under a lease, but the immediate freehold estate is still said to be vested "in possession". "Vested", used by itself, however, usually means vested in interest.

12–02 It is a basic feature of the doctrine of estates that estates vested in interest are valuable property rights, just like estates vested in possession, even though their immediate enjoyment is postponed.[1] These terms had their origin in common law estates. Under the Land and Conveyancing Law Reform Act 2009 ("LCLRA 2009"), future freehold estates (i.e. those vested in interest or contingent) can only exist as equitable interests under a trust of land.

12–03 To give an example before further definition:

to T and U[2] in fee simple in trust for A for life, remainder to B in fee simple at the age of 21.
(B is under 21 at the date of the gift.)

A's interest is vested in possession. B's interest is contingent on his becoming 21. If B becomes 21 in A's lifetime, his interest is said to become "vested in interest". Assuming B has become 21 in A's lifetime, when A dies then B's

---

[1] C. Fearne, *An Essay on the Learning of Contingent Remainders and Executory Devices*, 10th edn (London: Saunders & Benning, 1844), p.2; C. Harpum, S. Bridge and M. Dixon, *Megarry & Wade: The Law of Real Property*, 8th edn (London: Sweet & Maxwell, 2012), para.9–001.
[2] It is normally necessary for there to be at least two trustees of a trust of land under LCLRA 2009 s.21 in order for a purchaser to overreach the equitable interests.

interest "falls into possession", or becomes "vested in possession".[3] The practice of property lawyers is to use "vested" to mean "vested in interest". Where vested in possession is meant, then that will be stated.

12–04 To take another example:

> *to T and U in fee simple in trust for E for life, remainder to the first child*
> *of E in fee simple.*
> (E has no child at the time of the gift.)

Here, the interest is contingent because the person who is to take it is not ascertained. Hence, it can be said[4] that an interest is *vested in interest* if:

(a) the person or persons who are to take it are ascertained; and
(b) the only thing that prevents it taking effect in possession is the existence of the prior estate.

12–05 If either of these conditions is not satisfied, the interest is contingent. To take the first example above:

> *to T and U in fee simple in trust for A for life, remainder to B in fee simple*
> *at the age of 21.*

At the date of the grant, B's fee simple was prevented from vesting in possession not only by A's prior life estate but by the fact that B had not attained 21. B's interest was thus contingent.

12–06 The importance of the distinction between vested and contingent is as follows. If B dies under 21 in A's lifetime, the contingency (of B becoming 21) has not occurred and can no longer occur in future. The remainder cannot vest and although it was to be a fee simple, there is nothing which will pass on B's death to his testate or intestate successors. On the other hand, if B attains 21 in A's lifetime, the remainder vests in B and even if B then dies before A, the vested fee simple will pass to B's testate or intestate successors.[5]

12–07 But it is possible that a person could have a contingent interest which remains contingent at her death. This will occur if the contingency is not one which is to be satisfied by the donee. For example, in the limitation

> *to T and U in fee simple in trust for A for life, remainder to B in fee simple*
> *when C marries*

---

[3] *Bank of Ireland v Conmee*, unreported, High Court, McWilliam J., 8 December 1978.
[4] *Megarry & Wade: The Law of Real Property* (2012), para.9–002.
[5] Fearne, *Contingent Remainders* (1844), p.2; *Megarry & Wade: The Law of Real Property* (2012), para.9–001.

if B dies before A, and C is still unmarried at that time, the fee simple is still contingent. Those entitled to B's estate will inherit the contingent fee simple.[6] If C then marries in A's lifetime, the fee simple will vest in interest at that time, and when A dies it will vest in possession.[7]

12–08 A distinction between contingent and vested in interest is that where an interest is vested, the person so entitled will be entitled to the income of the property before it vests in possession, unless it is expressly granted to someone else, whereas in the case of a contingent interest, he or she is not.[8] This occurs more frequently in relation to personal property such as shares.

12–09 The fact that an interest is contingent does not mean that the "entitled" person has no rights at all. He or she has the present right to prevent the trustees from dissipating the fund (in the case of a trust of money or shares), or dealing with the land in breach of trust. This is because even though the condition may never be satisfied, if the trustees dissipate the fund they will deprive the intended beneficiary of the chance of ever receiving a vested interest.

12–10 In *Jacob v Revenue Commissioners*,[9] trustees held a discretionary trust of money. The trustees were to accumulate the income until the beneficiary became 33, and were then to pay the income to her. But they also had a power to appoint the capital to her. She was held to have the right to prevent them dissipating the fund.[10] The holder of a contingent interest, legal or equitable, would also have an action of waste against the holder of the prior estate in possession.[11]

12–11 In *Chaine-Nickson v Bank of Ireland*,[12] it was held that such a potential beneficiary had the right, at his or her own expense, to copies of the trust accounts and profit and loss accounts of a company in which trust funds had been invested. He or she also had the right to be informed as to who was in possession of land held by the trustees and as to outgoings of the land paid by trustees out of trust moneys. These are specific remedies in support of a contingent property interest in preventing dissipation of the trust fund.

---

[6] Fearne, *Contingent Remainders* (1844), p.364 and following; C. Sweet (ed.), *Challis's Law of Real Property*, 3rd edn (London: Butterworth, 1911), p.76n. At common law contingent remainders and contingent legal interests taking effect as executed uses were regarded as mere possibilities and so not alienable; but see *Challis's Law of Real Property* (1911), p.76n.

[7] If, in the example, C is still unmarried when A dies, the property would vest in the grantor by resulting trust until the contingency occurs. If C dies unmarried the remainder becomes void.

[8] *Re Murphy's Estate* [1964] I.R. 308 at 313; *McGredy v CIR* [1951] N.I. 155; *Ferguson v Ferguson* (1885) 17 L.R. Ir. 552. See also the rule in *Edwards v Hammond*, below.

[9] Unreported, High Court, McWilliam J., 6 July 1983.

[10] See also, *Love v Love* (1881) 7 L.R. Ir. 306.

[11] *Simpson v Simpson* (1879) 3 L.R. Ir. 308 (equitable tenant in tail).

[12] [1976] I.R. 393. See also, *Moore v McGlynn* [1894] 1 I.R. 74; *Moran v Moran* [1910] 1 I.R. 346; *Re Dunne, deceased*, unreported, Supreme Court, 26 November 1997.

12–12 In the case of a discretionary trust (where the trustees have a discretion to appoint property among a class of persons), each member of the class has a contingent interest in the trust property: contingent in this case upon the trustees exercising their discretion in favour of that member.

12–13 An interest can be contingent even if the event on which it depends is bound to occur:

> *to T and U in fee simple in trust for A for life, remainder to B in fee simple on the death of C.*

While A, B, and C are alive, B's interest is contingent. Nevertheless, although this is the traditional position it may no longer be the case at least where revenue statutes are concerned.[13]

12–14 In the limitation

> *to T and U in fee simple in trust for A and B for their joint lives, remainder to the survivor*

the remainder is contingent, whether the remainder is in fee simple[14] or for life.[15] Both A and B are bound to die, but it is uncertain which will be the survivor, so the person to take the remainder is unascertained.[16]

12–15 An interest may be vested although there is no certainty of it ever falling into possession. In the limitation

> *to T and U in fee simple in trust for A for life, remainder to B for life*

while A and B are alive, B's interest is vested even though B may die before A, in which case B's interest will never vest in possession. This is so even if A is 10 years old and B is 90. A may still die first. Personal characteristics are irrelevant.

12–16 An interest may be vested although the size of the interest has not been finally ascertained.[17] This occurs in the case of a class gift:

---

[13] See *IRC v Trustees of Sir John Aird's Settlement* [1983] 3 All E.R. 481.

[14] *Biggot v Smyth* (1628) Cro. Car. 102; *Quarm v Quarm* [1892] 1 Q.B. 184.

[15] *Whitby v von Luedecke* [1906] 1 Ch. 783; *Re Leigh's Estate* [1838] Ch. 39.

[16] It is contingent because the person to take is not ascertained, even though, in this example, it is true to say that the only thing that prevents it taking effect in possession is the existence of the prior estate.

[17] This point is true in relation to the common law remainder rules, and for the purpose of paying the income of a fund to those entitled to vested interests, but in the modern rule against perpetuities, an interest is not vested unless its size is also ascertained.

> *to T and U in fee simple in trust for A for life, remainder to such of B's children as attain 21 in fee simple.*

When a child of B becomes 21 in A's lifetime, his or her interest becomes vested despite the fact that it is liable to be reduced in size if and when later children become 21.[18] It is vested subject to being partially divested. But children under 21 have only contingent interests.[19]

12–17 An interest can be vested although it is subject to a condition subsequent. In the above example, a child who becomes 21 has a vested interest although it is liable to be partially divested later if other children become 21.[20] Vested conditional interests are also an example of this rule. On the other hand, if an interest is subject to a condition precedent it is necessarily contingent. Nevertheless, an interest may appear to contain a condition precedent, but be held not to do so. For example, in the limitation

> *to T and U in fee simple in trust for A for life, but if A dies, remainder to B in fee simple*

B has a vested fee simple. The phrase "but if A dies" adds no contingency which was not inherent in the natural determination of A's life estate.[21]

ASSIGNABILITY

12–18 The Statute of Wills 1634[22] was interpreted liberally to mean that future interests could be left by will, and this was confirmed by the Wills Act 1837.[23] The provision was repealed and replaced by ss.10 and 76 of the Succession Act 1965. Section 11(9) of the LCLRA 2009 now provides that all estates and interests in land, legal or equitable, may be disposed of. Thus, a contingent interest may be left by will, but may not take effect. In the example already given,

> *to T and U in fee simple in trust for A for life, remainder to B in fee simple at the age of 21*

B may make a will leaving his contingent interest by will, but if he then dies under 21, there is no longer an interest at his death to pass under his will.

---

[18] *Re Lechmere and Lloyd* (1881) 18 Ch. D. 524.

[19] *Rhodes v Whitehead* (1865) 2 Dr. & Sm. 532; *Megarry & Wade: The Law of Real Property* (2012), para.9–004.

[20] Again, this was not so for the purpose of applying the perpetuity rule.

[21] *Megarry & Wade: The Law of Real Property* (2012), para.9–004.

[22] 1540 in England.

[23] J.C.W. Wylie, *Irish Land Law*, 5th edn (Haywards Heath: Bloomsbury Professional, 2013), para.5.11. Real Property Act 1845 s.6 made future interests alienable *inter vivos* in England, but it was doubtful whether it had the same effect in Ireland.

Types of Future Interests before LCLRA 2009

12–19 Future interests under the old law were of the following kinds:

1. Reversions.
2. Future *estates* other than reversions:
   (a) Common law remainders;
   (b) Legal executory interests (executed uses);
   (c) Future trusts (future equitable interests).
3. Possibilities of reverter at common law.
4. Rights of entry for condition broken at common law.
5. Legal executory interests corresponding to 3 and 4.
6. Equitable interests corresponding to 3 and 4.

Future Interests under LCLRA 2009

12–20 Under the LCLRA 2009, the only freehold estate that can exist as a legal interest is a "fee simple in possession",[24] although this includes determinable fees[25] and fees simple subject to a right of entry or re-entry.[26] The interests which therefore may exist if the event of condition occurs, i.e. possibilities of reverter and rights of entry or re-entry, although not regarded as estates, are still legal interests. All other estates can only exist under a trust as equitable interests. This has produced a simplified scheme of future interests, as follows:

1. Future estates.
2. Possibilities of reverter at common law.
3. Rights of entry or re-entry for condition broken at common law.

Interests of types 2 and 3 have already been dealt with and the rest of this chapter is concerned with type 1.

Reversions and Remainders

12–21 If one considers common law estates, a reversion arose when the grantor failed to dispose of the whole of his interest by a grant, as when A, the holder of a fee simple, makes a grant to B for life. A retains the reversion in fee simple.

12–22 A remainder is part of the grantor's estate which is granted away and is that part which is postponed to an estate granted in possession at the same time.

---

[24] LCLRA 2009 s.11(1) and (2).
[25] LCLRA 2009 s.11(1) and (2)(a).
[26] LCLRA 2009 s.11(1) and (2)(b). Section 11(2)(c) also includes fees simple subject to a power of revocation.

It follows that a reversion arose by operation of law, whereas a remainder arose by a grant. A reversion was always vested in the grantor, although he or she might alienate it later, whereas a remainder was vested in someone other than the grantor. There could only be one true reversion,[27] whereas there could be several remainders. Reversions were necessarily vested,[28] whereas remainders could be vested or contingent.

12–23 Now that future estates take effect in equity under a trust of land, there are no true reversions, although the term is sometimes used to refer to a resulting trust. Now, if A has a fee simple and wants to give a life estate to B, he must convey the fee simple to trustees to hold on trust for B for life. If A creates no equitable remainder, when B dies the trustees hold the fee simple on resulting trust for the grantor, A.[29]

THE LCLRA 2009

12–24 Under the LCLRA 2009 future interests may exist only in equity under trusts of land. This has greatly simplified the law of future interests and has removed the need to consider the common law remainder rules, the rule in *Purefoy v Rogers*[30] and the Contingent Remainders Act 1877.[31] These rules never applied to equitable interests and so they were unnecessary in the new scheme.[32] Equitable interests had to comply with the old rule against perpetuities (the rule in *Whitby v Mitchell*[33]), the modern rule against perpetuities and the rule against accumulations, but the LCLRA 2009 has also abolished these.[34] The LCLRA 2009 abolished these old rules retrospectively, with a necessary qualification which may give rise to problems and which will be discussed in the next chapter.

FUTURE INTERESTS IN WILLS

12–25 In the past, when a person died intestate his or her real property vested automatically in the heir-at-law. If a person died leaving a will, the real property vested automatically in the devisee. If legal estates had been created by the will, they took effect at once. There were many reasons why this could

---

[27] When a quasi-settlement was created out of a lease for lives renewable forever there was both a reversion in fee and a "reversion for lives", but the latter was only a quasi-reversion.

[28] *Rae v Joyce* (1892) 29 L.R. Ir. 500 at 509.

[29] A is then entitled to the equitable fee simple and the situation is that of a bare trust. If of full age and an adult, A may call for the trustees to convey the legal fee simple back to him.

[30] (1671) 2 Wms. Saund. 380.

[31] For a discussion of these rules and the historical development of future interests at common law, see previous editions of this book.

[32] LCLRA 2009 s.16.

[33] (1890) 44 Ch. D. 85.

[34] LCLRA 2009 s.17.

lead to inconvenience and so the law was reformed so that the legal estate in a deceased person's land now vests initially in the personal representatives, i.e. the executors or administrators. This change was brought about in Ireland by the Administration of Estates Act 1959, and is now found in s.10 of the Succession Act 1965.

12–26 The effect is that the personal representatives hold the legal estate in trust for the persons entitled to the estates created by the testator in the will. When they administer the estate and distribute the property, they will confer estates on those entitled. If a testator attempted to give a legal life estate to A, on his or her death the fee simple vests in the personal representatives on trust to confer an equitable life estate to A, and A will necessarily receive an equitable life estate under a trust of land, since life estates can no longer exist as legal estates.

THE RULE IN EDWARDS V HAMMOND

12–27 In determining whether an interest was vested or contingent, a special rule at common law, known as the rule in *Edwards v Hammond*,[35] applied to wills. The rule was to the effect that where property, real or personal, is given in a will to a person on his or her attaining a certain age and a gift over is given on the event of that person *not* attaining the age, the primary gift is construed as *vested* and not contingent, but liable to be divested if the person fails to attain the age.

12–28 For example, in the limitations

to A in fee simple when he becomes 21, but if he dies under that age, to B in fee simple

to X for life, remainder to A in fee simple when he becomes 21, but if he dies under that age, to B in fee simple

the fee simple to A is vested, subject to being divested on A's failure to reach 21. The rule probably originated as a way of preventing common law limitations failing under the contingent remainder rules. In the first example, the gift to A would be an attempt to create a springing interest and would be void. In the second example, if A was under 21 at X's death, the remainder would fail under the wait-and-see rule. However, by the 19th century the courts had extended the rule beyond common law remainders to personal property[36] and

---

[35] (1684) 3 Lev 132. See *Bromfield v Crowder* (1805) 1 Bos. & P.N.R. 313; *Doe d Willis v Martin* (1790) 4 Term Rep. 39; *Finch v Lane* (1870) L.R. 10 Eq. 501; *Re Kilpatrick's Policies Trusts* [1965] 2 All E.R. 673 (affirmed (CA): [1966] Ch. 730 at 747); *Phipps v Ackers* (1842) 9 Cl. & Fin. 583; *Re Young's Settlement Trusts* [1959] 2 All E.R. 74; *Re Penton's Settlements* [1968] 1 W.L.R. 248; *Brotherton v Inland Revenue Commissioners* [1978] 2 All E.R. 267.
[36] *Re Heath* [1936] Ch. 259.

to equitable interests.[37] The modern explanation of the rule is that the grantor intends to dispose of the property either to A or to B, so that anything not taken by B should be taken by A.[38] In the case of a trust, if A's interest were treated as contingent, then A would not be entitled to the income before attaining the age and if B's interest were also treated as contingent, neither would B, so that the income would not be disposed of at all, would fall into residue and either go to a residuary legatee or on a partial intestacy, which was probably not what the testator intended.

12–29 The rule was examined by Kenny J. in *Re Murphy's Estate*.[39] The testator in the case devised his freehold farm in trust for his wife for her life and after her death in trust "for my son", S, "absolutely provided he has attained the age of twenty-five and in the event of my said son", S, "predeceasing my said wife or dying before reaching the said age of twenty-five years then in trust for my son", M, "provided he attains the said age of twenty-five years".

12–30 The will contained a residuary clause. The testator died in 1935. His widow died in 1937. S attained 25 years in 1956. The issues were: (a) did S take a vested estate on the death of the testator's widow in 1937, or on his attaining 25 in 1956? (b) Who was entitled to the income arising from the farm between the two dates? Kenny J. commented on the rule[40]:

> "The reasoning on which the rule was based is plainly fallacious when there is a residuary clause as it is then probable that the testator intended that the income of the property devised on condition should form part of the residuary estate until attainment of the specified age. The rule did not have its origin in the reasoning which was subsequently developed in its defence but in the common law doctrine that the seisin and the legal estate in freehold lands had to have an owner so that the subsequent estate which was contingent would not be destroyed by not having a particular estate to support it."

12–31 The judge held that, whatever may have been the case in the past, the rule was now merely one of construction. It may possibly be useful in some cases, but it is arguable that it no longer serves any real purpose.

12–32 On the facts the judge held that the property passed to S in 1956, when he attained the age of 25. He further held that the income of the farm between the two dates was held by the trustees on the trusts declared by the residuary clause of the will. The judge noted that the limitation before him not only made the gift to S dependent on his attaining 25, but also made the gift over to

---

[37] *Phipps v Ackers* (1842) 9 Cl. & F. 583.

[38] In *Phipps v Ackers* (1842) 9 Cl. & F. 583, the opinions in the House of Lords were given after the advice of 11 common law judges had been heard.

[39] [1964] I.R. 308 at 313; *McGredy v Inland Revenue Commissioners* [1951] N.I. 155; *Ferguson v Ferguson* (1885) 17 L.R. Ir. 552.

[40] [1964] I.R. 308 at 311.

M subject to a similar age qualification. The judge held this to be an additional factor in holding both interests to be contingent, a decision which he found was consistent with precedent. It would seem that today it is always a matter of construction and there is no fixed rule of law.

Gifts Over

After a Conditional or Determinable Estate

12–33 The only kind of "gift over" one could create at common law was a remainder after a determinable life estate. The limitation

> *to A for life or until she becomes a solicitor, then [in trust] to B and his heirs*

creates a determinable life estate and a valid gift over. After the LCLRA 2009 there is no reason why there cannot be a gift over after a conditional life estate. The life estate would take effect in equity and if the gift over is a fee simple, since it is a future interest, it must also take effect in equity. When the life estate comes to an end, B's fee simple vests in possession, initially as a bare trust, B being entitled to call for the legal fee simple.

12–34 Gifts over following legal determinable and conditional fees may be created, but gifts over, as future interests, take effect in equity under a trust, since only fees simple in possession (including determinable and conditional ones) can exist as legal estates.[41]

After a Fee Simple Absolute

12–35 Given that the common law remainders and the rules that applied to them have been abolished, prima facie there seems no reason why a fee simple remainder should not be limited to follow a fee simple in possession:

> *to A and his heirs, remainder [in trust] to B and his heirs.*

The fee simple in possession could take effect as a legal estate, but the fee simple remainder could only take effect under a trust.

12–36 The reason often given for the common law rule was that the fee simple is the largest interest that it is possible to have in real property, so that the grantor, in conferring a fee simple on A, has disposed of his entire interest and has nothing left to give to B. The result is supposed to be a logical conclusion drawn from some metaphysical quality inherent in the fee simple estate. This is a reifying explanation, detached from reality. The real explanation had a great deal to do with class relations within feudal society. The real reason was that if

---

[41] Possibilities of reverter and rights of entry and re-entry can exist as "legal interests", i.e. lesser interests than estates.

A died without heirs, the tenure would escheat in favour of A's lord who could then re-grant the land, probably for a higher rent. If, however, an estate in fee simple could be limited to take effect upon the happening of that event, the lord would be deprived of the escheat and its economic value. Since this reason is now obsolete it does not constitute an objection to the limitation.

12–37 But is there some lingering objection to the idea that the grantor could somehow create a "new" fee simple, i.e. not only confer his own one on some-one else, but create a "new" one in the form of the remainder to B? If so, it can be argued that there is no remainder after A's fee simple, merely an expression of intention or hope on the part of the grantor.

12–38 There is also a more direct objection. Section 73(1) of the Succession Act 1965 provides that in default of any person taking the estate of an intestate, the State takes the estate as ultimate intestate successor. Section 73 means that after 1 January 1967, a fee simple absolute never comes to an end. There is one possible exception to this. Section 73(2) provides that the Minister for Public Expenditure and Reform may waive the right of the State in favour of such person and on such terms as he thinks proper. Presumably, in the case of such a limitation, the State might wish to waive its right in favour of B. Even then, it is arguable that in that case the State confers the original fee simple on B.

CHAPTER 13

Class Gifts and Rules against Remoteness

A gift consists not in what is done or given, but in the intention of the giver or doer.

— Seneca, *Moral Essays* (Vol.iii)

THE CLASS-CLOSING RULES

13–01 A class gift[1] is a gift or limitation in favour, not of an individual, but of a number of persons by some form of description. So, for example, a limitation "to A" is an individual gift to the person called "A", whereas a gift to "my children" is a class gift to such persons who are children of the donor. An obligation on trustees to employ the trust funds for the benefit of members of a class at the trustees' discretion, i.e. a discretionary trust, is not a gift to a class.[2] The class-closing rules were developed to define the membership of a class in the absence of a precise definition by the donor. Before the Land and Conveyancing Law Reform Act 2009 ("LCLRA 2009") class gifts as *inter vivos* equitable interests or in wills had to comply with the modern rule against perpetuities. Since that rule has been abolished, the further complexities which this produced fortunately no longer apply.

13–02 It is a matter of construction as to whether a particular gift is to a class or to an individual, or individuals. In *Re Ramadge*,[3] a gift in a will was to "my four cousins, A, B, C and D". Did this create a class gift or a gift to four designated persons? The testator had more than four cousins at the date of death. When the will was made the four named cousins had a factor in common in that they were the only cousins on the Ramadge side of the family. Three other Ramadge cousins were born later. Lowry J. decided that it was not a class gift but a gift to the four designated cousins. He held that naming them pointed to that result. Furthermore, two of the four named belonged to the same *stirpes*, so the will itself made for an uneven division between persons in the same relation to the testator. Since the testator had discriminated between the named cousins

---

[1] A.J. Casner, "Class Gifts Other Than to 'Heirs' or 'Next of Kin': Increase in the Class Membership" (1937) 51 Harv. L.R. 254; J.H.C. Morris, "The Rule Against Perpetuities and the Rule in *Andrews v Partington*" (1954) 70 L.Q.R. 61; A. Lyall, "Class-Closing Rules and Future Interests in Freeholds: Law and Political Economy" (1985) 20 Ir. Jur. 66.

[2] *Re Davoren's Estate* [1994] 2 I.L.R.M. 276.

[3] [1969] N.I. 71.

and her other cousins, it was reasonable to suppose that she did indeed intend
to include those cousins and to exclude all other cousins.

The Modern Class-closing Rules
13–03 Whenever there is a gift to a class, such as "to the children of A", there
is the question of who is included in the gift. Does it mean the children of
A born at the time when the testator was writing the will? Or born by the time
of the testator's death? Or whenever born, i.e. even after the testator's death?
The modern class-closing rules were developed to solve these problems.

Policies: The Market versus Family Solidarity
13–04 The rules are usually described as rules of construction, used when
the donor's intention is unclear. They therefore are said to yield to a contrary
expressed intention.[4] It can be argued that the validity of these rules rests on
the principle of implied intent, and that the courts' role is limited to discovering
what the donor would have done if he or she had thought about it. On the other
hand, courts in such cases may actually be applying social policies.[5] Two main
social policies seem to be at work: early vesting and kinship solidarity.

Early Vesting
13–05 First, the rules generally have the effect of closing the class at the earliest possible moment, which is when a member of the class becomes entitled
to an interest vested *in possession*.[6] The notion here is that when someone
becomes entitled to an interest in possession, he or she should actually receive
the property at that point, and should not have to wait until others qualify later.
The rules therefore promote the efficient working of a market economy, arguably at the expense of more communal values which support the cohesion of
the family or other social unit by seeking to include as many of its members in
a class gift as possible.

Kinship Solidarity
13–06 A second, and often conflicting, concern detectable in the rules is not
to discriminate between members of the same kinship group in the distribution of the property and to avoid any animosities that might consequently arise
between members of a group of relatives. This favours the communal values
of the cohesion of the kinship group. As will be seen, the policy of maintaining the kinship unit is usually carried into effect only if it will not hinder the
policy in favour of the early vesting of property, which is therefore the dominant policy.

---

4   *Re Bleckly* [1951] Ch. 740 at 749.
5   See *Williamson v Williamson* [1974] N.I. 92.
6   *Donoghoe v Mooney* (1891) 27 L.R. Ir. 26 at 34; *Re Smith* (1862) 2 J. & H. 594 at 601.

The Rule in Andrews v Partington

13–07 The basic modern rule is known as the general rule in *Andrews v Partington.*[7] The general rule contains two distinct propositions.

1. The *time of distribution* (of the property) is the point at which the *first* member of the class qualifies for an interest *in possession* (not in interest only). It is at this point that a person becomes entitled to consume or deal with the property.[8]
2. The class *closes* at the time of distribution.

13–08 The four most common kinds of class gifts[9] are:

(a) Simple class gift. An example would be, in a will:
to the grandchildren of X in fee simple.[10]

(b) Class gift at a prescribed age or other event. An example would be, in a will:
to the grandchildren of X at 21 in fee simple.[11]

(c) Class gift after a prior estate. An example would be, in a will:
to A for life, remainder to the grandchildren of B in fee simple.[12]

(d) Class gift at a prescribed age or other event after a prior estate. An example would be, in a will:

---

[7] (1791) 3 Bro. C.C. 401.

[8] *Re Smith* (1862) 2 J. & H. 594 at 601.

[9] These are analysed in more detail in A. Lyall, "Class-Closing Rules and Future Interests in Freeholds: Law and Political Economy" (1985) 20 Ir. Jur. 66.

[10] If there are grandchildren of X when the instrument takes effect the class closes then. It includes grandchildren born up to that time and still in existence. This has now been altered where the class consists of the children or remoter issue of the testator: Succession Act 1965 s.98. It excludes later-born grandchildren: *Warren v Johnson* (1673) 2 Rep. Ch. 69; *Heathe v Heathe* (1740) 2 Atk. 121; *Sprackling v Ranier* (1761) Dick. 344; *Singleton v Gilbert* (1784) 1 Cox 68; *Hill v Chapman* (1791) 1 Ves. 405; *Davidson v Dallas* (1808) 14 Ves. 576; contra *Cook v Cook* (1706) 2 Vern. 545.

[11] The general rule of construction closes the class when the first grandchild obtains an interest vested in possession, in this case, when he or she reaches 21: *Gilbert v Boorman* (1805) 11 Ves. Jun. 238. The "class" would then include, of course, only the first grandchild to become 21. However, it seems unfair to exclude other grandchildren born before the class closes but still under the age specified, and so the courts have modified the general rule to include them as *potential* members, who will take when and if they reach the specified age: *Gilmore v Severn* (1785) 1 Bro. C.C. 582; *Andrews v Partington* (1790) 2 Cox 223. So, if at the testator's death there is a grandchild aged 21 and one or more under 21, the class closes then and includes those under age who will take if and when they become 21: *Re Chapman, deceased* (1922) 56 I.L.T.R. 32. Grandchildren born *after* the first grandchild becomes 21 are excluded: *Crone v O'Dell* (1811) 1 Ball. & B. 449; *Ellison v Airey* (1748) 1 Ves. Sen. 111.

[12] The general rule of construction would close the class when the first grandchild becomes entitled to an interest in possession. In this example, this will happen when the prior estate ends or when the first grandchild of B is born, if that is later: *Finch v Hollingsworth* (1855) 21 Beav. 112; *Reid v Swann* [1911] 1 I.R. 405 at 410 and *Re Gun* [1915] 1 I.R. 42.

to A for life, remainder to the grandchildren of B at 21 in fee simple.[13]

THE ABOLITION OF THE RULES AGAINST REMOTENESS

13–09 Section 16 of the LCLRA 2009 abolishes the following rules:

(a) the rule known as the rule in *Whitby v Mitchell*[14] (also known as the old rule against perpetuities and the rule against double possibilities);
(b) the rule against perpetuities;
(c) the rule against accumulations.

13–10 It should be noted that the *rule against inalienability* has not been abolished. It is discussed at the end of this chapter.

Retrospective Effect

13–11 In a provision that may prove problematic, s.17 of the LCLRA 2009 attempts to make the change retrospective:

"17.—Section 16 applies to any interest in property whenever created but does not apply if, before the commencement of this Part, in reliance on such an interest being invalid by virtue of the application of any of the rules abolished by that section—

(a) the property has been distributed or otherwise dealt with, or
(b) any person has done or omitted to do any thing which renders the position of that or any other person materially altered to that person's detriment after the commencement of this Part."

13–12 Retrospective abolition raised the following potential problem. Suppose that property had been given to A, and B was to take by default. The gift to A was thought to be void under one of the rules and in reliance on that, the property had vested in B. If the rule was abolished retrospectively without any saving, then A or A's successors might make a claim to the property which B had received in good faith under a rule of law valid at the time. This would almost certainly be unconstitutional as an unjust attack on the property rights of B. Section 17(a) attempts to meet this objection by exempting B from

---

[13] In this example, the general rule of construction would close the class when the first grandchild of B becomes entitled to an interest in possession. This cannot occur while A is alive, for even if a grandchild of B becomes 21 during A's life, its interest will be vested in interest but not in possession. The class will close when the life estate comes to an end, or when the first of B's grandchildren becomes 21, if that is later: *Kevern v Williams* (1832) 5 Sim. 171; *Re Canney's Trusts* (1910) 101 L.T.R. (ns) 905; *Re Chartres* [1927] 1 Ch. 466. Cases where the first member reaching the age was the later event were: *Bartlett v Hollister* (1757) Amb. 334; *Re Emmet's Estate* (1880) 13 Ch. D. 484; *Caldbeck v Caldbeck* [1911] 1 I.R. 144.

[14] (1890) 44 Ch. D. 85.

the retrospective effect if the property had already been "distributed" to B. The phrase "or otherwise dealt with" suggests that "distributed" is intended to mean something in addition to the property simply vesting in B. But if the property had *vested* in B, then regardless of the circumstances set out in (a) and (b), B had already become entitled to a vested property interest, and the objection on constitutional grounds would apply. As Mee has pointed out,[15] the thinking behind the provision, contained in the Law Reform Commission Report,[16] appears to be flawed. Mee cites the example given in the Report of a disposition which violates the modern rule against perpetuities[17]:

> *to A for life, remainder to the first of my grandchildren to become a doctor.*

13–13 The rule is outlined below, but one can make the point as to retrospective effect without further knowledge at this point. In an *inter vivos* conveyance[18] the remainder to the grandchildren would be void. Suppose X was to take by default. Mee asserts, surely correctly, that if A was already dead at the date the LCLRA 2009 took effect, so that X's interest had vested in possession, then s.17 must at least mean that X could keep the property. But if A were still alive, the intention in the Report is that X would lose his property. The Report explains that it would be preferable to honour the settlor's intention rather than fulfil "(at most) the expectation of a windfall, which X (on the basis of a law which to most lay people and many lawyers would seem antiquated and irrational) entertained". But to describe X as receiving a "windfall" when his interest vests in possession is incorrect. As Mee says, "X does not 'expect' to receive an interest – he already has a property interest vested in him."[19] It would just be as sensible to say that if a grandson of the settlor became a doctor in A's lifetime, the grandson would receive nothing of value until A died. Not so. It is a basic characteristic of the doctrine of estates that a property right vested in interest gives rise to present rights.

Reliance
13–14 A second problem might arise from the phrase "in reliance". What would constitute a justifiable reliance? Let us assume that the gift to A was held to be void (for perpetuity, etc.) by the decision of a court. That would surely constitute a valid reliance, and B's property would not be at risk. But suppose the executors of the will (or whoever) had acted in reliance on the opinion of counsel. Would that be sufficient? If not, then a court in future would still have

---

[15] J. Mee, "From Here to Eternity? Perpetuities Reform in Ireland" (2000) 7 D.U.L.J. 91.

[16] Law Reform Commission, *Report on the Rule against Perpetuities and Cognate Rules* (LRC 62-2000).

[17] Law Reform Commission, *Report on the Rule against Perpetuities and Cognate Rules* (LRC 62-2000), p.63.

[18] Mee also points out that one must assume that this is an *inter vivos* conveyance since if it occurred in a will it would be valid in some circumstances, i.e. if the testator had no surviving children. In that case the grandchildren would be a closed class at the testator's death and the event would be bound to occur, if it occurred at all, in their lifetime.

[19] J. Mee, "From Here to Eternity? Perpetuities Reform in Ireland" (2000) 7 D.U.L.J. 91 at 100.

itself to apply the relevant rule to determine whether A's gift was indeed void. This is probably unlikely to happen, and so the old rules will be discussed here as briefly as possible. Some discussion is necessary, apart from other reasons, to indicate what limitations are now possible which would not have been before, and to examine what problems they might pose.

THE OLD RULE AGAINST PERPETUITIES

13–15 This rule, although sometimes known as the rule in *Whitby v Mitchell*,[20] or the rule against double possibilities,[21] was of considerable age and probably developed in the early 17th century at the time when entails became barrable.[22]

Application

13–16 The rule applied to legal remainders and to legal executory interests and future trusts if the last two mentioned resemble legal remainders,[23] but not to shifting or springing uses or trusts.[24] It thus differed in scope from the modern rule against perpetuities which did not apply, in this jurisdiction, to legal remainders. The rule was abolished by s.16(c) of the LCLRA 2009.[25]

The Rule

13–17 The rule was that

if an interest in real property was given to an unborn person, then any further grant to his or her issue, however described, was void together with all subsequent limitations.

13–18 Take the following example:

to X for life, remainder to his eldest son for life, remainder to that son's eldest son for life ... (etc.)
(X had no son at the date of the gift.)

---

[20] (1890) 44 Ch. D. 85. See also, W.S. Holdsworth, *The History of English Law* (London: Methuen and Sweet & Maxwell, 1966 repr.), Vol.vii, p.209; C. Sweet, "The Rule in *Whitby v Mitchell*" (1905) 25 L.Q.R. 385; J.H.C. Morris and W. Barton Leach, *The Rule against Perpetuities* (London: Stevens & Sons, 1956), Ch.10; A.W.B. Simpson, *A History of the Land Law* (Oxford: Clarendon Press, 1986), p.216.

[21] *Whitby v Mitchell* (1890) 44 Ch. D. 85. The rule does not prohibit double possibilities as such, but only gifts to the unborn issue of unborn issue.

[22] Simpson, *A History of the Land Law* (1986), p.215 states that this position was reached by 1614 in *Mary Portington's Case* (1614) 10 Co. Rep. 35b. See *Re Rosher* (1884) 26 Ch. D. 801 at 812.

[23] *Re Nash* [1910] 1 Ch. 1.

[24] As to which, see Ch.12 of the third edition of this work.

[25] It has also been abolished in Northern Ireland: Perpetuities Act (Northern Ireland) 1966 s.15.

The second remainder in favour of the grandson of X was void together with all subsequent remainders. Another example is provided by *Bank of Ireland v Goulding*,[26] in which a limitation in a will was in the following form:

> *to my grandson (B) for life, remainder to his eldest son for life, provided he is born within 21 years of my death,*[27] *but if he is not, then to him absolutely, and in case of failure of male issue of such [great-grandson], remainder to the second or other of my grandsons for life ...*

B was living at the testator's death. The gift to B's eldest son, a great-grandson of the testator, was valid, but the gift on failure of male issue of that great-grandson was void as contrary to the rule.[28]

13–19 The original reason for the rule dates back to the time when entails became barrable. This meant that landowners were no longer able to keep land within their families by means of the entail. Their lawyers therefore attempted to create a succession of contingent life estates to each generation of the family in a form similar to the limitation above. This was known as a "perpetual freehold". If successful, this new device would have achieved the same result as an unbarrable entail, and so the courts reacted by creating the rule.

13–20 In *Bevan v White*,[29] the limitation was:

> *to A for life, remainder to his first and every other son in succession for life, and in default to B for life, remainder to his first and every other son in succession for life ...*

It was held to give rise to a valid series of life estates. All the sons mentioned were the sons of A or B, both of whom were in existence. There was no gift to the unborn issue of an unborn person.

13–21 For the rule to apply it was not sufficient that there merely be a gift to the unborn issue of an unborn person. There had first to be a *gift* to an unborn person followed by another *gift* to that unborn person's issue. For example, in the limitation

> *[in trust] for A for life, remainder in trust in fee simple for the first-born grandson of A born within 21 years of A's death*
> (A has no son)

---

[26] Unreported, Supreme Court, 14 November 1975.

[27] The drafter of the deed evidently thought that it was necessary to limit the gift in this way, although a limitation to 21 years from the death of B would have been sufficient.

[28] The majority held that the cy-pres doctrine could not be applied as the gift concerned was one of personalty.

[29] (1845) 7 Ir. Eq. R. 473.

the rule did not invalidate the remainder to the first-born grandson. The rule only applied if there was a grant of a property interest to an unborn issue, followed by a grant of a property interest to his or her issue. In the above example, no remainder is given to the first-born grandson's parent, i.e. A's unborn son.

Perpetual Freehold or Unbarrable Entails

13–22 The abolition of the rule now means that there is nothing to prevent a grantor creating, under a trust, a succession of life estates to unborn persons in each future generation. In the past, such a limitation would also have offended against the modern rule against perpetuities, but that has also been abolished by the LCLRA 2009.[30] It is rather odd, in view of abolition and conversion of the fee tail, that by abolishing the old rule against perpetuities, it should at the same time allow the so-called perpetual freehold or unbarrable entail[31] to be created, which the old rule prevented. They can, of course, only be created as equitable interests under a trust. The remedy provided by the LCLRA 2009, if at any time in future it was thought desirable to sell the fee simple, and the equitable interests are such as to prevent sale, would be for an "appropriate person" to apply for a variation of trust. Section 24 provides for an extended variation of trusts jurisdiction. An "appropriate person" is a trustee or a beneficiary or any other person that the court considers to be appropriate. However, the old rule at least avoided such trouble and expense. It should also be noted that the rule against inalienability, which is retained by the LCLRA 2009, does not seem to prevent such limitations, since it applies to the *duration* of *vested* interests, not to the vesting of contingent interests.

Cy-pres

13–23 The cy-pres doctrine,[32] which is also found in relation to charitable trusts, was developed by the courts to mitigate the harshness of the rule in *Whitby v Mitchell*. It allowed the court a limited jurisdiction to rewrite the limitation so as to conform to the rule while carrying out the intentions of the grantor as far as the law allowed. Where, for example, the limitation was in the form

to A for life, remainder to the first son of A for life, remainder in tail male to the first and every other son of such son and their issue male successively [with remainders over if A should die without male issue of his body]
(A had no sons at the date of the gift)

the remainders to the sons of A's sons were void. The court could redraft the limitation as a grant to A for life with remainder to his sons successively in

---

[30] Some limitations were void under the old rule but not under the modern rule: Morris and Barton Leach, *The Rule against Perpetuities* (1956), p.256.

[31] *East v Twyford* (1853) 4 H.L.C. 517; *Parfitt v Hember* (1867) L.R. 4 Eq. 443.

[32] Law French meaning "near to it", and pronounced "see pray" or "sigh pray".

tail male.[33] The redrafted limitation had to give interests only to those persons who would have been entitled under the original limitation.[34] Obviously, this jurisdiction no longer applies, since the main rule has gone, and also since fees tail can no longer be created.

THE MODERN RULE AGAINST PERPETUITIES

Introduction

13–24 If land is subject to a contingent interest then the marketability of the land is reduced. If the interest is contingent because the person entitled to it is not ascertained, then the whole fee simple cannot be sold. The persons entitled to the various estates cannot join together to sell the fee simple because the owner of the contingent estate is unknown. In the case of legal contingent remainders this situation could not continue for long because the common law rules had the effect of limiting the period during which interests could remain contingent. However, equity, before the Statute of Uses 1634, recognised contingent interests in uses and did not subject them to the old feudal common law rules.[35] It was therefore necessary to develop a new rule which would directly control the vesting of such contingent interests. Take the example of an equitable limitation:

> *to T and U in fee simple in trust for A for life, remainder to his eldest grand-*
> *child in fee simple at the age of 21.*

If A has no grandchild at the date the instrument takes effect, then the fee simple cannot be sold, because the owner of the contingent interest is unknown and there is no one to join with A to sell the fee simple in possession. A contradiction exists, therefore, even within a system of land law which rejects outmoded feudal rules. The contradiction is between an ideology which asserts the freedom of owners of property in land to do what they will with it, including the right to create whatever interests in it they wish, and an ideological position which favours the efficiency of a capitalist economy in which interests in land are a commodity which can be bought and sold. The latter supports the mechanism of this economy in redistributing land ownership towards those with money to invest and away from owners of impoverished or inefficiently-run estates. The latter position also stresses freedom: the freedom of those with money to be able to use the market mechanism. The modern rule against perpetuities was a compromise between these contradictory freedoms. The period is a long one and this could be seen as a compromise which therefore favoured the landowners, in allowing them to keep land in their families and off the market for quite a long time. The basis of the rule was laid down

---

[33] *Peyton v Lambert* (1858) 8 Ir. L.R. 485. It may be noticed that the first remainder was valid, but is necessarily affected by the application of the cy-pres doctrine.

[34] *Peyton v Lambert* (1858) 8 Ir. L.R. 485.

[35] See earlier editions of this work.

by Lord Nottingham in *Duke of Norfolk's Case*[36] at the end of the 17th century. The rule against perpetuities applied to equitable interests (and to legal executory interests under the Statute of Uses 1634[37]), and also to contingent interests in personal property.

The Perpetuity Period
13–25 The rule is to the effect that

> a contingent interest in property is valid only if it is certain from the beginning to vest, *if it vests at all*, within the period of a life or lives in being when the instrument takes effect and 21 years thereafter. If there are no such lives, the period is 21 years.

13–26 A good example of the application of the rule is the case of *Smithwick v Hayden*.[38] A somewhat eccentric testator by the name of John Hayden had no children of his own, but had a sister and a friend, Edward Fleming. The testator left all his property to trustees to pay the income to his sister for life, then after her death to Edward Fleming, and after Edward Fleming's death to "any female niece or relative" of Edward Fleming who should marry "a person by the name of John Hayden who should reside in Tipperary", where the testator's ancestors apparently came from, and who should be "born and reared a Roman Catholic". Any person by the name of John Hayden would do, provided he satisfied the other tests. Hayden is a Tipperary name and no doubt the testator believed that such a person might be related to him. However, it might be hundreds of years before a female relative of Edward Fleming married a person of that name, even though they might have had some incentive to do so. What defeated the gift was there was no one at the date of the gift of whom it could be said that within 21 years of his or her death a female relative of Edward Fleming was bound to marry a man called John Hayden.

Some Features of the Rule
No Wait-and-See
13–27 The common law perpetuity rule was not a wait-and-see rule.[39] One cannot wait to see if the contingency does in fact occur within the period. The limitation is void if it is possible that it *may not* do so. So, in *Smithwick v Hayden*,[40] one could not wait to see if a female relative of Edward Fleming married a man called John Hayden within 21 years of his sister's death. The gift was void because the event was not certain to happen within the period.

---

[36] (1681) 3 Chan. Cas. 1. See T.F.T. Plucknett, *A Concise History of the Common Law*, 5th edn (Boston: Little Brown, 1956), pp.563–565; S.A. Siegal, "John Chipman Gray, Legal Formalism and the Transformation of Perpetuities Law" (1982) 36 Miami L.R. 439.

[37] Since the latter were converted equitable interests. See *Abbiss v Burney* (1880) 17 Ch. D. 211.

[38] (1887) 19 L.R. Ir. 490.

[39] *Exham v Beamish* [1939] I.R. 336.

[40] (1887) 19 L.R. Ir. 490.

13–28 The reason for this approach was no doubt to maintain the character of the rule as one which a lawyer could apply to a limitation at the time the instrument took effect and be able to say at that time whether it was valid or void. However, the courts applied the logic of "no wait-and-see" to the extent of holding that even if, by the time the limitation came before a court, the contingency had occurred within the period, that had to be ignored so that the limitation would still be void if, at the time the instrument took effect, there was no certainty that events would occur in this way.[41] This aspect of the rule has been much criticised as leading to absurdity and attempts at reform in other jurisdictions, such as Northern Ireland,[42] often introduce a wait-and-see principle.

Applied to Contingent Interests Only

13–29 The perpetuity rule only required it to be certain that *contingent* interests should vest *in interest* within the period. It was immaterial that they might vest *in possession* outside the period.[43] Take the following limitation:

> *[in trust] for A for life, remainder in trust for her children for their joint lives, remainder in trust for B in fee simple.*
> (A has no children.)

The ultimate trust to B was valid. Although it would not vest in *possession* until after the perpetuity period if A's children survive her for more than 21 years, it is a vested interest from the beginning. The rule also had no application to the duration of vested interests.[44] If it had, then all fee simple estates would have been void.

13–30 The fact that a contingent interest might never vest at all was immaterial. Many contingencies are of the kind that may never occur at all. Take the following limitation:

> *[a trust] to A in fee simple, but if B marries C, in trust for B in fee simple.*

B may never marry C, but the contingent fee simple to B was valid, because it was absolutely certain from the beginning that *if* B did marry C, she would necessarily do so in her own lifetime and B was a life in being. If B died without marrying C, then it became clear at that point that the contingent interest could not vest, but the gift was not void for *perpetuity* and so not void from the beginning.

---

[41] *Exham v Beamish* [1939] I.R. 336. It was clear at the time of the case (1939) that William and Anne Thompson had not in fact had more children after the date of the *inter vivos* deed, i.e. 1865. Gavan Duffy J. held that that did not save the gift.

[42] Perpetuities Act (Northern Ireland) 1966.

[43] *Craig v Stacey* (1794) Ir. Term. Rep. 249; *Bank of Ireland v Gaynor*, unreported, High Court, Macken J., 29 June 1999.

[44] *Stevens Mineral Co v State of Michigan* 164 Mich App 692; 418 NW 2d 130 (1987).

Lives in Being, Express or Implied

13–31 The measuring lives were either those expressly mentioned in the instrument or referred to by implication. For example, a gift in a will

to my grandchildren who shall reach the age of 21 in fee simple

was a valid gift. All the grandchildren of the testator had to be born in the lives of their parents, the testator's children. The testator's children were lives in being by implication.

13–32 But in the same gift in a deed *inter vivos*, the contingent interest was void. The grantor might have more children after the date of the instrument and so it was possible that a grandchild who became 21 might not be the child of a person alive at the date of the instrument. The possibility rendered the gift void.

Human Lives Only

13–33 Lives in being had to be human lives. In *Re Kelly*,[45] there was a bequest of a sum of money out of which £4 a year was to be spent "on the support of my dogs" and this was followed by a contingent gift over to charity of any balance remaining "on the death of my last dog". The contingent gift as it was drafted could only be upheld if one could take the life of the surviving dog as a life in being for the purpose of the perpetuity rule. Meredith J. held, in an elegant judgment, that this was not permissible. Accordingly, the contingent gift of the balance of the fund was void for remoteness.[46] The preference for human lives was not based upon any assumed moral or religious superiority of human lives as against other forms of life. It was merely that if the lives of animals or plants were to be allowed, the rule would be rendered pointless. Conveyancers would simply insert an express clause limiting the contingency to the lives of a class of particularly long-lived species of plant or animal life, such as giant tortoises or California Redwood trees.

Express Limitation of Gifts to the Perpetuity Period

13–34 A contingency that would otherwise be void could be saved by expressly limiting it to the perpetuity period by reference to a life or class of lives. In *Re Villar*,[47] a testator who died in 1926 made a contingent gift in favour of

---

[45] [1932] I.R. 255.
[46] As to the *vested* gift of the fund, the rule against perpetuities did not apply, but the rule against inalienability, which has the same "perpetuity" period (discussed below), did do so. The vested fund would have been void if inalienable for longer than the perpetuity period. In applying that rule the judge felt able to uphold the vested gift as valid under the rule for each year the dogs lived up to a maximum of 21 years.
[47] [1929] 1 Ch. 243.

> *all my descendants who shall be living 21 years after the death of the survi-*
> *vor of all the lineal descendants of Queen Victoria living at my death.*

It was held to be a valid gift. Any number of lives could be chosen so long as they are not so numerous as to be completely unascertainable. But the court did not say that an attempt to ascertain the class membership had to be made.[48] After the case the clause became known as a "Royal lives clause", but there was of course no need for the lives to be those of royalty.

No Valid Lives

13–35 If there are no valid lives in being, the perpetuity period was 21 years.[49] The 21-year period, with or without lives, was a period "in gross", i.e. unrelated to the minority of any person.[50] It was not therefore affected by the reduction of the age of majority to 18 years.[51]

The "Surviving Spouse" or "Unborn Widow/Widower" Trap

13–36 This was a common mistake made in drafting limitations. For example:

> *[a trust] to A [unmarried] for life, remainder to any husband she may marry*
> *for life, remainder to the children of the marriage alive at the death of the*
> *survivor of A and her husband in fee simple.*[52]

The remainder to the children was void. It was possible that A might marry someone who was not alive at the date the instrument took effect, and so was not a life in being. If he survived A for more than 21 years the contingent interest to the children of the marriage would vest outside the period. This possibility rendered the remainder to the children void.

13–37 The mistake was to insert the words "alive at the death of the survivor of A and her husband". Even without those words, the gift would not vest *in possession* until that point, but the words have the effect of postponing the vesting *in interest* until the death of the survivor of A and her husband. There is no reason why vesting in *interest* should be postponed to that point. Since the LCLRA 2009, there would be nothing to invalidate the remainder to the children.

---

[48] The case has been criticised on the ground that the particular limitation in the case did not satisfy the test laid down. It was probably impossible to ascertain, even in the equivocal sense used by the court, whether all of Victoria's descendants had survived.

[49] *Palmer v Holford* (1828) 4 Russ. 403.

[50] *Palmer v Holford* (1828) 4 Russ. 403; *Re Kelly* [1932] I.R. 255.

[51] *Re Hooper* [1932] 1 Ch. 38; Age of Majority Act 1985.

[52] *Re Frost* (1889) 43 Ch. D. 246.

The Presumption of Fertility

13–38 In *Jee v Audley*,[53] an English court took the view that in considering possibilities, the common law refused to recognise that a person was too old or too young to have children. It was not a presumption, but a rule of law.

13–39 This was contrary to common sense and has been attacked as so absurd as bringing the law into disrepute. It did have some justification, however; *Jee v Audley* attempted to preserve the logical precision of the rule so that a lawyer looking at a limitation could advise with certainty as to its validity or invalidity without the need for expensive litigation. If evidence on the point was admissible, such as age or more direct medical evidence, then no such certain advice could be given, quite apart from the distress that such evidence might cause in some cases.

13–40 The cost of such logical certainty was the absurdity produced in some cases, especially when combined with the "no wait-and-see" rule. These cases were ridiculed by Barton Leach who referred to them as the "Fertile Octogenarian" and "Precocious Toddler" cases.[54]

13–41 Irish courts refused to apply the rule in *Jee v Audley*, and replaced it instead with a *presumption* in favour of fertility. In *Exham v Beamish*,[55] the deed was *inter vivos* and the issue was whether Anne Thompson had to be presumed capable, in accordance with *Jee v Audley*, of having another child in 1865, even though it was clear by 1938 that she had not. Gavan Duffy J. accepted that the no-wait-and-see rule applied in Ireland, but declined to follow *Jee v Audley*. He held instead that if modern medical science would regard as absurd the possibility that a given person could have a child, then the court was not required to regard it as possible. The effect of *Exham* was to replace the rule in *Jee v Audley* with a mere presumption to that effect, rebuttable by evidence. The hearing in *Exham* was adjourned, the judge indicating that he was prepared to hear evidence as to the possibility of further children being born to the settlors in 1865.[56]

13–42 Gavan Duffy J.'s decision in *Exham v Beamish* may accurately be described as a tour-de-force. It is bold and self-confident in its rejection of an absurd rule and sensible in its framing of an alternative approach. Nevertheless, when one attempts to unravel the absurdities of the perpetuity rule at common

---

[53] (1787) 1 Cox Eq. Cas. 324.

[54] W. Barton Leech, "The Rule Against Perpetuities and Gifts to Classes" (1938) 51 Harv. L.R. 1329. See *Re Dawson* (1888) 39 Ch. D. 155. See also, *Ward v Van der Loff* [1924] A.C. 653; *Re Gaite* [1949] 1 All E.R. 459.

[55] [1939] I.R. 336.

[56] It is interesting to note that historical evidence shows Anne Thompson was in fact 46 years old in 1865: L.G. Pine (ed.), *Burke's Genealogical and Heraldic History of the Landed Gentry of Ireland*, 4th edn (London: Burke's Peerage Ltd, 1958), p.687. See also B. Burke, *Burke's Irish Family Records* (London: Burke's Peerage, 1976), p.94.

law, it is not easy to justify stopping at any particular point. The judge, for example, accepted that the law in this jurisdiction did not allow wait-and-see in the common law perpetuity rule. It was possible, and not actual, events which had to be taken into account and the possibilities which existed must be those at the date of the settlement.[57] However, the absurdity of *Jee v Audley* was only replaced by the absurdity of inquiring into the ability of someone over 70 years before to have a child, when it was known that she had not in fact done so.[58]

Administrative Contingencies

13–43 These occurred where a contingent gift was made to take effect on the happening of an event of an administrative kind.

13–44 There was a similar absurdity in such cases. In *Re Wood*,[59] the testator owned some gravel pits and wanted them to be operated until exhausted, at which time the land was to be sold and the proceeds distributed to his issue. Evidence showed that at the normal rate of working, the pits were expected to last another four years. In fact, they lasted six years. The court held that the actual period was irrelevant, as there was no wait-and-see. The court held that as there were no lives in being by reference to whom the contingency was limited, the period was 21 years. Adopting a similar approach to *Jee v Audley*, the court held there was nothing necessarily to confine the life of the pits to this period either, and so the gift was void for remoteness. Barton Leach termed this case "the Magic Gravel Pit".[60] Again, *Exham v Beamish* could possibly have been extended to such cases.

Cy-pres

13–45 Courts in Ireland and England refused to recognise that there was a cy-pres rule in the modern rule against perpetuities.[61]

Exceptions to Perpetuity Rule

13–46 There were numerous exceptions to the perpetuity rule which added to the complexity of applying it. These have been discussed in the second edition of this work and only four need be mentioned here.

---

[57] It had been so decided by O'Loghlen M.R. in *Smith v Dungannon* (1841) Fl. & K. 638, upheld in the House of Lords, sub nom *Dungannon (Lord) v Smith* (1845) 12 Cl. & F. 546.

[58] J. Mee, "Return of Fertile Octogenarians" (1992) 14 D.U.L.J. 69, pointed out that the effect of the Status of Children Act 1987 appeared to have negated the effect of *Exham* as to dispositions after the Act. Under s.27(4)(b), in the absence of a contrary intention, an adopted child is entitled to take as if he or she had been born to his or her adoptive parents at the date of an adoption order. Moreover, there is no upper age limit on eligibility to adopt, so, he argued, the possibility existed in relation to any adult person, no matter how old, that he or she might have a child by adoption.

[59] (1894) 3 Ch. D. 381.

[60] W. Barton Leach, "The Rule Against Perpetuities and Gifts to Classes" (1938) 51 Harv. L.R. 1329.

[61] R.H. Maudsley, *The Modern Law of Perpetuities* (London: Butterworths, 1979), p.81.

Possibilities of Reverter

13–47 In *Attorney General v Cummins*,[62] Palles C.B. held that such interests were not subject to the perpetuity rule.[63] Thus, in the limitation

> *to A and her heirs until the land ceases to be used as a school*

even before the LCLRA 2009, a possibility remained in the grantor, no matter how remotely it might occur.

Rights of Entry for Condition Broken

13–48 Palles C.B. in the same case held obiter that rights of entry for condition broken following a conditional fee were not subject to the perpetuity rule either.

Possibilities of Resulting Trust

13–49 In the Northern Ireland case of *Walsh v Wightman*,[64] the court held that a possibility of resulting trust was not subject to the perpetuity rule.[65] Thus, a gift

> *[in trust for] the B school in fee simple so long as the land is used as a school*

created a possibility of a resulting trust in favour of the grantor if the land ceased to be used as a school at any time in the future.

Certain Gifts to Charities

13–50 The general rule was that a contingent gift to a charity was subject to the rule in the same way as other contingent gifts.[66] But if there was a gift to one charity followed by a gift over to another charity on a certain event, the gift over was not void merely because the event could occur outside the perpetuity period.[67] So if property was given to Charity A, but if Charity A failed to maintain the testator's tomb in repair, the property was to go to Charity B, the contingent gift over was valid.[68]

---

[62] [1906] I.R. 406.

[63] In the case itself quit rents were granted in fee simple until the recipient or his heirs were paid a lump sum.

[64] [1927] N.I. 1.

[65] The same rule operates in the United States. See *Commerce Union Bank v Warren County* 707 SW 2d 854 (1986).

[66] C. Harpum, S. Bridge and M. Dixon, *Megarry & Wade: The Law of Real Property* (London: Sweet & Maxwell, 2012), para.9–138.

[67] *Megarry & Wade: The Law of Real Property* (2012), para.9–138.

[68] *Re Tyler* [1891] 3 Ch. 252, but doubted in *RSPCA of NSW v Benevolent Society of NSW* (1960) 102 C.L.R. 629. The decision in *Re Tyler* was difficult to justify in principle. See below.

Gifts Over

13–51 Take the following example:

[in trust] for O and her heirs so long as the land is used for agriculture
[then over to P and her heirs].

Before the LCLRA 2009 the words in square brackets created no valid interest. The gift over was void for perpetuity, leaving a possibility of a resulting trust in the grantor. Now, the remainder to P would be valid, however remotely it might occur in future.

REFORM OF THE RULE AGAINST PERPETUITIES

13–52 Few common law jurisdictions have adopted the radical reform of outright abolition of the rule against perpetuities.[69] The English Report[70] noted that Scotland has never had a rule against perpetuities, but it is not a common law jurisdiction, at least as far as land law is concerned. The Perpetuities and Accumulations Act 1964 in England and Wales and the Perpetuities Act (Northern Ireland) 1966 reformed the rule by introducing various modifications, which have since been further reformed by the Perpetuities and Accumulations Act 2009.[71]

13–53 Abolishing the rule without any replacement raises the possibility that contingent interests in land may be created which will remain contingent over a long period and therefore remove the land from the market. However, after the LCLRA 2009 these will necessarily exist only as equitable interests under a trust, the legal fee simple being vested in the trustees. If the equitable interests are such as to prevent sale, the remedy under the LCLRA 2009 is for an "appropriate person" to apply for a variation of trust. An "appropriate person" is a trustee or a beneficiary or any other person that the court considers to be appropriate. The fondness of the drafters of the LCLRA 2009 for this technique—of putting the onus on the individual to bring an action in court, with all the anxiety and expense that would entail—in order to resolve possible problems arising from the reforms, is regrettable.

THE RULE AGAINST ACCUMULATIONS

13–54 There was certainly a rule at common law which controlled accumulations of income from land or from a fund consisting of personal property

---

[69] See J. Mee, "From Here to Eternity? Perpetuities Reform in Ireland" (2000) 7 D.U.L.J. 91.

[70] Law Commission, *The Rules against Perpetuities and Excessive Accumulations* (Law Com No. 251) (London: Stationery Office, 1998), p.22.

[71] This applies to England and Wales, and provides for a mandatory 125-year period, with wait-and-see, etc.

such as money or stocks and shares. However, the nature of the rule was open to question. Some writers regarded the supposed rule as similar to the rule against inalienability in that it applied to vested interests, in this case the vested fund, and limited its duration.[72] Stated in this way, the rule laid down that a direction to trustees to accumulate funds was void if the accumulation could endure beyond a period identical to the period of inalienability, i.e. a life or lives in being plus 21 years. It is certainly the case that charitable trusts were an exception. They could always accumulate funds for the charitable purpose indefinitely. It will be seen that a similar exception for charities still exists in the rule against inalienability.

13–55 In England, the Accumulations Act 1800[73] cut down drastically the period during which income could be accumulated in a fund. It was a result of the famous case of *Thellusson v Woodford*.[74] The testator in that case, Mr Thellusson, directed in his will that the income from all his property was to be accumulated during the lives of his sons, grandsons and great-grandchildren living at his death, and that on the death of the survivor the accumulated fund should be divided among specified descendants. Since the period of accumulation was limited to lives in being, the court upheld the validity of the direction under the supposed "common law rule". This caused an outcry and demands in Parliament for reform. It was felt to be grossly unfair that a testator could deprive his immediate descendants of all benefit from his fortune, and confer a vast fortune on remoter and as yet unascertained descendants, in order to satisfy a desire that his own remote posterity should become prominent in society, from a motive of what might be described as posthumous greed. The Accumulations Act 1800 therefore sought to cut down the period in which accumulations should take place.[75] The 1800 Act was passed in England just before the Union[76] and so never applied to Ireland, but the Accumulations Act 1892 was, curiously and apparently by an oversight, applied to Ireland. The LCLRA 2009 both abolished the common law rule[77] and repealed the 1892 Act.[78]

---

[72] *Megarry & Wade: The Law of Real Property* (2012), para.9–162.
[73] Sections 164–166 of the English Law of Property Act 1925 and s.13 of the Perpetuities and Accumulations Act 1964 have been repealed by ss.13 and 15 of the Perpetuities and Accumulations Act 2009. See *Megarry & Wade: The Law of Real Property* (2012), para.9–162.
[74] (1799) 4 Ves. Jun. 227.
[75] The period was the life of the settlor or grantor, or 21 years from the death of such person or testator, or the minorities of persons living or in the womb at the death of the grantor, etc., or the minorities of persons who under the limitation would be entitled, if of full age, to the accumulated fund: *Megarry & Wade: The Law of Real Property* (2012), para.9–163.
[76] The Union came into effect on 1 January 1801.
[77] LCLRA 2009 s.16(e).
[78] LCLRA 2009 s.8(3) and Sch.2, Pt 4.

THE RULE AGAINST INALIENABILITY

13–56 A confusing aspect of the laws against remoteness is that there is a rule which appears similar to the modern rule against perpetuities and which has the same period and is even sometimes referred to also as "the rule against perpetuities" but which is quite distinct. The rule against inalienability, as it is now generally called, has not been abolished by the LCLRA 2009. It applies to *vested* gifts and controls how long the subject matter can remain inalienable. The rule against inalienability arises in the context of non-charitable "purpose" trusts. In order to see why this is so, it is necessary to examine how alienability is dealt with in other property contexts.

The Control of Alienability

13–57 Since the Statute *Quia Emptores* 1290, there has been a basic principle that property should not be rendered inalienable by a disposition by a fee simple owner. As to legal estates, the principle is realised by various rules which have essentially the same result.

13–58 As to fee simple estates, *Quia Emptores* 1290 provided that the freehold tenant had the power of free alienation and the courts have struck down attempts to limit the power to any extensive degree. The rule is indeed restated by s.9(4) of the LCLRA 2009.[79] The types of clause struck down have generally been those which attempt to restrict alienation in terms of the description of people to whom the land can be sold or not sold, but a condition which attempted to prevent *any* alienation for a given period would also be void on this ground.

13–59 Life estates can be alienated to an extent consistent with the tenant's original interest by creating an estate *pur autre vie*. The Settled Land Acts 1882–1890 gave most limited owners the power to sell the fee simple estate. Under the LCLRA 2009 settlements under the Settled Land Acts are replaced by trusts of land in which the fee simple is vested in trustees who have power to deal with the fee simple in the interests of the beneficiaries under the trust.[80] Therefore, as to legal estates, it can be said that the principle of alienability is satisfied.

The Rule

13–60 The rule requires that the trust fund in the hands of trustees should not be rendered inalienable in their hands for an infinite period. The fact that the assets represented by the fund, e.g. stocks and shares, may be bought and sold by the trustees does not satisfy the rule, which is concerned with the trust

---

[79] "A fee simple remains freely alienable."
[80] LCLRA 2009 Pt 4.

property itself.[81] The trust fund itself will be rendered inalienable if there is a direction to employ the income from the fund for a given purpose for an infinite period, and so such a direction is void.[82] Thus, a trust in which the income is to be used to provide a cup for the best yachtsman in a sailing club is void if not limited to the period.[83] A trust to provide a prize for students in an educational establishment on the other hand would fall within the exception to the rule in favour of charitable trusts, being for educational purposes.[84]

The Period of Inalienability

13–61 The rule incorporates a period the same as that in the former modern perpetuity rule, namely a life or lives in being plus 21 years. This may be called the "period of inalienability". However, the former rule against perpetuities applied to contingent interests and determined the period within which they had to vest in interest, whereas the rule against inalienability applies to *vested* interests and determines the period within which they may remain inalienable.

Exception: Charitable Trusts

13–62 One exception to the rule is charitable trusts. The income from the fund may be used by the trustees for the charitable purpose for an infinite period without rendering the trust void.[85] In policy terms this may be said to be the case because the definition of charity incorporates public benefit and the benefit to the public resulting from the charitable purpose outweighs the disadvantage of removal of property from the market.[86]

Non-charitable Trusts

13–63 Non-charitable trusts are subject to the rule. Where there are human beneficiaries it would be rare for the rule to be invoked. In the past, the Settled Land Acts ensured that a "tenant for life" or person having the powers of a "tenant for life", which included nearly all cases where there was a trust of land, where his or her interest was in possession, could alienate the fee simple

---

[81] This is an interesting distinction which some find artificial. If the fund is wholly invested in stocks and shares, they represent the entire fund and they may be bought and sold, but they are all held in the name of the trust and "the fund" is held by the trustees in the sense that the income is paid to and then distributed by the trustees.

[82] *Boyle v Boyle* (1877) I.R. 11 Eq. 433.

[83] *Re Nottage* [1895] 2 Ch. 649.

[84] The fact that the trust fund, as opposed to assets in which it is invested (which will be alienable in accordance with provisions as to trust of land or as trustee investments), will have to be retained to give effect to the beneficial interests, does not in itself invalidate the trust: *Re Gage* [1898] 1 Ch. 506.

[85] See R. Keane, *Equity and the Law of Trusts in the Republic of Ireland*, 2nd edn (Haywards Heath: Bloomsbury Professional, 2011), paras 7.20 and 11.01.

[86] See now the definition of charity in s.3 of the Charities Act 2009. Charitable purposes are the prevention or relief of poverty or economic hardship, the advancement of education, the advancement of religion and "any other purpose that is of benefit to the community". Public benefit is the overriding test.

in the land. There was no problem in the case of a bare trust, i.e. a trust not involving successive interests, where the beneficiaries are of full age. The rule in *Saunders v Vautier*[87] ensures that beneficiaries who are absolutely entitled can put an end to the trust at any time and have the legal estate conveyed to them. A condition which attempted to exclude the rule would not be enforced. As to a trust of land under the LCLRA 2009, the fee simple is vested in trustees who have the powers, subject to any powers of the tenant for life.

13–64 The rule therefore comes into play as to non-charitable trusts where there are no human beneficiaries, the so-called "purpose trusts", for the upkeep of buildings, grave stones or monuments, or the maintenance of animals, etc. In *Re Fossit's Estate*,[88] the testator left one-third of his residuary estate to the Orange Institution of Ireland "for the upkeep of the Orange Hall, 10 Rutland Square, Dublin". It was held void as contrary to the rule.

13–65 The question is often one of interpretation, and courts have been generous in their interpretations. In *Re Byrne*,[89] the gift was "for the absolute use and benefit of the Jesuit Order of Ireland". It was held valid, on the ground that the members of the order could dispose of the fund at any time.[90] In *Re Conner*,[91] a testator by her will bequeathed £1,000 to a cemetery company "to be applied for the maintenance and care" of her family vault. There was no reference either to the investment of the sum, or to the income accruing, nor was there any gift over in the event of the cemetery company's failure to maintain or take care of the vault. Haugh J. held that the gift was an outright bequest of £1,000 to the cemetery company, which vested in the company on the death of the testator, and that it was a valid non-charitable gift which did not infringe the rule against inalienability.[92] Gifts have also been upheld on the ground that they are to the members that make up the institution at the date of the gift rather than to the institution.[93] If the gift includes future members, it would be void unless limited to the period, or, as in the *Byrne* case, the members for the time being were empowered to alienate it at their discretion.

Maintenance of Tombs
13–66 Many trusts that fell foul of the rule were gifts to trustees for the purpose of maintaining a tomb. The courts came to the aid of such trusts in *Re Tyler*[94] by upholding a gift to Charity A with a proviso that the fund should shift to Charity B if Charity A failed to maintain the testator's tomb. They

---

[87] (1841) Cr. & Ph. 240.
[88] [1934] I.R. 504.
[89] [1935] I.R. 782.
[90] See also *Re Keogh's Estate* [1945] I.R. 13.
[91] [1960] I.R. 67.
[92] Nor, at the time, the rule against perpetuities.
[93] *Re Byrne* [1935] I.R. 782.
[94] *Re Tyler* [1891] 3 Ch. 252, but doubted in *RSPCA of NSW v Benevolent Society of NSW* (1960) 102 C.L.R. 629.

interpreted the condition as not imposing a trust to maintain the tomb, but a bare condition.[95] The first, vested, gift was within the exception to the inalienability rule as to charities. The courts held that the contingent gift over to Charity B did not infringe the perpetuity rule as it fell within an exception in favour of gifts over from one charity to another. Then, probably because of doubts about the principle behind the *Re Tyler* device, a statutory exception to the inalienability rule was provided for by s.50 of the Charities Act 1961 which laid down that a gift for the indefinite upkeep of a tomb was valid if the income was not over IR£60 (now €76.18) per year or the capital was not over IR£1,000 (now €1,250). As to gifts for the maintenance of tombs in excess of the amounts, they had to be limited to 21 years or, possibly, given its dubious nature, the *Re Tyler* device.

13–67 After the LCLRA 2009, gifts for the maintenance of tombs would have to fall within s.50 or be limited to the period, unless a version of the charity-to-charity device is still valid. That device depends on a gift being given as a gift for charitable purposes to Charity A, subject to a condition subsequent with a gift over to Charity B. But *Re Tyler* always rested on dubious reasoning. How could the initial gift be said to be for the charitable purposes of Charity A, and so not subject to the inalienability rule, if it was to be divested as soon as Charity A ceased to use it for the non-charitable purpose? And if it did use it for the non-charitable purpose, how would that not compromise its charitable status?

13–68 Since the perpetuity rule and its exceptions have now been abolished by the LCLRA 2009, it would seem that, even assuming such a device is still valid, although the initial gift must still be in favour of a charity (in order to fall within the exception to the inalienability rule), there is nothing now to require the contingent gift over to be in favour of a charity—in which case the rule against inalienability could easily be flouted, without any necessary public benefit, which was the supposed justification for the device. That is, unless a charity-to-charity device similar to the old one is approved in future by the courts. Alternatively, the monetary limits in the Charities Act 1961 need to be increased.

Maintenance of Animals
13–69 There was no similar exception in the Charities Act 1961 for trusts for the upkeep of animals, and so the device of the gift-plus-gift-over, if still available, would still have to be used in such a case, or, if a trust for maintenance, the gift limited to the period.

---

[95] *Re Davies* [1915] 1 Ch. 543 upheld the device even though there would be no surplus left over for Charity A.

13–70 In *Re Kelly*,[96] there was a bequest of a fund out of which £4 a year was to be spent "on the support of my dogs". There was no express limit as to time. It was argued that the dogs' lives could be taken as lives in being for the purpose of the rule. Meredith J. held that for the purpose of the inalienability rule, the lives must be human lives. In the absence of such lives the period was 21 years. This should have rendered the gift of the fund void for inalienability, because there was nothing else by which to limit the gift to the 21-year period. The judge nevertheless felt able to uphold the gift as valid for each year the dogs lived up to a maximum of 21 years. This may have been in accordance with common sense, but seems open to the objection that it introduced both a cy-pres doctrine, and possibly also a wait-and-see rule,[97] into the rule against inalienability, neither of which had been recognised before in this jurisdiction.[98]

Cy-pres

13–71 The case law in Ireland and England does not support the view that there is a cy-pres jurisdiction in the rule against inalienability, with the exception of *Re Kelly* itself. Meredith J. did not refer to the doctrine by name but an alternative way of looking at the case, i.e. apart from its being wrong on the point, is to regard it as a precedent for cy-pres in the inalienability rule.

---

[96] [1932] I.R. 255.

[97] Because the number of years is not ascertainable unless one takes into account when the surviving dog dies.

[98] It also makes it more difficult to appreciate why the judge also struck down the contingent gift over to charity, under the rule against perpetuities, since it depended on the same contingency.

CHAPTER 14

Powers

[A]ll power is a trust ... we are accountable for its exercise ...

— Benjamin Disraeli, *Vivian Grey* (1826)

14–01 A power is "an individual personal capacity of the donee of the power to do something."[1] It is an authority given by one person, the donor, to another person, the donee, so that the donee may determine the legal relations affecting him- or herself, or between him- or herself and other persons, or between other persons.[2] In the context of property law powers, the word "power" is usually used to described a person's authority to dispose of or deal with property which she does not herself own.[3]

14–02 Part 6 of the Land and Conveyancing Law Reform Act 2009 ("LCLRA 2009") implements recommendations of the Law Reform Commission in relation to powers of appointment, but Pt 6 is wider in scope. Part 6 also applies to powers created or arising before or after the LCLRA 2009.[4]

CLASSIFICATION

14–03 Powers may be classified in a number of different ways. In the modern law the major distinction is between those powers which are fiduciary and those which are not, but in the past powers have been subject to a number of different schemes of classification.

Powers Collateral, in Gross and Appurtenant

14–04 The first method of classification focuses on whether the donee of the power has an interest in the property affected by the power. Powers "simply collateral" are those where the donee of the power is not given any estate or interest in the property. At common law, such powers could not be released, i.e. given up.[5] Section 27 of the LCLRA 2009 allows powers to be released,

---

[1] *Re Armstrong, Ex p. Gilchrist* (1886) 17 Q.B.D. 521 at 531.
[2] See J.C.W. Wylie, *Irish Land Law*, 5th edn (Haywards Heath: Bloomsbury Professional, 2013), para.11.01.
[3] G. Thomas, *Thomas on Powers*, 2nd edn (Oxford: Oxford University Press, 2012), p.2.
[4] LCLRA 2009 s.25.
[5] *Re Dunne's Trusts* (1878) 1 L.R. Ir. 516 (MR).

unless they are in the nature of a trust or other fiduciary power.[6] Section 28 allows any power to be disclaimed, i.e. renounced at the beginning.[7] On disclaimer, the power may be exercised by any other person or persons, or the survivor or survivors of such person, to whom the power is given, subject to the terms of the instrument creating the power.[8]

14–05 Powers in gross are those in which the donee has an interest in the property but the exercise of the power cannot affect that interest, as in the following limitation in a will:

> *to A for life and after his death to his children for such interests as he may appoint.*

14–06 Powers appurtenant or appendant are those in which the donee has an interest in the property and which can be affected by the exercise of the power, as in this limitation in a will:

> *to such of the children of X for such interests as X shall by deed or will appoint.*

Common Law and Equitable Powers

14–07 The second method of classification depends on whether a power is equitable or legal in nature. A limited range of powers were recognised at common law.[9] These included powers of sale and attorney but did not extend to a power of appointment. The Court of Chancery developed a wider range of equitable powers, including the power to revoke old uses and appoint new ones. After the passage of the Statute of Uses 1634, powers which had arisen under uses were executed by the Statute and common law courts began to develop rules regarding powers that had, theretofore, arisen in equity only. It remained (and remains) possible for equitable powers to arise under a trust or in relation to another equitable interest. The repeal of the Statute of Uses by the LCLRA 2009 means that a legal power of appointment can be created without the need for a use.

POWERS OF SALE

14–08 A testator may give executors a power to sell his or her land after the testator's death. The executors in such a case have power to vest the freehold estate in a purchaser although they do not have the estate themselves. In the

---

[6] Re-enacting s.52 of the Conveyancing Act 1882.
[7] Re-enacting s.6 of the Conveyancing Act 1882.
[8] LCLRA 2009 s.28(2).
[9] See W.S. Holdsworth, *The History of English Law* (London: Methuen and Sweet & Maxwell, 1966 repr.), Vol.vii, p.149.

past, real property would pass automatically to the heir-at-law on the death of a testator. Until the exercise of the power, the estate remained vested in the heir.[10] Statutory powers of sale have long been used to make land more alienable; prior to their repeal by the LCLRA 2009, the Settled Land Acts conferred a range of powers on a tenant for life.[11]

POWERS OF APPOINTMENT

History

14–09 Equity recognised powers of appointment before the Statute of Uses 1634 but such powers could only affect equitable interests in land. After the Statute of Uses 1634 it became possible to create legal powers of appointment affecting the legal estate by means of a use executed by the Statute. For example:

> *to X and his heirs to the use of A for life, remainder to such uses as A shall appoint, and in default of and until appointment, to the use of the children of A in fee simple in equal shares.*

The uses to A and the children of A were executed. A had a legal life estate, and there was a vested legal estate in the children of A, who were expressly entitled in default of appointment, subject to being divested[12] by a proper exercise by A of her power.

14–10 The LCLRA 2009 did not convert legal powers into equitable powers.[13] Although powers of sale, appointment and attorney are not listed in s.11(4) as "legal interests", s.11(8), which was added during the Bill's passage through the Seanad,[14] provides:

> "(8) Subject to this Act, a power of attorney, power of appointment or other power to dispose of a legal estate or interest in land operates with the same force and effect as such powers had before the commencement of this Part."

14–11 Furthermore, it seems that despite the repeal of the Statute of Uses 1634, legal powers may still be created, since s.62(2) of the LCLRA 2009 provides that "[a] deed executed after the commencement of this Chapter is fully effective for such purposes without the need for any conveyance to uses".

---

[10] R. Megarry and H.W.R. Wade, *The Law of Real Property*, 4th edn (London: Stevens, 1975), p.462.

[11] For example, the power of a tenant in tail to disentail under the Fines and Recoveries (Ireland) Act 1834, which included a power to convey a fee simple to a purchaser or to feoffees to the use of the tenant.

[12] *Re Earl of Kingston's Estate* (1880) 5 L.R. Ir. 169.

[13] J.C.W. Wylie, *The Land and Conveyancing Law Reform Acts: Annotations and Commentary*, 2nd edn (London: Bloomsbury, 2017), [42], n.54.

[14] Wylie, *Annotations and Commentary* (2017), [42], n.54.

The section then continues, "… and passes possession or the right to possession of the land, without actual entry, unless subject to some prior right to
possession", which could be taken to mean that the subsection applies only to
deeds which would have the effect of passing immediate possession, which the
creation of a power, as distinct from the exercise of it, would not. Nevertheless,
it may be that the rest of the subsection, from the words "and passes possession
…", only refers to deeds which pass possession and which in the past would
have required actual entry. The fact that Pt 6 of the LCLRA 2009 was intended
to consolidate the previous law gives support to this view.[15]

14–12 Given the other changes brought about by the LCLRA 2009, a legal
power of appointment could only be exercised to give a legal interest if that
interest were a fee simple in possession. So in the limitation

> *to A for life, remainder to such of the children of B as A shall by deed or
> will appoint*

if A made an appointment in her lifetime, it would necessarily take effect as a
future interest under a trust of land, and on A's death would presumably continue as a bare or other trust. If A appointed a fee simple by will, it could take
effect in the example as a legal fee simple in possession.

14–13 Equitable powers can still be created:

> *to T and U in fee simple in trust for A for life, remainder in trust as A shall
> by will [or "by deed" or "by deed or will"] appoint.*

A can appoint equitable life estates, or equitable life estates and the equitable
fee simple in remainder, or just a fee simple in remainder.

General and Special Powers
14–14 Powers of appointment may be general or special.

General Powers
14–15 Where the donee, i.e. the person to whom the power is given, can
confer interests in property to which the power relates on anyone, including
him- or herself, the power is a general power.[16] In the limitation

> *to A in fee simple for such trusts as B may by deed or will appoint and in
> default of and until appointment in trust for C in fee simple*

---

[15] Wylie, *Annotations and Commentary* (2017), [59], n.2.
[16] E. Sugden, *A Practical Treatise of Powers*, 8th edn (London: H. Sweet, 1861), p.102; *Bishop
of Oxford v Leighton* (1700) 2 Vern. 376.

B has a power. B is not required to appoint among a specified class and so may appoint to himself, i.e. it is a general power. C takes a vested estate subject to divesting by B. Clearly, a general power is akin to ownership of the fee simple. Hence, general powers form part of a deceased's estate at his or her death vesting in the personal representatives of the deceased when the power was exercised by will.[17]

Special Powers

14–16 If the donee of the power may not appoint to him- or herself then the power is special. Such a donee will have a power to appoint among a class of persons, the "objects of the power", or to one person. The essential difference between special and general powers is that the donee of a general power may appoint to him- or herself, for it is this feature that makes a general power akin to ownership in fee simple. It follows that a power to appoint to anyone in the world *except* oneself is a special power. If the donee of a general power exercises it in favour of X, then it is a gift from the donee to X, for the donee has given away his or her own property, whereas if the donee of a special power exercises it in favour of X, it is a gift from the *donor* of the power.

Certainty

14–17 For a power to be valid a test of certainty must be satisfied. There must be criteria in the grant which are sufficiently clear so that it can be said in relation to any claimant that they come within the power or not.[18] It is not required, however, that a complete list of all the objects be capable of being drawn up.[19] In *Re the Estate of Bayley*,[20] the Supreme Court held that the phrase "my Irish relatives" satisfied the test.

Non-testamentary Powers

14–18 The Law of Property Amendment Act 1859, which is now repealed by the LCLRA 2009,[21] required the exercise of a non-testamentary power (i.e. one otherwise than in a will) to be by deed attested by two or more witnesses, which was not required in an ordinary deed. Section 26 of the LCLRA 2009 dispenses with this additional requirement and provides that an appointment by deed after 1 December 2009 is valid if it complies with s.64 of the LCLRA 2009. Section 64 lays down the formalities of a deed and dispenses with the need for a seal, or the need for the authority to deliver a deed to be by deed. Section 26(1) does not prevent a donee from making a valid appointment in some other way expressly authorised by the instrument creating the power,

---

[17] Succession Act 1965 s.10(4); it is also therefore available for a claim under s.117 of the Succession Act 1965: *Reidy v McGreevy*, unreported, High Court, Barron J., 19 March 1993.
[18] *Kelly v Spears* (1952) 86 I.L.T.R. 81.
[19] *Re the Estate of Bayley* [1945] I.R. 224; *Re Parker's Will* [1966] I.R. 309.
[20] [1945] I.R. 224.
[21] LCLRA 2009 s.8(3) and Sch.2.

nor does it relieve the donee from complying with directions in the instrument requiring the consent of any person or other requirements as to the validity to any appointment.[22]

Entitlement in Default

14–19 If there is no express gift in default of appointment the objects of the power are impliedly entitled.[23] Moreover, equality is equity and they are entitled equally.[24] If the power is to appoint the whole interest of the estate subject to the power, then the gift in default, whether express or implied, cannot be less than that which might have been appointed by the exercise of the power.[25]

14–20 Consider again the example given previously:

> *to A in fee simple for such trusts as B may by deed or will appoint and in default of and until appointment in trust for C in fee simple.*

Suppose that B exercises the power by deed. If B appoints the land

> *in trust for D in fee simple*

B has created an equitable fee simple. The exercise of the power is read with the original limitation, so that it is as if that limitation had been:

> *to A in fee simple in trust for D and her heirs.*

D has a vested estate in fee simple. C's estate comes to an end: it is divested by the exercise of the power.

Formalities: Defective Execution

14–21 Such formalities as are required by the donor[26] and general law[27] must be complied with. If the donee fails to do so, the exercise of the power is said to be "defective". Section 26 of the LCLRA 2009 now provides that s.64, which lays down the formalities for deeds, applies to the execution of non-testamentary powers.[28]

---

[22] LCLRA 2009 s.26(2).

[23] *Sinnott v Walsh* (1880) 5 L.R. Ir. 27. See also, *Mill v Mill* (1877) I.R. 11 Eq. 158; *Re Kieran* (1916) 50 I.L.T.R. 175.

[24] *Doyley v Attorney General* 4 Vin. Abr. 485 pl. 16, 2 Eq. Cas. Abr. 194; *Sinnott v Walsh* (1880) 5 L.R. Ir. 27, App.

[25] *Crozier v Crozier* (1843) 3 Dru. & War. 353 at 373.

[26] *Reid v Thompson* (1854) 2 Ir. Ch. R. 26 (settlement required exercise to be in writing, sealed and delivered in the presence of two witnesses).

[27] LCLRA 2009 s.64.

[28] The Leases Acts 1849 and 1850 validated leases in Ireland which, when they were made, exceeded the terms of the powers under which they were made. The Acts were repealed by the LCLRA 2009: Wylie, *Irish Land Law* (2013), para.11.17.

Excessive Execution

14–22 An excessive execution of a power is one which exceeds the terms of
the power of appointment, as where a donee attempts to appoint to persons
who are not objects of the power. For example, in *Hennessey v Murphy*,[29] a
testator had a testamentary power of appointment over property in favour of
her children only. She purported to appoint the property by will to two of her
grandchildren, who were not objects of the power. Her will also contained a
residuary gift in favour of her son. It was held that as the purported express
exercise of the power was invalid, the residuary gift operated as an appointment to her son.

14–23 Excessive executions may not be wholly void. Where possible courts
try to save the valid part and discard the invalid. Where the donee exercises the
power in favour of some objects and some non-objects, the courts will uphold
the exercise of the power as to the objects.[30]

Illusory Appointments

14–24 Equity made a distinction between what it termed exclusive powers, in which the intention of the donor was that some of the objects might
not take anything at all, and non-exclusive powers, where the intention was
that each object should obtain something. In the latter case, if the donee
appointed a purely token amount to one or more objects, the courts of equity
set it aside as an "illusory appointment", i.e. an appointment creating the illusion that the power had been complied with, while in substance it had not.[31]
The doctrine proved difficult to apply in practice and led to the passing of
the Illusory Appointments Act 1830[32] which provided that the appointment
of a nominal amount was not to be invalid unless the terms of the power
expressly provided otherwise. Then the Powers of Appointment Act 1874
provided that every power of appointment was to be construed as an exclusive power so that the donee could make no appointment at all to one or
more objects, unless the terms of the power expressly provides otherwise.
Farwell commented that "[t]he Act of 1830 enabled an appointor to cut off
any object of the power with a shilling: the Act of 1874 enables him to cut
off the shilling also."[33]

14–25 The LCLRA 2009 repealed both the 1830 and the 1874 Acts and
replaced them with the provisions in s.29 which essentially consolidates the
two Acts and reproduces their combined effect:

---

[29] (1953) 87 I.L.T.R. 29.

[30] *Crozier v Crozier* (1843) 3 Dru. & War. 373; *Re Shekleton's Trusts* [1945] I.R. 115.

[31] *Gibson v Kinven* (1682) 1 Vern. 66.

[32] It applied to Ireland and England.

[33] G. Farwell, *A Concise Treatise on Powers*, 2nd edn (London: Stevens and Sons, 1893), p.374.

"29.—(1) No appointment made in exercise of any power to appoint any
property among two or more persons is invalid on the ground that—
   (a) an insubstantial, illusory or nominal share only is appointed to or left
        unappointed to devolve on any one or more of those persons, or
   (b) any such person is altogether excluded, whether by way of default of
        appointment or otherwise.
(2) This section does not affect any provision in the instrument creating
the power which specifies the amount of any share from which any such
person is not to be excluded."

Fraud on a Power

14–26 The doctrine applies to special powers only, i.e. in which the donee
may not appoint to him- or herself. The basic principle is that persons entitled
in default of an appointment have vested interests until the exercise of the
power divests them of those interests. An appointment for improper motives is
therefore a fraud on those entitled in default of appointment.[34]

Prior Agreement

14–27 Unless the donee is a person entitled in default of appointment, the
appointment is fraudulent if it is made under an agreement between the donee
and the appointee whereby a person other than an object of the power, such as
the donee, is to benefit.[35]

Intention Only

14–28 Even if there is no agreement, if the predominant intention is that a
non-object (who is not entitled in default either) is to benefit, then there is a
fraud.

Benefit to Appointer

14–29 An appointment to the benefit of the donee (i.e. the appointer) is fraudulent, unless the donee is entitled in default.[36] Thus, in *Duggan v Duggan*,[37] the
tenant for life, a mother, had power to appoint to her children. She had incurred
debts, admittedly for the benefit of the family, and for the upkeep of the farm
which was the family home. She appointed the fund to the children on condition that they bought her a life estate and paid the price out of the appointed
fund. The Court of Appeal in Ireland held that the appointment was a fraud on
the persons entitled in default. The primary purpose and only certain effect was
to confer a personal benefit on the mother by discharging her debts. Retention
of the farm might also benefit the children, but that was not the immediate
intention.

---

[34] *Heron v Stokes* (1842) 4 Ir. Eq. R. 285.
[35] *Hutchins v Hutchins* (1877) I.R. 10 Eq. 453.
[36] *Hutchins v Hutchins* (1877) I.R. 10 Eq. 453.
[37] (1880) 7 L.R. Ir. 152.

14–30 In *Kiely v Kiely*,[38] the owner of the power exercised it in favour of his own child who was dying of tuberculosis, so that the parent would inherit the property. The court set aside the appointment.

Acquiescence

14–31 If all the objects of the power agree or confirm the exercise of the power then they cannot later challenge it on the ground of fraud unless there is undue influence.[39]

Release

14–32 The doctrine of fraud on a power does not apply to the release of a power by the donee, i.e. a deed by which the donee relinquishes the power. A release of the power benefits the persons entitled in default and so cannot be a fraud. It is not a fraud on the objects of the power because the donee owes no duty to them to exercise it. A power is unlike a trust in this respect.

Revocation

14–33 The doctrine of fraud on a power does not apply to a revocation of an appointment by the donee. The donee owes no duty to the appointees deprived by the revocation. The donee is free to make another appointment.

The Effect of Fraud

14–34 The fraud affects the whole appointment. Nevertheless, the donee is free to make a new appointment. The fraud does not disqualify the donee from making further appointments[40] but the burden of proof shifts to those asserting the validity of the new appointment to show that it is proper.[41] Fraud has a different effect at common law and in equity. At common law a fraudulent appointment of a legal interest is only voidable by the aggrieved party, and so is valid until avoided. A fraudulent appointment of equitable interests is void ab initio.[42]

14–35 A bona fide purchaser (from an appointee) for value of the legal estate without notice of the fraud takes free of it and obtains a good title.[43] Notice in this instance must be actual, not constructive, if it is to affect the purchaser.[44] Equity recognises that a legal estate obtained for value prevails where there are two innocent parties. A bona fide purchaser (from the appointee) for value

---

[38] (1843) 5 Ir. Eq. R. 442.
[39] *Skelton v Flanagan* (1867) I.R. 1 Eq. 362 at 369. Presumably persons entitled in default are in the same position.
[40] *Hutchins v Hutchins* (1877) I.R. 10 Eq. 453.
[41] *Hutchins v Hutchins* (1877) I.R. 10 Eq. 453.
[42] *Cloutte v Storey* [1911] 1 Ch. 18.
[43] *Hamilton v Kirwan* (1845) 2 J. & L. 393; *McQueen v Farquhar* (1805) 11 Ves. 467.
[44] *McQueen v Farquhar* (1805) 11 Ves. 467; *Skelton v Flanagan* (1867) I.R. 1 Eq. 362.

of an *equitable* interest without notice of the fraud still obtains no title. Where the equities are equal, the first in time prevails. However, if there is anything in the conduct of those defrauded to alter the "balance" of equity, the scales will tip towards the later equity.

POWERS OF ATTORNEY

14–36 A power of attorney is an authority given by one person, the donor, to another person, the attorney or donee, to perform legal acts on behalf of the donor which the donor has power to perform.[45] Formerly they were governed in Ireland by the Conveyancing Acts 1881[46] and 1882.[47] These provisions were replaced by the Powers of Attorney Act 1996 (the "1996 Act").[48]

14–37 Powers of attorney are used for two main purposes: elderly people often wish to give powers of attorney to a trusted relative or friend to deal with their affairs when they feel they are becoming unable to deal with them themselves; and powers of attorney are also used when a person is buying or otherwise dealing with foreign property.

Enduring Powers of Attorney

14–38 In relation to powers of attorney granted by the elderly, in the past the problems often arose because of the rule of law that a power of attorney automatically became void as soon as the donor ceased to have mental capacity.[49] The 1996 Act introduced the *enduring* power of attorney which remains effective even if the donor later develops incapacity.[50] An enduring power of attorney may confer a general or a limited authority on the attorney, a general authority being the power to do any act which the donor could perform.[51] It may also confer on the attorney the power to make "personal care" decisions on the donor's behalf.[52]

14–39 There is an obvious danger that enduring powers of attorney could be abused and advantage could be taken of elderly people by unscrupulous relatives or others. For this reason the 1996 Act provides a number of safeguards, including a process of registration of powers of attorney by the court.[53]

---

[45] Wylie, *Irish Land Law* (2013), para.11.32.

[46] Conveyancing Act 1881 Pt XI.

[47] Conveyancing Act 1882 ss.8 and 9.

[48] In Northern Ireland by the Powers of Attorney (NI) Act 1971; Wylie, *Irish Land Law* (2013), para.11.29.

[49] Wylie, *Irish Land Law* (2013), paras 11.32 and 11.48.

[50] In England and Wales they were replaced by "lasting powers of attorney" under the Mental Capacity Act 2005. See C. Harpum, S. Bridge and M. Dixon, *Megarry & Wade: The Law of Real Property*, 8th edn (London: Sweet & Maxwell, 2012), para.36–027.

[51] Powers of Attorney Act 1996 s.6.

[52] Powers of Attorney Act 1996 s.6(6) and (7).

[53] Powers of Attorney Act 1996 Pt II.

An attorney must give notice to the donor's relatives where possible before applying for registration. The court has powers, both before and after registration, aimed at ensuring that advantage or the danger of it is not being taken of the donor. A purchaser of land is entitled to a certified copy of any power of attorney.[54]

Foreign Law

14–40 If a person is buying, selling or otherwise dealing with property in a foreign country, it is usually convenient to give a power of attorney to a person in that country, usually a local lawyer, to deal with the property on behalf of the donor of the power.[55] This is often still the case even when the donor has a solicitor in Ireland. Apart from saving the time and effort of possibly repeated trips abroad, and language difficulties, the foreign lawyer is in a far better position to advise and deal with the law in the foreign jurisdiction. In many cases, the donor will be required to sign the power of attorney in the presence of a notary public.[56] The notary public signs and attaches his or her seal to the document. Not all foreign lawyers, especially those in some European Union countries, require such a formality.

14–41 In order to prove the genuineness of a notary's signature, documents signed by a notary have to be authenticates either by *legalisation* or by an *apostille*.

14–42 Legalisation consists of an unbroken chain of verifying signatures, linking the notary to the registrar of the Supreme Court, then Consular Section of the Department of Foreign Affairs in Dublin, and then the consular representative in Dublin (or London) of the foreign country.

14–43 This laborious process is replaced, in the case of signatories to the Hague Convention of 5 October 1961[57] by apostille. Ireland ratified the Convention in 1999. The document is presented to the Department of Foreign Affairs, and the apostille certificate is stamped on or attached to the public document.

Revocation

14–44 At common law a power of attorney was automatically revoked by the donor's death, insanity, marriage or bankruptcy. The donor could also revoke

---

[54] Powers of Attorney Act 1996 s.23.

[55] See *http://www.notarypublic.ie/powers-of-attorney/* [accessed 4 March 2018].

[56] E. Rory O'Connor, *The Irish Notary; A Treatise on the Law and Practice of Notaries in Ireland* (Abingdon: Professional Books Ltd, 1987); Eamonn G. Hall and E. Rory O'Connor, *The Supplement to O'Connor's The Irish Notary* (Dublin: Faculty of Notaries Public in Ireland, 2007).

[57] Convention of 5 October 1961 Abolishing the Requirement of Legalisation for Foreign Public Documents.

the power unless it was "coupled with an interest", as where it was given to the donee as a part of a security for the payment of money[58]; for example, where a power was given to an equitable mortgagee (the donee) to sell the legal estate if the mortgagor (the donor) defaulted on the mortgage.[59] In this case the power was part of the mortgagee's security and it would be fraudulent for the donor to revoke it.

14–45 Under the 1996 Act, where a power of attorney is expressed to be irrevocable and is given to secure a proprietary interest of the donee of the power, or the performance of an obligation owed to the donee, then, so long as the donee has that interest or the obligation remains undischarged, the power cannot be revoked by the donor without the consent of the donee, or by the death, incapacity or bankruptcy of the donor or, if the donor is a body corporate, by its winding-up or dissolution.[60] The provisions apply whenever the power was created.[61]

Protection of the Attorney

14–46 The attorney or donee does not incur liability to the donor or to a third party if the donee does not know that the power has been revoked.[62] However, if the donee knows of an event, such as the death of the donor, which has the effect of revoking the power, the donee is deemed to know that the power has been revoked.[63]

Protection of Third Parties

14–47 Under the old provisions contained in ss.8 and 9 of the Conveyancing Act 1882, a distinction was made between: (a) powers of attorney given for valuable consideration and expressed to be irrevocable; and (b) powers of attorney "whether given for valuable consideration or not" and expressed to be irrevocable for a fixed time not exceeding one year.

14–48 These provisions were unsatisfactory on a number of grounds.[64] It was not clear why there was a distinction between powers given for valuable consideration and those that were not. They did not reflect the more valid distinction at common law between powers coupled with an interest, mentioned above, and those that were not so coupled.

---

[58] Wylie, *Irish Land Law* (2013), para.11.38. See *Walsh v Whitcomb* (1797) 2 Esp. 565; *Re Parkinson's Estate* (1864) 10 Ir. Jur. (ns) 82; *Tingley v Muller* [1917] 2 Ch. 144.

[59] Wylie, *Irish Land Law* (2013), para.11.42.

[60] Powers of Attorney Act 1996 s.20.

[61] Powers of Attorney Act 1996 s.20(3).

[62] Powers of Attorney Act 1996 s.18(1).

[63] Powers of Attorney Act 1996 s.18(5).

[64] Wylie, *Irish Land Law* (2013), paras 11.41–11.43.

14–49 The 1996 Act again recognises this distinction in a modified form. Section 20(1) provides:

"(1) Where a power of attorney is expressed to be irrevocable and is given to secure—
  (a) a proprietary interest of the donee of the power, or
  (b) the performance of an obligation owed to the donee,
then, so long as the donee has that interest or the obligation remains undischarged, the power shall not be revoked—
  (i) by the donor without the consent of the donee, or
  (ii) by the death, incapacity or bankruptcy of the donor or, if the donor is a body corporate, by its winding-up or dissolution."

The distinction is between powers of attorney expressed to be given for security and powers of attorney which are not. In either case the provisions in the 1996 Act apply whenever the power was created.[65]

Powers Given for Security

14–50 It follows that a third party is only protected if the power is *expressed* to be irrevocable *and* to be given for security.[66] A third party is not protected if the power was in fact given for security, but the instrument does not expressly say so. For the third party to be protected, the power must be expressed to be given for security, even if, in fact, it was not, unless the third party knows it was not, in which case he or she is not protected.[67] Furthermore, the third party in this case is protected unless he or she actually knows that the power had been revoked, i.e. that it was in law revocable and the third party knows it had in fact been revoked.[68]

Powers Not for Security

14–51 As to powers of attorney *other* than those given for security, where the power has been revoked, then as to a third party dealing with the donee of the power, "the transaction between them shall, in favour of that person, be as valid as if the power had then been in force".[69] The third party is entitled to assume that the power is fully operative, unless he or she knows it has been revoked.[70] In this case, if the donee knows of an event which has the effect of revoking the power, the donee is deemed to know that the power has been revoked, a more stringent requirement than in the case of powers given for security.[71]

---

[65] Powers of Attorney Act 1996 s.20(3).
[66] Powers of Attorney Act 1996 s.18(3).
[67] Powers of Attorney Act 1996 s.18(3) ("unless the person dealing with the donee knows that it was not in fact given by way of security"). See Wylie, *Irish Land Law* (2013), para.11.41. The latter qualification would seem to be necessary, otherwise the form could become a pure fiction.
[68] Powers of Attorney Act 1996 s.18(3).
[69] Powers of Attorney Act 1996 s.18(2).
[70] Powers of Attorney Act 1996 s.18(2).
[71] Powers of Attorney Act 1996 s.18(5).

CHAPTER 15

Trusts of Land

What between the duties expected of one during one's lifetime and the duties exacted from one after one's death, land has ceased to be either a profit or a pleasure. It gives one position and prevents one keeping it up. That is all that can be said about land.

— Oscar Wilde, *The Importance of Being Ernest*, Act 2, Lady Bracknell

INTRODUCTION

15–01 Under the Land and Conveyancing Law Reform Act 2009 ("LCLRA 2009"), successive estates in land can no longer exist as legal estates, and now take effect in equity only. This change meant that major alteration to the law of settled land was inevitable. However, the LCLRA 2009 implements the radical recommendation of the Law Reform Commission to replace the Settled Land Acts 1882–1890 entirely, even as to existing settlements, with the simpler scheme of trusts of land. It is worth noting that this contrasts with the reform scheme adopted in England and Wales by the Trusts of Land and Appointment of Trustees Act 1996 ("TLATA 1996"), under which existing settlements continue to be governed by the English Settled Land Act 1925.[1]

15–02 There is something to be said in favour of each approach. The English scheme reduces interference in private arrangements, an inhibition which is not evident in the LCLRA 2009, and it can be argued that in the sphere of private property rights, the less the State interferes, the better. The Irish scheme has the advantage of simplifying the law, which seems to be an almost overriding concern in the LCLRA 2009. Since all successive estates are equitable,[2] there is a strong case for bringing all trusts of land within a single rational scheme.

---

[1] TLATA 1996 s.2; See generally, C. Harpum, S. Bridge and M. Dixon, *Megarry & Wade: The Law of Real Property*, 8th edn (London: Sweet & Maxwell, 2012), Ch.12 and App. The TLATA 1996 applies retrospectively in England and Wales to trusts for sale (express or implied) and bare trusts created before 1997, but not to land which was settled land under the English Settled Land Act 1925 prior to 1997. (Land subject to an "immediate binding trust for sale" was excluded from the Settled Land Act 1925.) *Megarry & Wade: The Law of Real Property* (2012), paras 10–014, 12–002 and A–054.

[2] This change was made in England in 1925. The successive estates in settlements after 1925 in England and Wales were therefore equitable, and subject to the Settled Land Act 1925, although the fee simple was actually vested in the tenant for life, as trustee for the other beneficiaries, in addition to his or her life estate beneficially.

The English provisions still require fairly complex rules to determine whether what was a settlement is still a settlement or has become a trust of land.[3]

15–03 The more radical Irish scheme can be accused of being overzealous in its interference with existing family arrangements. Its retrospective aspect mainly affects a minority in Irish society, namely old landed families.[4] The primary justification for that is the simplification of the law. Convenient though it may be for judges, legal practitioners and law students, simplification hardly amounts to a compelling public benefit. On the other hand, it should be pointed out that the Settled Land Acts had already significantly undermined family settlements. It may even be that the new scheme, complete with the abolition of the remoteness rules, could strengthen the position of those who wish to enter new settlements in the future.

15–04 Another contrast between the two law reform schemes is that the TLATA 1996 is much more detailed in its provisions as to the new institution of trusts of land. Part 4 of the LCLRA 2009 is sparse indeed and will need to be filled out either by further legislation or by the courts. Partly for this latter reason, some account of the old law in Ireland is still useful to outline the problems or issues that may arise under Pt 4 of the LCLRA 2009. The old law may also provide useful guidance should the courts be asked to exercise their inherent jurisdiction, which may have survived the LCLRA 2009 to imply powers and authority for salvage payments into settlements. Finally, settlements and settled land had a prominent place in Irish land law for several centuries and an educated property lawyer should have some knowledge of their origin and operation before the LCLRA 2009.

THE OLD LAW: SETTLEMENTS

History

15–05 The history of settlements of land is the history of the resolution, both by legislators and judges, of conflicting desires: first, landowners' desire to keep their landed estates within their own families for generation after generation; and secondly, the recognition of the importance of maintaining and preserving a market in land and preventing landowners establishing and maintaining a monopoly over land ownership. The first policy led to the evolution of methods of tying up the title of land in family settlements involving successive freehold estates. The aim of these arrangements was to ensure that in each generation the freeholder in possession had only limited powers to deal with the land, and was, in particular, unable to sell the fee simple. The second policy favoured the free alienation of land and limited the ability of landowners to tie up land in this way. By the late 19th century, the Settled Land Acts 1882–1890

---

[3] *Megarry & Wade: The Law of Real Property* (2012), para.A–054.
[4] An attitude which is also evident in the conversion of all existing fees tail.

had largely vindicated the latter policy by conferring a power of sale on the tenant for life in possession.

15–06 The fee simple became freely alienable after *Quia Emptores* 1290 and was as such not a secure form in which to retain land within a family for future generations. The passing of the statute *De Donis* marked a victory for the feudal lords, establishing the fee tail as an inalienable estate and so enabling landowners to retain land in their family. In the succeeding centuries, however, the rise of capitalism saw the emergence of financial and commercial classes who possessed money and often wished to buy landed estates, either for industrial production as part of the industrial revolution, or for commercial agriculture.[5] There were also cultural factors which meant that the newly-rich wished to acquire the superior social status which still paradoxically was accorded to the traditional landowning classes. The increasing social influence of the commercial and financial classes had its effect on the legal system. It led to the development of fines and recoveries as a means whereby a previously inalienable entail could be barred to produce a fee simple, thus transforming landed estates into commodities available to be sold to those with the money to buy them. However, the old judicially-developed forms were expensive and cumbersome to use until they were placed on a statutory footing by the Fines and Recoveries (Ireland) Act 1834.

15–07 The problem of family settlements took a particularly acute form in Ireland. The landowning class was distinct from the majority of tenants, not simply by income and social position but by religion and what could be called ethnicity. It had been established over centuries by grants to Catholic immigrants in the first plantations, but increasingly, after the Reformation, to Protestant immigrants. The Penal Laws, with their aim of creating a Protestant landowning class, accelerated this trend.[6]

15–08 By the 18th century, Irish tenant farmers had been reduced by the "Eviction Codes" to a status virtually akin to that of tenants at will, whilst landowners had become increasingly impoverished and thereby unable, even if willing, to expend capital on the improvement of agriculture on their estates. These problems, however, paled in comparison to the disaster which befell the rural population in the Great Famine of the 1840s,[7] which saw the end of the landed estate with tenant farmers as a viable system of landholding in Ireland.

---

[5] See M.R. Chesterman, "Family Settlements on Trust: Landowners and the Rising Bourgeoisie" in G.R. Rubin and D. Sugarman (eds), *Law, Economy and Society 1750–1914: Essays in the History of English Law* (Abingdon: Professional Books, 1974).

[6] See C.I. McGrath, "Securing the Protestant Interest: the Origins and Purpose of the Penal Laws of 1695" (1996) 30(117) I.H.S. 25; L. Cullen, "Catholics Under the Penal Laws" (1986) 1 Eighteenth-Century Ir. 23; S.J. Connolly, *Religion, Law and Power: The Making of Protestant Ireland 1660–1760* (Oxford: Clarendon Press, 1992).

[7] See J. Crowley, J. Smyth and M. Murphy, *Atlas of the Great Irish Famine* (Cork: Cork University Press, 2012).

Development of Methods of Settlement

15–09 An early method of settling land[8] was for a landowner to make the following disposition when his son married:

to [the settlor] for life, remainder to [his son] in tail.

15–10 This was not very effective. When the father died the son, if of full age, could bar the entail and obtain the fee simple. An alternative was to make a grant on the son's marriage:

to [the settlor] for life, remainder to [his son] for life, remainder to [his son's eldest son - unborn] in tail ...

15–11 This depended on the development of a new kind of interest, the contingent remainder, which was recognised from about the 14th century. Contingent remainders had a more precarious existence than vested estates. After the settlor died, the son, because he then had seisin, could execute a feoffment in fee simple. This feudal conveyance was accorded an almost mystical power by the common law. The son, in executing the conveyance, was committing a wrong, a tort on the remaindermen and the reversioner, but a feoffment in fee simple nevertheless passed the fee simple to the purchaser, or to the son if he used the device of a conveyance to a feoffee to his own use. This could be challenged, but in the case of the contingent interest there was no one to challenge it. The contingent remainder was destroyed. This was known as the *artificial destruction* of contingent remainders. Thus, if the father died before the son himself had a son, the settlement was vulnerable.

15–12 Another method to create a succession of life estates to present and future generations would have removed the land permanently from the market and was struck down by the courts under what became known as the rule in *Whitby v Mitchell*,[9] which had its origin in *Chudleigh's Case*.[10]

15–13 The weakness of the settlement still lay in the destructibility of contingent remainders. In the 17th century conveyancers invented the key device known as *trustees to preserve contingent remainders*, recognised as effective by *Duncomb v Duncomb*.[11] The final development was the passing of the Real Property Act 1845[12] which provided that if a prior estate was destroyed by surrender, forfeiture or merger, that would not prevent the contingent remainder

---

[8] See F. Pollock, *The Land Laws* (London: Macmillan, 1883), pp.106–121.

[9] (1890) 44 Ch. D. 85.

[10] (1595) 1 Co. Rep. 113b at 138.

[11] (1695) 3 Lev. 43. It was not finally settled until *Smith d Dormer v Packhurst* (1740) 3 Atk. 135. See also, Lord Hardwicke in *Garth v Cotton* (1753) 1 Ves. Sen. 546; *Lemon v Mark* [1899] 1 I.R. 445; L. Bonfield, *Marriage Settlements, 1601–1740: the Adoption of the Strict Settlement* (Cambridge: Cambridge University Press, 1983).

[12] Real Property Act 1845 s.8.

taking effect. If the father and son were alive at the date of the settlement, it was then legally possible to remove land from the market until the point in time when the father was dead, the son had died and the grandson had attained his majority, since the grandson on coming of age could bar the entail and produce a fee simple.

Pin Money, Jointures and Portions

15–14 It was usual for settlements to make provision for various payments to members of the family charged on the land.[13] An annual sum would be provided for the wife of the settlor or of the tenant for life during the joint lives of the spouses, as "pin money" to provide the wife with an independent income. After the death of the tenant for life the settlement would provide for the widow or widows by periodic payments, called *jointures*, also secured by rentcharges. The younger members of the family would be provided for by lump sums, called *portions*. Since these were not annual sums they could not be secured by rentcharges. Instead, the settlement created long terms of years, typically 1,000 years, of part of the estate and vested them in trustees. The trustees could raise the lump sums by sale or mortgage[14] of the terms.

Resettlement

15–15 In the example above, when the grandson came of age he might well wish to have a sizeable income. In return for an annuity charged on the land his father might induce him to join with him in barring the entail so as to produce a fee simple and then to execute a new settlement under which he and his father would take life estates with a contingent entail to the grandson's unborn son. The land was thus removed from the market for another generation.

The Problem with Settlements

15–16 The existence of legal settlements and the pattern of resettlement in each generation meant that landed estates were unable to respond to economic and social change. In the early 19th century, the Napoleonic wars were followed by agricultural depression and this was particularly acute in Ireland. The legal restrictions affecting estates gave rise to three particular problems.

Alienability

15–17 The process of settlement and resettlement meant that the person entitled in possession to the land normally only had a life estate. He or she could not sell the fee simple. The life tenant also had only a limited ability to grant leases which would outlast his own life.

---

[13] For an account of the position of women with respect to property in the 19th century, see K. Costello, "Married Women's Property in Ireland 1800–1900" in N. Howlin and K. Costello (eds), *Land and the Family in Ireland, 1800–1950* (London: Palgrave, 2017).

[14] *Kelly v Lord Bellew* (1707) 4 Bro. P.C. 495; *Townsend v O'Callaghan* (1856) 4 Ir. Ch. R. 511.

Management

15–18 The management of the estate was hampered by the difficulty of raising money. The life tenant could only mortgage his own life estate which was not worth as much for security as the fee simple. Furthermore, unless he was made unimpeachable of waste by the settlement, the tenant for life was impeachable for voluntary waste and so could not cut timber or open mines.

Indebtedness

15–19 The existence of portions and jointures often meant that the estates passed from one generation to another burdened with debt. Often these had been incurred to supply an income to individuals and not from productive investment in improving the economic efficiency of the land. As capitalism developed, investments in stocks and shares offered a mechanism to generate income without burdening agricultural production by charging the land. Some settlements gave the tenant for life power to appoint or sell the fee simple during his life, and if he did so the other interests under the settlement were to be *overreached*, i.e. they would become corresponding interests in the purchase money raised by sale of the land and would no longer affect the title. The tenant for life could also be given power to create leases which would continue after his death. The usual period was 21 years for agricultural leases and 90 years for building leases. While these possibilities could alleviate some of the problems associated with settlements, settlors and their lawyers were often cautious about giving powers to the tenant for life which he might use to dissipate the estate.

15–20 Where debts incurred by successive generations had led to impoverished and run-down estates, the only solution at first was to procure a private Act of Parliament, which was an expensive procedure. The long-term solution was for Parliament to intervene by giving all tenants for life greater control over the estate. Because the problem was particularly acute in Ireland, the earliest legislation was applied here, starting with the Mines Act 1723.[15] The Incumbered Estates Acts 1848 and 1849 allowed settled land to be sold by a special court set up by the Acts—the Incumbered Estates Court. The instrument of sale was executed by the court.

15–21 The next stage in the development of the legislation was to allow the tenant for life to sell the land with the court's consent and this was done by the Settled Estates Acts 1856 and 1876, replaced by a single Act in 1877. Other transactions normally required the consent of the other persons entitled under the settlement, i.e. the remaindermen or reversioner and this proved to be the weakness of the Act. The other persons entitled to the settled land often wanted to retain it in the family even if the estate and the farms on the estate would be more efficiently run by a buyer with capital to develop them.

---

[15] 10 Geo I c 5 (Ir). See J.C.W. Wylie, *Irish Land Law*, 5th edn (Haywards Heath: Bloomsbury Professional, 2013), para.1.36.

15–22 The final stage was to give the tenant for life full powers of dealing with the land without the consent of the court or of the other persons entitled under the settlement. This was achieved by the Settled Land Acts 1882–1890.

The Settled Land Acts 1882–1890
15–23 The basic principle behind the Settled Land Acts 1882–1890 was to vest in the person whose interest under the settlement was in possession, usually a life tenant, full powers to deal with the land including the right to convey the fee simple, even though, in the latter case, the fee simple was not vested in that person. Having given such extensive powers to someone who normally had only a life estate, the rest of the Acts were concerned mainly to protect the interests of the other persons entitled under the settlement.

15–24 There were basically four problems inherent in such a statutory scheme:

(a) The limited owner to whom the powers are given might abuse them. Since he or she was not entitled to keep all the proceeds of a sale, there was no real interest to obtain the best price for the land. Also, the limited owner might try to abscond with the purchase money.

(b) A purchaser had to be able to tell whether the land was settled land and whether the person who purported to exercise the statutory powers had them vested in him.

(c) The interests of the other persons entitled under the settlement had to be cleared off the title so that the purchaser could acquire the unencumbered fee simple.

(d) A purchaser had to be protected if he or she acted in accordance with the provisions of the Acts.

The Definition of Settled Land
15–25 There were three cases where land came within the Acts:

1. where there were successive interests, legal or equitable[16];
2. where land was held by a minor[17]; and
3. where there was a trust for sale of land and the beneficial interests were held for successive interests.[18]

15–26 In the first two there was a problem of alienability, in 1. because there was no one who could dispose of the fee simple, and in 2. because although a

---

[16] Settled Land Act 1882 s.2(1).
[17] Settled Land Act 1882 s.59.
[18] Settled Land Act 1882 ss.2(1) and 63.

minor could hold land[19] and make a conveyance of the fee simple,[20] he or she could repudiate a conveyance on coming of age.[21] The third case was anomalous because there was no problem of alienability where there was a trust for sale.

Successive Interests

15-27 Section 2(1) of the Settled Land Act 1882 (the "1882 Act") provided that a settlement existed where under any "deed, will, agreement for a settlement or other instrument", or any number of instruments, land "stands for the time being limited to or in trust for any persons by way of succession". Section 2(2) amplified the definition by providing further that an estate or interest in remainder or reversion was an interest forming part of the settlement, so that the grant of a single life estate, or single fee tail, coupled with a reversion or remainder in fee simple was sufficient to constitute a succession of estates and therefore a "settlement", in the broader sense, within the 1882 Act.

Successive Legal Estates

15-28 "[L]imited to" in s.2(1) indicates that the statute applied to successive legal estates, created either as common law estates or, more usually, legal executory interests under the Statute of Uses 1634. This was the classic "strict settlement" and would also incorporate legal powers, also under the Statute of Uses 1634, and jointures and portions, etc. for other members of the family. Since the legal fee simple had been split up into successive lesser estates, there were no trustees of the land, i.e. holding the whole fee simple, but it was common to appoint "trustees of the settlement" who were trustees of certain powers under the settlement.[22]

15-29 Thus, under the law before 1 December 2009, settlements and the Settled Land Acts 1882–1890 included cases where there were successive interests but no trust, and cases where there was a trust. From 1 December

---

[19] The land was settled land and the minor deemed tenant for life when his or her title was absolute, i.e. a fee simple: *Re Price; Leighton v Price* (1884) 27 Ch. D. 552, or subject to being divested on death under 21.

[20] Before 1 December 2009, a minor could hold a legal estate in land, although it came within the Settled Land Acts 1882–1890. From 1 December 2009, the fee simple is subject to a trust of land and the fee simple will vest in the trustees, but see below. J.C.W. Wylie, *The Land and Conveyancing Law Reform Acts: Annotations and Commentary*, 2nd edn (London: Bloomsbury, 2017), [52], nn.20 and 21.

[21] *Megarry & Wade: The Law of Real Property* (2012), para.36–012. It was voidable at the option of the minor but not of the grantee (*Zouch d. Abbot v Parsons* (1765) 3 Burr. 1794), on attaining majority or within a reasonable time thereafter (*Carnell v Harrison* [1916] 1 Ch. 328). Since it was voidable, not void, it became binding on the minor after that period (*Edwards v Carter* [1893] A.C. 360).

[22] In the past there might be trustees as part of the device to preserve contingent remainders: see below.

2009 there is a trust of land, and trustees of the land, in all cases of successive interests, which simplifies the law.

Successive Equitable Estates

15–30 The phrase "… or in trust for" indicated that the land was also settled land where the legal fee simple was vested in trustees and those entitled under the settlement had equitable interests. This was sometimes referred to as a "holding trust", to distinguish it from a trust for sale which is discussed below.

"Instrument"

15–31 A disposition of land, in order to come within s.2(1), had to be contained in an "instrument", i.e. it had to be in writing. It was not necessary that *all* the estates which made up the succession of interests had to be contained in or granted by the instrument, since s.2(2) expressly included reversions.

15–32 However, there was a problem as to constructive trusts. If X held land in fee simple, but circumstances arose in which equity would regard X as holding the legal estate on trust for Y for life under the doctrine of constructive trusts or proprietary estoppel, then if equity acted on *oral* promises or representations by X, it was thought that the situation did not fall within the Settled Land Acts, since there was no "instrument". On the other hand, if the doctrine of constructive trusts or proprietary estoppel was applied on the basis of *written* undertakings or promises, then the written evidence might constitute an "instrument" for the purposes of s.2, the land was settled land, and the tenant for life would automatically have all the powers in the Settled Land Acts, including the right to sell the fee simple under the Acts, which was almost certainly not what the parties intended.[23] This was one of the faults in the legislation.

Tenants for Life and Persons with Powers of a Tenant for Life

15–33 Another awkward feature of the Settled Land Acts 1882–1890 was that, instead of a single definition of a statutory tenant for life, s.2(5) of the 1882 Act defined a tenant for life[24] and then s.58 contained a list of persons having "the powers of a tenant for life" under the Act. That definition was more specific and narrower than the definition of "settlement" within s.2. It was and remained unclear in cases in which there was a succession of interests within s.2 but which were excluded from s.58, whether this meant: (a) that the land was settled land falling within the Acts, but there was no one with the powers

---

[23] In *National Bank Ltd v Keegan* [1931] I.R. 344, a written agreement was held by the Supreme Court to have created a life estate, but the court did not consider whether the situation came within the Settled Land Acts. The situation had been considered by the courts in England: see *Bannister v Bannister* [1948] 2 All E.R. 133; *Binions v Evans* [1972] Ch. 359, where, however, the statutory provisions differ. The courts there avoided the conclusion that the situation fell within the Settled Land Act 1925.

[24] As "the person who is for the time being ... beneficially entitled to possession of settled land for his life …".

of a tenant for life, which would have been awkward (since there would be no one who could exercise the powers); or (b) the land was not settled land at all and fell outside the Acts altogether. Judicial opinion was not entirely consistent on the issue.

15–34 On the other hand, common law determinable and conditional interests which fell outside s.58 were treated as falling outside the Acts altogether,[25] on the bases that possibilities of reverter and rights of entry or re-entry were not "estates" forming a succession.

15–35 Since the LCLRA 2009 has now repealed the Settled Land Acts, and all settlements are effectively converted into trusts of land under the LCLRA 2009, there is no point now in entering into a detailed discussion of the definition of persons having the powers of a tenant for life under s.58. Should any issue arise, reference should be made to the second edition of this work.

Tenant in Tail after Possibility of Issue Extinct

15–36 Section 58(2)(vii) included a tenant in tail after possibility of issue extinct whose entail was unbarrable under the Fines and Recoveries (Ireland) Act 1834. Such a tenant had the powers of a tenant for life under the Settled Land Acts. This is not surprising as his or her interest resembled a life estate.

Estate Plus Power of Appointment

15–37 An instrument which grants a life estate followed by a power of appointment creates a succession of interests because the remainder after the life estate is vested in those entitled in default of appointment until a valid exercise of the power divests them and vests it in an object of the power. Thus, in *Re Bective Estate*,[26] R devised land to his wife for life, with remainder as she should by will appoint. It was held that the land was settled land within the Act.

Land Held by a Minor

15–38 If land was held by a minor, or by a minor as a co-owner with an adult,[27] even for a fee simple estate, then the land came within s.59 of the 1882 Act, provided the minor was "in his own right seised of or entitled in possession to land".[28] Under s.59 the minor was deemed to be the tenant for life, but s.60 provided that in such a case the powers of the tenant for life "may" be exercised on the infant's behalf by the trustees of the settlement. In *Re Conroy's Trusts*,[29]

---

[25] Settled Land Act 1882 s.58(1)(ii).
[26] (1891) 27 L.R. Ir. 364.
[27] *Re Greenville's Estate* (1882) 11 L.R. Ir. 138 (land held by partners descended to minor on death of one partner).
[28] Settled Land Act 1882 s.59; *Re Scally* (1952) 86 I.L.T.R. 171.
[29] [1938] Ir. Jur. Rep. 26.

the court, by a gloss on the Act, read the section as *requiring* the trustees to act in such a case.

Trusts for Sale

15–39 An anomaly of the 1882 Act was that trusts for sale were specifically deemed to be settled land by s.63 where the beneficial interests were successive. It would have been wiser to exclude them, since no problem of alienability arose under a trust for sale.[30] In the case of a trust for sale there was a special definition of "tenant for life" under s.63.

Interests outside the Acts
Bare Trusts

15–40 Where both the legal estate and the beneficial interest were held in fee simple there was no succession of interests and so the land was not settled land[31] unless the beneficiary, or one of them, was a minor.

Rights of Residence

15–41 Wills in Ireland sometimes confer on a person, often an elderly relative, the right to reside on the land for his or her life with other associated rights. It would have entirely defeated the purpose of such an interest if the holder had the powers of a tenant for life under the Settled Land Acts. However, there was no specific provision within the Acts. The better view was that a right of residence did not make the land settled land.

Fee Simple Subject to Family Charges

15–42 This situation could arise when land which was once subject to a strict settlement had become vested in a person in fee simple, but family charges, i.e. jointures or rentcharges, still remained. In *Re Blake's Settled Estates*,[32] the Supreme Court held that the existence of family charges did not make the land settled land. They did not create any successive interests.[33]

Fee Farm Grants

15–43 Since the estate under a fee farm grant is a fee simple there is no element of succession and so the land was not settled land under s.2.

---

[30] They are excluded from the Settled Land Act 1925 (England and Wales).

[31] *Re British Land and Allen's Contract* (1900) 44 S.J. 593.

[32] [1932] I.R. 637, departing from *Re Bective Estate* (1891) 27 L.R. Ir. 364.

[33] Although the incumbrances could not therefore be cleared off the title by a sale under the Settled Land Acts, under s.5 of the Conveyancing Act 1881 (which is not repealed by the LCLRA 2009), the owner of land subject to an incumbrance, which included a jointure or rentcharge, could sell the land free of it by obtaining the permission of the court to lodge a sum of money in court, the sum being sufficient to provide an income, after investment in government securities, to pay the annual amount.

Leases for Lives Renewable Forever

15–44 Section 58(2)(v) included in the definition of persons having the powers of a tenant for life "a tenant for the life of another, not holding merely under a lease at a rent ...". Leases for lives perpetually renewable at commercial rents were commercial holdings and not family settlements and there was not a particular problem with alienability. Even though there was an element of succession within s.2, and a reversion under s.2(2), it had long been assumed that the intention behind s.58(1)(v) was to exclude such interests from the operation of the Acts.[34]

The Tenant for Life

15–45 The main problem addressed by the Settled Land Acts was the problem of alienability. The solution was to confer extensive powers on the tenant for life. This contained an inherent danger. The tenant for life might be tempted to abuse his powers to the detriment of the remaindermen. The Acts therefore contained mechanisms to prevent this.

Sale

15–46 Under s.4 of the 1882 Act the land had to be sold by private treaty or auctioned at the best price reasonably obtainable. Exchange or partition had to be for the best consideration in land or money reasonably obtainable. The tenant for life could not buy the land by private treaty, but could bid at the auction. Again, this was to prevent a tenant for life buying the land at an under value which would be a fraud on the other persons entitled under the settlement.

Power to Lease

15–47 A tenant for life had a general power to create leases up to 35 years under s.65(10).[35] Building leases could be created for up to 99 years under s.6.[36] Mining leases could be created for up to 60 years under s.6.

Power to Mortgage

15–48 One of the problems with settlements was that the land could become burdened with debt. It was not therefore the policy of the Acts to grant extensive powers of mortgaging to the tenant for life. Unless the settlement otherwise

---

[34] By 1882 such tenants had the power to demand a fee farm grant from the lessor and so did not require the powers for that reason either.

[35] In England the maximum was 21 years, but the special provision for Ireland was to bring the Act into conformity with the powers of "limited owners" under s.25 of the Land Law (Ireland) Act 1881. See also, s.25 of the Landed Property (Ireland) Improvement Act 1860; *Re Casey's Estate* (1878) 1 L.R. Ir. 481. The general power was extended by s.43 of the Landlord and Tenant Act 1931 to 99 years, where required under the Act, but the 1931 Act was repealed by the Landlord and Tenant (Amendment) Act 1980.

[36] This was extended to 150 years for urban land by s.62 of the Landlord and Tenant Act 1931 but that extension was abolished as to dwellings by the Landlord and Tenant (Ground Rents) Act 1978 and the whole of the 1931 Act was repealed by the 1980 Act.

provided, the tenant for life could, apart from the Acts, only mortgage his own estate, usually a life estate. Section 18 of the 1882 Act conferred a limited power on the tenant for life to create mortgages binding the remainders for the purpose of equality of exchange of land or partition. The tenant for life could convey the fee simple or a term of years as security. On the other hand, the money so raised had to be treated as capital money, i.e. it had to be paid to the trustees of the settlement under s.22 and applied by them. Section 11 of the Settled Land Act 1890 (the "1890 Act") extended the powers to mortgage in order to pay off incumbrances.

Improvements

15–49 Section 25 of the 1882 Act authorised the expenditure of capital money for the purpose of effecting improvements, including the purchase of other land.

Qualifications
Mansion House

15–50 The 1882 Act, passed under Gladstone's Liberal Administration, made few concessions to the sentimental attachment of landed families to their ancestral estates. The government changed in 1886 with the election of the Conservatives and this saw an increased reassertion of the influence of landed families. The 1890 Act introduced a concession by limiting the power of the tenant for life or person having such powers to dispose of the mansion house and ornamental garden that such estates frequently included. Under s.10 the mansion house and ornamental garden could not be sold without the consent of the trustees of the settlement under the Acts or of the court.

15–51 The weakness of the provision was revealed by *Re Marquess of Ailesbury's Settled Estates*,[37] in which the tenant for life applied to the court for consent to sell the estate to Lord Iveagh, the heir to the Guinness fortune. Had the court refused, the tenant for life could have sold the estate without the house and garden, without the necessity for any consent. The House of Lords in granting consent took this into account and the fact that, had they refused, the estate might have remained unsold. This would have reduced the efficiency of the entire estate, given that the proposed purchaser was in a position to invest considerable sums in improvements to the agriculture of the tenant farms on the estate. The court held that this latter factor was a legitimate consideration to be taken into account in granting consent to the sale of the whole estate. The case therefore also indicates that the judges at this time were more concerned with the efficient economic running of the estate and the tenant farms rather than the sentimental attachments of the landed aristocracy.

---

[37] [1892] A.C. 356.

Heirlooms

15–52 The 1882 Act did contain one concession to the landed interest. Section 37 provided that heirlooms could not be sold without a court order.

The Position of the Tenant for Life
Exercise of the Powers

15–53 Section 53 provided that a tenant for life in exercising any power under the 1882 Act had to have regard to the interests of all parties entitled under the settlement and in relation to the *exercise* of the powers was deemed to be a trustee for those parties. On the other hand, ss.50 and 51 invalidated any attempt by the settlor to restrain the exercise of the powers. The courts interpreted this to mean that the tenant for life could decide whether or not to sell or otherwise deal with the property in his own interest. The court would restrain the tenant for life from selling at a gross undervalue,[38] but would not restrain him merely because his motive was selfish, such as to pay off his debts or to provide a more comfortable existence for himself.[39] Nor would he be restrained because "he was selling out of ill will or caprice, or because he does not like the remainderman, because he desires to be relieved from the trouble of attending to the management of land, or from any other such object, or with any such motive".[40]

No Restriction on the Statutory Powers

15–54 Section 50 provided that the powers could not be assigned or released by the tenant for life, even if he alienated his estate in the land.[41] A contract by a tenant for life not to exercise the powers was void.[42] Section 51 rendered void any attempt by a settlor to insert into a settlement any restriction on the powers of the tenant for life, whether directly or by way of an inducement not to exercise them.[43]

Grant of Greater Powers

15–55 There was nothing to prevent a settlor conferring additional powers on the tenant for life,[44] provided they did not conflict with the provisions of the Acts, so that, for example, the settlor, having granted a life estate, could not

---

[38] *Wheelwright v Walker (No.1)* (1883) 23 Ch. D. 752.
[39] *Wheelwright v Walker (No.1)* (1883) 23 Ch. D. 752; *Middlemas v Stevens* [1901] 1 Ch. 574, seems wrongly decided: See contra, *Gilbey v Rush* [1906] 1 Ch. 11 (lease by husband to wife held in good faith).
[40] *Cardigan v Curzon-Howe* (1885) 30 Ch. D. 531 at 540.
[41] But see *Re Bruen's Estate* [1911] 1 I.R. 76. Wylie J. held, on a limitation in the form "to A for life, remainder to B for life, remainder to C in tail …", that an assignment by A of his life estate to B, which caused a merger, made the statutory powers exercisable by B. The court left open the question as to whether the powers could still be exercised by A.
[42] Settled Land Act 1882 s.50(2).
[43] *Re Fitzgerald* [1902] 1 I.R. 162; *Re Richardson* [1904] 2 Ch. 777; *Re Haynes* (1887) 37 Ch. D. 306.
[44] Settled Land Act 1882 s.57(1).

exempt the life tenant from the provisions requiring that the proceeds of sale must be paid to the trustees of the settlement.[45]

Notice

15–56 Under s.45 of the 1882 Act a tenant for life, when intending to exercise his powers under the Acts of sale, exchange, partition, leasing, mortgaging, etc. had to give at least one month's notice to the trustees for the purposes of the Acts if the dispositions were to bind those entitled in remainder.[46] If there were no trustees for the purposes of the Acts, then application had to be made to the court to appoint them.[47] By s.5(1) of the Settled Land Act 1884, notice could be of a general intention.[48]

Power to Give Directions

15–57 Another important power of the tenant for life was to give directions to the trustees of the settlement as to how the capital money arising from the exercise of powers under the Acts was to be invested.[49] This was an important distinction between the position of the tenant for life under the Acts and a beneficiary under an ordinary trust, for in such a trust the trustees did not generally have to accept directions from the beneficiaries.[50] This reflected the basic strategy of the Settled Land Acts in concentrating the powers in the tenant for life under the Acts. The tenant for life, as the trustee of his powers under s.53, in giving directions, had to have regard to the interests of the other persons entitled under the settlement, and the court on application by the trustees could restrain an unwise investment.[51]

Trustees of the Settlement

15–58 Before the LCLRA 2009 settlements of land might have been created by a succession of equitable estates, but also, and more usually in the case of the "strict" family settlement, by a succession of legal estates. In such a case there were no trustees of the land. Nevertheless, the operation of the Settled Land Acts required there to be *trustees of the settlement* within the meaning of the Settled Land Acts, since, for example, capital money arising from a sale or other dealing had to be paid to them and not to the tenant for life.

15–59 The settlement could confer on the trustees of the settlement powers such as a power to sell the settled land, but under s.56 of the 1882 Act they could not exercise such powers without the consent of the tenant for life.

---

[45] *Re the Estate of Kenny, Deceased; Roberts v Kenny* [2000] 1 I.R. 33.
[46] *Hughes v Fanagan* (1891) 30 L.R. Ir. 111; *Re Naper* (1952) 86 I.L.T.R. 106.
[47] *Hughes v Fanagan* (1891) 30 L.R. Ir. 111; *Re Naper* (1952) 86 I.L.T.R. 106; *Marlborough (Duke) v Sartoris* (1886) 32 Ch. D. 616 at 623.
[48] *Re Naper* (1952) 86 I.L.T.R. 106.
[49] Settled Land Act 1882 s.22(2).
[50] For the position under trusts of land under the LCLRA 2009, see below.
[51] *Re Hunt's Settled Estates* [1905] 2 Ch. 418.

Again, this was consistent with the policy of the Acts in concentrating the powers in the tenant for life.

Who Were the Trustees of the Settlement?

15–60 There were four tests to define the persons who were the trustees of the settlement under the Settled Land Acts. They were:

(a) the persons who, under the settlement, were trustees with power of sale of the settled land or power to consent to the exercise of the power of sale.[52]

If there were no such persons, then they were:

(b) persons declared by the settlement to be trustees of the settlement for the purposes of the 1882 Act.[53]

Two additional tests were added by the 1890 Act[54]:

(c) persons who, under the settlement, were trustees with power of or upon trust for sale of other land in the settlement, or power to consent to the exercise of such a power.

If there were none, then:

(d) the persons under the settlement with a future trust or power of sale or with power to consent to such a power.

If there were still no persons who qualified, then the tenant for life or any other person with an interest in the settlement could apply to the court under s.38 of the 1882 Act for trustees to be appointed. They had to do so before a sale, etc. as the purchase money had to be paid to the trustees. Under s.39(1), capital money had to be paid to two trustees unless the settlement provided otherwise.[55]

Powers of the Trustees of the Settlement

15–61 Although the trustees of the settlement may have had important powers conferred on them by the settlement, they could not exercise such powers

---

[52] Settled Land Act 1882 s.2(8).
[53] Settled Land Act 1882 s.2(8).
[54] Settled Land Act 1890 s.16, as a result of *Wheelwright v Walker* (1883) 23 Ch. D. 752.
[55] In the case of a settlement by will, there was no need to go to court as s.50(3) of the Succession Act 1965 provides that the personal representatives proving the will were for all purposes deemed trustees of the settlement until trustees were appointed.

without the consent of the tenant for life.[56] The trustees' main role was to protect the interests of those entitled in remainder.[57] The powers are as follows.

Notice

15–62 The trustees of the settlement had to receive notice by the tenant for life of his or her intention to exercise the powers under the Acts to the trustees,[58] which under s.5 of the Settled Land Act 1884 could be of a general intention, as previously mentioned. Under s.45(3) of the 1882 Act a purchaser in good faith of settled land dealing with the tenant for life was not obliged to inquire whether notice had been given to the trustees. However, in *Hughes v Fanagan*[59] it was held that this did not avail a purchaser who actually knew that there were no trustees.[60]

Mansion House

15–63 The consent of the trustees or of the court was necessary for a sale of the "principal mansion house" or the ornamental garden on an estate.[61]

Capital Money

15–64 Capital money arising under the 1882 Act had to be paid to the trustees of the settlement or into court.[62] This was one of the principal protections of the remaindermen and other persons having an interest in the settlement, since it prevented a dishonest tenant for life absconding with the money.

Rent

15–65 Rent arising under a lease made by the tenant for life was not capital money but belonged to the tenant for life,[63] but in the case of a mining lease, since mining diminished the capital value of the land and so would affect the value of the remainders, a proportion of the rent was retained as capital money.[64]

Improvements

15–66 Capital money could be expended on improvements to the land. Section 25 of the 1882 Act contained a list of such authorised improvements and s.13 of the 1890 Act added a number of items to the list. No further details are given here and reference may be made to previous editions of this work.

---

[56] Settled Land Act 1882 s.56.
[57] *Hughes v Fanagan* (1891) 30 L.R. Ir. 111.
[58] Settled Land Act 1882 s.45.
[59] (1891) 30 L.R. Ir. 111.
[60] There were no trustees for the purposes of the Settled Land Acts in *Hughes* at the time.
[61] Settled Land Act 1890 s.10.
[62] Settled Land Act 1882 s.22.
[63] *Re Wix* [1916] 1 Ch. 279.
[64] Settled Land Act 1882 s.11.

Salvage

15–67 Where an expenditure was not specifically authorised the court asserted an inherent jurisdiction to sanction the use of capital money as salvage, i.e. to avoid an imminent loss to the estate.[65] This applies where the property would otherwise be damaged.[66]

15–68 In *Re Lisnavagh Estate*,[67] the tenant for life of the settled estate applied to the court for authorisation to be given to the trustees to raise and to expend capital monies in demolishing a wing, constituting about one-half of the mansion house, and in reconstructing the remainder. There was no electric light in the house and the acetylene plant lighting some of the rooms was worn out. The rooms were large with high ceilings. It was impossible to heat the house adequately as it was too large for the tenant for life and his family. The tenant for life, William McClintock, Baron Rathdonnell, nevertheless wanted to continue to live on the estate on which his family had resided for about 300 years. Section 13 of the 1890 Act only sanctioned expenditure up to half the annual rental of the land which would be insufficient for the scheme. The court allowed the extra expenditure of capital money as salvage. Dixon J. allowed the expenditure as it would not only prevent a loss but would enhance the value of the estate as a whole.

15–69 The salvage principle was used to sanction expenditure on repairs[68] and, as in *Re Lisnavagh*, partial demolition[69] "so as to make the mansion house, as it exists at present, more suited to modern requirements and the size and value of the estate to which it is now attached".[70]

Borrowing Money

15–70 The trustees could be given express power in the settlement to borrow money. In *Re O'Reilly*,[71] it was held by the High Court that such a power could be implied in some instances. In that case a settlement created by trust vested wide powers in the trustees as to the management of a family farming business. The settlement referred to the trustees' powers "as if beneficially entitled to the land". Kenny J. held that this was enough to imply a power to borrow.

---

[65] *Neill v Neill* [1904] I.R. 513; *De Vere v Perceval and Cole* [1845] Ir. Jur. Rep. 9.

[66] *Re Johnson's Settlement* [1944] I.R. 529.

[67] [1952] I.R. 296.

[68] *Re Johnson's Settlement* [1944] I.R. 529.

[69] *Re Dunham Massey Settled Estates* (1906) 22 T.L.R. 595; *Re Windham's Settled Estate* [1912] 2 Ch. 75. In the latter, the rebuilding was due to the unhealthy and ruinous condition of the old house, and for the purpose of making it habitable. The erection of completely new wings was sanctioned.

[70] *Re Walker's Settled Estate* [1894] 1 Ch. 190 at 192.

[71] (1975) 109 I.L.T.R. 121.

Overreaching Effect of Sale

15–71 One of the principal aims of the Settled Land Acts was to ensure that the land could be sold so that the purchaser would obtain a fee simple freed of the interests under the settlement. This was achieved by the process of "overreaching" those interests, i.e. they were transformed on sale from being interests in the land to being interests in the purchase money. The word itself was not used in the Settled Land Acts, but it is now used in the LCLRA 2009 as to trusts of land.

15–72 The 1882 Act provided that a deed executed under the 1882 Act was effectual to pass the land "conveyed … discharged from all the limitations, powers and provisions of the settlement".[72] Excepted from this were leases, easements, etc. created by the tenant for life and also interests "having priority to the settlement", such as a fee farm rent created out of the fee simple before it was settled.[73]

15–73 The beneficiaries were protected by providing that, for all purposes, capital money from the sale was to be considered as land and was to be held for the same interests successively and in the same way as the land would have been held.[74] This created a fiction of "non-conversion" in relation to the purchase money. Thus, if there were fees tail under the settlement, they continued to exist in relation to the purchase money despite the fact that personal property could not normally be entailed.

Trusts for Sale

15–74 The definition of "settlement" in s.2(1) on the face of it would have included trusts for sale of land where there were successive interests, since it refers to land "limited … in trust for any persons by way of succession". While the 1882 Act was in the process of being enacted, s.63 was introduced by an amendment to make it clear that trusts for sale of land were indeed to be within the scope of the 1882 Act. It was quite unnecessary to subject trusts for sale of land to the provisions of the 1882 Act since there is no problem of alienability. The section applied to trusts for sale only where the beneficial interest was for a limited period. Where there was a trust for sale of land *not* for a limited period, i.e. the beneficiaries had a fee simple, but one or more of them was a minor,[75] it would seem that the land was settled land, but under s.59, not s.63. Where there was a trust for sale of land for beneficiaries all of whom were of full age and they had a fee simple, the land was a bare trust for sale and outside the Acts.[76]

---

[72] Settled Land Act 1882 s.20(2).

[73] Settled Land Act 1882 s.20(1)(i).

[74] Settled Land Act 1882 s.22(5).

[75] *Re Greenville* (1882) 11 L.R. Ir. 138.

[76] *Re Earle and Webster's Contract* (1883) 24 Ch. D. 144.

15–75 The effect of the section was to give control of the land not to the trust-ees for sale but to the tenant for life. This was unnecessary as the trustees had power in any case to sell and to confer on the purchaser a fee simple freed from the other interests under the trust.

15–76 The Settled Land Act 1884 attempted to reform the position. Section 6 provided that the trustees for sale could exercise their powers without the consent of the tenant for life, thus reversing s.56 of the 1882 Act in relation to trusts for sale, and by s.7 the tenant for life could not exercise his or her powers under the Acts without leave of the court. The result was that the trustees had full power of sale unless the tenant for life had obtained such an order under s.7. However, they had no power of leasing or mortgaging or other powers, apart from sale, unless the trust for sale expressly or impliedly conferred these on them.[77] The tenant for life was not entitled to an order, but had to satisfy the court that the contemplated sale would benefit all parties.[78]

15–77 These provisions were invoked in *Re Naper*.[79] The plaintiff was entitled for life to the income from certain freehold property devised to trustees in trust for sale. The trust conferred wide powers of management upon the trustees until sale. Dixon J. held that the court, in the exercise of its judicial discretion, was entitled, upon the plaintiff giving proper undertakings for the protection of the estate and the trustees, to let the plaintiff into possession of the settled land, and that the plaintiff was thereupon entitled to exercise all the powers conferred by the Acts on a tenant for life, provided only that she should not be entitled to exercise the power of sale or exchange without the consent of the trustees.

The Need for Reform
15–78 The second edition of this work noted that the Settled Land Acts 1882–1890 created a confusing and paradoxical body of law which was, among other disadvantages, difficult for lawyers to explain to lay clients, and noted further that

> "a possible solution is to remove trusts for sale from the operation of the Settled Land Acts altogether, or, as has recently been done in England, to create a single statutory régime of trusts of land.[80] In Ireland, however, suc-cessive estates may still exist as legal estates, not under a trust, and so the latter reform would have to be part of a more radical reform whereby suc-cessive estates could in future only exist under a trust."[81]

---

[77] *Re Bellinger* [1898] 2 Ch. 534.
[78] *Re Tuthill* [1907] 1 I.R. 305.
[79] (1952) 86 I.L.T.R. 106.
[80] See the TLATA 1996.
[81] A. Lyall, *Land Law in Ireland*, 2nd edn (Dublin: Round Hall Sweet & Maxwell, 2000), p.414.

15–79 This has now been done, but the sparseness of Pt 4 of the LCLRA 2009 which deals with the new concept of trust of land will pose some problems, especially as it applies to existing settlements, previously governed by the Settled Land Acts, which at least were quite detailed in their provisions.

TRUSTS OF LAND

Definition
15–80 The definition of "trust of land" is contained in s.18 of the LCLRA 2009:

"18.—(1) Subject to this Part, where land is—
  (a) for the time being limited by an instrument, whenever executed, to persons by way of succession without the interposition of a trust (in this Part referred to as a 'strict settlement'), or
  (b) held, either with or without other property, on a trust whenever it arises and of whatever kind, or
  (c) vested, whether before or after the commencement of this Part, in a minor,
there is a trust of land for the purposes of this Part.
(2) For the purposes of—
  (a) subsection (1)(a), a strict settlement exists where an estate or interest in reversion or remainder is not disposed of and reverts to the settlor or the testator's successors in title, but does not exist where a person owns a fee simple in possession,
  (b) subsection (1)(b), a trust includes an express, implied, resulting, constructive and bare trust and a trust for sale.
(3) Subject to this Part, a trust of land is governed by the general law of trusts.
(4) Conversion of a life estate into an equitable interest only does not affect a life owner's liability for waste.
  ...
(7) In dealing with an action under subsection (6), the court may make such order as appears to it to be just and equitable in the circumstances of the case.
(8) Any party to a conveyance shall, unless the contrary is proved, be presumed to have attained full age at the date of the conveyance.
(9) This Part does not apply to land held directly for a charitable purpose and not by way of a remainder."

Included Interests
Settlements
15–81 Section 18(1)(a) indicates that *all* settlements, even those previously taking effect under the old law as successive legal estates ("strict settlements"), take effect under the LCLRA 2009 as trusts of land. The other provisions of

the LCLRA 2009 converted the legal estates to equitable ones, but s.18 makes it clear that they then come within Pt 4 of the LCLRA 2009. Section 18(2)(a) repeats the provision of s.2(2) of the 1882 Act in providing that a reversion in the grantor was sufficient to constitute a succession of estates. Thus, the grant of a single life estate brought it and the reversion within the Settled Land Acts, and now takes effect in equity as a trust of land.

For the Time Being

15–82 This is the same phrase as that in s.2(2) of the 1882 Act. It is somewhat superfluous, since if in the course of time the successive beneficial interests cease to exist, due to the deaths of life tenants, leaving an ultimate remainder in fee simple, the trust becomes a bare trust, but is still a "trust of land" within s.18(2)(b).

By an Instrument

15–83 Section 18 repeats the words of s.2 of the 1882 Act, and the purpose of the phrase seems to be to make it clear that s.18(1)(a) includes settlements whether created *inter vivos* or by will.[82] It is important to note that an "instrument" is not necessary to constitute a trust of land other than in the case of the old settlements, since, as provided by s.18(1)(b), "trust of land" includes "a trust whenever it arises and of whatever kind" and s.18(2)(b) expressly provides that implied, resulting and constructive trusts of land are "trusts of land" within Pt 4.

Whenever Executed

15–84 The operation of the LCLRA 2009 is therefore retrospective, and the Settled Land Acts 1882–1890 are repealed.[83]

Trusts
With or Without Other Property

15–85 Where the trust property consists of land alone or land and other property, the trust is a trust of land within s.18(1)(b).

General Law of Trusts

15–86 The general law of trusts applies, subject to the provisions of Pt 4.[84]

---

[82] Wylie, *Annotations and Commentary* (2017), para.51, n.8.

[83] LCLRA 2009 s.8(3) and Sch.2, Pt 4. Section 8(2)(a) nevertheless provides that any reference in an enactment to the Settled Land Acts "shall be construed as a reference to this Act or to the equivalent or substituted provision of this Act, as may be appropriate".

[84] LCLRA 2009 s.18(3).

Whenever It Arises

15–87 Section 18 includes in the definition of "trust of land" trusts of all kinds, whether they were created in the past by successive equitable interests, or not, or created after the LCLRA 2009 by such a succession, or not. The phrase "whenever it arises" might appear to refer only to the future but it is clear this is not so from the earlier phrase "held", i.e. held at the time the LCLRA 2009 came into force on 1 December 2009, or later.

15–88 In contrast to trusts for sale, which are also within s.18, trusts for successive interests were "settlements" in the broader sense, and were sometimes referred to as "holding trusts" since the intention was that the person entitled to the immediate equitable interest for the time being should be in occupation of the premises. This point will be referred to later in relation to the powers of the trustees and restrictions on their powers.

Implied, Resulting and Constructive Trusts

15–89 It has been seen that one of the problems with the Settled Land Acts was that, as a result of the doctrine of constructive trusts, a settlement within the Acts might inadvertently be created. An owner of a legal fee simple might be held in equity to hold it as a trustee to give effect to an equitable interest, such as a life estate, and if this was on the basis of written evidence ("an instrument") then the situation might fall within the Settled Land Acts so that the equitable tenant for life would acquire under the 1882 Act the power to sell the fee simple under the Acts, which would give the tenant for life a much greater interest in the land than was necessary to protect the equitable claim. Although now all implied, resulting or constructive trusts fall within Pt 4 of the LCLRA 2009, the powers of sale are vested by the LCLRA 2009 in the trustees and not the tenant for life, and so this problem will no longer arise.

15–90 The problem as to whether constructive trusts arising orally before 1 December 2009 fell within the Settled Land Acts is now solved, since they are all now trusts of land within s.18(2)(b).

Equitable Interests by Proprietary Estoppel

15–91 Part 4 of the LCLRA 2009 does not specifically mention equitable interests arising through the application of the doctrine of proprietary estoppel. Nevertheless, proprietary estoppel gives rise to an equity and if a court decided to satisfy it by an equitable interest, that would necessarily give rise to a trust, the holder of the legal fee simple holding the land on trust for the claimant, and all trusts fall within s.18 in any case.

Bare Trusts

15–92 Section 18(2)(b) specifically includes bare trusts as trusts of land. Such a situation is governed by the principle of *Saunders v Vautier*,[85] under which the person or persons entitled to the beneficial interests, if all of full age and absolutely entitled, may demand the legal fee simple from the trustees and so put an end to the trust.

Discretionary Trusts

15–93 Discretionary trusts did not fall within the Settled Land Acts but now come within the definition of trusts of land.[86] Discretionary trusts usually occur where property held on trust consists of stocks and shares or money, but s.18 applies where land is held on trust "either with or without other property".[87]

Trusts for Sale

15–94 Trusts for sale are also now trusts of land by virtue of s.18(2)(b), thus solving the awkward problems arising from the inclusion of trusts for sale within the Settled Land Acts and the paradox by which the land subject to such trusts could actually be more difficult to sell or deal with than settlements.

Concurrent Ownership Trusts

15–95 In co-ownership equity will impose a constructive trust where a fee simple is held by a single owner or by joint tenants. Where the subject matter is land the trust will be a trust of land within s.18 and Pt 4, since it applies to "a trust whenever it arises and of whatever kind". Special provisions in the LCLRA 2009 apply to such trusts, but they will be discussed in the chapter on co-ownership.

Purchaser's Equity

15–96 If A enters into a contract to sell an estate to B, usually a legal fee simple, then between contract and the conveyance A holds the fee simple on a kind of trust for the purchaser, B. This purchaser's equity is a special type of trust in equity.[88] The vendor is a trustee for most, but not all, purposes. The vendor has his or her own interests which he or she is entitled to protect, e.g. if the property is let out to a tenant, then the vendor and not the purchaser is entitled

---

[85] (1841) Cr. & Ph. 240.

[86] Wylie, *Annotations and Commentary* (2017), [51], n.16.

[87] LCLRA 2009 s.18(1)(b); Wylie, *Annotations and Commentary* (2017), [51], n.14.

[88] Wylie, *Annotations and Commentary* (2017), [51], n.16, calls it a bare trust. That is true where the estate agreed to be sold is a fee simple and to the extent that the purchaser can thereby call for the legal fee simple to be conveyed, but in view of the qualifications mentioned above, it must at least be considered a special case of bare trust.

to the rent between contract and conveyance.[89] In *Lysaght v Edwards*,[90] Jessel M.R. stated the doctrine of the purchaser's equity with precision:

"[T]he effect of a contract for sale has been settled for more than two centuries; certainly it was completely settled before the time of Lord Hardwicke ... What is that doctrine? It is that *the moment you have a valid contract for sale* the vendor becomes in equity a trustee for the purchaser of the estate sold, and the beneficial ownership passes to the purchaser, the vendor having a right to the purchase money, a charge or lien on the estate for the security of that purchase money, and a right to retain possession of the estate until the purchase money is paid, in the absence of express contract as to the time of delivering possession. Consequently ... then, *although the purchase money is unpaid*, the contract is valid and binding; and being a valid contract, it has this remarkable effect, that it converts the estate, so to say, in equity; it makes the purchase money a part of the personal estate of the vendor, and it makes the land a part of the real estate of the vendee ..." (emphasis supplied).[91]

15–97 The judge went on to mention the qualifications on the "trusteeship" of the vendor:

"[I]s the vendor less a trustee because he has the rights which I have mentioned? I do not see how it is possible to say so. If anything happens to the estate between the time of sale and the time of completion of the purchase it is at the risk of the purchaser ..."[92] In the same way there is a correlative liability on the part of the vendor in possession. He is not entitled to treat the estate as his own. If he wilfully damages or injures it, he is liable to the purchaser; and more than that, he is liable if he does not take reasonable care of it. So far he is treated in all respects as a trustee, subject of course to his right to being paid the purchase money and his right to enforce his security against the estate. With those exceptions, and his right to rents till the day of completion, he appears to me to have no other rights."[93]

15–98 The majority of the Supreme Court in *Tempany v Hynes*[94] held that this trust only arose if part of the purchase money was paid and that the equity was proportionate to the amount of purchase money paid at any time. This attracted

---

[89] *Lysaght v Edwards* (1876) 2 Ch. D. 499 at 507–508.

[90] (1876) 2 Ch. D. 499.

[91] (1876) 2 Ch. D. 499 at 506–507. See also, Lord Westbury L.C. in *Holroyd v Marshall* (1861–62) 10 H.L.C. 191 at 209–210: "a contract for valuable consideration passes at once the beneficial interest, provided the contract is one of which a court of equity will decree specific performance. In the language of Lord Hardwicke, the vendor becomes a trustee for the vendee; subject, of course, to the contract being one to be specifically performed."

[92] But notice that the vendor is under a duty of care to maintain the premises in repair: *Lyons v Thomas* [1986] I.R. 666.

[93] (1876) 2 Ch. D. 499 at 507–508.

[94] [1976] I.R. 101.

criticism[95] in that it was inconsistent with earlier decisions, and insofar as the equity entitled the purchaser to call for the legal estate as against those who might later have entered into contracts with the vendor, a "partial equity" was meaningless.[96] Section 52 has now reversed *Tempany v Hynes* by providing that the entire equitable interest passes to the purchaser on entering into the contract and also gives statutory force to the qualifications on the trust:

> "52.—(1) Subject to subsection (2), the entire beneficial interest passes to
>   the purchaser on the making, after the commencement of this Chapter, of
>   an enforceable contract for the sale or other disposition of land.
>   (2) Subsection (1) does not affect—
>   (a) the obligation of the vendor to maintain the land so long as posses-
>   sion of it is retained, or
>   (b) the liability of the vendor for loss or damage under any contractual
>   provision dealing with such risk, or
>   (c) the vendor's right to rescind the contract for failure by the purchaser
>   to complete or other breach of the contract, or
>   (d) any provision to the contrary in the contract."

15–99 The section does not specifically mention the vendor's right to retain rent, but presumably that would still apply on the basis of case law.

Minors
15–100 Before 1 December 2009, a minor could hold a legal estate in land, but the land was settled land within s.2 of the 1882 Act and the minor was the "tenant for life" (s.59), even though the minor might have the legal fee simple vested in him. Nevertheless, the powers of management were exercised by the trustees of the settlement (s.60).

15–101 From 1 December 2009, under s.18(1)(c) "where land is vested, whether before or after the commencement of [Part 4], in a minor",[97] i.e.

---

[95] LCLRA 2009 Explanatory Memorandum, p.28; A. Lyall, "The Purchaser's Equity: an Irish
      Controversy" (1989) 7 I.L.T. 270; Law Reform Commission, *Report on Interests of Vendor
      and Purchaser in Land during the Period between Contract and Conveyance* (LRC 49-1995).
[96] *Re Hamilton; Hamilton v Hamilton* [1982] I.R. 466.
[97] Persons subject to other disabilities were not included in s.62 of the Settled Land Act 1882 and
      are not within s.18 of the LCLRA 2009. Persons suffering from a mental incapacity should
      be dealt with under the wards of court jurisdiction: J. Costello, "Wards of Court—A General
      Guideline of the Procedures Involved" (1993) 78 Gaz. L. Soc. Ir. 143; Law Reform Commis-
      sion, *Consultation Paper on Reform and Modernisation of Land Law and Conveyancing Law*
      (LRC CP 34-2004), para.4.16, fn.74.

someone under the age of 18 and unmarried,[98] the land is a trust of land.[99] Section 19(1)(a)(i) of the LCLRA 2009 (which is general and not concerned specifically with minors) defines the trustees in the case of a settlement existing at the date of the LCLRA 2009 as including the tenant for life. Section 19 does not expressly exclude a minor. Is the minor automatically a trustee together with the other persons defined by s.19?

15–102 It is questionable whether that was the intention of the LCLRA 2009, but there is nothing, apart from the provisions of Pt 4, which expressly prevents a minor holding a legal estate in land, or being a trustee,[100] although he or she might lack capacity to act as a trustee in terms of judgement or discretion.[101]

15–103 The other relevant provision is s.19(1)(c), which is concerned specifically with minors, and says that in the case of land vested in a minor before the LCLRA 2009, or "purporting so to vest after such commencement", the trustees are the persons defined in s.19(1)(b) in the case of an express trust of land. Section 19(1)(c) does say "purporting" to vest, which could imply that *from* 1 December 2009, an instrument does not vest land in a minor, but it could alternatively mean that it does not vest in the minor alone.

15–104 What about instruments executed *before* 1 December 2009 and converted by the LCLRA 2009? Section 19(1)(c), dealing specifically with the case of a minor under an old settlement, defines the trustees of the trust of land as

"… the persons who would fall within paragraph (b) if the instrument vesting the land were deemed to be an instrument creating a trust of land."

All the sub-paragraphs of para.(b) of s.19(1) expressly refer to persons mentioned in a "trust instrument", which does not literally apply to an instrument before 1 December 2009, vesting a legal fee simple in a minor. However, "trust instrument" must be construed, in this context, in the light of s.19(1)(c) which says "if the instrument vesting the land [in the minor] were *deemed to be* an instrument creating a trust of land" (emphasis supplied). So for this purpose "trust instrument" in s.19(1)(b) must be read as if it said "instrument creating the settlement".

---

[98] Age of Majority Act 1985 ss.2(1) and 4(1); a person attains majority on attaining the age of 18 or marrying under that age. Under s.31 of the Family Law Act 1995, a person must be 18 in order to marry, unless an exemption is granted by either the Circuit Court or the High Court; Wylie, *Annotations and Commentary* (2017), [52], n.19.

[99] There is also now a presumption that any party to a conveyance has attained full age at the date of the conveyance, unless the contrary is proved: s.18(8).

[100] See s.21(2)(a)(iii) which refers to "land vested in or held on trust for a minor". Can land be vested in a minor?

[101] *Hearle v Greenbank* (1749) 3 Atk. 695; *Re Barry* (1844) 2 Jo. & Lat. 1; *Moore v Grogan* (1846) 9 Ir. Eq. R. 472. And a conveyance by a minor trustee would be voidable at the instance of the minor on attaining majority.

15–105 The next question is: do any of the persons mentioned in s.19(1)(b) (as trustees) refer to the tenant for life? The only relevant expression would seem to be in s.19(1)(b)(ii), i.e. "any person on whom the trust instrument confers a present or future power of sale of the land, or power of consent to or approval of the exercise of such a power of sale ...". So if the settlement instrument gave such a power or powers to the minor, it would then follow that he or she is a trustee of the trust of land. But not otherwise. However, it would not seem possible for the legal estate to be vested in the minor, but not as a trustee, while other persons would hold it with him as trustees, i.e. the trustees of the trust of land defined by s.19. It would also be odd, since minors are not precluded technically from acting as trustees under the general law of trusts, if they were to be precluded in the case of a trust of land. It seems inevitable therefore that a minor holding a legal fee simple under the Settled Land Acts becomes, from 1 December 2009, a trustee of the trust of land, together with the other trustees. This would also be consistent with express trusts of land made after 1 December 2009. But it would have been better to say so directly.

15–106 Indeed, it would seem preferable to reform the law as has been done in at least one other jurisdiction[102] and to provide specifically that a minor may no longer hold a legal estate in land or act as a trustee.

Excluded Interests
Charitable Trusts
15–107 An important exception to the general scheme of trusts of land is that charitable trusts are excluded by s.18(9). The view was taken that charitable trusts are subject to a special statutory regime, now mainly contained in the Charities Act 2009.[103] The exception only applies where the charity currently holds the land, and not where it is entitled in remainder after a prior estate currently held by a non-charity.[104]

Rights of Residence
15–108 It has been seen that the only freehold estate that can exist as a legal estate is a fee simple in possession under s.11(2), which also defines that phrase as including a fee simple subject only to a right of residence which is not an exclusive right over the whole land.[105]

---

[102] For example, Law of Property Act 1925 s.1(b) (England and Wales). A purported conveyance of land to a minor operates as a declaration of trust in favour of the minor.

[103] Amending the Charities Act 1961. See also the Charities Act 1973; Wylie, *Annotations and Commentary* (2017), [51], n.43.

[104] LCLRA 2009 s.18(9); Wylie, *Annotations and Commentary* (2017), [51], nn.44 and 45.

[105] LCLRA 2009 s.11(2)(c)(iii).

Tenant for Life as a Trustee

15–109 One possible area of controversy is the position of a tenant for life of a trust of land who is also a trustee. It has been seen that s.19 automatically makes the tenant for life of a former settlement a trustee of the trust of land (apart from the issue of whether that applies where the tenant for life is a minor).

15–110 As to trusts of land created expressly after 1 December 2009, there is nothing to prevent the settlor making the tenant for life a trustee, since s.19(1)(b)(i) includes as a trustee "any trustee nominated by the trust instrument".

15–111 Generally it would seem undesirable to nominate a tenant for life as a trustee because of possible conflicts of interest between the role of the tenant for life as beneficiary and as trustee.

Tenant for Life versus Other Beneficiaries or Trustees

15–112 There may also be conflicts between the tenant for life as beneficiary and other beneficiaries, i.e. those entitled in remainder, or between the tenant for life as beneficiary and the trustees. The tenant for life may wish to sell the land in order to provide money for more suitable accommodation and also, with the surplus invested, to increase his or her income from the resulting life interest in the investments (as in *Wheelwright v Walker*[106]), whereas the other beneficiaries may wish to retain the land. Or the tenant for life may wish to retain the land while the trustees or other beneficiaries wish to sell.

15–113 The answer to such possible conflicts is provided by the LCLRA 2009 in the dispute procedure in s.22 by which "any person having an interest in a trust of land, or a person acting on behalf of such a person, may apply to the court in a summary manner for an order to resolve a dispute". However, that again involves an application to the court with its attendant expense and stress on all concerned, and yet again the LCLRA 2009 seems ready to resort to the courts instead of providing more detailed provisions. Even if the settlor gives an express power of sale to the tenant for life, or a power of consent or refusal to sale, it is not clear at present whether that would give a "trump card" to the tenant for life in a dispute or how it would affect the dispute procedure under s.22.

Trustees

Definition

15–114 Part 4 of the LCLRA 2009 has also quite an elaborate definition of the trustees of a trust of land.

---

[106] (1883) 23 Ch. D. 752.

Former Settlements

15–115 As to former settlements, they are the tenant for life and the persons who were trustees or trustees of the settlement under the Settled Land Acts, as already discussed.[107]

Express Trusts of Land

15–116 As to trusts of land created expressly, they are defined by s.19(b):

"(b) in the case of a trust of land created expressly—
  (i)   any trustee nominated by the trust instrument, but, if there is no such person, then,
  (ii) any person on whom the trust instrument confers a present or future power of sale of the land, or power of consent to or approval of the exercise of such a power of sale, but, if there is no such person, then,
  (iii) any person who, under either the trust instrument or the general law of trusts, has power to appoint a trustee of the land, but, if there is no such person, then,
  (iv) the settlor or, in the case of a trust created by will, the testator's personal representative or representatives."

Implied, Resulting, Constructive or Bare Trusts of Land

15–117 In the case of land the subject of an implied, resulting, constructive or bare trust, the trustee is a person in whom the legal title to the land is vested.[108]

Appointment

15–118 Under s.19(3) nothing in s.19 affects the right of any person to obtain an order of the court appointing a trustee of land or vesting land in a person as trustee. Furthermore, the court has inherent power to appoint a trustee.[109]

Powers

15–119 Section 20 gives a trustee of land "the full power of an owner to convey or otherwise deal with the land" subject to the duties of a trustee and "any restrictions imposed by any statutory provision (including this Act) or the general law of trusts or by any instrument or court order relating to the land". Such powers would include, for example, the power to insure the trust property.[110]

---

[107] LCLRA 2009 s.19(1)(a)(i).

[108] LCLRA 2009 s.19(1)(d).

[109] Wylie, *Annotations and Commentary* (2017), [52], n.27; *Pollock v Ennis* [1921] 1 I.R. 181; Trustee Act 1893 ss.25 and 36; Law Reform Commission, *Report on Trust Law: General Proposals* (LRC 92-2008), paras 2.105–2.11.

[110] Wylie, *Annotations and Commentary* (2017), [53], n.9; A. Lyall, "Life Tenants and Insurance" (2008) 13(2) C.P.L.J. 26; *Re Kingham* [1897] 1 I.R. 170.

15–120 The power of a trustee includes the power "to permit a beneficiary to occupy or otherwise use the land on such terms as the trustee thinks fit",[111] and "to sell the land and re-invest the proceeds, in whole or in part in the purchase of land, whether or not situated in the State, for such occupation or use". The LCLRA 2009 does not contain, as the English Act does, a specific power for the trustees to delegate their functions to the tenant for life.[112] But the settlor's general power to impose restrictions may include the power to give trustees a power to delegate.

Restrictions

15–121 This is another area where the LCLRA 2009 makes a significant change to the regime of the Settled Land Acts. Under the Settled Land Acts, as part of the policy of concentrating powers in the tenant for life, there was a strong principle that the powers of the tenant for life under the Acts could not be cut down or restricted in any way and any attempt to do so was void.

15–122 The LCLRA 2009, on the other hand, vests the legal fee simple in the trustees, but there is no prohibition on a settlor imposing restrictions in an express trust of land.[113] This may include the power to give trustees the power to delegate their powers to beneficiaries.

15–123 It is unclear how express restrictions in the trust instrument affect disputes between the trustees and a tenant for life. One possible view is that if an express power of consent to sale is given to the tenant for life and the tenant for life later refuses to sanction a proposed sale by the trustees, that may not fall within the dispute procedure in s.22, since the settlor had in effect determined in advance how such a dispute should be resolved. The proper course of action for trustees who believe there is an overwhelming need to sell, as where the house is in danger of becoming derelict, is probably for them to apply for a variation of the trust under Pt 5 of the LCLRA 2009. What they would be attacking would be the provision in the trust instrument giving a decisive power to the tenant for life.

Trusts for Occupation

15–124 One advantage of a general scheme for trusts of land is that it allows, and ought to allow, for trusts to be created by settlors for different purposes. Some trusts may be intended to provide accommodation for the tenant for life for the rest of his or her life if he or she so wishes. The question is how this can be achieved under Pt 4.

---

[111] LCLRA 2009 s.20(2)(a).
[112] TLATA 1996 s.9(1); *Megarry & Wade: The Law of Real Property* (2012), para.12–024.
[113] Wylie, *Annotations and Commentary* (2017), [53], n.7.

15–125 The trustees, apart from being subject to the duties of trustees generally, under s.20(2)(a) have a *power* to permit a beneficiary to occupy the premises, but they have no positive duty to do so, unless that is specifically imposed on them. They must also consider the rights of all beneficiaries. However, under s.20(1)(b) they must comply with "any restrictions imposed by any statutory provision (including this Act) or the general law of trusts or by any instrument or court order relating to the land". It would seem then that a settlor could impose a *duty* on the trustees to allow the tenant for life to occupy the premises if he or she wishes and for as long as he or she wishes. Trustees have a power of sale, but no duty to sell (if the trust is a "holding trust" and not a trust for sale). There also seems no reason to suppose that the settlor could not give the trustees power to delegate their powers to one or more of the beneficiaries.[114]

Overreaching

15–126 The Settled Land Acts provided for the interests of those entitled beneficially under the settlement to be overreached on sale of the fee simple, i.e. their interests (legal or equitable) would be cleared off the legal title to the land and they would have corresponding interests in the capital money held by the trustees of the settlement. The word "overreaching" or "overreached" was not, however, used in the Acts.

15–127 Beneficial interests under a trust for land are necessarily equitable and s.21 of the LCLRA 2009 sets out provisions for them to be overreached on a sale of the land and this process is now expressly referred to as overreaching.[115] A purchaser is not affected by them if the LCLRA 2009 is complied with, even if he or she has notice of them.[116]

15–128 For overreaching to be effective the conditions in s.21 have to be complied with. Where the land comprises a (former) strict settlement, a trust, including a trust for sale, of land held for successive interests, or land vested in a minor, the money must be paid to at least two trustees or a trust corporation.[117] In the case of other trusts, payment to a single trustee or owner of the legal estate is sufficient.[118] The latter case would arise, for example, where equity holds a legal owner A to hold as trustee for himself and B as beneficiaries where B has contributed to the purchase price of the land.

Exceptions to Overreaching

15–129 Overreaching does not apply in the following cases.

---

[114] TLATA 1996 s.9 (England and Wales) gives express power to trustees to delegate their powers.

[115] LCLRA 2009 s.21(5).

[116] LCLRA 2009 s.21(1). Subject to qualification below as to the rights of persons in actual occupation of land.

[117] LCLRA 2009 s.21(2)(a).

[118] LCLRA 2009 s.21(2)(b).

A Conveyance for Fraudulent Purposes

15–130 Overreaching does not apply to a conveyance for fraudulent purposes of which the purchaser has actual knowledge or to which the purchaser is a party.[119]

Any Equitable Interest to which the Conveyance Is Expressly Made Subject[120]

Protected by Deposit of Documents Relating to the Legal Estate or Interest[121]

15–131 This refers to the former practice of creating equitable mortgages by deposit of the title deeds, or in the case of registered land, of the land certificate. This practice has been overtaken, in the case of registered land, by other developments, namely "eConveyancing" and s.73 of the Registration of Deeds and Title Act 2006 ("RDTA 2006") by which, since 1 January 2007, the Property Registration Authority has ceased to issue land certificates and charge certificates.[122] Section 73(2) of the RDTA 2006 provides that such certificates cease to have effect on the expiration of three years after s.73 came into effect. The evidence of title of registered land is now the entry on the electronic database held by the Land Registry.

15–132 An equitable mortgage by deposit of such certificates existing at the date of the RDTA 2006 had to be protected by a lien registered by 31 December 2009, as a burden under s.69 of the RTA 1964.[123] Where a holder of such lien has suffered loss by not applying for registration of the lien as a burden, he or she may apply to the court for compensation, on notice to the Minister for Public Expenditure and Reform.[124] Other forms of equitable mortgage may still be created, as for example, a charge over an equitable interest, or an attempt to create a legal mortgage by one of the old methods abolished by the LCLRA 2009.[125]

15–133 As to unregistered land, title deeds are still evidence of title, of course. Equitable mortgages by deposit of title deeds have become less common in recent years, but they may still be created.[126]

---

[119] LCLRA 2009 s.21(3)(a).

[120] LCLRA 2009 s.21(3)(b)(i).

[121] LCLRA 2009 s.21(3)(b)(ii); Wylie, *Annotations and Commentary* (2017), [54], n.29.

[122] Registration of Deeds and Title Act 2006 (Commencement) (No. 2) Order 2006 (S.I. No. 511 of 2006).

[123] Wylie, *Annotations and Commentary* (2017), [54], n.29; RDTA Act 2006 s.73(2) and (3), and see Registration of Title Act 1964 s.90, substituted by RDTA 2006 s.63.

[124] RDTA 2006 s.73(4).

[125] LCLRA 2009 s.89(6).

[126] LCLRA 2009 s.89(6) and s.21(3)(b)(ii).

Trusts within Section 21(2)(b)[127]

15–134 This refers to "other trusts" mentioned above, where payment to a single trustee is sufficient to overreach the equity. Overreaching does not apply:

- where the equitable interest is protected by registration prior to the date of the conveyance.

  In the case of unregistered land, it would have to be registered in the Registry of Deeds, or in the case of registered land, in the Land Registry.[128] This situation would include the case of a single owner holding a fee simple subject to an equity arising by virtue of the doctrine of constructive trusts or proprietary estoppel, unless he or she is in actual occupation of the land, as mentioned in the next paragraphs. If he or she is not registered, then the equity would be overreached on a sale by the single owner. This could cause problems in the normal case where the owner is held subject to an equity arising by constructive trust or proprietary estoppel because until the court makes such a finding, the person entitled to the equity will not be aware that he or she has one. For example,[129] suppose A, a farmer, owns the legal fee simple in a farm. He has employed B, a young relative, for many years as a farm worker and later manager. A has no children of his own. On several occasions before witnesses he has said that he will leave the farm to B by will. B had abandoned his education to work for A and gives up other opportunities to pursue other careers, relying on A's assurances. Several years later, A, unknown to B, leaves the farm to X. Assuming that B is entitled to equity through proprietary estoppel, what right has B against X? He would hardly have been able to protect it by registration, since he would not be aware of his rights until a court decided on them. If B was "in actual occupation" of the farm, his right is protected even though not registered and is not overreached, and he can obtain the farm if X had notice of his right: the doctrine of notice continues to apply. Is the test satisfied if B lived in a room in A's farm house rent-free? Or if he lived in a house or cottage on the farm? If he did not live on the farm, his right would in any case be overreached under s.21 of the LCLRA 2009 and the most he would be entitled to would be the value of the farm.
- Where the equitable interest is a burden under s.72(1)(j) of the RTA 1964 ("the rights of persons in actual occupation or in receipt of the rents and profits thereof, save where, upon enquiry made of such person, the rights are not disclosed").
- In the case of unregistered land, the equitable interest would take effect as a burden under s.72(1)(j) of the RTA 1964 if the land were registered land, i.e. rights of persons in actual occupation. This was formerly the

---

[127] LCLRA 2009 s.21(3)(b)(iii).
[128] Wylie, *Annotations and Commentary* (2017), [54], nn.31–33.
[129] The example is based on the facts of *Gillett v Holt* [2000] 2 All E.R. 289.

principle of *Hunt v Luck*[130] and *Hamilton v Lyster*.[131] The equitable principles in the case law are replaced by the corresponding wording of s.72(1)(j).

Family Home Protection Act 1976

15–135 Overreaching does not affect the requirement that the consent of a "non-owning" spouse is necessary to a conveyance of a family home under the Family Home Protection Act 1976.[132]

Interests Having Priority to the Trust of Land

15–136 It was seen in relation to the Settled Land Acts that overreaching did not affect "interests having priority to the settlement", such as a fee farm rent created out of the fee simple before it was settled.[133] Presumably the same applies under s.21 of the LCLRA 2009, i.e. overreaching would not apply to such interests created before the land became subject to the trust of land.[134] Section 21 does not apply to legal interests, such as fee farm rents, and applies expressly only to equitable interests. Possibly, although admittedly not expressly, it only applies to equitable interests created after the trust of land, although there remains a doubt on that point.

Purchasers

15–137 Where a purchaser pays the money to two trustees, where that is required under the provisions discussed above, or to one trustee in other cases, the purchaser obtains a good title freed of the equitable interests of the beneficiaries under the trust of land and whether the purchaser had notice of them or not,[135] subject to the exceptions just discussed, which includes where the purchaser has actual notice that a conveyance is fraudulent.[136] "Fraud unravels all."[137] Constructive notice, as modified by s.86 of the LCLRA 2009, is not enough in this context. To that extent, overreaching abolishes the doctrine of notice.

---

[130] [1902] 1 Ch. 428.

[131] (1844) 7 Ir. Eq. R. 560.

[132] LCLRA 2009 s.21(6); Wylie, *Annotations and Commentary* (2017), [54], n.38.

[133] Settled Land Act 1882 s.20(1)(i).

[134] Fee farm rents existing at law at the date the LCLRA 2009 came into force are preserved: s.12(6).

[135] LCLRA 2009 s.21(1).

[136] LCLRA 2009 s.21(3)(a).

[137] Wylie, *Annotations and Commentary* (2017), [54], n.23; *Lazarus Estates Ltd v Beasley* [1956] 1 Q.B. 702 at 712: "No court in this land will allow a person to keep an advantage which he has obtained by fraud. No judgment of a court, no order of a Minister, can be allowed to stand if it has been obtained by fraud. Fraud unravels everything. The court is careful not to find fraud unless it is distinctly pleaded and proved; but once it is proved, it vitiates judgments, contracts and all transactions whatsoever." *HIH Casualty and General Insurance Ltd v Chase Manhattan Bank* [2003] UKHL 6: "[F]raud is a thing apart. This is not a mere slogan. It reflects an old legal rule that fraud unravels all: *fraus omnia corrumpit*."

15–138 Wylie mentions that the Law Reform Commission wished to extend overreaching to all conveyances, even where a person might have a claim based on resulting or constructive trusts or proprietary estoppel. The Bill was nevertheless amended in the Dáil at Select Committee stage to restrict the overreaching provision. This seems wise, since the equities raised by such doctrines would not necessarily be satisfied by an interest in a sum of money and real injustice could have been done. Nevertheless, such interests are only exempt from overreaching where (apart from registration) the person entitled is in actual occupation.

15–139 "Purchaser" includes persons acquiring other interests in land, such as leases or mortgages, and "conveyance" has a similarly extended meaning.[138] "Purchaser" means a person acquiring an interest in the land for valuable consideration and there is no reference to "good faith" or "notice".[139]

Disputes

15–140 Section 22 of the LCLRA 2009 sets out the procedure for settling disputes as to trusts of land. Section 22(1) provides:

> "Any person having an interest in a trust of land, or a person acting on behalf of such a person, may apply to the court in a summary manner for an order to resolve a dispute between the—
> (a) trustees themselves,
> (b) beneficiaries themselves,
> (c) trustees and beneficiaries, or
> (d) trustees or beneficiaries and other persons interested,
> in relation to any matter concerning the—
> (i) performance of their functions by the trustees, or
> (ii) the nature or extent of any beneficial or other interest in the land, or
> (iii) other operation of the trust."

15–141 The court may make whatever order and direct whatever inquiries it thinks fit in the circumstances of the case,[140] subject to its having regard to the interests of the beneficiaries as a whole and, subject to those, to the purposes which the trust of land is intended to achieve, the interests of any minor or other beneficiary subject to any incapacity, the interests of any secured creditor of any beneficiary, and any other matter which the court considers relevant.[141] "Person having an interest" includes a mortgagee or other secured creditor, a

---

[138] LCLRA 2009 s.3.
[139] LCLRA 2009 s.3.
[140] LCLRA 2009 s.22(2).
[141] LCLRA 2009 s.22(3).

judgment mortgagee or a trustee.[142] Nothing in s.22 affects the jurisdiction of the court under s.36 of the Family Law Act 1995.[143]

Variation of Trusts

15–142 The changes to the law of future interests by the LCLRA 2009 mean that it becomes possible for settlors to create trusts of land which could postpone the point where the fee simple could be sold for a long time in the future. The abolition of the rule in *Whitby v Mitchell* means that a settlor could, for example, create a trust giving life estates not only to his living son or daughter, but to his unborn grandchildren, and then his unborn great-grandchildren, and so on, creating in effect an interest similar to an unbarrable entail. The abolition of the modern rule against perpetuities has a similar effect, allowing the creation of contingent future interests, so that, while the recipient remains unascertained, all the people entitled to interests in the land cannot come together to consent to a sale. The solution provided by the LCLRA 2009 is the provisions of Pt 5 which confer an extended jurisdiction on the courts to vary the trust if in the future there is a need to do so. Variation of trusts is beyond the scope of the present work and reference should be made to Wylie's commentary on the LCLRA 2009.[144]

---

[142] LCLRA 2009 s.22(4).
[143] LCLRA 2009 s.22(5).
[144] Wylie, *Annotations and Commentary* (2017), [56]–[59].

CHAPTER 16

The Irish Land Purchase Acts

Partiality, one-sidedness, and partisanship, as between classes, were not nice things in themselves, but they were the very life and essence of the statute which they were considering. Its avowed purpose and policy were to take large masses of the land value of Ireland away from the landlord class and hand it over to the tenant class ... He was not saying that it was wrong, or that it was right; he was merely stating that it was the fact. There might be social mischiefs or social crises so grave as to require that those things to which the lawyers were in the habit of paying, perhaps, a superstitious reverence — namely, the sacredness of property and the inviolability of contracts, should give way to the exigencies of a great public policy; and the present might be an occasion of that kind. He could not tell. He was no judge of high politics.

— Lord Justice Christian in *Shearman v Kelly* (1878) 12 I.L.T.S.J. 98 at 99

GENERAL EFFECT OF THE ACTS

16–01 The Irish Land Commission was created by the Land Law (Ireland) Act 1881 enacted during William Gladstone's administration. It was the means of resolving the "Land Question",[1] i.e. the chronic agricultural unrest caused by the Irish land tenure "system" whose main features were:

1. absentee landlords who had little or no interest in their Irish estates beyond collecting rent;
2. tenants with little or no security of tenure and little incentive or ability to improve the land;
3. a system of tenure which required tenants to make all improvements, including the erection of their own cottages, but which held the landlord entitled to them at the end of the tenancy or on eviction;
4. the eviction of tenants unable to pay rent, resulting in their total destitution;
5. the attempt to replace evicted tenants with landless people from the local community, resulting in great bitterness on the part of the dispossessed

---

[1] For a historiographical reflection of this and other Irish "land questions", see F. Campbell and T. Varley, *Land Questions in Modern Ireland* (Manchester: Manchester University Press, 2013).

and imposing a cruel dilemma on those offered the chance to replace them;

6. the reaction of agricultural tenants to their situation which took various forms, from the Whiteboys of the 18th century to the boycotts, Land War and Land League of the 19th century.[2]

16–02 The Land League had been established in 1879 by Michael Davitt in Co. Mayo and soon became a national movement led by Charles Stewart Parnell.[3] It campaigned in Ireland and in the British Parliament for reduction of rents and the right of tenants to purchase the freehold of their holdings. Part of the campaign involved ostracism of tenants who had taken over holdings from evicted tenants and it organised the refusal of agricultural workers to assist in bringing in the harvests on landlords' estates. This form of protest came to be known as a boycott, from the name of the manager of one such estate, Captain Boycott, and added a new word to the English language, and other European languages, in the process.[4] In the North of Ireland, a campaign urged the enactment of legislation to establish the "Three F's": fixity of tenure, fair rents and free sale.[5]

16–03 Gladstone's 1881 Act, which replaced the less effective Act of 1870,[6] was based on the policy of the "Three F's". The Act gave security of tenure to tenants, provided a means of fixing fair rents and gave tenants the right to assign their tenancies without the landlord's consent.[7] The Act also compelled the landlord to compensate the tenant fully for disturbance in his occupancy, and for any improvements he may have effected on the holding. These measures were described as "dual ownership", in that the rights of ownership were split between landlord and tenant, and were denounced by some at the time as an expropriation of the landlords' property rights.[8] Landlords who wished to do so could, as an alternative, sell the fee simple to the tenant. The Act established the Irish Land Commission as an intermediary, providing an advance to

---

[2] See S. Clark, *Social Origins of the Irish Land War* (Princeton, N.J.: Princeton University Press, 1979).

[3] J.C.W. Wylie, *Irish Land Law*, 5th edn (Haywards Heath: Bloomsbury Professional, 2013), para.1.47.

[4] OED: "boycott". See Wylie, *Irish Land Law* (2013), para.1.47, for references to academic studies of the Land Purchase Acts.

[5] For an account of the Land Purchase Acts and their economic effects, see C.F. Kolbert and T. O'Brien, *Land Reform in Ireland: A Legal History of the Irish Land Problem and Its Settlement* (Cambridge: University of Cambridge Department of Land Economy, 1975).

[6] The Landlord and Tenant (Ireland) Act 1870. The first land purchase Act was in fact the Irish Church Act 1869 which disestablished the Church of Ireland. It vested the considerable land holdings of the church in the Church Temporalities Commissioner and gave them power to sell the land to the church tenants: Wylie, *Irish Land Law* (2013), para.1.51.

[7] For a detailed discussion, particularly of the financial provisions of the Irish Land Acts, see Wylie, *Irish Land Law* (2013), paras 1.44–1.68.

[8] See D. Hogan, "Arrows Too Sharply Pointed: the relations of Lord Justice Christian and Lord O'Hagan, 1868-1874" in J.F. McEldowney and P. O'Higgins (eds), *The Common Law Tradition: Essays in Irish Legal History* (Dublin: Irish Academic Press, 1990).

the tenant of three quarters of the purchase price for the purchase of the land and recovering the loan from the erstwhile tenant by an annuity charged on the land.[9] The Irish Land Commission was also given power to acquire land by agreement for resale to tenants. While the 1881 Act provided a mechanism for land purchase, the scheme was only a voluntary alternative to "dual ownership". It did not provide sufficient assistance to tenants to purchase and was only partially successful.

16–04 The Purchase of Land (Ireland) Act 1885 (the "Ashbourne Act", named after the Irish Lord Chancellor at the time) improved the position by empowering the Irish Land Commission to advance the whole purchase price to the tenant and extended the repayment period for land purchase annuities to 49 years.

16–05 The Purchase of Land (Ireland) Act 1891 and the Land Law (Ireland) Act 1896 (the "Balfour Acts") saw the Conservatives converted to the notion of land purchase. The 1891 Act introduced the Congested Districts Board with special powers to deal with land in "congested districts" in which the particular problem was small uneconomic holdings. Most of the counties in the West of Ireland were defined as congested, from Donegal in the north to Cork and Kerry in the south. The 1891 Act replaced the system of advances with a system of payment by land stock and later land bonds.[10] When the price of government stock fell, landlords became reluctant to sell and tenants also found it difficult to calculate the amount of the annual payments each year under the scheme. The situation was only partly relieved by the 1896 Act.

16–06 The Irish Land Act 1903 (the "Wyndham Act", after George Wyndham, Secretary of State for Ireland), re-introduced cash payment and provided for the sale of whole estates, supervised by the Irish Land Commission's own land agents, the Estates Commissioners.[11] The Act was a great success in accelerating the process of land transfer to the tenants, and it can be argued that it was the most successful of all the Irish Land Acts.[12] Before it, most land was in the hands of landlords: within a few years after it, most had passed into the hands of the tenants. The Evicted Tenants (Ireland) Act 1907 introduced compulsory acquisition for the first time, for the re-instatement of evicted tenants or their sons.[13] The Irish Land Act 1909 ("Birrell's Act") extended compulsory acquisition to congested districts and congested estates.

16–07 The Land Act 1923, the first land purchase Act enacted by the newly independent government, introduced compulsory land purchase in Ireland for tenanted land for the first time. The Land Act 1933 extended the compulsory

---

[9]   Based on the so-called "Bright Clauses" in the 1870 Act, called after the English economist John Bright who had drafted the earlier clause in the Irish Church Act 1869.
[10] Wylie, *Irish Land Law* (2013), para.1.53.
[11] Wylie, *Irish Land Law* (2013), para.1.55.
[12] Wylie, *Irish Land Law* (2013), para.1.56.
[13] Wylie, *Irish Land Law* (2013), para.1.56.

powers of the Irish Land Commission and removed many of the restrictions which had previously applied to acquisition.[14]

16–08 After 1922 the annuities accumulated in a fund were still paid to the British government as repayment for the financial advances under the schemes before 1922; but the Land Act 1933 allowed the Minister for Finance to divert the annuities for local government projects. This caused retaliation by the British government in the form of economic sanctions from 1933–1938, and was resolved by a one-off payment of £10 million to the United Kingdom in 1938.

16–09 The Irish Land Commission, having operated for over 100 years, had completed its work by 1992. Some 13.5 million acres of land had been transferred to tenants.[15] The Irish Land Commission (Dissolution) Act 1992 provided for its abolition.[16] It was brought into force by order on 31 March 1999.[17] The Act provides that the powers of the Irish Land Commission to acquire land, except for the purposes of exchange of holdings, and to resume holdings, parcels or tenancies, are abolished.[18] Other powers are transferred to the Minister for Agriculture and Food.[19]

16–10 The Irish Land Purchase Acts represented probably the most extensive system of acquisition of land in Europe carried out by legal means. Their social effects were immense. Their technical legal effect on titles was also profound, more radical in many ways than that of the Settled Land Acts.

16–11 From a technical perspective the Land Purchase Acts had an overreaching effect similar in some ways to the Settled Land Acts, and so they remain important from a conveyancing point of view.

Like the Settled Land Acts
16–12 The Land Purchase Acts applied to most instances where land was held for freehold interests other than an unencumbered fee simple estate.

16–13 The effect of a sale was to "overreach" other interests in the land, termed "superior interests" in the Land Purchase Acts, such as future freehold estates or landlords' reversions, i.e. to convert them into interests in the purchase money and to convey to the purchaser, the former tenant farmer, a fee simple estate free of these interests.

---

[14] See T. Dooley, *The Land for the People: The Land Question in Independent Ireland* (Dublin: UCD Press, 2004).

[15] Land Bill 2004 Explanatory and Financial Memorandum, p.1.

[16] Irish Land Commission (Dissolution) Act 1992 s.4.

[17] S.I. No. 75 of 1999. Individual functions were transferred before that date: *O'Cleirigh v Minister for Agriculture, Food and Forestry* [1998] 2 I.L.R.M. 263.

[18] Irish Land Commission (Dissolution) Act 1992 s.2(2).

[19] Irish Land Commission (Dissolution) Act 1992 s.4.

Powers of the Irish Land Commission

16–14 The Land Purchase Acts vested the powers in the Irish Land Commission, not in a tenant for life or any other private individual.

16–15 The operation of the powers in relation to any given piece of land was a once-and-for-all exercise. Under the Settled Land Acts, the powers could be invoked more than once in relation to a given piece of land, namely, at any time it was the subject of a settlement.

16–16 Overreaching under the Land Purchase Acts was more radical than under the Settled Land Acts. Under the Settled Land Acts interests "having priority to the settlement" were not overreached, whereas under the Land Purchase Acts virtually all interests affecting the land, except easements and an important category of sporting rights, were overreached. A sale under the Land Purchase Acts thus had the effect of curing defects in the title to the fee simple. This is considered in more detail below.

16–17 A vesting deed executed by the Irish Land Commission is not only a "good root of title", but is one of the best proofs of title in fee simple it is possible to have. It is proof that "superior interests" affecting the title were cleared off the title at the time of the vesting deed. A conveyance in fee simple under the Settled Land Acts is proof that other interests under the settlement were cleared off the title but it does not clear off interests having priority to the settlement, i.e. created before the land was settled.

OVERREACHING EFFECT

16–18 Section 31 of the Land Law (Ireland) Act 1896 provided for the overreaching of "superior interests" when the fee simple was vested by the Irish Land Commission in a purchaser[20]:

> "31.—(1) Where any land has been sold under the Land Purchase Acts ... or where land is sold by the Land Judge to the tenant thereof, and an advance under the Land Purchase Acts is made for the purpose of such sale, or where a lessor or grantor has signified his consent to the redemption of a rent under the Redemption of Rent (Ireland) Act 1891, the sale of such land ... or the redemption ... shall be made discharged from all superior interests as defined by this section, or from any of them, and in every such case the land shall be vested accordingly in the purchaser in fee simple, and such superior interests, or the value thereof, shall become a lien upon, and be redeemed or satisfied out of, the purchase money of such land.

---

[20] Replacing Landlord and Tenant (Ireland) Act 1870 s.35. See also Irish Land Act 1903 s.98 and Irish Land Act 1909 s.23(5).

(2) [Vesting order is subject to such exceptions and reservations as specified in the order.]"

16–19 Section 16 of the Irish Land Act 1903 provided that, when the Irish Land Commission agreed to purchase land, the Commission could vest the land in itself prior to sale in certain cases, and in such a case the section provides for overreaching to take effect when the fee simple vested in the Irish Land Commission rather than when it vested in a purchaser:

"16.—(1) The Land Commission may, where they agree to purchase any land, make a vesting order which shall be effectual to vest in the Commission the fee simple of the land purchased, subject—
(a) to any public rights affecting the land;
(b) to any sporting rights reserved by the vendor;
(c) to any maintenance charge under the Public Works Acts; and
(d) to any interests of the tenants on the land, or of persons having claims upon those interests, and to any easements, rights and appurtenances mentioned in section thirty-four of the Act of 1896; [see below] but save as aforesaid and subject to the provisions of this Act with respect to minerals, discharged from the claims of all persons who are interested in the land, whether in respect of superior or intervening interests or incumbrances or otherwise, and all such claims shall, as from the date of the vesting order, cease as against the land and attach to the purchase money, in like manner as immediately before the date of the order they attached to the land."

16–20 A holding vested in a purchaser was still to be subject, as the section says, to "easements, rights and appurtenances; and any privilege previously in fact enjoyed, whether by permission of the landlord or otherwise" under s.34 of the 1896 Act, and to certain sporting rights, which are considered below.

Superior Interests
16–21 Section 31(8) of the Land Law (Ireland) Act 1896 contained a wide definition of the "superior interests" overreached by a vesting order:

"(8) The expression 'superior interest' shall include any rent, rentcharge, annuity, fees, duties, services, payable to or to be rendered in respect of the land sold to any person, [including the Crown] and any estates, exceptions, reservations, covenants, conditions, or agreements, contained in any fee-farm grant, or other conveyance in fee, or lease, under which such land is held, and, if such land is held under a lease for lives or years renewable forever, or for a term of years of which not less than 60 are unexpired at the date of the sale, shall include any reversion or estate expectant on the determination of such lease or expiration of such term, and notwithstanding that such reversion or estate may be vested in the [State]."

16–22 "Superior interest" also includes any reversion expectant on the determination of an estate tail or a base fee, whether or not vested formerly in the Crown.[21]

16–23 The more radical effect of overreaching under the Land Purchase Acts can be seen here, in that it actually cures defects in the title to the fee simple. If the title purchased and conveyed to a former tenant was really a base fee, the section nevertheless had the effect of overreaching it and therefore, in effect, converting the base fee into a full fee simple. This got rid of one of the possible defects in a title which would not be entirely cured by the Statute of Limitations 1957.

16–24 The definition does not include a reversion expectant on a life estate, but s.31(7) of the 1896 Act provides that where the superior interest is settled land within the Settled Land Acts, the person who is tenant for life or has the powers of tenant for life of the interest has the power to consent to the sale being made discharged from such interest. Section 16 of the Irish Land Act 1903 applies not only to "superior interests" but to the claims of "all persons who are interested in the land".[22]

16–25 This section was extended by s.2 of the Congested Districts Board (Ireland) Act 1899 to cases where the land was sold by the Congested Districts Board.

16–26 Superior interests vesting in the Irish Land Commission under the Land Act 1923 were converted to personalty for the purpose of determining their "destination" or of the redemption money.[23]

Intervening Interests
16–27 The Irish Land Commission had power to vest the fee simple in a subtenant rather than the tenant. The policy of the Acts was generally to vest the fee simple in the person substantially occupying the land and farming it, and where there was a sub-tenancy the subtenant was likely to be that person. The provisions were in the Irish Land Act 1903:

> "15.—(1) In the case of the sale of an estate the Land Commission may, if they think fit, declare that any person who, as a subtenant, is in the exclusive occupation of a parcel of land comprised in the estate shall be deemed the tenant of that parcel, and the parcel shall be deemed to be a holding.

---

[21] Irish Land Act 1903 s.98(2); State Property Act 1954 s.21.
[22] This section replaced the earlier provision contained in s.35 of the Landlord and Tenant (Ireland) Act 1870.
[23] Land Act 1931 s.32(2).

(2) The Land Commission shall in such case redeem the interests (in this Part of this Act referred to as 'intervening interests') intervening between the owner of the estate and the person in such exclusive occupation as aforesaid, at a price which [in default of agreement] shall be fixed by the Land Commission and the redemption money shall be paid out of the purchase money of the estate ... provided that, if the Land Commission are of opinion that any intervening interest is of no appreciable value, they shall by order declare that interest to be extinguished."

Sporting Rights
16–28 Many sporting rights of the vendor were exempted from the overreaching effect of the Acts and so remained vested in the former owner.

Resumption of Holding
16–29 Where the Irish Land Commission "resumed" a holding[24] there was a separate overreaching provision in s.12 of the Land Act 1953, but sporting rights were further preserved from the effect of that section[25] where they were vested in someone other than the tenant.

REGISTRATION OF VESTING ORDERS

16–30 Registration of vesting orders was provided for by s.16(3) of the Irish Land Act 1903, i.e. for registration under the Local Registration of Title (Ireland) Act 1891. The section was replaced by s.31 of the Land Act 1931 ("as full owner"), which was repealed by s.5 of the Registration of Title Act 1964 ("RTA 1964"). Vesting orders now come within the compulsory registration provision of s.23 of the RTA 1964 ("where the land has been, or is deemed to have been, at any time sold and conveyed to or vested in any person under any of the provisions of the Land Purchase Acts"), and s.26(1) of the RTA 1964 provides that where land has been so sold, conveyed or vested before 1 January 1892, the person appearing to the Land Commission to be in possession shall be registered as the owner.

LAND PURCHASE ANNUITIES

16–31 The form of land purchase as it evolved in the legislation was that the Irish Land Commission paid the landowner the purchase price of the land as an advance and then recovered the money over a period of time from the former tenant and successors in title by attaching to the land a land purchase annuity. Under s.20 of the Land Law (Ireland) Act 1887 such an annuity had priority over all existing and future estates, interests and incumbrances created either

---

[24] See Land Act 1939 s.54; Land Act 1953 s.18; Land Act 1965 s.14.
[25] Land Act 1953 s.12(6).

by the landlord or the tenant with the exception of a quit rent, other charges incident to the tenure, other charges for public money, and, where the land was subject to a fee farm rent or a lease reserving a rent, to such a rent. The annuity is an incorporeal hereditament separate from and paramount to the estate of the owner.[26]

16–32 Land purchase annuities are registered as a burden against registered land under s.72(1)(c) of the RTA 1964. Under s.2 of the Land Act 2005 land purchase annuities, where the annual sum payable was not more than €200 on 13 July 2004, were discharged.[27]

---

[26] *Re Parkinson* [1898] 1 I.R. 390.
[27] The cost of collecting such annuities, even if paid on time, approximately equalled the amount received. About 4,200 farmers fell into the category: Land Bill 2004 Explanatory and Financial Memorandum, p.3.

CHAPTER 17

Co-ownership

In Nature's state ... Man walk'd with beast, joint tenant of the shade.

— Alexander Pope, *An Essay on Man* (1733), Vol.iii, p.152

INTRODUCTION

17–01 Interests in land may be held by more than one person at the same time, which implies some form of co-ownership. The common law recognised four forms of co-ownership: joint tenancy, tenancy in common, coparcenary and tenancy by entireties. Prior to the Land and Conveyancing Law Reform Act 2009 ("LCLRA 2009"), coparcenary could occur only in the case of the fee tail and since such estates are converted by the LCLRA 2009 to fees simple, it can no longer arise. Tenancy by entireties is likewise obsolete.

17–02 The term "tenancy" in the titles of the forms of co-ownership can cause confusion. Tenancy in this context should be taken to denote the holding of an estate or other interest. It does not imply the relationship of landlord and tenant.

JOINT TENANCY

17–03 Joint tenancy describes a situation in which two or more people are treated "vis-à-vis the outside world, as one single owner."[1] The characteristics of joint tenancy are the principle of survivorship and the four unities.

Survivorship (Ius Accrescendi)
General
17–04 The basic principle is that when one joint tenant dies, his or her interest in the land ceases and the surviving joint tenants hold the property among themselves. If a joint tenant's death leaves only one remaining owner, then co-ownership ceases and the sole survivor holds the estate alone. It follows from this that the principle of survivorship takes precedence over a gift of his or her interest by a joint tenant by will.[2] Section 4(c) of the Succession Act 1965 confirms this:

---

[1] *Hammersmith and Fulham LBC v Monk* [1992] 1 A.C. 478 at 492.
[2] Co Litt 185b.

"(c) the estate or interest of a deceased person under a joint tenancy where any tenant survives the deceased person shall be deemed to be an estate or interest ceasing on his death …".

17–05 If land is held in fee simple by A and B as joint tenants and A leaves his interest by will to X, then the result depends on whether A survives B or not. If A survives B, then A has become sole owner and the gift in the will can take effect. If A dies before B, then at A's death, when the will takes effect, A has ceased to have any interest in the land and the gift in his will fails.[3]

17–06 The principle of survivorship developed in the feudal period, possibly because the class of feudal lords wished to ensure that the tenements held from them did not become divided up among an ever-increasing number of tenants. If that had been allowed to occur, the enforcement of feudal services would have become more difficult. It also corresponded with social relations between family members who would be likely to want the property on their death to be held by remaining family members. The rule has survived to the present day because it has come to perform a different requirement. It is a convenient mode of holding for trustees. When one trustee dies the property vests automatically in the remaining trustees without the necessity of a deed vesting it in them.

17–07 The principle of survivorship is the main reason why the interest of a joint tenant is not spoken of as an "undivided share" as is the case with a tenancy in common. But this conceptual distinction is rather artificial. If A, B and C hold land in joint tenancy, A has something which she can sell to a third party, X. (A major change brought in by the LCLRA 2009 is that after 1 December 2009, A must obtain the consent of B and C, as will be discussed below.) If A does sell her interest, this has the effect of creating a tenancy in common between X on the one hand and B and C on the other. X has a one-third share as tenant in common. So A really had something in the nature of an inchoate one-third share for this purpose. Equally, if A, B and C had decided to sell the land, A would have been entitled to one-third of the proceeds.[4]

Commorientes: Simultaneous Death

17–08 One special problem that arises on the death of joint tenants is that of *commorientes* (those dying together), i.e. when two or more joint tenants all die in the same accident or catastrophe. Those claiming the estates of the various joint tenants could only succeed by showing that the one whose estate they claimed had survived the others. Usually this could not be done due to lack of

---

[3] A in her lifetime may convey to a third party, the effect being to sever the joint tenancy as between the other joint tenancy and the third party. Such a conveyance now needs the consent of the other joint tenants under the LCLRA 2009.

[4] *Re Wilks* [1891] 3 Ch. 59. In the absence of a mutual intention to sever, the money is held on joint tenancy until divided: *Byrne v Byrne*, unreported, High Court, McWilliam J., 18 January 1980; *Re Hayes' Estate* [1920] 1 I.R. 207.

evidence.[5] In such a case the common law treated the heirs of deceased joint tenants as themselves holding on joint tenancy. Thus, there was, in effect, a presumption of simultaneous death.[6] Section 5 of the Succession Act 1965 now provides as follows:

> "5.—(1) Where, after the commencement of this Act, two or more persons have died in circumstances rendering it uncertain which of them survived the other or others, then, for the purposes of the distribution of the estate of any of them, they shall all be deemed to have died simultaneously."[7]

17–09 The implication of this was that the position was the same as at common law, i.e. none of those who held the property could take by survivorship. The personal representatives of the deceased held the property collectively on trust for the persons entitled under the will or on intestacy.[8] Whereas the personal representatives held the legal estate as joint tenants, it was unclear how the equitable interests were held, i.e. by the successors of those dying together.[9]

17–10 Section 5 was amended by the Civil Law (Miscellaneous Provisions) Act 2008 so that where two or more persons immediately before their death held property as joint tenants and then die simultaneously, or are deemed to have done so under s.5, then they are deemed to have held the property immediately before their deaths as tenants in common in equal shares.[10] The shares will then pass to their respective separate estates.[11]

Unlawful Killing

17–11 The unlawful killing of one joint tenant by another raises a complex problem for the law of survivorship. Public policy requires that the wrongdoer be prevented from deriving any benefit from his criminality—an argument which suggests that the right of survivorship will require modification in such cases so as to prevent the wrongdoer from acquiring enlarged rights over the land. It is also necessary to consider what the effect of the unlawful killing

---

[5] Uncertainty was still held to exist in *Kennedy v Kennedy*, unreported, High Court, Kearns J., 31 January 2000, a case of a car plunging into water, despite the fact that there was evidence that one person may have died almost immediately of a heart attack, while the other died minutes later from drowning. According to the pathologist, the heart attack could also have been caused by a struggle to open the car door.

[6] *Wing v Angrave* (1860) 8 H.L.C. 183.

[7] Apparently taken from the German Civil Code (Art.20), as amended in 1951. See also Art.32 of the Swiss Civil Code.

[8] Succession Act 1965 s.10.

[9] The second edition of this book stated at this point: "It may be the case that ... the equitable interest is held by those entitled to it as tenants in common, so that simultaneous death causes a severance in equity."

[10] Succession Act 1965 s.5(2), as inserted by Civil Law (Miscellaneous Provisions) Act 2008 s.68(b).

[11] Succession Act 1965 s.5(3), as inserted by Civil Law (Miscellaneous Provisions) Act 2008 s.68(b).

should be on the killer's own share. Section 120(1) of the Succession Act 1965 provides that a person who has been convicted of the murder, attempted murder or manslaughter of another is precluded from taking any share in his victim's estate. Section 120(5) provides that any affected share is to be distributed as if the wrongdoer had predeceased the victim. Were a similar rule to be applied to property held under a joint tenancy, the wrongdoer would be deprived of any interest in the property—a result which is arguably unduly punitive in light of the abolition of forfeiture as a penalty for crime.[12]

17–12 The effect of unlawful killing on survivorship was considered by the High Court in *Cawley v Lillis*,[13] in which the defendant had been convicted of the manslaughter of his wife, who had been survived by their daughter. Prior to her death, the deceased and the defendant had been joint tenants of two properties. The plaintiffs argued that the court should apply the survivorship principle on the basis that the defendant had predeceased his wife, by analogy with the Succession Act 1965—a result which would have vested sole ownership of the properties in the deceased's estate. Laffoy J. declined to adopt this approach as to do so would be to interfere with the defendant's existing rights in the properties at the date of the crime, something which she felt the court had no power to do in the absence of an appropriate legislative provision. Two other solutions were then canvassed by the court: the severance of the joint tenancy in equity as a result of the unlawful killing, or the imposition of a constructive trust over the deceased's share in favour of her estate. Severance of the joint tenancy in equity has attracted support in England and Wales,[14] whilst other Commonwealth jurisdictions appear to have adopted the position that the right of survivorship will vest sole legal title to the property in the wrongdoer, but that that legal title is impressed with a constructive trust as to the deceased's share.[15] Laffoy J. concluded that severance did not occur on the killing of the deceased but that any joint assets which had accrued to the defendant by virtue of survivorship were held by him on a constructive trust for the deceased's estate.

17–13 *Cawley v Lillis* was decided on the basis of the pre-LCLRA 2009 law and its conclusion must therefore be approached with caution as the changes to severance introduced by s.30 of the LCLRA 2009 may allow the court's reasoning to be distinguished in future cases. The Law Reform Commission

---

[12] See Forfeiture Act 1870 s.1.

[13] [2012] 1 I.R. 281.

[14] *Re K (deceased)* [1986] 1 Ch. 180; *Dunbar v Plant* [1988] Ch. 412 (defendant had been convicted of aiding and abetting the suicide of a joint tenant). See also, *Chadwick v Collinson* [2014] EWHC 3055 (Ch). C. Harpum, S. Bridge and M. Dixon, *Megarry & Wade: The Law of Real Property*, 8th edn (London: Sweet & Maxwell, 2012), para.13–049, suggest that in spite of these cases, the question is not conclusively settled and that there is much to be said for the constructive trust approach.

[15] See *Re Pechar (deceased)* [1969] N.Z.L.R. 574; *Rasmanis v Jurewitsch* (1979) 70 S.R. (NSW) 407; *Schobelt v Barber* (1966) 60 D.L.R. (2d) 519.

has published an issues paper which addresses survivorship in unlawful killing situations, which may result in further developments in this area.[16]

The Four Unities

17–14 In order that a joint tenancy can exist, there must be the four unities. These are the unities of possession, interest, title and time.[17]

Possession

17–15 This unity is a characteristic shared by all forms of co-ownership. Each co-owner is entitled to possession of the whole premises. A co-owner who evicts another co-owner from the premises is therefore liable in trespass.[18] Acts which destroy the enjoyment of the property in common can amount to ouster.[19] However, liability for ouster seems to apply only if the "ousting" tenant remains in possession. If one joint tenant of a leasehold tenancy gives notice to quit to the landlord, the House of Lords held in *Hammersmith and Fulham LBC v Monk*[20] that the effect was to terminate the tenancy as to both of them. The parties in the case were cohabiting joint tenants under a periodic tenancy of local authority housing. When their relationship broke down, the female tenant gave notice to quit to the local authority and vacated the premises. The local authority successfully sought possession from the remaining male tenant. The House of Lords held that the tenancy required the consent of both tenants and when one withdrew her consent, the tenancy was terminated, even though in that case it caused the male tenant to become homeless. The human rights issues raised in the subsequent case of *Harrow LBC v Qazi*[21] have been discussed in Ch.1.

17–16 At common law a co-owner who had not been ousted had no action against another co-owner, so that if the property had been rented out in his absence he had no action to recover his part of the rent if it had been retained

---

[16] Law Reform Commission, *Issues Paper on Review of Section 120 of the Succession Act 1965 and Admissibility of Criminal Convictions in Civil Proceedings* (LRC IP 7-2014). The paper identifies New Zealand's Succession (Homicide) Act 2007, which provides that the deceased's estate, the wrongdoer and any other interested person take as tenants in common, as one possible option in this area. The Succession (Amendment) Bill 2015 was introduced in the Seanad in 2015 but did not progress beyond the first stage. It proposed to insert new ss.120A and 120B into the Succession Act 1965.

[17] *A.G. Securities v Vaughan* [1990] 1 A.C. 417 at 431.

[18] *Beaumont v Kinsella* (1859) 8 Ir. C.L.R. 291; J.C.W. Wylie, *Irish Land Law*, 5th edn (Haywards Heath: Bloomsbury Professional, 2013), para.8.08; E.H. Burn and J. Cartwright, *Cheshire and Burn's Modern Law of Real Contract*, 18th edn (Oxford: Oxford University Press, 2011), p.494. See s.3 of the Housing (Miscellaneous Provisions) Act 1997, under which a tenant of a housing authority who is a joint tenant may obtain an exclusion order against another joint tenant. Barring orders made under s.3 of the Domestic Violence Act 1996 would also seem to apply to joint tenants.

[19] *Beaumont v Kinsella* (1859) 8 Ir. C.L.R. 291.

[20] [1992] 1 A.C. 478; *Notting Hill Housing Trust v Brackley* [2002] EWCA Civ 601.

[21] [2003] UKHL 43.

by the other co-owner. The Administration of Justice Act 1707[22] gave a co-owner the right to sue for an account against a co-owner who received more than his share of rent or profit. This has now been replaced by s.31(2)(d) of the LCLRA 2009, by which a co-owner at law or in equity can apply to the court for "accounting adjustments" to be made between the co-owners.[23]

17–17 There are problems with the unity of possession which do not seem to have been resolved by case law, probably because the concept depends upon co-owners resolving disputes between themselves. If each co-owner has the right to possession of the whole premises, can one have no exclusive right to a bedroom? Can one not exclude the others from the bathroom while the one is actually using it, without being liable for trespass? The law seems an inadequate forum to resolve disputes in this area.

17–18 In *Lahiffe v Hecker*,[24] Lynch J. had to grapple with some of these problems in a situation complicated by an attempt to give one of the joint tenants an additional right of residence. The testator left a house to his three daughters, A, B and C, and to his son, D, as joint tenants, subject to a right of residence in C "until she marries". A, B and D were married. The parties subsequently severed the joint tenancy by an assent, which vested the house in them as tenants in common in equal shares.

17–19 Lynch J. held that, while C was not entitled to exclude the other tenants in common from possession, they, on the other hand, could not exercise their right to possession so to overcrowd the property as to render C's right of residence ineffective. C, while "not legally entitled to the exclusive use of any particular part of the house", would be entitled to choose one of the three bedrooms in the house for her exclusive use, "to enable her properly to enjoy her general right of residence in the house". He further held that the right of residence did not inhibit the discretion of the court to order a sale on an application under the Partition Acts (now replaced by the LCLRA 2009). The judge also held that on sale, C would be entitled to an additional fractional share in respect of her right of residence. One might note that the intention of the testator may well have been to ensure C's right to possession rather than to give her an extra share of money. It seems unfortunate that the courts have been unwilling, with at least one exception,[25] to give effect to this intention behind rights of residence and to hold that they may be overreached.

---

[22] 6 Anne c 10 (Ir), s.23; *Dawson v Baxter* (1887) 19 L.R. Ir. 103. The repeal of s.23 by s.3 of the Common Law Procedure Amendment Act (Ireland) 1853 was held to apply only to procedure and the jurisdiction was held to remain by *Keaney v Kearney* (1861) 13 Ir. C.L.R. 314 at 322–323; A. Dowling, "The Baby and the Bathwater: The Administration of Justice (Ireland) Act 1707, s 23" (1996) 47 N.I.L.Q. 428. The 1707 Act was repealed by LCLRA 2009 Sch.2.

[23] H. Conway, *Co-Ownership of Land: Partition Actions and Remedies*, 2nd edn (Haywards Heath: Bloomsbury Professional, 2012), Ch.11.

[24] Unreported, High Court, Lynch J., 28 April 1994.

[25] *Johnston v Horace* [1993] I.L.R.M. 594.

Interest

17–20 Every joint tenant must have an identical interest in the land. If one co-owner has a freehold interest and another a leasehold interest, they do not hold as joint tenants. Moreover, they must have the same estates, e.g. both fees simple or both life estates. The unity of interest is not affected if one joint tenant has an additional interest in the land created at the same time (or possibly before) the joint tenancy:

[in trust for] X and Y for life, remainder to X in fee simple.

X and Y still have a joint tenancy for their joint lives.[26]

Title

17–21 Joint tenants must take by the same title, e.g. the same deed, or will or the same act of adverse possession.[27] If A conveys land to B and C jointly and then C sells his interest (now with B's consent) to D, B and D are not joint tenants. B's title derives from the conveyance by A, and D's from the conveyance by C. It is a common situation in rural Ireland for members of a family to remain in possession of land after the owner's death without the estate being administered. In such a case the members of the family who remain acquire by adverse possession the interests of those who are absent. They acquire them as joint tenants so that, as between those who remain, the principle of survivorship applies.[28] The courts may support the notion not only that those who have left should be excluded, but also that those who remain constitute a new family unit as to which survivorship rightly applies.

Time

17–22 Joint tenants must also take vested interests at the same time. At common law if land was granted

to A for life, remainder to the heirs of B and C

and B and C died in A's lifetime, the heirs of B and C were tenants in common.[29] Although the heirs of B and of C took by the same title, their interests

---

[26] Contrast subsequent acquisition of an interest by a joint tenant.

[27] *Maher v Maher* [1987] I.L.R.M. 582; *Gleeson v Feehan* [1997] 1 I.L.R.M. 522.

[28] *Maher v Maher* [1987] I.L.R.M. 582; *Gleeson v Feehan* [1997] 1 I.L.R.M. 522. Where two or more persons are entitled to a share of a deceased estate they acquire their own prospective "shares" as joint tenants: Succession Act 1965 s.125, reversing *Smith v Savage* [1906] 1 I.R. 469; *Gleeson v Feehan* [1997] 1 I.L.R.M. 522.

[29] *Megarry & Wade: The Law of Real Property* (2012), para.13–008.

vested at different times. The common law principle was not satisfied by the interests vesting *in possession* at the same time.[30]

17–23 In the example above, the interests would now take effect as a trust of land. Trusts were an exception to the common law rule before the LCLRA 2009. Such interests often arose in family settlements. Equity was less stringent than the common law once was. The explanation seems to be that joint tenancy is a more appropriate form in the case of limitations to members of the same family. As a result of successive interests now taking effect in equity under the LCLRA 2009, the exception would now seem to have become the rule, at least where a single group of close relatives is concerned.

17–24 In *O'Hea v Slattery*,[31] a settlement was made of tenancies from year to year (and personal chattels) to trustees on trust for the settlor until his intended marriage and then on trust for the settlor, his wife and the children of the present marriage and that of his previous marriage. The court held that the intention was that the settlor, his wife and the children should hold as co-owners. Furthermore, they held as joint tenants. Later-born children would take interests when they were born, existing joint tenants being divested of their interests to the extent necessary to provide such interests. Unity of time was not required.[32]

TENANCY IN COMMON

No Survivorship
17–25 The principle of survivorship does not apply to tenancies in common. When one tenant in common dies his or her interest passes to the devisee or legatee under his or her will or to the persons entitled on intestacy. Therefore, land held on tenancy in common is said to be held in "undivided shares". Each tenant has a claim to a share in the property which will not be destroyed by their death.

Unity of Possession
17–26 The only unity that need be present for a tenant in common to exist is the unity of possession.

---

[30] Co litt 188a; Bl Comm ii. 181. In the example, if B and C were not related, then it may be that "the heirs of B" would take between themselves as joint tenants, and the heirs of C similarly, but that the two *groups* would be tenants in common in relation to each other. This may be what Coke meant (Co Litt 188a) when he speaks of "one moiety" vesting at one time and the other moiety at a different time.

[31] [1895] 1 I.R. 7.

[32] A similar exception existed in the past in relation to executory devises, so that in a limitation in a will "to A for life, remainder to her children in fee simple", the children took as joint tenants although their interests vested in interest at different times. It is suggested that the exception now applies to all gifts in wills, because they take effect as equitable interests, the legal estate vesting initially in the personal representatives.

Legal Tenancies in Common and Multiple Ownership

17–27 Legal tenancies in common potentially create a problem of alienability because they allow the possibility of dividing the legal title into many separate shares. Suppose a legal tenancy in common was originally vested in A, B and C in equal shares. Suppose that A, B and C have now died. A left his share by will to D, E and F. B died intestate, leaving children G and H. C also died intestate, leaving children I, J, K and L. D, E and F now have one-ninth of the legal interest each. G and H both have one-sixth. I, J, K and L each have one-twelfth. All these people will have to join together to convey the whole fee simple in the land, since they must all be parties to the deed. Underhill,[33] who investigated the law of property in England before the 1925 legislation, found a case of a house the title to which had become divided among 17 people, each entitled to 1/70th or multiples of that fraction. This had resulted from two relatively simple wills.[34] The English Law of Property Act 1925 therefore changed the law to prohibit the creation in future of legal tenancies in common and also prohibit the severance of a legal joint tenancy so as to produce a tenancy in common.

17–28 Such a change was considered, but rejected, by the Law Reform Commission.[35] The English provisions have not proved universally popular, one reason being that wherever land is conveyed to or held by two or more persons beneficially, whether as joint tenants or tenants in common, a statutory trust for sale is imposed.[36] Practitioners who were consulted did not report problems with fragmentation of ownership. Large groups of investors in commercial property made representations to the effect that they preferred to hold the legal title as tenants in common which gave them distinct individual shares, and would not be content if the legal title was held by a few trustees as joint tenants on trust for all the investors who would only have equitable interests. Also, where joint tenants died, or were deemed to have died, simultaneously in an accident (*commorientes*) no survivorship took place, but it was uncertain how the equitable interests were held by their estates. The law had already been changed in 2008, as will be seen below, to implement the recommendation of the Law Reform Commission so that they are deemed to have held the property immediately before their deaths as tenants in common in equal shares.

---

[33] A. Underhill, *Acquisition and Valuation of Land Committee, Fourth Report* (London: HMSO, 1919), p.30.

[34] A man had devised the house by will to his wife for life, remainder to his children in fee simple. He had 10 children, one of whom died in the widow's lifetime, leaving seven children and a widow and a similar will.

[35] Law Reform Commission, *Consultation Paper on Reform and Modernisation of Land Law and Conveyancing Law* (LRC CP 34-2004); Law Reform Commission, *Report on Land Law and Conveyancing Law: (1) General Proposals* (LRC 30-1989), pp.11–12; J.C.W. Wylie, *The Land and Conveyancing Law Reform Acts: Annotations and Commentary*, 2nd edn (London: Bloomsbury, 2017), [65], n.1.

[36] Law of Property Act 1925 ss.34 and 36.

If tenancies in common could no longer exist at law, the problem would have re-occurred.

CREATION OF JOINT TENANCY AND TENANCY IN COMMON

At Law

17–29 At common law there is a presumption in favour of a joint tenancy rather than a tenancy in common. Thus, if land is conveyed

> *to A and B in fee simple*

prima facie they hold the legal title as joint tenants.[37] It might also be noticed that the common law preferred to regard the relationship as a non-market one. In the feudal period co-tenants were assumed to be family members as between whom survivorship was appropriate. In fact, co-tenants in the feudal period would be more likely to be members of the same family or kin group, and so the presumption also corresponded with social reality. The common law presumption is rebutted by the following.

Lack of One of the Four Unities

17–30 If one of the four unities is absent there can be no joint tenancy at law, although exceptions to the unity of time were allowed in equity.

Words of Severance

17–31 Certain words used in a limitation have been held to rebut the presumption of a joint tenancy and to indicate that a tenancy in common is intended. Words such as "in equal shares", "share and share alike",[38] "share and share among them",[39] "equally",[40] "between"[41] and "respectively"[42] suggested an undivided share rather than the interest of a joint tenant. Where the words are equivocal or contradictory the modern tendency is to construe the document as a whole so that "as joint tenants in common in equal shares" may be construed

---

[37] *McDonnell v Jebb* (1865) 16 Ir. Ch. R. 359; *Kennedy v Ryan* [1938] I.R. 620.

[38] *Hayes v Ward* (1788) 2 Ridg. P.C. 85; *Clarke v Bodkin* (1851) 12 Ir. Eq. R. 492; *Re Dennehy's Estate* (1865) 17 Ir. Ch. R. 97.

[39] *Lessee of Scully v O'Brien* (1839) 1 Ir. L.R. 287.

[40] *Lewen v Dodd* (1595) Cro. Eliz. 443; *Lewen v Cox* (1599) Cro. Eliz. 695; *Lambert v Browne* (1871) I.R. 5 C.L. 281.

[41] *Crozier v Crozier* (1843) 3 Dru. & War. 373.

[42] *Stephens v Hide* (1734) Ca. t. Talb. 27; *Flemming v Flemming* (1857) 5 Ir. Ch. R. 129. But see *Re Newsom's Trusts* (1878) 1 L.R. Ir. 373 ("sole and separate use of herself and her daughters" in a will held to give joint tenancy).

as creating either a joint tenancy or a tenancy in common, depending on the circumstances.[43]

Bodies Corporate

17–32 If land was conveyed to a body corporate to hold with other persons or a corporation, the common law held them to be tenants in common and not joint tenants.[44] The common law refused to recognise that survivorship could apply to a body that never literally "died".[45] The Bodies Corporate (Joint Tenancy) Act 1899 therefore provided that a corporation could hold any property in a joint tenancy as if it were an individual. This became important when banks began to act as trustees.[46] Section 32 of the LCLRA 2009 replaces the 1899 Act without substantial amendment.[47] If a body corporate is a joint tenant of any property and is dissolved, then the property vests in the other surviving joint tenants.[48]

In Equity

17–33 Equity tends to favour a tenancy in common rather than a joint tenancy: "equity leans against survivorship". Equity reveals here again its preference for commodity relationships in which survivorship would be inappropriate. There is, however, no general presumption in equity. There are instead a number of situations in which equity intervenes and presumes an intention to create a tenancy in common, subject to proof to the contrary. A trust based on presumed intention is usually referred to as a resulting trust or, somewhat superfluously, as a presumed resulting trust, as distinct from a constructive trust in which equity intervenes on proof of certain facts, although constructive trusts are really a residual category.[49]

17–34 In situations where equity intervenes, the single legal owner or the legal joint tenants will hold the legal title on trust for the beneficiaries as tenants in common. Thus, if A, B and C hold the legal title as joint tenants in circumstances in which equity would infer a tenancy in common, they will hold the legal title as trustees for themselves as tenants in common in equity. Survivorship operates as to the legal title but not as to the beneficial interest. Thus, if

---

[43] *Martin v Martin* (1987) 54 P. & C.R. 238 (held a tenancy in common); *Joyce v Barker Bros (Builders) Ltd* (identical words held a joint tenancy); *Megarry & Wade: The Law of Real Property* (2012), para.13–019.

[44] *Fisher v Wigg* (1700) 1 Ld. Raym. 622 at 627; *Law Guarantee, etc Society v Bank of England* (1890) 24 Q.B.D. 406.

[45] Wylie, *Annotations and Commentary* (2017), [68], n.2; *Megarry & Wade: The Law of Real Property* (2012), para.13–003.

[46] *Megarry & Wade: The Law of Real Property* (2012), para.13–003.

[47] The 1899 Act says "any real or personal property", while s.32 says "any property". Law Reform Commission, *Consultation Paper on Reform and Modernisation of Land Law and Conveyancing Law* (LRC CP 34-2004), paras 6.15 and 6.16.

[48] LCLRA 2009 s.32(3); Wylie, *Annotations and Commentary* (2017), [68], n.6.

[49] *Megarry & Wade: Real Property* (2012), para.11–017.

C dies, the legal title is then held by A and B alone, since they are the surviving joint tenants, but C's beneficial interest will pass to whoever becomes entitled to C's estate on his death. The key to understanding equity's role is to consider the legal title separately from the equitable interest: first, apply the rules of the common law discussed above as to the legal title, and then consider whether there are grounds for equity to intervene as to the beneficial interest.

Multiple Title
Equal Contribution

17–35 If two or more people hold the legal title to property as joint tenants, and the purchase money is provided by them in equal shares, then equity presumes that there is nothing to displace the common law position and the parties hold the beneficial interest as well as the legal title as joint tenants: "equity follows the law". In this instance equity does not intervene at all unless there is proof of intention.[50]

17–36 The presumption can be rebutted by evidence of an actual intention to the contrary. In *O'Connell v Harrison*,[51] there was such evidence. A number of shares were purchased and put in the joint names of two sisters, MW and EW. There was no evidence as to the proportion in which the purchase price was provided, although the judge was prepared to assume that it was in equal shares. EW became of unsound mind and MW was appointed her legal committee. MW died not long after and was survived by EW, who died two years after her sister. The personal representative of EW claimed that the shares were held in joint tenancy and that EW's estate was entitled to them by survivorship. Kennedy C.J. held that the sisters held the shares as tenants in common in equity. There were three pieces of evidence which pointed to this conclusion. The sisters had inherited a business and some other shares from their father and had later executed a deed declaring that these were held as beneficial tenants in common. They had themselves bought other shares which, although taken in their joint names, were declared by deed to be held as tenants in common. Finally, MW, while she was the committee of EW, had declared that EW was entitled to half the shares and asked that they be applied to her maintenance.

17–37 Where the parties are or were married, issues as to beneficial interests in the family home now occur in the context of family law legislation.[52]

---

[50] If there is, then the trust should probably be called a constructive trust, but it is not universally accepted terminology.

[51] [1927] I.R. 330.

[52] For example, *BD v JD*, unreported, High Court, McKechnie J., 5 December 2003, p.71: "This case in my opinion is not a company law case, or a trust action or a case where a declaration as to beneficial ownership is appropriate ... Therefore I don't propose to approach the division of assets in any manner other than in accordance with section 16 [of the Family Law Act 1995, as amended by s.52 of the Family Law (Divorce) Act 1996] as interpreted and applied by the authorities above mentioned ...".

Unequal Contribution

17–38 If the legal title is in the name of more than one person as joint tenants but the purchase money is provided by them in unequal shares, equity presumes that the person who provided the greater share did not intend to make a gift of the excess amount to the other party or parties, and therefore that they hold the beneficial interest as tenants in common. Thus, if A and B buy property and A provides £6,000 and B provides £4,000, then if they were to be beneficial joint tenants, if the joint tenancy were to be put to an end by partition, each would receive half the proceeds. A would, by his initial contribution, have made a gift to B of a proportion of the property initially represented by £1,000. The presumption in equity, however, is that A did not intend to make a gift to B and so they hold the joint tenancy in trust for themselves as tenants in common in proportion to the amounts contributed.[53] Equity shows its commodity-oriented aspect here. The relationship that it assumes is one in which the parties seek to maximise their own advantage and so only part with something in order to obtain a corresponding benefit. The presumed trust is subject to proof of a contrary intention.[54]

Single Title

17–39 It may be that, although the legal title is held by one person only, more than one person has contributed to the purchase of the property. Equity presumes that the holder of the legal title holds it on trust for himself or herself and the other party as tenants in common in equity. Equity presumes that the party who contributed, but who does not hold the legal estate, did not intend to make a gift of the money to the titleholder, but intended to acquire some interest in the property in return.

17–40 In *Bull v Bull*,[55] the plaintiff and his mother bought a house to be a home for themselves. The son provided most of the purchase money and the conveyance was taken in his name alone. The court held that the mother did not intend to make a gift of the money to him. The son later married and it was agreed that the mother should occupy two rooms in the house and the son and his wife the rest of the house. Differences of opinion arose between the mother and her daughter-in-law and the son gave his mother notice to quit. When she refused to leave, he sued her for possession. Denning L.J. in the English Court of Appeal held that the provision by the mother of part of the purchase price had made her a tenant in common with the son in equity. As such she was entitled to remain in possession concurrently with the son. Although this conclusion had the effect of securing the mother's possession, it ignored the fact that the agreement entered into on the son's marriage gave her possession of only two rooms in the house. Ignoring the fact did have the advantage of

---

[53] *Lake v Gibson* (1729) 1 Eq. Ca. Abr. 290 at 291.

[54] *Megarry & Wade: The Law of Real Property* (2012), para.13–022.

[55] [1955] 1 Q.B. 234. See also, *Lloyds Bank plc v Rosset* [1991] 1 A.C. 107.

avoiding the awkward conclusion, which would seem to be inevitable, that the agreement had caused a partition in equity.

17–41 In *Jones v Jones*,[56] a father bought a house near his own home for his son. The son moved into the house with his wife and family, having given up a job in a different town in order to do so. The son gave his father money equal to a quarter of the price of the house. The son understood from his father that the house was to be his. The father then died and the house vested in the plaintiff, who was the son's stepmother. The English Court of Appeal held that the son was a tenant in common and could not be evicted. In the reported proceedings the stepmother sued for rent, but it was held that, as with joint tenants, one tenant in common could not claim rent from another unless the claimant had been ousted from possession.[57]

Mortgage Loans

17–42 In the past it was not uncommon for private persons to invest money by advancing it on the security of a mortgage. If two or more people lent money on the mortgage of property, whether in equal or unequal shares, then even if the legal interest which they took in the property mortgaged to them was a joint tenancy, equity presumed a beneficial tenancy in common. Since it was a commercial transaction the assumption was readily made that survivorship was not an appropriate principle to apply.

Partnership

17–43 Since partnership is a commercial relationship then, even if the legal estate in property vested in partners is a joint tenancy, equity presumes that partnership assets are held *as between the partners themselves*[58] in a tenancy in common.

17–44 *Reilly v Walsh*[59] is an instance of the presumption being rebutted. In that case a partnership was carried on by two brothers. One of the brothers became mentally ill and took little part in the business from then on. He was later discharged from hospital as recovered and left a will in which he purported to leave his share of the assets to the plaintiff. It was held that the assets were held beneficially as joint tenants and so the gift in the will was defeated by survivorship. The result was due in part to the fact that the deceased brother had taken little part in the business and the augmentation of the assets. It may also have been because the partners were also brothers.

---

[56] [1977] 2 All E.R. 231.
[57] The facts were held also to have given rise to a claim under the doctrine of proprietary estoppel and that the stepmother was bound by the claim.
[58] *Hayden v Carroll* (1796) 3 Ridg. P.C. 545 at 620.
[59] (1849) 11 Ir. Eq. R. 22.

Other Situations

17–45 The above situations are not exhaustive of the instances in which equity will intervene to find a tenancy in common.

17–46 In *Twigg v Twigg*,[60] the testator directed trustees to sell the residue of his estate and to hold the money on trust for his nephews and nieces. He then strongly recommended, without imposing a trust to that effect, that the nephews and nieces should expend the money on the education of their children. Some of the beneficiaries were unmarried. It was held that the money was held in tenancy in common in equal shares. The testator could not be taken to have intended that the unmarried beneficiaries should contribute out of a joint fund for the education of the married beneficiaries' children.

17–47 In *L'Estrange v L'Estrange*,[61] the testator devised the residue of his estate to trustees for six of his children with power to advance such sums for the education and "advance in life" of the children as the trustees thought fit. Lord Ashbourne L.C. held that the power of advancement was inconsistent with a joint tenancy. It showed that they were treated as having different needs and so were intended to take separate interests. The children were held to be tenants in common of the residue.

17–48 In *Malayan Credit Ltd v Jack Chia MPH Ltd*,[62] two businessmen took a lease of the seventh floor in an office block in Singapore. There was no lump sum to be paid, but they agreed to divide the rent and the floor space in the same unequal proportions. The Privy Council held that they were tenants in common in equity.

Presumption of Advancement

17–49 Sometimes the normal presumption is replaced by the presumption of advancement. This applies in certain relationships in which equity recognises that one person owes an obligation to provide for another, such as a father for a son[63] or a grandfather for a grandson.[64] If, for example, a mother and daughter both contribute to the purchase of property, the title to which is put in the daughter's name, the presumption is that the mother made an advancement, i.e. a gift, to the daughter and the mother does not obtain a beneficial interest in equity.

17–50 The presumption of advancement used to apply between husband and wife, in that a husband was regarded as being under an obligation to provide

---

[60] [1933] I.R. 65.
[61] [1902] 1 I.R. 467.
[62] [1986] 1 All E.R. 711.
[63] *Redington v Redington* (1794) 3 Ridg. P.C. 201; *Scroope v Scroope* (1663) 1 Chan. Cas. 27; *Grey (Lord) v Grey (Lady)* (1666) 1 Chan. Cas. 296; *Elliot v Elliot* (1677) 2 Chan. Cas. 231.
[64] *Ebrand v Duncer* (1680) 2 Chan. Cas. 26; *Stileman v Ashdown* (1737) 2 Atk. 477; *Taylor v Taylor* (1737) 1 Atk. 386.

for his wife, but the increasing recognition of equality of the sexes has led the courts to reduce the strength of the presumption of advancement in the case of married couples.[65]

17-51 In *RF v MF*,[66] Henchy J. treated it as still applying to some degree where a wife adopts the traditional role of homemaker, but as weak and easily rebutted when both parties go out to work and provide for the family out of their own income. This may equally apply where one spouse in a same-sex marriage adopts the homemaker role. However, there is said to be no presumption that a wife owes an obligation to provide for her husband.[67]

Express Declaration of Trust
17-52 Is an express declaration by the parties as to their respective beneficial interests conclusive? One view derives from a political attitude which supports the idea that the market mechanism should operate as free from State intervention or interference as possible. This view asserts that parties are the best judges of their own interests. They are also assumed to be equal in their economic strength, and so it is also assumed that the agreement is a free one. Thus, on these assumptions, equity's role is limited to spelling out the intentions of the parties only where they have not made them clear. This being the case, any express declaration by the parties as to their intentions is treated as conclusive and renders the intervention of equity unnecessary.[68]

17-53 An alternative approach is based upon a political attitude to the market which regards it as producing injustice in that it does not satisfy human needs unless the subjects have the means to pay for the goods to satisfy them. This approach is prepared to question the assumptions of the "free market" approach and in particular to question whether the terms of the agreement represent the interests of both parties, or merely those of the stronger.[69] Irish courts have tended to find that an express declaration ousts the inference of a tenancy in common in equity, but without stating categorically that it is always conclusive.[70]

SEVERANCE OF JOINT TENANCY

17-54 Severance of a joint tenancy does not put an end to the co-ownership but converts the joint tenancy to a tenancy in common. Essentially, therefore,

---

[65] *RF v MF*, unreported, Supreme Court, Henchy J., 24 October 1985; *Heavey v Heavey* (1977) 111 I.L.T.R. 1; *McGill v S* [1979] I.R. 283; *Parkes v Parkes* [1980] I.L.R.M. 137; *Pettit v Pettit* [1970] A.C. 777.
[66] Unreported, Supreme Court, Henchy J., 24 October 1985.
[67] *Containercare v Wycherley* [1982] I.R. 143 at 152.
[68] *Goodman v Gallant* [1986] 1 All E.R. 311.
[69] See *Bedson v Bedson* [1965] 3 All E.R. 307.
[70] See *W v W* [1981] I.L.R.M. 202; *Containercare Ltd v Wycherley* [1982] I.R. 143 at 147.

it means that survivorship ceases to apply. Logically, since it is possible to have a tenancy in common with all the four unities, severance does not necessarily require the destruction of one of the four unities, but for severance to take effect at law, i.e. to sever the legal title, the common law does require some objective transaction which has this effect. On the other hand, since it is not possible for a joint tenancy to continue if one of the four unities is absent, destruction of any one of them, at law or in equity, will cause a severance. There are two exceptions to this, however. Since the unity of possession is essential both to a joint tenancy and to a tenancy in common, destruction of this unity will put an end to the co-ownership altogether. This is known as *partition* and is dealt with later. The unity of time is a pre-condition. Either it is present at the beginning or it is not. Severance, where it is caused by the destruction of one of the unities, therefore concerns the unities of interest and of title.

17–55 Section 30 of the LCLRA 2009 implements the Law Reform Commission's recommendation[71] that severance of a joint tenancy at law or in equity should no longer be possible, as it was at common law, without the consent of the other joint tenants.

17–56 There were a number of arguments for and against this "radical"[72] change. Unilateral severance meant that a joint tenant could "opt out" of survivorship and obtain a definite share. It therefore deprived the other joint tenants of the chance of benefiting by survivorship. Suppose there are three joint tenants, A, B and C. A is 80 years old, while B is 70 and C is 60. A is likely to die before B and C. This of course is by no means certain, but A might wish to sever unilaterally so that he would have a definite share to leave by will. If A can do so without the consent of B and C, he has deprived B and C of the chance that the survivor of them would end up with the whole property. But what sort of interest is the chance of benefiting from survivorship? After all, there is also a chance of losing by it, and depending on the relative ages, health, etc., possibly a greater chance. Is it a property right, or a mere expectation or *spes successionis*?[73] The common law did not seem to regard it as a property right, since it allowed A to sever unilaterally. Another argument against unilateral severance is that joint tenancy often occurs between family members or spouses and it is an inappropriately aggressive way of solving

---

[71] Law Reform Commission, *Report on Reform and Modernisation of Land Law and Conveyancing Law* (LRC 74-2005), Ch.6; Law Reform Commission, *Consultation Paper on Reform and Modernisation of Land Law and Conveyancing Law* (LRC CP 34-2004); Law Reform Commission, *Report on Land Law and Conveyancing Law* (LRC 30-1989); Law Reform Commission, *Report on Land Law and Conveyancing Law (7): Positive Covenants over Freehold Land and Other Proposals* (LRC 70-2003), para.5.02; Law Reform Commission, *Consultation Paper on Judgment Mortgages* (LRC CP 30-2004).

[72] Wylie, *Irish Land Law* (2013), para.8.29.

[73] H. Conway, "When is a Severance Not Actually a Severance?" (2009) 16 Aust. Prop. L.J. 278.

disputes in such situations, and that the parties should be encouraged to resolve their differences by agreement.[74]

17–57 The Law Reform Commission[75] gave as a reason for the change, the following:

"Under the present law, one joint tenant can act independently in a manner which affects the property rights of the other joint tenants. This is so even where, originally, the parties have all agreed to hold as joint tenants and where discrepancies in their ages may have made the right of survivorship particularly significant. Yet this flies in the face of the basic idea of contract law (possibly because this area of property law developed long before the law of contract became established), which is also a basic moral principle, namely that agreements freely entered into should be honoured."

17–58 However, Mee[76] has pointed out that

"[t]his reference to contract law and to 'basic moral principle' seems to overlook an essential point. The nature of a joint tenancy is, and has been for centuries, that it is capable of severance. This is what the parties sign up for when they create a joint tenancy. The creation of a joint tenancy creates no contract or obligation not to sever. On the contrary, the law currently regards the right to sever unilaterally as an essential protection against the possible hardship caused by the 'odious' right of survivorship."

17–59 Another objection was that it could be difficult to obtain consent, as where a co-owner is elderly or incapacitated, or even impossible where the relationship between co-owners has become antagonistic, and that it would be sufficient to have a requirement that the joint tenant intending to sever should merely notify the others.[77] The LCLRA 2009 did not adopt this course, but met the argument by providing that consent may be dispensed with by the court.

---

[74] Wylie, *Annotations and Commentary* (2017), [66], n.1; U. Woods, "Unilateral Severance of Joint Tenancies – the Case for Abolition" (2007) 12(2) C.P.L.J. 47.

[75] Law Reform Commission, *Report on Land Law and Conveyancing Law (7): Positive Covenants over Freehold Land and Other Proposals* (LRC 70-2003), para.5.07.

[76] J. Mee, "The Land and Conveyancing Law Reform Bill 2006: Observations on the Law Reform and a Critique of Selected Provisions – Part II" (2006) 11(4) C.P.L.J. 91 at 93.

[77] J. Mee, "The Land and Conveyancing Law Reform Bill 2006: Observations on the Law Reform and a Critique of Selected Provisions – Part II" (2006) 11(4) C.P.L.J. 91; Wylie, *Annotations and Commentary* (2017), [66], n.1. This is the course taken in the England and Wales reform: Law of Property Act 1925 s.36(2), by which a joint tenancy may sever unilaterally in equity by a notice in writing to the others: *Megarry & Wade: The Law of Real Property* (2012), para.13-044. Severance of a legal joint tenancy was not permitted after 1925 in England and Wales.

Consent

17–60 Under s.30 of the LCLRA 2009 a conveyance or contract for a conveyance of land held on joint tenancy or acquisition of another interest in the land by a joint tenancy without the consent of the other joint tenants is void at law and in equity, unless consent is dispensed with by the court.[78] "Consent" (except in the case of severance in equity[79]) means the prior consent in writing of the other joint tenant or joint tenants,[80] a wording which recalls the provisions of the Family Home Protection Act 1976 as to consent of a non-owning spouse. Under s.31, "a person having an estate or interest in land" may apply to the court for an order dispensing with consent where it is being unreasonably withheld.[81] It is for the courts to develop the test for unreasonableness. Wylie has suggested that "the obvious analogy" is the court's power to declare that a landlord is unreasonably withholding consent to a tenant who wishes to alienate.[82] The section does not, however, give discretion to the court where a joint tenant finds it difficult to obtain consent because he or she is elderly or incapacitated. Powers of attorney may provide a solution in such a case.

Severance at Law

17–61 To cause a severance, the common law required some transaction or dealing which destroys one of the unities. Mere intention of the parties, whether mutual or unilateral, was not enough. There are possibly two reasons why the common law took this view. First, the common law developed when legal tests took a relatively primitive form, in that they relied on external acts that were clearly present or not present, rather than states of mind which were more difficult to assess. Secondly, the feudal common law favoured joint tenancies over tenancies in common and was not disposed therefore to make it easy to put an end to a joint tenancy.

17–62 In addition to a conveyance, the LCLRA 2009 now also requires the consent of the other joint tenant or tenants.[83] Also, one may note that a contract is insufficient to sever at law, even if preceded by a written consent.

Subsequent Acquisition of Another Interest

17–63 The fact that an interest is given to a number of persons as joint tenants and *at the same time* an additional interest is given to one of them does not prevent the joint tenancy taking effect as such.[84]

---

[78] LCLRA 2009 s.30(1). The provision as to dispensing with consent was introduced in the Seanad Committee Stage on the Bill: Wylie, *Annotations and Commentary* (2017), [66], n.10.

[79] LCLRA 2009 s.30(4). A court may find that joint tenants have severed by mutual agreement or by the conduct of them all. See below.

[80] LCLRA 2009 s.30(2).

[81] LCLRA 2009 s.31(1) and (2)(e).

[82] Wylie, *Annotations and Commentary* (2017), [67], n.12. See *Whyte v Cosgrave* [2016] IEHC 190.

[83] LCLRA 2009 s.30(1).

[84] Although it may exacerbate problems raised by the unity of possession: see *Lahiffe v Hecker*, unreported, High Court, Lynch J., 28 April 1994.

17–64 If a legal joint tenant acquires an additional interest in the property at a later time, with consent under the LCLRA 2009 or if consent is dispensed with, it destroys the unity of interest and produces a severance.[85]

17–65 Such was the primitive concern of the feudal common law with form rather than substance, that the effect of a transaction depended on technical distinctions between different forms of deed, such as a conveyance and a release, the latter being normally the correct deed to use in transferring interests between joint tenants. So in the limitation

> *to X, Y and Z in fee simple*

if X *releases* his interest to Y, it causes a severance in relation to X's interest only. Y holds a one-third share as tenant in common with Z, representing X's interest. Y and Z hold the other two-thirds as joint tenants.

17–66 Under the LCLRA 2009, Z's consent would be required and arguably this is reasonable, since the severance affects Z in that Z now holds as tenant in common with Y in relation to X's share.

17–67 If, on the other hand, X *conveys* his interest to Y, Y has obtained an additional interest and this causes a severance between Y and Z, but again, only now with Z's consent.[86] Y and Z take as tenants in common. This distinction follows from the purely technical distinction between the effect of a release and a conveyance at common law, but whether modern courts would treat these rules as immutable is open to question. On the other hand, if Z consents, this then accords with Z's wishes and so there seems no reason why it should not operate in this way.

Alienation by One Joint Tenant

17–68 Alienation by one joint tenant of his or her interest to a third party destroys unity of title and causes a severance.[87] So, if land is conveyed "to A, B, and C in fee simple" and A later sells to X, X is a tenant in common as to one-third in relation to B and C and they are tenants in common as to two-thirds in relation to X, but B and C are still joint tenants in relation to each other.[88] Thus, if X dies, her interest passes to those entitled to her estate, but if B dies then C takes the two-thirds by survivorship from him. The explanation of these rules seems to be that sale introduces a market or commodity relationship into what was otherwise an extra-market relation and the law reflects this by severance. It does not, however, affect the relationship between the original joint tenants.

---

[85] *Connolly v Connolly* (1866) 17 Ir. Ch. R. 208; *Flynn v Flynn* [1930] I.R. 337.
[86] Co Litt 183a, 192a.
[87] Co Litt 185a; *Re Gilburn*, unreported, High Court, Kenny J., 9 July 1975, p.2.
[88] Co Litt 189; See also, *Stephen v Beall et Ux* 89 US 329 (1874).

17–69 Other forms of alienation, such as a lease or mortgage, have the same effect, since they give a right to possession, but not a mere incumbrance, such as a rentcharge.[89]

Unilateral Dealing

17–70 Before the LCLRA 2009 a joint tenant could bring about a severance vis-à-vis the others by a conveyance to feoffees. If A, B and C were joint tenants, and A conveyed to F in fee simple to hold to the use of A in fee simple, the Statute of Uses would execute the use, giving A back her interest, but this time as a tenant in common, since the conveyance caused a severance.

17–71 Since the Statute of Uses 1634 has been repealed, this is no longer possible. A could convey her interest (with the consent of B and C) to a trustee to hold in fee simple back to A, which would create a bare trust (which would be a trust of land) and then A could demand a conveyance of the legal estate.[90] This would take two deeds. There seems to be a need here for a statutory reform expressly allowing a joint tenancy to sever in his or her own favour by a single deed, signed also by the other consenting parties.

Act of a Third Party under Statutory Powers

17–72 Before the LCLRA 2009 the effect of the registration of a judgment mortgage against *unregistered* land was to transfer the estate or interest of the judgment debtor to the judgment mortgagee (the creditor)[91] and therefore where the debtor was a joint tenant it had the effect of severing the joint tenancy.[92] In *Containercare v Wycherley*,[93] the court held that this effect was not prevented by s.3 of the Family Home Protection Act 1976 since that section only prevented conveyances by a spouse without the consent of the other spouse and the registration of a judgment mortgage was a conveyance not by a spouse but by a third party. On the other hand, it did not have that effect in *registered* land.[94] It merely created a charge on the interest of the debtor.

17–73 This state of the law was considered unsatisfactory by the Law Reform Commission, not only because there was an anomalous difference between registered and unregistered land, but because it ran counter to the new rule requiring consent to a unilateral severance.[95] Section 30(3) of the LCLRA 2009 now provides that the registration of a judgment mortgage against the estate

---

[89] Co Litt 286.
[90] Under the principle in *Saunders v Vautier* (1841) Cr. & Ph. 240.
[91] Judgment Mortgage (Ireland) Act 1850 s.7; repealed by LCLRA 2009 s.8 and Sch.2, Pt 4.
[92] *McIlroy v Edgar* (1881) 7 L.R. Ir. 521; *Containercare v Wycherley* [1982] I.R. 143; *Murray v Diamond* [1982] I.L.R.M. 113.
[93] [1982] I.R. 143. See also, *Murray v Diamond* [1982] I.L.R.M. 113; *McIlroy v Edgar* (1881) 7 L.R. Ir. 521.
[94] *Mahon v Lawlor* [2008] IEHC 284; *Irwin v Deasy* [2006] IEHC 25.
[95] Wylie, *Annotations and Commentary* (2017), [66], n.16.

or interest of a joint tenancy does not sever the joint tenancy. Furthermore, if the joint tenancy remains unsevered, the judgment mortgage is extinguished on the judgment debtor's death.[96] The reason is that now, if nothing else causes a severance of the joint tenancy, and the judgment debtor predeceases the others, his or her interest also ceases by survivorship on his or her death.[97] On the other hand, if the judgment debtor turns out to be the sole survivor, what then? Should it still cease, even though the survivor's interest survives for his or her estate?

Severance in Equity

17–74 A characteristic of equity which has already been noted is that, in contrast to the concern of the common law for objective formalities, it paid greater regard to the subjective intentions of the parties to a transaction. While, therefore, equity recognised the methods of severance at common law as severing the beneficial interest, it also recognised that joint tenancy tenants could sever by mutual agreement.

17–75 Section 30(4) of the LCLRA 2009 specifically provides that "[n]othing in this section affects the jurisdiction of the court to find that all the joint tenants by mutual agreement or by their conduct have severed the joint tenancy in equity." This preserves the discretion of the court to find that a severance has occurred in equity.[98] The Law Reform Commission took the view that there was no objection to the jurisdiction of equity so long as the words or actions were evidence of mutual consent of all the joint tenants.

17–76 Page Wood V-C in *Williams v Hensman*[99] stated three ways in which severance could occur in equity and this has become a classic formulation of the position:

> "A joint-tenancy may be severed in three ways: in the first place, an act of any one of the persons interested operating upon his own share may create a severance as to that share. ... Secondly, a joint-tenancy may be severed by mutual agreement. And, in the third place, there may be a severance by any course of dealing sufficient to intimate that the interests of all were mutually treated as constituting a tenancy in common. When the severance depends on an inference of this kind without any express act of severance, it will not suffice to rely on an intention, with respect to the particular share, declared only behind the backs of the other persons interested. You must find in this class of cases a course of dealing by which the shares of all the parties to the contest have been effected, as happened in the cases of *Wilson v. Bell* [(1843) 5 Ir. Eq. R. 501] and *Jackson v. Jackson* [(1804) 9 Ves. Jun. 591]."

---

[96] LCLRA 2009 s.30(3).
[97] Wylie, *Annotations and Commentary* (2017), [67], n.17.
[98] Wylie, *Annotations and Commentary* (2017), [67], fn.18.
[99] (1861) 1 J. & H. 546 at 557.

17–77 The first method is the same as at common law, the other two are peculiar to equity.

Mutual Agreement

17–78 An express or implied mutual agreement between the co-owners may sever a joint tenancy. In *Burgess v Rawnsley*,[100] it was held that an agreement between the parties by which one agreed to convey an interest in the property to another need not be enforceable as a contract in order to sever the joint tenancy in equity. It was not therefore necessary that it should be evidenced in writing under the Statute of Frauds or accompanied by an act of part performance. The significance of the agreement was what it showed as to the intention of the parties, not whether one could have enforced it on the other. Mr H, a widower, had the tenancy of a house. The owner offered to sell the freehold to Mr H. Mr H wanted to marry Mrs R and had evidently persuaded himself that she also wanted to marry him. Mrs R never had such an intention. Mr H suggested to Mrs R that they buy the house together. She agreed, but only because she intended to occupy the upstairs flat while Mr H occupied the lower one. Mr H told his solicitor to put the conveyance in the joint names of himself and Mrs R, because of his belief that they were to be married. Mrs R contributed half the purchase price. Mrs R refused to marry Mr H as a result of which he refused to allow her to move into the house. They remained otherwise on friendly terms. Subsequently, Mr H agreed orally with Mrs R to buy her interest in the house for £750. Mrs R later changed her mind, saying that she wanted £1,000. The matter rested there until Mr H died. The house was then sold and the plaintiff, Mr H's daughter, claimed that, as Mr H's administrator, she was entitled to a half share in the house. Mrs R claimed that the house remained held on a joint tenancy at Mr H's death and that she had become entitled to the whole interest by survivorship.

17–79 The English Court of Appeal held that the oral agreement, which had never been completed and was unenforceable, since it did not satisfy the Statute of Frauds, nevertheless had the effect of severing the joint tenancy prior to Mr H's death. The plaintiff's claim therefore succeeded. The agreement established that the parties no longer intended their interest to be a joint tenancy. The fact that the agreement was later repudiated did not affect the matter.

17–80 Section 30(4) of the LCLRA 2009 preserves the jurisdiction of the court to find severance in the circumstances of *Burgess*. Prior written consent in writing under s.30(1) is not required in equity.

Course of Dealing

17–81 The phrase "course of dealing" includes not only negotiations falling short of an agreement but also the way in which the property in question has been dealt with by those concerned. Section 30(4) of the LCLRA 2009 contemplates that a court may find that joint tenants by their "conduct" have shown a mutual intention that the property should in future be held in undivided shares. In other words, the word "mutual" in s.30(4) qualifies "conduct" as well as "agreement".

17–82 *Wilson v Bell*[101] concerned the residue of personal estate left by a testator. The residuary legatees had dealt with the property in various transactions, including a marriage settlement and a will, as if it were held in tenancy in common. The court held that the property had been severed in equity:

> "[I]f the acts and dealings of the parties in respect of the joint tenancy indicate an intention to treat it as property held in common and not jointly, the court will, from those acts and dealings, infer an agreement to sever the joint tenancy."[102]

17–83 In *Re Wallis' Trusts*,[103] the testator gave property to his sons "in equal shares" and also appointed them residuary legatees. It was held that they held the property as residuary legatees in joint tenancy, since there were no words of severance as to the residue, but the fact that dividends arising from the residue had been paid to the sons as residuary legatees in equal shares, and after their deaths to the personal representatives of each, was a course of dealing from which a subsequent severance of the joint tenancy could be inferred. The solution is not without problems. A "course of dealing" implies more than one transaction, but the court seems to have meant that the first of such payments to the sons during their joint lives caused the severance. If it were otherwise, another problem would arise: at what point in a series of transactions does the severance occur?

17–84 What exactly is meant by a "course of dealing"? In *Burgess v Rawnsley*,[104] Sir John Pennycuick considered that an offer by one joint tenant to another followed by a counteroffer by the other would not be sufficient, whereas the other judges did not specifically adopt this view. An offer followed by a counteroffer is, in any case, typical of negotiations. But must the negotiations have arrived at the point whereby some agreement has been reached and if so, about what? Conway points out that "negotiations (which come to nothing) for the purchase of one co-owner's interest, or its partition or sale to a third party and the division of proceeds, do not amount to a course of dealing".[105]

---

[101] (1843) 5 Ir. Eq. R. 501.
[102] (1843) 5 Ir. Eq. R. 501 at 507.
[103] (1889) 23 L.R. Ir. 460 (MR).
[104] [1975] 1 Ch. 429.
[105] Conway, *Co-Ownership of Land: Partition Actions and Remedies* (2012), para.13.29; *Saleeba v Wilke* [2007] QSC 298. Conway notes that courts in other jurisdictions are more willing to find a course of dealing arising from inconclusive negotiations between joint tenants.

17–85 What is required in such a case is not so much explicit agreement about severance, which is unlikely to occur, but evidence that the relations between the parties have changed from one in which each would be content for the property to pass to the other on the death of one party to one in which this is no longer the case.[106]

Unilateral Notice

17–86 Before the LCLRA 2009 an unresolved point was whether a unilateral notice given by one joint tenant to the others was sufficient to sever the joint tenancy in equity.[107]

17–87 The LCLRA 2009 has now resolved the issue by providing that severance in equity must be mutual on the part of all joint tenants.[108]

Contract by One Joint Tenant

17–88 Before the LCLRA 2009 if one joint tenant entered into a contract to sell his or her interest to a third party, that was not a conveyance and so caused no severance at law, but in equity it gave rise to a purchaser's equity and an equitable interest in the property in the purchaser's favour. This caused a severance of the beneficial interest, but under s.30(4) of the LCLRA 2009 no severance can be caused without the mutual agreement of all the joint tenants.

Contract by All Joint Tenants

17–89 In *Byrne v Byrne*,[109] all the joint tenants entered into a contract of sale together to sell to a third party. One joint tenant then died. A conveyance was executed after his death. The question was whether the contract had severed the joint tenancy prior to his death. If so, then survivorship would have meant that the deceased joint tenant no longer had an interest at his death. The High Court held the contract had not caused a severance, as there was no evidence of intention to sever between themselves. Under s.30(4) of the LCLRA 2009 it would still be open to a court to conclude that there was no mutual intention to sever. In other circumstances the contract may be part of evidence of a mutual intention to sever.[110]

Simultaneous Death

17–90 Under s.5 of the Succession Act 1965 where two or more joint tenants die simultaneously, or are deemed to have done so, then they are deemed to

---

[106] But see *Gore v Carpenter* (1990) 60 P. & C.R. 456 (course of dealing not alone enough in England and Wales: must be mutual intention).

[107] The English Law of Property Act 1925 specifically provided by s.36(2) that a unilateral notice in writing by one joint tenant to the others was to be sufficient.

[108] LCLRA 2009 s.30(4).

[109] Unreported, High Court, McWilliam J., 18 January 1980.

[110] See also *Re Hayes' Estate* [1920] 1 I.R. 207.

have held the property immediately before their deaths as tenants in common in equal shares.[111]

COPARCENARY

17–91 Before the Succession Act 1965, the rules of intestacy were still based on primogeniture, so that where there were males of equal degree to the intestate, the eldest took to the exclusion of the others. If there were no males, then females inherited, but they did so jointly as coparceners. They were considered to take as if they were a single heir.[112] The old rules of descent were replaced in the 1965 Act by the new scheme, but the Act expressly retained the old rules in the case of estates tail.

17–92 The LCLRA 2009 has now converted all fees tail to fee simple, so coparcenary can no longer occur. Coparcenary was discussed in the second edition of this work, but there is no longer any reason to do so.

TENANCY BY ENTIRETIES

Origin
17–93 At common law a conveyance to A and B which, if they were not married to each other, would create a joint tenancy, would instead, if A and B were married to each other, create a tenancy by entireties as between themselves.[113] If O conveyed "to A, B and C in fee simple" and A and B were married at the date of the conveyance, A and B held in tenancy by entireties between themselves but C held as joint tenant, i.e. in relation to C, A and B were joint tenants, but were tenants by entireties as between each other.[114] An express statement that they were to take as joint tenants had no effect. The law thus imposed the legal form regardless of the intention of the donor. This clearly indicates that the rules were imposing a policy to which was ascribed a higher value than the intention of donors, and that policy appears to have been the subjection of wives to the authority of their husbands.

17–94 At common law husband and wife were regarded as a single person, although that single person was, in effect, the husband. There were no "undivided shares". There was "complete unity". The husband was entitled to the whole of the rents or profits during the joint lives of the spouses.[115] But if H and

---

[111] As amended by Civil Law (Miscellaneous Provisions) Act 2008 s.68.

[112] J. Reeves and J.F. Finlason, *Reeves' History of English Law, From the Time of the Romans, to the End of the Reign of Elizabeth* (London: Reeves & Turner, 1869), Vol.i, p.76.

[113] *Crofton v Bunbury* (1854) 2 Ir. Ch. R. 465; *Re Tyrell* [1894] 1 I.R. 267; *Kennedy v Ryan* [1938] I.R. 620 at 625.

[114] *Back v Andrew* (1690) 2 Vern. 120.

[115] *Re Tyrell* [1894] 1 I.R. 267.

W were married and held by entireties and one of them died, the survivor took the whole, not by the principle of survivorship, as in joint tenancy, but by virtue of the original limitation, so the law held. Tenancy by entireties, unlike joint tenancy, was not severable. Neither the husband nor the wife could sell without the concurrence of the other in the conveyance.[116]

Abolition

17–95 The effect of the Married Women's Property Act 1882[117] was generally held to be that it prevented the creation of new tenancies by entireties after 1882.[118] The Act provided for the wife's separate estate, which she could control and dispose of, apart from her husband. The courts extended this by interpretation, in the light of the policy behind the Act, to mean that in future conveyances to husbands and wives would take effect as joint tenancies.

ENDING CO-OWNERSHIP

17–96 The relationship of both joint tenancy and tenancy in common may be ended so that the result is separate ownership vested in the former co-owners.

Partition and Sale
Introduction

17–97 Partition is the legal division of the property so that each co-owner occupies and owns a separate part of the property. Partition ends the unity of possession and therefore puts an end to co-ownership.

History
Agreement

17–98 At common law co-owners could put an end to their relationship by agreement in such a manner as they might agree, by partition, or by sale to a third party and division of the proceeds. But one joint tenant or tenant in common could not force a partition on the others. He or she could sell his or her own interest, but this would be likely to be less valuable than a share of the proceeds from selling the entire property to a purchaser and also less attractive to purchasers.

17–99 More significantly, one joint tenant or tenant in common could not force a *sale* of the property on another such tenant against his or her will. This meant less land available for sale, but the common law was more concerned to

---

[116] *Crofton v Bunbury* (1854) 2 Ir. Ch. R. 465.

[117] See K. Costello, "Married Women's Property in Ireland 1800–1900" in K. Costello and N. Howlin (eds), *Law and the Family in Ireland, 1800–1950* (London: Palgrave, 2017), pp.68–86.

[118] *Kennedy v Ryan* [1938] I.R. 620; C. Sweet (ed.), *Challis's Law of Real Property*, 3rd edn (London: Butterworth, 1911), pp.378–379; *Thornley v Thornley* [1893] 2 Ch. 229.

protect the possession of land by those who wished to retain it than to advance the cause of the market economy.

The Act of 1542 and Equity

17–100 An Act of 1542[119] allowed one party to force a legal *partition* of the property.[120] The Act itself expressly conferred jurisdiction on the common law courts, but courts of equity soon asserted that they possessed a similar jurisdiction.[121] It seems that the equitable jurisdiction to partition survived until the Judicature Act and, since after that date it could be exercised in any court, the Act of 1542 had become obsolete.[122] The Act of 1542 was therefore repealed by the Statute Law Revision (Pre-Union Irish Statutes) Act 1962.[123]

Partition Acts

17–101 It was only by the Partition Acts 1868 and 1876 that the court was given power to order *sale* of the property on application by one of the parties.[124] The 1868 Act gave a co-owner the right to a sale *in lieu of* partition, if the court considered it to be more beneficial than partition.[125] Where an application was made by parties whose interest was "a moiety or upwards" the court had to order sale unless the other parties agreed to purchase.[126] However, the Act was unclear as to whether there were circumstances in which the court had jurisdiction to refuse both.[127] One view was that the equitable jurisdiction replicated in equity the one conferred on common law courts by the 1542 Act, that it thus gave a right to partition, and that the Partition Acts had modified this only to the extent of giving a right to sale in the alternative. An alternative view was that all equitable remedies are discretionary and, at least since 1962 when the 1542 Act was repealed in Ireland, partition had been discretionary and so also the statutory alternative of sale. Whatever the true position may have been,

---

[119] 33 Hen VIII c 10 (Ir). The equivalent English Act is 32 Hen VIII c 32, 1540.

[120] Since this was usually inconvenient, it probably had the indirect effect of making reluctant joint tenants and tenants in common agree to a sale and indeed some of the instances of absurd partitions may be instances of the courts deliberately using the Act indirectly to force a sale: *Turner v Morgan* (1803) 8 Ves. Jun. 143 (owner of two-thirds given all the chimneys and fireplaces and the only stairs); *Lewis v Maddocks* (1803) 8 Ves. Jun. 150 at 157.

[121] This passage in the second edition, until the end of the paragraph, was cited with approval in *Irwin v Deasy* [2004] 4 I.R. 7 (HC) by Finlay Geoghegan J.

[122] Wylie, *Annotations and Commentary* (2017), [68], n.32; J. Mee, "Partition and Sale of the Family Home" (1993) 15 D.U.L.J. 78; Conway, *Co-Ownership of Land: Partition Actions and Remedies* (2012).

[123] *O'D v O'D*, unreported, High Court, Murphy J., 18 November 1983; *FF v CF* [1987] I.L.R.M. 1 (HC) (Circuit Court appeal), Barr J. (equitable jurisdiction survived).

[124] The court was not the vendor; the solicitor having carriage of the sale was agent for all parties: *Blackall v Blackall*, unreported, High Court, Finnegan J., 6 June 2000; *Re Bannister; Broad v Munton* (1879) 12 Ch. D. 131.

[125] Partition Act 1868 s.3.

[126] Partition Act 1868 ss.4 and 5.

[127] *Drinkwater v Ratcliffe* (1875) L.R. 20 Eq. 528 (Jessel M.R.); *Re Whitwell's Estate* (1887) 19 L.R. Ir. 45; *CH v DG O'D* (1980) 114 I.L.T.R. 9.

Irish courts, at least where the parties were husband and wife, asserted a discretion to refuse sale even if no partition was to be ordered.[128] Section 36(1) of the Family Law Act 1995[129] then provided that a husband or wife may apply to the court in a summary manner to determine any question between them as to the title to or possession of any property. The court may make such order as it thinks proper, including an order for sale or partition of the property.[130]

Subdivision

17–102 Formerly under s.12 of the Land Act 1965, no agricultural land in the Republic of Ireland could be subdivided without the consent in writing of the Minister, but s.12 was repealed by s.12 of the Land Act 2005. In Ireland, in the past, agricultural land was often subdivided among family members producing uneconomic holdings but those conditions have ceased to be significant.

LCLRA 2009

17–103 The LCLRA 2009 provides, in s.31, an extensive jurisdiction to the court (the Circuit Court having concurrent jurisdiction with the High Court) to resolve issues of partition and sale.

17–104 Any person having an estate or interest in land which is co-owned, whether at law or in equity, may apply to the court for any of the orders under the section. The orders include an order for partition,[131] for sale,[132] an account of incumbrances,[133] for accounting adjustments between co-owners,[134] for dispensing with consent to a severance[135] as required by s.30 where consent is unreasonably withheld, or any order relating to the land as appears to the court to be just and reasonable in the circumstances of the case.[136] The court may make an order with or without conditions, make no order, or combine more than one order.[137] The courts' wide discretion in reconciling the competing

---

[128] *O'Neill v O'Neill*, unreported, High Court, Barron J., 6 October 1989; *First National Building Society v Ring* [1992] 1 I.R. 375 (jurisdiction under Partition Acts wholly discretionary). In *AL v JL*, unreported, High Court, Finlay P., 27 February 1984, it was held that where the property was a "family home", a sale could not be ordered unless the other spouse consented or the court could dispense with consent under s.4 of the Family Home Protection Act 1976. However, in *Nestor v Murphy* [1979] I.R. 326, the Supreme Court held that s.3 of the 1976 Act did not require a separate consent of a spouse to a conveyance if the spouse's consent was in any case essential to that conveyance. The case did not concern an application under the Partition Acts, but it was questionable whether *AL v JL* was correct in extending the Family Home Protection Act 1976 to co-owning spouses where a spouse applied for partition under the Partition Acts.

[129] As amended by Family Law (Divorce) Act 1996 s.52.

[130] Family Law Act 1995 s.36(2)(a).

[131] LCLRA 2009 s.31(2)(a).

[132] LCLRA 2009 s.31(2)(c). See *Quinns of Baltinglass Ltd v Smith* [2017] IEHC 461.

[133] LCLRA 2009 s.31(2)(b).

[134] LCLRA 2009 s.31(2)(d).

[135] LCLRA 2009 s.31(2)(e).

[136] LCLRA 2009 s.31(2)(f).

[137] LCLRA 2009 s.31(3).

interests of parties in partition proceedings was underlined in *Yippi Trading Ltd v Costello*.[138] The case concerned a car park held by the parties in fee simple as tenants in common in equal shares. The plaintiff sought partition of the car park in the context of a general falling-out between the co-owners following disruptive building work on the defendants' property. The application under s.31 was refused: as well as pointing out the many practical implications of severance, Ryan J. emphasised that the co-owners had signed an agreement in 1980 regulating the use and management of the shared property, and that this required them to co-operate. He emphasised that partition must be both legally and practically feasible for a s.31 order to be made.

17–105 A "person having an estate or interest in land" includes a mortgagee or other secured creditor, a judgment mortgagee or a trustee.[139] The former equitable jurisdiction to order partition is abolished.[140]

17–106 Section 32(5) specifically preserves the jurisdiction of the court under the Family Home Protection Act 1976, the Family Law Act 1995 and the Family Law (Divorce) Act 1996.

17–107 The effect of these changes in the case of spouses is that, where the legal title is vested in one party alone, and the other has no interest at law or in equity, the consent of the other to a conveyance, which includes a mortgage, etc. is necessary under the Family Home Protection Act 1976, unless the court is asked to dispense with it and does so under s.4.

17–108 If the legal title is held as co-owners, the consent of both is necessary at common law to a conveyance in favour of a third party, but if one applies for partition or sale under s.31 of the LCLRA 2009, the court has discretion to order partition or sale.

17–109 If one holds the legal title alone, he or she may nevertheless hold it on trust for the other where the other has an equitable claim, as on a resulting trust, and the beneficial interest is therefore held as co-owners and the consent of the spouse with a beneficial interest is necessary in equity to a conveyance, including a mortgage, etc. to a third party. But again, if one applies for partition or sale under s.31, the court would have a discretion.

17–110 The court also has discretion to make property adjustment orders in the case of judicial separation[141] or divorce.[142]

---

[138] [2013] IEHC 564.
[139] LCLRA 2009 s.31(4)(a).
[140] LCLRA 2009 s.31(6); Wylie, *Annotations and Commentary* (2017), [68], n.32.
[141] Family Law Act 1995 s.9; Wylie, *Annotations and Commentary* (2017), [67], n.30.
[142] Family Law (Divorce) Act 1996 s.14; Wylie, *Annotations and Commentary* (2017), [67], n.31.

17–111 Where partners are not married, and the property is vested in one alone, the doctrine of constructive trust may still produce co-ownership in equity. Civil partners are dealt with by the Civil Partnership and Certain Rights and Obligations of Cohabitants Act 2010, as amended.

Partition of Commonage

17–112 It has been seen that commonage, i.e. pasture rights held in common, is a traditional form of landholding akin to a separate form of tenure. It can also be regarded as a form of co-ownership, although it has not been dealt with as such since it is not really part of the common law categories.

17–113 In some areas where land purchase was not carried out, commonage remained. Section 24 of the Land Act 1939[143] provides that where some, but not all, owners of land held in commonage wish to partition it they may apply, formerly to the Irish Land Commission, now to the Minister,[144] for the compulsory partition of the holding. The Minister[145] may then prepare a scheme for partition of the land. After objections have been invited and heard, the Minister may then approve, modify or cancel the scheme. Appeal lies to the High Court.[146]

17–114 In *Re Commonage at Glennamaddoo*,[147] Carroll J. held that the interests of those who wanted partition, those who wanted to continue in commonage, and the objectors to the original scheme of total partition could be accommodated by a new scheme. The new scheme partitioned only sufficient land to satisfy those who wanted partition, leaving a commonage area for those who wanted to continue the common rights. The new scheme would also allow public access to the land, which would meet one of the objections made to the original plan.

Union in a Sole Tenant

17–115 Tenancy in common and joint tenancy may also be terminated by one party buying out interests of the others, or in the case of joint tenancy, by survivorship resulting in a sole survivor.

---

[143] As amended by Land Act 1950 s.25, Land Act 1953 s.23, and Land Act 1965 s.41.

[144] Irish Land Commission (Dissolution) Act 1992 s.4, in force from 31 March 1999: S.I. No. 75 of 1999. Individual functions were transferred before that date.

[145] Irish Land Commission (Dissolution) Act 1992 s.4.

[146] Irish Land Commission (Dissolution) Act 1992 s.3.

[147] [1992] 1 I.R. 297.

CHAPTER 18

Family Property

I've been so bothered with my property, that I'm tired of it, and don't mean to save up any more, but give it away as I go along, and then nobody will envy me, or want to steal it, and I shan't be suspecting folks and worrying about my old cash.

— Louisa May Alcott, *Little Men* (1871), Ch.15

INTRODUCTION

18–01 Property disputes in the context of the family or other intimate relationships have led to the development of statute law and common law rules. These in turn must be considered against the background of the Irish Constitution, the European Convention on Human Rights (ECHR) and the ECHR Act 2003. The relevant provisions will be considered before examining the ordinary or common law in these areas.

THE FAMILY AND THE HOME

The Constitution
18–02 The Irish Constitution recognises the family in Art.41.1 as "the natural and fundamental unit group of society", possessing "inalienable and imprescriptible rights", and guarantees to protect it "in its constitution and authority" as "the necessary basis of social order and as indispensable to the welfare of the Nation and the State". Article 41 further provides that "[t]he State pledges itself to guard with special care the institution of Marriage, on which the Family is founded, and to protect it against attack." The Thirty-Fourth Amendment of the Constitution (Marriage Equality) Act 2015 added a new Art.41.4, which states that "[m]arriage may be contracted in accordance with law by two persons[1] without distinction as to their sex." The Fifteenth Amendment of the Constitution Act 1995 also amended Art.41 by providing for the dissolution of marriage.[2]

---

[1] For an examination of legal aspects of polygamy, see A. Cryan, "Changing Demographics: Legal Responses to Polygamy and the Challenges Ahead for Ireland" (2016) 19(4) I.J.F.L. 82.

[2] Replacing Art.41.3.2°, which had specifically precluded the legislature from providing for the dissolution of marriage.

18–03 The Constitution does not explicitly define the family, although the phrase "Marriage, on which the Family is founded" has been interpreted by the courts to mean that the family protected by Art.41 is exclusively one based on marriage.[3] The concept of the family "based on marriage" does not appear to require there to be a subsisting marriage, since a widow living with her children, or widower with his, would seem still to constitute a constitutional family, but further than that it is less certain. Is there still a constitutional family if both parents are dead and adult brothers or sisters continue to live in the family home without children?

18–04 As to adoption, s.58 of the Adoption Act 2010, as amended by the Adoption (Amendment) Act 2017, provides that on an adoption order being made,[4] "the child concerned shall be considered, with regard to the rights and duties of parents and children in relation to each other as the child of the adopter or adopters."[5] This essentially makes these constitutional families. In these cases the family relationship has been specifically approved and, indeed, constituted by the State.

18–05 Practices such as donor-assisted human reproduction (DAHR) and surrogacy arrangements have blurred these lines somewhat when it comes to defining parent-child relationships. The Supreme Court in *MR and DR v An t-Ard-Chláraitheoir*[6] ruled that the genetic mother in a surrogacy arrangement was not entitled to be registered as the mother for the purposes of civil registration. Legislation now identifies the legal parents to a child born as a result of DAHR. Section 5 of the Children and Family Relationships Act 2015 provides that the parents of a donor-conceived child born as a result of DAHR are the mother and the mother's spouse, civil partner or cohabitant, as the case may be. The donor of a gamete or embryo is not the child's parent.[7]

18–06 Regarding property rights, Art.41 may only require that the family based on marriage should not be treated less favourably than other relationships. It does not necessarily require it to be treated more favourably. Such an interpretation would also have the merit of reducing the possibility of a conflict between the Constitution and the ECHR, even though the courts are not required to adopt such an interpretation.

---

[3] *State (Nicolaou) v An Bord Uchtála* [1966] I.R. 567 at 622.

[4] Or on the recognition of an intercountry adoption.

[5] Section 58 does not apply where the person adopting the child is his or her step-parent. In such cases the child is considered to be the child of the adopter and his or her spouse, civil partner or cohabitant, as appropriate: s.58A.

[6] [2014] IESC 60.

[7] Children and Family Relationships Act 2015 s.5(5), (6) and (7), as amended by the Marriage Act 2015.

The ECHR and ECHR Act 2003

18–07 Article 8 of the ECHR[8] states:

"1. Everyone has the right to respect for his private and family life, his home and his correspondence.

2. There shall be no interference by a public authority with the exercise of this right except such as is in accordance with the law and is necessary in a democratic society in the interests of national security, public safety or the economic well-being of the country, for the prevention of disorder or crime, for the protection of health or morals, or for the protection of the rights and freedoms of others."

18–08 The European Court of Human Rights (ECtHR) has adopted a "factual test" of "home" under the ECHR.[9] In *Gillow v United Kingdom*,[10] Mr and Mrs Gillow had sold their house in the UK and built a home in Guernsey[11] where Mr Gillow had a job. He and his wife satisfied the residence requirements of the States of Guernsey. Mr Gillow later resigned his post and from then on worked abroad with various agencies and they let out the Guernsey house on lease for the next 19 years. He then retired and he and his wife intended to take up residence in Guernsey but they were refused a licence to occupy the house by the authorities, a licence being required by those who no longer had residence qualifications. The Gillows argued that the house was their "home" under Art.8 and the refusal to allow them to occupy it was a violation of their rights under Art.8. They had no home in the UK and had retained strong connections with Guernsey. The ECtHR agreed. In *Buckley v UK*,[12] the ECtHR laid down what has become known as the factual test, namely, that whether or not a habitation is a "home" under Art.8 depends upon "the existence of sufficient and continuous links". It does not therefore depend upon issues of ownership or current residence, although residence at some time would seem to be relevant.

Discrimination

18–09 Article 14 of the ECHR further provides that

"[t]he enjoyment of the rights and freedoms set forth in [the] Convention shall be secured without discrimination on any ground such as sex, race, colour, language, religion, political or other opinion, national or social origin, association with a national minority, property, birth or other status."

---

[8] See F. de Londras and C. Kelly, *European Convention on Human Rights Act: Operation, Impact and Analysis* (Dublin: Round Hall, 2010).

[9] F. de Londras, *Principles of Irish Property Law*, 2nd edn (Dublin: Clarus Press, 2011), p.203.

[10] [1986] ECHR 14 (24 November 1986).

[11] Guernsey is not part of the UK, although the UK is responsible for its external affairs. The Human Rights (Bailiwick of Guernsey) Law 2000 incorporated the ECHR into Guernsey law.

[12] (1996) 23 E.H.R.R. 101.

18–10 Despite this seemingly categorical requirement, the extensive qualification in relation to private family life in Art.8.2 could significantly reduce the effectiveness of Art.14 in that context. Nevertheless, the ECtHR tends to give it a narrow interpretation given that the purpose of the article is to protect individual and, indeed, family rights.[13] The ECtHR has used it to allow contracting states a "margin of appreciation"[14] or discretion, recognising differences of social attitude in different contracting states. However, it has also applied a test of proportionality in determining whether a derogation from Art.8.1 is justified.

18–11 As to the family, the ECtHR in *Keegan v Ireland*[15] noted that "family" in the ECHR is not confined to families based on marriage, and "may encompass other de facto 'family' ties where the parties are living together outside of marriage." Nevertheless, the ECtHR in *Mata Estevez v Spain*[16] held that long-term homosexual relationships do not fall within the scope of the Art.8 right to respect for family life. However, in *Karner v Austria*[17] the ECtHR cited *Mata Estevez v Spain* as authority for the view that "protection of the family in the traditional sense is, in principle, a weighty and legitimate reason which might justify a difference in treatment" for same-sex couples, but held that it remained "to be ascertained whether, in the circumstances of the case, the principle of proportionality has been respected".

Domestic Law

18–12 The ECHR is an international treaty and is not part of the domestic law of Ireland.[18] Therefore, if there is a conflict between the provisions of the ECHR and the Irish Constitution, the Constitution prevails. The ECHR Act 2003 nevertheless provides in s.2(1) that,

> "[i]n interpreting and applying any statutory provision or rule of law, a court shall, in so far as is possible, subject to the rules of law relating to such interpretation and application, do so in a manner compatible with the State's obligations under the Convention provisions."

And further, s.3(1) provides that,

> "[s]ubject to any statutory provision (other than this Act) or rule of law, every organ of the State shall perform its functions in a manner compatible with the State's obligations under the Convention provisions."

---

[13] De Londras and Kelly, *European Convention on Human Rights Act* (2010), pp.140–141.
[14] See below, *Mata Estevez v Spain* [2001] ECHR 896.
[15] (1994) 18 E.H.R.R. 342 at para.44.
[16] [2001] ECHR 896.
[17] [2003] ECHR 395.
[18] *Re Ó Laighléis* [1960] I.R. 93 at 124–125.

18–13 An "organ of the State" is defined in s.1 of the ECHR Act 2003 and excludes the President, the Oireachtas and the courts. In *T v O*,[19] McKechnie J. stated that the High Court should

> "apply the provisions of the Convention, in the interpretation and application of any statutory provision or rule of law, insofar as it is possible to so do in accordance with the established canons of construction and interpretation."

18–14 In the 1990s there seemed to be some moves towards recognition of de facto families in the Irish courts in the context of guardianship and access.[20] However, the Supreme Court in *McD v L and M*[21] apparently retreated from this development and refused to recognise de facto families as a legal institution,[22] not only in the constitutional context but in the context of guardianship and a same-sex relationship.[23] The applicant father in the case was a homosexual man who had acted as sperm donor to enable two female same-sex partners to have a child, and then sought to be appointed guardian of the child. The female partners had entered into a civil union under the law of the UK. The biological father had never in any sense been a member of the de facto family and the court held that in any case the child's interests were paramount. Denham J. noted the ECtHR's decision in *Mata Estevez v Spain*,[24] and did not find that the attitude of the ECtHR had changed since that case. The court held that the father did not have a right to be appointed guardian, although he had a right to apply, but did not find that would be in the child's best interests. It held that access could be allowed and remitted the case to the High Court to decide that issue.

18–15 It could be objected that the statements in the judgments in *McD v L and M* denying recognition to de facto families went beyond what was necessary in the context of the case. To a certain extent, these issues have since been addressed by the legislature, in the form of the Children and Family Relationships Act 2015, discussed below, although not all provisions of that Act have been commenced.

18–16 In a purely property context, the High Court in the past in two cases[25] has shown a willingness to modify the general rule of resulting trusts in equity in relation to unmarried couples. Section 5 of the Family Law Act 1981[26] also

---

[19] [2007] IEHC 326 at para.36.

[20] *JK v VW* [1990] 2 I.R. 437; *W O'R v EH* [1996] 2 I.R. 248.

[21] [2009] IESC 81.

[22] This was despite strong support for the recognition of de facto families by Hedigan J. in the High Court: [2008] IEHC 96.

[23] The court recognised that the issue of a de facto family was not directly before it.

[24] [2001] ECHR 896.

[25] *McGill v Snodgrass*, sub nom *McGill v S* [1979] I.R. 283; *Power v Conroy* [1980] I.L.R.M. 31.

[26] As clarified by Family Law Act 1995 s.48.

extends the concept of indirect contributions to the purchase of property by engaged couples, which also puts them in a distinct legal category.

The Matrimonial Home

Property Rights

18–17 Before the intervention of statute law, property issues between spouses tended to arise where the legal title to the home was in the husband's name and the wife claimed a beneficial interest in it through contributions to its purchase or otherwise. The courts were therefore called upon to apply equitable doctrines. Where the legal title to property is vested in one person and another contributes to the cost of purchasing it, equity presumes that the title holder holds it on a resulting trust for the contributing party who has a beneficial interest proportionate to his or her contribution. Where two people live together in the premises, the non-legal owner's contribution to the purchase of the property will take the form of contributions to paying off the mortgage, or more indirect contributions. The study of how courts dealt with these issues is therefore the study of the extent to which they were willing or reluctant to adapt the general principle of equity to these specific circumstances. Before considering these issues in detail it is necessary to examine statutory schemes for the adjustment of property on the dissolution of intimate relationships.

Family Law Act 1995 s.36

18–18 Section 36(1) of the Family Law Act 1995 (the "1995 Act") provides that either spouse may apply to the Circuit Court or High Court[27] in a summary manner to "determine any question arising between them as to the title to or possession of any property".[28] The court may make such order, with respect to the property in dispute and as to costs, as the court thinks proper, including an order for sale or partition of the property.[29] Hence, the 1995 Act gave the courts a discretion in recasting property interests where the parties are married. The similar provision in s.12 of the Married Women's Status Act 1957, which the present provision replaced, was interpreted by the courts as conferring on them power to resolve disputes according to existing principles of law and equity, extended where they deemed necessary. Significantly, the court did not use the previous section to confer property rights to the matrimonial home on the "homemaker" wife. The position may be different under the 1995 Act, although s.16, which specifies factors to be taken into account in making property adjustment orders and other orders under various sections in the 1995 Act, does not specifically apply to s.36. Section 36 may be intended merely to provide a summary procedure for settlement of disputes rather than

---

[27] Family Law Act 1995 s.38.
[28] See *JD v DD*, unreported, High Court, McGuinness J., 14 May 1997.
[29] Family Law Act 1995 s.36(2)(a).

altering substantive law, although it refers to the partition jurisdiction which is considered below.

Judicial Separation

18–19 The 1995 Act, which replaced[30] the property provisions in the Judicial Separation and Family Law Reform Act 1989[31] (the "1989 Act"), provides for various orders affecting property to be made on the grant of a decree of judicial separation.[32]

Property Adjustment Orders

18–20 Section 9 of the 1995 Act[33] gives the court jurisdiction, when granting a decree of judicial separation, or at any time thereafter, to make a property adjustment order. The order may include an order that a spouse shall transfer to the other spouse, to any dependent child of the family or to another person for the benefit of the child, property belonging to the first-mentioned spouse, either in possession or reversion. Property may also be settled[34] for the benefit of the other spouse or dependent members of the family, and a settlement may be varied.[35]

18–21 Section 16 specifies that in deciding whether to make a property adjustment order or one of the other orders[36] in the 1995 Act, and in determining the provisions of such an order, the court "shall endeavour to ensure that such provision is made for each spouse concerned and for any dependent member of the family concerned as is adequate and reasonable having regard to all the circumstances of the case".[37]

18–22 Section 16 lays down several factors which a court must consider if making a property adjustment order or one of the other orders. They are essentially identical to the factors in the case of property adjustment orders on divorce and so they will be considered together in the section below. They notably include contributions, both financial and "by looking after the home or caring for the family". The court is therefore obliged, in making a property

---

[30] See *JD v DD*, unreported, High Court, McGuinness J., 14 May 1997.

[31] *TF v Ireland, the Attorney General and MF* [1995] 2 I.L.R.M. 321 (upheld constitutionality).

[32] *O'D v O'D* [1998] 1 I.L.R.M. 543.

[33] As amended by the Civil Partnership and Certain Rights and Obligations of Cohabitants Act 2010, the Civil Law (Miscellaneous Provisions) Act 2008 and the Family Law (Divorce) Act 1996. Section 9 replaced s.15 of the 1989 Act. The new section contains no equivalent of s.15(2) of the 1989 Act, which provided that the court could consider whether to make an order "on one occasion only" unless a spouse had concealed information.

[34] Family Law Act 1995 s.9(1)(b).

[35] Family Law Act 1995 s.9(1)(c) and (d).

[36] Under Family Law Act 1995 ss.7, 8, 9, 10(1)(a), 11, 12, 13, 14, 18 or 25, as amended.

[37] The test of "adequate and reasonable" may be contrasted with the "proper provision" test under s.20 of the Family Law (Divorce) Act 1996. The test of "proper provision" is also used in relation to children of a deceased testator: Succession Act 1965 s.117.

adjustment order, to consider the contribution of a "homemaker", which courts declined to do on the traditional basis of an equity acquired by contributions to the purchase of the house.

18–23 Several cases illustrate the courts' approach since these provisions came into force. In *JC v CC*,[38] Barr J. awarded a 50 per cent share in a family home to a wife who had made direct contributions and ordered the husband to continue making the annual mortgage and insurance payments in respect of the property. In *VS v RS*,[39] Lynch J. granted a declaration that the family home vested in the husband and wife as tenants in common in equal shares without a review of contributions by the wife.

18–24 In *AS v GS*,[40] a wife instituted proceedings against her husband seeking, inter alia, a property adjustment order. The husband had become indebted to the bank which, in the meantime, had obtained judgment against him. The bank, which had actual notice of the proceedings instituted by the wife, sought to register a judgment mortgage against the property in priority to any property adjustment order the wife might obtain in those proceedings. Geoghegan J. held that the wife's *claim* to the order was itself a *lis pendens* binding on a purchaser or mortgagee of the property if the *lis pendens* was registered under s.10 of the Judgments (Ireland) Act 1844,[41] if the purchaser or mortgagee had actual notice of the proceedings. Hence, it was already too late for the bank to gain priority over any order that might be made.

Order for Sale
18–25 On granting a decree of judicial separation the court may also make an order for sale of the family home[42] subject to such conditions as the court may specify. Where the court makes a lump sum order, a secured periodic payments order or a property adjustment order, it may also order a sale of property vested in, or in which a beneficial interest is vested in, either or both of the spouses.[43]

Right to Occupy
18–26 On an application for judicial separation the court may make an order conferring on one spouse "for life[44] or for such other period (definite or contingent) as the court may specify the right to occupy the family home to the exclusion of the other spouse".[45]

---

[38] Unreported, High Court, Barr J., 15 November 1991.

[39] Unreported, High Court, Lynch J., 10 June 1991.

[40] [1994] 1 I.R. 407.

[41] See Land and Conveyancing Law Reform Act 2009 ss.121 and 125.

[42] Family Law Act 1995 s.10, as amended.

[43] Family Law Act 1995 s.15, as amended.

[44] Family Law Act 1995 s.10(1)(a)(i); *JC v CC*, unreported, High Court, Barr J., 15 November 1991.

[45] Presumably the right is binding on third parties, although the last phrase is somewhat ambiguous.

Divorce

18–27 Divorce was introduced by the amendment to Art.41.3.2° of the Constitution which now provides that a court may grant divorce where spouses have
lived apart for four out of the previous five years, where there is no reasonable
prospect of reconciliation and where proper provision is made for the spouses
and children and any other person prescribed by law. Any further conditions
may also be prescribed by law. The constitutional requirement is therefore the
general one of "proper provision".

18–28 The Family Law (Divorce) Act 1996 (the "1996 Act") provides that
on granting a decree of divorce, the court may make a property adjustment
order,[46] which, like such an order made on judicial separation, may provide for
the transfer of property belonging to one spouse to the other or a dependent
member of the family, or its settlement. The court may also confer a right to
occupy the family home, for life or other period (definite or contingent) on a
spouse[47] or for the sale of the family home.[48]

Property Adjustment Orders

18–29 Section 20 of the 1996 Act sets out in some detail the factors which
the court is obliged to take into account when making a property adjustment
order under s.14 (as amended), or one of the other orders under the 1996 Act.[49]
In deciding whether to make an order and in determining the provisions of
such an order, the court "shall ensure that such provision as the court considers proper having regard to the circumstances" either already exists or will
be made for the spouses and any dependent member of the family concerned.
The factors to be taken into account, which are essentially the same as those in
the case of a property adjustment order on judicial separation, are considered
below. Again, they include contributions, both of a financial nature and "by
looking after the home or caring for the family", i.e. of a "homemaker" spouse.
The Supreme Court has stated that the division of assets between spouses is
based on principles of fairness and not equality.[50]

18–30 Under s.20(3) in deciding whether to make an order and in determining
the provisions of such an order, the court is to have regard to the terms of any
separation agreement which has been entered into by the spouses and is still
in force.

---

46 Family Law (Divorce) Act 1996 s.14(1).
47 Family Law (Divorce) Act 1996 s.15(1)(a).
48 Family Law (Divorce) Act 1996 s.15(1)(a).
49 Family Law (Divorce) Act 1996 s.12, 13, 14, 15(1)(a), 16, 17, 18 or 22; *DT v CT* [2002] 3 I.R.
   334.
50 *MK v JP (otherwise SK) and MB* [2001] 3 I.R. 371.

Factors to Be Taken into Account in Property Adjustment Orders
18–31 The factors to be taken into account in making any orders under the 1996 Act, including property adjustment orders, are as follows[51]:

(a) the income, earning capacity, property and other financial resources which each spouse concerned has or is likely to have in the foreseeable future;

(b) the financial needs, obligations and responsibilities which each of the spouses has or is likely to have in the foreseeable future (whether in the case of the remarriage of the spouse, registration in a civil partnership, or otherwise);

(c) the standard of living enjoyed by the family concerned before the proceedings were instituted or before the spouses separated, as the case may be;

(d) the age of each spouse and the length of time during which the spouses lived together;

(e) any physical or mental disability of either of the spouses;

(f) the contributions which each of the spouses has made or is likely in the foreseeable future to make to the welfare of the family, including any contribution made by each of them to the income, earning capacity, property and financial resources of the other spouse and any contribution made by either of them by looking after the home or caring for the family;

(g) the effect on the earning capacity of each of the spouses of the marital responsibilities assumed by each during the period when they lived together and, in particular, the degree to which the future earning capacity of a spouse is impaired by reason of that spouse having relinquished or foregone the opportunity of remunerative activity in order to look after the home or care for the family;

(h) any income or benefits to which either of the spouses is entitled by or under statute;

(i) the conduct of each of the spouses, if that conduct is such that in the court's opinion it would in all the circumstances of the case be unjust to disregard it;

(j) the accommodation needs of either of the spouses;

(k) the value to each of the spouses of any benefit (for example, a benefit under a pension scheme) which by reason of the decree of judicial separation concerned that spouse will forfeit the opportunity or possibility of acquiring;

(l) the rights of any person other than the spouses but including a person to whom either spouse is remarried.

---

[51] Family Law (Divorce) Act 1996 s.20(2); Family Law Act 1995 s.16(2).

Order for Sale

18–32 On granting a decree of divorce the court may make an order for sale of the family home, in addition to other orders.[52] However, if a right to occupy is granted, that is effectively a bar on sale.[53]

Right to Occupy

18–33 On granting a decree of divorce, or at any time thereafter, the court on application by either of the spouses concerned or by a person on behalf of a dependent member of the family, may, during the lifetime of the other spouse or, as the case may be, the spouse concerned, make an order conferring on one spouse, "either for life or for such other period (whether definite or contingent)" as the court may specify, the right to occupy the family home to the exclusion of the other spouse.[54] This is in addition to any order under the Family Home Protection Act 1976 or for partition under s.31 of the Land and Conveyancing Law Reform Act 2009 ("LCLRA 2009"), etc., but if the right to occupy is granted it effectively precludes an order for sale.[55]

The Equity Based on Contributions

18–34 The statutory provisions as to judicial separation and divorce have replaced, so far as those jurisdictions are concerned, the earlier case law developed by the courts when disputes arose as to the ownership of a matrimonial home on the basis of the presumed resulting trust in equity. That case law would seem now only to be relevant in an action by a spouse under s.36 of the 1995 Act, or otherwise, where the spouse claims an equity by contributions. Given that the jurisdiction on judicial separation (or divorce) is much wider and has largely made good the defects and limitations in the old equitable jurisdiction, it would seem preferable for a spouse to apply for judicial separation if the relationship has reached that point.

Direct Contributions

18–35 Where a spouse contributes directly to the purchase of the house, by paying part of a lump sum, or more usually, contributing to the mortgage repayments, the spouse in whose name the house is held holds the legal title on trust for them both as tenants in common in equity, the proportional shares being the same as the proportions in which the actual contributions to the purchase price are made.[56]

---

[52] Family Law (Divorce) Act 1996 s.15(1)(a)(ii).
[53] *AK v JK* [2008] IEHC 341.
[54] Family Law (Divorce) Act 1996 s.15(1)(a)(i).
[55] *AK v JK* [2008] IEHC 341.
[56] *C v C* [1976] I.R. 254.

18–36 In *HD v JD*,[57] the family house had been purchased in the husband's sole name. The wife's earnings were paid into a family pool out of which the mortgage payments were made. At one stage the husband had bought a pub and the wife took a major part in running it. She did the work without pay. It was held that both forms of contribution gave her equity in the house.

Indirect Contributions

18–37 Significant problems were posed by what were called indirect contributions to the purchase of the house. The problem here was to establish and define a link between the payment and the purchase of the house. Even if there was a link, a further issue was whether it was necessary for there to be some agreement between husband and wife that indirect contributions by the wife would give her an equity in the house, or whether that was to be presumed. To require an agreement would be to refuse to extend the presumed resulting trust and rely instead on an express trust or declaration of trust. Furthermore, if it was necessary to show evidence of agreement, then wives would usually fail to establish a claim. Parties in a domestic situation often do not enter into a precise agreement as to their respective rights and obligations, as they would in a business transaction. Originally in Ireland there seems to have been a divergence of views in the High Court as to the basis of liability and two lines of cases developed.

18–38 The first line of cases took the view that indirect contributions by a wife did give rise to an equity in her favour without any evidence of express agreement. This line can be traced to the dictum of Lord Reid in the House of Lords case of *Gissing v Gissing*.[58] The dictum was taken up by Lord Denning in a line of cases in the English Court of Appeal.[59] This approach was also adopted in Ireland in *FG v PG*.[60] In that case the wife contributed money to a joint account. No money from the pool was used to pay off the mortgage. Finlay P. nevertheless held that the wife was entitled to a share of the equity. The payments into the pool were indirect contributions relieving the husband of expenses he would otherwise have had to bear. There are also dicta of Kenny J. in *Heavey v Heavey*[61] to the effect that it is unrealistic to look for an agreement as between husband and wife where each has made contributions. The same judge in *C v C*[62] did not distinguish between direct and indirect contributions. He said it was "futile" to try to infer an agreement where the wife had made payments or undertaken expenses.

---

[57] Unreported, High Court, Finlay P., 31 July 1981.
[58] [1971] A.C. 886.
[59] *Falconer v Falconer* [1970] 3 All E.R. 499; *Hargrave v Newton* [1971] 3 All E.R. 866; *Hazell v Hazell* [1972] 1 All E.R. 923 at 926; *Kowalczuk v Kowalczuk* [1973] 2 All E.R. 101.
[60] [1982] 2 I.L.R.M. 155.
[61] (1977) 111 I.L.T.R. 1.
[62] [1976] I.R. 254.

18–39 The other line of cases can be traced to the majority judgment of the House of Lords in *Gissing*.[63] In that case the house was in the husband's sole name. There had been no direct contributions by the wife but she paid for household items and the cost of laying the lawn. She went out to work and paid for her own clothes and those of their son. All the judges agreed that she did not have equity in the house, but the majority so held on the ground that an indirect contribution was not enough in itself to raise a trust. There had to be an "agreement or arrangement" to that effect.

18–40 Some Irish High Court cases followed the majority in *Gissing*. In *MG v RD*,[64] the house was in the husband's sole name. The wife continued to work as an air hostess after the marriage as she had done before. She had a separate bank account. The husband had suggested several times that they operate a joint account, but she refused. The husband made the mortgage repayments. The wife bought food and household items, and a car which they both used. There was no evidence of any express agreement between them. Keane J. held that the wife did not have equity in the house. *R v R*[65] also held that an agreement was necessary.[66]

18–41 The Northern Ireland Court of Appeal in *McFarlane v McFarlane*[67] also followed the majority in *Gissing* to the effect that an "agreement or arrangement" was necessary, although the position has been attenuated by the Northern Ireland High Court finding an equity on the basis of a "tacit understanding" or where the parties "took it for granted" that they both "owned the house".[68]

18–42 In *W v W*,[69] the husband bought a farm subject to mortgages. Both spouses applied their savings to stocking and improving the farm. The wife claimed that her contributions increased the income of the farm and effectively contributed to paying off the mortgages. Finlay P. accepted that contributions to a general family fund made during a period when mortgages were being paid off by the husband could not be distinguished in principle from direct contributions to mortgage instalments. He held that the wife's contributions during the period when the mortgages were being redeemed gave her an equity amounting to 50 per cent. He stated principles which were generally approved in the Supreme Court in *McC v McC*, considered below.

---

[63] [1971] A.C. 886.
[64] Unreported, High Court, Keane J., 28 April 1981.
[65] Unreported, High Court, McMahon J., 12 January 1979.
[66] See also *CMCB v SB*, unreported, High Court, Barron J., 17 May 1983. Barron J. held that the wife's contributions gave her an equity because of an intention that they should do so.
[67] [1972] N.I. 59 at 78.
[68] *Northern Bank Ltd v Beattie* (1982) 18 N.I.J.B. 1.
[69] [1981] I.L.R.M. 202.

18–43 The conflict of authority in the High Court was resolved by the Supreme Court in *McC v McC*.[70] The husband and wife in that case lived in Dublin. The husband sold the family home when his employer transferred him to Cork. The sale price was £5,000 and after paying off the mortgage there was £1,800 left over. It was agreed that, since the wife had contributed one-third of the purchase price of the house, she was entitled to one-third of that sum, i.e. £600. She agreed to allow her husband to use the money in connection with buying the new home in Cork. The husband obtained a 100 per cent mortgage to purchase the house and spent the £1,800 left over from the sale of the Dublin house on furniture and other fittings for the house in Cork. In the High Court, Costello J. held that the wife was entitled to one-third of the furniture and fittings. A single judgment was delivered in the Supreme Court by Henchy J. without dissent. Referring to Kenny J. in *C v C*,[71] Henchy J. said that since then it had become "judicially accepted" that

> "[w]here the matrimonial home has been purchased in the name of the husband, and the wife has, *either directly or indirectly*, made contributions towards the purchase price or towards the discharge of mortgage instalments the husband will be held to be a trustee for the wife of a share in the house roughly corresponding with the proportion of the purchase money represented by the wife's total contribution. Such a trust will be inferred when the wife's contribution is of such a size and kind as will justify the conclusion that the acquisition of the house was achieved by the joint efforts of the spouses.
>
> When the wife's contribution has been *indirect* (such as by contributing, by means of her earnings to a general family fund) the court will, *in the absence of any express or implied agreement to the contrary*, infer a trust in favour of the wife, on the ground that she has to that extent relieved the husband of the financial burden he incurred in purchasing the house."[72]

18–44 Here, the £600 due to the wife was not used in purchasing the new house in Cork because of the 100 per cent mortgage. The court therefore found that the wife had failed on the facts to prove that she had made indirect contributions. There was apparently no suggestion that the wife had contributed to household expenses and so there were no indirect contributions in that form. The payment for the furniture was not considered an indirect contribution, even though it relieved the husband of expenses which he would otherwise have to bear, presumably because the contributions were traceable to one item, taking the furniture as a whole, and the court took the view that it could be adequately compensated for by ownership of the furniture. This illustrates that the kind of contributions which are held indirect contributions to the acquisition of the house are those which do not give any immediate interest in other property.

---

[70] [1986] I.L.R.M. 1.
[71] [1976] I.R. 254.
[72] [1986] I.L.R.M. 1 at 2 (emphasis supplied).

18–45 Henchy J.'s assertion that it had become "judicially accepted" that contributions to the purchase of a house give rise to an equity in the absence of an agreement to the contrary is intriguing. He can hardly have been referring to the High Court bench, since the cases there were conflicting. The phrase seems carefully chosen to indicate that the Supreme Court judges had decided that this was the correct approach. The fact that there was no dissenting judgment must strengthen this view. Viewed restrictively, the judge's formulation could be said to be obiter since the wife was not found to have made contributions to the purchase of the house on the facts, but there is really no distinction to be drawn between obiter dictum and ratio decidendi in the final appeal court, since the court was evidently indicating what it would decide if the appropriate facts came before it.

18–46 In the wider context of equity, *McC v McC*[73] marks a milestone in that it recognises that the social and legal context itself, in this case the institution of marriage, and not any particular conduct by the parties involved, gives rise to an equity unless it can be proved to be unjust in the particular case. Given the social context, the courts have held as a matter of principle that it would be inequitable for indirect contributions *not* to give rise to an equity.

18–47 Some cases immediately after *McC v McC* show that the High Court was slow to realise the significance of the case. For example, in *CR v DR*[74] the High Court may not have applied the correct test. In that case, the wife was denied an equity because there was no evidence that her contributions had relieved the husband of expenses which he would have been unable to bear. However, the Supreme Court in *McC v McC* did not lay down that the husband must have been *unable* to bear the cost on his own, but merely that the wife's contribution "to that extent relieved the husband of the financial burden he incurred in purchasing the house".[75] Again, according to Henchy J., the test is whether the property was acquired through "the joint efforts of the spouses".[76]

---

[73] [1986] I.L.R.M. 1.

[74] Unreported, High Court, Lynch J., 5 April 1984.

[75] See also *R v R*, unreported, High Court, McMahon J., 12 January 1979; *MB v EB*, unreported, High Court, Barrington J., 19 February 1980. Both these cases treat the test as being whether the payments by the wife relieved the husband of expenses he would otherwise have had to bear.

[76] See also *B v B*, unreported, High Court, McKenzie J., 22 April 1986, which appears to be wrongly decided. The judge held that the wife's indirect contributions did not give rise to an equity unless there was evidence that the spouses intended that the legal relations should be altered, following Keane J. in *MG v RD*, unreported, High Court, 28 April 1981 and Finlay P. in *W v W* [1981] I.L.R.M. 202, cases which had been overruled by *McC v McC*. A similar objection could be raised against Barron J.'s judgment in the High Court in *EN v RN* [1990] 1 I.R. 383.

Improvements

18–48 In *W v W*,[77] a High Court decision before *McC v McC*, Finlay P. proposed a distinction between, on the one hand, contributions to the acquisition of property by the other spouse and, on the other, contributions to the improvement of property which had already been acquired in the other spouse's name, either by immediate payment or by paying off mortgages. In the case of improvements the judge considered that the spouse who was not the legal owner would have no claim to an equity "unless she established by evidence that from the circumstances surrounding the making of it she was led to believe (or of course that it was specifically agreed) that she would be recompensed for it". Such a distinction may not reach a fair result in all cases, especially where the contribution is to a physical extension of the property, in money or in kind, or arguably to its total value, and which is therefore a contribution to acquiring a part of the property or a proportion of the value of the completed whole. Also, the phrase "led to believe" suggests that the judge considered that some evidence, apart from merely the circumstances and perhaps the elements of proprietary estoppel, was necessary before the non-owning spouse could become entitled to a beneficial interest in the house.

18–49 The judge further took the view that "[e]ven where such a right to recompense is established either by an express agreement or by circumstances in which the wife making the contribution was led to such belief it is a right to recompense in monies only and cannot and does not constitute a right to claim an equitable share in the estate of the property concerned".[78] It is questionable whether this will stand the test of time. If a non-owning spouse contributes to improvements in money or labour which results in the value of the property being increased, it is by no means clear why he or she should be held to have made a gift of it to the other spouse in the absence of evidence to the contrary.

18–50 In *NAD v TD*,[79] a case between married partners after *McC v McC*, Barron J. followed *W v W* in treating contributions to improvements as in a separate category. In that case the husband bought a vacant site and built a house on it using his own labour and supervising hired labour. The wife sought a declaration as to the ownership of the first house. She claimed she had supported the family on her income while the husband was building the house and had paid sums in cash while the building was in progress. Barron J. cited *McC v McC*[80] for the proposition that indirect contributions to the acquisition of the property give rise to the presumption of an equity. He then went on essentially to follow *W v W* as to improvements. He held that the sums in cash were direct contributions to the purchase of the house, but discounted the expenditure by the wife in maintaining the family, even though he found that if she had not

---

[77] [1981] I.L.R.M. 202 at 204–205, cited in *CD v WD and Barclays Bank plc*, unreported, High Court, McGuinness J., 5 February 1997.

[78] [1981] I.L.R.M. 202 at 205.

[79] [1985] I.L.R.M. 153 (10 May 1984).

[80] [1986] I.L.R.M. 1.

done so it would have cost the husband an extra £500. He discounted these payments because he found no evidence of conduct on the part of the husband leading the wife to believe she would have an interest or a right to compensation. The wife therefore failed on the facts.

18–51 On the question of improvements, the judge cited Finlay P. in *W v W*[81] and Kenny J. in *Heavey v Heavey*,[82] although in the latter case Kenny J. drew no distinction between "purchase or improvements", as Barron J. acknowledged. The distinction is not found in *McC v McC*.[83] McWilliam J. in *Power v Conroy*[84] did not seek to discount that part of the claim which was based upon improvements.

18–52 Contributions to the purchase price of property have long been recognised as a case of the intervention of equity and a source of equitable interests quite apart from marital situations. Improvements to property, on the other hand, have generally only been recognised in the context of proprietary estoppel. Nevertheless, given the special definition of "indirect contributions" as laid down by *McC v McC*,[85] a clear distinction between acquisition and improvement may not survive that case where the total value of the property at the end of a period is attributable to the joint efforts of both spouses.

Express Declarations
18–53 The principle expounded by Henchy J. in *McC v McC*[86] is subject to agreements or arrangements to the contrary, and so the parties retain the right to exclude the presumption of equity. Such a situation occurred in *GK v EK*.[87] In that case the wife had made direct contributions to the purchase of the house in the form both of down payments and mortgage repayments. Both were considerably larger than those of the husband. The conveyance of the house was nevertheless taken in their joint names. O'Hanlon J. held that the parties intended the house to be in their joint ownership with equal rights to the beneficial interest, but his view was not based on the mere fact that the property was put in their joint names, but also on evidence given by the wife that they intended equal beneficial ownership.[88]

18–54 In *AL v JL*,[89] the parties bought a house before they were married. W was under the age of majority at the time of marriage. Both contributed to the purchase. They had agreed that the house should be put into their joint

---

[81] [1981] I.L.R.M. 202.
[82] (1977) 111 I.L.T.R. 1.
[83] [1986] I.L.R.M. 1.
[84] [1980] I.L.R.M. 31.
[85] [1986] I.L.R.M. 1.
[86] [1986] I.L.R.M. 1.
[87] Unreported, High Court, O'Hanlon J., 6 November 1985.
[88] See also, *AL v JL*, unreported, High Court, Finlay P., 27 February 1984.
[89] Unreported, High Court, Finlay P., 27 February 1984.

names, but their solicitor advised (incorrectly) that W could not take a conveyance in her name as she was under age. The property was conveyed to the husband alone. When the wife came of age they went back to the solicitor to have
a new deed executed putting the house in their joint names, but, on learning the
cost, they decided against doing so. Later, their relationship broke down and
the wife left the house. The husband remained in possession. The issue arose
as to the interests existing in the house. The court held that the wife had a half
"share"[90] in equity, their intention being to hold the property jointly. In view
of this manifest intention the court felt that it was unnecessary to go into the
question of contributions.

The Wife's Domestic Work

18–55 In *C v C*,[91] Kenny J. stated that a wife's domestic work in the home
did not count as an indirect contribution to the acquisition of the matrimonial
home:

> "When the matrimonial home is purchased in the name of the husband,
> either before or after marriage, the wife does not as wife become entitled to
> any share in its ownership either because she occupies the status of wife or
> because she carries out household duties."[92]

18–56 If this were to be so, the law would encompass a great anomaly.
The wife who goes out to work and is thus able to contribute financially to the
acquisition of the home is rewarded by a property interest in it, whereas the
wife who adopts the traditional role and stays at home would obtain no financial security by so doing. Yet such a position does not arise by chance. Law in
a society dominated by the economic phenomenon of the market finds it easy to
ascribe property rights on the basis of the expenditure of money and leans naturally against the notion that an expenditure of money is a gift: in a market no
one parts with cash unless he or she obtains some tangible asset in return. This
is the law's assumption. Indeed, there may be something in the nature of law
itself that makes it easier to translate value in terms of the market into value in
property rights, rather than to translate the more intangible and indeterminate
obligations of family and kinship into property interests.[93]

---

[90] In other words, she was entitled to half the proceeds if the land were sold. Strictly speaking a
joint tenant does not have an undivided share, because of the principle of survivorship.
[91] [1976] I.R. 254.
[92] [1976] I.R. 254 at 257.
[93] See in this context the difficulties involved in erecting the "deserted wife's equity". Lord Denning M.R. in the English Court of Appeal had attempted to create such an equity in a series of
cases, but it was struck down by the House of Lords, among other reasons because it would be
terminable on divorce and the court found it difficult to accept that a property interest in land
should terminate on such an event.

18–57 In *BL v ML*,[94] Barr J. in the High Court found that a wife had acquired a 50 per cent interest in the equity in the house through her contributions to the running of the home and family. Applying the then existing principles of equity, the judge said "the conclusion is inescapable that the wife is not entitled to a beneficial interest in the family home or farm because she has made no contribution in money or money's worth, directly or indirectly, towards the acquisition of either property".[95] As to the wife's work in the business, the judge concluded that the wife had not contributed significantly to the work of the farm or the business, such that it could be said that she had relieved the husband wholly or in part of the financial burden of acquiring the house. Despite this, the judge held that there was another line of reasoning stemming from the Constitution which would justify the conclusion that the wife was entitled to a beneficial interest in the home. The judge referred to Art.41.2 of the Constitution:

> "1° In particular, the State recognises that by her life within the home, woman gives to the State a support without which the common good cannot be achieved.
>
> 2° The State shall, therefore, endeavour to ensure that mothers shall not be obliged by economic necessity to engage in labour to the neglect of their duties in the home."[96]

18–58 Applying the Article to the case before him, the judge held that it was capable of justifying the court finding that the wife had acquired a beneficial interest in the home.

> "It is also in harmony with that philosophy to regard marriage as an equal partnership in which a woman who elects to adopt the full-time role of wife and mother in the home may be obliged to make a sacrifice, both economic and emotional, in doing so."[97]

18–59 The judge considered it to be consistent with the philosophy behind the Article that in return for the "voluntary sacrifice" of the wife which the Constitution recognises as being in the interest of the common good, she should receive some reasonable economic security within the marriage. Her role as wife and mother would prevent her from contributing, directly or indirectly, to the acquisition of the home and its contents, and so "her work as home maker and in caring for the family should be taken into account in calculating her contribution towards that acquisition - particularly, as such work is of real monetary value."[98]

---

[94] [1992] 2 I.R. 77.

[95] Cited by Finlay C.J. in the Supreme Court: [1992] 2 I.R. 77 at 103.

[96] See judicial comment on the Article in *De Burca and Anderson v Attorney General* [1976] I.R. 38; *W v Somers* [1981] I.R. 126.

[97] [1992] 2 I.R. 77 at 98.

[98] [1992] 2 I.R. 77 at 98–99.

18–60 The size of the share in the beneficial interest thus acquired should depend on the "nature, quality and duration" of the wife's domestic work. The judge felt that such a wife's share of the beneficial interest, bearing in mind that marriage is an "equal partnership", should not exceed 50 per cent unless there were exceptional circumstances. He also considered that since her interest was based upon her position as wife and mother, it was confined to the home itself and did not extend to other property owned by the husband, such as, in this case, the farm.

18–61 Barrington J. in *H v H*[99] followed Barr J.'s judgment but other High Court judges declined to follow *BL v ML*,[100] namely Barron J. in *EN v RN*,[101] whose view was subsequently upheld in the Supreme Court,[102] and Lardner J. in *JF v BF*.[103] Lardner J. stated that Art.41 was not intended to confer property rights or to confer a specific jurisdiction on the court to determine property disputes in accordance with its principles. In the judge's view, any change in the law should be left to the legislature.

18–62 After these judgments were delivered, the appeal in *BL v ML*[104] was decided by the Supreme Court, which allowed the appellant's appeal. All the judges appeared to have accepted the inconsistency and unfairness which existed between the position of a wife who contributes financially and the wife who performs unpaid domestic work. They also agreed: (a) that existing precedent precluded them from finding that a homemaker wife acquired equity in the home; and (b) that it was inappropriate to use Art.41 to remedy the defect in the law. More specifically, Finlay C.J. found that

> "[n]either sub-s. 1 nor sub-s. 2 of s. 1 of Article 41 purports to create any particular right within the family, or to grant to any individual member of the family rights, whether of property or otherwise, against other members of the family, but rather deals with the protection of the family from external forces."[105]

18–63 The judge accepted that the judiciary was one of the organs of the State, and that therefore the obligation on the State to endeavour to ensure that mothers should not be obliged by economic necessity to engage in labour outside the home to the neglect of their duties was an obligation imposed on the judiciary as well as on the legislature and the executive. However, he was satisfied that there was no warrant for interpreting the duty on the judiciary as granting to it jurisdiction to award to a wife and mother any particular interest in the family

---

[99] Unreported, High Court, ex tempore, 20 June 1989.
[100] [1992] 2 I.R. 77.
[101] [1992] 2 I.R. 116.
[102] [1992] 2 I.R. 116.
[103] Unreported, High Court, Lardner J., 21 December 1988.
[104] [1992] 2 I.R. 77.
[105] [1992] 2 I.R. 77 at 108.

home, where that would be unrelated to the question of her being obliged by economic necessity to engage in labour to the neglect of her duties.[106] The judge found that Art.41 would be relevant in assessing the alimony or maintenance payable by a husband to a wife and mother and a court may act on the duty "by refusing to have any regard to a capacity of the wife to earn herself, if she was in addition to a wife a mother also, and if the obligation so to earn could lead to the neglect of her duties in the home".[107]

18–64 McCarthy J. agreed that precedent was against the acquisition of equity by a homemaker wife.[108] He also found that to use Art.41 would be to create new anomalies. Article 41.2.2° refers not to women in general but to "mothers". To found property rights upon it would be to introduce a discrimination on grounds of gender, since "no complementary role is accorded a father, although such a role reversal is, nowadays, by no means uncommon".[109] The Article would not avail a wife who had not borne children.

18–65 The whole concept of a constitutionally preferred role for women is open to question and is regarded by many as outdated, if not offensive.[110] Many women today aspire to the same economic and intellectual challenges and rewards as men. Women played little or no role in drafting Art.41. There is no corresponding constitutionally preferred role for men and this conflicts with the assertion of equality in Art.40. The Constitution should be seen as providing a framework of rights within which individuals may freely choose their own mode of life.

18–66 Egan J. concluded, as to the state of the law at the time regarding equities acquired by wives[111]:

> "Present case law is based on long-standing equitable principles as a result of which trusts are implied in favour of a contributing spouse. These principles have been extended to their permissible limit."

18–67 *BL v ML*[112] was decided before the 1995 and 1996 Acts, which replaced the old equitable jurisdiction as far as property adjustment orders on judicial separation and divorce are concerned.

---

[106] [1992] 2 I.R. 77 at 108.

[107] [1992] 2 I.R. 77 at 109.

[108] [1992] 2 I.R. 77 at 110.

[109] [1992] 2 I.R. 77 at 111.

[110] In 2013, for example, the Constitutional Convention voted by a majority of 88 per cent in favour of amending Art.41.2: Vote on Amending the Clause on the Role of Women in the Home (17 February 2013), available at: *https://www.constitution.ie/AttachmentDownload.ashx?mid=cee1b183-0b79-e211-a5a0-005056a32ee4* [accessed 1 August 2017].

[111] [1992] 2 I.R. 77 at 115.

[112] [1992] 2 I.R. 77.

Comment

18–68 It is open to question whether the domestic work of a wife had been so decisively dealt with by precedent as the court appeared to think in *BL v ML*. The only clear statement positively rejecting the homemaker equity was by one judge in the High Court, namely Kenny J. in *C v C*,[113] a decision which was not binding upon the Supreme Court. Such an important point should not have been considered as settled by anything less than a full bench of the Supreme Court and it is difficult to see why the judges of the Supreme Court treated the statement by a single judge with such deference. McCarthy J. cited *McC v McC*,[114] commenting that "the decision is entirely related to monetary contribution", but it could equally be viewed as not excluding contributions in money's worth. In fact, Henchy J., in delivering the court's judgment in that case, referred to indirect contributions and added "such as by contributing, by means of her earnings to a general family fund". This is not unequivocal and it could be that the judge was giving contributions in money as an *example* of indirect contributions, not necessarily as the only kind. There are examples, as will be seen below, of judges accepting that unpaid work by a wife in a family business can give rise to an equity. The judges have developed the original equity by including within its scope indirect contributions in money, so a further extension to include unpaid domestic work which is part of a joint undertaking and which could be valued in money, would not seem unwarranted.

An Attempt at Reform

18–69 If the position in *BL v ML*, that no account could be taken of the contributions of a homemaker wife, were indeed the case then the law would have produced the odd anomaly that a wife who adopted the so-called constitutionally preferred role of homemaker would actually be at a disadvantage as against a wife who had a career and contributed in money to the acquisition of the family home.

18–70 The Matrimonial Home Bill 1993 was an attempt to redress the anomaly of the homemaker wife. The Bill proposed to vest a joint tenancy in equity in the matrimonial home and household effects in both spouses regardless of the state of the legal title. After being passed by both Houses of the Oireachtas, it was referred by the President to the Supreme Court under Art.26 of the Constitution.[115] The Supreme Court took the view that the imposition of a joint tenancy in equity interfered to an unjustified degree with the relationship between husband and wife and Clause 6 did not avoid this result, and indeed may even have aggravated it, by requiring one of the parties to seek redress in the courts. The Bill would also give a non-owning spouse a beneficial interest regardless of how long the marriage had lasted and irrespective of contributions. A less ambitious approach might have been simply to provide by statute that the

---

[113] [1976] I.R. 254.
[114] [1986] I.L.R.M. 1.
[115] *Re Matrimonial Home Bill, 1993* [1994] 1 I.L.R.M. 241.

courts in assessing the beneficial interest in the house could take account of the contributions of a homemaker wife. This has now been done in relation to property adjustment orders on separation or divorce.

Partition

18–71 Where the application is for partition under the LCLRA 2009, the court has a wide discretion under s.31 in ordering partition, or a sale and division of the proceeds. The section applies where any person has an interest in land whether at law or in equity.[116] The court may order accounting adjustments to be made as between co-owners which includes "any other adjustment necessary to achieve fairness between co-owners".[117] A spouse who is not a joint owner of the legal title could therefore nevertheless claim an equity in such an action and the section gives jurisdiction to the courts to take into account indirect contributions by a spouse in any form, including, arguably, as a homemaker.

18–72 There is one High Court case in which a judge considered such contributions, under the former Partition Acts 1868 and 1876. In *M(B) v M(A)*,[118] the house had been a local authority house rented to the parents of the wife. The house was than acquired by the parents under a tenant purchase scheme. By that time the house was occupied by the husband and wife, but purchase by the parents was sanctioned by the local authority and it was accepted that the husband and wife would actually discharge the repayments under the transfer order. In fact, they were paid by the husband, since he was the sole breadwinner. The husband and wife raised five children in the house. The legal title had been in the names of the wife's parents. The wife's mother died and the wife's father left the house to the husband and wife jointly. The wife later obtained a divorce in England. Although the legal title was in their joint names, it was argued by the husband that the wife held her interest on a resulting trust for the husband since he had made the monetary contributions towards paying for the property. Peart J., in making an order for sale and distribution of the proceeds, noted that the inference of a resulting trust could be rebutted, and particularly where the person into whose name the property was conveyed was the wife of the person advancing the money under the doctrine of advancement. He therefore found it necessary to assess the relative beneficial interests of husband and wife and in so doing took into account the wife's contribution as homemaker. He referred to Finlay P. in *AL v JL*,[119] commenting:

> "I have already concluded that Mrs Murphy made an indirect contribution to the household by her involvement at home in the rearing of the children and her running the house, as it were, and this replaces the reference in the

---

[116] LCLRA 2009 s.31(1).

[117] LCLRA 2009 s.31(4)(b)(v).

[118] Unreported, High Court, Peart J., 3 April 2003; de Londras, *Principles of Irish Property Law* (2011), para.9-126.

[119] Unreported, High Court, 27 February 1984.

above case to both the husband and the wife contributing to a joint pool from which the mortgage repayments were made."

18–73 It does not appear that the Partition Acts 1868 and 1876 gave any extended jurisdiction as to the assessment of beneficial interests, and so the judge's comments in that case were something of a bold extension of the traditional equity jurisdiction. However, it is otherwise under the LCLRA 2009, s.31 of which expressly confers an extended jurisdiction, as has been seen.

18–74 Section 31 does not affect the jurisdiction of the court under the Family Home Protection Act 1976, Family Law Act 1995 and the Family Law (Divorce) Act 1996.[120] As to the Family Home Protection Act 1976, the Act requires the consent of the "other spouse" to a conveyance by the spouse holding the legal title, or that the court dispense with the consent in accordance with the Act. However, the "other spouse" may have a beneficial interest in the family home by contributions, and so the home is held in co-ownership.[121] This was the case under the previous law. In *AL v JL*,[122] in which the wife was held to have a beneficial interest in equity, the court held that the husband could not succeed in a claim for partition and sale under the Partition Acts 1868 and 1876 unless the other spouse consented or the court could dispense with her consent under s.4 of the Family Home Protection Act 1976.

Work in Spouse's Business

18–75 In *HD v JD*,[123] a wife's work in the husband's public house was held by Finlay P. to be a contribution entitling her to equity in the matrimonial home. Other judges have been less willing to recognise such work as giving rise to equity in the family home. The authority of these cases is affected adversely by the fact that many different reasons have been given by the judges for the result, and none of them are particularly convincing.

18–76 In *BL v ML*,[124] Barr J. drew a distinction between work in the home, which he felt to be specially protected by Art.41, and work on the farm which he necessarily discounted as not protected by Art.41. He maintained this distinction in *CM v TM*,[125] this time on the ground that the claim was outside the scope of s.12 of the Married Women's Status Act 1957 because the section related to the *title* to property and the wife's claim was properly only one to remuneration. The wife apparently claimed "compensation" which the judge interpreted as a claim to a money sum. He seems to have regarded this as an alternative to a property interest in the *business* and therefore to have discounted the claim

---

[120] LCLRA 2009 s.31(5).
[121] J.C.W. Wylie, *The Land and Conveyancing Law Reform Acts: Annotations and Commentary*, 2nd edn (London: Bloomsbury, 2017), [67], n.29.
[122] Unreported, High Court, Finlay P., 27 February 1984.
[123] Unreported, High Court, Finlay P., 31 July 1981.
[124] [1992] 2 I.R. 77.
[125] Unreported, High Court, Barr J., 30 November 1989.

as one to an interest in the matrimonial home. This appears to be inconsistent with the reasoning of Finlay P. in *HD v JD*.[126]

18–77 In *CR v DR*,[127] Lynch J. discounted the work of the wife in helping in the husband's business and on the family farm, holding that it was not related to the acquisition of the property.[128] One of the implications of *McC v McC*[129] is that work of the type contributed by the wife in *CR v DR*[130] cannot be so readily discounted in future. Since no agreement is required there need be nothing to link the wife's contribution and the acquisition of the house other than the circumstance that her spouse was in fact thereby relieved to some extent of the expense of acquiring it, and whether or not he or she could have borne the extra expense without that relief. The High Court decision in *B v B*[131] appears to be *per incuriam* on the point, and Lynch J. in *CR v DR*[132] appears to have misinterpreted Henchy J. in *McC v McC*.[133] The Supreme Court more recently in *EN v RN*[134] took into account the wife's indirect contribution to the repayment of a mortgage used to convert the house into rented flats. The wife managed the rented flats and the rental income was used to pay off the mortgage.

Presumption of Advancement
18–78 This is an equitable principle which is based on the notion that where one party is under an obligation to provide financially for another, then if the person who is under the obligation transfers property to the other it is presumed to be in discharge of the obligation and so the transferor will not retain any interest by trust or use in the property. It used to be the case that a husband was regarded as being under the obligation of providing for his wife and the presumption would apply in such a case. This position is clearly based upon assumptions about the social role of parties to a heterosexual marriage, and specifically on the assumption that it is the husband who has the role of being the breadwinner, the party who has a job and a career, while the wife is seen as performing the role of remaining at home and doing domestic work. Today these assumptions can no longer be as readily made in the past (not least because of the introduction of same-sex marriages) and many married women also seek to fulfil themselves in a paid job or career. Not surprisingly, therefore, the courts have had to examine the application of the presumption

---

[126] Unreported, High Court, Finlay P., 31 July 1981.
[127] Unreported, High Court, Lynch J., 5 April 1984.
[128] See also *Grant v Edwards* [1986] 2 All E.R. 426, in which domestic work of a de facto wife was apparently taken into account.
[129] [1986] I.L.R.M. 1.
[130] Unreported, High Court, Lynch J., 5 April 1984.
[131] Unreported, High Court, McKenzie J., 22 April 1986.
[132] Unreported, High Court, Lynch J., 5 April 1984.
[133] [1986] I.L.R.M. 1.
[134] [1992] 2 I.R. 116.

of advancement to marriage in a sceptical light.[135] In *W v W*,[136] Finlay P. suggested obiter that the presumption still applied. The statement was obiter because in that case the house was in the husband's name. The judge said that where property is in the wife's sole name and the husband contributes, there is a rebuttable presumption that it was an advancement and gives the husband no interest in the house.

18–79 In *CC v SC*,[137] the husband and wife operated a joint account in the bank and this account had been used to pay for the matrimonial home. McMahon J. held that in the absence of evidence to rebut the presumption, they were beneficial as well as legal joint owners. Even if the husband had in fact put more into the account than the wife, the additional amount was presumed to be an advancement. They were not, therefore, tenants in common in proportion to their contributions. Hence they were also beneficial joint tenants of a house bought with the fund.

18–80 In *JC v JHC*,[138] the house was paid for by the husband but conveyed to the husband and wife as joint tenants. Keane J. held that the husband and wife were beneficial joint tenants. The presumption of advancement had not been rebutted. On the contrary, the evidence was that the husband intended to make a gift to the wife and that she should have the property if he predeceased her. The judge noted that the House of Lords in *Pettit v Pettit*[139] had said that the presumption was inappropriate today between husband and wife and although it still applied, it would be rebutted by comparatively slight evidence. But here, the evidence supported it. The changing social context of the presumption of advancement was memorably described by Lord Diplock in *Pettit v Pettit*:

"The consensus of judicial opinion which gave rise to the presumptions of advancement and resulting trust in transactions between husband and wife is to be found in cases relating to the propertied classes of the nineteenth century and the first quarter of the twentieth century among whom marriage settlements were common, and it was unusual for the wife to contribute by her earnings to the family income. It was not until after World War II that the courts were required to consider the proprietary rights in family assets of a different social class. The advent of legal aid, the wider employment of married women in industry, commerce and the professions and the emergence of a property-owning, particularly a real-property-mortgaged-to-a-building-society-owning, democracy has compelled the courts to direct their attention to this during the last 20 years. It would, in my view, be an abuse of the legal technique for ascertaining or imputing intention to apply to

---

[135] See *RF v MF*, unreported, Supreme Court, Henchy J., 24 October 1985; *Parkes v Parkes* [1980] I.L.R.M. 137; *M v M* (1980) 114 I.L.T.R. 46. See also *Lynch v Burke* [1990] 1 I.R. 1.
[136] [1981] I.L.R.M. 202.
[137] Unreported, High Court, McMahon J., 2 July 1982.
[138] Unreported, High Court, Keane J., 4 August 1982.
[139] [1970] A.C. 777.

transactions between the post-war generation of married couples presumptions which are based on inferences of fact which an earlier generation of judges drew as to the most likely intentions of earlier generations of spouses belonging to the propertied classes of a different social era."[140]

18–81 The Supreme Court in *RF v MF*[141] further qualified the circumstances in which the presumption operates. The husband in that case bought a house and put it in the joint names of himself and his wife. He did so at the suggestion of his wife and with the aim of reviving their strained relationship. The wife then refused to move into the new house and continued to live in their original family home. She nevertheless claimed that she was entitled to a half share because it was jointly owned. Henchy J. held:

"The equitable doctrine of advancement, as applied to transactions between husband and wife, has the effect that when a husband (*at least where the circumstances show that he is to be expected to provide for his wife*) buys property and has it conveyed to his wife and himself jointly, there is a presumption that the wife's paper title gives her a beneficial estate or interest in the property. Unless the presumption is rebutted by evidence showing a contrary intention on the part of the husband at the time of the transaction, he will be deemed to have entered into the transaction for the purpose of conferring a beneficial estate or interest on the wife. That estate or interest is treated in law as an advancement, that is to say, a material benefit in anticipation of the performance by the husband of his duty to provide for the wife."[142]

18–82 More recently the Irish courts appear to have moved away from the notion that the presumption of advancement applies to gifts from husbands to wives alone. In *DPP v B*,[143] Feeney J. described the doctrine as anachronistic and questioned whether it was capable of application in light of the constitutional status of spouses and the guarantee of equality. In Northern Ireland the presumption as between husband and wife and as between fiancées has been abolished.[144] Section 199 of the Equality Act 2010 provided for the outright abolition of the presumption of advancement throughout the United Kingdom, apparently on the basis that the then government was of the view that the presumption violates Art.5 of the 7th Optional Protocol to the ECHR, but this section has never been commenced.[145]

---

[140] [1970] A.C. 777 at 824.

[141] Unreported, Supreme Court, 24 October 1985. See also, *Lynch v Burke*, unreported, Supreme Court, 7 November 1995; *Parkes v Parkes* [1980] I.L.R.M. 137.

[142] Unreported, Supreme Court, 24 October 1985, p.6 (emphasis supplied).

[143] [2009] IEHC 196.

[144] Law Reform (Miscellaneous Provisions) Order 2005 (S.I. No. 1452 of 2005), r.16.

[145] The section was not well drafted; see J. Glister, "Section 199 of the Equality Act 2010: How Not to Abolish the Presumption of Advancement" (2010) 73 M.L.R. 807.

18–83 The presumption of advancement has been altered in other ways to take account of contemporary social conditions. In *Pecore v Pecore*, the Supreme Court of Canada held that the presumption of advancement is not confined to gifts as between father and child but that it should equally apply to gifts from a mother to her child.[146] In a further nod to changing social conditions, the court held that the presumption in respect of parental gifts is confined to gifts given to minor children and does not apply where the child is an adult. Rothstein J. even went so far as to suggest that a where a gift is given by a parent to an adult child, there should be "a rebuttable presumption that the adult child is holding the property in trust for the ageing parent to facilitate the free and efficient management of that parent's affairs."[147] In *Lau Siew Kim v Yeo Guan Chye Terence*, the Court of Appeal in Singapore similarly rejected the notion that the presumption of advancement was confined to gifts from father to child on the basis that it embodies "archaic patriarchal concepts of the family", though the court did not follow *Pecore's* suggestion that a gift from parent to child might attract the presumption.[148]

A Right to Possession?

18–84 It has already been seen that the court has a wide discretion in making orders under the Family Law Act 1995 and the Family Law (Divorce) Act 1996, including an order giving the right to possession of the family home to one spouse to the exclusion of the other.

18–85 Apart from this, where the legal title to a matrimonial home is in one spouse's name but the other spouse has an equity and is in occupation of the house, the question frequently arises as to whether the second spouse has a right to retain possession. The first spouse may still be in possession with the second spouse, or he or she may have left and a third party, often a judgment mortgagee, may have an equitable interest vested in it. Generally speaking a beneficiary under a trust only has possession of the land with the consent and at the discretion of the trustees, since possession is a right at common law primarily vested in the common law owner. On the other hand, it is clear that one co-owner has no right to evict the other.[149] Where one spouse holds the legal estate on trust for him- or herself and the second spouse as co-owners in equity, the courts would seem to have had a choice as to whether they regard the first spouse as a trustee or as a co-owner in relation to the second spouse. In fact, they have generally chosen to regard the first spouse as a co-owner for this purpose and therefore unable unilaterally to evict the other spouse.

---

[146] (2007) 279 D.L.R. (4d) 513 at para.31.

[147] (2007) 279 D.L.R. (4d) 513 at para.36.

[148] [2008] 2 S.L.R. 108 at para.63.

[149] *Beaumont v Kinsella* (1859) 8 Ir. C.L.R. 291.

The Effect of Domestic Violence

18–86 Barring orders made under s.3 of the Domestic Violence Act 1996 (as amended)[150] have the effect of suspending the right to possession of one spouse or civil partner to the family home, and where that spouse or civil partner has a property interest in it, they suspend the right to possession. Barring orders may also now be made where the parties are not married or in a civil partnership, provided they have lived together in an intimate and committed relationship for six months in a nine-month period before the application.[151] A parent may also apply for a barring order against a child of full age who is not a dependent person in relation to the parent.[152] Where the applicant is not married to or in a civil partnership with the respondent, or is the parent, no barring order can be made if the respondent has a legal or beneficial interest in the house and the applicant has an interest less than that of the respondent.[153]

18–87 A tenant of a housing authority may apply under s.3 of the Housing (Miscellaneous Provisions) Act 1997 for an exclusion order in respect of the house let to the tenant excluding a person from the house on the ground of "anti-social behaviour", which includes the possession of drugs or threatening or violent behaviour.

18–88 Domestic violence may also have other effects. In *Dennis v McDonald*,[154] a woman contributed to the acquisition of a house in which she and her partner lived. She was forced to quit because of the man's violence. It was held that they were tenants in common in equity, and that the man had ousted her from possession. Since a tenant in common is not entitled to exclusive possession as against a co-tenant, he had to pay her rent. Had she left voluntarily he would not have been obliged to pay her rent.

Family Home Protection Act 1976

18–89 The purpose of the Family Home Protection Act 1976 (the "1976 Act") is to protect a spouse who does not have the legal title to the matrimonial home vested in him or her, against being deprived of his or her security in the home through the other spouse conveying or creating other interests in the home, such as a mortgage, to a third party. It seeks to give this protection to the non-conveying spouse whether or not that spouse has a beneficial interest in the matrimonial home. The means it adopts is to require the spouse's consent

---

[150] Replacing the Family Home (Protection of Spouses and Children) Act 1981 s.2. See also the Domestic Violence (Amendment) Act 2002 and the Civil Law (Miscellaneous Provisions) Act 2011 s.60.

[151] Domestic Violence Act 1996 s.3(1)(b).

[152] Domestic Violence Act 1996 s.3(1)(c).

[153] Domestic Violence Act 1996 s.3(4).

[154] [1982] 1 All E.R. 590.

to a "conveyance" executed by the other spouse. Section 3(1) of the 1976 Act provides as follows:

"Where a spouse, without the prior consent in writing of the other spouse, purports to convey any interest in the family home to any person except the other spouse, then, subject to subsections (2) and (3) and section 4, the purported conveyance shall be void."

18–90 Subsection (2) provides that subs.(1) shall not apply to a conveyance if it is made by a spouse in pursuance of an enforceable agreement made before the spouses' marriage. Subsection (3), discussed in detail below, basically provides that a conveyance shall not be rendered void under subs.(1) if it is made to a "purchaser for full value". "Full value" means such value as "amounts or approximates to the value of that for which it is given".[155]

18–91 Section 4 provides that a court may dispense with the consent of a spouse if it is unreasonably withheld. As can be seen from the provisions, the protection of the family home is not absolute in the case of lack of consent to a conveyance. The provisions represent a compromise between protecting the family home, or rather, the security of tenure in the family home of the spouse and children, on the one hand, and protecting innocent purchasers of property on the other. The policy of protecting the family home is balanced against the protection of the commercial market in land.

The Meaning of "Conveyance"

18–92 Section 1(1) of the 1976 Act defines "conveyance" as including

"a mortgage,[156] lease, assent, transfer, disclaimer, release and any other disposition of property otherwise than by a will or a *donatio mortis causa* and also includes an enforceable agreement (whether conditional or unconditional) to make any such conveyance, and convey shall be construed accordingly".

18–93 The section makes it clear that the 1976 Act applies to contracts as well as conveyances. Most conveyances of land are carried out in two stages: a contract to convey a title, followed by the actual conveyance of the title. The section does not require two consents, one for the contract and one for the conveyance. In *Kyne v Tiernan*,[157] the wife consented to the contract. Then the husband and wife agreed to separate. The wife then refused to sign a consent

---

[155] Family Home Protection Act 1976 s.3(5). See also, *Bank of Ireland v Carroll*, unreported, High Court, Hamilton P., 10 September 1986.

[156] Including an equitable mortgage by deposit of title deeds: *Bank of Ireland v Purcell* [1990] I.L.R.M. 106.

[157] Unreported, High Court, McWilliam J., 15 July 1980. See also, *Lloyd v Sullivan*, unreported, High Court, McWilliam J., 6 March 1981.

contained in the deed of conveyance. McWilliam J. held that the wife's consent to the contract was a consent to the entire transaction.

18–94 Consent is required for mortgages, but in *National Irish Bank Ltd v Graham*[158] the Supreme Court held that where a conveyance and a mortgage are, in reality, part of a single transaction, consent to the conveyance also operates as consent to the mortgage. The court held that different considerations would apply where land was acquired under a conveyance and was then, within a short time, subsequently mortgaged so as to provide the purchase price which up to then had been supplied by means of a bridging loan.[159]

18–95 The 1976 Act applies to disclaimers or releases, so that where the family home was vested in a company and the husband merely had a licence to occupy, any release of his licence would be a "conveyance" and would be void without consent.[160]

"Family Home"
18–96 Section 2(1) defines "family home" as meaning,

"primarily, a dwelling in which a married couple ordinarily reside. The expression comprises, in addition, a dwelling in which a spouse whose protection is in issue ordinarily resides or, if that spouse has left the other spouse, ordinarily resided before so leaving."

18–97 In *LB v HB*,[161] it was stated that the couple did not have to be living "as husband and wife", i.e. having regular sexual intercourse. It was enough if they both resided on the premises. The 1976 Act is often invoked when the relationship between the spouses has deteriorated.

18–98 The definition does not depend on ownership: even if the title to a house is vested in a company,[162] a trust, or in someone other than one of the spouses, it can still be a family home under the 1976 Act. The 1976 Act cannot be avoided by putting a family home in a company's name.

18–99 The definition does depend on residence, and an intention to reside is not enough. If a spouse enters into a contract to buy a house, which the spouses intend to be their future home, the mere fact that they intend to reside there, or that the purchasing spouse acquires a purchaser's equity by virtue of the

---

[158] [1994] 2 I.L.R.M. 109. See also, *Kyne v Tiernan*, unreported, High Court, McWilliam J., 15 July 1980; *Lloyd v Sullivan*, unreported, High Court, McWilliam J., 6 March 1981.

[159] [1994] 2 I.L.R.M. 109 at 114.

[160] *Walpoles Ltd v Jay*, unreported, High Court, McWilliam J., 20 November 1980. The case is discussed in A. Lyall, "The Family Home Protection Act 1976 and Conveyances Other Than by Spouses" (1984) 6 D.U.L.J. (ns) 158.

[161] [1980] I.L.R.M. 257.

[162] *Walpoles Ltd v Jay*, unreported, High Court, McWilliam J., 20 November 1980.

contract, does not confer rights on the non-purchasing spouse under the 1976 Act.[163] He or she only acquires such rights when he or she takes up residence.

18–100 The land comprised in a conveyance may consist of a family home together with other land, such as a farm, which is not part of the family home in the normal sense of that phrase. Before 1996 the issue arose in several cases in which no valid consent was held to have been given to such a conveyance, as to whether the court could notionally sever the land and uphold the transaction in relation to the land not forming part of the family home.[164] Section 2(2) of the 1976 Act has now been amended by s.54 of the Family Law Act 1995, as follows:

> "In subsection (1), 'dwelling', means any building or part of a building occupied as a separate dwelling and includes any garden or other land usually occupied with the dwelling, being land that is subsidiary and ancillary to it, is required for amenity or convenience and is not being used or developed primarily for commercial purposes, and includes a structure that is not permanently attached to the ground and a vehicle, or vessel, whether mobile or not, occupied as a separate dwelling."

Consent Required at Common Law or in Equity

18–101 In *Nestor v Murphy*,[165] the Supreme Court held that s.3 of the 1976 Act does not require a separate consent of a spouse to a conveyance if the spouse's consent is in any case essential to that conveyance. Henchy J. said that what has been called a "schematic or teleological approach" must be adopted in interpreting s.3(1) of the 1976 Act,[166] meaning that it is to be "given a construction which does not overstep the limits of the operative range that must be ascribed to it",[167] having regard to the legislative scheme of the 1976 Act as a whole. Therefore, the words of s.3(1) "must be given no wider meaning than is necessary to effectuate the right of avoidance given when the non-participating spouse has not consented in advance in writing to the alienation of any interest in the family home."[168] It was held that in this case the wife's consent was not required under the 1976 Act because they were legal joint tenants and therefore any conveyance or contract would be ineffective without her participation.[169]

---

[163] *National Irish Bank Ltd v Graham* [1994] 2 I.L.R.M. 109.

[164] *Hamilton v Hamilton and Dunne* [1982] I.R. 466 at 490. The High Court, on appeal from the Circuit Court, ordered a severance in *Bank of Ireland v Slevin*, unreported, High Court, Johnson J., 16 February 1989—a case cited by Blayney J. in the Supreme Court in *Bank of Ireland v Smyth* [1996] 1 I.L.R.M. 241. Blayney J. left the point open. See *Allied Irish Banks plc v O'Neill*, unreported, High Court, Laffoy J., 13 December 1995.

[165] [1979] I.R. 326.

[166] [1979] I.R. 326 at 329. See also, *AIB v O'Neill*, unreported, High Court, Laffoy J., 13 December 1995.

[167] [1979] I.R. 326 at 329.

[168] [1979] I.R. 326 at 329.

[169] Since in that case the wife was a party to the contract, the court could still order specific performance of the contract.

18–102 A close reading of subs.(1) supports Henchy J.'s view. It refers to a spouse who conveys ("conveys" includes "contracts") and "the other spouse" who, impliedly, is not conveying. Where both spouses must convey the legal title, it is therefore arguable that there is no "other spouse" within the meaning of the section, but in that case the consent of both is required at common law. Where a spouse has only an equitable interest, the courts have held that consent is required under the 1976 Act,[170] so that "other spouse" includes such a spouse, and his or her consent is required. Section 21 of the LCLRA 2009, which otherwise now overreaches equitable interests, preserves spouses' rights under the 1976 Act.[171] Moreover, s.21 also preserves the rights of a person in occupation from overreaching.[172]

"Interest"

18–103 Section 3 applies to the conveyance "of any interest" in the family home. "Interest" is defined by the 1976 Act as meaning "any estate, right, title or other interest, legal or equitable".[173]

18–104 In *Bank of Ireland v Purcell*,[174] the plaintiff held an equitable charge over the defendant's lands by virtue of the deposit of title deeds to secure present and future advances. The lands included the family home, within the meaning of the 1976 Act, of the defendant and his wife, but the deposit was made before the 1976 Act came into force. Further advances were made to the defendant on security of the deposit after the 1976 Act came into force but no consents to these advances were obtained from the defendant's wife. Barron J. granted a declaration that no security was created in favour of the plaintiff over the family home in respect of advances made after the date on which the 1976 Act came into force. All the advances made after the 1976 Act came into force required the consent of the defendant's wife since, although the bank obtained an estate in the lands, the word "interest" in the 1976 Act is defined more widely than a reference to an estate and the fact that an estate had been conveyed need not prevent a subsequent transaction from conveying an "interest" in the lands. The judge referred to Kenny J.'s definition of an equitable mortgage in *Allied Irish Banks v Glynn*[175] and continued:

> "Each time there is a further advance the amount which is being charged on the lands is altered and accordingly the interest of the mortgagor in those lands is altered. I have no doubt that future further advances are the conveyance of an interest in the lands for the purposes of s 3 of the Act."[176]

---

[170] *AL v JL*, unreported, High Court, Finlay P., 27 February 1984.
[171] LCLRA 2009 s.21(6).
[172] LCLRA 2009 s.21(3)(b)(iii).
[173] Family Home Protection Act 1976 s.1(1).
[174] [1990] I.L.R.M. 106.
[175] [1973] I.R. 188 at 191.
[176] *Bank of Ireland v Purcell* [1988] I.L.R.M. 480 at 482.

The ratio was upheld in the Supreme Court.[177]

"Prior"

18–105 The consent must be "prior" in that it must be given before the "conveyance" purports to take effect. In the case of a deed, that point is the delivery of the deed.[178] In the case of registered land, it is the time of entry on the register.

18–106 In the case of a deposit of title deeds or a land certificate creating an equitable mortgage, the time is not necessarily the time when the title deeds or land certificate are left with the intending mortgagee. In *Bank of Ireland v Hanrahan*,[179] the husband had gone to the bank with the land certificate intending to leave it on deposit as security for a loan. The bank told him that his wife's consent was required under the 1976 Act. He left the certificate with the bank, and returned later with his wife who then executed a consent form. O'Hanlon J. held that the 1976 Act's requirement of prior consent by the wife to the equitable deposit had been complied with. There was a tacit agreement that the bank held the certificate as mere custodian in the period before the wife executed her consent, and that the character in which the bank held the certificate changed once she executed it to that of equitable mortgagee. While the distinction between the two different types of possession provides a sophisticated rationale, it can nevertheless be objected that the reasoning leads only to the conclusion that the execution of the consent and the change in the nature of the bank's possession coincided in point of time, whereas the 1976 Act requires the consent to precede the possession as mortgagee. It must be assumed that there is a fictional fraction of a second in time, between the moment of execution of the consent and the change in the character of possession.

Consent

18–107 It seems that the court may scrutinise the reality of consent by a non-owning spouse with particular care. The onus is on the third party to ensure that the non-conveying spouse's consent is a real one.[180]

18–108 In *Bank of Ireland v Smyth*,[181] the wife had signed a deed of charge in favour of the plaintiff over registered land owned by her husband. The land consisted of a farm and included the family home. The family home had been built with the aid of a loan secured by a mortgage on the farm. When she signed

---

[177] *Bank of Ireland v Purcell* [1990] I.L.R.M. 106.

[178] *AD v DD and Irish Nationwide Building Society*, unreported, High Court, McWilliam J., 8 June 1983.

[179] Unreported, High Court, O'Hanlon J., 10 February 1987. See also, *Bank of Ireland v Smyth* [1996] 1 I.L.R.M. 241.

[180] *Bank of Ireland v Smyth* [1996] 1 I.L.R.M. 241.

[181] [1996] 1 I.L.R.M. 241. See also, *Barclay's Bank v O'Brien* [1992] 4 All E.R. 983, where the court scrutinised the reality of consent given by a married woman to a charge by her husband.

the consent to the present mortgage, the wife believed, incorrectly, that this circumstance meant that the present bank would have no right to obtain possession of the family home. The wife argued, inter alia, that her consent was invalid since she did not have a proper understanding of what she was signing. Geoghegan J. agreed with this submission and held the charge void on the ground that the plaintiff had failed to take reasonable steps to ensure that the wife understood the nature and effect of the charge or, alternatively, to advise her to obtain independent advice. The judge described married women as a "protected class" because of the probability of influence by their husbands and the probability of reliance on their husbands.

18–109 The Supreme Court upheld the decision, but on somewhat narrower grounds. It noted that the purpose of the 1976 Act was not merely to protect the non-conveying spouse, but to protect the family. The consent must be "fully informed". The onus was on the bank to prove a valid consent had been given.[182] As it had not discharged this onus, the consent was invalid and the charge was void. The bank should have made inquiries of the wife to discover the state of her knowledge as to the effect of the proposed charge. Since it had failed to do so, it had "constructive notice" of what it would have discovered and therefore her apparent consent was unreal.

18–110 The judge also held that the bank should have advised the wife to obtain independent advice, but rejected the notion that this stemmed from a duty owed by the bank to the wife. It was in the bank's own interest to ensure that a real consent had been obtained, because if it did not, the consequence was that the charge was void.[183]

18–111 Consent by a spouse, or the circumstances surrounding it, may also operate to prevent a third party obtaining constructive notice, in the equitable sense, of a spouse's equity obtained by contributions or otherwise. In *Hibernian Life Association Ltd v Gibbs*,[184] the defendant, the husband, was assignee of a lease in the house subject to a first mortgage. The husband later entered into a second mortgage with the plaintiff. In relation to that transaction the husband and the wife made a statutory declaration which declared that they were married and that the husband was the owner of the house. The mortgage was in the ordinary standard form. It recited that the leasehold property which was being mortgaged was "vested in the borrower", that is the husband, for the residue of the term granted and that the defendant "as beneficial owner" demised to the plaintiff the house for the mortgage term, but subject to the first mortgage. The wife executed a consent to the mortgage under the 1976 Act. The husband defaulted in the repayments under the second mortgage and the

---

[182] Contrast undue influence in equity, where the party alleging it generally has to prove it: see *Bank of Nova Scotia v Hogan* [1997] 1 I.L.R.M. 407.

[183] Contrast the position in equity, where a third party who has constructive notice takes a title, but subject to the equity.

[184] Unreported, High Court, Costello J., 23 July 1993.

plaintiff obtained an order declaring the second mortgage to be well-charged. In 1989 the wife instituted proceedings against her husband under the provisions of the Married Women's Status Act 1957, claiming a beneficial interest in the premises. McKenzie J. in the High Court held that the wife had a 100 per cent beneficial interest in the property. The wife then applied to discharge the well-charging order. The husband was joined as a second defendant in the proceedings. The plaintiff then sought a declaration that any interest which the wife enjoyed in the premises was held subject to the plaintiff's prior rights under its mortgage. The plaintiff claimed it was a purchaser for value without notice of the wife's interest in the lands. The defendants argued that the plaintiff had constructive notice. Costello J. did not agree. Initially a joint loan to husband and wife was contemplated but when it was found that the husband alone was the lessee, it was decided, without any demur on the part of husband or wife, that the loan should be made to the husband alone. The wife had thus consented to a loan to the husband alone on the basis that he alone held the beneficial interest.

Right of Veto, Not a Property Right

18–112 The 1976 Act does not confer any property right on the spouse.[185] It is merely a statutory right of veto.[186] The right of veto is not, therefore, one of the "unregistered rights" referred to by s.74(1) of the Registration of Title Act 1964, subject to which a judgment mortgage takes effect on registration, because that phrase refers to property rights only.[187]

18–113 A spouse may have acquired a share of the beneficial interest through contributions, direct or indirect, to the acquisition of the house, but that is an entirely distinct issue. A spouse who has acquired such an equitable interest will have both proprietary rights in the home and, in addition, rights under the 1976 Act. A spouse who has not acquired equity will still be able to rely on his or her rights under the 1976 Act.

18–114 Although the right of a spouse under the 1976 Act is not a positive property right, it may create a defect in title with which third parties need be concerned. Yet the line between this necessary result of the statutory provisions and the personal nature of the right in some contexts needs to be carefully drawn. In *Bank of Ireland v Carroll*,[188] G conveyed a house to C and C was registered as owner. On the same day, he mortgaged it to the bank. G's wife had consented orally to the conveyance, but not in writing as required by the 1976 Act. C was made bankrupt. The official assignee sought to establish that

---

185 In the High Court in *Bank of Ireland v Smyth* [1993] 2 I.R. 102, the judge referred to the right of veto as "quasi-proprietary", but this language was not repeated in the Supreme Court: [1996] 1 I.L.R.M. 241.

186 *Guckian v Brennan* [1981] I.R. 478.

187 *Murray v Diamond* [1982] I.L.R.M. 113.

188 Unreported, High Court, Hamilton P., 10 September 1986.

the conveyance was void for lack of consent. Hamilton P. held, citing *Nestor v Murphy*,[189] that the basic purpose of the 1976 Act is to protect the home by giving a right of avoidance to the spouse who was not a party to the conveyance, and "this means that section 3 must be given a construction that does not overstep the limits of the operative range that must be ascribed to it". The section must be given no wider meaning than "necessary to effectuate the right of avoidance". This, the judge felt, meant that only the wife could impugn the transaction, and she did not wish to do so here.

18–115 Although the point taken by the judge disposed of the issue before the court, it must still be the case that an intending purchaser may object to a title proffered by a vendor in the case of a family home on the ground that the non-conveying spouse has not consented to the transaction, or has only consented orally, and that consequently no title can pass. Lack of consent is a fatal flaw in the title.

Time Limit
18–116 Section 3(8)(a)(i) of the 1976 Act provides that proceedings shall not be instituted to have a conveyance declared void by reason only of s.38(1)[190] after the expiration of six years from the date of the conveyance.

18–117 This, however, does not apply where a spouse has been in actual occupation of the land from immediately before the expiration of six years from the date of the conveyance concerned until the institution of the proceedings. This also is without prejudice to any right of the spouse otherwise to seek redress under s.38(1). Furthermore a conveyance shall be deemed "not to be and never to have been void" by reason of s.3(1) unless it has been declared void by a court by reason of subs.(1) in proceedings instituted either before the passing of the Family Law Act 1995, or on or after such passing and complying with para.(a), or, subject to the rights of any other person concerned, it is void by reason of subs.(1) and the parties to the conveyance or their successors in title so stated in writing before the expiration of six years from the date of the conveyance.

18–118 The section was intended to give greater certainty to titles where a conveyance had been executed, and left unchallenged for a considerable time.

Consent to Future Conveyances
18–119 Section 3(9) of the 1976 Act permits a spouse to give "a general consent in writing to any future conveyance of any interest in a dwelling that is

---

[189] [1979] I.R. 326.
[190] Inserted by Family Law Act 1995 s.54(1)(b).

or was the family home of that spouse".[191] A deed executed after such consent
is valid.

Registered Land
18–120 Under s.72(1)(j) of the Registration of Title Act 1964, the rights of
persons in actual occupation of the land bind a transferee of registered land
even though they do not appear on the register. The right of veto under the
1976 Act is not, however, an interest within the section. It refers to property
rights only.[192] A spouse may, however, make an entry in the Land Register or
the Registry of Deeds under s.12 of the 1976 Act, noting the power of veto
under s.3 of the 1976 Act.

18–121 In *Murray v Diamond*,[193] it was held, following *Tempany v Hynes*,[194]
that the effect of a judgment mortgage is similar to a voluntary conveyance in
that the effect of registering it is to charge the interest of the judgment debtor,
subject, under s.71(4) of the Registration of Title Act 1964, to all unregistered
rights subject to which the judgment debtor held the interest. But the court
went on to hold that "rights" under s.71(4) refers to property and does not
include the spouse's statutory right of veto under the 1976 Act. The spouse's
right of veto under the 1976 Act is not protected against creditors of the other
spouse if they obtain a judgment mortgage.

Mortgages
General
18–122 Section 7(1) of the 1976 Act provides as follows:

> "Where a mortgagee or lessor of the family home brings an action against
> a spouse in which he claims possession or sale of the home by virtue of
> the mortgage or lease in relation to the non-payment by that spouse of
> sums due thereunder, and it appears to the court—
> (a) that the other spouse is capable of paying to the mortgagee or lessor
>   the arrears (other than arrears of principal or interest or rent that do
>   not constitute part of the periodical payments due under the mort-
>   gage or lease) of money due under the mortgage or lease within a
>   reasonable time, and future periodical payments falling due under
>   the mortgage or lease, and that the other spouse desires to pay such
>   arrears and periodical payments; and
> (b) that it would in all the circumstances, having regard to the terms of
>   the mortgage or lease, the interests of the mortgagee or lessor and the
>   respective interests of the spouses, be just and equitable to do so,

---

[191] Inserted by the Family Law Act 1995.
[192] *Murray v Diamond* [1982] I.L.R.M. 113.
[193] [1982] I.L.R.M. 113.
[194] [1976] I.R. 101.

the court may adjourn the proceedings for such period and on such terms as appear to the court to be just and equitable."

18–123 Under s.97 of the LCLRA 2009 a mortgagee now can no longer take possession of the mortgaged property without a court order granted under the section, unless the mortgagor consents in writing not more than seven days before.

Judgment Mortgages

18–124 If one spouse gets into debt the creditor may wish to register a judgment mortgage against that spouse's property. Judgment mortgages are now registered pursuant to s.116 of the LCLRA 2009, which replaces the Judgment Mortgage (Ireland) Act 1850.

18–125 There are two questions: (a) Does the 1976 Act prevent the registration of a judgment mortgage without the other spouse's consent? (b) What effect, once registered, does a judgment mortgage have, bearing in mind any property rights which the other spouse may have acquired in the home?

18–126 The first question was answered in *Containercare (Ireland) Ltd v Wycherley*.[195] Carroll J. held, first, that a judgment mortgage could be registered by a judgment creditor as to premises which are a family home within the meaning of s.3(1) notwithstanding the absence of consent by the other spouse. A judgment mortgage took effect by operation of law.[196] It was not a "conveyance by a spouse" within s.3 of the 1976 Act. Secondly, she held that the proceedings could not be adjourned under s.7 of the 1976 Act (allowing the non-conveying spouse to pay off the mortgage) because s.7 referred only to mortgages repayable by instalments and a judgment mortgage was not so repayable.[197]

18–127 As to the second question, under the 1850 Act, the effect of the registration of a judgment mortgage over unregistered land was to transfer the interest of the judgment debtor in the land to the judgment creditor and the judge held that this therefore had the effect of severing the joint tenancy[198] of the husband and wife in the premises and that henceforth the judgment creditor and the wife held the premises as tenants in common.

18–128 The LCLRA 2009 reformed the law and prevented this effect by s.30(3) which provides that "registration of a judgment mortgage against the

---

[195] [1982] I.R. 143.

[196] At the time, under s.7 of the 1850 Act.

[197] See K. O'Sullivan, "Judgment Mortgages and the Family Home Protection Act 1976: A Renewed Call for Reform" (2014) 17(3) I.J.F.L. 77.

[198] The title being unregistered. In registered land the registration of a judgment mortgage does not vest the judgment debtor's interest in the judgment mortgagee.

estate or interest in land of a joint tenant does not sever the joint tenancy and if the joint tenancy remains unsevered, the judgment mortgage is extinguished upon the death of the judgment debtor". This is consistent with the general position under the LCLRA 2009 whereby joint tenancies cannot be unilaterally severed. Under s.117(1) registration of a judgment mortgage under s.116 "operates to charge the judgment debtor's estate or interest in the land with the judgment debt and entitles the judgment mortgagee to apply to the court for an order under this section or section 31 [i.e. partition and sale]".

18–129 These provisions mean that a judgment mortgage therefore no longer operates to transfer the estate of the judgment debtor to the creditor. A judgment creditor may apply for partition or sale under s.31 but subs.(5) provides that nothing in the section affects the jurisdiction of the court under the 1976 Act, the Family Law Act 1995 and the Family Law (Divorce) Act 1996 under which Acts the court has a discretion as to granting property adjustment orders.

Notice
The Effect of Notice under the Act
18–130 Under s.3(3)(a) of the 1976 Act, a "purchaser for full value" takes a good title despite lack of consent by the non-conveying spouse. "Purchaser" is defined by s.3(6) as a purchaser "in good faith".

18–131 In *Somers v Weir*,[199] it was held that the expression "in good faith" imports a doctrine of notice into s.3 and in *Allied Irish Banks plc v Finnegan*,[200] the Supreme Court held that the plaintiff "purchaser" in that case had to establish that it did not have any actual or constructive notice of the possible invalidity of the consent. The doctrine is not identical with, but is analogous to, the doctrine of notice in equity. It is also quite different in its effect. In equity a bona fide purchaser without notice of a legal estate will take the legal title free of the equity. A purchaser with notice of the equity will nevertheless still obtain the legal title by the conveyance, but will take it subject to the equity. The intervention of equity does prevent the passing of the common law title. Under the 1976 Act, by contrast, the question of notice determines whether the purchaser acquires any title at all. A purchaser who takes without notice of the non-conveying spouse's rights under the 1976 Act takes a good title. A purchaser *with* notice takes no title at all: the purported conveyance is rendered void by s.3.

Constructive Notice
18–132 A purchaser of a home today must inquire of the vendor whether it is a "family home" within the 1976 Act. If the answer is that it is, then the purchaser will require the vendor to obtain the non-disposing spouse's consent

---

[199] [1979] I.R. 94.
[200] [1996] 1 I.L.R.M. 401.

under s.3, or if that cannot be obtained, then the vendor must apply to the court under s.4 for an order dispensing with the consent on the ground that it is being unreasonably withheld. Section 4 will be considered later.

18–133 What is the position of the purchaser if the conveying spouse denies that the house is a family home? Can the purchaser rely on that? Can he or she accept the plain statement itself? Or should the purchaser obtain a statutory declaration setting out the facts which, if true, would make it a correct answer? Is even that enough? Or can the purchaser insist on a second declaration corroborating the first?

18–134 In *Reynolds v Waters*,[201] in answer to the purchaser's inquiry the vendor replied that it was not a family home and, after a further inquiry from the purchaser as to the facts, informed him that he was separated from his wife who had deserted him before he took up residence in the house which he was now selling. He said that he and his wife were now divorced and that his wife had never lived in the house. A draft statutory declaration was included. The purchaser asked for the consent in writing of the wife or a joint declaration with reasons attached. The vendor refused and then applied to the High Court for a declaration that the wife's consent was not required. It was granted. The sale was eventually closed. The question now was as to whether the purchaser was liable to pay interest on the money from the date when the vendor replied. He would be so liable if he should have accepted a statutory declaration on that basis. It was held as follows:

1. The purchaser's solicitor had been too cautious. There was no general principle that a prudent purchaser should not accept the uncorroborated statutory declaration of a vendor merely because the vendor had a financial interest in the transaction.
2. If the statement later turned out to be incorrect due to fraud or carelessness then the purchaser is said to have acquired the property in good faith and, if for full value, the conveyance is then valid under s.3(3)(a).[202]
3. The court suggested that it might be otherwise if the purchaser's solicitors had reason to doubt the truth of the statement.

18–135 If the High Court's decision is correct, then it secures the position of purchasers but leaves some spouses vulnerable. To say that if one spouse commits a fraud, the purchaser is unaffected by notice, is little comfort to the second spouse. It is unclear why the loss in those circumstances should fall on the non-owning spouse. The court seems more concerned to reduce the risk to purchasers, rather than to protect the non-owning spouses whom it was the avowed aim of the legislation to protect. If the non-owning spouse is in actual occupation of the house, does that in itself put a purchaser on notice? In other

---

[201] [1982] I.L.R.M. 335.
[202] See *Stephenson v Royce* (1856) 5 Ir. Ch. R. 401; *Jones v Smith* (1843) 1 Phil. 244.

words, is the doctrine of *Hamilton v Lyster*[203] imported into s.3? That of course would not protect the non-owning spouse in all circumstances because a house can still be a family home even though not occupied by the spouse at the relevant time. Furthermore, in *Reynolds* there was a statement of the facts on which the husband's assertion was based. But is the purchaser fixed with notice if he or she asks if it is a family home and the vendor executes a statutory declaration simply saying that it is not?

18–136 In *Somers v Weir*,[204] the defendant wife lived in a house in Dublin with her husband. The husband had a lease of the premises. The wife claimed that she had helped to buy the lease. In 1973 she was, she said, compelled to leave the house and moved into a council house with their children for some time. In 1976 the husband entered into a contract to sell the house to the plaintiff. The plaintiff's solicitor asked for the defendant's written consent. The husband's solicitor replied that she had left the house some years ago and was no longer relying on it as a family home, that the husband was abroad, and that the defendant's address was unknown. When the husband returned to Dublin he made a statutory declaration to the effect that the defendant had not relied on the house as a family home since they had separated. He also stated that by virtue of their separation agreement she had no interest in the house. The separation agreement, which was not produced, did not mention the house. The plaintiff, relying on the declaration, paid the balance of the purchase money and the husband assigned the lease to her (the plaintiff). In 1977 the plaintiff decided to sell the house.

18–137 The new purchaser negotiated a mortgage with a building society. The plaintiff's solicitors, in order to satisfy the building society, traced the whereabouts of the defendant wife and asked her to consent to the original sale by the husband. She refused. The plaintiff sought a High Court order dispensing with the defendant's consent under s.4 of the 1976 Act, on the ground that she was withholding her consent unreasonably. Doyle J. granted the order.

18–138 The Supreme Court held, first, that the court had no jurisdiction under s.4 to dispense with consent after the conveyance (from the husband to the plaintiff) had been executed. Secondly, it held that, nevertheless, the plaintiff had constructive notice both of the defendant's prima facie valid claim to a proprietary interest in the premises in equity and of her statutory right to refuse consent.

18–139 As to the proprietary interest, Henchy J. noted that the wife claimed that she had paid a deposit on the lease and had pooled her wages with those of her husband. The plaintiff's solicitor knew of the existence of a separation agreement and should have obtained a copy of it. The plaintiff had gone to the

---

[203] (1844) 7 Ir. Eq. R. 560; *Hunt v Luck* [1902] 1 Ch. 428.
[204] [1979] I.R. 94.

Free Legal Advice Centre where the agreement was drawn up and the plaintiff's solicitor was told that a copy could not be supplied because the centre was closed for the holidays. The court held that he should not have accepted the excuse. Had he seen the agreement he would have seen that there was no reference to a claim by the wife and that would have put him on notice.

18–140 It seems that a purchaser in these circumstances gets notice in either event. He or she gets notice if there is a reference to a claim or if there is not. What the court may mean is that knowledge that the vendor is married but separated gives notice that the other spouse may be claiming an equity, in which case there is no need to examine the separation agreement because knowledge of its existence alone is enough to put the party on notice. Alternatively, the court thought that the statutory declaration itself, in referring even negatively to a claim, put him on notice.

18–141 As to the defendant's statutory right to refuse consent under s.3(3)(a) of the 1976 Act, the statute allows a conveyance to escape being void under that section if it is made to a purchaser for full value and "purchaser" is defined by s.3(6) as a person who acquires property in "good faith". The Supreme Court decided that this imports a doctrine of notice. It was also led to this conclusion because subs.(7) specifically refers to s.3 of the Conveyancing Act 1882 which gave statutory form to the equitable doctrine of notice and extended it to some extent.[205] It was held that the conveyance was void. The plaintiff had failed to discharge the onus, which fell on her under s.3(4), of proving that the conveyance was valid.

18–142 The Supreme Court in *Bank of Ireland v Smyth*[206] held that the consent under s.3 of the 1976 Act must be an informed consent and that consequently a bank obtained constructive notice of a wife's lack of understanding that a mortgage was intended to give the bank the right to sell the family home.

Registration
18–143 The only real protection of a spouse is provided by s.12 of the 1976 Act which says that a spouse may register under the Registry of Deeds Acts or under the Registration of Title Act 1964 a notice stating that she is married to a person being a person having an interest in such property or land. However, it is doubtful if many spouses are aware of, or use, the section.

Third Parties
18–144 A question of considerable importance is the effect of the 1976 Act on dealings with a family home.[207] Section 3(1) provides that where a spouse,

---

[205] Replaced by LCLRA 2009 s.86. On notice, see *Northern Bank v Henry* [1981] I.R. 1.
[206] [1996] 1 I.L.R.M. 241.
[207] See A. Lyall, "The Family Home Protection Act 1976 and Conveyances Other Than by Spouses" (1984) 6 D.U.L.J. (ns) 158.

without the prior consent in writing of the other spouse, purports to convey any interest in the family home to any person except the other spouse, then "subject to subsections (2) and (3) and section 4, the purported conveyance shall be void". Section 3 continues:

"(2) Subsection 1 does not apply to a conveyance if it is made by a spouse in pursuance of an enforceable agreement made before the marriage of the spouses.

(3) No conveyance shall be void by reason only of subsection (1)—
   (a) if it is made to a purchaser for full value,
   (b) if it is made, by a person other than the spouse making the purported conveyance referred to in subsection (1), to a purchaser for value, or
   (c) if its validity depends on the validity of a conveyance in respect of which any of the conditions mentioned in subsection (2) or paragraph (a) or (b) is satisfied.

(4) If any question arises in any proceedings as to whether a conveyance is valid by reason of subsection (2) or (3), the burden of proving that validity shall be on the person alleging it.

(5) In subsection (3), 'full value' means such value as amounts or approximates to the value of that for which it is given.

(6) In this section 'purchaser' means a grantee, lessee, assignee, mortgagee, chargeant or other person who in good faith acquires an estate or interest in property."

Initial Transaction

18–145 The phrase "initial transaction" is not one found in the 1976 Act but what is meant here is the first actual or purported transaction dealing with the legal title to a house or flat, etc. after it has become a "family home" within the meaning of the 1976 Act. The initial transaction may be made by a spouse or by some other person. It will be made by some other person if the legal title to the home is vested in someone other than the spouses, for example, if it is vested in a company.

18–146 If the initial transaction is, properly, made by someone other than a spouse, then it cannot be rendered void by s.3. Section 3 only applies to conveyances *by spouses*. This is a loophole in the 1976 Act.[208]

18–147 If the initial transaction is made by a spouse, then it is void if made without the prior consent in writing of the other spouse, unless, within s.3(3)

---

[208] *Containercare (Ireland) Ltd v Wycherley* [1982] I.R. 143; *Walpoles v Jay*, unreported, High Court, McWilliam J., 20 November 1980; A. Lyall, "The Family Home Protection Act 1976 and Conveyances Other Than by Spouses" (1984) 6 D.U.L.J. (ns) 158.

(a), it is made to a "purchaser for full value", in "good faith"[209] and without notice,[210] in which case such a purchaser will take a good title.

Subsequent Transaction
The Prima Facie Position

18–148 If the conveyance is a subsequent transaction, i.e. transaction following an initial transaction dealing with a family home, then the import of s.3 is that if the initial transaction is void under the 1976 Act, then any subsequent transaction is prima facie void. The prima facie position will then be displaced if it falls within one of the exceptions set out in s.3(3)(b) and (c). When s.3(3) says "[n]o conveyance shall be void by reason only of subsection (1)", etc., it must be taken not only to refer to initial transactions expressly made void by s.3(1), but also to incorporate the principle that a transaction which follows a transaction void under s.3(1) is also void—prima facie. This principle may be regarded either as implied in s.3(1) or an application of the *nemo dat quod non habet* rule,[211] i.e. that a person who has no title cannot confer it on another. This, it must be said, is nowhere expressly stated in s.3, although it is assumed, the authors would argue, by s.3(3)(b). It is an unfortunate aspect of the drafting of the 1976 Act that this is not stated explicitly, but the assumption appears sound as a matter of law, independent of the 1976 Act, and appears to be the only one which would give any meaning to s.3(3)(b).

18–149 If a family home is owned by a spouse, H, who purports to transfer it to P1, but without obtaining the consent of W, the other spouse, the transaction to P1 is prima facie void. This is the position taking into account s.3(1), the prima facie position as to initial transactions. If P1 then purports to convey the house to P2, that transaction is also prima facie void under general principles of law. If P1 had no title, he has nothing to transfer to P2.[212]

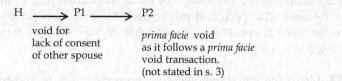

18–150 To see if the prima facie position is displaced one must look at s.3(3). There are logically four possible situations.

---

[209] Section 3(6) defines purchaser as a person who "in good faith" acquires an estate or interest in property.

[210] *Somers v Weir* [1979] I.R. 94.

[211] In the law of sale of goods, although there are many exceptions to it, so that the exceptions are now in reality the rule, the *nemo dat* principle is still the prima facie position.

[212] This, as careful observers will note, is a reifying explanation. The point is that it is the principle which seems to have been in the minds of the draftsmen of the 1976 Act.

P1 Has Notice, P2 Does Not

18–151 What is the position if P2 does not have notice of these matters? This is the subject matter of s.3(3)(b). There is a problem with interpreting s.3(3)(b). It is that s.3 begins by saying that "[n]o conveyance shall be void by reason only of subsection (1)" and then s.3(3)(b) refers to a transaction by a person *other* than a spouse. But s.3(1) only makes void certain transactions *by spouses*, i.e. it does not make a transaction by a person *other than a spouse* void in any case. It is therefore arguable that if s.3(3)(b) is to have any meaning at all, the phrase "void by reason only of subsection (1)", in relation to s.3(3) (b), must assume that a *consequential* effect of s.3(1) is not only to make void without consent an initial transaction, but also, prima facie, to make void a *subsequent* transaction by a person other than a spouse.

18–152 The conveyance is made "by a person (P1) other than the spouse making the purported conveyance referred to in subsection (1)". It refers to where there has been a purported conveyance by a spouse, followed by a conveyance by a non-spouse. In this instance the conveyance is valid if made in favour of a purchaser for value (P2). The prima facie position is displaced.

18–153 McWilliam J. remarked in *Walpoles v Jay*[213] that s.3(1) does not appear to make any subsequent transactions void. Nevertheless, s.3(3)(b) only makes sense if s.3(1) is taken to imply that a subsequent transaction would be prima facie void if the initial transaction is made void by s.3(1).

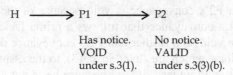

	H ⟶ P1 ⟶ P2
	Has notice. No notice.
	VOID VALID
	under s.3(1). under s.3(3)(b).

18–154 It may also be noticed that while s.3(3)(a) speaks of "purchaser for full value", s.3(3)(b) only uses the phrase "purchaser for value". The only apparent reason for this difference is that subs.(a) refers to an initial transaction when the price paid to the spouse can be compared at least approximately to the price for which the house was bought, while subs.(b) refers to subsequent transactions which may occur long after the original purchase of the family home and therefore it would be unrealistic to require a comparison to be made.

18–155 This situation raises a conveyancing problem: how does P2 acquire a title if P1 did not have one? There is a break in the chain of title deeds because the conveyance to P1 was void, even though the conveyance from P1 to P2 is valid. There are circumstances in the law of real property where a person acquires a title from a person who did not have one to give. Many of the reforms of the law have been brought about by this means: disentailment under

---

[213] Unreported, High Court, McWilliam J., 20 November 1980.

the Fines and Recoveries (Ireland) Act 1834, a conveyance by a tenant for life under the Settled Land Acts, and tortious feoffments at common law until the Real Property Act 1845. But in all those cases it could be seen from the type of document that it had this effect.

18–156 This situation also raises another interesting question: if P1 makes a profit on the transaction, can he keep it? P2 will be quite content with matters as they are—he has paid the purchase price and has a good title. The conveying spouse, H, has the money from the void sale to P1. He is quite content also. The aggrieved party is the non-conveying spouse. Does she have an action against P1 to recover the profit? Or against H? Could H claim the profit? The non-conveying spouse would seem to have an action against the conveying spouse under s.5(2) of the 1976 Act on the basis that the spouse "has deprived the applicant spouse or a dependent child of the family of his residence in the family home by conduct that resulted in the loss of any interest therein or rendered it unsuitable for habitation as a family home". The conveying spouse's conduct in conveying to P1 did have the effect of depriving the other spouse or a child of their residence because, as a result of the further conveyance to P2, P2 obtained a title good against them.

Both P1 and P2 Have Notice
18–157 In this case P2 does not gain a good title. This may be called the "*Somers v Weir*[214] situation", since it occurred in that case. The position appears to be that P2's conveyance is void because of the unstated assumption of s.3(1) that a conveyance that follows a prima facie void conveyance is also prima facie void, and further that P2's conveyance does not fall within any of the exceptions, which are stated in s.3(3), to the assumed position. P2's conveyance is not valid under s.3(3)(a) because he is not a purchaser for full value without notice. Nor does s.3(3)(b) apply because P2 is not a purchaser for value in good faith and without notice. Nor can he take advantage of s.3(3) (c). It would only apply if P1's conveyance was valid under s.3(2) or 3(3)(a) or 3(3)(b). Assume that s.3(2) is not satisfied. The validity of P2's conveyance depends on the validity of P1's conveyance in prima facie terms, but P1's conveyance does not satisfy s.3(3)(a) because it is not made to a purchaser for full value without notice and it does not satisfy s.3(3)(b) because it is not made to a purchaser for value without notice.

Neither P1 nor P2 Has Notice
18–158 In this case P2 obtains a good title under s.3(3)(c). This seems to be the situation contemplated by s.3(3)(c). Since P2's conveyance is a subsequent transaction its validity depends, prima facie, on the validity of P1's conveyance and P1's conveyance is valid because it satisfies para.(a), being made to a purchaser for full value without notice, P1.

---

[214] [1979] I.R. 94.

18–159 On the other hand, it is true that as s.3 assumes that a subsequent conveyance which follows a prima facie void conveyance by a spouse is also prima facie void, then one can arrive at the same conclusion under s.3(3)(a). P2's conveyance is not made void under subs.(1) because, as s.3(3)(a) provides, it is made to a purchaser for full value, P2. However, one should avoid this route because it requires one to show that, regardless of P1's position, P2 acquired for full value.

P1 Has No Notice, P2 Has Notice
18–160 In this case P2's position also falls within s.3(3)(c), but despite having notice here, P2 obtains a good title. This may be termed the *"Re Stewart's Estate*[215] situation" or *"Wilkes v Spooner*[216] situation", since it is analogous to those cases. P1, who does not have notice that the house is a family home, conveys to P2 who does have notice. The somewhat surprising result is that P2 obtains a good title despite the fact that he has notice. This also falls within s.3(3)(c). P2's conveyance depends for its validity on that of P1, on the assumption of the prima facie situation, i.e. that if P1's conveyance is prima facie void, then so is P2's. Section 3(3)(c) specifies that it will nevertheless be valid if conditions (a) or (b) in subs.(3) are satisfied by P1's conveyance. P1's conveyance does satisfy (a) because he is a purchaser for full value without notice.

18–161 This seems to be an odd result, but the reason for it may be similar to the rationale of *Wilkes v Spooner*.[217] When P1 bought the land without notice of the wife's rights, he presumably paid the market price for the property. In capitalist society courts try to ensure that an innocent buyer on the market can at least sell the commodity he or she has bought. In the case of land "the commodity" consists of a number of rights defined by the law of property. If P1 could only sell the same title he had acquired by finding a buyer who also, like himself, did not have notice, the wife could prevent this happening by advertising her right, or in this case, by registering it under s.12 of the 1976 Act.

18–162 Where two innocent parties, in the sense of not having notice, are concerned, the law has to make a choice between them. That choice will also be informed by the social policies that each one in a sense represents or personifies. To favour the buyer on the market is to favour the efficient working of the market as a mechanism for distributing wealth and to deny the validity of other considerations. To favour the non-property-owning wife is to reject the market as the sole mechanism and to assert that society, through the law, has a responsibility to protect those who cannot defend their interests through

---

[215] (1893) 31 L.R. Ir. 405 at 415; *Re Stapleford Colliery Co (Barrow's Case)* (1880) 14 Ch. D. 432.
[216] [1911] 2 K.B. 473.
[217] [1911] 2 K.B. 473.

that mechanism. The law in this case has evidently chosen the "free market" approach.

Conduct Depriving the Spouse of an Interest
18–163 Section 5 of the 1976 Act provides as follows:

> "5.—(1) Where it appears to the court, on the application of a spouse, that the other spouse is engaging in such conduct as may lead to the loss of any interest in the family home or may render it unsuitable for habitation as a family home with the intention of depriving the applicant spouse or a dependent child of the family of his [or her] residence in the family home, the court may make such order as it considers proper, directed to the other spouse or to any other person, for the protection of the family home in the interest of the applicant spouse or such child.
>
> (2) Where it appears to the court, on the application of a spouse, that the other has deprived the applicant spouse or a dependent child of the family of his [or her] residence in the family home by conduct that resulted [in the loss of any interest, etc.] … the court may order the other spouse or any other person to pay the applicant spouse such amount as the court considers proper to compensate the applicant spouse and any such child for their loss or make such other order … as may appear … just and equitable."

Future and Past Conduct
18–164 Subsection (1) contemplates that the conduct referred to has not yet resulted in the loss of an interest but "may" do so in future. It permits any order to be made, and not merely compensation as in subs.(2), so that the court could order the transfer of an interest in the land to be made. Furthermore, such an order can be directed not only against the other spouse but against any third party who might have acquired an interest in the family home. Subsection (2), on the other hand, is in the past tense. It refers to conduct which has already had the effect of depriving the spouse of his or her residence in the family home by causing the loss of an interest in it or rendering it unsuitable as a family home. But the difference is not merely as to the future or past tense. The conduct in subs.(1) is conduct which may either (a) lead to a loss of any interest, or (b) render it unsuitable as a family home. It need not affect, or be likely to affect, residence. Residence in subs.(1) is relevant to intention, not to conduct. The conduct in subs.(2), on the other hand, is conduct which is relevant to residence.

18–165 Subsection (1) does not require that the conduct may lead to a loss of an interest vested in the other spouse. Conduct by spouse A which may lead to the loss of an interest vested in spouse A is within the section. Thus, if spouse A, who has a beneficial interest in the house, gets into debt, and this results in creditor X obtaining a judgment mortgage against A's interest, that may be conduct within the section. Strictly speaking, therefore, conduct which has already led to the loss of an interest in the family home, such as indebtedness, which has resulted in the registration of a judgment mortgage, but which has not yet resulted in loss of residence is neither within subs.(1) nor (2). If the section had been applied literally this would be a major loophole in the 1976 Act, since the issue of one spouse's indebtedness and its effect upon the residence of the other spouse usually comes before the court at precisely this point. But it does not seem that the courts have been so strict in their application of the words of the section. They seem to have taken the view that where an interest has been lost, as by a judgment mortgage, but residence has not yet been affected, the other spouse can apply under subs.(1), while, if residence has already been lost, that still does not preclude a spouse bringing an action under subs.(1) if the reason for the loss of residence was attributable to the other spouse, as where the applicant spouse had been driven from the home by the violence of the other spouse.[218] Thus, on this aspect of the section, the judges have adopted a liberal interpretation.

Intention to Deprive

18–166 Subsection (1) specifically provides that the conduct must be accompanied by an "intention of depriving" the spouse of his or her residence in the family home. Subsection (2) does not require intention at all.

18–167 The cases interpreting "intention" in subs.(1) have taken a restrictive view of it, requiring a subjective test of intention. This, it must be said, is usually to the advantage of husbands, since it is more usual for wives to apply under the section than husbands.

18–168 In *ED v FD*,[219] a husband left the wife and children and went to live in London to work as a television journalist. He spent extravagantly on fast cars, holidays in expensive hotels and other luxuries and entertained lavishly. He failed to make maintenance payments in accordance with an interlocutory maintenance order, although he had recently made some attempt to do so. The wife brought proceedings to commit him for contempt of court and to fix future maintenance payments. She also asked for an order under s.5 transferring the family home into her name. The defendant had substantial debts in Ireland. Ejectment proceedings had been instituted by the mortgagees[220] of his family home. Costello J. held that the discretion under s.5 was "very wide", but that it could only be exercised where the court was satisfied that the spouse was acting with the intention of depriving the applicant spouse or a dependent child of the family of his or her residence in the family home. The court noted that the defendant had certainly acted in "a most improvident way" but there was no evidence that he had the necessary intention to deprive the wife of an interest.

---

[218] *AD v DD and Irish Nationwide Building Society*, unreported, High Court, McWilliam J., 8 June 1983. The judge noted the point, but did not have to decide it on the facts.

[219] Unreported, High Court, 23 October 1980.

[220] The judgment says "mortgagors".

No order was made for committal. Leave was given to renew the application under s.5, but in the meantime an order was made under s.11 of the Guardianship of Infants Act 1964, which contains wide powers for the protection of children's welfare, requiring him to enter into negotiations with his creditors and the Revenue Commissioners with a view to reducing his debts.

18–169 In *DC v AC*,[221] the family home was purchased in the joint names of the husband and wife. It was purchased by a mortgage, a gift from the wife's father and a loan from the husband's father. Both parties were described as young and immature when they married, although the wife had become rather more mature through looking after the two children of the marriage. She had supported the children on her earnings after the husband left home. He had used violence towards the wife and a barring order was granted.[222]

18–170 The husband had also run up some debts. Only two mortgage payments were made. The building society obtained an order for possession in other proceedings, but delayed execution of it pending the outcome of the present proceedings. In the earlier proceedings, the father had offered to repay all the arrears and future mortgage instalments, provided the house was transferred to the wife, his daughter, with a clear title. Carroll J. held that "conduct" includes inactivity as well as activity, so that the husband's failure to pay the mortgage instalments was conduct such as might lead to the loss of an interest in the family home, but the judge refused an order under the section transferring the family home to the wife on the ground that it would divest the husband of his share of the equity of redemption at a time when he had considerable debts.

18–171 The judge indicated the terms of the order she would make if the house were to be sold. First, £4,000 would be distributed to the wife in respect of her contribution (i.e. her father's gift). The husband contributed nothing and so was not entitled to any sum under this head. Secondly, the wife would receive such a sum as would represent any proportionate increase in the value of the house attributable to her contribution, so that if the value of the house had doubled, the wife would receive another £4,000. Thirdly, any balance remaining was at common law the joint property of the husband and wife, since the legal title to the house was in their joint names, but since the wife would have to find accommodation for herself and the children and maintain them, she would be allowed at her option to withdraw sufficient funds from the balance to repay debts in her name, their joint names and to repay the husband's father's loan. Fourthly, any balance then remaining would be used, at the husband's option, to pay off his debts. Fifthly, if there was still a balance remaining, it would be divided between the wife and the husband. Carroll J. felt that

---

[221] [1981] I.L.R.M. 357.
[222] Under the Family Law (Maintenance of Spouses and Children) Act 1976. See also the Civil Law (Miscellaneous Provisions) Act 2011.

as the wife's father had offered to pay off the arrears of the mortgage, the wife might, with her father's help, be able to put down a deposit on a smaller house.

18–172 The reason given by the judge in *DC v AC* for refusing an order under s.5, standing on its own, seems to be excessively restrictive. It will usually be the case that the conduct which has put the existing property interests in the house in jeopardy is one spouse getting into debt. It is probable, however, that the judge meant that debt was a sufficient reason for refusal *in the absence of the intention* to deprive the other spouse of an interest. It also seems probable that other factors influenced the refusal, namely the need to reimburse the husband's father and the fact that the wife could manage with a smaller house.

18–173 In *CP v DP*,[223] the defendant husband was an architect and had a reasonably successful business in partnership with another person. A recession in the building industry affected the business adversely. Arguments took place between the partners and the partnership was dissolved. In order to secure an overdraft with the bank, the husband had deposited the title deeds of the family home with the bank. The wife did not know of this transaction. The husband had other debts also. The plaintiff wife alleged that the defendant's conduct was such as could lead to the loss of the family home with the intention of depriving the wife and dependent children of their residence in it. It was also claimed that in those circumstances, s.5(1) of the 1976 Act gave the court a discretionary power to direct the husband to transfer the entire legal and beneficial ownership in the family home to the plaintiff wife. It was submitted that the word "intention" in the section should be construed so as not to be equivalent to notice, but rather with the "intention" which could be imputed to any person as to the natural and probable consequences of their conduct. This would clearly be a less stringent test. Finlay P. held first that the mortgage was void without the wife's consent, but that this was a theoretical point because the decision in *Containercare (Ireland) Ltd v Wycherley*[224] meant that the bank could still sue the husband for the money on the facts of the case as there was no claim by the wife for an equity in the house.[225]

18–174 He then went on to say that before a court could impute, in s.5, the intention which can arise from the natural and probable consequences of an act or omission, there must first be an element of deliberate conduct involved. The evidence did not sustain the assertion that there was sufficient premeditation as was required to constitute "intention" in s.5. He therefore refused to countenance a test which would have made it easier for, generally, wives to establish conduct within s.5. The judge argued that this result followed from the wording of the subsections. He noted that subs.(1) refers to intention whereas subs.(2) does not use the word at all. If intention could be inferred

---

[223] [1983] I.L.R.M. 380.
[224] [1982] I.R. 143.
[225] The registration of a judgment mortgage would not affect a prior unregistrable equity.

from consequences alone, he reasoned, then the distinction would be unnecessary. There is some force in this argument, even if one takes into account the
fact that the consequences in subs.(1) have not occurred, and are therefore
speculative, while in subs.(2) they are actual. Finlay P. in *CP v DP*[226] found on
the facts that there was insufficient evidence to support the element of deliber-
ateness of the conduct.

18–175 In *S v S*,[227] the court came to a similar conclusion, finding that the loss
of an interest would have been a natural and probable consequence on the facts,
but declined to find that s.5 had been satisfied. In that case the wife sought an
order transferring the home into her name. The home had been purchased in the
joint names of the husband and the wife. The husband incurred debts. A creditor approached the wife and told her that the home would have to be sold. This
was the first she knew of the husband's debts. The husband then disappeared.
The court dismissed the wife's claim, finding that the husband's conduct was
improvident and possibly dishonest but did not disclose an outright intention
of depriving the wife and children of their residence.

18–176 The cases in which s.5 has been held to be satisfied do not, unfortunately, provide any consistent guide as to evidence of deliberate intention.
In *CMCB v SB*,[228] the parties had married in England and bought a house there.
They were both employed at the time and the house was purchased through
their joint efforts, both wife and husband contributing to a lump sum which
partly paid for the house, the rest being raised by borrowing. In 1970 the parties
returned to Ireland. The house in England was sold and part of the surplus left
over after paying off the loan was used to buy the house in Ireland, although
the conveyance of this house was taken in the husband's name.

18–177 Barron J. in the High Court held that the wife was entitled to an equitable interest in the house. The parties separated in 1982 and from then on the
husband's financial position went from bad to worse. He had a hamburger stall
which caught fire on more than one occasion. He failed to make maintenance
payments to the wife. He said that he had "plant and machinery" stored in the
garage next to the house and tried to get access to it despite a barring order
which had been granted against him. The wife was supported partly by her own
job and by payments to her by the husband's sister, but these were not made
on the husband's behalf. The judge held that the terms of the section had been
satisfied, but made no order under it as he had not been asked to do so.

18–178 In *GP v IP*,[229] the husband obtained an order under s.4 of the 1976
Act dispensing with the wife's consent to a disposition of the family home on
the basis that he needed to raise money on a mortgage to start his own business.

---

[226] [1983] I.L.R.M. 380.
[227] [1983] I.L.R.M. 387.
[228] Unreported, High Court, Barron J., 17 May 1983.
[229] Unreported, High Court, O'Hanlon J., 19 October 1984.

The order specified that he was to use the money to discharge a debt he owed to a bank and to keep the wife's solicitors informed as to repayments of the mortgage debt. He did neither, nor did he start a business. This was held to be conduct sufficient to satisfy s.5. The court ordered the husband to transfer his interest in the house to the wife, not to raise loans and added a declaration that until the conveyance was executed by the husband, the wife was deemed to be the beneficial owner subject only to the mortgage. In *D v D*,[230] the court also found the intention proved and ordered the family home to be transferred into the wife's name.

18–179 It is difficult to see how the intention was proved in these cases while it had failed in earlier ones. The factor that stands out in *CMCB v SB*[231] and *GP v IP*[232] is that the husband had either misled the court or had violated its orders. A realistic approach to the case law suggests that this factor is likely to overcome the general reluctance of the judges to find the necessary intention in s.5.

Nature of the Order

18–180 Another difference between subs.(1) and subs.(2) of s.5 is that under subs.(1), the court may make "such order as it considers proper, directed to the other spouse or to any other person" for the protection of the family home, whereas under subs.(2) the court may order the other spouse or any other person "to pay the applicant spouse such amount as the court considers proper to compensate the applicant spouse and any such child for their loss or make such other order ... as may appear ... just and equitable." Thus, subs.(2) allows the award of compensation whereas subs.(1) does not contemplate such an award. One reason for the difference is no doubt that subs.(1) refers to conduct that has not yet resulted in a loss of an interest in the home and so no interest will have become vested in a third party. On the other hand, where subs.(2) is invoked, this may already have occurred. If the third party is one who, under s.3, obtains a good title, it would create a conflict in the 1976 Act if s.5 were to sanction an order transferring an interest from such a party back to an applicant spouse. Compensation is therefore a more appropriate remedy. It has already been seen that s.5 is drafted in wide enough terms to permit an order directed to an owner/spouse to transfer his or her interest in the family home to the other spouse.[233]

18–181 The section has been held not to require an absolute transfer of the interest of the errant spouse in favour of the claimant spouse or children. In *O'Neill v O'Neill*,[234] both spouses had beneficial interests in the family home. The wife left and went to live with another man. The husband and two

[230] Unreported, High Court, Costello J., 16 December 1981. The case is only noted in *S v S* [1983] I.L.R.M. 387.

[231] Unreported, High Court, Barron J., 17 May 1983.

[232] Unreported, High Court, O'Hanlon J., 19 October 1984.

[233] *GP v IP*, unreported, High Court, O'Hanlon J., 19 October 1984; *D v D*, unreported, High Court, Costello J., 16 December 1981. The latter case is noted in *S v S* [1983] I.L.R.M. 387.

[234] Unreported, High Court, Barron J., 6 October 1989.

children of the marriage continued to live in the house. The wife borrowed money from a bank to buy furniture and when she became unable to pay the instalments on the loan, she sought to obtain an order of sale in lieu of partition. This was refused. The bank obtained judgment against her for the amount due and registered a judgment mortgage against her interest in the family home. Barron J. found that she had put the residence of the husband and children at risk by not making efforts to pay off the judgment mortgage. He ordered her beneficial interest to be transferred to trustees until such time as she discharged the judgment mortgage.[235] The judge felt that a court would be unlikely to order a sale of the property until the children were grown up.

Minor Spouses
18–182 In *Lloyd v Sullivan*,[236] the defendant entered into a contract to sell a farm to the plaintiff. The defendant's wife consented to the sale. She was under age at the time. The plaintiff brought an action under the Vendor and Purchaser Act 1874 claiming a declaration that good title had not been shown. It was held that the same principles apply under the 1976 Act as in the law of contract. The minor was dealing with a valuable right and agreeing to surrender it without consideration. If the transaction was not shown to be to her advantage, she would be entitled to repudiate it on coming of age.[237] In the meantime a good title had been shown.

18–183 As result of the case, s.10 of the Family Law Act 1981 was passed. It provides that consent under the 1976 Act "shall not be invalid by reason only that the spouse is under age". This formulation still leaves a doubt. *Lloyd* did not hold that the consent was invalid by reason only of the spouse being under age. The case held that the consent of a minor is valid unless and until avoided on coming of age. If it is invalid, it is so because (a) being under age at the time of consent, he or she had the power to repudiate it on coming of age, and (b) on coming of age he or she did repudiate it.

Partition and the Family Home Protection Act 1976
18–184 It has already been seen that where a spouse has a beneficial interest in equity, and the other spouse holds the legal title, then the beneficial owner's consent, i.e. the "other spouse", must be obtained or dispensed with before an order can be made under s.31 of the LCLRA 2009.

---

[235] Assuming the title to the house to be unregistered, the effect of registration of the affidavit would be to transfer the interest of the judgment mortgagor to the mortgagee, leaving the wife with a type of equity of redemption expectant upon the discharge of the mortgage. It was presumably this interest which was ordered to be vested in trustees.

[236] Unreported, High Court, McWilliam J., 6 March 1981.

[237] Irish case on infant contracts: *Allen v Allen* (1842) 4 Ir. Eq. R. 472.

Bankruptcy

18–185 Where the owning spouse is bankrupt, the Bankruptcy Act 1988 provides that a family home cannot be sold without the prior sanction of the court.[238] The court has power to order postponement of the sale of the family home and may have regard to the interests of the spouse and dependants of the bankrupt as well as the creditors' interests.[239]

CIVIL PARTNERSHIP

Introduction

18–186 The Civil Partnership and Certain Rights and Obligations of Cohabitants Act 2010 ("CPA 2010") came into effect in 2010. It allowed same-sex couples to register as civil partners. Since the Marriage Act 2015, no new civil partnerships can be entered into, but existing civil partnerships remain valid and civil partners continue to enjoy the same rights as before.[240] Therefore it is still important to have regard to the legal rights and obligations of civil partners.

Definitions

18–187 Under s.3 a civil partner is either of two persons of the same sex who are either:

(a) parties to a civil partnership registration that has not been dissolved or the subject of a decree of nullity; or
(b) parties to a legal relationship "of a class that is the subject of an order made under section 5 that has not been dissolved or the subject of a decree of nullity".

18–188 There is no explicit requirement that civil partners be homosexual, but merely that they be of the same sex. However, although the provisions in the CPA 2010 as to civil partners do not expressly mention it,[241] it appears to assume an intimate relationship of a sexual nature, since civil partnership:

---

[238] Bankruptcy Act 1988 s.61(4) and (5).
[239] *Rubotham (Official Assignee) v Duddy*, unreported, High Court, Shanley J., 1 May 1996 (sale postponed for 10 years); *Rubotham (Official Assignee) v Young*, unreported, High Court, McCracken J., 23 May 1995.
[240] F. Ryan, "The Rise and Fall of Civil Partnership" (2016) 19(3) I.J.F.L. 50, observes that "civil partnership will gradually fade into history less than a decade after its inception".
[241] Contrast the provisions as to cohabitants which, under s.172, only apply to cohabitants "who live together as a couple in an intimate and committed relationship", and s.172(3) which provides that "[f]or the avoidance of doubt a relationship does not cease to be an intimate relationship for the purpose of this section merely because it is no longer sexual in nature". "Intimate relationship" is not used in the sections as to civil partners. Although there is nullity in relation to civil partnership, there is no concept of non-consummation. Non-consummation may still be a ground for nullity of marriage.

(a) is subject to the prohibited degrees of blood relationship (called *consanguinity*) which have their origins in the avoidance of sexual relations between near relatives[242]; and

(b) is not available to relationships definitely not of a sexual nature, such as closely related persons who in fact cohabit and share their lives, such as brother and sister, two brothers, or two sisters, or a mother and son, father and son, etc.

Affinity

18–189 As Ryan points out, in relation to marriage the law prohibits marriage not only between parties who are related by blood (relationships of consanguinity) but also between parties who are related by a prior marriage (relationships of *affinity*)[243]:

> "The Marriage Act 1835, section 2, renders a marriage void when it is contracted between persons within both the prohibited degrees of consanguinity *and* those based on affinity.[244] Thus, for instance, a man may not marry his former wife's daughter or mother, (though he may marry her sister, even after divorce[245])."

18–190 Ryan further points out that there is no comparable provision in the CPA 2010 as to civil partnership, and also that both the Law Reform Commission and the Law Reform Committee of the Law Society of Ireland have recommended that restrictions on marriage founded on affinity should be abolished.

General Comments

18–191 Apart from setting the general context, it is beyond the scope of this work to deal with aspects of civil partnership other than as to property. There were originally significant differences between civil partnership and marriage, although some of these have since been legislatively remedied. The provisions of the CPA 2010 demonstrated an absence of the recognition of civil partners

---

[242] As to the criminal law, incest is a crime confined to parties of opposite sex. Incest was made a crime by the Punishment of Incest Act 1908. There is no such crime in Ireland, at present, of homosexual incest. Homosexual incest was made an offence in the UK by s.64 of the Sexual Offences Act 2003.

[243] F. Ryan, *Civil Partnership and Certain Rights and Obligations of Cohabitants Act 2010 (An Annotation)* (Dublin: Round Hall, 2011), para.2.4.1.

[244] The1835 Act did not set out the prohibited degrees, which are detailed in the Marriage Act 1537 (as amended). These proscriptions are in turn based on biblical proscriptions set out in the Book of Leviticus. See Lev. 18:6 and 18:16–18.

[245] The Deceased Wife's Sister's Marriage Act 1907 (a man may marry his deceased wife's sister); the Deceased Brother's Widow's Marriage Act 1921 (a woman may marry her deceased husband's brother). In *O'Shea v Ireland*, unreported, High Court, Laffoy J., 6 November 2006, Laffoy J. ruled that the former legal restriction on a woman marrying her divorced husband's brother was unconstitutional.

in the role of parents. As originally enacted, there was no provision allowing civil partners jointly to adopt a child so that it was the child of both partners. Section 16 of the Adoption (Amendment) Act 2017 amends s.33 of the Adoption Act 2010 so that civil partners and cohabiting couples can jointly adopt.[246]

Nullity and Property Adjustment Orders
18–192 Grounds of nullity of a civil partnership are set out in s.107 and are a slightly expanded version of the impediments to a civil partnership set out above. There is no express provision in the CPA 2010 for property adjustment orders on nullity, although s.108(2) provides somewhat cryptically that "[t] he rights of a person who relied on the existence of a civil partnership which is subsequently the subject of a decree of nullity are not prejudiced by that decree." An application could also be made under s.106, dealt with in the next paragraph.

Application under Section 106
18–193 Section 106 is the equivalent to s.36(1) of the Family Law Act 1995 in that either civil partner may apply to the court in a summary manner to determine a question arising between them as to the title to or possession of property and the court may make the order it considers proper with respect to the property in dispute, including an order that the property be sold or partitioned, etc.

Separation
18–194 The CPA 2010 contains no equivalent of judicial separation in civil partnership and so no provision for property adjustment orders in such a case. As Ryan points out, although partners must make a declaration that they will live together, there appears to be no legal means to enforce this, as there is not as to marriage. There is nothing to prevent partners separating; this might lead to dissolution. Although courts have been reluctant to enforce agreements that contemplate a future separation, an agreement providing for immediate separation of married couples is enforceable, and the same may be the case as to civil partners.[247]

Dissolution
Grounds
18–195 On an application to the court by either of the civil partners, the court may grant a decree of dissolution of a civil partnership if it is satisfied that,

> "(a) at the date of the institution of the proceedings the civil partners have lived apart from one another for a period of, or periods amounting to, at least two years during the previous three years, and

---

[246] It also allows for adoption by parents, step-parents and other relatives.
[247] Ryan, *Civil Partnership* (2011), para.5.1.

(b) provision that the court considers proper having regard to the circumstances exists or will be made for the civil partners and any dependent child of the civil partners."[248]

The court may also adjourn the proceedings so that there may be an attempt at reconciliation, if the partners so wish.[249] On a grant of a decree of dissolution, the court may, where appropriate, give such directions as it considers proper[250] regarding the best interests, custody or right of access to any dependent child of the civil partners.[251] When the decree of dissolution has been granted, the civil partnership is dissolved and either civil partner may register in a new civil partnership or marry.[252] A civil partnership subsisting between two persons immediately before their marriage to each other is dissolved on the date of the marriage.[253]

Domestic Violence
18–196 Part 9 of the CPA 2010 applies the provisions of the Domestic Violence Act 1996 to civil partnerships and therefore a barring order under s.3 of the 1996 Act may be issued.

Property Adjustment Orders
18–197 Section 118 of the CPA 2010, as amended by the Children and Family Relationships Act 2015, provides for the granting of property adjustment orders on dissolution of a civil partnership. The provisions are less detailed than those on divorce in relation to marriage. The court on application to it by either of the civil partners (or by a person on behalf of a dependent child of one of them) may, "during the lifetime of either of the civil partners", make one or more of the following orders: (a) an order transferring specified property in which a civil partner has an interest either in possession or reversion from that civil partner to the other, to a dependent child of the civil partners, or any or all of such persons; (b) an order settling specified property in which a civil partner has an interest either in possession or reversion for the benefit of the other, to a dependent child of the civil partners or any or all of such persons, to the satisfaction of the court; (c) an order varying an ante-registration or post-registration settlement made by the civil partners, including one made by will or codicil, for the benefit of one of the civil partners; and (d) an order extinguishing or reducing the interest of either of the civil partners under such a settlement.

---

[248] CPA 2010 s.110.
[249] CPA 2010 s.111.
[250] Under the s.11 of Guardianship of Infants Act 1964.
[251] CPA 2010 s.110(2)
[252] CPA 2010 s.113.
[253] CPA 2010 s.109A.

18–198 There is no specific mention of taking into account contributions towards the purchase of the home, etc. or to work in the home as "home-maker", as may be the case especially where there are children, but the general power under (a) appears to be sufficient to allow such contributions to be taken into account.

Shared Home Protection
Prior Consent in Writing

18–199 These provisions of the CPA 2010 are the equivalent of the Family Home Protection Act 1976 as to marriage and are in similar terms. Section 28(1) provides as follows:

> "Where a civil partner, without the prior consent in writing of the other civil partner, purports to convey an interest in the shared home to a person except the other civil partner, then, subject to subsections (2), (3), and (8) to (14) and section 29, the purported conveyance is void."

18–200 Section 28(2) provides that subs.(1) does not apply to a conveyance if it is made by a civil partner in pursuance of an enforceable agreement made before the civil partners' registration of their civil partnership, and subs.(3), similarly to the 1976 Act, provides that a conveyance is not void by reason only of subs.(1) if: (a) it is made to a purchaser for full value; (b) it is made by a person other than the civil partner to a purchaser for value; or (c) its validity depends on the validity of a conveyance in respect of which a condition mentioned in subs.(2) or (a) or (b) above is satisfied.

18–201 "Full value" means "value that amounts or approximates to the value of that for which it is given",[254] as in the 1976 Act, and "purchaser" means a grantee, lessee, assignee, mortgagee, etc. or other person who in good faith acquires an estate or interest in property.[255]

18–202 "Conveyance" has the same meaning as in the 1976 Act and includes a mortgage, lease, assent, transfer, disclaimer, release, etc.[256] It is to be assumed that the case law on the equivalent provisions in the 1976 Act would be applied to s.28 of the CPA 2010.

18–203 "Shared home" has a similar definition to "family home" in the 1976 Act and "dwelling" has a similar definition also.[257]

---

[254] CPA 2010 s.28(5).
[255] CPA 2010 s.28(6).
[256] CPA 2010 s.27.
[257] See CPA 2010 s.27.

Dispensing with Consent

18–204 Under s.29 a court may dispense with the consent on grounds similar to s.4 of the 1976 Act. The court may dispense with the consent if it considers it unreasonable for the civil partner to withhold consent, taking into account all the circumstances,[258] including (a) the respective needs and resources of the civil partners and any dependent children of the civil partners, and (b) in a case where the civil partner whose consent is required is offered alternative accommodation, the suitability of that accommodation having regard to the respective degrees of security of tenure in the shared home and the alternative accommodation.

18–205 What could be described as a glaring and surprising omission is the absence of any requirement that the court consider the needs of any children either of the non-disposing partner or indeed of the disposing partner. The CPA 2010 withholds recognition of civil partnership as constituting a family, but in this case it seems to have gone a step too far in maintaining this position, at the cost of the needs of children. In theory, a court could deem alternative accommodation to be suitable for the non-disposing partner even if it was unsuitable for the rearing of children.[259] Ireland signed the UN Convention on the Rights of the Child on 30 September 1990 and ratified it, without reservation, on 21 September 1992. Article 3 states: "The best interests of children must be the primary concern in making decisions that may affect them. All adults should do what is best for children. When adults make decisions, they should think about how their decisions will affect children. This particularly applies to budget, policy and law makers."

Conduct

18–206 Section 30 deals with conduct leading to loss of a shared home, equivalent to s.5 of the 1976 Act.

COHABITANTS

In General

18–207 Questions also arise as to direct and indirect contributions to the acquisition of property where two people are living together who are not married to each other. Before the CPA 2010 the case law in this area was concerned exclusively with opposite-sex couples living together.

18–208 Where direct contributions are made to the purchase price of property, it has already been seen that a presumed resulting trust arises in equity, regardless of whether the parties are living together in the property or not. Where married partners are living together in the property it has been seen

---

[258] CPA 2010 s.29(2).
[259] Ryan, *Civil Partnership* (2011), para.4.1.4.

that the rules are modified to include indirect contributions. Arguably, this was necessary simply in order to recognise that where parties are living in the same household and sharing expenses the contributions will take a different form from where they are not, but it was certainly the case in the past that the development was also attributed to recognition of marital status and its place within the Constitution.

Before the CPA 2010

18–209 The case law before the CPA 2010 was concerned with opposite-sex cohabitants. If the case law shows any modification of the general position where parties who are not married are living together, it would show that there is some recognition in ordinary law of a "home" or a de facto family.

18–210 In *McGill v Snodgrass*,[260] Gannon J. held:

> "[I]n the case of two persons who are not spouses, evidence of consensus derived from words or conduct and intended to have legal consequences would support a trust expressed or implied or constructive …".[261]

But he did not think that the mere fact of the unmarried couple in this case living together was sufficient to create a trust. In so far as it discriminated against the party concerned, as against all other contributors, this decision appears inconsistent with Art.14, the non-discrimination clause of the ECHR. It also, paradoxically, means that the judge put such relationships in a special category distinct from the ordinary presumed resulting trust situation in equity and to that extent gave some legal recognition to a de facto relationship.

18–211 However, there is an example of the general rule as to resulting trusts being modified in relation to an unmarried couple with a more positive outcome. In *Power v Conroy*,[262] another case involving an unmarried couple, the property was purchased in the male partner's name, while the female partner contributed towards the deposit, the building cost, and the upkeep of the household. McWilliam J. took into account indirect contributions to the acquisition of the property, which arguably went beyond the general presumed resulting trust in equity.

18–212 Indirect contributions are only likely to occur where the property is occupied by the contributor. He did not treat the situation in this respect as different from that of a married couple and the concept of indirect contributions were in fact later recognised in the context of marriage by the Supreme Court in *McC v McC*.[263]

---

[260] Reported sub nom *McGill v S* [1979] I.R. 283.
[261] [1979] I.R. 283 at 289.
[262] [1980] I.L.R.M. 31.
[263] [1986] I.L.R.M. 1.

18–213 One English case has treated labour expended on a house as giving rise to an equity through a constructive trust. In *Cooke v Head*,[264] the defendant man and the plaintiff woman planned to build a bungalow in which they would live. The woman's work on the house consisted of demolishing a building, removing rubble, using a cement mixer and painting. They both saved as much money as they could each week from their earnings. They pooled these savings and used the money to pay off the mortgage. When the bungalow was near completion they separated. The defendant lived in it alone and continued to pay the mortgage. The plaintiff claimed a declaration that the house was owned jointly by them. The Court of Appeal assessed her interest as one-third. Lord Denning M.R. stated that whenever two parties "by their joint efforts acquired property to be used for their joint benefit, the courts may impose or impute a constructive or resulting trust."[265] The judge perhaps regrettably did not clearly define whether this was an example of a presumed resulting trust, or a constructive trust based on evidence of intention. Lord Denning M.R. said that the constructive trust doctrine applied "to husband and wife, to engaged couples, and to a man and mistress, and maybe to other relationships too".[266] The beneficial interest was not to be determined according to the parties' separate contributions but the value of the equity at the time the parties separated and then divided between them as the circumstances merited.

18–214 The English case of *Pascoe v Turner*,[267] dealing with unmarried partners, treated the facts as coming within the doctrine of proprietary estoppel. P, a wealthy man, had told T, a widow with whom he had lived for some years, that the house in which they lived and which he had bought, would be hers together with everything in it. T spent money on repairs and improvements and furniture in reliance on this assurance, to the knowledge of P. The Court of Appeal held that the assurance and the reliance upon it raised an equity which would only be satisfied by P transferring the fee simple to T. The facts of such cases seem to exert a pressure towards adopting different doctrinal approaches to the solution. In *Pascoe*, the facts certainly were highly suggestive of proprietary estoppel and *were* so treated by the court. But where no assurances or acts of reliance upon them are present, judges have tended to look to the constructive trust principle instead. Yet, if the approach in *Power v Conroy*[268] and *Cooke v Head*[269] is adopted it would seem to make reference to proprietary estoppel unnecessary. The presumed resulting trust arises from the situation in which the parties have placed themselves and not upon any specific assurances. If the trust arises, similarly to the case of married partners, in the absence of agreement or understandings to the contrary, this excludes the need to resort to estoppel. The overlap in decisions on proprietary estoppel and constructive

---

[264] [1972] 1 W.L.R. 518.
[265] [1972] 1 W.L.R. 518 at 520.
[266] [1972] 1 W.L.R. 518 at 520.
[267] [1979] 1 W.L.R. 431.
[268] [1980] I.L.R.M. 31.
[269] [1972] 1 W.L.R. 518.

trusts in these cases may indicate that judges find proprietary estoppel a more satisfactory basis where the facts justify such an inference, but where they do not, the constructive trust provides a concept of next, if not last, resort.[270]

The CPA 2010
Cohabitant
Definition

18–215 Part 15 of the CPA 2010 deals with the rights of cohabitants. Since the provisions are intended to deal with a de facto situation, there is no requirement that the relationship between cohabitants be registered. In fact, Pt 15 deals with the relationship of cohabitation insofar as it qualifies an *individual* as a cohabitant within Pt 15. It is for the court to decide on the facts whether a person is a cohabitant within Pt 15.

18–216 A cohabitant is defined in s.172 as

> "one of two adults (whether of the same or the opposite sex) who live together as a couple in an intimate and committed relationship and who are not related to each other within the prohibited degrees of relationship[271] or married to each other or civil partners of each other."

18–217 Thus, a person cannot be a "cohabitant" within s.172 if the two parties concerned are married to or in a civil partnership with each other.[272] But a person can be a "cohabitant" within s.172 even if he or she is married to a third party or in a civil partnership with a third party,[273] but is not a "qualified cohabitant" for the purposes of Pt 15.

Intimate and Committed Relationship

18–218 Since "intimate and committed relationship" is not a precise definition, s.172(2) provides that in determining whether or not two adults are cohabitants, the court is to take into account "all the circumstances of the relationship" and in particular:

---

[270] The English case of *Grant v Edwards* [1986] 2 All E.R. 426 seems to express this uncertainty in attempting to straddle both concepts.

[271] They are within the prohibited degrees if they would be prohibited from marrying each other in the State or their relationship is one of those set out in the Civil Registration Act 2004 Sch.3, inserted by CPA 2010 s.26; CPA 2010 s.172(4).

[272] Since in that case their mutual rights and obligations will be governed by that relationship.

[273] Since Pt 15 includes within its scope the situation where a married person or civil partner has left their spouse or civil partner and entered a relationship with another party.

"(a) the duration of the relationship;
(b) the basis on which the couple live together;
(c) the degree of financial dependence of either adult on the other and any agreements in respect of their finances;
(d) the degree and nature of any financial arrangements between the adults including any joint purchase of an estate or interest in land or joint acquisition of personal property;
(e) whether there are one or more dependent children;
(f) whether one of the adults cares for and supports the children of the other; and
(g) the degree to which the adults present themselves to others as a couple."

18–219 These seven factors are not to be considered as conclusive as to the nature of a relationship, but rather as indicative of the nature of the relationship.[274] Baker J. in *DC v DR*[275] points out that the statutory test for an "intimate and committed relationship" is broad, and that "[t]he basis of a relationship involves a number of interconnected elements such as the degree of shared activities that persons enjoy, such as shared meals, especially evening meals and breakfast, shared activities, shared division of household chores and shared holidays."[276] The various "indices of the relationship and the public presentation of that relationship" ought to be considered "as a whole and in the context of the social mores and perhaps even the age of the participants in the relationship".[277]

18–220 According to Baker J., "intimacy" requires that "a relationship must have been at some point in time a sexual relationship".[278] She adds that "the intimacy that is intended is a sexual intimacy and not merely the intimacy of close friendship."[279] Section 172(3) provides that "[f]or the avoidance of doubt a relationship does not cease to be an intimate relationship for the purpose of this section merely because it is no longer sexual in nature". The CPA 2010 therefore seems to assume that co-habitation originated in a sexual relationship, but does not apply a test other than the existence of an "intimate and committed relationship".

18–221 In assessing whether the couple were in a "committed" relationship, the court will have regard to the degree to which the couple presented themselves to others as a couple. However, this is not limited to, for example, "expressions of physical affection in public".[280]

---

[274] *DC v DR* [2016] 1 I.L.R.M. 178.
[275] [2016] 1 I.L.R.M. 178.
[276] [2016] 1 I.L.R.M. 178 at 202.
[277] [2016] 1 I.L.R.M. 178 at 205.
[278] [2016] 1 I.L.R.M. 178 at 198.
[279] [2016] 1 I.L.R.M. 178 at 198.
[280] [2016] 1 I.L.R.M. 178 at 202.

18–222 Cohabitants as such (apart from qualified cohabitants under Pt 15) have certain limited rights, such as the right to sue for wrongful death of a deceased cohabitant, the right to succeed to a statutory protected residential tenancy,[281] and the right to various orders, including a barring or safety order under the Domestic Violence Act 1996.[282]

Cohabitants' Agreement

18–223 Under s.202 of the CPA 2010, "notwithstanding any enactment or rule of law", cohabitants may enter into a cohabitants' agreement to provide for financial matters during the relationship or when the relationship ends, whether through death or otherwise. It is only valid if the cohabitants have each received independent legal advice before entering into it, or have received legal advice together and have waived in writing the right to independent legal advice, and the agreement is in writing and signed by both cohabitants, and it complies with the general law of contract.

18–224 Under s.202(3), subject to subs.(4), a cohabitants' agreement may provide that neither cohabitant may apply for an order for redress referred to in s.173, or an order for provision from the estate of his or her cohabitant under s.194. Under subs.(4) the court may vary or set aside a cohabitants' agreement in exceptional circumstances, where its enforceability would cause serious injustice. Subsection (5) provides that an agreement that meets the other criteria of the section shall be deemed to be a cohabitants' agreement under the section even if it was entered into before the cohabitation began.

Qualified Cohabitant

18–225 In order to apply for relief under the CPA 2010, a cohabitant has to satisfy the tests of a "qualified cohabitant" which means an adult who was in a relationship of cohabitation with another adult and who, immediately before the time that that relationship ended, whether through death or otherwise, was living with the other adult as a couple for a period:

"(a) of 2 years or more, in the case where they are the parents of one or more dependent children, and

(b) of 5 years or more, in any other case."[283]

18–226 An adult who would otherwise be a qualified cohabitant is not a qualified cohabitant if

---

[281] CPA 2010 s.203, amending Residential Tenancies Act 2004 s.39(3)(a)(ii).
[282] CPA 2010 Pt 9.
[283] CPA 2010 s.172(5).

"(a) one or both of the adults is or was, at any time during the relationship concerned, an adult who was married to someone else, and

(b) at the time the relationship concerned ends, each adult who is or was married has not lived apart from his or her spouse for a period or periods of at least 4 years during the previous 5 years."[284]

These provisions evidently aim to protect the marriage relationship. A court cannot grant an order in respect of a cohabitant which would affect the right of a person to whom either cohabitant is or was married.[285] There is no such qualification in relation to a person who is a civil partner of a cohabitant.

Succession

18–227 Under s.194 a qualified cohabitant may, after the death of his or her cohabitant but not more than six months after representation is first granted under the Succession Act 1965 in respect of that cohabitant's estate, apply for an order under this section for provision out of the net estate. In considering such an application in the case of *DC v DR*,[286] the High Court considered the jurisprudence under s.117 of the Succession Act 1965 to be helpful, because the CPA 2010 forms part of "the nexus of family and succession legislation".[287]

18–228 There are restrictions on the right to apply for provision, and the test in s.194 is different from the test in s.117 of the Succession Act 1965. The right to make a claim under s.194 is not founded on the mere fact of the relationship between the applicant and the deceased, as is the case with an application under s.117. A qualified cohabitant shall not apply for an order under this section where the relationship concerned ended two years or more before the death of the deceased, unless the applicant (a) was in receipt of periodical payments from the deceased, or (b) had, not later than two years after that relationship ended, made an application for an order under other provisions of the CPA 2010 and the proceedings were pending or the order had not yet been executed.[288]

Qualified Financially Dependent Cohabitant

18–229 A qualified cohabitant may apply for one or more of the several orders under Pt 15 of the CPA 2010.[289] Some orders may only be made in favour of financially dependent cohabitants, and so there is a third category of cohabitant: the qualified financially dependent cohabitant (QFDC). A cohabitant who claims to be financially dependent on the other cohabitant has to satisfy the tests in s.173(3).

---

[284] CPA 2010 s.172(6).

[285] Ryan, *Civil Partnership* (2011), para.7.7.

[286] [2016] 1 I.L.R.M. 178.

[287] [2016] 1 I.L.R.M. 178 at 211.

[288] CPA 2010 s.194(2).

[289] CPA 2010 s.173(1).

18–230 A QFDC is most likely to qualify as financially dependent if he or she has no career or earned income of his or her own and adopts the role of homemaker.

Orders
18–231 On being satisfied of the financial dependence of a cohabitant, the court may grant one or more of the several orders specified in ss.174, 175 and 187.

Just and Equitable Test
18–232 In determining whether or not it is just and equitable to make an order in all the circumstances, the court shall have regard to[290]:

"(a) the financial circumstances, needs and obligations of each qualified cohabitant existing as at the date of the application or which are likely to arise in the future,

(b) subject to subsection (5), the rights and entitlements of any spouse or former spouse,

(c) the rights and entitlements of any civil partner or former civil partner,

(d) the rights and entitlements of any dependent child or of any child of a previous relationship of either cohabitant,

(e) the duration of the parties' relationship, the basis on which the parties entered into the relationship and the degree of commitment of the parties to one another,

(f) the contributions that each of the cohabitants made or is likely to make in the foreseeable future to the welfare of the cohabitants or either of them including any contribution made by each of them to the income, earning capacity or property and financial resources of the other,

(g) any contributions made by either of them in looking after the home,

(h) the effect on the earning capacity of each of the cohabitants of the responsibilities assumed by each of them during the period they lived together as a couple and the degree to which the future earning capacity of a qualified cohabitant is impaired by reason of that qualified cohabitant having relinquished or foregone the opportunity of remunerative activity in order to look after the home,

(i) any physical or mental disability of the qualified cohabitant, and

(j) the conduct of each of the cohabitants, if the conduct is such that, in the court's opinion, it would be unjust to disregard it."

The Orders
18–233 The orders include property adjustment orders requiring[291]:

---

[290] CPA 2010 s.173(3).
[291] CPA 2010 s.174.

"(a) the transfer by either of the cohabitants to or for the benefit of the other, of specified property in which the cohabitant has an interest either in possession or reversion;

(b) the settlement of specified property in which the cohabitant has an interest either in possession or reversion, for the benefit of the other cohabitant or of a dependent child;

(c) the variation for the benefit of either of the cohabitants or of a dependent child of a cohabitants' agreement, section 202 ... or another settlement (including one made by will or codicil) made on the cohabitants; and

(d) the extinguishment or reduction of the interest of either of the cohabitants under [a cohabitants' agreement]."

Variation
18–234 The court may also vary, suspend either temporarily or permanently, revive a suspended order, or further vary an already varied order.[292]

ENGAGED COUPLES

18–235 The Family Law Act 1981[293] introduced certain changes in the law as to engaged couples. This has not been expressly amended by the Marriage Act 2015, which introduced same-sex marriage. However, it is to be presumed that the provisions described below apply equally to all engaged couples.

18–236 Section 3 provides that where two people have agreed to marry one another and any property is given as a wedding gift to either or both of them by any other person, it is presumed, in the absence of evidence to the contrary, that the property is given to both of them as joint owners and subject to the condition that it will be returned at the request of the donor or his or her personal representative if the marriage does not take place "for whatever reason". There is one obvious difficulty in interpreting this section. It creates a presumption of joint ownership where property is given to "either or both" of the parties to the engagement, subject to evidence to the contrary, and yet if property was given to one of them, rather than both jointly, that in itself would seem to constitute evidence that it was not intended that they be joint owners.

18–237 Section 4 deals with gifts from one engaged person to another. It is presumed, subject to evidence to the contrary, that gifts are subject to the condition that they will be returned at the request of the donor or his or her personal representative if the marriage does not take place for any reason other than the death of the donor.

---

[292] CPA 2010 s.173(6).
[293] As amended by s.48 of the Family Law Act 1995.

18–238 Section 3 applies to "any property" and therefore includes land and buildings attached to land. Section 4 does not include the phrase "any property" and so it could be argued that the omission is deliberate and that the section only refers to personal property, such as engagement rings, which is commonly the type of gifts given by one engaged person to another. On the other hand, land is not excluded, and "gift" is apt to include it. If land is within the section, then there would seem to be some overlap with the provisions of s.5.

18–239 Section 5 is a general provision applying where the agreement to marry is terminated. It says that the rules relating to the rights of spouses relating to property in which either or both of them has or have a beneficial interest shall apply to any property, in which either or both of the parties to the agreement had a beneficial interest, while the agreement was in force in the same way as they apply to property in which spouses have a beneficial interest.[294] This provision clearly seems to apply to engaged couples the law as to direct and indirect contributions by one spouse to the acquisition of property held in the other spouse's name. Thus, where a house is being purchased on mortgage by one party to an engagement, the other may acquire an equitable interest in it as tenant in common by contributions. Unlike gifts given to the couple by a third party, there is no presumption of joint tenancy in equity. The contributions may be included in a later assessment after the marriage has taken place, and even if the engagement is called off, a claim to an equity would still be possible, since there is no equivalent provision in this section to the conditions presumed in ss.3 and 4.

---

[294] Section 48 of the Family Law Act 1995 declares that s.5 of the 1981 Act does not apply to rights of spouses under the Succession Act 1965, the Family Home Protection Act 1976, the Judicial Separation and Family Law Reform Act 1989 or the Family Law Act 1995.

CHAPTER 19

Licences, Estoppel and Constructive Trusts

Past events provide context and background for the interpretation of subsequent events and subsequent events throw retrospective light upon the meaning of past events. The owl of Minerva spreads its wings only with the falling of the dusk.

— Lord Hoffmann in *Thorner v Major* [2009] 1 W.L.R. 777 at para.8

INTRODUCTION

19–01 A licence is a form of permission granted by the owner of an interest in land to a person to enter or enjoy the land in some way. Licences arise in many contexts and some of the complexity in the law of licences derives from the multiplicity of uses to which the licence concept is put. Licences are frequently encountered in commercial relationships, often as a supplement or even as an alternative to the relationship of landlord and tenant. Licences also arise in relation to domestic relationships. Judges have also used the concepts of proprietary estoppel and constructive trusts to resolve issues in this area. It is therefore appropriate to deal with these three concepts in the same chapter.

LICENCES

19–02 The common law has jealously guarded, as a fundamental liberty, the right of a private owner to determine who may or may not enter his or her land.[1] This has been not only to prevent private intrusions but also those by the State.[1] In *Entick v Carrington*[2] in 1765 Lord Camden C.J. observed that "[b]y the laws of England every invasion of land, be it ever so minute, is a trespass. No man can set his foot upon my ground without my licence."

19–03 A licence, at its simplest, is a permission given by an owner of an interest in land to another person to enter his or her land, which entry would

---

[1] As Coke C.J. said in *Semayne's Case* (1604) 5 Co. Rep. 91a, "[t]he house of every one is his castle ... It is not lawful for the sheriff ... at the suit of a common person, to break the defendant's house ... to execute any process at the suit of a subject."

[2] (1765) 19 St. Tr. 1029 at 1066: "Our law holds the property of every man so sacred, that no man can set his foot upon his neighbour's close without his leave; if he does he is a trespasser, though he does no damage at all."

otherwise be a trespass. The definition given by Vaughan C.J. in *Thomas v Sorrell* in 1674[3] is frequently quoted as the classic formulation: "A dispensation or licence properly passeth no interest nor alters or transfers property in any thing, but only makes an action lawful, which without it had been unlawful."[4] This formulation, handed down prior to the Judicature Act, is now heavily qualified.

Bare Licence
Private Land
19–04 A licence may be "bare", i.e. not supported by consideration, or not intended to give rise to legal relations, such as an invitation to dinner. There is no contract and thus there is nothing to prevent such a licence being revoked or its terms being altered at will by the licensor. Apart from contract, however, courts have been prepared to hold that a licence cannot be revoked so as to leave the licensee with no opportunity to avoid committing a trespass. Thus even a gratuitous licence granted by A to allow B to cross A's field cannot be revoked while B is still part of the way across.[5] Expenditure in reliance on a licence can render it irrevocable[6] or possibly only revocable if the licensor can put the party in the position he or she was in before the licence was entered into.[7] Some such situations may today be indistinguishable from proprietary estoppel giving rise to an enforceable licence, but at least one Irish case has held such licences to be irrevocable at common law.[8] Since proprietary estoppel is now capable of giving rise to legal interests, the distinction is of little importance.

19–05 The law also recognises implied licences to enter property on routine business. Thus, members of the public, including members of An Garda Síochána, benefit from an implied licence to enter premises, including dwelling houses, from the front gate or entrance up to the front or back door on legitimate business. Implied licences of this kind can be revoked at will by a clear indication of the occupier's intent.[9] Mere vulgar abuse may not be sufficient for this purpose.[10]

---

[3] (1674) Vaugh. 330.
[4] (1674) Vaugh. 330 at 351.
[5] *McDonald v Bord na gCon* [1965] I.R. 217 (HC).
[6] *Armstrong v Sheppard & Short Ltd* [1959] 2 All E.R. 651; *Blood v Keller* (1861) 11 Ir. C.L.R. 124.
[7] *Blood v Keller* (1861) 11 Ir. C.L.R. 124.
[8] *Blood v Keller* (1861) 11 Ir. C.L.R. 124.
[9] *Lambert v Roberts* [1981] 2 All E.R. 15.
[10] *Snook v Mannion* [1982] Crim L.R. 601 (police pursued a motorist into his driveway; the police officers were told to "f**k off", and it was held to be a matter for magistrates to decide in all the circumstances whether the licence had been revoked); *Gilham v Breidenbach* [1982] R.T.R. 328 (Justices are entitled to interpret the phrase "f**k off you planks" to police officers as coarse abuse, rather than as a request to leave premises). See also, *Lambert v Roberts* [1981] 2 All E.R. 15 and *Robson v Hallet* [1967] 2 Q.B. 939.

Quasi-Public Space

19–06 It has been argued that there is now a new type of land use called "quasi-public space".[11] Shopping centres, leisure centres and sporting grounds, for example, are generally open to the public, and indeed the public are invited in the interests of the owners. Can it be said that the owner's right to terminate a person's licence to enter cannot be exercised arbitrarily, but is subject to a test of "reasonable behaviour" or some such test?[12] English courts have refused so far to recognise this, although some courts in the United States have. The trend over recent years in Europe has been that many town centres are increasingly dominated by shopping centres owned by private companies. The refusal to recognise this as a significant social development and develop the law in response to it would constitute a serious restriction on civil liberty. The extension of a law developed in the past in the context of private houses and land to the new context of quasi-public spaces cannot be justified as judicial caution. New uses of land require a rethinking of traditional legal institutions. Although in their original context they protect civil liberties, when extended to quasi-public areas they actually threaten other civil liberties which are equally important to protect.

19–07 In *CIN Properties Ltd v Rawlins*,[13] the owner of a shopping centre in a town excluded a group of unemployed teenagers. He alleged that they constituted a nuisance. Criminal prosecutions failed. The youths then sued for an injunction to prevent the owner excluding them. The High Court granted the injunction. The judge recognised the quasi-public nature of the space. He held that the owner could only withdraw the licence if the youths' behaviour was unreasonable. The shopping centre was a main amenity in their home town.

19–08 The English Court of Appeal considered the case against the background of the law at the time (the case predates the UK Human Rights Act 1998) and took account of the fact that the UK had not ratified Protocol 4 to the European Convention on Human Rights (ECHR), guaranteeing freedom of movement, because of anti-terrorism legislation. The court held that as the shopping centre was private property, the owner had an absolute right to withdraw the implied licence to the public without giving reasons. Balcombe L.J., however, observed that there might come a time for change in law but that it was a matter for Parliament. Further leave to appeal was refused. This potentially meant that the youths could be made the subject of a lifelong ban.

---

[11] K. Gray and S. Gray, "Civil Rights, Civil Wrongs and Quasi-Public Space" [1999] E.H.R.L.R. 46. In sociological literature, these are often referred to as "third places".

[12] See K. Gray and S.F. Gray, *Land Law*, 7th edn (Oxford: Oxford University Press, 2011), paras 10-028–10-031; K. Gray and S. Gray, "Civil Rights, Civil Wrongs and Quasi-Public Space" [1999] E.H.R.L.R. 46; K. Gray and S.F. Gray, *Elements of Land Law*, 5th edn (Oxford: Oxford University Press, 2009), para.10.6.10.

[13] [1995] 2 E.G.L.R. 130. N. Roberts, "Access to Quasi-Public Spaces – Whose Visitor?" [2007] Conv. 235, presents an alternative analysis of the case, arguing that applying the law of easements to the facts in this case might result in a de facto acceptance of a right of access to quasi-public spaces in English property law.

Balcombe L.J. pointed out that if the local authority had entered into a "walk-ways" agreement with the company, i.e. created public rights of way within the shopping centre, then the teenagers might have had rights under byelaws regulating their use. No such agreement had been reached. The shopping centre owners were also subject to race relations legislation in making the decisions to exclude persons from access to the centre.

19–09 The teenagers then brought a case before the European Commission of Human Rights.[14] It again refused relief. The Commission declined to develop the ECHR case law which it noted had not, to date, indicated that freedom of assembly "is intended to guarantee a right to pass and re-pass in public places, or to assemble for purely social purposes anywhere one wishes". The Commission also held there had been no infringement of freedom of assembly or association, on the ground that it comprised, in the Commission's view, only a right for individuals to associate "in order to attain various ends". The Commission noted that the applicants had "no history of using the [Swansgate] Centre for any form of organised assembly or association", although it added a broad hint that the applicants' case might have been more appropriately presented as an alleged violation of liberty of movement within the territory of a State.

19–10 The notion of quasi-public space also has implications for rights to freedom of speech and freedom of assembly. In *Appleby v UK*,[15] the applicants had set up stalls at the entrance to a town centre owned by a private company, but which had originally been built by a government agency and funded in part by public money. A local college had obtained outline planning permission to build on an open area, a playing field, near the centre. The applicants had formed a protest group to bring to the attention of local residents the impending loss of amenity. They were told to remove the stalls by the company. The ECtHR held that owners can exclude campaigners, but held that States may have to modify property law where the bar on access to land has the effect of preventing any effective exercise of freedoms of expression, assembly and association, e.g. in a "company town". Maruste J. delivered a strong dissenting judgment. The judge observed that the area "in its functional nature and essence is a *'forum publicum* or quasi-public' space." It was "a new creation where public interests and money were and still are involved". In his view, "the situation [was] clearly distinguishable from the 'my home is my castle' type of situation". The judge continued[16]:

"It is in the public interest to permit reasonable exercise of individual rights and freedoms, including the freedoms of speech and assembly on the property of a privately-owned shopping centre, and not to make some

---

[14] *Anderson v UK* [1998] E.H.R.L.R. 218.
[15] (2003) 37 E.H.R.R. 783.
[16] (2003) 37 E.H.R.R. 783 at 797.

public services and institutions inaccessible to the public and participants in demonstrations."

19–11 In *Browne v Dundalk Urban District Council*,[17] the council had agreed to hire a hall to Sinn Féin for its annual conference. The council later passed a resolution to prevent it because Sinn Féin at the time supported violence. Members of Sinn Féin brought judicial review proceedings to quash the council's resolution. O'Hanlon J. in the High Court held that the council had entered into a valid and binding contract to hire the hall. Such a contract would not ordinarily be subject to judicial review, but the court was satisfied that the council's resolution, which had procured a breach of contract, was politically motivated and constituted a reviewable exercise of public power. The court did not consider *CIN* or the related cases, preferring to focus on the fact that the council's resolution had procured a breach of contract. It held that the applicant was entitled to enforce the contract by judicial review and made orders quashing the resolution and restraining the council from frustrating or otherwise refusing to fulfil the contract.

Licence Coupled with an Interest

19–12 When an interest such as a *profit à prendre* is granted (for example, the right to extract minerals from land, or to hunt or fish on it), a licence to enter and remain in the land for the purpose of giving effect to the rights granted is normally granted at the same time. It has long been recognised that such a licence is irrevocable while the property right to which it attached continues in being.

19–13 In *Woods v Donnelly*,[18] an agreement provided that the defendant was to have the right to "draw sand and gravel … as long as he requires it". It was also specified that "James Donnelly only … is hereby authorised" and that he was to make full and prompt payment for the sand and gravel each month. Hutton J. in the Northern Ireland Chancery Division held, inter alia, that the licence was not revocable except in accordance with the contract. The court further held that the agreement was a licence coupled with an interest, namely a *profit à prendre*, which together were valid for the life of the defendant, so that they could not be revoked during that life. But the right was expressly limited to the defendant and so would not pass to his personal representatives after his death.

Contractual Licences

19–14 The history of contractual licences is made difficult by procedural fallacies and by the generally well-founded reluctance of most judges to allow

---

[17] [1993] 2 I.R. 512.
[18] [1982] N.I. 257.

individuals to create burdens that would affect future owners of land at will and without restraint of any kind.

19–15 It has never been in doubt that A can make a contract with B, whereby A gives B the right to enter and remain on A's land for a certain period. What has given rise to confusion in the past are the circumstances in which such an arrangement ceases to be simply a matter of contract and becomes a property right.[19]

19–16 Traditionally, the English courts took the view that a contractual licence was not an interest in land and as such was revocable at will.[20] The courts initially took the position that the landowner had a right of revocation even where doing so amounted to a breach of contract.[21] In part, this position was driven by procedural concerns—prior to the Common Law Procedure Amendment Act (Ireland) 1856 common law courts had no power to grant injunctions and thus there was no common law mechanism to enforce a contractual licence. Following the procedural reforms of the 1850s, Irish courts did show a willingness to prevent the revocation of contractual licences, at least in some circumstances.[22]

19–17 The absurdity of the traditional position was illustrated by *Hurst v Picture Theatres Ltd*.[23] The plaintiff had paid for a cinema ticket which he surrendered to the usher upon entering the auditorium. The plaintiff was wrongly accused of having entered without paying and was forcibly ejected during the performance. Since a breach of contract action could not have obtained more than the price of the ticket in damages, the plaintiff sued for assault and battery, arguing that his ejection had been unlawful since purchasing a ticket had conferred on him a licence to remain in the auditorium during the performance. The Court of Appeal held that there was an implied term in the contract that the plaintiff would not be ejected until the performance had concluded. The licence was said to be founded on the contract and the court held that the plaintiff had no property right in the land itself. In *Winter Garden Theatre (London) Ltd v Millennium Productions Ltd*,[24] Greene M.R. in the Court of Appeal confirmed

---

[19] The development of these themes through case law has been considered at length in earlier editions of this work: *Atkinson v King* (1878) 2 L.R. Ir. 320; *Blood v Keller* (1861) 11 Ir. C.L.R. 124; *Hurst v Picture Theatres Ltd* [1915] 1 K.B. 1; *Winter Garden Theatre (London) Ltd v Millennium Productions Ltd* [1948] A.C. 173; *London Borough of Hounslow v Twickenham Garden Developments Ltd* [1971] Ch. 233; *Woods v Donnelly* [1982] N.I. 257; *Gale v First National Building Society* [1985] I.R. 609.

[20] *Wood v Leadbitter* (1845) 13 M. & W. 838; *Atkinson v King* (1878) 2 L.R. Ir. 320.

[21] *Hurst v Picture Theatres Ltd* [1915] 1 K.B. 1.

[22] *Blood v Keller* (1861) 11 Ir. C.L.R. 124, though see also *Smith v Earl of Howth* (1861) 10 Ir. C.L.R. 125.

[23] [1915] 1 K.B. 1.

[24] [1946] 1 All E.R. 678. The House of Lords reversed the Court of Appeal decision on the interpretation of the terms of the licence but the principle was left intact: [1948] A.C. 173. See also, *London Borough of Hounslow v Twickenham Garden Developments Ltd* [1971] Ch. 233.

that an injunction can be obtained to restrain a breach of contract where a contractual licence is revoked in breach of its terms.

19–18 The effect of licences on third parties has also proved controversial. The traditional position was set out by the House of Lords in an Irish appeal in *King v David Allen and Sons (Billposting) Ltd.*[25] In July 1913, the parties agreed that David Allen would have an exclusive licence to erect advertising boards on the side of a cinema which King was proposing to develop on the site. A company was incorporated to undertake the development and operation of the cinema and King granted a lease of the land to a trustee for the company. The lease made no mention of the licence which had been granted to David Allen. The House of Lords held that the licence did not bind the company and that the contract created nothing more than a personal obligation on King which he had, in breach of that contract, rendered himself unable to perform. A number of other decisions from this period illustrate a similar approach to the third party effect of licences.[26]

19–19 In *Errington v Errington and Wood*,[27] Denning M.R. suggested that the licences might have a broader effect. The plaintiff's husband had purchased a house in his own name for his son and daughter-in-law with the aid of a mortgage from a building society. The plaintiff's husband agreed that his son and daughter-in-law could live in the house so long as they paid the mortgage instalments and that when the mortgage was fully repaid the house would be theirs. The husband died and the house passed to the plaintiff under his will. Later the son's marriage broke down and he left the house. The plaintiff then sought to revoke the defendants' licence, claiming that it was revocable at will.

19–20 Denning M.R. advanced a bold theory that the effect of the fusion of law and equity under the Judicature Acts was to convert contractual licences into a form of equitable interest in land:

> "This infusion of equity means that contractual licences now have a force and validity of their own and cannot be revoked in breach of the contract. Neither the licensor *nor anyone who claims through him* can disregard the contract except a purchaser for value without notice."[28]

19–21 While the outcome of Denning M.R.'s judgment is no doubt a just one, it cannot be reconciled with *King v David Allen and Sons Billposting Ltd.*[29]

---

[25] [1916] 2 A.C. 54.
[26] *Daly v Edwardes* (1900) 83 L.T. 548; *Frank Warr & Co Ltd v London County Council* [1904] 1 K.B. 713; *Clore v Theatrical Properties Ltd* [1936] 3 All E.R. 483 at 491.
[27] [1952] 1 K.B. 290.
[28] [1952] 1 K.B. 290 at 299 (emphasis added).
[29] [1916] 2 A.C. 54.

It must also be acknowledged that the same result could have been achieved using any one of a range of narrower (and more conventional) grounds.[30]

19–22 In *Binions v Evans*,[31] the English Court of Appeal considered the revocation of a licence granted to an elderly widow which permitted her to remain in her late husband's cottage for her lifetime. The land upon which the cottage stood had been sold by the original licensor to a third party who took with notice of the licence and who paid a reduced price for the cottage in consequence. Denning M.R. held that by taking a conveyance of the land, with notice of and expressly subject to the rights of the widow, the purchaser was bound in equity not to interfere with the widow's rights. He thus imposed a constructive trust on the purchaser.

19–23 In *Ashburn Anstalt v Arnold*,[32] the English Court of Appeal sought to return to the earlier notion of equity acting on the conscience of the third party. The court held: (a) that a contractual licence would not, without more, be binding on a third party even though he or she took with notice of it; but (b) that appropriate facts might give rise to a constructive trust. Irish courts have not adopted the *Errington* approach, and such cases are likely to be resolved using the doctrines of estoppel or constructive trusts.

Domestic Arrangements
19–24 The concept of licence has frequently been invoked in order to characterise domestic arrangements when it is clear that the parties did not consider what legal rights would exist or did not consider what rights would exist in the circumstances which subsequently arose. Courts have sometimes found difficulty in such cases in defining when such a licence may be terminated or revoked.[33]

RIGHTS OF RESIDENCE

Nature of the Right
19–25 A right of residence is a right peculiar to Irish land law and consists of a personal right[34] to occupy a house or a room or rooms in a house and often includes also the right of support or maintenance out of the profits of the land,

---

[30] Including a purchaser's equity (*National Provincial Bank v Ainsworth* [1965] A.C. 1175 at 1239), or proprietary estoppel (*Re Basham* [1986] 1 W.L.R. 1498; *Smyth v Halpin* [1997] I.L.R.M. 38).

[31] [1972] 1 Ch. 359.

[32] [1989] Ch. 1.

[33] See, e.g. *Tanner v Tanner* [1975] 1 W.L.R. 1346; *Chandler v Kerley* [1978] 1 W.L.R. 693.

[34] The Court of Appeal in *Bank of Ireland v O'Donnell* [2016] IECA 227 confirmed that a right of residence is a personal right.

by provision of food, fuel or other products.[35] Nevertheless, the nature of the right is still in some doubt as the case law is somewhat vague and inconclusive on the subject.

19–26 The Land and Conveyancing Law Reform Act 2009 ("LCLRA 2009") provides that the only freehold legal estate in land which may be created or disposed of is a fee simple in possession and that includes a fee simple "subject only to a right of residence which is not an exclusive right over the whole land".[36] The nature of a right of residence will now be examined in the light of case law.

Special and General Rights
19–27 Kennedy C.J. in the Supreme Court in *National Bank v Keegan*[37] described the right as follows:

"The residential rights, which are so commonly given in farm holdings in this country, especially by way of testamentary provision for testator's widows, also frequently by the reservations to parents of rights in settlements made on the marriage of sons, are of two types, namely, the type which is a general right of residence charged on the holding usually coupled with a charge of maintenance; and the type which is a particular right of residence created by reserving or giving the right to the exclusive use during life of a specified room or rooms in the dwelling-house on the holding. The general right of residence charged on a holding is a right capable of being valued in moneys numbered at an annual sum, and of being represented by an annuity or money charge."[38]

19–28 The judge went on to hold that the instrument in the present case created the special type of interest and further held that it amounted to a life estate, apparently in the specified part of the land. If this distinction between a general and a special right of residence is correct, then the two forms are really quite different. The special right would then not be a distinct interest in land at all, but merely a method of granting a life estate.

19–29 In *Lahiffe v Hecker*,[39] Lynch J. held that the holder of a right of residence in a house was entitled to choose one of the three bedrooms in the house for her exclusive use, "to enable her properly to enjoy her general right of residence in the house". The judge nevertheless treated it as a general right in that he held that it was not a life estate, did not confer the powers of a tenant for

---

[35] B.W. Harvey, "Irish Rights of Residence—The Anatomy of a Hermaphrodite" (1970) 21 N.I.L.Q. 389 at 391.
[36] LCLRA 2009 s.11(2)(c)(iii).
[37] [1931] I.R. 344.
[38] [1931] I.R. 344 at 354.
[39] Unreported, High Court, Lynch J., 28 April 1994.

life under the Settled Land Acts 1882–1890 on the holder, and did not inhibit the power of the court to order a sale.

Rights of Maintenance

19–30 The right or "charge" of maintenance has often taken eccentric forms. Among the things to be provided have been "the grass of a donkey wet and dry on the said lands and stabling therefor",[40] "a quart of new milk daily, one quart of sour milk daily, two eggs daily, a pound of butter weekly, 10 horse rails of turf annually to be cut saved and delivered by my son, ten pecks of good table potatoes yearly",[41] etc.

19–31 It would come naturally to someone living in the largely subsistence economy of rural Ireland to express an amount needed to maintain a person in use values, i.e. in actual produce with its useful qualities, rather than in exchange value, i.e. money. The advantage of use value as an expression is that it need not be "index-linked": a pound of butter remains a pound of butter no matter what happens to prices. But in other cases, the right of maintenance was subordinate to the right of residence and there is a dominant intent to give the donee the right to reside on that particular piece of land, usually for the rest of his or her life. This may be particularly so where the donee is elderly and has already lived in the house for many years. The intention is to secure his or her residence in a familiar house and to give effect to his or her evident reluctance to move.

19–32 It may be noticed that Kennedy C.J. in *National Bank v Keegan*[42] suggests that a right of maintenance is only granted with a general right of residence and not a special one. This is far from being established.

Money Charge or Right to Reside?

19–33 The implication of Kennedy C.J.'s judgment in *National Bank v Keegan* is that the special type, unlike the general right, is not a money charge on the land but amounts to a life estate.

19–34 The view that there is some distinction between the general and special right is now backed by statutory authority, since it has found its way into s.40 of the Statute of Limitations 1957:

"An action in respect of a right in the nature of a lien for money's worth in or over land for a limited period not exceeding life, such as a right of support or a right of residence, not being an exclusive right of residence in or on a

---

[40] B.W. Harvey, "Irish Rights of Residence—The Anatomy of a Hermaphrodite" (1970) 21 N.I.L.Q. 389 at 391.

[41] B.W. Harvey, "Irish Rights of Residence—The Anatomy of a Hermaphrodite" (1970) 21 N.I.L.Q. 389 at 391.

[42] [1931] I.R. 344.

specified part of the land, shall not be brought after the expiration of twelve years from the date on which the right of action accrued."

19–35 If the special right of residence was in effect a life estate it would have given rise to some awkward, even absurd, results and ones which would not accord with the donor's intention. If the grant was contained in an "instrument" it fell within the Settled Land Acts 1882–1890 and it would have conferred on the recipient the powers under the Acts, including the power to convey the fee simple. The life estate itself would have been overreached by a sale by the donee under the Acts: it would have been converted into a life interest in the capital produced in the unlikely event of a sale. If, as appears to be the case, the life estate was only over the specified room or rooms in the house, then the donee would have had the right to sell the fee simple in those rooms separately from the rest of the house. Under the LCLRA 2009 it would create an equitable life estate under a trust of land, the power of sale being vested in the trustees. However, s.11(2)(c)(iii) of the LCLRA 2009 contemplates that a right of residence over part of the land can, or does, exist as a legal interest attached to the legal fee simple.

19–36 Some grants of rights of residence specify that it is to be a charge while others do not. It is not clear whether these different formulations express two different forms of the right or not. Some judicial statements, such as Kennedy C.J. in *National Bank v Keegan*,[43] suggest that a general right of residence is a mere charge, while a "particular" or special right of residence is not. There is also authority for the view that the court has a *discretion* whether to convert the right to reside in the house into a money charge, or interpret it to be one ab initio. Johnson J. in the High Court in *National Bank v Keegan* considered a voluntary promise in writing to grant to the defendant "during her life the exclusive use of the drawing room and the bedroom … with fuel and support and maintenance" of property in County Westmeath. The judge said[44]:

> "It is well settled that a general right of residence and support in a house or upon a farm does not amount to an estate in the land, but is a mere charge in the nature of an annuity upon the premises in respect of which it exists and when it becomes necessary to sell such property a Court of Equity has power and authority to ascertain the value of such charge, so that the purchaser may get the property discharged from the burden."

19–37 *Ryan v Ryan*[45] was the first Irish case on the right. The testator's will contained the statement: "I also order that my beloved wife shall have her diet and lodging in this my house … as long as the lease of it will last, provided she will wish to remain in it with my aforesaid nephew Patrick Ryan …".

---

[43] [1931] I.R. 344.
[44] [1931] I.R. 344 at 346.
[45] (1848) 12 Ir. Eq. R. 226.

The widow at first lived in the house with the nephew but then left when he married. She later wished to return to the house and when the nephew refused to allow her to do so, she sued for the benefit under the will. Brady L.C. held that she was entitled to relief, and that the devise created an obligation. He said that whether it created a trust was immaterial.

> "It would be very difficult to lay down a rule as to the quantity of diet the legatee should have, or the room in the house which she should get; but it is perfectly plain she is entitled to have some diet or lodging, and there is no insuperable difficulty in enforcing that right ... [P]robably the best course will be to decree the plaintiff entitled in the words of the will, and leave her then to work out that declaration if she is dissatisfied with the way in which it is obeyed."[46]

19–38 In *Kelaghan v Daly*,[47] a farm was assigned to Catherine Kelaghan's son in consideration of natural love and affection and included a covenant by the son, his executor, administrators or assigns "to clothe, support, maintain and keep the said Catherine Kelaghan and her daughter Lizzie during their joint lives and the life of the survivor of them in a manner suitable to their condition in life; and will permit ... them to use, occupy and enjoy the dwelling house on the said farm in the same manner as they now occupy and enjoy the same". The property was then mortgaged and sold by the mortgagees subject to "all rights which may now be vested in Lizzie Kelaghan", Catherine Kelaghan having died. The covenant therefore created what Kennedy C.J. would call a general right of residence. Boyd J. held there was a lien on the land binding on the purchaser since he "had express notice of the rights of the plaintiff". This suggests that the "lien" was equitable. The judge then went on to note:

> "It has been admitted on the argument before me that the covenant, so far as relates to the occupation of the said house, affects land, and that the vendor's lien in respect thereof is operative; but it has been contended that the rest of the covenant is merely personal and does not run with the lands."[48]

19–39 The judge apparently did not consider whether the right created a life estate in the mother and daughter. This may have been an oversight, or the argument may not have been made, but it seems this omission may be the basis of the supposed distinction in the later case law, especially evident in *National Bank v Keegan*,[49] between the special right, which is in effect a life estate, and the general right which is said to be a mere charge. Secondly, it is questionable whether the right can be captured by the concept of a vendor's lien. Those who took the benefit of the lien were not the mortgagee-vendors but the mother and daughter.

---

[46] (1848) 12 Ir. Eq. R. 226 at 228.
[47] [1913] 2 I.R. 328.
[48] [1913] 2 I.R. 328 at 330.
[49] [1931] I.R. 344.

19–40 The court in *Re Shanahan*[50] also decided that the general right created a charge on the land. If the right is a charge on the land, then under s.5 of the Conveyancing Act 1881 the owner of land subject to an incumbrance, which includes a rentcharge, may sell the land free of it by obtaining the permission of the court to lodge a sum of money in court, the sum being sufficient to provide an income, after investment in government securities, to pay the annual amount.[51] If this is correct, then the general right does not secure the donee's occupation on the land.

19–41 In *Leonard v Leonard*,[52] the court found that a right of residence created an implied trust. An ante-nuptial settlement contained a covenant to "support, maintain and clothe and keep in a suitable and proper manner in his house on the said farm [TL] and his wife and family…". Holmes J. found that the covenant was not merely personal but created a trust. In some cases judges have shown a reluctance to infer a trust where words in a will do not expressly impose a trust but merely a wish or desire as to the use of the property in the hands of the donee.[53]

19–42 General rights of residence were considered by the Court of Appeal in the recent decision in *O'Donnell v Bank of Ireland*. In that case, O'Donnell J. held that a general right of residence is a right "touching on or concerning property and perhaps more importantly has an economic value", though he ultimately concluded that rights of residence are personal and cannot be assigned by those entitled to them.[54]

Registered Land
19–43 Section 81 of the Registration of Title Act 1964 states:

> "A right of residence in or on registered land, whether a general right of residence on the land or an exclusive right of residence in or on part of the land, shall be deemed to be personal to the person beneficially entitled thereto and to be a right in the nature of a lien for money's worth in or over the land and shall not operate to create any equitable estate in the land."

19–44 The declaration that a right of residence is personal to the holder presumably means that it is not alienable. The further declaration that it is "in the nature of a lien for money's worth" is not entirely clear, but a lien in general is a right to possession until money is paid. The sentence might imply that the

---

[50] [1919] 1 I.R. 131.
[51] *Re McGuinness's Contract* (1901) 35 I.L.T.R. 65.
[52] (1910) 44 I.L.T.R. 155; *Gallagher v Ferris* (1881) 7 L.R. Ir. 489; *Re Butler* (1925) 59 I.L.T.R. 166.
[53] *Lefroy v Flood* (1854) 4 Ir. Ch. R. 1; *McAlinden v McAlinden* (1877) I.R. 11 Eq. 219; *Bradshaw v Bradshaw* [1908] 1 I.R. 288; *Berryman v Berryman* [1913] 1 I.R. 21; *Re Blackwood* [1953] N.I. 32.
[54] *O'Donnell v Bank of Ireland* [2016] 2 I.L.R.M. 441 at 464–465.

right can be "bought off", but the courts have rather sought to discover the testator's intention. The second part of the sentence may indicate that the purpose of the section was to avoid the awkward consequences, already mentioned, of a life estate.

19–45 In *Johnston v Horace*,[55] Lavan J. considered a right of residence created over registered land. He said that the role of the court is to find the testator's intention and if that was to secure the donee's occupation, the court will give effect to it. The testator, PK, had appointed his daughter, BH, as sole executor and beneficiary of his estate subject to a right of residence in favour of his son, Edward, who had since died, his other daughter, TJ, who was the plaintiff in the case, and her daughter, the second plaintiff. The latter was struck out of the action before trial. The defendant was the son of BH and had inherited the property on her death, subject to the right of residence. The plaintiff alleged that after the death of Edward the defendant began a campaign of bullying and oppressive behaviour towards her. This eventually led to her leaving the house against her will and moving in with her daughter. It seems that this was probably the object which the defendant wished to achieve. Lavan J. held that the right was a general one, giving the plaintiff the right to share with the others the use and occupation of the premises, and although she had the personal use of one bedroom in a three-bedroom cottage, she had not been granted any exclusive right. The judge valued the right at a one-third interest in the cottage. However, the testator had not intended to create a mere charge—he had intended to provide for "a roof over their heads for life, and a security that same would be available until the end of their days - that is a right of residence for life."[56] Lavan J. held that it would not be appropriate to make a monetary award in respect of the right:

> "I consider the suggestion of valuing the right of residence unreal. Where I have to value same, I take the view that it would have to be on an actuarial basis, having regard to the defendant's conduct and his ability to pay. In addition, I take the view that a secured right of residence would otherwise become an unsecured right with no certainty that periodic payments would or could be made."[57]

19–46 The judge went on to hold that although a right of residence could be voluntarily abandoned expressly or by efflux of time, the plaintiff had not abandoned the right as she had left the premises under duress. The court would require "strong cogent evidence" from a party seeking to defeat the right while it remained a burden on the register. The judge granted the plaintiff injunctions restraining the defendant from preventing the plaintiff exercising her right of

---

[55] [1993] I.L.R.M. 594; P. Coughlan, "Enforcing Rights of Residence" (1993) 11 I.L.T. 168.
[56] [1993] I.L.R.M. 594 at 600.
[57] [1993] I.L.R.M. 594 at 601.

residence and ordering the defendant to supply a key to the cottage. He also awarded £7,500 damages for interference with the right of residence to date.

19–47 This judgment may indicate a growing willingness to use the discretion of the court, mentioned in earlier cases, even in the case of a general right of residence, to secure the occupation of the donee.

Reform

19–48 There is a need in land law for a form of right which confers on the recipient, usually an elderly member of a family, a right to reside in a house for the rest of his or her life, or until incapacity requires other arrangements. The right should be personal to the recipient in the sense that he or she cannot alienate it, but it should be secure against third parties. The uncertainty of the rights conferred by a right of residence in Ireland means that it does not fulfil that requirement. Licences, on the other hand, may be insecure against third parties, while life estates if created expressly are now liable to be overreached under the LCLRA 2009. The legislature might therefore consider creating a statutory form of right which could be conferred in such cases. There is no doubt a concern that such a right should not withdraw land from the market for an unduly long time, but that could be met by restricting it in some way, perhaps by providing that it could only be conferred on recipients above a certain age.

PROPRIETARY ESTOPPEL

Introduction

19–49 Proprietary estoppel, or estoppel by reliance, has become an important way in which rights in land may be acquired in equity. From its origins as an equity recognised in a number of limited situations, it has developed into a more general principle whose limits are still being explored. In many respects, proprietary estoppel is similar to another equitable doctrine, the constructive trust. However, while proprietary estoppel may result in the imposition of a constructive trust, it may also result in an order that the legal owner of the land must convey the legal estate to the plaintiff. Constructive trusts, on the other hand, are wider in the situations to which they apply.

19–50 As Gray and Gray put it, in "the ill-defined and chaotic circumstances of everyday life – especially in the family context – problems of entitlement arise for which the relatively orderly framework of structural property principles provides no convenient answer. It is here that proprietary estoppel has emerged as a dramatic source of rights".[58]

---

[58] Gray and Gray, *Land Law* (2011), para.9-047.

19–51 In general terms to establish a claim to proprietary estoppel, three elements—representation, reliance and detriment—must be present:

1. An owner of property (the representor) must have encouraged, by promises or assurances intended to be relied on, or must have acquiesced in, the belief by a non-owner (the representee or claimant) that the claimant either has, or expects to obtain, a property interest in the owner's land.
2. The claimant, in reliance on the assurance or the belief, must have acted so as to change his or her position.
3. The acts of reliance or change of position must be such that if the representor repudiated the promise or assurances the claimant would suffer a detriment.

As to the remedy, a fourth element may be added:

4. The detriment can only adequately be remedied by the court by awarding the representee a property interest in the representor's land. If this element is not present, the court may still award a remedy by way of damages or restitution by *quantum meruit*,[59] etc. but then it would not be characterised as *proprietary* estoppel, but as promissory estoppel, or estoppel by representation, etc.[60]

19–52 The overall test is that the court must be satisfied that it would be unconscionable for the representor to repudiate the assurances or act inconsistently with the representee's belief. The three elements are in fact an attempt by equity to capture the circumstances in which it would be unconscionable for the representor to act in that way. A more succinct definition of the elements was given by Lord Neuberger of Abbotsbury M.R. in a lecture[61]:

1. a statement or action (which can include silence or inaction) by the defendant, who ought to appreciate the claimant will rely on it;
2. an act by the claimant in the reasonable belief that he has or will get an interest in land, induced by that statement or action; and
3. consequent detriment to the claimant if the defendant is entitled to resile from his statement or action.

Origins
19–53 The principle of proprietary estoppel has its origins in four strands of case law.[62] These are:

---

[59] Latin, "as much as he deserved".
[60] For a comparative analysis of remedies for proprietary estoppel, see H. Biehler, "Remedies in Cases of Proprietary Estoppel: Towards a More Principled Approach?" (2015) 54(2) Ir. Jur. 79.
[61] Lord Neuberger, "The Stuffing of Minerva's Owl? Taxonomy and Taxidermy in Equity" (2009) 68 Camb. L.J. 537.
[62] These are discussed in detail in earlier editions of this book.

1. lease surrendered in reliance on void lease[63];
2. equitable extensions to the rules as to improvements to land by tenants[64];
3. exceptions to the rule that equity would not perfect an imperfect gift[65]; and
4. the circumstances in which a licence to occupy land may become irrevocable.[66]

The Development of the Modern Doctrine
From Promissory to Proprietary Estoppel
19–54 In *Central London Property Trust v High Trees House Ltd*,[67] the plaintiff property company had entered into a lease of High Trees House with the defendant, a subsidiary company in 1937. In 1940 the tenant company found that it could not pay the rent reserved due to the wartime conditions. The plaintiff company agreed that it would not insist on the full rent payable under the lease. The tenant paid the reduced rent while the wartime conditions continued. In 1945 those conditions ceased to apply. The plaintiff company had in the meantime gone into receivership, and the receiver demanded the full rent, including arrears. In the subsequent friendly action, however, the receiver claimed only the full rent from the end of wartime conditions, i.e. the last two quarters of 1945. The defendant, in its defence, pleaded that the agreement had been for the full term of the lease, and that the plaintiff was estopped from claiming the full amount. Denning J. held: (a) that, on the facts, both sides had understood the reduction of rent to apply to the period of wartime conditions, and that the plaintiff was therefore entitled to the increased rent for the quarters claimed; and (b), obiter, that the plaintiffs would have been estopped in equity from claiming arrears of rent. The judge held that there were cases since the Judicature Acts in which "a promise was made which was intended to create legal relations and which, to the knowledge of the person making the promise, was going to be acted on by the person to whom it was made, and which was in fact so acted on",[68] and in such case the promise was held to be binding. Although there was earlier authority[69] for a new branch of estoppel known as "promissory estoppel", this case gave it general recognition. Nevertheless, the new doctrine was thought to have its dangers, since it recognised that promises could be binding other than by the law of contract and this might threaten to

---

[63] See *Nowland v Bagget* in A. Lyall (ed.), *Irish Exchequer Reports: Reports of Cases in the Courts of Exchequer and Chancery in Ireland 1716–1734*, Publications of the Selden Society Vol.125 (London: Selden Society, 2008), pp.cxxxii, clxi, 230–231.

[64] See *Kenney v Browne* (1796) 3 Ridg. P.C. 462 (Irish HL) and *Ramsden v Dyson* (1866) L.R. 1 H.L. 129.

[65] See *Dillwyn v Llewelyn* (1862) 4 De G.F. & J. 517.

[66] See *Blood v Keller* (1861) 11 Ir. C.L.R. 124.

[67] [1947] K.B. 130; and see now *Brikom Investments Ltd v Carr* [1979] Q.B. 467 at 482f.

[68] [1947] K.B. 130 at 134.

[69] *Hughes v Metropolitan Railway Co* (1877) 2 App. Cas. 439.

undermine the law of contract itself.[70] It was therefore thought that the principle of promissory estoppel was "a shield and not a sword". It was available as a defence to an action to enforce a contract, but did not found an independent cause of action.

19–55 The 19th century cases of *Dillwyn v Llewelyn*[71] and *Ramsden v Dyson*[72] and the principle which underlay them had largely been forgotten until *Inwards v Baker*.[73] In that case a father allowed his son to build a bungalow on the father's land. The son went into occupation of the bungalow and remained there in the belief, which the father had encouraged, that he would be able to remain there for the rest of his life. The father died without having granted the son any interest in the property or making any contract to do so and did not leave the property to his son in his will. The trustees under the will attempted to evict the son, but the court refused to allow them to do so. They held that the expenditure by the son had entitled him to an equity in the land in the form of a licence.[74] Lord Denning M.R. said:

> "If the owner of land requests another, or indeed allows another, to expend money on the land under an expectation created or encouraged by the landlord that he will be able to remain there, that raises an equity in the licensee such as to entitle him to stay … All that is necessary is that the licensee should, at the request or with the encouragement of the landlord, have spent the money in the expectation of being allowed to stay there."[75]

19–56 The view which developed after *Inwards v Baker* in England was that promissory estoppel was a doctrine of contract law which provided a defence to an action to enforce a contractual right: it was a "shield and not a sword". Proprietary estoppel, on the other hand, was a cause of action which gave rise to property interests: proprietary estoppel was a sword and not merely a shield.[76]

---

[70] Promissory estoppel had been recognised in the United States as a "sword" supplying a lack of consideration, but it was pointed out in *Waltons Stores (Interstate) Ltd v Maher* (1987) 164 C.L.R. 387, by the High Court of Australia, that consideration in the United States is based on a narrower "bargain" theory not found in Australia or England.

[71] (1862) 4 De G.F. & J. 517.

[72] [1866] L.R. 1 H.L. 129 at 141.

[73] [1965] 2 Q.B. 29. See R.H. Maudsley, "Note" (1965) 81 L.Q.R. 183.

[74] The case also appears to have decided that the licence bound not only the father and his personal representatives but also successors in title except bona fide purchasers for value of the legal estate without notice. This is now doubtful in view of the decision in *Ashburn Anstalt v Arnold* [1989] Ch. 1, which held, as an alternative ratio, that a *contractual* licence is not binding on third parties in the absence of a constructive trust binding the third party. This, however, is a problem as to the nature of licences and not as to the nature of the equity which gives rise to them.

[75] [1965] 2 Q.B. 29 at 36–38.

[76] *Dillwyn v Llewelyn* (1862) 4 De G. F. & J. 517; *Pascoe v Turner* [1979] 1 W.L.R. 431 at 436.

19–57 An early Irish authority on proprietary estoppel is *Cullen v Cullen*.[77] The plaintiff lived with his family on premises that comprised the family residence, the business premises and some other land. His son, M, had joined him in the business after leaving school. At one point the plaintiff had given money to M to buy land of his own and this he had done. The father began to show signs of mental health problems and, in an attempt to avoid being committed to a psychiatric hospital, agreed to transfer the business and house to his wife in return for her promise not to have him committed. About the same time his wife won a portable house in a competition. She gave this house to her son, M. M began to prepare a site for it on his own land, but the wife suggested to his father that M should erect the house on the land where the family house and business was situated. The father said that as he was transferring the place to her she could do as she wished. M therefore erected the house on the land near the family business. Later, the father decided to resume control of his affairs and told M to remove his house. He brought the present action claiming, inter alia, an injunction to restrain the defendant from trespassing on the property. M counterclaimed that he was entitled to the house and the land on which it stood.

19–58 Kenny J. held that the plaintiff had granted a licence (either to the wife, or to the son through the wife) and that he had revoked it. The judge awarded a lump sum of damages to the plaintiff against M for trespass. However, he went on to hold that the plaintiff was estopped from asserting his title against M. He could therefore not succeed in his claim to an injunction against M. The judge declined to hold that M could require the plaintiff to execute a conveyance of the site of his house. The judge considered that he did not have jurisdiction on the existing authorities. He nevertheless suggested that if the son remained in possession for 12 years, which the father could do nothing to prevent, the son could then register his title with the Land Registry.

19–59 One criticism of the case is that, while denying that he had the power to order a transfer of the fee simple, the judge reached a result that virtually amounted to the same thing. However, the result conferred only a possessory title on the son. If the father managed to retake possession of the land by stealth before the 12 years had expired, the son could not recover his possession.

19–60 The case should clearly now be considered in the context of its time. In 1962 there was no judicial consensus in favour of the view that proprietary estoppel was a distinct doctrine from promissory estoppel. It is clear that Kenny J. thought that he was applying a principle derived from the *High Trees* case. He felt bound to treat the estoppel as a shield and not a sword.

19–61 The solution found by the judge also seems unsatisfactory in that the plaintiff could revoke the licence but was left without an adequate remedy.

---

[77] [1962] I.R. 268. See also *McMahon v Kerry County Council* [1981] I.L.R.M. 419.

He was unable to evict the son by an equitable remedy and the judge seems to have ignored the point that trespass is a continuing tort which should have allowed the father to bring successive actions until the son left. It is also unclear why the judge held that the plaintiff was estopped from enforcing his title against M, but was not estopped from revoking the licence in the first place.

19–62 More recent cases have shown a greater willingness to give a positive remedy. In *Haughan v Rutledge*,[78] the plaintiffs claimed that the defendant had encouraged them to believe that they would be granted a 20-year lease of the defendant's land on which to establish a horse racing track. Blayney J. found there was no foundation for their belief, nor had the defendant done anything to create such an expectation. The plaintiffs had merely been let into occupation on a trial basis for one year. The judge nevertheless cited with approval the often-quoted formulation of Lord Kingsdown in *Ramsden v Dyson* and also the four conditions stated in the 28th edition of Snell's *Principles of Equity*[79] which he described as a "correct statement of the law" and which were not disputed by counsel for the defendant. The four conditions are: (a) detriment; (b) expectation or belief; (c) encouragement; and (d) there must be no bar to the equity. He found that the claim failed to satisfy the second and third conditions. They could not have believed they were to obtain a 20-year lease since there had been no agreement for such a lease. They had also argued that even if no definite interest had been agreed, so that the matter had been left vague, they nevertheless believed that they would obtain some interest. Blayney J. rejected this because none of them had testified to any belief other than that they were to get a lease for 20 years. Neither had the plaintiffs encouraged any such belief. The judge quoted Lord Cranworth L.C. in *Ramsden v Dyson*,[80] who said:

"It follows as a corollary from these rules, or, perhaps it would be more accurate to say that it forms part of them, that if my tenant builds on land which he holds under me, he does not thereby, in the absence of special circumstances, acquire any right to prevent me taking possession of the lands and buildings when the tenancy has determined.

He knew the extent of his interest, and it was his folly to expend money upon a title which he knew would or might soon come to an end."[81]

19–63 The judge said that in his view that statement of the law applied in the present case. He found no special circumstances in the case. The difficulty here is that if the more extensive work in making a permanent track was to be regarded as compensation for past use of the land, then there was no need to

---

[78] [1988] I.R. 295
[79] E.H.T. Snell, P.V. Baker and S.J.H. Langan, *Snell's Principles of Equity*, 28th edn (London: Sweet & Maxwell, 1982), p.558.
[80] (1866) L.R. 1 H.L. 129.
[81] (1866) L.R. 1 H.L. 129 at 141.

consider whether it was performed in expectation of an interest in the land in future.

19–64 In _Crabb v Arun District Council_,[82] the plaintiff sold part of his land without reserving a right of way for the retained part because he had been led to believe by a representative of the district council that they would allow him to construct and use an alternative access over their land. The plaintiff constructed and used the alternative access and the district council then tried to prevent him from so doing. Lord Denning M.R. said that if a person,

> "by his words or conduct, so behaves as to lead another to believe that he will not insist on his strict legal rights—knowing or intending that the other will act on that belief—and he does so act, that again will raise an equity in favour of the other; and it is for a court of equity to say in what way the equity may be satisfied."[83]

19–65 Scarman L.J. accepted Lord Kingsdown's formulation in _Ramsden v Dyson_,[84] approved Fry J.'s judgment in _Willmott v Barber_,[85] deprecated the distinction between proprietary and promissory estoppel, and stated that equity would interfere if it would be "unconscionable and unjust to allow the defendants to set up their undoubted rights against the claim being made by the plaintiff."[86]

19–66 A strong example of proprietary estoppel as a sword was _Pascoe v Turner_.[87] A businessman, P, lived with T, a widow living on an invalidity pension. P bought a house and they moved in together as a couple. Seven years later P started an affair with another woman. T stayed in the house, and P told her the house and everything in it was hers. In reliance, T spent money on repairs and improvements and furniture, to the knowledge of P. P moved out in the same year in which he started the affair with the other woman. Three years later he told her to leave.

19–67 The English Court of Appeal held that the assurances he gave to her and her reliance on them raised an equity in her favour. It was for the court to decide how that equity could best be satisfied. The court considered conferring a licence on T, but felt that would not allow her to raise money for other improvements which might be necessary. It held that the equity could only be satisfied here by the conveyance of the fee simple to her. The court also commented on the ruthlessness with which P had sought to avoid his obligations

---

[82] [1976] Ch. 179.
[83] [1976] Ch. 179 at 188.
[84] [1866] L.R. 1 H.L. 129 at 170.
[85] (1880) 15 Ch. D. 96.
[86] [1976] Ch. 179 at 195.
[87] [1979] 1 W.L.R. 431.

and to evict his erstwhile companion from the house,[88] and held that the transfer of the fee simple was necessary to protect her against this ruthlessness in the future.

19–68 Academic criticism of the decision tended to the view that the court conferred on the widow a greater interest than her contributions justified.[89] But the court's decision was not based upon the monetary contributions so much as on the unfulfilled promise to convey the house to the widow. The case may therefore belong rather to the "perfecting an imperfect gift" class of case than to the type of case in which the court is recompensing a person for an outlay of money. This is consistent with the language of the court which spoke of "compelling the plaintiff to give effect to his promise and her expectations".[90] It is also consistent with Lord Kingsdown's statement in *Ramsden v Dyson* when he said that "a court of equity will compel the landlord to give effect to such promise or expectation".

Towards a General Principle

19–69 In the 1970s and 80s, doubts were appearing as to whether the distinction between promissory estoppel and proprietary estoppel could be maintained.[91] In *Taylors Fashions Ltd v Liverpool Victoria Trustees Co Ltd*,[92] Oliver J. reviewed all the authorities and in a statement which he repeated in the Court of Appeal in *Habib Bank Ltd v Habib Bank AG Zurich*,[93] concluded:

> "[T]he more recent cases indicate, in my judgment, that the application of the *Ramsden v Dyson*, LR 1 HL principle - whether you call it proprietary estoppel, estoppel by acquiescence or estoppel by encouragement is really immaterial - requires a very much broader approach which is directed rather at ascertaining whether, in particular individual circumstances, it would be unconscionable for a party to be permitted to deny that which, knowingly, or unknowingly, he has allowed or encouraged another to assume to his detriment than to inquiring whether the circumstances can be fitted within the confines of some preconceived formula serving as a universal yardstick for every form of unconscionable behaviour."[94]

19–70 In *Re Basham*,[95] discussed below, an English court was prepared to enforce an unperformed promise to make a will where the party to whom the promise had been made had acted in reliance on it. It is also clear from *Dillwyn*

---

[88] [1979] 1 W.L.R. 431 at 438f.
[89] See B. Sufrin, "An Equity Richly Satisfied" (1979) 42 M.L.R. 574.
[90] [1979] 1 W.L.R. 431 at 439B. A "rule-sceptic" might also stress that P was a relatively wealthy man, while T had only limited financial resources.
[91] For example, *Holiday Inns Inc v Broadhead* (1974) 232 E.G. 951.
[92] [1982] Q.B. 133.
[93] [1981] 1 W.L.R. 1265 at 1285.
[94] [1982] Q.B. 133 at 151.
[95] [1986] 1 W.L.R. 1498.

v Llewelyn[96] and other authorities that a court in similar circumstances will perfect an imperfect *inter vivos* gift. If estoppel can perfect an imperfect gift, can it also perfect an imperfect contract? There was ample authority for the view that it would do so where the parties were already landlord and tenant and the landlord had encouraged the tenant to believe that a new lease would be granted at the end of the present one and there was detrimental reliance by the tenant.[97] In *JT Developments v Quinn*,[98] Ralph Gibson L.J. rejected a distinction in this context. It was now possible to argue that where parties were negotiating to create a property interest, promissory estoppel was no longer a mere defence, and that equity would confer rights where the law of contract had failed for some reason. In the landlord and tenant situation there was already an existing legal relationship between the parties. Yet it did not seem that this could found a valid distinction. Where the elements of the equity were present it was no less unconscionable for the party creating the expectation to resile from it.

Incomplete Agreements and Failed Contracts

19–71 Where parties are negotiating an agreement it may be that one party begins to act, to the knowledge of the other, upon the expectation that an agreement will be reached, and spends money or otherwise alters his or her position so that if, as it turns out, the negotiations fail to produce a binding contract, the party who has already "jumped the gun" will suffer a detriment. This situation raises some issues particular to it. In other situations, the person to whom representations are made (the representee) acts on the belief that the representor may, by a unilateral act, confer on him or her the property interest he or she expects. In the case of negotiations preliminary to an agreement, it takes both the representor and representee to act, that is, to agree. Also, the case usually involves business persons who may be expected to be aware of the law of contract or be advised by lawyers who do, and therefore the reliance may be less understandable, and therefore less likely to found a claim, than in the case of those inexperienced in business. It also may be the case that judges are uncomfortable with the notion that proprietary estoppel might be an alternative ground of action in situations previously governed by the law of contract and are more restrictive in applying the general test of proprietary estoppel in such situations.

Australian Cases

19–72 In *Waltons Stores (Interstate) Ltd v Maher*,[99] the High Court of Australia considered a case where there was no prior lease, but parties were negotiating to enter into one. The owners of a developed site proposed to demolish existing buildings and erect a new one suitable for a supermarket. The owners

---

[96] (1862) 4 De G.F. & J. 517.
[97] *Kenney v Browne* (1796) 3 Ridg. P.C. 462 at 518 (Irish HL); *Taylors Fashions Ltd v Liverpool Victoria Trustees Co Ltd* (Note) [1982] Q.B. 133. See *Haughan v Rutledge* [1988] I.R. 295.
[98] (1990) 62 P. & C.R. 33.
[99] (1987) 164 C.L.R. 387. See also *Commonwealth v Verwayen* (1990) 170 C.L.R. 394.

proposed certain amendments to the draft lease and were told verbally by the company's solicitors that the amendments were acceptable. The company returned an amended, but unexecuted, copy of the lease. The owners executed the lease and returned it to the company "by way of exchange". The company, which had become aware that the demolition was proceeding, then told the owners that it did not wish to proceed with the lease.

19–73 Brennan J. reformulated the doctrine of estoppel, which he did not characterise as "promissory" or "proprietary":

> "In my opinion, to establish an equitable estoppel, it is necessary for a plaintiff to prove that (1) the plaintiff assumed that a particular legal relationship then existed between the plaintiff and the defendant or expected that a particular legal relationship would exist between them and, in the latter case, that the defendant would not be free to withdraw from the expected legal relationship; (2) the defendant has induced the plaintiff to adopt that assumption or expectation; (3) the plaintiff acts or abstains from acting in reliance on the assumption or expectation; (4) the defendant knew or intended him to do so; (5) the plaintiff's action or inaction will occasion detriment if the assumption or expectation is not fulfilled; and (6) the defendant has failed to act to avoid that detriment whether by fulfilling the assumption or expectation or otherwise. For the purposes of the second element, a defendant who has not actively induced the plaintiff to adopt an assumption or expectation will nevertheless be held to have done so if the assumption or expectation can be fulfilled only by a transfer of the defendant's property, a diminution of his rights or an increase in his obligations and he, knowing that the plaintiff's reliance on the assumption or expectation may cause detriment to the plaintiff if it is not fulfilled, fails to deny to the plaintiff the correctness of the assumption or expectation on which the plaintiff is conducting his affairs."[100]

19–74 The High Court of Australia upheld an award of damages for the "concluded agreement by way of exchange" which the judge found to exist between the parties and so was not called upon to order the execution of the lease. In these circumstances the word "proprietary" may indeed not have been appropriate. But the judgments indicate that there is no reason in principle why a conveyance should not have been ordered in appropriate circumstances and

---

[100] (1986) 5 N.S.W.L.R. 407 at 428–429.

the members of the court agreed that the equivalent of the Statute of Frauds in force in New South Wales would not have been a bar to doing so.[101]

19–75 In the later case of *Commonwealth v Verwayen*,[102] Brennan J. stated the doctrine in the context of unfulfilled promises:

> "Equitable estoppel or, as I prefer to call it, an equity arising by estoppel precludes a person who, by a promise, has induced another party to rely on the promise and thereby to act to his detriment from resiling from the promise without avoiding the detriment."[103]

Cobbe v Yeoman's Row

19–76 In *Cobbe v Yeoman's Row Management Ltd*,[104] C, an experienced property developer, spent considerable time and effort to obtain planning permission for the development of land owned by Yeoman's Row Management Ltd ("Yeoman's Row"). The parties had discussions as to finance, implementing the development and profit sharing if and when planning permission was granted. C was to buy the property for £12 million, then develop and sell it and share the proceeds in excess of £24 million equally with Yeoman's Row. However, they decided not to enter into an agreement until planning permission was obtained. C assumed that he had reached an understanding, binding in honour only, with Yeoman's Row, that, if permission was granted, he and Yeoman's Row would enter into such an arrangement on a legally binding basis. Yeoman's Row also understood this to be the state of affairs and continued to do so until the last three months of C's application to obtain planning permission. Three months before planning permission was obtained, the anticipated profit of the project had increased to such an extent that Yeoman's Row decided to resile from the understanding. But it did not tell C this until after planning permission had been obtained. It then offered him a much less financially attractive arrangement than had been discussed. He rejected that offer, and started proceedings. Initially he alleged there was a contract but that was an unsustainable claim on the facts and was dropped. He later raised a claim in proprietary estoppel.

---

[101] Brennan J. held that s.54A of the Conveyancing Act 1919 (NSW) did not preclude the enforcement of the agreement on the ground that equitable estoppel does not create a contract to which the section applies, even where the equity is satisfied by treating the defendant as though a contract had been made. Deane J. so held on the ground that estoppel precluded the denial of a valid and enforceable agreement, so that the estoppel outflanked s.54A; Gaudron J. so held on the ground that the fact that the company was estopped from denying that the exchange had taken place involved an assumption that the agreement was duly executed by the company; and by Mason C.J. and Wilson J. for the reasons given by the other members of the court.

[102] (1990) 170 C.L.R. 394.

[103] (1990) 170 C.L.R. 394 at 422.

[104] [2008] UKHL 55. See also, Lord Neuberger M.R., "The Stuffing of Minerva's Owl? Taxonomy and Taxidermy in Equity" (2009) 68(3) Camb. L.J. 537.

19–77 While deprecating Yeoman's Row's conduct, the House of Lords held C was only entitled to a *quantum meruit* for the work he had done in obtaining planning permission. There was no "certain interest in land" which C could say he was anticipating, and any arrangement he relied on was subject to contract. Both Lord Scott and Lord Walker cited Deane J. in the leading Australian case of *Muschinski v Dodds*,[105] who observed that "proprietary rights fall to be governed by principles of law and not by some mix of judicial discretion, subjective views about which party 'ought to win' and 'the formless void' of individual moral opinion". Lord Neuberger M.R., commenting on the case extra-judicially,[106] cited Lord Cranworth L.C. in *Ramsden v Dyson*[107]:

"If anyone makes an assurance to another ... that he will do or abstain from doing a particular act, but he refuses to bind himself, and says that for the performance of what he has promised the person to whom the promise has been made must rely on the honour of the person who has made it, this excludes the jurisdiction of courts of equity no less than of courts of law."

19–78 There is no doubt that Yeoman's Row behaved dishonourably, but that did not mean that there was a remedy in equity when both parties, who were experienced in business, knew that there was no binding contract. C could have ensured that the agreement was reduced to writing[108] with the condition that it should take effect if and when planning permission was obtained.

The Death of Commercial Proprietary Estoppel?
19–79 Macfarlane and Robertson[109] suggested that *Cobbe* sounded the death knell of proprietary estoppel, at least in the commercial context. It is unusual for judges to engage directly with academics in a debate, but in an interesting and unusual response, Lord Neuberger of Abbotsbury M.R. commented on this assertion in a lecture[110]:

"[Macfarlane and Robertson] suggested that *Cobbe* represented 'the death of proprietary estoppel,' not so much because the decision was wrong but because the reasoning precluded a proprietary estoppel claim unless the claimant believed that he had a legally enforceable claim. I agree – and, at least in a commercial context, what's wrong with it?"

---

[105] (1985) 160 C.L.R. 583 at 616.
[106] Lord Neuberger M.R., "The Stuffing of Minerva's Owl?" (2009) 68(3) Camb. L.J. 537 at 541.
[107] (1866) L.R. 1 H.L. 129 at 145–146.
[108] A. Goymour, "Cobbling Together Claims Where a Contract Fails to Materialise" (2009) 68(1) Camb. L.J. 37 at 39.
[109] B. Macfarlane and A. Robertson, "The Death of Proprietary Estoppel" (2008) 4 L.M.C.L.Q. 449.
[110] Lord Neuberger M.R., "The Stuffing of Minerva's Owl? Taxonomy and Taxidermy in Equity" (2009) 68(3) Camb. L.J. 537.

19–80 However, Lord Neuberger in *Thorner v Major*[111] recognised that the decision in *Cobbe* was confined to contractual negotiations, or failed contracts, and was not, or not necessarily, a guide to the response of the courts in other situations.[112] *Thorner v Major* was a different type of case, concerning a promise to leave a farm by will.

19–81 In a case after *Cobbe* in the Court of Appeal, Wilson L.J. found proprietary estoppel to be established in a case between businessmen, which did not involve s.2 of the Law of Property (Miscellaneous Provisions) Act 1989, where there was an agreement in writing containing the essential terms. The judge observed that "the law requires that the promisor should make clear not that the promise cannot be revoked but that it will not be revoked". He also quoted the words of Mummery L.J. in *Cobbe*, that "the crucial element is that the defendant has created or encouraged the belief on the part of the claimant that the defendant will not withdraw from the assurance, arrangement or understanding".

19–82 *Cobbe v Yeoman's Row* was recently followed by the Irish High Court in *Prunty v Crowley*.[113] In that case, the parties were in contractual negotiations for the sale of a property belonging to the plaintiff. The plaintiff argued that the correspondence between the parties amounted to a concluded contract, and that the defendants were estopped from denying the existence of the contract. The High Court held, however, that there was no concluded agreement between the parties. Nevertheless, O'Malley J. considered that it would be unconscionable in the circumstances to allow the defendants to deny the existence of a contract, and she made an order for specific performance.

The Relevance of the Statute of Frauds

19–83 The judges in *Waltons Stores (Interstate) Ltd v Maher*[114] did not consider that the Australian equivalent of the Statute of Frauds was a bar to proprietary estoppel.

19–84 In Ireland, s.2 of the Statute of Frauds 1695, with minor changes, was replaced as to contracts concerning land by s.51 of the LCLRA 2009[115]:

> "51.—(1) Subject to subsection (2), no action shall be brought to enforce any contract for the sale or other disposition of land unless the agreement on which such action is brought, or some memorandum or note of it, is

---

[111] [2009] 1 W.L.R. 776.

[112] [2009] 1 W.L.R. 776 at 804, para.100.

[113] *Prunty v Crowley* [2016] IEHC 293.

[114] (1987) 164 C.L.R. 387 at 545, n.165.

[115] J.C.W. Wylie, *The Land and Conveyancing Law Reform Acts: Annotations and Commentary*, 2nd edn (London: Bloomsbury, 2017), [94]. The original s.2 remains in force as to other contracts, such as contracts of guarantee and in consideration of marriage: Wylie, *Annotations and Commentary* (2017), [94], n.1.

in writing and signed by the person against whom the action is brought
or that person's authorised agent.

(2) Subsection (1) does not affect the law relating to part performance or
other equitable doctrines."

19–85 The 1695 statute, like the original English one, exempted from the
operation of s.2 implied, resulting and constructive trusts, but did not mention
proprietary estoppel. Section 51 goes further and exempts "equitable doctrines". This makes it clear that the section is no bar to proprietary estoppel.

19–86 The issue was the subject of controversy in England and Wales.[116]
The Statute of Frauds was re-enacted in England by s.40 of the Law of
Property Act 1925, but s.40 was itself replaced by s.2 of the Law of Property (Miscellaneous Provisions) Act 1989, unwisely, in the view of many.[117]
The 1989 section, which is not a model of the draftsman's art, declares that
any contract purporting to create or dispose of an interest in land can only
be made in writing, not merely *evidenced* in writing, and if not, it is not
merely unenforceable, but void. It therefore abolished the doctrine of part
performance.[118] Section 2(5) sets out certain exceptions, including implied,
resulting and constructive trusts, but does not mention proprietary estoppel.
Lord Scott's statement in *Cobbe* that his "present view" was that "proprietary
estoppel cannot be prayed in aid in order to render enforceable an agreement
that statute has declared to be void",[119] might seem to mean the end of proprietary estoppel at least in the case of oral agreements in England. Nevertheless,
Lord Scott appeared to have accepted the decision in *Crabb v Arun District
Council* as correct.[120] In *Crabb* there was no agreement because there was
no *consensus ad idem*. Nor is it clear in England that if there is a concluded
agreement, the section excludes proprietary estoppel as an alternative to writing. Lord Neuberger also pointed out that insofar as proprietary estoppel can
give rise to a constructive trust, the doctrine would seem still to be applicable
under the English statute[121] and Robert Walker L.J. in *Yaxley v Gotts* considered that the 1989 section did not prevent the intervention of equity where "a
supposed bargain has been so fully performed by one side, and the general
circumstances of the matter are such, that it would be inequitable to disregard
the claimant's expectations, and insufficient to grant him no more than a

---

[116] *Yaxley v Gotts* [2000] Ch. 162; *Kinane v Mackie-Conteh* [2005] EWCA Civ 45; C. Harpum,
S. Bridge and M. Dixon, *Megarry & Wade: The Law of Real Property*, 8th edn (London:
Sweet & Maxwell, 2012), paras 15–014 and 15–015; M. Dixon, "Invalid Contracts, Estoppel,
and Constructive Trusts" [2005] Conv. 207; B. McFarlane, "Proprietary Estoppel and Failed
Contractual Negotiations" [2005] Conv. 501.

[117] *Courtney v Clorp Ltd* [2006] EWCA Civ 518 at para.1; Lord Neuberger M.R., "The Stuffing
of Minerva's Owl?" (2009) 68(3) Camb. L.J. 537 at 546.

[118] *Megarry & Wade: The Law of Real Property* (2012), para.15–015.

[119] [2008] 1 W.L.R. 1752 at para.29.

[120] Lord Neuberger M.R., "The Stuffing of Minerva's Owl?" (2009) 68(3) Camb. L.J. 537 at 546.

[121] Lord Neuberger M.R., "The Stuffing of Minerva's Owl?" (2009) 68(3) Camb. L.J. 537 at 545.

restitutionary remedy".[122] Furthermore, the section only applies to contracts and if essential terms have not been agreed, or there is a misunderstanding as to what they are, then it is arguable that there is no *consensus ad idem* and the section does not apply.

19–87 In Ireland the decision was made not to adopt the change made in England in 1989, which was motivated by a concern to deal with "gazumping", i.e. vendors resiling from contracts in order to take advantage of rapid increases in property prices, which was a temporary phenomenon caused by market conditions in the 1980s.[123] Later the view was that formalities for contracts to convey land would have to be reviewed before electronic conveyancing was introduced, but no change should be made before that development.[124]

Promises to Leave Property by Will
19–88 Quite a different context, as the courts have recognised,[125] is the case of a farmer's employee or relative who assists him or her in the management and work of the farm. These are cases where the employee or relative is given assurances or promises or is led to believe by the farmer that the farmer will leave the farm to the employee or relative in his or her will; and then the farmer either makes a will in favour of someone else, or dies intestate, whereby the farm will pass to someone else, or even announces in his or her lifetime an intention to leave the farm to someone else.[126]

Irish Cases
19–89 In *Reidy v McGreevy*,[127] the plaintiff stayed at home and worked his father's lands between 1962 and 1969, and again for approximately a year, prior to his father's death. He claimed that on both occasions he did so as the result of promises by his father that if he did so, the father would exercise a special power of appointment vested in him in favour of the plaintiff. The father died leaving his own property to his widow, the plaintiff's mother, and exercised the power of appointment in favour of his widow and his three daughters. The plaintiff claimed, inter alia, that the committee of the widow and the daughters held the property which was the subject of the power of appointment on trust for him. Barron J. observed that the nature and extent of such claims depends on the facts:

---

[122] [2000] Ch. 162 at 180.

[123] Law Reform Commission, *Report on Gazumping* (LRC 59-1989), paras 3.18–3.21; Wylie, *Annotations and Commentary* (2017), [94], n.1.

[124] Law Reform Commission, *Report on Land Law and Conveyancing Law (6): Further General Proposals Including the Execution of Deeds* (LRC 56-1998); Wylie, *Annotations and Commentary* (2017), [94], n.1.

[125] Lord Neuberger M.R. in *Thorner v Major* [2009] 1 W.L.R. 776 at para.100; Lord Walker in *Cobbe v Yeoman's Row Management Ltd* [2008] 1 W.L.R. 1752 at para.66.

[126] As in *Gillett v Holt*: see below.

[127] Unreported, High Court, Barron J., 19 March 1993.

"What may be unconscionable upon one set of facts may not be upon another set. So, depending upon the facts, the Plaintiff may be entitled to an estate in the property; to a charge over it; or to nothing. But whatever the facts, the claim could not be maintained until the death of the testator because it could not have been ascertained until then that he had failed to honour his promise. Of course, if he had repudiated his promise during his life-time, this would have given rise to a cause of action at that stage. That, however, is not the case here."

19–90 In other words, since the breach of the promise alleged in the case consisted of the failure to exercise the power in the plaintiff's favour, that had not occurred until the testator's death and the claim was not statute barred. The obiter dictum is an interesting one, since it asserted that liability may arise in estoppel, or constructive trust, if a promise or expectation which has been relied upon, is departed from by an "anticipatory breach". The same point was later accepted by the English Court of Appeal in *Gillett v Holt*.[128]

19–91 In *Smyth v Halpin*,[129] Geoghegan J. recognised proprietary estoppel in the context of succession. The father, who owned a house and farm, made a will in which he had left the property to his wife for life with remainder to the plaintiff, his son, subject to the rights of his two daughters who were each to be entitled to choose a half-acre plot on which to build a house. The plaintiff became engaged to be married and asked his father for some land on which to build a house. The father replied that "this place is yours after your mother's day – what would you be doing with two places?" The father then suggested that the plaintiff build an extension to the family home. It was designed by an architect who took into account that the plaintiff would eventually own the whole house. The site on which the extension was to be built was conveyed to the plaintiff so that he could use it as security for a loan to finance the extension. The extension was built. In a later will the father left the land to his wife for life with remainder to the plaintiff absolutely and the house to his wife for life with remainder to one of the plaintiff's sisters absolutely. The father died. The plaintiff sought a declaration that he was entitled to the remainder interest in the house after the life estate. Geoghegan J., citing *Dillwyn v Llewelyn*[130] and *Pascoe v Turner*,[131] granted the declaration and ordered the execution of a conveyance transferring the remainder to the plaintiff. The case is important in that it held in Ireland, (a) that the equity raised may require the conveyance of the legal fee simple, and (b) that the doctrine may displace a will.[132]

---

[128] [2000] 2 All E.R. 289.

[129] [1997] I.L.R.M. 38.

[130] (1862) 4 De G.F. & J. 517.

[131] [1979] 1 W.L.R. 431.

[132] In *Re Basham* [1986] 1 W.L.R. 1498 the promisor died intestate.

19–92 In *McCarron v McCarron*,[133] the Supreme Court recognised the principle. The plaintiff had helped the deceased with the management and operation of his farms over a period of 16 years, since the deceased had an accident which limited his mobility. The plaintiff's late father was a first cousin of the deceased. The plaintiff claimed that the deceased had entered into a contract with him to remunerate him for the work he did on the farm by leaving the farm to him by will, and sought specific performance of it. In the alternative he claimed he was entitled to the farm by proprietary estoppel. The defendant did not plead the absence of any note or memorandum in writing as required by the Statute of Frauds 1695. Little discussion took place between the plaintiff and the deceased as to the form of remuneration. On one occasion the deceased had asked whether he, the plaintiff, was wondering about some compensation for his work and the plaintiff replied, "I suppose I will not be forgotten", to which the deceased responded, "[w]ell, you will be a rich man after my day." At a later date the deceased said that he would soon have to take to a wheelchair and that he wanted the plaintiff to look after him and that he and the plaintiff's father would draw up "some class of an agreement". The plaintiff replied, "I will not put you out of house or home, George", and the deceased replied, "[r]ight, we will leave it at that." Murphy J. in the Supreme Court commented:

> "What is noticeable from the transcript and in particular the evidence of the plaintiff was that natural courtesy (which John Millington Synge associated with the west of Ireland) which often results in an unwillingness to pursue discussion to a logical and perhaps harshly expressed commercial conclusion. In other parts of Ireland the concept of a person working long hours over a period of four years before any discussion takes place in relation to remuneration or reward might be unthinkable ...I would merely conclude that in some, particularly rural areas, a meeting of minds can be achieved without as detailed discussion as might be necessary elsewhere."

19–93 He found that such nuances should be left to the trial judge. The Supreme Court therefore upheld the High Court order for specific performance and did not have to decide the issue of proprietary estoppel. Murphy J. nevertheless commented:

> "If successfully invoked this doctrine would permit the Plaintiff to claim in equity an estate in the lands of the Deceased irrespective of any testamentary disposition by the latter."

19–94 He then went on to cite *Plimmer v Wellington Corporation*[134] and continued:

---

[133] Unreported, Supreme Court, 13 February 1997.
[134] (1884) 9 App. Cas. 699.

"In principle I see no reason why the doctrine should be confined to the expenditure of money or the erection of premises on the lands of another. In a suitable case it may well be argued that a plaintiff suffers as severe a loss or detriment by providing his own labours or services in relation to the lands of another and accordingly should equally qualify for recognition in equity. In practice, however, it might be difficult to determine the extent of the estate or interest in land for which a plaintiff might qualify as a result of his personal efforts. Perhaps a claim of that nature would be adequately compensated by a charge or lien on the lands for a sum equivalent to reasonable remuneration for the services rendered."

19–95 *CF v JDF*[135] was a case of judicial separation and the only issue relevant to proprietary estoppel was that the applicant wife argued that a stud farm which her husband had developed was part of his assets in that he had acquired a beneficial interest in it by proprietary estoppel. The husband came from a farming background in County Wicklow. In 1989 he bought a farmhouse from his aunt. In 1992, the couple moved into the farmhouse. The applicant's businesses went through a somewhat troubled period and were sold without profit in the early 1990s. In 1998, the husband's employment was terminated and he received a settlement from his employers. Around this time he established a stud farm business. Since there was no land attached to the parties' family home in Wicklow, the husband operated the stud farm on 22 acres of land adjacent to the family home which was part of the farm owned by his father, JF senior. Although the husband used this land for his stud farm, the land remained in the ownership of his father. The husband from time to time assisted his father on his farm, and it appears that the father, though now elderly, also at times assisted his son. The trial judge held that they had a close relationship.

19–96 The applicant petitioned the High Court for a decree of judicial separation and certain ancillary orders. The applicant argued that the land on which the stud farm was operated, including that portion on the respondent's father's farm, formed part of the family home or of the matrimonial assets. In May 2002, the High Court (O'Sullivan J.) granted the decree of judicial separation and made certain ancillary orders, including an order that the land on which the stud farm was operated formed part of the family home.

19–97 It was held by the Supreme Court (McGuinness, McCracken and Kearns JJ.) that in order to establish the existence of a beneficial interest on the basis of promissory or proprietary estoppel, there must be some clear evidence of an actual promise, inducement or representation, and that it was not sufficient that a situation was permitted to happen or that a third party would think a particular outcome was likely. The crucial issue in determining whether an interest in property had arisen on the basis of proprietary estoppel was the quality of the assurances which had been given. The court therefore held that

---

[135] [2005] IESC 45.

the husband had not acquired a beneficial interest in the father's farm. McGuinness J. observed:

"In order to establish a beneficial interest accruing to the son by means of a proprietary or promissory estoppel there must be at least some clear evidence of an actual promise, inducement or representation by the father to the son that he intended the son to be the owner of the land. Inferences from conduct are not sufficient, particularly if they are not supported by the evidence at the trial."

19–98 The English case of *Gillett v Holt*[136] was cited to the court where a similar claim succeeded, but the crucial difference seems to have been that in *CF v JDF* there was no evidence, even by such oblique or elliptical statements, such as occurred in *Gillett* (and the later case of *Thorner*, discussed below), that the father had induced or encouraged a belief in the son that the father would transfer the farm to him. The father, who "at least to some extent [was] motivated by hostility to his daughter-in-law", testified that he intended the farm to pass to his wife after his death, and on her death to his son for life only, and then to his grandchildren. The father's will was produced, which indeed contained such provisions. It was not of course in the son's interest to argue that the farm was part of his assets for the purpose of calculating his wealth in the making of a separation order.

English Cases

19–99 In *Re Basham*,[137] the plaintiff lived at her stepfather's house from the age of 15 until her marriage. She helped her mother and stepfather run the stepfather's business. She was never paid for this but understood that she would inherit the stepfather's property when he died. He purchased a tenanted cottage with money provided largely by the plaintiff's mother. When the mother died the stepfather moved into the cottage which had become vacant. He told the plaintiff that the cottage was hers. The plaintiff and her family lived near the stepfather, and the plaintiff's husband provided food for him, kept the garden in order and helped the plaintiff with work about the house. The plaintiff bought carpets for it and laid them herself and regularly prepared meals for him. She was told by her stepfather that she would lose nothing by doing those acts for him. A few days before his death he indicated that he wanted to make a will leaving money to the plaintiff's son and that she was to have his house. He died intestate and the plaintiff claimed a declaration against the administrators of his estate, that she was absolutely and beneficially entitled to the house and other property. The English Chancery Division held that she was entitled to the declaration.

---

[136] [2000] 2 All E.R. 289.
[137] [1986] 1 W.L.R. 1498.

19–100 *Re Basham* was followed by the English Court of Appeal in *Wayling v Jones*.[138] In that case the plaintiff went to live with the deceased when the plaintiff was 21, and the deceased 56. The plaintiff helped him to run his businesses in return for living expenses and pocket money. The plaintiff was promised that he would inherit a particular hotel. The deceased made a will leaving the hotel to the plaintiff but by the time of his death had sold the hotel. The gift of the hotel had therefore been adeemed. The plaintiff nevertheless claimed that he was entitled to the proceeds of sale of the hotel by proprietary estoppel. The claim failed at first instance on the ground that the plaintiff had been unable to prove in cross-examination that the promises of the deceased influenced him to remain with the deceased. The Court of Appeal upheld the appeal. Balcombe L.J.[139] stressed the following:

"(1) There must be a sufficient link between the promises relied upon and the conduct which constitutes the detriment … (2) The promises relied upon do not have to be the sole inducement for the conduct: it is sufficient if they are an inducement[140] … (3) Once it has been established that promises were made, and that there has been conduct by the plaintiff of such a nature that inducement may be inferred then the burden of proof shifts to the defendants to establish that he did not rely on the promises …".[141]

19–101 In *Taylor v Dickens*,[142] it was suggested that the fact that it is common knowledge that wills are revocable until death, restricted the application of proprietary estoppel in that context. In that case, an elderly lady promised to leave her house to her gardener, T. T thereafter refused to accept payment for his work. The lady made the will as she had promised, but soon afterwards T began to behave as if the house were already his, by leaving his things in sheds on the property. The testator found this both disturbing and unacceptable. Without telling T, she made a new will under which the house was left to a married couple who were friends of hers. She told a friend that she was apprehensive about telling T of the new will and that she had "taken the coward's way out". There was also evidence that T's wife had told him he should not "count his chickens before they were hatched".

19–102 Weeks J. held there was no equity raised in T's favour. He considered that it is well known that a testator can revoke his or her will and so it was not sufficient for A to believe that he was going to be given a right over B's property if he knew[143] that B had reserved the right to change his mind. In that

---

[138] [1995] 2 F.L.R. 1029.

[139] (1996) 69 P. & C.R. 170 at 173.

[140] Citing *Amalgamated Property Co v Texas Bank* [1982] Q.B. 84 at 104–105.

[141] Citing *Greasely v Cooke* [1980] 1 W.L.R. 1306.

[142] [1998] 1 F.L.R. 806.

[143] It is doubtful if the judge intends this to be an additional requirement, since he noted that it is common knowledge and, one might add, a matter of law on which T could have informed himself by taking legal advice at the time of the assurance.

case, A must also show that B created or encouraged a belief on A's part that B would not exercise that right.

19–103 While the decision seems correct in not giving the claim priority over the testator's power of revocation on the facts, it is difficult to accept that an equity was not raised in T's favour by the fact of his declining to accept payment for his work, the testator's acceptance of that situation, and her later failure to inform him of her change of mind, which would have enabled him to claim the lost wages. Surely he should have been at least entitled to his wages? She acquiesced in his reliance on her promise. Moreover, the case has been criticised as wrong in principle in so far as the judge held that a promise to make a will in someone's favour is inherently revocable, or is revocable unless the testator expressly tells the intended donee that he or she has renounced the right to revoke the will. A will is indeed always revocable until death, but equity may still attach to the property in the hands of personal representatives or beneficiaries. What makes the promise irrevocable is that the person, to the knowledge of the deceased, relied on the assurance to his or her detriment.[144]

19–104 This point was also emphasised in the English Court of Appeal in *Gillett v Holt*.[145] In that case G, who was then 12-years-old, became friendly with H, a 38-year-old farmer. G left school at 16, at H's suggestion, and went to work on H's farm in 1956, giving up the prospect of further education. G continued to work for H until 1995. He became effectively the manager of the farm. At one point G and his wife sold the house they were living in and went to live in a house and farm acquired by H's company, spending money on repairs and improvements. Over the years H indicated to G that he intended to leave most of his estate to G, and executed a number of wills giving effect to the intention. H also announced his intention on seven separate occasions before family and friends. G had urged H to give him some immediate interest in the farm but H did not do so. By 1995 the personal and working relationship between G and H had broken down and H made a new will, in favour of the second defendant, which entirely excluded G. G brought an action against H based on proprietary estoppel claiming that he had devoted his entire working life to H's service on the understanding, fostered by H, that he would inherit his estate and that therefore H was under an obligation to leave the bulk of his estate to him.

19–105 The Court of Appeal held that the plaintiff had succeeded. Robert Walker L.J. held that proprietary estoppel could not be divided into separate compartments of expectation or assurance, reliance and detriment. The nature and quality of the assurances could influence the issue of reliance and detriment. The overall test was one of unconscionability. He found there was

---

[144] W.J. Swadling, *"Taylor v Dickens"* (1998) 6 Rest. L. Rev. 220, cited in the Court of Appeal in *Gillett v Holt* [2000] 2 All E.R. 289.
[145] [2000] 2 All E.R. 289.

ample evidence of detrimental reliance, based on repeated assurances given. The judge also accepted the criticism of *Taylor v Dickens*.

19–106 In *Thorner v Major*,[146] D lived with his parents and worked on his father's farm. P, his father's childless cousin, also had a farm and when P became a widower D also helped with the work on that farm also. From 1986, after D's father gave up farming, D worked full-time on P's farm until P's death in 2005. D not only worked on P's farm, but looked after the paper-work and also provided D with emotional support. Over the years the farm varied in size as P bought additional land to farm or sold parcels of land for development. D continued to live with his parents. At no time was the claim-ant ever paid for his work and his only income was pocket money from his father. By the time of P's death D had worked on P's farm for 30 years. Dur-ing that time various oblique remarks were made by P which led the claimant at first to hope and later to expect that he would inherit the farm on P's death. P was a man of few words, rather in the same mould as the farmer in *McCar-ron v McCarron*, but his few indirect remarks on the subject were attested to by witnesses. On one occasion in 1990, P handed the claimant an insurance bonus notice, relating to two policies on his life, and said: "That's for my death duties." In 1997 P made a will in which he left pecuniary legacies totalling £225,000 and the whole of his residuary estate to the claimant, who was also named as sole executor. Later, P fell out with one of the pecuniary legatees and destroyed the will. He never made a new will and died intestate. The claimant sought a declaration that the defendants, P's personal representatives, held his estate on trust for the claimant.

19–107 The Court of Appeal held that P's implicit statement of 1990 did not amount to a "clear and unequivocal" representation by P upon which he had intended the claimant to rely. The claimant appealed. On the appeal the defen-dants raised the additional issue that, given P's buying and selling of land over the years, the property which was the subject of the alleged estoppel lacked certainty.

19–108 The House of Lords reversed the Court of Appeal on the ground that whether representations were sufficient depended on the context. They found the court had given insufficient weight to the context in which the statements were made which was that of two taciturn men who communicated obliquely but understood each other well. As Lord Hoffmann elegantly observed[147]:

"I do not think that the judge was trying to pinpoint the date at which the assurance became unequivocal and I think it would be unrealistic in a case like this to try to do so. There was a close and ongoing daily relationship between the parties. Past events provide context and background for the

[146] [2009] UKHL 18.
[147] [2009] 1 W.L.R. 777 at para.8.

interpretation of subsequent events and subsequent events throw retrospective light upon the meaning of past events. The owl of Minerva spreads its
wings only with the falling of the dusk.[148] The finding was that David reasonably relied upon the assurance from 1990, even if it required later events
to confirm that it was reasonable for him to have done so."[149]

19–109 The House of Lords rejected the argument that the extent of the farm
was uncertain. The judge found that there had been an assurance by P that the
claimant would inherit "the farm", that both parties had known that the extent
of the farm was liable to fluctuate, with sales and purchases of parcels of land
from time to time; but it was clear that the assurances given by P related to the
extent of the farm as it would exist at the time of his death.

Recent Irish Cases
19–110 Recent Irish cases have, like many of the cases discussed above,
concerned the disposition of farmland. In *Naylor v Maher*,[150] the plaintiff had
worked, unpaid, on the deceased's farm for many years. *Thorner v Major* was
accepted as "persuasive authority" by O'Keeffe J., and the plaintiff was able to
establish that a proprietary estoppel had arisen in his favour.[151]

19–111 In *Finnegan v Hand*,[152] the plaintiff had worked on the defendant's
farm from the age of 12 in 1971 until the death of the defendant in 2009.
He lived in substandard accommodation close to the defendant's property,
and at one point turned down an offer of social housing because it would have
inconvenienced the defendant if he were to move further away. The defendant
died intestate in 2009 and the plaintiff, who had expected to be named as a
beneficiary in the deceased's will, brought a case based on proprietary estoppel
or, in the alternative, a constructive trust.

19–112 White J. found on the evidence that the plaintiff had "worked on the
farm for 28 years to an extent way beyond that required of an employee, that
he was substantially underpaid and made a significant sacrifice in giving up
social housing in 1987." The court also found that "on different occasions,
the deceased both directly and obliquely led the plaintiff to believe that he
would, at least, name the beneficiary in his will." The court was satisfied that
the plaintiff had relied on the deceased's assurances to his detriment. White J.
found that "[w]hile the court can hold that proprietary estoppel arises, because

---

[148] The reference is to the German philosopher, G.W.F. Hegel, who held that philosophy could
only describe the world and that philosophy comes to understand a historical condition just as
it passes away: G.W.F. Hegel, *Elements of the Philosophy of Right* (Berlin, 1820), Preface.

[149] The judge expressed the same thought when in the Court of Appeal in *Walton v Walton*, unreported, 14 April 1994.

[150] [2012] IEHC 408.

[151] In *Coyle v Finnegan* [2013] IEHC 463 the plaintiff had similarly worked on the deceased's
farm for around 13 years without being paid.

[152] *Re Gartlan; Finnegan v Hand* [2016] IEHC 255.

of the uncertain nature of the promises made as to the future intentions of the deceased, the court is of the opinion that a constructive remedial trust arises."[153] The court expressly relied on *Thorner v Major* in relation to the finding of the constructive remedial trust.

Mistake

19–113 Some of the early cases on what would now be seen as proprietary estoppel were cases in which a person, in the mistaken belief that a plot of land belonged to him or her, built on it, or made improvements to it, while the true owner, knowing of his or her mistake, stood idly by and then, when the building was complete or the improvements made, sought to assert his legal title.

19–114 In *Willmott v Barber*,[154] Fry J. set out five *probanda* which were intended to define the grounds of intervention of equity in such cases:

1. the claimant must have made a mistake as to his or her rights;
2. the claimant must have "expended some money or must have done some act … on the faith of … the mistaken belief";
3. the owner of land must know of his own right which is inconsistent with the right claimed;
4. the owner must know of the claimant's mistaken belief; and
5. the owner must have encouraged the claimant in his expenditure or other acts.

19–115 For a time it seemed that the mistake cases were a significant instance of equitable estoppel and a guide to other situations, but more recently the mistake cases have been found to be relatively rare. Furthermore, there have been criticisms of Fry J.'s *probanda* as being too strict, most notably in *Taylor Fashions Ltd v Liverpool Victoria Trustees Co Ltd*,[155] in which doubts were expressed as to *probandum* 3. Also, *probanda* 2 and 5 required a positive act on the part of the relier or of the owner, whereas inaction on the part of the relier, as in *Greasley v Cook*,[156] would seem to justify equitable intervention, as would inaction by the owner in the knowledge of the mistake.

19–116 In *McMahon v Kerry County Council*,[157] the court characterised the facts as a case of mistake, perhaps controversially, but certainly in unusual circumstances. The plaintiffs acquired a plot of land in 1964 for the purpose of building a secondary school. The defendant, a local authority, had assented to this. Later the plaintiffs decided that it would not be feasible to build a school and abandoned their plan. They did not visit the site again until 1968 and

---

[153] [2016] IEHC 255 at para.70.
[154] (1880) 15 Ch. D. 96.
[155] [1982] Q.B. 133.
[156] [1980] 1 W.L.R. 1306.
[157] [1981] I.L.R.M. 419.

discovered that employees of the defendant local authority were preparing to build on it. Upon complaint being made the work ceased. The plaintiffs never fenced or marked off the site. Beginning in 1972, the local authority built two houses on the site. In 1973, the plaintiffs discovered this situation and after some delay began proceedings to recover possession of the site. In the same year the local authority put tenants in the two houses. The plaintiffs claimed possession of the site and the houses. The local authority submitted that the court should exercise its equitable jurisdiction and refuse an order for possession in the circumstances. The judge quoted the passage in *Ramsden v Dyson*[158] as to circumstances in which a person mistakenly erects buildings on land belonging to another:

> "But it will be observed that to raise such an equity two things are required, first, that the person expending the money suppose himself to be building on his own land; and, secondly, that the real owner at the time of the expenditure knows that the land belongs to him and not to the person expending the money in the belief that he is the owner. For if a stranger builds on my land knowing it to be mine, there is no principle of equity which would prevent my claiming the land with the benefit of all the expenditure made on it. There would be nothing in my conduct, active or passive, making it inequitable in me to assert my legal rights."[159]

19–117 There was no question of the plaintiffs remaining wilfully passive when the defendant began to build on their land since the judge was satisfied on the evidence that the plaintiffs did not know of such building until December when they immediately made a complaint to the County Council. However, the judge considered that the plaintiffs had contributed to the "second mistake", if that is what it was, when the local authority later built houses on the site. The judge then went on to list the factors which led him to conclude that it would be unjust to allow the plaintiffs to recover possession of the land. They were:

1. the plaintiffs secured possession of the site for the express purpose of building a school, which purpose was never realised;
2. the plaintiffs never secured the site nor did they keep it under surveillance;
3. there was no intrinsic value in the site so far as the plaintiffs were concerned;
4. the defendant's mistake was excusable;
5. if given possession the plaintiffs would realise a large profit without having expended any effort or money; and
6. the houses were now in the occupation of needy persons.

---

[158] (1866) L.R. 1 H.L. 129 at 140–141. See also *Sheridan v Barrett* (1879) 4 L.R. Ir. 223.
[159] See also *East India Co v Vincent* (1740) 2 Atk. 83 at 84.

19–118 The combination of these factors persuaded the judge that it would be unconscionable and unjust for the plaintiffs to recover possession. He held they were nevertheless entitled to the market value of the site, without the houses, and to damages. Citing *Cullen v Cullen*,[160] the judge said that at the expiration of 12 years the defendant could apply to have itself registered as owner of the plot. The continuing influence of *Cullen* is therefore apparent.

19–119 If the plaintiffs had recovered possession of the land and title to the houses, they would have received a considerable benefit at public expense, but it is less easy to explain the decision in terms of legal principle. The judge described the conduct of the defendant local authority as "excusable" even though they were well-placed to know the true position since they had approved the proposed use of the site and, as a local authority, had ready access to the relevant plans of the site. The judge emphasised the conduct of the plaintiffs and the fact that they had not kept the site under surveillance. The law does indeed provide that an owner may lose his or her rights by failing to pursue them, but that is only after the limitation period has expired, and here it had not done so. It is difficult to see why a mere lack of surveillance, in the absence of the requisite period of adverse possession, should lead to a loss of ownership. A usual formulation of the doctrine today is to speak of "encouragement" of a "belief or expectation". Can it really be said that the plaintiffs encouraged the mistaken belief of the local authority?

An Imaginative Remedy

19–120 In *Re JR, a Ward of Court*,[161] JR, who suffered from mental illness, was made a ward of court and a committee appointed of his person and estate. He later entered a psychiatric hospital for treatment. While there he formed a relationship with the respondent, a temporary patient in the hospital. JR invited her to live with him in his house and told her that he would look after her and that she would be sure of a home for the rest of her life. The respondent moved into JR's house. The judge had no evidence before him of where she was living at the time she was admitted to the hospital and met JR, but held that the court was entitled to assume she had a house or flat which she had given up in order to move in with JR. In 1988 JR made a will leaving all his property to the respondent. He handed the will to her saying "it's not my house now, it's our house and eventually it will be your house". The couple lived in the house for another two years. JR, who was then 71 years old, was readmitted to hospital as his mental health had deteriorated and it was found that he would need institutional care for the rest of his life. The respondent continued to live in the house which had fallen into an advanced state of disrepair. The committee of JR sought an order for sale of the house to pay for medical and other expenses. The respondent claimed she had an interest in the premises due to representations made by JR.

---

[160] [1962] I.R. 268.
[161] [1993] I.L.R.M. 657.

19–121 Costello J. in the High Court held that the respondent had established an estoppel as she had acted to her detriment on JR's representations at the time he invited her to stay in his house. The judge found, citing *Maharaj v Chand*,[162] that the detriment consisted of her leaving her existing home on the faith of the assurance that she would have another in its place. The judge found that the respondent had an equity in the house on the basis that it would be inequitable for JR to deny that she had a right to live in his house rent free for as long as she wished. It was then for the court to decide how that equity was to be satisfied. The judge found that it would be unreasonable to authorise the use of JR's meagre resources to put the house in good repair, which he estimated would cost about £34,000. The judge ordered that the house be sold provided that another dwelling suitable to the respondent's needs be purchased in JR's name in which the respondent would be free to live as long as she wished.

19–122 In coming to his decision the judge found that the respondent did not acquire a distinct interest by virtue of the representations made by JR in 1988 and the fact of his handing her his will because (a) the respondent had not acted on them to her detriment, and (b) JR had not intended to give her expressly an immediate beneficial interest because, had he done so, he would have transferred the house to her or to them both jointly. He intended only that she should have "a right to reside in the house during his life" and, secondly, ownership of it after his death. The respondent had nevertheless acquired an equity by "promissory estoppel" at the time she moved in.[163] In arriving at this decision the judge distinguished between promissory and proprietary estoppel. Speaking of promissory estoppel he said:

> "If the subject matter of the representation is land, no right or interest in the land results from this estoppel—a personal right is vested in the representee which will preclude the representor from enforcing a title to the land. A proprietary estoppel is different in a number of ways. When it relates to land it may result in the creation of rights in or over land."[164]

19–123 The judge cited *Re Basham*[165] and *Greasley v Cook*[166] as examples of the latter. The judge clearly considered the case before him to be one of "promissory" estoppel. This seems to be because he considered that the remedy he awarded created a personal licence and not a property interest. In fact there is nothing in the judgment to indicate that there was any other difference in the judge's view between the two doctrines, in which case there is little difference at all. No third parties were involved and so a property interest was probably not necessary to secure the respondent's position until JR's death, when she would in any case acquire one under the will. However, she had acquired by

---

[162] [1986] A.C. 898.
[163] [1993] I.L.R.M. 657.
[164] [1993] I.L.R.M. 657 at 663.
[165] [1986] 1 W.L.R. 1498.
[166] [1980] 1 W.L.R. 1306.

the estoppel something in the nature of a personal licence which, on the *Ashburn* principle,[167] could give rise to a constructive trust binding on third parties during JR's life.

19–124 The case is novel in that it decides that the personal licence is available not only against the property originally occupied in response to the representation, but attaches to property to be acquired later by the representor, and this was no doubt an appropriate remedy on the facts. However, merely because the judge decided that the "minimum equity" necessary on the facts of the case was a personal licence should not have led to the estoppel being classified as "promissory".[168] It would be more flexible to regard the estoppel as raising an equity of an indeterminate kind and the issue of how it is to be satisfied on the facts, to determine whether a personal licence would be sufficient or some interest of a proprietary nature binding on third parties. It is also not easy to see why JR's statement in 1988 that "it's not my house now, it's our house" was not a declaration of trust. The ghost of *Cullen* may still have been evident.

The Elements of Estoppel
Detriment
19–125 Some judges have treated the requirement of detriment in proprietary estoppel as if it were the same as detriment in the doctrine of consideration in the law of contract, i.e. as if it required some actual expenditure of money, or money's worth, the value of which would be lost if no corresponding benefit were received.[169] This restricted sense of detriment, however, fails to address the different basis of proprietary estoppel and has proved inadequate to reach the number of situations in which the estoppel requires a remedy.

19–126 Several cases indicate that other judges prefer to use the term "prejudice"[170] or "change of position"[171] to "detriment".[172]

19–127 In proprietary estoppel the detriment consists not of the acts done in reliance, because reliance may consist of inaction, but in the prospective loss that would occur to the party if the expectation were to be defeated. When a court grants the remedy it is to prevent this prospective detriment occurring in fact. Working unpaid on a farm for a number of years has been clearly

---

[167] *Ashburn Anstalt v Arnold* [1989] Ch. 1.

[168] The case widens the definition of "promissory" estoppel since there was no prior contractual relationship between the parties.

[169] *Ramsden v Dyson* (1866) L.R. 1 H.L. 129 at 170; *Willmott v Barber* (1880) 15 Ch. D. 96 at 105f; see the second of Fry J.'s five tests of estoppel.

[170] *Watts v Story* [1983] CAT 319.

[171] *E R Ives Investments Ltd v High* [1967] 2 Q.B. 379 at 405F; *Re Basham, dec'd* [1986] 1 W.L.R. 1498 at 1504D; *Bhimji v Salih*, unreported, Court of Appeal, 4 February 1981; *Grundt v Great Boulder Pty Gold Mines Ltd* (1937) 59 C.L.R. 641 at 674.

[172] *Grundt v Great Boulder Property Gold Mines Ltd* (1937) 59 C.L.R. 641.

recognised as a detriment,[173] and the English Court of Appeal has suggested that the representor need not necessarily be aware of the relier's detriment.[174]

19–128 These points were brought into focus in *Greasley v Cook*.[175] The defendant, C, claimed a declaration that she had the right to occupy a house rent-free for life. She had come to live in the house at the age of 16 as a live-in maid. The owner was a widower with four children. At first she was paid a weekly wage, but after eight years she began a relationship with K, one of the sons of the owner. For the next 30 years she looked after various members of the family, including a mentally disabled daughter of the owner. She received no wages during this long period. C gave evidence that she had not asked for payment because she had been encouraged by members of the family, including one of the present plaintiffs, to believe that she could look upon the house as her home for the rest of her life. When both the owner and K died, other family members brought the present proceedings to evict her. The county court judge refused to find proprietary estoppel on the ground that she had not expended money on the property. This decision was reversed by the Court of Appeal. Lord Denning M.R. held that expenditure was not essential for estoppel.[176]

19–129 However satisfactory the result in *Greasley*, the treatment of the issue of conduct and detriment is less convincing. The judge appears to create a presumption in favour of both when, in the sense used by the judge, neither were present. The defendant did not "act" in reliance on the expectation of residential security. She did nothing. Yet that was precisely the behaviour which such an expectation was likely to produce. She was, to use the cliché, lulled into a false sense of security. Had she not been under the impression that she would have been able to stay in the house for the rest of her life, she might have made some financial provision for her accommodation after retirement, or she might have revived her claim to be paid wages. The detriment in *Greasley* was the same as in any other case involving the doctrine. It was the *reliance* which was "negative".

19–130 This is not to say that there is no problem of proof in cases of "negative reliance". What a person *might* do, or *might have done*, or been forced to do, cannot be proved in the same way as what he or she did in fact do. But a court can still be persuaded that a person desisted from conduct, or even failed to consider it at all, because of assurances he or she had been given. The editor of *Snell* in formulating the first of the conditions specified that the person claiming "must have incurred expenditure or otherwise have prejudiced himself or acted to his detriment".[177]

---

[173] *McCarron v McCarron*, unreported, Supreme Court, 13 February 1997; *Naylor v Maher* [2012] IEHC 308.

[174] *Joyce v Epsom and Ewell Borough Council* [2012] EWCA 1398 at para.39.

[175] [1980] 1 W.L.R. 1306.

[176] [1980] 1 W.L.R. 1306 at 1311f.

[177] E.H.T. Snell, P.V. Baker and S.J.H. Langan, *Snell's Principles of Equity*, 28th edn (London: Sweet & Maxwell, 1982).

19–131 It may also be the case that in the "mistake" type of case, where the conduct on the part of the property owner is of a negative or inactive kind, reliance in the form of expenditure of money may be required to raise the equity. It is, after all, difficult to imagine circumstances in which an equity would be raised by a person acquiescing in another doing nothing. But this is arguably still a question of reliance. In such a case the reliance is that of the mistaken party relying on his or her own mistaken view of his or her rights, a reliance fortified by the knowing failure of the property owner to correct it.

19–132 If this is so, a further question arises as to the necessary elements in prejudice. Does it imply an element of irrevocability? In *Greasley* it was too late for the old lady to make provision for accommodation by the time she was given notice to quit. That was why it would be inequitable to deny her a remedy. There is one suggestion in the Irish authorities that irrevocability may be an element in the conduct of the relier. In *Cullen* Kenny J. found that there was no equity in favour of the mother because she could readily reimburse herself for the money she had spent in running the business. Nevertheless, it may simply depend on what a court sees as necessary to satisfy the equity. It may be that in some cases, even though the relier could be compensated or could recover his or her position in other ways, the equity would not be satisfied short of a property interest.

Reliance

19–133 Proprietary estoppel is often formulated in terms of reliance on an assurance to the detriment of the relier. Reliance has thus been sometimes treated as a separate element in the doctrine to detriment. Problems which have been perceived as one of detriment may really be problems of reliance. It is the act of reliance, or failure to act induced by reliance on the assurance, which gives rise to the equity. A party relies on an assurance or a mistaken impression of his or her rights when he or she alters his or her position on the faith of the assurance or impression emanating from the other party, or desists from some course of action which he or she would otherwise have undertaken in the absence of such an assurance or impression; and this action or lack of it means that he or she would be worse off than if no such assurance or impression had been created or encouraged. Patten L.J. in the English Court of Appeal said in *Lester v Woodgate*[178] that what a court must determine is whether the actions or words of the representor would reasonably convey to the relier an assurance which it would be reasonable to rely on.

Expectation or Belief

19–134 The doctrine of proprietary estoppel has frequently been invoked when the representor (or estoppee) has acted in some way to induce an expectation or belief in the other party that he or she is to have, or does have, some

---

[178] [2010] EWCA Civ 199 at para.26.

property interest.[179] In *McMahon v Kerry County Council*,[180] there was no element of wilful knowledge of a mistaken belief in the owner of the land. If the case is to be explained in terms of what it decided about the conduct of the owner of the land then it can only be justified by accepting that negligence in discovering that a mistake has been made is sufficient to deprive an owner of his or her land. It stands for the proposition that the price of ownership is eternal vigilance.

Third Parties

19–135 The estoppel, or perhaps more accurately the equity raised by the estoppel, binds not only the original estoppee whose conduct gave rise to it, but also third parties who would be bound in equity, namely all those except a bona fide purchaser of the legal estate without notice of the equity.

19–136 The point that the equity raised by the estoppel binds the personal representatives of the estoppee had already been decided by *Inwards v Baker*,[181] but the implications of the cases are interesting. The cases make it clear that although the doctrine raises an equity, the equity may in some circumstances only be satisfied by the conferment of a legal estate. This was the case in *Pascoe v Turner*,[182] in which the man was ordered to convey the legal fee simple to the widow. In that case no third party was involved. In *Re Basham*,[183] a third party was involved, but one who would have been bound in equity in any case. Nevertheless, the situation could arise in which the third party involved was not someone who would be bound in equity, but only if the interest conferred was a legal estate, i.e. a purchaser of the legal estate without notice. Would a court order such a party to convey the legal estate to the relier in order to satisfy the equity? If, in *Pascoe v Turner*,[184] the man had conveyed the legal estate to a third party and the third party had tried to evict the widow, would the widow have succeeded? The answer seems clearly "no". Proprietary estoppel is a doctrine of equity and so long as a legal estate had not passed to the relier by order of the court, only those third parties are bound who are bound in equity.

19–137 In *Re Sharpe (A Bankrupt)*,[185] these issues were brought into focus. J was an elderly woman. She had contributed much of the purchase price of a lease in a shop and maisonette bought by her nephew, S. In order to increase her contribution, J had sold her existing home and had moved into the maisonette with S and his wife on the understanding that she would be able to remain there for as long as she wished. S later became bankrupt. J, acting on

---

[179] For the position in estoppel by representation, see *Doran v Thompson* [1978] I.R. 223.
[180] [1981] I.L.R.M. 419.
[181] [1965] 2 Q.B. 29. Or was it the licence which bound them?
[182] [1979] 1 W.L.R. 431.
[183] [1986] 1 W.L.R. 1498.
[184] [1979] 1 W.L.R. 431.
[185] [1980] 1 W.L.R. 219. See G. Woodman, "Note" (1980) 96 L.Q.R. 336; J. Martin, "Recent Cases: Constructive Trusts and Licensees; Re Sharpe" [1980] Conv. 207.

her solicitor's advice, then obtained a promissory note from S for £15,700. S's trustee in bankruptcy contracted to sell the lease to a purchaser, P, with vacant possession. When S's trustee in bankruptcy sought vacant possession, J argued that she had an interest in the premises. Browne-Wilkinson J. declined to hold that she had an equitable interest by way of what he termed a "resulting trust", and held that the money contributed by her was primarily intended to be a loan. He took the promissory note to be evidence of this. She had "something less than an aliquot share of the equity in the premises" which was the right to remain in occupation until the loan was repaid. Referring to *Ramsden v Dyson*,[186] he went on:

> "[I]t is now established that, if the parties have proceeded on a common assumption that the plaintiff is to enjoy a right to reside in a particular property and in reliance on that assumption the plaintiff has expended money or otherwise acted to his detriment, the defendant will not be allowed to go back on that common assumption and the court will imply an irrevocable licence or trust which will give effect to that common assumption."[187]

19–138 He held that the right, "whether it be called a contractual licence or an equitable licence or an interest under a constructive trust", was binding not only upon S but also upon S's trustee in bankruptcy, who was essentially in the same position as S. This was sufficient to dispose of the issue before the court, but the judge was clearly concerned as to whether the right would be binding on P. He observed that P would not necessarily be bound by it "as a purchaser without express notice" and that he might take priority over it if he sued for specific performance of the contract. The judge clearly did not find this satisfactory, since if it were to occur, J's right would be at an end and she would be left with only the right to sue S who was, in any case, bankrupt. The judge said that he found this area of the law "very confused and difficult to fit in with established equitable principles". He expressed the hope that the whole question would soon receive full consideration in the Court of Appeal so that, "in order to do justice to the many thousands of people who never come into court at all but who wish to know with certainty what their proprietary rights are, the extent to which these irrevocable licences bind third parties may be defined with certainty".

19–139 *Re Sharpe* illustrates the problems which arise in this area of the law where the doctrines of proprietary estoppel, constructive trust and, at least in this case, contractual licence, overlap. Was the issue in *Re Sharpe* as to the circumstances in which:

(a) a contractual licence binds third parties? or
(b) a third party is bound as constructive trustee? or
(c) the equity raised by proprietary estoppel binds third parties?

---

[186] (1866) L.R. 1 H.L. 129 at 141.
[187] [1980] 1 W.L.R. 219 at 223.

19–140 The judge seems far from clear. The doctrines are liable to intersect and become confused where, as in this case, the result of applying proprietary estoppel is to find that the equity so created should be satisfied by a licence, especially if it is termed, oddly, a "contractual licence".[188] The problem was compounded by the judge apparently holding that the equity raised by proprietary estoppel can only be satisfied by a licence or a "trust". The issue will have to be disentangled from the quite separate issue of the extent to which a contractual or occupational licence can be binding on third parties. In *Ashburn Anstalt v Arnold*,[189] Fox L.J. in the English Court of Appeal suggested, as an alternative ratio, that a *contractual* licence is not binding on third parties in the absence of a constructive trust. But the court arrived at this conclusion having already held that a contractual licence was not an equitable interest in itself. Hence, a third party was not bound merely by notice of it. However, the *equity* raised by proprietary estoppel is not to be confused with the further interest which an owner may be required to convey as a result of it, whether by way of licence or fee simple or something else. The equity raised by proprietary estoppel is, it is submitted, an equitable interest and as such should bind third parties with notice of it. It will, of course, be necessary to decide what degree of knowledge or constructive knowledge the third party must have in order that the test of notice is satisfied. It is suggested tentatively that it should be a knowledge of all the elements which gave rise to the proprietary estoppel, unless the relier is in occupation, in which case that fact should put the third party on notice.

CONSTRUCTIVE TRUSTS

19–141 A constructive trust arises by operation of law, usually as a result of the conduct, rather than the intention of parties.[190] As Biehler observes, there may be some overlap between constructive and resulting trusts, but "from a practical perspective it makes little difference whether a trust is described as resulting or constructive"[191]—both are exempt from the formalities of express trusts.

19–142 In the past there was some discussion over whether a constructive trust was a remedy given at the discretion of the court to avoid unconscionable behaviour, or if it arises "by operation of law as from the date of the circumstances which give rise to it".[192] In other words, whether the constructive trust

---

[188] The equity arising under proprietary estoppel may be satisfied by a licence, but it is hardly "contractual". If there was a contract it would not be necessary to invoke proprietary estoppel.
[189] [1989] Ch. 1.
[190] For a more comprehensive examination of constructive trusts, see H. Biehler, *Equity and the Law of Trusts in Ireland*, 6th edn (Dublin: Round Hall, 2015), Ch.8.
[191] Biehler, *Equity and the Law of Trusts in Ireland* (2015), p.228.
[192] *Westdeutsche Landesbank Girozentrale v Islington LBC* [1996] A.C. 669 at 714; *Megarry & Wade: The Law of Real Property* (2012), para.11–017.

is to be viewed as remedial or institutional. Deane J. in *Muchinski v Dodds*[193] described the modern constructive trust as "a remedial institution"; it then follows that whether or not the imposition of the trust is retrospective is a matter of discretion. Under an institutional model, it would not be a matter of discretion.

Situations Where Constructive Trusts May Arise
Existing Fiduciary Relationship
19–143 A fiduciary relationship is one in which one party has "undertaken to act for or on behalf of another in a particular matter in circumstances which give rise to a relationship of trust and confidence."[194] Where there is no existing trust but there is an existing fiduciary relationship, there is a general principle that no one in a fiduciary position may benefit from their position. This is known as the doctrine of *graft*. It applies not only to trustees but to other fiduciary relationships as well.[195] It has always been seen in Ireland as an example of the constructive trust.[196] In England the doctrine is not known by the name of graft and is simply part of the doctrine of constructive trusts.[197] The leading English case is *Keech v Sandford*.[198] It is questionable whether there are any significant differences between the Irish and English doctrines, although the doctrine in Ireland has found expression in statute law for specific purposes.[199]

Existing Trust
19–144 Examples of constructive trusts where there is an existing trust are:

(a) A trustee, or trustees, convey the legal title to a third party. Equity will treat the third party as holding the property on trust unless the third party

---

[193] (1985) 160 C.L.R. 583 at 614.

[194] *Bristol and West Building Society v Mothew* [1998] Ch. 1, approved in *McMullen v McGinley* [2005] IESC 10.

[195] There are some categories of fiduciary relationship which are well-recognised, such as the relationships between trustee and beneficiary, or agent and principal, and there is evidence of some judicial reluctance to further extend the categories, as expressed by Hogan J. in *Irish Life and Permanent plc v Financial Services Ombudsman* [2012] IEHC 367 at para.45.

[196] See *Gabbett v Lawder* (1883) 11 L.R. Ir. 295 at 299.

[197] A. Underhill and D.J. Hayton, *Law Relating to Trusts and Trustees*, 14th edn (London: Butterworths, 1987), Ch.7, Article 33, pp.301–325.

[198] (1726) Sel. Cas. Ch. 61.

[199] Section 14(3) of the Land Law (Ireland) Act 1887 (retained by the Schedule to the Statute Law Revision Act 2007) provides that any tenant has power to enter into an agreement for purchase of the holding and any interest conveyed to the tenant under such an agreement "shall be deemed to be a graft on the previous interest of the tenant" in the holding. See also now s.74 of the Landlord and Tenant (Amendment) Act 1980 which applies to a person entitled to an interest in land the title to which interest originated under a lease for lives renewable forever which was created prior to 1 August 1849 and was not converted into a fee farm grant. Section 74 provides that such a person "shall from the commencement of this Act hold the land for an estate in fee simple" and that "the said estate shall be deemed to be a graft upon the previous interest".

can make the plea of bona fide purchaser for value of the legal estate without notice of the equity. In the case of registered land this is now modified to the extent already discussed in that chapter. This is the *proprietary* remedy against third parties.

(b) A third party has received trust property, or has received it but has subsequently parted with it, or has not actually received the trust property but assists in a breach of trust. Equity will hold the third party personally liable as a constructive trustee if he or she has been a party to a fraudulent use of trust property or has knowingly interfered with it in other ways inconsistent with the trust.[200]

Agreement to Make Mutual Wills
19–145 This is dealt with in the chapter on succession.

Purchaser's Equity
19–146 This is dealt with in the chapters on equity and registration of deeds and title.

Common Intention
The Scope
19–147 Where there is no existing trust, the courts may impose a constructive trust where one party has acted to his or her detriment in reliance on a common intention that he or she will acquire an interest in property. This most often occurs where A acquires the legal title to property but B has contributed either directly or indirectly to its acquisition or improvement. This most commonly occurs in the context of family or intimate relationships. Equity in this area has been substantially encroached upon by legislation. Where the parties are not in such a relationship, direct contribution to the purchase of the property has always been characterised as a presumed resulting trust, and courts do not always care to distinguish resulting from constructive trusts in this area. Where contributions are indirect, as between husband and wife, in the *McC v McC*[201] situation, it is arguable that this should be classified as a constructive trust based on implied or imputed intention. Constructive trusts in this area also overlap or intersect with proprietary estoppel and this has already been commented upon.

19–148 However, as Megarry and Wade[202] point out, there are situations outside family law, civil partnership and cohabitant legislation where constructive trusts may still be deployed:

---

[200] *Megarry & Wade: The Law of Real Property* (2012), para.11–019.
[201] [1984] IESC 1.
[202] *Megarry & Wade: The Law of Real Property* (2012), para.11–024.

(a) on the death of a spouse, etc., or otherwise, in deciding what property passes with his or her estate;

(b) in assessing the assets of a party to a marriage, civil partnership or cohabitation;

(c) on the insolvency of a spouse, etc. in determining what property is available to creditors;

(d) where co-owners mortgage land and the mortgage is held not to be binding on one of them for lack of consent, in determining the extent of the interest that is bound by the mortgage. Where the parties are married, consent is governed by the Family Home Protection Act 1976 and in the case of civil partners by the equivalent provisions in the Civil Partnership and Certain Rights and Obligations of Cohabitants Act 2010; and

(e) other miscellaneous cases, either not covered by legislation or outside the typical family context.

19–149 It seems that in a domestic or intimate relationship situation, the courts are prepared to impute an intention on the part of both parties that direct and indirect contributions to the acquisition or improvement of the occupied property, stemming from the relationship itself, do not require evidence of specific acts or representations. However, where less intimate relations are involved, some evidence of conduct in the form of representations must be shown. If classification is required, then it would seem more appropriate to regard a trust arising from the fact of the relationship itself as a presumed trust, and therefore a presumed resulting trust. If the trust will only be found to arise on proof of conduct, by representations or otherwise, that could be regarded as a constructive trust.

Irish Cases
19–150 Detrimental reliance, or some form of it, based on a claimed common intention may be the subject of a claim in other cases, as where a landowner reneged on an informal promise to allow the vendor to remain in a cottage rent-free.[203]

19–151 On the other hand, there are some cases in which the constructive trust has been imposed on the general ground of "unconscionability" which, without the elements of detrimental reliance or some other articulated principles, seems lacking in legal precision. It is here that Deane J.'s comment in *Muschinski v Dodds* is well-founded.

19–152 One controversial instance is *Murray v Murray*,[204] which is open to the criticism that the basis for the constructive trust was unclear. In that case the plaintiff, the defendant's nephew, had lived in a property with his aunt, EM, the defendant's sister, since he was a child. The defendant had financed

---

[203] *Bannister v Bannister* [1948] 2 All E.R. 133.
[204] [1996] 3 I.R. 251.

the building of the house through a mortgage and he paid a deposit equal to a quarter of the cost from his own resources. He originally intended to move into the house with his wife, but never did. Instead, he and his wife exchanged the house for his parents' house and went to live in theirs. In fact, the first resident was the defendant's sister, EM, who continued to reside in the house until her death in 1988. During her life EM discharged the mortgage instalments and paid rent and rates. The defendant paid the insurance. In 1962, the defendant's parents also moved into the house, with the plaintiff who was then two-and-a-half years old. The plaintiff was the son of another sister of the defendant. When the defendant's parents died, the defendant's solicitors prepared documents transferring the house to EM, but EM never executed them. In 1988, the defendant indicated that he would execute a transfer to EM if she discharged the balance of the mortgage and certain other charges. EM did so, but died before the deed of transfer had been executed. The nephew continued to live in the house, but a dispute arose between them and the defendant then asked the nephew to pay rent. The nephew never paid rent. The defendant took out letters of administration and drew up a schedule of her assets which did not include the house. The nephew, who was her next of kin, claimed to be entitled to the beneficial interest, on the basis that it would be unconscionable for the defendant to rely on his legal title.

19–153 If the familiar rule as to presumed resulting trust were to apply, the aunt would have been entitled at her death to the beneficial interest which would then presumably have passed to her nephew. Barron J., however, found that the presumption had in effect been rebutted by the evidence that the aunt had refused a conveyance of the legal title from her brother. It may be that she trusted her brother to allow the nephew to remain after her death, or maybe she never considered the further implications. There was no evidence of her intentions beyond the fact of the refusal. The controversial aspect of the decision is that Barron J. then went on to find that there was a constructive trust in the aunt's favour which passed to the nephew and that he was entitled to three-quarters of the beneficial interest.

19–154 The difficulty is that it is not clear why, if the resulting trust, based on presumed common intention, was rebutted by the evidence, there was not a similar objection to the constructive trust.[205] It could not be said to be unfair or unconscionable in relation to the aunt, since there was no evidence that she intended to benefit and furthermore, to put it plainly, she was dead. Also, if the nephew had a claim, it was based on inheritance. The nephew did not apparently argue that he had an independent claim based upon an expectation, created or encouraged by the defendant, that he was to have an interest in the property, since there was no such evidence. Nor was it alleged that he had contributed to the purchase or the value of the property himself. The nephew

---

[205] See J. Mee, "Palm Trees in the Rain: New Model Constructive Trusts in Ireland" (1996) 1(1) C.P.L.J. 9 at 13.

may have expected to live in the property for as long as he wished, rent-free, or to have some interest in it, but the defendant did not appear to have made any representation to that effect. Silence in the mistake type of case, where the mistaken party builds on the land and the owner knows of the other party's mistake, may be enough, but if the claim concerns expectation, then, as McGuinness J. pointed out in *CF v JDF*,[206] there must be a representation of some kind. Also, it was not alleged that the nephew had done or refrained from doing anything that would amount to detrimental reliance.

19–155 *Kelly v Cahill*[207] is another case which has attracted criticism.[208] The deceased had made a will leaving some property to his nephew. Later, he changed his mind, and told his solicitor that he wished to alter his will and that he wished to leave all his property to his wife. His solicitor advised him to transfer his property into the joint names of himself and his wife, which would avoid probate tax. The solicitor through inadvertence did not include all the property in the deed of transfer. The deceased executed the deed, believing, as did his wife and the solicitor, that it included all his property. The land that was not included in the transfer would pass on his death under his will, which he had not altered by the time of his death, to his wife and his brother jointly for life and then to the nephew, subject to the wife's legal right to one-half of the land concerned. The issue was whether there was a constructive trust as to the lands not transferred in favour of the wife.

19–156 Barr J. observed that the evidence established that the testator had a clear intention to transfer all the land, that he took the appropriate steps to do so and indeed believed he had done so. The judge also noted that the nephew was neither aware of nor had any responsibility for the error, but considered that to be irrelevant. He considered that "a 'new model' constructive trust ... the purpose of which is to prevent unjust enrichment is an equitable concept which deserves recognition in Irish law".[209] "Justice and good conscience" required that the nephew should not inherit the property. He held that the remainder in the will was subject to a constructive trust in favour of the wife. Barr J. cited with approval a passage from Keane's *Equity and the Law of Trusts in the Republic of Ireland*[210]:

"In recent years, there has been much discussion in other jurisdictions as to whether a constructive trust can be said to arise in any circumstances where permitting the defendant to retain the property would result in his being 'unjustly enriched'. This, it has been said, effectively means treating the

---

[206] [2005] IESC 45.

[207] [2001] 1 I.R. 56.

[208] E. O'Dell, "Unjust Enrichment and the Remedial Constructive Trust" (2001) 23 D.U.L.J. 71; M. Hourican, "The Introduction of 'New Model' Constructive Trusts in this Jurisdiction" (2001) 6(2) C.P.L.J. 49.

[209] [2001] 1 I.R. 56 at 62.

[210] 1st edn (London: Butterworths, 1988), p.186.

constructive trust as a form of remedy intended to restore property to a person to whom in justice it should belong rather than as an institution analogous to the express or resulting trust. The constructive trust, in its additional traditional form, arises because of equity's refusal to countenance any form of fraud: in this wider modern guise it is imposed by law 'whenever justice and good conscience require it'."

19–157 As Barr J. noted, the latter quotation was from Lord Denning M.R.'s judgment in *Hussey v Palmer*[211] which is considered below. Lord Denning's attempt to establish the "new model" constructive trust as a general discretionary remedy without more precise definition has fallen somewhat out of favour in England, but judgments such as that in *Kelly v Cahill* may indicate that it commands greater approval in Ireland than in England and Wales. *Re Custom House Capital Ltd*[212] may perhaps indicate greater scepticism on the part of contemporary judges. Finlay Geoghegan J. suggested that the constructive trust is best confined to situations where there has been fraud.

19–158 While the result in *Kelly* may be satisfactory in that it gave effect to the wishes of the deceased, it is more difficult to find a more precise and therefore predictable principle on which the case is based. The deceased never changed his will and the decision undermines the law of wills in an unpredictable way. It also, in O'Dell's view, collapses the distinction between unjust enrichment as a personal remedy and the constructive trust as a proprietary one.[213] The alternative might have been for the wife to sue the nephew in a personal claim for unjust enrichment at common law[214] or the solicitor in professional negligence.

Institution or "New Model" Remedy?
19–159 In North America the constructive trust is seen as a general remedial device, rather than as an institution, and this development appears to date to before similar ideas emerged in England. It is a solution which judges impose on situations which are impossible to categorise, rather than a concept which can be seen to arise on the basis of some special set of facts common to the instances in which the trust has been found to exist. The North American model imposes a constructive trust wherever it would be unjust for the holder of the legal title to property to take all its benefits. As Cardozo J. put it:

> "When property has been acquired in such circumstances that the holder of the legal title may not in good conscience retain the beneficial interest, equity converts him into a trustee."[215]

---

[211] [1972] 1 W.L.R. 1286.
[212] [2014] 1 I.L.R.M. 360.
[213] E. O'Dell, "Unjust Enrichment and the Remedial Constructive Trust" (2001) 23 D.U.L.J. 71.
[214] E. O'Dell, "Unjust Enrichment and the Remedial Constructive Trust" (2001) 23 D.U.L.J. 71 at 95.
[215] *Beatty v Guggenheim Exploration Co* 225 NY 380 (1919) at 386.

19–160 The starting point of the "new model" in England was arguably[216] the judgment of Lord Denning M.R. in *Hussey v Palmer*.[217] He expressed the view that a constructive trust is imposed by law whenever justice and good conscience require it:

> "It is a liberal process, founded upon large principles of equity to be applied in cases where the legal owner cannot conscientiously keep the property for himself alone, but ought to allow another to have the property or the benefit of it or a share in it. The trust may arise at the outset when the property is acquired, or later on, as the circumstances may require."[218]

19–161 In the case itself a mother-in-law had paid for the construction of an extra bedroom in a house which belonged to her son-in-law. It was to provide a home for her in her old age. She later moved out after disagreements with the son-in-law. Lord Denning held it "entirely against conscience" that the son-in-law should keep the whole interest in the enlarged house. However, there were elements in *Hussey* that could have suggested some greater precision in defining why it was unconscionable. The mother-in-law had expended a considerable amount of money in expectation of a benefit which did not materialise. True, its failure was not due to any action on the part of the son-in-law but to the mother-in-law's decision to move out, but here there is also an element of a common intention which had been defeated, and a gratuitous benefit to the son-in-law was never part of it.

19–162 In *Cook v Head*,[219] Lord Denning M.R. stated the equitable treatment of domestic situations in these terms:

> "[W]henever parties by their joint efforts acquire property to be used for their joint benefit, the courts may impose or impute a constructive or resulting trust."[220]

19–163 Lord Denning considered that the constructive trust doctrine applied generally to domestic situations, not merely to husband and wife. In *Cook* itself a woman who had contributed labour and financial savings to the building of a house in which she and her male partner planned to live was awarded a one-third beneficial interest in it.

---

[216] An academic argument had been made for what became known as the "new model" by D.M. Waters, *The Constructive Trust: The Case for a New Approach in English Law* (London: Athlone Press, 1964).

[217] [1972] 1 W.L.R. 1286.

[218] [1972] 1 W.L.R. 1286 at 1290.

[219] [1972] 1 W.L.R. 518.

[220] [1972] 1 W.L.R. 518 at 520.

19–164 In *Eves v Eves*,[221] the English Court of Appeal awarded a one-quarter interest in the beneficial interest in a house to the female partner. Lord Denning said that "a few years ago" the court would not have provided a remedy, but that "things have altered now". He traced the new departure to Lord Diplock's judgment in *Gissing*:

> "Equity is not past the age of child bearing.[222] One of her latest progeny is a constructive trust of a new model. Lord Diplock brought it into the world and we have nourished it."[223]

19–165 In fact, Lord Diplock in the House of Lords in *Gissing v Gissing*[224] had formulated a rather more limited principle[225]:

> "A resulting, implied or constructive trust – and it is unnecessary for present purposes to distinguish between these three classes of trust – is created by a transaction between the trustee and the *cestui que trust* in connection with the acquisition by the trustee of a legal estate in land, whenever the trustee has so conducted himself that it would be inequitable to allow him to deny to the *cestui que trust* a beneficial interest in the land acquired ...".

19–166 The reference to "conduct" is more limiting than Cardozo J.'s formula, especially in intimate relationships. Referring more specifically to the case before him, Lord Diplock went on to formulate a more limited rule. A person, he said,[226]

> "will be held so to have conducted himself if by his words or conduct he has induced the *cestui que trust* to act to his own detriment in the reasonable belief that by so acting he was acquiring a beneficial interest in the land."

19–167 The specific case before the court concerned indirect financial contributions by a wife over 25 years to the discharge of a mortgage on the matrimonial home, the legal title to which was vested in the husband alone. The majority of the court found that the wife failed. In the court's view, she would have had to produce some evidence, if not of an agreement between them, then at least that they had consciously contemplated the legal consequences of their respective contributions in relation to the house, and this evidence was lacking. This is the approach which was rejected in Ireland in the domestic context in *McC*

---

[221] [1975] 1 W.L.R. 1338.

[222] In *National Provincial Bank v Ainsworth* [1965] A.C. 1175, the House of Lords rejected the notion, fostered by Lord Denning, that there was such a thing as a deserted wife's equity to remain in the matrimonial home. In his judgment Lord Hodson dismissed the notion with the words: "Equity may not be past the age of child-bearing, but an infant of the kind suggested would lack form or shape."

[223] [1975] 1 W.L.R. 1338 at 1341.

[224] [1971] A.C. 886.

[225] [1971] A.C. 886 at 905.

[226] [1971] A.C. 886 at 905.

v McC[227] as unrealistic, and no longer represents the law in England. Lord Denning in *Eves v Eves* quoted Lord Diplock's more general statement, but apparently chose to ignore the limiting factor of proof of conduct.

19–168 The House of Lords in *National Provincial Bank v Ainsworth*[228] had rejected Lord Denning M.R.'s attempt to establish the doctrine of the "deserted wife's equity", that is, a licence which was automatically binding in equity on third parties. This did not appear to constrain Lord Denning in contractual licence cases where the "new model" was deployed in such cases as *Binions v Evans*,[229] but in *Ashburn Anstalt v Arnold*[230] this development was constrained by the Court of Appeal. The court held that a contractual licence would not, without more, be binding on a third party even though he or she took with notice of it. More specific grounds would be required before the court would impose a constructive trust. The third party's conscience would only be affected by proof that he or she, (a) had expressly undertaken to be bound by the contractual licence, or (b) impliedly, in that he or she had paid less for the legal title because of the licence.

19–169 More recently the constructive trust has had something of a resurgence in the domestic context with the House of Lords, no doubt reflecting changing social attitudes, in *Stack v Dowden*.[231] The majority indicated that: (1) "people living together in an intimate relationship"[232] would be treated as in the same category (whether married, unmarried or lesbian/gay); (2) the resulting trust, based on the narrow ground of monetary contributions, was less suitable a concept in that context than a constructive trust based on (implied) shared intentions in the light of their "whole course of conduct" in relation to it; and (3) different considerations applied where the parties were "at arm's length" where the resulting trust based on a calculation of financial contributions was still appropriate.[233] Lord Neuberger of Abbotbury dissented from this view, supporting the more traditional position in support of resulting trust and calculation in the absence of parliamentary authority, whether the relationship was "sexual, platonic, familial, amicable or commercial".[234]

19–170 Constructive trusts in the commercial sphere have seen the emergence of "the *Pallant v Morgan* equity"[235] which made a resurgence in *Banner Homes*

---

[227] [1984] IESC 1.

[228] [1965] A.C. 1175.

[229] [1972] 1 Ch. 359. See also *DHN Food Distributors Ltd v Tower Hamlets LBC* [1976] 1 W.L.R. 852.

[230] [1989] Ch. 1.

[231] [2007] UKHL 17; [2007] 2 A.C. 432.

[232] [2007] UKHL 17 at para.42.

[233] [2007] UKHL 17 at para.31.

[234] [2007] UKHL 17 at para.107.

[235] [1953] Ch. 43; *Chattock v Muller* (1878) L.R. 8 Ch. D. 177. See also *Baynes Clarke v Corless* [2010] EWCA Civ 338.

Group plc v Luff Developments Ltd.[236] In the *Pallant* case, A and B orally agreed that B would not bid at an auction against A in return for the promise that A, if successful, would sell a part of the land to B. A succeeded in buying the land in the auction and then refused to sell the part to B. B sued for specific performance. A asserted in defence the fact that essential terms had not been agreed.[237] The court held that to allow the defence to succeed would be to sanction a fraud and held that they were joint tenants, and ordered an inquiry as to the price, etc. In *Banner Homes*, the Court of Appeal imposed a constructive trust in similar circumstances, and did not regard that, as a contract, the agreement was unenforceable. The imposition of a constructive trust in such circumstances now looks uncomfortably like the position in *Cobbe*, and open to a similar objection to a remedy—that one businessman chose to trust another rather than reduce the agreement to an enforceable contract. It is no doubt also that different judges take a different view of fraud.

19–171 It has been pointed out, however, that since the *Banner Homes* decision, *Pallant v Morgan* constructive trusts have been "more notable for instances of … rejection, rather than … successful application."[238]

The Relationship between Constructive Trusts and Proprietary Estoppel
19–172 Both constructive trusts and proprietary estoppel are applications of "the equitable principle that a party should not be allowed to enforce his strict legal rights when it would be inequitable to do so on the basis of the dealings which have taken place between the parties."[239] Both doctrines allow for the creation of informal interests in land.

19–173 In *Re Basham*,[240] proprietary estoppel was said to give rise to a constructive trust, and a number of Irish cases have seen similar statements.[241]

19–174 In *Thorner v Major*,[242] Lord Scott noted "the extent to which proprietary estoppel and constructive trust have been treated as providing alternative and overlapping remedies". This was considered by White J. in the Irish High Court in *Finnegan v Hand*.[243] The plaintiff, who had worked on the deceased's farm without payment for many years, sought relief either on the basis of

---

[236] [2000] Ch. 372.

[237] It seems to have been taken for granted in *Pallant* that the agreement did not comply with s.40 of the Law of Property Act 1925 (Statute of Frauds).

[238] N. Hopkins, "The *Pallant v Morgan* 'Equity' – Again" [2012] Conv. 327.

[239] Biehler, *Equity and the Law of Trusts in Ireland* (2015), p.873.

[240] [1986] 1 W.L.R. 1498.

[241] For example, *Reidy v McGreevy*, unreported, High Court, Barron J., 19 March 1995, p.5; *Prendergast v McLaughlin* [2009] IEHC 250; *An Cumann Peile Boitheimeach Teoranta v Albion Properties Ltd* [2008] IEHC 447. See also, A. Keating, "A Re-Formulated Proprietary Estoppel and Remedial Constructive Trusts" (2016) 31(1) I.L.T. 174.

[242] [2009] UKHL 18 at para.14.

[243] *Re Gartlan; Finnegan v Hand* [2016] IEHC 255.

proprietary estoppel or a constructive trust. White J. based his decision on the unconscionability of denying relief. He viewed *Thorner v Major* as an "evolutionary step in the development of proprietary estoppel and, in particular, its overlap with constructive trust or constructive remedial trust."[244] He held that in this case, while a proprietary estoppel could be said to arise in favour of the plaintiff, a remedial constructive trust arose instead, owing to the uncertain nature of the promises made as to the deceased's future intentions.

CHAPTER 20

Landlord and Tenant

The manufacture of a five-pronged implement for manual digging results in a fork even if the manufacturer, unfamiliar with the English language, insists that he intended to make, and has made, a spade.

— Lord Templeman in *Street v Mountford* [1985] 1 A.C. 809 at 819

THE RELATIONSHIP IN IRELAND

20–01 The basis of modern landlord and tenant relations was fundamentally affected by the Landlord and Tenant Law (Amendment) Act (Ireland) 1860, commonly known as "Deasy's Act".[1] This was a conservative measure aimed at increasing landlords' power over their tenants and it remains something of an anomaly, both in the curiosity of its provisions and in the fact of its being retained on the statute book at all. The most radical section of Deasy's Act is s.3 which defines the relationship of landlord and tenant:

"The relationship of landlord and tenant shall be deemed to be founded on the express or implied contract of the parties and not upon tenure or service, and a reversion shall not be necessary to such relation, which shall be deemed to subsist in all cases in which there shall be an agreement by one party to hold land from or under another in consideration of any rent."

20–02 The section would seem to have the effect of reducing all tenancies to mere contracts rather than property interests, but this has not been literally applied in all its logical consequences and probably was never intended to be. Deasy's Act itself, for example, provides for the running of covenants between successors to the original contracting parties, thereby assuming that some interest is created by the contract which can be alienated in the first place. If the agreement was only a contract and nothing more this would not be the case. It is therefore necessary to examine each aspect of the landlord and tenant relationship to see how it has been affected by the Act.

20–03 The Draft General Scheme of Landlord and Tenant Law Reform Bill 2011 ("LTLRB 2011") purports to amend significantly the existing legislative framework governing the relationship between landlords and tenants.

---

[1] After Rickard Morgan Deasy, the Attorney General for Ireland who introduced it.

For example, it proposes to repeal Deasy's Act in its entirety, and replaces the definition in s.3 as follows:

"(1) The relationship of landlord and tenant continues in all cases to be based on the express or implied agreement of the parties and not upon tenure or service.

(2) An obligation to pay rent is necessary in all cases for creation of a tenancy.

(3) The grant of a tenancy without a reversion after the commencement of this Part is void both at law and in equity."[2]

20–04 Restating the contractual basis of the landlord-tenant relationship, this largely re-enacts the provisions of s.3 of Deasy's Act, with some modifications, which will be discussed below.

20–05 More broadly, the LTLRB 2011 proposes to:

- repeal 35 pre-1922 statutes, as well as more recent statutory provisions;
- improve protection for tenants, in particular by clarifying the obligations on both landlords and their tenants; and
- abolish ancient "eviction" remedies available to landlords, and replace them with an updated statutory redress scheme.

However, over a decade after the publication of the Law Reform Commission's report on the law of landlord and tenant,[3] at the time of writing, the LTLRB 2011 has yet to be enacted.[4]

INTERESSE TERMINI

20–06 At common law a tenant had no estate until he or she entered the land. Until actual entry the tenant had merely an *interesse termini*, an "interest in the term" and a right of entry.[5] The absence of an estate caused problems for tenants who had not entered under the lease.[6] It is arguable that s.3 of Deasy's Act abolished this common law doctrine, since it provides that the relationship of landlord and tenant arises as soon as the contract is formed.

---

[2] LTLRB 2011, Head 10.

[3] Law Reform Commission, *Report on the Law of Landlord and Tenant Law* (LRC 85-2007).

[4] According to the Government's legislative work programme for 2018, the Heads of the Bill have been approved, and "work is continuing".

[5] The doctrine was abolished in England, as to all leases, whether made before or after 1925, by the Law of Property Act 1925 s.149(1) and (2).

[6] Merger could not occur, nor could the tenant surrender to a reversioner: *Doe d Rawlings v Walker* (1826) 5 B. & C. 111.

REVERSION

20–07 One effect of s.3 of Deasy's Act is that a reversion need not be retained on the grant of a leasehold interest in order that the relationship of landlord and tenant is created. The notion that a reversion has to be retained on the grant of a leasehold term if it is to be a sublease and not an assignment of the landlord's interest, is in fact a misconception with its origin in freehold tenure.[7] Section 3 reaffirmed the pre-existing Irish position[8] following a period of uncertainty.[9]

20–08 The LTLRB 2011 provides that "[t]he grant of a tenancy without a reversion after the commencement of this Part is void both at law and in equity."[10] Thus, if enacted, this will change the position which currently pertains under Deasy's Act.

20–09 It is notable that s.3 of Deasy's Act only recognises the relation of landlord and tenant for the purposes of the Act where a rent is reserved. Leasehold terms where no rent is reserved would seem to be governed by the law as it stood immediately before Deasy's Act, i.e. a reversion would still be required on a sub-grant. This position remains unchanged by the LTLRB 2011. A similar observation applies to a lease made "for a term which is uncertain" within the meaning of s.11(3)(c) of the Land and Conveyancing Law Reform Act 2009 ("LCLRA 2009").[11]

CONCURRENT LEASES

20–10 At common law, landlord L, having granted a lease to A, can still grant a lease to take effect at the same time to B. This is known as a *lease of the reversion* or a *concurrent lease*. The effect in terms of tenure was to insert B between L and A, making B the new landlord of A and the new tenant

---

7   The misconception that the retention of a reversion was in some way necessary to create tenure arose in England in relation to freehold tenure. This was because there were no exceptions to *Quia Emptores* in England, unlike in Ireland. In Ireland, on the other hand, since the misconception had never taken root in relation to freeholds, it was never applied to leaseholds.

8   *Gordon v Phelan* (1881) 15 I.L.T.R. 70.

9   *Pluck v Digges* (1832) 5 Bligh N.S. 31; *Lessee of Fawcett v Hall* (1833) Al. & Nap. 248; *Cremen v Hawkes* (1846) 8 Ir. Eq. R. 153; *Lessee of Walsh v Feely* (1835) 1 Jones 413, following *Lessee of Coyne v Smith* (1826) Batty 90.

10   LTLRB 2011, Head 10. The Law Reform Commission had originally recommended retention of a provision along the following lines: "A reversion is not necessary to the relationship." However, this was queried by the Department of Justice on the grounds, (i) that fee farm grants can no longer be created under the Land and Conveyancing Law Reform Act 2009 s.12, and (ii) that "middlemen" grants were no longer desirable. The Law Reform Commission indicated agreement with the proposed change.

11   See also A. Lyall, "Leases, Time Certain and the 2006 Bill: A Comment" (2007) 12(1) C.P.L.J. 31.

of L.[12] It operates as a disposition by the landlord of his or her reversion.[13] The purpose is to confer on B the position of landlord and not to disturb the possession of A.

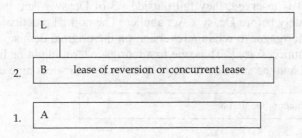

Hence L can no longer give notice to quit to A.[14] There is authority for the proposition that B's concurrent lease may be of the same duration[15] as the original lease to A and some authority for the view that it may even be shorter.[16] B may collect rent from A and enforce the covenants in A's lease.[17] In such a case there would have been tenure between A and B, although B did not have a "reversion" in the sense of a longer estate than A. This is not consistent with the general rule followed in England, but it is consistent with the view held in Ireland before Deasy's Act.

20–11 Concurrent leases are usually created in favour of investors. It is unusual for concurrent leases to occur in leases which grant the right to occupy, but such leases do occur in mortgages by demise and sub-demise created prior to the LCLRA 2009.[18] In such terms a rent is not normally reserved, since it is not intended that the mortgagee should pay rent to the mortgagor. Where the granting landlord has the freehold, then on the grant of a lease he or she will always retain a reversion since a freehold estate is notionally greater than

---

[12] *McKeague v Hutchinson* (1884) 18 I.L.T.R. 70; *Beamish v Crowley* (1885) 16 L.R. Ir. 279 at 290.

[13] *Neale v Mackenzie* (1836) 1 M. & W. 747. But note the older cases say that the concurrent lease had to be by deed and the first tenant had to attorn, i.e. accept the grantee as landlord: *Neale v Mackenzie* (1836) 1 M. & W. 747. In *Jones v Wrotham Park Settled Estates* [1980] A.C. 74, an attempt was made, unsuccessfully, to use a concurrent lease as a means to prevent the original tenant from acquiring the landlord's reversion.

[14] *Wordsley Brewery Co v Halford* (1903) 90 L.T. 89.

[15] *Burton v Barclay* (1831) 7 Bing. 745 at 746, citing *Hughes v Robotham* (1593) Poph. 30. The power to create concurrent leases, even where possession is granted, was expressly preserved in England by the Law of Property Act 1925 s.149(5). C. Harpum, S. Bridge and M. Dixon, *Megarry & Wade: The Law of Real Property*, 8th edn (London: Sweet & Maxwell, 2012), para.17–134.

[16] *Neale v Mackenzie* (1836) 1 M. & W. 747; *Watt v Maydewell* (1628) Hut. 105; *Re Moore & Hulm's Contract* [1912] 2 Ch. 105 (mortgage terms, second one the same length as first, second held valid). *Megarry & Wade: The Law of Real Property* (2012), para.17–134, fn.578.

[17] *Burton v Barclay* (1831) 7 Bing. 745 at 746.

[18] LCLRA 2009 s.89(2) prohibits the creation of a legal mortgage henceforth other than by way of a charge by deed.

leasehold. But where the landlord has only a leasehold, it may be questioned whether he or she must retain a reversion on the original lease if he or she is later to grant a concurrent lease. The better view as to mortgage terms is that, since no rent is reserved, they fall outside s.3 of Deasy's Act, therefore the law immediately before Deasy's Act applies. The normal practice was for the "landlord"/mortgagor to retain a reversion on the original demise, although it is probably unnecessary.[19] Thus, the first mortgage term might be for 99 years less 10 days, and the second mortgage term for 99 years less nine days.

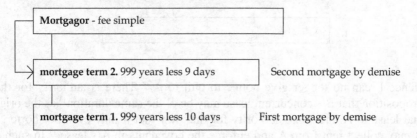

20–12 The LTLRB 2011 proposes to clarify the law relating to concurrent leases. As the explanatory note points out, case law on concurrent leases is scarce and lacking in clarity. Head 19 defines "concurrent tenancy" as "a tenancy of premises granted to a person other than the tenant of a pre-existing tenancy of the same premises to run concurrently with and subject to that pre-existing tenancy." A "pre-existing tenancy" is "a tenancy of premises to which a concurrent tenancy of the same premises is subject". It provides:

> "19(1) Upon the grant of a concurrent tenancy by the landlord of premises subject to a pre-existing tenancy, the concurrent tenant becomes in relation to those premises the successor in title to that landlord during the concurrent tenancy and Heads 16 and 17 apply to the landlord, the concurrent tenant and the pre-existing tenant accordingly."[20]

---

[19] Landlord and Tenant (Amendment) Act 1980 s.80 refers to the "normal reversion" where a lessee mortgages by sub-demise. A reversion was necessary prior to the LCLRA 2009 to ensure that the Satisfied Terms Act 1845 applied.

[20] In the rare situation where the concurrent tenancy relates to part only of the landlord's interest in the premises, the rent and other payments under the pre-existing tenancy and all other obligations and provisions relating to that interest are apportioned and enforceable in accordance with Head 18. Head 18 seeks to provide a clear set of "default" provisions to operate, in the absence of provisions otherwise agreed by the parties, where the landlord or tenant assigns part only of his or her interest or otherwise severs it. Head 18(1) provides that upon severance of either the landlord's or tenant's interest, the rent and other payments under the tenancy and all other provisions and obligations will become severed as between the severed parts of the premises and enforceable accordingly.

EXCLUSIVE OCCUPATION

20–13 The right to exclusive occupation means the general right to exclude all others from the premises, including the landlord. The right of exclusive occupation is an essential component of a lease or tenancy, especially when determining whether an agreement is a tenancy or a licence. The right of exclusive occupation may still exist even if the agreement includes terms which give the landlord or his or her agents the right to enter the premises from time to time for specific purposes, such as to inspect or carry out repairs. Indeed, the view has been expressed that the existence of such terms may positively indicate that exclusive possession has been granted since the grant of a right to the landlord to enter for specific purposes implies that in general the landlord has otherwise no right to do so.[21]

SUBLETTING

20–14 There is no provision in Deasy's Act which expressly authorises subletting, apparently on the principle that subletting creates a new contract between the sub-landlord and the sub-tenant and so is governed by the Act like any other lease. Subletting does not require the consent of the head-landlord unless the lease contains a provision to that effect.[22]

LEASE OR LICENCE?

A Question of Substance, Not Form
20–15 Land may be a commodity under capitalism, but unlike most other commodities, its supply is necessarily limited. Ownership of it confers a monopoly control over a scarce resource. Landlords have often used this power to extract terms in leases and tenancies which would be more beneficial to them than those they could extract in the case of a free market. Over time, the State intervened to reduce the monopoly power of those whose income is derived from rent. The resulting statutes were phrased so as to apply to leases or tenancies. Landlords often tried to evade these Acts by calling tenancies or leases "licences" instead. Courts have therefore had to consider whether devices to avoid the rent control legislation would be recognised or not. If the terminology used were to be taken at face value, the landlords would virtually have restored their monopoly position despite the aims of democratic legislatures. Courts have generally chosen not to accept

---

[21] *Irish Shell v Costello (No.1)* [1981] I.L.R.M. 66.

[22] If the subletting is made with the landlord's consent, Deasy's Act s.19 provides that the receipt of the sub-landlord of the rent paid by the sub-tenant is a full discharge of the latter as against the head-landlord. However, if the sub-landlord is in arrears with his or her rent to the head-landlord, the head-landlord can give notice under s.20 to the sub-tenant to pay the rent or part of it directly to him or her.

the terms used by the parties, but tend to scrutinise the agreements and create their own tests so as to determine whether a tenancy or licence has been created.

20–16 In *Irish Shell v Costello (No.1)*[23] the Supreme Court held that an agreement under which an oil company allowed the other party to occupy a service station was a tenancy in law although it was described in the agreement itself as a licence. Griffin J. cited Lord Denning M.R. in *Shell-Mex v Manchester Garages*,[24] to the effect that:

> "Although a document may be described as a licence it does not necessarily follow that, merely on that account, it is to be regarded as amounting only to a licence in law. Whether the transaction is a licence or a tenancy
>
>> does not depend on the label which is put on it. It depends on the nature of the transaction itself: see *Addiscombe Garden Estates Ltd v Crabbe* [1958] 1 QB 513. Broadly speaking, we have to see whether it is a personal privilege given to a person (in which case it is a licence), or whether it grants an interest in land (in which case it is a tenancy). At one time it used to be thought that exclusive possession was a decisive factor. But that is not so. It depends on broader considerations altogether. Primarily on whether it is personal in its nature or not."

20–17 Griffin J. applied these tests in *Irish Shell*. The premises occupied by the so-called licensees were used by them as a lock-up garage, in which they provided a full garage business, with mechanics, workshop apprentice, and petrol pump attendants. The petrol pumps were locked and the owner of the premises did not have a key to them. A right to inspect equipment, generally exercised no more than once a month by a representative of the "licensor", had to be provided for in the contract: otherwise there would have been no right to enter. If such a right had inhered in the "licensor", there would have been no need to provide for it. There was agreed removal, in renewals of the contract, of clauses which had provided that there was not to be interference "with the possession and user of the premises" by the owner and that nothing was intended to confer on the licensee the right of exclusive possession. This showed "that it was intended that the defendants should have the right to occupy the premises and that this was intended to be a right to exclusive occupation and possession".[25]

---

[23] [1981] I.L.R.M. 66; followed in *National Maternity Hospital v McGouran* [1994] 1 I.L.R.M. 521.

[24] [1971] 1 W.L.R. 612 at 615; *Gatien Motor Co v Continental Oil* [1979] I.R. 406.

[25] [1981] I.L.R.M. 66 at 70.

20–18 Griffin J. went on to find that the payments in the agreement which ostensibly were for the hire of equipment were in fact rent and their being described otherwise did not prevent them being held to be rent.[26]

20–19 Some of the uncertainty now existing in this area is illustrated by *Irish Shell v Costello (No.2)*,[27] which concerned the nature of the relationship between the parties after their 1974 agreement had been terminated. O'Higgins C.J. in the majority cited Scarman L.J. in *Heslop v Burns*[28] and found that it was a tenancy at will which had been terminated by the letter of 5 November 1974, following which the defendants had become trespassers. Henchy J., also in the majority, held that had the defendants stayed on and paid a monthly rent they would have been monthly tenants, but the payment was said to be a "licence fee" and not rent and had been accepted as such. They were tentative interim payments pending negotiations. This rebutted the presumption at common law of a monthly tenancy. The judge concluded therefore that they were licensees following the end of the 1974 agreement. After the expiry of this licence they had become trespassers. McCarthy J., dissenting, found that they were monthly tenants and that the tenancy still continued.

20–20 Peart J.'s decision in *Smith v CIÉ and Iarnród Éireann*[29] represents a re-affirmation of the approach adopted by the Supreme Court in *Irish Shell v Costello (No.1)* in the pre-eminent weight it attached to the objective substance of the terms agreed between the parties, and their overall legal character, as opposed to the label which they had chosen to place upon the relationship. In this case, the plaintiff had taken a licence for a 10-year term to operate a newsagent and confectionery shop in one of the arches under Tara Street railway station in Dublin. The agreement contained an elaborately worded clause to the effect that a tenancy was not intended to be created nor exclusive possession granted, the defendant being influenced by the need not to submit any of its available space at such a vital railway station to the risk of statutory renewal rights. Peart J. noted that the defendant had not retained a key to the premises occupied by the plaintiff and tended never to undertake inspections of repair work there. Security and storage of stock were entirely a matter for the plaintiff. According to Peart J., the approach to be adopted was as follows:

"The entire document must be looked at … in order to see what the legal consequences of the document may be. This is not simply a question which arises solely from the expressed intention of the parties. It is in essence a matter of law. For a tenancy to exist, there is no doubt that exclusive possession of the premises is a pre-requisite, but … the fact that there is exclusive possession does not preclude the agreement from being a licence."

---

[26] [1981] I.L.R.M. 66 at 70–71.
[27] [1984] I.R. 511.
[28] [1974] 3 All E.R. 406.
[29] [2002] IEHC 103.

20–21 According to Peart J., with the sole exception of the one clause which purported to characterise the agreement as a licence rather than a lease, the thrust of the entire agreement was consistent with a commercial letting if what he termed the "licence labels" were taken out and replaced with "tenancy labels".[30]

Exclusive Occupation

20–22 While the absence of exclusive occupation means that the agreement is not a tenancy, the mere fact that exclusive occupation is granted will not resolve the issue of whether a particular agreement constitutes a lease or a licence.

20–23 Previously, judges were apt to say that the presence of exclusive occupation would negative the existence of a licence.[31] The courts have since departed from this position and no longer hold the fact of exclusive possession to be decisive.[32] In *Ó Síodhcháin v O'Mahony*,[33] Kearns J. held that a lease did not exist, despite the appearance of exclusive possession, where other indicia of a lease, such as landlord and tenant covenants and the reservation of rent, were absent and there was, furthermore, evidence of undue influence which would have rebutted the intention of the grantors to part with an estate in their property.

Intention of the Parties or Policy?

20–24 It is now clear that the courts no longer pursue the vexed question of the intention of the parties in deciding whether an agreement is a lease or a licence, since the reason for the intervention of parliament was that landlords frequently inserted provisions designed to avoid the legislation and intending tenants had no choice but to accept them if they wished to obtain accommodation.

20–25 The LTLRB 2011 seeks to provide some clarity in this area. Head 11 of the draft bill states:

"(1) Subject to Head 10, in determining whether a tenancy has been created the court shall—

(a) give effect to any express provision relating to the matter, and

(b) presume that each party had received independent legal advice in relation to it.

(2) Where it is established that a party had not received such advice, the court may disregard any such express provision if satisfied that to give

---

[30] However, see *Clear Channel UK Ltd v Manchester City Council* [2006] L. & T.R. 7.
[31] For example, *Lynes v Snaith* [1899] 1 Q.B. 486.
[32] *Heslop v Burns* [1974] 3 All E.R. 406.
[33] [2002] 4 I.R. 147.

effect to it would not reflect the true intention of that party and would prejudice that party."

20–26 This would implement the Law Reform Commission's recommendation[34] and requires courts in future to give effect to the parties' express agreement, provided they have each had the benefit of independent legal advice. This is expressly subject to Head 10, so that the parties must still create the relationship of landlord and tenant and reserve a rent or other consideration. Subhead (2) confirms that where it is established that no advice had been received, it is open to the court to disregard an express provision if satisfied that it does not reflect the true intention of the party in question and that its enforcement would prejudice that party.

Commercial Agreements

20–27 Courts may permit a licence to be used to avoid statutory control, at least where the parties are, in the court's view, on equal terms.

20–28 In *Gatien Motor Co Ltd v Continental Oil*[35] the occupier of premises would have been entitled, after three years' occupation as a tenant, to a new tenancy of the premises. In order to prevent the occupier acquiring this right the grantor inserted a term which made the occupier a "caretaker" for a two-week period immediately preceding the expiry of the three years. The Supreme Court held that a caretaker agreement was not a tenancy, despite the fact that it also conferred the right of exclusive possession on the "caretaker". It may be that the court considered that the parties had contracted on an equal footing and the grantee had acted in its own interests in contracting out of its rights in order to secure a new tenancy at the end of the caretaking period. In *Irish Shell v Costello (No.1)*[36] the Supreme Court held an agreement to be a tenancy, which was to the tenant's advantage, despite its description as a licence, in a commercial context; namely, an agreement between an oil company and the operator of a service station, in which the station operator is generally considered to be at a disadvantage. Similarly, in *Smith v CIÉ and Iarnród Éireann*[37] Peart J. held that the preponderance of a commercial agreement between two business parties constituted it a tenancy, notwithstanding the attempt by the grantor to designate it a licence.

---

[34] Law Reform Commission, *Consultation Paper on General Law of Landlord and Tenant* (LRC CP 28-2003), para.1.31.

[35] [1979] I.R. 406.

[36] [1981] I.L.R.M. 66; followed in *National Maternity Hospital v McGouran* [1994] 1 I.L.R.M. 521. In this case, one particular clause which provided that the grantor could substitute other premises within the hospital building for that licensed to the defendant proved to be crucial to a finding by Morris J. that exclusive possession had not been granted, despite the existence of several provisions in the agreement consistent with a lease.

[37] [2002] IEHC 103.

20–29 Against this developing trend, the decision in *Gatien Motor Co Ltd v Continental Oil* may seem something of an anomaly, explicable perhaps on the basis that the transitional caretaker arrangement was deemed by the court to be a reasonable price to pay by the former tenant in order to secure a new tenancy which otherwise would not have been granted. It is also significant that during the two-week term of the caretaker agreement there was a suspension of payment of rent.

Residential Agreements

20–30 In agreements involving the occupancy of residential property, the courts are more concerned to protect the interests of the perceived vulnerable occupier where the occupancy is designated as a licence and exclusive possession is found to have been granted. The courts will hold the occupancy to be a tenancy unless the circumstances demonstrate that an intention to create a tenancy could not have existed.

20–31 This is clearly demonstrated by the House of Lords in *Street v Mountford*[38] in which the emphasis was once again shifted back to exclusive possession as indicating a tenancy rather than a licence where residential accommodation is concerned. In that case the landlord granted the appellant the right to occupy a furnished room under a written agreement which stated that the appellant had the right to occupy the room "at a licence fee of £37 per week", that "this personal licence is not assignable", that the "licence may be terminated by 14 days' written notice", and that the appellant understood and accepted that "a licence in the above form does not and is not intended to give me a tenancy protected under the Rent Acts". The appellant had exclusive possession of the room. Some months after signing the agreement the appellant applied to have a fair rent registered in respect of the room. The landlord then applied for a declaration that the appellant occupied the room under a licence and not a tenancy.

20–32 The House of Lords held that this agreement was a lease. Lord Templeman held that where the occupier of residential accommodation had been granted exclusive possession of the accommodation for a fixed or periodic term at a stated rent, the interest was presumed to be a tenancy and not a licence. The presumption could be rebutted by proving special circumstances which would negative a tenancy; for example, where from the outset there was no intention to create legal relations or where the possession was granted pursuant to a contract of employment. The intention of the parties, as manifested in the agreement, that they intended only to create a licence (and expressed the agreement to be a licence), and that they agreed not to be bound by the Rent Acts, was irrelevant. In the memorable words of the judge: "The manufacture

---

[38] [1985] 1 A.C. 809. In *Smith v CIÉ and Iarnród Éireann* [2002] IEHC 103, Peart J. experienced no difficulty in applying *Street v Mountford* to a case of a commercial, as opposed to a residential, agreement.

of a five-pronged implement for manual digging results in a fork even if the manufacturer, unfamiliar with the English language, insists that he intended to make and has made a spade."[39] Accordingly, since the effect of the agreement between the appellant and the landlord was to grant the appellant exclusive possession for a fixed term at a stated rent, and no circumstances existed to negative the presumption of a tenancy, it was clear that the appellant was a tenant. The appeal was therefore allowed.[40]

20–33 In *AG Securities v Vaughan* and *Antoniades v Villiers*,[41] two appeals heard together, the House of Lords refined and qualified the principles in *Street v Mountford*. In the first appeal, the occupants of a four-bedroom flat had entered into separate agreements at different times and for different monthly payments. The agreements, which expressly were called licences, granted the exclusive right to use the flat in common with three other occupants who had or might from time to time be granted a similar right. The landlords sought a declaration in the county court that the four occupants were licensees and not tenants of the flat. The House of Lords held that the agreements did not grant exclusive occupation to any of the occupants—principally because the agreements included a clause whereby if any one of the occupants terminated his or her agreement those that remained were obliged to find a replacement flat-mate, and, if they failed to do so, the owner could require them to accept someone of his choice. The House of Lords also held that the occupants could not be joint tenants holding under a tenancy since each signed agreements at different times, and so the four unities requisite to the existence of a joint tenancy were not present.

20–34 In the second appeal, two occupants of a one-bedroom flat who were living as a couple had each signed separate agreements, also called "licences", at the insistence of the landlord. The agreements included clauses which purported to give the landlord the right to grant to other prospective occupants the right to live in the flat and also reserved to himself the right to move into and share the flat with the two original occupants. The landlord, who represented himself in court, said that he had inserted the latter provision so that, if his own house burned down or was otherwise destroyed, he would have somewhere to live. The court found that neither clause was intended to be implemented and had been inserted for the sole purpose of avoiding the Rent Acts. The court held that the two agreements signed by the occupants separately should be construed as a single document and that the occupants were tenants holding with exclusive occupation.

20–35 However, if it is apparent that a clause in a residential occupancy agreement which purports to deny exclusive possession to the occupant, is genuinely

---

[39] [1985] 1 A.C. 809 at 819.
[40] [1985] 2 All E.R. 289 at 290.
[41] [1990] A.C. 417.

intended to have and actually does have that effect, then a licence and not a tenancy will be held to exist. Accordingly, in *Westminster City Council v Clarke*,[42] the House of Lords, in a case which involved a council-run hostel for the homeless, found that an occupier was not entitled to occupy any particular room and that the council's staff could enter "at any time" they pleased; in these circumstances the council had clearly retained possession and the occupant did not have a tenancy. This is to be contrasted with *Aslan v Murphy*[43]—a case on its facts not dissimilar to *Antoniades v Villiers*—in which a clause that the putative licensee would have to vacate between 10.30am and noon every day was deemed not to represent the "true bargain" between the parties which instead was held to constitute a tenancy.

20–36 Section 3 of Deasy's Act, as we have seen, defines the relationship of landlord and tenant as deriving from "an agreement by one party to hold land from or under another in consideration of any rent", which purportedly implies it may just be an agreement between two parties, and impliedly recognises the concept of tenancy by estoppel. As to third parties, Deasy's Act then extends the concept beyond contract by providing that the grantor and grantee may assign their interest, and so recognises that the relationship of landlord and tenant can (and normally does) give rise to a proprietary interest affecting third parties. But Deasy's Act does not seem to require that the grantor has a proprietary interest before creating an arrangement between grantor and grantee. Such an arrangement is a contract between them to hold land at a rent, and in that sense can be called a "lease", without necessarily affecting third parties.[44]

Rent
20–37 If no rent is reserved does this mean that the agreement is not a lease? It would seem that while rent is a requirement of a landlord and tenant relationship within s.3 of Deasy's Act, if no rent is reserved the relationship may still exist, but is not governed by the Act. The courts have taken the view that a lease which is made orally can exist as an equitable lease under the doctrine of *Walsh v Lonsdale*,[45] provided it is enforceable as a contract. Thus, such a lease, lacking one of the requirements of Deasy's Act, can exist apart from the statute, but only in equity. Therefore, the existence or otherwise of rent does not of itself resolve the issue of whether an agreement is a licence or a lease.

20–38 In *Gatien Motor Co Ltd v Continental Oil*[46] Kenny J. held that the caretaker agreement was not a tenancy and gave among a number of reasons the fact that no rent was paid, citing s.3 of Deasy's Act. Had rent been decisive no other reasons would have been required, but the judge mentioned a number of

[42] [1992] A.C. 288.
[43] [1990] 1 W.L.R. 766.
[44] See also *Bruton v London and Quadrant Housing Trust* [2000] 1 A.C. 406.
[45] (1882) 21 Ch. D. 9.
[46] [1979] I.R. 406.

other factors, including the "surrounding circumstances".[47] Kenny J., dissenting in *Irish Shell v Costello (No.1)*,[48] suggested that rent was a requirement of a lease in Ireland, but the majority did not decide the point. They found that the periodic payments were rent, even though disguised as periodic payments for hire of equipment.

20–39 In *Bellew v Bellew*[49] the majority in the Supreme Court held that a licence had been granted by the plaintiff son to the father. The majority held the case was one of family arrangement, quoting Scarman L.J. in *Heslop v Burns*.[50] No rent had been reserved but the court did not decide the case on that ground. Section 3 of Deasy's Act did not repeal s.3 of the Real Property Act 1845 (the "1845 Act") insofar as it concerned leases. The 1845 Act required leases which previously had to be in writing to be by deed. Although s.3 of the 1845 Act has been repealed by s.8(3) of the LCLRA 2009, s.62(1) of the latter Act provides that, with limited exceptions, "a legal estate or interest in land may only be created or conveyed by a deed". Thus, if there are leasehold terms outside Deasy's Act, it remains the case that they would have to be created by deed.

20–40 The LTLRB 2011 provides that "[a]n obligation to pay rent is necessary in all cases for creation of a tenancy." If enacted, this would implement the Law Reform Commission's recommendations[51] that it should be made clear that there is a universal rule that reservation of rent or other consideration is necessary to creation of the relationship of landlord and tenant. The definition of "rent" in Head 3 of the Bill includes:

"(i) any sum or other payment in money or money's worth or any other consideration,
(ii) any payment specified as rent under the terms of the tenancy,
(iii) any sum payable or refundable to the landlord on a recurring or regular basis under the terms of the tenancy."

This is wider than the definition of "valuable consideration" in the LCLRA 2009.

Time Certain

20–41 The main distinction between leaseholds and freeholds at common law was that leaseholds are for a time certain, i.e. for a definite time, either in years,

---

[47] In the earlier case of *Davies v Hilliard* (1967) 101 I.L.T.R. 50, an agreement was held to be a caretaker agreement even though exclusive possession was granted and the "caretaker" paid sums termed "rent". However, this was in the context of interim occupation pending completion of negotiations for a lease.
[48] [1981] I.L.R.M. 66.
[49] [1982] I.R. 447.
[50] [1974] 3 All E.R. 406.
[51] Law Reform Commission, *Consultation Paper on General Law of Landlord and Tenant* (LRC CP 28-2003), para.1.23.

months, weeks, days etc. Thus, a lease granted for "the duration of the war" has been held void.[52]

20–42 The law was comprehensively reviewed in England in *Prudential Assurance Co Ltd v London Residuary Body*.[53] In that case a purported lease had been granted in 1930 at a rent of £30 a year to last until the land was required for road widening. By the 1990s it had become extremely unlikely that the land would ever be required for road widening, and so if the uncertain term had been upheld the tenant would have had the benefit of a virtually per-petual lease at a minimal rent which could not be reviewed; something neither party had contemplated at the time of the grant. The uncertain term was held void. Since the tenant had gone into possession and paid rent referable to a year, the court held that there was a tenancy from year to year terminable by notice.[54] Lord Templeman stated: "A grant for an uncertain term does not create a lease. A grant for an uncertain term which takes the form of a yearly tenancy which cannot be determined by the landlord does not create a lease."[55] In the case of periodic tenancies, if the right of either party to determine the tenancy is suspended, the maximum period of suspension must be certain at the time the tenancy is created. Hence, a suspension for a period of five years *unless* an uncertain event occurs in the meantime is valid, but a suspension *until* an uncertain event occurs, without a term, is void. So is a provision that prevents either party from terminating the tenancy at any time.

20–43 In Ireland, the common law has long been displaced by Deasy's Act. Section 3 provides that the relation of landlord and tenant "shall be deemed to exist in all cases where there is an agreement by one party to hold land from another in consideration of any rent". Irish courts have held that this allows the relation of landlord and tenant to be created in Ireland where the estate granted is freehold, such as a fee simple. Freehold estates are not definite periods of time and so the question arises as to whether a landlord and tenant relationship can be created in Ireland for an indefinite period of time which is not a freehold estate, such as "for so long as the present Taoiseach remains in office" or "until the land ceases to be used as a school", etc. Prior to the LCLRA 2009, the clearest light on this issue was shed by s.4 of Deasy's Act. Section 4 requires leases or tenancies to be in writing if they are to create the legal[56] relation of landlord and tenant "for any freehold estate or interest, or for

---

[52] *Lace v Chantler* [1944] K.B. 368. An attempt had been made in *Great Northern Railway v Arnold* (1916) 33 T.L.R. 114 in the First World War to make an exception in the case of leases granted for the duration of the war.

[53] [1992] 2 A.C. 386.

[54] Lord Templeman held *Charles Clay & Sons Ltd v British Railways Board* [1971] 1 All E.R. 1007 and *Ashburn Anstalt v Arnold* [1989] Ch. 1 to have been wrongly decided.

[55] [1992] 2 A.C. 386 at 395. The majority concurred with Lord Templeman.

[56] Oral grants may nevertheless create equitable leases: see below "Agreements for a Lease: *Walsh v Lonsdale*".

any definite period of time not being from year to year or any lesser period". This contemplates two types of lease, i.e.

(a) one granted for a freehold estate; and
(b) one granted for a definite period of time or successive definite periods, i.e. periodic tenancies.

20–44 In addition, hybrid interests granted for a combination of (a) and (b) could also exist, such as leases for lives and years.[57] It seems clear that leases for successive definite periods, such as tenancies from week to week or year to year, come within Deasy's Act but can be made orally. However, the implication of s.4 is that there is no *third* category of leases for indefinite periods which are not freehold estates.

20–45 This throws up a particular complication in relation to s.11(3) of the LCLRA 2009 which provides that

"a 'leasehold estate' means ... the estate which arises when a tenancy is created for any period of time or any recurring period and irrespective of whether or not the estate—

...

(c) is for a term which is uncertain or liable to termination by notice, re-entry or operation of law or by virtue of a provision for cessor on redemption or for any other reasons."

20–46 On the face of it, this provision displaces the application of *Prudential Assurance Co Ltd v London Residuary Body*[58] in Ireland and must be so interpreted. Accordingly, it is now possible for a lease for an uncertain term, which does not constitute a freehold estate, to be created in Ireland. How is this so? It is scarcely conformable to the parliamentary intention behind the enacting of s.11(3) that such a lease can be granted orally, simply because it does not create a freehold estate, and is not a lease for a definite time or for a recurring period as envisaged by s.4 of Deasy's Act. A more reasonable interpretation is that a lease for an uncertain or indefinite term is a lease to which Deasy's Act does not apply at all and that a legal estate in such a lease can only be granted by deed as stipulated by s.62 of the LCLRA 2009. As against that, s.3 of Deasy's Act does not expressly require a lease or tenancy to be for a certain period and in fact the provision of the section that landlord and tenant relationships depend upon the contract of the parties could be taken as a contrary indication. Whether or not the provisions of Deasy's Act[59] can be construed as applying to a lease made for an uncertain or indefinite term, it is clear that s.14(c) of the

---

[57] After 1 December 2009, LCLRA 2009 s.14 prohibits the creation of either a lease for lives, or of a lease for lives and years, or a lease of any description which comes to an end upon death.
[58] [1992] 2 A.C. 386.
[59] Of particular interest in terms of the implication of covenants and the enforcement of covenants against third parties.

LCLRA 2009 prohibits the creation of a lease for a determinable life estate, which was permissible in the past under s.3 of Deasy's Act.

20–47 Leases which fall outside Deasy's Act because they fail to reserve rent will continue to be governed by the common law and by the terms expressly contained in or necessarily implied into the particular lease.

PERIODIC TENANCIES

20–48 The common law recognised that tenancies could be created for successive definite periods, as from week to week, month to month, year to year, etc. In such periodic tenancies, each period is automatically renewed and the tenancy is therefore terminable by notice. The periods of notice were laid down by the common law and have been modified by statute.

20–49 The traditional requirement of "time certain" could be said to have been satisfied in that at the end of each period the tenancy is renewed for another certain period unless terminated by notice.[60]

TENANCY AT WILL

20–50 A tenancy at will is an ancient common law concept used to categorise situations which did not easily fall within any other category of property right. Nevertheless, the tenancy at will itself does not easily fall within the conventional category of tenancies. Tenancies at will are without rent by definition, for if rent is payable weekly, or monthly, etc., the relation is not a tenancy at will but a weekly or monthly tenancy. Such tenancies are outside of Deasy's Act. Tenancy at will is a concept that has long been declining in importance.[61] Lord Scarman in *Heslop v Burns*[62] suggested that the concept of a licence now performed the function that used to be covered by tenancies at will. In *Bellew v Bellew*[63] the majority in the Supreme Court preferred the concept of licence to that of tenancy at will in the context of family arrangements.

20–51 Section 17 of the Statute of Limitations 1957 provides that a tenancy at will is deemed to end one year after it begins unless previously determined. The tenant's possession then becomes adverse to that of the landlord, and time begins to run against him or her.[64] This rule was first adopted in 1833[65] and can be regarded as favouring the development of land, perhaps reflective of the

---

[60] *Prudential Assurance Co Ltd v London Residuary Body* [1992] 2 A.C. 386.
[61] *Binions v Evans* [1972] Ch. 359.
[62] [1974] 3 All E.R. 406.
[63] [1982] I.R. 447.
[64] See O'Higgins C.J. dissenting in *Bellew v Bellew* [1982] I.R. 447.
[65] Real Property Limitation Act 1833 s.7.

ideas of the Industrial Revolution. The LCLRA 2009 does not include a tenancy at will within the definition of a lease set out in s.11(3), and so the tenancy at will has consequently been abolished by that statute.[66] The LTLRB 2011 expressly excludes tenancies at will from the definition of tenancies.[67]

TENANCY AT SUFFERANCE

20–52 This was the interest that arose if a tenant continued in possession at the end of a lease or tenancy without continuing to pay rent and without the landlord's consent or dissent. Riddled with anomalies, a tenancy at sufferance was classified by the common law with common law tenancies although it has little in common with leaseholds. A tenant at sufferance differs from a trespasser in that the original entry is lawful and from a tenant at will in that occupation is without the landlord's consent. Tenants at sufferance are liable to pay not rent, but compensation for the use of the land. Exclusive possession continues until the landlord terminates the tenancy. Thus, the landlord cannot sue other trespassers until he or she terminates the tenancy at sufferance.

20–53 Before 1833 a tenant for years who held over after the termination of the tenancy and without paying rent was not in adverse possession against the landlord or those claiming under him. The former tenant's possession was deemed to be possession by the landlord.[68] One of the aims of the Real Property Limitation Act 1833 was to do away with these cases of deemed possession and replace it by the test of actual possession. Time would then begin to run from the moment that a right of action to oust the possession accrued to some other party. A tenant at sufferance after 1833 is in adverse possession and the landlord has 12 years from the expiry of the previous tenancy within which to bring an action for possession.[69]

20–54 Under s.5 of Deasy's Act, the landlord has the option to treat the tenant holding over as a tenant from year to year where the original lease was in writing and it was for a term. The yearly tenancy is at the old rent and subject to such of the terms of the old tenancy as may be applicable.

20–55 Like a tenancy at will, a tenancy at sufferance has been silently abolished by s.11(3) of the LCLRA 2009, so that such an occupant will henceforth

---

[66] In this regard the commentary in the Explanatory Memorandum to the LCLRA 2009 (pp.6–7) is instructive and broadly reflects the commentary offered above.

[67] LTLRB 2011, Head 3.

[68] *Howard v Sherwood* (1832) Al. & Nap. 217.

[69] Real Property Limitation Act 1833 s.5; Statute of Limitations 1957 s.15. The rule is implied from the general provisions of the sections which provide that the right of action shall accrue to the owner of an estate in reversion when it falls into possession, subject to other provisions. Section 17 of the Statute of Limitations 1957 does not apply to a tenancy at sufferance since a tenant at sufferance is in adverse possession *ab initio*.

be regarded in law as a trespasser. The LTLRB 2011 expressly excludes tenancies at sufferance from the definition of tenancies.[70]

PERPETUALLY RENEWABLE LEASES FOR YEARS

20–56 A lease for years which contains a clause providing for the renewal of the term constitutes a perpetually renewable lease. In *McDermott v Caldwell*[71] a lease was granted for 50 years from 1754 with a clause providing for renewal for further terms, each of 31 years, during a total term of 1,000 years. This was held to fall within the Tenantry Act 1779 (the "1779 Act"), thereby attracting an equity to renew the term under s.1 of that Act even after the previous term would have expired. The preamble to the 1779 Act expressly refers only to leases for lives with covenants for perpetual renewal, but perpetually renewable leases for years may well have been within the scope of the "old equity" applied by courts of equity in Ireland before the statute's enactment. Strictly speaking, *McDermott v Caldwell*[72] itself concerned a lease which was not perpetual, since the renewals were limited to a total term of 1,000 years.[73]

20–57 Perpetually renewable leases for years clearly fall within the Renewable Leaseholds Conversion Act 1849 (the "1849 Act").[74] Section 1 of this Act refers only to a "lease in perpetuity" but s.38 provides that that phrase

"... shall be taken to apply to all cases where any hereditaments have been or shall be ... demised, leased, or granted, for one or more lives, with or without a term of years, or for years determinable upon one or more life or lives, *or for years absolute*, with a covenant or agreement ... for the perpetual renewal of such lease or contract." [emphasis supplied]

20–58 A lease for a term containing a covenant that at the end of the term the lessor is to grant a new lease which will include the same covenants as the original lease, and also the covenant for renewal, has been held to be a perpetually renewable lease.[75]

---

[70] LTLRB 2011, Head 3.
[71] (1877) I.R. 10 Eq. 504.
[72] (1877) I.R. 10 Eq. 504.
[73] The case was criticised in *Hussey v Domville* [1900] 1 I.R. 417; *Hussey v Domville (No.2)* [1903] 1 I.R. 265.
[74] *Re Gore* (1859) 8 Ir. Ch. R. 589. The lease in this case was created out of a lease for lives renewable and the term was to be renewed with the lives, but the same would seem to apply to a normally renewable term.
[75] *Bridges v Hitchcock* [1715] Bro. P.C. 6.

Granted after 1 August 1849

20–59 If granted after 1 August 1849, the purported grant of a "lease in perpetuity" operated automatically as a fee farm grant, subject to the covenants in the lease with the exception of the covenant for renewal.[76]

20–60 It is open to question whether a lease in the terms of the one in *McDermott v Caldwell*[77] would fall within the 1849 Act. It is certainly not perpetual in a literal sense, so that, ideally, it would have taken effect according to its terms and the tenant could have claimed the right to renew under the 1779 Act after the expiry of any one term.

Subsisting on 1 August 1849

20–61 If the "lease in perpetuity" was subsisting on 1 August 1849, the 1849 Act vested in the tenant a power to demand a fee farm grant.[78] Section 74 of the Landlord and Tenant (Amendment) Act 1980 (the "1980 Act") provides that a person holding under a lease for lives renewable forever, who had not sought to convert that lease into a fee farm grant under the 1849 Act, shall instead hold a fee simple estate, which is deemed to be a graft upon the previous interest and subject to any rights and equities that arise from that fact. Section 74 does not apply to perpetually renewable leases for years, since it expressly refers only to leases for *lives*. As pre-1849 leases for years renewable forever had been interpreted as also coming within the 1779 Act, the tenant had an equity to renew the lease even after a term has expired. The tenant therefore had a choice: either to renew the term under the 1779 Act or to exercise the power under the 1849 Act to demand a fee farm grant.

The LCLRA 2009

20–62 Section 12(1) of the LCLRA 2009 prohibits the creation of a fee farm grant. Subsection (2) provides that any instrument executed after 1 December 2009 purporting to grant either a fee farm grant or a lease for lives or years that is perpetually renewable will operate instead to grant the fee simple. All covenants, excepting that to pay rent, which are deemed to be consistent with a fee simple, contained in the purported fee farm grant or perpetually renewable lease, will continue in force.[79] According to the general repeal provisions of s.8(3) of the LCLRA 2009 the 1779 Act stands repealed, as also does the 1849 Act. On that basis, there would now appear to be no statutory foundation for the extension or enlargement of a lease for years renewable forever, except through the possible application of the ground rents legislation or the invocation, if found still to exist (which is unlikely), of the "old equity" applied by the pre-Union Court of Chancery in Ireland. Section 74 of the 1980 Act, which served to convert all leases for lives renewable forever which stood

---

[76] Section 37.

[77] (1877) I.R. 10 Eq. 504.

[78] Renewable Leaseholds Conversion Act 1849 s.1.

[79] LCLRA 2009 s.12(3).

unconverted at the enacting of the 1980 Act into fees simple, is unaffected by the LCLRA 2009.

TIMESHARE LEASES

20–63 Timeshare leases arose in the 20th century in the context of holiday accommodation. The typical timeshare lease[80] grants the right to occupy a holiday home for one or two weeks at the same time each year for a specified number of years. Timeshare leases were often sold by unscrupulous developers using high-pressure sales techniques. In order to protect the unwary purchaser, the European Union enacted legislation[81] which provides that purchasers must be given a document containing certain essential information as to the property, and allowed the right to withdraw from the contract without giving reasons within 10 days; with, furthermore, the right to withdraw altogether within three months if the information specified as being required to be provided is not provided.[82]

20–64 Judges have been in some doubt as to how to treat such leases.[83] An obvious question here is whether, in order to fall within the phrase "definite period" in s.4 of Deasy's Act, the term has to be a continuous one. If so, then timeshare leases would fall outside the Act.

20–65 In *An Application of O'Sullivan, Folio 27742 Co Cork*[84] D'Arcy J. considered a lease granted under a holiday timeshare scheme which granted "week no 25 in each year" for a term of 1,100 years. The applicant applied for registration of the lease as a burden under s.69(1)(g) of the Registration of Title Act 1964. This section refers to "any lease where the term granted is for a life or lives, or is determinable on a life or lives, or exceeds twenty-one years, or where the term is for any less estate or interest but the occupation is not in accordance with the lease".[85] D'Arcy J. held that the phrase "twenty one years" meant a continuous period of that length and that any change to accommodate timeshare leases was a matter for the Oireachtas.

20–66 The decision is unfortunate. The total term of 1,100 years was no doubt chosen because 1,100 weeks divided by 52 equals just over 21 years.

---

[80] See J. Edmonds, *International Timesharing* (London: Services to Lawyers, 1984).

[81] Directive 94/47/EC [1994] OJ L280/83.

[82] The Directive has been implemented in Ireland by the European Communities (Contracts for Time Sharing of Immovable Property – Protection of Purchasers) Regulations 1997 (S.I. No. 204 of 1997).

[83] See *Cottage Holiday Associates v Customs & Excise* [1983] 1 Q.B. 735.

[84] Unreported, High Court, D'Arcy J., 24 March 1983.

[85] If it is in accordance with the lease and the term exceeds 21 years then the lease is a registrable interest under s.27(c).

Fitzgerald[86] suggests that any amending legislation should classify such interests as s.72 burdens under the Registration of Title Act 1964 so that a note of their existence could then be entered on the register under s.72(3). It is open to question as to whether it follows from D'Arcy J.'s judgment that a timeshare term is not within s.72(1)(i) as being a tenancy "created for any term not exceeding twenty-one years or for any less estate or interest, in cases where there is an occupation under such tenancies". The section the judge was considering certainly also includes the phrase "any less estate or interest" but the judge's mind seems to have been directed towards the length of the term primarily. It is also arguable that there is occupation under the tenancy, namely during the specified occupational week.

20–67 A more intriguing question is whether a timeshare is within s.72(1)(j) as the right of a person in "actual occupation of the land or in receipt of the rents and profits thereof, save where, upon enquiry made of such person, the rights are not disclosed". Such interests are binding even without registration. Is the tenant in "actual occupation"? If a lease grants "week 25 in each year" to a tenant and a prospective purchaser of the registered title inspects the land in week 25, he or she may well find the holiday-makers in residence. But if they inspect it during any other week in the year, they will not. But another tenant might be in occupation in that week. Would this be sufficient to bind the purchaser not only as to the tenancy granted for that week, but also put him or her on notice that there is a timeshare scheme in operation and so also that other leases exist? In unregistered land the doctrine of notice may act in this way, but the doctrine of notice has been replaced in the case of registered land by the provisions of the Act.

FORMALITIES

Certain Leases to Be in Writing
20–68 Section 4 of Deasy's Act lays down the formalities to be satisfied by a lease if it is to fall within the provisions of the Act:

> "Every lease[87] or contract with respect to lands whereby the relation of landlord and tenant is intended to be created for any freehold estate or interest, or for any definite period of time not being from year to year or any lesser

---

[86] B. Fitzgerald, *Land Registry Practice* (Dublin: Round Hall, 1989), p.252. But this sensible suggestion has been taken up neither by the Registration of Deeds and Title Act 2006 nor by the LCLRA 2009.

[87] Section 4 may apply to leases or terms without a rent which do not otherwise fall within Deasy's Act. The alternative view, that such terms fall outside Deasy's Act altogether, because they are outside s.3, would mean that no formalities apply to them, since Deasy's Act repealed the Real Property Act 1845, which required a deed, except as to feoffments, exchanges and partitions. If no formalities were required, it then also follows that there would be no scope for *Walsh v Lonsdale* to apply in relation to such terms.

period, shall be by deed executed, or note in writing signed by the landlord or his agent thereunto lawfully authorized in writing."

20–69 It is also necessary that certain basic terms be agreed between the parties. These have been set out by Finnegan P. in *Cosmoline Trading Ltd v DH Burke and Co Ltd and DHB Holdings Ltd*[88] and include, principally:

- the parties[89];
- the premises[90];
- the term[91];
- the commencement date[92]; and
- the rent.[93]

20–70 Depending on the particular circumstances, there may be additional terms to be agreed; for example, the date of commencement of an increased rent following a review of rent after a new lease has been granted[94]; respective responsibilities where part only of a building is being let, with the landlord retaining the other part[95]; or covenants in relation to support and protection where a portion of a multi-storey building is being let.[96]

20–71 The LTLRB 2011 retains the requirement that leases be in writing, stating that "a tenancy[97] shall be created at law only in a document signed by (a) the landlord, or (b) an agent authorised in writing by the landlord."[98] It is worth noting that Head 12 of the LTLRB 2011 is concerned with the express creation of legal rights to a tenancy as opposed to equitable rights.[99] It is also worth pointing out that Head 12 does not refer to a deed on the basis that

---

[88] [2006] IEHC 38.

[89] *Silverwraith Ltd v Siúcre Éireann*, unreported, High Court, 8 June 1989. This also supports the proposition that, in the absence of a clearly identified commencement date, a lease can be deemed to commence on the date that the premises are available for occupation.

[90] *Law v Murphy*, unreported, High Court, 12 April 1978.

[91] *Crane v Naughton* [1912] 2 I.R. 318; for present purposes the word "term" also includes the nature of the recurrent period where the lease has not been granted for a term certain.

[92] *O'Flaherty v Arvan Properties Ltd*, unreported, Supreme Court, 12 July 1977; see also *Silverwraith Ltd v Siúcre Éireann*, unreported, High Court, 8 June 1989, above.

[93] *Shannon v Bradstreet* (1803) 1 Sch. & Lef. 52.

[94] *Ormond v Anderson* (1813) 2 B. & B. 363.

[95] *Dore v Stephenson*, unreported, High Court, 24 April 1980.

[96] *Cosmoline Trading Ltd v DH Burke and Co Ltd and DHB Holdings Ltd* [2006] IEHC 38. Finnegan P. (at para.72) observed: "... in the case of a multi-occupancy building involving retail, office and residential portions one would expect to find a management structure and indeed provision for a service charge".

[97] Under the LTLRB Bill 2011, a "tenancy" excludes tenancies at will and tenancies at sufferance.

[98] LTLRB 2011, Head 12.

[99] Such equitable rights cannot be registered in the Land Registry and must be protected by registration of a notice or caution if they are to be enforceable against a purchaser for value. Similarly, such equitable rights in unregistered land are not enforceable against a bona fide purchaser of a legal interest in the same land without notice of them. They may be protected by registering a memorial of any document relating to them in the Registry of Deeds.

writing can take any form, including engrossment in a document intended to operate as a deed.

20–72 The requirement of writing contained in Head 12 of the LTLRB 2011 does not apply to a tenancy for a recurring period not exceeding one year, or a tenancy for a fixed period not exceeding one year unless the grant includes provision for a renewal or extension which, if exercised, would result in the period, as renewed or extended, exceeding one year.

Agreements for a Lease: Walsh v Lonsdale

20–73 An equitable tenancy may arise through the doctrine of *Walsh v Lonsdale*.[100] In that case the parties had failed to create a legal lease through failure to comply with the necessary formalities. It was held that equity would treat the failed lease as an agreement to create a lease, provided that the formalities required for entering into a contract were complied with. Furthermore, provided that it was a contract which equity could enforce by specific performance, equity would treat "that as done, that which ought to be done" and would treat it as already a lease in equity. The principle applies in Ireland.

20–74 When may a lease fail to be a legal lease because of lack of formalities, but the agreement complies with the formalities required of a contract to create an interest in land? Such situations occur where an agreement fails to be a valid legal lease because it fails to comply with the formalities for a grant under s.4 of Deasy's Act, but still satisfies the requirements of a contract under the Statute of Frauds or of part performance in equity. Section 2 of the Statute of Frauds (Ireland) 1695[101] reads:

> " ... no action shall be brought whereby to charge ... any person ... upon any contract or sale of lands, tenements, or hereditaments, or any interest in or concerning them ... unless the agreement upon which such action shall be brought, or some memorandum or note thereof, shall be in writing, and signed by the party to be charged therewith, or some other person thereunto by him lawfully authorised."

20–75 The statute has been replaced as to contracts concerning land by s.51 of the LCLRA 2009, with minor changes. The phrase "signed by the party to be charged" has been changed to "signed by the person against whom the action is brought." Section 51 does not affect "the law relating to part performance or other equitable doctrines" (subs.(2)).[102]

---

[100] (1882) 21 Ch. D. 9.

[101] *Walsh v Lonsdale* (1882) 21 Ch. D. 9. See L.A. Sheridan, "*Walsh v Lonsdale* in Ireland" (1952) 9 N.I.L.Q. 190.

[102] In the rest of this section on *Walsh v Lonsdale*, s.51 or s.2 are referred to as "the Statute of Frauds".

20–76 The courts of equity in the past considered that the Statute required a certain kind of evidence, namely the note or memorandum, but that they could, in order to avoid fraud, accept an alternative form of evidence. This gave rise to the doctrine of *part performance*. Part performance of a contract for the sale of land will make it enforceable in the same way as if a memorandum existed.

20–77 It is crucial, however, that an actual agreement be found to exist. If the parties are not *ad idem* on fundamental terms, there is no agreement and the doctrine of part performance cannot arise, even if either or both of the parties are under the impression that they had reached agreement. As Finnegan P. observed in *Cosmoline Trading Ltd v DH Burke*[103]:

> "Where there is no contract part performance does not arise and if in reliance on an incomplete contract a party performs some or more of the matters on which agreement has indeed been reached that will not cause the negotiations which were otherwise incomplete to mature into a completed contract. Where ... there was no consensus on material and essential terms there cannot be a contract."

20–78 The following are the cases to be considered under s.4 of Deasy's Act.

Tenancy from Year to Year or Any Lesser Period
20–79 This type of agreement is outside s.4 and there are no formalities that apply, so that it can be made orally and still operate as a legal lease. Accordingly, there is no scope for the application of *Walsh v Lonsdale*.[104] The *assignment* of such a tenancy must be in writing under s.9 of Deasy's Act.

20–80 What if the lease is for one year? In *Wright v Tracey*[105] the court had to decide whether a term of one year was "less than a tenancy from year to year" for the purpose of s.62(2) of the Landlord and Tenant (Ireland) Act 1870. By a majority of 4:3 the court held that it was not. A tenancy from year to year was essentially for one year certain renewed automatically. This suggests that a tenancy for one year certain is included in the first (but not the second) part of the phrase "tenancy from year to year or any lesser period" and so is outside s.4 of Deasy's Act and can be made orally.[106]

Term Greater than from Year to Year
20–81 The doctrine of *Walsh v Lonsdale*[107] applies where the agreement is for a term greater than from year to year in the following situations, i.e. where the

---

[103] *Cosmoline Trading Ltd v DH Burke and Co Ltd and DHB Holdings Ltd* [2006] IEHC 38 at para.21.
[104] (1882) 21 Ch. D. 9.
[105] (1874) I.R. 8 C.L. 478.
[106] See also, *Brew v Conole* (1875) I.R. 9 C.L. 151; *McGrath v Travers* [1948] I.R. 122.
[107] (1882) 21 Ch. D. 9.

agreement falls within the terms of s.4 but does not comply with it, and yet *does* comply with the Statute of Frauds.

Where the Agreement Is in Writing Signed by the Landlord's Orally Authorised Agent
20–82 This fails as a lease under s.4 because the landlord's agent was not authorised in writing. Under the Statute of Frauds the agreement must be signed by the person against whom the action is brought. The tenant can sue the landlord in any case, since it has been signed by the landlord's agent.[108]

Where the Agreement Is in Writing Signed by the Tenant
20–83 In this case it is enforceable only by the landlord.

Where the Agreement Is in Writing Signed by the Landlord's Orally Authorised Agent and By the Tenant
20–84 There could also be a combination of the two above in which the agreement is in writing, and signed by the landlord's orally authorised agent and by the tenant. This agreement would be enforceable both by the landlord and by the tenant since both parties have signed the agreement under the Statute of Frauds.

Where the Agreement Is Oral, but Written Evidence of it Exists or Comes into Existence Later
20–85 The agreement is enforceable against the party or parties by whom or by whose agent the written evidence is signed.

20–86 In *Craig v Elliot*[109] the defendant landlord entered into a verbal agreement to grant the plaintiff a lease of a house for a term of years. The draft lease was sent by the plaintiff tenant's solicitors to the defendant landlord's solicitors. The defendant's solicitors signed the draft on behalf of their client and returned the draft lease. The defendant later wrote to the plaintiff complaining that the draft lease had not been engrossed, and later refused to carry out the agreement. The plaintiff tenant sued for specific performance of the agreement. It was held that the letter signed by the defendant—the "party to be charged"—contained a sufficient reference to the draft lease to connect them together so as to form the memorandum required by the Statute of Frauds.

20–87 In *Babington v O'Connor*[110] the intending tenant executed the draft lease. The landlord had not done so, but it was he who sued the tenant under a covenant in the draft to pay rent in advance. The defendant tenant had gone

---

[108] *McAusland v Murphy* (1881) 9 L.R. Ir. 9.
[109] (1885) 15 L.R. Ir. 257.
[110] (1887) 20 L.R. Ir. 246.

into possession and paid rent. The landlord was held entitled to the rent in advance. The court did not refer to *Walsh v Lonsdale* although the facts are almost the same. The tenant was holding as a tenant in equity bound by the covenants in the agreement.

The Agreement is Oral, but Is Subsequently Partly Performed

20–88 *Babington v O'Connor* could also be seen as an example of this situation since there was clearly part performance in that case. It used to be said that the act of part performance had to be "unequivocally referable" to the contract. In *Steadman v Steadman*[111] the House of Lords reviewed the law on part performance and modified it somewhat: the acts relied on did not have to refer to specific terms. Also, contrary to what was previously the case, they held that payment of money can be an act of part performance.[112]

20–89 The principles applicable to part performance were set out by the Supreme Court in *Mackey v Wilde*.[113] The doctrine is based upon principles of equity. There are three things to be considered:

- the acts on the part of the plaintiff said to have been in part performance of a concluded agreement;
- the involvement of the defendant with respect to such acts;
- the oral agreement itself.

20–90 It is obvious that these considerations only relate to a contract of a type which the courts will decree ought to be specifically performed. Each of the three elements is essential. Ultimately it is essential that:

- there was a concluded oral contract;
- the plaintiff acted in a way that showed an intention to perform that contract;
- the defendant induced such acts or stood by while there were being performed; and
- it would be unconscionable and a breach of good faith to allow the defendant to rely upon the terms of the Statute of Frauds to prevent performance of the contract.

20–91 Granting possession can be an act of part performance, but permitting a party already in possession to remain in possession will not.[114] In *Sweeney v Denis*,[115] a tenant was in possession under an existing lease which was due to end. He entered into an agreement for a new lease at an increased rent, but

---

[111] [1976] 2 All E.R. 977.

[112] H. Wallace, "Part Performance Re-examined" (1974) 24 N.I.L.Q. 453.

[113] [1998] I.L.R.M. 449 at 458.

[114] *Sheridan v The Louis Fitzgerald Group Ltd and Burston Ltd* [2006] IEHC 125 at para.9.

[115] (1883) 17 I.L.T.R. 76.

remained in occupation, paying the old rent. This did not amount to part performance as he was not doing anything which he had not done before.

20–92 There is one possible further case where the doctrine of *Walsh v Lonsdale* may apply.

Future Lease

20–93 This situation arises where an agreement conforms to s.4 of Deasy's Act but it is for a lease to begin at a future date. *Walsh v Lonsdale* could then apply if it could be said that the agreement did not create a lease to begin in future (i.e. a future interest) but created only a contract to grant a lease in future to take effect at the date specified. If the doctrine applied there would be a lease in equity immediately, to take effect at the future date, but no legal lease.

20–94 There seem to be two difficulties in the way of coming to this conclusion. The first is that it is not clear whether it is possible in Ireland to have an agreement to create a lease in future which does not immediately give rise to a lease, albeit a future legal lease. Section 3 of Deasy's Act appears to lay down that a lease is no more than a contract and that a contract within the terms of the section is a lease.

20–95 The second difficulty is that a contract to grant a lease in future would be a contract to enter into a contract. Such a contract is not binding at common law. What is it a contract to do? To negotiate in good faith?[116] In the case of contracts for leases these problems may be less significant than in other cases. If the parties agree on the duration, the premises, and the rent, the law implies other terms. In *Union v McDermott*[117] an agreement for a weekly tenancy to begin in future was held not to be a mere agreement to make a letting in future. It was a legal tenancy to take effect in future, but the court said that it held this on the facts of the case and did not purport to lay down a general rule.

20–96 Finally, an agreement may comply neither with s.4 of Deasy's Act *nor* with the Statute of Frauds *nor* be capable of being rescued by the doctrine of part performance. Where the doctrine of equity cannot apply, so that an interest in land is incapable of being held to exist, it would seem that no more

---

[116] *May & Butcher v King* [1934] 2 K.B. 17 (contract to contract is a nullity). Sheridan, in *"Walsh v Lonsdale* in Ireland" (1952) 9 N.I.L.Q. 190, says that if this is so one cannot enter into a contract to create a lease in future. One can only enter into a legal lease to take effect at a future date.

[117] (1921) 55 I.L.T.R. 194.

than a licence[118] (although perhaps a contractual licence) may result. In *Ward v Ryan*[119] an oral agreement purporting to grant a term of years was held to create a tenancy at will. Tenancies at will have now in effect been abolished by s.11(3) of the LCLRA 2009 so the application of this decision post the LCLRA 2009 is uncertain.

Is an Agreement for a Lease as Good as a Lease?

20–97 Where the doctrine of *Walsh v Lonsdale* applies, it is sometimes said that "an agreement for a lease is as good as a lease". This is misleading because a lease in equity suffers from the following defects as compared to a legal lease:

Discretionary Remedies

20–98 The doctrine gives rise only to a lease in equity, and so depends on the discretionary remedy of specific performance. If for some reason that remedy cannot be granted the doctrine cannot apply.[120] Where, for example, the grant of the lease was subject to a condition precedent which remains unperformed by the proposed tenant and has not been waived by the landlord, there is no lease in equity.[121]

Not a "Conveyance"

20–99 Statutory provisions that apply to "conveyances" do not apply to an equitable lease under the doctrine, so that, for example, s.71 of the LCLRA 2009[122] would not apply to equitable leases arising under the doctrine.[123]

Prior Equities

20–100 Equitable tenants cannot plead purchase of a legal estate without notice in order to take free of prior equities. The situation can still arise under the Registration of Deeds system where the prior equity is not registrable because it is not created by deed, as for example, an interest under a resulting

---

[118] In *Ó Síodhcháin v O'Mahony* [2002] 4 I.R. 147, Kearns J. held a licence, rather than a lease, to exist, where, despite the presence of several indicia consistent with a lease, it was clear that the putative grantor had not the requisite intention to part with an estate for the principle in *Walsh v Lonsdale* to be invoked. In addition, the party seeking to call in aid the principle had brought undue influence to bear upon the other, and it is a maxim of equity that one who seeks its relief "must come with clean hands".

[119] (1875) I.R. 9 C.L. 54 at 55, on appeal I.R. 10 C.L. 17 at 20.

[120] *Kingswood Estates v Anderson* [1963] 2 Q.B. 169.

[121] *Cornish v Brook Green Laundry Ltd* [1959] 1 Q.B. 394.

[122] LCLRA 2009 s.71 provides that a conveyance of land conveys and includes (a) all buildings, erections, fences, etc. forming part of the land, as well as (b) all easements, *profits à prendre*, etc. which appertain to the land.

[123] *Borman v Griffith* [1930] 1 Ch. 493 at 497f.

trust. In relation to such interests the equitable doctrine of notice still applies. A similar situation can also arise in the case of registered land.

Liable to Be Defeated

20–101 Like all equitable interests, equitable tenancies are liable to be defeated by a later purchaser of the legal estate without notice of them. In the case of registered title an equitable tenant in actual occupation may be protected as having a s.72 interest. If not in actual occupation, the tenancy would need to be protected by an entry on the register as a minor interest.

Outside Deasy's Act?

20–102 The requirements of s.4 of Deasy's Act are necessary if "the relation of landlord and tenant" is to be created. This presumably must be construed as meaning *for the purposes of the Act*. If so, then on the face of it leases in equity within the *Walsh v Lonsdale* principle are valid but not governed by Deasy's Act. An alternative view is that the equitable doctrine treats such agreements as if specific performance had been granted in which case they would notionally comply.

IMPLIED TENANCIES

Section 5 of Deasy's Act

20–103 Implied tenancies may arise under s.5 of Deasy's Act:

"5. In case any tenant or his representative, after the expiration or determination of the term agreed upon in any lease or instrument in writing, shall continue in possession for more than one month after demand for possession by the landlord or his agent, such continuance shall, at the discretion of the landlord, be deemed to constitute a new holding of the lands from year to year, subject to the former rent and to such of the agreements contained in the lease or instrument as may be applicable to the new holding."

20–104 In *O'Keefe v Walsh*[124] O'Keefe was a tenant for life. He created a tenancy from year to year in favour of the defendant. Then he died. For 15 months the defendant remained in occupation. He assumed that the plaintiff, who was entitled in remainder after O'Keefe, did not want to alter the arrangement. He offered rent and it was refused. The question was whether the defendant was entitled to notice to quit, i.e. had the tenancy continued after the death of the tenant for life? It could only have done so if it had been adopted by the remaindermen and it was held on appeal that there was insufficient evidence that they had done so.

---

[124] (1880) 8 L.R. Ir. 184.

20–105 Section 5 presupposes a previous term which has expired and therefore deals with overholding by an existing tenant. Nevertheless, it is clear that s.5 is not exhaustive of the situations in which courts in Ireland may find implied tenancies. The next section deals with these.

Outside Section 5

20–106 Tenancies under the doctrine of *Walsh v Lonsdale*[125] are valid apart from the section,[126] although it is arguable that they are not really "implied" but rather result from equity providing a remedy to avoid an otherwise unfair result.

20–107 The courts have also held there to be an implied tenancy even though there was a prior valid term which had expired but the situation did not fall within s.5 of Deasy's Act. In *Phoenix Picture Palace Ltd v Capitol & Allied Trustees Ltd*[127] there was a lease for three years at a weekly rent with an option to renew for another two years. The three years came to an end. The tenants did not exercise their option, but continued in possession paying a weekly rent. During the three-year term by agreement between the parties, rent had been paid in quarterly instalments of 13 times the weekly rent. After the three years were up, the tenants paid rent weekly. The court held that there was only a weekly and not a yearly tenancy. Even if s.5 were wide enough to include the present case, its application was excluded by the circumstance that the express words of the section provided for the landlord to treat the tenant only as a yearly tenant.

20–108 Under s.40 of the 1980 Act, a tenant entitled to a reversionary lease to begin at the end of his or her present tenancy is entitled to remain in possession. Under ss.27 and 28, so is a person entitled under statute to the fee simple or to a new lease, i.e. long-term residents of residential or business premises who have made substantial improvements.[128] What interest do they have in the meantime? In *Cooke v Dillon*[129] a tenant was entitled to a new tenancy. He remained in possession and paid rent as he had done before, which was on a monthly basis. The court refused to imply a tenancy from year to year. He was held to be a monthly tenant.

---

[125] (1882) 21 Ch. D. 9.

[126] *Kennan v Murphy* (1880) 8 L.R. Ir. 285.

[127] [1951] Ir. Jur. Rep. 55.

[128] For discussion of the rights and obligations of the tenant in such situation, see *Harrisrange Ltd v Duncan* [2003] 4 I.R. 1; *Crofter Properties Ltd v Genport Ltd* [2007] 2 I.L.R.M. 528.

[129] (1959) 93 I.L.T.R. 48.

TENANCIES BY ESTOPPEL

20–109 Tenancies can also arise through the operation of estoppel.[130] As between the parties to an agreement, an estoppel is no more than a matter of evidence or procedure, but it requires more than that to extend the binding effect to third parties. Various attempts have been made to do so. The common law doctrine of "feeding" the estoppel produces the result that the tenancy is a legal estate. The doctrine of proprietary estoppel produces an "equity" which may nevertheless only be satisfied by the vesting of a legal estate in the person relying on representations. Tenancies by estoppel need not be in writing, and this principle is continued by the LTLRB 2011, Head 12.

Original Parties
20–110 If A, who has no interest in a piece of land, purports to grant a lease in it to B, then each is estopped, as against the other, from denying that the relationship of landlord and tenant exists between them.[131]

20–111 In *Keenan v Walsh*[132] K executed a mortgage on his house. Afterwards he sublet two rooms in the house to Walsh. The tenant was not satisfied with the rent and brought an action under the then Rent Restrictions Act 1946. The mortgage contained a clause prohibiting subletting without the consent of the mortgagees. It was held that the tenancy, even though contrary to the mortgage, was valid between the parties. It was a tenancy by estoppel that neither party could dispute.

20–112 A similar outcome arose in *Morton v Woods*.[133] The owner of a factory had granted a mortgage by way of conveyance. He then purported to grant a second mortgage to a different mortgagee, also by conveyance. The existence of the prior mortgage was recited in the second conveyance. By way of additional security, the mortgagor created the relationship of landlord and tenant between them, with the mortgagee becoming the landlord. This made it easier for the mortgagee, as landlord, to enter into possession and to levy distress on goods and chattels in the event of default by the mortgagor. When this eventuality later occurred, the mortgagor protested that the second mortgagee could not exercise a right of distress as the legal estate had not vested in it. The court held that the mortgagor was estopped from denying the second mortgagee's title.[134]

---

[130] *Sturgeon v Wingfield* (1846) 15 M. & W. 224; *Gowrie Park Utility Society Ltd v Fitzgerald* [1963] I.R. 436.

[131] This can also arise where a lease is not purported to be created, but exclusive possession is granted and the party in occupation pays rent, as in *Bruton v London and Quadrant Housing Trust* [2000] 1 A.C. 406.

[132] (1951) 85 I.L.T.R. 86.

[133] (1868–1869) L.R. 4 Q.B. 293.

[134] (1868–1869) L.R. 4 Q.B. 293 at 304.

20–113 Although approving the principle enunciated in *Morton v Woods*, the House of Lords in *Bruton v London and Quadrant Housing Trust*[135] introduced an interpretative refinement in the case of a dispute between original contracting parties. Where the relationship between the parties, in particular the giving of exclusive possession, conforms to that of landlord and tenant, then such a relationship will be found to exist between them, regardless of whether the grantor was seized of an estate, and regardless of whether that fact was recited in the agreement with the grantee.[136] In Hoffmann L.J.'s view, estoppel only arises strictly at the point when one of the parties denies that a particular obligation, necessary to the holding of land, has arisen. The original arrangement, so long as neither denies an element of it, cannot, in the judge's view, therefore depend on the concept of estoppel. It might be objected, however, that this is overly precise reasoning. The agreement binds the parties as a contract, but what binds the parties to further obligations and incidents flowing from an agreement to hold or occupy land is the *possibility* of estoppel. But the main point, if one interprets the judge's remarks correctly, is that an arrangement exists between the parties which can be called a "lease", with its necessary incidents binding on both, quite apart from any effect it might or might not have as to third parties.

Feeding the Estoppel

20–114 The common law held that if A, who had no estate, purported to grant a tenancy to B, then if A later acquired an estate in the land granted, the tenancy which had operated by estoppel between A and B became a full legal estate.[137] Later cases referred to the estoppel as being "fed" by the legal estate.

20–115 Lord Hoffmann's remarks in *Bruton v London and Quadrant Housing Trust*[138] may have undercut the concept of estoppel as to the original arrangement, i.e. that it is better to regard it simply as a lease or tenancy existing as between the two parties. "Tenancy by estoppel" may be regarded simply as a short way of referring to such a "lease" or tenancy existing between two persons by contract.

20–116 One of the earliest cases in which an estoppel was held to bind a third party is the Irish case of *Jones v Kearney*.[139] It was said that if a person who has not got an estate enters into a contract in respect of it, then if he or she afterwards acquires the estate, it will be bound by the contract. In *Church v Dalton*,[140] A, a tenant at will of B, purported to grant a lease to C. A later obtained a lease from B. It was held that the grant from B to A operated

---

[135] [2000] 1 A.C. 406.

[136] [2000] 1 A.C. 406 at 416.

[137] *Webb v Austin* (1844) 7 Man. & G. 701; *Sturgeon v Wingfield* (1846) 15 M. & W. 224; *Church v Dalton* (1847) 9 Ir. C.L.R. 355.

[138] [2000] 1 A.C. 406.

[139] (1841) 4 Ir. Eq. R. 82.

[140] (1847) 9 Ir. C.L.R. 355.

retrospectively, turning the "estoppel" created between A and C into an estate at law.[141]

20–117 In *Universal Permanent Building Society v Cooke*[142] a purchaser entered into a contract to buy a shop with a flat over it. Before the legal estate was conveyed to her the purchaser let the flat to her sister. The sister went into possession and paid rent. The premises were then conveyed to the purchaser in fee simple. The next day she mortgaged the premises to the building society. Three years later the mortgagor went into default. The building society claimed that it was entitled to vacant possession, i.e. not subject to the tenancy. It was held that in the absence of evidence that the conveyance and mortgage were all one transaction, there was an interval of time during which the mortgagor was the owner of the fee simple not subject to the mortgage, and as a result the tenancy by estoppel of the sister was "fed" by the legal estate, thereby giving her a legal tenancy before the mortgage was executed which accordingly bound the mortgagee.

20–118 In *Woolwich Equitable Building Society v Marshall*[143] it was held that even when the conveyance and the mortgage are executed on the same day there was a presumption that the conveyance was executed first, as legally it ought to be, and the estoppel was still fed.[144] In *Abbey National Building Society v Cann*[145] a considerable restriction was placed on the doctrine by the House of Lords in holding that it was inequitable for a person to claim a tenancy by estoppel if that person knew at the time of the conveyance that a mortgage was to be entered into by the "grantor" and that the building society would not grant a mortgage if there was a tenancy already in existence. In *First National Bank plc v Thompson*[146] the English Court of Appeal held that the doctrine did not depend on a representation by the grantor, but on the common law principle that a grantor could not deny his or her own title.[147]

Proprietary Estoppel

20–119 In *Haughan v Rutledge*,[148] the plaintiffs claimed a lease based on proprietary estoppel. The judge cited a passage from Snell's *Principles of Equity*[149] setting out the test of proprietary estoppel and he described this as a "correct statement of the law", though on the facts the court held that proprietary estoppel had not been made out.

---

[141] See also *Eyre v Sadleir* (1865) 15 Ir. Ch. R. 1; *Sexton v McGrath* (1872) I.R. 6 Eq. 381; *Ward v Ryan* (1875) I.R. 10 C.L. 17.

[142] [1952] Ch. 95.

[143] [1952] Ch. 1.

[144] See also *Church of England Building Society v Piskor* [1954] Ch. 553.

[145] [1991] 1 A.C. 56.

[146] [1996] Ch. 231.

[147] See also *Goodtitle d Edwards v Bailey* (1777) 2 Cowp. 597.

[148] [1988] I.R. 295.

[149] E.H.T. Snell, *Principles of Equity*, 28th edn (London: Sweet & Maxwell, 1982), p.558.

20–120 In *Law v Murphy*[150] a claim to a tenancy by estoppel also failed. A licence had been granted to remove gravel. The owner of the land then offered the licensees a lease. It was held that there was an insufficient memorandum to satisfy the Statute of Frauds because there was no reference to the area to be leased or to the term. McWilliam J. held that there could be no lease by estoppel because the licensees had suffered no detriment. They merely continued excavating on the land, which they had previously been doing under the licence.

ASSIGNMENT AND SUBLETTING AND OTHER EXPRESS COVENANTS

20–121 The question of whether a tenant has an estate in land is largely meaningless in view of Deasy's Act. The attributes of the leasehold relationship in this respect are governed by the statute, not by the common law. Section 9 of Deasy's Act provides that the "estate or interest" of any tenant in any lands under any lease or contract of tenancy shall be assignable by deed or instrument in writing signed by the assignor or his or her agent lawfully authorised in writing, or by devise or bequest (i.e. a will) or by operation of law, and not otherwise. "And not otherwise" indicates that if the assignment is in writing it must be signed by the assignor or his or her agent lawfully authorised in writing. Thus, in *McIlherron v McIlherron*[151] it was held that an oral agreement to assign followed by an actual change of possession is not enough without the landlord's consent to effect an assignment by operation of law.

20–122 Section 9 also applies to tenancies that can be created orally under s.4 of Deasy's Act, i.e. tenancies "from year to year or any lesser period". The death of the tenant causes an assignment by operation of law.[152] Section 11 provides that the assignee is subject to all the agreements in respect of assignment or subletting to the same extent as the assignor.

20–123 The LTLRB 2011 purports to re-enact the substance of s.9 of Deasy's Act. It provides that a tenancy is assignable only in a document signed by the assignor, or an agent authorised in writing by the assignor.[153] The definition of "tenancy" in Head 3 of the Bill, when read with Head 12, makes it clear that Head 14(1) covers both tenancies created in writing and oral tenancies. Head 14(1) does not affect:

(a) devolution of a tenancy on the death of the tenant;
(b) transmission of a tenancy by act and operation of law; or
(c) the doctrine of estoppel or other equitable principles.

---

[150] Unreported, High Court, McWilliam J., 12 April 1978.
[151] (1892) 27 I.L.T.R. 62, and see Lawson J. in *Bourke v Bourke* (1874) I.R. 8 C.L. 221 at 223.
[152] *Wallis v Wallis* (1883) 12 L.R. Ir. 63.
[153] LTLRB 2011, Head 14.

The Running of Covenants at Common Law
Assignees of the Tenant

20–124 In *Spencer's Case*[154] it was held that an assignee of the tenant could enforce against the landlord an express covenant in the lease conferring a benefit on the tenant, provided the covenant "touched and concerned the land", i.e. was for the benefit of the land and did not confer a purely personal benefit on the tenant.[155] The benefit of such a covenant "ran with the land", i.e. passed to the person in possession of the land under the lease. *Spencer's Case* also held that the burden of covenants touching and concerning the land ran with the land. Thus, if the original lease contained a covenant binding the tenant to keep a wall in repair, assignees of the original tenant could be sued by the landlord if they failed to repair the wall.

Assignees of the Reversion

20–125 At common law an "assignee of the reversion", i.e. an assignee of the landlord's interest, could sue on covenants implied in the relationship of landlord and tenant by the general law, such as the covenant by the tenant to pay rent, but had no right to enforce express covenants in the lease entered into between the original parties.[156] Following the dissolution of the monasteries the grantees of monastic lands wished to enforce covenants in leases entered into by the monasteries with their tenants and so the Grantees of Reversions Act 1540 was passed to enable them to do so.[157] It also made them liable to be sued on express covenants by tenants. A similar Act was passed in Ireland in 1634.[158] The statutes were regarded as having changed the law to allow *all* grantees of reversions to sue and be sued on express covenants which "touched and concerned" the land.[159]

20–126 The relationship between assignees of the original landlord and assignees of the original tenant came to be called "privity of estate".[160] Between the original landlord and the original tenant there was privity of contract, and all covenants were binding within the limits of the law. Between assignees of the original parties there was privity of estate and those covenants were binding which touched and concerned the land.

---

[154] (1583) 5 Co. Rep. 16.

[155] *Mayor of Congleton v Pattison* (1808) 10 East 130 at 135: "[it] affected the nature, quality, or value of the thing demised, independently of collateral circumstances; or if it affected the mode of enjoying it."

[156] E.H. Burn and J. Cartwright, *Cheshire and Burn's Modern Law of Real Property*, 18th edn (Oxford: Oxford University Press, 2011), p.309.

[157] 32 Hen VIII c. 34, 1540.

[158] 10 Chas. I sess. 2 c.4 (Ir), 1634, repealed by Deasy's Act 1860 s.104 & Sch.

[159] *Cheshire and Burn's Modern Law of Real Property* (2011), p.309.

[160] *Berney v Moore* (1791) 2 Ridg. P.C. 310.

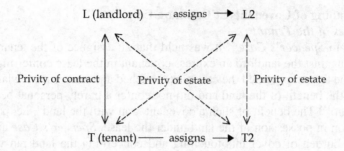

Touching and Concerning: Examples

20–127 The following are examples from the case law of covenants which have been held to touch and concern the land:

By the lessor	By the lessee
To supply the premises with pure water.[161]	To pay rent.[162]
Not to build on adjoining land.[163]	To repair the property or fixtures on it.[164]
To renew the lease.[165]	To insure against fire.[166]
Not to determine a periodic tenancy during its first three years.[167]	To use as a private dwelling house only.[168]
	To pay a sum of money towards redecorating on quitting.[169]

The Running of Covenants under Statute
Benefit and Burden of Covenants

20–128 Sections 12 and 13 of Deasy's Act replaced the common law concept of privity of estate. They provide that the benefit and burden of covenants and agreements contained or implied in leases or tenancies are enforceable by and against successors to the original landlord and tenant.

20–129 The sections do not include the common law qualification that the covenants only bind successors if they "touch and concern" the land. However,

---

[161] *Jourdain v Wilson* (1831) 4 B. & Ald. 266.

[162] *Parker v Webb* (1693) 3 Salk. 5.

[163] *Ricketts v Enfield Churchwardens* [1909] 1 Ch. 544.

[164] *Matures v Westwood* (1598) Cro. Eliz. 599; *Williams v Earle* (1868) L.R. 3 Q.B. 739 at 751f.

[165] *Chandos (Duchess) v Brownlow* (1791) 2 Ridg. P.C. 345 at 409; J. Lyne, *A Treatise on the Leases for Lives, Renewable for Ever* (Dublin: Hodges and Smith, 1837), p.123. Every assignee can take advantage of it and every person who comes lawfully by the term: Lyne, *Treatise on Leases for Lives, Renewable for Ever* (1837), p.123; *Hyde v Skinner* (1723) 2 P.W. 196.

[166] *Vernon v Smith* (1821) 5 B. & Ald. 1.

[167] *Breams Property Investment Co Ltd v Stroulger* [1948] 2 K.B. 1.

[168] *Wilkinson v Rogers* (1864) 2 De G.J. & S. 62.

[169] *Boyer v Warbey* [1953] 1 Q.B. 234.

Lyle v Smith[170] placed a similar qualification on the sections. The court held that "covenants not capable of vicarious performance" do not bind, nor would "collateral agreements", but that covenants which "touch and concern"[171] the land will bind under Deasy's Act.[172] *Lyle v Smith* therefore confirms that Deasy's Act does not consistently treat the parties to leases as being in fictional terms in the same position as the original contracting parties.

20–130 Head 16 of the LTLRB 2011 would replace ss.12 and 13 of Deasy's Act, as well as the identical provisions in ss.10 and 11 of the Conveyancing Act 1881. It provides:

"(1) Subject to subhead (2), the holder for the time being of the landlord's or the tenant's interest under a tenancy is—

    (a) entitled to enforce the benefit of all provisions,

    (b) bound by all obligations.

(2) Subhead (1) does not apply to—

    (a) a successor in title to the landlord or tenant in respect of the benefit of any provision or an obligation expressed to be personal to the original or another holder of the landlord's or tenant's interest, or

    (b) any obligation contained in a collateral or other agreement separate from the tenancy agreement unless the holder of the interest in question had actual knowledge of the obligation at the time the interest was acquired."

20–131 Head 16 assimilates the position of landlord and tenant so that the successors of either party are in the same position; they step fully into the position of their predecessors in title, subject to certain limitations.

Liability under Covenants

20–132 At common law, if the landlord assigned only a part of the reversion, the assignee of the part could not sue on the covenants. In *Liddy v Kennedy*[173] it was observed that Deasy's Act was intended to remove technical difficulties that stood in the way of justice. The House of Lords held that s.12 abolished the common law rule so that where a landlord constituted himself or herself and another as the landlord, then both together had the benefit of the covenants.

20–133 Section 16 of Deasy's Act provides that the assigning tenant is released from future liability on the covenants when he or she assigns the lease with the landlord's consent. At common law the original tenant would remain

---

[170] [1909] 2 I.R. 58.
[171] [1909] 2 I.R. 58 at 79.
[172] Overruling *Borrowes v Delaney* (1889) 24 L.R. Ir. 503.
[173] (1871) L.R. 5 H.L. 134.

liable on the covenants even after assigning the lease unless he or she had contracted with the landlord only to be liable while he or she retained an interest
in the land. This was seen as a matter of privity of contract and parties could
contract to be liable to whatever extent they had agreed. Deasy's Act alters this
so that the tenant's liability ends with his or her parting with the interest in the
land. In this respect the Act, far from treating leases like contracts, removes the
position of the original parties from the realm of contract and links continued
liability under covenant with ownership of a property interest.

20–134 Section 14 of Deasy's Act provides that the assignee of a tenancy is liable only in respect of breaches of covenant that occurred while he or she was a
tenant, i.e. while there is what at common law would be called privity of estate.
Here the Act merely declares what was the position at common law. Between
an assignee and the landlord, whether the original landlord or a new one, there
was no privity of contract, and therefore the assignee of the tenant was only
liable to the extent that there was privity of estate. But notice that under s.14
the assignee only ceases to be liable on assigning his or her interest if he or she
gives written notice to the landlord. Also, the assignee can only take the benefit
of the covenants while an assignee, so that if the covenant was broken before
he or she became tenant the assignee cannot sue for the breach at that time.[174]

20–135 Sections 14 and 16 of Deasy's Act would be replaced by Head 17 of
the LTLRB 2011. This drops the distinction drawn between the original tenant
and subsequent assignees of the tenant's interest. This distinction was probably
significant in an age when the rent was usually paid in arrears but in modern
times it is invariably payable in advance. Head 17(1) provides as follows:

"17(1) … on the passing, whether by assignment or otherwise, of the landlord's or the tenant's interest under a tenancy, the assignor or previous
holder of that interest—

(a) ceases to be entitled to enforce the benefit of provisions,
(b) is not liable for any breach of obligation which occurs after the date
of such passing of the interest.

(2) Subhead (1)(b) does not apply—

(a) in the case of assignment of the tenant's interest unless, whether
required or not by the terms of the tenancy, the consent of the landlord to the assignment has been given in writing,
(b) in all cases until notice in writing of the passing of the interest is
given to the landlord or tenant, as appropriate."

20–136 The principle in Head 17(1) is subject to limitations. It does not
affect the right of an assignee or other successor in title to enforce a breach
of obligation which occurred before the passing of the interest and remained

---

[174] *Doyle v Hart* (1880) 4 L.R. Ir. 455 at 467.

unremediated at the date of such passing.[175] Nor does it affect the liability of an assignee or other successor in title for the continuing breach of an obligation where the breach commenced before and continued after such passing of the interest. Thus a successor in title would remain liable for continuing breaches of obligation which occur while he or she holds the interest in question.[176]

Waiver

20–137 Sections 18 and 43 of Deasy's Act provide that no act of a landlord is a waiver of a breach of covenant, unless the landlord or his or her authorised agent signifies agreement in writing.[177] Section 22 provides that agreement by a landlord to a particular subletting is not a general waiver of the covenant, as it would be at common law.[178] The provisions in Deasy's Act as to waiver have been construed as clear and unambiguous, to be strictly followed.[179] The words "any breach" in relation to a covenant, condition or agreement in a lease signify that a waiver by a landlord must relate to a specific breach, rather than to breaches generally, and it must be in writing.[180]

20–138 Head 47 of the LTLRB 2011 seeks to clarify and simplify the law relating to waiver. It replaces s.43 of Deasy's Act, providing that "a general release of a landlord or tenant obligation or a waiver of a particular breach of such an obligation shall be in writing signed by the party releasing or waiving or by that party's agent authorised in writing." Under Head 47(2),

"[w]here—

(a) the landlord gives consent to the tenant in a particular instance to do any thing which under a tenant's obligation requires consent or which would otherwise be a breach of obligation by the tenant, or

(b) the landlord or tenant waives a particular breach of obligation by the other party to the tenancy,

such consent or waiver is confined to that particular instance or breach of obligation and is not a general release of the obligation."

Payment for Consent

20–139 Section 3 of the Conveyancing Act 1892 provides that no fine (lump sum) or similar sum is to be payable for the landlord's consent unless the lease

---

[175] As the explanatory guide to the Heads of Bill states, there is authority that this is the position under the Conveyancing Act 1881 s.10, but it is difficult to reconcile with Deasy's Act s.14.

[176] This continues to reflect the position in *Doyle v Hart* (1880) 4 L.R. Ir. 455 at 467.

[177] *O'Toole v Lyons* [1948] I.R. 115 (acceptance of rent).

[178] Section 22 duplicates in Ireland ss.1 and 2 of the Law of Property (Amendment) Act 1859 and s.6 of the Law of Property (Amendment) Act 1860, which are to the same effect.

[179] *Foley v Mangan* [2009] IEHC 404.

[180] *Crofter Properties Ltd v Genport Ltd*, unreported, High Court, McCracken J., 15 March 1996.

provides for it. However, the 1980 Act[181] modifies this in relation to covenants prohibiting alienation[182] and change of user,[183] discussed below, to the extent that, as to such covenants, a landlord may only require payment of a reasonable sum to cover legal and other expenses. In a tenancy to which the Residential Tenancies Acts 2004–2016 apply, s.17(3) of that Act provides that where a tenant seeks the landlord's consent, either to an assignment or sub-letting, to alterations or improvements, or to a change of use, then, regardless of whether the landlord consents to such application, the landlord will be entitled to be reimbursed by the tenant for "any costs or expenses reasonably incurred by him or her in deciding" upon the application.

Covenants Restricting Assignment or Subletting

20–140 In other areas of property law there is a conflict between two objectives or policies, both of which derive from the relations of a society based on the market. One is that people should be free to make their own bargains without intervention by the State. This has an ideological aspect, in that it may be assumed or asserted that the freedom exists regardless of the factual position of the parties. Without factual equality there can be no freedom in the market, a point often ignored by those who advocate the market as a mechanism of distribution. The other objective is that interests in land should be freely marketable like other commodities. If a lease contains terms which absolutely prohibit assignment, the land is rendered unmarketable during the continuance of the lease. Alternatively, the covenant may give the landlord the right to refuse consent to an assignment or subletting, which may both be the result of the fact that the landlord was able to insist on the term being included through his or her unequal economic position and also confer on the landlord a power to restrict, in his or her own interests, the marketability of the leasehold interest.

20–141 Statutory controls were contained originally in Deasy's Act[184] but these have now[185] been replaced by s.66 of the 1980 Act.[186] Section 66(1) of the 1980 Act applies to covenants in leases of "tenements" made before or after the commencement of the Act which absolutely prohibit or restrict alienation of the tenement either generally or in a particular way.[187] It provides that such prohibition or restriction shall take effect as a covenant against alienation

---

[181] And see the earlier Landlord and Tenant Act 1931, repealed by the 1980 Act. Section 3 of the Conveyancing Act 1892 was not repealed by the Landlord and Tenant Act 1931, nor by the LCLRA 2009.

[182] 1980 Act s.66.

[183] 1980 Act s.67.

[184] Deasy's Act ss.10 and 18. Before this, there was statutory control of subletting in the "Subletting Act", i.e. the Landlord and Tenant (Ireland) Act 1826 (7 Geo IV c.29) (see below). See *Robinson v Wakefield* (1892) 30 L.R. Ir. 547.

[185] Previously by s.56 of the Landlord and Tenant Act 1931.

[186] The section did not, oddly, repeal ss.10 and 18. Sections 10 and 18 of Deasy's Act were not repealed until 1967 by s.35 of the Landlord and Tenant (Ground Rents) Act 1967.

[187] N. Dawson, "Covenants 'Against' Subletting" (1983) 34 N.I.L.Q. 56.

without the landlord's consent. Section 5 of the Act defines "tenement" in such a way as to include land mostly covered by buildings, and where the land is not wholly covered by buildings the part not covered is subsidiary and ancillary to the part that is.

20–142 Section 66(2) applies to three situations, of which the first two are by far the most common, i.e.:

(a) leases containing covenants not to alienate without the landlord's consent;

(b) leases containing covenants not to alienate at all which, by virtue of s.66(1), take effect as covenants not to alienate without the landlord's consent;

(c) leases or agreements for leases made between 1 June 1826 and 1 May 1832,[188] and which (by the Landlord and Tenant (Ireland) Act 1826) are for less than 99 years and contain no reference to subletting. This was the result of the Landlord and Tenant (Ireland) Act 1826[189] which was repealed with saving by s.104 and Sch.B of Deasy's Act. The former Act rendered void any subletting made without the landlord's consent.[190]

20–143 Section 66(2) provides that in the above cases there is implied a proviso, notwithstanding any express provision to the contrary, that the consent shall not be unreasonably withheld. If the landlord could not reasonably have refused consent, then an assignment or subletting is deemed to be "with consent" for this purpose, regardless of whether an application was made for consent and was refused or whether it was not sought at all.[191] Such an assignment is valid and effective.

20–144 The implied proviso contained in s.66(2) of the 1980 Act does not apply to a tenancy which falls within the ambit of the Residential Tenancies Acts 2004–2016. Section 16(k) of the Residential Tenancies Act 2004 ("RdTA 2004") requires the tenant not to "assign or sub-let the tenancy without the written consent of the landlord (which consent the landlord may, in his or her discretion, withhold)".[192] There is no express restriction that the landlord shall not unreasonably withhold consent. However, in the event that the landlord does withhold the sought consent, s.186 of the RdTA 2004 provides that

---

[188] The Landlord and Tenant (Ireland) Act 1826 was repealed by the Assignment of Leases (Ireland) Act 1832, but only as to leases made after 1 May 1832.

[189] 7 Geo IV c.29.

[190] *Penney v Gardner* (1833) Al. & N. 345; *Meares v Redmond* (1879) 4 L.R. Ir. 533, affirmed on appeal (not reported).

[191] Note under (c) above the Landlord and Tenant (Ireland) Act 1826 does make a subletting void: *Meares v Redmond* (1879) 4 L.R. Ir. 533.

[192] This does not apply in respect of a dwelling the subject of a tenancy referred to in RdTA 2004 s.3(4).

the tenant can give notice to terminate the tenancy regardless of any contrary clause in the agreement.[193]

Effect of Lack of Consent

20–145 Does s.66 make an assignment or subletting "without consent" void? It follows from the above that an assignment "without consent" means an assignment or subletting where it would *not* be unreasonable for the landlord to refuse consent and either the landlord has in fact refused consent to an application or no application was made.

20–146 At common law an assignment or subletting without consent did not prevent the passing of an estate, although the landlord could forfeit the lease where the covenant against assignment or sub-letting was made a condition of the lease; or, if the lease was subject to a proviso for re-entry for breach of covenant, the landlord could re-enter and put an end to the lease. In *UDC of Tralee v McSweeney*[194] a lessee sublet part of the premises without the landlord's consent. The lessee later tried to recover possession of the premises. The sub-lessee applied to the landlord for consent to the sub-lease, and the landlord granted it. Even so, the lessee obtained an order for possession in the High Court. The Supreme Court upheld the judgment. The sub-lease was inoperative until the consent of the landlord had been obtained, but became operative after that,[195] so that all previous acts of the parties had the effect they would have had if the consent had been obtained at the time of execution of the sub-lease.[196] These retrospectively validated acts, however, included the notice to quit given by the lessee to the sub-lessee, which was in accordance with the terms of the sub-lease. An assignment or subletting made without consent is ineffective unless and until it is subsequently ratified by the landlord, the ratification retrospectively validating earlier acts, provided that this does not prejudice innocent third parties.[197]

20–147 In *Meagher v Luke J. Healy Pharmacy Ltd*[198] the Supreme Court considered the following remedies to be potentially available where a lessor unreasonably refuses consent to an assignment of the lease:

---

[193] Sections 66 (covenant against alienation), 67 (covenant against change of use) and 68 (covenant against improvements) of the Landlord and Tenant (Amendment) Act 1980 are disapplied from tenancies to which the Residential Tenancies Acts 2004–2016 apply by RdTA 2004 s.193(d), and are replaced by the tenant's statutory obligations specified in that Act: see RdTA 2004 s.16(k) (alienation), (l) (carrying out of improvements), and (m) (change of use).

[194] [1954] I.R. 233.

[195] *Scott v Redmond* (1880) 6 L.R. Ir. 374; following *Davis v Davis* (1827) 4 Ir. L.R. 353; *Tobin v Cleary* (1872) I.R. 7 C.L. 17 at 22.

[196] This essentially follows earlier cases on s.10: *Butler v Smith* (1864) 16 I.C.L.R. 213; *Whyte v Sheehan* (1943) Ir. Jur. R. 38; *Scott v Redmond* (1881) 8 L.R. Ir. 112, App. See also *Manning v Saul* (1890) 25 L.R. Ir. 640.

[197] *Scott v Redmond* (1880) 6 L.R. Ir. 374; *Davis v Davis* (1827) 4 Ir. L.R. 353; *Tobin v Cleary* (1872) I.R. 7 C.L. 17 at 22.

[198] [2010] IESC 40.

1. The lessee may make an application to court for a declaration that the lessor's consent has been unreasonably withheld, and, in the event of the court granting the declaration, the lessee may then proceed to assign without the lessor's consent.
2. The lessee may proceed to assign the lease in any event, without application to court, and both lessee and assignee can raise as a defence to any action brought by the lessor for breach of the covenant against alienation the unreasonable refusing by the lessor of consent contrary to s.66(2).
3. The assignment having taken place despite the lessor's refusal of consent, the assignee may seek a declaration that the lessor's consent was unreasonably refused and raise this as a defence in any proceedings brought by the lessor for breach of covenant.
4. In the event that the court finds the withholding by the lessor of consent to the assignment *not* to have been unreasonable, the assignee may seek relief from the court against forfeiture of the lease.[199]

20–148 The court also considered that s.66(2) of the 1980 Act, which incorporates into a covenant against alienation a proviso that the consent of the lessor to such alienation is not to be unreasonably withheld, could not be construed as implying a further covenant on the part of the lessor that consent to assignment would not be unreasonably withheld.[200] On this basis, the court held that s.66 could not be interpreted as conferring on the lessee a right to seek damages from the lessor for the lessor's unreasonable withholding of consent, although there was nothing to prevent the parties to a lease from making specific provision for this right by way of covenant in the lease.[201]

Conacre

20–149 It has been pointed out that conacre, which typically allows for use of the land for 10 or 11 months per year is a "useful informal tool ... particularly in relation to land that has little economic value".[202] Conacre agreements were considered by the courts before Deasy's Act not to constitute "sub-leasing" and therefore did not fall within the scope of covenants which prohibited subleasing without the lessor's consent.[203] Indeed they were also held not to amount to "parting with possession" or "ceasing to occupy" in express covenants that required the lessee to maintain possession.[204] Section 2 of the Land Act 1946,[205]

---

[199] Pursuant to the Conveyancing Act 1881 s.14, as amended by Landlord and Tenant (Ground Rents) Act 1967 s.35(1).

[200] Finnegan J. followed a consistent line of English case law, including *Treloar v Bigge* (1874) L.R. 9 and *Rendell v Roberts and Stacey* (1960) 175 E.G. 265.

[201] Finnegan J. declined to follow *Kelly v Cussen* (1954) 88 I.L.T.R. 97.

[202] G. Brennan, "Renewal Rights for Agricultural Tenants – Who Cares?" (2017) 22(2) C.P.L.J. 30 at 31.

[203] *Dease v O'Reilly* (1845) 8 Ir. L.R. 52; *Booth v McManus* (1863) 12 Ir. C.L.R. 418.

[204] *Booth v McManus* (1863) 12 Ir. C.L.R. 418 (conacre agreement to grow oats and to cut the crop).

[205] Formerly s.2 of the Land Law (Ireland) Act 1881.

which prohibits the subletting of land sold under the Land Purchase Acts, specifically excludes conacre and agistment from this prohibition. Conacre is not mentioned in the LTLRB 2011, and the explanatory note to Head 5 makes it clear that a conacre agreement is not to be considered a tenancy.

Covenants Restricting User

20–150 Many leases contain covenants restricting user of the premises, for example, to that of a dwelling house, or not for trade or business or not to sell alcohol. Section 67 of the 1980 Act modifies these in a similar way to covenants as to assignment and subletting, so that a covenant absolutely prohibiting alteration of user shall have effect as if it were a covenant prohibiting a change of user without the landlord's consent, with the stipulation that the landlord's consent shall not be unreasonably withheld. Similarly, this proviso that a landlord shall not unreasonably withhold consent has no application to a tenancy falling within the Residential Tenancies Acts 2004–2016. Section 16(m) of the RdTA 2004 obliges a tenant not to use the dwelling for any purpose except as a dwelling without the landlord's consent, which consent the landlord in his or her discretion may withhold. There is no incorporated requirement of reasonableness to the withholding of consent.

The Test of Reasonableness

20–151 What constitutes being "unreasonable" in withholding consent to an assignment or subletting or change of user? This has been the subject of considerable case law and some general categories of considerations have emerged.

General Commercial Considerations

20–152 In *Rice v Dublin Corporation*,[206] a case involving similar provisions in the Landlord and Tenant Act 1931,[207] the Supreme Court held that the onus is on the tenant to prove that a refusal of consent is unreasonable, apparently on the general principle that the person who asserts must prove.[208] A plaintiff tenant would have to establish at least a prima facie case of unreasonableness. The court went on to hold that the onus was not shifted even if the landlord originally gave no reason for the refusal at all. It was open to a landlord to state the reason at the trial of the action. This could, however, put a tenant at a disadvantage. If no reasons are given at the trial stage then the refusal must be unreasonable, otherwise the statutory provisions would be nullified.

---

[206] [1947] I.R. 425.
[207] Section 57.
[208] *White v Carlisle Trust* [1976–77] I.L.R.M. 311; *Egan Film Service v McNamara* (1952) 86 I.L.T.R. 189; *Shanley v Ward* (1913) 29 T.L.R. 714; *Pimms Ltd v Tallow Chandlers in the City of London* [1964] 2 All E.R. 145 at 147.

20–153 In *Rice v Dublin Corporation* the tenant was the plaintiff. If a landlord sues to enforce a covenant against a tenant who has changed the user without applying for consent, is the onus then on the landlord, as plaintiff, to establish not only the existence of the covenant, but also, in accordance with the statutory provisions, that had an application been made by the tenant it would have been reasonable to refuse it? The assumption in *Rice* seems to be that it is not; that it is for the tenant to plead the statute and make a prima facie case.[209]

20–154 A criticism of *Rice* is that it puts tenants in a less favourable position than landlords for no apparent reason. The legislation was intended to prevent landlords from acting on arbitrary or capricious grounds and probably also now on discriminatory grounds. There seems no good reason why the onus should always be on the tenant in every case to establish unreasonableness rather than for the landlord to establish that his or her act was reasonable.

20–155 In *White v Carlisle Trust*[210] McWilliam J. held that a landlord was acting arbitrarily if he or she refused consent solely on the ground of the effect which a change of user would have on other tenants. It was argued by them that a change of user from a hatter's to a confectionery shop would compete with their trade as confectioners. McWilliam J. considered whether the change would affect them or not, but concluded that no effect could be shown, as the shops of the other tenants were in central Dublin and although they were near the applicant's shop there was no demonstrable effect on their business of the applicant's intended change of user. The judge, however, held that a detriment to one of the landlord's other tenants would not be a reasonable ground for refusal of consent without showing some consequential effect on the landlord's own financial position.

20–156 In *Green Property Co Ltd v Shalaine Modes*[211] it was held that a lessor can legitimately consider his or her own financial interests in refusing consent.[212] This concerned a shopping centre with more than one toy shop. The premises in dispute, plots 45 and 46, had originally been used as a hardware store in accordance with a term in the lease. The lessee's interest was assigned to the defendant, Shalaine Modes, with the consent of the plaintiff lessor but without a specific application for consent to a change of user. Shalaine Modes traded as a boutique selling women's clothes without the specific consent of the lessor but also without objection by the lessor. In 1977, before Christmas of that year, the premises were sublet to B who had a toy shop elsewhere in the centre and who used the windows of 45 and 46 to display toys. B was the tenant of the premises next door, plot 47. Again, the lessor did not

---

[209] In *Green Property Co Ltd v Shalaine Modes* [1978] I.L.R.M. 222, discussed below, the lessor was the plaintiff but did not raise the issue of reasonableness as such.

[210] [1976–77] I.L.R.M. 311.

[211] [1978] I.L.R.M. 222.

[212] This was also held to be a valid ground in *Crowe Ltd v Dublin Port & Docks Ltd* [1962] I.R. 194, in relation to subletting.

object to the change of user and no application was made by B for consent. In a subsequent year plots 45 and 46 were sublet to C to sell toys in the weeks before Christmas. B then objected to the landlord.

20–157 The High Court upheld the right of the landlord to enforce the covenant. McWilliam J. considered that the lessor in the case of a shopping centre has a legitimate interest in maintaining a "tenant mix", i.e. a variety of different shops, in order to attract customers. The lessor's own interest in this was that the more attractive the shopping centre was to would-be shoppers, the higher the rents the lessor could charge for tenancies in the centre. This would seem to be the distinction between *Shalaine* and *White*, and also to constitute shopping centres as a special legal regime in the sense that this factor of "tenant mix" and its capacity to generate lucrative tenancies is not present in other situations,[213] such as that in *White* itself. It would seem that the one thing a landlord must not be is altruistic. It could be argued that the effect of such cases as *White* and *Shalaine* is that tenants cannot take advantage of the supposedly random factor that they have the same lessor as against a tenant who wishes to change the user of his or her premises in a way which will compete with their businesses. Tenants of separate landlords could not restrain what would be normal market competition by a change of user in a nearby shop, in the absence of restrictive covenants, and it is arguable that tenants should be in no better position because they happen to have the same landlord. Their remedy, if any, must lie in their bargain with their own landlord. In the shopping centre context it is possible that they may bargain for a term in their lease to control or specify the number of other businesses in the shopping centre which may compete directly with theirs. In the absence of this the court in *Shalaine* appeared unwilling to interfere in what are in essence landlord-focused commercial decisions.

20–158 The court in *Shalaine* notably refused to apply any form of estoppel. It had been argued on the basis of *Shaw v Applegate*[214] that the failure of the lessor to object in the past had created an expectation that he would not object on this occasion. The court did not, however, accept that a failure to enforce a covenant in one year could reasonably raise an expectation that it would not be invoked in a subsequent year, any more than the grant of permission in one year would constitute a general waiver of the covenant as to the future. Nor would consent to a change of user in one year constitute a general waiver of the term for future years, binding the landlord to consent if a similar application were made in a subsequent year. It was simply left to the lessor's discretion. This is not to say, of course, that an Irish court may not apply concepts of acquiescence such as were raised in *Shaw v Applegate*.

---

[213] A point addressed by Murphy J. in *Meagher v Luke J. Healy Pharmacy Ltd* [2005] IEHC 120.
[214] [1978] 1 All E.R. 123. See also, *Attorney General v Guardian Newspapers* [1990] A.C. 109; *Westland Savings Bank v Hancock* [1987] 2 N.Z.L.R. 21; *British Leyland Motor Corp v TI Silencers Ltd*, unreported, Chancery Division, 17 October 1984.

20–159 In *OHS Ltd v Green Property Co Ltd*[215] a plot in a Dublin shopping centre was used as a fruit and vegetable store. The lease in the plot, which was subject to a covenant that it should continue to be used as a fruit and vegetable store, was held by the plaintiff. After a supermarket was opened in the centre the plaintiff found it increasingly difficult to make its business pay. It found a building society which was willing to take over the site and applied to the defendant for permission to change the user. The defendant refused on the ground that a building society was "dead frontage". By this the defendant meant that it had been shown that potential customers of the shopping centre were not attracted to it by commercial premises of that kind, although they might make use of such premises once they were there. The defendant also argued that the shopping centre already had a higher proportion of "dead frontage" than other centres in Dublin and that the reason for refusal of the requested change of use was in order to avoid an excessive amount of such frontage. The plaintiff conceded that this was a valid reason, but argued as to the weight to be attached to it. Lynch J. accepted the argument of the defendant and held that it had acted reasonably on "valid estate management grounds".[216]

20–160 In the English case of *International Drilling Fluids Ltd v Louisville Investments (Uxbridge) Ltd*[217] it was held that, although in general a lessor was bound only to consider his or her own relevant interests when deciding whether to refuse consent to an assignment of a lease, it was nevertheless unreasonable for a landlord not to consider the detriment which would be suffered by the tenant who applied for a change of user if consent were to be refused and if that detriment would be extreme and disproportionate in relation to the benefit gained by the landlord.

20–161 Where a covenant in a lease that prohibits change of user without the landlord's consent identifies particular grounds of which "full account would be taken", the reasonableness or otherwise of any refusal by the landlord will be measured against the extent to which the stated grounds were in fact considered. The application of such a clause fell to be examined in *Dunnes Stores (ILAC Centre) Ltd v Irish Life Assurance plc and O'Reilly*.[218] The plaintiff was a long-term tenant in a Dublin shopping centre and applied to the landlords for change of use to a "high quality food hall". Consent was refused on the standard ground of "good estate management" which, upon a challenge by the tenant to the reasonableness of the landlords' refusal, was elaborated to confirm that the plaintiff's proposed use was inconsistent with the defendants' overall "vision and image" for the relevant part of the centre, primarily as a retail fashion area. The clause in the lease that prohibited change of use without the landlords' consent required full account to be taken of a number of items, including the maintenance of diversity among retail outlets in the centre. Clarke J. held

[215] [1986] I.R. 39. See also *Wanze Properties v Mastertron Ltd* [1986] I.R. 39.
[216] [1992] I.L.R.M. 746.
[217] [1985] 1 Ch. 513.
[218] [2008] IEHC 114.

that the eventually adduced ground for withholding consent seemed designed
to have the reverse effect, i.e. to diminish the prospect of diversity in the centre,
and on that account alone was unreasonable.

20–162 Clarke J. also considered the genuineness of the grounds offered by
the landlord for its refusal of consent to change of use. A refusal of consent
based upon an improper consideration, or one not contemplated by the lease,
would not be permissible.[219] The plaintiff had alleged that the real reason for
the landlords' refusal of consent was that they wanted to exert pressure upon
the plaintiff to surrender its lease. To this, Clarke J. observed that the sought
surrender of a tenant's lease might well be a permissible commercial objective
if pursued through orthodox methods of negotiation, but that a refusal of consent to a change of use could not be justified on this basis.[220]

20–163 Haughton J. in *Perfect Pies Ltd and Farrell v Chupn Ltd*[221] noted
that "a practice of refusing or declining consent for an improper motive, and
then later attempting to rely on a 'good' reason, is something that the courts
should not encourage or permit". Here, the landlord was held to have an ulterior motive for withholding consent. Haughton J. commented that "a landlord
surely cannot be permitted to deliberately keep secret from the tenant what it
claims to be the real reason for declining consent and later produce it like a rabbit out of the hat and rely on it in court." The decision in *Perfect Pies* strength-
ens the position of tenants in relation to unreasonable withholding of consent.
A landlord's ability to retrospectively justify a withholding of consent, where
no valid reason had initially been put forward, has been curtailed. Usefully,
Haughton J. noted that the general principles to be considered were as follows:

1. The purpose of a covenant against assignment is to protect the landlord
   from having his or her premises used or occupied in an undesirable way,
   or by an undesirable tenant or assignee.
2. A landlord cannot refuse consent on grounds unrelated to the landlord
   and tenant relationship in regards to the lease.
3. The onus of proving consent has been unreasonably withheld is on the
   tenant.
4. The landlord does not need to prove that the conclusions leading to a
   refusal were justified, rather, that a reasonable man could have arrived at
   them in the circumstances.
5. It may be reasonable to refuse consent to an assignment on the grounds of
   the purpose to which the proposed assignee intends to use the premises,
   even though that purpose is not forbidden by the lease.
6. While a landlord need usually only consider his or her own interests,
   if there is a disproportion between the benefit to the landlord and the

---

[219] Clarke J. cited *Bromley Park Garden Estates Ltd v Moss* [1982] 1 W.L.R. 1019 and *Design
Progression Ltd v Thurloe Properties Ltd* [2005] 1 W.L.R. 1, as authority for this proposition.
[220] [2008] IEHC 114 at p.118.
[221] [2015] IEHC 692.

detriment to the tenant if the landlord witholds consent to assignment, it could be the case that the refusal is unreasonable.

7. Subject to the proposition set out above, it is, in each case, a question of fact, depending on the circumstances, whether the landlord's consent to an assignment is being unreasonably withheld.[222]

20–164 It is clear from both *Dunnes Stores* and *Perfect Pies* that the reasonableness of the landlord's withholding of consent will be considered on a case-by-case basis, with the latter case being described as representing a "pro-tenant shift".[223]

Competition

20–165 The provisions of ss.66 and 67 of the 1980 Act and the case law on them are now subject to the provisions of the Competition Act 2002. A tenant whose landlord refuses consent on the ground that the proposed user would not provide a sufficiently attractive mixture of shops can appeal to the Competition and Consumer Protection Commission under the Act on the basis that these grounds of refusal are incompatible with the aim of free competition which is the policy of the Act. On the other hand, a landlord whose tenant took this course of action might argue that competition should be judged *as between* shopping centres and not merely between units within one particular shopping centre.

Human Rights

20–166 Constitutional rights and rights under the European Convention on Human Rights may be involved in the application of s.67. In the notorious case of *Schlegel v Corcoran*,[224] Gavan Duffy J. held that it was reasonable for a landlady to refuse consent to an assignment because the assignee was Jewish and she was, in her own estimation at least, a Christian. A distinction needs to be made between the constitutional issue raised and the specific statutory test. It may be that a ground would satisfy the statutory test as reasonable but violate constitutional rights. It could also be the case that a ground does not violate constitutional rights, but fails to satisfy the statutory test of reasonableness. As to the statutory test, McWilliam J. in the High Court[225] has taken the view that "reasonable" is to be distinguished from "arbitrary and capricious". A refusal on the ground of race or religion arguably falls within the latter category. As to constitutional rights, Art.40.1 guarantees the equality of citizens as "human persons". The case law supports the view that this introduces a distinction between discrimination on grounds of human attributes, which is proscribed, and discrimination on some ground not related to a person's human

---

[222] These are largely based on *International Drilling Fluids v Louisville Investments (Uxbridge) Ltd* [1985] 1 Ch. 513.

[223] See D. Dwyer, "A Pro-Tenant Shift in the Balance of Unreasonable Withholding of Consent to Assignment – *Perfect Pies v Chupn Ltd*" (2016) 21(1) C.P.L.J. 12.

[224] [1942] I.R. 19.

[225] In *White v Carlisle Trust* [1976–77] I.L.R.M. 311.

qualities, such as economic or commercial grounds, which is not proscribed. It may also be the case that there is a "private" area where the Article does not protect even against discrimination on grounds of human qualities.

20–167 The ground offered for the landlord's refusal to consent to assignment of the lease in *Schlegel v Corcoran* would now fall foul of the Equal Status Acts 2000–2015.[226] Section 6 of the principal Act prohibits discrimination in relation to:

- the disposal of an estate,
- the termination of a tenancy or other interest, or
- the provision or denial of accommodation or of amenities or services relating to accommodation[227]

in premises for any one of 10 specified and proscribed grounds of discrimination set out in s.3,[228] which include religious grounds.[229] However, s.6(2), as amended, excepts from the general scheme of prohibited discrimination a number of specific situations, such as shared accommodation where "embarrassment or infringement of privacy" may reasonably be expected to arise on gender grounds.[230] Among these exceptions is where accommodation is being provided in part of a person's home which is not separate and self-contained or where the "provision of accommodation affects the person's private or family life or that of any other person residing in the home …".[231] Accordingly, the extent to which the particular facts (as opposed to the actual ground of refusal) which underpinned the decision in *Schlegel v Corcoran* would prohibit the discrimination practised in that case with reference to the Equal Status Acts 2000–2015 remains debatable.[232]

20–168 There also appears to be what may be called a loophole in the Acts as to advertising. Under s.12(1), "[a] person shall not publish or display or cause to be published or displayed an advertisement which indicates an intention to engage in prohibited conduct or might reasonably be understood as

---

[226] Council Directive 2000/43/EC, which implements the principle of equal treatment between persons irrespective of racial or ethnic origin, prohibits direct or indirect discrimination on racial or ethnic grounds, including in relation to access to housing "available to the public".

[227] Equal Status Acts 2000–2015 s.6(1)(a). Subsection (3) provides that references in subs.(2) to disposal of an estate or the provision of accommodation or associated services or amenities include references to the termination of a tenancy.

[228] Amended by the Equality Act 2004 s.48.

[229] The other grounds are: (i) gender, (ii) marital status, (iii) family status, (iv) sexual orientation, (v) age, (vi) disability, (vii) race, (viii) membership of the Traveller community, (ix) victimisation for having relied on or for seeking to rely on the facilities for redress under the Act, for opposing acts rendered unlawful by the Act, or for having given evidence in related civil or criminal proceedings.

[230] Equal Status Acts 2000–2015 s.6(2)(e).

[231] Equal Status Acts 2000–2015 s.6(2)(d).

[232] On this point, see R. Cannon, "The Bigoted Landlord: A Re-Examination of *Schlegel v Corcoran and Gross*" (2005) 12 D.U.L.J. 248.

indicating such an intention." "Prohibited conduct" means "discrimination [under s.3] against, or sexual harassment or harassment of, or permitting the sexual harassment or harassment of, a person in contravention of this Act". However, as seen above, there are exceptions to prohibited conduct, as, for example, where accommodation is being provided in part of a person's home which is not separate and self-contained, etc. In those circumstances, it would not then be prohibited under s.12 to *advertise* such accommodation, including the discriminatory description. The purpose of the exemption in s.12 is to allow a *private* sphere in which an individual may discriminate, yet advertising is by definition making a public statement, which could cause gratuitous offence to innocent and otherwise unconcerned third parties.

Conditions in Lease

20–169 To what extent are specific conditions contained in the lease relevant to the question of the reasonableness of a landlord's withholding consent? Clearly, if a clause prohibits change of use without the landlord's consent and also requires certain considerations to be addressed, failure to take these considerations into account will render the refusal unreasonable.[233] However, if a landlord has not imposed a certain condition in the lease, is it then unreasonable of him or her to invoke the absent condition to justify refusing consent under a covenant which prohibits change of use without consent? One would think this is not unreasonable, since, if it were otherwise, all the possible reasons justifying refusal would have to be set out in advance in the lease. But one case held the absence of reference in the lease to the grounds justifying refusal to be fatal. In *Boland v Dublin Corporation*[234] the landlord was a local authority. It let a house under the Housing (Ireland) Act 1919 but had not required its maintenance as accommodation for members of the "working classes". The defendant refused to consent to an assignment to a person on the ground that he was not a member of the working class. This refusal was held to be unreasonable. However, it is arguable that the court was exercised by the particular nature of the property and inclined to the view that had the local authority intended it as a condition of the tenancy that the property be preserved for working class accommodation, it ought to have included that requirement expressly in the tenancy.

Covenants as to Commercial User: The Restraint of Trade Doctrine

20–170 If the premises are used for business purposes and the lease contains a restriction on user, then the common law doctrine of *restraint of trade* may be invoked. If the doctrine applies, the restrictions are void if they are not reasonable. If the doctrine does not apply, there is no test of reasonableness.

---

[233] *Dunnes Stores (ILAC Centre) Ltd v Irish Life Assurance plc and O'Reilly* [2008] IEHC 114.
[234] [1946] I.R. 88.

20–171 The general rule is that if A has an interest in a piece of land called Gortduff, and the interest is not subject to any covenant restricting trade, and then A enters into a contract or lease of the premises whereby his or her freedom of trade is restricted, the restraint of trade doctrine applies, and the restriction is only valid if it satisfies a test of reasonableness. On the other hand, if A has no interest in Gortduff, but then takes a lease of the land which contains a covenant restricting freedom to trade, the common law doctrine does not apply and there is no test of reasonableness. In the latter case there was no prior freedom to trade which could claim to have been diminished by the covenant.

20–172 The question of when the doctrine applied arose in *Irish Shell v Elm Motors*.[235] The plaintiff oil company owned a plot of land in Limerick. Some years later the defendants, who had been trading as garage proprietors, bought a plot of land immediately adjoining the plaintiff's land. They were given to understand that they would not obtain planning permission to develop their site as a petrol station. The defendants then asked the plaintiff oil company to lease them its plot and allow them to incorporate it into a combined site of a proposed new garage. The plaintiff agreed. The defendants then obtained planning permission to develop the combined site as a petrol station. A lease was granted by the plaintiff oil company to the defendants which contained a covenant whereby the defendants agreed, both as to their own plot and the plot demised to them, that they would buy only the petroleum products of the plaintiff oil company. Disagreements arose, and defendants notified the plaintiff oil company that they did not consider themselves bound by the covenants. The plaintiff sought an injunction. The Supreme Court held that the extensive review of the law of restraint of trade by the judge was unnecessary in an interlocutory application. The court held that there was a "fair case to be made" and that the balance of convenience lay in favour of granting the interlocutory injunction.

20–173 The issue of restraint of trade was dealt with in the High Court by Costello J. It is, despite the strictures of the Supreme Court, a useful exposition of the law on the subject. He referred to two English cases, *Esso Petroleum v Harper's Garage Ltd*[236] and *Cleveland Petroleum Ltd v Dartstone Ltd*,[237] and a Privy Council decision on appeal from Australia, *Amoco Australia Property Ltd v Rocca Bros Motor Engineering*.[238] According to Costello J.:

1. The effect of those decisions, with which he agreed in principle, was that the doctrine of restraint of trade applies only where a person who previously had unfettered freedom of trade enters into a contract or covenant whereby he or she restricts that freedom. In other words, it does not apply where a person buys or leases a plot of land already subject to a

---

[235] [1984] I.L.R.M. 200 at 220.
[236] [1968] A.C. 269.
[237] [1969] 1 W.L.R. 116.
[238] [1975] A.C. 562.

restriction because in that case he or she has not given up a freedom that he or she previously enjoyed.

2. In the instant case the principle was not limited to covenants as to user of the land—the covenant was to use the land as a petrol station—but also applied to covenants restricting trading activity as such, e.g. to buy only the plaintiff's products.

3. The present covenant could be regarded as positive or negative, but this made no difference. A positive covenant might be more onerous but this did not mean that the restraint of trade doctrine would necessarily apply to it.

4. In the instant case the covenant applied not only to the land the defendants had leased from the plaintiff but also to their own land which they owned free of the restriction. However, Costello J. held that the defendants could not have traded as a garage on their own land without obtaining planning permission and they had not obtained it without the additional lease from the plaintiff of the adjoining land; so, in effect, the defendants had not held their own land with freedom to trade. As a result, the defendants were not giving up an unfettered freedom to trade in relation to that land.

Thus, the restraint of trade doctrine applied neither to the land leased to the defendants nor to the land they had originally owned.

20–174 Does the *existence* of planning legislation mean that no one has freedom to trade on their own land any more until and unless they have obtained planning permission, so that the restraint of trade doctrine has effectively been abrogated? It seems not. In *Irish Shell v Elm Motors*[239] planning permission would probably have been refused without the additional plot and so it was possible to say that the defendants had no prior freedom to trade, but it might be otherwise if permission would possibly, or probably, have been obtained. The Supreme Court referred to two factors that might influence the outcome of the case on the substantive issue. First, although it was unlikely that the defendants would have obtained planning permission on their own plot alone, that situation might change over time. Secondly, although the covenant in the lease was to build the station on the premises demised to the defendants and on their own site, in fact the station was built on the defendants' land only. In other words, the scheme to include the leased land in the new application for planning permission looked like a mere device to ensure the granting of planning permission.

20–175 In *Amoco*,[240] considered by Costello J., the proprietor of the land built a service station on the land and then leased it to the oil company which then subleased it back to him. The High Court of Australia held that the covenants

---

[239] [1984] I.L.R.M. 200 at 220.
[240] *Amoco Australia Property Ltd v Rocca Bros Motor Engineering* [1975] A.C. 562.

were subject to the restraint of trade doctrine and were unreasonable. Costello J. in *Irish Shell v Elm Motors*[241] agreed with the application of the doctrine in such a situation. The lease-back arrangement was a device to evade the doctrine and would not succeed in this jurisdiction. The courts would look at the substance of the transaction, which was that a proprietor who had previously enjoyed a freedom to trade had given it up.

20–176 The principle here seems to be that the law protects the original free owner, but does not seek to confer a freedom on someone who had not acquired it for himself through the market, or inheritance, etc. The law takes the view that someone who had not previously enjoyed freedom of trade in relation to the land has, in theory, a free choice: he may reject the lease with the restriction if he wishes. What characterises this as ideology in support of the market mechanism is that the fact of freedom is asserted without a test as to whether it is actually present. Could an intending petrol station operator obtain a lease of another petrol station free of the restriction?

20–177 Costello J. dealt with a number of objections to the doctrine, in particular those raised by Heydon[242]:

1. The doctrine can lead to gross anomalies. For example, X owns two shops. He sells or leases one to A. A and X mutually covenant that neither shop should be used as a butcher's shop. The restraint of trade doctrine would apply to X's obligations, because he accepted a restraint on a freedom he previously enjoyed as owner, but not to A's, because he had no previous freedom to trade in relation to the shop he bought from X. So A may not be able to enforce X's obligations while X could enforce A's obligations. Absurd. But Heydon himself says that A might invoke the principle of *Halsall v Brizell*,[243] i.e. that X could not take advantage of a deed unless he was prepared to submit to its obligations.
2. The restraint of trade doctrine is undesirable because it could easily be avoided by sale with lease-back. Costello J. took the view that the courts would not accept the device.
3. If positive covenants are exempt from the restraint of trade doctrine it could impose onerous obligations on the covenantor. Costello J. rejected this objection as not being a sufficient reason to vitiate the exemption of these covenants from the principle.

Covenants of Repair
20–178 Section 65 of the 1980 Act applies where a tenancy includes an agreement by the tenant to put into repair or keep the premises in repair at the end of the tenancy. Damages for breach of the covenant are not the cost of repair.

---

[241] [1984] I.L.R.M. 200 at 220.
[242] J.D. Heydon, *The Restraint of Trade Doctrine* (London: Butterworths, 1971).
[243] [1957] Ch. 169.

Section 65(2) provides that the damages shall not exceed the amount by which the value of the reversion in the tenement is diminished.[244] Except where the want of repair is due to wilful damage or waste, no damages are recoverable for breach if it is shown that:

(a) in regard to the age and condition of the premises its repair is physically impossible;
(b) in regard to the age, condition, character, and the situation of the tenancy its repair would involve expenditure which is excessive in proportion to the value of the tenement; or
(c) in regard to the character and situation of the tenement the tenement could not when so repaired be profitably used, or could not be used unless it was rebuilt, reconstructed, or structurally altered to a substantial extent.

20–179 However, where a tenant has allowed a let property to become ruinous and uninhabitable by failing to comply with, and being financially unable to comply with, a covenant to repair contained in the lease, this constitutes "good and sufficient reason" to justify a landlord declining to grant a new lease at the end of the tenancy in accordance with s.17(1)(a)(v) of the 1980 Act.[245]

20–180 In *Trustees of St Catherine's Parish, Dublin v Alkin*[246] the plaintiff claimed damages for breach of a repairing covenant in a lease for 100 years which expired in 1981. The lease was of a number of houses. One of them had been demolished and as a result the flank wall of the next house had been exposed to the weather, causing it to decay. The front wall also had an incipient bulge which had deteriorated. Carroll J. held that the damage caused by the exposure of the flank wall was not the lessee's responsibility. It was for the landlord to seal the exposed wall. But the lessee was responsible for allowing the bulge to become worse—that was permissive waste. On the measure of damages, Carroll J. laid down the method of calculation to determine the amount by which the reversion is affected. This was:

1. estimate the annual rental value in its unrepaired state and multiply it by the multiplier (7 in this case);
2. estimate the annual rental value in its repaired state and multiply it by the multiplier (7.5 here);
3. take the difference between the two which is the amount by which the reversion is reduced; and
4. deduct the proportion of that sum for which the lessee is not responsible (10 per cent deducted here).

The amount so calculated was less than the cost of the repairs, as s.65 intended.

---

[244] Similar provisions had been contained in earlier legislation: Landlord and Tenant Act 1931 s.55(b). *Gilligan v Silke* [1960] I.R. 1 at 9.
[245] *McCarthy v Larkin* [2009] IEHC 75.
[246] Unreported, High Court, Carroll J., 4 March 1982.

20–181 In *Udarás na Gaeltachta v Uisce Glan Teoranta*,[247] O'Neill J. applied the well-established principle[248] that a tenant under a covenant to repair does not have to rebuild or carry out works to improve the premises beyond the state of repair enjoyed at the date of the demise. Accordingly, where already existing cracks in the ungrouted tiling of a porous floor caused aluminium sulphate to percolate into the soil, the tenant of a factory premises was not deemed to be in breach of a covenant to repair when what was termed a "ground heave" later occurred which caused internal structural damage. Apart from the fact that it had not been established that the aluminium sulphate was the most likely cause of the damage, O'Neill J. held that the tenant could not be regarded as in breach of the covenant to repair simply because the ground heave had occurred during its tenancy. This circumstance did not impose a liability on the tenant to repair the demised premises under the covenant to repair.

20–182 Where a landlord is found to be in breach of a covenant to repair, damages will be assessed under the normal principles that govern assessment of damages in tort, "so as to be appropriate compensation for the degree of discomfort or inconvenience suffered over the period during which the breach of covenant continues".[249]

IMPLIED COVENANTS, STATUTORY RIGHTS AND DUTIES

By the Landlord
20–183 Section 41 of Deasy's Act implies two covenants on the part of the landlord.

Good Title
20–184 Section 41 implies a covenant that the landlord has a good title to grant the lease. This is not a very significant provision since if there is a written contract, such a term would usually be included, and if the tenancy is one that is enforceable albeit oral, the common law implies such a term. However, it was held in *Leonard v Taylor*[250] that s.41 extended the common law, as it also applied to landlord and tenant relationships under Deasy's Act which could not exist at common law.

20–185 The LTLRB 2011 proposes to replace s.41 of Deasy's Act. Head 25 of the Bill states: "the landlord has an overriding obligation to give at or before the grant of the tenancy good title to the tenant sufficient to support the grant

---

[247] [2007] IEHC 95.

[248] Citing in support *Chaloner v Broughton* (1865–1866) II Ir. Jur. 112; *Lister v Lane and Neshan* [1893] 2 Q.B. 212; *Sotheby v Grundy* [1947] 2 All E.R. 761; and *Whelan v Madigan* [1978] I.L.R.M. 136.

[249] O'Neill J. in *Jiminez v Morrissey and McGrath* [2006] IEHC 18, following the test set out in *Wallace v Manchester City Council, Times Law Reports*, 23 July 1998.

[250] (1872) I.R. 7 C.L. 207.

of the tenancy."[251] Unlike s.41 of Deasy's Act, Head 25 of the LTLRB 2011 would apply to all tenancies and would not be confined to leases. The parties may still agree to proceed with the grant of a tenancy notwithstanding a defect in title which has been fully disclosed prior to the grant. A tenancy by estoppel may arise where a defect in title, whether or not disclosed, exists at the date of the grant.

Quiet Enjoyment

20–186 Section 41 implies a covenant that the lessee should have quiet and peaceable enjoyment of the premises without interruption by the landlord "or any person whatever" during the term and so long as the tenant performs his or her obligations. The tenant has another remedy which may overlap with this one in protecting quiet enjoyment and that is the tort of nuisance. In *O'Leary v Islington LBC*[252] it was held that there was no implied term in a tenancy at common law obliging the landlord of A to sue to enforce the covenant of another tenant, B, binding B not to cause a nuisance. A can bring an action for nuisance against B. But Deasy's Act says "any person whatever", so it would seem that in Ireland the landlord may be liable on his or her covenant to A if another tenant, B, causes a nuisance.

20–187 However, the ambit of what is understood by "quiet enjoyment" is limited by traditional legal interpretations. In *Southwark London Borough v Mills*[253] two tenants of pre-World War II properties which had been built without sound-proofing sought to invoke a covenant for quiet enjoyment to claim redress where the absence of insulation caused them to hear virtually all sounds that emanated from their neighbours' apartments even where the activities themselves were not exceptionally noise-creating, "not only the neighbours' televisions and their babies crying but their coming and going, their cooking and cleaning, their quarrels and their love-making". Understandably, this gave rise to "tension and distress". However, the House of Lords held that a covenant for quiet enjoyment could not be enlarged into a warranty as to the condition of the property, and that, since the absence of sound-proofing was an inherent feature when the letting was made, the tenants took the property with notice of its condition. In addition, according to Hoffmann L.J., the covenant for quiet enjoyment was prospective in its application and could not be taken as pertaining to the state of the property at the time of the letting even if that might have ongoing consequences for the tenant.

---

[251] This modifies the recommendation that the replacement of s.41 should be a "default" obligation, as stated in the Law Reform Commission, *Consultation Paper on General Law of Landlord and Tenant Law* (LRC CP 28-2003), para.6.03. According to the explanatory note to the Heads of Bill, the Law Reform Commission subsequently took the view that it should be an "overriding" obligation because it is confined to giving sufficient title to support the grant of tenancy.

[252] *The Times*, London, 5 May 1983.

[253] [1999] 4 All E.R. 449.

20–188 The LTLRB 2011 expressly incorporates the common law implied obligation by the landlord to give the tenant possession of the premises. It states that the landlord has an overriding obligation to:

"(a) give the tenant possession of the premises on the day the tenancy begins or on such other day as may be agreed,

(b) ensure that the tenant enjoys peaceful possession of the premises throughout the tenancy without interruption by the landlord or any person lawfully claiming through, under or in trust for the landlord."[254]

20–189 Under the LTLRB 2011, the obligation would be confined to the landlord and persons lawfully claiming through, under, or in trust for the landlord. A landlord would not be in breach of the peaceful enjoyment obligation where an interruption is a consequence of the exercise of a right conferred by the tenancy, e.g. the right of re-entry for breach of covenant by the tenant or right to inspect for damage. The same applies to interruption caused by performance of an obligation, e.g. entry in order to carry out maintenance or repairs for which the landlord is responsible. Also excluded is interruption by the landlord or other persons caused by action taken under statutory provisions, e.g. works carried out in order to correct an environmental or public health hazard or nuisance.[255]

Condition of the Premises
At Common Law
20–190 At common law there was, up to the dawn of the 19th century, no implied term in a lease of land that the land was fit for any particular purpose at the time the lease began. If the lessor was to be liable for any defect in the premises it could only be on the basis of an express term. In relation to vacant land this rule made some sense, because it could be said that the lessor should not be liable in the absence of some specific agreement as land could be used for a number of purposes. Even so, the courts were prepared to use their power to protect the economic interests of landowners, of agricultural land at any rate, and this can be seen in the rule that the absence of an implied term applied even to agricultural land where it was obvious that the land was to be used, for example, for pasture. So in *Sutton v Temple*[256] a lessor was held not liable where the tenant's cows died of lead poisoning in a contaminated field. The immunity was also extended to tort. Landlords were held to be immune from liability to the tenant's guests or customers for damage caused due to the condition of the premises at the time the lease or tenancy came into effect. The law at the time was summarised by Erle C.J. in *Robbins v Jones*[257]:

---

[254] LTLRB 2011, Head 26.
[255] LTLRB 2011, Explanatory Note.
[256] (1843) 12 M. & W. 52 at 65.
[257] (1863) 15 C.B.N.S. 221.

"A landlord who lets a house in a dangerous state is not liable to the tenant's customers or guests for accidents happening during the term: for, fraud apart, there is no law against letting a tumble-down house; and the tenant's remedy is upon his contract, if any."[258]

This can be seen as a classic statement of an extreme form of the ideology of freedom of contract, the expression in legal terms of an economic policy of "laissez-faire". It was false, in that it assumed equality between landlords and tenants, regardless of whether it existed in fact or not. Tenants were free to live in slums if they wished to do so.

20–191 By the early 19th century the industrial revolution had led to a movement of population to the towns. People who worked in the new factories and shops often lived in appalling conditions, which the law did little to alleviate. In one case the courts took a small step towards decent housing standards by creating a new exception to the old immunity of landlords. In *Smith v Marrable*[259] it was held that the immunity did not apply in the case of furnished accommodation. The distinction lacked any justification in principle, because although it could be said of furnished residential premises that they were evidently let with the intention that they should be occupied by human beings, the same could equally be said of unfurnished residential premises.

20–192 The main principle was nevertheless reaffirmed by the House of Lords in *Cavalier v Pope*[260] as late as 1906. That decision confirmed a number of earlier English decisions in the common law courts to the same effect, and also a decision of the Court of Appeal, *Lane v Cox.*[261]

20–193 The next development was the House of Lords' decision in *Donoghue v Stevenson*[262] on appeal from the Scottish Court of Session. This laid down both a general theory of the law of negligence liability, the so-called "neighbour principle", and also established an area of manufacturers' liability. The neighbour principle proposed that a person should be liable in negligence if, at the time he was acting, it was foreseeable that some other category of persons would be detrimentally affected by his actions if he did not take care.

20–194 Since the "neighbour principle" would, without more, make a lessor who let defective premises liable to a tenant who was injured due to the defect, the question arose as to whether the principle in *Cavalier v Pope*[263] had

---

[258] Cited in the House of Lords in *Cavalier v Pope* [1906] A.C. 428 at 430. See *McNerny v London Borough of Lambeth* (1989) 19 E.G. 77.
[259] (1843) 11 M. & W. 5 at 8f.
[260] [1906] A.C. 428 at 430.
[261] [1897] 1 Q.B. 415.
[262] [1932] A.C. 562.
[263] [1906] A.C. 428 at 430.

survived *Donoghue v Stevenson*.[264] At the time *Donoghue* was decided the House of Lords did not consider itself free to depart from its own decisions, and so could not have reversed *Cavalier* even if it had wished to do so. However, the principle of manufacturers' liability in *Donoghue* provided another exception to the general rule of immunity for lessors. It was held that if the lessor was also a manufacturer, i.e. the builder of the house, or the person who had financed the building, then manufacturers' liability prevailed over the immunity, and the lessor was liable.[265]

20–195 Thus, in England *Cavalier v Pope*[266] started to become something of an anomaly. It was nevertheless confirmed in *Rimmer v Liverpool City Council*[267] that the immunity in *Cavalier* survived in England except for furnished dwellings and where the lessor was the builder.

20–196 The decisions in *Cavalier v Pope*[268] and the cases which preceded it are open today to the criticism that they placed landlords as a class in a more favourable position than other subjects of the law and so violated notions of equality, if not specifically in the form of the constitutional right to equality as human persons, then in a more general political sense stemming from the nature of a democratic state. It is difficult to justify this blatant inequality by showing that the immunity confers some benefit on society generally or provides some compensating benefit to tenants. Instead, it appears to be an example of the law directly favouring a particular social class and doing so because of the superior influence which that class traditionally enjoyed on the process of law-making.

20–197 The common law as established in the English authorities considered above was reviewed as to its application in Ireland in *Siney v Dublin Corporation*.[269]

Emergence of an Irish Jurisprudence
20–198 In *Siney v Dublin Corporation* the issue arose as to whether the immunity accorded to lessors in *Cavalier v Pope* was part of Irish law. Mr Siney took a tenancy of a new flat from Dublin Corporation. After he moved in damp and fungus appeared due to insufficient ventilation and the condensation that resulted from it. The special factor in the relationship between landlord and tenant in this case was that the landlord was a local authority providing housing under the Housing Acts,[270] whose aim was to make available low-cost rented

---

[264] [1932] A.C. 562.
[265] *Anns v Merton London Borough Council* [1978] A.C. 728, and *Rimmer v Liverpool City Council* (1983) 12 H.L.R. 23.
[266] [1906] A.C. 428 at 430.
[267] (1983) 12 H.L.R. 23.
[268] [1906] A.C. 428 at 430.
[269] [1980] I.R. 400.
[270] Now collectively the Housing Acts 1966–2015.

accommodation on terms that the private market was not able to provide. The Supreme Court held that these special circumstances created in law an implied warranty by the defendant in the tenancy agreement that the flat was fit for human habitation at the date of the letting. The court also held that the provisions of s.114 of the Housing Act 1966, since repealed,[271] did not apply to a housing authority and that, accordingly, the implied warranty was neither excluded nor replaced by the more limited statutory warranty of fitness for human habitation created by s.114. The court also held the landlord liable in negligence, finding that the defendant owed the plaintiff a duty to take reasonable care in the special circumstances of the tenancy to ensure that the flat was fit for human habitation at the date of the letting.[272] While O'Higgins C.J. was prepared to hold that *Cavalier v Pope*[273] was not part of Irish law, Henchy J. held that the special circumstances of the letting on the facts before him provided yet another exception to the rule in *Cavalier v Pope* and preferred to leave the removal of whatever vestige remained of that rule to the Oireachtas. Kenny J. concurred with the other two judges while expressing no view on these issues. There was thus a majority in favour of Henchy J.'s more limited *ratio decidendi*.

20–199 In *Gallagher v N McDowell Ltd*,[274] which was reviewed by O'Higgins C.J. in *Siney*, the Northern Ireland Court of Appeal refused to regard the immunity as being one that attached to realty. In that case the court held that the builders were liable for injury to the wife of the tenant of a house let by the Northern Ireland Trust; the wife's injury had been caused by a defect in the house. O'Higgins C.J. then went on to quote as follows from the judgment in *Gallagher*[275]:

"In my opinion, the cases since *Donoghue v Stevenson* [1932] AC 562 show that the land-owner's immunities, which I have described as settled before that decision, have not been disturbed by it. But the fact that these immunities arise in relation to defects and dangers on land does not mean that the law imposes no neighbourly duty of reasonable care as respects defects and dangers of that kind. The immunities attach to land-owners as such, and I do not think one is at liberty to jump from that to saying that the law of negligence in relation to what is dangerous draws a clear distinction between what are chattels and what, by attachment or otherwise, form part of the realty. Why should it? Such a distinction does not justify itself, and it is not required by the immunities I have mentioned when one is not dealing with land-owners as such."

---

[271] By Housing (Miscellaneous Provisions) Act 1992 s.37 and Sch.

[272] *Donoghue v Stevenson* [1932] A.C. 562; *Batty v Metropolitan Realisations Ltd* [1978] Q.B. 554; and *Anns v Merton London Borough* [1978] A.C. 728 considered.

[273] [1906] A.C. 428 at 430.

[274] [1961] N.I. 26.

[275] [1961] N.I. 26 at 38.

O'Higgins C.J. continued:

"In that passage from his judgment, Lord MacDermott seems to assume a continuing immunity for land-owners, as such, from the rule in *Donoghue v Stevenson* [1932] AC 562 in respect of defects or dangers on their land. Such a view of the law is not consistent with the decisions of this Court in *Purtill v Athlone UDC* [1968] IR 205 and *McNamara v Electricity Supply Board* [1975] IR 1. In relation to their particular facts, those cases regarded the liability of the occupier of land (whether as owner or otherwise) in respect of defects or dangers found on the land as proper to be treated under the principles of *Donoghue v Stevenson* [1932] AC 562."

20–200 Henchy J., finding himself in the unusual position of being more conservative than O'Higgins C.J., preferred to leave the matter to the legislature to resolve.

20–201 The point has already been made that Deasy's Act purported to put landlord and tenant relations in Ireland on a contractual footing. This could have provided a basis for the courts refusing to apply English cases such as *Cavalier v Pope*[276] and assimilating instead the law of leaseholds to the law of contract and so reading into contracts of tenancy the same kind of implied terms as one would find in modern commercial contracts. The courts in the United States have adopted this approach and so have placed implied terms in leases on a more rational and defensible basis.

20–202 In *Coleman v Dundalk UDC*[277] the Supreme Court held that the implied warranty in *Siney* applied to a lease for 99 years. In *Burke v Dublin Corporation*,[278] the Supreme Court held, in the context of the installation of a heating system that later proved to be defective, that the implied warranty of a flat or house let pursuant to the Housing Act 1966 being fit for human habitation, was in the nature of an absolute guarantee and did not depend for its existence upon the discoverability of any defect. This warranty was not diminished by the fact that the let house was an old property. In *Siney*, the premises were a new flat. In addition, according to Finlay C.J., the implied warranty that a house or flat so let should be fit for human habitation was an ongoing obligation, and equally arose if a tenant later made the housing authority aware of a feature in the property, such as a heating system installed by the landlord prior to the letting, which rendered it unfit for human habitation. The implied warranty likewise applied where a house, having first been let, was later sold to a tenant, under the provisions of the Housing Act 1966, since both sale and letting were effected under the same statute and ostensibly for the same purpose. In such situation, the traditional principle of *caveat emptor* was displaced.

---

[276] [1906] A.C. 428 at 430.
[277] Unreported, Supreme Court, 17 July 1985.
[278] [1991] 1 I.R. 341.

However, the Supreme Court declined to extend the implied warranty to a case where a house originally let under the Housing Act 1966 was sold on to a person not in need of assisted housing. It is significant that, in considering the breadth of the implied warranty as to habitability, the Supreme Court took the view that the 12 listed matters that had to be taken into account in the Schedule to the Act were not exhaustive of the responsibility of the housing authority. Otherwise, the defendant could have justified itself in not considering matters other than those specifically set out.

Unfit Houses
20–203 Under s.66 of the Housing Act 1966, a housing authority has power to issue a repair notice or a demolition order in extreme cases where houses are unfit for human habitation.

Health and Safety Legislation
20–204 Various Acts deal with health and safety for residential as well as commercial premises. They include the Public Health (Ireland) Act 1878, the Factories Act 1955, the Safety in Industry Act 1980 and the Office Premises Act 1958.[279]

Rented Houses
20–205 In addition to the general provisions already discussed, the Housing (Miscellaneous Provisions) Act 1992 (the "1992 Act") (as amended) contains a number of measures which taken together constitute a "Housing Code" for privately rented houses and are mainly aimed at strengthening the position of tenants.[280] There is also a detailed list of landlord's obligations, in the context of properties let for residential purposes, set out in s.12 of the RdTA 2004.

20–206 The Residential Tenancies Acts 2004–2016 have effected an enormous transformation in many aspects of the law of landlord and tenant as these apply to properties let for residential accommodation. This is significant, as increasing numbers of households rent privately from landlords.[281] Section 3 provides that the Acts apply to every dwelling subject to a tenancy, apart from the following:

- A business tenancy.
- A dwelling to which Pt II of the Housing (Private Rented Dwellings) Act 1982 applies (i.e. a formerly rent-controlled dwelling).

---

[279] J.C.W. Wylie, *Landlord and Tenant Law*, 3rd edn (London: Bloomsbury, 2014), para.15.06.
[280] See Housing (Standards for Rented Houses) Regulations 2017 (S.I. No. 17 of 2017).
[281] According to the Central Statistics Office, renting has overtaken home ownership "to become the predominant tenure status in the urban towns and cities, rising from a share of 27% in 2006 to 36% in 2016." Central Statistics Office, *Census of Population 2016 - Profile 1 Housing in Ireland* (2017), *http://www.cso.ie/en/releasesandpublications/ep/p-cp1hii/cp1hii/tr/* [accessed 26 April 2018].

- A dwelling let to or by a local authority, including a dwelling provided by a public authority to an approved housing body other than a dwelling referred to in s.3(2A).[282]
- A dwelling approved for social housing purposes in accordance with s.6 of the 1992 Act and occupied by a person to whom s.9(2) of the Housing Act 1988 applies.
- A dwelling in respect of which the occupier is entitled to acquire the fee simple under Pt II of the Landlord and Tenant (Ground Rents) (No. 2) Act 1978.
- A dwelling occupied under a shared ownership lease.
- A holiday dwelling.
- A dwelling in which the landlord also resides.
- A dwelling in which the spouse, civil partner, parent or child of the land-lord resides and where there is no lease or tenancy agreement in respect of anyone resident in the dwelling: it follows that, where there *is* a written agreement in such a case, the Act *will* apply.
- A dwelling held under tenancy subject to an application for a statutory renewal of its term pursuant to the 1980 Act, or its predecessor of 1931, and in respect of which the matter was before the courts. The intention here was that a person so entitled would be able to renounce his or her right and instead claim the protections of the RdTA 2004 when it came into effect.[283] As of 1 September 2009, the right to a new tenancy under the 1980 Act no longer exists in the case of a tenancy to which the RdTA 2004 applies, unless the tenant had by that date applied for relief under the 1980 Act.[284]

20–207 For most purposes, a "dwelling" is defined as

"a property let for rent or valuable consideration as a self-contained residential unit and includes any building or part of a building used as a dwelling and any out office, yard, garden or other land appurtenant to it or usually enjoyed with it and, where the context so admits, includes a property available for letting but excludes a structure that is not permanently attached to the ground and a vessel and a vehicle (whether mobile or not)".[285]

20–208 A "lease" is "an instrument in writing, whether or not under seal, containing a contract of tenancy in respect of a dwelling." A "tenancy" "includes a periodic tenancy and a tenancy for a fixed term, whether oral or in writing or implied ..." and in certain cases can include an existing or a terminated

---

[282] This would be where a public authority provides a dwelling to an approved housing body under a contract or lease, and the dwelling concerned is the subject of a tenancy between the approved housing body and a household that qualifies for social housing support.
[283] RdTA 2004 s.191.
[284] RdTA 2004 s.192.
[285] RdTA 2004 s.4(1).

sub-tenancy.[286] The definition of tenancy has been amended by s.100 of the Housing (Miscellaneous Provisions) Act 2009 not to include a tenancy the term of which is more than 35 years.[287] A tenancy agreement is deemed to include an oral tenancy agreement. A "self-contained residential unit" includes a "bedsit".[288]

Notice to Quit

20–209 Section 16 of the 1992 Act provides that notice by a landlord or a tenant to the other to terminate the tenancy of a house let for rent or other valuable consideration is not valid unless it is in writing and is served not less than four weeks before the date on which it is to take effect. Exceptions are made for "tied" houses let in connection with employment, tenancies let for temporary convenience or necessity, holiday lettings and other tenancies prescribed by the Minister. These provisions no longer apply in the case of a tenancy to which the Residential Tenancies Acts 2004–2016 apply. Instead, s.66 of the Acts provides for a progressive scale of notice periods to be applied, in the case of intended termination of a tenancy by either the landlord or the tenant, of which the minimum is 28 days' notice for a tenancy that has lasted for less than six months.[289] An exception is provided for in s.67: where the tenancy is being terminated by the landlord on the grounds of defined "anti-social" behaviour by the tenant or where the tenant's behaviour is "threatening to the fabric" of the let property, the notice period required is only seven days, except in the case of Pt 4 tenancies, in which case the notice period is 28 days.

Rent Books

20–210 Landlords of rented houses must provide tenants with rent books.[290] The landlord must acknowledge all rent and other payments by the tenant in the rent book. The rent book must also contain details of the landlord and of the tenancy, including the rent reserved, any advance payments or deposits, the terms of the tenancy and details of furnishings and appliances supplied by the landlord for the use of the tenant. The rent book must also contain a basic statement of information for the tenant which is set out in the Schedule to the

---

[286] RdTA 2004 s.5(1).

[287] However, s.100(6) of the Housing (Miscellaneous Provisions) Act 2009 provides that the removal of a tenancy for longer than 35 years from the definition of "tenancy" for the purposes of the RdTA 2004 does not affect any matter referred for resolution to the Residential Tenancies Board, prior to the coming into effect of s.100 of the Residential Tenancies (Amendment) Act 2009.

[288] RdTA 2004 s.4(1).

[289] As noted above, the Residential Tenancies (Amendment) Bill 2018 purports to extend the notice periods by landlords.

[290] Housing Act 1992 s.17 and the Housing (Rent Books) Regulations 1993 (S.I. No. 146 of 1993).

Regulations. This statement must include a reference to the landlord's obligations under the Housing (Standards for Rented Houses) Regulations 2011.[291]

Housing Regulations

20–211 The Housing (Standards for Rented Houses) Regulations 2017 came
into effect on 1 July 2017, replacing previous regulations.[292] They were made
under s.5 of the Housing Act 1966, as amended. The Regulations impose
standards on rented houses as to structural condition, sanitary facilities, heating facilities, food preparation and storage facilities, laundry facilities, refuse
facilities, ventilation, fire safety,[293] lighting, gas, electricity and oil. These
Regulations have been described as "steps in the right direction",[294] but the lack
of a definition as to what constitutes "reasonable" repairs, and the fact that this
is dependent on *"the age, character and prospective life* of the house", limits
their usefulness from a tenant's point of view. They are also limited in their
scope, applying to houses let or available to let for rent or other valuable consideration. They do not apply to holiday lettings; nor do they apply to a house
let by the Health Service Executive or by an approved body, as accommodation
with sanitary, cooking or dining facilities provided for communal use within
the building which contains the house. They do not apply to caravans or mobile
homes let by local authorities.[295] O'Sullivan[296] and Kenna[297] have also pointed
out that there are problems with enforcing these Regulations.

20–212 A landlord must carry out, as may be required, any needed repairs
so as to ensure that the structure complies with the standards for houses prescribed by the Housing (Standards for Rented Houses) Regulations 2017.[298]
He or she must also ensure that the interior fittings of the premises are repaired
and replaced as may be needed "so that that interior and those fittings are
maintained in, at least, the condition in which they were at the commencement
of the tenancy and in compliance with any such standards for the time being
prescribed." The Residential Tenancies Board (RTB) may receive submissions
from relevant interested parties and then specify by regulation which parts of

---

[291] Housing (Rent Books) (Amendment) Regulations 2010 (S.I. No. 357 of 2010) reg.2. The
Housing (Standards for Rented Houses) Regulations 2008 (S.I. No. 534 of 2008) were replaced
by the Housing (Standards for Rented Houses) Regulations 2017 (S.I. No. 17 of 2017). The
Rent Books Regulations appear not to have been amended in light of these changes.

[292] Housing (Standards for Rented Houses) Regulations 2008 (S.I. No. 534 of 2008), Housing
(Standards for Rented Houses) (Amendment) Regulations 2009 (S.I. No. 462 of 2009).

[293] On the "unwieldy web of fire safety provisions" more generally, see M. Canny, "Fire Safety
Legislation and Regulation of Overcrowding in Private Rented Dwellings: The Complexities
Examined" (2018) 23(1) C.P.L.J. 17.

[294] K. O'Sullivan, "'A Lot Done, More to Do?': Local Authority Housing Standards in Ireland"
(2018) 23(1) C.P.L.J. 2.

[295] Housing (Standards for Rented Houses) Regulations 2017 (S.I. No. 17 of 2017) reg.3.

[296] K. O'Sullivan, "'A Lot Done, More to Do?': Local Authority Housing Standards in Ireland"
(2018) 23(1) C.P.L.J. 2 at 4.

[297] P. Kenna, *Housing Law, Rights and Policy* (Dublin: Clarus Press, 2011), p.755.

[298] RdTA 2004 s.12(1)(b).

a let premises are to be regarded as either the interior or the structure.[299] However, in a rare gesture of deference to the once favoured position of landlords, the RTB shall not make such a designation if, in the RTB's opinion, the effect of it will "result in unreasonably burdensome obligations being imposed on landlords".[300]

Distress

20–213 Section 19 of the 1992 Act prohibits levying the common law remedy of distress for any rent or rentcharge due in the case of premises let solely as a dwelling. Insofar as it applied to dwellings, the remedy may in any case offend against Art.40.5 of the Constitution which provides: "The dwelling of every citizen is inviolable and shall not be forcibly entered save in accordance with law." The levying of distress is "in accordance with law", but it seems that there is a degree of due process implied in this provision.[301] The remedy of distress has some similarities to the right of possession traditionally afforded to a legal mortgagee by conveyance prior to the LCLRA 2009. In *Irish Life & Permanent plc v Duff*,[302] Hogan J. suggested that the existence of such a remedy might have to be "re-examined" in light of Art.40.5. There seems to be no reason why the remedy of distress would be treated differently.

20–214 Section 58 of the RdTA 2004 responds to such concerns by providing that tenancies to which the Acts apply cannot be terminated by forfeiture or re-entry or by any other procedure not provided for in the Acts. In essence, such a tenancy can be terminated only by a notice of termination given in accordance with the Acts for the reasons which the Acts provide. Either party can seek redress through the RTB which, in appropriate cases, at the behest of the relevant party can seek an interim or interlocutory injunction from the Circuit Court.[303] A finding in a dispute by the RTB is embodied in a "determination order", which can be enforced through the Circuit Court.[304]

Registration

20–215 Part 7 of the Residential Tenancies Acts 2004–2016 provides for the compulsory registration of tenancies to which the Acts apply. It also obliges the RTB to maintain a confidential "residential tenancies register" for statistical and analytical purposes.[305] Selected extracts from this, containing details deemed by the RTB to be "useful to members of the public", are contained in a "published register" to which the public has access. However, this published register cannot disclose, or enable to be ascertained, the identity of either the

---

[299] RdTA 2004 s.13.
[300] RdTA 2004 s.13(2)(b).
[301] See *Damache v DPP* [2012] 1 I.R. 266 and *People (DPP) v Cunningham* [2013] 2 I.R. 631.
[302] [2013] 4 I.R. 96.
[303] RdTA 2004 s.189.
[304] RdTA 2004 s.124.
[305] RdTA 2004 s.127.

landlord or the tenant or the amount of the rent paid in respect of any dwelling.[306] The RTB can publish what are called "details of an aggregated nature … concerning the private rented sector" provided that these do not result in prohibited disclosures being made.[307]

20–216 A landlord must register details of a tenancy to which the Residential Tenancies Acts 2004–2016 apply no later than one month from the commencement of the tenancy.[308] Section 136 of the RdTA 2004 sets out the required details, as follows:

- The address of the dwelling.
- The name, address for correspondence and personal public service number (PPSN) (if any) of the landlord or his or her agent.
- If the landlord or agent is a company, the registered number and registered office of that company.
- The name and PPSN(s), of the tenant(s) (unless this cannot be ascertained by reasonable inquiry).
- The name of the housing authority in whose functional area the dwelling is situated.
- If the dwelling is one of a number of dwellings comprising an apartment complex, the name of the management company (if any) of the complex and the registered number and registered office of that company.
- A description of the dwelling, indicating whether it is a whole or part of a house, a maisonette, an apartment, a flat or a bedsitter and, in case it falls within the category of a house or maisonette, an indication as to whether the house or maisonette is detached, semi-detached or terrace.
- The number of bedrooms.
- The date the tenancy of the dwelling commenced.
- The amount of the rent payable under that tenancy, the frequency with which it is required to be paid and any taxes or other charges required to be paid by the tenant.
- If the tenancy is for a fixed term, the period of that term.
- Whether the tenancy consists of a sub-letting.
- The number assigned under s.135(3) in respect of a previous tenancy that was registered in respect of the dwelling.
- Such other matters as may be prescribed.

20–217 The landlord is obliged to notify the RTB of any variation in the rent payable under a tenancy, not later than one month after it occurs, stating the amount and from when it is payable.[309] The landlord may, at any time, notify

---

[306] RdTA 2004 ss.128 and 129.

[307] RdTA 2004 s.131.

[308] RdTA 2004 s.134. In the case of a dwelling provided by a public authority and let by a housing association to a household qualifying for social housing support, the registration may be carried out later: see RdTA 2004 s.134(2A).

[309] RdTA 2004 s.39.

the RTB in writing of any changes in respect of particulars entered in the register, or any additional particulars to be entered in the register.[310] If the landlord believes that a circumstance has emerged which causes the Act no longer to apply to a dwelling under tenancy, he or she must so notify the RTB of that opinion, and of the reasons for it: this must be done not later than one month from the time when, in the landlord's opinion, the tenancy ceased to be subject to the Act.[311] If the RTB accepts the submission of the landlord it will then delete the entry in the register, and so advise the landlord, although it may preserve some of the particulars of the tenancy for statistical, advisory, or general information purposes.[312]

Landlord's Statutory Duties in the Case of a Residential Tenancy
To the Tenant
20–218 In the case of a tenancy to which the Residential Tenancies Acts 2004–2016 apply, both landlord and tenant are subject to a number of implied covenants described as obligations. Landlords' obligations are set out in Ch.1 of Pt 2 of the Acts.

20–219 A landlord shall[313]:

- allow the tenant to have peaceful and exclusive occupation;
- save in cases where a tenant has damaged the dwelling beyond normal wear and tear, carry out such repairs as to ensure that the structure of the let dwelling complies with the standards for houses prescribed by regulations made under s.18 of the 1992 Act and that the interior and fittings are maintained in the same condition that they were in at the commencement of the tenancy and comply with any prescribed standards for interior and fittings;
- provide receptacles suitable for the storage of refuse outside the dwelling, save where the provision of such receptacles is not within the power or control of the landlord in respect of the dwelling concerned;
- insure the structure of the dwelling against destruction and damage, and insure the landlord to at least the amount of €250,000 against landlord's liability arising from the use, possession or ownership of the dwelling (provided that such insurance can be obtained at reasonable cost);

---

[310] RdTA 2004 s.139(7)(a).

[311] RdTA 2004 s.141(1).

[312] RdTA 2004 s.41(3) and (5).

[313] This list is drawn from the detailed requirements set out in s.12, modified in relation to the landlord's responsibility for repair and to return the tenant's deposit at the end of the tenancy by s.16(f) and (g) which limit the tenant's obligation "not to cause a deterioration in the condition the dwelling was in at the commencement of the tenancy" to deterioration greater than that which results from "wear and tear that is normal" having regard to the time elapsed since the commencement of the tenancy and the occupation of the dwelling reasonably foreseen by the landlord.

- return any deposit paid by the tenant upon agreeing to enter the lease or tenancy,[314] provided that any arrears of rent (or other charges or taxes payable by the tenant in accordance with the lease or tenancy[315]) or the cost of repairing any deterioration caused in the dwelling by the tenant beyond normal wear and tear do not exceed the amount of the deposit, and, to the extent that arrears of rent (or other charges or taxes payable by the tenant) or the costs of repairing damage caused by the tenant are less than the amount of the deposit, to return only the difference between the two;
- notify the tenant of the identity of the landlord's agent and of the contact details of either the landlord or the agent;
- reimburse the tenant vouched expenses reasonably incurred by the tenant in undertaking repairs for which the Act ascribes responsibility to the landlord, where the landlord has failed to carry out the repairs at the tenant's request and a postponement of them would have caused a health or safety risk to the tenant or other lawful occupants of the dwelling or a significant reduction in the quality of their living environment;
- where the dwelling is in an apartment complex, notify the management company of any complaint about the performance by it of its duties, in relation to the apartment complex, made by the tenant, and forward to the tenant any response by the management company, including a statement of any steps that the management company may already have taken to deal with the matter; and
- where the tenancy is of a dwelling in a rent pressure zone, furnish the tenant with a written statement of the amount of rent that was last set for the dwelling, the date at which this was set, and a statement as to how the rent has been calculated, having regard to s.19(4).

20–220 Section 14 prohibits a landlord from penalising a tenant for referring a dispute to the RTB, for giving evidence in a dispute, or for referring or threatening to refer a complaint in relation to occupation of a dwelling to the Garda Síochána or a public authority. A tenant is deemed to have been penalised if "subjected to any action that adversely affects his or her enjoying peaceful occupation of the dwelling concerned". This can arise even if the landlord is acting upon his or her rights, if

- the frequency or extent of the right being exercised, or
- the propinquity in time between the exercising by the landlord of his or her right and the act by the tenant alleged to have prompted the victimisation, or
- any other relevant circumstances

---

[314] In residential tenancies, a landlord commonly requires the tenant to pay a deposit, as an insurance against damage or default, which in most cases is equivalent to one month's rent.

[315] The addition given above in parenthesis was introduced by substitution by s.100 of the Housing (Miscellaneous Provisions) Act 2009.

make it a reasonable inference that the purpose of the landlord's action is to penalise the tenant. Any such alleged penalisation may be the subject of a complaint by the tenant to the dispute resolution mechanism presided over by the RTB and set up under Pt 6 of the RdTA 2004.[316]

To Third Parties

20–221 Section 15 of the Residential Tenancies Acts 2004–2016 provides that a landlord owes to "each person who could be potentially affected" a duty to enforce the tenant's obligations under the tenancy. Such a person is defined as being one "who, it is reasonably foreseeable, would be directly and adversely affected by a failure to enforce an obligation of the tenant were such a failure to occur", and also includes other tenants under the relevant tenancy. This provision is stated as not affecting any "duty of care", and remedies available for its breach, which otherwise arise. A complaint under s.15 can be made under the complaints resolution procedures established in Pt 6 of the RdTA 2004 only if the potential complainant has first endeavoured to resolve the issue with the relevant parties to the tenancy, but this does not require either the institution or threatened institution of proceedings.[317]

Rent Pressure Zones

20–222 In recognition of the housing crisis precipitated by rapidly rising rents in certain parts of the country, the Planning and Development (Housing) and Residential Tenancies Act 2016 amended the RdTA 2004 to provide for rent pressure zones. Under s.24A of the Residential Tenancies Acts 2004–2016, the Housing and Sustainable Communities Agency, following consultation with the relevant housing authority, may make a proposal in writing to the Minister that an area be prescribed by order as a rent pressure zone.[318] The Minister should then be furnished with a rent zone report demonstrating that the annual rate of increase in the average amount of rent for that area is more than 7 per cent in each of at least four of the preceding six quarters, and that the average rent for the area in the last quarter was above the average national rent. The Minister can then by order prescribe the area as a rent pressure zone for a specified period not exceeding three years. Such an order can be revoked by the Minister, having regard to the housing market, the rental market, or changes in rent levels. For the purposes of s.24A, "area" means either the administrative area of a housing authority, or a local electoral area within the meaning of s.2

---

[316] RdTA 2004 s.78(1)(o).

[317] RdTA 2004 s.77(2)(b).

[318] For example, administrative areas of the following local authorities are deemed to be rent pressure zones for three years from 24 December 2016: Cork City Council; Dublin City Council; Dún Laoghaire Rathdown County Council; Fingal County Council; and South Dublin County Council. RdTA 2004 s.24B, as inserted by Planning and Development (Housing) and Residential Tenancies Act 2016 s.36. Since then, a number of other areas have been designated rent pressure zones by the Minister. The updated list of designated zones can be found at *https://www.rtb.ie/rent-pressure-zones*. See, for example, S.I. Nos 18–29 of 2017; S.I. Nos 109, 113, 401 and 402 of 2017.

of the Local Government Act 2001.[319] The main effect of declaring an area to be a rent pressure zone is that the rents for dwellings in those areas can only rise according to a prescribed formula by a maximum of 4 per cent annually, as discussed below.

Amount of Rent

20–223 Rent controls have long been a matter of some controversy and debate,[320] and the constitutionality of the rent pressure zones has recently been questioned.[321] Part 3 of the Residential Tenancies Acts 2004–2016 makes provision for the monitoring and control of rents in a tenancy to which the Acts apply. Upon an initial setting of the amount of the rent in a lease or tenancy, or in a review of such rent, the rent reserved cannot be in excess of what is defined as the "market rent".[322] This is defined as

"… the rent which a willing tenant not already in occupation would give and a willing landlord would take for the dwelling, in each case on the basis of vacant possession being given, and having regard to:

(a) the other terms of the tenancy, and

(b) the letting values of dwellings of a similar size, type and character to the dwelling and situated in a comparable area to that in which it is situated."[323]

20–224 If the dwelling is located in a rent pressure zone, the rent cannot be higher than that which would be set using the calculation

$$R \times (1 + 0.04 \times t/m)$$

where "R" is the last rent set for the dwelling; "m" is 24 (where s.24C(1)(a) applies) or 12 (in all other cases), and "t" is the number of months between

"(a) (i) the date the current rent came into effect under a tenancy for the dwelling, or

(ii) where paragraph (a) does not apply but the dwelling was previously let, other than in circumstances to which [s.19(5)] applies, the date rent became payable under a tenancy for the dwelling as last so let,

and

---

[319] RdTA 2004 s.24A(10).

[320] See the discussion by D. O'Sullivan, "Rent, Regulation and the Public Interest in Ireland" (2016) 21(4) C.P.L.J. 74; G. Hogan, "The Constitution, Property Rights and Proportionality" (1997) 32(1) Ir. Jur. 373.

[321] D. Harnedy, "Constitutionality of Planning and Development (Housing) and Residential Tenancies Act 2016" (2017) 22(4) C.P.L.J. 73.

[322] RdTA 2004 s.19.

[323] RdTA 2004 s.24(1).

(b) the date the rent for the tenancy of the dwelling will come into effect after its determination under this subsection."[324]

20–225 Section 19(5) states that the formula set out above does not apply

- where a dwelling has not at any time been the subject of a tenancy during the period of two years prior to the date the area is prescribed as a rent pressure zone or deemed to be so prescribed; or
- if, in the period since the rent was last set under a tenancy for the dwelling, (i) a substantial change in the nature of the accommodation provided under the tenancy occurs, and (ii) the rent under the tenancy, were it to be set immediately after that change, would, by virtue of that change, be different to what was the market rent for the tenancy at the time the rent was last set under a tenancy for the dwelling.

20–226 Section 19A deals with the setting of rent for properties referred to in s.3(4)—that is, properties provided by local authorities to be let to households qualifying for social housing support. The rent for such tenancies shall be set in accordance with the terms of the contract or lease with the housing authority, or with the terms of the social housing assistance provided.

Rent Reviews
20–227 In cases where a lease or tenancy does not already provide for it, either party is deemed to have a right to seek a review of the rent.[325] A rent review includes any procedure whereby "a reduction or increase in the amount of rent for the time being payable" is determined, including the application of a formula or the exercise of a discretion "on the part of any person".[326] From this it is clear that a rent review may be upwards *or* downwards.

20–228 A rent review cannot take place more than once in any period of 12 months or in the first 12-month period following the commencement of the tenancy,[327] but an exception is permissible in the event of "a substantial change in the nature of the accommodation provided under the tenancy" if the effect of this is that the market rent, if set immediately after the substantial change, would be different from the market rent when last set.[328]

20–229 A review of the rent under the tenancy of a dwelling referred to in s.3(4) shall be carried out in accordance with the tenancy agreement relating to the tenancy of the dwelling. Where such a tenancy agreement does not include

---

[324] RdTA 2004 s.19(4).

[325] RdTA 2004 s.21.

[326] RdTA 2004 s.24(2)(a) and (b).

[327] The 12-month period is to be construed as a 24-month period between 4 December 2015 and 3 December 2019. RdTA 2004 s.20(4) as amended by the Residential Tenancies (Amendment) Act 2015 s.25(1).

[328] RdTA 2004 s.20(1) and (3).

provision for a rent review, then either party may require a rent review to be carried out for the purpose of setting the rent, provided this is not done more than once in a 12-month period.[329]

20–230 In order to effectuate a review of rent, the landlord must give the tenant not less than 90 days' notice, in writing, setting out the amount of the new rent and from when it is to be paid. The notice must also include:

- a statement that a dispute in relation to the setting of a rent pursuant to a review of the rent under a tenancy must be referred to the RTB before the date stated in the notice as the date from which that rent is to have effect, or before the expiry of 28 days from the receipt by the tenant of that notice, whichever is the later;
- a statement by the landlord that in his or her opinion the new rent is not greater than the market rent, having regard to the other terms of the tenancy, and letting values of dwellings of a similar size, type and character, situated in a comparable area to that in which the dwelling the subject of the tenancy concerned is situated;
- a statement of the amount of rent sought for three dwellings of a similar size, type and character situated in a comparable area;
- the date on which the notice is signed; and
- where the dwelling is in a rent pressure zone, a statement of how the rent set under the tenancy was calculated having regard to s.19(4) or, where s.19(4) does not apply, a statement of why it does not apply.

20–231 A dispute regarding the increased rent may be referred by the tenant to the RTB within the date set out in the notice or within 28 days of receiving the notice, whichever is the later.[330] Arrears of rent can be claimed under the dispute resolution procedures set out in Pt 6 of the Acts.[331]

By the Tenant
To Pay the Rent
General

20–232 In the past, the courts treated covenants in leases as separate property rights rather than as part of a contract, i.e. as part of a set of reciprocal obligations. This meant that a landlord could sue a tenant for unpaid rent even though the landlord had defaulted in some of his or her covenants in the lease. The tenant's remedy was to sue the landlord on the landlord's covenant. The tenant could not deduct money owed to him or her by the landlord in an action by the landlord to enforce the covenant to pay rent. The tenant's obligation to pay rent was absolute. Thus, in *Paradine v Jane*,[332] a tenant who had been dispossessed

---

[329] RdTA 2004 s.20A, as inserted by the Residential Tenancies (Amendment) Act 2015 s.7.
[330] RdTA 2004 s.22.
[331] RdTA 2004 s.23.
[332] (1647) Aleyn 26 at 27f.

by the forces of Prince Rupert during the English Civil War was held still liable to pay rent to the landlord for the period of dispossession. The rule was associated with the rule of the common law, based on the same property notion, that the doctrine of frustration in contract law did not apply to leases, although this has recently been held no longer to be the case. A tenant thus remained liable to pay rent even if the premises were destroyed by fire.[333] These rules probably indicate that judges in the past favoured the dominant landowning classes at the expense of tenants.[334]

20–233 Section 42 of Deasy's Act provides that the tenant and successors are obliged to pay the rent. The tenant is now entitled to make certain deductions from rent. This is discussed in the next section.

20–234 Head 38 of the LTLRB 2011 purports to implement the Law Reform Commission's recommendation that the implied obligation to pay rent in s.42 of Deasy's Act should be replaced by an overriding obligation[335]:

> "(1) The tenant has an overriding obligation to pay the rent provided for under the tenancy on the date when it falls due for payment.
> (2) The tenant has a default obligation to make such payment in advance."

Deductions and Set-off
Common Law
20–235 The traditional common law principle was that a tenant had in general no right to make deductions from the rent owing by him or her to the landlord. In *Corkerry v Stack*[336] it was held that the rule by which the tenant is not relieved from paying the rent because the landlord defaults on his or her tenancy obligations applied in Ireland. In *Shipsey v McGrath*[337] a tenant was sued for rent and successfully claimed the right to deduct sums spent by him or her on repairs; however, the court apparently accepted this on the ground that the landlord had allowed him or her to make such deduction in the past. On the other hand, there is also authority to the effect that the landlord's covenant of quiet enjoyment only bound the landlord if the tenant performed his or her obligations under the lease.[338]

20–236 In more recent decades the courts have demonstrated a tendency to depart from or whittle down the strict common law rules regarding set-off. It has been held in England that a tenant has the right to deduct from rent the

---

[333] *Balfour v Weston* [1786] 1 T.R. 310 at 312.

[334] In the United States, where landowners were less influential, the courts in the 19th century departed from these rules: e.g. *Graves v Berdan* (1868) 26 N.Y. 498.

[335] Law Reform Commission, *Consultation Paper on General Law of Landlord and Tenant* (LRC CP 28-2003), para.8.03.

[336] (1948) 82 I.L.T.R. 60.

[337] (1879) 31 I.L.T.R. 77.

[338] *Southwark LBC v Mills* [2001] Ch. 1 at 27D.

amount he or she has spent on repairs which were the responsibility of the landlord.[339] At common law, if a landlord is liable to undertake repairs and the failure to do so causes a legal nuisance, the tenant can sue for damages[340] or an injunction.

Statute
20–237 Section 48 of Deasy's Act provides:

> "All claims and demands by any landlord against his tenant in respect of rent shall be subject to deduction or set-off in respect of all just debts due by the landlord to the tenant."

Deasy's Act was seemingly consistent here in its aim, already noted, in shifting the landlord and tenant relationship from the property notion to the contract principle. Nevertheless, despite the apparently deliberate use of the word "deduction" in addition to the word "set-off", 19th century case law held that the section only conferred a right by the tenant to set off such debts in an action by the landlord to recover the rent, and did not provide a defence to an action for ejectment for non-payment of rent.[341] In other words, the tenant had no right to deduct sums at source, but could only plead the section in defence to a claim for the rent. Section 48 of Deasy's Act has been interpreted as applying to where a liquidated sum, rather than damages generally, is owed by the landlord to the tenant.[342]

20–238 More recently, and more specifically, s.87 of the 1980 Act provides:

> "(1) Where a landlord refuses or fails to execute repairs to a tenement which he is bound by covenant or otherwise by law to execute and has been called upon by the tenant to execute, and the tenant executes the repairs at his own expense, the tenant may set off the expenditure against any subsequent gale or gales of rent until it is recouped."

The section applies to "tenements" as defined in the Act. It is clear that in this section "set-off" includes a right to deduct rather than merely raise a defence of specified money owing by the landlord. This is reinforced by s.87(2) which provides that if the tenant validly "sets off" the amount of repairs against rent and provides the landlord with evidence that this has been done, the landlord

---

[339] *Parker v Izzet* [1971] 3 All E.R. 1099; *British Anzani (Felixtone) Ltd v International Marine Management (UK) Ltd* [1979] 2 All E.R. 1063; A. Waite, "Disrepair and Set-off of Damages against Rent: the Implications of *British Anzani*" [1983] Conv. 373.

[340] *Byrne v Martina Investments Ltd* [1984] IEHC 9.

[341] *Cahill v Kearney* (1868) I.R. 2 C.L. 498 at 500; *Dalton v Barlow* (1867) 1 I.L.T. 490; Wylie, *Landlord and Tenant Law* (2014), para.12.11.

[342] *MacCausland v Carroll* (1938) 72 I.L.T.R. 158 per Maguire P., approved in *Riordan v Carroll* [1996] 2 I.L.R.M. 263; *Harrisrange Ltd v Duncan* [2003] 4 I.R. 1; and *The Leopardstown Club Ltd v Templeville Developments and Smyth* [2006] IEHC 133.

is bound to give a receipt of the gale of rent as if the full rent "had been paid in money".

20–239 There are differences in procedure between: (a) a set-off in an action by the landlord, (b) a counterclaim, and (c) a right to deduct. A *set-off* is a defence. It means that the landlord's claim should be reduced in part or in whole in respect of the amount which the tenant can set off against it.[343] A *counterclaim* is an action which is independent of the landlord's action: a tenant can succeed on a counterclaim even if the landlord fails to prove his or her case. A *right of deduction* is the right on the part of the tenant to deduct sums of money from payments of rent, i.e. before any action arises.

20–240 The difference in normal legal language between a set-off and a right to deduct can be illustrated as follows. T is a tenant of landlord L. L has failed to make repairs which he is bound to do under the lease. T does the repairs herself and deducts the sums from the rent, paying the balance. If L sues T for the full amount, T may answer that the full amount has been paid. Carrying out the repairs, paying the bill, and tendering evidence of both, is an alternative way of paying the rent. The same would apply if, instead, in a tenancy not covered by the Residential Tenancies Acts 2004–2016,[344] L brings an action of ejectment for non-payment of rent. T can say she has paid it.

20–241 As to the cost of repairs which the landlord was bound to undertake, the tenant has a right to deduct at source under s.87. This section applies only to repairs required to be carried out by the landlord. As to other "just debts", there is merely a right of set-off under s.48 of Deasy's Act.

20–242 Head 48 of the LTLRB 2011 proposes to replace s.48 of Deasy's Act. It extends the right of set-off to any proceedings for breach of obligation (not just in respect of rent). Secondly, it applies to both landlords and tenants (not just tenants). Thirdly, it confines the right of set-off to its proper context, i.e. as a defence in court proceedings. It states:

"(1) ... in any proceedings by the landlord or the tenant against the other for breach of any obligation under the tenancy either party may set off any sum owed by the other in connection with the tenancy.

(2) For the purposes of subhead (1)—

(a) 'any sum owed' includes both a liquidated and, subject to subhead (3), an un-liquidated sum,

(b) the right of set-off applies equally where the sum owed was owed by the other party's predecessor in title and remains un-discharged."

---

[343] See *In the Matter of Irish Shipping Ltd* [1986] I.L.R.M. 518.

[344] RdTA 2004 s.58 provides that "a tenancy of a dwelling may not be terminated by the landlord or tenant by means of a notice of forfeiture, a re-entry or any other process or procedure not provided by this Part [Pt 5]".

20–243 Subhead (2) clarifies two issues with respect to the right of set-off: para.(a) reverses the approach taken by the Irish courts (but not the English courts in recent times) which confines the right to liquidated sums. Paragraph (b) clarifies a point on which there is some doubt in Ireland. The English courts have recently held that the right of set-off is personal in respect of sums owed by the existing landlord and cannot be invoked in respect of sums owed by the previous landlord and remaining un-discharged.[345] Paragraph (b) makes it clear that this limitation does not apply under this section.[346]

Equity

20–244 In *The Leopardstown Club Ltd v Templeville Developments and Smyth*,[347] O'Sullivan J. stated that an equitable right of set-off is likely to have survived s.48 of Deasy's Act. This would arise where there was a close connection between the respective demands of the landlord and the tenant (e.g. by arising out of the same contract) "such that the tenant's claim impeaches the title to the plaintiff's [landlord's] demand".

20–245 The possible application of this principle was seen in *Irish Life Assurance plc v Quinn*.[348] A landlord sued a surety of the tenant on foot of the tenant's failure to pay rent and service charges. The tenant ran a hair and beauty salon in the Irish Life Mall in Dublin for which purpose continuity of "footfall" (i.e. a regular throughput of potential customer traffic) in the mall was a necessity. The defendant surety claimed that the landlord had not acted in accordance with good estate management by failing to replace the mall's anchor tenant and also by suffering several of the retail units near the tenant's premises to remain empty. As a result, the surety claimed that the tenant had suffered an unquantified financial loss which ought to be set off against the rent.

20–246 According to Dunne J., in principle equitable set-off may have been available to the surety, notwithstanding the provisions of s.48 of Deasy's Act and despite the obligation in the tenancy agreement to pay the rent "without any deduction". The applicable principle had been articulated by Clarke J. in *Moohan v S & R Motors (Donegal) Ltd*[349]:

"… the test as to whether a cross claim gives rise to a defence in equity, depends on whether the cross claim stems from the same set of facts (such as the same contract) as gives rise to the primary claim. If it does, then an equitable set off is available so that the debt arising on the claim will be disallowed to the extent that the cross claim may be made out."

---

[345] *Edlington Properties Ltd v J H Fenner & Co Ltd* [2006] 3 All E.R. 1200.
[346] LTLRB 2011, Head 48, Explanatory Note.
[347] [2006] IEHC 133.
[348] [2009] IEHC 153.
[349] [2008] 3 I.R. 650.

20–247 The mere fact that the tenancy obliged payment of rent "without any deduction" did not imply that either the tenant or the surety had contracted out of the right to seek an equitable set-off against rent due arising independently of s.48 of Deasy's Act. However, evidence had not been offered that any attempt was made to raise with the landlord, in response to its demands for outstanding rent and unpaid service charges, the issue of non-replacement of the departed anchor tenant or the fact that one-third of the retail units were left unoccupied. Nor was any effort made to quantify the loss suffered by the tenant. Accordingly, the plea struck the judge as "very much a last ditch effort on the part of the defendant to avoid his obligations under the terms of the guarantee entered into by him", although she added, that "if this had been an issue raised in correspondence prior to the issue of these proceedings, one would attach more weight to the matter"—thereby permitting the theoretical prospect of seeking an equitable set-off against rent if raised in good time.

20–248 Head 48(4) of the LTLRB 2011 states that subhead (1) "displaces any right of set-off available under the general law." This makes it clear that the new statutory right also displaces any right (such as an equitable right) of set-off, which may exist outside of s.48 of Deasy's Act.[350]

To Give Up Peaceable Possession

20–249 The tenant is obliged to give up peaceable possession and leave the premises in good and substantial repair, subject to the tenant's right to remove fixtures and claim compensation for improvements under Pt IV of the 1980 Act.

Waste

20–250 At common law the tenant was liable, subject to agreement to the contrary, for permissive, voluntary, or equitable waste. In leasehold tenure the common law rules have been almost entirely replaced by the provisions of Deasy's Act.

20–251 Section 25 of Deasy's Act made fee farm grantees of Deasy's Act grants[351] made after 1 January 1861,[352] and lessees under perpetually renewable leases for lives or years, impeachable only for "fraudulent or malicious" waste.

20–252 Under s.26 of Deasy's Act tenants cannot open mines, quarries or cut trees without the landlord's consent, unless the land was leased for that purpose. The tenant can cut turf, but for domestic fuel use only, not for profit.

---

[350] This resolves the issues raised in *The Leopardstown Club Ltd v Templeville Developments Ltd* [2006] IEHC 133.

[351] Fee farm grants by virtue of the Renewable Leasehold Conversion Act 1849 are excluded.

[352] The section does not apply to renewals after the Act of leases originally granted before the Act, since that would alter the terms originally agreed.

Residential Tenancies

20–253   Residential tenancies are governed by the RdTA 2004. The RdTA 2004 sets out a range of duties[353] and designated obligations, on the part of a tenant of a dwelling to which the Act applies:

- to pay the rent and any charges or taxes which may lawfully be required of a tenant;
- to ensure that no act or omission of the tenant causes the dwelling to fall below the standard required in the pertinent regulations made under the Housing Acts; this obligation also applies in relation to acts done by anyone in the dwelling with the tenant's consent[354];
- to allow the landlord or his or her agent access upon reasonable request, for the purpose of inspection, on a date and at a time agreed in advance;
- to notify the landlord of any defects arising which it is the landlord's responsibility at law to repair and to allow reasonable access to the dwelling to persons duly authorised by the landlord to carry out the repairs;
- not to cause any deterioration to the dwelling beyond such wear and tear as is reasonable having regard, among other relevant matters, to the time that has passed since the tenancy commenced and the extent of the occupation of the dwelling which the landlord could reasonably have foreseen during that time; otherwise to take such steps as the landlord may reasonably require, or defray such costs as the landlord reasonably incurs, in rectifying any deterioration greater than permissible wear and tear[355];
- not to act, or allow other occupiers or visitors to act, in such a way as would invalidate the landlord's insurance; and, in the event that any action by the tenant or the tenant's occupiers or visitors occasions an increase in the landlord's insurance premium (this increase not being attributable to any other cause), to pay the difference between the normal insurance and the higher amount for as long as the insurance "loading" persists;
- not to "assign or sub-let the tenancy without the written consent of the landlord (which consent the landlord may, in his or her discretion, withhold)"; but in the event of such consent being withheld, regardless of whether the tenancy is for a fixed or periodic term, the tenant can give notice to terminate the tenancy[356];
- not to alter or improve the dwelling (which terms are defined as including the changing of the locks and adding to or altering the structure) without the consent of the landlord, which the landlord in his or her discretion may withhold, except in the case of repairing or repainting or decorating where the landlord's consent cannot be unreasonably withheld;

---

[353] RdTA 2004 ss.16–18, as amended.

[354] RdTA 2004 ss.16(b) and 17(2).

[355] RdTA 2004 s.16(f) and (g). Section 193(a) disapplies from a tenancy to which the RdTA 2004 applies the implied condition by the tenant in Deasy's Act s.42, to keep the property "in good and substantial repair and condition".

[356] RdTA 2004 ss.16(k) and 186. This is subject to the RdTA 2004 s.3A(4).

- not to use the dwelling for any purpose except as a dwelling without the landlord's consent, which consent the landlord in his or her discretion may withhold;
- to notify the landlord in writing of the identity of each person ordinarily resident in the dwelling, except in the case of a "multiple tenant"[357];
- "not [to] behave within the dwelling, or within the vicinity of it, in a way that is anti-social or allow other occupiers of, or visitors to, the dwelling to behave within it, or in the vicinity of it, in such a way."[358]

20–254 This important latter requirement derives from social housing legislation, and touches profoundly upon the landlord's stated duty, set out in s.15, to any "person who could be potentially affected" to enforce the tenant's obligations under the tenancy.

20–255 Section 17(1) provides three complementary definitions of what is meant by to "behave in a way that is anti-social":

(a) engaging in behaviour that constitutes an offence which is reasonably likely to affect directly the welfare or well-being of others;

(b) engaging in behaviour that causes, actually or potentially, fear or injury to any person lawfully in the dwelling subject to the tenancy or its vicinity; this includes, but is not limited to, "violence, intimidation, coercion, harassment, or obstruction of, or threats to, any such person"; or

(c) engaging persistently in behaviour that "prevents or interferes with the peaceful occupation" of his or her property by a person also living in the affected dwelling, or in another dwelling in the same property, or in a "neighbourhood dwelling" defined as being in the vicinity of the dwelling under tenancy or the property that contains it."

FRUSTRATION

20–256 Section 40 of Deasy's Act provides that where there is no express covenant to repair, the tenant may surrender his or her lease if the premises is destroyed or made uninhabitable through fire or other inevitable accident which is not due to the fault of the tenant. In other words, the risk of fire does not fall on the tenant. This partly reversed what was thought to be the common law rule that the doctrine of frustration did not apply to leases,[359] though as Clark points out the law is not fully clear as regards frustrating events falling outside of s.44.[360] In England the House of Lords has held that the doctrine of

---

[357] A "multiple tenant" is defined in s.48 as any one of two or more persons who are tenants of the dwelling (whether as joint tenants, tenants-in-common or under any other form of co-ownership).

[358] RdTA 2004 s.16(h).

[359] But see now *National Carriers v Panalpina (Northern) Ltd* [1981] A.C. 675.

[360] R. Clark, *Contract Law in Ireland*, 8th edn (Dublin: Round Hall, 2016), para.8–109.

frustration applies in principle to leases, although it may rarely be held to do so on the facts.[361] The circumstances of its application are not entirely clear. It was held not to apply where the only means of access to a warehouse, leased for 10 years, was closed after five years of the lease had elapsed.[362] But it may apply where the land is physically destroyed, e.g. by being washed away by the sea, or by fire before the term begins, or, possibly, shortly after the term begins. In *Irish Leisure Industries Ltd v Gaiety Theatre Enterprises Ltd*[363] the Irish Supreme Court held a lease of a theatre to be frustrated in circumstances where a previous tenant had obtained a statutory extension to his tenancy thus preventing the new lease from falling into possession. Clark notes that this authority is unsatisfactory because it is not clear that the contract was frustrated. The defendant may have been in simple breach of the lease agreement by failing to place itself in a position where it could perform its obligation as landlord.[364]

20–257 The LTLRB 2011 provides, in Head 60, that "[f]or the avoidance of doubt it is hereby provided that the doctrine of frustration of contract applies and always has applied to a tenancy." This reflects the view that s.40 of Deasy's Act has outlived its usefulness and should be regarded as replaced by the general doctrine of frustration of contract as developed by the courts.

FIXTURES

Common Law
20–258 At common law, anything attached to the soil by more than gravity became part of the land and belonged to the owner of the freehold.[365] Fixtures attached to the land at the tenant's expense were simply acquired free of charge by the landlords. It was a rule which favoured the landed class. With the rise of trade and the industrial revolution, the idea developed that the person who had invested their own labour or money in purchasing a commodity should be entitled to the monetary value of it. The courts began to recognise and develop categories of fixtures which tenants could "sever" and remove. Trade fixtures were probably the first to be recognised.[366] Today these would include such things as petrol pumps attached to tanks embedded in the ground,[367] or a shed used for the manufacture of concrete products and secured to the ground by bolts passing through holes in the bottom of the posts at each corner and

---

[361] See *National Carriers v Panalpina (Northern) Ltd* [1981] A.C. 675, accepted in *Neville Sons Ltd v Guardian Builders* [1995] 1 I.L.R.M. 1.

[362] *National Carriers v Panalpina (Northern) Ltd* [1981] A.C. 675.

[363] Unreported, Supreme Court, 12 February 1975.

[364] Clark, *Contract Law in Ireland* (2016), para.8–110.

[365] See *Holland v Hodgson* (1872) L.R. 7 C.P. 328; *Re Ross and Boal Ltd* [1924] 1 I.R. 129; *Maye v Revenue Commissioners* [1986] I.L.R.M. 377; *Ardfert Quarry Products v Moormac Developments* [2013] IEHC 572.

[366] *Poole's Case* (1703) 1 Salk. 368.

[367] *Smith v City Petroleum* [1940] 1 All E.R. 260.

through metal tags set in the floor.[368] The method of attachment is probably today no more than evidence of the intention as to the use of the fixture and its relative permanence. The amount of damage that would be caused by removing the claimed fixture is relevant to the issue of whether its removal by the tenant is permissible.[369]

20–259 In the late 19th century, the Irish Court of Appeal in *Cosby v Shaw*[370] showed its indulgence for trade fixtures by exempting from a clause in a lease, which restricted the right of a tenant to remove fixtures, trade fixtures that had been introduced "as scientific improvements to fulfil functions previously performed by manual labour...". The courts thus chose a result which favoured the introduction of scientific inventions. Next, the courts recognised that ornamental and domestic fixtures may be removed by a tenant.[371] But the English courts never recognised that agricultural tenants had the right to remove fixtures, and this refusal to develop the law in that direction may be taken as a concession to the landed class.

20–260 In 1803, in *Elwes v Maw*[372] a tenant farmer had built sheds and yards at his own expense. He removed them at the end of the lease, leaving the land in the same condition as at the beginning of the lease. He was held liable to the landlord in damages. The court held that, even if the sole purpose of annexation was to promote the use of the land by the tenant for agriculture, the annexed structures could not be regarded as trade fixtures. It refused to create a new category of fixture that the tenant could remove. This decision upheld the expropriation of the labour, or capital, of improving tenants and failed to extend the new category of trade fixtures to agricultural tenants. The position was remedied only by the Landlord and Tenant Act 1851 which gave agricultural tenants the right to remove fixtures, subject to the landlord's right to elect to buy them.

Deasy's Act s.17
20–261 Section 17 of Deasy's Act partially codified this area of the law in Ireland by providing as follows:

"Personal chattels, engines, and machinery, and buildings accessorial thereto, erected and affixed to the freehold by the tenant at his sole expense, for any purpose of trade, manufacture, or agriculture, or for ornament or for the domestic convenience of the tenant in his occupation of the demised premises, and so attached to the freehold that they can be removed without substantial damage to the freehold or to the fixture itself, and which shall

---

[368] *Webb v Bevis* [1940] 1 All E.R. 247.
[369] *Spyer v Phillipson* [1931] 2 Ch. 183.
[370] (1889) 23 L.R. Ir. 181.
[371] *Spyer v Phillipson* [1931] 2 Ch. 183.
[372] (1802) 3 East 38.

not have been so erected or affixed in pursuance of any obligation or in violation of any agreement in that behalf, may be removed by the tenant, or his executors or administrators, during the tenancy, or when the tenancy determines by some uncertain event, and without the act or default of the tenant, within two calendar months ... except so far as may be otherwise specially provided by the contract of tenancy; provided that the landlord shall be entitled to reasonable compensation for any damage occasioned to the premises by such removal."

20–262 Some points of difference with the common law position should be noted. The section only applies where the fixture is attached at the tenant's sole expense. Damage to the fixture itself is also relevant. It is unclear to what extent the common law still applies where Deasy's Act does not. It must do so to some extent since the Act does not define the terms used in the section and reference would probably have to be made to case law where words such as "affixed" or "domestic convenience" are employed in a tenancy agreement in the context of items claimed as removable fixtures.

20–263 Head 20 of the LTLRB 2011 provides that the "tenant's property" includes:

"any property, whether affixed or not,—

(a) brought onto,
(b) erected upon, or
(c) installed in, on or under, the premises by the tenant or the tenant's pre-decessor in title."

20–264 It goes on to state that "ownership of the tenant's property remains vested in the tenant but without prejudice to any hiring or leasing agreement or other agreement entered into by the tenant or the tenant's predecessor with the landlord or a third party with respect to such property." This reverses the common law rule that a tenant's fixtures belong to the landlord so long as affixed to the premises and until the tenant exercises the right of removal. Head 21 of the Bill provides that the tenant may exercise the "right of removal" at any time during the continuance of the tenancy, or at the latest upon vacation of the premises. This is subject to the tenant making good or compensating the landlord for any damage to the premises. Under the Bill, where the tenancy is, without act or default by the tenant, unexpectedly terminated, the right of removal may be exercised within two months after the date of such termination, or upon vacation of the premises before expiry of that period.

ENFORCEMENT OF COVENANTS

Original Parties
Action

20–265 As there is privity of contract between the original parties to the tenancy, each may sue the other in contract for a breach of covenants. In addition to this common law right, s.45 of Deasy's Act gives a statutory right to a landlord to sue for rent in arrears. Section 46 gives the right to a grantor of an interest in land, where no rent is specified, to sue for "reasonable satisfaction" for use and occupation. Under s.48, the tenant can set off in an action for recovery of rent "all just debts" owed him or her by the landlord.

20–266 The principle in s.45 of Deasy's Act is preserved in the LTLRB 2011.[373] The Bill extends and clarifies the law relating to "set-off" contained in s.48.

Distress

20–267 The remedy of distress traditionally vested in landlords is another example in the law of landlord and tenant of rules imported by analogy to the old law of freehold tenure. At common law the landlord has the right, if the tenant fails to perform his or her obligations, to enter the premises and seize the chattels of the tenant and hold them as a pledge until the tenant performs the tenancy obligations.

20–268 Under a combination of s.5 of the Distress for Rent Act 1741 and s.5 of the Distress for Rent Act 1751 the landlord can sell the goods after eight days if they are not redeemed by then. Section 51 of Deasy's Act provides that no distress for rent may be levied where the rent payment is overdue for more than one year before making the distress. There are other restrictions on the remedy of distress.[374] It is odd that Deasy's Act assumes in s.51 that the remedy continued to exist at all after its enactment, in view of s.3, which states that the landlord and tenant relationship in Ireland does not depend any longer on tenure but on contract. The remedy of distress applied to that relationship by analogy to freehold tenure and is therefore an incident of tenure. The constitutional concerns about the applicability of distress to dwelling houses have been considered above.

20–269 In line with these concerns, Head 41(1) of the LTLRB 2011 states that "[i]n so far as it survives, the remedy of distress for rent is abolished."

---

[373] LTLRB 2011, Head 41: "The landlord or other person entitled to rent may bring an action in court to recover (a) any arrears of rent still recoverable, (b) where a tenancy has ended, rent up to the date of actual recovery of possession of the premises."

[374] J.C.W. Wylie, *Irish Land Law*, 5th edn (Haywards Heath: Bloomsbury Professional, 2013), para.19.73.

Forfeiture

20–270 A tenancy may be forfeited on account of failure by the tenant to comply with a covenant in the lease in which case the landlord has the right to terminate it by entry or action.[375]

Ejectment

20–271 Ejectment is the general term for an action by a landlord to recover possession of the premises let to a tenant. It takes various forms.

Residential Tenancies

20–272 A tenancy of a dwelling to which the RdTA 2004 applies is prohibited by s.58(1) from being terminated by means of forfeiture or re-entry or any other "process or procedure" not provided for by Pt 5 of the Acts. Either of the original parties to a tenancy has a contractual right to enforce the covenants. Section 78(1)(d) and (e) provide for the respective rights of landlord and tenant to refer a dispute in relation to non-compliance by the other party with his or her obligations under the tenancy to the conflict determination mechanism of the RTB. If the outcome of the matter results in a "determination order" from the RTB, this can, if not implemented by the party against whom it is directed, be enforced through the Circuit Court for the area in which the dwelling subject to the tenancy is situated.

Successors in Title

20–273 The question whether successors in title can enforce covenants in the original lease depends upon ss.12 and 13 of Deasy's Act. Since the basic principle of the Act, contained in s.3, was to place landlord and tenant relations on the basis of contract rather than on tenure, it was felt necessary to provide expressly that successors should be bound by covenants and able to enforce those for their own benefit. In *Lyle v Smith*[376] it was effectively held that these sections meant that all covenants bound successors except those that were not capable of "vicarious performance". By this expression, the court may have meant simply to indicate a distinction between covenants which refer to the land and are for the benefit of it, and which "run" with it as part of the property interest, and those which refer to some personal agreement between the original parties which, though included in the lease, are not for the benefit of the land and so do not "run". If that is so, then it is difficult to see any real distinction between the first category and covenants covered by the phrase "touch and concern", which was the test for the running of covenants before 1860. On the other hand, covenants also exist which are capable of vicarious performance but which are still personal in the sense that they are not for the benefit of the land as such. Under the interpretation of

---

[375] *Bank of Ireland v Lady Lisa Ireland Ltd* [1992] 1 I.R. 404; *Serjeant v Nash, Field & Co* [1903] 2 K.B. 304.
[376] [1909] 2 I.R. 58.

Deasy's Act in *Lyle v Smith* these covenants also would run so that they could be enforced by and against successors of the original contracting parties.

20–274 Head 16 of the LTLRB 2011 proposes to replace the duplicate provisions in ss.12 and 13 of Deasy's Act and ss.10 and 11 of the Conveyancing Act 1881. It assimilates the position of landlord and tenant so that successors of either party are in the same position, i.e. they step fully into the position of their predecessors in title.

ENDING THE RELATIONSHIP OF LANDLORD AND TENANT

Residential Tenancies
General
20–275 In the case of a tenancy to which the Residential Tenancies Acts 2004–2016 apply, the landlord or the tenant can terminate the tenancy only in accordance with the procedures set out in Pt 5 of the Acts and subject to giving the requisite notice. The termination and notice provisions set out in Pt 5 apply to all tenancies that fall within the ambit of the Acts, regardless of whether they are affected by the provisions of Pt 4.

20–276 A residential tenancy cannot be terminated "by means of a notice of forfeiture, a re-entry or any other process or procedure not provided by this Part."[377] Accordingly, the mode of termination of a tenancy provided for in Pt 5 supersedes all existing legislation and rules of law.[378] This means that every tenancy which falls within the Act is deemed to have an implied term enabling its termination in accordance with, and only in accordance with, Pt 5.

20–277 However, except where the tenancy agreement itself expressly provides otherwise, a tenancy for a fixed term cannot be terminated by notice unless the party on whom the notice has been served is in default of his or her obligations under the tenancy.[379] Notice is deemed to commence on the date following the date on which it has been served. References to the duration of a tenancy are deemed to be from either the date on which the tenancy

---

[377] RdTA 2004 s.58(1).

[378] RdTA 2004 s.59.

[379] RdTA 2004 s.58(3). *Canty v Private Residential Tenancies Board* [2007] IEHC 243. According to Laffoy J. (at para.34), the objective of s.58(3) is "to ensure that contractual rights of a tenant which are more beneficial than the statutory rights conferred by the Act of 2004 are not interfered with, an objective which is also given effect to in s.26, which provides that nothing in Part 4 shall derogate from rights enjoyed by the tenant which are more beneficial for the tenant than Part 4 rights." However, Laffoy J. also held that the existence of a "break clause" which permitted a landlord to terminate the tenancy on the grounds that he or she wished to occupy the dwelling subject to the tenancy prevented its being a fixed-term tenancy for the purposes of the Act.

commenced, or 1 September 2004, whichever is the later, until the date on which the notice was served.[380]

20–278 Section 62 sets out the formalities that must be complied with in order for a notice of termination to be valid:

- It must be in writing and be signed by the party giving the notice or that party's agent.
- It must specify the date on which the notice is being served, provided that all steps required to be taken to effectuate service have been taken by that date; if they have not been, the notice of termination will be invalid.[381]
- It must be in such form as may be prescribed.
- It must state the reason for the termination where the termination is by the landlord and the tenancy has lasted for six months or more, or if the tenancy is a further Part 4 tenancy.
- It must specify the termination date (including the day, month and year) and state that on or before that date the landlord will require vacant possession, indicating that the tenant will have the whole period of 24 hours of the termination date to vacate possession; provided that the correct period of notice has been given, the termination notice need not specify what that notice period is, but merely confirm the termination date.[382]
- It must state that any issue in relation to the validity of the notice or of the landlord's or tenant's right to give it must be referred to the RTB within 28 days of the receipt of the notice.[383]

Period of Notice
20–279 Except in those cases where abridged notice is allowed to be given, because one party is in default of that party's obligations under the tenancy, the period of notice required to be given with reference to the length of the tenancy is as follows[384]:

Duration of tenancy	Notice period by landlord	Notice period by tenant
Less than 6 months	28 days	28 days
6 months to 1 year	35 days	35 days
1 year to 2 years	42 days	42 days

---

[380] RdTA 2004 s.61.
[381] RdTA 2004 s.64, in particular subs.(3) read with s.62(1)(c). Section 64A provides that a slip or omission in the notice of termination shall not of itself render the notice of termination invalid.
[382] RdTA 2004 s.65(2).
[383] RdTA 2004 s.62(1)(g).
[384] RdTA 2004 s.66.

Duration of tenancy	Notice period by landlord	Notice period by tenant
2 years to 3 years	56 days	56 days
3 years to 4 years	84 days	56 days
4 years to 5 years	112 days	84 days
5 years to 6 years	140 days	84 days
6 years to 7 years	168 days	84 days
7 years to 8 years	196 days	84 days
8 or more years	224 days	112 days

20–280 The Residential Tenancies (Amendment) Bill 2018 purports to amend s.66 of the RdTA 2004 by extending these notice periods with respect to termination by landlords.[385]

20–281 Where the tenant is alleged to be behaving "in a way that is anti-social", as defined in s.17,[386] or is engaging in action which threatens the fabric of the dwelling subject to the tenancy or of the property which contains the dwelling, the landlord is required to give only seven days' notice.[387] In the case of any other breach or default by the tenant, the landlord must give 28 days' notice. An exception arises where that breach or default constitutes failure by the tenant to pay rent; where this arises, the landlord must:

- give preliminary written notice to the tenant that an amount of rent has not been paid, and
- allow 14 days from the date of the notice for the amount outstanding to be paid

before giving notice of termination of the tenancy.[388]

---

[385] Residential Tenancies (Amendment) Bill 2018 s.2. At the time of writing, this had not been enacted. The proposed new notice periods are as follows:

Duration of Tenancy	Notice Period by Landlord
Less than 6 months	90 days
6 months to 1 year	90 days
1 year to 2 years	120 days
2 years to 3 years	120 days
3 years to 4 years	120 days
4 years to 5 years	120 days
5 years to 6 years	140 days
6 years to 7 years	168 days
7 years to 8 years	196 days
8 or more years	224 days

[386] But not as defined in sub-para.(c), which appears therefore implicitly to be regarded as a lesser degree of "anti-social behaviour".

[387] RdTA 2004 s.67(1) and (2)(a).

[388] RdTA 2004 s.67(2)(b) and (3). See *Canty v Private Residential Tenancies Board* [2007] IEHC 243 per Laffoy J. at para.9.

20–282 Where a tenant is giving notice of termination of a tenancy to the land-lord, the notice period will be seven days if the ground of termination is that the behaviour of the landlord "poses an imminent danger of death or serious injury or imminent danger to the fabric of the dwelling or the property containing the dwelling".[389] Otherwise, the notice period is 28 days, but the tenant must first notify the landlord in writing of the default and allow the landlord reasonable time to remedy it. This remedying can constitute either desisting from the behaviour complained of, or rectifying an omission, or compensating the ten-ant, or some combination of all three, depending on the circumstances.[390]

20–283 A lesser period of notice than that required in Pt 5 may be agreed between the landlord and tenant, but only *after* the one party has indicated to the other that he or she intends to terminate the tenancy. An agreement to give or accept such lesser notice cannot be contained in the lease or tenancy agreement. In other words, it is not possible to "contract out" of the minimum statutory notice periods prior to one party indicating that it wishes to terminate the tenancy.[391]

20–284 Nothing will prevent the parties to a tenancy from agreeing a greater period of notice than that specified in Pt 5, except that if the tenancy has lasted for less than six months, notice of more than 70 days cannot be required to be given.[392]

Sub-tenancies

20–285 If a landlord serves a notice of termination on a tenant, and the tenant's tenancy is subject to a sub-tenancy, the landlord must state in the notice of ter-mination whether he or she requires the tenant to terminate the sub-tenancy.[393]

Where the Landlord Requires the Sub-tenancy to Be Terminated

20–286 Where the landlord requires the tenant to terminate the sub-tenancy, a copy of the notice of termination served by the landlord on the tenant must also be served by the landlord on the sub-tenant.[394] If the tenant *does not* intend to refer a dispute regarding the termination to the RTB, the landlord must, within 28 days of receipt of notice of termination of the tenancy, serve on the sub-tenant a notice of termination of the sub-tenancy.[395]

20–287 However, if the head-tenant intends to refer the matter to the RTB, the head-tenant must in the notice which he or she serves on the sub-tenant

---

[389] RdTA 2004 s.68(1) and (2)(a).
[390] RdTA 2004 s.68(1), (2)(b), (3) and (4).
[391] RdTA 2004 s.69.
[392] RdTA 2004 ss.60 and 65(4).
[393] RdTA 2004 s.70(1) and (2).
[394] RdTA 2004 s.70(3).
[395] RdTA 2004 s.71.

terminating the tenancy, require the sub-tenant to notify the head-tenant, within 10 days of the receipt of that notice, whether the sub-tenant intends to refer any dispute regarding the termination to the RTB. If the sub-tenant does not comply with this requirement, the sub-tenant will be disentitled to refer such dispute.[396] Similarly, if the head-tenant does not require the sub-tenant to notify him or her of the sub-tenant's intentions, neither may the head-tenant refer a dispute regarding the termination to the RTB.[397]

Where the Landlord Does Not Require the Sub-tenancy to Be Terminated
20–288 Where the notice of termination served by the landlord on the tenant *does not* require termination of the sub-tenancy,[398] then:

- if the tenant *does not* refer a dispute regarding the termination to the RTB, he or she must, within 28 days of receiving the notice of termination, advise the sub-tenant of its contents;
- if the tenant *does* refer a dispute regarding the termination to the RTB, he or she must, within 28 days of receiving the notice of termination, advise the sub-tenant of its contents and also of the fact that a dispute has been referred to the RTB *and* also forward to the sub-tenant a copy of the RTB's "determination order" within 14 days of the tenant's receiving it.

Multiple Tenants
20–289 Section 48(1) of the RdTA 2004 defines "multiple tenants" as persons who are tenants with each other of a dwelling "whether as joint tenants, tenants-in-common or under any other form of co-ownership". The concept has particular relevance in the context of a "Part 4 tenancy".

20–290 Where a dwelling under tenancy is occupied by multiple tenants, a notice in writing, signed by one of the multiple tenants, purporting to be on behalf of himself or herself and all the other multiple tenants, and setting out the names of the other multiple tenants in the notice, will suffice to terminate the tenancy on behalf of all the multiple tenants.[399] However, if the tenancy is a periodic tenancy, and the multiple tenant or tenants who have not signed are either unaware of the notice of termination, or have not agreed to it, then the notice of termination will not be effective.[400]

Invalid Notice
20–291 A person who gives notice of termination of a tenancy which does not comply with the Pt 5 requirements, and then purports to act in reliance upon

---

[396] RdTA 2004 ss.62(2) and 81(2)–(4).
[397] RdTA 2004 s.81(5).
[398] RdTA 2004 s.72.
[399] RdTA 2004 s.73(1) and (2).
[400] RdTA 2004 s.73(3).

this invalid notice in a way that adversely affects the party to whom the notice is given, is guilty of an offence. A person is deemed to act in reliance upon an invalid termination notice if that person states that he or she is so acting or will so act, or under the circumstances acting in reliance upon the invalid notice may reasonably be inferred. It will be a defence to a prosecution that the party giving the notice could not reasonably have been expected to know that it was, in fact, invalid.[401]

Expiry

20–292 Where the tenancy is for a fixed term the relationship of landlord and tenant will naturally come to an end when the term expires. Periodic tenancies, on the other hand, will continue indefinitely unless terminated by notice to quit. Section 17 of the Statute of Limitations 1957 provides that a tenancy at will is deemed to terminate one year after it began.[402]

20–293 The same section deems a tenancy from year to year or for other successive periods "without a lease in writing" to terminate at the end of the first year or other successive period, at which time a right of action for possession accrues unless rent is paid subsequently.

20–294 In *Foreman v Mowlds*[403] a written agreement was made in 1907 creating a tenancy from year to year. Since 1922, M and later his successors in title had remained in possession without paying rent. The issue before the court was as to whether M or his successors had acquired title by adverse possession. They could only have done so if the periodic tenancy had terminated at least 12 years prior to action in the 1980s, after which the possession had become adverse to the landlord's title. Barrington J. found that the Statute of Limitations 1957 gave no assistance to the question. He held that M's successors had good title because the tenancy had ended "probably" in 1922 when M had stopped paying rent.

20–295 In *Sauerzweig v Feeney*[404] the parties entered into a weekly tenancy in writing. The tenant had not paid rent since 1950. In 1956 the tenant offered to pay rent but was dissuaded from doing so by the landlord's solicitor because the tenant was negotiating to buy the landlord's reversion. The landlord demanded rent on three occasions between 1977 and 1981. The tenant claimed he had acquired the landlord's title by adverse possession. The Supreme Court noted that s.17 did not apply to periodic tenancies in writing. *Foreman v Mowlds* was not cited. However, the Supreme Court in *Sauerzweig* held that the tenancy had not been abandoned in view of the landlord's repeated demands for rent and that it did not in fact end until the landlord served notice

---

[401] RdTA 2004 s.74.
[402] The tenancy at will and tenancy at sufferance were abolished by s.11(3) of the LCLRA 2009.
[403] Unreported, High Court, Barrington J., 28 January 1985.
[404] [1986] I.R. 224.

to quit in 1982. The court held that the landlord had lost the right to rent due for more than six years under s.28 of the Statute of Limitations. The rationale behind s.17 seems to be that, where there is a lease in writing the parties may provide for the original period to be renewed for a maximum number of times, or for some other ultimate term, but if they do not do so the tenancy may be terminated by notice to quit in any case. If the parties do not choose to insert an express provision the legislature seems to have taken the view that it is not necessary for statute law to intervene. The appropriate remedy of the landlord where the tenancy has expired and the tenant has not vacated the premises is an ejectment action for overholding. Section 72 of Deasy's Act provides that any tenant who "wilfully" holds over is liable to pay double rent for the period of overholding, but this is rarely claimed in practice.[405] Courts would be reluctant to hold that the overholding was "wilful".

Non-Payment of Rent and Adverse Possession

20–296 If the tenant fails to pay rent then this may give rise to a forfeiture, provided there is an express clause to that effect in the lease or tenancy agreement.

20–297 If a tenant holds over after the end of a lease for a fixed term, then he or she becomes what used to be called a tenant at sufferance and is in adverse possession.[406]

20–298 Termination can also arise where a tenant fails to pay rent and the landlord takes no action to seek forfeiture of the lease, so that the tenant's continued possession becomes adverse to the landlord's title and may in time extinguish it. There is judicial authority to the effect that when a tenant under a periodic tenancy ceases to pay rent, the law presumes that the tenancy has come to an end and that the tenant is thereafter in adverse possession. But the varying facts of decided cases do not make this proposition universal. For example, in *Re Shanahan*[407] the Supreme Court held that non-payment of rent had merely barred claims to the rent due for more than six years and did not make the possession of the tenant adverse to the title of the landlord. The parties had, however, remained in a debtor/creditor relationship for 20 years, which Ó Dálaigh C.J. held negated "any presumption of the determination of the tenancy that might otherwise arise from the non-payment of rent." *Re Shanahan* was cited to the court in *Foreman v Mowlds*[408] which distinguished it on the ground that in the instant case there were no circumstances to negate the presumption that non-payment of rent had rendered the tenant's possession adverse. This holding is an alternative *ratio* to the one found not to be applicable in *Sauerzweig*

---

[405] Deasy's Act s.76.
[406] Since 1833: *Doe d Bennett v Turner* (1840) 7 M. & W. 226; *Remon v City of London Real Property Co Ltd* [1921] 1 K.B. 49.
[407] Unreported, Supreme Court, 5 July 1968.
[408] Unreported, High Court, Barrington J., 28 January 1985.

v Feeney,[409] i.e. that the tenancy had determined under s.17 of the Statute of Limitations 1957. In *Sauerzweig* the court held that the tenancy had been determined by notice to quit and therefore, impliedly, not by adverse possession following from non-payment of rent, although there were grounds on which it could have held that the presumption of the tenant's possession becoming adverse following prolonged non-payment of rent had been negated: namely, the continued demands of the landlord. The court did not cite *Re Shanahan* or *Foreman*. Hence, despite the outcome in that case the presumption probably survives the decision in *Sauerzweig*.

20–299 Non-payment of rent over a long period may give rise to other presumptions, such as that the rent has been paid[410] or, in suitable cases, redeemed,[411] or the term enlarged, although the cases on these points may have to be reviewed in the light of *Re Shanahan* and *Sauerzweig*. In *Atkins v Atkins*[412] it was held that where rent in a lease had remained unclaimed for 40 years, the court could assume that it had been redeemed as a ground rent or under other applicable legislation.[413] The court refused to presume that the lease had been enlarged into a fee simple under s.65 of the Conveyancing Act 1881, even though there is authority to the effect that such a presumption can be made where the lease fell within the terms of the section either when rent ceased to be paid, or at some time during the period of non-payment of rent.[414]

Notice to Quit
20–300 A lease may provide for termination by notice by either party. When a tenancy is terminated by the landlord he or she is said to give the tenant notice to quit the premises. Since periodic tenancies will not terminate by expiry, the common law provided that they may be terminated by notice after certain established periods.

20–301 In the case of a weekly tenancy the period was one week,[415] and in the case of a monthly tenancy, one month. In the case of a yearly tenancy the period at common law was six months. However, s.1 of the Notice to Quit (Ireland) Act 1870 provides that in the case of agricultural or pastoral holdings[416] (which, as a result of the Land Purchase legislation, are now rare), the period of notice is one year, unless there is an agreement to the contrary.[417]

---

[409] [1986] I.R. 224.

[410] *Courtney v Parker* (1866) 16 Ir. Ch. R. 320 at 338.

[411] *Atkins v Atkins* [1976–77] I.L.R.M. 62.

[412] [1976–77] I.L.R.M. 62.

[413] Citing *Lefroy v Walsh* (1852) 1 Ir. C.L.R. 311.

[414] *Re Waugh* [1943] Ir. Jur. Rep. 50; *Blaiberg v Keeves* [1906] 2 Ch. 175.

[415] *Harvey v Copeland* (1892) 30 L.R. Ir. 412.

[416] Notice to Quit (Ireland) Act 1870 s.5. It also applies to partly agricultural and partly pastoral holdings.

[417] Except where the tenant has been adjudged bankrupt or has made an agreement with his or her creditors.

The year's notice must expire on any gale day of the calendar year in which the rent becomes due. The section also provides that the landlord, having given notice, may waive the right to possession by accepting rent after the period has expired. The section does not affect weekly or monthly tenancies or tenancies at will,[418] or yearly tenancies for other than agricultural or pastoral purposes. However, the 1992 Act, which primarily applies to social housing and so-called "shared ownership leases" between tenants and housing authorities, provides, in s.16(1):

> "Subject to *subsections (2)* and *(3)*, a notice by a landlord or a tenant to the other of termination of the tenancy of a house let for rent or other valuable consideration shall not be valid unless it is in writing and is served not less than four weeks before the date on which it is to take effect."

20–302 "House" includes "any building or part of a building used or suitable for use as a dwelling and any outoffice, yard, garden or other land appurtenant thereto or usually enjoyed therewith". Subsection (2) provides that the section shall not apply:

(a) to the tenancy of a house let to a person in connection with any office, appointment or employment;

(b) to a tenancy let *bona fide* for temporary convenience or to meet a temporary necessity;

(c) to a holiday tenancy; or

(d) to such other classes of tenancies prescribed by the Minister for the Environment under the section.

20–303 Nothing prevents any provision in a contract or other rule of law prescribing a greater period of notice.[419]

20–304 The effect of s.16 of the 1992 Act on the common law periods appears to be to lengthen the period of notice required in the case of a tenancy of residential premises to which the Act applies to one month where the period of notice would otherwise be less than one month, i.e. where the tenancy was for a period less than one month or was a periodic tenancy for periods less than one month.[420] Where such premises are let on a yearly basis, the common law period of six months still applies. Where the land is agricultural or pastoral, the one-year period in the Notice to Quit (Ireland) Act 1870 still applies unless, as the Act provides, there is agreement to the contrary. This appears to override an express term in a tenancy specifying any period of notice less than one

---

[418] Notice to Quit (Ireland) Act 1870 s.2.

[419] Housing (Miscellaneous Provisions) Act 1992 s.16(3).

[420] The period of notice at common law in respect of a monthly tenancy was already one month. The preponderance of residential tenancies to which the Housing (Miscellaneous Provisions) Act 1992 does not apply are covered, in terms of notice of termination, by the RdTA 2004 Pt 5.

month. Section 16 of the 1992 Act applies to a notice to terminate a tenancy by a landlord to a tenant as well as by a tenant to the landlord. An issue which may arise is whether a landlord or a tenant may waive his or her right to a month's notice. However, as has been noted, s.16 of the 1992 Act does not apply to a tenancy to which the RdTA 2004 applies.[421]

20–305 The appropriate remedy of the landlord where a tenant continues in occupation after a notice to quit is ejectment for overholding.

Surrender

20–306 Section 7 of Deasy's Act provides that a tenancy may be surrendered to the landlord by deed or writing signed by the tenant or his or her agent authorised in writing or by act or operation of law. Where a purported surrender does not comply with s.7 it may nevertheless operate as surrender by operation of law as the landlord or tenant may be estopped from pleading the absence of formalities. The broad basis on which this would be approached was succinctly set out by Brady C.B. in *Lynch v Lynch*[422]:

> "A surrender by act and operation of law I think may properly be stated to be a surrender effected by the construction put by the courts on the acts of the parties, in order to give to those acts the effect substantially intended by them; and when the courts see that the acts of the parties cannot have any operation, except by holding that a surrender has taken place, they hold it to have taken place accordingly."

20–307 Accordingly, surrender of a lease can be inferred by the simple expedient of the tenant vacating and the landlord taking possession[423]; or by the tenant vacating and returning the landlord's keys.[424] On the other hand, in the case of a commercial tenancy, even if the tenant has moved out a considerable amount of stock and equipment, a surrender cannot be inferred if the landlord does not understand that the tenant is indicating an intention to surrender. Nor if the tenant has indicated that it would be prepared to vacate the premises for a consideration, if the landlord has not indicated a willingness to pay for vacant possession.[425]

20–308 Head 53 of the LTLRB 2011 would retain the principle stated in s.7 of Deasy's Act.

---

[421] RdTA 2004 s.193(e).
[422] (1843) 6 Ir. L.R. 131.
[423] *Foley v Mangan* [2009] IEHC 404.
[424] *Cosmoline Trading Ltd v DH Burke and Co Ltd and DHB Holdings Ltd* [2006] IEHC 38.
[425] *Cosmoline Trading Ltd v DH Burke and Co Ltd and DHB Holdings Ltd* [2006] IEHC 38.

Forfeiture
Express Clause
20–309 If the lease contains a proviso for re-entry on breach of condition, or what is called a "forfeiture clause", then either a right of entry, which may be enforced either by actual entry on the premises or by legal action, will be created in the event of the breach, or a forfeiture will occur, which may be enforced by action. Regardless of how the clause is worded, the tenancy will not determine automatically on the breach of the term: the lease is merely voidable at the landlord's option. This is because a tenant cannot rely on his or her own breach to terminate the tenancy.

20–310 In *Bank of Ireland v Lady Lisa Ireland Ltd*[426] the plaintiff landlord had purported to determine a tenancy by serving on the tenant a "notice of re-entry and forfeiture" reciting that the rent due had not been paid. The defendant tenant contended that this was insufficient to determine the tenancy and this contention was upheld in the High Court. There must either be an *actual* entry, or some act which sets in motion an action for possession based on a valid claim. The judge cited Collins M.R. in *Serjeant v Nash, Field & Co*[427]:

> "There is a final determination of a tenancy under a lease when the lessor, by some final and positive act which cannot be retracted, treats a breach of covenant by the lessee as constituting a forfeiture".

20–311 O'Hanlon J. added that the ineffective notice "need not be fatal to the plaintiff's case if the procedure followed thereafter was effective of itself to forfeit the lease and set in motion a valid claim for an order for possession". He held further that the present proceedings, which were for possession on the ground of non-payment of rent under s.52 of Deasy's Act, and were by summary summons, were inappropriate where the landlord's claim was based on forfeiture.[428] In *Minister for Communications, Marine and Natural Resources v Figary Water Sports Development Co Ltd*,[429] the Supreme Court accepted these statements as a correct account of the law.

Condition Subsequent
20–312 The question can arise whether the term in the tenancy that has been broken is a condition subsequent. If it is interpreted as a condition subsequent, the position is analogous to a conditional fee. It is as if the grantor had granted the land

> *to A for N years, on condition that ...*

---

[426] [1992] 1 I.R. 404.
[427] [1903] 2 K.B. 304.
[428] Citing *Keating v Mulcahy* [1926] I.R. 214.
[429] [2015] IESC 74 at para.24. See also *McIlvenny v McKeever* [1931] N.I. 161 at 172.

The breach of the condition will give rise to a right of re-entry at common law or a "right" of forfeiture in equity, subject to the jurisdiction of equity to grant relief against forfeiture. A right of entry is an old-fashioned remedy since it relies on self-help by the landlord, which makes it open to abuse. For this reason a number of restrictions on the exercise of a right have been developed by the law to prevent abuse by the landlord.

20–313 Where a right of entry exists, s.14(1) of the Conveyancing Act 1881 provides that the lessor must serve notice on the lessee before the right is exercised, whether by actual entry or by action, such notice to specify the breach and require it to be remedied if possible, and also requiring the tenant to make monetary compensation for the breach.[430] It is not necessary for the forfeiture notice to claim a specific sum in compensation.[431] Reasonable time must be allowed to the tenant to rectify the alleged breach of covenant before forfeiture can occur; however, the notice to the tenant specifying the breach need not itself set out the time limit in which the breach is to be rectified.[432] Ideally, the relevant time period allowed for rectifying the alleged breach is that which elapses between the date of the forfeiture notice and the attempt by the landlord to enforce the forfeiture, whether by action or entry: if a time period set out in the notice is believed by the tenant to be too short, it is open to the tenant to protest that fact to the landlord and seek an extension of time or else to argue its inadequacy in an application to court for relief against forfeiture.[433] If, however, the tenant demonstrates an unwillingness to rectify the breach complained of within a reasonable period, or at all, the landlord will be deemed to have allowed sufficient time to elapse once it has become apparent that the tenant does not intend to rectify the breach.[434]

The Entry
20–314 A number of ancient statutes sought to prevent the use of force by the landlord in gaining entry to the land, but these have now been replaced by the Prohibition of Forcible Entry and Occupation Act 1971. Section 2 makes it a criminal offence to use force to enter land or a vehicle unless the person entering (a) is the owner of the land or vehicle, or (b) if he or she is not the owner, does not interfere with the use and enjoyment of the land or vehicle, or (c) has a bona fide claim of right. Section 1 provides that "owner" in relation to land includes, inter alia, the lawful occupier, every person lawfully entitled to the immediate use and enjoyment of unoccupied land, and any person having "an

---

[430] Section 14 does not apply to non-payment of rent. This is specified in subs.(8). Section 14 was retained by the LCLRA 2009.
[431] *McIlvenny v McGeever* [1931] N.I. 161; *Silvester v Ostrowska* [1959] 3 All E.R. 642; *Crofter v Genport* [2002] IEHC 94.
[432] *Campus and Stadium Ireland Developments Ltd v Dublin Waterworld Ltd* [2006] IEHC 200.
[433] *Foley v Mangan* [2009] IEHC 404 at paras 29–30.
[434] *Billson v Residential Apartments Ltd (No.1)* [1991] 3 All E.R. 265, cited with approval by Laffoy J. in *Foley v Mangan* [2009] IEHC 404.

estate or interest in land".[435] Section 1(5) provides that nothing in the Act shall be regarded as conferring on any person any right to entry upon or occupation of land which did not exist immediately before the Act. In *Dooley v Attorney General*[436] the Supreme Court held, interpreting the statute as a whole, that a person having an estate or interest only qualifies as an "owner" within the Act if he or she has an immediate right to possession of the land and hence a right to enter it. "Owner" does not include a mortgagee or a reversioner unless the mortgagee or reversioner enjoys such a right of entry.

Relief against Forfeiture

20–315 It has long been held in Ireland that a tenant has the right to invoke the jurisdiction of equity to grant relief against forfeiture of a lease.[437] In *Walsh v Wightman* Andrews L.J. explained that "the policy of the law in modern times has been against the enforcement of forfeitures when the breach relied upon can be remedied, pecuniary compensation awarded, and adequate undertaking given to prevent a recurrence of the breach".[438] If equity grants relief against the forfeiture then the common law right of entry cannot be enforced.

20–316 At common law a forfeiture of a lease also destroyed all sub-leases, even though the sub-lessees were not in breach of their covenants.[439] This result seems to have been purely the effect of reifying the concept of "estate". If the estate on which the sub-estates depended was destroyed, went the reasoning, so were the sub-estates. This outcome illustrates the dangers of reification in that it ignored the reality of property as a set of relations between persons and ignored also therefore the rights and wrongs of the issue. A sub-tenant could, however, obtain relief in equity, in the case of the tenant being sued in eject-ment for non-payment of rent, by paying the rent due.[440] Sections 4 and 5 of the Conveyancing Act 1892 reformed the law by providing that a sub-lessee has a statutory right to apply to the court for relief. The court may order the term of the lease to be vested in the sub-tenant.

20–317 Relief against forfeiture can also be sought by a tenant under s.14(2) of the Conveyancing Act 1881. This entitles a lessee to apply to court for relief against forfeiture where the lessor is seeking to enforce his or her right of re-entry or forfeiture by action or otherwise. It gives the court broad discre-tion when dealing with that application. The court may grant or refuse relief

---

[435] In *Sweeney v Powerscourt Shopping Centre* [1984] I.R. 501, the defendants entered premises let to a tenant using a master key, after a notice under the Conveyancing Act 1881 s.14 had been issued. Carroll J. held that they had not violated the law in doing so as they had entered peacefully.

[436] [1977] I.R. 205.

[437] *Malone v Geraghty* (1843) 5 Ir. Eq. R. 549 citing the Irish House of Lords in *Berney v Moore* (1791) 2 Ridg. P.C. 310; *Breaden v Fuller & Son* [1949] I.R. 290.

[438] [1927] N.I. 1 at 9.

[439] *Dowding v Commissioner of Charitable Donations and Bequests* (1862) 12 Ir. Ch. R. 361.

[440] *Berney v Moore* (1791) 2 Ridg. P.C. 310.

as it thinks fit "having regard to the proceedings and conduct of the parties under the foregoing provisions of this section, and to all other circumstances". Furthermore, the court may grant relief "on such terms, if any, as to costs, expenses, damages, compensation, penalty or otherwise, including the granting of an injunction to restrain any like breach in the future, as the Court, in the circumstances of each case, thinks fit".

20–318 According to Laffoy J. in *Foley v Mangan*,[441] even though

> "the relief is granted under statutory powers, it seems clear from the word-ing of the sub-section that the jurisdiction is discretionary and is to be exer-cised largely on the same principles as the general equitable jurisdiction to afford relief which may be invoked in cases of forfeiture for non-payment of rent".[442]

This is consistent with the overall approach taken by the courts, which is not to fetter the exercise of judicial discretion in relation to the granting of statutory relief against forfeiture by the introduction of rules or restrictions governing how the discretion is to be exercised. Otherwise, as explained by Lord Lore-burn L.C. in *Hyman v Rose*,

> "the free discretion given by the statute would be fettered by limitations which have nowhere been enacted. It is one thing to decide what is the true meaning of the language contained in an Act of Parliament. It is quite a dif-ferent thing to place conditions upon a free discretion entrusted by statute to the Court where the conditions are not based upon statutory enactment at all".[443]

20–319 In *Campus and Stadium Ireland Development Ltd v Dublin Water-world Ltd*,[444] Gilligan J. set out a number of factors to be taken into account in deciding whether or not to grant relief against forfeiture to a tenant:

> "I take the overall view that in order to exercise my discretion fairly, I must take into account the conduct of the parties, the wilfulness of any breach by the tenant, the general circumstances particular to the issue, the nature of the commercial transaction the subject matter of the lease, whether the essentials of the bargain can be secured, the value of the property, the extent of equality between the parties, the future prospects for their relationship, the fact that even in cases of wilful breaches it is not necessary to find an exceptional case before granting relief against forfeiture and then apply general equitable principles in reaching a conclusion."

---

[441] [2009] IEHC 404, citing J.C.W. Wylie, *Landlord and Tenant Law*, 2nd edn (Dublin: Blooms-bury Professional, 1998).
[442] *Foley v Mangan* [2009] IEHC 404 at para.41.
[443] [1912] A.C. 623 at 630.
[444] [2006] IEHC 200 at para.64.

20–320 The courts may adopt a more rigorous approach to the granting of relief against forfeiture in the case of a commercial tenancy "where the parties were on equal terms and each had the benefit of legal, financial and other material advice".[445] This was Murphy J.'s view in *Cue Club Ltd v Navaro Ltd*[446]:

"The nature of the discretion exercised by the Courts of Equity in granting relief against forfeiture is hardly applicable or applicable to the same extent, at any rate where the Court is dealing with substantial commercial transactions in which the lessor and lessee are on equal terms."

20–321 On the other hand, where the tenancy itself constitutes part only of a series of complicated commercial arrangements it is apt for the court to consider the *bona fides* of the landlord in seeking to forfeit the tenancy and resisting an application for relief by the tenant. In *Foley v Mangan*[447] the parties had an intricate commercial relationship, which involved, first, the sale of his land by the later lessee to the later lessor, and then the granting back to the vendor of a lease of the land for a term of less than five years, with an option by the lessee to re-purchase the land subject to strict compliance with conditions as to time limits provided also that the lease had not been forfeited. Accordingly, the granting of relief against forfeiture was of crucial importance to the lessee even though, at the time of the hearing, the term of the lease had expired. In Laffoy J.'s view, it was relevant to the question of the exercise of judicial discretion whether the lessor was genuinely motivated, in seeking to forfeit the lease, by anxiety to ensure compliance with covenants, or was instead seeking to deny to the lessee one of the necessary conditions for the exercise of the option to re-purchase the land under lease that had formerly been owned by him. As the evidence adduced was consistent with this consideration being at least a motivating factor, the court granted the sought relief, but on condition that the lessee complied strictly with the time limits for exercising the option, rectified all breaches of covenant and paid for the costs of the action. Relief against forfeiture may also be granted where the landlord has been guilty of laches in acting on the notice.[448]

20–322 The breadth of the court's discretion is well illustrated by Charleton J.'s decision in *The Leopardstown Club Ltd v Templeville Developments Ltd.*[449] There, the parties to a lease had undertaken a process of mediation to resolve a complex dispute between them. This resulted in a mediation agreement under which the defendant agreed to pay an increased rent on its lease. The plaintiff

---

[445] [2006] IEHC 200 at para.74.

[446] Unreported, Supreme Court, 23 October 1996, p.14. See also *Sweeney v Powerscourt Shopping Centre Ltd* [1984] I.R. 501.

[447] [2009] IEHC 404.

[448] *Minister for Communications v Figary Watersports Development Co Ltd* [2010] IEHC 541 at para.120. This judgment was appealed to the Supreme Court (see [2015] IESC 74), but the court did not decide the point.

[449] [2013] IEHC 526.

claimed that the defendant was in fundamental breach of the mediation agreement in a number of respects and in particular claimed that it had not paid rent due under the agreement to the plaintiff landlord. The defendant pursued a complex counterclaim which proved unsuccessful at first instance.[450] In considering the question of forfeiture of the defendant's lease, Charleton J. considered the corporate governance arrangements of the defendant company. Describing the company as "dysfunctional", Charleton J. granted the company a four-week stay of forfeiture in order to restructure the company's internal corporate governance arrangements. The court expressed the view that at least two new directors needed to be appointed to counteract the influence of one of the original directors and also expressed the view that the board should meet on at least a monthly basis. Subject to these matters being resolved, the court held that the forfeiture of the lease could be left in abeyance. In a subsequent judgment,[451] Charleton J. granted relief against forfeiture noting that the company had cleared the arrears of rent due and that "extra directors of excellent experience" had agreed to join its board.

Forfeiture for Non-Payment of Rent

20–323 At common law a landlord could only bring ejectment for failure to pay rent where the lease contained an express clause for forfeiture in this event.[452] The effect of the clause was to make the lease subject to a condition subsequent and the right to recover possession rested on the ending of the tenancy by the condition rather than from the failure to pay rent in itself.

20–324 In Ireland, a number of Acts were passed before Deasy's Act which strengthened the legal position of landlords as against tenants by imposing terms in tenancies favourable to landlords. The Acts were known collectively as the "Ejectment Code". The Ejectment Code "gradually removed every formality by which the old Common Law delayed and obstructed the forfeiture of the tenant's estate."[453] Courts of equity could nevertheless grant relief to tenants against ejectment under the code.[454] Landlords were given the right to bring ejectment proceedings after one whole year's rent was in arrears, regardless of whether the tenancy contained a clause for forfeiture, but the provision only applied where there was a written agreement.[455] This created an anomaly,

---

[450] This aspect of the judgment was successfully appealed to the Court of Appeal: see *Leopardstown Club Ltd v Templeville Developments Ltd* [2015] IECA 164. The Supreme Court ([2017] IESC 50) ultimately restored the High Court's decision holding that the Court of Appeal had exceeded its jurisdiction in overturning the findings of fact made by the trial judge. The forfeiture issues were not considered before the Court of Appeal or the Supreme Court.

[451] [2013] IEHC 529.

[452] Although, as was noted by Laffoy J. in *Foley v Mangan* [2009] IEHC 404 at para.21, this requirement was frequently dispensed with, by agreement between the parties, through inclusion in the re-entry clause of the words "whether formally demanded or not".

[453] C.F. Kolbert and T. O'Brien, *Land Reform in Ireland: A Legal History of the Irish Land Problem and its Settlement* (Cambridge: Cambridge University Press, 1975), p.31.

[454] *Berney v Moore* (1791) 2 Ridg. P.C. 310.

[455] 5 Geo II c 4 s.1 (Ir); 25 Geo II c 13 s.2 (Ir).

from the landlord's point of view, as to tenancies from year to year, which were a common form of holding in agricultural tenancies. Such tenancies would only come within the statutory ejectment code if they were in writing, and many were not. In such a case, the landlord could only determine the tenancy by notice to quit and he could lose two and a half years' rent.[456] A further statute[457] remedied this by extending statutory ejectment to landlords of holdings let orally for a low rent.

20–325 Deasy's Act replaced these provisions by an even more extensive one. Section 52 gives a statutory remedy of ejectment to a landlord where land is held under a fee farm grant, lease or other contract of tenancy or from year to year and whether by writing or otherwise. Thus, despite the pretensions of the Act to base tenancies on contract, it failed to do so when this would mean taking rights away from landlords, and here it actually extended them.

20–326 In *Chester v Beary*[458] it was held that the rent in arrears need not be an unbroken year's rent. It is enough that the total amount of rent due is equal to that of a year's rent. Section 53 provides that a demand by the landlord is not required here before the action is brought. Under ground rent legislation,[459] s.52 no longer applies where the tenant of a dwelling house has the right to acquire the fee simple, i.e. it no longer applies to a "ground rent" of a dwelling house as defined by statute. A tenant who has such a right is clearly in a different position to other tenants: the legal form here does not fit the social perception of them or their substantive rights. It would not be sensible to allow a landlord to evict a tenant who had the right to acquire the landlord's interest and therefore be put back in to possession within a short time. On the other hand, a tenant who exercises his or her right to acquire the fee simple is required to pay arrears of rent before the fee simple interest is vested in him or her.

20–327 Under s.7 of the Family Home Protection Act 1976, if a landlord brings an action under s.52 of Deasy's Act, and the premises are occupied by a married couple and one spouse is the legal tenant in arrears, then if the other spouse is able to pay the rent, the court can adjourn the proceedings.

20–328 The restrictions on forfeiture contained in the Conveyancing Acts 1881 and 1892 do not apply to a forfeiture or re-entry for non-payment of rent.[460] At common law the landlord has to make a formal demand for rent unless the lease dispenses with this requirement. The tenant may apply in equity for relief against the forfeiture or under s.14(2) of the Conveyancing Act 1881. Landlords often prefer to rely on s.52 of Deasy's Act. Previously

---

[456] A.G. Richey, *Irish Land Laws*, 2nd edn (London: Macmillan, 1881), p.41.
[457] 14 & 15 Vic., c.57, s.73.
[458] (1852) 2 Ir. C.L.R. 120.
[459] Landlord and Tenant (Ground Rents) (No. 2) Act 1978 s.27.
[460] Conveyancing Act 1881 s.14(8).

s.14 of the Conveyancing Act 1881 did not apply to a forfeiture under a cov-enant against assignment or subletting, but now it does so by virtue of s.35 of the Landlord and Tenant (Ground Rents) Act 1967.

20–329 Head 71 of the LTLRB 2011 clarifies the effect of a forfeiture notice. It purports to put in place a straightforward rule that forfeiture does not occur until the landlord obtains actual possession under a court order. This reverses the position under *Moffat v Frisby*[461] whereby the tenancy is deemed to be forfeited upon issue of possession proceedings.

Denial of Title
20–330 The law of landlord and tenant also followed the old law of freehold tenure in holding that a denial by a tenant of the landlord's title gives rise to a forfeiture.[462] The title of the tenant derives from that of the landlord and so the landlord can claim that the tenant has in effect denied his or her own title.

20–331 In *O'Reilly v Gleeson*[463] the Supreme Court held that a denial by a tenant of the landlord's title otherwise than in legal proceedings, i.e. by an act *in pais*, does not forfeit the lease. It may be that courts today are less inclined to treat the tenant as dependent or subservient to the landlord except in purely technical terms. To accept that a denial outside legal proceedings could cause a forfeiture would be to put the tenant in an invidious position as against the landlord in a social sense. The Supreme Court also held that denial or disclaimer of the landlord's title by a tenant would only disentitle the ten-ant to require the landlord to terminate the tenancy by serving a notice to quit where the tenancy is a periodic one but not where the tenancy is for a fixed term. The reason is that "in the case of a lease for a fixed term not terminable by notice to quit, the estate of the lessee in the land is not defeasible by mere disclaimer of title on his part".[464]

20–332 The appropriate remedy of a landlord where a forfeiture has occurred is ejectment on title. This is also called simply an action for possession and is brought where the landlord alleges that a forfeiture has occurred. It will also be the appropriate form where the land is occupied by a person having no title valid against the proprietor, i.e. someone in adverse possession.

---

[461] [2007] 4 I.R. 572.
[462] *Foot v Warren* (1861) 10 Ir. C.L.R. 1.
[463] [1975] I.R. 258.
[464] [1975] I.R. 258 at 272.

Satisfied Term
20–333 The Satisfied Terms Act 1845[465] applied to terms of years created under settlements to secure payment of portions. On payment of the money the term of years came to an end. The Act was repealed by the LCLRA 2009.[466]

Enlargement
20–334 This topic is dealt with in the next chapter.

[465] 8 & 9 Vict c 112.
[466] LCLRA 2009 s.8 and Sch.2, Pt 4.

CHAPTER 21

Statutory Control and Enlargement of Tenancies

*The rent of this cottage is said to be low; but we have it on very hard terms,
if we are to dine at the park whenever any one is staying either with them,
or with us.*

— Jane Austin, *Sense and Sensibility*, Ch.19

21–01 A number of legislative enactments contain provisions for extending
or renewing the term by the tenant, or which enable the enlargement of leases
and tenancies into a fee simple. The provisions which control specific terms
of tenancies, such as attempts to restrict alienability or subletting, have been
dealt with in the previous chapter. This chapter concerns statutory provisions
providing for continuation or extensions of the original term or its enlargement
into a fee simple. It also deals with provisions for compensation for improvements. The chapter is divided into sections according to the type of premises,
i.e. general, business, residential, etc., rather than conceptually according to
extension of the term, enlargement into a fee simple, etc.

CONVEYANCING ACT 1881

21–02 Section 65 of the Conveyancing Act 1881 (the "1881 Act") provides
for the enlargement of certain long leases into fees simple. The section applies
to tenants holding under leases for 300 years or more with a term unexpired
of 200 years "without any rent, or with merely a peppercorn rent or other
rent having no money value".[1] The tenant of such a lease may execute a deed
enlarging the lease into a fee simple.[2] The rent must be valueless in money
terms and so if the rent consists of money at all, however small the amount, it
would seem the lease may not be enlarged under the section.[3]

Covenants
21–03 The fee simple remains

---

[1] Conveyancing Act 1881 s.65(1) and Conveyancing Act 1882 s.11. Neither were repealed by
the Land and Conveyancing Law Reform Act 2009: see s.8(3) and Sch.2, Pt 4.

[2] Conveyancing Act 1881 s.65(2) and (3).

[3] *Re Smith & Stott* (1885) 29 Ch. D. 1009 (a lease with a rent of three shillings, infrequently
paid, is not within the section); *Blaiberg v Keeves* [1906] 2 Ch. 175 (a rent of one shilling was
assumed to take the lease out of the section); *Re Chapman & Hobbs* (1885) 29 Ch. D. 1007 (a
rent of one silver penny had the same effect).

"subject to all the same trusts, powers, executory limitations over, rights, and equities, and to all the same covenants and provisions relating to user and enjoyment, and to all the same obligations of every kind, as the term would have been subject to if it had not been so enlarged".[4]

This would seem to include the valueless rent, if any, and if so the enlarged fee simple would in theory be a fee farm grant. However, s.12 of the Land and Conveyancing Law Reform Act 2009 ("LCLRA 2009") provides that any instrument executed after 1 December 2009 purporting to create a fee farm grant operates instead to vest the fee simple. Hence, any deed executed by a tenant entitled to rely upon s.65 of the 1881 Act will vest in that tenant the full fee simple subject only to such "covenants or provisions...as [are] consistent with the nature of a fee simple".[5] Section 65 was capable of being used as a device to attach covenants to a fee simple the burden or benefit of which would not otherwise run under the rules as to the running of covenants between freehold owners.[6] However, the scope to achieve this result has probably been diminished by s.28 of the Landlord and Tenant (Ground Rents) (No. 2) Act 1978 (the "No. 2 Act of 1978") so that only certain types of covenants, namely those enhancing the amenities of the land, would survive enlargement.[7] Since s.65 of the 1881 Act does not provide for compensation it is arguably challengeable on constitutional grounds as an infringement of the property rights of those entitled to the reversion. A reversion on an unexpired term of 200 years and a valueless rent in the meantime is of minimal value to those alive today, and the terms of the section were probably drafted with this in mind, but the reversion could be of considerable value to their posterity. There is as yet no decision on the constitutionality of the section.[8]

Business Tenancies

History
21–04 The Town Tenants (Ireland) Act 1906[9] (the "1906 Act") gave two principal rights to business tenants in towns. First, it gave tenants of premises situated in towns or villages and used wholly or partly for business purposes a right to compensation for improvements on quitting the premises. Secondly, it gave tenants of premises wherever situated, but used wholly or substantially

---

[4] Conveyancing Act 1881 s.65(4).

[5] LCLRA 2009 s.12(3).

[6] *Re McNaul's Estate* [1902] 1 I.R. 114 held that covenants originally contained in a lease continued to affect the fee simple under the Renewable Leasehold Conversion Act 1849, even though they would have been invalid in the grant of an ordinary fee simple.

[7] See below.

[8] However, much of the observations made by Peart J. in *Shirley v O'Gorman* [2006] IEHC 27, regarding the constitutionality of the ground rents legislation, are undoubtedly also pertinent here. See discussion below.

[9] See J.C.W. Wylie, *Irish Land Law*, 5th edn (Haywards Heath: Bloomsbury, 2013), para.20.04.

for business purposes, a right to compensation for loss of goodwill and removal expenses on disturbance without good cause.

21–05 The weakness of the 1906 Act was that landlords could avoid its effect if they offered the tenant an extension of the existing tenancy or a new tenancy on reasonable terms. Landlords could also avoid the Act by designing leases which did not fall within its provisions. The Act was therefore largely a failure. The 1906 Act was repealed and replaced by the Landlord and Tenant Act 1931 (the "1931 Act"), which was itself repealed and replaced by the Landlord and Tenant (Amendment) Act 1980 (the "1980 Act"). The 1931 Act was not confined to business premises and applied also to residential premises where there had been occupation over a long period, giving such tenants the right to compensation for improvements and the right to a new tenancy.[10] Such provisions have been replaced by similar provisions in the 1980 Act but have now been effectively repealed, insofar as concerns the right to a new tenancy only, in the context of residential premises by s.192 of the Residential Tenancies Act 2004 ("RdTA 2004").

Landlord and Tenant (Amendment) Act 1980
Scope of the Act
21–06 The 1980 Act applies to "tenements". A "tenement" is defined as land wholly or partly covered by buildings or a defined portion of a building and if the land is only partly covered by buildings, the portion not covered must be subsidiary and ancillary to the buildings.[11] The Draft General Scheme of Landlord and Tenant Law Reform Bill 2011 ("LTLRB 2011"), which has yet to be enacted, proposes to drop this reference to "tenements". As recommended by the Law Reform Commission,[12] the Bill drops the need to have buildings on the land. It thus avoids the distinction, which is often difficult to draw, between land which is subsidiary and ancillary to buildings and land which is not.[13]

21–07 The land must be held by the occupier under a lease "or other contract of tenancy" express, implied or arising by statute. The tenancy must not be one made for the "temporary convenience" of the lessor or lessee. If granted since 1931, the nature of the temporary convenience must be stated in the

---

[10] See also the Landlord and Tenant (Reversionary Leases) Act 1958, repealed by the Landlord and Tenant (Amendment) Act 1980.

[11] *Terry v Stokes* [1993] 1 I.R. 204 (the significant factor is not the relative area or value but the use made by the tenant); *Dursley v Watters* [1993] 1 I.R. 224; *Lynch v Simmons* (1954) 88 I.L.T.R. 3; *Irish Glass Bottle Ltd v Dublin Port* [2005] IEHC 89 at para.6: "The relevant time is the time the application ... was made and it is a question of fact whether or not the portion of land not covered by the building at that time was subsidiary or ancillary to the building".

[12] Law Reform Commission, *Consultation Paper on Business Tenancies* (LRC CP 21-2000), para.3.16.

[13] LTLRB 2011, Head 80 and Explanatory Note.

lease.[14] "Lease" includes fee farm grant. The 1931 Act applied only to tenants in *occupation* of the premises[15] but this is no longer required by the 1980 Act. Section 3 of the 1980 Act extends "business" to include activities for providing "cultural, charitable, educational, social or sporting services" and also the public service and local authorities, health boards and harbour authorities carrying out their functions.[16]

21–08 Section 4 of the 1980 Act, on the other hand, restricts the operation of the Act by providing that it does not bind a State authority or the Central Bank[17] in its capacity as *lessor*. This seems to put the State in an unnecessarily favourable position as against private lessors. If a private lessee of the State has made improvements to the premises there seems no reason why they should be deprived of the rights they would otherwise have under the Act, such as compensation for improvements attributable to them. If the principle that a person should not benefit from expenditure which is not their own is a desirable one, on moral and economic grounds, then it is no less desirable where the lessor is the State. The point is re-enforced by the argument that it would be particularly unprincipled for the State to exempt itself, since it is the State which promulgated the principle by enacting legislation.

21–09 The practical, or, some would say, unprincipled objection might be made that the burden on public funds would be too great if many tenants, perhaps companies, suddenly claimed large sums as improvements, but in fact the 1980 Act requires the tenants to submit improvement notices before the improvement is made and the question as to whether the improvement should be made can be referred to the court. The Law Reform Commission has recommended that the State should no longer have blanket exemption as a landlord,[18] and this recommendation has been incorporated into the LTLRB 2011. Head 82 of the draft Bill applies to the State both as landlord and tenant save where

---

[14] In *Like It Love It Products Ltd v Dun Laoghaire Rathdown County Council* [2008] IEHC 36 it was held that the specific ground of the temporary convenience had been clearly set out in the original letting and the fact that this letting had been extended on the same terms did not detract from its overall ongoing character as a temporary convenience letting. However, it cannot invariably be assumed that a temporary convenience specified in an original letting will be deemed to apply to a subsequent renewal or renewals of that letting, on the basis that, as observed by Fitzgibbon L.J. in *McCutcheon v Wilson* (1891) 12 L.R. Ir. 151, "[e]very letting is in a sense for the convenience or to meet a necessity of one or other or both of the parties"; *O'Driscoll v Riordan* (1895) 16 L.R. Ir. 235; *Murphy v O'Connell* [1949] Ir. Jur. Rep. 1. In *Like It Love It Products Ltd*, there were issues of estoppel which affected the tenant's right to challenge the temporary convenience character of later lettings.

[15] Landlord and Tenant Act 1931 s.2.

[16] See *Rice v Dublin Corporation* [1947] I.R. 425.

[17] As amended by s.86 of the Central Bank (Supervision and Enforcement) Act 2013. Section 4(1A) now states that, subject to certain restrictions, the 1980 Act does not bind the Central Bank of Ireland in its capacity as lessor or immediate lessor of any premises.

[18] Law Reform Commission, *Consultation Paper on Business Tenancies* (LRC CP 21-2000), para.3.13.

the appropriate State authority is satisfied that this would not be in the public interest.

Compensation for Improvements

21–10 Under s.46 of the 1980 Act, a tenant of a "tenement" is entitled to compensation for certain improvements from the lessor on quitting the tenement. Under s.45, "improvement" means an addition or alteration to the building, including the installation of water, gas or electricity conduits, but excludes redecoration or repair. The tenant is entitled on quitting the premises to compensation from the lessor for improvements made by the tenant or any predecessor in title which is suitable for the character of the building and which adds to its letting value.[19] Compensation does not apply, however, if the tenancy is terminated by surrender or by the lessor for non-payment of rent.[20] In the case of surrender, a lessor does not have to accept it and so the parties can agree on the terms of a surrender. There is therefore no need to provide for compensation by statute. As to non-payment of rent, the statute, by excluding compensation for improvements in such a case, creates a new sanction for failure to pay the rent, but it can be questioned whether the "forfeiture" of improvements is appropriate. Even if a lessee has failed to pay rent, the moral principle behind the legislation, that a lessor should not gain from expenditure by the lessee, should still apply. It would be more appropriate for the rent owing to be deducted from the compensation, or vice versa, depending on which is greater than the other.

21–11 The amount of compensation is to be agreed between the parties or, in the absence of agreement, decided by the Circuit Court.[21] In the latter case s.47 provides for the assessment of compensation as the capitalised value of the addition to the letting value of the tenement at the termination of the tenancy attributable to the improvements. Deductions are to be made in respect of benefits received by the tenant or his or her predecessors, such as reduction in the rent expressly or impliedly in consideration of the improvements.[22] Part IV of the 1980 Act contains new provisions to give greater flexibility in some cases. Under s.60 a lessor can, in certain circumstances, obtain an order terminating an occupational tenancy where the buildings are obsolete or are in an "obsolete area".[23] The lease must be for a term of which not less than three and not more than 25 years remain unexpired.[24] The lessee is not able to

---

[19] Landlord and Tenant (Amendment) Act 1980 s.46. Compensation for improvements was described by McKechnie J. in *Harrisrange Ltd v Duncan* [2003] 4 I.R. 1, as "but a method by which a tenant may recoup his expenditure on the demised property, which expenditure has enhanced its value for the landlord but in respect of which the tenant no longer enjoys occupation".

[20] Landlord and Tenant (Amendment) Act 1980 s.46(1)(b).

[21] 1980 Act s.8.

[22] 1980 Act s.47(2).

[23] 1980 Act s.60(1).

[24] 1980 Act s.60(2).

take advantage of the Act unless he or she submits an "improvement notice" under s.48. The notice must contain a statement of the works proposed and their estimated cost. If the development is one for which planning permission is required, a copy of the permission must be attached. The landlord then has a choice of three courses of action. He or she can:

(a) consent to the improvement, (referred to in the Act as an "improvement consent");
(b) undertake as landlord to execute the improvement subject to an increased rent that is either specified or to be fixed by the court (an "improvement undertaking"); or
(c) object to the improvement (an "improvement objection").[25]

In the case of (a) the tenant has one year in which to execute the improvement.[26] In the case of (b) the tenant can object to the increased rent and bring an action in the Circuit Court to determine the new rent or to deal with the matter as an improvement objection.[27] In the case of (c) the tenant can bring an action in the Circuit Court[28] or withdraw the notice.[29]

21–12 An improvement objection can only be served on the ground that the tenant does not hold the tenement under a lease for a term of which at least five years are unexpired and furthermore that the tenant would not be entitled to a new tenancy under s.17(2)(a) of the 1980 Act. The principle here is that the lessor can only legitimately object on the ground that the tenant's interest is too slight to justify the improvement. Where the immediate landlord is a tenant of a superior landlord the improvement will affect the relationship between the immediate landlord and the superior one. Section 48 provides that in such a case, where the landlord on whom the notice is served holds from a superior landlord

• for a term of which less than 25 years is unexpired,
• under a lease for life or lives in being either without a concurrent term or with a concurrent term which has less than 25 years remaining unexpired, or
• under a tenancy from year to year or a lesser tenancy,

then the landlord has to serve notice on the superior landlord. In such a case, the superior landlord can serve on the landlord and the tenant, either an improvement consent or an improvement objection, but not an improvement undertaking. Where an improvement is carried out by the tenant then, under s.55, the landlord must issue, if asked, an improvement certificate certifying

---

[25] 1980 Act s.48(2).
[26] 1980 Act s.50.
[27] 1980 Act s.51.
[28] 1980 Act s.52.
[29] 1980 Act s.52(1)(a) and (2).

that the improvement has been made in accordance with the notice or order. This will assist the tenant in case the landlord or a successor challenges the improvement at a later time.

New Tenancies

21–13 Part II of the 1980 Act confers on tenants of certain tenements[30] the right to a new tenancy on satisfying certain conditions. Business tenants have the right to a new tenancy under s.13(1)(a) if they have been in continuous occupation of the premises for five years.[31] Subsections (b) and (c) are not confined to business premises. They give the same right to tenants of *other* premises, on proof of continuous occupation for 20 years, or of improvements carried out such that the tenant would, but for the section, have the right to compensation under the Act and that not less than half the letting value of the premises is attributable to the improvements. Section 192 of the RdTA 2004 withdrew the rights conferred by Pt II of the 1980 Act from tenancies to which the RdTA 2004 applies.[32] Tenancies in the Custom House Docks Area used for financial services are exempt from the renewal provisions of the 1980 Act.[33]

21–14 The LTLRB 2011 proposes to reform the law in relation to new tenancies for business tenants, in line with the Law Reform Commission's recommendations.[34] Head 84 of the Bill states that a tenant is entitled to a new tenancy beginning on the termination of the previous tenancy, provided that the premises have been continuously occupied by the tenant or his or her predecessors in title for the purposes of carrying on a business during the whole of a minimum period of five years immediately prior to that termination, or provided that the tenant has, without any breach of the terms of the tenancy, made improvements to the letting value of the premises which, at that termination, are worth not less than one-half of the letting value of the premises as improved.

Controlled Business Premises

21–15 Part II of the 1980 Act also applies to business premises formerly controlled under the Rent Restrictions Act 1946.[35] Although Pt II is headed "Right

---

[30] *Mason v Leavy* [1952] I.R. 40; *Hardiman v Galway County Council* [1966] I.R. 124; *McEvoy v Gilbeys of Ireland Ltd* (1962) 96 I.L.T.R. 143; *The Commissioners of Public Works v Kavanagh* [1962] I.R. 216.

[31] As amended by Landlord and Tenant (Amendment) Act 1994 s.3.

[32] A short-term exception applied in the case of any dwelling whose tenant prior to 1 September "served a notice of intention to claim relief under and in accordance with section 20 of the Act of 1980".

[33] 1980 Act s.13(3) and(4), inserted by the Landlord and Tenant (Amendment) Act 1989. The exemption originally applied for five years from the date of the Act (1 March 1989) but was extended to 10 years (S.I. No. 36 of 1994) and then 15 years (S.I. No. 52 of 1999), i.e. to 2013.

[34] Law Reform Commission, *Consultation Paper on Business Tenancies* (LRC CP 21-2000), paras 3.24–3.25, 3.30–3.31 and 4.11–4.14.

[35] 1980 Act s.14.

to New Tenancy" the part does not operate in relation to these controlled premises in quite that way. Rather than a *right* to a new tenancy, the Act confers a new tenancy on the tenant in the same terms as the old one in the same way that most rent Acts confer a statutory tenancy. Since in the present case the premises were formerly subject to a statutory tenancy, the effect of Pt II of the 1980 Act is to confer a new statutory tenancy, but subject to a term that the landlord may terminate the tenancy on three months' notice to quit.[36]

Break in Use

21–16 Under s.13(2) of the 1980 Act a "temporary break in the use" of a tenement can be disregarded if the court considers it reasonable to do so. The subsection expressly qualifies only s.13(1)(a), the section dealing with business premises. Where statutes give rights to tenants it is common for landlords to react by adopting devices to deprive the tenants of those rights. Avoidance of the Act is considered in the next section.

Avoidance of the Act

21–17 In *Gatien Motor Co Ltd v Continental Oil of Ireland Ltd*[37] the Supreme Court had to decide as to the validity of a device to avoid the application of the 1931 Act. The 1931 Act specified a qualifying period of three years for a tenant to be eligible to claim a new tenancy, but did not include any provision that entitled the court to disregard a period during which the applicant was not in occupation as tenant. However, s.42 of the 1931 Act declared to be void any contract which purported directly or indirectly to prevent an applicant acquiring a right to a new tenancy. In *Gatien* the respondent landlord let property to a tenant for three years from 6 February 1970, which the tenant used for the purposes of his business during that period. Before the expiration of the term, the tenant sought a renewal of his tenancy, but the landlord refused to grant a renewal unless the tenant surrendered possession of the tenement for a week. The tenant was unwilling to vacate the premises for the week since he believed that it would damage the goodwill of his business. Eventually it was agreed that the tenant would remain "in possession" of the tenement from 6–12 February 1973, as a caretaker for the respondent, and not as a tenant, and without payment of rent. The respondent was to grant to the applicant company (which had been set up by the tenant) a new tenancy for three years from 12 February 1973. The tenant was aware that this arrangement was designed to prevent the acquisition of a statutory right to a new tenancy under the 1931 Act. The caretaker's agreement and new tenancy agreement were executed by the parties, and the applicant used the tenement for business purposes as tenant. On the expiration of the new tenancy on 12 February 1976, the tenant claimed to be entitled to a new tenancy under the 1931 Act, contending that they had been in possession of the tenement as a tenant from 6–12 February 1973, and

---

[36] 1980 Act s.14(2).
[37] [1979] I.R. 406.

that, accordingly, the tenement had been used by the tenant for the time being
for a complete period of three years and three months immediately preceding
12 February 1976, as required by the Act to sustain entitlement to renewal of
the tenancy.

21–18 The Circuit Court held the tenant to be entitled to a new tenancy.
On appeal to the High Court, a case was stated to the Supreme Court asking
whether the caretaker's agreement had created a tenancy and, if not, whether
that agreement was void under s.42 of the 1931 Act on the ground that it indirectly deprived the applicant of a right to a new tenancy under that Act.

21–19 The Supreme Court held that the answer to both questions was "No".
The judges accepted the caretaker agreement at face value even though that
agreement had expressly conferred "possession" on the "caretaker".[38] Griffin
J. laid stress on the fact that there was no rent payable during the caretaker
period and that no rent had been paid. One might also point out that there is
another argument which runs almost exactly counter to this, and that is that if
the landlord had genuinely been employing the erstwhile tenant as a caretaker
it is customary to pay such a person for their services, but the agreement made
no mention of wages or salary and none was paid. Griffin J. went on to consider
the effect of s.42 of the 1931 Act. He held that, as no tenant of the tenement
had acquired a right to obtain relief under the 1931 Act, the provisions of s.42
of the 1931 Act did not apply. He justified this position in the following way:

> "Although it is not lawful to contract out of the Act of 1931, a distinction
> must be drawn between a provision which attempts to exclude the Act from
> a transaction to which it applies, and a transaction to which the Act has no
> application. Thus, in *Hardiman v Galway County Council* [1966] IR 124 this
> Court held that a covenant by a tenant not to claim compensation for distur-
> bance offended against section 42 of the Act of 1931 and was void. In that
> case the term of the lease was 20 years and the tenant would clearly have
> been entitled to a new tenancy on the expiration of the lease .... Although
> section 42 of the Act of 1931 avoids contracting out of the Act, it does not
> prevent the parties from so arranging matters that there is nothing to which
> the Act can apply. When the lease of 1970 expired, Coady was fully aware
> of the fact that he was not entitled to a new lease, and also that the respon-
> dents were not prepared to give him, or the company which he was in the
> process of forming, a new lease which would have the effect of giving the
> tenant rights under the Act of 1931 on its expiration ... The agreement was
> not for the purpose of evading the Act of 1931 but of preventing the provi-
> sions of the Act from applying or, in other words, of arranging a lease which
> would be outside the scope of the Act. In my opinion, that is not in breach
> of section 42 of the Act of 1931."

---

[38] *Shell-Mex v Manchester Garages* [1971] 1 W.L.R. 612 considered.

21–20 This is curious reasoning: the judge says that the applicant knew that the landlord was "not prepared to give him" a lease which would qualify under the 1931 Act, as if the application of the Act were a matter of choice for the landlord. If it were a matter of choice for landlords generally whether protective landlord and tenant legislation applied or not, it becomes difficult to explain why the legislature considered such Acts necessary at all.

21–21 Kenny J. agreed with the general trend of Griffin J.'s reasoning. The treatment of s.42 by the court amounts to sanctioning a device to avoid the 1931 Act and to render it almost useless except in relation to leases entered into before it took effect. It also requires an artificial reading of the section. The section states that a contract "by virtue of which a tenant would be directly or indirectly deprived of his right to obtain relief" under the Act "shall be void". The court read it to mean that before one can be deprived of a right one must first have a right. This reading does, admittedly, point to a mistake in the drafting of the section. The drafter of the section should have said "by virtue of which a tenant would ... have been deprived of a right which, but for the contract, they would otherwise have obtained". A court more disposed to protect rights which the legislature had evidently intended to confer on tenants would no doubt have interpreted the section in that way. It might be objected that, in that case, the argument could be made that even a lease for one year would be caught because, being for a term of less than three years, it operates to prevent the tenant from obtaining a right under the Act which he or she would otherwise have acquired. However, courts are capable of developing rules to distinguish between devices that effectively prevent the tenant acquiring rights to possession for periods to which the Act is intended to apply and agreements genuinely entered into for lesser periods. As to the facts of *Gatien* itself, the court indicated that it considered the tenant to be on an equal footing with the landlord and that he had accepted the new terms after independent legal advice. This suggests that perhaps the court did not intend to lay down a rule that the Act could be avoided in all cases by caretaker agreements.

21–22 It does not seem that s.13(2) of the 1980 Act, which provides that a temporary break in use of the tenement "shall be disregarded" if the court considers it reasonable to do so, is sufficient to reverse the effect of *Gatien*. A caretaker agreement does not necessarily involve a break in "use". Indeed, according to *Gatien*, it does not necessarily involve a break in *possession*. Section 85 of the 1980 Act states that any contract, whether made before or after the Act, which "provides that any provision of this Act shall not apply in relation to a person or that the application of any such provision shall be varied, modified or restricted in any way in relation to a person" shall be void. The wording is different from that in s.42 of the 1931 Act and is no doubt deliberately so. While it is still true that the agreement in *Gatien* did not expressly oust the provisions of the Act, the language of s.85 indicates a legislative intention that the provisions of the Act should not be avoided by agreement.

21–23 In *Bank of Ireland v Fitzmaurice*[39] a lease provided that from 1983 until 1986 the rent on the premises would be increased by an amount calculated in relation to the "Cost of Living Index" published by the Central Statistics Office. From June 1986 until May 1988 the increase would be calculated in a similar fashion, save that after ascertaining the "index-linked" increase, that figure would be multiplied by four to arrive at the new rent for the period in question. The defendant tenant asserted that this multiplier clause constituted a device to force him to surrender the tenancy and, as such, was in contravention of s.85 of the 1980 Act and was therefore void. He also alleged that certain representations had been made on behalf of the lessor prior to the execution of the lease to the effect that these clauses would not be enforced against him. It was claimed that the indexation clauses were incapable of operating since the cost of living index referred to in the lease was never published by the Central Statistics Office. Lardner J. held that by providing for a rent greatly in excess of that available in the open market, the plaintiff landlord intended to exercise a compelling pressure on the defendant to surrender his tenancy in order to escape liability for the increased rent. By surrendering the lease, the defendant would exclude himself from any right to claim a new tenancy under s.17(1)(a)(iii) of the 1980 Act. The judge held that the multiplier clause was, in effect, a provision which restricted the application of the provisions of the 1980 Act to the defendant and was therefore void as being in contravention of s.85. Thus, *Bank of Ireland v Fitzmaurice* is authority for the view that s.85 is contravened not simply by a provision which expressly purports to oust the application of the Act, but also by an agreement which has the effect of doing so. This conclusion impliedly casts doubt on the authority of *Gatien*.[40]

21–24 The need for complex or indirect contrivances to vitiate the application of s.13 of the 1980 Act to a tenancy used for a business purpose has been removed by s.47 of the Civil Law (Miscellaneous Provisions) Act 2008 (the "2008 Act"). This amends s.17 of the 1980 Act,[41] by adding a situation in which a tenant of a tenement, otherwise eligible to claim a renewal of tenancy, "has renounced in writing, whether for or without valuable consideration, his or her entitlement in the tenement and has received independent legal advice in relation to the renunciation". Section 48 of the 2008 Act provides that a renunciation within the terms of s.47 does not fall within the prohibition on contracting out of the Act contained in s.85 of the 1980 Act. The facility to renounce a potential right to a new tenancy contained in s.47 of the 2008 Act is an extension of an earlier facility contained in s.4 of the Landlord and Tenant (Amendment) Act 1994 which had been confined to where "the terms of the tenancy provided for the use of the tenement wholly and exclusively as an office". It furthermore required the renunciation to have been executed prior to the commencement of the tenancy. There is no such requirement in s.47

---

[39] [1989] I.L.R.M. 452.

[40] See also *Hardiman v Galway County Council* [1966] I.R. 124.

[41] The section which, as shown below, sets out the circumstances in which a right to a new tenancy does not arise.

of the 2008 Act, so that now it would appear that, subject only to securing independent legal advice and that the renunciation is in writing, the parties to a tenancy in which the "tenement" is *"bona fide* used wholly or partially for the purpose of carrying on a business" can with impunity, either prior to the granting of a tenancy or at any time during it, contract out of a tenant's right to a new tenancy under Pt II of the 1980 Act.[42]

21–25 Head 86 of the LTLRB 2011 purports to replace s.17 of the 1980 Act, including the amended "contracting out" provision in s.47 of the 2008 Act.

Disentitlement

21–26 Under s.17(1) of the 1980 Act the tenant has no right to a new tenancy if the tenancy has been terminated:

  (i) by ejectment for non-payment of rent, whether the action is so termed or not;
 (ii) by the landlord for breach of covenant by the tenant;
(iii) by the tenant by surrender or otherwise;
 (iv) by the landlord by notice to quit with "good and sufficient reason"; or
  (v) otherwise than by notice to quit and the landlord refused for "good and sufficient" reason to renew the lease, or would have had "good and sufficient" reason to refuse a renewal of the lease if he or she had been asked.

21–27 "Good and sufficient reason" means a reason based upon some action or conduct by the tenant which in the opinion of the court is a good and sufficient reason for terminating or refusing to renew the lease.[43]

21–28 Under s.17(2) the tenant is not entitled to a new tenancy:

  (i) if the landlord intends or has agreed to pull down and rebuild or reconstruct the buildings or part of them included in the tenement and has obtained planning permission to do so;
 (ii) if the landlord requires vacant possession in order to carry out a scheme of development and has planning permission to carry it out;
(iii) if the landlord is a planning authority and the area is an "obsolete area";
 (iv) if the landlord is a local authority and will require possession within five years under a compulsory purchase order; or

---

[42] See R. Cannon, "Section 47 of the Civil Law (Miscellaneous Provisions) Act 2008 and ss.191 and 192 of the Residential Tenancies Act 2004: New Developments in Relation to Contracting Out under the Landlord and Tenant (Amendment) Act 1980" (2008) 13(3) C.P.L.J. 68.

[43] 1980 Act s.17(1)(b). An example of what constitutes "good and sufficient reason" appears from *McCarthy v Larkin* [2009] IEHC 75, in which, notwithstanding a covenant to repair on the part of the tenant in a tenancy which came to an end in natural course, the tenant had allowed the house to become ruinous and uninhabitable and was also manifestly incapable of affording to restore the property to a habitable state or even to pay a full market rent.

(v) if for any reason the new tenancy would be inconsistent with good estate management.

21–29 In Head 86 of the LTLRB 2011, the restrictions contained in s.17 are re-cast into two broad categories: default or voluntary action by the tenant and an overriding need by the landlord.

Terms
21–30 The terms of the new tenancy are to be fixed by agreement, but failing that, by the Circuit Court. Where the terms are fixed by the court, s.23 lays down certain limits as to duration,[44] rent payable (not less than the landlord pays to his or her landlord: generally, the gross rent less the allowance for improvements), and an allowance for improvements.

21–31 The gross rent[45] is to be the rent which a willing tenant not already in occupation and a willing landlord would agree upon with vacant possession and without regard to goodwill.[46] The letting value of other tenements of similar character in comparable areas may also be taken into account under the section. The gross rent is reduced by the allowance for improvements where it applies.[47] The court can also order the tenant to carry out specified repairs before the new tenancy takes effect.[48]

Compensation for Disturbance
21–32 Where a tenant[49] would have been entitled to a new tenancy but for the application of any one of the disqualifying conditions set out in s.17(2), e.g. the landlord wishes to rebuild the premises,[50] the tenant has a right to compensation for disturbance. The measure of compensation is the pecuniary

---

[44] Thirty-five years generally, 20 years for business premises: 1980 Act ss.13 and 23, as amended by Landlord and Tenant (Amendment) Act 1994 ss.3 and 5.
[45] For discussion of the meaning of the term "gross rent" under the 1931 Act, see *Farrell v Caffrey* [1966] I.R. 170; *Byrne v Loftus* [1978] I.R. 211. See also, *Olympia Productions Ltd v Olympia Theatres Ltd* [1981] I.L.R.M. 424; *McGovern v Governors and Guardians of Jervis St Hospital* [1981] I.L.R.M. 197; *Gilsenan v Foundary House Investments Ltd* [1980] I.L.R.M. 273; *Caulfield v DH Bourke & Son Ltd* [1980] I.L.R.M. 223; *Rowan & Co Ltd v Bank of Ireland* (1973) I.L.T.R. 91. On overholding after the original tenancy expires, see: *Eamon Andrews Productions Ltd v Gaiety Theatre (Dublin) Ltd* [1973] I.R. 295; *Cook v Dillon* (1959) 93 I.L.T.R. 48.
[46] 1980 Act s.23(5).
[47] 1980 Act s.23(6).
[48] 1980 Act s.23(7).
[49] 1980 Act s.58(1)(b) originally confined the right to seek compensation for disturbance to business tenancies (as per s.13(i)(a)) only, but s.199(1) of the Residential Tenancies Acts 2004–2016 extended the application of the right to other tenancies (by including tenancies held under the 1980 Act s.13(1)(b)).
[50] See "Disentitlement", above. Compensation for disturbance was described by McKechnie J. in *Harrisrange Ltd v Duncan* [2003] 4 I.R. 1, as arising "where a tenant has satisfied all of the statutory preconditions for the obtaining of a new tenancy, but is denied such a tenancy because of the landlord's plans for the property".

loss, damage or expense which the tenant directly incurs or will directly incur by reason of quitting the premises.[51] The availability to a tenant of accommodation in other premises which are available for letting is a relevant factor in assessing compensation for disturbance.[52]

Notice

21–33 A claim by a tenant for relief under the 1980 Act must be preceded by service of a notice of intention to claim relief.[53] The court has power to extend the time within which such a notice must be given "on such terms as it thinks proper".[54] The court *must* extend the time "unless satisfied that injustice would be caused" where the failure was due to "disability, mistake, absence from the State, inability to obtain information or any other reasonable cause". This has been interpreted to mean that where a reasonable cause exists the time should be extended unless a clear injustice would be caused.[55]

Interim Occupation Rights by Tenant

21–34 Section 28 of the 1980 Act provides that where an application is pending for a new tenancy, or to fix the terms of such a tenancy, and the prior tenancy was not terminated either by ejectment or surrender, the tenant may "continue in occupation of the tenement" until the final outcome of the application, and in the meantime is subject to all the terms of the pre-existing tenancy, "but without prejudice to such recoupments and adjustments as may be necessary in the event of a new tenancy being granted" which will commence the termination of the previous tenancy.[56] This right of occupancy is a personal right, in the nature of a chose in action.[57]

> "[It] is personal to the pre-existing tenant and, quite unlike a contractual tenancy, does not create any estate or interest capable of being transferred or

---

[51] 1980 Act s.58(2).

[52] *Aherne v Southern Metropole Hotel Co Ltd* [1989] I.L.R.M. 693.

[53] 1980 Act s.20.

[54] 1980 Act s.83.

[55] On the discretion under s.45 of the 1931 Act, see Wylie, *Irish Land Law* (2013), para.20.12; *Bridgeman v Powell* [1973] I.R. 584; *Hayes v Kilbride* [1963] I.R. 185, doubted by O'Higgins J. in *Linders Garage Ltd v Syme* [1975] I.R. 161 (court should extend time "unless a clear injustice would be caused"); *Grey Door Hotel Ltd v Pembroke Trust Ltd* [1976–1977] I.L.R.M. 14 (court can therefore decide case anew on its merits); *H. Wigoder & Co Ltd v Moran* [1977] I.R. 112 (applicant gave correct instructions to its solicitor who through a mistake of law induced by wrong advice from a barrister failed to apply in time).

[56] It is not entirely clear whether a tenant may continue in occupation pending an application for extension of time within which to serve a notice of intention. Section 28 applies to an application "pending under this Part". Section 83, which provides for the court granting an extension of time, is not within that Part of the statute. Nevertheless, the discretion under s.83, which applies "[w]here a person fails to do any act or thing in the time provided for by or under this Act", may be wide enough to order that a tenant remain in possession until the application itself is dealt with.

[57] *Crofter Properties Ltd v Genport Ltd* [2007] IEHC 80 per Finlay Geoghegan J.

transmitted either *inter vivos* or on death ... [T]he right ... is a bare one, and, by itself, does not confer on the tenant any estate or interest in the land".[58]

21–35 Failure by the claiming tenant to comply with any term of the former tenancy does not of itself give rise to forfeiture of that tenancy: the landlord, however, retains a right of re-entry for breach of any term or condition, including non-payment of rent, which can be enforced upon application made to the court.[59] However, the landlord must await the granting of a new tenancy by the court, if one is granted, before he or she can seek to retrieve "recoupments and adjustments"[60] in the form of an increased rent; the landlord cannot seek an adjustment to the rent while the tenant remains in occupation pending the outcome of the application for a new tenancy.[61]

Right to Acquire the Fee Simple
21–36 In some circumstances the occupier of premises used for business purposes may be entitled to acquire the fee simple. The general powers are contained in Pt II of the No. 2 Act of 1978. They are discussed below, for the sake of convenience, in the section on residential and occupational tenancies. Part II of the No. 2 Act of 1978 contains a special procedure by which owners of dwelling houses could acquire the fee simple and such provisions have no application, of course, to business premises. There are in addition some restrictions affecting the general powers which apply to business premises specifically[62] and one factor affecting the determination of the purchase price by arbitration which applies specifically to business premises.[63]

---

[58] *Harrisrange Ltd v Duncan* [2003] 4 I.R. 1 at 13.
[59] *Crofter Properties Ltd v Genport Ltd* [2007] IEHC 80. In order to prevent "serious injustice to [the landlord]" through a possible continuance of "those breaches of the terms of the expired lease as found ... while [the tenant] remained in occupation under section 28", the order made by Finlay Geoghegan J. was that the tenant was to be restrained from continuing in occupation under s.28, with a stay placed upon the order provided there was full ongoing compliance by the tenant with the conditions of which it had been found to be in breach: the purpose of this was to prevent the landlord being put to the trouble of further litigation in the event of continued breaches by the tenant.
[60] As provided for in s.28.
[61] *Harrisrange Ltd v Duncan* [2003] 4 I.R. 1 at 15: "The plain meaning and understanding of the words [of s.28] can only convey the view that under this section a tenant must have been successful in his assertion for a new tenancy before there can be any question of recoupments or readjustments."
[62] No. 2 Act of 1978 s.16(2)(a).
[63] Landlord and Tenant (Amendment) Act 1984 s.7(3)(d).

RESIDENTIAL AND OCCUPATIONAL TENANCIES

Landlord and Tenant (Amendment) Act 1980
New Tenancies
General
21–37 It has already been mentioned that the right to a new tenancy is not confined to business premises, but the provisions of Pt II of the 1980 Act can no longer be claimed in respect of tenancies to which the Residential Tenancies Acts 2004–2016 apply.[64] As to non-business premises, s.13(1) of the 1980 Act specified a period of 20 years of continuous occupation by the tenant or his or her predecessors in title.[65] The alternative basis for a claim was that the tenant had made improvements which would, apart from s.13, entitle the tenant to compensation for improvements which amounted to not less than half of the letting value.[66] Section 13(2), which enables the court to disregard temporary breaks in the use of the premises, does not apply to non-business premises.

Controlled Dwellings
21–38 In the case of "controlled dwellings", which were subject to a statutory tenancy immediately before the Rent Restrictions (Amendment) Act 1967, they are now subject to a statutory tenancy on the same terms as the former statutory tenancy except that the landlord can terminate it on three months' notice to quit.[67]

Compensation for Improvements
21–39 It has already been seen that the provisions of Pt IV of the 1980 Act apply to residential premises as well as business premises. They entitle a tenant to compensation for improvements carried out by the tenant which add to the letting value of the premises at the end of the tenancy. These provisions have already been discussed.

---

[64] Except where notice of intention to claim relief pursuant to the 1980 Act was served prior to 1 September 2009.
[65] 1980 Act s.13(1)(b).
[66] 1980 Act s.13(1)(c).
[67] 1980 Act s.15.

Residential Tenancies Acts 2004–2016[68]

21–40 The Residential Tenancies Acts are a series of legislative measures intended to regulate residential tenancies.[69] They are of relatively limited scope, and do not apply, for example, to

- dwellings that could qualify under the "business equity" provisions of the 1980 Act;
- any dwelling governed by the Housing (Private Rented Dwellings) Act 1982;
- any dwelling let by or to a public authority;
- any dwelling in relation to which a tenant is entitled to acquire the fee simple under the Landlord and Tenant (Ground Rents) (No. 2) Act 1978;
- any dwelling occupied under a shared ownership lease;
- service occupancies (i.e. providing accommodation for an employee);
- holiday lettings;
- dwellings in which the landlord is also resident;
- any dwelling in which the spouse, parent or child of the landlord resides and no lease or tenancy agreement in writing has been entered into by any person resident in the dwelling; or
- any dwelling the subject of a tenancy granted under Pt II of the Landlord and Tenant (Amendment) Act 1980.

21–41 Part 2 of the 2004–2016 Acts sets out the rights and obligations of landlords and tenants. Part 3 deals with issues relating to rent, such as rent reviews and rent pressure zones. Part 4 introduces an entirely new system for the extension of a tenancy, which was in many respects an improvement for tenants on Pt II of the 1980 Act.[70] Part 5 deals with the termination of tenancies, setting out notice periods and procedural requirements. Part 6 inaugurates a new system of dispute resolution, featuring mediation and arbitration and an adjudicative body called the tenancy tribunal. Part 7 provides for the registration of

---

[68] The Acts included in this collective citation are the Residential Tenancies Act 2004; Residential Tenancies (Amendment) Act 2009; Housing (Miscellaneous Provisions) Act 2009; Residential Tenancies (Amendment) Act 2015 (other than s.1(3) and ss.15, 85 and 87); and the Planning and Development (Housing) and Residential Tenancies Act 2016. Note that at the time of writing, the Residential Tenancies (Amendment) Bill 2018 was passing through the Oireachtas. This purports to amend RdTA 2004 ss.66 and 151.

[69] References to the RdTA 2004 in this book refer to the amended Act, including all amendments up to 25 February 2018.

[70] Most noticeably, that protection can be claimed after a tenancy has endured for six months, whereas the so-called "long occupation equity" provided for in the 1980 Act s.13(1)(b) required continuous occupation as a tenancy for 20 years. However, there are also potential pitfalls for tenants: e.g. during every cycle of four years, the landlord is entitled to terminate the tenancy for any reason during the first six months, provided that the termination procedures specified in Pt 5 are followed.

private tenancies and Pt 8 establishes the Private Residential Tenancies Board (now named the Residential Tenancies Board (RTB)).[71]

Part 4 Tenancies
The Basic Concept
21–42 The principle which underlies the statutory protection of a tenancy conferred by Pt 4 of the Residential Tenancies Acts 2004–2016 is that, once a tenant has enjoyed six months' continuous occupation, he or she will be entitled to a six-year tenancy (including the initial six-month period) which can only be terminated by the landlord for specific limited reasons and in accordance with procedures set out in the Act.[72] Such a tenancy is called a Pt 4 tenancy.[73] If the tenancy has not been determined at the end of the six-year term, the tenant becomes entitled to a further six-year tenancy, except that during the first six months of the second period the tenancy can be terminated by the landlord for any reason, subject only to giving the proper notice in accordance with Pt 5. Provided that the tenancy has not been terminated, or notice of termination has not been given, in the first six months, then for the remainder of the next period of six years, the landlord can only terminate for specific limited reasons and in accordance with procedures. Thus, the cycle of Pt 4 tenancies is capable of continuing indefinitely, but will never at any one time confer on a tenant a statutory right to a longer term than six years.

Non-application of Part 4
21–43 Section 25 sets out certain circumstances in which the benefits conferred by Pt 4 cannot be claimed:

  (i) where the dwelling, originally built as one dwelling, at the relevant time contains two dwellings, the landlord lives in one dwelling and, at the commencement of the tenancy, has given written notice to the tenant of the other dwelling that he or she opts for Pt 4 not to apply;

 (ii) where the dwelling is let for student accommodation and the landlord is entitled to income tax relief on the costs of construction, conversion or refurbishment in accordance with the Taxes Consolidation Act 1997, as amended;

(iii) where the tenant is entitled to reside in the dwelling as part of his or her employment; and

(iv) where the dwelling is designated by the approved housing body for the use by it as a transitional dwelling, and the consent of the relevant public authority has been obtained by the approved housing body. A "dwelling" for this purpose is one which an approved housing body leases for

---

[71] The Private Residential Tenancies Board was re-named the Residential Tenancies Board under s.13 of the Residential Tenancies (Amendment) Act 2015, with effect from 7 April 2016 (S.I. No. 151 of 2016).

[72] The basic entitlement is set out in RdTA 2004 s.28.

[73] RdTA 2004 s.29.

periods not exceeding 18 months for the purposes of the approved housing body concerned.

21–44 Otherwise, nothing in any agreement "may operate to vary, modify or restrict in any way a provision" of Pt 4.[74] However, there is no prohibition on a landlord allowing more beneficial rights to the tenant than those provided for in Pt 4.[75]

The Operation of Part 4

21–45 Once a tenant has been in occupation of a dwelling for a continuous period of six months, on foot of a tenancy or tenancies, and no notice of termination of the tenancy has been served prior to the expiry of that time, the tenant is entitled to a tenancy for a six-year period, which will run from the commencement of the tenancy (or of the first tenancy if there has been more than one) (the "relevant date").[76] The continuous period of six months for the purpose of this reckoning must commence on or after the "relevant date".[77] However, if notice is served on the tenant that would expire *after* the term of the six-year tenancy, the tenancy will run until the expiry of the notice.[78] Where notice of the required amount is served on the tenant and expires after the term of the six-year tenancy, it can be for any reason: in other words, it need not be for one of the specified reasons that alone are permissible to terminate the tenancy in the case of notice given and expiring during the remaining five-and-a-half years of the six-year term.[79]

21–46 Subject to the right of the parties to vary the terms of a Pt 4 tenancy at any time, the terms of the Pt 4 tenancy will be the same as in the original tenancy that produced the qualifying occupation period of six months; a purported variation in the terms of the tenancy will not be effective if inconsistent with the Act.[80]

---

[74] RdTA 2004 s.54(1). The existence of a "break clause" permitting a landlord to terminate a tenancy on the basis that he or she intends to occupy the dwelling was held by Laffoy J. in *Canty v Private Residential Tenancies Board* [2007] IEHC 243 not to be an attempt to contract out of the Act.

[75] RdTA 2004 ss.26 and 54(2).

[76] RdTA 2004 s.28(1), (2) and (4), and s.31, as amended by s.37(1) of the Planning and Development (Housing) and Residential Tenancies Act 2016.

[77] RdTA 2004 s.27, as amended by s.4 of the Planning and Development (Housing) and Residential Tenancies Act 2016.

[78] RdTA 2004 s.28(2)(b).

[79] RdTA 2004 s.34(b). In *Dunivya v Private Residential Tenancies Board* [2016] IEHC 41, it was held that a termination notice under s.34(b) must state a reason for the termination.

[80] RdTA 2004 s.30.

Termination of Tenancy by the Landlord

21–47 Subject to s.35A, discussed below, a tenancy can be terminated, for any reason, by the landlord subject to giving the appropriate period of notice provided for in Pt 5, provided that notice

(i) is served during the original period of continuous occupation of six months before a right to a Pt 4 tenancy has yet been established;

(ii) is served during the currency of the first six months of any subsequent Pt 4 tenancy; or

(iii) expires on or after the term of a Pt 4 tenancy.[81]

21–48 Otherwise a tenancy can only be terminated, even when giving the correct period of notice and following the procedures set out in Pt 5, for one of the following reasons, which must be duly stated in the notice and is subject to the following conditions[82]:

1. Failure by the tenant to comply with his or her obligations under the tenancy, reasonable opportunity having first been allowed by the landlord to the tenant to remedy the default. This can include desisting from prohibited conduct, redressing an omission, or the payment of arrears of rent or paying compensation where the landlord has incurred financial loss; however, the pre-condition of allowing facility to redress the default does not arise in the case of a tenant behaving "in a way that is anti-social" as defined in s.17(1)(a) or (b).[83]

2. The dwelling subject to the tenancy is no longer suitable for occupation by reason of insufficiency of bed spaces in relation to "the size and composition of the occupying household".[84]

3. The landlord intends within three months after the termination of the tenancy to execute a contract for sale of his or her entire interest, "for full consideration", in the dwelling or in the property that contains the dwelling.[85] Section 35A(2) provides that the tenancy shall not be terminated where the landlord intends to enter into an enforceable agreement in respect of dwellings situated within the development concerned, for the transfer to another, during a relevant period of time, for full consideration, of the whole of his or her interest in 10 or more of those dwellings, each being the subject of such a tenancy. However, s.35A(2) does not apply where the landlord can show that the price to be obtained by

---

[81] RdTA 2004 s.34(b).

[82] RdTA 2004 s.34(a), Table.

[83] RdTA 2004 s.35(2) and (3), but it does apply in the case of the definition given in s.17(c).

[84] The notice of termination must be accompanied by a statement specifying the bed spaces in the dwelling and the grounds on which it is no longer suitable: s.35.

[85] This does not entitle a landlord to terminate a tenancy on account of an intention of the landlord to sell but where the landlord intends to bind himself or herself to a contract for sale within three months: *Hennessey v Private Residential Tenancies Board* [2016] IEHC 174. The notice of termination must be accompanied by a statutory declaration, the details of which are specified in RdTA 2004 s.35.

selling at market value is more than 20 per cent below the market value that could be obtained for the dwelling with vacant possession, and that the application of s.35A(2) would, having regard to all the circumstances of that case, be unduly onerous or cause undue hardship to that landlord.[86]

4. The landlord requires the dwelling, or the property that contains it, either for his or her own occupation, or occupation by a member of his or her family. Where this ground arises, the notice of termination must contain or be accompanied by a statutory declaration:

   i. specifying who is intended to occupy the dwelling and, if not the landlord, his or her relationship to the landlord;

   ii. specifying how long that person is intended to remain in the dwelling;

   iii. confirming that the landlord acknowledges the obligation to offer a tenancy to the tenant in the dwelling if the party in occupation vacates within six months of either the expiry of the notice period or the final resolution of a dispute referred to the RTB regarding the validity of the termination notice; and

   iv. setting out the statutory requirement that the obligation specified above is subject to the tenant, within 28 days of either the expiry of the notice period or the final resolution of a dispute referred to the RTB regarding the validity of the termination notice, notifying the landlord in writing of his or her contact details and subsequently of any changes in them[87] and provided, in addition, that the tenancy had not also been terminated on the basis of ground 1, 2, 3 or 6. A member of the landlord's family includes "any spouse, civil partner, child, stepchild, foster child, grandchild, parent, grandparent, step parent, parent-in-law, brother, sister, nephew or niece … or a person adopted by the landlord under the Adoption Acts 1952 to 1998".[88]

5. The landlord intends substantially to refurbish or renovate the dwelling, or the property that contains it, in a way that requires it to be vacated, and, if planning permission is required for the works, it has been obtained. The termination notice must contain or be accompanied by a written statement:

   i. specifying the nature of the intended works[89];

   ii. in a case where planning permission has been obtained, attaching a copy of the planning permission;

---

[86] RdTA 2004 s.35A(3). Section 35A(4) provides that where, before the commencement of s.40 of the Planning and Development (Housing) and Residential Tenancies Act 2016, a notice under s.34 of the RdTA 2004 has been served on a tenant specifying that the landlord intends within three months after the termination of the tenancy to execute a contract for sale, then s.34 shall continue to apply to that notice as if s.40 had not been enacted.

[87] RdTA 2004 s.35(5). This requirement also applies to the grounds of termination specified in paras 5 and 6 of the Table.

[88] RdTA 2004 s.35(4), as amended by the Civil Partnership and Certain Rights and Obligations of Cohabitants Act 2010.

[89] In a case where planning permission has been obtained, a copy of the planning permission is attached to the notice or statement, or if planning permission is not required, the name of the contractor who will carry out the works and the proposed dates for the works.

iii. confirming that planning permission is not required and he or she has complied with the requirements of s.35(9)(b);

iv. confirming that the landlord acknowledges the obligation to offer a tenancy to the tenant if the dwelling becomes available for reletting (unlike in the cases of grounds 4 and 6 there is no maximum time stipulation); and

v. setting out the statutory requirement specified in 4(iv) above, and provided, in addition, that the tenancy had not also been terminated on the basis of ground 1, 2, 3 or 6.

6. The landlord intends to change the use of the dwelling, or of the property that contains it, and, if planning permission is required for that change of use, it has been obtained; the termination notice must contain or be accompanied by a written statement:

i. specifying the nature of the intended use, attaching a copy of the planning permission (where obtained). Where works are to be carried out in respect of change of use, the landlord must specify details of those works, the name of the contractor, if any, employed to carry out such works, and the dates on which the intended works are to be carried out and the proposed duration of the period in which those works are to be carried out;

ii. confirming that the landlord acknowledges the obligation to offer a tenancy to the tenant if the dwelling becomes available for reletting within six months of either the expiry of the notice period or the final resolution of a dispute referred to the RTB regarding the validity of the termination notice; and

iii. setting out the statutory requirement specified in 4(iv) above, and provided, in addition, that the tenancy had not also been terminated on the basis of ground 1, 2 or 3.

21–49 Acceptance of an offer of a tenancy, as provided for in grounds 4, 5 and 6, within a reasonable period specified for acceptance, creates an enforceable agreement between the former landlord and tenant: occupation on foot of this tenancy will be deemed continuous with that under the terminated tenancy.[90]

21–50 Where a tenant has vacated possession on foot of a notice of termination given in accordance with any one or more of grounds 3, 4, 5 and 6 and

- in the case of ground 3, the contract for sale was not executed within three months following either the termination of the tenancy or the final resolution of a dispute referred to the RTB regarding the validity of the termination notice, or

- in the cases of grounds 4, 5 and 6, the occupation, refurbishment or change of use (as the case may be) did not take place within a reasonable time after service of the notice of termination, or the final resolution of

---

[90] RdTA 2004 s.35(6).

a dispute referred to the RTB regarding the validity of the termination notice, *or* the landlord failed to make the required offer of a new tenancy when the property again became available for letting,

in these circumstances, the tenant may refer a complaint to the RTB that he or she "has been unjustly deprived of possession of the dwelling concerned by the landlord".[91] An order directing repossession by the tenant or an award of damages, to a maximum of €20,000, may be made.[92]

21–51 Where the landlord has cited two or more of grounds 3, 4, 5 and 6 as justification for termination of the tenancy, any alleged statutory dereliction by the landlord will have to be established in respect of each of these grounds.[93]

21–52 A tenant is entitled, in a complaint to the RTB, "to put in issue, in a dispute in relation to the validity of the notice of termination … the bona fides of the intention of the landlord to do" the thing or things set out in the notice of termination.[94]

21–53 Section 184 states that any provision in a lease or tenancy which is designed specifically to facilitate termination by either party "for any reason that suits the interests of that party at the particular time rather than because the failure to comply has occurred" will be void.[95] An inference that any particular provision is designed to facilitate termination on such spurious grounds may be drawn:

- if the provision cannot be regarded as conferring any practical benefit on the party entitled to terminate for breach of it in relation to that party's interest in the dwelling;
- if compliance with the provision is likely to be impracticable; or
- if the provision is so couched that compulsory compliance with it is arbitrary.[96]

21–54 A tenancy or sub-tenancy created with a view to facilitating the collusive termination of a further sub-tenancy will be void, but the further sub-tenancy will continue to subsist for its agreed term (and no longer), on the basis that the sub-tenant holds from the party who created the tenancy or sub-tenancy found void.[97]

---

[91] RdTA 2004 s.56(1)–(3).
[92] RdTA 2004 ss.115(3) and 182(1).
[93] RdTA 2004 s.56(5).
[94] RdTA 2004 s.56(6)(b).
[95] RdTA 2004 s.184(1) and (2).
[96] RdTA 2004 s.184(3).
[97] RdTA 2004 s.184(4) and (5).

Termination of Tenancy by the Tenant

21–55 A tenant may terminate a Pt 4 tenancy by giving notice to the landlord in accordance with Pt 5.[98] A tenancy will be deemed to have been terminated by a tenant if:

(i) either the tenant vacates having served insufficient notice and before expiry of the notice served the rent has fallen into arrears; or

(ii) the tenant vacates after rent has been in arrears for 28 days and has not served notice at all.[99]

In these circumstances the landlord is entitled to possession and the tenant remains liable for the rent.[100] However, the concept of "deemed termination" does not apply if the tenancy has been assigned or sub-let.[101] The provisions in relation to "deemed termination" by a tenant also apply to a tenancy to which Pt 4 either does not apply, by reason of its falling within one of the excluded categories,[102] or in respect of which the minimum time for the establishment of a Pt 4 tenancy has not passed.[103]

21–56 Regardless of whether a tenancy has been created for a fixed term, and regardless of any provision to the contrary in the lease or tenancy, the with-holding by the landlord of consent to an assignment or sub-letting entitles the tenant to terminate the tenancy by giving the appropriate notice specified in Pt 5.[104]

21–57 A Pt 4 tenancy terminates on the death of a tenant. However, the tenancy can be continued if the tenant's spouse, civil partner or qualified cohabitant,[105] or a child, stepchild, foster child, or adopted child, any such child being at least 18 years old, or the tenant's parent, elects in writing to become a tenant. In such event the original Pt 4 tenancy continues.[106]

Assignment of Tenancy

21–58 If a tenant, with the landlord's consent, assigns a Pt 4 tenancy to a person other than a sub-tenant of the property, the original Pt 4 tenancy comes to an end. It is converted into a periodic tenancy, but a new Pt 4 tenancy can come into existence once the assignee has been in occupation, under the tenancy, for

---

[98] RdTA 2004 s.36.

[99] RdTA 2004 s.37(1) and (2).

[100] RdTA 2004 s.37(4).

[101] RdTA 2004 s.37(3).

[102] See discussion of these above.

[103] RdTA 2004 s.194.

[104] RdTA 2004 s.186.

[105] Within the meaning of s.172 of the Civil Partnership and Certain Rights and Obligations of Cohabitants Act 2010.

[106] RdTA 2004 s.39, as amended by s.203 of the Civil Partnership and Certain Rights and Obligations of Cohabitants Act 2010.

a continuous period of six months.[107] An assignment cannot be made of part only of a dwelling subject to a Pt 4 tenancy and any such purported assignment is void.[108]

Sub-letting

21–59 If a tenant, with the landlord's consent, assigns a Pt 4 tenancy to his or her sub-tenant, the sub-tenant is deemed to become a tenant of the landlord under the terms of the original Pt 4 tenancy (unless they had been varied by agreement between the original landlord and tenant) and the assignee's sub-tenancy merges with the Pt 4 tenancy.[109] A sub-tenancy cannot be created out of part only of a dwelling subject to a Pt 4 tenancy; any such purported sub-tenancy is void.[110]

21–60 Where a tenant intends to create a sub-tenancy in a dwelling, he or she must, prior to granting the sub-tenancy or entering into an agreement to create it, inform the prospective sub-tenant that it is a sub-tenancy that is being created.[111] Failure to do so renders the tenant guilty of an offence, and any agreement to grant a sub-tenancy unenforceable by the tenant.[112]

21–61 Where a sub-tenancy is created out of a Pt 4 tenancy, with the written consent of the landlord, s.32 and the Schedule to the Acts extend to such sub-tenancy the protections applicable to a tenant in a Pt 4 tenancy for as long as the tenancy continues to exist. References in Pt 2 to the respective duties of landlord and tenant apply, with appropriate modifications, to landlord and subtenant. If the landlord gives notice of intention to terminate the tenancy, but does not require the sub-tenancy to be terminated, or if the tenant gives notice of intention to terminate the tenancy, the sub-tenant shall become a direct tenant of the landlord, under the same terms as the sub-tenancy, except that the duration of the Pt 4 tenancy will be the same as that of the original tenancy if it had not been terminated.[113] Liabilities between original contracting parties are unaffected.[114]

21–62 Where a sub-tenant has vacated possession on foot of a notice of termination given on the basis that the tenant ("head-tenant") requires the dwelling, or the property containing the dwelling (either for his or her own occupation, or for occupation by a member of his or her family)[115] *and* the occupation did not take place within a reasonable time after service of the notice of termination,

---

[107] RdTA 2004 s.38(1)(a).

[108] RdTA 2004 s.38(4) and (5).

[109] RdTA 2004 s.38(1)(b) and (2).

[110] RdTA 2004 s.32.

[111] RdTA 2004 s.185(1).

[112] RdTA 2004 s.185(2) and (3).

[113] RdTA 2004 Sch., paras 5 and 6.

[114] RdTA 2004 Sch., paras 4(3) and 7.

[115] As defined in s.35(4); see above.

or the final resolution of a dispute referred to the RTB regarding the validity of the termination notice, *or* the head-tenant failed to make the required offer of a new tenancy when the property became again available for letting, the sub-tenant may refer a complaint to the RTB that he or she "has been unjustly deprived of possession of the dwelling concerned by the head-tenant." An order directing payment of damages by the head-tenant to the sub-tenant may be made. A sub-tenant will be entitled, in any complaint made to the RTB, "to put in issue, in a dispute in relation to the validity of the notice of termination … the bona fides of the intention of the head-tenant to do" what he or she purported to do in the notice of termination.[116]

21–63 Regardless of whether the tenancy is for a fixed term, and despite any provision to the contrary contained in it, if a landlord refuses consent to an assignment or a sub-letting, the tenant may serve on the landlord notice of termination of the tenancy.[117]

Further Part 4 Tenancies

21–64 If a Pt 4 tenancy comes to the end of its term without notice of termination having been served either by the landlord or the tenant, a new tenancy called a "further Part 4 tenancy" comes into being on the same terms, with effect from the expiry date of the previous Pt 4 tenancy.[118] However, this will not happen if the landlord gives notice for the correct period (not necessarily for any one of the listed causes in the Table to s.34) which expires either on or after the end of the Pt 4 tenancy, in which event the tenancy will end on the date mentioned in the notice.[119]

21–65 The rights arising under a further Pt 4 tenancy are described as being "of a rolling nature"[120]: each Pt 4 tenancy is progressively followed by each subsequent one unless the landlord takes the permissible steps to prevent this from happening. The terms of any Pt 4 tenancy can be varied by the parties, by agreement, provided that any such variation is consistent with the provisions of the RdTA 2004.[121]

Multiple Tenants

21–66 Special provisions apply in relation to what are called "multiple tenants." Section 48 defines "multiple tenants", in relation to a dwelling, as persons who are tenants of it "whether as joint tenants, tenants-in-common or under any other form of co-ownership". Where a dwelling is occupied, either by multiple tenants or by one or more multiple tenants and their licensee or

---

[116] RdTA 2004 Sch., para.8.
[117] RdTA 2004 s.186.
[118] RdTA 2004 s.41(1)–(3).
[119] RdTA 2004 ss.34(b) and 41(4)(c).
[120] RdTA 2004 s.43.
[121] RdTA 2004 s.46.

licensees, a Pt 4 tenancy is deemed to come into existence once the earliest of the occupiers has been in occupation, on foot of the tenancy, for a continuous period of six months without notice of termination having been served within that time.[122]

21–67 Once a tenant has been in lawful occupation of a dwelling subject to a Pt 4 tenancy, in respect of which there are multiple tenants, for a period of six months (regardless of whether part of that occupation was as licensee rather than tenant), that tenant will be entitled to the protections conferred on a tenant in a Pt 4 tenancy.[123] In reckoning the period of six months' continuous occupation, any period of occupancy as a licensee is deemed to be continuous with that as a tenant immediately subsequent to it.[124] However, a separate Pt 4 tenancy in relation to the dwelling is not deemed to be created in favour of each tenant: the Pt 4 tenancy comes into existence once the *first* tenant completes six months' continuous occupation of the dwelling.[125]

21–68 A licensee of a tenant or of multiple tenants, during a Pt 4 tenancy, may apply to the landlord to be accepted as a tenant and the landlord may not unreasonably refuse the request.[126] The landlord's acceptance can be signified by a simple written acknowledgement. The former licensee will then hold the dwelling on the same terms as the existing multiple tenants, modified as appropriate.[127] A modification, through adjustment of the division of the rent, for example, may arise if the licensee is accepted in addition to, rather than as a replacement for, any of the multiple tenants.

21–69 Any act or omission by one or more multiple tenants, which ordinarily would either have the effect of determining the tenancy or of rendering the tenancy liable to be determined by the landlord, will not cause termination to occur if the landlord is entitled reasonably to conclude that such act or omission was without the consent of the other multiple tenant or tenants.[128] A landlord may reasonably conclude that the act or omission was without the consent of those multiple tenants who provide the landlord with such "information or assistance as he or she may reasonably need" to ascertain by whom the act was done and who agreed to it. If, on the other hand, the other multiple tenant or tenants do not co-operate with such a request, the landlord can conclude that they consented to what was done or omitted to be done.[129] Where other multiple tenants co-operate with a request for assistance from the landlord, the

---

[122] RdTA 2004 s.49.
[123] RdTA 2004 s.50(1)–(4).
[124] RdTA 2004 s.50(5).
[125] RdTA 2004 s.53.
[126] RdTA 2004 s.50(6)–(8). This does not apply to licensees of a tenant or of multiple tenants: s.3B, as inserted by Residential Tenancies (Amendment) Act 2015 s.3.
[127] RdTA 2004 s.50(4) and (8).
[128] RdTA 2004 s.51(1).
[129] RdTA 2004 s.51(2).

Pt 4 tenancy and the rights arising under it will not be determined in relation to those multiple tenants, but will or may be in the case of any tenant or tenants responsible for the act or omission or who consented to it.[130]

21–70 Once a Pt 4 tenancy has been established in respect of a dwelling occupied by multiple tenants, neither the death of the tenant whose continuous occupation for six months first gave rise to the establishment of the Pt 4 tenancy, nor the vacating by that person of possession of the dwelling, deprives the other multiple tenants of Pt 4 protection.[131]

Overholding
21–71 A tenant in occupation of a dwelling pursuant to a fixed-term tenancy for a term of at least six months, who intends to continue in possession, on whatever basis, including by assertion of a claim to a Pt 4 tenancy, must notify the landlord of his or her intention so to do, *not earlier than* three months before the expiry of the term of the tenancy and *not later than* one month before the expiry of the term of the tenancy.[132]

Dispute Resolution under the Residential Tenancies Acts 2004–2016
Disputes and Disagreements
21–72 The most comprehensive provisions of the Residential Tenancies Acts 2004–2016 are contained in Pt 6, which provides for a dispute resolution mechanism to replace that formerly exercised by the courts. A wide range of tenancy-related disputes or disagreements, including those which affect licensees, neighbours and sub-tenants may be referred to the RTB[133] which will arrange for their being dealt with either by a mediator (if the parties so choose), or an adjudicator or a three-person tenancy tribunal.[134]

21–73 A "dispute" is deemed to comprehend a "disagreement", which can include:

- an issue arising with regard to compliance with landlord and tenant obligations under the tenancy;
- "any matter with regard to the legal relations between the parties that either or both of them requires to be determined (for example, whether the tenancy has been validly terminated)"; and

---

[130] RdTA 2004 s.51(3).

[131] RdTA 2004 s.52.

[132] RdTA 2004 s.195(1)–(3). However, subs.(4) provides that failure to give the required notice does not disentitle the tenant to a Pt 4 tenancy but enables a landlord to seek damages for any loss accruing from the tenant's failure to give the required notice.

[133] In *Doyle v Private Residential Tenancies Board* [2015] IEHC 724, the tenant argued in the High Court that the Board did not have jurisdiction to deal with the dispute as the tenancy had not been registered. However, this argument had not been raised at first instance, and so could not be relied upon on appeal.

[134] RdTA 2004 s.75(1).

- a claim by a landlord for arrears of unpaid rent which the tenant has failed to contend that he or she is not obliged to pay.[135]

A "dispute" also includes the following categories of complaint:

- by the tenant, that he or she has been "unjustly deprived of possession" by reason of the landlord's having falsely or covinously invoked one of the permitted grounds of termination set out in the Table to s.34[136];
- by a licensee of a multiple tenant or tenants lawfully in occupation of the dwelling, that the landlord has unreasonably refused an application to grant that licensee a tenancy[137];
- by a "person who could be potentially affected", that he or she has been directly and adversely affected by a failure by the landlord to enforce any of the tenant's obligations under the tenancy[138];
- by a landlord, for loss or damage arising from the fact that a tenant in possession under a fixed-term tenancy of not less than six months failed to give the required notice of his or her intention to remain in occupation[139];
- by a sub-tenant, that he or she has been "unjustly deprived of possession" by reason of unlawful termination of the tenancy by the head-tenant on the basis of an alleged but false requirement by the head-tenant for him or her or a member of the head-tenant's family to occupy the dwelling.[140]

21–74 References to a "party" to a dispute include, in appropriate cases, his or her personal representatives.[141] Section 76(1) provides: "Either or both of the parties to an existing or terminated tenancy of a dwelling may, individually or jointly, as appropriate, refer to the Board for resolution any matter relating to the tenancy in respect of which there is a dispute between them." A landlord may refer to the RTB a dispute relating to the dwelling between the landlord and "another, not being the tenant but through whom the other person claims any right or entitlement".[142]

21–75 Section 77 sets out requirements for a "person who could be potentially affected" who wishes to refer to the RTB a complaint that he or she has been directly and adversely affected by the landlord's failure to enforce a tenancy obligation by the tenant. The person affected must first take all reasonable steps

---

[135] RdTA 2004 s.75(3). The issue of rent arrears arose in *Doyle v Private Residential Tenancies Board* [2015] IEHC 724.

[136] RdTA 2004 ss.56(2) and 75(2).

[137] RdTA 2004 s.75(2) and 76(4).

[138] RdTA 2004 s.15, 75(2) and 77.

[139] RdTA 2004 ss.75(2) and 195: such a tenant, if intending to remain in occupation, on whatever basis he or she may be permitted to do so, must give notice of that intention to the landlord, *not earlier* than three months before, and *not later* than one month before, the expiry of the period of the tenancy.

[140] RdTA 2004 s.75(2) and Sch., para.8(2).

[141] RdTA 2004 s.75(4)(b) and (c).

[142] RdTA 2004 s.76(3).

to try and resolve the matter, short of threatening or instituting proceedings, by attempted communication with the parties. In the case of a tenant who engages in anti-social behaviour, the person affected may request an owners' management company, residents' association or similar group to communicate with the landlord or former landlord. The RTB can advise the potential complainant of the name and address of the landlord or of the landlord's agent if the RTB takes the view that the party seeking this information may make a complaint.

21–76 Section 78(1) sets out a non-exhaustive list of subject matters for complaint that may be referred to the RTB, which include:

- the retention or refund of a deposit;
- the amount of rent and timing of rent reviews;
- an alleged failure by either a landlord or tenant to comply with obligations contained in the lease or tenancy agreement or required by statute;
- disputes in relation to termination of a tenancy,[143] e.g. that:
  — the termination of a Pt 4 tenancy is not for one of the permissible reasons set out in the Table to s.34, or, if so, that it does not comply with the requirements that govern such termination;
  — the termination of a tenancy (not necessarily a Pt 4 tenancy) does not comply with the procedures or notice set out in Part 5;
  — the alleged ground of termination was not valid; or
  — the tenancy has been terminated despite absence of notice by the tenant, in a case where the tenant has allegedly vacated;
- an alleged failure by a tenant or sub-tenant to yield vacant possession upon the expiry of a validly served notice of termination;
- a claim for recovery of costs or damages by either a landlord or tenant for breach of a contractual or statutory obligation by the other;
- a claim by a landlord for arrears of rent or other charges;
- an allegation by a tenant that the landlord has penalised him or her, contrary to s.14, for relying upon his or her rights under the Act;
- an allegation by a tenant that the landlord has not offered a new tenancy following a termination where that termination was by reason of anticipated occupation of the dwelling by the landlord or a member of his or her family, *or* substantial refurbishment *or* change of use, and the dwelling *has* become available for reletting under the circumstances envisaged within grounds 4, 5 and 6 of the Table to s.34; and
- an alleged failure to comply with a "determination order" made by the RTB.

21–77 Section 82 enables a party who has referred a matter to the RTB to withdraw it at any stage by notice in writing. If the matter is being dealt with by a mediator, an adjudicator, or the tenancy tribunal, oral communication will suffice. However, inquiry must be made of the other party to the dispute, and

---

[143] For example, *O'Shaughnessy v Private Residential Tenancies Board* [2015] IEHC 401.

if that other party objects to the withdrawal, the adjudicating body may direct the party withdrawing the matter to pay such of the other party's incurred costs and expenses as it determines.

Specific Provision for Sub-tenants

21–78 A sub-tenant may refer a dispute to the RTB regarding the termination of a head-tenancy, despite the absence of a referral by the head-tenant[144] and "shall have standing to put in issue any matter relating to the notice of termination concerned", even if the head-tenant fails to do so or has represented to the landlord that he or she would not refer a dispute.[145]

21–79 If the landlord serves notice of intention to terminate a tenancy subject to a sub-tenancy and requires the tenant to terminate the sub-tenancy, a copy of that notice must also be served on the sub-tenant by the landlord.[146] Then, if the tenant intends to refer a dispute regarding the termination to the RTB:

  (i)   the tenant must serve notice of termination of the sub-tenancy on the sub-tenant;

 (ii)   in this notice of termination, the tenant must require the sub-tenant to inform the tenant, within 10 days of receipt of the notice of termination, whether the sub-tenant intends to refer a dispute to the RTB;

(iii)   if the tenant does not comply with this requirement, the tenant may not refer a dispute relating to the termination of the tenancy to the RTB;

(iv)   if the sub-tenant does not indicate his or her intention, within the 10 days specified, to refer a dispute to the RTB, he or she may not refer a dispute; and

 (v)   if the sub-tenant *does* comply with the notification requirement, within the 10 days specified, the tenant may not refer a dispute to the RTB until 15 days have elapsed from the date of service of notice of termination on the sub-tenant.[147]

21–80 If the landlord serves notice of intention to terminate a tenancy subject to a sub-tenancy and requires the tenant to terminate the sub-tenancy, *and* a dispute regarding the termination of the head-tenancy is *not* referred to the RTB, the tenant, no later than 28 days from receipt of the notice of termination, must serve a notice of termination of the sub-tenancy on the sub-tenant.[148]

---

[144] RdTA 2004 s.78(2).
[145] RdTA 2004 s.78(3).
[146] RdTA 2004 s.70(3).
[147] RdTA 2004 s.81.
[148] RdTA 2004 s.71.

Grounds for Residential Tenancies Board to Decline Hearing a Dispute

21–81 The RTB may charge a fee for dealing with a dispute and shall decline to deal with it until the fee has been paid.[149] In the case of a dispute referred by a landlord, the RTB will not deal with it if the tenancy has not been registered in accordance with Pt 7.[150] In this event, if the RTB draws the failure to register to the landlord's attention, and the landlord rectifies the omission within a reasonable time, the matter can proceed to be dealt with.[151]

21–82 If the RTB is of opinion, in relation to any dispute referred to it, that

- (i) the dispute, had it come before the ordinary courts, would have been statute-barred,
- (ii) the issues concerned are frivolous or vexatious,
- (iii) the dispute concerns a dwelling to which the RdTA 2004 does not apply, or
- (iv) the dispute does not fall within the RTB's jurisdiction, perhaps due to failure to comply with a procedure requisite for its effective referral,

the RTB must serve a notice on the party who referred the dispute, stating the opinion formed by it and allowing that party opportunity to make submissions, within a specified period, "that the opinion is not well founded."[152] Unless the RTB is persuaded that the opinion formed by it is not well founded, it will decline to deal with the matter. If the RTB forms the view that its original opinion was not well founded, it will so advise, in writing, the other party to the dispute, and also furnish, upon request, that other party with a copy of the written submissions made by the party referring the dispute or a written summary of the submissions if the submissions were orally made.[153] Either party may appeal a finding of the RTB on this issue to the Circuit Court for the circuit in which the dwelling is situated.[154]

21–83 If an adjudicator or the tenancy tribunal forms the view that one of the grounds which entitle the RTB to decline to deal with a dispute applies to any particular dispute, the adjudicator or tenancy tribunal shall not deal with that dispute.[155] However, if the RTB had already formed such an opinion in relation to the dispute, and, upon submissions being made, subsequently decided that the initial opinion was not well founded, or if the Circuit Court on appeal to

---

[149] RdTA 2004 s.83(1).
[150] RdTA 2004 s.83(2). See *Snochowski v Private Residential Tenancies Board* [2017] IEHC 165, where it was held that the landlord was entitled to appeal the adjudicator's decision to the Tenancy Tribunal even though he was not entitled to refer the dispute to the RTB. This was because he had failed to register the tenancy, because the tenant had referred the dispute to the RTB and there is no qualification of the right to appeal under the RdTA 2004 s.100.
[151] RdTA 2004 s.83(3).
[152] RdTA 2004 s.84(1)–(3) and (7).
[153] RdTA 2004 s.84(4).
[154] RdTA 2004 s.84(5) and (6).
[155] RdTA 2004 s.85(1).

it had directed the RTB to deal with the matter, the adjudicator or the tenancy tribunal must do so.[156]

Time Limits

21–84 In the case of a tenancy that has already been terminated, a dispute in relation to the amount of the rent may not be referred to the RTB by the former tenant later than 28 days after the termination.[157] Similarly, where the dispute relates to the validity of a notice of termination, it may not be referred to the RTB more than 28 days after the date of receipt of the notice.[158]

21–85 However, the RTB, upon application made to it, may extend any relevant time limit, but it "shall not" do so "unless the applicant for the extension shows good grounds for why the time should be extended." The RTB's decision either to grant or refuse a requested extension of time can be appealed to the Circuit Court for the circuit in which the dwelling is situated. A time limit includes not only the time within which a referral is to be made, but also the time within which any condition precedent required for a referral to be effective must be met.[159]

Status of Disputed Matters and Alternative Remedies

21–86 Once a matter has been referred to the RTB, subject to the determination when made, and *provided* that the matter is not withdrawn prior to adjudication *or* that the RTB, for one of the permitted causes considered above, declines to deal with it,

- rent (including rent under a sub-tenancy) will continue to be paid unless there is agreement to suspend it;
- if the dispute concerns the amount of the rent, the rent cannot be increased unless the relevant parties agree; and
- the tenancy cannot be terminated, *unless* notice of termination was served prior to the referral of the dispute to the RTB *or*, if served after the referral of the dispute, the notice required to terminate the tenancy was 28 days or less and has been given—*except* where the dispute relates to the validity of the notice of termination or the right of the relevant party to serve it, in which event the tenancy cannot be terminated prior to the adjudication of the dispute.[160]

21–87 Section 87 prevents a party to a terminated tenancy who is alleged to be in default from mending his or her hand prior to hearing, by providing that, if a dispute relates to termination of a tenancy on account of default in the

---

[156] RdTA 2004 s.85(2).
[157] RdTA 2004 s.76(2).
[158] RdTA 2004 s.80.
[159] RdTA 2004 s.88.
[160] RdTA 2004 s.86.

tenancy obligations by either party, "any remedial action taken by the other party subsequent to the receipt of the notice of termination shall not be taken into account" by either the RTB or the relevant adjudicating body.

21–88 An arbitration agreement cannot prevent a dispute that could otherwise be referred to the RTB from being so referred, unless the tenant, at or subsequent to the arising of the dispute, consents to its being referred to arbitration.[161] However, if a party entitled to refer a dispute to the RTB has an alternative remedy available and "takes any steps to avail" of that alternative remedy, that party may not refer the dispute to the RTB.[162] In the event that the party entitled to avail of and electing to avail of the alternative remedy is not the party who referred the dispute, the RTB or the relevant adjudicating body may take account of the existence of the alternative remedy, to the extent that the RTB or the adjudicating body thinks just, in determining any relief that should be granted.[163]

Preliminary Procedural Steps
21–89 Several of the arrangements established in Pt 6 are clearly designed to head off taking up time in the hearing of disputes. Accordingly, s.92 provides that, when a dispute is referred to the RTB, the RTB may communicate with the parties to ensure that they are fully aware of the issues involved, and, in the event that it believes that the issue between the parties derives from a misunderstanding in relation to basic rights and obligations, seek "to have the issue or issues between the parties resolved by agreement between them without recourse being needed to the other procedures in this Part".[164] This communication by the RTB may "where it would be of assistance to the parties, include an indication by the Board, based on appropriate assumptions stated to the parties, of the typical outcome of issues of the kind concerned being determined under this Part."[165] Naturally, the RTB must communicate such views as fully to one party as to the other party and at all times remain cognisant of each party's right to invoke the full dispute procedures provided for in Pt 6 of the Act.[166]

21–90 If the parties have not already reached agreement as a result of any preliminary steps taken by the RTB, the RTB then will ask each of them whether they consent to the dispute becoming the subject of mediation.[167] If both parties agree, the RTB will refer the dispute to a mediator appointed from a panel of mediators.[168] If either party fails to respond or indicates that he or she objects to mediation, the RTB will refer the dispute to an adjudicator appointed from

[161] RdTA 2004 s.90.
[162] RdTA 2004 s.91(1).
[163] RdTA 2004 s.91(2).
[164] RdTA 2004 s.92(1) and (2).
[165] RdTA 2004 s.92(3).
[166] RdTA 2004 s.92(4).
[167] RdTA 2004 s.93(1).
[168] RdTA 2004 s.93(2).

a panel of adjudicators.[169] However, if the RTB has, at the behest of one of the parties, made application on behalf of that party to the Circuit Court for interim or interlocutory relief,[170] the RTB need not refer the dispute to mediation, but rather instead to an adjudicator or the tenancy tribunal. Likewise, in relation to any dispute, "if, in all the circumstances, [the RTB] considers it would be more appropriate for it to refer the dispute to the Tribunal and refers it accordingly".[171]

Mediation

21–91 Where a dispute has been referred to mediation by the RTB, the mediator "shall inquire fully into each relevant aspect of the dispute concerned, provide to, and receive from, each party such information as is appropriate and generally make such suggestions to each party and take such other actions as he or she considers appropriate" to enable the parties to resolve the issue between themselves without further recourse to the Pt 6 procedures.[172] At the end of the mediation process, the mediator forwards to the director of the RTB a report which includes:

- a statement of relevant facts agreed by the parties;
- a summary of any other pertinent matters agreed to by the parties, whether or not they go in whole or in part to resolving the dispute, which is to be signed by each of the parties and acknowledged as agreed; and
- a summary of the conduct of the mediation, including the number of sessions and those attending and also the documents submitted to the mediator, but not disclosing the contents of any of these documents.[173]

21–92 The director then forwards to the RTB only the summary of pertinent matters other than facts agreed between the parties, or a statement that there have been no such matters agreed, but no other part of the report.[174] Either party can notify the mediator and the RTB within 10 days of completion of the mediation that they no longer agree with the agreement and do not wish to be bound by it.[175]

21–93 Following receipt of the mediator's report, if 10 days have elapsed without either party rescinding the agreement, the RTB prepares a determination order[176] in respect of the dispute. The determination order is binding on the

---

[169] RdTA 2004 s.93(3).

[170] As it is empowered to do under s.189.

[171] RdTA 2004 s.94.

[172] RdTA 2004 s.95(1)–(3).

[173] RdTA 2004 s.95(4) and (5).

[174] RdTA 2004 s.95(6).

[175] RdTA 2004 s.95(5A).

[176] The determination order contains the terms of the agreement, determination or direction concerned: s.121.

parties.[177] Where the report furnished to the RTB states that there is no agreement between the parties, the dispute has not been resolved, or the agreement was made but rescinded, the RTB can refer the dispute to the tribunal.[178]

Adjudication

21–94 If the parties refuse mediation or the RTB elects to refer the matter to adjudication, it will be considered by an adjudicator appointed from a panel, who "shall inquire fully into each relevant aspect of the dispute concerned and provide to, and receive from, each party such information as is appropriate".[179] The adjudicator may require each party to furnish documents and information and, at his or her discretion, allow a party to be represented. The adjudicator will determine the matter, either by reaching a decision or by adopting as a determination a decision arrived at by the parties, with the assistance of the adjudicator, in resolution of it.[180]

21–95 Where an adjudicator "considers it would be of practical benefit" he or she "may provide assistance to the parties with a view to the parties themselves reaching a decision in resolution of the matter concerned; such assistance may include the adjudicator's stating to the parties any provisional conclusion he or she has reached in relation to any of the issues concerned."[181] This must be accompanied by a statement from the adjudicator that it is provisional only and that the matter will continue to be determined impartially and with procedural fairness. The adjudicator will not express a provisional conclusion in relation to any issue of fact in dispute between the parties unless they expressly request it; nor until all documents have been submitted and initial oral submissions made been considered by the adjudicator.[182]

21–96 Before adopting for his or her determination a decision arrived at between the parties, the adjudicator must allow them a 10-day "cooling off" period, in which to decide whether their decision still stands. The adjudicator must also advise the parties that, if at the end of that period, the decision taken by them still stands, that decision cannot be appealed to a tenancy tribunal and will become binding on them once embodied in a determination order communicated to them by the RTB. If, however, during the 10-day period, one or more of the parties advises the adjudicator that he or she no longer accepts the decision made by them, the adjudicator shall make a decision, having properly concluded the investigation.[183]

---

[177] RdTA 2004 s.123(1).
[178] RdTA 2004 s.96(1) and (2).
[179] RdTA 2004 s.97(2).
[180] RdTA 2004 s.97(1)–(4) and (7).
[181] RdTA 2004 s.97(5).
[182] RdTA 2004 s.97(6).
[183] RdTA 2004 s.98.

21–97 Once the adjudicator has made a determination he or she submits to the RTB a report which contains:

- a statement of relevant facts agreed by the parties;
- a summary of any other pertinent matters agreed to by the parties, whether or not they go in whole or in part to resolving the dispute;
- the terms of the adjudicator's determination, and, if that determination is based on the adjudicator's own decision rather than that of the parties, a summary of the reasons for it; and
- a summary of the conduct of the adjudication, including the number of sessions and those attending and also the documents submitted.[184]

21–98 The RTB then serves on each party a copy of the adjudicator's report, together with a statement to the effect that, unless an appeal is made by either party to the tenancy tribunal, within the time limit, against a determination by the adjudicator based upon his or her own decision (but not upon a decision of the parties), the RTB will proceed to make a determination order.[185] The time limit for appealing to the tenancy tribunal a determination made by an adjudicator is 10 working days from the date the RTB has served on that party the adjudicator's report and the RTB's accompanying statement.[186]

The Tenancy Tribunal
21–99 A dispute can be referred to a three-person tenancy tribunal where:

- the RTB has formed the view that the matter is not appropriate for either mediation or adjudication[187];
- mediation has failed to resolve the issue[188]; or
- an appeal is made against a determination of an adjudicator.[189]

21–100 Each tenancy tribunal has three members, appointed by the RTB from its "dispute resolution committee".[190] One of the tribunal members is chosen by the RTB as the chairperson.[191] A decision of a majority of the tenancy tribunal suffices.[192] Once the tenancy tribunal is seised of a dispute, it gives notice to all parties of the date, time, venue and purpose of the hearing, an outline of the matter to be dealt with and of the statutory and regulatory procedures to be followed.[193] The notice will include a statement that, unless substantial grounds

---

[184] RdTA 2004 s.99(1) and (2).
[185] RdTA 2004 s.99(3) and (4).
[186] RdTA 2004 s.100.
[187] RdTA 2004 ss.94 and 104(1)(a).
[188] RdTA 2004 ss.96(6) and 104(1)(b).
[189] RdTA 2004 ss.100 and 104(1)(c).
[190] RdTA 2004 ss.103(1)–(3) and 159.
[191] RdTA 2004 s.103(4).
[192] RdTA 2004 s.103(7).
[193] RdTA 2004 s.104(3) and (4)(a)–(d).

urge otherwise, the tribunal will deal with the matter despite the absence or non-participation of any party.[194] The notice period is 21 days commencing on the date of giving it. A lesser time may be specified by the RTB where one party requests it and the other party agrees, or where the alleged behaviour of either party threatens death or serious injury or serious danger to the fabric of the dwelling or of the property that contains it, or if one or more of the parties requests the RTB to specify such a period on the grounds of alleged financial or other hardship.[195]

21–101 Each party can be represented and can call witnesses. In the case of an appeal from the determination of an adjudicator, the tribunal may have regard to the adjudicator's report. The tribunal may adjourn a hearing and can arrange for more than one hearing in relation to a particular dispute.[196] Evidence is taken on oath. The tribunal can compel the attendance of witnesses and production of documents in the power or control of a witness. Each witness is liable to cross-examination. A witness before the tenancy tribunal has the same immunities and privileges as a witness before the High Court. Witness expenses can be paid either before or after the hearing. Any person, to whom witness expenses have been tendered, who fails to attend before the tribunal when summoned, or who having attended fails either to take the oath, or to produce any document lawfully required, or to answer any question lawfully put, or otherwise acts in a way that would have been in contempt of court were the tribunal a court, is guilty of an offence.[197]

21–102 Proceedings before the tribunal shall be in public, but in certain circumstances the RTB can order that the identity of a particular party or parties not be disclosed. Anyone contravening such an order is guilty of an offence.[198] As soon as its hearing is complete, the tribunal shall make a determination and notify it to the RTB.[199]

General Procedures
21–103 The procedures to be followed by the mediator, the adjudicator and the tenancy tribunal will be in accordance with rules made by the RTB with the consent of the relevant Minister.[200] These may include a fee to be paid for referring a dispute, the forms to be used and notifications to be made, and the application of various time limits at different points throughout the process, including for the making of determinations and determination orders and for the RTB to seek to enforce a determination order if advised that it has not

---

[194] RdTA 2004 s.104(4)(e) and (f).
[195] RdTA 2004 s.104(5).
[196] RdTA 2004 s.104(2), (6) and (7), and s.107.
[197] RdTA 2004 s.105.
[198] RdTA 2004 s.106.
[199] RdTA 2004 s.108.
[200] Under the Planning and Development (Housing) and Residential Tenancies Act 2016, the Minister for Housing, Planning, Community and Local Government.

been complied with. In the absence of any specific provision for a time limit where one is permitted, the relevant thing will be construed as being required "to be done as soon as practicable after the doing of the thing that immediately precedes it".[201]

21–104 A party's title may not be brought into question in any dispute.[202] A mediator, or adjudicator, or a member of the tenancy tribunal or of the RTB, may inspect any dwelling to which a dispute relates, even if that dwelling is occupied by a person not party to the dispute. In this event, at least 24 hours' notice must be given, unless the occupant otherwise consents. The power of inspection may be delegated in writing to an expert in the field of activity that the dispute concerns. It is an offence to obstruct or impede a lawfully authorised inspection.[203] An offence is also committed by a party who makes a statement or supplies information, either to a mediator, an adjudicator, the tenancy tribunal, or the RTB itself, in relation to a dispute, where the statement or information is false or misleading, in a material respect, and the party knows it to be so.[204]

Redress
21–105 The power conferred upon an adjudicator and the tenancy tribunal to make a determination is stated as including a power to make "declarations" and to give "directions" so as to provide appropriate relief to the relevant parties.[205] These can include, but are not confined to the following[206]:

- a direction that rent or other charge be paid from a certain date;
- a declaration as to whether rent complies with the definition of "market rent" in s.19, and, if not, the amount of rent that would so comply;
- a direction as to the return or repayment of a deposit, or part of it;
- a declaration regarding the validity of a notice of termination;
- a direction that a dwelling be quitted by a certain date[207];
- a direction that a term of a lease or tenancy is void, under s.184, as facilitating a termination on spurious grounds or as facilitating a collusive termination of some other lease or tenancy;
- a declaration in relation to a right to return to a dwelling, which can include a direction disregarding any interruption in possession;
- a direction that specified costs or damages be paid; except with the consent of the RTB and in "exceptional circumstances", the costs and

---

[201] RdTA 2004 s.109.
[202] RdTA 2004 s.110.
[203] RdTA 2004 s.111.
[204] RdTA 2004 s.113.
[205] RdTA 2004 s.115(1).
[206] RdTA 2004 s.115(2).
[207] This can also include quitting by a sub-tenant: s.116.

expenses awarded by an adjudicator or the tenancy tribunal cannot include legal or professional or technical witness costs[208];

- a direction in relation to interim relief, provided that this is expressly stated as not necessarily being indicative of the final determination. This is to be reduced to writing as soon as given and forwarded immediately to the RTB[209];
- "in the special circumstances of a dispute heard under this Part, a direction that the whole or part of the costs or expenses incurred by the adjudicator or the Tribunal in dealing with the dispute shall be paid by one or more of the parties."[210]

21–106 Excluding costs and expenses, the maximum award that can be made either by the adjudicator or the tenancy tribunal is, either or both of, €20,000 for damages, or, in relation to arrears of rent or other charges, €20,000 or an amount equal to twice the annual rent, whichever is the higher; but in any case not exceeding a maximum of €60,000 in relation to arrears of rent or other charges.[211]

21–107 If the adjudicator or the tenancy tribunal forms the view that a determination which contains a direction that a party is entitled to resume possession of a dwelling would cause "hardship or injustice" to a person in possession of it, the determination may, instead of directing repossession, contain a declaration that the first party was wrongfully deprived of possession together with a direction that the landlord pay an amount of damages to that person. The person actually in possession has the right to make submissions. In deciding whether a direction of repossession would cause "hardship or injustice" to a person in possession of a dwelling, the adjudicator or the tenancy tribunal will have regard to the length of time the person in possession has been there, any involvement he or she may have had with the first party's becoming dispossessed and any knowledge regarding the existence of a dispute about the first party's right to possession.[212]

21–108 A determination stipulating an amount of rent to be paid by a tenant to a landlord may also contain a stipulation that the amount be *decreased* by any debts owing for improvements or sums due in compensation by the landlord to the tenant and may have set off against it any expenditure on repairs which the tenant is entitled to claim; conversely, such amount may be stipulated to be *increased* by any costs (not exceeding €1,000) incurred by the landlord in quest of the arrears of rent, or by damages. In either case, the adjudicator or tenancy tribunal shall "indicate how the amount was calculated".[213] In the case of any

---

[208] RdTA 2004 s.5(3) and (4).
[209] RdTA 2004 s.117.
[210] RdTA 2004 s.115(2)(i).
[211] RdTA 2004 s.115(3).
[212] RdTA 2004 s.118.
[213] RdTA 2004 s.119.

dispute relating to either the amount of the rent or the timing of a rent review, the financial or other circumstances of either the landlord or the tenant are not to be taken into account.[214]

Equitable Relief and the Role of the Courts

21–109 In the case of a dispute which might otherwise be referred to the RTB, proceedings cannot be brought before any court, unless for damages of in excess of €20,000, or for arrears of rent or other charges which exceed either €60,000 or twice the annual rent if twice the annual rent would be less than €60,000.[215]

21–110 If the circumstances of a dispute are such that, were it being litigated before the courts, a party might apply for interim or interlocutory relief, the RTB, upon being requested by that party, may apply to the Circuit Court for interim or interlocutory relief.[216] The RTB may have regard to the perceived strengths of the requesting party's case and the amount of damages potentially payable to a defendant on foot of an undertaking as to damages, but notwithstanding these factors may accede to the request to seek interim or interlocutory relief if it forms the view that it ought to be sought.[217] The RTB will not be deterred from making an application by the prospect of an award of damages on foot of an undertaking, if the party requesting the RTB to seek relief undertakes to defray any damages to which it may become liable and manifestly has the means to comply with the undertaking.[218]

Determination Orders: Communication, Appeals and Enforcement

21–111 Once the statutory dispute resolution process (to whichever level it has been taken) has been exhausted, the eventual agreement, determination or direction is enshrined by the RTB and issued to the parties in a written record called a "determination order".[219] The following are capable of being recorded in a determination order:

- an agreement between the parties included in a mediator's report, after the RTB has given the parties the 10-day facility to retract or renounce it[220];
- a determination contained in an adjudicator's report, which incorporates either a decision arrived at by the parties (following expiry of the "cooling off" period) or a decision arrived at by the adjudicator which has not

---

[214] RdTA 2004 s.120.
[215] RdTA 2004 s.182.
[216] RdTA 2004 s.189(1)–(3).
[217] RdTA 2004 s.189(4).
[218] RdTA 2004 s.189(5). Section 190 confirms the power of the Circuit Court to make an interlocutory order.
[219] RdTA 2004 s.121(1).
[220] RdTA 2004 ss.96(1) and 121(1)(a).

been appealed to the tenancy tribunal or in respect of which any appeal initiated has been abandoned[221];

- a determination of the tenancy tribunal[222];
- a direction by an adjudicator or the tenancy tribunal in respect of costs concerning a dispute that has been withdrawn[223];
- a direction by an adjudicator or the tenancy tribunal in relation to the granting of interim relief.[224]

21–112 The determination order is then issued to the parties under the seal of the RTB. The RTB may vary, in terms of how it is expressed, the agreement, determination or direction, as it deems appropriate, so as "to remove any ambiguity that the Board considers exists" in it "or to clarify, generally, those terms in a manner that it considers will be of benefit to the parties or will facilitate compliance". In so doing, the RTB shall have regard to the original wording of the report of an agreement or determination, and may also consult with, "as appropriate, the mediator, the adjudicator, or the Tribunal and with the parties themselves".[225]

21–113 If the RTB is of opinion that the determination of a tenancy tribunal is "not consistent with previous determinations of the Tribunal in relation to disputes of a similar nature to the dispute concerned", then, subject to giving the members of the tribunal the opportunity to make submissions, and after consulting with the parties to the dispute, the RTB may, *either* if the parties so consent, *or* if the RTB having considered the parties' representations, in any case deems it appropriate, direct the tribunal to rehear the matter and make a fresh determination. One dispute is deemed to be of a similar nature to another "if the issues involved in each of them are the same and the facts that gave rise to each of them, as appearing from any record kept by the Tribunal in relation to its proceedings or any other record available to the Board, are the same in all material respects".[226]

21–114 A determination order embodying the report of an agreement by a mediator or a determination by an adjudicator is binding on the parties once issued by the RTB.[227] A determination order embodying a determination of the tenancy tribunal may be appealed, not later than 21 days after it has been issued to the parties, to the High Court, on a point of law only: the determination of the

---

[221] RdTA 2004 ss.99 and 121(1)(b).
[222] RdTA 2004 ss.108 and 121(1)(c).
[223] RdTA 2004 ss.82(5) and 121(1)(d).
[224] RdTA 2004 ss.117 and 121(1)(d).
[225] RdTA 2004 s.121.
[226] RdTA 2004 s.122.
[227] RdTA 2004 s.123(1).

High Court is final and conclusive.[228] An appeal to the High Court cannot open the determination order on its merits, nor seek to set aside a finding of fact by the tenancy tribunal unless there is an absence of evidence to support it.[229] Neither can an application be brought by way of judicial review against a decision of the RTB in relation to extension of a time limit or other procedural matters where the proper course is to appeal on a point of law under the RdTA 2004.[230] The High Court may cancel or vary the original determination order. The definition of "determination order" for enforcement purposes includes a determination order as approved or varied by the High Court.[231]

21–115 A determination order can be enforced through the Circuit Court for the circuit in which the dwelling is situated, by either the party intended to benefit or the RTB, against the party allegedly in default. If the party seeking to enforce the determination order is not the RTB, the respondent, if opposing the application, must notify the RTB which is then entitled to appear in the action.[232] Once satisfied that the party is in default, the Circuit Court will direct compliance with the terms of the determination order, unless the court considers or the party allegedly in default establishes that:

- there was an absence of procedural fairness in the proceedings;
- a material consideration was not taken into account or account was taken of a consideration that was not material;
- there was a "manifestly erroneous decision in relation to a legal issue"; or
- the determination was "manifestly erroneous" on the evidence.[233]

21–116 If the Circuit Court is satisfied from "credible testimony" that the respondent will be unable to meet the applicant's costs, should his or her challenge to the fairness of the proceedings that led to the determination order fail, the court may require security for costs. Furthermore, if the determination order required a dwelling to be vacated on the basis that the tenancy had been validly terminated for non-payment of rent due, the Circuit Court may require the respondent to pay to the applicant, or to lodge in court, an amount equal to the arrears of rent together with a further amount for continued occupation.[234]

21–117 If the RTB or the Circuit Court is satisfied that there are "good and substantial reasons" why a party failed to appear at a hearing by an adjudicator or by the tenancy tribunal, it may, upon application by that party, cancel the

---

[228] RdTA 2004 s.123(2), (3), (4) and (8), although in *Canty v Private Residential Tenancies Board* [2008] 4 I.R. 592, Kearns J. in the Supreme Court seemed to leave open the possibility that in certain circumstances an award of costs could involve a point of law capable of constituting the subject of an appeal.

[229] *Canty v Private Residential Tenancies Board* [2007] IEHC 243.

[230] *O'Connor v Private Residential Tenancies Board* [2008] IEHC 205.

[231] RdTA 2004 s.123(5) and (6). The RTB may also publish its determination orders: s.123(7).

[232] RdTA 2004 s.124(1), (6) and (9).

[233] RdTA 2004 s.124(2) and (3).

[234] RdTA 2004 s.124(4) and (5).

determination order and direct that the matter be fully re-heard. The Circuit Court can direct security for costs and payment of arrears of rent or a sum to represent ongoing occupation. Either the RTB or the Circuit Court may impose conditions analogous to those imposed by the High Court when setting aside a judgment made in the absence of a relevant party. Before exercising its power to direct a re-hearing, the RTB must allow the other party to be heard.[235] A person who fails to comply with any term of a determination order is guilty of an offence, but shall not be sentenced to imprisonment if he or she can demonstrate that failure to comply was due to limited financial means.[236]

General Responsibilities of Residential Tenancies Board

21–118 The principal functions of the RTB relate to dispute resolution, the registration of tenancies, the provision of advice to the Minister about the rental sector, the making of reports and the publication of statistics, the development of guidelines, the collection and provision of information in relation to the rental sector, and the conducting of research into the rental sector.[237] It may also carry out such other functions as the Minister may assign.[238]

21–119 Section 152 provides that the RTB may, in developing guidelines for good practice, publish a precedent model lease, which will "contain provisions best calculated to ensure harmonious relations between the parties to the lease as regards their conduct towards one another in their capacity as such parties".[239] In this regard, textbook authors, practitioners, students and general readers will gladly endorse, if with but modest optimism, the objective set out in subs.(2)(b), that such precedent lease "shall ... be worded, so far as practicable, in plain language".

Ground Rents Legislation
Ground Rent

21–120 "Ground Rent" has no common law definition[240] but is generally understood to mean a rent which is charged in respect of the soil, or ground, itself. It is either, or both, (a) the rent charged on vacant land, or (b) the rent charged on land with buildings on it, but is then that part of the rent which is not attributable to the value of the buildings.[241] The statutory definition is

---

[235] RdTA 2004 s.125.

[236] RdTA 2004 s.126.

[237] RdTA 2004 s.151(1).

[238] RdTA 2004 s.151(1)(h), (2) and (3).

[239] RdTA 2004 s.152.

[240] In *Shirley v O'Gorman* [2006] IEHC 27, Professor J.C.W. Wylie, as an expert witness, described a "ground rent" as, not a term of art, but a phrase which means "a rent which is reserved on a long-term lease which is relatively low because all that is being leased is the ground, in other words it does not reflect any buildings because it is contemplated those buildings will be added later". See further below and W. Walshe, "From Riches to Rags: Expropriation by the Ground Rents Acts" (2014) 19(2) C.P.L.J. 40.

[241] See Ground Rents Commission, *Report on Ground Rents* (Dublin: Stationery Office, 1964).

complex due to its attempt to include the various circumstances in which such a rent exists or arguably exists.

Ground Rents Acts

21–121 The main provisions are now contained in the Landlord and Tenant (Ground Rents) Act 1967 (the "1967 Act"), the Landlord and Tenant (Ground Rents) Act 1978 (the "No. 1 Act of 1978") and the No. 2 Act of 1978. The two Acts passed in 1978 are to be construed together as one.[242] Other relevant legislation, now repealed, is contained in the 1931 Act and the Landlord and Tenant (Reversionary Leases) Act 1958 (the "1958 Act"). A Private Member's Bill was introduced in the Seanad in 2017 to amend ss.9 and 10 of the No. 2 Act of 1978.[243]

History

21–122 The 1967 Act gave certain persons the right to enlarge their leasehold interest into a fee simple. The No. 1 Act of 1978 attempted a more radical technical solution to ground rents by providing that leases which attempted to create ground rents should be void, thus making it impossible to create them. A purported tenant who had paid consideration for the void lease was to have the right to acquire the fee simple instead.[244] However, this has the disadvantage that many purported grantees under void leases might continue in possession unaware of their right to obtain the fee simple and whose title would therefore consist only of a statutory right to the fee simple rather than the fee simple itself. The No. 2 Act of 1978 amended the 1967 Act and the No. 1 Act of 1978 and contains a new definition of leases in respect of which the lessee would have the right to acquire the fee simple, i.e. the statutory definition of a ground rent.

Problem

21–123 Unfortunately, the No. 2 Act of 1978 created a problem in that it appears to have removed the prohibition on the future creation of a ground rent provided for in s.2 of the No. 1 Act of 1978:

> "2.—(1) Subject to subsection (2), a lease of land made after the passing of this Act shall be void if the lessee would, apart from this section, have the right under section 3 of the Act of 1967 to enlarge his interest into a fee simple and the permanent buildings are constructed for use wholly or principally as a dwelling.

---

[242] No. 2 Act of 1978 s.1(2). The effect of such a provision is that every part of each of the two Acts is to be construed as if it were contained in one Act, unless there is some manifest discrepancy making it necessary to hold that the later Act has modified something in the earlier Act: *Bank of Ireland v Kavanagh*, unreported, High Court, Costello J., 19 June 1987; *Canada Southern Railway Co v International Bridge Co* (1883) 8 App. Cas. 723.

[243] Landlord and Tenant (Ground Rents) (Amendment) Bill 2017.

[244] No. 1 Act of 1978 s.2(4).

(2) Subsection (1) shall not apply where the lease is a reversionary lease under the Act of 1958."

21–124 The No. 2 Act of 1978, however, while it did not repeal s.2 of the No. 1 Act of 1978, repealed s.3 of the 1967 Act.[245] Part II of the No. 2 Act of 1978 contains a new definition of leases as to which the lessee has the right to acquire the fee simple, but there is nothing to connect that with s.2 of the No. 1 Act of 1978, and therefore no express provision that such leases granted after the No. 2 Act of 1978 are to be void. It is true that the No. 2 Act of 1978 provides in s.1(2) that "the collective citation, the Landlord and Tenant Acts 1931 to 1978, shall include this Act and those Acts and this Act shall be construed together as one Act" but it would seem to be going beyond the bounds of statutory interpretation for a court to hold that the reference in s.2 of the No. 1 Act of 1978 to "section 3 of the Act of 1967" is to be read as if it said "Part II of the Landlord and Tenant (Ground Rents) (No. 2) Act 1978" without an express provision to that effect, especially as it would render certain leases void.[246] Preventing the creation of certain types of leases is a restriction on the rights of ownership and there is a strong argument to be made that the Constitution requires that to be done by express words. The No. 2 Act of 1978 could simply have substituted a new s.3 in the 1967 Act, which it did not, in any case, wholly repeal. Moreover, the repeal of s.3 of the 1967 Act does not leave s.2 of the No. 1 Act of 1978 without any meaning. It would still render void leases created after the No. 1 Act of 1978 which fell within the definition in the then s.3 but granted before the No. 2 Act of 1978 came into effect.

21–125 It may be noted here that if the prohibition does survive the No. 2 Act of 1978, by importing the definition of the right to acquire the fee simple in Pt II into s.2 of the No. 1 Act of 1978, then the restrictions on Pt II would also be imported, so that, for example, a lease of a building divided into not less than four self-contained flats with the specified type of rent review clause would not be void if granted after the No. 2 Act of 1978 even if it otherwise fell within Pt II.

21–126 If the effect of the No. 2 Act of 1978 is to remove the prohibition contained in the No. 1 Act of 1978, the result would be as follows:

1. If a lease is granted after the No. 2 Act of 1978 to a person coming within the conditions laid down in Pt II of the No. 2 Act of 1978, the lease is not void but the person has the right to enlarge it into a fee simple under the No. 2 Act of 1978.
2. If a lease was granted before the No. 1 Act of 1978 and it came within the definition of ground rent in the 1967 Act, the lease was valid and the

---

[245] Section 7(1) repealed s.3 except for subs.(5) which refers to rateable valuation certificates.
[246] In fact, the definition section of the No. 2 Act of 1978 provides on the contrary that "the Act of 1967 means the Landlord and Tenant (Ground Rents) Act, 1967".

tenant had the right to acquire the fee simple. If the tenant had not exercised that right by the time the No. 2 Act of 1978 came into force, he or
she retains the same rights, but the right to acquire the fee simple is now
governed by Pt II of the No. 2 Act of 1978 (by virtue of s.73 of the 1980
Act).

3. There is a residual category of leases, namely those granted after the No.
   1 Act of 1978 came into force but *before* the No. 2 Act of 1978 came
   into force, i.e. between 16 May and 28 June 1978. Where such a lease
   was granted to a person who would have been entitled to enlarge his or
   her lease into a fee simple under the 1967 Act, the lease is void, but if the
   person has paid consideration for the void lease, he or she has a right to
   a conveyance of the fee simple.

Policy
21–127 The provisions which allow a tenant to acquire the fee simple (which
certainly apply to leases within the definition that were granted prior to the
No. 1 Act of 1978), or a reversionary lease, apply where the situations outlined below exist. There are restrictions, so that not everyone who falls into
the broad descriptive categories will necessarily be entitled to the fee simple.
Obviously, few people would be interested in acquiring a reversionary lease if
they could acquire the fee simple, but there are fewer restrictions that apply to
the acquisition of reversionary leases than to the acquisition of the fee simple,
which would make this course attractive to some. The three basic situations to
which the provisions apply are:

1. where a lease is what used to be called a "building lease" or "proprietary
   lease", i.e. the buildings were erected at the expense of the lessee. In this
   situation, the old common law rule that fixtures belong to the landlord
   would not reflect the economic reality. Statutory provisions providing
   compensation for improvements are an inadequate remedy in such cases.
   Economic development would be discouraged. Legal relations should
   reflect economic ones, so that the person at whose expense the buildings
   were erected should have the fee simple;
2. where a person has bought a house in a housing estate, but instead of
   acquiring the fee simple has been given a long lease, with the developer
   or management company retaining a reversion, to ensure that covenants
   as to user etc. would be enforceable. This arrangement avoided problems
   that would have arisen if the covenants were freehold (the burden of positive covenants not running at common law, etc.), but it also frequently
   involved the payment by house "buyers" of a "ground rent" to the devel-
   oper/lessor. Since a buyer would have paid, or raised on mortgage, a
   sum that was little less than would have been paid for the freehold and
   looked upon the transaction as "buying their own home", he or she would
   understandably resent continuing to pay rent; and
3. where a tenant is not entitled to the fee simple, he or she may be entitled
   to a reversionary lease (discussed below). This is commonly the case

where the letting is of business premises or of residential premises[247] "divided into not less than 4 separate and self-contained flats".

Right to Acquire the Fee Simple

21–128 The general right to acquire the fee simple is conferred by s.8 of the No. 2 Act of 1978. It certainly applies to leases falling within the definition that were granted before the No. 1 Act of 1978. It is also applied retrospectively by s.73 of the 1980 Act in order to preserve similar rights under the 1967 Act. The persons entitled to acquire the fee simple are listed in ss.9 to 16 of the No. 2 Act of 1978 and are discussed below. The unrepealed sections of the 1967 Act continue to apply to such persons, so that, for example, a county registrar can determine disputes in regard to the acquisition of the fee simple.[248]

21–129 A person entitled to acquire the fee simple also has the right to acquire intermediate interests.[249] If a person does not have the right to acquire the fee simple, he or she has no right to acquire intermediate interests.[250] There is no right to acquire the fee simple in a lease in a horizontal layer above the ground.[251]

21–130 Part II of the No. 2 Act of 1978, which deals with the right to purchase the fee simple, does not apply to a person holding a house under a shared ownership lease pursuant to the Housing (Miscellaneous Provisions) Act 1992 since that is a separate scheme for acquiring the fee simple in a house from a housing authority. Section 26 of the No. 2 Act of 1978 gives a tenant of a housing authority, other than a tenant under a shared ownership lease, the right to acquire the fee simple under the section.

Business Premises

21–131 Although the problem of ground rents arose mainly, in social and political terms, in relation to residential premises, Pt II of the No. 2 Act of 1978 is capable of applying to business premises also.

Dwelling Houses

21–132 Since the main objection to ground rents arose in relation to dwelling houses, the No. 2 Act of 1978, in addition to general powers applying to

---

[247] No. 2 Act of 1978 s.16.
[248] *Heatons Wholesale Ltd v McCormack* [1994] 2 I.L.R.M. 83.
[249] No. 2 Act of 1978 s.8.
[250] *Metropolitan Properties v O'Brien* [1995] 2 I.L.R.M. 383.
[251] *Metropolitan Properties v O'Brien* [1995] 2 I.L.R.M. 383 at 391. The judge held that the legislature did not contemplate the situation.

the acquisition of the fee simple, contained a special scheme in Pt III which is applicable only to dwelling houses.[252]

21–133 Under Pt III of the No. 2 Act of 1978 the Property Registration Authority,[253] upon application made by a lessee, if satisfied that the lessee is entitled to acquire the fee simple, whether with or without the consent of the lessor, where the lessor is known, can issue a "vesting certificate" under s.22 which has the effect of vesting the fee simple in the applicant. The Property Registration Authority must be satisfied that the purchase price has been paid to the person entitled to the fee simple or deposited with the Authority,[254] but can proceed to act as arbitrator if necessary.

Conditions
21–134 Section 9 of the No. 2 Act of 1978 sets out the conditions to be satisfied by a lease if the person entitled is to have the right to purchase the fee simple. All the following conditions in s.9 have to be fulfilled:

(a) There are permanent buildings on the land and the portion of the land not covered by buildings is subsidiary and ancillary[255] to them (i.e. residential and office sites).
(b) The permanent buildings are not an "improvement" defined in subs.(2) as "any addition to or alteration of the buildings ... but does not include any alteration or reconstruction of the buildings so that they lose their original identity".
(c) The buildings were not in breach of a covenant in the lease.

In addition, one of the alternative conditions in s.10 must be complied with:

1. The buildings were erected by the lessee or the person entitled to the lessee's interest.
2. The lease is for a term of 50 years or more *and* the rent is less than the rateable valuation *and* the permanent buildings were not erected by the lessor: it is presumed in this case that they are not unless the contrary is shown.

---

[252] It was originally designed to run for five years from the date the No. 2 Act of 1978 came into force (1 August 1978): No. 2 Act of 1978 s.18. It was extended: Landlord and Tenant (Ground Rents) (Amendment) Act 1983 s.1; Landlord and Tenant (Ground Rents) (Amendment) Act 1984 s.2; but the restriction was later removed: Landlord and Tenant (Ground Rents) (Amendment) Act 1987 s.1.

[253] Formerly the Registrar of Titles: the Property Registration Authority was granted its powers in relation to Pt III of the No. 2 Act of 1978 by the Registration of Deeds and Title Act 2006 s.10(1)(c).

[254] No. 2 Act of 1978 s.22(2).

[255] For discussion of the meaning of "subsidiary and ancillary", see *A. O'Gorman & Co Ltd v JES Holdings Ltd* [2005] IEHC 168; *Digital Hub Development Agency v Keane* [2008] IEHC 22; and W. Walshe, "From Riches to Rags: Expropriation by the Ground Rents Acts" (2014) 19(2) C.P.L.J. 40.

3. Where the lease was granted by the lessor to the nominee (i.e. the buyer or tenant) of a builder to whom the land was demised for the purpose of erecting the buildings under an agreement between the lessor and the builder, whereby the builder, after contracting to sell the buildings, would surrender his or her lease in consideration of the lessor granting a new lease to the builder's nominee.

4. Where the lease was granted by the lessor to the nominee (i.e. the buyer or tenant) of the builder under an agreement between the lessor and the builder whereby, on the erection of the buildings by the builder, the lessor would grant a lease to the builders' nominees (same as 3, but the builder has no lease).

5. The lease was granted, either at the time of, or subsequent to, the expiration or surrender of a previous lease[256]:

   (a) at a rent less than the rateable valuation of the property at the date of the grant of the lease, or

   (b) to the person entitled to the lessee's interest under the previous lease, provided that the previous lease would have been a lease to which Pt II would have applied had the No. 2 Act of 1978 been in force and provided that it shall be presumed, until the contrary is proved, that the person to whom the lease was granted was so entitled (i.e. it is a lease granted in renewal of a previous lease and the previous lease would have entitled the lessee of it to enlarge it into a fee simple had the Act then been in force).

6. The lease is a reversionary lease granted after 31 March 1931 to a person entitled to it under the 1931, 1958 [or 1980] Acts.[257]

7. The lease is for a term of not less than 50 years and made:

   (a) partly in consideration of a sum of money other than rent paid by the lessee before the grant of the lease, which is deemed to include money paid in redemption of rent (whenever paid);

   (b) partly in consideration of the expenditure of a sum of money, other than on decoration, by the lessee on the premises; or

   (c) both (a) and (b);

   where the sum is not less than 15 times the yearly amount of the rent. A lease for a term of not less than 50 years[258] shall be deemed to comply with condition 7, if:

   (a) it was granted partly in consideration of the lessee undertaking to carry out specified works on the premises;

   (b) the amount to be spent on the works was not specified;

   (c) works were carried out by the lessee; and

   (d) the reasonable cost of the works taken alone or together with any fine or other payment mentioned in condition 7 is not less than 15 times the yearly rent or the greatest rent reserved, whichever is the lesser.

---

[256] Amended by Landlord and Tenant (Amendment) Act 1980 s.71.
[257] Reference to the 1980 Act was added by s.30(2)(c) of the 1980 Act.
[258] No. 2 Act of 1978 s.12.

21–135 Condition 7 has been extended by the 1980 Act to cover leases for *less* than 50 years.[259] A person entitled to such a lease has the right to acquire the fee simple if, in addition to one of the above, *all* the following conditions are complied with:

(a) It is a *sub-lease* under a (superior) lease to which Pt II of the 1978 Act applies.
(b) The land demised in the sub-lease is the whole or part of the land demised in the superior lease.
(c) The term equals or exceeds the lesser of the following: 20 years or two-thirds of the term of the superior lease, and in any case expires at the same time as, or not more than 15 years before, the expiration of the superior lease.
(d) The other requirements of condition 7 are fulfilled (i.e. 7(a) or 7(b) or 7(c)).

21–136 In *Walsh v Registrar of Titles*[260] the premises consisted of a dwelling house, shop, offices, and a slaughter house store. It had been used for business purposes for some years. The Registrar of Titles refused a vesting certificate on the ground that he was not satisfied that the buildings were constructed wholly or principally as a dwelling house. The Circuit Court held that the premises were deemed to be a dwelling house within the meaning of s.19 of the No. 2 Act of 1978. In *Eastern Health Board v O'Beirne*[261] a lease granted in 1899 for 99 years contained a covenant that the property was to be used as a dispensary. At the time of the proceedings the lease was held by the Eastern Health Board which wished to enlarge it. The owner of the fee simple resisted the application. The Circuit Court upheld the decision of the Registrar that the buildings were not constructed wholly or principally as a dwelling house.

Restrictions

21–137 The No. 2 Act of 1978 contains restrictions on the right to acquire a fee simple under the Act. A person declared under s.15(1)[262] of the 1958 Act not to be entitled to a reversionary lease of the land under that Act, and who is in possession of the land under a lease or tenancy, or by virtue of s.15(2), is not entitled to acquire the fee simple.[263] Section 15(1) of the 1958 Act applied where the lessor of such a person had a reversion of at least 15 years and the lessor intended to develop the property.[264] Section 15(1) of the 1958 Act is in almost identical terms to s.33(1) of the 1980 Act which continues the restriction in

---

[259] Landlord and Tenant (Amendment) Act 1980 s.72, extends condition 7 in ss.10 and 12 of the No. 2 Act of 1978.
[260] Unreported, Southern Circuit Court, Record No. E 309/84, 24 October 1984.
[261] Unreported, Circuit Court, Wicklow, Record No. 5/83, 17 April 1984.
[262] Continued by s.3(4)(a) of the 1967 Act, now repealed by s.7 of the No. 2 Act of 1978.
[263] No. 2 Act of 1978 s.16(1).
[264] Section 15 of the 1958 Act was continued by s.3(4)(a) of the 1967 Act, but this was then repealed by s.7 of the No. 2 Act of 1978.

relation to reversionary leases. Section 16 of the No. 2 Act of 1978 provides that a person is not entitled to acquire the fee simple under s.8 if the lease:

(a) is used for business purposes or includes a building divided into not less than four self-contained flats with a rent review clause allowing the rent to be altered within 26 years of the beginning of the lease, not being a clause that allows for the alteration of the rent once only and within five years from the beginning or upon erection of buildings or upon breach of covenant in the lease[265];

(b) was granted before the 1967 Act, for business purposes where the lessee is restricted to dealing in commodities supplied by the lessor (e.g. a "solus" agreement where the land is used as a garage, service station, etc.); or

(c) contains a covenant requiring the lessee to erect buildings on the land if and for so long as the covenant has not been complied with.

21–138 Section 16(2) of the No. 2 Act of 1978 contained two other cases where a person would be disqualified:

(a) if the lease was made by the Commissioners of Irish Lights; or

(b) if the lease was made by a harbour authority within the meaning of the Harbours Act 1946.

21–139 Section 4 of the No. 2 Act of 1978 provided that that Act did not bind a Minister of the Government or the Commissioners of Public Works or the Irish Land Commission. This absolute disqualification was amended by the 1980 Act[266] so that it now only applies if the appropriate State authority, or under s.16, the Minister for Transport, is satisfied that the acquisition of the fee simple would not be in the public interest. The list of official entities not bound by the No. 2 Act of 1978, set out in s.4, was amended by s.2 of the Landlord and Tenant (Ground Rents) Act 2005 to remove the now defunct Land Commission and to include the Industrial Development Agency (Ireland), the Shannon Free Airport Development Company and Udarás na Gaeltachta.[267]

---

[265] Amended by Landlord and Tenant (Amendment) Act 1984 s.8: the right to acquire the fee simple is not to be excluded by reason only of a provision in a reversionary lease granted after the 1984 Act for review of the rent.

[266] 1980 Act s.70.

[267] The amendment was by way of substituting a new s.4 into the No. 2 Act of 1978. In *Digital Hub Development Agency v Keane* [2008] IEHC 22, O'Neill J., considering the applicable principles of statutory interpretation, concluded that it was beyond doubt that the identified State agencies could not have the ground rents legislation applied against them but could seek to avail of it. "Manifestly, in my view if one of the State organs mentioned in section 4 avails of the provisions of the Act to claim a fee simple they could only be so entitled if they demonstrate compliance with the conditions set out in the Act for entitlement to a conveyance of the fee simple."

Purchase Price

21–140 The original provisions for the determination of the purchase price of the fee simple[268] were found to be unworkable in *Gilsenan v Foundry House Investments Ltd*.[269] A new formula has therefore been introduced by s.7 of the Landlord and Tenant (Amendment) Act 1984 (the "1984 Act"). This retains the overriding principle of the price which an arbitrator believes a willing purchaser would pay and a willing vendor would accept, but links it to several price-pertinent factors, such as existing and prospective rents, interest yields on government securities, costs and expenses incurred, and also "if the land is used for the purposes of business, or exceeds one acre in area and is not used for the purposes of business, the area and nature of the land, its location and user and the state of repair of any buildings or structures thereon". This latter indicator, where the permanent buildings on the land have reached the end of their useful life and contribute little if anything to the overall value of the ground, can be treated as broadly synonymous with the site's potential development value.[270] In *Digital Hub Development Agency v Keane*,[271] it was held that, where the fee simple owners' expected right to occupation, on account of the application of renewal rights to existing tenancies, was likely to be deferred by more than half a century, the value of the site based on its development value could be discounted by as much as 95 per cent.[272]

Deasy's Act Grants

21–141 "Lease" in the No. 2 Act of 1978 is defined as including a fee farm grant[273] and so a Deasy's Act grant which complies with the conditions in Pt II would appear to come within the provisions, even though the tenant would already have a fee simple. Nevertheless there is good ground for believing that such an existing interest is enlargeable under the Act because the acquisition of the fee simple under the No. 2 Act of 1978 has important effects on the covenants. Although the estate would remain the same, the interest of the tenant is enlarged in the sense that his or her rights of ownership are greater than before. Section 12 of the LCLRA 2009 prohibits the creation of a fee farm grant and provides that any instrument purporting to create one will have the effect of vesting the fee simple in the grantee.

---

[268] Originally contained in s.18 of the 1967 Act, replaced by s.17 of the No. 2 Act of 1978.

[269] [1980] I.L.R.M. 273. In *Byrne v Loftus* [1978] I.R. 211, the Supreme Court had adopted a formula for determining the "gross rent" under the 1931 Act for a new tenancy, but the same court in *Gilsenan* pointed out that in *Loftus* the formula was based on a much shorter 21-year period.

[270] [2008] IEHC 22.

[271] [2008] IEHC 22.

[272] O'Neill J. concluded that this discounted sum should be added to the price originally fixed by the County Registrar to arrive at the definitive purchase price.

[273] No. 2 Act of 1978 s.3.

Yearly Tenants

21–142 Provisions as to yearly tenants are contained in s.15 of the No. 2 Act of 1978 as amended by s.9 of the 1984 Act. This applies where the land:

(a) is mostly covered by buildings[274] which were not erected by the lessor[275];

(b) is held under a yearly tenancy; and

(c) has been so held by the tenant or by his or her predecessors in title for 25 years prior to the service of notice by the tenant of intention to acquire the fee simple under s.4 of 1967 Act[276] and where the rent is less than the rateable value[277] and the letting is not of a "tied" accommodation, i.e. dependent on a person continuing to hold a particular job.[278]

Sporting Leases

21–143 The Landlord and Tenant (Amendment) Act 1971 (the "1971 Act") had as its objective the extension of the rights to reversionary leases under the 1958 Act to clubs and societies that used land for recreational purposes, such as tennis, football or athletic clubs, etc. The 1980 Act substituted for references in the 1971 Act to the 1958 Act references to the 1980 Act. This had the effect of giving such clubs the right, in addition, to acquire the fee simple in their premises under the No. 2 Act of 1978.

21–144 One problem in relation to sports clubs was whether, in terms of the above conditions, the area of land not covered by buildings was "subsidiary" to the land covered by buildings, bearing in mind that the area used for sport, such as a golf course, was likely to be more extensive in area than the land covered by buildings, such as the club house.

21–145 In *Fitzgerald (Trustees of Castleknock Tennis Club) v Corcoran*[279] the plaintiffs held the premises under lease for a term of 99 years from 1973. It was a sporting lease within the meaning of the 1971 Act, granted to them by the landlord by virtue of a High Court order. The trustees brought an application to enlarge their interest in the property to a fee simple under s.4 of the 1967 Act. Lardner J. in the High Court held that the words "permanent buildings" in the Act could not be construed as including a hard tennis court and car park, which were part of the premises, and that the tennis courts could not be considered as being subsidiary or ancillary to the club house. The judge rejected the trustees' application to acquire a fee simple in the whole of the leased premises and stated a case to the Supreme Court to determine whether the club was entitled to acquire the fee simple in the club house and such ground as was "subsidiary

---

[274] No. 2 Act of 1978 s.15(1)(a).

[275] No. 2 Act of 1978 s.15(1)(d).

[276] No. 2 Act of 1978 s.15(1)(c).

[277] No. 2 Act of 1978 s.15(1)(d).

[278] No. 2 Act of 1978 s.15(1)(g).

[279] [1991] I.L.R.M. 545.

and ancillary" thereto. The Supreme Court held that the trustees were entitled to invoke s.14 so as to entitle them to acquire the fee simple interest in the club house and such ground as was subsidiary and ancillary to it, the balance of the ground being deemed to be a vacant lease within the meaning of s.14(2).

21–146 Referring to s.14(2), Finlay C.J. held:

"The reference in that subsection to 'so much of the land as is subsidiary and ancillary' in subclause (a), and the reference to 'the residue of the land' in subclause (b) makes it abundantly clear that the true meaning of the words 'not wholly subsidiary and ancillary,' contained in section 14(1), must be referring to a portion of land held under a lease, some area of which is subsidiary and ancillary, and some area of which is not."

21–147 Finlay C.J. concluded that the provisions of s.14 applied to sporting leases and that therefore the fiction of a "partly-built lease" allowed the sporting lease to qualify within the conditions for the acquisition of the fee simple.

The Effect on Covenants: Section 28
21–148 Section 28(1)[280] and (2) of the No. 2 Act of 1978 provide as follows:

"(1) Subject to subsection (1A), where a person to whom Part II of this Act applies acquires the fee simple in land under the Act of 1967 or Part III of this Act—

(a) covenants (except any of those specified in subsection (2)) affecting the land in the lease under which the person held the land thereupon cease to have effect, and

(b) no new covenant affecting the land shall be created when the fee simple is being conveyed, except with the person's agreement.

(1A) Subsection (1) has effect where the fee simple in the land concerned is acquired on or after 27 February 2006, unless before that date—

(i) a notice of intention to acquire the fee simple was served by the person in accordance with section 4 of the Act of 1967, or

(ii) an application was made by the person to the Registrar of Titles under Part III of this Act.

(2) In the case of a covenant—

(a) which protects or enhances the amenities of any land occupied by the immediate lessor of the grantee, or

(b) which relates to the performance of a duty imposed by statute on any such person, or

(c) which relates to a right of way over the acquired land or a right of drainage or other right necessary to secure or assist the development of other land,

---

[280] As substituted by s.77 of the Registration of Deeds and Title Act 2006.

the covenant shall, notwithstanding anything contained in this Act, continue in full force and effect and shall be enforceable as follows:

(i) in the case of a covenant which does not relate to a right of way, right of drainage or other right aforesaid, by any such person or his personal representatives or successors in title, as if their acquisition had not occurred, and

(ii) in the case of a covenant which does so relate, by any person aggrieved by breach of the covenant."

Scope of the Section

21–149 As enacted, s.28 of the No. 2 Act of 1978 applied "where a person having an interest in land acquires the fee simple in the land". This enabled it to be invoked in order to extinguish covenants where the former tenant had acquired the fee simple by any means, including by voluntary disposition or conveyance for value or through the application of various statutory provisions. However, the amended section, in confining its application to where the fee simple has been acquired under the ground rents legislation, has considerably diminished its scope. On the other hand, the amended s.28 enables a new covenant to be entered into upon the acquiring of the fee simple with the agreement of the person acquiring it, whereas the unamended section had contained a blanket prohibition on the creation of covenants in conveying the fee simple. Similarly, the former s.28 had the effect of extinguishing "all covenants subject to which he held the land", whereas the amended s.28 applies only to "covenants...affecting the land in the lease". Any potential significance to be attached to this difference in wording has to be tempered against the unlikelihood of a covenant that does not affect the land being enforceable against a successor in any event, and the facility afforded by s.49(6)(b) of the LCLRA 2009 which enables parties to an instrument creating a covenant to agree that its application is personal to the parties and does not affect the land.

Third Party Covenants

21–150 One question that arises is whether s.28 can be interpreted as discharging restrictive covenants the benefit of which is vested not in the former landlord or former tenant, but in a third party under the doctrine of *Tulk v Moxhay*.[281] These covenants will be referred to as "third party covenants". In *Whelan v Cork Corporation*[282] Murphy J., upheld by the Supreme Court,[283] held that the section did discharge such covenants.

21–151 In *Whelan* the freehold owner of land granted a lease for 99 years in 1908. In 1948 the lessee was granted a further term, commencing in 2007, by a reversionary lease of the same land. In 1937 the lessee sublet part of the land,

---

[281] (1848) 2 Ph. 774. Pringle J. in *Williams & Co Ltd v LSD and Quinnsworth*, unreported, High Court, 19 June 1970, p.16.
[282] [1991] I.L.R.M. 19.
[283] There was an unsuccessful appeal to the Supreme Court.

known as Instow, to a sublessee. The sublease of Instow contained a covenant, binding the lessors, not to build, erect or permit or suffer to be built or to be erected on any part of the lands retained by the lessors (in effect the sublessor) any building or erection of a greater height than 12 feet from the existing ground level. "Lessors" was defined in the sublease of Instow to mean the persons for the time being entitled to receive rent under it. In 1989 the sublease of 1937 became vested in the plaintiffs by assignment. The assignment was expressly subject to covenants contained in the sublease. In 1948 the lessee under the 1908 lease granted a second sublease of a different part of the land to another sublessee. This part of the land became known as Riverside Cottage. The 1948 sublease of Riverside Cottage contained a covenant, in similar terms to that contained in the 1937 sublease of Instow. In 1984 the sublessee under the 1948 sublease of Riverside Cottage assigned his interest to the defendants, subject to the covenants. In 1989 the defendants also acquired the sublessor's interest in Riverside Cottage under the leases of 1908 and 1948 and a few days later obtained a conveyance of the freehold in Riverside Cottage. The conveyance was stated as being subject to the intent that the leases should merge with and be extinguished in the freehold reversion. The defendants, Cork Corporation, began roadworks involving the construction of a fly-over which would exceed 12 feet in height. The plaintiffs sought an injunction claiming that the roadworks would be in breach of the covenant in the 1937 sublease of Instow which had been repeated in the 1948 sublease of Riverside Cottage. The issue was whether the defendants were bound by the covenant.

21–152 The defendants argued that they were not "lessors" within the meaning of the 1937 sublease and so were not expressly bound by the covenant (i.e. in privity of estate), also that they were not bound under the principle of *Tulk v Moxhay* because they had no notice of the covenant, and that, in any case, when they had taken a conveyance of the fee simple to the Riverside Cottage land, the covenant had ceased to affect them by virtue of s.28 of the No. 2 Act of 1978.

21–153 Murphy J. held, first, that the defendants were "lessors" under the 1937 sublease if the word were given an extended interpretation. That expression, he held, was intended to identify not simply the immediate lessors, but in addition those persons who were also entitled to an interest in the Riverside land and able to burden it with a similar covenant. The judge then went on to apply *Tulk v Moxhay* and held that the defendants had constructive notice of the covenant at the time they acquired the fee simple in the Riverside land. They had acquired the fee simple in order to free themselves of the burden of covenants contained in the leases of the Riverside land and so it would have been reasonable for them to make inquiries as to whether any third parties could claim the benefit of other covenants affecting that land. Thus, apart from s.28, the judge held that the covenant would have bound the defendants in equity. Despite these findings the judge finally decided that the covenant had ceased to bind the defendants under s.28 of the No. 2 Act of 1978 when they acquired the fee simple. The judge found that the covenants which, with a "very limited number of exceptions", ceased to have effect under s.28 were not only those contained in the lease formerly held by the enlarging lessee, but also third-party covenants. The judge did not decide, as a constitutional issue, whether this contravened Art.40.2 as an unjust attack on property rights since the Attorney General did not appear to argue the issue.

21–154 The Supreme Court upheld Murphy J. on the same terms in an ex tempore judgment. It is, however, difficult to see how the defendants were "lessors" of the Instow land (that granted by the sublease of 1937) in any sense at all. Not only were they never entitled to receive rent in respect of Instow, but they never acquired any interest in it. All they acquired was an interest in the Riverside land. Even if "lessor" in the 1937 sublease of Instow is taken to mean someone who had, or later acquired, an interest in the original 1908 or 1948 leases, those leases referred to the entire land and the interests acquired by the defendants through them related only to the Riverside part of the land. Furthermore, if they were indeed "lessors" in a literal sense, they would have been bound by the covenant in the 1937 sublease under s.13 of Deasy's Act, or in privity of estate, to use the common law expression.

21–155 It is open to question whether s.28 ought to be able to destroy not only covenants binding between the former landlord and the former tenant, but also third party covenants. The evident purpose of the section was to relieve the new fee simple from the burden of covenants contained in the original lease which might have been appropriate between landlord and tenant but which would unduly restrict a fee simple. But it is a far wider proposition to suggest that the fees simple created under the No. 2 Act of 1978, which was concerned with enlarging leases into freeholds, should be freer of covenants than ordinary fees simple. After *Whelan* it seems that in relation to third parties s.28 exempts very few covenants from the generally destructive effect of the section. It therefore follows that the section provides some scope for use as a means of destroying restrictive covenants. An ampler facility for seeking extinguishment of covenants has been established by s.50 of the LCLRA 2009, but this requires an application to court and the obtaining and registering of a court order. It should also be noted that s.28(4) of the No. 2 Act of 1978 amends s.72 of the Registration of Title Act 1964 by adding, to the list of interests which bind a purchaser of registered land without registration, covenants preserved by s.28. It seems unfortunate that the No. 2 Act of 1978 did not instead require such covenants to be noted on the register at the time the fee simple is acquired under that Act or the 1967 Act or (until the section's amendment by the Registration of Deeds and Title Act 2006) by any other means. Most interests coming within s.72 are of the kind which could be discovered, although not without difficulty in some cases, by inspecting the land itself, but one could hardly expect this to glean evidence of s.28 covenants unless, perhaps, they relate to a right of way and there is a visible path on the land. Where a covenant is extinguished following an application to court under s.50 of the LCLRA 2009, the order as to extinguishment, including any conditions attaching to it, is to be registered, as the

case may be, in either the Land Registry or the Registry of Deeds.[284] It should
be noted that the amended s.28 of the No. 2 Act of 1978 would not have extinguished the covenant in *Whelan v Cork Corporation*, had it then been enacted,
as the amended section requires for extinguishment that the fee simple have
been acquired pursuant to the ground rents legislation, and the fee simple of the
Riverside land in *Whelan* had been acquired by conveyance.

Constitutionality of Section 28

21–156 The issue of constitutionality was left unresolved by *Whelan*. It had
been argued that if the section rendered ineffective covenants which had
previously affected the land under *Tulk v Moxhay*, then it would be unconstitutional, given the absence of compensation; and that a court, faced with
a choice between alternative interpretations, one of which would render the
section unconstitutional and one of which would not, should, in accordance
with the decision in *East Donegal Co-operative Livestock Marts Ltd v Attorney-General*,[285] choose the constitutional interpretation. That decision also
recognised, however, that where words were clear and unambiguous, the court
should give effect to them even if that rendered a statute void as being unconstitutional. Murphy J. considered that the words were clear and unambiguous
so that there was no real choice to be made:

> "It is difficult to escape the wide net cast by the words 'all covenants'[286]
> subject to which the land was held and any argument that the comprehensive
> expression should be limited to the relationship between the lessee and those
> entitled to the superior interests would be inconsistent with the subsequent
> provisions of the section which provide that certain covenants which do not
> cease to have effect may be enforced 'by any person aggrieved by breach of
> the covenant'. The Oireachtas clearly recognised that the covenants which
> were ceasing to have effect (subject to a very limited number of exceptions)
> included covenants for the benefit of a wide range of covenantees and not
> only the lessor or owner of a superior interest. In my view the Oireachtas has
> shown a clear and unambiguous intention to eliminate a wide range of cov-
> enants, including those for the benefit of third parties, where the fee simple
> is acquired under the provisions of the 1978 Act. This does not necessarily
> render the section unconstitutional. Indeed it would be impossible to reach
> such a conclusion without the benefit of hearing argument from the Attorney
> General to the contrary."[287]

---

[284] LCLRA 2009 s.50(4).
[285] [1970] I.R. 317.
[286] The original s.28(1) had provided for extinguishment of "all covenants subject to which he
held the land". In the amended subsection the word "all" was dropped.
[287] *Whelan v Cork Corporation* [1991] I.L.R.M. 19 at 27–28.

21–157 In arriving at this conclusion the judge did not consider that the literal meaning was necessarily unconstitutional.[288]

21–158 It could certainly be argued in future that s.28 is unconstitutional, in so far as it affects covenants which are property interests, as an "unjust attack" on such interests under Art.40.3.2°.[289] The effect of *Tulk v Moxhay* is that restrictive covenants are not merely contracts but a species of equitable property interest, and the section deprives third parties of the ability to enforce such covenants and provides no compensation for the loss.

Reversionary Leases

21–159 The grounds for obtaining a reversionary lease are the same as for enlargement of a lease into a fee simple, but fewer restrictions apply to persons entitled to a reversionary lease. The topic is dealt with by Pt III of the 1980 Act as amended by ss.3 and 4 of the 1984 Act.

Right to Reversionary Lease

21–160 The right to a reversionary lease, i.e. a lease to take effect immediately after the determination of the current lease, is contained in s.30 of the 1980 Act. Sections 9, 10 to 12, and 14 of the No. 2 Act of 1978 apply and the conditions in them must be complied with.[290]

Restrictions

21–161 It should be noted that the restrictions set out in s.16 of the No. 2 Act of 1978 do *not* apply to reversionary leases. The applicable restrictions are contained in s.33 of the 1980 Act. A person is not entitled where an interested party proves that:

(a) he or she has an interest in the reversion that is either a freehold or is for a term of not less than 15 years; and

(b) (i) he or she intends or has agreed to pull down and rebuild and has planning permission to do so,

(ii) he or she needs vacant possession to carry out a scheme of development, or

(iii) the grant of a reversionary lease would not be consistent with good estate management,[291]

---

[288] *Whelan v Cork Corporation* [1991] I.L.R.M. 19 at 28.

[289] In this regard, it should be noted that s.50 of the LCLRA 2009, which enables certain covenants to be extinguished pursuant to a court order following an application, also provides for the payment of compensation where "compliance with an order ... will result in a quantifiable loss to the dominant owner or other person adversely affected by the order": subs.(3).

[290] No. 2 Act of 1978 s.30(2).

[291] 1980 Act s.33(1).

or a planning authority shows that the land is in an "obsolete area" in the development plan.[292]

21–162 Under s.33(3) a local authority may refuse a reversionary lease where it is in relation to business premises and the local authority will require possession within five years of the termination of the existing lease for a purpose for which it could acquire the land compulsorily.

Damages
21–163 Section 33(5) provides that if the successful objector to the reversionary lease does not carry out the intention upon which the objection was based, the court can award punitive damages.

Terms
21–164 The lease is for a term of 99 years.[293] The rent is not to be less than the rent under the previous lease and if fixed by the court is one-eighth[294] of the "gross rent" as defined in s.36. The rent can be reviewed by the court under s.3 of the 1984 Act. It had been held in *Gilsenan v Foundry House Investments Ltd*[295] that the previously existing provisions as to the determination of rent in reversionary leases were unworkable.

Reversionary Lease a "Graft"
21–165 Section 39 of the 1980 Act provides that a reversionary lease shall be a graft on the previous lease "for all purposes" and is subject to the same rights and equities as affected the previous lease. The section applies to reversionary leases "whether granted on terms settled under this Part or negotiated between the parties". The words seem capable of applying to all reversionary leases, not merely those to which the tenant is entitled under the Act.

HUMAN RIGHTS

General
21–166 The question may arise as to whether legislation that gives a right to acquire a freehold reversion to a tenant contravenes the right to property of the owner of the reversion. This question has been answered in the negative by the European Court of Human Rights (ECtHR) in *James v United Kingdom (The Duke of Westminster's Case)*[296] in which English leasehold enfranchisement legislation was upheld.

---

[292] 1980 Act s.33(2).
[293] 1980 Act s.34(2).
[294] 1980 Act s.35(1).
[295] [1980] I.L.R.M. 273.
[296] Sub nom *James v United Kingdom* (1986) 8 E.H.R.R. 123.

21–167 The decision of the ECtHR in *James v United Kingdom* was in its turn relied upon by the Irish High Court in *Shirley v O'Gorman*,[297] a case in which the statutory scheme, under which a landlord can be disenfranchised from his or her reversion on the payment of compensation, was challenged with reference to Art.1 of Protocol No. 1 to the European Convention on Human Rights (ECHR) and Art.43 of the Constitution.

21–168 Section 2(1) of the European Convention on Human Rights Act 2003 (the "ECHR Act 2003") provides:

"In interpreting and applying any statutory provision or rule of law, a court shall, in so far as is possible, subject to the rules of law relating to such interpretation and application, do so in a manner compatible with the State's obligations under the Convention provisions."

21–169 "Convention provisions" in s.1 is defined as including the provisions of the Paris Protocol of 1952, Art.1 of which states:

"Every natural or legal person is entitled to the peaceful enjoyment of his possessions. No one shall be deprived of his possessions except in the public interest and subject to the conditions provided for by law and by the general principles of international law. The preceding provisions shall not, however, in any way impair the right of the State to enforce such laws as it deems necessary to control the use of property in accordance with the general interest or to secure the payment of taxes or other contributions or penalties."

21–170 In *Shirley v O'Gorman*, the defendant tenant was the proprietor of retail shops in Carrickmacross, Co. Monaghan. While it was accepted that the overall purpose of the ground rents legislation was to improve the position of tenants, generally perceived as being a disadvantaged class, the case for the plaintiff was that the preferring of the interest of this particular tenant in being able to acquire the freehold on advantageous terms discriminated against the plaintiff's right to the reversion contrary to Art.1 of Protocol No. 1 to the ECHR and the qualified protection of private property rights guaranteed by Art.43 of the Constitution. Referring to the decision of the ECtHR in *James v UK*, Peart J. distinguished between the overall objective of the ground rents legislation, which was to ease the position of tenants, "and the effect which its implementation may have in some instances", so that it could not be regarded as "unreasonable for [the legislature] to determine that landlords should be deprived of the enrichment which would otherwise ensue on reversion of the property, even if in a number of cases 'undeserving' tenants thereby benefited". As a result of this rationale

---

[297] [2006] IEHC 27.

"the operation of the legislation in practice and the scale of the anomalies under it did not render it unacceptable under Article 1, nor did it place an excessive burden on the applicants over and above the disadvantageous effects for landlords generally".[298]

21–171 Peart J. noted that Art.43 of the Constitution acknowledges the right of private ownership in property, which the State guarantees not to abolish, subject to the principle that the exercise of private property rights "ought, in civil society, to be regulated by the principles of social justice", so that "[t]he State, accordingly, may as occasion requires delimit by law the exercise of the said rights with a view to reconciling their exercise with the exigencies of the common good."[299]

21–172 The principle of "distributive justice" requires that, even though in some cases "so-called wealthy or prosperous tenants" can acquire the freehold of valuable commercial property through the ground rents legislation, this "cannot...disturb the integrity of the social justice principles pursued by the legislation, and the presumption of constitutionality in that regard". According to Peart J., one had to consider the ground rents legislation as part of an overall social policy in ease of tenants, which went back to the foundation of the State and earlier. Disadvantage is no more to be judged in purely economic terms than is the concept of ownership itself absolute. In the opinion of Peart J., legislation which diminishes the otherwise uncompromising effect of covenants that restrict assignment, sub-letting and change of use, as with the ground rents legislation, can likewise be considered "as pursuing a social justice objective, which is apart and distinct from any question of wealth redistribution".

21–173 The constitutional requirement that private property rights be balanced by the State in "the exigencies of the common good" postulates something less than absolute necessity as justification and is not displaced by an occasional anomaly, so that a situation where "some persons already prosperous and even wealthy, are entitled to purchase at a fair price the residual interest of the landlord, as well as poorer persons, does not take the scheme outside of a common good exigency". Merely because such exigencies can ease with the passage of time does not mean that the common good is no longer being served when that happens.[300] Likewise, the applicable principle of proportionality (which is that infringements of constitutional rights will be to the minimum extent necessary to satisfy the exigencies of the common good) is not offended by apparent randomness regarding rateable valuations for similar premises in different locations, with the result that in many instances it can be a question of chance whether the rent is less than the rateable valuation.[301] In this regard,

---

[298] [2006] IEHC 27 at para.158.
[299] Article 43.2.
[300] *Tuohy v Courtney* [1994] 3 I.R. 1.
[301] Landlord and Tenant (Ground Rents) (No. 2) Act 1978 s.10, condition 5, as one of the alternative prerequisites that must be satisfied in order to acquire the fee simple, discussed above.

Peart J. noted that often where the rent starts out being more than the rateable valuation, in time the rateable valuation is adjusted to exceed the rent because of works carried out on the property by the tenant or his or her predecessors. Also relevant to the issue is that very frequently the landlord would never be entitled to possession of the property, so that his or her only "residual interest" is the income stream resulting from the rent. In such event, the principle that any person deprived by legislation of his or her otherwise constitutionally protected rights must "be fully compensated at a level equivalent to at least the market value of the acquired property"[302] applies. Peart J. concluded that "simply because the scheme throws up an anomaly or anomalies in this way is insufficient to render it unconstitutional". He said that where there is a general statutory scheme which includes a large number of premises, and "certain criteria are decided upon by the Oireachtas for eligibility into the scheme, it is reasonable that a certain margin of appreciation[303] be permitted to the Oireachtas in the manner in which the scheme is devised."[304]

21–174 The Norwegian ground rents scheme was considered by the ECtHR in *Lindheim v Norway*.[305] Six landowners had entered ground lease arrangements for plots of land. The leases were generally for 99 years. Legislation provided that the lessee could extend the agreement subject to the lessor's right to introduce new contractual conditions.[306] Further legislation placed limits on the amount of rent that lessors could demand, and granted lessees the right to extend their agreements, upon their expiry, on the same terms as previously negotiated and for an indefinite duration.[307] The ECtHR was asked to consider whether there had been a breach of Art.1 of Protocol No. 1 to the ECHR. The court accepted that the legislation pursued a legitimate aim—protecting the interests of lessees who had limited financial means. The court pointed out that states have a wide margin of appreciation in implementing social and economic policies. However, when considering the proportionality of the laws, the court held that a "fair balance" had not been struck between the general interest of the community and the person's rights under Art.1 of Protocol No. 1. There were five reasons proffered for why the "fair balance" had not been struck:

---

[302] *Re Article 26 and Part V of the Planning and Development Bill 1999* [2000] 2 I.R. 321 at 350.

[303] "Margin of appreciation", in the sense of a discretionary scope, is a concept frequently alluded to by the ECtHR in the context of a state's capacity to balance the application of Convention-ensured rights against collective duties owed by the State to its citizens, as demonstrated in recent case law regarding repossession procedures in relation to social housing and "the right to respect for ... family life [and] home" guaranteed by Art.8.

[304] [2006] IEHC 27 at para.200. On appeal to the Supreme Court, the appellant sought to challenge the constitutionality of a number of provisions in the 1967 Act and the No. 2 Act of 1978. The Supreme Court applied the double-construction rule of constitutional interpretation and the presumption of constitutionality to find that the appellant lacked standing to challenge the constitutionality of the No. 2 Act of 1978 s.10(2): *Shirley v O'Gorman* [2012] IESC 5.

[305] (2015) 61 E.H.R.R. 29

[306] Ground Lease Acts 1975 and 1996.

[307] Ground Lease Act 2004 s.33.

1. It was not apparent that Norway had specifically assessed whether s.33 of the Ground Lease Act (as amended) had struck a fair balance between the interests of the lessors and lessees.
2. There were no demands to the general or public interest which could justify the notably low level of rent that was received by lessors under the amended Ground Lease Act.
3. Section 33 most likely went much further than simply addressing potential financial hardship and social injustice. Section 33 applied to contracts of a certain age which were up for renewal, irrespective of the lessees' financial means.
4. Agreements were to be extended indefinitely and rent could not be adjusted beyond inflation-indexed levels. Section 15(2)(1) of the Ground Lease Act excluded the possibility of taking account of the value of the land in rent adjustments.
5. Any increase in the value of the land would be reflected in a sale of the lease with dwellings to third parties—a value accruing only to the lessee. If lessors were to sell their rent entitlements to third parties, the sale price could only reflect the value of the rent received at the controlled amounts.

It could not, therefore, be said that there was a fair distribution of the social and financial burdens created by the amended Ground Lease Act.[308]

Articles 6 and 8 of the ECHR

21–175 Certain rights guaranteed under the ECHR, and the extent to which these are protected in Irish law through the ECHR Act 2003, have fallen to be considered in a number of cases decided by the High Court in the context of repossession procedures under social housing legislation. In each case shades of distinction both in the facts as they affect the respective housing agreements and the ambit of redress sought by particular applicants have been crucial to the outcome arrived at by the court. Of at least equal relevance is a corresponding jurisprudence on rights affecting the home from the ECtHR and the judicial notice taken of these decisions as required by s.4 of the ECHR Act 2003.

21–176 Article 6 of the ECHR provides that "[i]n the determination of his civil rights and obligations...everyone is entitled to a fair and public hearing within a reasonable time by an independent and impartial tribunal established by law". Article 8 states:

"1. Everyone has the right to respect for his private and family life, his home and his correspondence.
2. There shall be no interference by a public authority with the exercise of this right except such as is in accordance with the law and is necessary in a democratic society in the interests of national security, public safety or the economic well-being of the country, for the prevention of disorder

---

[308] (2015) 61 E.H.R.R. 29 at paras 128–134 and 136.

or crime, for the protection of health or morals, or for the protection of the rights and freedoms of others."

21–177 The ECtHR jurisprudence on Art.8 has developed in a piecemeal or incremental manner,[309] as has that of the courts in the UK and Ireland. Because the ECHR has not been incorporated into domestic Irish law by the ECHR Act 2003,[310] the obtaining of a "declaration of incompatibility" under s.5(1) of the Act can represent something of a pyrrhic victory. Subsection (2) goes on to provide that a declaration of incompatibility "shall not affect the validity, continuing operation or enforcement of the statutory provision or rule of law in respect of which it is made", although it may be relied upon by a party to the action that has resulted in its being made in any proceedings brought before the ECtHR. A court order containing a "declaration of incompatibility" must be laid before each House of the Oireachtas within 21 days after the making of the order and a party to the relevant proceedings is entitled, by application to the Attorney General, to seek an *ex gratia* compensation payment from the State. The Government may request an appointed adviser to recommend the amount of any award that it may consider making, and in so doing the adviser "shall take appropriate account of the principles and practice" applied by the ECtHR "in relation to affording just satisfaction to an injured party under Article 41 of the Convention".[311]

21–178 Despite its capacity to make a "declaration of incompatibility", the court cannot creatively re-interpret the law in order to ensure that its application is compatible with the ECHR. This is because s.2(1) of the ECHR Act 2003 provides that the obligation on a court to interpret the law in accordance with the State's obligations under the ECHR is "subject to the rules of law relating to such interpretation and application", which means that the standard principles of statutory interpretation, with their inherent limitations, must continue to apply.[312] Furthermore, although s.3(1) of the ECHR Act 2003 requires every organ of the State to perform its obligations in a manner compatible with the State's obligations under the ECHR, the definition of "organ of the State" in s.1 excludes a court.

Section 62 of the Housing Act 1966
21–179 A number of cases have come before the Irish courts relating to s.62 of the Housing Act 1966 (the "1966 Act"), as amended. This section allowed for a summary procedure, following expiry of notice to quit, by which the District

---

[309] See I. Loveland, "Twenty Years Later: Assessing the Significance of the Human Rights Act 1998 to Residential Possession Proceedings" [2017] 3 Conv. 174.

[310] *Dublin City Council v Fennell* [2005] 1 I.R. 604.

[311] ECHR Act 2003 s.5(3)–(5).

[312] In *Dublin City Council v Gallagher* [2008] IEHC 354, O'Neill J. noted that the equivalent UK statute, the Human Rights Act 1998, was couched in terms which gave the courts greater freedom to interpret a statute in a Convention-compliant manner. On the principles of statutory interpretation, see discussion in *Whelan v Cork Corporation* [1991] I.L.R.M. 19.

Court could grant an order for possession to a housing authority, on being satisfied as to certain prescribed proofs, but without considering the merits of the termination or any mitigating factors adduced by the tenant. It should be pointed out that s.62 has now been repealed by the provisions of s.13(8) of the Housing (Miscellaneous Provisions) Act 2014, which requires the District Court to be satisfied that "recovery of possession by the housing authority is a proportionate response to the occupation of the dwelling by the person concerned." However, it is worth considering the line of jurisprudence which this provision gave rise to, as it has wider significance for the interpretation of ECHR rights.

21–180 The High Court considered four such cases in 2008–2009. In the first, *Leonard v Dublin City Council*,[313] the plaintiff was a tenant from week to week of the defendant housing authority, whose tenancy had been terminated by a notice to quit. She sought a declaration, under s.5(1) of the ECHR Act 2003, that s.62 of the 1966 Act was incompatible with a number of articles of the ECHR, in particular Arts 6 and 8. This contention was based on the fact that s.62 did not allow the District Court, in granting a possession order, to entertain a submission by the occupant, nor to consider anything other than whether the formal proofs required have been satisfied. The plaintiff's tenancy agreement with the defendant had included a clause which provided that her tenancy could be terminated if her former partner, who was alleged to have drug-related and anti-social problems, visited the house held by her under the present tenancy. The agreement included an undertaking by the tenant to keep her former partner out of the house. As a result of several breaches of this undertaking, the defendant, after a number of meetings and warnings, decided to terminate her tenancy. Following expiry of the notice to quit, the defendant sought an order for possession, under s.62 of the 1966 Act, from the District Court. This was granted and the plaintiff's appeal to the Circuit Court was dismissed.

21–181 According to Dunne J., the case had not been established for making a declaration of incompatibility. Referring to several decisions of the ECtHR and relying upon the UK decisions in *Harrow London Borough Council v Qazi*[314] and *Sheffield City Council v Smart*,[315] Dunne J. concluded that Art.8 of the ECHR could not apply if an applicant's right of occupancy to what had been his or her home had been brought to an end in accordance with law. She noted that in *Chapman v United Kingdom*,[316] the ECtHR had acknowledged that national authorities had a margin of appreciation as they were better placed

---

[313] [2008] IEHC 79.
[314] [2003] 3 W.L.R. 792. The court held that Art.8 had been intended to prohibit arbitrary intrusion by the State or public authorities into a person's home life and was not intended as an enhancement of any country's social housing legislation, so that the right guaranteed by the article ceased to apply if a tenant did not have a continuing right to occupy what once had been his or her home.
[315] [2002] L.G.R. 468.
[316] (2001) 33 E.H.R.R. 138.

"to evaluate local needs and conditions". Dunne J. also noted the decision in *Blečić v Croatia*,[317] which had recognised that states must make judgments as to where the boundary lies between the rights of particular classes, not least where a scarce resource needs to be sensibly and strategically apportioned as is the case with social housing.

21–182 In the context of the right to fair procedures, as safeguarded by Art.6, Dunne J. recorded that this had been interpreted in the UK as requiring, not that an administrative decision be reviewable on its facts, but that a court must be satisfied as to the legality of the manner in which that decision was arrived at. To go further, according to the judge, would be to interfere with the process of democratic accountability. On this account, and because all the proofs necessary to secure a possession order under s.66 of the 1966 Act were in order, the proper course would have been to seek judicial review of the housing authority's decision if it were felt to have been procedurally defective.

21–183 *Donegan v Dublin City Council*[318] was decided six weeks after *Leonard v Dublin City Council*,[319] and represented a significant shift in the courts' attitude to the issuing of a declaration of incompatibility. Like the plaintiff in *Leonard*, the plaintiff in *Donegan* was a tenant of the defendant housing authority and challenged the ECHR compatibility of the summary repossession procedures in s.62 of the 1966 Act. In *Donegan*, the possession order had not yet been enforced and the plaintiff disputed the defendant's holding that he had been in breach of his tenancy agreement.[320]

21–184 Laffoy J. noted the ECtHR's decisions in *Blečić v Croatia*[321] and *Tsfayo v United Kingdom*.[322] She distinguished *Leonard v Dublin City Council*[323] from the present case, because in *Leonard* there had been no factual dispute between the parties regarding the ground entitling the council to terminate the tenancy. In *Donegan*, there was a factual dispute between the outcome of a Garda investigation into the house and the plaintiff's argument that his son was not a drug pusher. Laffoy J. found that the plaintiff's Art.8 rights would

---

[317] (2005) 41 E.H.R.R. 13.

[318] [2008] IEHC 288.

[319] [2008] IEHC 79.

[320] The plaintiff lived in the house with his son. A Garda raid had discovered illicit drug material in the son's bedroom as a result of which the conclusion had been formed that the son was a drug pusher. The defendant several times encouraged the plaintiff to seek an exclusion order against his son, to which the plaintiff repeatedly replied that his son was not a drug pusher, but a drug user who was taking steps to battle against his addiction.

[321] (2005) 41 E.H.R.R. 13. Laffoy J. analysed in considerable detail the ECtHR decision in *Connors v United Kingdom* (2005) 40 E.H.R.R. 9, a case involving a gypsy caravan site operated by a local authority and the summary revocation of a licence, interpreting it, notwithstanding a strong focus in the case itself, as being of more pervasive application than in the confined context of gypsy rights. This wider reading has subsequently been followed by the ECtHR also.

[322] [2006] ECHR 981. This had not been opened to the court in *Leonard*.

[323] [2008] IEHC 79.

not be likely to be protected through the device of seeking a judicial review of the council's decision to issue a notice to quit. In the judge's opinion, any such judicial review would have had no prospect of success, because the court cannot substitute its own views for those of the housing authority on an issue of fact found by it. Accordingly, Laffoy J. held that the premises was the applicant's home within the meaning of Art.8[324] and that enforcing a s.62 possession order would be in violation of his Art.8 rights.

21–185 It was held that the summary nature of the s.62 facility displayed a disproportionate bias in favour of the housing authority being able to secure possession with comparative ease, by denying to the plaintiff any effective method of challenging a disputed question of fact on which the decision to serve notice to quit was based, before either the District Court or an independent tribunal. Laffoy J. issued a declaration of incompatibility under s.5(1) of the ECHR Act 2003.[325]

21–186 *Dublin City Council v Gallagher*[326] also concerned a possession order under s.62. The plaintiff argued that the defendant's late mother had been its tenant, and the defendant was not deemed to have satisfied the requirement of being in continuous occupation with the sitting tenant for two years prior to her death, so as to be eligible to be accepted as a tenant in accordance with the plaintiff's house allocation policy. The defendant argued that he had been living with his mother for the requisite time, a contention accepted by the District Court which then stated a case to the High Court in relation to the correct interpretation of s.62 so as to render it compliant with the State's obligations under the ECHR. O'Neill J. held that this was a proper utilisation of s.2 of the ECHR Act 2003, to which the following principles of interpretation should apply:

> "[I]t seems clear to me that the starting point in attempting to construe this section in a Convention compatible way is to first determine the correct construction without regard to the Convention and having done that to then see whether it is possible to impose or intertwine a different meaning where that is necessary to avoid incompatibility with the Convention. Where it is not possible to achieve this without breaching the rules of law relating to interpretation, and where there is an evident breach of a Convention right

---

[324] In *Donegan*, the plaintiff was still in possession because the order granted by the District Court had not been enforced. Laffoy J. did not pursue the line of authority adopted by Dunne J. in *Leonard v Dublin City Council* [2008] IEHC 79, that a property was incapable of being a person's home, within the meaning of Art.8, if he or she was no longer lawfully in possession of it.

[325] The potential alternative route, signalled by s.2, of endeavouring to interpret the law in a Convention-compliant manner was rendered otiose by the section's requirement that the exercise be effected "subject to the rules of law relating to such interpretation and application", as it would not have been possible to secure the desired interpretation without doing violence to the plain wording of s.62, which s.2(1) of the ECHR Act 2003 equally plainly prohibited.

[326] [2008] IEHC 354.

resulting from what is a correct interpretation of the law in question, the proper solution to that problem is a declaration of incompatibility under section 5 of the Act of 2003."[327]

21–187 O'Neill J. pointed out that the court had to adhere to existing rules of interpretation, meaning that "effect must be given to the will of Parliament, such intent being derived from the natural and ordinary meaning of the language used in the law concerned."[328] O'Neill J. also noted that the emerging jurisprudence of the ECtHR tended to regard a premises as capable of being a person's "home" even if the occupation of it is not in accordance with law,[329] so that "[t]he right to respect for one's home is to be viewed as an extension of the right to respect for one's private life." In this regard, the ECtHR had established that "in the realm of eviction proceedings there should, in principle, be an opportunity for an independent tribunal to adjudicate on the proportionality of the decision to dispossess".[330] O'Neill J. drew a distinction between the right to fair procedures (Art.6), and the right to respect for the home (Art.8), in the specific context of a summary possession order under s.62 of the 1966 Act. The procedure adopted by the District Court did not in itself give rise to a finding of incompatibility in relation to fair procedures under Art.6. One had to look to the specific provisions of the ECHR Act 2003. Section 1 excluded the court from the definition of "organ of the State", which s.3 obliged to "perform its functions in a manner compatible with the State's obligations under the Convention provisions." Similarly, the court's obligation, under s.2, to interpret and apply the law with a view to ensuring the same objective, was expressly stated as being "subject to the rules of law relating to such interpretation and application", so that the court had no discretion to amend the language of legislation in order to ensure that it was Convention-compliant. In effect, the District Court had no discretion at all except to state a case to the High Court, as it had done.

21–188 The breach of the defendant's Art.6 right to fair procedures was occasioned by the plaintiff's failure to implement an impartial and effective system whereby disputes in relation to fact, on the basis of which a decision to serve a notice to quit is formed, could be independently challenged and reviewed. A judicial review would probably have merely remitted the issue back to the plaintiff council to reconsider the matter in accordance with procedural fairness. Instead, the council ought in advance to have established procedures to deal with potential questions of contested fact which can result in applications being made to the District Court for possession under s.62.[331]

---

[327] [2008] IEHC 354.
[328] [2008] IEHC 354.
[329] A flagrant departure from the directly opposite conclusion arrived at by Dunne J. in *Leonard v Dublin City Council* [2008] IEHC 79.
[330] O'Neill J. placed considerable reliance on the decision of the ECtHR in *Connors v United Kingdom* (2005) 40 E.H.R.R. 9.
[331] [2008] IEHC 354.

21–189 O'Neill J. acknowledged a certain supererogation in his granting of a declaration of incompatibility under s.5(1) of the ECHR Act 2003, in light of the fact that this had already been done by Laffoy J. in *Donegan*, but said that it was necessary for the court also to make such a declaration in *Gallagher*, so that the absence of such declaration might not prejudice any application the defendant might make to the State for *ex gratia* compensation on the basis of the granting of such a declaration as provided for by s.5(4) of the ECHR Act 2003.

21–190 *Pullen v Dublin City Council*[332] was similar to *Donegan*; notice to quit had been served on the plaintiff tenants of one of the defendant's social housing properties on the basis of alleged anti-social behaviour, and the allegations were vigorously contested. There were, however, some differences. In *Pullen*, each plaintiff suffered from a disability. Although the s.62 possession order had been deferred pending the current proceedings, the plaintiffs had been put out of their house by the hostile enterprise of neighbours. There was also a different emphasis in the pleadings. In *Donegan*, *Leonard*[333] and *Gallagher*, the vehicle of challenge had been the seeking of a declaration of incompatibility on the part of the impugned statutory provision with the State's obligations under the ECHR. In *Pullen*, the relief primarily sought was an order that the defendant, in resorting to the summary possession procedure under s.62, had as an "organ of the State" failed to perform its functions in a Convention-compliant manner. *Leonard v Dublin City Council*[334] could thus be distinguished. In *Pullen*,[335] the plaintiffs' challenge focused on the defendant's failure to seek some less drastic method of requiting its statutory obligation as a provider of social housing, twinned with the absence of any independent and impartial forum in which the plaintiffs could challenge the defendant's conclusion of fact which had informed its decision to serve a notice to quit and then seek to enforce it summarily.[336] A consequence of the plaintiffs being made homeless through enforcement of this possession order was that they would be deemed to have rendered themselves "voluntarily homeless". The effect of this was that they would have no priority claim for alternative housing and would therefore be likely to remain homeless.

21–191 Irvine J. took judicial note of *Blečić v Croatia*,[337] *Tsfayo v United Kingdom*[338] and *McCann v United Kingdom*.[339] The latter stated that a person

---

[332] [2008] IEHC 379.

[333] [2008] IEHC 79.

[334] [2008] IEHC 79.

[335] [2008] IEHC 379.

[336] Irvine J. regarded the process embarked upon by the housing authority as, in effect, an "in-house investigation" which was clearly inadequate to the demonstrated need for impartiality and the seriousness of the potential consequences involved for the tenants.

[337] (2005) 41 E.H.R.R. 13.

[338] [2006] ECHR 981. Irvine J. noted that this decision had not been opened to the court in *Leonard v Dublin City Council* [2008] IEHC 79.

[339] [2008] ECHR 385.

at risk of losing their home "should in principle be able to have the proportionality of the measure determined by an independent tribunal in the light of the relevant principles under Article 8 of the Convention, notwithstanding that, under domestic law, his right of occupation has come to an end." Based on this, Irvine J. set out guidelines for determining in any one case whether the requirement of proportionality had been satisfied:

21–192 A public authority seeking to show that an interference is proportionate must, on the authorities, satisfy the court regarding four matters, namely:

(a) that the objective of restricting the right is so pressing and substantial that it is sufficiently important to justify interfering with a fundamental right;
(b) that the restriction is suitable: it must be rationally connected to the objective in mind so that the limitation is not arbitrary, unfair or based on irrational considerations;
(c) that the restriction is necessary to accomplish the objective intended. In this respect the public authority must adopt the least drastic means of attaining the objective in mind, provided the means suggested are not fanciful; and
(d) that the restriction is not disproportionate. The restriction must not impose burdens or cause harm which is excessive when compared to the importance of the objective to be achieved.

21–193 In *Pullen*, the requirements of an impartial hearing on the disputed facts, and the use of a procedure potentially less disastrous to the tenants, were facilitated by the existence in the letting agreement of a re-entry clause. This would have permitted the defendant to make an application to the court for forfeiture of the lease in accordance with s.14 of the Conveyancing Act 1881. This would have enabled a court to make an assessment as to the grounds on which the re-entry provision was being invoked: this opportunity was denied to the District Court under s.62 of the 1966 Act. In this regard, Irvine J. noted

"that the jurisprudence of the ECtHR suggests that when a defendant seeks to assert that its interference with a particular right was proportionate in all of the circumstances it must be in a position to demonstrate that it adopted the least drastic means of attaining its objective. This is something the defendant has failed to demonstrate in the present case."[340]

21–194 The obligation to use such an alternative procedure was mandated by s.3 of the ECHR Act 2003 and the forfeiture route provided for by s.14 of the Conveyancing Act 1881 presented just such an appropriate alternative procedure.[341]

---

[340] [2008] IEHC 379.
[341] Irvine J. further held the plaintiffs' property rights safeguarded by Art.1 of Protocol No. 1 to the ECHR could be deemed to be subsumed in the primary breach of the right to protection of the home safeguarded under Art.8.

21–195 In *Byrne v Dublin City Council*[342] the facts were similar to those in *Leonard, Donegan* and *Pullen*.[343] The issue was whether the court could award an interlocutory injunction on the basis that enforcement of a District Court possession order would be in breach of the requirement of ensuring respect for the plaintiff's private life under Art.8 of the ECHR. The difficulty with this proposition as simply stated was that the granting of an injunction could be construed as, in reality, seeking to nullify the effect of s.62 of the 1966 Act, which the ECHR Act 2003 did not empower a court to do. Murphy J. noted that Art.13 of the ECHR required the availability of an effective domestic remedy to ensure compliance with ECHR rights, but that it did not oblige the suspension or invalidation of domestic law. No provision of the ECHR could be invoked before the Irish courts to bring about a result contrary to the intention of the Oireachtas as expressed in the ECHR Act 2003.[344] On this general point, Murphy J. observed that

"the Oireachtas has not, through the medium of the [ECHR Act 2003], purported to empower the courts to disapply any statutory provision or rule of law by reference to the Convention: see s. 5(2)(a). It is at least highly questionable whether it could have done so without thereby effecting an impermissible delegation of the legislative powers vested in it by Article 15.2.1°...No injunction can be granted based on a violation of her [the plaintiff's] Convention rights inherent in the statutory provision itself."[345]

21–196 Murphy J. set out the essence of the problem confronted by the court:

"It is clear from the provisions of section 5(2) ... that the power to rectify such incompatibilities is expressly reserved to the Oireachtas. The courts are empowered to draw the attention of the Oireachtas to the problem, but it is then for the Oireachtas to determine both whether it will amend the impugned provision and, if it does, the content of that amendment."[346]

21–197 The recourse primarily open to the court, where injunctive relief is sought, is to draw a distinction between:

* the existence of legislation on foot of which action *may* be taken which *could* violate a Convention-ensured right; and
* the execution of measures by an administrative "organ of the State" pursuant to that legislation, which the court could seek to restrain as being in breach of the obligation imposed on that "organ" to "perform its

---

[342] [2009] IEHC 122.
[343] [2008] IEHC 379.
[344] In this regard, Murphy J. derived comfort from the judgment of O'Neill J. in *Dublin City Council v Gallagher* [2008] IEHC 354.
[345] [2009] IEHC 122.
[346] [2009] IEHC 122.

functions in a manner compatible with the State's obligations under the Convention's provisions" by s.3 of the ECHR Act 2003.[347]

21–198 From this perspective, Laffoy J.'s decision in *Donegan* was explicable on the basis that the judge had not deemed it necessary to consider granting an injunction as the plaintiff had been allowed to remain in possession even after the making of the District Court order. An injunction in that case, therefore, would have been tantamount to suspending the operation of s.62 of the 1966 Act, which the ECHR Act 2003 does not permit.[348] Irvine J. in *Pullen v Dublin City Council* had indicated that the duty imposed by s.3 of the ECHR Act 2003, on an organ of the State to perform its functions in a manner compatible with the State's obligations under the ECHR, can be interpreted as limiting "the right of a local authority to resort to a particular procedure notwithstanding that it is one provided for by statute, at least insofar as there is another means of attaining the legitimate objective being pursued". That "other means" was the forfeiture procedure under s.14 of the Conveyancing Act 1881 which would enable the court, upon application made, to consider the merits of the grounds on which the re-entry clause in the letting had been invoked. On this basis there could be said to be a serious question to be tried, as to whether the order for possession had been sought and obtained unlawfully by the defendant (albeit not granted unlawfully),[349] so that, if enforced, there would have been a breach of the right of the plaintiff to respect for her home as safeguarded by Art.8. This being so, and having regard to the clear thrust of the balance of convenience, an interlocutory injunction was granted.

21–199 The appeals in both *Donegan* and *Gallagher* were heard together in the Supreme Court in 2012.[350] McKechnie J. referred to the ECtHR cases of *Connors v United Kingdom*[351] and *McCann v United Kingdom*.[352] He emphatically rejected submissions that in this jurisdiction judicial review provides an adequate safeguard for Art.8 rights: "judicial review is not, in any meaningful sense, a forum to which recourse can be had in the presenting circumstances." McKechnie J. pointed out that a s.62 possession order was a lawful

---

[347] "Since [the ECHR Act 2003] makes clear that Irish law continues to operate even where it is incompatible with the Convention, clearly no injunction can issue to restrain the operation of domestic law. However ... that is not to say that administrative as distinct from legislative action is immune from the application of the Convention." *Byrne v Dublin City Council* [2009] IEHC 122.

[348] Murphy J. seems to have been of the view that the decision of Laffoy J. in *Donegan v Dublin City Council* [2008] IEHC 288 was primarily about the summary nature of the proceedings before the District Court "rather than a breach [of the plaintiff's Convention-safeguarded rights] flowing from discretionary administrative action"—an interesting observation, since this was largely the basis on which Laffoy J. indicated that the case before her was capable of being distinguished from that decided by Dunne J. in *Leonard v Dublin City Council* [2008] IEHC 79.

[349] The court not being an "organ of the State" and so not subject to the s.3 duty.

[350] [2012] IESC 18.

[351] (2005) 40 E.H.R.R. 9.

[352] [2008] ECHR 385.

interference with Art.8 rights, and that therefore Art.8 is engaged. In determining whether an interference is Art.8 compliant, the regulatory framework
within which the measure has been established and operates will be assessed.
Questions to determine proportionality might be: (i) is the framework procedure sufficient to afford true respect to the interests safeguarded by the
article?; (ii) is the decision-making process fair in such a way as to respect
that right?; (iii) has the affected person an opportunity to have any relevant
and weighty arguable issues tested before an independent tribunal?; and (iv)
has that person an opportunity to have such an issue considered against the
measure? Where any one or more of these requirements is absent, it may be
considered that the safeguards necessarily attendant on Art.8 for the purposes
of its vindication have not been satisfied. A violation in such circumstances
may follow. While no relief was granted in relation to *Gallagher*, a declaration
of incompatibility was issued in relation to *Donegan*. This represented the first
time the Supreme Court made a declaration of incompatibility pursuant to s.5
of the ECHR Act 2003. McKechnie J. emphatically rejected the argument that
to make such a declaration would "open the floodgates" and render housing
authorities unable to carry out their duties. The court refused to accept that
additional administrative burdens would justify a violation of ECHR rights
remaining in existence without remedy.

21–200 A declaration of incompatibility does not render a legislative provision invalid, so s.62 remained operable until it was repealed in 2014.[353] Housing authorities could also still avail of other methods generally available to
landlords to recover possession.[354]

21–201 *McCauley v Fergus*[355] also concerned s.62 of the 1966 Act.[356] An order
for possession was affirmed by Fergus J. in the Circuit Court, and judicial
review of this decision was refused by the High Court.[357] As with the cases
discussed above, the tenant argued that the summary nature of the proceedings
under s.62 infringed his rights under Art.8 of the ECHR. However, no declaration of incompatibility was sought in this case. The main issue to be considered
was whether there had been a breach of s.2 of the ECHR Act 2003. The tenant
contended that in order to be ECHR-compatible, s.62[358] of the 1966 Act should
be read as requiring an independent adjudication of whether the dwelling
was, in fact, the applicant's home within the meaning of Art.8. If so, an order
for possession should only then be made in the council's favour where this
was proportionate. The court considered whether such an interpretation was

---

[353] Housing (Miscellaneous Provisions) Act 2014 s.13(8).
[354] See generally, Ú. Ní Chatháin, "Section 62 of the Housing Act 1966 and the Implications of
the Decision in *Donegan*" (2012) 17(3) C.P.L.J. 54.
[355] [2018] IECA 30.
[356] The case was initiated before the relevant provisions of the Housing (Miscellaneous Provisions) Act 2014 had been commenced.
[357] [2015] IEHC 825.
[358] The judgment refers to s.66 in several instances but this appears to be a typo.

"reasonably open" in respect of s.62. It was argued that it ought to be possible to construe s.62 of the 1966 Act in light of the interpretative rules contained in s.2 of the ECHR Act 2003 in order to provide for an independent external mechanism which would determine (i) whether the property in question was the applicant's "home" within the meaning of Art.8 ECHR, and (ii) whether the making of a possession order would amount to a disproportionate interference with such rights. However, Hogan J. in the Court of Appeal held that "such a construction would be at odds with all established case law on the construction of this section."

21–202 Section 62(3) of the 1966 Act has now been superseded by s.13(8) of the Housing (Miscellaneous Provisions) Act 2014 which now requires the District Court to be satisfied that "recovery of possession by the housing authority is a proportionate response to the occupation of the dwelling by the person concerned."

RENT RESTRICTION

Introduction
21–203 The Housing (Private Rented Dwellings) Act 1982 (the "1982 Act"), as amended,[359] provides for the control of rents and security of tenure in relation to certain tenancies. The Act is a successor to earlier legislation, in particular the Rent Restriction Acts 1960 to 1981, and, although the 1982 Act repealed the earlier legislation, reference must still be made, by virtue of the later Act, to the earlier legislation in order to determine whether or not a particular dwelling comes within the 1982 Act. Furthermore, certain dwellings were decontrolled under the earlier Acts and the 1982 Act also contains decontrolling provisions.

21–204 The occasion for the passing of the 1982 Act was the decision of the Supreme Court in two appeals heard together, *Blake v Attorney General* and *Madigan v Attorney General*.[360] The appeals held that provisions of the rent restriction legislation then in force were unconstitutional in that they were based on rent levels in 1941, or in some cases in 1914, that there was no provision for review of the rents, and that the restrictions on the recovery of possession by the landlords unfairly restricted their property rights.

---

[359] Housing (Private Rented Dwellings) (Amendment) Act 1983.
[360] [1982] I.R. 117. The first Bill, the Housing (Private Rented Dwellings) Bill 1981, was referred by the President to the Supreme Court under Art.26. In *Re The Housing (Private Rented Dwellings) Bill, 1981* [1983] I.R. 181, the Supreme Court held the Bill to be unconstitutional. The Bill provided for a five-year period in which landlords were to receive the market rent reduced by a percentage. It was held to be an unjust attack on property rights. A new Act was passed, the Housing (Private Rented Dwellings) Act 1982, and this time the President signed it without referring it to the Supreme Court.

21–205 The law in this area is complicated and what follows is a summary of the main features.[361]

Definition of Controlled Dwellings

21–206 Section 8(1) of the 1982 Act provides as follows:

> "Subject to subsection (2), this Part applies to every dwelling which would, at the commencement[362] of this Act, be a controlled dwelling within the meaning of the Rent Restriction Acts, 1960 to 1981, if those Acts had full force and effect at such commencement, other than such a dwelling held at such commencement under a contract of tenancy for greater than from year to year during such period as it is so held."

The provision therefore requires continued reference to the earlier legislation. The meaning of the obscure last phrase is considered under the heading "Let" below.

Dwellings

21–207 The 1982 Act applies only to a "dwelling" which is defined by s.2(1) of the Act as "a house let ... or part so let, of any house". One of the effects of the continued reference to the earlier legislation is that the 1982 Act applies to premises which are not exclusively residential, since such premises came within the earlier Acts, and so premises partly used for business purposes are a "dwelling" for the purposes of the 1982 Act.[363] There must be some residential use, however.[364] On the other hand, premises which are mainly used for business but which have been used temporarily for residence for a night or two have been held not to constitute a "dwelling".[365]

21–208 In *Foley v Galvin*[366] the Supreme Court held that the fact of residence need not be continuous for the Acts to apply and it is sufficient if there is occupation by a member of the tenant's family or a caretaker or a person "who, though not at the moment in actual occupation, does in fact require the dwelling-house for his own use".[367]

---

[361] A more detailed treatment is to be found in J.C.W. Wylie, *Landlord and Tenant Law*, 3rd edn (Dublin: Bloomsbury, 2014), Ch.29.

[362] 20 July 1982.

[363] *Mullane v Brosnan* [1974] I.R. 222; *Foley v Johnson* [1988] I.R. 7 (licensed premises with living accommodation above); *Walsh v Coyne* [1958] I.R. 233 (ditto); *Hardwicke Ltd v Byrne* [1963] I.R. 52 (dwelling accommodation plus cobbler's business).

[364] Rent Restrictions Act 1960 s.4.

[365] *Bradley v McGowan* [1951] I.R. 72.

[366] [1932] I.R. 339.

[367] [1932] I.R. 339 at 361–362; *Walsh v Coyne* [1958] I.R. 233.

Let

21–209 The 1982 Act applies only if the dwelling is "let", i.e. if the relation of landlord and tenant has been created or exists between the parties. This would include any such relation within Deasy's Act 1860, which is necessarily at a rent.[368] It has been held that the Rent Restriction Acts did not apply to tenants at will.[369] Section 3 of Deasy's Act provides that the relation of landlord and tenant "shall be deemed to subsist in all cases in which there shall be an agreement by one party to hold land from or under another in consideration of any rent" and so it is arguable that "let" in the 1982 Act is governed by that provision, so that whenever those elements are present the premises are "let". Apart from that, s.8(1) of the 1982 Act specifically excludes "such a dwelling held at such commencement [of the Act] under a contract of tenancy for greater than from year to year during such period as it is so held". It is not clear what the phrase "during such period as it is so held" is intended to mean. A fixed-term tenancy seems clearly to be excluded from control, but the phrase suggests, as Wylie points out,[370] that this is so only in so far as a tenant holds under such a tenancy at the commencement of the Act, thereby implying that it is otherwise if the same tenant continues in occupation after the end of the term (on, for example, a monthly tenancy), at some time after the commencement of the Act. This would mean that a tenant who was not protected at the date of commencement of the Act would later become protected. It is doubtful whether the Act was intended to have such an effect, as its whole purpose was merely to continue control over dwellings that were already controlled. However, it is difficult to see what other meaning this rather obtuse language can be made to bear.

Separate

21–210 Section 2(1) of the 1982 Act requires the house or part of the house to be let as a separate dwelling. Prima facie this means that the tenant must have exclusive possession of the whole of the house, or part of the house, which constitutes the dwelling. Nevertheless, the section goes on to say: "whether or not the tenant shares with any other persons any portion thereof or any accommodation, amenity or facility in connection therewith". While this allows certain types of shared accommodation to come within the control provided by the Act, the requirement of "letting" means that the tenant would have to have exclusive possession in some sense, otherwise there is no landlord and tenant relationship and therefore no control.[371]

Valuation Limits

21–211 The 1982 Act, as has already been pointed out, controls only dwellings that were controlled under the earlier legislation at the date the 1982

---

[368] Deasy's Act 1860 s.3.

[369] *Delany (Blanchardstown Mills Ltd) v Jones* [1938] I.R. 826; *Irish Soldiers' and Sailors' Land Trust v Donnelly* [1944] I.R. 464.

[370] Wylie, *Landlord and Tenant Law* (2014), para.29.08.

[371] Wylie, *Landlord and Tenant Law* (2014), para.29.09.

Act came into force. Since the control under that earlier legislation[372] was based on valuation limits set in the past, the valuation limits under the 1982 Act are low and the number of dwellings coming under the control is consequently small. The limits are:

(1) In the county borough of Dublin and borough of Dún Laoghaire:
    a house £40
    a separate and self-contained flat £30
    other dwelling £60
(2) Elsewhere:
    a house £30
    a separate and self-contained flat £20
    other dwelling £40

21–212 The figures represent the estimated annual income produced from rent. If the rateable valuation is increased above the limit for the dwelling in question, the dwelling remains controlled until the landlord recovers possession.[373] This is an important provision, because in most cases the most usual way in which the valuation increases is by the Rent Tribunal, discussed below, fixing a new rent for the property in question above that fixed in the past.

21–213 The limits set out above were introduced by the Rent Restrictions (Amendment) Act 1967 and the effect was to decontrol many dwellings. The Rent Restrictions (Amendment) Act 1967 also decontrolled any house with a rateable value exceeding £10 of which a person being a bachelor or spinster over the age of 21 and under 65 became tenant.[374] Such property remains decontrolled under the 1982 Act. There is at least one case where property which had been decontrolled under earlier legislation is recontrolled by the 1982 Act, namely, where parts of dwelling houses had been let and the dwelling house itself had not been decontrolled.[375] Nevertheless, the 1982 Act applies only to tenants in possession at the date of the coming into force of the Act and the dwelling ceases to be controlled when that possession comes to an end. It is, in fact, tenants that are protected rather than dwellings. It follows that once the protected possession comes to an end, so also does control and it will not revive.

---

[372] Rent Restrictions Act 1960 s.3(2)(a), as amended by s.2(1) of the Rent Restrictions (Amendment) Act 1967.

[373] Rent Restrictions Act 1960 s.3(4), as amended by s.2(1) of the 1967 Act; Rent Restrictions Act 1960 s.3(7), as amended by s.2(5) of the 1967 Act.

[374] Rent Restrictions (Amendment) Act 1967 s.2(4). The provision could possibly be challenged on constitutional grounds as infringing the guarantee of equality as human persons.

[375] *Donnelly v O'Neill* [1935] I.R. 286; *Logan v Donoghue* [1938] I.R. 427; Wylie, *Landlord and Tenant Law* (2014), para.29.10.

Land other than Site

21–214 A dwelling is not controlled if it is let with land "other than the site of the dwelling", and where the rateable valuation exceeds the lesser of:

(1) half the rateable valuation of the site including the building or buildings thereon; or

(2) (i) in the case of a dwelling situated in the county borough of Dublin or the borough of Dún Laoghaire, £10; and

    (ii) in any other case, £5.[376]

21–215 "Site" means only the ground on which the dwelling and outhouses are built and not surrounding land.[377]

Date of Construction

21–216 A dwelling is not controlled if it was erected after, or was in the course of being erected on, 7 May 1941.[378] "Erected" includes the conversion of existing premises to a dwelling.[379]

Repossession by Landlord

21–217 It was noted under "Valuation Limits" above that if the rateable valuation is increased above the limit for the dwelling in question, the dwelling remains controlled until the landlord recovers possession. As to dwellings under the limits, repossession by the landlord after 8 June 1966 decontrols the dwelling.[380] The Rent Restrictions (Amendment) Act 1967 also decontrolled separate and self-contained flats *not* forming part of a building reconstructed by conversion into flats.[381] "Possession" means actual possession and not possession by a new tenant with the landlord's consent.[382] Under the 1982 Act a dwelling also is decontrolled when the rights of the tenant to retain possession "cease to subsist"[383] and where a landlord recovers possession under s.16.[384]

Assignment, Subletting by Tenant

21–218 The 1982 Act ceases to apply if the tenant assigns or sublets the tenancy.

---

[376] Rent Restrictions Act 1960 s.3(2)(h); *McGrane v Wills* (1930) 65 I.L.T.R. 86; *Mason v Leavy* [1952] I.R. 41; *O'Reilly v Acres* [1974] I.R. 454.

[377] See above, especially *O'Reilly v Acres* [1974] I.R. 454 at 460.

[378] Rent Restrictions Act 1960 s.3(2)(b).

[379] *Somers v Hutchinson* (1930) 64 I.L.T.R. 103; *Keeler v Brangan* (1930) 64 I.L.T.R. 213; *McDonagh v Mulholland* [1957] Ir. Jur. Rep. 4.

[380] Rent Restrictions (Amendment) Act 1967 s.2(2).

[381] Rent Restrictions (Amendment) Act 1967 s.2(3).

[382] *Griffin v Kennedy* (1965) 99 I.L.T.R. 199.

[383] 1982 Act s.8(3)(a).

[384] 1982 Act s.8(3)(c).

Wholly Excluded Lettings

Public Housing
21–219 Dwellings let or deemed to be let[385] under the 1966 Act are excluded from control.[386] The 1982 Act may nevertheless apply where the dwelling is owned by the State, e.g. the Commissioners for Public Works.[387]

Unfit Housing
21–220 The control provisions cannot be relied on where a housing authority takes action against an "unfit" house by means of a repair notice, a closing order or a demolition order.[388]

Furnished Lettings
21–221 The Rent Restrictions Act 1960 excluded from control furnished lettings and those where the rent included payment for services such as board, or heating, hot water, fuel, electricity, or other services, unless the portion of the rent attributable to the dwelling alone was equal to or exceeded three-quarters of the total reserved rent.[389] The court must apportion the rent between payment for the dwelling and payment for the services.[390] An agreement between the parties apportioning the rent is not binding on the court.[391] The time for making the apportionment is the date when the issue is raised in court.[392] "Services" for the purpose of the Acts are those provided by the landlord, and not, for example, by another tenant.[393]

Owner-Occupied Houses
21–222 The 1982 Act has no application to owner-occupied houses. The Rent Restrictions Acts were designed to protect tenants and so excluded such houses.[394]

Separate Self-Contained Flats
21–223 A separate and self-contained flat in a building "reconstructed by way of conversion" into such flats after the coming into force of the Rent

---

[385] For example, housing provided under the Labourers Acts or the Housing for the Working Classes Acts.

[386] Rent Restrictions Act 1960 s.3(2)(c).

[387] Wylie, *Landlord and Tenant Law* (2014), para.29.14.

[388] Housing Act 1966 s.66(17).

[389] Rent Restrictions Act 1960 s.3(2)(d).

[390] As above; *Hanratty v Hardy* [1947] Ir. Jur. Rep. 42; *Parkinson v O'Malley* [1940] I.R. 498.

[391] *Parkinson v O'Malley* [1940] I.R. 498.

[392] *Fridberg v Doyle* [1981] I.L.R.M. 370.

[393] *Elkinson v Cassidy* (1975) 110 I.L.T.R. 27.

[394] Rent Restrictions Act 1960 s.3(2)(e). For this purpose, the Act defines "owner" as including a person holding under a long lease, i.e. "any estate or interest in a house except under a tenancy not being for more than twenty-one years": s.3(6). However, the 1982 Act excludes all fixed-term tenancies from control.

Restrictions Act 1960 was also excluded from control.[395] Repair necessary to make the building once again fit for human habitation does not constitute "reconstruction" and so such repair will not decontrol the flat.[396] Substantial refurbishment may not have this effect either.[397]

Partially Excluded Lettings
Service Letting
21–224 The 1982 Act partially excludes from control, as did earlier legislation, dwellings let to a person "in connection with his continuance in any office, appointment or employment."[398] Such dwellings are only excluded from those parts of the Act which entitle the tenant to retain possession and restrict the landlord's right of recovery. The Act does not prevent a tenant of such a dwelling from applying to have the terms of the tenancy determined. Such a right is, however, unlikely to be effective since the tenancy is not otherwise protected.

Temporary Convenience Letting
21–225 The 1982 Act also partially excludes, as did earlier legislation, dwellings let "*bona fide* for the temporary convenience or to meet a temporary necessity of the landlord or the tenant".[399] Such dwellings again are only excluded from those parts of the Act which entitle the tenant to retain possession and which restrict the landlord's right to recovery. As with a service letting, the Act does not prevent the tenant applying to have the terms of the tenancy fixed, but without the other protections, the right is hardly significant.

Fixing the Terms of Tenancies
Rent Tribunal
21–226 In default of, or notwithstanding, agreement between landlord and tenant the terms of the tenancy can be fixed by the Rent Tribunal,[400] established by the Housing (Private Rented Dwellings) (Amendment) Act 1983 (the "1983 Act"). Under the 1982 Act the jurisdiction had been vested in the District Court. The Rent Tribunal consists of a chairperson, several vice-chairpersons and ordinary members whose period of office is not to exceed three years.[401] Members are part-time.

---

[395] Rent Restrictions Act 1960 s.3(2)(g); *Boyle v Fitzsimons* [1926] I.R. 378; *Broadhead v Knox* (1974) 109 I.L.T.R. 116.

[396] *Gore-Grimes v Foley* (1930) 64 I.L.T.R. 52; Wylie, *Landlord and Tenant Law* (2014), para.29.20. As to partial conversion: *Connolly v Gleeson* [1942] I.R. 68; *Downes v Kennedy* (1976) 110 I.L.T.R. 25.

[397] *Noyk v O'Brien* (1941) 76 I.L.T.R. 66; *O'Sullivan v Cullen* (1925) 29 I.L.T.R. 133.

[398] 1982 Act s.8(2)(a).

[399] 1982 Act s.8(2)(b).

[400] Housing (Rent Tribunal) Regulations 1983 (S.I. No. 222 of 1983).

[401] 1983 Act s.2(2). Housing (Rent Tribunal) Regulations 1983 (S.I. No. 222 of 1983).

21-227 Some are lawyers, while others have experience in valuation of property. The Tribunal sits in divisions usually consisting of the chairperson or one of the vice-chairpersons and two other members. Any party can appear in person or be represented.[402] Either landlord or tenant may apply to the Rent Tribunal to fix the terms of the tenancy regardless of any agreement already entered into between them.[403]

Fixing the Rent

21-228 The Rent Tribunal may fix the rent for the dwelling.[404] The statutory rent is defined by s.13 of the 1982 Act as the "gross rent" reduced by an amount in respect of "improvements" made by the tenant.[405] The gross rent is the rent which in the opinion of the Tribunal is a

> "...just and proper rent having regard to the nature, character and location of the dwelling, the other terms of the tenancy, the means of the landlord and the tenant, the date of purchase of the dwelling by the landlord and the amount paid by him therefor, the length of the tenant's occupancy of the dwelling and the number and ages of the tenant's family residing in the dwelling."[406]

21-229 The "gross rent" as defined is clearly not the same as market rent since it may be fixed by reference to the criteria laid down in s.13. In *Quirke v Folio Homes Ltd*[407] McCarthy J. in the Supreme Court divided the criteria into three categories:

> "...the first of them objective—the nature, character and location of the dwelling and the other terms of the tenancy; the second personal but potentially common to both sides and the third matters capable of exact detail and touching upon the second category."[408]

21-230 The judge went on to comment in a typically ironic but somewhat cryptic fashion:

> "Whilst there is much appeal in the philosophy — 'From each according to his ability, to each according to his need,' (Karl Marx - Criticism of the Gotha Programme) it is not an aid to statutory construction."

This was apparently intended as a rejection of the view that the relative means of the landlord and the tenant were always relevant, so that a disparity in their

---

[402] Housing (Rent Tribunal) Regulations 1983 reg.10(1)(b).
[403] 1983 Act s.5.
[404] 1982 Act s.13, as amended by s.9(2) of the 1983 Act.
[405] 1982 Act s.13(1).
[406] 1982 Act s.13(2).
[407] [1988] I.L.R.M. 496.
[408] [1988] I.L.R.M. 496 at 499.

means would invariably entitle a poor tenant to a reduction of rent. In the judge's view the categories were not an "automatic check list" all of which had to be considered in every case. Although the factors in the first category were always relevant, those in categories 2 and 3 were not necessarily so and should be considered only when deemed relevant. In the instant case the landlord company had stated before the Tribunal that its income was greater than that of the tenant. The Tribunal had refused the tenant's demand for information as to the means of the shareholders or directors of the landlord company. The Supreme Court held that the means of the landlord were only relevant when the landlord sought to counter a claim by the tenant to hardship by showing hardship to itself.

21–231 In *Dowd v Pierce*[409] the dwelling was in a state of disrepair due to the landlord's failure to repair and this in turn had meant that the tenant was unable to effect internal repairs. The Circuit Court held that the proper course of action was to adjourn the landlord's application to fix the rent until the landlord had carried out the repairs. If the landlord failed to do so, the housing authority could be informed that the dwelling was unfit for human habitation. If the application had been made by the tenant a similar procedure would have been adopted.[410]

Rent Allowances

21–232 Since the rents of properties affected by the 1982 Act had been fixed at an unrealistically low level, the effect of the Act was to raise the rents of many controlled properties by a substantial amount. Section 23 of the Act sought to offset any hardship on tenants that arose from this by enabling tenants to claim rent allowances.[411]

Registration

21–233 Where a dwelling is controlled and a new rent is fixed, either by agreement or by the Rent Tribunal, the landlord is under a duty to inform the housing authority which must enter the details in their register maintained under s.20 of the Housing (Miscellaneous Provisions) Act 1992.[412] Registration is not required where the new rent is less than the previous one.

Rent Review

21–234 Where a rent has been fixed by the District Court under the 1982 Act or the Rent Tribunal under the 1983 Act, no new application can be made

---

[409] [1984] I.L.R.M. 653.

[410] [1984] I.L.R.M. 653 at 655.

[411] Social Welfare (Rent Allowance) Regulations 1998 (S.I. No. 188 of 1998).

[412] Housing (Private Rented Dwellings) Regulations 1982 (S.I. No. 217 of 1982) reg.7, as substituted by reg.4 of the Housing (Private Rented Dwellings) (Amendment) Regulations 1983 (S.I. No. 286 of 1983).

until the expiration of four years and nine months from the date when it was previously fixed.[413]

Appeals

21–235 The landlord or tenant may appeal to the High Court within three months of a decision of the Rent Tribunal, or within such longer period as the court allows. Strictly speaking, the appeal is on a point of law, but some latitude is allowed and appeals on issues of mixed fact and law have been entertained.[414]

Recovery of Possession

21–236 One of the constitutional objections to the original legislation was that it unduly restricted the right of the landlord to recover possession. The 1982 Act therefore gives to the tenant a more restricted liberty to retain possession.

Tenant

21–237 "Tenant" for the purpose of the 1982 Act is the person:

(a) who would have been defined as being protected if the Rent Restrictions Acts 1960 and 1967 had been in force at the date of coming into force of the 1982 Act;

(b) who was in possession at that date; and

(c) provided no order for possession had been made under the Rent Restrictions (Temporary Provisions) Act 1981.[415]

21–238 Included in category (a) are, as a result of the earlier legislation, statutory tenants, i.e. tenants whose contractual tenancy had expired but whose security of possession was protected under the earlier Acts; also the spouse or family member of a protected tenant who had inherited the right to retain possession on the death of the protected tenant, and in some circumstances an assignee of the protected tenant.[416]

21–239 The Supreme Court has held[417] that it is sufficient if there is occupation by a member of the tenant's family or a caretaker or a person "who, though not at the moment in actual occupation, does in fact require the dwelling-house for his own use".[418]

---

[413] 1983 Act s.5(3).

[414] Wylie, *Landlord and Tenant Law* (2014), para.29.37.

[415] 1982 Act s.7(1).

[416] Rent Restrictions Act 1960 ss.31 and 32; *Jordan v O'Brien* [1960] I.R. 363; Wylie, *Landlord and Tenant Law* (2014), paras 29.40–29.44.

[417] *Foley v Galvin* [1932] I.R. 339.

[418] *Foley v Galvin* [1932] I.R. 339 at 361–362; *Walsh v Coyne* [1958] I.R. 233.

Order for Possession
21–240 Section 16(1) of the 1982 Act sets out the grounds on which the District Court may grant an order for possession, provided it considers it reasonable to do so.

Breach of Tenancy
21–241 The landlord may apply for an order for possession if the tenant fails to pay the rent or commits some other breach of the terms of the tenancy.[419] Where the amount due was small a court has declined to grant an immediate order on condition that the tenant pay the arrears.[420]

Nuisance
21–242 "Nuisance or annoyance" to the landlord, his or her agent, or adjoining owners, is a ground for possession, and so also is the use of the premises for "any immoral or illegal purpose" regardless of whether or not there has been a conviction arising out of the use.[421]

Deterioration
21–243 The landlord may seek possession if the condition of the dwelling deteriorates due to waste, neglect or default of the tenant or of any person residing in the dwelling.[422]

Required by Landlord
21–244 The landlord may seek possession if he or she bona fide requires the dwelling:

(a) for occupation as a residence for the landlord or any person bona fide residing or to reside with him or her;

(b) for occupation as a residence for a person in the full-time employment of the landlord; or

(c) in the interests of good estate management.[423]

21–245 The landlord must pay into court such a sum as the court considers reasonable to meet the tenant's expenses in leaving the dwelling and a sum not exceeding three years' rent of alternative accommodation which is "reasonably suited to the residential and other needs of the tenant, his spouse and his family

---

[419] Housing (Private Rented Dwellings) Act 1982 s.16(1)(a).
[420] *Boyle v Fitzsimons* [1926] I.R. 378.
[421] 1982 Act s.16(1)(b).
[422] 1982 Act s.16(1)(d).
[423] *Hardwicke Ltd v Byrne* [1963] I.R. 52.

bona fide residing with him in the dwelling".[424] There is no express requirement under the new legislation that the accommodation should be available.[425]

Scheme of Development

21–246 A landlord may also seek possession where he or she requires vacant
possession in order to carry out a "scheme of development"[426] which includes
the dwelling and has planning permission for the scheme.[427] The same requirement of paying money into court to cover the tenant's expenses and the rent of
alternative accommodation applies as in the preceding section.

21–247 Even if the landlord establishes one or more of the above grounds the
District Court may only grant an order for possession if it considers it "reasonable" to do so.[428] In exercising this discretion the court may consider the
conduct of the landlord and the extent to which it "contributed to the existence
of the grounds upon which he relies in support of his application for recovery
of possession".[429] Motive has also been found relevant in refusing an order for
possession, as where the landlord's real purpose is to replace the present tenant
with a new one.[430]

---

[424] 1982 Act s.16(1).
[425] Contrast the earlier 1960 Act s.29(1)(e)(ii), (f) and (g).
[426] 1982 Act s.16(4).
[427] 1982 Act s.16(1)(e).
[428] 1982 Act s.16(1).
[429] 1982 Act s.16(2). *Fitzsimons v Parker* [1949] Ir. Jur. Rep. 59.
[430] *Westport Harbour Commissioners v McBride* [1931] L.J. Ir. 50.

CHAPTER 22

Covenants

As soon as one promises not to do something, it becomes the one thing above all others that one most wishes to do.

— Georgette Heyer, *Venetia* (1958)

INTRODUCTION

Terminology
Positive and Negative
22–01 Covenants, i.e. binding promises, may be *positive* (covenants to do something) or *negative* (covenants to refrain from doing something). It has always been a basic principle that the burden of positive covenants does not run at law. The burden of negative covenants may run in equity, and so *restrictive covenants* are a special type of equitable interest in land. The traditional rules of common law and equity relating to the enforcement of covenants by and against successors of freehold property have been replaced by ss.48 and 49 of the Land and Conveyancing Law Reform Act 2009 ("LCLRA 2009"). These provisions establish a statutory scheme in which the benefit and burden of covenants, both positive and negative, which relate to freehold property, are enforceable between successors. This heralded a significant transformation in the established principles for the enforcement of covenants between successors to the original covenanting parties. The effect of the relevant provisions of the LCLRA 2009 goes a long way towards removing the traditionally recognised distinction between easements, as incorporeal interests affecting land, and covenants, which have tended to be regarded as a vestige of contract law to which the intervention of equity[1] has ascribed certain proprietorial characteristics.

Burden and Benefit
22–02 Does the benefit or burden of a covenant pass to another party? If A promises B that A will use the land he has purchased from B only for residential purposes, then A has undertaken the burden, the disadvantage, of the covenant, and B has obtained the benefit of it. If B assigns the interest in the land she has retained to X, the question arises as to whether the benefit of the covenant has passed to X, so that he can sue A to enforce it.

---

[1] Especially through the emergence and development of the rule in *Tulk v Moxhay* (1848) Phil. 774.

Types of Covenant

22–03 Covenants may exist in three forms: first, they may be contractual terms; secondly, they may be contained in leases or tenancies; and thirdly, they may exist between independent owners of separate plots of land. In order to see whether one party is able to enforce a covenant against another party, or is bound to perform the covenant at the behest of another party, it is necessary to identify which of these three relationships exists and then apply the appropriate rules. Accordingly, three questions have to be asked:

1. Is there privity of contract? i.e. are the parties contracting parties? If the answer is "yes", the extent to which the benefit or burden of the covenant can be enforced is governed by the law of contract.[2]
2. If the answer to 1 is "no", is there tenure (or privity of estate), either freehold or leasehold, between the parties? If there is a leasehold relationship, the extent to which covenants run is governed by Deasy's Act and the interpretation of it in *Lyle v Smith*.[3] If there is freehold tenure between the parties, which would be rare, the extent to which covenants run would be governed by the, now obscure, rules of the common law which broadly applied the test of whether the covenant "touched and concerned" the land and was not purely personal.
3. If the answer to 2 is "no", the issue concerns the law of covenants as it applies between independent owners or, at least, between persons whose relationship is not that of landlord and tenant. Such owners could themselves have either freehold or leasehold interests. It is this subject which is the main concern of this chapter.

PRIVITY OF CONTRACT

22–04 Here the parties are the original contracting parties to the conveyance. The law of contract applies. The promisee can enforce the covenant against the promissor unless the promisee has assigned the benefit.

22–05 Who are contracting parties? At common law, no one could claim a benefit under a contract unless they were named as parties to it. Section 5 of the Real Property Act 1845 provided, as to deeds taking effect after 1 October 1845:

"An immediate estate or interest in any tenements or hereditaments, and the benefit of a condition or covenant respecting any tenements or hereditaments, may be taken although the taker thereof be not named as a party to the same indenture."

---

[2] LCLRA 2009 s.49(6)(a)(i) expressly confirms that the enforcement of a covenant under the doctrine of privity of contract has not been affected.

[3] [1909] 2 I.R. 58.

22–06 This section has now been repealed and replaced by s.70 of the LCLRA 2009, subs.(1) of which provides:

> "Where a deed is expressed to confer an estate or interest in land, or the benefit of a covenant or right relating to land, on a person, that person may enforce the deed whether or not named a party to it."

22–07 Subsection (2) confirms that nothing in the section otherwise affects the doctrine of privity of contract. Hence, a person can take the benefit of a covenant although not named in the deed that contains it. Section 5 of the 1845 Act was expressly limited to covenants "respecting any tenements or hereditaments", which Irish cases had taken to imply an intended limitation to covenants affecting the land as property and so not extending to purely personal covenants.[4] *Beswick v Beswick*[5] held on the corresponding s.56 of the English Law of Property Act 1925, that the section did not fundamentally affect the law of privity of contract. The matter has been put beyond doubt in s.70 of the LCLRA 2009, since subs.(1) limits its effect to "the benefit of a covenant or right relating to land" and subs.(2) preserves as inviolable the doctrine of privity of contract.

22–08 It used to be assumed that if there is privity of contract, a party may be able to sue even though he or she has no land capable of benefiting—a clear statement of promissory liability.[6] But the law has long shown unequivocal signs of moving away from promissory liability towards a property notion, so that where a covenant is for the benefit of land rather than being personal, the original contracting party will no longer be liable after he or she has parted with the interest in the land, in the absence of evidence to the contrary.[7]

PRIVITY OF ESTATE

22–09 Privity of estate,[8] or tenure, can exist in two forms: freehold and leasehold.

---

[4] *Lloyd v Byrne* (1888) 22 L.R. Ir. 269; *Monroe v Plunket* (1889) 23 I.L.T.R. 76; *Grant v Edmondson* [1931] 1 Ch. 1.

[5] [1968] A.C. 58 at 104–105.

[6] *London County Council v Allen* [1914] 3 K.B. 642.

[7] *London & County Ltd v Wilfred Sportsman Ltd* [1970] 2 All E.R. 600 (covenant in a lease). LCLRA 2009 s.49(2)(b)(ii) provides for enforcement of a freehold covenant affecting land against a former owner of the land subject to the covenant "but only in respect of a breach of covenant which occurred during the period when that person was such owner".

[8] Textbooks on this subject usually use the phrase "privity of estate" in dealing with covenants instead of the more usual word "tenure", although there appears to be no difference in meaning.

Freehold

22–10 Prior to the abolition of feudal tenure by s.9 of the LCLRA 2009, one example of freehold tenure in fee simple in Ireland had survived, i.e. fee farm grants by feudal tenure *non obstante Quia Emptores*. Since *Quia Emptores* 1290 only forbade subinfeudation in fee simple, a grant of an estate less than a fee simple could also create freehold tenure and contain covenants falling into this category. In Ireland, it was usual to include covenants in a grant of a lease for lives. Such covenants theoretically were governed by the rules as to covenants in freehold tenure but the law in this area is now obscure and the judges seemed to have treated these covenants as being governed by the same rules as leasehold covenants.

Leasehold

22–11 Deasy's Act replaced the concept of privity of estate at common law with ss.12 and 13, although it is still a convenient term to use. If L and T are the original contracting parties to a lease or tenancy, privity of contract exists between them. If T has assigned to T2, then privity of estate, but no privity of contract, exists between L and T2. If L has assigned his reversion to L2 but T has not assigned his interest, privity of estate would exist between L2 and T. If both L and T have assigned their interests, privity of estate would exist between L2 and T2.

NEITHER PRIVITY OF CONTRACT NOR OF ESTATE

Description

22–12 The rest of this chapter is concerned with the situation where there is neither privity of contract nor privity of estate. Prior to the enactment of the LCLRA 2009, there were separate rules at common law and in equity, for equity here developed ways by which the benefit and burden could run even though they did not at common law. In considering these developments one must distinguish between the burden and the benefit of the covenant, as it is possible in any one case, where neither party to the covenant has retained an interest in the properties respectively affected, for either the benefit or the burden of the covenant to be enforceable but not the other. In examining the issue, therefore, one must look to ensure that, in any one case, both the benefit and the burden can be enforced.

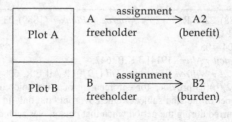

22–13 In this example, B covenants with A to use Plot B only for residential purposes. The burden of the covenant affects Plot B, i.e. it restricts the use of Plot B. The benefit accrues to Plot A, in that the use of Plot A is enhanced by the covenant. The situation in which a covenant affects the land of two independent owners usually arises when A, who originally owns Plot A and Plot B, sells off Plot B to B, retaining Plot A. In the case of a housing estate, A will be a developer who sells each plot in turn to the various house buyers. A2 can enforce the covenant against B2 only if the benefit of the covenant has passed to A2 and the burden has passed to B2.

22–14 There is another situation in which a party may seek to enforce a covenant against another party where there is neither privity of contract nor privity of estate, and that is between head landlord and sub-tenant. If HL is the landlord of T and T has sub-let to ST, then neither privity of contract nor privity of estate exists between HL and ST and some other method must be found of making the covenant enforceable.

The Historical Trend

22–15 The old rules, particularly the common law rules, began by treating covenants as purely personal obligations, affecting only those parties who originally entered into them. Sometimes the common law, and more frequently equity, went beyond this and began to recognise covenants as property rights. As such they could bind successors to the original parties between whom there was no privity of contract. Finally, equity in some cases went even beyond the recognition of covenants as private property rights and began to recognise them as a form of planning law.

22–16 Thus, before the advent of modern planning legislation, the courts had developed covenants into a species of enforceable planning obligations as a means of maintaining land for a particular use, usually residential. Private law may not be best adapted for functions which properly belong in the public domain and subject to public and democratic scrutiny, but the law of covenants can be seen as a response to a genuine social need. Property covenants may also function today to govern matters outside the normal planning rules or to deal with issues too detailed for attention by public planning law. For example, when developers sell plots of land in a housing estate it is usual to include in the deed of conveyance a covenant on the part of the purchaser promising not to erect television aerials. There is probably a sufficiently strong public interest (in avoiding unsightly additions to buildings) to bring the matter within the realm of planning law, but those immediately affected are the residents of the area and so the issue is dealt with by restrictive covenants in the purchase deeds.

Burden
At Law
22–17 The general rule at common law is that the burden of freehold covenants does not pass at all. This is clearly a contractual principle. Privity of contract involves the notion that parties to a contract cannot by their agreement impose liabilities on a third person who is not a party to that agreement.[9] The next stage in the development of the law was that devices were developed to avoid the rule. These are as follows.

Chain of Covenants
22–18 A covenantor remains liable on the covenant to the covenantee even after parting with his or her interest in the land,[10] unless they contract otherwise. Thus, if A promises B, for consideration or under seal, that no television aerial shall be erected on plot X, this promise will bind A even after A sells plot X to someone else—unless A has been careful to qualify the promise by specifying that the promise is only to apply so long as A owns plot X. This follows from general principles of contract law. Hence, one method of making the burden pass at law is for the covenantor to take an indemnity from P1 to indemnify him or her if the covenantor is sued by the covenantee. In due course, P1 does the same with P2.

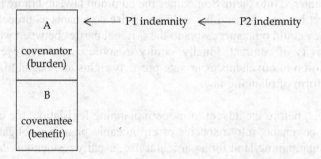

22–19 P1 similarly remains liable on his or her indemnity to the covenantor even after he or she has sold the land to P2. Thus, if P2 erects a television aerial on the land, the covenantee can sue the covenantor who in turn joins P1 in the action, pleading the indemnity, and P1 in turn joins P2 who will be liable on the indemnity entered into with P1. Thus, P2 will be ultimately liable. The problem with this solution, however, is that if any person in the chain fails to insist on the new purchaser taking an indemnity, the burden fails to pass to the next purchaser.

---

9   *Austerbury v Corporation of Oldham* (1885) 29 Ch. D. 750.
10 *Belmont Securities Ltd v Crean*, unreported, High Court, O'Hanlon J., 17 June 1988.

The Principle of Reciprocity

22–20 This principle was applied in the English case of *Halsall v Brizell*.[11] It is to the effect that if a person takes the benefit of a corresponding covenant, he or she must be subject to the burden of the covenant in issue. This refers to the moral principle that would condemn a person for insisting that some benefit is rightfully due to him from X while refusing himself to confer the same benefit on Y who is in the same position in relation to him as he is to X.

22–21 In *Halsall v Brizell,* the vendor sold off a series of plots to A, B and C in turn. The plots fronted onto a road which provided access to each of the plots.

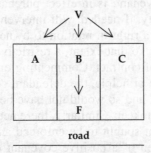

A, B and C covenanted to contribute to the cost of repair of the road. F purchased B's plot and later refused to contribute to the cost of repair of the road. F argued that the burden of the covenant had not passed to him.

22–22 Upjohn J. in the English High Court held that if F wanted the benefit of the covenants entered into by A and C, he had to accept the burden of B's covenant, although he endorsed the general principle that the burden of a covenant could not be enforced against a party who had not covenanted. In this case it was clear that F would take the benefit of those covenants since he occupied a plot between plot A and plot C. But the judge admitted that there was a flaw in the doctrine. If F did not derive any benefit from the other covenants, or was willing to forego it, he would not be bound. Thus, if F had bought a plot on the edge of the estate and either did not use, or undertook not to use, the road running past the other plots, the principle would not be sufficient to impose the burden on him.

22–23 More recently, the House of Lords in *Rhone v Stephens*[12] has clarified, and potentially narrowed, the reciprocity principle enunciated in *Halsall v Brizell*. In the later case, the owner of a conjoined house and cottage, when selling off the cottage, had covenanted with the purchaser to maintain in wind and watertight condition the roof of the house that overhung the bedroom

---

[11] [1957] Ch. 169. It is known in England as the rule in *Halsall v Brizell*. See also *Tito v Waddell (No.2)* [1977] Ch. 106.

[12] [1994] 2 W.L.R. 429; applied in *Davis v Jones* [2009] EWCA Civ 1164.

of the cottage. The appellant was the current owner of the cottage to whom the benefit of the covenant had been expressly assigned. The respondent as the current owner of the house was the successor of the covenantor. Lord Templeman held that the burden of a positive covenant cannot be enforced against a successor of the covenantor either by common law or equity "without flatly contradicting the common law rule that a person cannot be made liable upon a contract unless he was party to it".[13] Accordingly, enforcement of a positive covenant is a matter of contract and cannot be sought against a party who has not contracted.[14] A negative or restrictive covenant is different: a person who purchases property subject to a restrictive covenant, and has notice of the covenant, is in effect purchasing property subject to a restriction; and so equity, if needed, will intervene to prevent that person from seeking to exercise a right in relation to ownership of property which he or she never acquired. To that extent, a restrictive covenant is a property right rather than a facet of contract. Commenting on *Halsall v Brizell*, Lord Templeman noted that, in principle, the defendant could have elected not to enjoy the use of the road, and so would not have been liable under the covenant to contribute to its upkeep. Similarly, there needed to be some connection between the covenant sought to be enforced and the covenant claimed to be enjoyed. The burden of a positive covenant could not artificially be made to run by the contrivance of linking it as a condition to the enjoyment of the benefit of another covenant which had no discernible connection with it. In *Rhone v Stephens,* the purchaser of the cottage had covenanted with the owner of the house that the house could continue to be supported by the cottage. An attempt by the appellant to link this covenant to the respondent's original predecessor's covenant to maintain the overhanging roof failed. The two were unrelated. Lord Templeman stated:

"It does not follow that any condition can be rendered enforceable by attaching it to a right nor does it follow that every burden imposed by a conveyance may be enforced by depriving the covenantor's successor in title of every benefit which he enjoyed thereunder. The condition must be relevant to the exercise of the right."[15]

22–24 In *Cardiff Meats Ltd v McGrath*,[16] Murphy J. in the Irish High Court cited with approval the interpretation of Lord Templeman's speech in *Rhone v Stephens* as expressed by Peter Gibson L.J. in *Thamesmeade Town Ltd v Allotey*[17]:

"The reasoning ... suggests that there are two requirements for the enforceability of a positive covenant against a successor in title to the covenantor.

---

[13] [1994] 2 W.L.R. 429 at 433.

[14] This is consistent with the principle of indemnity under the chain of covenants.

[15] [1994] 2 W.L.R. 429 at 437.

[16] [2007] IEHC 219. See *McGrath v Reddy Charleton McKnight* [2017] IEHC 210.

[17] (1998) 30 H.L.R. 1052.

The first is that the condition of discharging the burden must be relevant to the exercise of the rights which enable the benefit to be obtained. In *Rhone v Stephens* the mutual obligation of support was unrelated to and independent of the covenant to maintain the roof. The second is that the successors in title must have the opportunity to choose whether to take the benefit or, having taken it, to renounce it, even if only in theory, and thereby to escape the burden and that the successors in title can be deprived of the benefit if they fail to assume the burden. On both these grounds *Halsall v Brizell* was distinguished."[18]

Right of Entry

22–25 Another method of enforcing the burden of a covenant against a successor is for the vendor to reserve a right of entry exercisable for condition broken, the condition being the performance of the covenants. Since a right of entry is an interest in land it could pass to that person's successors who could enforce it against the purchaser's successors.[19] One problem in some jurisdictions is that such a right is subject to the rule against perpetuities. This is so, for example, in England where there is the further disadvantage that after 1925 such a right can exist only in equity and not at law. In Ireland, however, if created as a conditional fee at common law, a right of entry is both legal and (up to its abolition) immune from the perpetuity rule.[20] However, the usefulness of this expedient is somewhat attenuated by the fact that if its utilisation resulted in a forfeiture, equity might grant relief from it.

Enlarged Leases

22–26 These instances of the burden of covenants passing at law to successors in title are the result of statutory reforms whose main purpose was to enlarge certain kinds of leases into fee simple estates. The statutes provide that certain covenants which were contained in the leases before enlargement continue to bind after the tenant's interest becomes a fee simple. They are therefore instances of where the burden of a covenant will bind all successors in title of the land "at law", which really means regardless of notice, since the burden passes by express statutory provision. Before the LCLRA 2009, these statutes were apt to be used as a device by someone who wished to attach the burden of covenants to land so that the burden would affect all successors in title to the land. The core of this device was, depending on the effect of the particular statute, either deliberately to create a leasehold which, under statute, could be enlarged into a fee simple, with the lessee then so enlarging it, or to create a leasehold which would be automatically enlarged from the outset.

---

[18] [2007] IEHC 219 at para.8.4.

[19] *Shiloh Spinners Ltd v Harding* [1973] A.C. 691.

[20] The situation was somewhat different in Northern Ireland: see *Walsh v Wightman* [1927] N.I. 1 and s.13(1) of the Perpetuities Act (Northern Ireland) 1966.

Conveyancing Act 1881 s.65

22–27 The section applies to tenants holding under leases originally for 300 years or more with an unexpired term of not less than 200 years "without any rent, or with merely a peppercorn rent or other rent having no money value".[21] It applies to such leases whether the reversion is freehold or not, but does not apply to a term liable to be determined by re-entry for condition broken or a term created by sub-demise out of a term which could not itself be enlarged.[22] The tenant of such a lease may execute a deed enlarging the lease into a fee simple.[23]

22–28 The apparent facility of using the section to attach covenants affecting the user of the land to a fee simple into which a qualifying lease is enlarged is, on closer examination, subject to important qualifications. First, the rent must be valueless in money terms and so if the rent consists of money at all, however small the amount, it would seem that the lease may not be enlarged under the section.[24] This should not be a problem as to the term which is created in order to be enlarged, since it could be made for a valueless rent, but since the term out of which it is created must also qualify, if that term were for a valuable rent the section could not be used. Secondly, if a third party is entitled to claim the benefit of covenants, the burden of which affected the demised land while it was a lease, the issue might arise as to whether the burden of such covenants continues to bind the land after the lease has been enlarged into a fee simple. Section 65(4) of the Conveyancing Act 1881 provides that the fee simple remains "subject to all the same trusts, powers, executory limitations over, rights, and equities, and to all the same covenants and provisions relating to user and enjoyment, and to all the same obligations of every kind, as the term would have been subject to if it had not been so enlarged." On the face of it these words are wide enough to continue the burden of covenants that affect the enjoyment of the land.

Landlord and Tenant (Ground Rents) (No. 2) Act 1978

22–29 This Act applies to dwelling houses where a ground rent, as defined, is created and gives a right to the tenant to acquire the fee simple. Section 28(1), as substituted by s.77 of the Registration of Deeds and Title Act 2006, provides that "covenants (except any of those specified in subsection (2)) affecting the land in the lease under which the person held the land thereupon cease to have effect", and that "no new covenant affecting the land shall be created when the

---

[21] Conveyancing Act 1881 s.65(1) (not repealed by the LCLRA 2009: see LCLRA 2009 s.8(3) and Sch.2, Pt 4).

[22] Conveyancing Act 1882 s.11 (not repealed by the LCLRA 2009: see LCLRA 2009 s.8(3) and Sch.2, Pt 4).

[23] Conveyancing Act 1881 s.65(2) and (3).

[24] *Re Smith & Stott* (1883) 29 Ch. D. 1009; *Blaiberg v Keeves* [1906] 2 Ch. 175; *Re Chapman & Hobbs* (1885) 29 Ch. D. 1007.

fee simple is being conveyed, except with the person's agreement."[25] Section 28(2) preserves covenants which protect or enhance the amenity of the land occupied by the immediate lessor of the grantee, covenants which relate to the performance of a statutory duty by such a person, or which relate to a right of way over the acquired land or a right of drainage "or other right necessary to secure or assist the development of other land". A covenant which does not relate to a right of way, etc., can be enforced by "any such person" or personal representatives or successors in title as if the acquisition of the fee simple had not occurred. Where it does so relate, it can be enforced by any person aggrieved by a breach of the covenant.[26]

22–30 There are several problems with using the section to attach covenants to the freehold. First, the statutory definition of "ground rent" is complex and care would have to be taken to ensure that the lease created for the purpose of being enlarged actually did qualify within the provisions. Secondly, the covenants would have to be of a type that would qualify within s.28(2). That subsection may be restrictively interpreted in view of the general purpose of the section which is to free the fee simple from covenants that had previously affected the land. Thirdly, the section has been held to apply not only to covenants which previously bound because of privity of estate but also to covenants in favour of third parties which bound the land under the doctrine of *Tulk v Moxhay*.[27] Such covenants, if they are within s.28(1), cease to have effect. This might constitute an objection, similar to that discussed under s.65 of the Conveyancing Act 1881, to the use of the section as a device to attach covenants to the freehold. Fourthly, the amended s.28 applies only to cases where the fee simple has been acquired through invoking the ground rents legislation, which potentially limits its usefulness in a situation where a lease may have been created for the primary purpose of enabling its enlargement into a fee simple so as to preserve the enforceability of former leasehold covenants against that fee simple. In any event, as discussed below, the necessity for utilising a contrived lease to ensure future enforcement of covenants has been obviated by ss.48 and 49 of the LCLRA 2009.

Deasy's Act Grant
22–31 A grant of a fee simple under Deasy's Act was also capable of creating leasehold tenure as a fee farm grant, if granted at a rent. Covenants contained in the grant would bind as leasehold covenants. However, where the land concerned is a house plot, the rent would be likely to qualify as a ground rent and so the fee farm grantee would acquire a "right to a fee simple" under the

---

[25] Subsection (1A) provides that the amended s.28 applies where the fee simple is acquired on or after 27 February 2006, unless the requisite machinery under the ground rents legislation was activated to acquire the fee simple before that date.

[26] Landlord and Tenant (Ground Rents) (No. 2) Act 1978 s.28(2).

[27] [1848] 2 Ph. 774; *Whelan v Cork Corporation* [1991] I.L.R.M. 19; *Williams & Co Ltd v LSD and Quinnsworth*, unreported, High Court, Pringle J., 19 June 1970, p.16; *Power Supermarkets Ltd v Crumlin Investments Ltd*, unreported, High Court, Costello J., 22 June 1981.

Landlord and Tenant (Ground Rents) (No. 2) Act 1978, which would presumably mean the right to a fee simple free of leasehold tenure. The effect in such a case would be to put the grantee in the same position as the last device and nothing would be gained by granting a fee farm grant originally rather than a lease subject to a ground rent. Section 12 of the LCLRA 2009 prohibits the future creation of a fee farm grant at law or in equity, providing that any attempt to create a fee farm grant after 1 December 2009 vests in the purported grantee or lessee a fee simple estate. Where this occurs, subs.(3) states that the resultant fee simple "is freed and discharged from any covenant or other provision relating to rent, but all other covenants or provisions continue in force so far as consistent with the nature of a fee simple". This harmonises with the provisions of ss.48 and 49 of the LCLRA 2009 which transform the pre-existing common law in relation to the mutual enforcement of covenants affecting freehold land by and against successors of the original covenanting parties.

Renewable Leasehold Conversion Act 1849

22–32 This Act gave a power to tenants holding under leases for lives renewable forever granted before it came into force (on 1 August 1849) the right to demand a grant in fee farm from the owner of the reversion on the lease for lives in substitution for that lease. The Act has now been repealed under the general repeal provision in s.8(3) of the LCLRA 2009, s.14 of which also prohibits the creation of a lease for lives.

In Equity
Tulk v Moxhay

22–33 In the leading case of *Tulk v Moxhay*,[28] it was held that the burden of a *restrictive*, i.e. negative, covenant binds the covenantor's land—what might be called, to borrow an expression from the law of easements,[29] the "servient tenement"—in equity. The applicable principle was explained by Pringle J. in *Williams & Co Ltd v LSD and Quinnsworth*[30] in the following terms:

> "The principle established in the well-known case of *Tulk v Moxhay* [is] that a negative bargain, as for instance a covenant against a particular use of land retained on a sale or lease of part of an estate, may be enforced by any person entitled in equity to the benefit of that bargain against any person bound in equity by notice of it, either express or to be imputed at the time of acquisition of his title."

---

[28] [1848] 2 Ph. 774; *Whelan v Cork Corporation* [1991] I.L.R.M. 19; *Williams & Co Ltd v LSD and Quinnsworth*, unreported, High Court, Pringle J., 19 June 1970, p.16; *Power Supermarkets Ltd v Crumlin Investments Ltd*, unreported, High Court, Costello J., 22 June 1981.

[29] Now itself borrowed in LCLRA 2009 s.48.

[30] Unreported, High Court, Pringle J., 19 June 1970, p.16, cited by Murphy J. in *Whelan v Cork Corporation* [1991] I.L.R.M. 19.

22–34 A restrictive covenant is therefore an equitable interest in land, and like other equitable interests it binds all except a *bona fide* purchaser for value of the legal estate in the affected property without notice of the restrictive covenant. The registration of deeds system in Ireland means that it is unlikely that lack of notice could be shown.

22–35 The 19th century case of *Luker v Dennis*[31] had suggested that notice, actual or constructive, was sufficient *in itself* to bind successors to the land subject to the restrictive covenant. However, this inclination was halted in *London & South Western Railway v Gomm*,[32] which established as a further condition that the person attempting to enforce the benefit of the covenant against the party subject to the burden must show that he or she has an interest in land capable of being benefited. The basis of the rule is the preservation of the value of the covenantee's land—the land benefited by the covenant—which cannot occur if the covenantee possesses no land that can be benefited. A personal interest is not sufficient. In this respect restrictive covenants are like easements: they are enforced against one piece of land for the benefit of another piece of land. They do not exist "in gross".

22–36 The principle that *Tulk v Moxhay*[33] applies only to restrictive covenants, not to positive covenants, was confirmed in *Haywood v Brunswick Permanent Building Society*.[34] Nevertheless, if a covenant has both positive and negative aspects, the positive can be severed from the negative and the negative part enforced.[35] The test of whether a covenant is positive or negative is one of substance, not form, so that merely because a covenant is phrased negatively will not mean that the burden of it will pass if the covenant is in substance positive. A covenant "not to allow the building to fall into disrepair" is in essence a positive covenant to repair: positive because it requires expenditure of money to comply with it, and hence is not enforceable against a successor under the principle of *Tulk v Moxhay*. A covenant "to use the premises for residential purposes only", despite its positive language, is in fact negative because it impliedly prohibits other uses, and arguably does not involve expenditure *which exceeds* that associated with other uses. This is not to say that expenditure of money is the only test: expenditure of labour also constitutes a positive covenant. A covenant not to permit a path to become overgrown is positive because it imposes a positive duty to clear the path, either through spending money to employ someone to do so, or by the owner of the property burdened by the covenant doing so through his or her own labour. The policy in not allowing the burden of positive covenants to run is a policy against increasing

---

[31] (1877) 7 Ch. D. 227.

[32] (1882) 20 Ch. D. 562 at 583 (Jessel M.R.); *Power Supermarkets Ltd v Crumlin Investments Ltd*, unreported, High Court, Costello J., 22 June 1981.

[33] [1848] 2 Ph. 774.

[34] (1881) 8 Q.B.D. 403, and further affirmed in *Rhone v Stephens* [1994] 2 W.L.R. 429.

[35] *Shepherd Homes Ltd v Sandham (No.2)* [1971] 1 W.L.R. 1062.

the burdens on the land. In *Re Fawcett & Holmes Contract*,[36] it was held that the deed creating the restrictive covenant must show an intention that the burden of it should run.

Development or Building Schemes

22–37 As will be seen below, a special situation arises when it is established that a building scheme, or "scheme of development", exists in law. The doctrine was developed in relation to the passing of the *benefit* and in that context is discussed in detail below, but it should not be forgotten that the judges in the cases which established a regime of enforceability for restrictive covenants in building schemes speak of successors in title being able to sue and *be sued* by owners of other plots. However, it is worth pointing out in relation to the passing of the *burden* of a restrictive covenant, that it does not seem that the concept of a building scheme constitutes a separate method for the burden to run. If it did, then the burden would run, in effect, "at law", which it does not. One of the fundamental principles established by *Tulk v Moxhay* is that the burden of restrictive covenants runs only in equity, not at law. On the other hand, it is also true that if a building scheme is present then the requirements of *Tulk v Moxhay* are almost certainly met.

Benefit
At Law
Automatic Running

22–38 At first the common law did not recognise that the benefit of a contract could be assigned, since contracts created purely personal rights. But from an early date[37] the common law accepted that the benefit of covenants affecting land would pass to successors in title of the covenantee. Thus, the common law began to regard such contracts as not being purely personal but as having some of the characteristics of a property right. When such contracts are contained in deeds conveying interests in land the common law recognises that the benefit of covenants will run with the land, i.e. will pass automatically to successors in title of the land, provided that the following four conditions are fulfilled.

Concern Covenantee's Land

22–39 The covenant must benefit the land of the covenantee—the person to whom the promise was made.[38] The common law enforces the benefit, but only if the covenant has the characteristic of a property interest. In *Gaw v CIÉ*,[39] the covenant was to keep the path clear of undergrowth, i.e. positive acts. The benefit of the covenant was held to pass at law to the successor in title of the covenantee together with a right of way over the path. Another example

---

[36] (1889) 42 Ch. D. 150.

[37] *The Prior's Case* (1369) YB 42 Edw III Pl 14 fol 3A.

[38] *Newton Abbot Coop Society v Williamson* [1952] Ch. 286.

[39] [1953] I.R. 232.

of the benefit of a positive covenant passing at law, in that case a covenant to supply water to a bungalow, is afforded by *Shayler v Woolf*.[40]

Legal Estate
22–40 For the benefit to pass at common law, the successor to the original covenantee has to show that he or she has a common law estate.[41]

Same Estate
22–41 The successor must not only show that he or she has a legal estate, but that it is the *same* legal estate as that of the original covenantee.[42]

Intention that Benefit Will Run
22–42 There must also be an intention, either express or necessarily to be inferred, that the benefit will run with the land. Such an intention is now presumed as a result of s.58(1) of the Conveyancing Act 1881. Under that section covenants are deemed to be made with "the covenantee, *his heirs and assigns*" as if the heirs and assigns had been expressly mentioned. At first it was thought that the section had a more radical effect: that it extended the passing of the benefit at law to all "heirs and assigns", including those who did *not* take the same estate as the original covenantee. The case law, however, took a more restrictive view of the section, holding that it merely saved the use of some words in a deed.[43] It would seem that its effect is to presume the required intention in the absence of evidence to the contrary, but not to relieve compliance with the other requirements mentioned above.

22–43 In England, s.58 was replaced by s.78 of the Law of Property Act 1925 which contains the wider phrase "successors in title and the persons deriving title under him or them". In *Federated Homes Ltd v Mill Lodge Properties*,[44] following *Smith and Snipes Hall Farm Ltd v River Douglas Catchment Board*,[45] the English Court of Appeal held that this had a wider effect than s.58 of the 1881 Act. It held that the effect of s.78 was to annex the benefit of covenants to the land. It can be argued that this abolishes in England the requirement that

---

[40] [1946] Ch. 320.
[41] *Webb v Russell* (1789) 3 T.R. 393. This is no longer required in England after 1925.
[42] *Gaw v CIÉ* [1953] I.R. 232.
[43] *Westhoughton UDC v Wigan Coal & Iron Co Ltd* [1919] 1 Ch. 159.
[44] [1980] 1 All E.R. 371.
[45] [1949] 2 K.B. 500.

the successor in title, in order to enforce the benefit, must have the same estate as the original covenantee.[46]

22–44 However, in *Roake v Chadha*,[47] the English High Court impliedly modified the effect of *Federated Homes*. It held that the benefit did not automatically pass where it was expressly stated that the covenant would not inure for the benefit of successors without express assignment. While under *Federated Homes* implied assignment extended to successors regardless of their estate, according to *Roake v Chadha* implied assignment could in any case be ousted by an express term to the contrary: it was only a presumption as to the parties' intention and so could be rebutted. Thus, while *Federated Homes* had removed one impediment, *Roake* held that the new widened doctrine was only a presumption and could yield to an express term.[48] The court in *Roake* took the "market-oriented" view that the role of law is not to extend the benefit of covenants as a matter of policy, but is confined to spelling out the intention of the parties to a bargain. *Federated Homes*, on the other hand, tends to the view that the benefit of covenants should be extended as a matter of general law and that those in a stronger bargaining position should not be able to use it to prevent a weaker party obtaining the benefit, or passing it on. Behind the technical dispute, the more basic dispute is about the role of law in relation to the market.

22–45 English cases after 1925 contrasted the more radical effect of s.78 with the earlier s.58 of the 1881 Act and in so doing accepted the English case law on s.58 before 1925. However, there is a possibility that the courts in Ireland will not necessarily follow either set of English decisions and may hold that the earlier s.58 is not a mere "word-saving" provision. One cannot therefore categorically state that the law in Ireland, for covenants to which ss.48 and 49 of the LCLRA 2009 do not apply, is the same as that set out in the English cases on s.58 of the 1881 Act. It has also been held in England that for a successor to enforce the benefit at law, he or she must demonstrate being a successor to the *whole* of the land and not merely a part. "At law, the benefit could not be assigned in pieces."[49] There is no decision in Ireland on the point. If this statement is correct as to Irish law, then a successor would have to resort to the rules of equity as to the passing of the benefit. The situation in relation to covenants entered into after the coming into force of the LCLRA 2009 on 1 December 2009 is eased by the fact that the definition of "land" in s.3 includes

---

[46] D.J. Hurst, "The Transmission of Restrictive Covenants" (1982) 2(1) L.S. 53; D. Hayton, "Revolution in Restrictive Covenants Law?" (1980) 43 M.L.R. 445; G.H. Newsom, "Universal Annexation?" (1981) 97 L.Q.R. 32; G.H. Newsom, "Universal Annexation? A Postscript" (1982) 98 L.Q.R. 202; P.N. Todd, "Annexation after Federated Homes" [1985] 3 Conv. 177; E.H. Scamell, "Positive Covenants in Conveyances of the Fee Simple" [1954] 18 Conv. 546 at 553–556; L.A. Sheridan, *Survey of the Land Law of Northern Ireland* (Belfast: HMSO, 1971), para.180.

[47] [1983] 3 All E.R. 503.

[48] See also *Sainsbury plc v Enfield London Borough Council* [1989] 1 W.L.R. 590 and *Crest Nicholson Residential (South) Ltd v McAllister* [2004] 1 W.L.R. 2409.

[49] *Re Union of London* [1953] Ch. 611 at 630.

"any part of land", which seems to place beyond doubt the proposition that in future a covenant affecting or attaching to land is to be interpreted as affecting or attaching to all or any part of that land. The conditions for the benefit to pass at law do *not* include:

(a)   that the covenant must be negative. The benefit of positive covenants can pass at law[50];
(b)   that the covenant should affect land owned by the *covenantor*.[51] The rules concerning the running of the benefit of a covenant are bound up only with the land of the covenantee.

Express (Statutory) Assignment

22–46 The benefit of a contract can be expressly assigned as a chose in action under s.28(6) of the Judicature (Ireland) Act 1877.[52] As to covenants affecting land, this provision presents no particular difficulty where the defendant, i.e. the bearer of the burden, is the original covenantor or his or her personal representative (and so liable at law), but the better view seems to be that the statute does not permit an express assignee of the benefit of a covenant to enforce it against a successor to the original covenantor except within the limits of the rule in *Tulk v Moxhay*.[53] It would not, therefore, enable an express assignee to enforce the benefit against a successor who is a *bona fide* purchaser of the land without notice of the covenant. If this is correct the section does not create a separate statutory form of assignment that overrides the rules of equity.

In Equity

22–47 In the diagram below, A and B are two adjoining plots of freehold land. In the past they were also owned by A and B respectively. A and B entered into a covenant restricting the use of plot B. A could enforce it in contract. If A sells his plot to A2, can A2 enforce the benefit of the covenant?

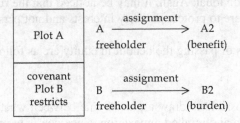

---

[50]   E.H. Scamell, "Positive Covenants in Conveyances of the Fee Simple" [1954] 18 Conv. 546; A. Pritchard, "Making Positive Covenants Run" [1973] 37 Conv. 194.

[51]   *Smith and Snipes Hall Farm Ltd v River Douglas Catchment Board* [1949] 2 K.B. 500.

[52]   Replaced in England by s.136 of the Law of Property Act 1925.

[53]   [1848] 2 Ph. 774.

It has been seen that the benefit of covenants can run at common law and so A2 can often rely on the common law rules. But there are situations where the common law rules are inadequate, because one or more of the conditions discussed above is/are lacking, namely:

(i) A2 wants an equitable remedy. This will frequently be the case because an injunction is usually the best remedy to enforce a covenant affecting the use of land.

(ii) A2 or the person from whom he or she bought the land is or was an equitable owner, e.g. a mortgagor having only an equity of redemption.[54] This is not uncommon in Ireland because mortgages, prior to the abolition of the method by s.89 of the LCLRA 2009, were capable of being created by conveyance of the fee simple, so that the mortgagor did not retain any legal estate in the land.

(iii) Where A2 does not have the same estate as A.

(iv) If *Re Union of London*,[55] which provides that the benefit of a covenant can pass only with the *entirety* of the land that it affects, applies in this jurisdiction (to covenants entered into prior to the coming into effect of the LCLRA 2009 on 1 December 2009), and A has conveyed only part of the land.

(v) Where A2 relies on express assignment under s.28 of the Judicature (Ireland) Act 1877 and the statute has not been complied with; for example, notice was not given to the covenantor, or the assignment was not made under the hand of the assignor.

22–48 The benefit can pass in equity by three methods. However:

(a) these apply only to restrictive, not positive covenants;

(b) the plaintiff must show that he or she is the current owner of the land. Equity only enforces the benefit on the basis that it benefits *land*, not a particular individual. Again it may be noticed that the rule in equity was developed here to protect property interests and not personal ones.

The three methods of passing the benefit in equity are as follows.

Annexation

22–49 It is not possible to draw a precise line between what courts may call express annexation and implied annexation, since courts have laid down general tests to determine when the benefit may be said to have been annexed; but one may at least distinguish between the fairly clear tests set out to establish the fact of annexation and the residual category of cases which may be termed "implied" annexation.

---

[54] *Rogers v Hosegood* [1900] 2 Ch. 388.
[55] [1953] Ch. 611.

Express Annexation

22–50 Here the person claiming the benefit has to show:

(i) that there was an intention to benefit the land of the covenantee and his or her assigns and to burden the land adjacent to it. Such an intention has been held to be present when the phrase used was "with intent that the covenant may inure to the benefit of the vendors, their successors and assigns and others claiming under them *to all or any of their lands adjoining*".[56] These rules again show that equity attempts to confine its intervention to the protection of property interests;

(ii) the land benefited must be ascertainable from the language of the conveyance or by parol evidence;

(iii) the covenant must be capable of benefiting the land;

(iv) there must have been no separation between the title to the covenant and the title to the land.

22–51 The reason for this latter rule is said to be that if a covenantee sold the land without the benefit of the covenant, then the covenant is not needed because the whole purpose of the covenant was to benefit the land. Equity protects the covenantee's property interest. It is also said to be a requirement that if part of the land is assigned and is to have the benefit, then the covenant must have been taken with the intention of benefiting each part of the land as well as the whole of the land.[57] This is, however, a somewhat subjective, contractual type of test and it is arguably doubtful today as to whether it would be applied. It is probable that once a covenant is assigned in equity, it becomes annexed to the land, i.e. in future the benefit automatically passes in equity.[58]

Implied Annexation

22–52 The English case of *Marten v Flight Refuelling Ltd*[59] took the view that the benefit of a covenant is impliedly annexed where to ignore it would not only cause injustice but would depart from common sense. It is suggested that the first reason on its own is sufficient.

---

[56] *Rogers v Hosegood* [1900] 2 Ch. 388.

[57] *Marquess of Zetland v Driver* [1939] Ch. 1; D. Hayton, "Revolution in Restrictive Covenants Law?" (1980) 43 M.L.R. 445.

[58] *Re Pinewood Estate* [1958] Ch. 280 assumed that one would have to show a chain of assignments but later cases contain *dicta* to the opposite effect, e.g. *Stilwell v Blackman* [1968] Ch. 508. H.W.R. Wade, "Restrictive Covenant—Benefit—Assignment—Building Scheme" (1957) 15(2) Camb. L.J. 146.

[59] [1962] Ch. 115 at 133. See also *Shropshire County Council v Edwards* (1982) 46 P. & C.R. 270.

Assignment
Express Assignment
22–53 The difference between assignment and annexation is that assignment, at least in the first instance, confers the benefit on a person: annexation confers it on the land, or rather, so as to avoid reifying the concept, confers it on all the owners of the land for the time being. For a person to show that he or she has the benefit of the covenant by assignment, that person should show a complete chain of assignments from the original covenantee to him or her. However, there are arguments that this is not in fact necessary:

1. The cases suggest that the courts may be prepared to dispense with this strict requirement by holding that once the benefit of a covenant has been assigned in equity, this has the effect of permanently annexing it to the land so that from then on the benefit of the covenant will pass in equity without express assignment.[60]
2. It can be argued that s.71 of the LCLRA 2009 (which replaces s.6 of the Conveyancing Act 1881) acts as a kind of statutory assignment. Under the section, "a conveyance of land includes, and conveys with the land, all ... advantages, easements, liberties, privileges, *profits à prendre* and rights appertaining or annexed to the land".[61]

22–54 The key question is whether the benefit of a covenant is a right or advantage pertaining to the land. On the face of it, if it "touches and concerns" the land, it should.[62] The argument was considered in *Roake v Chadha*,[63] which had to address the equivalent s.62 of the English Law of Property Act 1925, but was rejected on the ground that there was an express provision in the original conveyance that the covenant should not pass except by express assignment, which had not occurred. The probable outcome in the absence of such express words did not fall for decision.

Implied Assignment
22–55 If the covenant was annexed to the land when it was created, or, possibly, if the benefit was subsequently assigned, then the benefit of the covenant will pass *automatically* on subsequent conveyances. For this to happen it must be shown that:

---

[60] *Stilwell v Blackman* [1968] Ch. 508. *Re Pinewood Estate* [1958] Ch. 280 assumed that one would have to show a chain of assignments but *Stilwell* contains *dicta* to the opposite effect. H.W.R. Wade, "Restrictive Covenant—Benefit—Assignment—Building Scheme" (1957) 15(2) Camb. L.J. 146.

[61] LCLRA 2009 s.71(1)(b). Subsection (2)(b) is in identical terms, but includes also "houses or other buildings" in addition to "land".

[62] See *PUK and A. Swift Investments v Combined English Stores Group plc* [1988] 3 W.L.R. 313.

[63] [1983] 3 All E.R. 503.

1. words in the deed creating the covenant demonstrate an intention to benefit the land,[64] as, for example, where the covenant is made with X, as owner for the time being of Gortduff;
2. the land benefited must be ascertainable;
3. the covenant must be capable of benefiting the land; and
4. it may be the case that if the benefit is annexed only to the whole of the land, only an assignee of the whole land can take the benefit.[65] If the covenant is annexed to the whole *or any part* of the land, then an assignee of part of the land can benefit.[66]

Development or Building Schemes

22–56 The above discussed rules extended the situations in which the benefit of covenants could be found to run with the land. Even so, there were still situations which fell outside the scope of the rules. One such situation can be illustrated as follows:

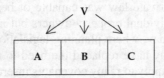

This is one situation. There may be others. In this example, V is the original covenantee. She sells separate plots first to A, then to B, then to C. All the purchasers enter into covenants with V as they buy their plots, for example, to use the land for residential purposes only. Can A enforce the covenant entered into by B with V since the amenity of plot A will be reduced if the covenant is broken? A cannot do so at common law because when V sold to B she had already parted with plot A. V could not covenant for the benefit of plot A because she no longer owned plot A. The covenant may have benefited the land of the covenantee, V, but plot A was not part of that land when V took the covenant from B. Nor can A enforce the benefit in equity for the same reason. V could not have annexed the benefit of the covenant to plot A, and although it is possible for V to have assigned to A the benefit of her covenant taken from B, this is unlikely to have occurred in practice.

22–57 One way of avoiding this problem was for V not to sell the fee simple in the plots but to sell long leases instead, thus retaining a reversion on all the plots. This was, however, unpopular with purchasers who usually wished to acquire the fee simple. Another method was for V to induce B to contract directly with A. There would thus be privity of contract between A and B. But this only works by the later purchaser contracting with the earlier one. It does not work

---

[64] *Rogers v Hosegood* [1900] 2 Ch. 388.
[65] *Re Ballard's Conveyance* [1937] Ch. 473.
[66] *Marquess of Zetland v Driver* [1939] Ch. 1.

the other way round. Suppose V sells plot C to C. Can C enforce the benefit of the covenant between V and B, or between V and A? A and B cannot contract with C at the time they buy their plots because C was not ascertained then. Could the covenants have been assigned or annexed to C's plot? True, it was part of land retained by V at the time the covenants were created, but at common law part of the benefit cannot be assigned. In equity the problem may be that the covenant was annexed only to the whole of V's retained land or, frequently, that plot C was not capable of benefiting from the covenant at the time because no house had yet been built on it.[67]

22–58 Problems such as this could lead to unfortunate results, particularly in housing estates. In housing estates land has been laid out for residential purposes and its satisfactory use by all residents depends upon the observance of restrictions on land use by all residents. This is a problem which today is largely provided for by planning legislation and conditions as to user attached by the planning authority to the planning permission. The law of covenants shows how in the past private law was capable of being developed to serve not only the needs of individual property owners but more general needs of a social character. Even today, where planning legislation and conditions made under such legislation may have replaced the need to rely on the law of covenants, this law will still apply to many covenants inserted by the developer for the general benefit of the estate which have not been included in the planning conditions. A common example is a covenant not to erect television aerials in estates where cable television is available. This is intended simply to preserve the aesthetic appeal of the land and the buildings. Housing estates, "schemes of development", or "building schemes", as they are variously known, have been recognised as special cases for in excess of a century.

22–59 In *Elliston v Reacher*,[68] Parker J. held that a scheme of development creates a special legal regime in relation to the enforcement of restrictive covenants (but not positive covenants) that affect the estate. Each purchaser of a plot, and that purchaser's successors in title, can sue and be sued by every other purchaser and his or her successors in title on foot of restrictive covenants entered into by each original purchaser of a plot with the vendor. The scheme of development creates a kind of "local law" for the estate. Parker J. laid down a number of tests to determine when a scheme of development would be held to exist:

1. the plaintiff and defendant must derive title from a common vendor;

---

[67] It could be argued that in this situation, a reverse of the rule in *Halsall v Brizell* (discussed above) applies, so that if C is bound by his covenant with V which is for the benefit of A and B, then he should be able to claim the benefit of their covenants and enforce the burden against them.

[68] [1908] 2 Ch. 374 at 384.

2. the vendor must have laid out the land for sale in plots subject to restrictions intended to be imposed on all the plots or consistent only with such a scheme;
3. the vendor must have intended the restrictions to benefit all the plots sold;
4. the plots must have been purchased on the basis that the restrictions should benefit all the plots sold.

One more test was added later:

5. the area of the scheme must be defined.[69]

22–60 The basis of this latter principle is that there cannot be reciprocity of obligation if any one purchaser has not been made aware of the total area affected by the covenants intended to be mutually enforceable by and against all the purchasers in the scheme.[70] An instance of the application of this is afforded by the advice of the Privy Council in *Emile Elias and Co Ltd v Pine Groves Ltd,*[71] a case that came before it from the Court of Appeal in Trinidad and Tobago. The development, which was of a limited and purportedly exclusive character, had been hived off from the surplus ground of St Andrew's Golf Club. Five plots only were involved, and the purchaser of the fourth plot was also the purchaser of the fifth. The existence of the fifth plot had not been indicated on the site plan attached to the deeds of their plots to the first three purchasers. The Privy Council held that the necessary ingredients for an estate scheme had not been satisfied, by reason of the fact that the first three purchasers had not been made aware of the entire area to be affected. The result was that the restrictive covenants could not be mutually enforced among any of the purchasers.

22–61 English courts in recent decades have tended to hold that the tests in *Elliston* were too restrictive and have now extended the definition of "scheme of development" to such an extent that it closely resembles planning restrictions detached from the notion of property rights created by mutual agreement. In *Baxter v Four Oaks Property,*[72] there was no antecedent division into plots by the vendor, although there was a deed of mutual covenant among all the purchasers. A scheme of development was nevertheless held to exist. In *Re Dolphin's Conveyance,*[73] there was no common vendor, but the same principle was nevertheless applied. The court found that there was a common intention by the several vendors to create such a scheme. In *Brunner v Greenslade,*[74] one of the plots had been subdivided, so that the plaintiff and defendant were not even successors in title to the two original contracting parties. No covenant had

---

[69] *Reid v Bickerstaff* [1909] 2 Ch. 305.
[70] *Reid v Bickerstaff* [1909] 2 Ch. 305 at 319.
[71] [1993] 1 W.L.R. 305.
[72] [1969] Ch. 816.
[73] [1970] Ch. 654.
[74] [1970] 3 W.L.R. 891.

ever been expressly created as between the two parties in contention. Nevertheless, they were held to be bound by covenants similar in nature to those that bound other plots in the development. This is quite significant, for it shows that enforcement of freehold restrictive covenants in an estate scheme had become detached from contractual principles. Even so, Megarry J. strenuously denied he was creating a new equity.

22–62 It is questionable whether the special regime of the development scheme enunciated in *Elliston v Reacher* was capable of being construed in the context of commercial developments. In *Belmont Securities Ltd v Crean*,[75] the first plaintiff was the developer of a small shopping complex, comprising three units. The third and fourth plaintiffs were the occupiers of the shop designated in the original scheme as a grocer's shop. The plaintiffs brought an action against the defendants, who were occupiers of the shop designated as a newsagent, claiming damages for breach of a covenant contained in the original scheme which restricted the use of that shop to the business of a newsagent, and claiming that the defendants were carrying on business as a grocer as well. The defendants argued that they had been carrying on business as a grocer since the beginning of the term and that it would be inequitable to enforce the covenant after such a lapse of time. O'Hanlon J. held that the covenant was not enforceable by the third and fourth plaintiffs because it had not been shown that the covenant was inserted in the original lease either for their benefit or for the benefit of the particular parcel of land that they occupied. The first plaintiff, as original covenantee, was entitled to enforce the covenant, but as it had not retained any land, it had only established a technical breach (of contract) and was entitled to no more than nominal damages of £5. O'Hanlon J. quoted Cozens-Hardy M.R. in *Reid v Bickerstaff*[76] on the definition of a development scheme:

> "What are some of the essentials of a building scheme? In my opinion there must be a defined area within which the scheme is operative. Reciprocity is the foundation of the idea of a scheme. A purchaser of one parcel cannot be subject to an implied obligation to purchasers of an undefined and unknown area. He must know both the extent of his burden and the extent of his benefit. Not only must the area be defined but the obligations to be imposed within that area must be defined. A building scheme is not created by the mere fact that the owner of an estate sells it in lots and takes varying covenants from various purchasers. There must be notice to the various purchasers of what I may venture to call the local law imposed by the vendors upon a definite area. If on a sale of part of an estate the purchaser covenants with the vendor, his heirs and assigns, not to deal with the purchased property in a particular way, a subsequent purchaser of part of the estate does not take the benefit of the covenant unless (a) he is an express assignee of

---

[75] Unreported, High Court, O'Hanlon J., 17 June 1988.
[76] [1909] 2 Ch. 305 at 319.

the covenant, as distinct from assignee of the land, or (b) the restrictive covenant is expressed to be for the benefit and protection of the particular parcel purchased by the subsequent purchaser ... Unless either (a) or (b) can be established, it remains for the vendor to enforce or abstain from enforcing the restrictive covenant."

22–63 This is a somewhat outmoded definition of a building scheme in view of the later English cases, and, indeed, under the revised definition of "scheme of development" in s.48 of the LCLRA 2009, there is now no justification for denying the application of the more flexible principles associated with an estate scheme to commercial as well as to residential properties, while recognising that the overall thrust and purpose of such schemes are more obviously relevant to the latter than the former.

LCLRA 2009
Basic Provisions
22–64 Chapter 4 of Pt 8 of the LCLRA 2009 addresses the enforceability of covenants affecting freehold land by and against successors in a way which, to a large extent, approximates the law in this regard to those governing easements. Accordingly, a freehold covenant is defined as being "a covenant attaching to dominant land and servient land" which has been entered into after 1 December 2009.[77] Dominant land "means freehold land with the benefit of a covenant to which other freehold land is subject" and servient land "means freehold land which is subject to a covenant benefiting other freehold land". Dominant and servient owners are those holding an estate in the respective lands and those, as defined, deriving title from or under them. In the case of a servient owner, the definition excludes "a tenant for a period of less than 5 years", from which must be inferred that a tenant for a period of longer than five years falls *within* the definition and that a tenant for any period is covered within the definition of a person deriving title from a dominant owner. In the case of a restrictive covenant,[78] the definition of servient owner includes a licensee "or other person in occupation of the land with or without the consent of that owner". Hence, restrictive covenants are enforceable against both licensees of the servient owner and trespassers on the servient land.

22–65 Section 49 of the LCLRA 2009 sets out the basic, and seemingly simple, rules regarding the enforcement of freehold covenants among successors. The existing rules of common law and equity (expressly stated as including the rule in *Tulk v Moxhay*) "are abolished to the extent that they relate to

---

[77] LCLRA 2009 s.48: the principles of law and equity discussed above continue to govern the enforceability among successors to the original covenanting parties of freehold covenants entered into prior to 1 December 2009.

[78] Appropriately described as "a covenant which is restrictive in substance".

the enforceability of a freehold covenant".[79] Instead, "any freehold covenant which imposes in respect of servient land an obligation to do or refrain from doing any act or thing is enforceable" by the current dominant owner, or by a former dominant owner in respect only of breaches occurring while he or she was dominant owner, against the current servient owner in respect of breaches occurring during that person's term as servient owner or which occurred before but were not rectified when he or she became servient owner, or against a former servient owner in respect only of breaches that occurred while that servient owner was servient owner.[80]

22–66 Where the servient land has been subdivided, all covenants, positive and negative, are to be appropriately apportioned among the subdivided parts and their respective owners as if the covenants had first been entered into in respect of each subdivided part separately. Disputes in this regard are referred to the High Court which can order an apportionment in relation to the applicability of any covenant.[81]

22–67 The enforcement of any covenant under the traditional principle of privity of contract remains unaffected.[82]

Non-application
22–68 The new rules established by the LCLRA 2009 apply only where both sets of land affected are held in freehold estate, although the definition of "persons deriving title from or under" both dominant and servient owners impliedly includes lessees.[83] Sections 12 and 13 of Deasy's Act, as interpreted by the courts, continue to govern the enforcement of landlord and tenant covenants by and against successors. It is axiomatic from the introduced concepts of dominant and servient land that the provisions of the LCLRA 2009 do not apply at all where the covenant does not affect land and is personal only. Significantly, s.49(6)(b) provides that the section "takes effect subject to the terms of the covenant or the instrument containing it". This means that the original covenantor and covenantee can agree in the instrument that creates the covenant that it is not to be enforceable by and against successors, although a later agreement to that effect, whether entered into by the original covenanting parties or *by* the successors of either or both of them, will not serve to displace the operation of the section.

---

[79] LCLRA 2009 s.49(1).
[80] LCLRA 2009 s.49(2).
[81] LCLRA 2009 s.49(4) and (5).
[82] LCLRA 2009 s.49(6)(a)(i). Earlier drafts of the equivalent of this section in Bill form had, arguably, left this matter in some doubt.
[83] With the exception of a tenant for less than five years in the case of a servient owner.

Scheme of Development

22–69 The effect of the LCLRA 2009 on a scheme of development appears in the main to be the adoption of the regime of flexibility introduced by *Elliston v Reacher* and the extension of it to positive covenants and to all schemes falling within the statutory definition, commercial as well as residential.

22–70 Section 48 defines a scheme of development as "a development of land under which—

(a) the land is, or is intended to be, subdivided into 2 or more parts for conveyance in fee simple to each owner of a part;

(b) there is an intention as between the developer and the owners of parts to create reciprocity of covenants in accordance with section 49(3);

(c) that intention is expressed in each conveyance to the owners of parts or implied from the covenants in question as they relate to the parts and the proximity of the relationship between their owners".

22–71 Section 49(3) provides, where a scheme of development as defined exists, that the new statutory rules for the enforcement among successors of covenants affecting freehold dominant and servient land apply "so as to render covenants which are capable of reciprocally benefiting and burdening the parts of land within the scheme enforceable by and against the owners for the time being of such parts", and also by and against former owners in relation to breaches occurring when they were such owners. From this, it is clear that only covenants capable of affecting the various plots within the scheme of development will "run", but that, subject to this, there is no restriction on the type of covenants that may be enforced or the type of estate scheme within which they may be enforced, provided that both dominant land and servient land are involved.

Potential Difficulties

22–72 While it is indisputable that the new statutory regime for the enforcement of covenants among successors substantially simplifies the former intricate labyrinth of rules at law and in equity, with their frequently differing application to positive and negative covenants, certain elements cry out for attention and may prove to be pitfalls for the unwary.

1. The new rules apply only to covenants affecting freehold land which have been entered into after 1 December 2009. Any covenants entered into prior to that date are still subject, in terms of enforcement among successors, to the pre-existing rules of law and equity.

2. Chapter 4 of Pt 8 of the LCLRA 2009 applies only to covenants affecting dominant and servient land where both parcels of land are held in freehold. In terms of leasehold covenants, ss.12 and 13 of Deasy's Act 1860 continue to govern enforcement of covenants by and against successors to the landlord and the tenant respectively. However, as demonstrated

in *Lyle v Smith*,[84] even in the case of leasehold covenants there remains a judicial tendency to consider their enforceability among successors against the more rigorous rubrics of the common law. In consequence, it is possible that henceforth it will be seen as easier to cause to run a covenant "attaching to" (the expression used in the definition of "freehold covenant" in s.48 of the LCLRA 2009) freehold property than one attaching to a lease unless in due course the words "attaching to" are interpreted by the courts as meaning the same thing as is understood by the traditional expression "touching and concerning".

3. The confining of the regime of enforcement of covenants by successors established in the LCLRA 2009 to cases where the covenant affects both land of the covenantee (dominant land) and of the covenantor (servient land) represents an important qualification to its effect. Not all covenants heretofore found enforceable at law have necessarily involved two parcels of land. To situations of this kind Ch.4 of Pt 8 of the LCLRA 2009 will not apply. Potentially, a further complication would have been caused by the blanket abolition of the existing "rules of common law and equity" in s.49(1), which would have left situations not covered by the LCLRA 2009 to be decided without the benefit of precedent. However, since this abolition is stated as applying only to "the enforceability of a freehold covenant", and a freehold covenant is defined as "a covenant attaching to dominant land and servient land which has been entered into after the commencement of this Chapter", the result is that the statutory abolition of the pre-existing rules does not apply to covenants that fall outside Ch.4 of Pt 8 of the LCLRA 2009, to which instead the rules of law and equity that formerly applied to them will continue to apply.

4. If the parties to a covenant which affects land owned by each of them intend that the covenant is not to pass to or be enforced against successors, this intention must be made clear in the instrument that contains the covenant.[85] A subsequent agreement or waiver it seems will be ineffective to reverse the operation of the LCLRA 2009, although s.50(2) (g) provides that a servient owner may apply to court for an order discharging or modifying a covenant on the ground that it constitutes an unreasonable interference with the use and enjoyment of the servient land, where "the dominant owner has agreed, expressly or impliedly, to the covenant being discharged or varied". It is suggested that the need for recourse to a court order, in the context of a regime intended to ease the overall law of covenants, seems an unnecessarily cumbrous requirement in order to remove a covenant that the parties who are respectively entitled to enforce and have enforced are prepared to agree either to discharge or to confine to themselves without its being enforceable between their successors.

---

[84] [1909] 2 I.R. 58.
[85] LCLRA 2009 s.49(6)(b).

5. The previous point touches on a more fundamental one which perhaps is the most profound objection to the new system of covenant enforceability introduced by the LCLRA 2009. This is the interpolation from the law of easements of the concept of dominant land and servient land with the consequential likely blurring or obliterating of the distinction between covenants and easements. Traditionally, covenants were rights in contract to which separate developments at law and in equity gave in certain instances proprietorial attributes. Easements are appurtenant land rights which by their very nature involve two properties and also in order to exist must contain certain defining characteristics. Rights sought to be attached to property which did not comply with the requisite ingredients for an easement were safeguarded, to the limited extent possible, by being made the subject of a covenant.[86] It may be that one of the overall results of Ch.4 of Pt 8 of the LCLRA 2009 will be the proliferation of the range and type of burdens capable of being enforced against property.

DISCHARGE AND MODIFICATION

Freehold Covenants

22–73 Prior to the enactment of the LCLRA 2009, one of the problems associated with covenants in Ireland was that there was no really effective method of dealing with obsolete specimens. In the case of registered land, s.69(3) of the Registration of Title Act 1964 provides that the Property Registration Authority[87] can modify or discharge a covenant with the consent of all persons interested in its enforcement. It follows from this that one such person can prevent the discharge of the covenant or demand a large sum of money for his or her consent. If all the persons interested in the covenant's enforcement consent, the Property Registration Authority can modify or discharge the covenant provided that this exercise is "beneficial" to such persons.[88]

---

[86] Examples include the right to preservation of a view, the right to a throughput of a particular quality of air, the right of exclusive access to percolating water in the soil, which, generally on account of their unduly burdensome and indeterminate character, were incapable of being ranked as easements.

[87] Formerly the Registrar of Titles: Registration of Deeds and Title Act 2006 s.4.

[88] In *Re an Application by Edwards* [1983] R.V.R. 94, the covenant prohibited the use of the land for business purposes. The English Lands Tribunal held that the covenant was not obsolete, but impeded the reasonable use of the land. The injury to objectors was slight and compensation would be awarded. In *Gilbert v Spoor* [1982] 2 All E.R. 576, it was held that the objectors were not affected and consequently there was jurisdiction to refuse. In *Re 6, 8, 10 & 12 Elm Avenue, New Milton* [1984] 3 All E.R. 632, the land was voluntarily acquired by a local authority. It was held that the restrictive covenant could not be enforced so as to restrict the statutory purposes for which the land was acquired. This did not amount to discharge of the covenant.

22–74 Section 50 of the LCLRA 2009 provides for the modification or discharge of any freehold covenant, regardless of when entered into.[89] However, application must be made to the High Court by the owner of the servient land (the land burdened by the covenant) in order for the covenant to be modified or discharged. The grounds of such application must be "that continued compliance with it [the covenant] would constitute an unreasonable interference with the use and enjoyment of the servient land".[90] In determining whether, and on what terms, an order should be made, "the court shall have regard as appropriate" to various matters set out in s.50(2):

- when, how and why the covenant was entered into;
- any changes in the meantime in the character of the dominant land and the servient land and their neighbourhood, taking into account the development plan for the area under the Planning and Development Act 2000 and the granting and refusing of planning permissions in the vicinity;
- whether the covenant confers any practical benefit, and, if so, of what kind and to what extent;
- in the case of a positive covenant, whether compliance with it has become unduly onerous in comparison with the corresponding benefit;
- "whether the dominant owner has agreed, expressly or impliedly, to the covenant being discharged or varied";
- representations made by interested parties;
- "any other matter which the court considers relevant".

22–75 The court can order compensation to be paid either to the dominant owner "or other person adversely affected by the order" where it is satisfied that "quantifiable loss" will occur and can make the payment of such compensation a condition of the order.[91] Any order made "shall be registered in the Registry of Deeds or Land Registry, as appropriate."[92]

22–76 Overall, s.50 of the LCLRA 2009 introduces a welcome new facility for the removal of an otiose or over-burdensome covenant, without giving a right to demand extortionate payment for its discharge to a party entitled to enforce the covenant, which is a clear latent weakness in s.69(3) of the Registration of Title Act 1964. Allowing the court to attach payment of compensation as a condition of the granting of an order of discharge or modification

---

[89] To this extent, s.50 modifies the definition of freehold covenant in s.48 which limits itself to a covenant "which has been entered into after the commencement of this chapter." In the draft of the equivalent of s.50 in Bill form, the parenthesised words "(whether created before or after the commencement of this Chapter)" had not been included. Clearly, the legislative intention was that the new regime for the modification or extinguishment of covenants affecting freehold land should apply to all freehold covenants immediately.

[90] LCLRA 2009 s.50(1).

[91] LCLRA 2009 s.50(3).

[92] LCLRA 2009 s.50(4). It is not specifically stated whether failure to register the modification or discharge means that the order is unenforceable. Presumably, an action could not be taken for its enforcement unless the registration requirement of the section had been complied with.

provides appropriate protection to a party who would otherwise be at risk of gratuitous denial of his or her property rights. On the other hand, the necessity of making an application to court may provide a disincentive to the use of the section. As noted above, an application for modification or discharge of a covenant under s.50 will henceforth be the only way of ensuring the removal of a covenant that otherwise attaches to and runs with the properties which it affects in the event of failure by the original covenanting parties to agree otherwise in the instrument creating the covenant. This aspect of things can scarcely be seen as a desirable development.

Leasehold Covenants

22–77 At present there is no effective method of removing a moribund or excessively burdensome leasehold covenant short of seeking to utilise (with their marked inherent limitations) the enfranchisement statutes previously discussed. In *Whelan v Cork Corporation*,[93] it was held that one of the results of a lessee's acquiring the fee simple of land subject to a ground rent under s.8 of the Landlord and Tenant (Ground Rents) (No. 2) Act 1978 was to discharge the burden of restrictive covenants binding the land. This included not only those binding in privity of estate, i.e. as between the former tenant and the landlord, but also those binding under the doctrine of *Tulk v Moxhay*. Murphy J. in the High Court did not decide, as a constitutional issue, whether this contravened Art.40.2 as an unjust attack on property rights, since the Attorney General did not appear to argue the issue.

22–78 The Supreme Court upheld Murphy J. on the same terms in an ex tempore judgment. It seems likely that the provision is unconstitutional to the extent that it deprives third parties, without compensation, of the ability to enforce a covenant in equity under *Tulk v Moxhay*. Such a result also appears to go beyond the evident purpose of the section which was to relieve the new fee simple from the burden of covenants contained in the original lease which might have been appropriate between landlord and tenant but which might unduly restrict a fee simple.

HUMAN RIGHTS

22–79 Covenants which attempt to impose restrictions on *alienation* to particular groups, whether religious, social, or of any other description, will, if they affect the fee simple estate, be liable to be held void as contrary to the principle of free alienation embodied in *Quia Emptores* 1290, and now stated in s.9(4) of the LCLRA 2009, quite apart from human rights or constitutional implications.

22–80 Covenants which attempt to restrict *ownership* or *occupation* of land to members of a particular religious, racial, or other restricted social group are

---

[93] [1991] I.L.R.M. 19.

open to challenge on constitutional grounds as violating the right to equality as human persons under Art.40.1 of the Constitution. The Irish courts have yet to address the issues raised by racial or religious restrictions in the context of freehold covenants.

22–81 EU Council Directive 2000/43/EC,[94] which implements the principle of equal treatment between persons irrespective of racial or ethnic origin, prohibits direct or indirect discrimination on racial or ethnic grounds, including in relation to access to housing "available to the public".

22–82 The Equal Status Act 2000, which was not passed specifically to implement the EU Directive, but was amended in 2004, provides in s.6[95] that a person shall not discriminate, on the grounds specified in the Act, in "disposing of any estate or interest in premises". The grounds are wider than the Directive and include: gender; marital status; family status; sexual orientation; religion; age (except where a person is under the age of 18[96]); disability; race, colour, nationality or ethnic or national origins; membership of the traveller community; and victimisation, i.e. where a person has applied for redress on any of the above grounds.[97] Section 6, however, exempts disposal by will or gift,[98] which are not excluded by the Directive.

---

[94] 29 June 2000.
[95] As amended by s.49 of the Equality Act 2004.
[96] Equal Status Act 2000 s.3.
[97] Equal Status Act 2000 ss.2 and 3.
[98] Equal Status Act 2000 s.6(2)(a).

CHAPTER 23

Easements and Profits

INCORPOREAL HEREDITAMENTS INTRODUCED

23–01 Incorporeal hereditaments can broadly be defined as interests in land which do not include the right of possession. In feudal times the dominant legal concept in relation to land was seisin. Feudal law was obsessed with seisin because physical possession of land was necessary to the feudal method of extracting tribute from the villeins. Their surplus labour was extracted by force, or the threat of force, not through, in Adam Smith's phrase, the "invisible hand" of the market. The hand of the feudal lord, or his agents, was eminently visible. Hence it was important to distinguish between interests in land which conferred seisin and those which did not. Incorporeal hereditaments were interests which did not entitle the owner of them to seisin.

23–02 Incorporeal hereditaments were "hereditaments" in that they were, and are, inherited under the rules of succession. They were said to be "incorporeal" because they did not give seisin itself, which was seen as "corporeal", i.e. having a *corpus*, a body, or in other words, being a physical thing. Incorporeal hereditaments fell into the definition of what is known as real property, but were not land in the tangible sense. Blackstone, writing just before the Industrial Revolution, described incorporeal hereditaments as not "the object of sensation, can neither be seen nor handled, are creatures of the mind, and exist only in contemplation".[1]

23–03 The traditional importance of seisin was also evident in the formalities as to its transfer. A feoffment with livery of seisin was necessary to transfer corporeal rights, but a simple deed sufficed to transfer incorporeal interests. As the agricultural basis of society gave way to an industrial one, the importance of physical possession of land also declined. Force yielded to the market and tribute yielded to wage labour. Seisin declined as a legal concept, and after the enactment of the Real Property Act 1845 "corporeal" rights could be transferred by grant. Incorporeal hereditaments are now understood as interests in land which do not include the right of possession. Sometimes they are described as "rights over the land of another person". Accordingly, the subject of this chapter is rights that fall under the general heading of incorporeal

---

[1] W. Blackstone, *Commentaries on the Laws of England*, Vol.II, 1st edn (London: Clarendon Press, 1765–69), p.17.

hereditaments: easements (such as rights of way), *profits à prendre* (such as shooting or fishing rights), rentcharges, and other miscellaneous rights.

INCORPOREAL HEREDITAMENTS AS THE SUBJECT OF ESTATES

23–04 Incorporeal hereditaments are held for estates: freehold or leasehold. Leasehold easements can be granted, and, in Ireland, can be acquired by tenants by such methods as prescription.

23–05 Although an incorporeal hereditament is held for an estate, the hereditament itself, if deemed appurtenant to land, attaches to the land. An easement affects the land both of the party to be benefited (the dominant tenement) and of the party subject to the burden of the easement (the servient tenement). By contrast, a *profit à prendre* can in certain instances benefit its holder personally, or exist "in gross".

23–06 In *Wall v Collins*[2] a right of way had been granted a century earlier to the holder of a leasehold interest in property for a term of 999 years. The English Court of Appeal held that the subsequent acquisition by an assignee of the lease of the freehold reversion did not occasion extinguishment of the right of way. Carnwath L.J. asserted the basic proposition as follows: "An easement must be appurtenant to a dominant tenement, but not necessarily to any particular interest for the time-being." Here, the leasehold interest had clearly merged into the fee simple, as evidenced by the assignee's consenting to the deletion of any reference to the erstwhile lease in the Land Registry entry for the folio of his property. However, according to Carnwath L.J.,

> "merger of the lease into a larger interest in the dominant tenement is not in itself fatal to the continued existence of the easement, for the period for which it was granted. The dominant tenement remains unchanged and there is no legal impediment to the continued enjoyment of the easement by the occupier for the time-being of that tenement."[3]

23–07 In Carnwath L.J.'s opinion, it offended common sense to suggest that a grantee should be worse off, as regards an easement annexed to his or her land, for no better reason than that he or she had acquired a superior interest in the dominant tenement.

23–08 The Law Commission of England and Wales[4] criticised this decision, and recommended that the decision in *Wall v Collins* be reversed by statute. However, it also recommended that such statute "should provide a mechanism

---

[2] [2007] EWCA Civ 444.

[3] [2007] EWCA Civ 444 at para.16.

[4] The Law Commission, *Making Land Work: Easements, Covenants and Profits à Prendre* (327/2011), paras 3.252–3.255.

to enable the reversioner, on merger and surrender, (or the tenant, where there is a surrender and re-grant) to elect to keep the benefit of interests appurtenant to the lease surrendered or merged."[5]

CATEGORIES NOT CLOSED

23–09 Some easements have been recognised since feudal times, such as the right of way. The Industrial Revolution, with its mass movement of population to towns and cities and the new industrial uses of land, created a need for different types of easements to be recognised. This caused a legal controversy in the early 19th century. Resistance to the creation of many new types of easements was expressed by Lord Brougham in *Keppel v Bailey*.[6] Lord Brougham was a progressive judge, to the extent that he saw the need for land to be freely alienable as a commodity, but was nonetheless concerned that owners ought not to be able to put any restrictions they liked on user that would make land subject to easements less easily saleable. There was also a suggestion that the categories of easements should be taken as fixed, but this was opposed by Lord St Leonards in *Dyce v Hay*.[7] He said that the categories of easements "must alter and expand with the changes that take place in the circumstances of mankind." The solution was not to refuse to recognise new easements but to develop tests to control them. These tests were extensively discussed in *Re Ellenborough Park*,[8] which essentially summed up 19th century developments of the doctrine. These are embodied in the several tests set out below.

EASEMENTS

23–10 An easement was defined by Monaghan C.J. in *Hamilton v Musgrove*[9] as

"an incorporeal right which may be defined to be a privilege, not conferring any right to a participation in the profits of the land over which it is exercised, which the owner of one tenement has over the neighbouring tenement, by which the owner of the servient tenement is obliged to suffer something to be done, or refrain from doing something, on his own land for the advantage of the dominant tenement. It must be imposed for the benefit of corporeal property, and imposed upon corporeal property."

---

[5] The Law Commission, *Making Land Work*: *Easements, Covenants and Profits à Prendre* (327/2011), para.3.255. It was announced in 2016 that a draft Law of Property Bill would be brought forward, based on the Commission's recommendations, but no legislation has been passed.

[6] (1834) 2 My. & K. 517 at 535.

[7] (1852) 1 Macq. 305.

[8] [1956] Ch. 131.

[9] (1870) I.R. 6 C.L. 129.

Tests
Dominant and Servient Tenement
23–11 An easement is a property right in land, sometimes called an "appurtenant right". The person who acquires or holds it does not do so for his or her personal benefit but for the benefit of a piece of land in which he or she has an estate. An easement cannot exist "in gross", i.e. it cannot exist as a benefit not connected to land. It must both confer a benefit on some land, known as the dominant tenement, and constitute a burden upon, i.e. reduce the usefulness of, some other land, known as the servient tenement.

23–12 While there must be some physical proximity between the dominant and servient tenements in order for one property to be able to confer a benefit on the other, it has been held that the two need not be immediately adjacent. In *Latimer v Official Co-operative Society*[10] there were three attached houses in a row which belonged to A, B and C in that order. A's house was demolished and rebuilt. Subsequently the wall of B's house, which supported C's adjoining wall, detached itself from C's wall causing it to crack. The evidence was that the new building on A's site had settled down after construction, probably because it was heavier than the former building. It had pulled B's house with it, causing B's house to detach itself from that of C. The Court of Common Pleas held A liable to C without proof of negligence. An easement of support had been acquired over time, by prescription, for the benefit of C's house from A's land.

23–13 If the dominant tenement is not specified, but an attempt is made to reserve the right to nominate in future unspecified land as the dominant tenement, the purported grant cannot be an easement.[11] If the potential dominant and servient tenements are ascertained, then a right to create an easement in future is capable of being valid as a property right exercisable by a third party.[12]

Must Accommodate Dominant Tenement
23–14 The fact that other persons may benefit from enjoyment of the right is not relevant to its status as an easement. However, it is not enough, for it to be an easement, that the right enhances the value (price) of the dominant tenement. It must enhance its use value; making it, in effect, a "better" property. This is really a test aimed at restricting the number of possible new easements and reflects the 19th century controversy mentioned above. New easements are to be recognised to meet *social* needs, in order to take account of new uses of land.

---

[10] (1885) 16 L.R. Ir. 305.
[11] *London & Blenheim Estates Ltd v Ladbroke Retail Parks Ltd* [1993] 4 All E.R. 157.
[12] *London & Blenheim Estates Ltd v Ladbroke Retail Parks Ltd* [1993] 4 All E.R. 157.

Ownership in Different Persons

23–15 At common law, at least as it developed in England, ownership of the dominant and servient tenements had to be vested in different persons. This rule was modified in Ireland because of the prevalence in the past of agricultural tenancies and is now dealt with by s.36 of the Land and Conveyancing Law Reform Act 2009 ("LCLRA 2009").

Capable of Forming the Subject Matter of a Grant

23–16 All the methods of acquiring easements discussed below are based on the notion of grant. This can be an express grant, or one arising by implication, or what has come to be known as a presumed grant. In order to be recognised as an easement a right must be capable of being described in a deed of grant and so it must not be too vague. It must also be of such a nature that it is possible to tell if it has been interfered with by the owner of the servient tenement. In *Cochrane v Verner*[13] it was held that there was no such easement as a right to shade and shelter for cattle provided by a hedge. It was too vague.

23–17 A grant intended to create an easement must not amount to effective ownership or possession of the supposed servient tenement.[14] In *Copeland v Greenhalf*[15] a landowner utilised a strip of his neighbour's land to store vehicles on which he carried out repairs. This was held not to be an easement, as it was tantamount to joint possession of the land. Such usage might create a contractual licence or a tenancy, but not an easement. Similar considerations have operated to prevent certain claimed car-parking rights from constituting an easement. Where land was granted "for the purpose only of exercising troops thereon" it was held[16] that it was the grant of a fee simple and not an easement.

Negative Factors

23–18 Even if the above tests are satisfied the court is still unlikely to recognise an asserted right as an easement if:

1. it involves expenditure by the servient owner.[17] No recognised easement, with one exception, imposes such a burden. The exception is the easement to fence land. It is exceptional because it was recognised in the medieval period before the modern tests were developed[18];
2. it is purely negative, i.e. it stops the servient owner doing something. But this limitation as simply stated is dubious because of the existence of two exceptions: easements to light and easements of support; or

---

[13] (1895) 29 I.L.T. 571.
[14] *London & Blenheim Estates Ltd v Ladbroke Retail Parks Ltd* [1993] 1 All E.R. 307.
[15] [1952] Ch. 488.
[16] *White v Baylor* (1846) 10 Ir. Eq. R. 43.
[17] *Regis Property v Redman* [1956] 2 Q.B. 612.
[18] *Crow v Wood* [1971] 1 Q.B. 77.

3. it is contrary to public policy. In *Blackburne v Somers*[19] it was held that a right could not be acquired by prescription to pollute a stream in a way injurious to public health. In *Lanigan v Barry*[20] Charleton J. held that a right to create a nuisance by noise could not be acquired by prescription. These are examples of the common law protecting the environment.

23–19 A person claiming an easement not only has to show that it satisfies the positive and negative tests described above: he or she must show that the easement has been acquired by one of the methods discussed below, i.e. by express, implied or presumed grant. It is not inherent, and, as such, is to be distinguished from a "natural right" discussed below.

Specific Easements
List of Examples
23–20 The following have been held to be capable of being easements:

(a) a right to throw spoil onto a neighbour's land[21];
(b) a right acquired by prescription to a higher degree of light required for the normal use of a greenhouse and the benefit of the rays of the sun needed to grow plants[22];
(c) a right, acquired after 20 years' user, to the greater amount of light entering a new room which replaced an older one[23];
(d) a right to run telephone lines over neighbouring land[24];
(e) a right to use an airfield[25];
(f) a right to use a lavatory and tap water for making tea on the servient tenement, a cinema, for the benefit of the dominant tenement, a shop in the cinema, exercisable by the lessee of the shop and her staff[26];
(g) a right to store eel tanks on a river bed for the benefit of eel weirs reserved by a conveyance and of which the parties claiming the right were lessees[27];
(h) a right to water cattle[28];

---

[19] (1879) 5 L.R. Ir. 1. See also, *Goldsmid v The Tunbridge Wells Improvement Commissioners* (1865) L.R. 1 Eq. 161 at 169; *Attorney General v Richmond* (1866) L.R. 2 Eq. 306 at 311; *The Staffordshire and Worcestershire Canal v The Birmingham Canal* (1866) L.R. 1 H.L. 254.

[20] [2008] IEHC 29.

[21] *Middleton v Clarence* (1877) I.R. 11 C.L. 499.

[22] *Allen v Greenwood* [1980] Ch. 11.

[23] *Mackey v Scottish Widows Insurance Co* (1877) I.R. 11 Eq. 541.

[24] *Lancashire & Cheshire Telephone Exchange Co v Manchester Overseers* (1884) 14 Q.B.D. 267.

[25] *Dowty Boulton Paul Ltd v Wolverhampton Corporation (No.2)* [1976] Ch. 13.

[26] *Jeffers v Odeon (Ireland) Ltd* (1953) 87 I.L.T.R. 187. See also *Miller v Emcer Products* [1956] Ch. 304 at 316.

[27] *Ingram v Mackey* [1898] 1 I.R. 272.

[28] *Re the Estate of Harding* (1874) I.R. 8 Eq. 620; *Re Tibbotstown and Cloneen Water Arbitration* (1897) 31 I.L.T. 380.

(i)   a right to dump lime and manure on another's land[29];

(j)   a right to use a shoeing stone on the servient tenement for the benefit of a horse shoeing forge, the dominant tenement.[30]

Rights of Way

23–21 This is probably the most common easement.[31] A right of way may be by foot only and a grant of a right of way does not automatically carry with it the right to use vehicles. This is a matter of construction of the instrument that grants it, or of implication from the words used or the circumstances in which the easement is granted, as to the extent of the right.[32] Where a right of way is established for a particular purpose, it cannot normally be expanded into a different or broader purpose although such a broader purpose could be acquired over time by prescription.[33] A vehicular right of way, however, has been held in certain circumstances to include the right to park for the time necessary to load and unload vehicles.[34] A right of way that included passage by vehicles in favour of a dominant tenement which was a restaurant, in a situation where there was adequate room for this to happen, has been held to include as a necessary corollary a right on the part of patrons of the restaurant to park their cars outside while dining there.[35]

Right to Light

23–22 A right to light that descends vertically from the sky is an incident of the ownership of property. A right to light that passes horizontally over other property must be acquired as an easement, with the property over which the light passes constituting the servient tenement. The nature of the easement is the right to have the light pass unencumbered over the servient tenement so that it can reach an aperture in the dominant tenement. In the nature of things, a right to light is rarely the subject of an express grant and is most often acquired by prescription. The traditional common law position, reflected in s.3 of the Prescription (Ireland) Act 1858, is that, for the purposes of a right to light, the dominant tenement must be a building. Access to the dominant tenement must be to a window or windows "or apertures in the nature of windows and not to apertures with doors in them, which were primarily constructed for the purpose

---

[29]   *Redmond v Hayes*, unreported, High Court, Kenny J., 7 October 1974.

[30]   *Calders v Murtagh* (1939) 5 Ir. Jur. Rep. 19.

[31]   *Head v Meara* [1912] 1 I.R. 262; *Dunne v Rattigan* [1981] I.L.R.M. 365; *Flanagan v Mulhall* [1985] I.L.R.M. 134.

[32]   *Gogarty v Hoskins* [1906] 1 I.R. 173; *Cannon v Villars* (1878) 8 Ch. D. 415 (see Jessel M.R. at 420–421); *Bulstrode v Lambert* [1953] 2 All E.R. 728; *Doolan v Murray*, unreported, High Court, Keane J., 21 December 1993.

[33]   *Byrnes and Neylon v Meakstown Construction Ltd* [2009] IEHC 123.

[34]   *Bulstrode v Lambert* [1953] 2 All E.R. 728.

[35]   *Redfont Ltd and Wright's Fisherman's Wharf Ltd v Custom House Dock Management Ltd and Hardwicke Property Management Ltd* [1998] IEHC 206.

of being closed and thus excluding light".[36] In *Colls v Home and Colonial Stores Ltd*,[37] the House of Lords decided that in order for deprivation of the easement of light to give rise to a cause of action, the extent of its diminution had to be actionable as a nuisance, on the basis of the amount of light required by the dominant tenement for its ordinary use, whether domestic or commercial.[38] What has been called an "extraordinary quantity of light" is capable of being acquired by prescription provided that this quantity of light can be shown as necessary for the particular use to which the dominant tenement has been put throughout the prescriptive period.[39]

Right of Support

23–23 It is an incident of the ownership of land that that land has a right to be supported in its natural state by the land adjacent to it. However, a right to have any building erected on land supported by that adjacent land must be acquired as an easement.[40] Where a right of support for a building by adjacent land has been acquired by prescription, a cause of action lies against the owner of the adjacent soil if he or she disturbs his or her own land so as to take away the lateral support to which the right to its continuance had been acquired.[41] A right of support to a building by a building on adjacent land is also capable of being acquired as an easement.[42]

Right to Park Cars

23–24 In *London & Blenheim Estates Ltd v Ladbroke Retail Parks Ltd*[43] the English High Court held[44] that the right to park cars may exist as an easement, provided that it is a general right to park within a designated area and not a right to park in a specific parking place only, which would leave the servient

---

[36] *Levet v Gaslight and Coke Co* [1919] Ch. 24 at 27, approved by Teevan J. in *Walsh v Goulding*, unreported, High Court, 31 July 1968.

[37] [1904] A.C. 179.

[38] This formulation has been adopted in a number of Irish cases, including *Smyth v Dublin Theatre Co Ltd* [1936] I.R. 692; *Gannon v Hughes* [1937] I.R. 284; *McGrath v Munster and Leinster Bank Ltd* [1959] I.R. 313.

[39] *Lanfranchi v Mackenzie* (1867) L.R. 4 Eq. 421; *Allen v Greenwood* [1980] Ch. 119.

[40] *Green v Belfast Tramways Co* (1887) 20 L.R. Ir. 35.

[41] *Dalton v Angus* (1881) 6 App. Cas. 740.

[42] *Gately v A & J Martin Ltd* [1900] 2 I.R. 269. In *Latimer v Official Co-operative Society* (1885) 16 L.R. Ir. 305, the right acquired was in respect of a building on a terraced row, not beside the servient tenement, but two houses away. The servient tenement, however, was the land beneath the reconstructed building as it was in respect of this land that the easement of support arose.

[43] [1993] 1 All E.R. 307.

[44] The decision was upheld by the Court of Appeal, but on other grounds: [1993] 4 All E.R. 157. See also *Bilkus v London Borough of Redbridge* (1968) 207 E.G. 803.

owner without any reasonable use of that piece of land.[45] In *Newman v Jones*[46] it was said that "a right for a landowner to park a car anywhere in a defined area nearby is capable of existing as an easement." In *Batchelor v Marlow*[47] the English Court of Appeal held that an exclusive right to park cars for over nine hours a day each working day could not rank as an easement, since the servient owner's "right to use his land is curtailed altogether for intermittent periods throughout the week", in such a way as effectively to "make his ownership of the land illusory." The Irish Supreme Court has held that a right to park is capable of constituting an easement.[48] Regardless of the scope of the right and its effect on the servient tenement, a right of car-parking cannot be an easement unless it accommodates, or is appurtenant to, a dominant tenement. On the other hand, outside the realm of property law, a right to park in a specific parking place could, of course, exist as a contractual right, as, for example, between employer and employee.

Right to a View

23–25 The right to a view has been held not to exist as an easement, on the ground that it is too vague.[49] Nevertheless in *Gilbert v Spoor*[50] it was held that a view may be relevant in the discharge of a restrictive covenant, i.e. a court may not discharge the covenant if the result would be the loss of a view.

Right to Protection from Weather

23–26 The English Court of Appeal in *Phipps v Pears*[51] held that the right to have a wall of a house protected against the weather by the owner of the adjoining property could not exist as an easement, apparently on the ground that the right was too vague. On the other hand, an easement of support gives the owner of the dominant tenement the right to support of buildings on the dominant tenement from the servient tenement. However, weather proofing of adjoining buildings could be a condition of planning permission.

---

[45] Against the background of subsequent developments, the decision in *Esso Petroleum v Epps* [1973] 1 W.L.R. 1071, to the effect that a right to park cars was not an overriding interest in registered land because it could not exist as an easement, must now be regarded as of unlikely authority.

[46] Unreported, English Chancery Division, 22 March 1982, quoted in *Handel v St Stephen's Close* [1994] 1 E.G.L.R. 70.

[47] [2003] 1 W.L.R. 764; see also *Montrose Court Holdings v Shamash* [2006] EWCA Civ 251.

[48] *AGS (ROI) Pension Nominees Ltd v Madison Estates Ltd*, unreported, Supreme Court, Keane C.J., ex tempore, 23 October 2003.

[49] *Phipps v Pears* [1965] 1 Q.B. 76. The original case on the point denied the easement on the ground that a view was a matter of pleasure only: *William Aldred's Case* (1610) 9 Co. Rep. 57b: "the law does not give an action for such things of delight." However, *Re Ellenborough Park* [1956] Ch. 131 held a *jus spatiandi* (right to walk about for recreation) to be an easement although pleasure is a large element in such a right.

[50] [1982] 2 All E.R. 576.

[51] [1965] 1 Q.B. 76.

23–27 In *Treacy v Dublin Corporation*[52] a local authority issued a statutory notice to demolish a dangerous building to the first-floor level. The owner of the adjoining land sought an injunction to restrain the local authority from exercising the power to demolish the dangerous building on the ground that an easement of support existed for the benefit of his building which bound the owner of the land on which the dangerous building stood. He argued that the statutory powers did not authorise the local authority to interfere with this property right. Costello J. in the High Court granted an injunction restraining the local authority from demolishing the building without providing a means of support for the adjoining building. The judge further ordered that the local authority could not proceed without providing wind and weather protection for the adjoining owner's building. The statute created duties as well as a power. This order was upheld in the Supreme Court, which nevertheless approved of *Phipps v Pears*, i.e. that the right to protection from the weather for the benefit of a building could not exist as an easement. According to Finlay C.J., it would be unrealistic for the local authority to shore up the support it had removed from the building with replacement materials that would be insufficient to withstand buffeting from the elements.[53]

Easements in High-rise Buildings

23–28 In *Liverpool City Council v Irwin*[54] a local corporation was the owner of a tower block, which contained some 70 dwelling units including the maisonette of which the appellants were tenants. Access to the various units was provided by a common staircase together with two electronically operated lifts. Over the course of years the condition of the block deteriorated badly, including (a) continual failure of the lifts, (b) lack of proper lighting on the stairs, and (c) blockage of the rubbish chutes. The appellants together with other tenants protested against the condition of the block by refusing to pay rent to the corporation. The corporation sought an order for possession of the appellants' premises and the appellants counterclaimed against the corporation alleging, inter alia, a breach on the part of the corporation of implied covenants for repair and for the appellants' quiet enjoyment of the property; also that there was an implied obligation on the corporation to keep the staircase and corridors of the block in repair and the lights in working order, and that the corporation was in breach of this obligation.

---

[52] [1993] 1 I.R. 305.

[53] In *Tapson v Northern Ireland Housing Executive* [1992] N.I. 264, Carswell J. applied the neighbour principle in tort to hold an adjoining house owner liable for damage caused to the property next door by seepage that arose from bomb damage 10 years earlier to the adjoining house which its owner had failed to rectify. In *Rees v Skerrett* [2001] 1 W.L.R. 1541, the English Court of Appeal held that a duty to protect a neighbour's house from the elements arose where the demolition of a terraced house had removed the party wall between it and the house adjoining.

[54] [1977] A.C. 239.

23–29 The House of Lords held that easements for the use of the stairs, lifts, and rubbish chutes were implied in the tenancy agreements. Lord Wilberforce said:

> "There can be no doubt that there must be implied (i) an easement for the tenants and their licensees to use the stairs, (ii) a right in the nature of an easement to use the lifts and (iii) an easement to use the rubbish chutes."[55]

23–30 The court also held that in the nature of the circumstances, the obligation to repair the common parts fell on the landlord, even though the owner of the servient tenement is normally not obliged to keep the subject matter of the easement under repair. Lord Wilberforce quoted Bowen L.J. in *Miller v Hancock*[56]:

> "The tenants could only use their flats by using the staircase. The defendant, therefore, when he let the flats, impliedly granted to the tenants an easement over the staircase ... for the purpose of the enjoyment of the flats so let. Under those circumstances, what is the law as to the repairs of the staircase? It was contended by the defendant's counsel that, according to the common law, the person in enjoyment of an easement is bound to do the necessary repairs himself. That may be true with regard to easements in general, but it is subject to the qualification that the grantor of the easement may undertake to do the repairs either in express terms or by necessary implication ... It appears to me obvious, when one considers what a flat of this kind is, and the only way in which it can be enjoyed, that the parties to the demise of it must have intended by necessary implication, as a basis without which the whole transaction would be futile, that the landlord should maintain the staircase, which is essential to the enjoyment of the premises demised, and should keep it reasonably safe for the use of the tenants, and also of those persons who would necessarily go up and down the stairs in the ordinary course of business with the tenants ... ."

23–31 The House of Lords in *Liverpool* further held, that while it was not open to the court to imply terms simply because they were reasonable, the subject-matter of the agreement, i.e. a high-rise building in multiple occupation, and the nature of the relationship of landlord and tenant, necessarily required implication of the obligations by the corporation. There was an implied term by the landlord/local authority to take reasonable care to maintain the common parts in a state of reasonable repair and efficiency. The obligation was not, however, absolute, and required no more than was necessary or reasonable in the circumstances. The court concluded that it had not been shown that the local authority had failed in its obligation to maintain the common parts.

---

[55] [1977] A.C. 239 at 254.
[56] [1893] 2 Q.B. 177 at 180–181.

23–32 In *Heeney v Dublin Corporation*[57] (the "Ballymun lifts case"), O'Flaherty J. in an ex tempore judgment went further than the *Liverpool* case. Referring to Art.40.5 of the Irish Constitution, which provides that "[t]he dwelling of every citizen is inviolable and cannot be forcibly entered save in accordance with law", the judge suggested that "the corollary of that guarantee must be that a person should be entitled to the freedom to come and go from his dwelling provided he keeps to the law". It is arguable that such a "constitutional easement", if it exists, is available only against the State, although Art.40.5 is not expressly so directed.

23–33 In *Sweeney v Duggan*[58] Murphy J. in the Supreme Court noted that Lord Wilberforce in *Liverpool* "preferred to describe the different categories which he identified as no more than shades on a continuous spectrum."

23–34 Although judges still use the language of consensual contract, the particular characters of high-rise buildings, and other special forms of land use, such as shopping malls, are giving rise to modern regimes of property enjoyment in which the general law as enunciated by the courts, rather than the contract between the parties, imposes the terms.

Future Easements
23–35 If V conveys land to P and a covenant in the conveyance gives P the right, on buying additional land from V, to create an easement for the benefit of P's newly-acquired land (future dominant tenement) over V's land (future servient tenement), then:

1. the agreement is binding between V and P under the law of contract, even though the dominant tenement is left unspecified;
2. the contract is capable of creating an interest in land, i.e. an option, enforceable by P against successors in title of V, or by successors in title of P against V or V's successors in title, but only if:
   (a) according to the English Court of Appeal in *London & Blenheim Estates Ltd v Ladbroke Retail Parks Ltd*,[59] the dominant tenement of the possible future easement is ascertained before V sells his or her land to a successor in title. The land in the hands of V's successor in title cannot be subject to an easement as to which the dominant tenement is unascertained: it would be tantamount to allowing an easement in gross[60] and would place undue burdens on land ownership; and

---

[57] *The Irish Times*, 18 August 1998.
[58] [1997] 2 I.L.R.M. 211.
[59] [1993] 4 All E.R. 157.
[60] *Voice v Bell* (1993) 68 P. & C.R. 441.

(b) formerly, the exercise of the option to create the easement had to be limited to the perpetuity period, because the contract created a contingent interest in property.[61]

23–36 The abolition of the perpetuity rule by the LCLRA 2009 has removed this latter test 2(b), but arguably 2(a) must still be satisfied, since it is not concerned with the perpetuity rule as such, but with the nature of an easement.

PROFITS À PRENDRE

23–37 A *profit à prendre* (Law French for "to take") is the right to take something from another's land. The most usual examples are the right to fish[62] or shoot game[63] and remove the caught and killed spoils of such sport. Other examples are the right to dig and extract turf[64] or minerals such as gravel. Unlike easements, certain *profits à prendre* may exist "in gross", i.e. for the benefit of an individual person and not for the benefit of a dominant tenement.[65] The owner may bequeath the profit by will, sell it, or deal with it like any other property right. Many shooting and fishing rights survived the Land Purchase legislation and continue to constitute qualifications on titles in Ireland in some areas.

Right of Turbary

23–38 The right to cut turf for fuel was formerly of great importance in Ireland, as judges have recognised,[66] since people depended upon it to heat their houses and cook their food.

23–39 The right to cut turf may exist in a number of forms, only one of which is strictly a *profit à prendre*, i.e. a right vested in a person, or a number of identified persons, to cut turf on land the title to which is vested in another person. Prima facie the grant of a right of turbary includes the right to cut turf for fuel only, and not to sell it.[67] A right to cut turf for sale must be expressly granted.[68] When vested in more than one person the right is referred to as a *common of turbary*. Such rights have arisen in various ways. When an estate was sold under the Land Purchase Acts to a number of former tenants, there might be bog land on one of the purchaser's plots. The practice of the Irish

---

[61] *Dunn v Blackdown Properties Ltd* [1961] Ch. 433. A possible exception was an option in a lease to create an easement in conjunction with an option to renew the lease, the easement to last for the renewal period.

[62] *Moore v Attorney General* [1934] I.R. 44.

[63] *Radcliffe v Hayes* [1907] 1 I.R. 101.

[64] *Convey v Regan* [1952] I.R. 56; *Re Bohan* [1957] I.R. 49.

[65] *Chesterfield (Lord) v Harris* [1911] A.C. 623.

[66] *Chambers v Betty* (1815) Beatty 488; *Re Scott's Estate* [1916] 1 I.R. 180 at 198.

[67] *Lifford (Lord) v Kearney* (1883) 17 I.L.T.R. 30; *Douglas v McLaughlin* (1883) 17 I.L.T.R. 84.

[68] *Copinger v Gubbins* (1846) 9 Ir. Eq. R. 304; *Stevenson v Moore* (1858) 7 Ir. Eq. R. 462.

Land Commission was in some cases to create commons of turbary vested in the other adjoining purchasers, while in other cases the Irish Land Commission conveyed the bog in trust to be distributed among the purchasers.[69]

23–40 At common law a tenant has the right to cut turf for fuel where the land demised includes bog.[70] Section 29 of Deasy's Act 1860 gave a statutory right to tenants to cut turf on their holdings for fuel.[71]

23–41 A right of turbary comprises the right to use bog turf for fuel and for other reasonable purposes such as to improve the soil,[72] but does not include the right to scrape off "scraws", i.e. surface turf,[73] or to deplete the soil remaining after the turf has been cut away.[74]

Sporting Rights

23–42 Wild game and fish belong to no one so long as they remain at large, but at common law a landowner has the privilege of capturing and killing fish and game on his or her land.[75] This right can be severed from the other rights of ownership and vested in a person other than the owner of the land, in which case it becomes a *profit à prendre*. Since Deasy's Act 1860, sporting rights had always been reserved, on the grant of a lease, to the owner of the realty.[76]

23–43 The vendor's sporting rights[77] could be exempted from the overreaching effect of sale under the Land Purchase Acts by s.16 of the Irish Land Act 1903 (the "1903 Act"). Section 13(2) of the 1903 Act defines sporting rights as including "any right of hunting, shooting, fishing and taking game[78] or fish on any land ... ." The rights could, by agreement, either be conveyed to the purchaser or expressly reserved to the vendor. In the absence of agreement they vested in the Land Commission and this "default" position means that

---

[69] *Hickson v Boylan*, unreported, High Court, Carroll J., 25 February 1993; P. Bland, *Easements*, 3rd edn (Dublin: Round Hall, 2015), para.17–03.

[70] *Howley v Jebb* (1859) 8 Ir. C.L.R. 435; *McGeough v McDermott* (1886) 18 L.R. Ir. 217.

[71] *Dobbyn v Somers* (1860) 13 Ir. C.L.R. 293; *Lifford (Lord) v Kearney* (1883) 17 I.L.T.R. 30; *Bruce v Jackson* [1936] N.I. 192.

[72] *Dawson v Baldwin* (1832) H. & J. 24; *Fitzpatrick v Vershoyle* [1913] 1 I.R. 8; *Hutchinson v Drain* (1899) 33 I.L.T.R. 147.

[73] *Jameson v Fahey* [1907] 1 I.R. 411.

[74] *Hutchinston v Drain* (1899) 33 I.L.T.R. 147; *Walsh v Johnston* (1913) 47 I.L.T.S.J. 231; *Jameson v Fahey* [1907] 1 I.R. 411. It may be otherwise in England.

[75] *Radcliffe v Hayes* [1907] 1 I.R. 101.

[76] Bland, *Easements* (2015), para.19–02.

[77] Subject, under s.13(1) of the 1903 Act, to the Ground Game Act 1880.

[78] "Game" has the same meaning as in s.5 of the Land Law (Ireland) Act 1881 and means "hares, rabbits, pheasants, partridges, quails, landrails, grouse, woodcock, snipe, wild duck, widgeon and teal" (s.5(5)) and s.13(2) of the 1903 Act adds "deer"). Rabbits were not included in earlier legislation: see T. De Moleyns, *The Landowner's and Agent's Practical Guide*, 8th edn (Dublin: E. Ponsonby, 1899), p.177.

many fees simple in rural Ireland remain subject to such rights. Sporting rights were also preserved on the resumption of a holding by the Land Commission.[79]

23–44 Where the title to land is registered, as it would be where a sale took place under the Land Purchase Acts, there is provision for extinguishing sporting rights other than fishing rights where these were reserved to a person who is not the registered owner.[80] Where such rights have not been exercised during a 12-year period after the coming into force of the Land Act 1965 the Property Registration Authority may cancel the entry on the Register on application by any person interested in the land.[81]

Fishing Rights

23–45 The grant of an exclusive right to fish, i.e. including the right to exclude the owner of the riverbed, is called a *several fishery*.[82] The owner of a several fishery may or may not also own the soil of the riverbed,[83] but even if he or she does not, he or she may exclude the owner of the soil from fishing.[84] If the owner grants only the right to fish in common with the owner, or in common with others, it is known as a *common of fishery* or *common of piscary*.

23–46 *Gannon v Walsh*[85] confirmed the existence of a presumption that the grant of a several fishery carried with it the ownership of the riverbed up to its mid-point.[86] Although there are many decisions[87] in favour of the presumption, Coke[88] expressed a contrary opinion, on the basis that it was illogical to presume that what appeared to be the grant of a mere incorporeal hereditament should carry with it ownership of the soil itself.[89]

23–47 The practical enjoyment of fishing rights has been controlled for many years by legislation and bye-laws.

---

[79] The Land Commission was dissolved on 31 March 1999 and its functions transferred to the Department of Agriculture and Food: Land Commission (Dissolution) Act 1992 and S.I. No. 75 of 1999.

[80] Land Act 1965 s.18.

[81] Land Act 1965 s.18(c).

[82] *Foster v Wright* (1878) L.R. 4 C.P.D. 438 at 449 per Lord Coleridge; *Malcomson v O'Dea* (1863) 10 H.L.C. 593. See generally, R. Longfield, *The Fishery Laws of Ireland* (Dublin: Ponsonby, 1863).

[83] *Malcomson v O'Dea* (1863) 10 H.L.C. 593.

[84] Co Litt 122a. The holder of the right of fishing may give the owner of the soil permission to participate in the fishing, but such owner's facility so to participate is dependent entirely upon the permission given which may be withdrawn: *Agnew v Barry* [2009] IESC 45.

[85] [1998] 3 I.R. 245. See *Inland Fisheries Ireland v O'Baoill* [2012] IEHC 550.

[86] Applied in *Agnew v Barry* [2009] IESC 45. See A. Power, *Intangible Property Rights in Ireland*, 2nd edn (Haywards Heath: Tottel, 2009), p.257.

[87] See Bland, *Easements* (2015), para.19–10.

[88] Co Litt 4b.

[89] See also *Hindson v Ashby* [1896] 2 Ch. 1.

ANALOGOUS RIGHTS

Natural Rights
Common Law Right of Support

23–48 A landowner enjoys, as part of the rights of ownership, a natural right of support for his or her land from adjoining land. The common law right affects land only in its natural state, so that if an adjoining landowner causes the soil on the neighbouring land to subside, the neighbour has a cause of action.[90] But there is no natural right to the support of buildings from adjoining buildings or soil. Such a right can exist only as an easement.[91]

23–49 The common law rule developed in a predominantly agrarian society and the rule confining liability to subsidence caused by land in its natural state may have worked satisfactorily in such a context. However, it is less satisfactory in urban settings where it may not be clear whether the building on the subsided land was partly responsible for the subsidence or whether the land subsidence would have happened anyway.[92] Moreover there is a legal issue as to damages. Even if it could be proved that the affected land would have subsided regardless of the building on it, are damages to be confined to damage to the land, or do they extend to damage to buildings on the affected land? Easements of support may be acquired at common law[93] as to "ancient" buildings and by statutory prescription. It has been held that an easement of support may be breached not only by subsidence on the servient land but also by piling stones on it which causes cracks to appear in buildings on the dominant land.[94]

23–50 The traditional principle, anchored in *Dalton v Angus*,[95] that an easement of support for a building on land cannot be established other than by grant or prescription, was departed from by the Singapore Court of Appeal in *Xpress Print Pte Ltd v Monocrafts Pte Ltd.*[96] In a case where damage had been done, both to the access road to a high-rise building and the pipes that serviced it, by land subsidence which resulted from construction works carried out on adjoining land, the court held that the proper approach was to regard a right of support for buildings on land from neighbouring land as arising once the buildings were erected. The right in effect was a right to ongoing support from the soil of the adjoining land, which translated into an obligation on the part of the owner of that land to ensure that in carrying out construction or excavation

---

[90] *Atkinson v King* (1878) 2 L.R. Ir. 320; *Backhouse v Bonomi* (1861) 9 H.L.C. 503.

[91] *State (McGuinness) v Maguire* [1967] I.R. 348; *Latimer v Official Co-operative Society* (1885) 16 L.R. Ir. 305; *Treacy v Dublin Corporation* [1992] I.L.R.M. 650 (sanitary authority's statutory duty to demolish dangerous structures includes duty to support and protect adjoining buildings from weather).

[92] C. Berger, *Land Ownership and Use*, 3rd edn (Boston: Little, Brown, 1983), p.585.

[93] *Latimer v Official Co-operative Society* (1885) 16 L.R. Ir. 305.

[94] *Green v Belfast Tramway Co* (1887) 20 L.R. Ir. 35.

[95] (1881) 6 App. Cas. 740.

[96] [2000] 3 S.L.R. 545.

works on his or her land sufficient alternative support was provided. The Singapore court further held that an action arising from withdrawal of support was equivalent to a claim in nuisance and that the appropriate level of damages was all foreseeable loss caused by the wrongful act of withdrawing and not replacing the support. There is no suggestion that such a significant departure from established principle is likely to take place in Ireland, although developments in relation to the "neighbour principle" in tort suggest that a cause of action may not simply be defeated by the blanket defence that an easement of support had not been granted or had not yet accrued.

Water Rights

23–51 Owners of land have as one of the common law rights of ownership certain rights over water flowing in a defined channel[97] through the land. More extensive rights may, however, be acquired as easements.[98]

Negligence

23–52 If an easement is not found to exist, a party may have to rely upon the tort of negligence to seek redress for injury caused. An example is where an easement of support cannot be established.[99] The injured party may establish a duty of care to support the building, a breach of the duty and resultant damage.[100]

23–53 In *Kempston v Butler*[101] a jury found that there was a custom in Dublin in the building trade that if a builder demolished a house he was under a duty of care to support adjoining houses, but the Court of Common Pleas held such a custom to be unreasonable and void. The custom may have developed because of the many Georgian terraces in Dublin consisting of tall houses supported on both sides by adjoining houses.[102] Today, such a duty would seem to be both reasonable and desirable. A suggestion that it might exist appears from *Daly*

---

[97] *Thompson v Horner* [1927] N.I. 191.

[98] *Pullan v Roughfort Bleaching and Dyeing Co Ltd* (1888) 21 L.R. Ir. 73; *Hanna v Pollock* [1900] 2 I.R. 664.

[99] In *Munnelly v Calcon Ltd* [1978] I.R. 387, damages in negligence were awarded for the removal of a support even though an easement of support had not been established.

[100] In *Bond v Nottingham Corporation* [1940] Ch. 429, Lord Greene M.R. held that where two houses support each other and one has fallen into disrepair, the owner of that house cannot undertake repairs in such a way as to remove support from the other house without replacing it with equivalent support.

[101] (1862) 12 Ir. C.L.R. 516.

[102] *Bradburn v Lindsay* [1983] 2 All E.R. 408. The defendant allowed her semi-detached house to become derelict and accumulate dry rot. It was vandalised. The local authority demolished it by order. A conveyance of the adjoining house described the party wall as repairable by each owner in equal shares. The adjoining house was damaged. The defendant was held liable. There was a duty of care. The defendant should have foreseen the danger of dry rot and lack of support. See also, *Holbeck Hall Hotel Ltd v Scarborough Borough Council* [2000] Q.B. 836; *Rees v Skerrett* [2001] 1 W.L.R. 1541.

v McMullan.[103] Property damage had been caused by soil slippage, and the Circuit Court held that there was a qualified duty on the owner of land to take reasonable steps to prevent damage to his or her neighbour's land which arises from either natural hazards or those caused by human agency and which was reasonably foreseeable.

Party Walls

23–54 At common law there are four categories of party walls[104]:

(a) a wall of which two adjoining owners are tenants in common;
(b) a wall divided down its length into two, the half on one side belonging to the owner of the land on that side, and the half on the other to the owner of the land on that side[105];
(c) a wall belonging entirely to the owner of land on one side, but subject to an easement of support in favour of the owner of the land on the other side;
(d) a wall divided down its length into two, the half on one side belonging to the owner of the land on that side, and the half on the other to the owner of the land on that side, but subject in each case to an easement of support in favour of one owner affecting the other.

23–55 The most usual forms are (a) and (d). There is a presumption at common law in favour of (a), i.e. co-ownership, which may be rebutted by evidence, for example, that the boundary line runs down the middle of the wall, which results in situation (b), or that the wall belongs to one owner alone.[106]

23–56 Chapter 3 of Pt 8 of the LCLRA 2009, while it does not address the issue of ownership of party walls, provides a new statutory power for the owner of property (described as a "building owner") to carry out works on a party structure between that owner's property and an adjoining or adjacent property. Section 43 defines "party structure" as any

"arch, ceiling, ditch, fence, floor, hedge, partition, shrub, tree, wall or other structure which horizontally, vertically or in any other way—

(a) divides adjoining and separately owned buildings, or
(b) is situated at or on or so close to the boundary line between adjoining and separately owned buildings or between such buildings and unbuilt-on lands that it is impossible or not reasonably practical to carry out works to the structure without access to the adjoining building or unbuilt-on land,

---

[103] [1997] 2 I.L.R.M. 232, following *Leakey v National Trust* [1980] 1 All E.R. 17.
[104] *Bond v Nottingham Corporation* [1940] Ch. 429.
[105] *Hutchinson v Mains* (1832) Alc. & Nap. 155; *Ingram v Mooney* (1870) I.R. 5 C.L. 357.
[106] *Hutchinson v Mains* (1832) Alc. & Nap. 155. See *Jones v Read* (1876) I.R. 10 C.L. 315.

and includes any structure which is—

(i) situated entirely in or on one of the adjoining buildings or unbuilt-on lands, or

(ii) straddles the boundary line between adjoining buildings or between such buildings and unbuilt-on lands and is either co-owned by their respective owners or subject to some division of ownership between them."

23–57 A wide range of works is permitted to be carried out, which includes alterations, decorations, demolitions, improvements, and work on ditches, drains, verdure, pipes, sewers and cables. These are to be carried out for one or more specified purposes, including compliance with a statutory requirement, undertaking an exempted development or a development for which planning permission has been required, preservation of the party structure or of any building or land of which it is part, and also work which will not cause damage or inconvenience to the adjoining owner, or if so causing damage or inconvenience, is yet reasonably necessary to be carried out.[107]

23–58 The building owner is required to make good all damage caused to the adjoining owner by the carrying out of the works, or else reimburse that person appropriately. The building owner must also pay the adjoining owner "the reasonable costs of obtaining professional advice with regard to the likely consequences of the works" together with reasonable compensation for inconvenience caused. However, the building owner is entitled to seek from the adjoining owner, or to deduct from any reimbursement of expenses or compensation payable, a sum that takes into account the proportionate use and enjoyment that the adjoining owner makes from the party structure or can reasonably be assumed to be likely to make.[108]

23–59 Where a dispute arises in relation to the intended works, the building owner may apply to the District Court for a "works order". In deciding whether to grant a works order, and, if so the conditions that should be attached to it, the court will consider the statutorily permitted grounds for undertaking the works "and may take into account any other circumstances which it considers relevant".[109] The works order will specify the conditions under which the works are to be undertaken, including conditions as to indemnification against damage, but it "shall not authorise any permanent interference with, or loss of, any easement of light or other easement or other right relating to a party structure".[110] The court may modify or discharge a works order, on such terms as it thinks appropriate, following application by any part affected by it.[111]

---

[107] LCLRA 2009 s.44(1).
[108] LCLRA 2009 s.44(2) and (3).
[109] LCLRA 2009 s.45.
[110] LCLRA 2009 s.46.
[111] LCLRA 2009 s.47.

Public Rights
Navigation
23–60 The public has the right at common law to navigation in the tidal part of a river.[112] In the non-tidal part of rivers the public only has the right to navigation if it has been dedicated as a public right and accepted as such right by the public (long use creating a presumption to that effect) or if it has been conferred by statute.[113]

Fisheries
23–61 The right to fish in the sea, i.e. territorial waters, and in tidal rivers belonging at common law to the Crown, is now vested in the State.[114] This means that the public has the right to fish in these waters unless the State by legislation has vested them in some other body.[115] The public's right may be curtailed by the grant of aquaculture licences.[116]

23–62 The medieval common law recognised that the Crown could grant the right to fish in river estuaries and tidal waters to individuals or groups. However the Crown lost this right by Magna Carta 1215,[117] which is construed as having prohibited such grants after the date of the charter. Such privately-granted fisheries as can be proved to have been granted before Magna Carta (or "put in defence by the Crown", to use the technical expression) still exist today.[118]

23–63 The public has no right to fish in non-tidal rivers or lakes.[119] The Crown did not at common law have a right to the soil or a right to fish in the large non-tidal lakes of Ireland, which right prima facie is vested in the riparian owners, subject to any fishing rights granted as *profits à prendre*.[120] As to non-tidal rivers, the right to fish is vested in the owner of the river bed. The presumption is that the owner of the adjoining land owns the bed of the river *usque ad*

---

[112] *Attorney General v Tomline* (1880) 14 Ch. D. 58; *Evans v Godber* [1974] 1 W.L.R. 137. For the purposes of the law of public rights, navigation includes swimming.

[113] *Orr-Ewing v Colquhoun* (1877) L.R. 2 App. Cas. 839.

[114] *R. (Moore) v O'Hanrahan* [1927] I.R. 406; *Whelan v Cork Corporation* [1991] I.L.R.M. 19; *Foyle and Bann Fisheries Ltd v Attorney General* (1949) 83 I.L.T.R. 29.

[115] *The Case of the Royal Fishery of the Banne* (1610) Davies 149.

[116] Fisheries (Amendment) Act 1997; Fisheries and Foreshore (Amendment) Act 1998. Previous legislation was the subject of scrutiny in *Madden v Minister for the Marine* [1997] 1 I.L.R.M. 136.

[117] Cap 16. *The Case of the Royal Fishery of the Banne* (1610) Davies 149 denies this point but is erroneous: *Moore v Attorney General* [1934] I.R. 44.

[118] *Little v Cooper* [1937] I.R. 1 (several pre-Magna Carta fishery in River Moy, Co. Mayo: discusses history of the *Magna Carta Hiberniae*); *Moore v Attorney General* [1934] I.R. 44 (several pre-Magna Carta fishery, River Erne, Co. Donegal).

[119] *Murphy v Ryan* (1868) I.R. 2 C.L. 143; *Bloomfield v Johnson* (1868) I.R. 8 C.L. 68; *Bristow v Cormican* (1878) 3 A.C. 641 at 651; *Johnston v O'Neill* [1911] A.C. 552; *Toome Eel Fishery (Northern Ireland) Ltd v Cardwell* [1966] N.I. 1.

[120] *Bristow v Cormican* (1878) 3 A.C. 641 per Lord Cairns L.C. Lord Blackburn doubted whether the ownership of a small frontage on a lake would carry with it a strip of the soil of the lake out to the mid-point.

medium filum aquæ, i.e. up to the mid-point of the river.[121] The owner may grant the right to fish to another person, in which case this right becomes separated from the other rights of ownership and exists as a *profit à prendre.* Where this occurs, any power to fish enjoyed by the owner of the land adjoining the river will be based upon permission from the holder of the *profit à prendre* rather than upon the landowner's ownership of the soil.[122]

Public Rights of Way

23–64 A public right of way may be acquired by statute or by dedication to and acceptance by the public.[123] As stated by the Supreme Court in *Walsh and Cassidy v Sligo County Council*:

"A public right of way can arise in a number of ways: it may be shown to arise from use from time immemorial or may be created by statute. Finally, a public right of way may be established by proof of long user by the public as of right, leading to express or implied dedication by the owner of the ground over which it passes and acceptance of such dedication by the public."[124]

23–65 If a public right of way is of ancient origin it may be presumed to have been so dedicated in the distant past.[125] There is no legal presumption of dedication; it is a question of fact[126] and may be inferred from the circumstances. In making such inference, courts will consider "the duration, extent, nature and context of public user, and the possibility of inferring or presuming that the landowner has dedicated the way to the public."[127] Mere proof of public user does not of itself create the right, although "user may provide compelling evidence of dedication to the public, or may more properly be ascribed to tolerance or liberality of the landowner."[128]

23–66 A public right of way is treated by the common law as a highway,[129] and "confers the unrestricted right of the general public to pass and repass at all times of the day or night, and at all seasons without notice to, or permission

---

[121] *Welsh National Water Development Authority v Burgess* (1974) 28 P. & C.R. 378 at 383; *Gannon v Walsh* [1998] 3 I.R. 245.

[122] *Agnew v Barry* [2009] IESC 45. Keane J. in *Gannon v Walsh* [1998] 3 I.R. 245 regarded the presumption that the holder of the fishing rights has ownership of the soil of the river bed up to its meridian point as displacing the like presumption in relation to the ownership of land adjacent to a river.

[123] *Neill v Byrne* (1878) 2 L.R. Ir. 287; *Smeltzer v Fingal County Council* [1998] 1 I.R. 279; *Fortin v Delahunty* [1999] IEHC 82; *Walsh and Cassidy v Sligo County Council* [2014] 2 I.L.R.M. 161.

[124] *Walsh and Cassidy v Sligo County Council* [2014] 2 I.L.R.M. 161 at para.52.

[125] *Carroll v Sheridan* [1984] I.L.R.M. 451.

[126] *Walsh and Cassidy v Sligo County Council* [2014] 2 I.L.R.M. 161 at para.73.

[127] *Walsh and Cassidy v Sligo County Council* [2014] 2 I.L.R.M. 161 at paras 6–7.

[128] *Walsh and Cassidy v Sligo County Council* [2014] 2 I.L.R.M. 161 at para.6.

[129] *Walsh and Cassidy v Sligo County Council* [2014] 2 I.L.R.M. 161 at para.52.

from, the landowner over whose land the way runs."[130] Planning authorities have power to create and extinguish public rights of way.[131]

23–67 A private right of way is a right to pass from one "terminus", i.e. entry or exit point, to another, although where land is under tillage or for other reasons the servient owner may direct a variation of the course from time to time.[132] In general a public right of way is a right in the public to pass from one public place to another public place, but may not be restricted to such a case.[133]

23–68 In *The Giant's Causeway Case*[134] a landowner granted a lease of the Giant's Causeway to a company set up to exploit it commercially. The company put a fence around the area and charged for admission. One issue was whether it was necessary for a public right of way to have a terminus at either end. It was accepted in argument that a cul de sac could be the subject of a public right in towns,[135] but the court did not expressly decide that such could not be the case in the country, and held that any right over the causeway had failed through lack of evidence of dedication to the public. However, in *Collen v Petters*,[136] O'Leary J. accepted as good law that there was no need for a *terminus ad quem* (or point of exit) when the claim was based on dedication to the public use and the destination is a place of natural beauty.

23–69 That a right to walk about or "promenade" could exist as a public right was doubted in *Abercromby v Town Commissioners of Fermoy*.[137] In that case a stretch of land called "The Barnane Walk" was held to be subject to the right of the inhabitants of Fermoy to walk about for recreation, as had long been customary practice. Such a right could be acquired by custom or possibly dedication, but the court seems to have based its decision on a local customary right because it doubted that such a right could exist as a species of public right.[138]

---

[130] *Walsh and Cassidy v Sligo County Council* [2014] 2 I.L.R.M. 161 at para.3.
[131] Local Government (Planning and Development) Act 1963 ss.48 (creation) and 76 (extinguishment). Where an authority intends to extinguish a public right of way it must advertise its intention by notice in a newspaper and hear objections: Roads Act 1993 s.73.
[132] *Donnelly v Adams* [1905] I.R. 154; *Flanagan v Mulhall* [1985] I.L.R.M. 134.
[133] (1905) 5 N.I.J.R. 301.
[134] (1905) 5 N.I.J.R. 301. N. Dawson, "The *Giant's Causeway Case*: Property Law in Northern Ireland 1845–1995" in N. Dawson, D. Greer and P. Ingram (eds), *One Hundred and Fifty Years of Irish Law* (Dublin: Round Hall Sweet & Maxwell, 1996). The Giant's Causeway is now owned by the National Trust.
[135] As demonstrated in *Connell v Porter*, Supreme Court, 8 December 1972, reported at [2005] 3 I.R. 601.
[136] [2007] 1 I.R. 790. See also *Moser v Ambleside Urban District Council* (1925) 89 J.P. 118.
[137] [1900] 1 I.R. 302.
[138] It is now generally accepted that there cannot be a public right to wander and that for a public right of way to exist, it must be exercised along a specific route between definite ascertainable points: *Smeltzer v Fingal County Council* [1998] 1 I.R. 279; *Murphy v Wicklow County Council*, unreported, High Court, Kearns J., 19 March 1999.

23–70 Both these cases may have been affected by the decision in *Re Ellen-borough Park*[139] which held that a *jus spatiandi*, the right to walk about for recreation, can exist as a private right, which had previously been thought not to be the case.[140] However, more recently, Costello J. stated *obiter* in *Smeltzer v Fingal County Council*[141] that a *jus spatiandi* could not exist as a public right.

23–71 Any determination of whether a public right of way exists necessitates a balancing of public and private interests. These are,

> "on the one hand, the rights of the public to continue to use without obstruction a way or road over which there are established public rights and, on the other, those of the owner of the land, over which the public wish to pass, to the uninterrupted enjoyment of his or her property."[142]

Local Custom

23–72 Local customary rights are recognised at common law if they satisfy the tests of being ancient, certain, reasonable and continuous.[143]

23–73 "Ancient" means, at common law, proven to exist since "time immemorial", i.e. since 1189, but, as in the case of the acquisition of easements by prescription at common law, user for not less than 20 years[144] will give rise to a presumption of user since 1189, which can be rebutted by showing a modern origin. They will also be void if contrary to statute.[145] Nor can there be a customary right to take anything off the land, on the basis that the uncontrolled enjoyment of this right would lead eventually to total depletion of the commodity.[146]

23–74 Local customary rights must be local in the sense of being vested in the local community or sections of it, unlike public rights which are vested in the public in general.[147] As against that, local customary rights are capable of permitting a wider range of modes of enjoyment than public rights which are confined to rights of way, navigation and fishing.

---

[139] [1956] Ch. 131.

[140] The English Court of Appeal in *Re Ellenborough Park* overruled Farwell J. in *Attorney General v Antrobus* [1905] 2 Ch. 188 and *International Tea Stores Ltd v Hobbs* [1903] 2 Ch. 165.

[141] [1998] 1 I.R. 279.

[142] *Walsh and Cassidy v Sligo County Council* [2014] 2 I.L.R.M. 161 at para.54.

[143] *Daly v Cullen* (1958) 92 I.L.T.R. 127.

[144] *Daly v Cullen* (1958) 92 I.L.T.R. 127, applying *Bright v Walker* (1834) 1 Cr. M. & R. 211 at 217; *DPP (Long) v McDonald* [1983] I.L.R.M. 223.

[145] *Merttens v Hill* [1901] 1 Ch. 842.

[146] *Mullen v Irish Fish Meal Co*, unreported, High Court, Kenny J., 9 November 1970; *Adair v National Trust* [1998] N.I. 33.

[147] *Abercromby v Town Commissioners of Fermoy* [1900] 1 I.R. 302.

METHODS OF ACQUISITION OF EASEMENTS AND PROFITS

Express Grant

23–75 An express grant occurs if V sells land to P and V grants an easement to P over land which V retains. Such a grant in the case of a freehold estate must be by deed.[148] Prior to the coming into effect, on 1 December 2009, of the LCLRA 2009, words of limitation were necessary for an *inter vivos* transaction: the grantor needed to use the words "and his/her heirs" or "in fee simple" to grant the easement in fee simple.[149] Now, s.67(1) of the LCLRA 2009 provides:

> "A conveyance of unregistered land with or without words of limitation, or any equivalent expression, passes the fee simple or the other entire estate or interest which the grantor had power to create or convey, unless a contrary intention appears in the conveyance."

23–76 If the easement is to be for a leasehold estate within Deasy's Act 1860 it must comply with the Act, i.e. it must be at a rent (s.3), in writing and signed by the grantor or his or her agent authorised in writing, unless it is from year to year or a lesser period, in which case it may be made orally (s.4). One should remember that these formalities only apply in practice to easements expressly granted because where an easement is claimed on other grounds, such as prescription or estoppel, it will be presumed that the formalities were complied with, or the other party will be estopped from denying compliance with them, or may be bound to execute a valid grant.

23–77 If a purported grant of a leasehold easement fails to comply with Deasy's Act 1860 but is supported by a memorandum under the Statute of Frauds (Ireland) 1695 or is partly performed, then it may be an easement in equity.

Express Reservation

23–78 The common law distinguished between exceptions and reservations in grants.[150] A grantor could *except* a physical part of the land, such as mines, minerals, stones or quarries ("things *in esse*") or a pre-existing right over it, and this is commonly done.[151] The common law used the word "reservation" to refer to a right which had not previously existed and which was intended to come into existence on the making of the grant. The general rule was that a grantor could not make a reservation in his or her own favour. Thus, if

---

[148] LCLRA 2009 s.62(1).

[149] An easement, being an incorporeal hereditament, is included in the definition of "land" in s.3 of the Registration of Title Act 1964 and so can pass by way of transfer which does not use words of limitation.

[150] Co Litt 47a.

[151] *McDonnell v Kenneth* (1850) 1 Ir. C.L.R. 113; *Quinn v Shields* (1877) I.R. 11 C.L. 254.

V granted part of Gortbane to P, V could not reserve an easement over the part conveyed in favour of the part he retained. The common law saw a logical objection: such a right could only come into existence[152] once P had acquired the interest in the land, which would be *after* the grant had taken effect. The common law did, however, allow a category of new rights to be reserved, namely those that "issued" out of the land granted, so that, for example, on a grant of Gortbane by V to P, V could reserve a rentcharge in his own favour charged on Gortbane.[153] This was probably because the feudal common law regarded rent as almost a physical attribute of land and therefore more in the nature of an exception.[154]

Before the LCLRA 2009

23–79 In the case of deeds executed prior to the coming into effect of the LCLRA 2009 on 1 December 2009, there were two ways to avoid the general rule against reservations. First, if the conveyance was executed by the purchaser of the land as well as the grantor the conveyance had a dual operation: it operated as a conveyance by V of the estate in the land to P, and as a grant by P of the easement to V.

23–80 A second method was for the vendor to convey the land to a feoffee to uses to the use that the purchaser should have the land subject to the use and that the vendor should have the easement. The Statute of Uses 1634 then executed the use vesting a legal estate in the land in the purchaser and the legal estate in the easement in the vendor. There was a doubt about the effectiveness of this device before 1881, since the objection could be made that the Statute only operated where a person was seised to the use of another and it was doubted if the feoffee could be said to be "seised" of the easement before the conveyance was executed. To remove this doubt, s.62(1) of the Conveyancing Act 1881 (the "1881 Act") provided that a conveyance of freehold to the use that a person should have an easement shall operate to vest the easement in that person.

LCLRA 2009

23–81 In the case of a reservation made after 1 December 2009, the necessity for either the deed to be executed by the grantee or the creation of a use is removed by s.69 of the LCLRA 2009. This provides that the reservation of a legal estate or interest in a conveyance serves to vest that estate or interest in the grantor or any other person for whose benefit it has been made, and will also annex it to the relevant land, without the need for execution of the conveyance by the grantee or execution of a deed of regrant. A reservation is

---

[152] While the land was still vested in V it could only exist as a quasi-easement: *O'Donnell v Ryan* (1854) 4 Ir. C.L.R. 44 at 59–60.

[153] Co Litt 143a.

[154] The income of the land, which is the source of the rent, is a thing in existence at the time of the grant.

also deemed to arise where the estate or interest to which the conveyance is expressed to be subject is itself created by the conveyance.

Construction

23–82 Where a question arises as to the meaning or scope of a grant or reservation, the relevant principle of construction is that a grant is generally construed against the grantor, on the basis that a grantor may not derogate from his or her grant. This has been described as "a principle which merely embodies in a legal maxim a rule of common honesty".[155] Where a reservation of an easement is made in the form of a re-grant by one of the methods described above, the courts have traditionally construed the re-grant of the easement against P, the purchaser of the land, on the basis that P is the grantor of the easement.[156] Nevertheless, this has been criticised.[157] The argument looks like sophistry rather than principle, since the whole deed is usually drafted by the vendor of the land.[158] Recognition of this reality is reflected in s.69(3) of the LCLRA 2009 which provides that, for the purpose of construing the effect of a conveyance of land, "a reservation shall not be treated as taking effect as a regrant". The principal purpose of this provision appears to be to ensure that, in the case of any ambiguity, the deed will be construed against the grantor (and also its likely drafter) in terms both of the land that is granted and any easement or other right that is reserved.

Implied Grant

23–83 Easements may arise by implied grant as part of an express grant of land, for a grant is construed in favour of the grantee and against the grantor. This follows from the principle that a grantor may not derogate from his or her grant and will arise in circumstances where on a grant of land a particular easement can be construed as intended as being part of the grant.[159] Not only may the original grantor not derogate, but those claiming through him or her are similarly barred and so the principle can give rise to a property interest.[160] Barrett J. in *The Square v Dunnes Stores* noted that "what one is looking for

---

[155] *Harmer v Jumbil (Nigeria) Tin Areas Ltd* [1921] 1 Ch. 200 at 225.

[156] *Neill v Duke of Devonshire* (1882) 8 A.C. 135 at 149; *Dwyer Nolan Developments Ltd v King-scroft Developments Ltd* [1999] 1 I.L.R.M. 141.

[157] Bland, *Easements* (2015), para.4–06; Land Law Working Group (NI), *Final Report* (London: HMSO, 1990) (recommended reversal of the rule).

[158] In *Doolan v Murray and Dun Laoghaire Corporation*, unreported, High Court, Keane J., 21 December 1993, the judge quoted J.C.W. Wylie, *Irish Land Law*, 2nd edn (Dublin: Butterworths, 1986), para.6.058: "a grant of an easement will be construed against the grantor, whereas a reservation, being treated as a re-grant by the grantee, will be construed against him in favour of the grantor", but then the judge went on to construe the re-grant against the vendor of the land.

[159] *Swanton v Gould* (1860) 9 Ir. C.L.R. 234; *Donegall v Templemore* (1860) 9 Ir. C.L.R. 374; *Lalor v Lalor* (1879) 4 L.R. Ir. 350, [1879] Q.B. 678 (appeal); *Ewart v Belfast Poor Law Guardians* (1880) 5 L.R. Ir. 536; A. Lyall, "Non-Derogation from a Grant" (1988) 6 I.L.T. 143; D.W. Elliott, "Non-Derogation from a Grant" (1964) 80 L.Q.R. 244.

[160] *Ewart v Belfast Poor Law Guardians* (1880) 5 L.R. Ir. 536.

when testing for derogation from grant is actual or likely deprivation of a grantee's reasonable enjoyment of existing rights as a grantee."[161]

23–84 In *Connell v O'Malley*[162] the defendant had a site near a river for sale with outline planning permission. Access was by a road, part of which ran over the defendant's land. The defendant entered into an agreement to sell the land to the plaintiff. The defendant then refused to go through with the sale. After protracted litigation resulted in the defendant being ordered to execute a conveyance, he erected two gates across the road and a cattle grid. Barron J. held that he was not entitled to do so as it would be a derogation from the grant. Both parties knew that the sold land was intended to be developed into dwelling houses and in order for these to be saleable it was necessary for the local authority to take over the maintenance of the access road. This would not occur if the access road were subject to obstructions by the owner of the land over which it passed, which would effectively set at naught the known purpose for which the purchaser acquired the land. Barron J. continued:

"Since [the doctrine] depends upon the presumed intention of the parties it cannot apply to a situation which could not have been anticipated. While the grantor must have knowledge of the particular purpose for which the property is acquired before any obligation arises, nevertheless he cannot have imputed to him more than ordinary knowledge of what such purpose was."

23–85 If the grantor anticipated or ought to have anticipated that the land would be rendered unfit or materially less fit for the purpose for which it was acquired, then conduct on his or her part which would have that effect would constitute a derogation.[163] However, if knowledge of a particular purpose for which the purchaser intends to put the land, or of necessary physical conditions attaching to that particular purpose, cannot reasonably be imputed to the vendor, the doctrine of non-derogation from grant will not apply, nor will an implied easement be deemed to arise.[164] The principle of non-derogation from grant was approved by Keane C.J. in *William Bennett Construction Ltd v Greene*,[165] but found not to arise on the facts. In addition, the Chief Justice held that the principle applied only in cases where at the time of the grant there was a defined right of way over the land retained by the grantor in favour of the land granted and its obstruction by the grantor rendered that land significantly less

---

[161] *The Square Management Ltd, National Asset Property Management Ltd and Indego v Dunnes Stores Dublin Co* [2017] IEHC 146 at para.71. See also *Dunnes Stores (Bangor) Ltd v New River Trustee Ltd* [2015] NI Ch 7.

[162] Unreported, High Court, Barron J., 28 July 1983; A. Lyall, "Non-Derogation from a Grant" (1988) 6 I.L.T. 143.

[163] In the case itself the issue was between the two parties to the agreement. The judge did not expressly decide that an easement had been granted, but that would seem to be the unavoidable inference from his decision.

[164] *Robinson v Kilvert* (1889) 41 Ch. D. 88.

[165] [2004] 2 I.L.R.M. 96.

capable of development.[166] Section 40 of the LCLRA 2009, which abolishes
the rule known as the rule in *Wheeldon v Burrows*, provides in subs.(3)(b) that
this does not affect the operation of the doctrine of non-derogation from grant.

23–86 Easements arose in the past under various doctrines which are now
regarded for the most part as examples of implied grant. It is now questionable
whether the following categories, or the first two at any rate, are any longer
distinct.

Easements of Necessity

23–87 If a grant is made of a plot of land and as a result the plot would become
land-locked, a court will find that a right of way is created in favour of the
grantee as an easement of necessity. Although the principle generally concerns
rights of way it does not appear to be limited to such rights.[167] The grantee
must choose a convenient route and must not thereafter vary it.[168] Easements
of necessity also arise where V sells part of his land to P and it is found that
V's plot has become landlocked.

23–88 The English High Court held in *Nickerson v Baraclough*[169] that the
doctrinal basis of easements of necessity was not the implied intention of the
parties but a public policy in favour of the development of land, or against land
being rendered unusable. The Court of Appeal rejected this view and asserted
that the doctrine of easements of necessity was founded purely on the implied
intention of the parties. It would follow from the latter position that such a
right could be excluded by express agreement and that such an easement could
only arise on a voluntary grant of land and not, for example, on escheat[170] or
adverse possession.[171]

23–89 Irish authorities even before *Nickerson* favoured the view that the
doctrine is based on the intention of the parties. O'Connor L.J. in *Maguire v
Browne*[172] said:

"[A] right of way of necessity rests on the supposed intention of the parties; that the law presumes that a man owning a parcel of land, and granting
away all the land surrounding it, would not be so foolish as to leave himself

---

[166] [2004] 2 I.L.R.M. 96 at 102. For application of the principle of non-derogation from grant in
the context of landlord and tenant, see *Conneran v Corbett and Sons Ltd* [2004] IEHC 389,
approved by Barrett J. in *The Square Management Ltd, National Asset Property Management
Ltd and Indego v Dunnes Stores Dublin Co* [2017] IEHC 146, and *Camiveo Ltd v Dunnes
Stores* [2017] IEHC 147.
[167] See *Wong v Beaumont Property Trust* [1965] 1 Q.B. 173.
[168] *Donnelly v Adams* [1905] 1 I.R. 154.
[169] [1981] 2 All E.R. 269.
[170] *Procter v Hodgson* (1855) 10 Exch. 824.
[171] *Wilkes v Greenway* (1890) 6 T.L.R. 449.
[172] [1922] 1 I.R. 23.

entirely land-locked...; that, accordingly, it was taken that in such a case the parties would have understood or agreed that the owner of the otherwise land-locked land was to have a right of way... ."[173]

23–90 *Dwyer Nolan Developments Ltd v Kingscroft Developments Ltd*[174] reaffirmed that the basis of the doctrine is the intention of the parties.[175] In holding that the vendor in that case was entitled to a way of necessity, Kinlen J. held that the court should take into account what each of the parties knew, all of the contractual terms concerning the conditions affecting the development, and the area itself. The relevant factors in the case were that both vendor and purchaser were developers and knew that the land was intended for development.

23–91 In *Wong v Beaumont Property Trust*[176] three cellars in a house were let by B's predecessors in title to W's predecessors in title as a Chinese restaurant. Statutory regulations provided that no premises could be used as a restaurant unless it had a ventilation system. This could only be installed by fixing a duct to the outside wall of B's retained upper floors of the building. The English Court of Appeal held that W was entitled to an easement to affix and maintain a duct on the wall. The court classified this as an easement of necessity, although it was not a physical, but a legal, necessity.

23–92 Can the extent of an easement of necessity be greater than the actual user of the servient tenement at the time of the grant? If V sells part of his land to P, and P's plot would become landlocked, can P claim not only the use of a footpath over V's retained land, but a right to use it for vehicles also? On principle it should be possible to imply such an extended user, depending upon the purpose of the grant and the understanding of the parties, for the basis of the doctrine is implied *grant*, and therefore the question is what was intended to be granted, not what use the vendor made of the land before the grant. Although it is possible to infer some support for this view from Powell J.'s decision at first instance in the Irish case of *Maguire v Brown*,[177] the Court of Appeal in that case held that the prior usage of the relevant land must determine the nature of an easement alleged to arise out of necessity.[178] This more narrow construction was not followed in *Dwyer Nolan Developments Ltd v Kingscroft Developments Ltd*[179] which instead looked to the common intention reasonably to be

---

[173] [1922] 1 I.R. 23 at 169.

[174] [1999] 1 I.L.R.M. 141.

[175] The judge cited *London Corporation v Riggs* (1880) 13 Ch. D. 798 and *Browne v Maguire* [1922] 1 I.R. 23.

[176] [1965] 1 Q.B. 173.

[177] [1921] 1 I.R. 148, the differing interpretations being based upon differing assessments as to the facts of the case in relation to how the principle enunciated by Jessel M.R. in *London Corporation v Riggs* (1880) 13 Ch. D. 798 bore upon them. See Power, *Intangible Property Rights in Ireland* (2009), pp.55–59.

[178] *Maguire v Browne* [1921] 1 I.R. 148.

[179] [1999] 1 I.L.R.M. 141.

imputed to the parties and their mutual awareness of the purpose to which the land was to be put.

Common Intention

23–93 Easements have also been held to arise even where they are not strictly necessary in the sense that the land could be used without them. In such cases the basis is usually said to be that they give effect to a presumed or implied common intention of the parties.[180]

23–94 In *Latimer v Official Co-operative Society*[181] a conveyance selling one of two semi-detached houses was held to imply an easement of support in favour of the house sold, even though the house could be used without the easement so long as the other house stood. As suggested above, there is now probably little practical difference between an easement of necessity and an easement arising from the common intention of the parties. Kinlen J.'s decision in *Dwyer Nolan Developments Ltd v Kingscroft Developments Ltd*,[182] though presented as based upon necessity, is equally consistent with a common intention reasonably attributable to a pair of building companies which were grantor and grantee in the case. Further evidence of conflation of the two principles can be seen in s.40(3)(a) of the LCLRA 2009 which provides that that section, abolishing the rule in *Wheeldon v Burrows*, does not otherwise affect "easements arising by implication as easements of necessity or in order to give effect to the common intention of the parties to the disposition."

23–95 In *Palaceanne Management Ltd v Allied Irish Banks*,[183] the Court of Appeal had to consider whether a right of way was enjoyed by implication of law (including the rule in *Wheeldon v Burrows*), by necessity or by inference. The plaintiff was the management company of a block of nine apartments, and the defendant bank held a mortgage over two unsold apartments and had been granted possession of them in 2009. The dispute concerned easements to the common areas of the block. In the High Court, it was held that on the basis of the mortgage deed, the bank did not have any entitlement to the use of rights including a right of way over the common areas, except for access to a site beside the block. This effectively rendered the bank's properties "landlocked", and Clarke J. in the High Court commented on the resulting unsatisfactory situation. However, on appeal to the Court of Appeal it was argued by the bank that the argument in the High Court, and ultimately the judgment, had proceeded on

---

[180] *Pwllbach Colliery Co Ltd v Woodman* [1919] A.C. 634, approved by Shanley J. in *Redfont Ltd and Wright's Fisherman's Wharf Ltd v Custom House Dock Management Ltd and Hardwicke Property Management Ltd* [1998] IEHC 206. See also *Conneran v Corbett and Sons Ltd* [2004] IEHC 389.

[181] (1885) 16 L.R. Ir. 305.

[182] [1999] 1 I.L.R.M. 141.

[183] [2017] IECA 141.

a mistaken understanding by the parties of a crucial deed of 2009.[184] The Court of Appeal found that the right of way was expressly provided for in the deed of 2009. Furthermore, it was "irresistible that a right arises by necessity or by implication of law or under the rule in *Wheeldon v. Burrows*".[185]

Section 40 of the LCLRA 2009

23–96 Section 40 abolished and replaced the rule in *Wheeldon v Burrows*.[186] The rule expressed in that English case was to the effect that,

> "where an owner of land grants part of the land there will pass to the grantee all those quasi-easements which are continuous and apparent or which are reasonably necessary to the reasonable enjoyment of the property granted and which have been and are at the time of the grant used by the owner of the whole property for the benefit of the part granted."

Thus, if V owned two adjacent properties, A and B, and used a path across A for the benefit of B and then sold B, the conveyance passed a right of way over A without express mention in the deed. The right could not exist as an easement before the conveyance since both properties were within the owner-ship of V and his use of the path was no more than the exercise of the rights of an owner,[187] hence it was called a "quasi-easement". It may be doubted whether the fiction of the "quasi-easement" was at all useful. American courts adopted a similar rule but as an easement "implied from prior use".[188] "Con-tinuous" could not be taken to mean incessant use as otherwise rights of way, for example, would be excluded. "Apparent" implies that there must be some physical evidence of use. Thesiger L.J. in *Wheeldon v Burrows* seems to have intended the phrase "reasonably necessary to the reasonable enjoyment of the property granted" to be an alternative to "continuous and apparent", but it has since been taken as an additional test to be satisfied.

23–97 In *Sovmots Investments v Secretary of State for the Environment*[189] the House of Lords held that the rule applied only to voluntary (i.e. in the sense of being at the free will of parties) conveyances. The facts concerned the Centrepoint building in London. Built in 1967 as an investment property, the

---

[184] Ryan P. in the Court of Appeal noted: "The parties presented their cases in the High Court on an erroneous basis and the judgment is expressly predicated on the same understanding as to the provisions of the conveyance. My view is that this Court must review the judgment in light of the agreed fact that the terms of the conveyance were misunderstood in the High Court. It is not possible in the very unusual circumstances of this case to decide the appeal properly without reference to the unquestionably material deed."

[185] [2017] IECA 141 at para.68.

[186] (1879) 12 Ch. D. 31 at 49. The rule is obiter even in England as the case itself involved implied reservation to which the rule does not apply.

[187] *Head v Meara* [1912] 1 I.R. 262.

[188] *Romanchuk v Plotkin* (1943) 215 Minn. 156; and see R. Cunningham, W. Stoebuck and D. Whitman, *The Law of Property* (St Paul, Minnesota: West Publishing Co, 1984), pp.444–446.

[189] [1979] A.C. 144.

complex had remained unoccupied for many years. It included 36 maisonettes on the second-floor level. The local authority issued a compulsory purchase order acquiring the 36 maisonettes in order to carry out its statutory duty of providing houses for the homeless. A schedule attached to the order claimed various ancillary rights which included rights of support and passage of water, sewage etc. The House of Lords held that the order concerning ancillary rights was in excess of statutory powers. It also held that the ancillary rights had not passed under the rule in *Wheeldon v Burrows* as this did not apply to a compulsory purchase order. The rule was based on the principle that a grantor may not derogate from the grant because the grant was a voluntary act, whereas in this case the acquisition was based on compulsory purchase under statutory powers. The judgments indicate an attitude unfavourable to local authorities exercising compulsory powers aimed at providing housing for the homeless.

23–98 Section 40 of the LCLRA 2009 abolishes the rule in *Wheeldon v Burrows* and replaces it with the following formula, which seems intended to anchor the rule as a further manifestation of the principle against non-derogation from a grant[190]:

> "Where the owner of land disposes of part of it or all of it in parts, the disposition creates by way of implication for the benefit of such part or parts any easement over the part retained, or other part or parts simultaneously disposed of, which—
>
> (a) is necessary to the reasonable enjoyment of the part disposed of, and
> (b) was reasonable for the parties, or would have been if they had adverted to the matter, to assume at the date the disposition took effect as being included in it."

23–99 Despite its ostensible purpose, in many respects the new rule seems suspiciously similar to that which it has abolished. First, the new rule, like the rule in *Wheeldon v Burrows*, applies only to cases of implied grant, not implied reservation; in other words, it does not apply to benefit land retained by the grantor even if that land is immediately afterwards disposed of by the grantor to another party. The rule in s.40 does not apply to an easement of necessity, although the easement in order for it to arise under s.40 must be "necessary to the reasonable enjoyment of the part disposed of" (in *Wheeldon v Burrows* the language used was "reasonably necessary to the reasonable enjoyment of the property granted": hence, the new formulation demands a more absolute test). By contrast, however, with the original rule, there is now an additional requirement to be satisfied: that the parties, if they had thought about it, would reasonably have assumed the passing of the easement. This introduces an element of judgement which may present difficulties in practice.

---

[190] As recommended by the Law Reform Commission, *Consultation Paper on Reform and Modernisation of Land Law and Conveyancing Law* (LRC CP 34-2004).

23–100 There is no express requirement of prior usage, as in the rule in *Wheeldon v Burrows*; however, in practice, courts may look to evidence of prior usage in order to satisfy the above requirement of assumed intention based on happenstance advertence. The requirement that the enjoyment of the quasi-easement be "continuous and apparent" no longer applies.

23–101 An easement can be deemed to arise by implication under the new rule, not only where part of the grantor's property is disposed of and part retained (the part being disposed of becoming the dominant tenement, the part remaining the servient tenement), but where *all* the grantor's property is disposed of in parts simultaneously, with all of these parts becoming either dominant or servient tenements or both. The rule does not apply to benefit any part retained by the grantor where the grantor does not dispose of all his or her property in parts simultaneously, because that in effect would create an implied reservation to which neither the new rule nor the old rule applies.[191]

Section 71 of the LCLRA 2009

23–102 Section 71 of the LCLRA 2009 replaces s.6 of the 1881 Act, which read:

"A conveyance of land ... shall be deemed to include and shall ... operate to convey with the land ... all ... buildings, erections, fixtures, commons, hedges, ditches, fences, ways, watercourses, liberties, privileges, easements, rights and advantages whatsoever appertaining or reputed to appertain to the land, or any part thereof, or at the time of the conveyance demised, occupied, or enjoyed with, or reputed or known as part or parcel or appurtenant to the land or any part thereof."[192]

23–103 Section 6(4) of the 1881 Act provided that the section "applies only if and as far as a contrary intention is expressed in the conveyance".[193] Section 6 of the 1881 Act was in some ways more extensive than the rule in *Wheeldon v Burrows* and in other ways more restricted.

23–104 The section had the same effect as the rule in *Wheeldon v Burrows* in that it did not operate to create new kinds of right, i.e. rights had to satisfy existing tests of property rights, so that, if the section were relied on to claim

---

[191] In *Close v Cairns* [1997] N.I.J.B. 70, Girvan J. in the Northern Ireland High Court applied the rule in *Wheeldon v Burrows* to a case in which the two parcels of land comprising the dominant and servient tenements had been disposed of at the same time by will.

[192] Subsection (2), which applied where the land contains a building, sets out a list of various constructions and works that, in the absence of express provision to the contrary, are taken as included in a conveyance of the land.

[193] The "contrary intention" had to be express, not required to be drawn by inference: *Steele v Morrow* (1923) 57 I.L.T.R. 89.

an easement, the easement needed to satisfy the usual tests.[194] This requirement
has not changed.

23–105 Section 6 had a *wider* ambit than the rule in that:

1. it applied to all kinds of rights, not only easements;
2. easements did not have to be continuous and apparent to fall within its
   scope[195]; and
3. nor did they have to be shown as reasonably necessary for the reasonable
   enjoyment of the property. For example, if a landlord granted a renewal
   of a lease to a tenant, s.6 operated to convert any licences or privileges
   which the landlord had allowed the tenant to exercise in the past into
   easements or *profits à prendre*, if they were capable of qualifying as such
   in law.[196]

23–106 It was *narrower* in its scope than the rule in *Wheeldon v Burrows* in
that:

1. it applied only to conveyances made since 1881;
2. it applied only to conveyances and not to contracts[197];
3. it may also not have applied to an equitable lease under the doctrine of
   Walsh v Lonsdale since that is not a "conveyance"[198]; and
4. there is authority in England for the proposition that the section applied
   only where there was a separation between the ownership and occupation
   of the two parts before the conveyance,[199] i.e. it did not apply to rights
   which could *only* have been quasi-easements because they were enjoyed
   by the former owner of the property as an incident of that person's
   ownership of the whole; in other words, that prior to the conveyance
   the owner of the land had not also been the owner or occupier of *both*
   parts claimed to be affected by an easement. This position was restated
   in the Court of Appeal in *Sovmots Investments v Secretary of State for*

---

[194] *Phipps v Pears* [1965] 1 Q.B. 76. Right to protection of a wall from the weather did not pass
under s.62 of the Law of Property Act 1925, because it could not exist as an easement.

[195] *Tichmarsh v Royston Water Co Ltd* (1899) 81 L.T. 673; *Long v Gowlett* [1923] 2 Ch. 177. As
seen above, easements are not now required to be "continuous and apparent" to fall within s.40
of the LCLRA 2009, which abolishes and replaces the rule in *Wheeldon v Burrows*.

[196] *International Tea Stores Ltd v Hobbs* [1903] 2 Ch. 165; *Jeffers v Odeon (Ireland) Ltd* (1953)
87 I.L.T.R. 187.

[197] *McDonagh v Mulholland* [1931] I.R. 110 at 122; *Peilow v O'Carroll* (1972) 106 I.L.T.R. 29.

[198] *Borman v Griffith* [1930] 1 Ch. 493.

[199] *Long v Gowlett* [1923] 2 Ch. 177, but see C. Harpum, "*Long v Gowlett*: A Strong Fortress"
[1979] Conv. 113; C. Harpum, S. Bridge and M. Dixon, *Megarry & Wade: The Law of Real
Property*, 8th edn (London: Sweet & Maxwell, 2012), para.28–033.

the Environment,[200] but the point was not argued in the House of Lords although dicta of Lord Wilberforce[201] appear to support it.

23–107 However, the principle requiring separation of ownership and occupation was recognised as being subject to at least two exceptions: where the right in question was a right to light[202] and where the enjoyment had been continuous and apparent.[203] Continuous and apparent quasi-easements were also regarded as an exception to the principle that a person could not exercise "rights" over his or her own land.[204]

23–108 With effect from 1 December 2009, s.6 of the 1881 Act has been replaced by s.71 of the LCLRA 2009. Subsection (1) provides:

"A conveyance of land includes, and conveys with the land, all—

  (a) buildings, commons, ditches, drains, erections, fences, fixtures, hedges, water, watercourses and other features forming part of the land,

  (b) advantages, easements, liberties, privileges, *profits à prendre* and rights appertaining or annexed to the land."

23–109 Subsection (2) deals with land which contains a building and sets out a list of physical adjuncts which are to be regarded as included in a conveyance of such land.

23–110 Subsection (3) states that the section:

"(a) does not on a conveyance of land (whether or not it has houses or other buildings on it)—

  (i) create any new interest or right or convert any quasi-easement or right existing prior to the conveyance into a full interest or right, or

  (ii) extend the scope of, or convert into a new interest or right, any licence, privilege or other interest or right existing before the conveyance,

(b) does not—

---

[200] [1979] A.C. 144, see above, interpreting s.62 of the Law of Property Act 1925, which was a re-enactment of s.6 of the Conveyancing Act 1881.

[201] *Sovmots Investments v Secretary of State for the Environment* [1979] A.C. 144 at 169. Approved by Shanley J. in *Redfont Ltd and Wright's Fisherman's Wharf Ltd v Custom House Dock Management Ltd and Hardwicke Property Management Ltd* [1998] IEHC 206 and by Keane C.J. in *William Bennett Construction Ltd v Greene* [2004] 2 I.L.R.M. 96, but in neither case was the disputed right found to have been enjoyed by the owner of the two properties prior to conveyance.

[202] *Broomfield v Williams* [1897] 1 Ch. 602.

[203] *Watts v Kelson* (1870) 6 Ch. App. 166; *Bayley v GWR* (1883) 26 Ch. D. 434 at 456; *Barkshire v Grubb* (1881) 18 Ch. D. 616.

[204] C. Harpum, "*Long v Gowlett*: A Strong Fortress" [1979] Conv. 113 at 114 et seq; M.P. Thompson, "Paths and Pigs: Case Comment" [1995] Conv. 239 at 241.

    (i) give to any person a better title to any land, interest or right referred
        to in this section than the title which the conveyance gives to the land
        expressed to be conveyed, or

    (ii) convey to any person any land, interest or right further or other than
        that which could have been conveyed to that person by the grantor,

  (c) takes effect subject to the terms of the conveyance."

23–111 The omission from s.71(1) of "reputed" rights and rights "enjoyed
with" the land, present in the former s.6, together with the uncompromising
terms of subs.(3), makes it clear that henceforth such ephemeral entitlements
will not pass on a conveyance of land that formerly enjoyed them. In order
for a right to be claimed as an easement subsequent to a conveyance of land
it must have been enjoyed as an easement prior to that conveyance. The continuing requirement for diversification of ownership and occupation of the
relevant lands is represented by the prohibition against a quasi-easement being
converted into a full easement, as a quasi-easement by definition exists where
the enjoyment has been had as an incident of the ownership of both sets of
land involved. From 1 December 2009 onwards a quasi-easement, if it is to
become a full easement upon a conveyance of land to which it refers, will
arise as an implied grant under s.40 of the LCLRA 2009—instead of under
the now abolished rule in *Wheeldon v Burrows*—provided that it falls within
the terms of that section. Furthermore, unlike s.6(4) of the 1881 Act, which
required the intention to exclude operation of the section to be "expressed in
the conveyance", s.71(3)(c) of the LCLRA 2009 merely states that the section
"takes effect subject to the terms of the conveyance". As this arguably includes
implied terms and terms arising by inference, it may be easier in the future
(although this should *not* be assumed), than under the 1881 Act, to contend
that a conveyance on a proper interpretation of its terms intended the section
not to apply.

Implied Reservation
23–112 It is more difficult to establish easements by implied reservation due
to the principle that a grantor should not derogate from his or her grant. Barron
J. in *Connell v O'Malley*[205] expressed the view that if a grantor wished to retain
the benefit of quasi-easements for the land retained he or she would have to
reserve them expressly, but there are examples of easements of necessity and
easements of common intention arising by way of implied reservation.

Common Intention
23–113 One Northern Ireland case found that such an easement had arisen,
although for the benefit not of the grantor but of his tenant. In *Re Flanagan and*

---

[205] Unreported, High Court, Barron J., 28 July 1983. A similar view was expressed by Thesiger
L.J. in *Wheeldon v Burrows* (1879) 12 Ch. D. 31 at 49.

McGarvey and Thompson's Contract[206] a person had two adjoining houses, A and B. He held B on a 989-year lease which he let out on a quarterly tenancy. A path led from a road across the land attached to house A to the back door of the sub-let B. The path was convenient but not essential to the enjoyment of house B. The executors of the owner entered a contract, which did not mention the path, to sell house A to a purchaser. They claimed that they were entitled to reserve an easement for themselves over the path for the duration of the 989-year lease.

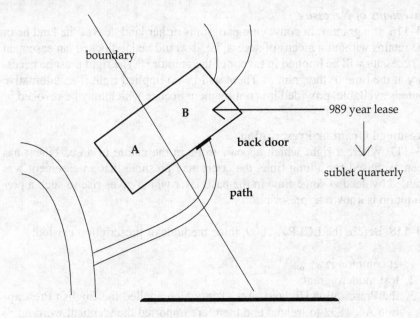

23–114 It was held by the High Court of Northern Ireland that they were not entitled to do so, but that they *were* entitled to reserve a right of way for the benefit of the quarterly tenancy over house B and any statutory tenancy that might arise on its determination.

23–115 An explanation of the result in the case which does not involve an exception to the rule against derogating from a grant, is that when the sub-tenancy was granted over house B the "quasi-easement" over the path became an easement for the duration of the tenancy. As a legal right the tenant could have enforced it against third parties, including the present purchaser, regardless of notice. Thus, the purchaser of A would be bound by it whether there was any mention of it in his contract or not and without any need to imply a reservation. The only right over A which the executors had power to convey to a purchaser was subject to a legal easement for the benefit of the sub-tenancy. On the other hand, this was not the reason given by the court for its decision and the case may therefore be some authority for the view that while a grantor cannot in general impliedly reserve easements for his or her own benefit, there may be circumstances in which this may be done for the benefit of the grantor's tenants.[207] *Dwyer Nolan Developments Ltd v Kingscroft Developments Ltd*[208] also seems to indicate that courts are more willing than in the past to find such easements and to regard them as based on a re-grant by the purchaser of the land in favour of the vendor.

Easements of Necessity

23–116 If a grantor, in conveying part of his or her land, leaves the land he or she retains without a means of access, i.e. it would be landlocked, an easement of necessity will be implied in favour of the grantor.[209] The right must be necessary at the time of the grant.[210] There will be no implied right if an alternative route is available, provided it is not by mere licence which may be revoked.[211]

Presumed Grant or Prescription

23–117 Where a right which appears to be in the nature of an easement has been exercised for a long time, the court may presume that an easement was granted by deed at some time in the past. User which gives rise to such a presumption is known as prescription.

23–118 Before the LCLRA 2009, three methods of prescription existed:

1. at common law;
2. lost modern grant;
3. the Prescription (Ireland) Act 1858 which applied the English Prescription Act 1832 to Ireland and therefore imported the identical wording.[212]

23–119 These have now been abolished[213] by the LCLRA 2009 and a new system of statutory prescription has been introduced. However, s.38(b) provides that in respect of a claim brought before 1 December 2012, the new provisions will "not apply to any claim based on a user period under the law applicable prior to the commencement of this Chapter and alleged to have commenced prior to such commencement ...". This means, in effect, that up to and including 30 November 2012, a claim by prescription in proceedings will have

---

[207] *Thomas v Owen* (1887) 20 Q.B.D. 225 disapproved.

[208] [1999] 1 I.L.R.M. 141; *Geraghty v Quinn* [2008] IEHC 166.

[209] *Browne v Maguire* [1922] 1 I.R. 23; *Maude v Thornton* [1929] I.R. 454; *Re Flanagan and McGarvey and Thompson's Contract* [1945] N.I. 32 at 42; *Palaceanne Management Ltd v Allied Irish Banks plc* [2017] IECA 141.

[210] *Geraghty v McCann* (1872) I.R. 6 C.L. 411; *Browne v Maguire* [1922] 1 I.R. 23.

[211] *Barry v Hasseldine* [1952] Ch. 835.

[212] The English Prescription Act 1832 applied only to England and Wales: s.9.

[213] The first two by s.34 of the LCLRA 2009; the Prescription (Ireland) Act 1858 by LCLRA 2009 s.8 and Sch.2, Pt 4.

reference either to prescription at common law, the doctrine of lost modern grant, or under the Prescription (Ireland) Act 1858.

General Tests

23–120 Certain requirements exist if a claim to an easement by prescription is to succeed. While these have been built up over a long period by the common law, their continued relevance has been effectively ensured by s.33 of the LCLRA 2009 which defines "user as of right" as "use or enjoyment without force, without secrecy and without the oral or written consent of the servient owner".

User as of Right

23–121 Gilligan J. in *Zopitar Ltd v Jacob*[214] explained that "[u]ser as of right" means "without force, secrecy, and without oral or written consent of the servient owner."[215] He continued:

> "The important question is whether the use would suggest to a reasonably careful and prudent owner of the land that a casual use only of the land was being made dependant for its continuance upon the tolerance and good nature of such servient owner, or would it put such servient owner on notice that an actual right of way was being asserted. It cannot therefore be secret, clandestine or surreptitious. The use also cannot be forced upon the servient owner, for prescription theory demands acquiescence in order for a right to be established. Finally, for the Court to be satisfied that there has been acquiescence to the establishment of a right, the necessary use cannot be referable to a consent, permission or licence. It cannot be precatory, in the sense of being precarious, that is, subject to the will of the servient owner and capable of being interrupted. The determination as to whether a case falls on either side of the acquiescence/toleration divide depends on its particular facts."[216]

23–122 To succeed in a claim based on prescription the claimant must show that he or she has exercised the easement as if entitled to it under a grant. This is why prescription is sometimes known alternatively as presumed grant. Prescription may be contrasted here with acquiring title to land by adverse possession. Unlike adverse possession, the user on which a claim to prescription is based must be lawful in origin. Adverse possession, it is true, is possession which is "as of right" in one sense, i.e. a right which is inconsistent with the right of the original owner but which, because of the concept of relativity of title in real property, is a right good against later possessors. Prescription is "as of right" in the sense of a right consistent with the owner having granted

---

[214] [2015] IEHC 790 at para.81.

[215] *Nec vi, nec clam, nec precario.* Derived from the Roman law of praedial servitudes.

[216] [2015] IEHC 790 at para.81. See also, *Lynn Shellfish Ltd v Loose* [2016] UKSC 14 at para.37; *Winterburn v Bennett* [2016] EWCA Civ 482.

the right to the claimant of the easement and which is not therefore exercised merely by permission or at the will of the owner of the servient tenement which can be withdrawn.

Without Force

23–123 A claim to an easement by prescription cannot succeed if the servient owner has objected to the use continually and unmistakably.[217] In order for an easement to accrue the servient owner must have acquiesced in the use in the sense that he or she had knowledge of the acts constituting user, had the power to prevent them by his or her own acts or by suing in respect of them, and had abstained from doing so.

Without Secrecy

23–124 The servient owner cannot acquiesce without knowledge of the user. Using a path only in the dead of night will not establish a right of way.

Without Mere Permission

23–125 The user must be consistent with a grant of a right. If user is by virtue of a bare licence then it is clearly precarious in that permission may be withdrawn by the owner of the land. User under a contract can be said to be as of right, but the right is then personal and is inconsistent with a right of property available against all owners of the land which is the kind of right conferred by a grant.[218] If user is under an express grant, user is, of course, as of right, but in that situation the easement will have been granted, so that the claimant has no need to resort to prescription. Nevertheless, if user is under the mistaken belief that an express grant was made in the past that does not prevent user being "as of right."[219]

23–126 As Charleton J. stated in *The Leopardstown Club v Templeville Developments*, "the essential quality of prescriptive rights must arise by reference to right and not by reference to permission."[220] A similar point was made by the Supreme Court in *Walsh and Cassidy v Sligo County Council*:

> "User by permission of the owner is not user as of right. At the same time, user without express permission is not necessarily user as of right. Whether particular acts of user are to be described as being as of right requires account to be taken of all the circumstances. Acts may be tolerated or

---

[217] *Dalton v Angus* (1881) 6 App. Cas. 740 at 773; E.H. Burn and J. Cartwright, *Cheshire and Burn's Modern Law of Real Property*, 18th edn (Oxford: Oxford University Press, 2011), p.668.

[218] *Lowry v Crothers* (1870) I.R. 5 C.L. 98 (right to cut turf enjoyed by permission for the whole of 60-year period. Tenant of the servient tenement who made the agreement had died before the period began).

[219] *Bridle v Ruby* [1988] 3 All E.R. 64.

[220] [2013] IEHC 526 at para.20.

indulged by a landowner vis-à-vis his neighbours without being considered to be the exercise of a right."[221]

23–127 In *The Square v Dunnes Stores*,[222] the defendant had express permission to allow its customers to use a car park outside a Dublin shopping centre. The express permission or licence meant that a claim to have an easement by prescription failed.

Continuous User

23–128 User must be continuous and not intermittent, but the meaning of continuous will depend on the type of easement claimed. A right to light is enjoyed uninterruptedly, at least while light is available, but the use of a right of way is necessarily from time to time and not constant. In *Orwell Park Management Ltd v Henihan*[223] Herbert J. stated, in the context of a claimed right of way, that continuous use was not to be equated with incessant use: "what the law requires is that the use be such as would clearly indicate to a servient owner that a continuous right to do what would otherwise amount to a trespass was being asserted ... ." The judge drew a distinction between casual use "dependent for its continuance upon the tolerance and good nature of the servient owner", which would not enable an easement to be claimed by prescription, and use of a kind which "would put such servient owner on notice that an actual right to do these things was being asserted", which *could* accrue into an easement. The right being claimed must itself have sufficient certainty and uniformity surrounding its enjoyment in order for it to be capable of being identified and also interrupted.[224]

Prescription at Common Law

23–129 To succeed in a claim to an easement by prescription at common law the claimant had to show user from "time immemorial", described by Coke[225] as a "time whereof the memory of men runneth not to the contrary".[226] This is also known as the time of "legal memory"[227] and was specified in the Statute of Westminster 1275 as commencing in 1189, the year of the coronation of

---

[221] [2013] IESC 48.

[222] *The Square Management Ltd, National Asset Property Management Ltd and Indego v Dunnes Stores Dublin Co* [2017] IEHC 146 at para.71.

[223] [2004] IEHC 87.

[224] *Lanigan v Barry* [2008] IEHC 29, which held that a right to create a nuisance by noise could not be acquired by prescription. Charleton J. said that "in terms of its duration, its intrusiveness, its intensity and its character ... it has come and gone away in a manner which could not give rise to any valid prescription plea", also relying upon B. McMahon and W. Binchy, *Law of Torts*, 3rd edn (Dublin: Butterworths, 2000), paras 24.99–24.100.

[225] Co Litt 114b at 170. Coke also calls it "time out of mind".

[226] The phrase is used in the preamble to the Prescription Act 1832.

[227] *Knox v Earl of Mayo* (1858) 7 Ir. Ch. R. 563.

King Richard I.[228] A plaintiff in an action claiming an easement at common law could not rely on facts prior to 1189 but, since user had to be continuous, he or she had to establish continuous user *since* 1189, or at least facts from which it could be inferred. Equally, a defendant to an action could successfully challenge the claim if it could be proven that user began at any time after 1189. This continued to be the law until the abolition of prescription at common law in s.34 of the LCLRA 2009.

23–130 As time went by and it became increasingly impossible to prove user back to 1189, the judges adopted a second rule, consistent with the general principle of proof from time immemorial. They *presumed* user from 1189, on proof of user for as far back as the memory of living witnesses would go.[229] Later still a third rule was adopted by analogy to a statute[230] of James I which laid down a limitation period of 20 years for possessory actions. The courts thereafter presumed that the prescriptive right had existed from 1189 on proof of 20 years' user.[231]

23–131 An obvious weakness of common law prescription was that 20 years' user raised only a *presumption* of user since 1189, rather than creating a legal fiction that user had endured since that date. The presumption could be rebutted by showing that user could not have been continuous since the late 12th century. This made it particularly easy to resist a claim to a right of light based on the common law period. All one needed to show was that the building purporting to be the dominant tenement, or any predecessor structure with identically placed window apertures, did not date back to 1189, or that the land had not been built upon until some time since then.

23–132 A claim to a right of way based on prescription at common law succeeded in *Carroll v Sheridan and Sheehan*.[232] The plaintiffs owned land abutting a mile-long ancient path which linked two public roads—the main Dublin to Dundalk road and a road leading from Dundalk to nearby Blackrock. The path was shown on a number of old maps, one dating from 1777. The ancient name of the path was "An Bóthar Maol" and according to folklore Queen Maeve traversed it in the course of her legendary cattle-raid on Cooley. The path was overgrown, and it was no longer practicable to travel along it from end to end. The defendants, owners of land at one end of the lane, asserted that any right of way which may formerly have existed in favour of

---

[228] The time laid down was the limitation period of a writ of right and it was later relied upon by the courts by way of analogy in prescription claims: Co Litt 170.

[229] *Angus v Dalton* (1881) 3 Q.B.D. 104. T. Carson, *Carson's Real Property Statutes*, 2nd edn (London: Sweet & Maxwell, 1910), p.21.

[230] 1623, 21 Jas. I c.16.

[231] *Daly v Cullen* (1958) 92 I.L.T.R. 127 (Circuit Court, Wexford, Judge Deale), applying *Bright v Walker* 1 Cr. M. & R. 211 at 217; *DPP (Long) v McDonald* [1983] I.L.R.M. 223.

[232] [1984] I.L.R.M. 451.

the plaintiffs' land had been extinguished by non-user. The plaintiffs sought a declaration that they were entitled to a right of way over the length of the lane.

23–133 O'Hanlon J., granting the declaration, held (i) that the evidence established that there was from time immemorial a road or lane, (ii) that the owners of the soil had dedicated the way to the use of the abutting landowners if not to the public in general, and (iii) that the plaintiffs had not originally claimed that the path was a public right of way, and so could not amend their pleadings on appeal.

Lost Modern Grant

23–134 Because prescription at common law could be defeated so easily in many cases, the courts created another fiction. If user could be shown for a considerable period they were prepared to presume that a grant had been made of an easement in modern times but had subsequently been lost. Twenty years' user has been held to be sufficient to raise the doctrine.[233] Some cases have held that the doctrine could not be defeated by showing that no grant was in fact made.[234] More recently[235] the English Court of Appeal held that user under the mistaken belief that a grant had been made in the past was not inconsistent with user as of right and so did not rebut the presumption of lost modern grant. Even so, it was less than clear what part the supposed lost grant played in the operation of the doctrine. There is authority to the effect that the doctrine could be defeated by showing that during the period there was no person capable of making a grant[236] or that a grant would have contravened a statute.[237]

23–135 The doctrine of lost modern grant enjoyed a continuing life in Ireland even after the enactment of the Prescription (Ireland) Act 1858. This was partly because it could be used to get around certain restrictions contained in the statute. The Prescription (Ireland) Act 1858 required that the period of continuous enjoyment have taken place immediately before the commencement of litigation in relation to the claimed right.[238] Accordingly, the doctrine of lost modern grant could be pleaded to establish an easement where there had been a significant gap between the period of provable continuous enjoyment and

---

[233] *Tisdall v McArthur Steel & Metal Co Ltd* [1951] I.R. 228.

[234] *Hanna v Pollock* [1900] 2 I.R. 664; *Tehidy Minerals Ltd v Norman* [1971] 2 Q.B. 528.

[235] *Bridle v Ruby* [1988] 3 All E.R. 64.

[236] *McEvoy v Great Northern Railway Co* [1900] 2 I.R. 325 per Palles C.B.; *Oakley v Boston* [1976] Q.B. 270.

[237] *McEvoy v Great Northern Railway Co* [1900] 2 I.R. 325; *Neaverson v Peterborough RDC* [1902] 1 Ch. 557.

[238] Prescription (Ireland) Act 1858 s.4. A similar requirement is now contained in LCLRA 2009 s.35(2), with a facility for discretionary modification in subs.(3), which may prove problematic.

the commencement of litigation.[239] Furthermore, Irish courts have held that the doctrine of lost modern grant could apply between tenants even holding under a common landlord,[240] so taking a line at variance with that of the English Court of Exchequer in a case decided two years after the enactment of the Prescription Act 1832 in Great Britain.[241]

The Prescription (Ireland) Act 1858

23–136 The Prescription (Ireland) Act 1858 provided that the Prescription Act 1832, which had been confined to England and Wales, should apply in Ireland from 1 January 1859. The purpose of the Prescription (Ireland) Act 1858 was to set out alternative periods of prescription to those at common law or under the doctrine of lost modern grant. The Act established different treatment for, on the one hand, easements other than of light and also *profits à prendre* and, on the other hand, easements of light.

23–137 As to easements other than of light and *profits à prendre*, there were two statutorily defined periods, the "shorter period" and the "longer period". Depending on which period applied different consequences would follow. In the case of the shorter period, oral or written permission given during it would defeat the claim. In the case of the longer period, oral permission would never defeat it. It could only be defeated by showing written permission given during the period. In either case, permission, written or oral, given before the period began was not relevant.

Easements other than of Light and Profits à Prendre
The Shorter Period

23–138 Sections 1 and 2 applied here. The "shorter period" in the case of easements other than of light was 20 years, for *profits à prendre* 30 years. In either case, where the requisite duration of user was proved the claim could not be defeated simply by showing that user began at some time since 1189 but before the start of the user period. In other words, the relevant period of user was shortened to the duration of the shorter statutory period. A claim could be

---

[239] As occurred in *Orwell Management Ltd v Henihan* [2004] IEHC 87 (last proven use 30 years prior to action) and was potentially capable of occurring in *Agnew v Barry* [2009] IESC 45 (oral consent to use of fishing given for more than 30 but less than 60 years, so failing to satisfy s.1 of the Prescription (Ireland) Act 1858), except that the Supreme Court refused to allow lost modern grant, not pleaded earlier, to be introduced on appeal. Of the doctrine, Geoghegan J. observed: "The prescription for the purposes of that doctrine is not required to terminate at the date of the commencement of the proceedings. In other words it could be an earlier period."

[240] *Timmons v Hewitt* (1888) 22 L.R. Ir. 627; *O'Kane v O'Kane* (1891) 30 L.R. Ir. 489; but lost modern grant could not apply where the supposed dominant and servient owners were tenants of the same landlord in such a way as subsequently to bind the fee simple: *Lord MacNaghten v Baird* [1903] 2 I.R. 731. However, see s.8 of the Prescription (Ireland) Act 1858, discussed below.

[241] *Bright v Walker* (1834) 1 Cr. M. & R. 216, which had held that prescriptive enjoyment had to be shown as capable of binding all estates in the servient tenement.

defeated by proving an "interruption" as defined and discussed below. A claim could also be defeated by showing that the claimed right could not qualify as an easement, or by showing that its enjoyment had been objected to by the owner of the land claimed to be the servient tenement, or that it was in secret, or that it was, during the period, exercised only by the mere permission or licence of the owner rather than as of right.

The Longer Period

23–139 This was also covered by ss.1 and 2. The longer period was, in the case of easements other than of light, 40 years and for *profits à prendre*, 60 years. In either case, if the requisite duration was proved the right was "deemed absolute and indefeasible" unless enjoyed by *written* consent. Oral consent was not sufficient to prevent acquisition of the easement or *profit à prendre* where enjoyment had been for the longer period. However, proof of enjoyment for either period could be attenuated by reason of the statutory definition of "deductions".

"Next Before Action"

23–140 Section 4 of the Prescription Act 1832 stated that both the longer and the shorter periods must be "next before ... action", i.e. the periods could not be any periods in the past but must immediately precede the bringing of the action in which the right is asserted or disputed. The significance of this appears in the context of interruptions as defined in the Act.

Interruptions

23–141 In order for an easement to be claimed under the Prescription Act 1832 the period of enjoyment must not have been "interrupted" within the meaning of s.4, which stated:

> " ... no act ... shall be deemed to be an interruption, within the meaning of this statute, unless the same shall have been or shall be submitted to or acquiesced in for one year after the party interrupted shall have had or shall have notice thereof, and of the person making or authorizing [the interruption]."

23–142 An interruption had to be factual in terms of the actual stopping of user, by, for example, a barrier being erected across a right of way, but to qualify as an "interruption" within the meaning of the Act the factual interruption must also have been "submitted to or acquiesced in" for a period of one year. Furthermore, the one year did not start to run until the claimant was aware of the interruption and of the identity of the person interrupting or causing or permitting interruption. In *Glover v Coleman*[242] it was held that in order not to acquiesce in an interruption the claimant did not have to go so far as to remove

---

[242] (1874) 10 C.P. 108.

the factual interruption by, for example, forcibly taking away a barrier, or even suing the interrupter. It was enough to communicate his or her objection to the interruption to the interrupter with sufficient force and clarity.

Action, Based on Actual User, Not Hypothetical

23–143 In *Reilly v Orange*[243] an English court held that the requirement of "next before ... action" referred to an action based on actual user, not hypothetical user. Thus, if X prescribed for 19 years and five days and was then interrupted by Y, X could not claim the easement immediately on the argument that Y would be unable to complete the necessary one year's interruption before the 20 years expired. X had to wait another 360 days and then bring an action. It could also be argued that, were it otherwise, then X could claim an easement after only 19 years and five days, which would be contrary to the Act, which required 20 years of actual user.

23–144 But it has been pointed out that this had the anomalous result that X then had only five days within which to bring his action. If he delayed longer than that, Y would by then have completed the one-year interruption.[244] Equally, if X prescribed for 19 years and one day and was then interrupted by Y, X would have to wait another 364 days to bring his claim, but would then only have one day in which to start a successful action. If X began the action before that time he would not be able to show 20 years' user "next before ... action": if he delayed until after the day has passed, Y could establish a one-year interruption and so defeat X's claim under the Act.

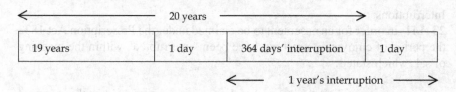

23–145 It would also follow that if X was interrupted after exactly 19 years he could not claim an easement at all, because he had to wait another 365 days, but by then Y would also have established a full one-year interruption. However, these hypothetical situations were not so serious an obstacle as might at first appear, because X could stop the interruption at any time by indicating that he did not acquiesce in it. On the other hand, it would seem that if a servient owner issued a writ before the shorter period of user had elapsed, it did not rank as an "interruption" but would stop the period running (as enjoyment would no longer be "as of right") and so prevent the claim from succeeding.[245]

---

[243] [1955] 2 Q.B. 112.
[244] G.C. Cheshire and E.H. Burn, *Cheshire and Burn's Modern Law of Real Property*, 13th edn (London: Butterworths, 1982), p.520.
[245] *Reilly v Orange* [1955] 2 Q.B. 112.

23–146 In *Wilson v Stanley*,[246] Pigot C.B. stated that the effect of s.4 of the Prescription Act was to require evidence of actual enjoyment on the part of the claiming dominant owner within the period of the last year before the action was brought, or otherwise the delay of more than a year in bringing the action from the last demonstrated enjoyment of the right would cause a forfeiture of the potential benefit of all preceding enjoyment no matter how long had elapsed since its commencement.

Deductions

23–147 The Prescription Act 1832 also allowed deductions to be made from the relevant periods of enjoyment. These deductions did not count as interruptions, nor as user. Their effect was arithmetic and had reference to the amount of time that could be computed for the purposes of enjoyment within ss.1 and 2. The period during which a deduction applied could simply be deducted and the remaining periods of user added together to make up the relevant period of user for the purpose of either the "longer period" or the "shorter period".

23–148 Section 7 applied where the period of enjoyment was not such as to create an "absolute and indefeasible" right; in effect, it applied only to easements (other than of light) where the enjoyment had been for 20 years, and to *profits à prendre* where the enjoyment had been for 30 years. It provided that periods were to be automatically deducted from this shorter period during which the servient owner was a minor, or mentally ill or was a tenant for life. So was a period during which an action is pending and has been "diligently prosecuted". Section 7 did not apply where the servient tenement was held under a lease.

23–149 Section 8 applied only to easements (other than of light) and not to *profits à prendre*.[247] It provided that periods were to be deducted from the longer period during which the servient tenement was held for "a term of life, or any term of years exceeding three years from the granting thereof", provided that the claim was resisted by a reversioner on the term within three years after its expiry or earlier determination. Section 8, in other words, provided (unlike s.7) for periods during which the servient tenement was held on leasehold to be deducted, but not automatically or invariably. Such periods could be deducted only if the landlord resisted the claim to an easement within three years following the end of the lease. Accordingly, as explained by the Irish Court of Appeal in *Beggan v McDonald*,[248] s.8 of the Prescription Act 1832 introduced a "defeasible inchoate right",[249] which, if resisted by the reversioner within

---

[246] (1861) 12 I.C.L.R. 345.

[247] Section 8 applied in the case of a "way or other convenient watercourse or use of water", but it appears that "convenient" was a misprint for "easement", hence s.8 applied to all easements other than of light: *Laird v Briggs* (1881) 19 Ch. D. 22 at 33. Section 2 had the phrase "any way or other easement, or to any watercourse, or the use of any water".

[248] (1877) I.R. 11 C.L. 362.

[249] (1877) I.R. 11 C.L. 362 at 572.

three years following the end of the term, could not bind the fee simple, but otherwise would, thereby becoming a full "absolute and indefeasible" right.

23–150 The historical operation of the sections can be seen by taking some examples. If a path over land had been used by D, an adjoining owner, for 15 years while the land was held in fee simple, then for 10 years while it was held by a tenant for life, and then for another two years while it was held in fee simple again, the claim to an easement would fail. Only the shorter period could be relied on and, under s.7, the period while the servient land was held by a tenant for life must be deducted. This left 15 years which could be joined to the two years when it was again held by a tenant in fee simple, but this still did not add up to 20 years' user. If, however, user were to have continued for another three years while the land remained held in fee simple the claim would succeed, for the 15 years could be added to the five years making up the required 20 years' user, provided that this was, for the purpose of the Act, 20 years' user "next before action".[250]

23–151 If D had used a right of way against S's land for 10 years and then S became mentally ill, while user continued for another 12 years, the claim of D would fail, for only s.7 could be relied on and under that section the period of insanity must be deducted. But if user were to have continued for 30 years after S became insane, S remaining in this condition throughout, the claim would succeed under s.8 because the enjoyment would have been had for the longer period of 40 years and the term of insanity was not deductible under s.8, so enabling an absolute and indefeasible right to an easement to be asserted.

23–152 The only provision for deducting leasehold terms was under s.8. If user continued for 15 years while the land was held in fee simple, then for 10 years while held under a lease, and then for a further three years while the land was held in fee simple, the claim would succeed under s.7 since leasehold terms are not deductible under that section. However, s.7 only applied to the shorter period, where the right was not absolute and indefeasible, and so enabled the claim to be defeated on any of the grounds by which it could have been defeated at common law, except on the ground that enjoyment had commenced sometime after 1189 but not less than 20 years before the claim was made. It may be that the relevant period had to begin while the land was held in fee simple and also end while held in fee simple.[251]

Is the Longer Period "Absolute and Indefeasible"?
23–153 It seems that s.8 may work in a way which casts doubt on whether the longer period gives rise to a right "deemed absolute and indefeasible". Suppose X prescribes for 33 years while the land is held in fee simple, then 10 years while under a lease, and then a further two years while the land is held in fee

---

[250] *Clayton v Corby* (1842) 2 Q.B. 813.
[251] *Palk v Shinner* (1852) 18 Q.B. 568; *Pugh v Savage* [1970] 2 Q.B. 373.

simple. If the reversioner on the term sues after seven years of the lease have run, he or she will fail, for under s.8 the leasehold term cannot be deducted unless he or she sues within three years of the end of the lease. It would then seem that the prescriber has established the 40-year term which gives a right "deemed absolute and indefeasible". But if the reversioner sues during the later two-year period, he or she will defeat a claim under s.8 because then the leasehold term is deducted. Section 8 therefore seems to detract from the general rule in s.2.[252]

23–154 It may be thought that the prescriber could succeed under s.7 in either case, but it may be that such a claim would be defeated because of an oral permission given during the period, which is not an objection to the longer period. It seems that the principle which s.8 seeks to apply is that the longer term should not give rise to an easement against the reversioner on a term of years until the reversioner has had the opportunity, after the end of the term, of resuming occupation and challenging the use. Until that occurs the completion of the longer period only gives a right which is "absolute and indefeasible" against the tenant under the term of years.

Easements of Light

23–155 Section 3 provided that when the access and use of light to a dwelling house, workshop, or other building[253] has been "actually enjoyed" for a period of 20 years without interruption the right was "deemed absolute and indefeasible", any local custom notwithstanding, unless it was enjoyed by some consent or agreement expressly made or given by deed or writing. Thus, an oral consent given during the period would not defeat the claim.

23–156 It seems that the effect of s.3 was to make a 20-year period of enjoyment in the case of a right to light the equivalent of the longer period in the case of all other easements.

23–157 Section 3, in contrast to ss.1 and 2, used the phrase "actually enjoyed" without the further qualification that it must be by a person "claiming right thereto". It seems therefore that the only element of "as of right" which applied under the Prescription Act 1832 in the case of an easement of light was that a claim would be defeated by written consent during the period. It has been held that the Act abolished the presumption of a grant in the case of easements of

---

[252] *Beggan v McDonald* (1878) 2 L.R. Ir. 560.
[253] The section's coverage was construed as including a greenhouse in *Allen v Greenwood* [1980] Ch. 119, which held that the dominant owner may acquire by prescription a right to an additional amount of light which is reasonably required for the use of a greenhouse, this being known to the servient owner.

light,[254] although Irish authorities took the view that an easement of light could still be claimed on the basis of lost modern grant.[255]

23–158 There was no deduction under either s.7 or s.8 for any of the grounds specified in those sections, because s.7 did not apply where the right claimed is "absolute and indefeasible" and s.8 applied only where the requisite period of enjoyment is 40 years.

23–159 Light which is refracted through glass remains "light" within the meaning of the Act and the refraction does not constitute an "interruption" as understood by s.4.[256]

23–160 Unlike ss.1 and 2, s.3 did not refer to the Crown and so it was not possible to acquire an easement of light under the Act over Crown land, but there is no legal presumption that the State is not bound by a statute.[257]

LCLRA 2009 s.33
A New Statutory Prescription

23–161 The acquisition of easements and *profits à prendre* by prescription is dealt with in Ch.1 of Pt 8 of the LCLRA 2009. Section 33 defines "dominant land" as "land benefited by an easement or *profit à prendre* to which other land is subject or in respect of which a relevant user period has commenced", and gives a corresponding definition of servient land as being "land subject to an easement or *profit à prendre* or in respect of which a relevant user period has commenced". The critical concept of a relevant user period is defined as "a period of user as of right without interruption by the person claiming to be the dominant owner or owner of *profit à prendre* in gross" for a minimum of 12 years where the servient owner is not a State authority and of 30 years where it is a State authority. The prescription period is 60 years where the servient land is the foreshore. Consistently with the common law principles discussed above, "user as of right" is defined as "use or enjoyment without force, without secrecy and without the oral or written consent of the servient owner."

23–162 Unlike the Prescription (Ireland) Act 1858, there is no difference as to periods between categories of easement or between easements and *profits à prendre*. The only difference is where the servient land is State-owned or the foreshore. Otherwise the relevant user period is 12 years in all cases.

---

[254] *Jordeson v Sutton, Southcoates & Drypool Gas Co* [1898] 2 Ch. 614 at 626, affirmed on appeal: [1899] 2 Ch. 217.

[255] *Hanna v Pollock* [1900] 2 I.R. 664; *Tisdall v McArthur & Co (Steel & Metal) Ltd* [1951] I.R. 228 at 241 although the Supreme Court did not decide the point on appeal: 246–248. It was suggested in the English case of *Tapling v Jones* (1865) 11 H.L.C. 290, that the Act had abolished the doctrine as to easements of light.

[256] *Tisdall v McArthur* [1951] I.R. 228.

[257] *Howard v Commissioners of Public Works* [1994] 1 I.R. 122.

23–163 Section 35 of the LCLRA 2009, as amended, introduces a new method of acquiring easements or profits by prescription. Section 49A of the Registration of Title Act 1964[258] now provides for the establishment and registration of non-contentious claims in prescription for easements and profits, by application to the Property Registration Authority. This was enacted following concerns about the effects of s.35(1) of the LCLRA 2009,[259] and has been described as a "novel and practical reform".[260] Under s.49A easements may be registered in the Land Registry where the Property Registration Authority is satisfied that the applicant has either (a) fulfilled the requirements of the Prescription Acts or (b) a right to an easement at common law or under the doctrine of lost modern grant. Although the language of s.49A does not expressly require that the servient tenant holder assent to the application, the s.49A scheme is not designed to deal with disputed cases.[261]

23–164 Section 35(2) provides that, in an action to establish or dispute the acquisition by prescription of an easement "the court shall make an order declaring the existence of the easement or *profit à prendre* if it is satisfied that there was a relevant user period immediately before the commencement of the action." This is similar to the "next before ... action" requirement in s.4 of the Prescription Act 1832. However, subs.(3) provides that the court may make such an order even if "the relevant user period was not immediately before the commencement of the action if it is satisfied that it is just and equitable to do so in the circumstances of the case". One must presume that this saver is designed to apply primarily to marginal cases, where the claimed right can be shown to have been enjoyed for a long time but there is insufficient evidence of such enjoyment in the period immediately preceding the action.[262] An easement or *profit à prendre* can be acquired at law by prescription only upon registration of the court order[263] in either the Land Registry of the Registry of Deeds, as appropriate.[264]

---

[258] Inserted by s.41 of the Civil Law (Miscellaneous Provisions) Act 2011.

[259] See P. Bland, "A 'Hopeless Jumble': the Cursed Reform of Prescription" (2011) 16(3) C.P.L.J. 54.

[260] Bland, *Easements* (2015), para.7–01.

[261] See Property Registration Authority, "Practice Direction, Easements and Profits à Prendre Acquired by Prescription under Section 49A" (February 2013), para.9.

[262] This provision was not included in the equivalent section of the Land and Conveyancing Law Reform Bill 2006. It can hardly be envisaged as applying to the kind of situation that arose in *Orwell Park Management Ltd v Henihan* [2004] IEHC 87, where there was almost three decades of non-proven user prior to action, especially in light of the abolition of lost modern grant by s.34. However, the legislative intention may have been to mitigate the immediate effect of this abolition by providing for some judicial latitude. The absence from the legislation of any structure or context other than the requirement of the exercise of the discretion being "just and equitable in the circumstances of the case" is likely to prove a source of lawyerly tussling in the times ahead.

[263] LCLRA 2009 s.35(1). Presumably, following the court order, and until registration, the declared easement or *profit à prendre* has effect in equity.

[264] LCLRA 2009 s.35(4).

Interruption

23–165 The new scheme of statutory prescription retains the concepts of "interruption" and "deductions" contained, respectively, in ss.4 and 7 of the Prescription Act 1832. However, somewhat confusingly, both concepts are defined as being an "interruption" which is then stated as having different consequences in different contexts. Primarily, an "interruption" has the effect, as in s.4 of the Prescription Act 1832, of stopping the flow of enjoyment giving rise to the claimed right so that it must commence all over again. The relevant user period "means a period of user as of right without interruption" by the claimant. Section 33 defines interruption as

"interference with, or cessation of, the use or enjoyment of an easement or *profit à prendre* for a continuous period of at least one year, but does not include an interruption under section 37(1)."

23–166 This first and principal strand of this definition is similar to s.4 of the Prescription Act 1832 in that an act of interruption lasting for a year has the effect of terminating the period of enjoyment in terms of the prospective accrual of a property right. However, there are several points of divergence:

- Interruption constitutes a factual interference, and does not require to have been submitted to or acquiesced in by the aspirant dominant owner.
- There is no requirement, as there had been, that for the interruption to be effective the party claiming the right shall have had notice of it and of the identity of the person making or authorising the interruption.
- The definition of interruption as also including cessation means that not in every case will the putative servient owner or any other party be involved: cessation of enjoyment of the right for a continuous period of one year will be an interruption for the purpose of the Act.[265]

23–167 To the extent of these considerations, it should henceforth be easier for an interruption in its new definition to terminate the process of acquisition of an easement or *profit à prendre* by prescription than under the Prescription Act 1832. However, to constitute an interruption, the interference or cessation must last for a "continuous" period of at least a year.

Deductions

23–168 The only statutory deduction permissible under the LCLRA 2009 is in the context of an interruption as that term is understood by s.37. Subsection (1) provides that this arises "where the servient owner is incapable, whether at the commencement of or during the relevant user period, of managing his or her affairs because of a mental incapacity", in which event "the running of that period is suspended until the incapacity ceases." However, the deduction

---

[265] This gives added force to the observations of Pigot C.B. in *Wilson v Stanley* (1861) 12 I.C.L.R. 345.

will not occur if at least 30 years have elapsed since the commencement of the relevant user period,[266] or where

"the court considers that it is reasonable, in the circumstances of the case, to have expected some other person, whether as trustee, committee of a ward of court, an attorney under an enduring power of attorney or otherwise, to have acted on behalf of the servient owner during the relevant user period".[267]

Tenancies

23–169 Section 36 deals with the situation where either or both of the dominant and servient tenements is held under a lease or tenancy. If the *dominant* tenement is held under tenancy, the easement or *profit à prendre* attaches to the land, the benefit of it passing to the landlord after the tenancy has ended. If the *servient* tenement is held under tenancy, the easement or *profit à prendre* ends once the tenancy ends, but it will attach to any renewal or extension of that tenancy for as long as that renewal or extension lasts, or to any superior interest in the land acquired by the servient owner. Where a tenancy against which an easement or *profit à prendre* had been acquired by prescription comes to an end, the relevant right can be acquired in turn against the landlord after he or she resumes possession, but on the basis of the commencement of a new relevant user period.

Transitional Arrangements

23–170 The effect of ss.34 and 38 is that prescription at common law and under the doctrine of lost modern grant were both abolished as methods of acquiring an easement or *profit à prendre* with effect from 1 December 2009. However, up until 30 November 2012, an action could be taken to establish a right to an easement or *profit à prendre* based upon either prescription at common law or the doctrine of lost modern grant or the Prescription (Ireland) Act 1858. Henceforth, a claim by prescription will be under Ch.1 of Pt 8 of the LCLRA 2009 only. Where user as of right, without either interruption or deduction has been established for a full period of 12 years after 1 December 2009, a claim can be mounted under the LCLRA 2009 regardless of for how little or how long the claimed right has been enjoyed prior to that date. In effect, this means that the earliest date on which a claim can be made to an easement or *profit à prendre* by prescription under the LCLRA 2009 is 2 December 2021, except in cases where a claim was made under the old law by 30 November 2012.

Estoppel

23–171 A small body of case law demonstrates that in certain circumstances a court may deem a party to be estopped from denying the grant of an easement

---

[266] LCLRA 2009 s.37(2)(b).
[267] LCLRA 2009 s.37(2)(a).

to another party, where an informal or unenforceable agreement is found to exist between the parties and the other party has acted to his or her detriment in reliance upon it.

23–172 In *Annally Hotel v Bergin*[268] the plaintiffs owned a hotel and the defendant an adjoining yard. The hotel had been erected on the site of an earlier building and its owners claimed "ancient lights", i.e. an easement to light acquired by presumed grant, in respect of windows overlooking the defendant's yard.[269] When the plans for the hotel building were drawn up they included two windows at a low level in the same position as windows in the earlier building. The plans were shown to the defendant's father, the then owner of the yard, who made no objection to them. However, when the construction reached the level of the proposed windows the defendant's father asked that they be put at a higher position in the wall as he might want to extend his own building in the yard at the lower level. The plaintiffs agreed although it caused them considerable inconvenience. They asked that the agreement be put in writing but the defendant's father refused. Later, the defendant erected screens which obscured the hotel windows which had been put at the higher position.

23–173 Teevan J., in the High Court, held that where there was an agreement, however informal, to allow a right to light and, relying on that agreement, a person proceeds without a deed of grant to erect, and spends money on erecting, the windows in a building which, to be serviceable, must have the claimed right to light, and the other person acquiesces in the acts of reliance, then the person who acquiesces will not be permitted to deny the right nor to rely on the absence of a grant.

23–174 The reason given by the judge is reason enough to justify an estoppel against the defendant's father, but not against the son. To explain that result one can only conclude that the estoppel gave rise to an equity, and specifically an easement of light applying to the windows at the higher level. The case should therefore be regarded as an instance of proprietary estoppel.

23–175 In *Crabb v Arun District Council*[270] the executors of A owned a 5½-acre plot. They divided it into a 3½-acre plot and a 2-acre plot and sold the 2-acre plot to the plaintiff, Crabb. It was proposed to build a new road between the two plots which would give access to the main road. The conveyance to Crabb granted him an access point (point A) on the boundary of the two plots, onto the new link road, and also a right of way over this to the main road. Later, the executors conveyed the 3½-acre plot to the defendant, Arun District Council, expressly reserving the right of way from point A. Crabb later decided to divide his plot into two and to sell the northern portion

---

[268] (1970) 104 I.L.T.R. 65.
[269] If such rights existed as to windows in the earlier building they would continue for the benefit of the present building as to windows in the same position.
[270] [1976] Ch. 179.

which contained point A. At a meeting with a representative of the defendant in 1967 he explained his plan and pointed out that he would need access to the new road at another point (point B) to serve the southern portion which he intended to retain. The defendant's representative gave the plaintiff an assurance that this would be acceptable to the defendant. Although no formal grant was made to the plaintiff of any exit at point B or easement of way over the new road from that point, the parties thereafter acted in the belief that he had been or would be granted such a right. In early 1968 the defendant erected the boundary fence and constructed gates at points A and B. The gates were clearly intended to be permanent. In September 1968 the plaintiff agreed to sell the northern portion. In the belief that he had a right of access to the southern portion at point B, he did not reserve for himself as owner of the southern portion any right of way over the link road where it ran alongside the northern portion.

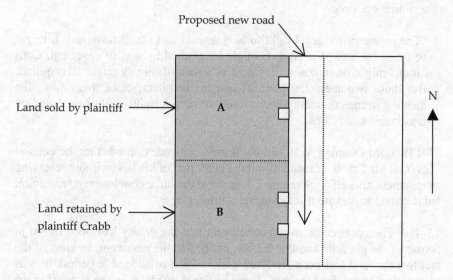

23-176 In January 1969, the defendant removed the gates at point B and closed up the access by extending the fence across the gap. It offered to grant a right of access and an easement of way along the link road on payment of £3,000 by the plaintiff. The plaintiff was unwilling to pay and so, without any access, the southern portion was rendered useless to him. In 1971 he began proceedings claiming a declaration that he was entitled to a right of way from the southern portion along the new road and an injunction restraining the defendant from interfering with his enjoyment of the right of way.

23-177 The trial judge held that, although there was "agreement in principle" at the meeting between Mr Crabb and the council, there was no contract to grant an easement and that, in any event, an oral contract would be unenforceable without written evidence under the English Land Act 1925 which replaced the Statute of Frauds.[271]

23–178 In the Court of Appeal Lord Denning M.R., Lawton and Scarman L.JJ. held that the absence of written evidence was not fatal to the plaintiff's claim. An assurance or expectation had been created by the council and the plaintiff had acted to his detriment in acting upon the belief so created that an easement would be granted. He had sold the other plot without reserving a right of way to point A. Lord Denning M.R. rejected the argument that the "agreement in principle" was conditional on a legal grant. Any such anticipated formality had, in effect, been dispensed with by the action of the defendant council in putting up the gates at point B at considerable expense to itself, which would have led the plaintiff to believe that it had agreed that he should have the right of access through point B without more ado.[272] Scarman L.J. was of a similar opinion:

"The nature of the legal right to be granted had to be determined. It might be given by way of licence. It might be granted by way of easement. Conditions might be imposed. Payment of a sum of money might be required. But those two men, the plaintiff and his architect, came away from the meeting in the confident expectation that such a right would be granted on reasonable conditions."[273]

23–179 Lord Denning M.R. did not think it was relevant whether the council knew that Mr Crabb intended to sell the other part of his land without reserving an easement himself.[274] Scarman L.J. came to the same conclusion on the point, but declined to elevate it into a general principle.[275]

23–180 The court came to the conclusion that the equity had been raised in favour of the plaintiff and that he was entitled to the easement. In view of the fact that the land had been rendered useless for a considerable period, he was not required to pay for the grant. There had been no claim by the plaintiff in the original action for damages for loss caused by the sterilisation of the land, and although it was held in later proceedings[276] before the Court of Appeal that the court would have had power to grant such damages, the court held that since the issue had not been raised at the trial or the appeal of the original action, it was now too late to do so.

---

[271] The Act 1925 s.40 has now been repealed in England by the Law of Property (Miscellaneous Provisions) Act 1989. Contracts for sale, etc. of land in England now have to be made by signed writing.
[272] [1976] Ch. 179 at 189.
[273] [1976] Ch. 179 at 196.
[274] [1976] Ch. 179 at 189.
[275] [1976] Ch. 179 at 198.
[276] *Crabb v Arun DC (No.2)* (1977) 121 S.J. 86.

23–181 Atiyah[277] criticised the case on the ground that it was unnecessary to decide it upon the basis of proprietary estoppel. In his view it could have been decided on the basis of contract. Was there really a difference between a verbal expectation or assurance intended to be acted upon and a promise? There had been, as the court found, an agreement between the parties in *Crabb*. The absence of written evidence should not have been fatal to this contract, on account of the doctrine of part performance, the alternative to the Statute of Frauds, which has traditionally been accepted by courts of equity.

23–182 Millet,[278] who appeared as one of the counsel for the plaintiff in *Crabb*, replied to Atiyah's criticism. Counsel for the plaintiff had conceded in both courts that there was no enforceable contract, he pointed out, and therefore, although one could criticise the wisdom of this concession, one could not legitimately criticise the judges who were bound by it. Millet argued that there were manifold difficulties with the contract proposition, namely (a) in establishing an agreement at all, (b) in proving consideration, (c) in establishing that there was either writing or an act of part performance and (d) on the issue of whether the officers of the defendant council had actual or ostensible authority as agents to bind the council. According to Millet, the action of Crabb in selling the upper plot without reserving an easement of way was not an act of part performance of the agreement, as it was no part of the agreement that Crabb sell the land.

23–183 The last point is no doubt correct, and to suggest otherwise is to confuse detrimental reliance in estoppel with part performance in contract. But it is arguable that there were other acts which constituted part performance, such as the use of point B by Crabb and possibly the attaching of a padlock to the gate. As to the other arguments, the Court of Appeal found that the parties' actions were only explainable if there was an agreement, that it had been agreed that Crabb should pay a reasonable amount and that therefore there was in fact consideration, even if the amount had not been precisely quantified. However, it remains questionable whether the parties in *Crabb* had reached an agreement as to the price to be paid for the grant that was sufficiently definite to form a contract, or, as Millet maintains, whether there was any agreement at all. Be that as it may, the case illustrates that the device of "estoppel as a sword" may inevitably begin to occupy some of the ground previously covered by contract. One should not in any event accept the assumption that merely because the case could have been decided in contract it could not also have been decided on the grounds of proprietary estoppel.

---

[277] P.S. Atiyah, "When is an Enforceable Agreement not a Contract? Answer: When it is an Equity" (1976) 92 L.Q.R. 174.

[278] P. Millet, "*Crabb v Arun District Council* - A Riposte!" (1976) 92 L.Q.R. 342. He later became a judge of the Chancery Division.

23–184 The principle in *Crabb* was applied by Gannon J. in *Dunne v Molloy*.[279] The plaintiff sought to assert a right of way over the defendant's land. Failing to satisfy the requirements necessary to acquire the easement by prescription or lost modern grant, he attempted to establish his right to an easement on the basis of estoppel by conduct. Gannon J. on appeal dismissed the claim on the ground that the plaintiff had not established that the defendant encouraged him to act to his detriment. More recently, the principles of estoppel enunciated in both *Annally Hotel v Bergin*[280] and *Crabb v Arun District Council*[281] have been cited with approval but found not to apply, in *Frank Towey Ltd v South Dublin County Council*,[282] another case of a claimed right of way.

EXTINGUISHING EASEMENTS AND PROFITS

By Statute Generally

23–185 There are a number of statutes which provide for the extinguishment of easements and *profits à prendre* by public bodies or officials. Section 18 of the Land Act 1965 gives power to the Property Registration Authority to cancel the registration of sporting rights, other than fishing rights, where they have not been exercised for 12 years after the Act came into force. It follows that there is no power under the Land Act 1965 to cancel the registration of such a right where a period of 12 years' disuse began after the Act came into force. This once-and-for-all effect of the provision is probably because it was seen as part of the land purchase legislation.

23–186 Section 29 of the Turf Development Act 1946 gives Bord na Móna power to terminate "any easement, wayleave, water right or other right whatsoever over or in respect of land or water" in connection with the acquisition of land for its statutory purposes.[283] There is a similar provision in s.19 of the Forestry Act 1946.

23–187 A *profit à prendre* may be extinguished where the servient tenement is designated as a Special Area of Conservation (SAC) under the European Communities (Natural Habitats) Regulations 1997.[284]

---

[279] [1976–77] I.L.R.M. 266.

[280] (1970) 104 I.L.T.R. 65.

[281] [1976] Ch. 179.

[282] [2005] IEHC 93.

[283] The constitutionality of the section was challenged, unsuccessfully, in *O'Brien v Bord na Móna* [1983] I.R. 255 at 314.

[284] S.I. No. 94 of 1997, made under the European Communities Act 1972, implementing Council Directive 92/43/EEC.

LCLRA 2009

23–188 Section 39 of the LCLRA 2009 introduces qualified extinguishment of easements and *profits à prendre* as a converse to the provisions in s.35 for their acquisition by prescription. Section 39(1) states:

"On the expiry of a 12 year continuous period of non-user of an easement or *profit à prendre* acquired by (a) prescription, or (b) implied grant or reservation, the easement or *profit à prendre* is extinguished except where it is protected by registration in the Registry of Deeds or the Land Registry, as appropriate."

23–189 Section 33 defines "period of non-user" as "a period during which the dominant owner ceases to use or enjoy the easement or *profit à prendre*". There is no requirement here of evidence of intention to abandon or the presuming of such intention. Once non-enjoyment has occurred continuously for the requisite period, extinguishment follows. This result is automatic and there is no stated requirement for a court order such as is necessary, in accordance with s.35, to acquire an easement or *profit à prendre* by prescription.

23–190 There are situations in which statutory extinguishment under the LCLRA 2009 will *not* occur, regardless of there being found to have elapsed a continuous 12-year period of non-user:

1. where the easement or *profit à prendre* has been acquired by express grant or reservation;
2. where the easement or *profit à prendre* has been acquired at law by prescription under the LCLRA 2009, except in accordance with the transitional arrangements where the old law applies in the case of an action instituted prior to 30 November 2012. This is because, in order for an easement or *profit à prendre* to be acquired at law by prescription under the Act, according to s.35(1) it must be on foot of a court order which is duly registered. In this situation, s.39 is expressly stated as not applying. Where an easement or *profit à prendre* has been acquired under the Act pursuant to a court order, but that court order has not been registered, an equitable easement or *profit à prendre* will have been acquired, the right to which is liable to be extinguished under s.39. This demonstrates that the statutory obligation to register the court order declaring the existence of the easement or *profit à prendre*, in either the Registry of Deeds or the Land Registry, is more than a mere cosmetic obligation. Failure to do so puts the right so acquired at risk of being automatically extinguished if there is subsequently a proven 12-year period of continuous non-user on the part of the dominant owner.

23–191 The rights of the dominant owners of easements or *profits à prendre* acquired by presumed grant or prescription or by implied grant or reservation prior to the coming into effect of the LCLRA 2009, on 1 December 2009, are tangentially protected by s.39(2) which provides that the section applies even in the cases of easements or *profits à prendre* earlier acquired provided that at least three years of the period of non-user take place after 1 December 2009. This means that the owners of rights at risk of being statutorily extinguished have the opportunity of anchoring their rights, either:

- by seeking to have them recognised under the "old law" through a court action taken not later than 30 November 2012, in accordance with s.38(b); or
- by resuming enjoyment in sufficient time to prevent application of the statutory definition of non-user in s.33 and so prevent the consequence of extinguishment stipulated in s.39.

23–192 Where the easement or *profit à prendre* has been acquired either by express grant or reservation, or by prescription under the LCLRA 2009 pursuant to a court order that has been duly registered, the provisions of s.39 will not apply, and extinguishment of the relevant right, if it occurs, can only be on the basis of the established principles of common law considered below. This is ensured by s.39(3) which provides that nothing in the section "affects the jurisdiction of the court to declare that an easement or *profit à prendre*, however acquired, has been abandoned or extinguished".

Implied Release
23–193 The law has long recognised that an easement may be held to have ceased to exist on account of sustained behaviour by the dominant owner inconsistent with its continuance. This can range from excessive user, such that the dominant owner is deemed to have destroyed the easement,[285] to prolonged non-user in circumstances indicative of an intention to abandon it. Technically, where an easement has been destroyed through over-use one speaks of extinguishment, whereas protracted non-use can occasion abandonment. In the latter situation, the courts look, not only to the length of time that the right has been continuously not enjoyed, but also to some demonstration on the part of the dominant owner, either never again to enjoy the easement on his or her own account or never to assign the right to enjoyment to another party.[286] Abandonment based on non-user buttressed by evidence of intention is sometimes known as implied release. It has not been found to arise where the period of non-enjoyment is less than 20 years.[287]

---

[285] *Craig v McCance* (1910) 44 I.L.T.R. 90; *White v Callan* [2006] 2 I.L.R.M. 92.
[286] *Cullen v Dublin Corporation*, unreported, Supreme Court, 22 July 1960; *Orwell Park Management Ltd v Henihan* [2004] IEHC 87.
[287] In *Mulville v Fallon* (1872) I.R. 6 Eq. 458, Chatterton V.C., at 463, stated that once there had been a cessation of user of the right, coupled with any act clearly indicative of an intention to abandon it, "if such intention be thus shown, the duration of the cesser need not be for twenty years or any other defined period."

23–194 In *O'Gara v Murray*[288] the parties were two adjoining owners of premises in Connolly Street in Sligo. Since commercial access to the defendant's licensed premises was prevented by its having been blocked off, the only service access was by the rear of the premises through use of a way to which the defendant at that time admitted having no title. A lease of 1912 showed a gap in the rear boundary wall and some form of way giving access to the rear. The right of way had been used until the 1950s since when it had fallen into disuse and become overgrown. Later, it was cultivated as a vegetable garden by the plaintiff. The defendant had at some time since 1912 enlarged the gap in the rear boundary wall without the permission of the plaintiff. The gap had been filled in after 1960. McCarthy J. stated the position as follows:

"A right of way or other easement may be released expressly or impliedly; such implied release may arise where it is established that there was an intention on the part of the owner of the easement to abandon it. Mere cesser of user may not be enough; cesser of user coupled with incidents indicating abandonment may well be enough."

23–195 Among the factors indicating abandonment in the instant case were: (a) the use as a vegetable garden of the area over which the right existed, (b) the filling in of the wall, and (c) the creation of a way along a different area. The judge held that whatever right of way existed in 1912 had been released by "cesser of use and surrounding circumstances".

23–196 In *Carroll v Sheridan and Sheehan*,[289] O'Hanlon J. held (i) that mere evidence of non-user is not sufficient to bring about the extinguishment of private rights of way,[290] and (ii) that a presumption of abandonment, which is not lightly to be inferred,[291] required to be supported by evidence of conduct or intention adverse to the exercise of the right.[292] He further held *obiter*[293] that public rights over highways cannot be lost by disuse. In the case of a public right of way, there was a presumption that "once a highway, always a highway", as the public is incapable of releasing its rights.[294] Hence, in a case where the sides of the way had become covered with furze and heath, and fir trees had grown during 25 years, the public could claim the right to have the verdure cleared.[295] On the other hand, where a road had been closed up for more than 60 years, the public excluded, and an alternative road laid, the court was prepared to presume that the procedures for statutory extinguishment had

---

[288] Unreported, High Court, McCarthy J., 10 November 1988.
[289] [1984] I.L.R.M. 451.
[290] *R. v Choley* (1848) 12 Q.B. 515.
[291] *Gotobed v Pridmore* (1970) 115 S.J. 78.
[292] *R. v Choley* (1848) 12 Q.B. 515; *Ward v Ward* (1852) 7 Ex. 838; *Crossley v Lightowler* (1867) 2 Ch. App. 478.
[293] The appellants had not alleged a public right of way in their pleadings and the judge refused to allow them to amend them on appeal.
[294] *Dawes v Hawkins* (1860) 8 C.B. (ns) 848.
[295] *Turner v Ringwood Highway Board* (1870) L.R. 9 Eq. 418.

been invoked.[296] In the case of a private right of way, the principle had been established that mere evidence of non-user was not sufficient to bring about the extinction of "discontinuous" easements (those, by their nature, not used incessantly, such as a right of way), abandonment in such situations only being treated as having occurred where the person entitled had demonstrated a fixed intention never at any time thereafter to assert the right himself or herself or to attempt to transmit it to anyone else.[297]

Unity of Ownership and Possession

23–197 If the dominant and servient tenements come into the same ownership then any easements and *profits à prendre* will cease to exist as separate rights and will merge into the general rights of an owner as to his or her own property.

RENTCHARGES

Introduction

23–198 A *rent-service* is a form of rent that is incidental to feudal tenure. The original form was a service of freehold tenure, but an analogous form was developed as to leaseholds, which is the form of rent most familiar to people today. The remedy of the feudal lord where a rent-service remained unpaid was distress, and since this was an attribute of tenure it did not have to be expressly granted, but applied automatically, i.e. by operation of law. This again was a feature of a pre-market economy that it did not leave to the parties the creation of remedies but imposed them by general law. A basic principle early recognised was that a rentcharge could only be charged on or attached to a corporeal hereditament. This is sometimes rendered by the maxim that there can be no rentcharge on a rentcharge.[298] Freehold rent-services continue to exist in Ireland by the creation of new tenures in fee simple since *Quia Emptores* 1290 under *non obstante* grants.

23–199 *Quia Emptores* has now been repealed by s.8(3) of the LCLRA 2009. Section 41 prohibits the creation of a rentcharge at law or in equity, except pursuant to a contract to do so made before 1 December 2009, or by order of the court or under a statutory provision. Most rent-services today, however, are rents attached to the modern landlord and tenant relationship created under Deasy's Act 1860, which can also apply to freehold estates.

23–200 Rents which were not the services of tenure, freehold or leasehold, were known as *rents seck*, or "dry" rents. They were "dry" because the remedy of distress did not automatically apply to them. Thus, if A conveyed a

---

[296] *Representative Church Body v Barry* [1918] 1 I.R. 402.

[297] *Tehidy Minerals Ltd v Norman* [1971] 2 Q.B. 528 at 533.

[298] *Re the Alms Corn Charity* [1901] 2 Ch. 750 at 759. In England since 1925 a rentcharge on a rentcharge is valid: Law of Property Act 1925 s.122.

fee simple to B and A reserved a rent for herself without creating the modern landlord and tenant relationship under s.3 of Deasy's Act 1860, that rent was a rentcharge. Rentcharges have existed in Ireland since the Middle Ages. At common law a person entitled to a rentcharge was not entitled to distress unless the right had been expressly granted. Statutory policy has undergone an evolution, from extending the right of distress to owners of rentcharges from the 17th century onwards, when legislation tended to embody the interests of landowners, towards a more recent and democratic tendency to restrict and finally eliminate the remedy. The most recent embodiment of this is s.42 of the LCLRA 2009 which provides that, subject to any other statutory provision, from 1 December 2009, a rentcharge can be enforced as a simple contract debt only. Section 44 of the 1881 Act which had provided for other enforcement mechanisms has been repealed.

Creation in the Past

23–201 Many rentcharges were created by statute, the most important examples in Ireland being rentcharges created for land drainage and improvements under the Landed Property Improvement (Ireland) Act 1847[299] and land purchase annuities under the Land Purchase Acts. In the case of creating a rentcharge *inter vivos*, appropriate words of limitation had to be used. Grants of rentcharges for legal estates had to be by deed,[300] but equitable rentcharges could be created by any of the methods recognised in equity, such as an agreement to create a legal rentcharge or by proprietary estoppel or constructive trust. Under s.94 of the Succession Act 1965, which replaces the same provision in s.28 of the Wills Act 1837, the whole interest in a rentcharge passes in a will without the use of special words of limitation.

Enforcement

23–202 The person liable to pay a freehold rentcharge is the *terre tenant* (from Norman French "terre" meaning land), i.e. the freeholder in possession.[301] "In possession" is used in the technical sense, meaning, in the old sense, the person who has seisin of the land, or as it would be expressed today, the holder of the immediate freehold estate. For example, if the land subject to a rentcharge in fee simple held by X is held by A in fee simple but has been let for 10 years to B, the *terre tenant* is A. A, not B, is liable to pay the rentcharge. X's action was originally one of the real actions and so lay against the *terre tenant* because he or she had seisin of the land. Furthermore, distress was levied against the person in actual occupation of the land. In freehold tenure the lord of a tenure could *lawfully* distrain against any goods he found on the land and when the remedy was extended to persons entitled to rentcharges the same

---

[299] The English statute is the Improvement of Land Act 1864.
[300] *Hewlins v Shippam* (1826) 5 B. & C. 221.
[301] *Swift v Kelly* (1889) 24 L.R. Ir. 478 at 485–486.

rules were applied, although of course the rentcharge owner was not the lord of the tenure.

23–203 The position as to rentcharges held for leasehold estates is less clear. If R holds land in fee simple and grants T a term of 99 years and reserves a rent, then the rent is a rent-service, not a rentcharge, but if the land in the hands of R was already subject to a rentcharge in favour of Y for a term of years, could Y seek to enforce the rentcharge against R or T, or both? If the answer is both, then Y would be in a more favourable position than if he or she had a freehold rentcharge, because then Y could seek to enforce only against R. There is some authority for the view that the owner of a leasehold rentcharge can proceed against the leaseholder of the land.[302] If so, then every person intending to enter into a lease or tenancy should ask whether the land is subject to any leasehold rentcharges or require the landlord to enter into an indemnity. A rentcharge can now be enforced only as a simple contract debt except in a case of express statutory provision to the contrary.[303]

Extinguishment

23–204 If a rentcharge remains unclaimed for 12 years the title to it is barred by s.13(2) of the Statute of Limitations 1957.[304] At common law if the possession or ownership of the land and the rentcharge vest in the same person the rentcharge is extinguished by merger, regardless of the intention of the parties. A rentcharge may be also released by deed.

23–205 In a case where a rentcharge qualifies as a "ground rent" under the Landlord and Tenant (Ground Rents) (No. 2) Act 1978 the owner of the land has the "right to acquire the fee simple" free of the rent.

FRANCHISES

23–206 The common law recognised that the Crown could grant exclusive rights, i.e. monopolies, to individuals, known as franchises. These were grants of part of the royal prerogative, such as the right to hold fairs or markets,[305] to

---

[302] *Re Herbage Rents* [1896] 2 Ch. 811.

[303] LCLRA 2009 s.42.

[304] Section 13(2) refers to "land" and s.2 defines "land" as including a rentcharge (but not other incorporeal hereditaments).

[305] *Waugh v Treasurer of The Grand Jury of Cork* (1847) 11 Ir. C.L.R. 451; *Russell v Beakey* (1846) 8 Ir. Eq. R. 559; *Cork Corporation v Shinkwin* (1825) Sm. & Bat. 395; *Midleton (Lord) v Power* (1886) 19 L.R. Ir. 1.

wrecks[306] and to treasure trove[307] and the right to fish in rivers and tidal waters. The right to grant fishing rights in rivers and tidal waters was taken away from the Crown by Magna Carta 1215 which prohibited such grants after the date of the charter. Any such fisheries as can be proved to have been granted before Magna Carta still exist today.[308]

OBSOLETE HEREDITAMENTS

23–207 Obsolete hereditaments include tithe rentcharges, advowsons and titles of honour.[309]

---

[306] *The Jeane Adolphe* (1857) 2 Ir. Jur. (ns) 285; W.N. Osborough, "Discoveries from Armada Wrecks" (1970) 5 Ir. Jur. (ns) 88; S. Dromgoole, "Protection of Historic Wreck: the UK Approach. Part 1: The Present Legal Framework" (1989) 4(1) I.J.E.C.L. 26; "Protection of Historic Wreck: the UK approach. Part 2: Towards Reform (1989) 4(2) I.J.E.C.L. 95. See now Merchant Shipping (Salvage and Wreck) Act 1993.

[307] *Attorney General v Trustees of the British Museum* [1903] 2 Ch. 598 at 608. The case is discussed in Ch.2 ("Land").

[308] *Little v Cooper* [1937] I.R. 1; *Moore v Attorney General* [1934] I.R. 44.

[309] These are discussed in earlier editions of this book.

CHAPTER 24

Mortgages

No one ... by the light of nature ever understood an English mortgage of real estate.

— Lord Macnaghten in *Samuel v Jarrah Timber & Wood Paving Corporation Ltd* [1904] A.C. 323 at 326

INTRODUCTION

24–01 A mortgage is a form of security interest which can be granted to a creditor in order to secure the performance of a contractual obligation (usually the repayment of a debt). The mortgage is an important mechanism for taking security in both commercial and residential property transactions. Irish mortgage law was substantially overhauled by the Land and Conveyancing Law Reform Act 2009 ("LCLRA 2009"). The intervening years have seen an increased interest in regulatory and legislative activity in this area. The Central Bank of Ireland has introduced regulations[1] and codes of practice[2] aimed at enhancing consumer protection in a number of different aspects of residential mortgages. The European Union has also introduced a directive in this area which has recently been implemented in Ireland.[3] Reform of personal insolvency and bankruptcy laws has also significantly impacted on this area.

HISTORY

24–02 Early feudal law regarded credit with suspicion. Making money out of money was religiously condemned as usury. As capitalism developed,

---

[1] Central Bank (Supervision and Enforcement) Act 2013 (Section 48) (Housing Loan Requirements) Regulations 2015 (S.I. No. 47 of 2015); Central Bank (Supervision and Enforcement) Act 2013 (Section 48) (Housing Loan Requirements) (Amendment) Regulations 2016 (S.I. No. 568 of 2016).

[2] Central Bank of Ireland, *Code of Conduct on Mortgage Arrears* (Dublin: Central Bank). The Code has been amended on several occasions.

[3] Directive 2014/17/EU of the European Parliament and of the Council of 4 February 2014 on credit agreements for consumers relating to residential immovable property and amending Directives 2008/48/EC and 2013/36/EU and Regulation (EU) No 1093/2010 [2014] OJ L60/34; implemented in Ireland by the European Union (Consumer Mortgage Credit Agreements) Regulations 2016 (S.I. No. 142 of 2016).

however, methods were found of avoiding the feudal prohibition.[4] The borrower would lease land to the lender who would go into possession. The lender could then obtain repayment from the income derived from the borrower's land. Such a transaction was known as a *vivum vadium* or living pledge. A second form of transaction was the *mortuum vadium*, or dead pledge, in which the lender went into possession of the borrower's land and used the income to pay off only the interest on the loan leaving the capital outstanding.[5] The dead pledge could lead to the borrower being unable to repay the capital sum, particularly if he was a small farmer or peasant and the land represented his main source of income.

24–03 A later practice created security over land through the manipulation of the ownership of estates. This took two main forms. The borrower could grant a lease of one kind or another to the lender (a mortgage by demise) or the borrower would convey his freehold estate to the lender with a covenant for reconveyance on the repayment of the loan.[6] These forms of mortgage could yield harsh results. The date set in the deed for the repayment of the loan, known as the *legal date of redemption*, was decisive. If the debtor did not repay the debt on that date, then the condition for reconveyance could not be enforced and the lender was left with the fee simple absolute. To remedy this situation, Chancery evolved the *equity of redemption*. Equity declared it unreasonable that the lender should retain for his own benefit what was intended as a mere security. Initially, equitable intervention was only available where the borrower would suffer some special hardship as a result of forfeiture, but by the early 17th century, it had become generally available. In 1675, Lord Nottingham held:

"In natural justice and equity the principal right of the mortgagee is to the money, and his right to the land is only as security for the money."[7]

24–04 By the 17th century, courts of equity had come to treat the equity of redemption as a form of equitable property right which could be dealt with by the debtor.[8]

FINANCIAL AND REGULATORY ASPECTS

24–05 The mortgage is a form of security for lending. The mortgage of real property can be, and is, used as a form of security for business and consumer

---

[4] See R.H. Tawney, *Religion and the Rise of Capitalism* (London: Murray, 1926), pp.36–55, 150–164, and 297, fn.69 for a description of devices to avoid the prohibition.

[5] 3 Bl Comm 156.

[6] A.W.B. Simpson, *A History of the Land Law*, 2nd edn (Oxford: Oxford University Press, 1986), pp.243–244.

[7] *Thornborough v Baker* (1675) 3 Swans. 628 at 630.

[8] See *Rosscarrick v Barton* (1673) 1 Ch. Cas. 217 and Simpson, *A History of the Land Law* (1986), pp.245–246.

lending. In the main, the terms of the underlying loan agreements are a matter of contract between the parties. Important terms of the loan agreement will include the loan amount, the term of the loan and the rate of interest to be charged.

24–06 Viewed from the perspective of the borrower, a short-term mortgage will typically be cheaper overall since less interest will accrue on the outstanding principal. On the other hand, where the loan is repaid on a monthly basis, a longer term will typically allow for a reduction in the amount to be repaid each month.

24–07 The maximum amount lent on the security of a mortgage will usually be connected to the value of the property which is to be offered to the lender as security. The lender will normally wish to ensure that the amount outstanding on the loan does not exceed the value of the property and will seek to build in a margin to allow for the possibility that the value of the property may fall, leaving the lender partially unsecured. The failure to make provision for the possibility of such a fall was a contributory factor in the collapse of the Irish banking sector during the financial crisis after 2008.[9] Where the value of the property is less than the amount outstanding on the loan, the borrower is said to be in "negative equity" since the proceeds of the property will not suffice to discharge the secured loan in the event of default. Negative equity was a significant feature of the Irish property market in the aftermath of the financial crisis, with one estimate suggesting that up to 64 per cent of mortgages drawn down between 2005 and 2012 were in negative equity in 2014.[10] Negative equity can produce unusual economic incentives for borrowers including the possibility of so-called "strategic default" where the borrower may, in certain circumstances, find it economically advantageous to default on loan repayments.[11]

24–08 In the aftermath of the financial crisis, the courts were asked on a number of occasions to consider whether individual borrowers might have any recourse against lenders for having engaged in "reckless lending". Such arguments have not met with success. In *ICS Building Society v Grant*,[12] Charleton J. held that the common law has no tort of reckless lending.[13] In *Healy v Stepstone Mortgages Funding Ltd*,[14] Hogan J. declined to further extend the law of torts to provide a remedy in such cases, holding that power

---

[9] Commission of Investigation into the Banking Sector in Ireland, *Misjudging Risk: Causes of the Systemic Banking Crisis in Ireland* (Dublin, 2011), paras 2.7.24 and 4.5.9–4.5.10. See also P. Honohan, *The Irish Banking Crisis: Regulatory and Financial Stability Policy 2003–2008* (Dublin, 2010), para.5.2.1.

[10] D. Duffy and N. O'Hanlon, "Negative Equity in Ireland: Estimates Using Loan-Level Data" (2014) 7(3) J. Eur. R.E.R. 327.

[11] G. Connor and T. Flavin, "Strategic Unaffordability and Dual-Trigger Mortgage Default in the Irish Mortgage Market" (2015) 28 J.H. Ec. 59.

[12] [2010] IEHC 117.

[13] Followed by Kelly J. in *McConnon v Zurich Bank Ireland* [2012] 1 I.R. 449.

[14] [2014] IEHC 134.

to develop wholly new categories of tortious liability rests with the Oireach-tas and not the courts. Although the legislature (through the Central Bank of Ireland) has now intervened to place limits on the amount of lending in the residential mortgage market, it is worth noting that breaches of these limits are not actionable by borrowers.

24–09 The key determinant of the cost of mortgage credit is the rate of inter-est to be charged. Again, this is a matter of contract for the parties to deter-mine, and mortgage lenders will normally offer a variety of options designed to attract customers to choose their services. Typically, loans may have fixed or variable rates of interest. Fixed interest rates may be applied for the entire duration of the loan term or for a portion thereof. A fixed interest rate may be to the borrower's advantage in circumstances where market interest rates rise while the interest rate is fixed. It also provides the borrower with a degree of certainty about the monthly cost of repayments. Where market rates fall dur-ing the fixed period, the arrangement will disadvantage the borrower. Where the interest rate is fixed, it is usual for the lender to charge a break fee/early redemption penalty should the borrower wish to repay the mortgage early. In the context of consumer borrowers, the amount of this fee is now controlled by the European Union (Consumer Mortgage Credit Agreements) Regulations 2016 (the "Consumer Mortgage Regulations"), reg.26 of which prohibits the imposition of any sanction on a consumer.[15]

24–10 Variable rate mortgage products permit the lender to vary the rate of interest. The lender's right to vary the interest rate may be capped at an upper rate or may be linked to a reference interest rate such as that set by the European Central Bank. The latter arrangement, known as a tracker mort-gage, became a common feature of the Irish residential mortgage market in the run up to the 2008 crisis. Tracker mortgages may pose a risk for lenders if their cost of borrowing money rises significantly above the reference rate. This problem was also cited as a causative factor in the Irish banking crisis.[16] Variable rate mortgages may be cheaper for the borrower, particularly where general interest rates remain low over the life of the mortgage. Generally, lend-ers do not charge early redemption fees where a variable rate mortgage loan is wholly or partially repaid during the mortgage term.

Housing Loans
24–11 In February 2015, the Central Bank of Ireland imposed limits on loans secured against residential property which can be granted by institutions

---

[15] European Union (Consumer Mortgage Credit Agreements) Regulations 2016 (S.I. No. 142 of 2016), reg.26. The regulations permit the lender to impose charges only where it incurs costs directly as a result of early repayment and caps early termination fees at the level of financial loss suffered by the lender.
[16] Commission of Investigation into the Banking Sector in Ireland, *Misjudging Risk: Causes of the Systemic Banking Crisis in Ireland* (Dublin, 2011), para.2.7.26.

regulated by the Central Bank.[17] These limits were subsequently amended in 2016 for transactions occurring after 1 January 2017.[18] A further amendment was made in December 2017 for transactions taking effect after 1 January 2018.[19]

24–12 The regulations limit the amount of money which can be advanced by banks in two ways. First, they prescribe a maximum loan-to-value ratio for different types of transaction. Where the borrower is a first-time buyer seeking to finance the purchase of a principal private residence, the ratio is capped at 90 per cent[20] Where the borrower is not a first-time buyer, the ratio is capped at 80 per cent,[21] while a 70 per cent limit is imposed where the property being acquired is not to be used as the borrower's principal residence.[22] The second limit imposed is that the mortgage amount may not exceed 3.5 times the borrower's gross annual income, though there is a degree of flexibility for financial institutions in applying these limits in individual loan applications and this limit does not apply where the loan is not for the purposes of financing the purchase of a principal private residence.[23]

Consumer Protection

24–13 Mortgage lending is the subject of a growing body of legislative and regulatory measures aimed at striking a balance between access to mortgage credit for consumers and the prevention of over-indebtedness and exploitative behaviour on the part of lenders. The law in this area is a complex mix of general consumer protection measures such as the European Communities (Unfair Terms in Consumer Contracts) Regulations 1995 (the "Unfair

---

[17] Central Bank (Supervision and Enforcement) Act 2013 (Section 48) (Housing Loan Requirements) Regulations 2015 (S.I. No. 47 of 2015).

[18] Central Bank (Supervision and Enforcement) Act 2013 (Section 48) (Housing Loan Requirements) (Amendment) Regulations 2016 (S.I. No. 568 of 2016).

[19] Central Bank (Supervision and Enforcement) Act 2013 (Section 48) (Housing Loan Requirements) Regulations 2017 (S.I. No. 559 of 2017).

[20] Central Bank (Supervision and Enforcement) Act 2013 (Section 48) (Housing Loan Requirements) Regulations 2015 reg.6(1)(b), as amended.

[21] Central Bank (Supervision and Enforcement) Act 2013 (Section 48) (Housing Loan Requirements) Regulations 2015 reg.6(1)(b), as amended.

[22] Central Bank (Supervision and Enforcement) Act 2013 (Section 48) (Housing Loan Requirements) Regulations 2015 reg.6(3).

[23] Central Bank (Supervision and Enforcement) Act 2013 (Section 48) (Housing Loan Requirements) Regulations 2015 reg.5, as amended. The Central Bank (Supervision and Enforcement) Act 2013 (Section 48) (Housing Loan Requirements) (Amendment) Regulations 2016 permitted banks to issue 20 per cent of first-time buyer and second and subsequent mortgages at a level which exceeded the 3.5 loan-to-income ratio. The Central Bank (Supervision and Enforcement) Act 2013 (Section 48) (Housing Loan Requirements) Regulations 2017 reduced this exception from 20 per cent to 10 per cent for second and subsequent mortgages.

Terms Regulations"),[24] and mortgage-specific measures such as Pt IX of the Consumer Credit Act 1995 (the "1995 Act") and the Consumer Mortgage Regulations.[25] Alongside the statutory layer of regulation, the Central Bank of Ireland has issued a number of codes of practice which impact mortgage lenders. A detailed examination of consumer protection is beyond the scope of this chapter and the reader is referred to more specialised works on the subject.[26]

24–14 Part IX of the 1995 Act imposes a variety of rules on mortgagors when offering housing loan mortgages.[27] These include an extensive list of pre-contractual information which must be provided to prospective customers in advance of a transaction.[28] Section 121 of the 1995 Act also created a right for the borrower to repay a mortgage loan or part thereof before the agreed time for repayment. This right was subject to an exception where the interest rate was fixed for the entire term, or for a period of more than one year or where the interest rate was subject to an upper limit not exceeding 2 per cent in excess of the rate agreed at the drawing down of the loan for a period of at least five years.

24–15 The requirements of the 1995 Act were later supplemented by the Central Bank of Ireland's Consumer Protection Code 2012. This Code, issued under the provisions of s.117 of the Central Bank Act 1989, imposed additional information requirements for consumer mortgages particularly in connection with arrears and incentives.[29] The Code also introduced information and warning requirements where the customer seeks to change from a tracker mortgage or where this option is offered to a customer by a regulated entity.[30]

24–16 Most recently, the Mortgage Credit Directive[31] was implemented in Ireland by the Consumer Mortgage Regulations. The Regulations apply to transactions in which the borrower is a consumer (i.e. a natural person acting

---

[24] European Communities (Unfair Terms in Consumer Contracts) Regulations 1995 (S.I. No. 27 of 1995), as amended by the European Communities (Unfair Terms in Consumer Contracts) (Amendment) Regulations 2000 (S.I. No. 307 of 2000); the European Communities (Unfair Terms in Consumer Contracts) (Amendment) Regulations 2013 (S.I. No. 160 of 2013); and the European Communities (Unfair Terms in Consumer Contracts) (Amendment) Regulations 2014 (S.I. No. 336 of 2014).

[25] S.I. No. 142 of 2016.

[26] M. Donnelly, *The Law of Credit and Security*, 2nd edn (Dublin: Round Hall, 2015), Ch.10; J. Breslin, *Banking Law in Ireland*, 3rd edn (Dublin: Round Hall, 2013), Chs 2 and 4.

[27] Housing loans mortgages are defined by s.2(1) of the Consumer Credit Act 1995, as inserted by s.33 and Sch.3, Pt 12 of the Central Bank and Financial Services Authority of Ireland Act 2004.

[28] See Donnelly, *Law of Credit and Security* (2015), para.10–175.

[29] Consumer Protection Code 2012, Chs 6 and 8.

[30] Consumer Protection Code 2012, paras 6.9–6.12.

[31] Directive 2014/17/EU of the European Parliament and of the Council of 4 February 2014 on credit agreements for consumers relating to residential immovable property and amending Directives 2008/48/EC and 2013/36/EU and Regulation (EU) No 1093/2010 [2014] OJ L60/34.

for purposes outside of his or her trade, business or profession).[32] The Regulations require lenders to operate in an honest, fair and transparent manner and to take account of the interests of consumers in designing credit products and in granting credit.[33] Lenders are required to ensure that their staff are properly qualified and trained to carry out their functions,[34] and must ensure that staff remuneration policies do not create an incentive for staff to act against the interests of consumers.[35] The Regulations impose restrictions and requirements on the marketing of mortgage products.[36]

24–17 From the consumer perspective, the Consumer Mortgage Regulations introduce two major new protections for borrowers. First, lenders are required to conduct a thorough assessment of the customer's creditworthiness in advance of making the loan.[37] Secondly, the Regulations introduce new requirements regarding the provision of pre-contractual information to the borrower. This must include supplying the consumer with a European Standardised Information Sheet (ESIS) in good time before the conclusion of a mortgage agreement in order to enable the consumer to compare different mortgage products on the market and to make an informed choice about the best product to suit his or her needs.[38] Breaches of the Regulations by a regulated financial institution may result in criminal prosecution.[39] The Central Bank may also enforce the Regulations via its administrative sanction powers under Pt IIIC of the Central Bank Act 1942.

24–18 The collapse in property prices and the subsequent mortgage arrears crisis experienced in Ireland from 2008 onwards has led to the introduction of a series of measures aimed at alleviating distressed borrowers and tackling the social problems caused by mortgage arrears. The centre-piece of this protection is the Central Bank's Code of Conduct on Mortgage Arrears (CCMA) which came into effect from 1 July 2013. The CCMA requires mortgage lenders to develop a Mortgage Arrears Resolution Process (MARP) and requires that the lender exhaust all reasonable alternatives before resorting to commencing possession proceedings against a mortgagor who is in default.[40]

---

[32] Consumer Mortgage Regulations reg.2.
[33] Consumer Mortgage Regulations reg.8.
[34] Consumer Mortgage Regulations reg.10.
[35] Consumer Mortgage Regulations reg.8(3)–(5).
[36] Consumer Mortgages Regulations regs 11–13. The Regulations are additional to the advertising provisions of the Consumer Protection Act 2007 but take precedence over the terms of the Consumer Credit Act 1995 to the extent that there is any conflict between the two regimes.
[37] Consumer Mortgage Regulations reg.19.
[38] Consumer Mortgage Regulations reg.15. The contents of the ESIS are specified in Sch.2 and cannot be modified by the lender.
[39] For the sentencing jurisdiction see reg.39(1). Continuing violations give rise to separate offences for each day in default: Consumer Mortgage Regulations reg.39(2).
[40] For a detailed account of the CCMA and its requirements, see N. Maddox, *Mortgages: Law and Practice*, 2nd edn (Dublin: Round Hall, 2017), paras 12–66 to 12–69.

24–19 Both the Consumer Protection Code and the CCMA are codes of practice issued under the Central Bank Act 1989. Failure to comply with the Codes exposes the mortgage lender to a variety of regulatory consequences. The Central Bank may issue a direction to a licensed institution requiring it to adopt certain practices where the Central Bank considers this necessary to secure the observance of a code of practice.[41] Failure to comply with such a direction is a criminal offence.[42] Contravention of a code of practice can also result in the imposition of administrative sanctions by the Central Bank under Pt IIIC of the Central Bank Act 1942.

24–20 The degree to which the Consumer Protection Code and the CCMA create rights for customers in civil litigation (usually in resisting actions for possession) has been the subject of a number of cases in recent years. In *Zurich Bank v McConnon*[43] the High Court considered an argument that the provisions of the Consumer Protection Code amounted to an implied term of a consumer loan contract and that the defendant was entitled to expect that the plaintiff bank would comply with the code in its dealings with him. Birmingham J., applying the traditional "officious bystander" test, took the view that it was "more than improbable" that an officious bystander would conclude that the provisions of the Code were terms of the contract. In *Irish Life and Permanent v Dunne*[44] Clarke J. rejected a similar implied terms argument in respect of the CCMA, noting that Codes are changed from time to time and that unlike, for example, the Sale of Goods Act, the Oireachtas has not provided for the Codes to operate as implied contractual terms.

24–21 In *Stepstone Mortgage Funding Ltd v Fitzell*[45] the High Court considered the significance of the CCMA in possession proceedings. There the plaintiff mortgagee had incorrectly informed the defendants that they were not entitled to appeal decisions taken by the mortgagee as a part of the MARP. Laffoy J. stated:

"I find it impossible to agree with the proposition that, in proceedings for possession of a primary residence by way of enforcement of a mortgage or charge to which the current code applies ... the plaintiff does not have to demonstrate to the court compliance with the current code. To take what is perhaps the best known provision of the current code, the imposition of a moratorium on the initiation of proceedings ... surely a court which is being asked to make an order which will, in all probability, result in a person being evicted from his or her home, is entitled to know that the requirement in provision 47, which has been imposed pursuant to statutory authority, is

---

[41] Central Bank Act 1989 s.117(3)(b).
[42] Central Bank Act 1989 s.117(4), as amended by Central Bank and Financial Services Authority of Ireland Act 2004 Sch.3.
[43] [2011] IEHC 75.
[44] [2016] 1 I.R. 92 at 110–111.
[45] [2012] 2 I.R. 318.

complied with. Moreover, it is likely that it would render the enforcement of provision 47 nugatory, if a lender did not have to adduce evidence to demonstrate that the moratorium period had expired."[46]

24–22 *Fitzell* was followed in *Irish Life & Permanent plc v Duff* albeit with some reluctance on the part of Hogan J., who raised the question of whether giving judicial effect to the Code by refusing to make possession orders poses constitutional difficulties, in that the Central Bank would effectively be exercising a power to change the law.[47] In *Freeman v Bank of Scotland (Ireland) Ltd*, Gilligan J. suggested that the status of the Central Bank Codes was unclear and that their application might vary from one case to another.[48]

24–23 The status of the Codes was clarified to some extent by the Supreme Court in *Irish Life & Permanent plc v Dunne*.[49] There, Clarke J. suggested that proceedings taken by a regulated entity which had contravened one or more of the requirements of the Consumer Protection Code or the CCMA are analogous to a situation in which an attempt is made to enforce a contract which is tainted by illegality. The law of contractual illegality was reviewed by the Supreme Court in *Quinn v Irish Bank Resolution Corporation* in which Clarke J. laid out five principles which should be applied where the court is asked to enforce a contract tainted by illegality.[50] The second of these principles applies where (as is the case with the Codes) the relevant statute is silent on whether a certain contract or class of contract is void or unenforceable, and is in the following terms:

"Where, however, the relevant legislation is silent as to whether any particular type of contract is to be regarded as void or unenforceable, the court must consider whether the requirements of public policy ... and the policy of the legislation concerned, gleaned from its terms, are such as require that, in addition to whatever express consequences are provided for in the relevant legislation, an additional sanction or consequence in the form of treating relevant contracts as being void or unenforceable must be imposed. For the avoidance of doubt it must be recalled that all appropriate weight should, in carrying out such an assessment, be attributed to the general undesirability of courts becoming involved in the enforcement of contracts tainted by illegality ... unless there are significant countervailing factors."[51]

24–24 Applying this test to the CCMA, Clarke J. noted that the Code contains a specific provision requiring the financial institution to observe a moratorium on the commencement of possession proceedings. Were a bank to commence

---

46 [2012] 2 I.R. 318 at 330.
47 [2013] 4 I.R. 96 at 117.
48 [2012] IEHC 371 at para.18.
49 [2016] 1 I.R. 92.
50 [2016] 1 I.R. 1 at 65–67.
51 [2016] 1 I.R. 1 at 65.

such proceedings in defiance of the Code, the court would be asked to entertain an application for the very outcome which the Code was intended to prevent. Clarke J. declared himself satisfied that the court could not properly consider an application for possession in such circumstances. In respect of other aspects of the Code, however, Clarke J. took a more cautious approach, arguing that the Oireachtas has not created a whole new jurisdiction for the courts "by the back door"[52] to evaluate the level of reasonableness, fairness or otherwise shown by mortgagees in their engagement with mortgagors who are in arrears.

The Unfair Contract Terms Directive

24–25 Recent cases have also highlighted the potential significance of the Unfair Contract Terms Directive (UCTD) in mortgage proceedings.[53] This Directive, which is of general application in consumer law, was implemented in Ireland by the Unfair Terms Regulations.[54] Article 3 of the UCTD provides that a contract term which, contrary to the requirement of good faith, creates a significant imbalance between the rights of the parties and which has not been individually negotiated shall be regarded as unfair.[55] The Annex to the UCTD contains a non-exhaustive list of terms which are regarded as unfair. Regulation 6(1) of the Unfair Terms Regulations provides that an unfair term is not binding on a consumer. Article 7 of the UCTD also imposes an obligation on member states to ensure that national law contains effective means to prevent the use of unfair terms in consumer contracts.

24–26 The Court of Justice has delivered guidance as to how a national court should apply the UCTD when considering contractual terms in consumer cases. In *Aziz v Caixa d'Estalvis de Catalunya*, the court held that national courts must, if necessarily of their own motion, assess "whether a contractual term falling within the scope of the directive is unfair, compensating in its own way for the imbalance which exists between the consumer and the seller or supplier, where it has available to it the legal and factual elements necessary for that task".[56] In *Allied Irish Banks plc v Counihan*[57] Barrett J. applied *Aziz* to summary proceedings for possession. He held that in such circumstances the court must, *of its own motion*, consider whether any of the terms of the mortgage agreement were unfair within the meaning of the Unfair Terms

---

[52] [2016] 1 I.R. 92 at 122.

[53] Council Directive 93/13/EEC of 5 April 1993 on unfair terms in consumer contracts [1993] OJ L95/29.

[54] European Communities (Unfair Terms in Consumer Contracts) Regulations 1995 (S.I. No. 27 of 1995), as amended by the European Communities (Unfair Terms in Consumer Contracts) (Amendment) Regulations 2000 (S.I. No. 307 of 2000); the European Communities (Unfair Terms in Consumer Contracts) (Amendment) Regulations 2013 (S.I. No. 160 of 2013); and the European Communities (Unfair Terms in Consumer Contracts) (Amendment) Regulations 2014 (S.I. No. 336 of 2014).

[55] Unfair Terms Regulations reg.3.

[56] (C-415/11) EU:C:2013:164 at para.44.

[57] [2016] IEHC 752.

Regulations and that should any such term give rise to an arguable defence, the matter should go to plenary hearing.

24–27 In *AIB Mortgage Bank v Cosgrave*,[58] the High Court considered the application of the Unfair Terms Regulations to a residential mortgage transaction. There the borrower argued that the mortgage was unenforceable on the basis, inter alia, that the mortgage contract contained terms relating to securitisation which would not have been intelligible to a borrower who lacked specialised knowledge of banking transactions. The plaintiff bank pointed to the fact that the recitals to the UCTD exclude "terms which describe the main subject matter of the contract" from the scope of the Directive.[59] The plaintiff argued that its application for possession of the mortgaged premises was based solely on the core terms of the bargain and that the defendant understood at the time of the contract that the monies advanced would have to be paid by him at the agreed intervals and that the premises would be charged accordingly. Faherty J., while not expressly accepting the bank's argument on the core terms of the bargain, held that the plaintiff's reliance on the securitisation clause could not give rise to a defence to an action for possession.[60]

Similar Interests

24–28 Mortgages are one of four different types of security interest arising in Irish property. The others include the pledge, the lien and the equitable charge. Pledges (or pawns, as they are known in the consumer context) involve the physical delivery of a chattel to a creditor. Pledges cannot be created over land. Liens give creditors the right to retain possession of property until a debt is discharged. Although the lien is classically concerned with personal, rather than real property, equitable liens play an important role in conveyances of real property.

Liens
24–29 A lien is a form of security which gives a creditor the right to retain possession of property or documents until a debt is discharged. Although liens can be created by contract, most liens arise by operation of law.[61]

At Common Law
24–30 A common law lien arises by operation of law and is a mere right to retain possession of property until a debt, owed by the owner of the property,

---

[58] [2017] IEHC 803.
[59] Similar language is also to be found in the operative provisions of the Directive: see UCTD Art.4.
[60] See *Harrold v Nua Mortgages Ltd* [2015] IEHC 15.
[61] *Tappenden v Artus* [1964] 2 Q.B. 185 at 194–195.

has been paid.[62] Unlike a mortgage or a pledge it carries with it no right to sell the property or indeed to deal with it in any other way. The retention of possession is simply a "lever" which the creditor has which may induce the debtor to pay up. Common law liens have been held to apply to repairers and improvers of goods giving them the right to retain goods until their bill for repair has been paid[63]; to the owner of horse stables[64]; and to ship owners for unpaid freight.[65] Solicitors have a lien over a client's documents while costs are unpaid.[66]

In Equity

24–31 An equitable lien arises in situations in which equity confers on a party a means of protecting their interest. The nature of equitable liens is somewhat vague, and it is difficult to identify a principle which clearly explains when and why they arise.[67]

24–32 A vendor of land enjoys a lien over the land for unpaid purchase money.[68] The lien arises as soon as the contract is entered into and continues until the purchase money has been paid in full. If the vendor has possession, which would normally be the case at least until the conveyance is executed, it may be retained,[69] but once possession has been given to the purchaser it cannot be reclaimed. Instead, the vendor is entitled to apply to court for the sale of the property and is entitled to recoup the debt from the proceeds of sale.[70] In *Tempany v Hynes*[71] the Supreme Court was divided on the nature of the vendor's lien. The case concerned a judgment mortgage which was registered after a contract for sale of land was entered into but before the purchaser was registered as the owner of the land. The question for the court was whether the vendor retained an interest in the land which was capable of being affected by the judgment mortgage. Kenny J., with whom O'Higgins C.J. agreed, held that the vendor retained beneficial ownership of the land to the extent that the purchase price was unpaid. Henchy J. on the other hand argued that the vendor's interest was by way of equitable lien only. The decision proved controversial because it exposed purchasers to the risk that the vendor might create interests in favour of third parties which would rank in priority to the purchaser between

---

[62] *Re Barrett Apartments Ltd* [1985] I.L.R.M. 679.

[63] *Green v All Motors Ltd* [1917] 1 K.B. 625; *Tappenden v Artus* [1964] 2 Q.B. 185.

[64] *Lee v Irwin* (1852) 4 Ir. Jur. (os) 372.

[65] *The Princess Royal* (1859) 5 Ir. Jur. (ns) 74; *Belfast Harbour Commissioners v Lawther* (1866) 17 Ir. Ch. R. 54.

[66] *Re Galdan Properties Ltd (In Liquidation)* [1988] I.L.R.M. 559 (SC); *Re Burrowes Estate* (1867) I.R. 1 Eq. 445 (equitable lien before Judicature Act).

[67] H. Beale, M. Bridge, L. Gullifer and E. Lomnicka, *The Law of Security and Title-Based Financing*, 2nd edn (Oxford: Oxford University Press, 2012), para.6.140.

[68] *Chapman v Tanner* (1684) 1 Vern. 276.

[69] *Shaw v Foster* (1872) L.R. 5 H.L. 321.

[70] *Hewett v Court* (1983) 149 C.L.R. 639.

[71] [1976] I.R. 101.

the time of the execution of the contract and the completion of the sale.[72] Section 52(1) of the LCLRA 2009 now provides that the beneficial interest in land passes to the purchaser on the making of an enforceable contract of sale between the parties. This appears to have the effect of reversing the majority decision in *Tempany*.

24–33 A purchaser of land has an equitable lien to secure the return of any part of the purchase money paid if the contract is unenforceable through no fault of his or her own.[73] The effect of this is to give the purchaser priority, as a secured creditor, over the other creditors of the vendor should the vendor become insolvent.[74] Such a lien is to be distinguished from the purchaser's equity which arises when a contract has been entered into and part of the purchase money paid[75] where the contract is enforceable. The purchaser's equity gives the purchaser an equitable interest or estate in the premises, and he or she can join third parties in an action for specific performance of the contract and so obtain a conveyance.[76]

24–34 It is normal today for an intending purchaser to pay a "booking deposit" to the developer of a housing estate so that the house will be reserved for the purchaser. The arrangement is conditional on a contract being signed. The Supreme Court in *Re Barrett Apartments Ltd*[77] refused to recognise that an intending purchaser had an equitable lien which would give the purchaser priority over the other creditors of the vendor. Equitable liens are the means by which the economic risks surrounding a market transaction are distributed by the legal system. If a policy is detectable behind the rules, it seems to be that parties to a land transaction are more favourably treated than other creditors once a contract for the sale of land has been entered into. Before a contract is formed, the intending purchaser has to take the same risk as other commercial creditors.

24–35 The purchaser's and vendor's liens can have important consequences for banks and other persons who provide finance for the purchase of property. The doctrine of subrogation may allow such a financier to step into the lienholder's shoes and exercise rights arising under an equitable lien. *Bank of Ireland Finance Ltd v DJ Daly Ltd*[78] provides an example. The plaintiff bank supplied finance to the defendant company for the purchase of land. It was a condition of the loan that the defendant would deposit the title deeds to the property with

---

[72] J.C.W. Wylie and U. Woods, *Irish Conveyancing Law*, 3rd edn (Dublin: Tottel, 2005), para.12.07.
[73] *Re Barrett Apartments Ltd* [1985] I.R. 350 at 356; *Tempany v Hynes* [1976] I.R. 101 (SC); *Rose v Watson* (1864) 10 H.L.C. 672, 11 E.R. 1187; and see Appendix A in the first edition of this work.
[74] *Re Barrett Apartments Ltd* [1985] I.R. 350 at 356 per Henchy J.
[75] *Tempany v Hynes* [1976] I.R. 101 (SC).
[76] *Rose v Watson* (1864) 10 H.L.C. 672; *Whitbread & Co Ltd v Watt* [1902] 1 Ch. 835.
[77] [1985] I.R. 350 at 356.
[78] [1978] I.R. 79.

the plaintiff as security for the loan. This was not done. The defendant paid over the loan amount to the vendor but failed to deposit the title deeds to the property. The plaintiff bank successfully argued that it was entitled to enforce the vendor's lien against the property by way of subrogation.

24–36 In *Highland Finance (Ireland) Ltd v Sacred Heart College Ltd; McEllin v Bank of Ireland*[79] the Supreme Court confirmed that the financier will not benefit from subrogation where to do so would confer additional rights beyond those provided for in the loan agreement.

Charges

24–37 A charge is an arrangement "whereby the charged property is appropriated to the discharge of an obligation without the transfer of ownership."[80] Section 89 of the LCLRA 2009 provides that a legal mortgage of land can only be created by a deed of charge. A legal charge over land is thus universally referred to as a mortgage. It is possible to create an equitable charge over land though this is uncommon.[81]

Judgment Mortgages

24–38 A judgment mortgage is a means of enforcing a debt due on foot of a court judgment. It enables a judgment creditor to register a mortgage against the judgment debtor's interest in land. Prior to the LCLRA 2009, judgment mortgages were governed by the Judgment Mortgages (Ireland) Acts 1850 and 1858. These Acts have now been repealed and replaced by a new regime for judgment mortgages under Pt 11 of the LCLRA 2009. Judgment mortgages will be discussed in detail below.

Welsh Mortgage

24–39 A Welsh mortgage was an ancient form of mortgage still found in some common law jurisdictions.[82] Its ancient and peculiar form is demonstrated by the characteristic that the mortgagee goes into occupation of the land. The lender is entitled to take the rent and profits of the land instead of interest on the loan. After the LCLRA 2009 a Welsh mortgage may not be created and an attempt to do so is void.[83]

---

[79] [1988] 2 I.R. 180.
[80] Beale, Bridge, Gullifer and Lomnicka, *The Law of Security and Title-Based Financing* (2012), para.6.17.
[81] *Bank of Ireland v Feeney* [1930] 1 I.R. 457.
[82] *Fidelity-Phoenix Fire Insurance Co v Garrison* 6 P.2d 47 (1931); *Humble Oil & Refining Co v Atwood* 150 Tex. 617 (1951).
[83] LCLRA 2009 s.89(7).

Islamic Mortgages

24–40 The old common law restrictions on usury are reflected in Islamic banking practices. Under the Qur'an, there is a prohibition of riba which is understood as a prohibition on any addition or increase received in repayment of any amount borrowed.[84] In order to facilitate banking transactions which are compliant with Islamic rules, s.39 of the Finance Act 2010 provides for banks to purchase property with a "borrower" on a joint venture basis or for the bank to purchase the asset which the borrower wishes to acquire and immediately convey it to its customer. The bank will demand a higher price from the customer than it paid for the property. The bank will also agree to accept payment by regular instalments from the customer for an extended period of time. This is a device to avoid the payment of interest, though in substance, the transaction in every other way resembles a term loan secured by a mortgage.

CREATION OF MORTGAGES

Unregistered Land

24–41 Following the recommendation of the Law Reform Commission, Pt 10 of the LCLRA 2009 simplifies the process by which mortgages are created over land.[85] Prior to the LCLRA 2009 a mortgage could be created over unregistered land using a variety of legal techniques. These will be considered below. Section 89 of the LCLRA 2009 provides that all mortgages now take effect by way of a legal charge over land. Any attempt to create a mortgage using the old forms is no longer effective to create a legal mortgage.[86] The old forms retain a limited degree of relevance in that they will appear in title deeds for some years to come. It should also be noted that s.89 does not apply to mortgages over property other than land. Thus, the old forms will continue to have relevance for mortgages taken over personal property.

Legal Mortgages
By Conveyance of the Fee Simple

24–42 Historically, a mortgage involved the conveyance of the fee simple estate to the mortgagee coupled with a covenant for the reconveyance of the fee simple upon the performance of the secured obligation. It was also possible to utilise modified fees simple such as a conditional fee to achieve the same effect.

24–43 Under such an arrangement, the legal date of redemption was typically set at six months from the date of the deed. Neither party intended the loan to

---

[84] M.M. Bilah, "The Prohibition of Riba and the Use of Hiyal by Islamic Banks to Overcome the Prohibition" (2014) 28 Ar. L.Q. 392 at 394.

[85] Law Reform Commission, *Consultation Paper on Reform and Modernisation of Land Law and Conveyancing Law* (LRC CP 34-2004), pp.140–142.

[86] LCLRA 2009 s.89(2)–(3).

be repaid, but the mortgagee could not sue on the debt until the legal date had passed on such a mortgage,[87] nor could the mortgagor redeem prior to this date.

24–44 The mortgagor retained the equity of redemption. The equity of redemption was not mentioned in the mortgage deeds but arose from cases in which the Court of Chancery insisted that the mortgagee be permitted to redeem the mortgage even after the expiry of the legal date of redemption.[88]

24–45 By the end of the 17th century, the equity of redemption had come to be recognised as a valuable interest in its own right.[89] Thus it may be used to secure the repayment of further loans or otherwise dealt with in its own right. The equity of redemption is a purely equitable interest and so any further mortgage or mortgages would necessarily be equitable as mortgages of an equitable interest. The theory is less explicit beyond this point, but it must be assumed that on a second mortgage, the mortgagor retains a new equity of redemption which, provided that the value of the property still exceeds the value of the existing mortgage debts, may itself be mortgaged, and so on.

By Demise or Sub-demise
24–46 Where the mortgagor had a fee simple a legal mortgage could be created by granting a lease to the mortgagee. This was usually for a long period, e.g. 10,000 years and subject to a clause ending the lease on repayment of the loan. The advantage was that the mortgagee was not liable under any covenants affecting the fee simple. This was especially important when mortgaging a fee farm grant to avoid the mortgagee becoming liable to pay the fee farm rent.[90] Since the mortgagor retained the legal fee simple in reversion it was possible to grant a subsequent legal mortgage of the mortgagor's interest. If the mortgagor had only a long lease and not the fee simple, then a mortgage would necessarily be created by conveying a term of years to the mortgagee.

(i) By Sub-demise
24–47 The sub-demise was usually a number of days less than the mortgagor's lease so that the mortgagor retained a reversion.[91] Subsequent mortgages could be legal, by leases of the reversion.

(ii) By Assignment
24–48 This was similar to a mortgage by conveyance of the fee simple where the mortgagor has a fee simple. The mortgagor conveyed his or her lease subject to a proviso for redemption. It was rare for this form to be adopted

---

[87] *Sinton v Dooley* [1910] 2 I.R. 162; *Bradshaw v McMullan* [1915] 2 I.R. 187.
[88] Simpson, *History of the Land Law* (1986), p.244.
[89] *Duchess of Hamilton v Countess of Dirlton* (1654) Rep. Ch. 165.
[90] *Re Sergie* [1954] N.I. 1.
[91] Mortgage terms, not being at a rent, would seem to be outside Deasy's Act s.3.

as the mortgagee would become liable under the covenants in the lease to the mortgagor's landlord.

Equitable Mortgages

24–49 The reforms of the LCLRA 2009 did not affect equitable mortgages over unregistered land.[92]

Mortgages of an Equitable Interest

24–50 Where the mortgagor only possesses an equitable interest in land, that interest may be made the subject of a mortgage. Such mortgages are necessarily equitable, as for example mortgages of an equity of redemption where a fee simple owner has created a legal mortgage by conveyance of the fee simple. Another example would be where a beneficiary under a trust mortgages his or her interest. Section 6 of the Statute of Frauds (Ireland) 1695 requires a written instrument for creation of such a mortgage, though in practice a deed is usually employed.

Agreement for a Legal Mortgage

24–51 A specifically enforceable contract to enter into a legal mortgage operates itself as a mortgage in equity.[93] This is an example of the maxim of equity that "equity regards as done that which ought to be done". In order to be enforceable, the contract must comply with s.2 of the Statute of Frauds 1695, i.e. there must be evidence of it in writing, signed by "the party to be charged", or alternatively there must be part performance.

24–52 Various arrangements have been held to amount to a contract to create a mortgage and, provided the contract is specifically enforceable, to create an immediate equitable mortgage. In *Re Stewart's Estate*[94] creditors held a judgment mortgage over a life estate held by the judgment debtor. When the land was sold by the Landed Estates Court, the judgment creditor agreed not to insist on immediate payment of the judgment debt provided that the judgment debtor continued to hold the fee simple. This agreement was held to give rise to a separate equitable mortgage of the land affecting the fee simple securing the repayment of the judgment debt.

Deposit of Title Deeds

24–53 The depositing of deeds evidencing an interest in land with a creditor by way of security creates an equitable mortgage over the land. On its face, the transaction has some similarity with a possessory pledge in that possession of the title deeds ensures that the mortgagor will be unable to deal with the land

---

[92] LCLRA 2009 s.89(6).

[93] *Card v Jaffray* (1805) 2 Sch. & Lef. 374; *Abbott v Stratten* (1846) 3 Jo. & Lat. 603; *Eyre v McDowell* (1861) 9 H.L.C. 619; *ACC Bank v Malocco*, unreported, High Court, Laffoy J., 7 February 2000.

[94] (1893) 31 L.R. Ir. 405.

without the mortgagee's consent. Similarities notwithstanding, a mortgage by deposit is not a pledge.[95] The title documents are considered to form a part of the land itself and, unlike the pledgee, the mortgagee does not acquire a special property in the land as a result of the transaction.

24–54 This type of mortgage has the advantage that it can be created without formality and in a simple manner. In particular, there is no requirement for its creation to be registered in the Registry of Deeds since there is no document which can be registered.[96] Nevertheless, as Hardiman points out, the very informality of the transaction can cause problems of its own which may result in litigation.[97] The continuing existence of the equitable mortgage by deposit is implicitly recognised by s.21(3)(b)(ii) of the LCLRA 2009 which ensures that the transaction is not vulnerable to being overreached on a sale by trustees.

24–55 The deposit of the title deeds must be done with an intention to create security. No equitable mortgage arises where deeds are deposited for safekeeping.[98] Not all of the title deeds must be deposited.[99] The deeds are usually, but not necessarily, deposited with the mortgagee. Deposit with the mortgagor's solicitor for the purpose of preparing a legal mortgage has been held sufficient, though it seems that deposit with a solicitor for the purposes of preparing an equitable mortgage is not, a distinction which appears to have no policy justification beyond reified conceptions of the nature of equitable interests.[100] If the mortgagee returns the deeds to the mortgagor before the loan is discharged the equitable mortgage is lost.[101] The mortgagee is liable for the safe custody of the deeds during the currency of the deposit.[102]

24–56 The equitable mortgage by deposit does not require a written memorandum; the deposit of the title deeds will suffice by itself.[103] One explanation for the mortgage by deposit is to regard it as an application of the equitable doctrine of part performance, with the deposit of title deeds serving to satisfy the evidentiary requirements of the Statute of Frauds.[104] Wylie, noting that there is no act of part performance on the part of the mortgagee, suggests that the mortgage by deposit should be better thought of as a species of equitable lien.[105]

---

[95] *Re Richardson; Shillito v Hobson* (1885) 30 Ch. D. 396.

[96] *Bank of Ireland v Purcell* [1989] I.R. 327 at 333.

[97] See D. Hardiman, "Deposit of Title Deeds" (1999) 6(1) C.L.P. 3.

[98] *Bank of Ireland v Coen*, unreported, High Court, Lynch J., 11 November 1985; *McKay v McNally* (1879) 4 L.R. Ir. 438; *Gilligan v National Bank Ltd* [1901] 2 I.R. 513.

[99] *Re Lambert's Estate* (1882) 13 L.R. Ir. 234.

[100] *Bulfin v Dunne* (1861) 11 Ir. Ch. R. 198 at 202, 204, citing *Ex Parte Bruce* (1810) 1 Rose 374.

[101] *Re Driscoll's Estate* (1867) I.R. 1 Eq. 285.

[102] LCLRA 2009 s.90(3); *Gilligan v National Bank* [1901] 2 I.R. 513.

[103] *Bulfin v Dunne* (1861) 11 Ir. Ch. R. 198; *Fullerton v Bank of Ireland* [1903] A.C. 309; *Russel v Russel* (1783) 1 Bro. C.C. 269.

[104] D. Hardiman, "Deposit of Title Deeds" (1999) 6(1) C.L.P. 3.

[105] J.C.W. Wylie, *Irish Land Law*, 5th edn (Dublin: Bloomsbury, 2013), para.12.45.

24–57 Although the deposit of title deeds is sufficient to create an equitable mortgage, the deposit may be accompanied by a written memorandum recording the fact that the deposit is intended to create security. Such writing should be approached with caution. The existence of a written note may be helpful, indeed vital, in proving that the deposit was made by way of security; however, there is a risk that a written note may be viewed as recording an agreement to create a mortgage and the deposit will be regarded as a step towards executing that agreement. Where the court takes this view, the memorandum must comply with s.51 of the LCLRA 2009 (replacing s.2 of the Statute of Frauds (Ireland) Act 1695); the written memorandum may be a registerable document for the purposes of Pt III of the Registration of Deeds and Title Act 2006 ("RDTA 2006") with the result that the mortgage may be void for non-registration under s.38(2) of that Act.[106] In *Paul v Nath Saha*, the Privy Council, sitting on an Indian appeal, held that the relevant question was whether the document constituted the agreement between the parties or was merely a record of an already completed transaction.[107]

Equitable Charge
24–58 Equity allows an owner of a property right to create a charge over it and this differs from an equitable mortgage properly so-called in that it does not have the effect of transferring an estate, legal or equitable, in the property.[108] In *Re Kum Tong Restaurant (Dublin) Ltd*,[109] a company borrowed money and agreed by letter to secure the loan by holding the purchase money from the sale of its land for the benefit of the lender. The letter was held to create an equitable charge over the purchase money.

Registered Land
Legal Mortgages
24–59 Under s.89(1) of the LCLRA 2009, a legal mortgage takes effect as a charge. Although such arrangements are often referred to as charges rather than mortgages,[110] s.89(1) of the LCLRA 2009 and s.62(6) of the Registration of Title Act 1964 ("RTA 1964") make clear that the terms mortgage and charge are synonymous for this purpose. For the sake of clarity, the term mortgage will be preferred throughout this chapter.

24–60 Section 62(1) provides that the registered owner of land may create a mortgage on the land by use of a written instrument in the prescribed form.

---

[106] *Fullerton v Bank of Ireland* [1903] A.C. 309.
[107] [1939] 1 All E.R. 737 at 739.
[108] *Shea v Moore* [1894] 1 I.R. 158 at 168; *Bank of Ireland v Feeney* [1930] I.R. 457.
[109] [1978] I.R. 446.
[110] See, for example, J. Deeney, *Registration of Deeds and Title in Ireland* (Dublin: Bloomsbury, 2014), Ch.21.

A person with a power to mortgage the land may also do so,[111] as may the personal representative of the registered owner.[112] The forms are set out in rr.52 and 105 of the Land Registration Rules 2012.[113]

24–61 A legal mortgage may be created by will without the use of the prescribed forms. This exemption is expressly provided for in s.62(2) of the RTA 1964. It would appear, however, that a mortgage of registered land made by will may not be made using the older forms developed in respect of registered land, i.e. it is not possible to create a mortgage by demise over registered land by will.[114]

24–62 A legal mortgage of registered land does not vest any interest in the land in the mortgagee until the charge is registered in accordance with s.62(2) of the RTA 1964. An unregistered charge, or a contract to create a charge, creates an unregistered right pending registration which can be protected by caution or inhibition.[115]

Equitable Mortgages
24–63 Section 105(5) of the RTA 1964 as originally enacted provided for the creation of equitable mortgages by deposit over registered land. This was achieved by lodging the land certificate or certificate of charge with the mortgagee by way of security. The effect of the section was to introduce a further departure from the "mirror principle" since the creation of such equitable mortgages was not disclosed in the Land Registry. The inclusion of equitable mortgages in registered land appears to have been justified on the basis of the cost and simplicity of the transaction.[116] Section 73 of the RDTA 2006 abolished the issuing of land certificates and with them, the possibility of future equitable mortgages by deposit over registered land. Section 73(1)(b) provided a temporary saver for equitable mortgages by deposit which existed at the time the RDTA 2006 entered into force but provided that such mortgages would cease to have any effect unless registered as a s.69 burden by 31 December 2009.[117]

By Agreement
24–64 Equitable mortgages may also arise, as in unregistered title, by an agreement to create a registered charge, or by a mortgage of an equitable

---

[111] RTA 1964 ss.62(4) and 76.
[112] Succession Act 1965 s.60(3). A mortgage for the improvement of land or buildings requires the consent of the beneficiaries.
[113] Land Registration Rules 2012 (S.I. No. 483 of 2012).
[114] This would appear to follow from s.89(2) of the LCLRA 2009 which does not contain any exclusion for wills.
[115] Maddox, *Mortgages: Law and Practice* (2017), para.2–03.
[116] J.L. Montrose, "Equitable Deposits of Title Deeds" (1940) 4 N.I.L.Q. 64; Wylie, *Irish Land Law* (2013), para.12.29.
[117] RDTA 2006 s.73(1). The practicalities of this process were described in the High Court in *Ulster Bank v Reaney* [2018] IEHC 43.

interest.[118] Such mortgages can only be protected by a caution entered by the person entitled to them. Mortgages of equitable interests are less frequently encountered in registered land because, since the creation of a legal charge does not transfer the legal title, subsequent charges can also be legal.

Mortgages by Estoppel

24–65 In *First National Bank plc v Thompson*[119] T, who was neither the registered proprietor of the registered land concerned, nor entitled to be at that time, purported to execute a charge in favour of the bank. T then became registered as proprietor. The bank then attempted to register its charge. The English Court of Appeal held that before T became registered as proprietor a charge by estoppel had been created in favour of the bank. When T became the registered owner, the estoppel was "fed" by the legal estate giving the bank a legal charge, which it was entitled to register.[120]

Priorities

24–66 It is not uncommon for the owner of an interest in land to grant multiple mortgages over the land to different lenders. Where the market value of the land is greater than or equal to the aggregate amount secured by multiple mortgages this poses no difficulty–should the mortgagor default on his or her obligations all of the mortgagees can be repaid in full from the proceeds of the land. By contrast, where the land is not sufficiently valuable to enable the full repayment of all of the mortgagees, an acute difficulty arises since the law must choose how the value of the land is to be divided among them. Such disputes are usually referred to as priority disputes. A party who fails to recover in a priority dispute is usually left to pursue an action against the mortgagor as an unsecured creditor. In many, if not most, such cases, the remedy will be illusory since the unsecured creditor will lack the resources to pay out on foot of a judgment. For this reason, priority disputes are particularly difficult since they require the law to make a choice which will result in the imposition of losses on one party.[121] The rules discussed below are a specialised application of the general rules of priority.

Unregistered Land
Registry of Deeds

24–67 Where a mortgage is created by a deed or other written instrument, it is usual to register that deed or instrument in the Registry of Deeds. The Registry

---

[118] RTA 1964 s.68(2).

[119] [1996] Ch. 231.

[120] The case was based upon ss.25 and 27 of the English Land Registration Act 1925, but ss.62 and 90 of the RTA 1964 are in similar terms.

[121] M. Mautner, "'The Eternal Triangles of the Law': Toward a Theory of Priorities in Conflicts Involving Remote Parties" (1991) 90 Mich. L. Rev. 95.

of Deeds is now governed by Pt III of the RDTA 2006. The key provision in determining priority in the Registry of Deeds is s.38 of the RDTA 2006. Section 38(1) provides that where both competing mortgages have been created by registered deed, priority is determined by the order of registration.[122] The date upon which the mortgages were created is not relevant. Questions of notice play no role in the resolution of disputes unless there has been fraud.[123]

24–68 Section 38(2) also provides that a mortgage created by a registrable but unregistered document is void as against a mortgage created by a registered instrument. In these cases, the date of creation of the mortgage is relevant. If the earlier transaction is registered while the later one is not, s.38(2) can apply in a straightforward manner and the registered (earlier) transaction is void.[124] Where a prior unregistered transaction is competing with a later registered transaction, additional qualifications apply to prevent the registration system being used to further a fraud:

(a) A knows that the land has been mortgaged to B under a prior registrable but unregistered document. A takes a conflicting mortgage and registers it in order to gain priority over B.

(b) A takes a mortgage over an interest in land without knowing at the time of advancing the money that B, under a prior registrable but unregistered document, has a conflicting mortgage of the same interest.

In scenario (a), the courts considered A to have acted fraudulently if she had actual[125] or imputed notice[126] of B's prior unregistered transaction. Thus, B had priority over A in spite of the fact that A was first to register her mortgage.[127] In scenario (b), the courts took the view that A was not acting fraudulently and was entitled to protect herself by prompt registration of her deed.[128] Section 38(3) provides for the continued operation of these rules under the modernised Registry of Deeds provided for by the RDTA 2006.

24–69 Not all mortgages are registrable in the Registry of Deeds. In particular, the equitable mortgage by deposit does not involve the generation of

---

[122] Strictly, priority is determined by serial numbers which are added in sequential order to documents as they arrive for registration: RDTA 2006 s.37.
[123] *Eyre v Dolphin* (1813) 2 Ball. & B. 290 at 300.
[124] *Re McDonagh's Estate* (1879) 3 L.R. Ir. 408; *Cleary v Fitzgerald* (1880) 5 L.R. Ir. 351.
[125] *Forbes v Deniston* (1722) 4 Bro. P.C. 189; *Delacour v Freeman* (1854) 2 Ir. Ch. R. 633; *Montgomery v McEvoy* (1857) 5 Ir. Ch. R. 126; *Clarke v Armstrong* (1861) 10 Ir. Ch. R. 263; *Re Flood's Estate* (1863) Ir. Ch. R. 312; *Agra Bank v Barry* (1874) L.R. 7 H.L. 135. On the possible shift of opinion on definition of actual notice, see *Workingmen's Benefit Society v Higgins* [1945] Ir. Jur. Rep. 38; *Re Fuller* [1982] I.R. 161.
[126] *Re Rorke's Estate* (1864) 14 Ir. Ch. R. 442 at 446; *Marjoribanks v Hovenden* (1843) 6 Ir. Eq. R. 238; *Espin v Pemberton* (1859) 3 De G. & J. 547 at 554.
[127] *Bushell v Bushell* (1806) 1 Sch. & Lef. 92; *Blades v Blades* (1727) 1 Eq. Cas. Abr. 358.
[128] *Reilly v Garnett* (1872) I.R. 7 Eq. 1 at 25.

a memorandum which is capable of registration. The priority position of an equitable mortgage by deposit will therefore depend on the equitable rules of priority.

Equitable Rules of Priority

24–70 Where the Registry of Deeds rules do not dispose of a priority conflict concerning registered land, the underlying common law rules and equitable principles must be considered.

24–71 In the context of mortgages these rules apply in three situations:

- One mortgage is registered while the other is unregisterable.
- Neither mortgage is registerable.
- Neither is registered.[129]

24–72 The priority rules governing transactions outside the Registry of Deeds vary depending on whether the mortgages are legal or equitable in nature. The basic principle is that the first in time prevails. This simple rule is modified in certain contexts by the equitable maxim "where equities are equal the first in time prevails".

24–73 Where there are two competing legal mortgages or two competing equitable mortgages, the basic rule is to rank them in order of their date of creation. The basic rule is subject to equitable modification. In cases of fraud,[130] estoppel[131] and gross negligence with respect to the title deeds,[132] the first mortgagee may be postponed behind a later mortgagee.

24–74 In a priority conflict between legal and equitable mortgages, the order of creation is important. If the legal mortgage is created first in time, it will generally take priority over the equitable mortgage. Where the equitable mortgage is created first in time, the holder of the legal mortgage will take priority if his or her mortgage was created bona fide, for value and without notice. Commonly, a later legal mortgagee will have notice (particularly of an equitable mortgage by deposit) if he or she fails to demand production of the title deeds.[133]

---

[129] Maddox, *Mortgages: Law and Practice* (2017), para.3–11.

[130] *Peter v Russell* (1716) Gilb. Eq. 122.

[131] *Dickson v Muckleston* (1872) 8 Ch. App. 155 at 160.

[132] *Re Greer* [1907] 1 I.R. 57. A first mortgagee who allows the mortgagor to retain the title deeds, thereby allowing a later mortgagee to be misled into believing that there is no prior mortgage, is grossly negligent unless he or she gives a plausible reason why the deeds are not produced: see *Re Ambrose's Estate* [1914] I.R. 123 and *Agra Bank v Barry* (1874) L.R. 7 H.L. 135.

[133] *Re Stephen's Estate* (1875) I.R. 10 Eq. 282.

Registered Land

24–75 Section 69(1)(c) of the RTA 1964 permits charges over registered land to be registered as burdens on the land. Section 74 provides that registered burdens rank in accordance with the date of their entry into the register. Section 68(3) of the RTA 1964 provides that registered charges are not subject to unregistered interests. Section 68(3) provides an exception for overriding interests as set out in s.72(1) of the RTA 1964. The abolition of the land certificate and the repeal of s.105(5) of the RTA 1964 by the RDTA 2006 has removed the possibility of conflicts between unregisterable mortgages and other interests in registered land.[134]

Salvage

24–76 There are a series of Irish cases which hold that the general principles of equitable priority can be displaced by salvage payments.[135] *Re Power's Policies* establishes three requirements which constitute a good salvage payment: (a) the payment must have had the effect of saving property which would otherwise have been lost for the benefit of all those interested in it; (b) the payment must be made by a person with an interest in or charge on the property; and (c) the payment must be made voluntarily and not in pursuance of some duty or obligation of the payor.[136] Examples include payments of rent to avoid the forfeiture of a leasehold interest[137]; the payment of renewal fines[138]; and payments made to preserve the property from an imminent risk of destruction.[139]

Tacking

24–77 Tacking allows a mortgagee, when there are several mortgages affecting land, to secure greater priority for the mortgage by attaching or "tacking" it onto an earlier mortgage in the series and gaining priority over intervening mortgages. At common law two forms of tacking developed: (1) *tabula in naufragio*, and (2) tacking further advances.

Tabula in Naufragio

Application

24–78 *Tabula in naufragio*[140] ("the plank in a shipwreck") applied in the following circumstances:

---

[134] For details, see the third edition of this work, pp.927–928.

[135] Maddox, *Mortgages: Law and Practice* (2017), paras 3–40 to 3–45; Wylie, *Irish Land Law* (2013), para.13.118.

[136] [1899] 1 I.R. 6 at 27.

[137] *Kehoe v Hales* (1843) 5 Ir. Eq. R. 497.

[138] *Hamilton v Denny* (1809) 1 Ball. & B. 199.

[139] *Re Cobden's Estate* [1923] 1 I.R. 1, holding that payments for ordinary maintenance are not salvage but payments for emergency works to prevent destruction by flooding do qualify. See Maddox, *Mortgages: Law and Practice* (2017), para.3–42.

[140] The phrase was said to be first used in *Brace v Duchess of Marlborough* (1728) 2 P. Wms. 491.

A takes a legal mortgage over land to secure a loan of €200,000. A sub-
sequent equitable mortgage is then given to B securing a loan of €50,000.
A second equitable mortgage, securing a loan of €50,000 is then granted to
C. The value of the property is €260,000.

The rule was that C could gain priority over B by acquiring the legal interest[141]
belonging to A.[142] The basis of the doctrine was said to be that an innocent
equitable mortgagee who acquires the legal estate can take advantage of the
principle that "where the equities are equal the law prevails".[143] For this reason,
tabula in naufragio could only operate where the equities were equal; thus if
C had notice of the existence of B's interest at the time he purchased from
A *tabula in naufragio* did not arise.[144]

24–79 The *tabula in naufragio* has been described as being "founded on technical and suspect reasoning".[145] The rule operated only in relation to unregistered land and even then only in cases where the equitable rules of priority,
as distinct from the Registry of Deeds priority rules applied.[146] It has had a
chequered career: it was abolished in Ireland and England by s.7 of the Vendor
and Purchaser Act 1874 but was then restored again in Ireland[147] by s.73 of the
Conveyancing Act 1881 (the "1881 Act"). It has now been abolished by s.111
of the LCLRA 2009 though the abolition does not affect rights acquired by
tabula in naufragio prior to the commencement of the Act.

Tacking Further Advances
24–80 Tacking further advances applies where a legal mortgagee lends more
money, i.e. makes further advances, intended to be on the same security,
unaware that another equitable mortgage has been created in the meantime.[148]

A grants a legal mortgage of land to B to secure an initial advance of
€100,000. A subsequently grants an equitable mortgage of the same land to
C to secure a further advance of €100,000. Later, B makes a fresh advance
to A of a further €100,000. The market value of the property is €250,000.

---

[141] *Tabula in naufragio* also operated if C obtained a better right to A's interest, e.g. if A held the
legal mortgage in trust for C. See *Wilkes v Bodington* (1707) 2 Vern. 599 at 600.

[142] *Marsh v Lee* (1671) 2 Ventr. 337; *Workingmen's Benefit Society v Dixon* [1908] 1 I.R. 582.

[143] *Basset v Nosworthy* (1673) Finch 102; *Chandos (Duchess) v Brownlow* (1791) 2 Ridg. P.C.
345 at 423; *Wortley v Birkenhead* (1754) 2 Ves. Sen. 571 at 574; *Bailey v Barnes* [1894] 1 Ch.
25 at 36.

[144] *Basset v Nosworthy* (1673) Finch 102.

[145] E.H. Burn and J. Cartwright, *Cheshire and Burn's Modern Law of Real Property*, 18th edn
(Oxford: Oxford University Press, 2011), p.879.

[146] *Tennison v Sweeney* (1844) 7 Ir. Eq. R. 511.

[147] It was restored in England by s.129 of the Land Transfer Act 1875, only to be abolished again
in England, as to competing mortgages only, by s.94(3) of the Law of Property Act 1925.

[148] *Morret v Paske* (1740) 2 Atk. 52 at 53.

In these circumstances, B can tack the second advance to his legal mortgage and thus gain priority over C's for the second advance. At common law, the rule only applied where equities were equal, thus A could not tack if, at the time of making the second advance, A had actual notice of the intervening equitable mortgage.[149]

24–81 Section 111 of the LCLRA 2009 now governs the tacking of advances in respect of registered land. It provides that where a mortgage is taken for the purpose of securing future advances, the mortgagee is entitled to tack such advances in priority to any subsequent mortgagee unless the first mortgagee has received "express notice in writing" of the second mortgage. There is some dispute about whether s.111 has changed the standard of notice which must be given to the first mortgagee. Wylie takes the view that the section merely codifies the existing position.[150] Donnelly has suggested that express notice in writing is a more exacting standard that the actual notice required pre-2009.[151] Wylie cites three cases in support of his contention,[152] but it is suggested these cases do not in fact support a requirement for written notice. The strongest of Wylie's cases is *Re O'Byrne's Estate* in which Naish L.C. suggested that the second mortgagee might have served a written notice on the first mortgagee[153]; however, the decision does not contain an express statement that actual notice must be given in written form. In two other cases, the courts held, on the facts, that the first mortgagee had actual notice of the second mortgage at the time of making their advance but did not decide a broader point. It seems therefore that Donnelly's view is to be preferred and that s.111 has narrowed the law of tacking future advances.

Other Cases of Tacking

24–82 Prior to the LCLRA 2009, there were other categories of tacking. In particular, where a legal mortgagee made an additional advance on the security of a further equitable mortgage, it was possible to tack the second mortgage to the first, and thus gain priority over an intermediary equitable mortgagee.[154] Section 111(3) of the LCLRA 2009 abolished this form of tacking though without prejudice to any existing rights.

---

[149] *Brown v Lynch* (1838) 2 Jo. 706; *Re Keogh's Estate* [1895] 1 I.R. 201; *Hopkinson v Rolt* [1899] 2 Ch. 355.

[150] J.C.W. Wylie, *The Land and Conveyancing Law Reforms Acts: Annotations and Commentary*, 2nd edn (London: Bloomsbury, 2017), [162].

[151] Donnelly, *Law of Credit and Security* (2015), para.13–99.

[152] *Re O'Byrne's Estate* (1855) 15 L.R. Ir. 373; *Re Macnamara's Estate* (1884) 13 L.R. Ir. 158; and *Re Keogh's Estate* [1895] 1 I.R. 201.

[153] *Re O'Byrne's Estate* (1855) 15 L.R. Ir. 373 at 378.

[154] *Morret v Paske* (1740) 2 Atk. 52 at 53.

Tacking Registered Land
Tabula in Naufragio
24–83 *Tabula in naufragio* cannot apply to registered land because there is no provision in the RTA 1964 to tack an unregistered charge onto a registered legal estate or charge.

Tacking Further Advances
24–84 Section 75(1) of the RTA 1964 expressly provides for future advances to be tacked onto a registered charge. The registered owner of the charge is entitled to priority to any subsequent charge, except where the further advance is made after the date of the subsequent charge and with "express notice in writing" of it.

THE POSITION OF THE PARTIES TO A MORTGAGE

24–85 The rights of the parties to a mortgage are primarily determined by the terms of the mortgage agreement. The mortgage contract is, however, overlain by an array of equitable principles, statutory provisions and, particularly in the case of housing loans, financial services regulations. Producing a clear statement of the rights of mortgagees and mortgagors is not, therefore, a straightforward task. As has been seen above Pt 10 of the LCLRA 2009 contains a variety of provisions regarding mortgages. Chapters 2–4 of this Part establish a number of rights for both mortgagee and mortgagor. Many of these provisions re-enact, with amendments, earlier law found in the Conveyancing Acts 1881–1911 which were partly repealed by the LCLRA 2009. The mortgage provisions of the Conveyancing Acts were designed to provide default rules for mortgages. Parties to specific transactions were entitled to, and commonly did, vary the application of the Conveyancing Acts or even exclude them entirely. Initially, it was proposed to make the mortgage provisions of the LCLRA 2009 mandatory for all mortgages.[155] The effect of this proposal was later narrowed so that the provisions of Pt 10 are only mandatory in respect of housing loan mortgages.[156] A housing loan mortgage is one which secures a loan for the purpose of purchasing, improving or constructing a principal residence for the borrower or the borrower's dependants.[157] For all other mortgages, it is necessary to carefully examine the mortgage agreement between the parties to determine the extent to which the provisions of the LCLRA 2009 may have been varied by agreement.

---

[155] See Land and Conveyancing Law Reform Bill 2006 cl.93.
[156] LCLRA 2009 s.96(3).
[157] Consumer Credit Act 1995 s.2(1)(ba), as amended by Central Bank and Financial Services Authority of Ireland Act 2004 Sch.3, Pt 12.

RIGHTS OF THE MORTGAGEE

24–86 A mortgage is ordinarily granted to the mortgagee as security for the repayment of a loan of money made to the mortgagor. If the loan is not repaid as agreed, the mortgagee has the option of suing the mortgagor for ordinary contract debt. This right exists in all loans, not merely those secured on land by way of mortgage and it is worth noting that the mortgagee's remedies are cumulative. It does not have to choose between suing in debt or on the mortgage.[158] The whole purpose of the mortgage is to enable the mortgagee to take control of the land, and satisfy the debt owed to it from the land, or from its proceeds. This section will explore the mortgagee's rights to enforce its security. Before doing so, however, it is necessary to examine a number of other rights which are conferred on the mortgagee as part of mortgage arrangements. Section 96(1)(c) of the LCLRA 2009 imposes a general restriction on the purposes for which the mortgagee's powers can be exercised. This section was a new innovation of the LCLRA 2009 and restricts the mortgagee to exercising its powers for the purposes of protecting the mortgaged property or enforcing the mortgagee's security. The potential effect of this section was illustrated in *Danske Bank v Ryan* where the High Court accepted that the appointment of a receiver could in principle be open to challenge if a receiver was appointed in bad faith or for some collateral purpose, though on the facts there was no evidence to support this allegation.[159]

Title Deeds

24–87 At common law the owner of an estate is entitled to possession of the title deeds. Thus prior to 2009, a first legal mortgagee is entitled to possession of the title deeds as the owner of the fee simple. Where the mortgage was created by demise, the mortgagee is entitled to the title deeds relating to the lease. Where a leasehold interest is mortgaged by assignment, the mortgagee will be entitled to the deed creating the lease. In the case of a mortgage by sub-demise, the common law entitlement is to the sub-lease only unless provision is made for the mortgagee to have possession of the main lease. Where an equitable mortgage is created by deposit, the mortgagee will obviously retain custody of the deeds. The equitable mortgagee by deposit's interest relates to the land itself rather than the title deeds, so it is possible for the mortgagee to be ordered to lodge the deeds in court.[160]

24–88 In respect of registered land, prior to the enactment of the RDTA 2006, the mortgagee of registered land was entitled to possession of a certificate of charge. It was also possible for registered land to be mortgaged by deposit of

---

[158] *Schoole v Sall* (1806) 1 Sch. & Lef. 176 at 177. Before the Judicature Act 1877, the mortgagee could sue on the common law debt and in equity at the same time, an exception to the general rule that one could not sue at law and in equity simultaneously.

[159] [2014] IEHC 236.

[160] *Re Girdwood's Estate* (1881) 5 L.R. Ir. 45.

the land certificate. Such certificates ceased to have any effect after 31 December 2009.

24–89 As noted above, mortgages created prior to 1 December 2009 operate by way of charge and thus the common law entitlement of the mortgagee to the possession of the title deeds as the legal owner of an estate in land does not apply. Section 90(2) confers a statutory right of possession of the title deeds on a first mortgagee which is equivalent to the right formerly enjoyed by a mortgagee whose security was created by conveyance of the legal estate prior to the enactment of the LCLRA 2009. Section 91 confers a right on the mortgagor to inspect the title deeds at reasonable times and upon payment of the mortgagee's costs and reasonable expenses in facilitating the exercise of this right.

24–90 In *Gilligan v National Bank Ltd*[161] the Irish courts held that there is no implied obligation on the part of the mortgagee to take reasonable care of the deeds and that the mortgagor had no right to compensation in the event of loss or damage to the deeds prior to redemption. This question was reconsidered by the court in *ACC Bank v Fairlee Property*[162] in which Finlay Geoghegan J. held that there was a common law duty of care on a mortgagee to take reasonable precautions to ensure that it could comply with a request to produce the deeds for inspection under the forerunner of s.91 of the LCLRA 2009.[163]

24–91 The reversal of *Gilligan* is now confirmed by s.90(3) of the LCLRA 2009 which provides that the mortgagee in possession of title deeds has the same responsibilities as if an undertaking for their safekeeping had been given under s.84 of the LCLRA 2009. This amounts to an obligation to keep them "complete, safe, uncancelled and undefaced". The undertaking must be specifically performed unless prevented by fire or inevitable accident and s.84(8) creates a right to damages for breach of undertaking.

Insurance
24–92 If property subject to a mortgage were to be damaged by fire or similar accident, the value of the security might fall to the point where the mortgagee might be unable to recover the money lent. Section 110 of the LCLRA 2009 confers a statutory right on the mortgagee to insure the property. This provision takes into account modern insurance practice by requiring the insurance to cover the full restatement cost of a damaged or destroyed property. The mortgagee can require that any money received under the insurance policy be applied either to the reinstatement of the property or the payment of the mortgage debt.

---

[161] [1901] 2 I.R. 513.
[162] [2009] 2 I.L.R.M. 101.
[163] Conveyancing Act 1881 s.16.

Fixtures

24–93 A mortgage of land includes all buildings and fixtures attached to the land.[164] The general test is that an article is prima facie a fixture if it is attached to the land by more than its own weight, unless it can be shown that it was not intended to be part of the land, and if it is only resting on the surface, it is prima facie not a fixture unless it can be shown that it was intended to be one. For details see Ch.2. Although a tenant may sever and remove the class of "tenant's fixtures" such as ornamental, trade and agricultural fixtures,[165] a similar exception does not apply to mortgagors.[166]

The Right to Possession

24–94 The right to possession is of vital importance to the mortgagee when it becomes necessary to enforce its security. There are a number of reasons for this. First, though it is not strictly necessary for the mortgagee to be in possession before exercising its right to sale, possession will usually be sought prior to sale in order to maximise the price obtained for the property. Secondly, possession may be necessary to protect the mortgaged property from damage owing to abandonment and the entry of trespassers. Thirdly, where it is proposed to appoint a receiver, it will usually be advantageous for the mortgagee to take possession of the property.

Mortgages Created Prior to 1 December 2009
Legal Mortgages

24–95 At common law, the legal mortgagee by conveyance had a right to possession following from the fact that it held the legal estate in the land.[167] Thus, strictly speaking, the mortgagee's right to possession did not require a default on the part of the mortgagor. As Harman J. put it in *Four-Maids Ltd v Dudley Marshall Properties Ltd*:

> "The right of the mortgagee to possession in the absence of some contract has nothing to do with default on the part of the mortgagor. The mortgagee may go into possession before the ink is dry on the mortgage unless there is something in the contract, express or by implication, whereby he has contracted himself out of that right. He has the right because he has a legal term of years in the property."[168]

24–96 Because the legal mortgagee's right to possession derived from its status as the holder of a freehold estate, the right to possession is a substantive

---

[164] LCLRA 2009 s.71 re-enacting, in amended form, ss.2 and 6 of the Conveyancing Act 1881.

[165] Deasy's Act 1860 s.17.

[166] *Climie v Wood* (1869) L.R. 4 Ex. 328.

[167] Unless the mortgagor had parted with the right before the mortgage was granted, as by granting a lease: *Moss v Gallimore* (1779) 1 Doug. K.B. 279 at 283. A lease granted after the mortgage would not bind the mortgagee.

[168] [1957] Ch. 317 at 320.

property right and not a remedy. The result is that in strict principle no court order is required for the mortgagee to take peaceable possession of mortgaged property.[169] In England, the extent of the mortgagee's right to possession has been the subject of controversy. In *Horsham Properties Group v Clark*[170] the original mortgagee transferred its interest in a defaulted mortgage to another company. The mortgagee's successor in title then utilised the mortgagee's right to possession as a basis to pursue trespass proceedings against a domestic mortgagor. This avoided the possibility of an application for an order for possession against the mortgagor being stayed under legislation designed to protect homeowners.[171] Such an approach is unusual and Briggs J. in the High Court conducted an extensive analysis of human rights arguments before ultimately concluding that the mortgagees did in fact enjoy a right of possession over the property.

24–97 It is less clear whether a mortgagee is entitled to take possession without a court order in Ireland. In *Gale v First National Building Society*,[172] Costello J. endorsed the proposition that a legal mortgagee has the right to take peaceable possession of the land without a court order. More recent decisions have taken a more ambiguous approach. In *Irish Life & Permanent v Duff*, Hogan J. suggested that "it is necessary to revisit the legal fiction underpinning a mortgage".[173] He went on to suggest that both "the ancient legal fictions" of the mortgage and the decision in *Gale* need to be "re-examined" in light of recent developments in constitutional law. Article 40.5 of the Constitution provides a guarantee of the inviolability of the dwelling house. In a series of cases, most notably *Damache v DPP*[174] and *People (DPP) v Cunningham*,[175] the Irish courts have held that Art.40.5 requires judicial oversight where the Gardaí seek a search warrant for the carrying out of searches of a dwelling house. By analogy, Hogan J. suggested that the mortgagee's right of possession must also require judicial oversight:

"This assurance of security and protection inherent in the guarantee of 'inviolability' would be fundamentally compromised if peaceable possession of a dwelling could be taken by a lender at almost any time other than by means of a court order without express notice to the borrower in the manner envisaged by Costello J. in *Gale v. First National Building Society* merely because the borrower was in default, even if this were to be contractually agreed by reason of the fictions which predate the Act of 2009 in respect of

---

[169] *Ropaigealach v Barclay's Bank plc* [2000] Q.B. 263.
[170] [2009] 1 W.L.R. 1255. See E. Dewhurst, "The Power of Sale without a Court Order: A Deprivation of Possession or a Contractual Right?" (2009) 14(1) C.P.L.J. 13.
[171] Administration of Justice Act 1970 s.36. See also S. Greer, "*Horsham Properties Group Ltd v Clark:* Possession – Mortgagee's Right or Discretionary Remedy?" [2009] Conv. 516.
[172] [1985] I.R. 609.
[173] [2013] 4 I.R. 96 at 110.
[174] [2012] 1 I.R. 266.
[175] [2013] 2 I.R. 631.

unregistered land we have just examined. Nor could this be assured if the determination as to whether the borrower was actually in default was to be left to the say so of the lender or whether there was an objective justification for the mortgagee taking possession of the dwelling without any independent determination of these questions by the judicial branch."[176]

24–98 The constitutional concerns raised by Hogan J. in *Duff* do not of course have any application to land which is not being used as a dwelling house. In *Moorview Developments Ltd v First Active plc*[177] the High Court upheld the actions of a receiver who had taken peaceable possession of mortgaged property in accordance with the mortgage agreement.

24–99 The mortgagee's right to take possession of the property is usually made conditional on a default in repayments by the mortgagor. The identification of a suitable event of default and the establishment of appropriate notification procedures are a matter of contract between the parties. For procedural reasons, it was the case in the past that mortgages commonly contained what was known as an attornment clause.[178] Under such a clause, the mortgagor declared himself or herself to be a tenant at will of the mortgagee, which in turn facilitated the use of ejectment actions available to landlords for the purposes of obtaining an order for possession of mortgaged land. In the absence of an express limitation on the mortgagee's right to possession, an implied limitation will not usually be found to exist. In *Esso Petroleum Co Ltd v Alstonbridge Properties Ltd*[179] the court held that the mere fact that the mortgage was to be repaid by instalments was not sufficient to justify the implication of a limitation.

Equitable Mortgages

24–100 In the case of an equitable mortgage, the mortgagee has no legal estate and so has no right to possession at common law. The mortgage agreement can confer a right to possession on the equitable mortgagee, but this would require the consent of any prior legal mortgagee. There is authority in Ireland for the view that an equitable mortgagee can claim possession in equity at least as against the mortgagor.[180] The mortgagee has a *remedy* of possession which is at the discretion of the court, as are all equitable remedies.[181]

---

[176] [2013] 4 I.R. 96 at 112.

[177] [2009] IEHC 214.

[178] See Maddox, *Mortgages: Law and Practice* (2017), para.5–11.

[179] [1975] 1 W.L.R. 1474.

[180] *Antrim County Land, Building and Investment Co Ltd v Stewart* [1904] 2 I.R. 357, and see *Re O'Neill* [1967] N.I. 129 at 135.

[181] *Bunyan v Bunyan* [1916] 1 I.R. 70; *Royal Bank of Ireland v O'Shea* (1943) 77 I.L.T.R. 4; *Irish Permanent Building Society v Ryan* [1950] I.R. 12; *Re O'Neill* [1967] N.I. 129.

Actions for Possession

24–101 Order 54 r.3 of the Rules of the Superior Courts creates a summary procedure for the recovery of possession by way of special summons. This process is available to both legal and equitable mortgagees. This replaced an older procedure whereby possession and sale of mortgaged property was sought by an action for a declaration that the mortgagor's interests were "well charged" with an order for sale if the mortgagor did not pay the principal or interest due within three months. The sale was by the court itself, which was a cumbersome and expensive process. In *Bank of Ireland v Slattery*, the High Court confirmed that the making of an order for possession can be made in isolation from an order for possession and sale in appropriate cases.[182] The courts' view of when an order for possession should be granted has, however, undergone some change. It seems that the court may be more willing to grant possession than was the case in the past.

24–102 In *Doran v Hannin*[183] possession was granted of licensed premises in order to prevent forfeiture of the licence; in *Bank of Ireland v Slattery*,[184] in order to effectuate a sale which was being frustrated by the interference of the mortgagor's family; and in *Bunyan v Bunyan*[185] where no payment of principal money had been made and there was a large amount of interest in arrears. In each case there was something unusual on the facts, but more recently in *Irish Permanent Building Society v Ryan*[186] a mortgagor had defaulted in repaying instalments of a building society mortgage and the High Court decided that possession would be granted merely on the ground that the property would fetch a higher price if sold with vacant possession, which is almost always the case. Gavan Duffy P. emphasised, however, that the mortgage itself contained a clause for possession when money was due and unpaid:

> "Mortgagees have seldom sought possession under Order 55 r 7, and the Court has been slow to make an order. Nevertheless, I am of opinion that applications such as the present should be encouraged, rather than discouraged, in suitable cases, in view of the great saving in costs so far as the defendant is concerned. Having regard to the position of the defendant, I think this is a suitable case. The defendant executed an indenture of mortgage which contained a special clause, carefully drafted, enabling the mortgagees to enter into possession of the mortgaged premises if the mortgagor should be in default for the space of three calendar months in the payment of some instalment of principal and interest due under the mortgage deed. In the present case the defendant has been in default for the space of twelve months in the payment of the instalments and, in fact, has never paid any of

---

[182] [1911] 1 I.R. 33 at 40, applying Rules of the Supreme Court (Ireland) 1905 Ord.55 r.7.
[183] (1906) 40 I.L.T.R. 185.
[184] [1911] 1 I.R. 33.
[185] [1916] 1 I.R. 70.
[186] [1950] I.R. 12.

the instalments due under the mortgage deed and has no prospect of paying any."[187]

A Discretion to Refuse Possession?

24–103 It is open to question whether the law should continue to distinguish between legal and equitable mortgages when it comes to determining whether there is a right to possession. The justification for the legal mortgagee's right to possession is derived from the fact that historically such mortgagees held a freehold estate in the land and thus enjoyed an inherent right of possession. This is a reifying explanation based on the supposed qualities of legal estates in land and which takes no account of the social function or economic substance of the mortgage transaction. By contrast, equity has long regarded the mortgagee's rights in other respects as accorded for the purpose of realising the security and not simply as an aspect of legal ownership as such. That is why equity allows redemption after the legal date of redemption has passed. Equity treats the mortgagor as the substantial owner of the property. Why should the right to possession be treated differently?

24–104 It is worth nothing that Lord Denning M.R. thought that there was a general discretion to refuse possession. In *Quennell v Maltby*[188] the owner of the fee simple in a house mortgaged it to a bank as security for a loan. In breach of the mortgage conditions, the homeowner then let the premises to university students. Some years later the students refused to leave the premises claiming that they had a statutory right to the premises under the English Rent Acts. The mortgagor tried unsuccessfully to persuade the bank to bring an action for possession as mortgagee. He then asked the bank to transfer the mortgage to his wife on her paying off the overdraft, which she agreed to do. The bank transferred the mortgage to the wife who then brought the action, claiming that as mortgagee she had an absolute right to possession.

24–105 The Court of Appeal refused to allow the Rent Acts to be evaded in this manner. Lord Denning M.R. pointed out that the wife had brought the action "simply for an ulterior purpose of getting possession of the house, contrary to the intention of Parliament, as expressed in the Rent Acts". Characteristically, he then went further and held that there was a more general discretion today in relation to a legal mortgagee:

> "[I]n modern times equity can step in so as to prevent a mortgagee, or transferee from him, from getting possession of a house contrary to the justice of the case."[189]

---

[187] [1950] I.R. 12 at 13–14.
[188] [1979] 1 W.L.R. 318.
[189] [1979] 1 W.L.R. 318 at 322.

24–106 As noted above Lord Denning's judgment in *Quennell* has not found favour with other English courts, and *Quennell* is now primarily read as an authority for the proposition that the right to possession must be exercised for the purpose of enforcing the mortgage and not for other unconnected reasons.[190]

Registered Land

24–107 A mortgagee of registered land has no estate in the land and thus no right to possession at common law.[191] As a result, the mortgagee (or chargee to use the language of the RTA 1964), had no right to possession (a state of affairs described as a "yawning gap" by Geoghegan J. in *Bank of Ireland v Smyth*)[192] until the passage of s.62(7) of the RTA 1964. This read as follows until its repeal by the LCLRA 2009:

"(7) When repayment of the principal money secured by the instrument of charge has become due, the registered owner of the charge or his personal representative may apply to the court in a summary manner for possession of the land or any part of the land, and on the application the court may, if it so thinks proper, order possession of the land or the said part thereof to be delivered to the applicant, and the applicant, upon obtaining possession of the land or the said part thereof, shall be deemed to be a mortgagee in possession."

24–108 Under s.62(7) it was clear that the court had a discretion as to whether to grant possession. In *Bank of Ireland v Smyth*[193] Geoghegan J. held that the court's discretion under s.62(7) amounted to no more than a requirement to apply equitable principles and did not entitle the court to take account of "sympathetic factors". A similar conclusion was reached in the High Court in *Anglo Irish Bank v Fanning*[194] and again in *Start Mortgages v Gunn*.[195] The judgment of Macken J. in *Dellway Investments v NAMA* suggests that the court's discretion might be somewhat broader than that suggested in *Smyth*:

"Critically, in the event of default, if a bank calls in a loan and wishes to sell, and does not enter into any arrangements of the types above mentioned, it must seek an order for possession from the court. On that application, again typically, a mortgagor will be entitled to argue against an order for possession, or may present to the court - and this often occurs even in domestic situations - a schedule or plan for its own sale of the premises. Provided the proposal is clear, certain and reasonable, a court may, and frequently will, exercise its discretion to refuse possession, by acceding to the plan, which

---

[190] See *Çukurova Finance International Ltd v Alfa Telecom Turkey Ltd (Nos 3 to 5)* [2016] A.C. 923 at 935 (Privy Council).
[191] *Northern Banking Co v Devlin* [1924] 1 I.R. 90.
[192] [1993] 2 I.R. 102 at 110.
[193] [1993] 2 I.R. 102 at 111–112.
[194] [2009] IEHC 141.
[195] [2011] IEHC 275.

may extend over a period in excess of a year, or more, provided, usually, that certain payments are made in the meantime to protect the mortgagee, and provided there is also remaining some underlying equity or 'free' element in the property for the mortgagor. In general, this application for possession will have been preceded by negotiations, sometime lengthy, between the parties. A mortgagor may or will therefore have significant protection from the court in such a situation."[196]

It is unclear how much weight should be attached to this paragraph. It is included in a broad summary of the general law of mortgages which was set out for the purposes of contrasting the special powers created by the National Asset Management Agency Act 2009 with the position of an "ordinary" bank. It is notable that the learned judge did not explicitly differentiate between registered and unregistered land in the passage. The mortgagee's right of possession was certainly not the key issue before the Supreme Court in *Dellway*, indeed there is no evidence from the law report that s.62(7) of the RTA 1964 was relied upon in argument, and *Bank of Ireland v Smyth* is not mentioned in any of the judgments in *Dellway*. The passage is clearly obiter and it is suggested that it was probably not intended to effect a change in the interpretation of s.62(7).

Repeal of Section 62(7)—Start Mortgages v Gunn

24–109 As a part of the simplification of the law of mortgages undertaken by the LCLRA 2009, s.62(7) of the RTA 1964 was repealed,[197] along with several of the mortgage provisions of the Conveyancing Acts 1881–1911. The intention was that s.62(7) would be replaced by the new mortgage provisions of the LCLRA 2009, though Pt 10 of the Act applies only to mortgages created after 1 December 2009. This left open the question as to the effect of the repeal of the section on proceedings in respect of mortgages created prior to that date.

24–110 As originally enacted, s.62 of the RTA 1964 was intended to align the rights and powers of a chargee of registered land with those of a mortgagee of unregistered land. The text adopted in s.62 contained complex provisions regarding the timing at which particular rights arose. Under s.62(6) the chargee obtained the powers of a mortgagee under the Conveyancing Acts (i.e. the power to appoint a receiver, the power of sale etc.) upon registration of the charge in the Land Registry. Section 62(7) conferred a right to apply for possession of the land at the date when the repayment of the principal monies secured by the charge fell due.

24–111 The consequences of the repeal of s.62(7) of the RTA 1964 were explored in *Start Mortgages v Gunn*.[198] The case involved a number of

---

[196] [2011] 4 I.R. 1 at 351.
[197] LCLRA 2009 s.8 and Sch.4.
[198] [2011] IEHC 275.

summary applications for possession of registered land on foot of mortgages created and registered prior to 1 December 2009. The mortgages in question all provided that the principal sum would become due upon the making of a demand of one kind or another by the lender and in each case the proceedings commenced after the repeal of s.62(7). This approach to drafting mortgage agreements is of recent origin and contrasts with the traditional approach which contained a "monies" clause designed to vest the mortgagee's remedies at or shortly after the date of the mortgage. The plaintiffs claimed that their right to seek possession under s.62(7) had been preserved by s.27(1)(c) of the Interpretation Act 2005. Section 27(1)(c) provides that where a statute is repealed, the repeal does not affect any "right, privilege, obligation or liability acquired, accrued or incurred under the enactment". The question therefore was whether the plaintiffs had a right to possession which had accrued under s.62(7) of the RTA 1964 prior to its repeal and which was thus capable of being preserved by the Interpretation Act 2005. Dunne J. rejected the contention that the right to possession had accrued under s.62(6) at the date of registration of the charge, holding instead that the right to possession was only preserved by the Interpretation Act 2005 if the principal sum of money secured by the charge had become due on or before 1 December 2009. Although this was the case in *Gunn*, in some of the other cases no formal demand had been made for payment prior to 1 December 2009.

24–112 The impact of *Gunn* was less dramatic than it has sometimes been portrayed. The "lacuna" identified in the decisions is fairly narrow and only affects mortgages where the documentation follows a particular pattern. In *Ulster Bank v McDonnell*,[199] for example, the mortgage agreement provided that the whole sum would become due without any requirement for the mortgagee to serve a valid letter of demand on the mortgagor; on the facts this enabled *Gunn* to be easily distinguished. In *GE Capital Woodchester v Reade*,[200] by contrast, the mortgage contract provided that the principal sum did not become due and owing until there had been (a) a default in payment and (b) the issue by the mortgagee of a letter of demand stating that the whole capital sum was due and owing. Secondly, it should be emphasised, as Laffoy J. did in *Reade* that *Gunn* does not invalidate pre-2009 mortgages or render them unenforceable. The sole effect of the repeal of s.62(7) of the RTA 1964 is to remove the right to apply for summary possession from the narrow class of mortgages within the scope of the *Gunn* decision.

24–113 *Gunn* has been criticised by Wylie.[201] First, he argues that Dunne J. should have considered the traditional form of mortgage and that had she done so she might have given broader meaning to the wording of s.27 of the Interpretation Act 2005. This criticism does not seem entirely fair, since the court was

---

[199] [2014] IEHC 69. See also *Ulster Bank v Carroll* [2013] IEHC 347 and *EBS v Gillespie* [2012] IEHC 243.
[200] [2012] IEHC 363.
[201] Wylie, *Irish Land Law* (2013), paras 14.25–14.26.

not presented with a traditional mortgage agreement in any of the cases before it. Secondly, Wylie suggests (with the support of Maddox)[202] that if *Gunn* is correct, the repeal of s.62(7) had the effect of stripping affected mortgagees of a valuable remedy retrospectively, an outcome which he and Maddox suggest is unconstitutional. This argument received a degree of judicial support from Hogan J. in *Irish Life & Permanent v Duff*, albeit on an obiter basis.[203]

24–114 It is worth noting that Feeney J. in *McEnery v Sheahan*[204] took a different approach to that adopted in *Gunn* when faced with determining the effect of the repeal of the mortgage provisions of the 1881 Act on the right to appoint a receiver. Feeney J. distinguished *Gunn* on the basis that the right to apply for possession on a summary basis is a procedural right rather than a substantive one (a distinction which is not perhaps entirely convincing[205]). He then held that the right to appoint a receiver was a substantive right which was acquired at the date of the mortgage and which was subsequently preserved as an acquired right under s.27(1) notwithstanding the repeal of s.19 of the 1881 Act. *McEnery* has been doubted by Wylie, who suggests that the decision has been "studiously ignored" by other High Court judges dealing with the consequences of *Gunn*.[206] The potential divergence between *Gunn* and *McEnery* was noted by Clarke J. in the Supreme Court in *Irish Life & Permanent v Dunne,* though Clarke J. explicitly refused to express a view on how that divergence might be resolved.[207]

24–115 The decision in *Gunn* caused significant concern for secured lenders and for wider policy makers, especially the EU/IMF/ECB Troika. In its Summer 2012 Report on the Economic Adjustment Programme for Ireland, the European Commission pointed to the need to "redress the legal gap which prevents creditors from exercising their right to collateral on defaulted loans in some circumstances."[208] As has been seen above, this concern was a little overstated—the *Gunn* judgment did not prevent creditors from enforcing their security over mortgaged land. Nonetheless, the Oireachtas responded to these concerns by passing the Land and Conveyancing Law Reform Act 2013 ("LCLRA 2013"). The LCLRA 2013 reverses the repeal of s.62(7) of the RTA 1964 and of the mortgage provisions of the Conveyancing Acts 1881–1911 and specifically applies those provisions to mortgages created before 1 December 2009 "as if those provisions had not been repealed".[209] Section 1(5) provided that the section did not apply to proceedings already in being

---

[202] Maddox, *Mortgages: Law and Practice* (2017), paras 5–53 to 5–54.
[203] [2013] 4 I.R. 96 at 108.
[204] [2012] IEHC 331.
[205] Wylie, *Irish Land Law* (2013), para.14.26.
[206] Wylie, *Irish Land Law* (2013), para.14.26.
[207] [2016] I.R. 96 at 129.
[208] European Commission, *Economic Adjustment Programme for Ireland Summer 2012 Review* (2012), pp.27–28.
[209] LCLRA 2013 s.1(2).

before the courts, but as Maddox points out, such proceedings could be discontinued and subsequently recommenced in order to take the benefit of the LCLRA 2013.[210]

Mortgages Created after 1 December 2009

24–116 Sections 97 and 98 of the LCLRA 2009 now govern the mortgagee's right to possession for mortgages created after 1 December 2009 regardless of their legal form. Section 97 provides that a mortgagee may not take possession without a court order unless the mortgagor consents in writing with at least seven days' notice prior to taking possession. Section 97(2) provides that the mortgagee may apply to court for an order for possession which may be granted on such terms and conditions as the court may think fit. The wording of this section is similar to s.62(7) of the RTA 1964. Section 101 requires the court to adjourn proceedings or stay an order for possession where there is a likelihood that the mortgagor will discharge arrears including interest under the mortgage. Other than in the context of housing loan mortgages,[211] there appears to be no reason, in principle, why the parties cannot contract out of these requirements.

24–117 Section 98 creates a jurisdiction for the District Court (or any other court seised of proceedings in relation to the mortgaged property) to permit a mortgagee to take possession where the mortgagor has abandoned the property or where urgent steps are necessary in order to prevent damage to the property on entry upon it by trespassers. The court has broad discretion to fix the terms of the mortgagee's possession, including its duration and can direct that the mortgagee's costs and expenses be added to the mortgage sum. This jurisdiction is separate to the mortgagee's general right to possession and under s.98(4) the mortgagee does not have an obligation of strict account whilst in possession on foot of an order under this section.

The Right to Possession and the Family Home

24–118 Section 7 of the Family Home Protection Act 1976 permits the court to adjourn proceedings for possession and sale in respect of a family home where the other spouse is capable of paying the arrears due and is willing to do so and where it would be just and equitable to do so having regard to all the circumstances. The duration of the adjournment and its terms and conditions can be set by the court. Section 32 of the Civil Partnership and Certain Rights and Obligations of Cohabitants Act 2010 provides a similar protection for the shared home of civil partners. There is a substantial overlap in this discretion with that afforded to the court under s.97 of the LCLRA 2009, but the two provisions are not quite identical in that the Family Home Protection Act 1976 and Civil Partnership and Certain Rights and Obligations of Cohabitants

---

[210] Maddox, *Mortgages: Law and Practice* (2017), para.5–55.
[211] LCLRA 2009 s.62(3).

Act 2010 discretions provide for the court to consider the ability of the spouse or partner of a mortgagor to discharge mortgage arrears whereas s.101 of the LCLRA 2009 seems to confine the analysis to the position of the mortgagor. Possession proceedings against family homes are also the subject of regulatory constraints which will be considered below.

The European Convention on Human Rights
24–119 Public authorities who wish to seek repossession of property may also have to take into account the impact of the European Convention on Human Rights Act 2003.[212] Possession may engage Arts 6 and 8 of the European Convention on Human Rights (ECHR). The ECHR issues may engage both the mortgagor and other occupiers of the home including children and other dependants.[213]

The Duty of Strict Account
24–120 A mortgagee in possession may recoup interest due from the rents or profits of the property, and may also apply any surplus to the repayment of capital.[214] For mortgages entered into prior to the LCLRA 2009, there was a statutory power to cut trees on the land.[215] This power has now been repealed, though as Wylie points out the discretion created under s.97(2) allowing the court to set the terms of the mortgagee's possession is wide enough to allow the court to make necessary orders in suitable cases.[216] Apart from these rights, the mortgagee must account strictly to the mortgagor, both for income actually received and for income which would have been received but for his or her default.[217]

24–121 Section 99 of the LCLRA 2009 imposes an obligation on a mortgagee in possession to sell or lease the property within a reasonable time after taking possession. Section 99(2) also eliminates an anomaly which existed in the pre-2009 law by providing that the mortgagee's possession is not adverse to the rights of the mortgagor.

The Mortgagee's Power of Sale
24–122 The mortgagee has a statutory power to sell the mortgaged property free of the mortgagor's equity of redemption. In the early development of the mortgage, mortgagees did not have the right to sell the land free of the

---

[212] See E. Dewhurst, "The Power of Sale without a Court Order: A Deprivation of Possession or a Contractual Right?" (2009) 14(1) C.P.L.J. 13.
[213] S. Nield and N. Hopkins, "Human Rights and Mortgage Repossessions: Beyond Property Law Using Article 8" (2013) 33 L.S. 431. See also Maddox, *Mortgages: Law and Practice* (2017), paras 5–81 to 5–85.
[214] *Nelson v Booth* (1858) 3 De G. & J. 119.
[215] Conveyancing Act 1881 s.19(4).
[216] Wylie, *Irish Land Law* (2013), para.12.82.
[217] *O'Connell v O'Callaghan* (1863) 15 Ir. Ch. R. 31.

mortgagor's equity of redemption.[218] In the early 19th century, a practice evolved of conferring a power on the mortgagee to sell the fee simple free of the equity of redemption and to recoup the capital, interest and costs from the purchase monies.[219] Section 19 of the 1881 Act[220] conferred a statutory power of sale on mortgagees created by deed. This was repealed by the LCLRA 2009 but was subsequently restored to the statute book by the LCLRA 2013 as regards mortgages created prior to 2009.[221]

24–123 The mortgagee will usually wish to exercise the power of sale after having gone into possession. This has the advantage that the mortgagee will be able to sell the property out of court and with the benefit of vacant possession. This course of action will generally result in a higher price for the property (since few purchasers will be prepared to purchase property where the mortgagor is still in possession) and also reduces the costs associated with a sale in court.

Power of Sale for Mortgages Entered into before 1 December 2009

24–124 Where a legal mortgage was created by deed before 1 December 2009, the power of sale will almost always be in accordance with s.19 of the 1881 Act.[222] Section 19 operates by implying terms into the mortgage contract and thus it is always necessary to check that the terms have not been varied by agreement between the parties. Where an equitable mortgage has been granted by deed the s.19 terms will be implied on the same basis. The power of sale under s.19 reads as follows:

"A power, when the mortgage money has become due, to sell, or to concur with any other person in selling, the mortgaged property, or any part thereof, either subject to prior charges, or not, and either together or in lots, by public auction or by private contract, subject to such conditions respecting title, or evidence of title, or other matter, as he (the mortgagee) thinks fit, with power to vary any contract for sale, and to buy in at an auction, or to rescind any contract for sale, and to re-sell, without being answerable for any loss occasioned thereby ...".

24–125 It is worth noting that an equitable mortgagee selling under this power cannot convey the legal estate in the land.[223] This problem can be avoided by

---

[218] *Croft v Powell* (1737) 2 Comyns 603.

[219] R.H. Coote, *A Treatise on the Law of Mortgages* (London: Butterworth, 1821), pp.126–127.

[220] The statutory power of sale was initiated by Lord Cranworth's Act 1860 (23 & 24 Vict c 145).

[221] See the previous section on *Start Mortgages v Gunn* [2011] IEHC 275. The restoration of s.19 of the Conveyancing Act 1881 appears to have been done *ex abundanti cautela* in view of the decision in *McEnery v Sheahan* [2012] IEHC 331.

[222] See Wylie, *Irish Land Law* (2013), para.14.56. Section 62(6) of the RTA 1964 provides that a charge on registered land confers the same powers as a mortgage by deed on the date of its registration.

[223] *Re Hodson and Howes' Contract* (1886) 31 Ch. D. 668.

granting the equitable mortgagee power of attorney to convey the legal estate or by declaring that the mortgagor holds the legal estate on trust for the mortgagee.[224] Where an equitable mortgage is created otherwise than by deed, e.g. an equitable mortgage by deposit, the mortgagee has no power of sale and must apply to the court for an order of sale.[225]

24–126 It is necessary to consider the distinction between the power under s.19 arising and it becoming exercisable. The importance of this distinction is that if the power has not arisen, then the mortgagee cannot give title to the property to a purchaser free of the mortgagor's right of redemption. If on the other hand, the power has arisen but has not become exercisable at the time of sale, the purchaser will take good title, but the mortgagee is liable in damages to the mortgagor.[226] The power of sale arises at the date when the legal date for redemption has passed. Where the mortgage is repayable by instalment, the power of sale will arise when there is default on the repayment of any instalment.[227]

24–127 Section 20 of the 1881 Act provides that the power of sale does not become exercisable unless:

  (i) notice requiring payment of the mortgage money has been served on the mortgagor and the mortgagor is in default of payment of the mortgage money, or of part thereof, for three months;

 (ii) interest is in arrears and unpaid for at least two months; or

(iii) there has been a breach of some provision contained in the mortgage deed or the Act, and on the part of the mortgagor other than payment of the mortgage money or interest.

24–128 The benefit which the purchaser enjoys here is that he or she need only satisfy himself or herself that the power has arisen, which in the past could be done by examining the mortgage deed to see if the legal date of redemption had passed without the mortgage being redeemed. He or she need not inquire into the mortgage accounts kept by the mortgagee. Nowadays, however, when most mortgages are repayable by instalments the purchaser will have to satisfy himself or herself that a payment is in arrears which will require some enquiry of the mortgagee/building society, although it need not be of the extensive kind which would be the case if he or she had to satisfy himself or herself that the conditions in s.20 were present. The courts have not allowed the 1881 Act to be used as a means of fraud and have held that the purchaser will not obtain title if he or she has actual knowledge of some irregularity.[228]

---

[224] *Re White Rose Cottage* [1965] Ch. 940; *Re Segie* [1954] N.I. 1.
[225] *Antrim County Land, Building and Investment Co Ltd v Stewart* [1904] 2 I.R. 357.
[226] For details, see the second edition of this work, pp.796–798.
[227] *Payne v Cardiff RDC* [1932] 1 K.B. 241.
[228] *Bailey v Barnes* [1984] 1 Ch. 25 at 30.

Mortgages Granted after 1 December 2009

24–129 The LCLRA 2009 simplifies the law of the mortgagee's power of sale. The provisions of the Act apply only to mortgages created by deed. Under s.96 of the LCLRA 2009, the powers of a mortgagee vest at the time when the mortgage is created, or at the time when the charge is registered in the case of registered land. This has the effect of eliminating the distinction between the power of sale arising and its exercise under s.19 of the 1881 Act.

24–130 Section 100 governs the exercise of the power of sale for a mortgage created after the LCLRA 2009. The exercise of the power of sale is still subject to the same three conditions provided for in s.20 of the 1881 Act, but the LCLRA 2009 has added a number of additional protections for the mortgagor. First, there is a general restriction under s.96 whereby the mortgagee's power can only be exercised for the purposes of protecting the property or enforcing the mortgagee's security. Secondly, s.100(1) requires that any exercise of the power of sale be preceded by the service on the mortgagor of a notice, in prescribed form,[229] of the possibility of a sale. Thirdly, the power of sale cannot be exercised without a court order unless the mortgagor consents in writing not less than seven days in advance of the exercise of the power.[230] The court has a discretion in disposing of such an application, which is in identical terms to the discretion in applications for possession.[231] A concurrent application can be made for both possession and sale simultaneously.[232]

24–131 The abolition of the distinction between the power of sale arising and becoming exercisable is a welcome simplification of the law and reduces the scope of inquiries which a purchaser buying from the mortgagee must make.[233] However, the court has an equitable jurisdiction to prevent a statute from being used as an engine of fraud. A purchaser who has knowledge of an irregularity in the exercise of the power of sale will not obtain good title to the land concerned.[234] The standard of knowledge required here is whether the purchaser "wilfully shut his eyes"[235] to the existence of an irregularity, which requires less vigilance on the part of purchasers than the principles of constructive notice.

24–132 Section 104 of the LCLRA 2009 provides that a sale gives the purchaser whatever estate or interest had been mortgaged. If the mortgage is

---

[229] Land and Conveyancing Law Reform Act 2009 (Section 100) Regulations 2010 (S.I. No. 653 of 2010).
[230] LCLRA 2009 s.100(3).
[231] LCLRA 2009 s.101.
[232] LCLRA 2009 s.100(4).
[233] In particular, there is no need for the purchaser to satisfy himself or herself that the legal date for redemption has passed.
[234] *Selwyn v Garfit* (1888) 38 Ch. D. 373; *Bailey v Barnes* [1894] 1 Ch. 25.
[235] *Bailey v Barnes* [1894] 1 Ch. 25 at 30.

over registered land, then the sale must be registered as a condition of its effectiveness.[236]

Exercising the Power of Sale

24–133 The advantage of the statutory power of sale is that the mortgagee has control of the sale and need not sell the mortgaged property through the court. In most cases this has advantages both in terms of saving court costs and in obtaining the best price for the mortgaged property since the mortgagee has a wide discretion in conducting the sale itself.[237] The mortgagee is entitled for example to impose restrictive covenants on the land.[238]

The Mortgagee's Duty of Care

24–134 A mortgagee in exercising the statutory power of sale is acting in its own interest in that it is recovering the mortgage debt due to it. The mortgagor and any other *puisne* mortgagees also have an interest in ensuring that the sale generates a good price since any surplus which is left after paying off the vendor mortgagee will be distributed to them. This conflict has given rise to controversy in the case law. In the early 19th century Lord Eldon held that the mortgagee was a trustee for the mortgagor in exercising the power of sale,[239] but this view has been decisively rejected by the Irish courts in recent times.[240] It is however the case that the mortgagee cannot sell the property to itself or to an agent acting on its behalf.[241]

24–135 Section 21 of the 1881 Act provides that the mortgagee is not liable for any involuntary loss occurring in the exercise of the power of sale.[242] This section remains relevant for mortgages created before 1 December 2009. Historically the courts had suggested that there was no need for the mortgagee to delay the sale where doing so might result in a better price being obtained.[243]

24–136 More recent Irish case law suggests that a mortgagee must act in good faith when exercising the statutory power of sale. In *Holohan v Friends Provident*[244] the mortgagees advertised the property as an investment and

---

[236] LCLRA 2009 s.104 applying RTA 1964 s.51.

[237] LCLRA 2009 s.102, re-enacting in substance s.19(1) of the Conveyancing Act 1881.

[238] LCLRA 2009 s.102; Conveyancing Act 1911 s.4.

[239] *Downes v Grazebrook* (1817) 3 Mer. 200.

[240] *Irish Life and Permanent plc v Financial Services Ombudsman* [2011] IEHC 439; *Irish Life and Permanent v Financial Services Ombudsman* [2012] IEHC 367 at paras 44–47.

[241] *Farrar v Farrars Ltd* (1888) 40 Ch. D. 395 at 408. On a sale to the mortgagee's agent, see *Hodgson v Deans* [1903] 3 Ch. 647.

[242] 1881 Act s.21, repealed by LCLRA 2009 ss.2, 8(3) and Sch.4, and restored by LCLRA 2013 s.1.

[243] *Farrar v Farrars Ltd* (1889) 40 Ch. D. 395 at 398. See also, *Haddington Island Quarry v Huson* [1911] A.C. 722 at 727; *Kennedy v De Trafford* [1896] 1 Ch. 762 at 772, affirmed in [1897] A.C. 180; *Belton v Bass, Ratcliffe and Gretton Ltd* [1922] 2 Ch. 449.

[244] [1966] I.R. 1.

without vacant possession. The mortgagor claimed that a higher price would be obtained if vacant possession were obtained and that parts of the premises should have been sold as separate lots. In the Supreme Court, Ó Dálaigh C.J. held that the mortgagees were under a duty to act as a reasonable person when exercising the power of sale.

24–137 Section 26(1) of the Building Societies Act 1989 places a statutory obligation on a building society to "ensure as far as is reasonably practicable that the property is sold at the best price reasonably obtainable". Section 439(1) of the Companies Act 2014 imposes a similar obligation on a receiver appointed under the Companies Act 2014 to "exercise all reasonable care to obtain the best price reasonably obtainable for the property as at the time of sale". Section 103(1) of the LCLRA 2009 imposes a similar statutory obligation on mortgagees exercising a power of sale for mortgages created after December 2009. It is worth noting that this duty is imposed regardless of any term in the contract and is thus the only provision of Pt 10, Ch.3 which is mandatory for all mortgages.

Proceeds of Sale
24–138 Although the mortgagee is not a trustee of the power of sale, s.21(3) of the 1881 Act and s.107 of the LCLRA 2009 provide that the mortgagee is a trustee of the proceeds of sale. The mortgagee must apply the proceeds of sale in the following order:

1. in discharge of prior incumbrances;
2. in payment of the costs and expenses of the sale;
3. in discharge of the mortgage money due under the mortgage;
4. in payment of the residue to the mortgagor, or if there is another mortgage, to the next mortgagee.

Effect of Sale
24–139 Section 21(1) of the 1881 Act and s.104 of the LCLRA 2009 provide that the sale of the mortgaged property under the Acts passes to the purchaser of the estate or interest in the mortgaged property "freed from all estates, interests and rights to which the mortgage has priority, but subject to all estates, interests and rights which have priority to the mortgage." Thus, where the mortgage was created by conveyance of the fee simple, the fee simple passes under the sale. Where the mortgage was by demise, or sub-demise, the term or sub-term passes. In the case of a mortgage by demise the mortgagor may declare the fee simple reversion to be held on trust for the mortgagee in case of sale so that the mortgagee may then sell it.[245] In the case of a mortgage by sub-demise a similar declaration of trust may be made of the head term held by the mortgagor.

---

[245] See *Re Sergie* [1954] N.I. 1.

Sale through the Court

24–140 Where a mortgagee cannot exercise the power of possession or cannot effectively sell the property without judicial assistance, the mortgagee may apply for an order of sale by the court. This approach will be necessary where the mortgage is not created by deed. The procedure involves an application by the mortgagee for a "well charging order". The court may direct that notice of the order be served on persons interested in the property who are not party to the proceedings and that such parties thereafter be bound by the court's order.[246]

24–141 Where a sale is ordered, the court may order that the sale by carried out by laying tenders before the court for its approval or out of court altogether. The court may not order a sale unless it is satisfied that all persons who have an interest in the land to be sold have been put on notice of the sale and will be bound by the court's order.[247] The court has power to set a reserve price.[248] The normal practice is for the court to appoint counsel to settle the conditions of sale and to investigate title if necessary.[249] If the sale is to be carried out with vacant possession then the mortgagee must apply separately to the court for an order of possession.[250] This procedure is generally avoided where possible as it involves considerable expenses.

Appointment of a Receiver

24–142 A mortgagee who takes possession of mortgaged property is strictly liable for rents and profits which might be obtained from the land. This can operate as a disincentive for mortgagees; however, if the mortgagor is left in possession, there is no obligation on him or her to apply rents and profits received from the land to the discharge of the mortgage debt. As a result, a conveyancing practice developed whereby clauses were added to mortgage deeds giving the mortgagee a power to call for the appointment of a receiver by the mortgagor. The receiver would take the profits of the land and apply them to the reduction of the mortgage debt. Since the receiver was technically an agent of the mortgagor, he or she was not liable to account as a mortgagee in possession.[251] Section 108 of the LCLRA 2009 and s.24 of the 1881 Act contain near-identical provisions governing the exercise of the power to appoint a receiver.

---

[246] Rules of the Superior Courts 1986 Ord.15 r.31.
[247] Rules of the Superior Courts Ord.51 r.3.
[248] Rules of the Superior Courts Ord.51 r.7.
[249] Rules of the Superior Courts Ord.51 r.9; *Sheridan v Gaynor* [2012] IEHC 410 at para.18.
[250] *Bank of Ireland v Waldrow* [1944] I.R. 303.
[251] Maddox, *Mortgages: Law and Practice* (2017), para.2–03.

Power to Appoint Receivers
Court-appointed Receivers
24–143 The power to appoint a receiver was developed by the Court of Chancery as an aspect of its inherent jurisdiction. This power was extended to the High Court by s.28(8) of the Supreme Court of Judicature (Ireland) Act 1877. This power is now controlled by Ord.50 r.6(1) of the Rules of the Superior Courts which provides that a receiver may be appointed by interlocutory order where it is just and convenient to do so. The jurisdiction is usually exercised where the appointment is necessary for the protection of the property for the benefit of those interested in it.[252] A receiver appointed in this way is an officer of the court and is subject to the control of the court.[253]

24–144 A receiver may also be appointed by the court as a means of enforcing a court judgment, an arrangement usually referred to as the appointment of a receiver by way of equitable execution. A receiver by way of equitable execution will not generally be appointed to payments which are to be received in the future,[254] nor can such an appointment be made where the debtor owns the legal interest in the property.[255]

Statutory Power to Appoint a Receiver
24–145 Section 19(1) of the 1881 Act and s.108 of the LCLRA 2009 provide a power to appoint a receiver. The two sections are for the most part identical, though it should be noted that for mortgages created after 1 December 2009, the power to appoint a receiver can only be exercised for the purposes authorised by s.96 of the LCLRA 2009. The power to appoint a receiver becomes exercisable on identical conditions as those which apply to the power of sale. Once the power has become exercisable, a receiver may be appointed by written instrument as a receiver of (i) the income of the mortgaged property or (ii) if the mortgage is of an interest in income, or a rent charge or period sum, the receiver may be appointed as a receiver of that income.

24–146 Section 19(1) of the 1881 Act was initially repealed by the LCLRA 2009 but has been restored to the statute book by s.1 of the LCLRA 2013. In *Kavanagh v Lynch*[256] and *McEnery v Sheahan*[257] attempts were made to suggest that the repeal of s.19 of the 1881 Act had undermined the right to appoint a receiver based on similar arguments to those advanced in respect of the right to possession in *Start Mortgages v Gunn*.[258] These arguments were not successful

---

[252] Breslin, *Banking Law in Ireland* (2013), para.15–05; *National Bank v Graham* [1994] 1 I.R. 215.

[253] *Marchioness of Downshire v Tyrrell* (1831) Hayes 254.

[254] *Ahern v Michael O'Brien & Co Ltd* [1991] 1 I.R. 421; *Clery & Co (1941) Ltd v O'Donnell* (1944) 78 I.L.T.R. 190.

[255] *Re Motor Racing Circuits Ltd*, unreported, Supreme Court, 31 January 1997.

[256] [2011] IEHC 348.

[257] [2012] IEHC 331.

[258] [2011] IEHC 275.

and the provisions of s.1 of the LCLRA 2013 would appear to preclude the possibility of future arguments succeeding on these grounds.

Appointment under the Mortgage Deed

24–147 With the exception of housing loan mortgages, the mortgage deed may alter the mortgagee's power to appoint a receiver. Modifications to the statutory provisions are a matter of contract between the parties. In particular in the context of corporate borrowers it is common to grant the receiver powers of management over the company's affairs.[259] It is critical to ensure that any formalities required by the contract on the appointment of a receiver are strictly complied with. In *Tyrell v Mahon* the High Court noted that a mortgagor is entitled to put a receiver on strict proof of all matters relating to the validity of his or her appointment.[260] The power must also be exercised in good faith and not for a collateral purpose.[261]

Functions of a Receiver

24–148 The basic function of a receiver is to collect income and rents arising from the property and to apply these to the reduction of the secured debt. Section 103(3) gives the receiver powers to demand and recover payment of such rents and to give effectual receipts for such payments. The proceeds recovered by the receiver must be applied in accordance with the order of priorities established by s.109 of the LCLRA 2009 or s.24(8) of the 1881 Act. Unlike a mortgagee in possession,[262] a receiver may charge a commission in priority to the repayment of the mortgage debt.

Receivers' Duties

24–149 Unlike a receiver appointed by the court, a receiver appointed by the mortgagee is deemed to be an agent of the mortgagor.[263] The receiver is not therefore regarded as taking possession on behalf of the mortgagee, who is relieved of its duty to account strictly to the mortgagor. This strikes a balance between ensuring that the mortgagee receives what is due to it and protecting the interest of the mortgagor. It should be noted that where a receiver is appointed to the property of a company, the Companies Act 2014 imposes more extensive duties on receivers including a duty of care to obtain the best price possible where the property is sold.[264]

---

[259] Breslin, *Banking Law in Ireland* (2013), para.15–09.
[260] [2017] IEHC 400 at para.3.
[261] *Downsview Nominees Ltd v First City Corp Ltd* [1993] A.C. 295.
[262] *Carew v Johnston* (1805) 2 Sch. & Lef. 280 at 301.
[263] LCLRA 2009 s.24(2); 1881 Act s.108.
[264] Companies Act 2014 s.439.

Foreclosure

24–150 Foreclosure is a remedy which arises in many common law jurisdictions whereby the mortgagor's right to redeem in equity comes to an end. Foreclosure was historically granted by the court on foot of a two-part procedure. First a decree nisi directed the drawing of accounts to determine the amount due to the mortgagee and any other incumbrancers and declared that the order would be made absolute unless these amounts were paid within a specified time period. The order forecloses the right of redemption, although the court had discretion to reopen a foreclosure order in certain circumstances.[265] Foreclosure was said to be a remedy that was never granted in Ireland,[266] though it was thought that the jurisdiction to foreclose was still extant prior to the LCLRA 2009 and that an order could be made in special circumstances.[267] Section 96(2) of the LCLRA 2009 abolishes the jurisdiction to grant foreclosure. It should be noted, however, that s.153 of the National Asset Management Agency Act 2009 allows the National Asset Management Agency (NAMA) and its group entities to apply to the court for a vesting order, a remedy which "bears comparison"[268] with foreclosure but which is confined to NAMA.

Consolidation

24–151 Megarry and Wade define the doctrine of consolidation as "the right of a person in whom two or more mortgages are vested to refuse to allow one mortgage to be redeemed unless the other or others are also redeemed".[269] The right of consolidation provides a useful protection to the mortgagee, particularly in a situation where there are changes to the underlying value of the mortgaged property. The potential difficulty can be demonstrated by the following example:

> A mortgages Blackacre and Whiteacre to B. Each mortgage secures a debt of €100,000 and each property has an estimated market value of €150,000. Assume that the value of Whiteacre falls to €75,000 while the value of Blackacre increases to €200,000.

In such a situation, equity regards it as unfair to permit A to render B under-secured by redeeming the mortgage on Blackacre but not that on Whiteacre. This is said to be an application of the maxim that "he who seeks

---

[265] *Campbell v Hoyland* (1887) 7 Ch. D. 166 at 169 and 172–175.

[266] *Re Power and Carton's Contract* (1890) 25 L.R. Ir. 459; *Clinton v Bernard* (1844) 6 Ir. Eq. R. 355; *Re Edwards* (1861) 11 Ir. Ch. R. 367; *Re O'Neil* [1967] N.I. 129; *Bruce v Brophy* [1906] 1 I.R. 611.

[267] In *Bruce v Brophy* [1906] 1 I.R. 611 at 619, Holmes L.J. appeared to suggest that an order might be made in an exceptional case where it was established that the land was worth less than the debt secured upon it though he did not decide the point.

[268] *Dellway Investments Ltd v National Asset Management Agency* [2011] 4 I.R. 1 at 366.

[269] C. Harpum, S. Bridge and M. Dixon, *Megarry & Wade: The Law of Real Property*, 8th edn (London: Sweet & Maxwell, 2012), para.25–055.

equity must do equity."[270] The doctrine of consolidation can apply to mortgages where one is of land and the other of personal chattels,[271] and applies regardless of whether the mortgages concerned are legal or equitable.[272]

24–152 For the right to consolidate to arise, the legal date of redemption must have expired on both mortgages.[273] Both mortgages must also have been originally created by the same mortgagor,[274] though the properties need not have initially been granted to the same mortgagee, provided that the same mortgagee holds the mortgages at the time when consolidation is sought.[275] Finally there must be a time when the right to both mortgages vested in one person, while at the same time the right to redeem both mortgages must have been vested in another person.[276]

Right Expressly Reserved

24–153 Consolidation was originally developed by courts of equity as a means of doing justice between the parties outside the bargain they had made. By the 19th century, with the development of a market economy, the notion took hold that parties should be left to themselves to bargain for what advantages they wished. Under s.17 of the 1881 Act the right to consolidate had to be expressly reserved in the mortgage deeds.[277] Section 17 was repealed by the LCLRA 2009[278] and is not one of the sections of the Conveyancing Acts which have been restored by the LCLRA 2013. Thus, it would appear that there is no longer a requirement that the right to consolidate be contained in the mortgage deeds. The extent to which the repeal of s.17 affects the consolidation of mortgages entered into prior to 1 December 2009 remains to be seen.

24–154 Section 92 of the LCLRA 2009 abolished the doctrine of consolidation to the extent that it applied to housing loan mortgages. The origin of this change lies in judicial criticism of consolidation noted by the Law Reform Commission

---

[270] *Cummins v Fletcher* (1880) 14 Ch. D. 699 at 708.

[271] *Tassell v Smith* (1858) 2 De F. & J. 713; *Watts v Smith* (1851) 3 De F.M. & G. 240.

[272] *Cracknell v Janson* (1877) 11 Ch. D. 1; *Tweedle v Tweedle* (1857) 23 Beav. 341.

[273] *AIB Mortgage Bank v O'Toole* [2016] IEHC 368 at para.11; *Cummins v Fletcher* (1880) 14 Ch. D. 699 at 709.

[274] *AIB Mortgage Bank v O'Toole* [2016] IEHC 368 at para.11; *Sharp v Richards* [1909] 1 Ch. 409.

[275] *Re Thompson's Estate* [1912] 1 I.R. 194.

[276] *Pledge v White* [1895] A.C. 187. It is worth noting that this requirement was not mentioned by the High Court in *AIB Mortgage Bank v O'Toole* [2016] IEHC 368 wherein Binchy J. substituted the additional requirement that both securities must be extant at the time that consolidation is sought. For useful examples of these principles in operation, see *Megarry & Wade: The Law of Real Property* (2012), paras 25–061 to 25–064; see also Maddox, *Mortgages: Law and Practice* (2017), para.8–43.

[277] The actual wording of the section was somewhat cumbersome in that the right to consolidate was removed "only if and as far as a contrary intention is not expressed in the mortgage deeds or any one of them".

[278] LCLRA 2009 s.8(2) and Sch.2.

in its 2004 Consultation Paper on what became the LCLRA 2009.[279] The doctrine of consolidation could lead to difficulties for a purchaser of mortgaged property who might find it difficult to discover that the vendor had mortgaged other property and that both mortgages were owned by a common mortgagee. This concern is referenced in a number of judgments.[280] The previous edition of this work argued that the operation of the Registry of Deeds may have made the problem less acute in the Irish context[281]; as against this it must be acknowledged that members of the judiciary have not indicated support for this suggestion.[282] The Law Reform Commission recommended the outright abolition of the doctrine of consolidation,[283] but s.92 affects only housing loan mortgages and in view of the repeal of s.17 of the 1881 Act the effect of the LCLRA 2009 may, ironically, be to extend the doctrine's application to a wider range of situations than was the case before its passage.

Marshalling

24–155 Marshalling is an equitable doctrine which applies where one person owns an interest in two properties and another person has an interest in one of them. The latter has the right in equity to require the owner of the two interests not to deal with them in such a way as to prejudice him or her. The remedy applies to the administration of the assets of a deceased person as well as to mortgages. The doctrine was explained by the English Court of Appeal in *Re BCCI (No.8)* as follows:

"The doctrine of marshalling applies where there are two creditors of the same debtor, each owed a different debt, one creditor (A) having two or more securities for the debt due to him and the other (B) having only one. B has the right to have the two securities marshalled so that both he and A are paid so far as possible. Thus, if a debtor has two estates (Blackacre and Whiteacre) and mortgages both to A and afterwards mortgages Whiteacre only to B, B can have the two mortgages marshalled so that Blackacre can be made available to him if A chooses to enforce his security against Whiteacre."[284]

---

[279] Law Reform Commission, *Consultation Paper on Reform and Modernisation of Land Law and Conveyancing Law* (LRC CP 34-2004), para.9.27.

[280] *AIB Mortgage Bank v O'Toole* [2016] IEHC 368 at para.12; *Pledge v White* [1896] A.C. 187 at 192.

[281] See the third edition of this work, pp.901–903.

[282] *Re Thompson* [1912] 1 I.R. 194 at 200 (Ross J.). See also the remarks of Lindley J. (as he then was) in *Chesworth v Hunt* (1880) 5 C.P.D. 266 at 271 who described the doctrine as a whole as "monstrous" and declined to extend its operation in the context of the Bills of Sale Acts 1878–1882.

[283] Law Reform Commission, *Consultation Paper on Reform and Modernisation of Land Law and Conveyancing Law* (LRC CP 34-2004), para.9.27.

[284] [1996] Ch. 245 at 271; affirmed by the House of Lords: [1998] A.C. 214 at 230–231.

24–156 Killip has described marshalling as "a slightly arcane doctrine".[285] Arcane though it may be, the doctrine's value from the perspective of a second incumbrancer is easily understood from the following example:

A mortgages Blackacre (market value €100,000) and Whiteacre (market value €100,000) to X to secure a loan of €150,000. A later grants a second mortgage over Whiteacre to Y in order to secure a loan of €40,000. If marshalling was not applicable, then X would enforce his security by selling both properties and deducting €75,000 plus interest and costs from the proceeds of each property. Since Y is secured on Whiteacre only, the value of his security would be reduced to no more than €25,000 leaving him significantly under secured. The doctrine of marshalling requires X to satisfy himself first from Blackacre and only then turn to Whiteacre. On these facts, X will take €50,000 from the sale price of Whiteacre, leaving Y to recover the full amount of his loan and a surplus of €10,000 which will go to A or any other encumbrancer.

24–157 Identifying the basis for the doctrine of marshalling is difficult. In *Highbury Pension Fund Management Co v Zirfin Investments*, Norris J. stated, "it is in truth difficult to know exactly what principle underlies the whole doctrine."[286] In *National Crime Agency v Szepietowski*, Lord Neuberger P.S.C. provided the following explanation:

"The principle behind the doctrine of marshalling has been identified by Joseph Story in his *Commentaries on Equity Jurisprudence*, 2nd ed (1892), pp 514–516, in these rather broad terms:

'The reason is obvious … [By] compelling [the first creditor with the two securities] to take satisfaction out of one of the funds no injustice is done to him … But it is the only way by which [the second creditor with one security] can receive payment. And natural justice requires, that one man should not be permitted from wantonness, or caprice, or rashness, to do an injury to another. In short we may here apply the common civil maxim: "Sic utero tuo ut non alienum laedas"; and still more emphatically, the Christian maxim, "Do unto others as you would they should do unto you."'

As I see it, there are also good practical reasons for equity adopting the doctrine, namely the unattractive and adventitious benefit which would otherwise be accorded to the first mortgagee. If marshalling was not available to the second mortgagee, the first mortgagee's free right to choose the property against which he enforced could have substantial value. In effect, he could auction that right as between the second mortgagee (who would be prepared to pay him to enforce against the other property) and the unsecured creditors

---

[285] J. Killip, "Marshalling - Nothing and then Two Come Along at the Same Time" (2015) 28 Insolv. Int. 114.
[286] [2014] Ch. 359 at 370.

of the mortgagor (who, especially where the mortgagor was actually or potentially insolvent, would be prepared to pay him to enforce against the common property)."[287]

24–158 There is some doubt about how the doctrine operates. On one view, which Ali refers to as the coercion theory of marshalling,[288] the doctrine operates by allowing *puisne* mortgagees to control the order in which paramount security holders realise their securities. Although there is support for this view in the early English cases,[289] the modern English authorities[290] favour what Ali refers to as the "post-realisation remedy".[291] On this view, marshalling does not "delay or defeat the creditor with several securities in the ... enforcement of his securities",[292] but simply directs the choice of fund from which the senior creditor can satisfy himself or herself. The Irish cases seem to favour the former view and suggest that if the creditor with two securities has already realised them, then the other creditor will be allowed to exercise the first creditor's rights via subrogation.[293]

24–159 Whatever the basis of the doctrine, its requirements can be stated with reasonable certainty. Lord Neuberger P.S.C. in *National Crime Agency v Szepietowski* summarised the requirements as follows:

> "Marshalling has thus been allowed to a creditor, in a case where (i) his debt is secured by a second mortgage over property ('the common property'), (ii) the first mortgagee of the common property is also a creditor of the debtor, (iii) the first mortgagee also has security for his debt in the form of another property ('the other property') (iv) the first mortgagee has been repaid from the proceeds of sale of the common property, (v) the second mortgagee's debt remains unpaid, and (vi) the proceeds of sale of the other property are not needed (at least in full) to repay the first mortgagee's debt. In such a case, the second mortgagee can look to the other property to satisfy the debt owed to him."[294]

24–160 A complication arises if the mortgagor later mortgages the plot of land subject only to the double mortgage to another mortgagee. Thus, if A mortgages Plots 1 and 2 to B, and then mortgages Plot 1 to C alone, and then mortgages Plot 2 to D alone, does C have a right to marshal against B, requiring B to resort first to Plot 2, even though that may now prejudice D?

---

[287] [2014] A.C. 338 at 350–351.
[288] P.A.U. Ali, *Marshalling of Securities* (Oxford: Oxford University Press, 1999), para.2.14.
[289] *Bovey v Skipwith* (1671) 1 Ch. Cas. 201; *Povye's Case* (1680) 2 Free. 51; *Lanoy v Duke and Duchess of Atholl* (1742) 2 Atk. 444; *Attorney General v Tyndall* (1764) Amb. 614.
[290] *Re Bank of Credit and Commerce International (No.8)* [1996] Ch. 245 at 272; *Highbury Pension Fund Management Co v Zirfin Investments* [2014] Ch. 359 at 367.
[291] P.A.U. Ali, *Marshalling of Securities* (Oxford: Oxford University Press, 1999), para.2.19.
[292] *Re Bank of Credit and Commerce International (No.8)* [1996] Ch. 245 at 272.
[293] *McCarthy v McCartie (No.2)* [1904] 1 I.R. 100.
[294] [2014] A.C. 338 at 349.

The law is unclear as to the application of the doctrine where such third parties are involved and as to the relevance of notice on the part of such third parties.

24–161 In *Re Archer's Estate*[295] Wylie J. held that C still has a right to marshal, on the ground that A should not be able to deprive C of his right to marshal simply by creating another mortgage over Plot 2. In that case, however, all the mortgagees had notice of prior mortgages, so that D could be taken to have had notice, not only of C's mortgage, but of C's right to marshal also.[296] Wylie J. expressly left open the question as to whether the same result would follow if D had no notice of the prior mortgages.

24–162 On the other hand, *Dolphin v Aylward*,[297] a decision of the House of Lords on appeal from Ireland, declined to recognise that the right to marshal could be exercised if it would prejudice a third party, such as D, whether the third party was a volunteer, i.e. had given consideration, or not. Later cases in Ireland seem to have ignored this decision, which was also inconsistent with earlier English authorities.[298]

24–163 In *Smyth v Toms*[299] Ross J. declined to follow *Re Archer's Estate*, which he held indistinguishable, and applied the English case of *Barnes v Racster*[300] holding that C only had a right to marshal against the mortgagor and those claiming as volunteers through him. Where, in the above example, D is not a volunteer, the judge held that B must resort to both plots rateably, i.e. in proportion to their values. The equity to marshal is thus apportioned between C and D and C has to be content with whatever surplus Plot 1 produces after paying off its proportionate part of B's security.

24–164 The latter cases suggest that the test of whether the taker of a later interest takes free of the right to marshal is one of consideration, and that those giving such consideration take free of the equity, whether or not they have notice. However, the normal rule in equity is that only purchasers of a legal interest for value and without notice take free of equitable interests, the further exception being, in the case of mere equities, that a purchaser of an equitable interest for value and without notice would also take free. Assuming that the right to marshal is a mere equity, it is submitted that the proper test should be that only those who take for value and without notice should be free of the right to marshal.

---

[295] [1914] 1 I.R. 285.
[296] See also *Re Mower's Trusts* (1869) L.R. 8 Eq. 110.
[297] (1870) L.R. 4 H.L. 486.
[298] *Averall v Wade* (1835) Ll. & Gt. Sug. 252 and *Barnes v Racster* (1842) 1 Y. & C.C.C. 401.
[299] [1918] 1 I.R. 338. See also *Re Lawder's Estate* (1861) 11 Ir. Ch. R. 346.
[300] (1842) 1 Y. & C.C.C. 401; *Tighe v Dolphin* [1906] 1 I.R. 305; and see *Flint v Howard* [1893] 2 Ch. 54 at 72; *Bugden v Bignold* (1843) 2 Y. & C.C.C. 377.

Purchasers from the Mortgagor

24-165 A owns Plot 1 and Plot 2 and mortgages them both to B. A then sells his equity of redemption in Plot 2 to P. It was held in *Ker v Ker*[301] that in certain circumstances P has a right to marshal against B. He or she can insist that B enforces his security first against Plot 1, the equity in which was retained by A. P has the right to marshal if A sold Plot 2 subject to a covenant against incumbrances, or a declaration that the estate was free of incumbrances, or "the nature of the dealings shows that the land is sold or settled *as if* free from incumbrances."[302] P would clearly have a remedy in damages against A for breach of covenant, but Christian L.J. in *Ker v Ker*[303] maintained that the court will specifically perform the covenant, even so as to affect B. The right to marshal would bind everyone claiming through A except a purchaser for value without notice.[304]

Judgment Mortgages

24-166 In *Re Lynch's Estate*[305] there was a first mortgage by deed of plots A and B. A judgment mortgage was then registered against plot A and, later, a further judgment mortgage was registered against plots A and B. The first mortgagee having enforced the security, the judgment mortgagee of plot A claimed the right to marshal as against the judgment mortgagee of plots A and B. It was held that the doctrine applied. The judgment clearly establishes that a judgment mortgagee has the right to marshal against a later judgment mortgagee, but Dobbs J. also held that a judgment mortgagee has the right as against all later charges, including ordinary mortgages, on the ground that registration enabled later chargees to discover the existence of the earlier judgment mortgage.

RIGHTS OF THE MORTGAGOR

The Right of Redemption

24-167 The central right of the mortgagor is to redeem the property upon performance of the secured obligation. This right arises under the mortgage itself in the form of the legal date for redemption; however, a mortgagor also enjoys a right in equity to redeem the mortgage after the legal date of redemption has passed. This right of redemption is "of the very nature and essence of a mortgage."[306] The law protects the mortgagee's right of redemption under a number of different headings. These include the equitable rule against "clogs

---

[301] (1870) I.R. 4 Eq. 15.

[302] (1870) I.R. 4 Eq. 15 at 30–31.

[303] (1870) I.R. 4 Eq. 15, and *McCarthy v McCartie (No.2)* [1904] 1 I.R. 100 at 115.

[304] *Averall v Wade* (1835) Ll. & Gt. Sug. 252 at 259; *McCarthy v McCartie (No.2)* [1904] 1 I.R. 100 at 119.

[305] (1867) I.R. 1 Eq. 396.

[306] *Manchester Sheffield and Lincolnshire Railway Co v North Central Wagon Co* (1888) 13 App. Cas. 554 at 568.

on the equity of redemption", the jurisdiction to relieve against unconscionable bargain and the common law rules on restraint of trade. For the purposes of clarity, these will be dealt with separately, but it is worth noting that the cases do not always fit neatly into schemes of categorisation.

The Rule against Clogs on the Equity of Redemption

24–168 The law of equity provides a right for mortgagors to redeem the mortgaged property even after the legal date for redemption has passed. Conveyancers acting for mortgagees responded to equitable intervention by inserting covenants into mortgage deeds aimed at restricting or eliminating the right to redeem. As is often the case in land law, such devices led to the creation of new rules aimed at ensuring a continuation of equity's protection of the mortgagee. The main principle was stated by Walker L.J. in *Browne v Ryan*:

> "When a transaction appears, or has been declared to be a mortgage, Courts of equity regard the instrument only as a security for the repayment of the principal, interest, and costs named and secured, and the mortgagor is entitled to get back his property as free as he gave it, on payment of principal, interest, and costs, and provisions inconsistent with that right cannot be enforced. The equitable rules, 'once a mortgage always a mortgage,'[307] and that the mortgagee cannot impose any 'clog or fetter on the equity of redemption,' are merely concise statements of the same rule."[308]

24–169 A provision in the mortgage deed which interferes with the right of the mortgagee to redeem the mortgage will be deemed void as being inconsistent with the nature of a mortgage.[309] The manner in which the provision is worded or described is not relevant—the court will examine the substance of the arrangement.

24–170 The following provisions in mortgages have been held void as clogs on the equity of redemption:

1. An option to purchase the reversion on the mortgage term or the equity of redemption given to the mortgagee on the creation[310] or assignment[311] of the mortgage. An option in a later transaction has been held valid, although the only consideration was a release of the mortgagor from the obligation to repay the mortgage loan.[312]

---

[307] *Seton v Slade* (1802) 7 Ves. 265 at 273.
[308] [1901] 2 I.R. 653 at 676.
[309] *Re Wells* [1933] Ch. 29.
[310] *Brown v Ryan* [1901] 2 I.R. 653; *Samuel v Jarrah Timber & Wood Paving Corp Ltd* [1904] A.C. 323.
[311] *Lewis v Frank Love Ltd* [1961] 1 W.L.R. 261; see *Kevans v Joyce* [1896] 1 I.R. 442 at 473.
[312] *Reeve v Lisle* [1902] A.C. 461.

2. A clause attempting to make the mortgage irredeemable.[313] The mortgagor will be allowed to redeem notwithstanding such a clause.
3. A clause confining the equity of redemption to the life of the mortgagor,[314] or providing that if the mortgagor died before his father, the property was to belong absolutely to the mortgagee.[315]

Postponement of Right to Redeem

24–171 From the point of view of the mortgagee, it may be commercially advantageous to prevent the mortgagor seeking an early redemption of the mortgage. Early redemption will lead to a reduced level of interest being paid on the underlying loan and may thus reduce the profitability of the transaction for the mortgagee. The basic rule is that a term which attempts to postpone the legal date of redemption beyond the customary six months, and which therefore attempts to postpone the equitable right to redeem, is not now[316] void unless it renders redemption illusory[317] or is otherwise unconscionable or oppressive.[318]

24–172 Modern cases demonstrate some reluctance to interfere with contractual terms merely on the ground that they postpone redemption. In *Knightsbridge Estates Trust Ltd v Byrne*,[319] Knightsbridge had mortgaged a number of houses and shops to secure a loan which was repayable on demand. The mortgage was subsequently refinanced with a term loan to be repaid over 40 years in biannual instalments and the mortgagee's right of redemption was suspended for this period. The English Court of Appeal upheld the validity of the agreement. Greene M.R. expressed the view that the agreement was "a commercial agreement between two important corporations experienced in such matters" and had "none of the features of an oppressive bargain where the borrower is at the mercy of an unscrupulous lender".[320] The agreement was "a proper business transaction" and any other result would place "an unfortunate restriction on the liberty of contract of competent parties who are at arm's length".[321]

24–173 In *Fairclough v Swan Brewery*[322] the mortgagor mortgaged a leasehold term of 17 years. Under the terms of the mortgage the right to redeem would only arise six weeks before the end of the lease. The Privy Council held that the term rendered the mortgage virtually irredeemable and was void.

---

[313] *Brown v Ryan* [1901] 2 I.R. 653 at 676.
[314] *Floyer v Lavington* (1714) 1 P. Wms. 268; 24 E.R. 384.
[315] *Salt v Northampton (Marquess)* [1892] A.C. 1.
[316] *Cowdry v Day* (1859) 1 Giff. 316 (postponed for 20 years, held "too long a period").
[317] *Fairclough v Swan Brewery* [1912] A.C. 565.
[318] *Knightsbridge Estates Trust Ltd v Byrne* [1939] Ch. 441, affirmed on other grounds in [1940] A.C. 613.
[319] [1939] Ch. 441.
[320] [1939] Ch. 441 at 455.
[321] [1939] Ch. 441 at 455.
[322] [1912] A.C. 565.

In *Sheehan v Breccia* the Irish High Court took a similar approach, holding that the right of redemption cannot be postponed to the extent that it would render the right of redemption illusory.[323] In *Breccia* the court also considered an alleged entitlement for the secured lender to include unagreed and untaxed legal costs within the amount the mortgagor was required to pay in order to redeem the mortgage. The court noted that these costs were contingent on the outcome of a complex modular trial before the High Court along with any subsequent appellate proceedings. Their inclusion in the redemption figure might thus delay the redemption of the mortgage.

Unconscionable Bargains

24–174 In equity there is a general jurisdiction to review unconscionable or oppressive bargains. Where parties to a contract are not on an equal footing that does not in itself invalidate the agreement or the unconscionable part of it, but the onus shifts to the dominant party to show that the agreement is fair and reasonable.[324] In *Chapple v Mahon*,[325] a covenant by a mortgagor to pay the mortgagee a commission of 5 per cent if the mortgage was paid off was held to be void as an unconscionable bargain and a clog on the equity of redemption. The jurisdiction of courts of equity to set aside unconscionable or oppressive bargains was independent of the usury laws and survived their repeal.[326] In modern times, however, the Irish courts have taken a more modest view of the judicial function in this area. In *Secured Property Loans Ltd v Floyd*,[327] the mortgagor had granted security to a sub-prime lender over her dwelling house. The mortgage secured a loan upon which the annual interest rate was 19.4 per cent. The mortgagor argued that the court should regard this rate as exorbitant and oppressive having regard to the much lower rates of interest being charged by mainstream financial institutions. Laffoy J. noted that the court had not been supplied with sufficient evidence to enable a comparative analysis of the interest rates charged by other lenders and that as such the court was not in a position to make a finding that the interest rate charged was unconscionable. Moreover, importantly however Laffoy J. appeared to doubt that there is jurisdiction to review interest rates in the first place, holding that "[a]ny regulation of interest rates charged by lenders to borrowers is a matter for the Oireachtas".[328]

---

[323] [2016] IEHC 67 at paras 179–207, citing with approval Wylie, *Irish Land Law* (2013), para.13.35.

[324] *Kevans v Joyce* [1896] 1 I.R. 442 at 463.

[325] (1870) I.R. 5 Eq. 225.

[326] *Chapple v Mahon* (1870) I.R. 5 Eq. 225; *Rae v Joyce* (1892) 29 L.R. Ir. 500 at 516 and 520; *Kevans v Joyce* [1896] 1 I.R. 442 at 463 and 473.

[327] [2011] 2 I.R. 652.

[328] [2011] 2 I.R. 652 at 667.

Penalties

24–175 Equity has long regarded clauses in contracts which impose a penalty on one party as being oppressive and has refused to enforce them. The sort of clause which will be regarded as a penalty has varied over time. It has been suggested that there is a distinction between clauses which provide that the normal interest is to be increased in the event of a default, and those which reduce the rate if the interest is paid on time, the former being void and the latter valid.[329] The distinction appears to be semantic and the cases are not unanimous on the point.[330]

Collateral Advantages

24–176 It is sometimes the case that the mortgage loan will attempt to confer some additional benefit on the mortgagee beyond the right to repayment of the capital sum, interest and costs secured. Such an advantage is known as collateral advantage. Prior to the repeal of the usury legislation in 1845,[331] courts tended to treat such an advantage as a disguised payment of unlawful interest. Since the repeal of this legislation a more liberal approach has been taken to collateral advantages. In *Biggs v Hoddinott*,[332] the court considered a "tied house" arrangement under which a brewery supplied finance to a publican on the security of a mortgage. The deed provided that the publican would source beer for the pub exclusively from the mortgagee during the currency of the mortgage. The court held that a collateral advantage is valid and enforceable unless it is oppressive, unconscionable or calculated to prevent or unduly hamper the redemption of the mortgage.

24–177 The new approach was further outlined in *Kreglinger v New Patagonia Meat & Cold Storage Co Ltd*.[333] There a meat company borrowed money from a firm of woolbrokers secured by a floating charge on the company's assets. The agreement included an option allowing the lenders to purchase any sheepskins the company had to sell for a period of five years. The company repaid the loan after two years, and claimed an entitlement to redeem the property free of the option.

---

[329] Wylie, *Irish Land Law* (2013), para.13.41.

[330] *Chapple v Mahon* (1870) I.R. 5 Eq. 225 but compare *Burton v Slattery* (1725) 5 Bro. P.C. 233. See generally the discussion in Maddox, *Mortgages: Law and Practice* (2017), paras 4–18 to 4–22.

[331] By the Usury Laws Repeal Act 1854 (17 & 18 Vict c 90). Statutes of the Parliament of Ireland repealed by the Act were: 10 Chas I sess. 2 c 22 (Ir); 2 Anne c 16 (Ir); 8 Geo I c 13 (Ir); 5 Geo II c.7 (Ir). See also, *National Bank of Greece SA v Pinios Shipping Co* [1989] 1 All E.R. 213; *Cityland & Property Holdings Ltd v Dabrah* [1968] Ch. 166; *Williamson v Williamson* (1869) 7 L.R. Eq. 542; *Mainland v Upjohn* (1889) 41 Ch. D. 126 at 136.

[332] [1898] 2 Ch. 307.

[333] [1914] A.C. 25.

24–178 The House of Lords held that the option was still valid as a free and independent bargain even though it was contained in the mortgage deed. Lord Parker declared that

> "there is now no rule in equity which precludes a mortgagee ... from stipulating for any collateral advantage, provided such collateral advantage is not either [*sic*] (1) unfair and unconscionable, or (2) in the nature of a penalty clogging the equity of redemption, or (3) inconsistent with or repugnant to the contractual and equitable right to redeem."[334]

24–179 In the past it had become the practice for banks to include a requirement that the mortgagor should insure the property with an insurance company which was linked to the mortgagor. Section 124 of the Consumer Credit Act 1995 prohibits this practice in the context of housing loans.

24–180 A collateral advantage may also be struck down if it contravenes the common law restraint of trade doctrine. A contract which imposes a restraint on the freedom of one of the parties to carry on his or her trade, business or profession in whatever manner he or she chooses is void at common law unless the restriction is justified both from the perspective of the parties to the contract and from the view of the interests of the public at large.[335] The fact that a restriction is contained within a mortgage transaction may be of assistance in arguing that a restraint of trade clause, which might otherwise be void, is valid. Collateral advantages may also fall to be considered under the s.4 of the Competition Act 2002 which renders void arrangements having the object or effect of distorting competition in trade for goods or services within the State.[336]

Terms of Redemption

24–181 A mortgagor may redeem out of court or by means of a redemption suit,[337] the latter being necessary if the mortgagee unjustifiably refuses the tender of the money due under the mortgage.

Who Can Redeem?

24–182 Redemption can be sought by any person interested in the equity of redemption,[338] such as assignees of the mortgagor or other successors in title,

---

[334] [1914] A.C. 25 at 61.

[335] *Kerry Co-Operative v An Bord Bainne* [1991] I.L.R.M. 851 at 867–869. See also *Esso Petroleum Co Ltd v Harper's Garage (Stourport) Ltd* [1968] 1 A.C. 269 at 300.

[336] A similar problem might arise at EU level under Art.101 of the Treaty on the Functioning of the European Union, although this seems unlikely in the mortgage context.

[337] See LCLRA 2009 s.94.

[338] *Tarn v Turner* (1888) 39 Ch. D. 456.

and subsequent mortgagees.[339] A lessee of the mortgagor may redeem where the lease itself is not binding on the mortgagee.[340]

Notice and Payment

24-183 The mortgagor may redeem on the legal date of redemption in the mortgage and need not give any notice of his or her intention to do so, since the mortgage itself contains the term. After the legal date of redemption has passed (and it is normally one day) the mortgagor only has an equitable right to redeem and so it must be exercised equitably, i.e. reasonably and fairly. The mortgagor must give reasonable notice, usually six months, or pay six months' interest instead.[341] This is to allow the mortgagee a reasonable opportunity to reinvest his or her capital. Nevertheless, reasonable notice is not required where the mortgage is temporary, which is usually the case with a mortgage by deposit,[342] or the mortgagee has demanded payment[343] or attempted to enforce the security.[344] The costs of the redemption fall on the mortgagor.[345]

Effect

24-184 Where only a single person is interested in the equity of redemption and the mortgage is the only incumbrance on the property, redemption discharges the mortgage and the property is then held free of it. Where more than one person is interested in the equity of redemption the effect of redemption is normally to transfer the mortgage to the person paying the money, as where property is mortgaged by A to X and Y and Y redeems X's mortgage. X will reconvey to Y, not A, and, since A still has the equity of redemption, Y still has a mortgage. Where there is more than one mortgage the first in order of priority has the best right to redeem.[346] Section 15 of the 1881 Act allowed a mortgagee who has the right to redeem to insist that the mortgagee conveys to a nominee of the mortgagor instead of to the mortgagor. This section has now been repealed by the LCLRA 2009 and replaced by s.93 which makes identical provision for mortgages executed post-2009.

"Redeem Up, Foreclose Down"

24-185 English law has a special principle which applies where there are a number of mortgages affecting property and one mortgagee wishes to redeem

---

[339] *Ocean Accident Corp v Collum* [1913] 1 I.R. 328.
[340] *Tarn v Turner* (1888) 39 Ch. D. 456.
[341] *Re Kennedy's Estate* (1889) 32 I.L.T.R. 115.
[342] *Fitzgerald's Trustee v Mellerish* [1892] 1 Ch. 385.
[343] *Edmonson v Copeland* [1911] 2 Ch. 301.
[344] *Re Alcock* (1883) 23 Ch. D. 372.
[345] *Webb v Crosse* [1911] 1 Ch. 323.
[346] *Teevan v Smith* (1882) 20 Ch. D. 724 at 730.

one of the other mortgages.[347] The rule only applies where a mortgage is redeemed through a redemption suit in court.[348] The principle is that a mortgagee who wishes to redeem a prior mortgage by action must not only redeem any other mortgages between its own mortgage and the one that is sought to be redeemed,[349] but must also foreclose all mortgages subsequent to its own mortgage and the mortgagor.[350] Thus, if property is mortgaged by X to A, B, C, D and E, the priority of those interested in the proceeds are, in order, A, B, C, D, E and X. X, as mortgagor, comes last because he is entitled to any surplus remaining after all the mortgages are paid off. The principle states that if D wishes to redeem B's mortgage then D must redeem C, who stands between himself and B, as well as B, and foreclose E. E can preserve his rights by paying off the other mortgages concerned in the action, but if he cannot, he will be foreclosed.

24–186 The basis of the principle is as follows. If B's mortgage is to be paid off, then C, D, and E are all concerned because they are affected by the account of whatever is found to be due to B, since they all rank after B and take what is left over. The court would therefore insist that they be made parties to the suit for redemption, so that they can be represented. A is not concerned because he will be paid first in any case. It would, however, be unfair on C and E to put them to the expense of joining the suit merely as observers and also since the same situation might occur again in relation to some of them if one of them seeks redemption of another mortgage.

24–187 It is unlikely that the principle ever applied in Ireland since the Irish courts did not grant foreclosure. The abolition of the foreclosure jurisdiction has probably removed any need to consider the rule in modern Irish law.

Sale

24–188 Section 94 of the LCLRA 2009 provides the court with a discretionary power to order a sale in a suit by the mortgagor for redemption. An early sale might be in the mortgagor's interest in circumstances where the property is in negative equity.[351] Prior to 2009, there was no statutory power for an Irish court to order a sale on redemption. Section 25 of the 1881 Act provided such a power in England, but the section did not extend to Ireland. Nonetheless the courts were regarded as possessing an inherent equitable jurisdiction to order a sale and Ord.54 r.3 of the Rules of the Superior Courts provides a procedural mechanism for such sales.

---

[347] See *Megarry & Wade: The Law of Real Property* (2012), paras 25–110 to 25–113. There is almost no modern English authority on the rule, however its continued existence was confirmed by the UK Supreme Court in *National Crime Agency v Szepietowski* [2014] A.C. 338 at 351.

[348] *Smith v Green* (1844) 1 Y. & C.C.C. 555.

[349] *Teevan v Smith* (1882) 20 Ch. D. 724 at 730.

[350] *Farmer v Curtis* (1829) 2 Sim. 466.

[351] See *Palk v Mortgage Services Funding plc* [1993] 2 All E.R. 481.

Title Deeds

24–189 Section 91 of the LCLRA 2009 confers on the mortgagee a right of inspection of the title deeds for so long as the right to redeem exists.

Actions

24–190 For so long as the mortgagor is in possession of the property, the mortgagor is entitled to protect that possession and may sue for trespass, nuisance etc. Prior to 2009, a difficulty could arise where leased property was mortgaged by assigning the lease to the mortgagee. Under such an arrangement the mortgagee would become the landlord of the lease and the mortgagor could not enforce leasehold covenants against the tenant without joining the mortgagee. Section 10 of the 1881 Act (which remains in force) permits the mortgagor who is entitled to possession to sue for rent, sign notices to quit and enforce all covenants in leases.

<h3 style="text-align:center">RIGHTS COMMON TO BOTH PARTIES: LEASES</h3>

Common Law
Mortgagor

24–191 At common law, the mortgagor may grant leases which will be binding between the mortgagor and the tenant by estoppel.[352] They will not, however, bind the mortgagee in the absence of provisions in the mortgage granting a power to lease to the mortgagor. Many mortgages prohibit the mortgagor from letting the premises without the consent of the mortgagee, since the mortgagee wishes to protect the right to enforce the security by sale with vacant possession. Where, in such a case, the mortgagor creates a letting of the premises with the mortgagee's consent, the lease binds the mortgagee and successors in title.[353]

24–192 The issue of a lease granted in breach of a mortgage term was considered in a number of recent decisions.[354] Charleton J. said of such a transaction in *Cussens v Brosnan*:

> "It is clear as between a mortgagor, as landlord, and a tenant to whom he lets the mortgaged property ... that there is ordinarily an agreement where both intend to create legal relations in respect of obligations which are certain and that there is consideration passing between both parties. There is thus ordinarily privity of contract. Yet, in those circumstances, if the tenancy arises only by virtue of the representation of the parties and the unfairness

---

[352] The following passages were quoted in *Cussens v Brosnan (Inspector of Taxes)* [2008] IEHC 169 at paras 15–16.

[353] *Roulston v Caldwell* [1895] 2 I.R. 136.

[354] *Cussens v Brosnan* [2008] IEHC 169; *ICC Bank plc v Verling* [1995] 1 I.L.R.M. 123; *The Wise Finance Co Ltd v O'Regan*, unreported, High Court, Laffoy J., 26 June 1998.

of allowing a mortgagor as landlord to deny the tenancy, the conditions for estoppel in these circumstances, it is clear that another legal factor stands between them which has upset the normal consequence of legal validity in a lease. This, in my judgment, is that having conveyed the legal interest in the property to the lending institution, the mortgagor has no legal title to alienate by way of lease. He or she holds the property in equity subject only to the right of redemption of the legal interest. Such a lease is void."

24–193 Charleton J. was considering a mortgage created by the conveyance of the legal estate. His reasoning, while impeccable, is based on a reified notion of the fee simple estate and the logical consequences of its transfer to the bank. As such, his judgment does not engage with the normative question of how the law *should* address the conflict of rights which these facts create between the lessor and the mortgagee. This is an important limitation on the scope of the *Cussens* judgment. In other forms of pre-2009 mortgage such as the mortgage by demise or the various forms of equitable mortgage, the mortgagee's rights are created by carving out an interest from that held by the mortgagor. In such cases, the rationale for the *Cussens* decision will not operate.

Mortgagee

24–194 A legal mortgagee, as holder of a legal estate, has, under the principles discussed above, the right to possession of the premises and, consistent with this, was treated at common law as having the right to create leases.[355] Such leases, however, are subject to the mortgagor's equity of redemption and so liable to be destroyed by the mortgagor's paramount right to redeem in equity.

Statute

24–195 Prior to the LCLRA 2009, s.18 of the 1881 Act resolved the insecurities of leases created at common law by mortgagor or mortgagee by giving power to either of them to create binding leases, depending upon which of them is in possession. Provided the lease complies with the provisions of the statute, a lease made by the mortgagor will bind every mortgagee and a lease made by the mortgagee will bind the mortgagor and prior mortgagees.

24–196 Section 112 of the LCLRA 2009 now governs all leases entered into after the commencement of the Act. The mortgagor has a general statutory right to grant a lease which must be exercised with the written consent of the mortgagee, although this consent may not be unreasonably withheld. The failure to obtain this written consent will only render the lease voidable at the insistence of the mortgagee if the lessee was actually aware of the mortgage and the mortgagee suffers prejudice by its grant. This power does not apply to assignees of the equity of redemption from the mortgagor.

---

[355] *Re O'Rourke's Estate* (1889) 23 L.R. Ir. 497.

24–197 The mortgagee's powers to lease the property must be consistent with the notion that the mortgage is security for the debt, i.e. to protect the security or preserve its value, or to reduce the amount of the mortgage debt. Otherwise the mortgagor must consent in writing or the lease must be made pursuant to an order of court. There is a general saving provision in s.112(3)(b) if the lease is an "appropriate" use of the land pending sale.

TRANSFER OF RIGHTS

By Mortgagor
Inter Vivos
24–198 A mortgagor may transfer his or her equity of redemption to another person. The mortgagor remains liable on the contractual covenant to pay the debt, unless there is agreement to the contrary.[356] The mortgagor would normally take an indemnity covenant from the assignee and such a covenant is implied in the case of an assignee for value.[357] A mortgagor may wish to sell the property free of the mortgage, as, for example, when a homeowner wishes to sell his or her existing property and buy another one. In such a case the mortgagor must redeem the existing mortgage. A mortgagor may also discharge the mortgage by paying money into court under s.5 of the 1881 Act.

On Death
24–199 It has been seen that the original mortgagor is normally liable on a personal covenant in the mortgage to pay the debt. Formerly, on the death of the mortgagor, the mortgagee could call upon the personal representatives of the mortgagor to repay the debt out of the estate of the deceased mortgagor, as in the case of other simple debts, since they "stood in the shoes" of the deceased. Legislation known as Locke King's Acts[358] curtailed the right. Now s.47 of the Succession Act 1965 provides that charges on the property of a deceased person are to be paid primarily out of the property charged.

By Direction of the Mortgagor
24–200 Section 93 of the LCLRA 2009 re-enacts the substance of s.15 of the 1881 Act, as amended by s.12 of the Conveyancing Act 1882. It entitles a mortgagor to require the mortgagee, in lieu of discharge on redemption, to transfer the mortgage to a third party on the mortgagor's direction. The right is also capable of being enforced by other encumbrancers on the property. A mortgagee in possession is exempted from the operation of the section by virtue of the fact that it is obliged to account strictly. Even if it subsequently gives up possession, it remains liable for the acts of the transferee, unless the court has directed the transfer.

---

[356] *Re Howard's Estate* (1892) 29 L.R. Ir. 266.
[357] *Adair v Carden* (1891) 29 L.R. Ir. 469.
[358] Real Estate Charges Acts 1854, 1867 and 1877.

By Mortgagee
Inter Vivos
Transfer

24–201 A mortgagee may transfer the debt or the mortgage security, or both, to a third person.[359] If the mortgagor does not join in the transfer then the transferee should give notice to the mortgagor, otherwise the transferee cannot complain if the mortgagor continues to pay money due to the transferor.[360] It is also advisable to obtain the concurrence of the mortgagor in order to obtain his or her agreement to the state of the accounts.[361] Where the mortgage is by way of a charge over registered land, s.64 of the RTA 1964 requires that the transfer be made using the prescribed form and the transferee acquires no interest until the transferee is registered as the owner of the charge. In *Kavanagh v McLoughlin,*[362] Laffoy J. in the Supreme Court considered the application of s.64 in circumstances where the chargee named on the folio had been merged with another bank in accordance with the European Communities (Cross-Border Mergers) Regulations 2008.[363] She held that the merged bank could not exercise the statutory powers of a chargee until such time as the bank had applied to become registered as the owner of the charge in accordance with s.64.[364] There are certain statutory exceptions to this requirement.[365]

Sub-mortgage

24–202 The mortgagee can create a mortgage of its mortgage, i.e. a sub-mortgage. Thus, a mortgagee by conveyance of the fee simple may create a sub-mortgage by conveying a term of years created out of the fee simple to a sub-mortgagee.[366] The sub-mortgagee thus accepts the mortgagee/sub-mortgagor's rights as security for the repayment of the new loan. The sub-mortgagee for most purposes stands in the place of the original mortgagee to enforce the security.[367]

On Death

24–203 Under s.10 of the Succession Act 1965 all the property of a deceased person devolves on his or her personal representatives and so both the debt,

---

[359] *Simmons v Montague* [1909] 1 I.R. 87.

[360] *Dixon v Winch* [1900] 1 Ch. 736 at 742.

[361] *Agnew v King* [1902] 1 I.R. 471.

[362] [2015] 3 I.R. 555.

[363] S.I. No. 157 of 2008.

[364] [2015] 3 I.R. 555 at 593–595.

[365] Central Bank Act 1971 s.36; Trustee Savings Banks Act 1989 s.51; Finance Act 1990 s.5; Asset Covered Securities Act 2001 s.58(10); National Asset Management Agency Act 2009 s.107; Credit Institutions (Stabilisation) Act 2010 s.40(1)(b); Central Bank and Credit Institutions (Resolution) Act 2011 s.50(1); European Union (Bank Recovery and Resolution) Regulations 2015 reg.76(1)(b). On the operation of the Central Bank Act 1971 s.36, see *KBC Bank Ireland plc v Wood* [2017] IEHC 164.

[366] *Feehan v Mandeville* [1890] L.R. Ir. 90; *Rossborough v McNeil* (1889) 23 L.R. Ir. 409.

[367] LCLRA 2009 s.3; Conveyancing Act 1881 s.2(vi).

which is personalty, and the mortgagee's interest in the property devolve on them in the same way. The Land Registration Rules make provision for an application to list the deceased's successor in title as the holder of a registered charge.[368]

DISCHARGE

24–204 Where the mortgagor has repaid the debt secured by the mortgage, the mortgage is discharged and the mortgagee's interest in the land ceases.

Unregistered Land
24–205 Where a mortgage of unregistered land is created by conveyance of the fee simple or assignment of a lease, the mortgage is discharged by reconveyance of the fee simple or reassignment of the lease, and the deed should contain a receipt for the mortgage redemption money. In the context of building societies, a statutory receipt endorsed on the mortgage deed operates both to discharge the mortgage and to reconvey the estate or interest without a formal reconveyance.[369]

24–206 Where the mortgage was created by demise or sub-demise, i.e. by a term of years created expressly for the purpose of mortgaging the land, the Satisfied Terms Act 1845 provided that where the purpose for which a term was created was fulfilled, it automatically merged with the reversion expectant upon it. The Satisfied Terms Act 1845 was repealed by the LCLRA 2009.[370] Section 106 of the LCLRA 2009 now provides that the receipt of the mortgagee discharges "any money or securities comprised in the mortgage". An equitable mortgage may be discharged by an ordinary receipt.[371]

Registered Land
24–207 A registered charge is discharged by the Registrar entering a note of satisfaction of the charge on the Register.[372] The Land Registration Rules also make provision for the cancellation of charges by electronic means.[373]

---

[368] Land Registration Rules 2012 (S.I. No. 483 of 2012) r.91.
[369] Building Societies Act 1989 s.23.
[370] LCLRA 2009 s.8 and Sch.2, Pt 4.
[371] *Firth & Sons Ltd v CIR* [1904] 2 K.B. 205.
[372] RTA 1964 s.65.
[373] Land Registration Rules 2012 (S.I. No. 483 of 2012) r.102. See Deeney, *Registration of Deeds and Title in Ireland* (2014), para.22.03.

JUDGMENT MORTGAGES

24–208 A judgment mortgage is a process of execution for enforcing a debt due on foot of a judgment. It enables a judgment creditor to register a mortgage against the judgment debtor's interest in land. Prior to the LCLRA 2009, this area was governed by the Judgment Mortgages (Ireland) Acts 1850 and 1858 (the "Judgment Mortgages Acts"). Section 6 of the Judgment Mortgages (Ireland) Act 1850 (the "1850 Act") governed the creation of judgment mortgages. It was a poorly drafted provision which gave rise to considerable scope for error and dispute in its application. Part 11 of the LCLRA 2009 has repealed and replaced this legislation with a simplified regime for judgment mortgages registered after 1 December 2009. The 19th century legislation still applies to judgment mortgages issued prior to that date.

Creation
Judgment Mortgages Registered prior to 1 December 2009
24–209 Under the Judgment Mortgages Acts, a judgment mortgage could be created on foot of a judgment from the superior courts. The regime was subsequently extended to judgments of the Circuit Court[374] and the District Court.[375] On obtaining a judgment, the judgment creditor would swear an affidavit averring the terms of the judgment and the fact that the judgment debtor held an interest in identified lands. The affidavit was then filed in the court which had issued the judgment and in either the Land Registry or the Registry of Deeds as appropriate. The Registrar of Deeds/Titles would then notify each party of the registration of a judgment mortgage.[376] Section 7 of the 1850 Act provided that this had the effect of giving the judgment creditor a mortgage by deed over the judgment creditor's interest in land. This included the power to appoint a receiver and a power of sale. In practice, however, judgment mortgages could only be enforced through a court-ordered sale.[377] This involved an application to court for a "well charging order" which confirmed that the judgment was "well charged" on the land and an order for the sale of the land within a specified period.[378]

24–210 The difficulty under the old law was that the affidavit which formed the foundation of the judgment mortgage had to comply with the provisions of s.6 of the 1850 Act. Under s.6, the affidavit had to contain:

---

[374] Circuit Court (Registration of Judgments) Act 1937.

[375] Courts Act 1981 s.24.

[376] Law Reform Commission, *Consultation Paper on Judgment Mortgages* (LRC CP 30-2004), para.2.01. See also N. Maddox, "The Law and Practice of Judgment Mortgages" (2006) 11 B. Rev. 189.

[377] *Irwin v Deasy* [2011] 2 I.R. 752 at 765.

[378] Wylie, *Irish Land Law* (2013), para.15.20.

(i) a clause indicating that the deponent was authorised to swear the affidavit;

(ii) the full name, title and record number of the cause of action upon which the judgment was obtained, the court in which judgment had been entered and the date of the judgment;

(iii) the name, the usual and last place of abode, and the trade, title and profession of the plaintiff and the defendant both at the time of judgment and at the date of the making of the affidavit;

(iv) the amount of the judgment debt including costs and interest accruing under the Courts Acts;

(v) an averment that the defendant is seised, possessed or has the power of disposition over certain lands to the knowledge and belief of the deponent; and

(vi) a description of the land. For registered land this had to include a reference to the folio. For unregistered land the description had to include the county, barony, town and parish as appropriate.[379]

24–211 Traditionally the courts demanded strict compliance with the requirements of s.6 with the result that technical defences, which alleged a failure to comply even where there was no prejudice or even potential prejudice to the defendant, traditionally enjoyed a good prospect of success. The most common challenges were based on the fact that the description of the parties, the lands or the costs were inaccurate. In *Allied Irish Banks v Griffin*[380] a reference to the judgment debtor as a widow (and a married woman when the judgment was entered), when in fact she was a farmer, was found to be non-compliant. In *Murphy v Lacey*[381] the description of the defendant farm labourers as "farmers" was sufficient to invalidate the judgment mortgage.

24–212 In *Irish Bank of Commerce v O'Hara*[382] a more flexible approach was taken. There Costello J. held that non-compliance would only make the mortgage void if it defeats the purpose of the Act. The court applied *Thorp v Brown*,[383] where it was held that the intention of s.6 with regard to the requirements for the description of the judgment debtor was "clearly for the purpose of distinguishing him from all other persons".[384] So long as the description was adequate to achieve this purpose, failure to comply with a statutory requirement would not render the affidavit void. The Supreme Court approved of the judgment of Kenny J. in *Credit Finance v Grace*[385] where it was held that an

---

[379] See N. Maddox, "The Law and Practice of Judgment Mortgages" (2006) 11 B. Rev. 189 at 190.
[380] [1992] 2 I.R. 70.
[381] (1896) 31 I.L.T.R. 42.
[382] Unreported, High Court, Costello J., 10 May 1989.
[383] (1867) L.R. 2 H.L. 220.
[384] (1867) L.R. 2 H.L. 220 at 232–233.
[385] Unreported, Supreme Court, 29 May 1972.

error in a judgment mortgage affidavit was not fatal unless it was likely to mislead.

24–213 However, *O'Hara* has been described as a "false dawn" by one commentator in light of the decision in *Allied Irish Banks v Griffin*.[386] Here the "title, trade or profession" of the defendant was misstated. Denham J. declined to follow *Thorp v Brown and O'Hara*, distinguishing them on the basis that they applied to the requirements for the description of lands and not to the description of the defendant. In light of this case, and of the archaic language of s.6, the Law Reform Commission had little difficulty in recommending the reform of judgment mortgages as a part of what became the LCLRA 2009.[387]

Judgment Mortgages Registered under the LCLRA 2009

24–214 Part 11 of the LCLRA 2009 greatly simplifies the process of registering judgment mortgages. It provides that where a person has obtained a judgment, a judgment mortgage can be registered against the judgment debtor's estate or interest in land by application to the Property Registration Authority (PRA). The application will then be registered in the Registry of Deeds or the Land Registry as appropriate. The form is prescribed in the Land Registration Rules 2012,[388] and must be accompanied by a certificate from a proper officer of the relevant court verifying that the judgment was in fact obtained. Where a judgment mortgage is sought against property owned by a company, a second set of particulars must be filed in the Companies Registration Office within 21 days of the receipt notification from the PRA of the creation of the judgment mortgage. Failure to do so renders the judgment mortgage void as against the liquidator and any creditor of the company.[389] Under s.51 of the Bankruptcy Act 1988 a judgment mortgage which is registered less than three months prior to the judgment debtor being adjudicated a bankrupt does not take priority over the bankrupt's unsecured creditors.

24–215 Under s.117 of the LCLRA 2009, the registration of a judgment mortgage charges the debtor's estate or interest in land with the judgment debt and entitles the judgment mortgagee to apply to the court for various remedies. This includes an order for the taking of an account of other incumbrances; an order for sale of the land; or such other order for the enforcement of the judgment as the court may deem fit. Section 117 expressly provides that the judgment mortgagee is entitled to apply for an order under s.31 of the LCLRA 2009 for the partition of the land, thus reversing the decision in *Irwin v Deasy*.[390]

---

[386] [1992] 2 I.R. 70. See C. Doyle, "Judgment Mortgages - A False Dawn" (1993) 87 Gaz. L. Soc. Ir. 297.
[387] Law Reform Commission, *Consultation Paper on Judgment Mortgages* (LRC CP 30-2004), para.2.27.
[388] Land Registration Rules 2012 (S.I. No. 483 of 2012) r.110.
[389] Companies Act 2014 s.413.
[390] [2011] 2 I.R. 752.

Priority of Judgment Mortgages

24–216 A judgment mortgagee was historically treated as having acquired an interest in land as a volunteer, i.e. as a person who was given no value for his or her interest.[391] As such, the judgment mortgage ranked in priority behind all equities affecting the land including a deed which was unregistered at the date of registration of the judgment mortgage.[392] This is now confirmed by s.117(3) of the LCLRA 2009. In respect of registered land, s.71(2) of the RTA 1964 provides that the judgment mortgage ranks in priority after registered burdens. s.72 burdens taking effect without registration, and any other unregistered burden to which the judgment debtor was subject at the time the judgment mortgage was registered.

JURISDICTION OF THE COURTS

24–217 Section 101(5) of the LCLRA 2009 provides that applications for possession and sale of land which is subject to a housing loan mortgage fall exclusively within the jurisdiction of the Circuit Court. Section 101(5) applies only to mortgages created after 1 December 2009. Section 3 of the LCLRA 2013 created exclusive Circuit Court jurisdiction in possession proceedings retrospectively for *some* mortgages over residential property created prior to 2009.[393] Confusingly, there is a difference between the definition of a housing loan mortgage in the LCLRA 2009 and the concept of residential property under the LCLRA 2013. The LCLRA 2009 imports by reference the definition of a housing loan set out in s.2 of the Consumer Credit Act 1995.[394] Under this definition, a loan is a housing loan if it is for the construction, improvement or acquisition of a principal private residence for the borrower *or his or her dependants.* Section 3 of the LCLRA 2013, by contrast, applies only to land upon which the principal private residence of the mortgagor or that of a spouse or civil partner of the mortgagor is built. Non-spousal dependants such as children, or partners falling outside the Civil Partnership and Certain Rights and Obligations of Cohabitants Act 2010, do not appear to be included within the provisions of the LCLRA 2013.

24–218 In *Bank of Ireland Mortgage Bank v Finnegan*[395] an issue arose with the jurisdiction of the Circuit Court to hear mortgage possession cases. There the defendant objected to possession proceedings being heard before the Cavan Circuit Court on the basis that the court lacked the jurisdiction to deal with the proceedings. The monetary jurisdiction of the Circuit Court to deal with land disputes was, prior to the Courts Act 2016, based on the rateable valuation

---

[391] RTA 1964 s.68(3); *Containercare Ltd v Wycherley* [1982] I.R. 143.
[392] *McAuley v Clarendon* (1858) 8 Ir. Ch. R. 121; *Re Jennings Estate* (1885) 15 L.R. Ir. 277.
[393] LCLRA 2013 s.3(3) grants jurisdiction to the judges of the circuit within which the land is situate.
[394] As inserted by Central Bank and Financial Services Authority of Ireland Act 2004 s.33 and Sch.3, Pt 12.
[395] [2015] IEHC 304.

of the land concerned. The Circuit Court's jurisdiction was limited to land disputes involving land with a rateable valuation of less than €253.95, though disputes in excess of this threshold could be dealt with by the asset of the parties.[396] Although domestic rates were abolished in Ireland in the late 1970s, the concept of rateable valuation was retained.[397] The Valuation Act 2001 provided a modern legislative basis for the conduct of valuations which are not now carried out on residential dwellings. Section 15 of the Valuation Act 2001 declared that a range of property types, including domestic dwellings, are not rateable. The defendant argued that since her property was not rateable, the jurisdiction of the Circuit Court could not be established. In the High Court, Murphy J. held that the defendant's home was neither rated nor rateable and agreed that this prevented the Circuit Court from hearing the proceedings. In the subsequent case of *Bank of Ireland Mortgage Bank v Hanley and Giblin*[398] Noonan J. came to a different conclusion, suggesting that the Circuit Court's jurisdiction does not depend on the production of proof of the rateable valuation of land and that under s.31 of the County Officers and Courts (Ireland) Act 1877, the court could "estimate" the rateable valuation of land in accordance with the valuation legislation.

24–219 The conflict of authority was taken up by the Court of Appeal in *Permanent TSB v Langan*[399] in which Hogan J., giving the judgment of the court, agreed that the Circuit Court's jurisdiction was ousted by virtue of the fact that the premises concerned was declared not to be rateable. On a further appeal to the Supreme Court, the Court of Appeal's judgment in *Permanent TSB v Langan* was reversed.[400] Clarke C.J. noted that s.67 of the Valuation Act 2001 permits the Valuation Commissioner to provide a value for any premises for a range of purposes even where that premises is not rateable and suggested that it is therefore possible to obtain a rateable valuation for the purposes of establishing the Circuit Court's jurisdiction.

24–220 Prior to the decision of the Supreme Court in *Langan*, the Oireachtas had, in apparent response to the Court of Appeal's decision, passed the Courts Act 2016 and the Minister for Justice and Equality commenced s.45 of the Civil Liability and Courts Act 2004 with effect from 11 January 2017.[401] The latter has the effect of conferring jurisdiction on the Circuit Court in land matters where the market value of such land is not greater than €3,000,000. The latter, which applies to all civil proceedings issued after 28 December

---

[396] Courts (Supplemental Provisions) Act 1961 s.22 and Sch.3 as amended by Courts Act 1971 s.2(1)(d) and Courts Act 1981 s.2(1)(d).

[397] Local Government (Financial Provisions) Act 1978 s.3 abolished domestic rates by providing certain categories of landholder with an "allowance" which was defined as being equal to the rates which would otherwise be payable.

[398] [2015] IEHC 738.

[399] [2016] IECA 229.

[400] [2017] IESC 71.

[401] Civil Liability and Courts Act 2004 (Commencement) Order 2017 (S.I. No. 2 of 2017).

2016, provides that where the Circuit Court's jurisdiction is limited by the value of land, then there is a rebuttable presumption that the land in question is below the value threshold.

CHAPTER 25

Adverse Possession

We think the world is ours forever, but we are little more than squatters.

— Alexander McCall Smith, *The Careful Use of Compliments* (2007), p.12

INTRODUCTION

25–01 The main principles of adverse possession have already been outlined in relation to freeholds. These are fundamental to understanding the concepts of possession and title to land under the common law system. This chapter considers some aspects of adverse possession in more detail and also considers its application to leaseholds. The law relating to acquisition of title by adverse possession is set out in the Statute of Limitations 1957. Many of the provisions are re-enactments of earlier legislation.

THE POLICY BASIS

25–02 Any system of law which sets as one of its goals the protection of private property needs a justification for rules which have the effect of depriving the original owner of his or her property.[1] A number of different rationales can be advanced for adverse possession.[2]

Individual Initiative
25–03 One justification is that those who have rights should actively pursue them. This means that it would be a misuse of the legal system to allow the holder of a right to be idle for many years until some accident or whim induces recourse to the judicial system. This argument is essentially procedural: if A is dispossessed by B, it would deny A an action to recover possession against

---

[1] M. Jordan, "Illegality and the Law of Fast-Fish and Loose-Fish" (2017) 57 Ir. Jur. 14 considers the significance of committing a criminal act whilst taking possession. He notes (at 32) that "[t] he historical development of the doctrine of adverse possession supports a distinction between the initial act of taking possession and ongoing possession. The common law prioritises the latter and tends to ignore the former, leading thereby to an unprincipled but pragmatic illegality blind spot."

[2] See also the Law Reform Commission, *Report on Title by Adverse Possession of Land* (LRC 67-2002), para.1.14 and *J.A. Pye (Oxford) Ltd v United Kingdom* (2008) 46 E.H.R.R. 1083 at paras 50–51.

B after a given period of time. However, if A were to get back into possession without resort to the courts, this argument would not justify preventing
A defending his superior title against B.

Quieting Titles

25–04 A second justification is that of "quieting of titles". This is the notion
that there ought to come a time when defects in a title are cured. This policy is
not so much concerned with securing the title of the squatter as with innocent
third parties who may buy titles in the market. This is a capitalist justification.
Securing the title of the squatter, who has successfully bucked the market and
gotten something for nothing, is seen on this theory as a *cost* of reducing the
risk to innocent purchasers. This argument goes further than the first and, in
the example taken, justifies the extinction of A's title after B had been in possession for the required period. The idea that A could recover possession and
then be able successfully to defend an action by B would run contrary to this
policy: after the period has run, B's title should be secure.

Development

25–05 A third justification is that the doctrine of adverse possession favours
the person who uses land at the expense of one who does not. The doctrine
thus furthers economic development. It favours the productive use of land
as a social goal. This approach looks at the effects on society as a whole and
implies that the law has a direct responsibility to further economic development. It can therefore be seen as a socialist or social democratic approach in
the sense that it ascribes to law a role in allocating resources or furthering
economic development.

Unadministered Estates

25–06 A fourth justification was alluded to by Griffin J. in *Perry v Woodfarm
Homes*[3]:

> "Until comparatively recent years, raising representation in the case of small
> farms was quite rare, the occupiers preferring to rely on the Statute of Limi-
> tations, and there must be very few agricultural holdings in this country in
> which at some time in the past 140 years a tenancy was not 'acquired' under
> the statute. Again, leases for 999 years ... are now quite common ...".[4]

25–07 To say that occupiers have "preferred" to rely on adverse possession
suggests a deliberate choice. There may well be cases in which such a choice
is made on grounds of costs; however, there seems little doubt that in many

---

[3] [1975] I.R. 104. See also *Gleeson v Feehan (No.2)* [1997] 1 I.L.R.M. 522 at 539, where Keane
J. noted the "traditional reluctance of small farmers in rural Ireland to make wills or raise
representation".

[4] [1975] I.R. 104 at 129.

cases, ignorance of the legal formalities is a more probable explanation for this pattern. This policy supports limitation for a specific purpose and to solve a particular social problem. Woods notes that applications continue to be made to the Land Registry for registration of possessory title in respect of adverse possession between family members.[5]

THE MOVEMENT OF POLICY

25–08 If one looks at the development of the law in Ireland, and indeed other common law countries, one can see that the law has moved from the first policy basis to the second: it has moved from a negative procedural approach to the notion of "quieting titles", reinforced by the fourth policy in judicial interpretation. The third approach has not been adopted in common law countries. The explanation is that this stems from the dominance of the market as a means of distributing not only the products of labour, but also means of production such as land. The second policy has prevailed since it is most appropriate to reduce the costs of those buying land in a market: purchasers should be assured of obtaining secure titles. In the words of Lord St Leonards:

"All statutes of limitation have for their object the prevention of the rearing up of claims at great distances of time when evidences are lost; and in all well-regulated countries the quieting of possession is held an important point of policy."[6]

25–09 This argument implies that it is more important to "quiet titles" than to protect that of the original owner. It is not surprising, therefore, that the adoption of this policy should have occurred in 1833 when the Industrial Revolution was beginning to have a major impact on society. However, in a capitalist economy the law limits itself to providing favourable conditions in which individual transactions can take place: it assumes that economic development is best attained by leaving the actors in a market to make their own bargains, and so the third justification is not adopted. Such a policy would be more appropriate for countries in which the market is less developed and where the State takes a more active role in promoting development.

THE EFFECT ON TITLE

25–10 Before 1833, if A possessed land adversely to the title of B and the limitation period had expired, the effect was to bar B's right to recover possession by action. However, it did not extinguish B's title. Thus, if B was able to regain possession without going to court, A could not recover possession.

---

[5] U. Woods, "Adverse Possession and Administered Estates: an Unfair Solution to a Redundant Irish Problem?" (2016) 67(2) N.I.L.Q. 137 at 148–149.

[6] *Dundee Harbour Trustees v Dougall* (1852) 1 Macq. 317 at 321.

This was unsatisfactory in a number of respects, principally that the adverse possessor's title was precarious. Although this might be quite acceptable in relation to the adverse possessor him or herself, it would be difficult for such a person or his or her successors in title to sell the land to a purchaser, and even if he or she did, the purchaser would acquire a precarious title. This would mean that the marketability of such land would be reduced. During the Industrial Revolution, it was regarded as desirable by those who made the law that land should be freely alienable through the market. One of the purposes of the Real Property Limitation Act 1833 was to render titles more secure. Thus, the 1833 Act provides that in future the effect of the expiry of the limitation period is to bar the title of the dispossessed party.

25–11 Section 24 of the Statute of Limitations 1957 (the "1957 Act") provides:

> "24.— Subject to section 25 of this Act and to section 52 of the Act of 1891, at the expiration of the period fixed by this Act for any person to bring an action to recover land, the title of that person to the land shall be extinguished."

Thus, if the dispossessed person re-enters after the period has expired, he or she is a trespasser.[7]

HUMAN RIGHTS

25–12 As described above, under the 1957 Act, after the 12-year period of adverse possession has expired, the paper owner's title is extinguished. At the turn of this century there was a growing body of opinion that this was a "deprivation" of property without adequate procedural protection or advance notice to the previous owner or payment of compensation.[8] On the one hand, the traditional view is that there must be a quieting of titles, that an owner of land must take action within a reasonable time to protect his or her rights, or lose them; that the onus is primarily on the individual to make use of remedies provided by the law to protect his or her property rights; and that it should not be for the State to protect the rights of someone who has failed after a reasonable time to protect them him or herself. On the other hand, there is a view that to deprive a person automatically of his or her property rights without payment of compensation and without an attempt to discover the original owner, or require a process before a court, is unjustified and disproportionate. Human rights law requires the striking of a balance between these competing views. Broadly, it requires that a person should not be deprived of his or her property without due process and that laws which seek to quiet titles must adopt proportionate means in this respect.

---

[7] *Incorporated Society for Protestant Schools v Richards* (1841) 4 Ir. Eq. R. 177.
[8] UK Law Commission, *Land Registration for the Twenty-First Century: A Conveyancing Revolution* (Law Comm. 271-2001), para.2.70.

25–13 In *J.A. Pye (Oxford) Ltd v Graham,*[9] the court had to apply the English law which then applied to the facts, namely that 12 years' adverse possession barred the title of the previous owner. That law had been described as "illogical and disproportionate" by the judge at first instance,[10] who found in favour of the squatter. This judgment was reversed on appeal by the Court of Appeal, which inquired closely into the state of mind of the squatter and held that the possession exercised was not "adverse".[11] The "squatter" in this case acquired an area of prime development land valued at about £10 million. The first-instance decision was restored by the House of Lords, but the senior law lord criticised the result as "apparently unjust".[12] The issue was referred to the European Court of Human Rights, and the first-instance Chamber ruled (by four votes to three) that the English law of adverse possession violated the European Convention on Human Rights (ECHR) guarantee of the "peaceful enjoyment" of possessions.[13] However, the Grand Chamber[14] (by 10 votes to seven) held that the English law did not violate the ECHR, and was proportionate. The majority held that the adverse possession provisions in the English Limitation Act 1980 did not upset the fair balance which the ECHR requires between an individual's "peaceful enjoyment" of his or her possessions and the demands of the public interest. The majority took the view that the limitation principle concerned only "control of use" and did not therefore require compensation, as opposed to "deprivation of possessions" which normally would have done. By protecting against stale claims, the limitation period pursued "a legitimate aim in the general interest" and that "even where title to real property is registered, it must be open to the legislature to attach more weight to lengthy unchallenged possession than to the formal fact of registration".[15]

25–14 English law, which had been amended in 2002 since the facts of *Pye,* out of concern for human rights challenges,[16] now provides that possession by an occupier for any length of time no longer bars the title of the previous owner.[17] As Lord Hope of Craighead noted in *Pye,* the new regime in the English 2002 Act makes it "much harder for a squatter who is in possession of registered land to obtain a title to it against the wishes of the proprietor".[18] In 2005 the Law Reform

---

[9] [2003] 1 A.C. 419.

[10] [2000] Ch. 676 at 710.

[11] [2001] Ch. 804.

[12] [2003] 1 A.C. 419 at para.2.

[13] *J.A. Pye (Oxford) Ltd v United Kingdom* (2006) 43 E.H.R.R. 43.

[14] (2008) 46 E.H.R.R. 1083.

[15] (2008) 46 E.H.R.R. 1083 at paras 70 and 74.

[16] Land Registration Act 2002; K.J. Gray and S.F. Gray, *Elements of Land Law*, 5th edn (Oxford: Oxford University Press, 2009), para.9.1.20.

[17] After 10 years of possession the occupier has to apply to the Land Registrar, and there is then a further period of two years in which the Registrar must notify the owner of the estate, or of any charge, who can then object to the application. If no compromise between the parties can be reached, the matter is referred to an adjudicator. An objection can be defeated by a successful claim to equitable estoppel, a reasonable mistake as to a boundary and other grounds.

[18] [2003] 1 A.C. 419 at para.73.

Commission recommended significant changes to the law on adverse possession in this jurisdiction.[19] However, the Land and Conveyancing Law Reform Act 2009 ("LCLRA 2009") which ultimately passed into law, although it has effected wide-ranging changes to the substantive law on real property, has only brought about a small number of changes to the law on adverse possession.[20]

25–15 In the period between the delivery of the first instance and the Grand Chamber decisions of the European Court of Human Rights in *Pye,* it appeared as if human rights considerations would necessitate a rebalancing of the law on adverse possession so as to afford a greater measure of protection to landowners.[21] However, as the compatibility with the ECHR of the pre-2002 English legislation on adverse possession has now been upheld by the European Court of Human Rights, the English Court of Appeal held in *Ofulue v Bossert*[22] that, in the absence of special circumstances (which had not been established), it was not open to a landowner to argue that his property rights were violated if a squatter extinguished his title to land by adverse possession.

THE "PARLIAMENTARY CONVEYANCE"

25–16 The earliest judicial view of the 1833 Act was, in the words of Parke B., that "[t]he effect of the Act is to make a parliamentary conveyance of the land to the person in possession after that period of twenty years [as it then was] has elapsed."[23] This view was upheld in Ireland in relation to leasehold land in *Rankin v McMurty*.[24] Holmes J. stated:

"Whatever the mode of transfer, I am of [the] opinion that the estate and interest the right to which is extinguished, so far as the original owner is

---

[19] Law Reform Commission, *Report on Reform and Modernisation of Land Law and Conveyancing Law* (LRC 74-2005). Under s.130 of the draft Land and Conveyancing Bill 2005, a person who claimed that he or she had acquired title to land by adverse possession would have to apply to court for a "vesting order" to vest title in him or her. The circumstances in which such an order would be made would be limited and the court would have jurisdiction to order that the squatter pay compensation to the dispossessed landowner.

[20] See LCLRA 2009 ss.99(2) and 119, amending ss.34 and 32 of the 1957 Act.

[21] *Beaulane Properties Ltd v Palmer* [2006] Ch. 79.

[22] [2009] Ch. 1, affirmed without reference to this point: [2009] 1 A.C. 990.

[23] *Doe d Jukes v Sumner* (1845) 14 M. & W. 39 at 42. See also, *Incorporated Society for Protestant Schools v Richards* (1841) 4 Ir. Eq. R. 177 at 197; *Scott v Nixon* (1843) 6 Ir. Eq. R. 8; *Tuthill v Rogers* (1849) 6 Ir. Eq. R. 429; *Burroughs v McCreight* (1844) 7 Ir. Eq. R. 49; *Trustees of Dundee Harbour v Dougall* (1852) 1 Macq. 317 at 321; E.B. Sugden, *An Essay on the New Statutes: Relating to Limitations of Time, Estates Tail, Dower, Descent, Operation of Deeds, Merger of Attendant Terms, Defective Executions of Powers of Leasing, Wills, Trustees and Mortgages* (London: S. Sweet, 1852), p.8; A.C. Meredith, "A Paradox of Sugden's" (1918) 34 L.Q.R. 253.

[24] (1889) 24 L.R. Ir. 290.

concerned, became vested in the person whose possession has caused such extinction."[25]

The judge felt that any other conclusion would cause uncertainty as to lease-hold titles in Ireland.

25–17 In England, the view of Parke B. and Sugden L.C. was rejected by the Court of Appeal in *Tichborne v Weir*,[26] a case on leaseholds. Lord Esher M.R. and Bowen L.J. held that the previous title was destroyed and not conveyed to the dispossessing tenant. The Irish decisions of Sugden L.C. were cited to the court but distinguished on the ground that they concerned freehold land.[27] Thus, even the court in *Tichborne* accepted the parliamentary conveyance theory in relation to freehold.

25–18 The rejection of the parliamentary conveyance theory in *Tichborne* seems to have been accepted obiter[28] by the Irish Court of Appeal in *O'Connor v Foley*.[29] The position in Ireland in relation to leaseholds has more recently been considered by the Supreme Court in *Perry v Woodfarm Homes Ltd*.[30] The majority of the Supreme Court in *Perry*, (a) did not accept that the ousted lessee retained an "estate" in the land, as opposed to contractual rights in rela-tion to the lessor, and further (b) did not accept the parliamentary conveyance theory applied to unregistered land. It impliedly rejected the distinction in *Tichborne* and *O'Connor* between leasehold and freehold in this respect.

25–19 There is, however, a suggestion in the judgment of Walsh J. in *Perry* that the parliamentary conveyance theory may apply in registered title. This view has been reinforced by the amendment to the definition of "leasehold interest" in s.3 of the Registration of Title Act 1964 which was effected by s.50 of the Registration of Deeds and Title Act 2006. The judgment in *Perry v Woodfarm Homes Ltd*[31] and the effect of adverse possession on leasehold interests are discussed further below.

25–20 In the case of freehold land it may not be easy to tell the difference between the parliamentary conveyance doctrine and a "new title" doctrine. The fact that the dispossessor's title is subject to rights which have not been extinguished is not consistent only with a conveyance having taken place. Equitable rights which bound the previous owner will bind the dispossessor because he or she, having taken by operation of law, is not a "purchaser" for

---

[25] (1889) 24 L.R. Ir. 290 at 301.

[26] (1892) 67 L.T. 735, followed in *Taylor v Twinberrow* [1930] 2 K.B. 16.

[27] (1892) 67 L.T. 735 at 737.

[28] In *O'Connor* the tenant was held to have become so by estoppel, not by adverse possession.

[29] [1906] 1 I.R. 20.

[30] [1975] I.R. 104.

[31] [1975] I.R. 104.

value,[32] but this would be so whether there was a conveyance of the previous title or not. On the other hand, under s.71 of the LCLRA 2009[33] or the rule in *Wheeldon v Boroughs*,[34] the new owner will not be able to claim advantages enjoyed by the ousted owner, since these rules have been held to apply only to voluntary conveyances.[35] This result would equally be unaffected by whether the title was held to pass by operation of law or whether a new title was created. An implication of adopting the parliamentary conveyance theory in relation to s.24 of the 1957 Act would seem to be that such advantages would pass under that section.

25–21 The problem with the "parliamentary conveyance" theory is that it did not fit well with fundamental common law property theory. In theory a squatter, from the first moment of dispossession, has a fee simple relative to everyone except the dispossessed title holder, or anyone with a better title than the dispossessed title holder. This is a possessory title distinct from the title of the dispossessed title holder. After the 12 years have expired, the title of the dispossessed title holder is barred, leaving the squatter with a fee simple less vulnerable than before, but a fee simple based on the same title he or she had from the first day he or she entered the land.

The Elements of Adverse Possession

Meaning of Possession
General Principles
25–22 The fundamental requirement of a claim of adverse possession is that the squatter be in possession of the property in question. Section 18(1) of the 1957 Act provides:

"No right of action to recover land shall be deemed to accrue unless the land is in the possession (in this section referred to as adverse possession) of some person in whose favour the period of limitation can run."

25–23 The additional requirement that the landowner be dispossessed, or discontinue his possession, contained in s.14(1) of the 1957 Act, is subsidiary to the question of whether, and if so, when, a squatter took possession of land. One possible exception exists in the case of land that is not at present capable of use and enjoyment, in which cases a number of *dicta* suggest that mere non-use will not by itself necessarily amount to discontinuance of possession.[36]

---

[32] *Re Nisbett & Pott's Contract* [1906] 1 Ch. 386.
[33] This section replaced s.6 of the Conveyancing Act 1881, with some alteration.
[34] (1878) 12 Ch. D. 31.
[35] *Sovmots Investments Ltd v Secretary of State for the Environment* [1979] 1 A.C. 144.
[36] See *Dundalk Urban District Council v Conway*, unreported, High Court, Blayney J., 15 December 1987, and *Battelle v Pinemeadow Ltd*, unreported, High Court, Finnegan J., 9 May 2002.

The relevance of future uses is considered further in the section on *animus possidendi*.

25–24 The question of what is required to establish possession of land is a question of fact and degree. As was stated by Lord O'Hagan in *The Lord Advocate v Lord Lovat*[37]:

"As to possession, it must be considered in every case with reference to the peculiar circumstances. The acts, implying possession in one case, may be wholly inadequate to prove it in another. The character and value of the property, the suitable and natural mode of using it, the course of conduct with the proprietor might reasonably be expected to follow with a due regard to his own interests - all these things, greatly varying as they must, under various conditions, are to be taken into account in determining the sufficiency of a possession."[38]

25–25 A further useful statement of what constitutes "possession", which has subsequently found favour in the House of Lords,[39] the High Court of Northern Ireland[40] and the Irish courts,[41] is that of Slade J. in *Powell v McFarlane*[42]:

"Factual possession signifies an appropriate degree of physical control. It must be a single and conclusive possession, though there can be a single possession exercised by several persons jointly.[43] Thus an owner of land and a person intruding on that same land cannot both be in possession of the land at the same time.[44] The question of what acts constitute a sufficient degree of exclusive physical control must depend on the circumstances, in particular the nature of the land and the manner in which land of that nature is commonly used or enjoyed."[45]

25–26 Acts such as grazing cattle might of themselves be equivocal in proving that possession had been taken of the land,[46] but if in addition fencing was erected or drainage works were carried out, this is likely to be sufficient

---

[37] (1880) 5 App. Cas. 273.

[38] (1880) 5 App. Cas. 273 at 288. This passage was quoted with approval by Costello J. in *Murphy v Murphy* [1980] I.R. 183 at 193 and by Gilligan J. in *Keelgrove Properties Ltd v Shelbourne Developments Ltd* [2007] 3 I.R. 1 at 8.

[39] Lord Browne-Wilkinson in *J.A. Pye (Oxford) Ltd v Graham* [2003] 2 A.C. 419 at 432 noted that the principles set out by Slade J. "cannot be improved upon".

[40] *McCann v McCann* [2013] NI Ch 7.

[41] See *Dooley v Flaherty* [2014] IEHC 528; *Dunne v Iarnród Éireann* [2007] IEHC 314; and *Dunne v Iarnród Éireann* [2016] IESC 47.

[42] (1977) 38 P. & C.R. 452.

[43] See *Murphy v Murphy* [1980] I.R. 183 at 195–196.

[44] If there are competing claims, the landowner would appear to have an easier test to satisfy: see the judgment of Clarke J. in *Dunne v Iarnród Éireann* [2007] IEHC 314 at paras 5.2–5.6.

[45] (1977) 38 P. & C.R. 452 at 470. See also *Doyle v O'Neill*, unreported, High Court, O'Hanlon J., 13 January 1995.

[46] *Convey v Regan* [1952] I.R. 56 at 59; *Dunne v Iarnród Éireann* [2007] IEHC 314.

to establish possession.[47] Acts involving dumping and temporary storage on waste ground are generally held not to be sufficient to establish possession,[48] but the position may be otherwise if these acts were carried out on land following the determination of a tenancy.[49] The carrying-out of repairs to the property can also amount to minimal acts of possession.[50] Maintaining cattle, farming the land, and applying for grants in relation to the land can also amount to possession.[51]

Animus Possidendi by Occupier

25–27 Section 18(1) of the 1957 Act requires that the property must be in the "adverse possession" of somebody before time will commence to run. This is frequently referred to as requiring that the squatter have *animus possidendi*. Beyond meaning that the possession must not be by consent, the phrase has a somewhat imprecise meaning. *Animus possidendi* does not imply that the possessor must be aware that a title exists as to which his or her own possessory title is adverse. A person who occupies land mistakenly believing it to be his or her own can extinguish the title of the owner.[52] Older cases which treat as relevant the issue of whether the use by the occupier is inconsistent with the use to which the owner intended to put the land in future must be treated with caution in view of the House of Lords decision in *J.A. Pye (Oxford) Ltd v Graham*.[53]

25–28 In *J.A. Pye (Oxford) Ltd v Graham*,[54] the House of Lords reviewed the meaning of "adverse possession" and held that since 1833 the proper view was that only "possession" had to be shown, and not some additional element of a special kind of possession "adverse" to the title of the owner of the paper title. This analysis was based partly on the language of the English Limitation Act 1980. However, Lord Browne-Wilkinson, in reviewing the history of limitation statutes, concluded that since 1833 the word "adverse" did not add anything to the word "possession".[55]

25–29 This was not always thought to be the case and there was a line of authorities which the House of Lords overruled on the issue, including *Leigh*

---

[47] *Murphy v Murphy* [1980] I.R. 183; *Seamus Durack Manufacturing v Considine* [1987] I.R. 677.

[48] *Doyle v O'Neill*, unreported, High Court, O'Hanlon J., 13 January 1995; *Tracey Enterprises MacAdam Ltd v Drury* [2006] IEHC 381.

[49] *Griffin v Bleithin* [1999] 2 I.L.R.M. 182.

[50] *Dooley v Flaherty* [2014] IEHC 528.

[51] *Hamilton v ACC Loan Management Ltd* [2016] IEHC 142.

[52] See Finlay P. in *McMahon v Kerry County Council* [1981] I.L.R.M. 419; *Ramsden v Dyson* (1866) L.R. 1 H.L. 129.

[53] See *Seamus Durack Manufacturing Ltd v Considine* [1987] I.R. 677; *Leigh v Jack* (1879) 5 Ex. D. 264.

[54] [2003] 1 A.C. 419. See also *Murphy v Murphy* [1980] I.R. 183 at 202–203.

[55] [2003] 1 A.C. 419 at paras 33–35.

v Jack,[56] which had held that there could be no adverse possession if the land-owner had no present use for the land, but had a future use for it. However, a lesser form of the same doctrine may retain some vitality, as Barron J. in *Seamus Durack Manufacturing Ltd v Considine*[57] held that knowledge that a landowner had no present use for the land, but had a future use for it, might lead to an inference that the squatter did not intend to possess the land abso-lutely, but instead merely for a temporary period.

25–30 There seems no reason to suppose the position under the 1957 Act is different from that as set out in *J.A. Pye (Oxford) Ltd v Graham*,[58] or that the 1957 Act intended to reintroduce the pre-1833 law. Indeed, the decision of the House of Lords is consistent with that of the Supreme Court in *Murphy v Murphy*.[59] In addition, the judgment of Clarke J. in *Dunne v Iarnród Éireann*[60] quoted with approval from the judgment of Slade J. in *Powell v McFarlane*,[61] which in turn was one of the main authorities relied upon by the House of Lords in *Pye*.[62]

Successive Adverse Possessors

25–31 Possession constitutes the most basic form of title. It follows from this that if a dispossessor transfers his or her possessory title to a third party, the period of possession of such a transferor constitutes part of the title of the transferee. Suppose X dispossesses O and then, before the limitation period has expired, passes his possessory title to Y by *inter vivos* conveyance, by will or on intestacy. Y is then sued by O. Y can add the period of X's possession to his own and if the two added together make up 12 years or more, O's title is extinguished.[63] However, if X abandons his possession and Y enters into possession of the land immediately after X's departure, Y cannot make use of X's period of possession.[64] In those circumstances, Y has not acquired X's possessory title.

---

[56] (1879) 5 Ex. D. 264 per Lord Bramwell: "Acts of user are not enough to take the soil out of the Plaintiff, and vest it in the Defendant; in order to defeat a title by dispossessing the for-mer owner, acts must be done which are inconsistent with his enjoyment of the soil, for the purposes for which he intended to use it." See also *Wallis's Cayton Bay Holiday Camp Ltd v Shell-Mex and BP Ltd* [1974] 3 All E.R. 575 at 580 per Lord Denning M.R.: "Possession by itself is not enough to give a title. It must be adverse possession ... There must be something in the nature of an ouster of the true owner by the wrongful possessor."

[57] [1987] I.R. 677; *Dunne v Iarnród Éireann* [2007] IEHC 314. To some extent this doctrine runs counter to the law as set out in *J.A. Pye (Oxford) Ltd v Graham* [2003] 1 A.C. 419.

[58] [2003] 1 A.C. 419.

[59] [1980] I.R. 183.

[60] [2007] IEHC 314.

[61] (1977) 38 P. & C.R. 452.

[62] [2003] 1 A.C. 419.

[63] Statute of Limitations 1957 s.15(4); *Clarke v Clarke* (1868) I.R. 2 C.L. 395; *Mount Carmel Investments Ltd v Peter Thurlow Ltd* [1988] 3 All E.R. 129.

[64] Statute of Limitations 1957 s.18(3).

THE LIMITATION PERIOD

Recovery of Land

25–32 The period laid down by the 1833 Act for actions to recover land was generally 20 years.[65] The Real Property Limitation Act 1874 reduced it to 12 years[66] and this is retained by the 1957 Act.[67] The general period does not apply to the State.

Recovery of Rent

25–33 The period for the recovery of a rent or of arrears of a rentcharge is six years.[68]

The State

25–34 Where the State seeks to recover land, the period is 30 years,[69] except for foreshore where it is 60 years.[70] Where land was once foreshore but has ceased to be so, the State has 60 years from the accrual of the right of action or 40 years from the date on which the land ceased to be foreshore, whichever first expires.[71]

Postponement of Period

25–35 Section 14(1) of the 1957 Act does not require knowledge of dispossession on the part of the dispossessed owner before the cause of action arises and time begins to run. The general rule is that time begins to run from when the adverse possessor enters into possession, which can take place without the knowledge of the landowner. Exceptions to this general rule exist in the case of fraud, fraudulent concealment and mistake.

Fraud and Fraudulent Concealment

25–36 Section 71(1) of the 1957 Act provides that where the dispossessed owner's right of action is based on fraud[72] or has been concealed by the defendant's fraud[73] or that of his or her agent, time does not begin to run until the

---

[65] Real Property Limitation Act 1833 s.2.
[66] Real Property Limitation Act 1874 s.1.
[67] Statute of Limitations 1957 s.13(2)(a).
[68] Statute of Limitations 1957 ss.27 and 28.
[69] Statute of Limitations 1957 s.13(1)(a).
[70] Statute of Limitations 1957 s.13(1)(b).
[71] Statute of Limitations 1957 s.13(1)(c).
[72] This requires that fraud be an essential element of the cause of action, such as a claim in deceit or fraudulent misrepresentation: see *Beaman v ARTS Ltd* [1949] 1 K.B. 550.
[73] This provision codifies the jurisdiction of the Courts of Equity in cases of equitable fraud and the requirements of such a plea are accordingly quite flexible: see *Cave v Robinson* [2003] 1 A.C. 384; *Heffernan v O'Herlihy*, unreported, High Court, Kinlen J., 3 April 1999; and *O'Sullivan v Rogan* [2009] IEHC 456.

dispossessed owner discovers the fraud or could with "reasonable diligence" have discovered it.[74]

25–37 Section 71(2) provides that nothing in subs.(1) shall enable any action to be brought to recover, or charge or set aside any transaction affecting property which has been purchased for valuable consideration after the transaction giving rise to the fraud by a person who did not know or have reason to believe that the fraud was made. Here again it can be seen that where a choice has to be made between two equally innocent parties, the modern law prefers the purchaser in the market to the original owner.[75]

25–38 The notion that modern capitalist systems protect private property has to be judged against this preference for those who act through the market.

Mistake

25–39 A mistake, such as a mistake as to where the true boundary lies, does not generally prevent time running against the dispossessed owner.[76] In fact, one of the purposes of the law on adverse possession is to ensure that de facto boundaries correspond with legal rights, even if mapping inaccuracies mean that one landowner is technically a squatter.[77]

25–40 The harshness of this rule is modified by s.72, which contains a limited defence of mistake, as follows:

"Where, in the case of any action for which a period of limitation is fixed by this Act, the action is for relief from the consequences of mistake, the period of limitation shall not begin to run until the plaintiff has discovered the mistake or could with reasonable diligence have discovered it."

25–41 The defence of mistake only applies where the basis of the action is relief from the consequences of the mistake, such as a claim for rectification of a deed, or of the register in the case of registered title. The wording of this provision can lead to unfair distinctions being drawn between functionally equivalent causes of action. For example, if moneys are overpaid by mistake, an action in unjust enrichment for moneys paid by mistake will fall within s.72(1), whereas if moneys are underpaid by mistake, an action for payment of the balance is an action for breach of contract that falls outside the section.[78] The test of reasonable diligence implies that time will still run against the dispossessed owner if he or she could have discovered the mistake with such

---

[74] See *Paragon Finance plc v D.B. Thakerar & Co (a firm)* [1999] 1 All E.R. 400.

[75] See *Eddis v Chichester Constable* [1969] 2 Ch. 345.

[76] *Re Jones' Estate* [1914] 1 I.R. 188.

[77] Law Reform Commission, *Report on Title by Adverse Possession of Land* (LRC 67-2002), para.1.14.

[78] See *Phillips-Higgins v Harper* [1954] 1 Q.B. 411.

diligence, whether or not the mistake was due to his or her fault or that of the dispossessor. Subsection (2) provides a similar exception as to innocent third parties to that in the case of fraud.

Disability

25–42 Where the dispossessed owner is under a disability,[79] such as being a minor[80] or of unsound mind,[81] the action may be brought within six years from the date when the owner ceased to be under the disability or dies, whichever first occurs, and this is regardless of whether the normal 12-year period has expired or not.[82] In the case of actions to recover land or money charged on land, there is a maximum limitation period of 30 years from the date the right of action accrued.[83]

Fresh Accrual

25–43 Certain actions may cause time to start running afresh.[84]

Acknowledgment

25–44 An acknowledgment will occur if a person in adverse possession of land indicates that he or she recognises that the dispossessed landowner has a better title to the land than he or she does.[85] There is no requirement that he or she acknowledge the landowner's precise interest in the land. The effect of an acknowledgment is, first, to destroy his or her possessory title up to that point, but secondly his or her possession does not cease to be adverse as to the future: time begins to run afresh against the dispossessed owner from that date. Examples of an acknowledgment include an offer to purchase a property[86] or an offer to take a lease of a property.[87] However, if the offer is made in without prejudice negotiations, it will not be admissible in evidence, and thus may not be relied upon.[88] The 1957 Act imposes formal requirements, namely that

---

[79] Statute of Limitations 1957 s.48.

[80] Statute of Limitations 1957 s.48(1)(a); Age of Majority Act 1985.

[81] Statute of Limitations 1957 s.48(1)(b); *Rohan v Bord na Móna* [1990] 2 I.R. 425; *Maga v Archbishop of Birmingham* [2010] 1 W.L.R. 1441.

[82] Statute of Limitations 1957 s.49(1)(a).

[83] Statute of Limitations 1957 s.49(1)(d).

[84] An acknowledgment or part payment must occur prior to the expiration of the limitation period to have any effect, as s.24 of the 1957 Act provides that a landowner's interest in land is extinguished when the limitation period expires.

[85] Statute of Limitations 1957 s.51. Acknowledgments also arise, inter alia, in cases involving mortgagees, mortgagors and debts secured on land: see Statute of Limitations 1957 ss.52–57.

[86] *Edgington v Clark* [1964] 1 Q.B. 367.

[87] *Rehman v Benfield* [2006] EWCA Civ 1392.

[88] See *Bradford & Bingley plc v Rashid* [2006] 1 W.L.R. 2066 and *Ofulue v Bossert* [2009] 2 W.L.R. 749.

the acknowledgment must be in writing and signed by the person making the acknowledgment.[89]

Part Payment

25–45 A part payment is a form of acknowledgment. Payment of part of a debt secured on land causes the limitation period to run afresh. Thus, if E is a mortgagee who has also acquired a right to enforce the security under the mortgage against R, the mortgagor, then if R pays part of the debt secured to E time begins to run against R afresh.[90] If E has gone into possession as mortgagee then any payment made by R on foot of the mortgage will set time running afresh as against M.[91]

Dispossessed Landowner Regaining Possession

25–46 If the dispossessed landowner re-takes possession at any time before the limitation period expires, this has the effect of causing the limitation period to run afresh, even if he or she only remains in possession temporarily. This occurred in *Dunne v Iarnród Éireann*,[92] where the defendant landowner carried out extensive repairs to a railway station situated on its land, and had repaired fencing around its land, prior to the limitation period expiring. While the station occupied only a small part of the lands, Clarke J. held that, as the lands were not divided in any way, it was not possible to say that the plaintiff had remained in possession of part of the lands.[93] He also approved of the statement of Slade J. in *Powell v McFarlane*[94] that "the slightest acts done by or on behalf of an owner in possession will be found to negative discontinuance of possession".[95]

PARTICULAR CASES

Future Interests
The General Rule

25–47 Adverse possession is possession adverse to some other possession, and so time does not begin to run against those entitled to future interests, whether in remainder or in reversion, until the interests vest in possession. At that point, they also cease to be future interests at all, and so in general it can be said that there is no special rule as to future interests. But in one sense there is.

---

[89] Statute of Limitations 1957 s.58. See *Good Challenger Navegante S.A. v Metalexportimport S.A.* [2003] EWCA Civ 1668.

[90] Statute of Limitations 1957 ss.62 and 68.

[91] Statute of Limitations 1957 s.64.

[92] [2007] IEHC 314.

[93] The decision of the High Court was upheld by the Supreme Court in *Dunne v Iarnród Éireann* [2016] IESC 47.

[94] (1977) 38 P. & C.R. 452.

[95] (1977) 38 P. & C.R. 452 at 472.

25–48 If the person entitled to a prior estate has been dispossessed, the owner of the future interest has no right of action until the prior estate has terminated, but when it does, the person entitled to the future interest has 12 years from when the adverse possession began, or six years from the end of the prior estate, whichever is longer.[96] Suppose land is settled on A for life, remainder to B in fee simple. X dispossesses A 10 years before A's death. B has six years from A's death in which to sue. If, on the other hand, X had dispossessed A three years before A's death, B would be able to sue at any time from A's death to a point nine years from that date, since the limitation period is measured as 12 years from the dispossession. This period is the correct one since it gives a longer period than six years from A's death.

25–49 If X completes 12 years' adverse possession before A dies, what then? Under the above rule A's title is barred, but not B's, and this is in accordance with principle. B has six years from A's death to bring an action against X. X extinguished A's title, but A's title was only a life estate. B claims by a title paramount to that of X. An interesting question is what estate did X acquire in the land? If the parliamentary conveyance theory applies, A's life estate would be conveyed to X, giving X an estate *pur autre vie* for the life of A. If not, then X would, as a squatter, have a relative fee simple which, after the 12 years, would be good against A, but not against B until six years after A's death.

25–50 If X had only taken possession after A's death, dispossessing B, B's interest would no longer be a future interest and the usual 12-year period would apply.

Interests after Fees Tail and Base Fees
25–51 In the past, there were exceptions to the preceding rules in relation to fees tail and base fees. The conversion of fees tail and base fees into fees simple by the LCLRA 2009 has done away with these exceptions.[97]

Equitable Interests
25–52 In general, the provisions of the 1957 Act apply to equitable estates and interests in land, including interests under a trust for sale, as they do to legal estates and interests.[98]

Strangers
25–53 The rule is modified where trust property is possessed adversely by a stranger. The stranger does not bar the trustee's title until the interest of all the

---

[96] Statute of Limitations 1957 s.15(2)(a).
[97] LCLRA 2009 s.13(1)–(3).
[98] Statute of Limitations 1957 s.25(1).

beneficiaries have been barred.[99] Thus, if T holds land on trust for A for life, with remainder on trust for B in fee simple, 12 years' adverse possession by X during A's lifetime bars A's life estate, but does not bar T's legal estate. Time does not run against B's future estate until it vests in possession at A's death. Under the 1957 Act, the same protection is given to T's estate: time does not run against T until A's death, and it will only be barred when B's estate is barred, i.e. six years after A's death.[100] Thus, after X has been in possession for 12 years, T holds the land in trust for X for the rest of A's life, then on trust for B. This result creates a major problem for purchasers of a title acquired by adverse possession. They must inquire whether the land was held in the past under a settlement by way of trust, including a trust for sale.

Trustees
25–54 In general trustees cannot bar the title of their own beneficiaries: there is no limitation period for an action by a beneficiary against his or her trustee to recover trust property where the claim is based upon fraud or for the recovery of property converted by the trustee to his or her own use.[101] If there is no fraud, such as a trustee paying money to the wrong person by mistake, the limitation period is six years.[102]

Beneficiaries
25–55 A beneficiary of land held on trust, including a trust for sale, cannot in general establish possession adverse to the trustees of the land or other beneficiaries.[103] An exception to this is where the beneficiary is entitled under a bare trust, i.e. where the beneficiary is solely and absolutely entitled to the whole beneficial interest.[104] In this case, time begins to run against the trustees from the moment the beneficiary is in possession. In such a situation, the beneficiary, under the principle in *Saunders v Vautier,*[105] is entitled to call upon the trustees to convey the legal estate to him. Thus, if land is held by T on trust for A for life and remainder to B in fee simple, if A dies and B enters into possession, time begins to run against T in B's favour and in 12 years B's estate will become a legal one, extinguishing that of T. In the meantime, B can in any case call upon T for the legal estate. Another possible case is that of a purchaser under a contract of sale of a fee simple where the purchaser goes into possession. Similarly, a vendor of land who lets a purchaser into possession after the

---

[99] Statute of Limitations 1957 s.25(2). For the former rule, see *Burroughs v McCreight* (1844) 1 Jo. & La T. 290.

[100] Statute of Limitations 1957 s.15(2)(a).

[101] Statute of Limitations 1957 s.44.

[102] Statute of Limitations 1957 s.43(1)(a).

[103] Statute of Limitations 1957 s.25(4).

[104] Statute of Limitations 1957 s.25(4).

[105] [1835–42] All E.R. 58.

contract is signed but prior to completion may be a bare trustee against whom time will run.[106]

Equitable Relief

25–56 The 1957 Act also contains a special provision for actions seeking equitable relief. Section 5 provides that nothing in the Act shall affect any equitable jurisdiction to refuse relief on the ground of acquiescence or otherwise. Equitable remedies may also, in equity, be refused on the ground of laches, i.e. undue delay in bringing the action.[107]

Mortgages

Mortgagors

25–57 Prior to the LCLRA 2009, a mortgagee who went into possession of land (a rare occurrence in any event) could bar the mortgagor's right to redeem the mortgage after 12 years. The mortgagee's possession was adverse provided that he or she did not acknowledge the mortgagor's title or received any payment of principal or interests during the period of possession.[108] For mortgages created after 1 December 2009, the mortgagee cannot take possession of the mortgaged property without the mortgagor's consent or a court order. Section 99(2) of the LCLRA 2009 provides that s.37 of the 1957 Act does not apply to a mortgagee in possession on foot of a court order, thus removing this anomaly.

Mortgagees

25–58 The mortgagee's[109] right to bring an action for sale or to sue for possession is barred after 12 years from the date when the repayment became due.[110] The mortgagee's title to the land then becomes extinguished.[111] The right to recover interest on principal is barred six years after the payment became due,[112] but the right to recover principal is barred after 12 years have expired

---

[106] *Bridges v Mees* [1957] Ch. 475. See also s.52 of the LCLRA 2009, which provides that the entire beneficial interest in land passes to the purchaser on the making of a contract for the sale of the land, reversing *Tempany v Hynes* [1976] I.R. 101.

[107] See, e.g. *Re Ffrench's Estate* (1887) 21 L.R. Ir. 283 at 311–312 and *Lindsay Petroleum Co v Hurd* (1873) L.R. 5 P.C. 221 at 239–240.

[108] Statute of Limitations 1957 ss.33, 34(1)(a), 54 and 64.

[109] A judgment mortgage is included within the definition of a mortgage contained in s.2 of the Statute of Limitations 1957.

[110] Statute of Limitations 1957 ss.32(2)(a) and 33. If the mortgagee is a State authority, the limitation period is 30 years: s.32(1). In the case of a judgment mortgage, time runs from the date the judgment became enforceable: s.32(3) of the 1957 Act, as inserted by s.119 of the LCLRA 2009.

[111] Statute of Limitations 1957 s.33. *Cotterell v Price* [1960] 1 W.L.R. 1097. Under s.36(1)(b) of the 1957 Act, the period is 30 years for certain mortgages, namely where interest on the mortgage is paid into the Church Temporalities Fund, a charge under s.31 of the Land Law (Ireland) Act 1881, and a charge under the Housing (Gaeltacht) Acts 1929 and 1934.

[112] Statute of Limitations 1957 s.37; *Re Huggard's Estate* [1930] I.R. 532.

from the time when it became due.[113] However, this rule does not apply in cases where a mortgagor seeks to redeem the mortgaged property,[114] or seeks payment from the surplus proceeds of sale,[115] in which cases no limitation period applies. Other mortgagees may[116] prove their claims in an action brought by one of them to realise the sum due on a mortgage sale of the property, as it is regarded as being for the benefit of all incumbrancers.[117]

Strangers

25–59 If a stranger is in adverse possession of the land at the time when a mortgage has been created, it has been held that if the stranger then completes the period, the title so acquired is valid not only against the mortgagor, but also against the mortgagee.[118]

Deceased Persons' Estates

25–60 It is not uncommon in Ireland, particularly in rural areas, for the estates of deceased persons to remain unadministered and for family members to remain in possession of the land after the death of the deceased. The limitation period for a claim against a personal representative in respect of any share or interest in the estate of a deceased person is six years, and three years for recovery of arrears of interest on a legacy, except for actions against personal representatives for fraud.[119] In *Gleeson v Feehan (No.1)*,[120] it was held by the Supreme Court that s.45 of the 1957 Act only contains the limitation period for claims by a beneficiary *against* a personal representative administering the estate, and not for claims brought *by* personal representatives. In the latter case, the ordinary limitation periods apply, e.g. the 12-year limitation period for actions seeking the recovery of land.

Personal Representatives

25–61 The social practice described above has influenced the development of the law in this area.[121] Personal representatives are trustees for the beneficiaries under the will or for the intestate successors.[122] As such, the rule was that they could not be in adverse possession as regards such persons. This caused a problem where a family member or members remained in occupation of land

---

[113] Statute of Limitations 1957 ss.36 and 39.

[114] *Holmes v Cowcher* [1970] 1 W.L.R. 834.

[115] *Lloyd v Lloyd* [1903] 1 Ch. 385.

[116] Time continues to run against those mortgagees who do not prove their claim in the action: *Allied Irish Banks plc v Dormer* [2009] IEHC 586; *Bank of Ireland v Moffitt* [2009] IEHC 545.

[117] See *Re Conclough's Estate* (1859) 8 Ir. Ch. R. 330 and the other cases discussed in *Allied Irish Banks plc v Dormer* [2009] IEHC 586.

[118] *Munster & Leinster Bank Ltd v Croker* [1940] I.R. 185.

[119] Statute of Limitations 1957 s.45, substituted by Succession Act 1965 s.126. In Northern Ireland, adverse possession is governed by the Limitation (Northern Ireland) Order 1989 and the Land Registration Act (Northern Ireland).

[120] [1993] 2 I.R. 113.

[121] See *Maher v Maher* [1987] I.L.R.M. 582.

[122] Succession Act 1965 s.10(3).

and then, when the situation became clear to them, they applied for and were granted letters of administration. They could not acquire title as adverse possessors against those family members who were not in possession. For some time, Irish courts followed the rule as to trustees,[123] but then underwent a change of heart and decided that personal representatives could bar the claims of beneficiaries or intestate successors.[124] Legislation in both parts of Ireland has given statutory effect to this change. Section 2(2) of the 1957 Act[125] now provides that a personal representative in that capacity is not a trustee for the purposes of the 1957 Act and this provision has now been replaced by a similar provision in s.123 of the Succession Act 1965.

Family Members in Possession
25–62 If family members are factually in possession of an unadministered estate, their possession is adverse[126] to the title of the President of the High Court.[127] After the expiry of the limitation period, the possessory title bars the title of the President of the High Court. They hold the possessory title as joint tenants and not as tenants in common.[128] This is so whether their own shares in the estate, or those of absent members, are equal or unequal.[129] Survivorship applies to the title of family members acquired by adverse possession and so when one of them dies, there is no share to pass to their successors. This simplifies title but at the expense of depriving other family members of a share.

Wives and Children
25–63 Suppose H and W, who are husband and wife, occupy a matrimonial home the title to which is vested solely in H. After disagreements, H leaves the house and remains absent for at least 12 years. Does the wife, or do the wife and children, acquire H's title by adverse possession?

25–64 In the past, the judicial acceptance of the inferior legal position of the wife tended to prevent the courts accepting that the wife could have a possession independent of and adverse to that of her husband. The decision of the

---

[123] *Nugent v Nugent* (1884) 15 L.R. Ir. 321; *Molony v Molony* [1894] 2 I.R. 1.
[124] *Vaughan v Cottingham* [1961] I.R. 184; similarly in Northern Ireland: *McNeill v McNeill* [1957] N.I. 10; *Fagan v McParland* (1977) 28 N.I.L.Q. 201.
[125] See also art.45(1) of the Limitation (Northern Ireland) Order 1989.
[126] In *Martin v Kearney* (1902) 36 I.L.T.R. 117, Palles C.B. had held that a family member in possession was an equitable tenant in common, not a "trespasser" (i.e. not in adverse possession), and would become a legal tenant in common when the estate was administered. However, this was overruled in *Gleeson v Feehan (No.2)* [1997] 1 I.L.R.M. 522 at 529–530, a decision reached *per incuriam Ruddy v Gannon* [1965] I.R. 283.
[127] Succession Act 1965 s.13; *Flack v President of the High Court*, unreported, High Court, Costello J., 29 November 1983.
[128] Succession Act 1965 s.125. The law in respect of pre-Succession Act 1965 intestacies is contained in *Maher v Maher* [1987] I.L.R.M. 582 and *Gleeson v Feehan (No.2)* [1997] 1 I.L.R.M. 522, but see *contra Ruddy v Gannon* [1965] I.R. 283.
[129] Succession Act 1965 s.125.

Supreme Court of the Irish Free State in *Keelan v Garvey*[130] is typical of this attitude. The tenant of a farm, having quarrelled with his wife, left the farm in 1897. A few days after leaving he wrote to his wife asking her to sell oats and pay some money he owed and also giving directions about the treatment of the land. The wife remained in sole possession until her death in 1923. At some time during that period and before 12 years had expired, the wife purchased the farm under the Land Purchase Acts. The husband never returned to the farm during the wife's lifetime and she remained in possession until she died in 1923.

25–65 Molony L.C.J. held that the wife had acquired the tenancy of the farm by adverse possession, but was reversed by the Supreme Court. O'Connor J. said:

"It is true that the old doctrine of unity of ownership and possession as between husband and wife has been abolished by the Married Women's Property Act, but there still remains a relationship between them arising out of the marriage tie, and the mutual duties and obligations thereby imposed, which must be taken into consideration when the question arises between them as to the exclusive possession by either of the property of the other ... It is the moral duty of the wife within certain limits to guard and manage her husband's property, and, in most cases, this is not merely recognised but cheerfully accepted and performed ... His actual possession would no doubt cease during his absence, but there would still remain a certain unity between them which would make the possession of the wife the possession of the absent husband."[131]

25–66 Some features of this example of reasoning are worth commenting upon. At the end of the passage the judge restates the concept of unity, despite the fact that it had been abolished by statute and this had been acknowledged by the judge at the beginning of his judgment. There is also an implied stricture against the wife for not having "cheerfully" performed her subordinate role of managing the husband's property without any contact or support from the absent husband for 26 years. The judge nevertheless admitted that the "unity" was not absolute. It could be "severed":

"For instance, if the husband announced to his wife that he did not intend to return, that he had abandoned her and his family and farm, or if the circumstances showed that such was his intention, then the conclusion might fairly be drawn that the previous unity which made the wife the mere bailiff or agent of her husband was severed, and that her subsequent possession was not his possession but her own."[132]

---

[130] [1925] 1 I.R. 1.
[131] [1925] 1 I.R. 1 at 9.
[132] [1925] 1 I.R. 1 at 9–10.

25–67 This passage points up another feature of the genre: the carefully crafted impression that the rules operate equally as to both parties, are reasonable and provide exceptions. In the first passage quoted, the judge speaks of the "exclusive possession by either of the property of the other" while the social facts at the time of the decision were almost universally that wives occupied property legally vested in their husbands. In the present quotation, the judge stresses the reasonable exception, and yet the key element is not the abandonment of the property by the husband, which would have given the wife title to the farm on the facts, but the intention to abandon expressed at the time the desertion took place, which would be highly unusual in most cases, and the effect of imposing this newly discovered test was to deprive the wife of the title on the facts. The husband's subsequent lack of interest in the land over the following 26 years was apparently regarded as irrelevant, although it could have been taken as evidence of an intention to abandon dating from his last contact or at some time thereafter. Surely it would have been reasonable to find that the husband had abandoned the farm at some time between his last contact and the start of a 12-year period expiring by the wife's death? The fact that the wife had purchased the freehold was also apparently irrelevant. The exception seems designed to justify a conclusion which is insupportable on the grounds of justice.

25–68 In *Re Daily,*[133] Andrews L.C.J. also had to consider the case of a husband who had left home after quarrels with his wife. In this case there were children also present in the house and they remained with the wife. They also contributed to the working and improvement of the farm. The husband left the house in 1928 and did not return. The wife brought an action after the limitation period had expired claiming that the register should be amended in her favour. Andrews L.C.J., delivering the judgment of the court, held that the husband's title had been extinguished by adverse possession, but not by that of the wife alone, but by that of the children as well, so that the wife and children had acquired title as joint tenants. *Keelan v Garvey*[134] was not binding upon the judge but he chose to distinguish it on the facts. He found that the Supreme Court in *Keelan* was influenced by factors not present in the present case, particularly (a) the fact that the husband had written letters in which he treated the wife as a mere agent, (b) that the wife had become (fee simple) owner of the farm before the limitation period had expired and so before she could have claimed to extinguish his title by adverse possession, and (c) that the judge found that there was an arrangement between the parties that the wife was to have the use of the farm during their separation and possibly for life. Andrews L.C.J. did not express any view as to when a wife's possession was still to be considered as that of the husband or whether social, or judicial, attitudes to the relationship had changed since *Keelan*.

---

[133] [1943] N.I. 1.
[134] [1925] 1 I.R. 1.

25–69 It seems clear that judicial attitudes have undergone considerable change since *Keelan* and even since *Re Daily*. The courts in a number of contexts have stressed that marriage is to be regarded as an equal relationship.[135] It seems more likely today that a court would hold that a wife, or a wife and children, can acquire by adverse possession the title to property vested in a husband.

Forfeiture or Breach of Condition
25–70 Section 16 of the 1957 Act provides that a right to recover land by virtue of a forfeiture or breach of condition shall be deemed to have accrued on the date on which the forfeiture was incurred or the condition broken.

25–71 Suppose land is given to A subject to two conditions by which if either of two events occurs the land is to be forfeit. Both events occur. If an action is brought a short time after the second event, but more than 12 years after the first event occurred, then the action is barred. The occurrence of the second event does not give rise to a separate cause of action.[136] When the first event occurred the possession of A became adverse and those affected had 12 years from that point in which to bring an action.

Leaseholds
Running of Time against Lessor
25–72 Where land is subject to a lease, time does not begin to run against the lessor until the termination of the lease.[137] When the lease comes to an end, the lessor has 12 years within which to recover the land. This still constitutes one of the defects which in theory can affect any title, at least in unregistered land, given that such titles in Ireland are investigated back for a limited period, usually 20 years. If V is selling land to P, the title deeds may indicate that V has a fee simple, but if the title deeds were searched back 150 years, they would show that V's title was in fact a lease for 160 years. There is thus a reversion outstanding on the term and it will fall into possession in 10 years' time. Time will not begin to run against the person entitled to the reversion until that time. Hence, V's title suffers from a defect which could destroy it.

Position of Dispossessor of Lessee
25–73 Where someone has dispossessed a lessee and has remained in possession for 12 years, does the dispossessor acquire the remainder of the term so that he or she holds on the same conditions as the ousted lessee, or is his

---

[135] *BL v ML* [1989] I.L.R.M. 528; *L v L* [1992] I.L.R.M. 115; *State (DPP) v Walsh* [1981] I.R. 412; *McKinley v Minister for Defence* [1992] 2 I.R. 333 (SC); *W v W* [1993] I.L.R.M. 294; *RF v MF*, unreported, Supreme Court, Henchy J., 24 October 1985.

[136] Statute of Limitations 1957 s.20. *Clarke v Clarke* (1868) I.R. 2 C.L. 395; *Doe d Hall v Moulsdale* (1847) 16 M. & W. 689.

[137] Statute of Limitations 1957 s.15(1).

or her possession more precarious? The landlord's right to possession is suspended until the termination of the lease. The lease may terminate by expiry or by breach of a condition or a forfeiture provided for in the lease. On the face of it, the answer should therefore depend on whether the dispossessor has performed the covenants in the lease during the 12-year period and whether the landlord has accepted this performance. If the landlord has done so, then he or she should be estopped from denying the tenancy.[138] Unfortunately the issue has not come before the courts in the leading cases in this straightforward form. A common case of adverse possession arises when A encroaches on the adjoining land of B, unknown possibly to both parties. If B holds the land under a lease, then B will continue to pay the rent and perform the other terms of the lease during the 12-year period. The lessor can of course bring an action for possession when the lease terminates and has 12 years from that point in which to do so. But the question is as to the rights of the parties while the term continues. The question is whether the dispossessor's title is precarious during this time.

The English Position in Fairweather

25–74 The House of Lords in *Fairweather v St Marylebone Property Co Ltd*[139] took the view that a dispossessor's title is precarious. In that case, A had a garden shed which straddled the boundary line between his land and that of B, which B held on a 99-year lease. The dispossessed lessee purported to surrender his "lease" to the lessor. The lessor claimed that this had given him an immediate right to possession in the lessor which he could therefore enforce at once and that he did not have to wait until the 99-year term had expired.

25–75 The majority of the court, Lord Morris dissenting, held that he was entitled to do so. They held that the title of the dispossessed lessee was extinguished as against the dispossessor but not in relation to the lessor. The title of the ousted lessee to the lease remained as between the lessor and the ousted lessee so that the ousted lessee could surrender it to the lessor. They went on to hold that the effect of this was that the lessor's right to possession was no longer postponed by the lease and, more surprisingly, that this was so not only in relation to the ousted lessee but in relation to the dispossessor as well. The result was that the dispossessed lessee, by "surrendering" the lease, and the lessor, by accepting the "surrender", could together oust the squatter even though the limitation period had expired.

25–76 *Fairweather* is open to the criticism that the result involves an inconsistency in theory. The court begins by adopting a "relative title" approach in holding that the title to the lease is extinguished in relation to the squatter but

---

[138] In *O'Connor v Foley* [1906] 1 I.R. 20 and *Ashe v Hogan* [1920] 1 I.R. 159, a squatter was held to be a tenant by estoppel, implying that a landlord could also be held bound to accept a squatter as a lessee on the same ground.

[139] [1963] A.C. 510.

not in relation to the lessor, but it ends by holding that a "surrender" of the lease by the lessee to the lessor can affect the squatter, which should only be so if it were an absolute title valid against all. It is also open to the criticism that it violates the provisions of the English Limitation Act 1939[140] which, just as the Irish Act, expressly says that after the limitation period has expired, the lessee has no title to the lease. It would seem to follow that if the lessee has no title to the lease, he or she cannot surrender it or otherwise deal with it. A result which is on the face of it inconsistent in reasoning and contrary to the plain meaning of a statute may indicate that the judges were unwilling to follow the logic of the statute to its result in the case at hand. In *Fairweather* the willingness of the court to accept the theoretical inconsistency may have been motivated by a reluctance as a matter of policy to accept that squatters can acquire a lease as against lessors. In urban areas in Britain, squatting in residential premises had become a growing consequence of homelessness.

25–77 The *Fairweather* case was extended in England by *Tickner v Buzzacott*,[141] which held that a lessor could forfeit the lease for non-payment of rent by the ousted lessee and this would give the lessor an immediate right to possession against the dispossessor. The court also held that the dispossessor had no right in equity to relief against forfeiture.

The Irish Position in Perry

25–78 The question was considered in Ireland by the Supreme Court in *Perry v Woodfarm Homes Ltd*.[142] The Irish judges did not accept the position in *Fairweather*. While they recognised that a contractual relationship can still exist between the ousted lessee and the lessor, they clearly held that the dispossessor's position is not as precarious as that in England after *Fairweather*. In *Perry,* the northern extremity of the plaintiff's property was bounded by a lane which ran from east to west. A narrow strip of ground adjoined the northern side of the lane. In 1955 the plaintiff entered into adverse possession of a portion of the strip and continued in possession without acknowledging the title of any person to the portion. At the time the plaintiff entered possession, the strip of ground was held, together with other land, by a lessee under a lease which created a term of 999 years from September 1947. In October 1970, the lessee purported to assign the lease to the defendant for the residue of the term. By that time, the plaintiff had clearly completed the 12-year period of adverse possession. A month later the lessors conveyed to the defendant the fee simple reversion in the land. The defendant claimed to be entitled to the possession of the strip of ground, including the portion possessed by the plaintiff. It argued that the leasehold interest in the portion of the strip had been determined by merger with the fee simple reversion when that had been acquired by the defendant. The plaintiff claimed an injunction restraining the defendant from

---

[140] The English Limitation Act 1980 is in similar terms.
[141] [1965] Ch. 426.
[142] [1975] I.R. 104 at 117.

entering upon the portion of the strip used by the plaintiff. O'Keeffe P. in the High Court granted a perpetual injunction.

25–79 The majority of the Supreme Court held on appeal as follows:

1. After the expiry of the 12-year period, the ousted lessee has no title to the lease and so no interest capable of being assigned.[143] Hence the purported assignment of the lease in October 1970 by Irish Life did not vest any estate in land in the defendant which could merge with the freehold reversion when it was conveyed in November 1970.[144]

2. An ousted lessee, whose leasehold interest has been extinguished by adverse possession, cannot surrender the lease to the lessor and so cannot confer an immediate right to possession on the lessor, because the ousted lessee no longer has title to the lease.[145] The Supreme Court did not follow the House of Lords in *Fairweather v St Marylebone Property Co Ltd*[146] on this point. It followed from this that the lessor and the ousted lessee could not collude in this way to evict the adverse possessor.

3. In unregistered[147] land there is no "parliamentary conveyance" of the lease from the ousted lessee to the adverse possessor.[148] On this point the Supreme Court followed the Irish Court of Appeal in *O'Connor v Foley*[149] and the English Court of Appeal in *Tichborne v Weir*,[150] Griffin J. observing that the latter case "has since been accepted as good law in England and as burying there, once and for all, the notion of a parliamentary transfer or conveyance".[151]

4. The leasehold estate, although not the ousted lessee's title to it, continues to exist in a negative sense in that it forms an "incumbrance" on the freehold suspending the lessor's right to possession.[152]

5. The lease still exists as a contract between the lessor and the ousted lessee and so, if the ousted lessee is an original contracting party,[153] unless the original lease expressly provided otherwise, the ousted lessee remains bound, contractually, to the lessor to perform the covenants in

---

[143] [1975] I.R. 104 at 119 and 130. Henchy J. expressed no view on assignment, but dissent would be consistent with his view on merger and surrender (at 124).

[144] [1975] I.R. 104 per Walsh J. at 119 and 121 upholding the decision of O'Keeffe P. in the High Court; Griffin J. at 130 and 132; Henchy J. dissenting at 124.

[145] [1975] I.R. 104 per Walsh J. at 119; Griffin J. at 130; Henchy J. dissenting at 124.

[146] [1963] A.C. 510.

[147] The law concerning registered land is discussed in the next section.

[148] [1975] I.R. 104 per Walsh J. at 120; Griffin J. at 128 and 129; Henchy J. at 122; overruling *Rankin v McMurtry* (1889) 24 L.R. Ir. 290.

[149] [1906] 1 I.R. 20 per Fitzgibbon L.J. at 26.

[150] [1891–4] All E.R. 449, followed in *Taylor v Twinberrow* [1930] 2 K.B. 16.

[151] [1975] I.R. 104 at 128.

[152] [1975] I.R. 104 per Walsh J. at 119; Griffin J. at 129; Henchy J. dissenting at 124.

[153] If he or she is not, then there is no privity of contract between the ousted lessee and the lessor and the lessee would not remain liable after parting with his or her estate: *Re Field* [1918] 1 I.R. 140. Deasy's Act s.14 provides that a landlord or tenant who is such by assignment is only to have the benefit of or to be liable on the covenants so long as he or she retains the estate.

the lease.[154] This follows from basic principles. A contract is a personal obligation not dependent upon the promissor having any estate in the land, unless the parties expressly say that it is.

25–80 The court is less clear as to the effect of the ousted lessee failing to perform the covenants in the lease. The court is clear that if the ousted lessee is an original contracting party, he or she remains liable in privity of contract to the original lessor. If the contract contained a forfeiture clause, then this would cause a "forfeiture of the lease" and the question then is as to the effect of this. Insofar as the lease remains a contractual obligation, on the face of it the only effect a forfeiture would have is to terminate this contract and release the parties to it from their mutual obligations. The adverse possessor would be unaffected. This result would also follow logically from the court's basic position that the ousted lessee's only remaining legal relations are in contract with the lessor. Griffin J. is, however, equivocal on the point, saying on the one hand that "it is not necessary for the purpose of this case to decide what right, if any, has been gained by the squatter by reason of the title of the lessee having been extinguished", but going on to say:

> "Nevertheless, it seems to me that, though there is no transfer or statutory conveyance to the squatter, what the plaintiff (as squatter) has gained is the right to possession of the premises in dispute as against the defendants (as fee-simple owners) for the unexpired portion of the term of the lease, subject to the risk and possibility of a forfeiture."[155]

But a forfeiture brought about by whom? Earlier in his judgment, speaking of the decision of the House of Lords in *Fairweather*, the same judge says:

> "[T]he effect of this decision is that by collusion between the lessee and the freeholder, the successors in title of a squatter on leasehold land can be ejected however long the lessee has been out of possession—be it 12 years, 120 years or 900 years. It seems to me that such a result would entirely defeat the object of the Statute of Limitations."[156]

This reasoning would seem to be as apt to the case of forfeiture as it is to assignment or surrender, but, again, later in his judgment the judge says:

> "In the present case, at the time when the purported assignment by Irish Life was made [i.e. in 1970], there had been no forfeiture and the plaintiff was accordingly entitled to remain in possession against the lessor."[157]

---

[154] [1975] I.R. 104 per Walsh J. at 119; Griffin J. at 130.
[155] [1975] I.R. 104 at 129.
[156] [1975] I.R. 104 at 129.
[157] [1975] I.R. 104 at 130.

The plaintiff had completed 12 years' adverse possession in 1967 and so this could be taken to suggest that the ousted lessee, if they had failed to perform the covenants between 1967 and 1970, could have brought about a forfeiture, but the meaning is far from clear.

25–81 Walsh J., the other judge in the majority, seems to be more firmly of the view that the erstwhile squatter can prevent a forfeiture by performing the covenants personally:

"[T]he squatter may be indirectly forced to carry out the covenants to preserve his possession from ejectment by forfeiture for non-observance of the covenants."[158]

Later he expresses the same view:

"But because of the threat of re-entry hanging over the squatter in the event of failure to pay rent or to observe the covenants, the lessor is effectively in no worse position than he would have been with the original lessee. In fact he may find himself in a stronger position in so far as he can hold the original lessee to the terms while at the same time he is in a position to enforce indirectly all the covenants against the squatter by the threat of re-entry, if the lease provides for re-entry in the event of failure to observe the covenants."[159]

25–82 Certainly, it must be correct that if the lessor has accepted the adverse possessor as a tenant, the lessor cannot at the same time seek to evict the adverse possessor on the ground that the ousted tenant has failed to perform the covenants. Two problems that present difficulty occur where an adverse possessor, S, has never performed the covenants in the lease, as where a strip was occupied and the adverse possessor only asserts a right after the expiry of the limitation period. Thus, neither S nor the lessor, L, has acted on the basis that S is a tenant of L. The problems are:

1. Can S force the lessor to accept performance from S?
2. What happens if S remains in possession and does not perform the covenants?
3. Can L force S to act as tenant and, if not, can S remain in possession free of rent for the rest of the term of the lease?

Neither judgment gives a definitive answer to these problems.

25–83 In 1., the problem is made more difficult by the equivocal nature of leases and tenancies generally: on the one hand they are property interests which

---

[158] [1975] I.R. 104 at 120.
[159] [1975] I.R. 104 at 120.

can be conveyed or transferred but on the other hand they may involve at the least the lessee paying rent to the lessor who therefore has a legitimate interest in determining whether a proposed tenant is creditworthy, and may involve a more personal relationship. Hence many leases provided for any assignment or subletting to be subject to the lessor's consent. It also underlines the unsatisfactory feature of the reasoning in *Perry* in following the English cases in holding that there is no "parliamentary conveyance" in the case of unregistered land, which must mean that the squatter is not automatically entitled to the benefit, or subject to the burden, of the leasehold interest. Registered land apart, it is difficult to see on what basis he or she could insist that the lessor accept him or her as the new tenant if the lessor is unwilling to do so and in the absence of a doctrine of a statutory conveyance.

25–84 Problem 2. points out a contradiction in the judgments in the Supreme Court. Both Walsh and Griffin JJ. agree that the lease continues to exist in a negative sense, suspending the right to possession of L until the end of the lease. In this case it is difficult to see what L can do if S fails to pay the rent or to perform the other covenants in the lease. Can it be that there is a kind of legal limbo in which S can remain for the remainder of the term of the lease and there is nothing either L or T can do about it? If L sues to enforce the terms of the lease, may S not say "but I am not a tenant: I am a squatter, and you cannot evict me because you have no right to possession until the lease comes to an end!"? Suppose also that S starts to commit what in a tenant would be waste. It may be that the odd equivocation on forfeiture on the part of Griffin J., and to a lesser extent on the part of Walsh J., may be due to their anticipating this type of problem. Griffin J. suggests that if T does not continue to perform the obligations, a forfeiture may occur affecting S, but this is surely inconsistent with the logic of the judgment. Walsh J. suggests that L may have a choice of seeking performance from either T or S, implying that L can force S to comply with the lease or face forfeiture. Again, in the absence of a doctrine of parliamentary conveyance it is not immediately obvious why he can do so. The answer may be that if S remains without performing the covenants, L will sue for possession. S will then attempt to plead that there is a lease outstanding in a negative sense suspending L's right to possession. In such a case the court is likely to take the view that S cannot plead the lease to his own advantage unless he is also prepared to undertake the burdens of tenant. S cannot have it both ways: he cannot approbate and reprobate.[160]

25–85 It remains to be decided whether in Ireland the acceptance of rent by the lessor from the adverse possessor is sufficient without more to estop the lessor denying that the adverse possessor is the new tenant. The English cases of *Tichborne v Weir*[161] and *Tickner v Buzzacott*[162] held that payment of a monthly

---

[160] *Corrigan v Irish Land Commission* [1977] I.R. 317; *O'Reilly v Gleeson* [1975] I.R. 258; *Re Deighton's Will Trusts* (1952) 86 I.L.T.R. 127.

[161] [1891–4] All E.R. 449.

[162] [1965] Ch. 426.

rent, for example, would only give rise to a monthly tenancy and Walker L.J. in *O'Connor v Foley*[163] refers to the point in an exposition of the effect of the *Tichborne* case, but without comment. Since, in unregistered land, there is no "parliamentary conveyance", the adverse possessor is not automatically liable on the covenants in the lease to the landlord. This was certainly the view of Fitzgibbon L.J. in *O'Connor v Foley*[164] who said:

> "It appears to me to decide only this, that the Statute of Limitations oper-
> ates by way of extinguishment, and not by way of assignment of the estate,
> which is barred; and that a person who becomes entitled to a leasehold inter-
> est by adverse possession for the prescribed period is not liable to be sued
> in covenant as assignee of the lease, unless he has estopped himself from
> denying that he is assignee."[165]

Nor is the lessor on expiry of the 12-year period automatically entitled to sue the adverse possessor for rent or on the other covenants.

The Special Position of Registered Land
25–86 Walsh J., in a dictum in *Perry v Woodfarm Homes Ltd*[166] which was not dissented from by the other judges, said that he considered registered land to be on a different footing from unregistered land, due to the provisions of the Registration of Title Act 1964. Section 49(2) of the 1964 Act provides that where any person claims to have acquired a title by possession to registered land, he or she may apply to the registrar to be registered as owner of the land and the registrar, if satisfied that the applicant has acquired the title, may cause the applicant to be registered as owner of the land with an absolute, good leasehold, possessory or qualified title. In discussing this subsection, Walsh J. stated:

> "This would appear to permit a squatter to have himself registered in the
> Land Registry as the owner of a leasehold, being registered land, where the
> squatter has dispossessed the registered owner of the leasehold."[167]

In fact, it can be argued that this is more than a mere dictum since the title to the land in *Perry v Woodfarm* was in fact registered.

25–87 In the years since *Perry v Woodfarm Homes Ltd*, the practice of the Land Registry, and now Property Registration Authority, was to allow a squat-ter who had adversely possessed a registered leasehold interest to apply to be

---

[163] [1906] 1 I.R. 20 at 33.
[164] [1906] 1 I.R. 20.
[165] [1906] 1 I.R. 20 at 26.
[166] [1975] I.R. 104.
[167] [1975] I.R. 104 at 121.

registered as owner of that interest in place of the registered owner.[168] As the jurisprudential basis for this practice was uncertain,[169] the Law Reform Commission, in its *Report on Title by Adverse Possession of Land*,[170] sought to clarify this area of law and made recommendations for statutory reform. This led to the passing of s.50 of the Registration of Deeds and Title Act 2006, which extended the definition of "leasehold interest" in s.3 of the Registration of Title Act 1964, to include the following:

> "[T]he right or interest of a person who has barred, under the Statute of Limitations 1957, the right of action of a person entitled to such leasehold interest."

25–88 This amendment has been interpreted by the Property Registration Authority as confirming the propriety of its former position,[171] and also as extending it to cases where the dispossessed tenant's leasehold interest was not registered,[172] but only in cases where there are 21 years left unexpired on the leasehold interest, which is an additional element of the definition of "leasehold interest" in s.3 of the 1964 Act. The section does not provide any means for the squatter to obtain a copy of the lease, and unless he or she can obtain a copy from other sources,[173] he or she will not know the nature of the covenants contained in the lease. The practice of the Property Registration Authority is not to allow a first registration if the squatter is unable to ascertain the terms of the lease,[174] which is the one area where the law falls short of effecting a de facto parliamentary conveyance.

Tenancy from Year to Year
25–89 Section 17(2) of the Statute of Limitations 1957 provides:

---

[168] Prior to the passing of the Land Registration Act 2002, English law reached the same result but relied on the mechanism of a statutory trust in favour of the squatter: see *Spectrum Investment Co v Holmes* [1981] 1 W.L.R. 221 and *Central London Commercial Estates Ltd v Kato Kagaku Ltd* [1998] 4 All E.R. 948.

[169] See U. Woods, "Adverse Possession of Unregistered Leasehold Land" (2001) 36 Ir. Jur. 304.

[170] Law Reform Commission, *Report on Title by Adverse Possession of Land* (LRC 67-2002).

[171] See the Property Registration Authority's practice direction on "Title by Adverse Possession to Registered Land" (1 December 2009), para.16.1. An interpretation of s.50 of the 2006 Act that would only have allowed a squatter on a leasehold interest to register a bare right to possess the property until the determination of the lease is also consistent with the language used: see U. Woods, "Registration of Deeds and Title Act 2006" in *Irish Current Law Statutes Annotated 2006* (Dublin: Thomson Round Hall, 2006), pp.12–38 to 12–41.

[172] See the Property Registration Authority's practice direction on "Title by Adverse Possession to Registered Land" (1 December 2009), para.16.4. The application for first registration is made pursuant to r.17 of the Land Registration Rules 2012 (S.I. No. 483 of 2012).

[173] Such as a memorial of the lease which may have been registered at the Registry of Deeds.

[174] See the paper delivered by John Murphy, Examiner of Titles, to the Cavan Bar Association on 26 March 2010 entitled "Compulsory First Registration and First Registration of Title based on Documentary Title and on Possession".

"(2) (a) A tenancy from year to year or other period, without a lease in writing, shall, for the purposes of this Act, be deemed to be determined at the expiration of the first year or other period.

(b) The right of action of a person entitled to land subject to a tenancy from year to year[175] or other period, without a lease in writing, shall be deemed to have accrued at the date of the determination of the tenancy,[176] unless any rent or other periodic payment has subsequently been received in respect of the tenancy, in which case the right of action shall be deemed to have accrued on the date of the last receipt of rent or other periodic payment."

25–90 The section is a modified version of s.8 of the Real Property Limitation Act 1833.[177] The phrase "without a lease in writing" clearly indicates that such leases are outside the section, presumably because where the parties have reduced a periodic tenancy to writing the written agreement will normally provide for the termination of the lease by notice. Nevertheless, if the parties omit to make such a provision the section is of no avail, with the result that non-payment of rent, even for a very lengthy period, does not cause the possession exercised by the tenant to become adverse to the landowner's rights.[178]

25–91 One question which might arise is whether a document which fails to create a periodic tenancy at common law, but is effectual in equity under the doctrine of *Walsh v Lonsdale*,[179] counts as a "lease in writing" for the purpose of the section. There is authority on the 1833 Act to the effect that it is not.[180] At common law such a tenant was a tenant from year to year or other period according to how the rent was paid, but in equity such a person holds under the terms contained in the document, and this rule now prevails.[181] Time will not therefore run against such a tenant until the term in the document has expired.[182]

---

[175] A tenancy "for a year and so on from year to year" cannot be determined by notice until the end of the second year: *Doe d Chadborn v Green* (1839) 9 Ad. & E. 658. It is a tenancy for one year followed by a periodic tenancy. It is probable that such a tenancy does not terminate under the section until the end of the second year.

[176] This phrase is equivocal, since a periodic tenancy is renewed automatically at the end of the first period. The *tenancy* therefore continues until terminated by notice. In view of the sections of other statutes cited below, on which the section is evidently based, it would seem that it means the end of the first year or other period.

[177] 3 & 4 Wm IV c 27.

[178] *Sauerzweig v Feeney* [1986] I.R. 224; *Foreman v Mowlds*, unreported, High Court, Barrington J., ex tempore, 28 January 1985.

[179] (1882) 21 Ch. D. 9.

[180] *Archbold v Scully* (1861) 9 H.L.C. 360; *Drummond v Sant* (1871) L.R. 6 Q.B. 763.

[181] *Walsh v Lonsdale* (1882) 21 Ch. D. 9.

[182] *Archbold v Scully* (1861) 9 H.L.C. 360; 11 E.R. 769; *Drummond v Sant* (1871) L.R. 6 Q.B. 763.

Tenancy at Will

25–92 Section 17 of the 1957 Act provides that a tenancy at will is deemed to end one year after it begins unless previously determined. This means that after a year the possession of the tenant becomes adverse to that of the landlord, and time begins to run against him.[183] O'Higgins C.J., dissenting, in *Bellew v Bellew*[184] applied the provision to the facts of the case and held that a deserted family who remained in possession of a family home and lands with the permission of the absent husband, did so as tenants at will whose possession was adverse after the expiration of one year from the granting of that permission. The majority of the court preferred to regard the facts as having given rise to a licence.

Licences

25–93 A licence to occupy land, although it may imply more than this today, is at least a permission to occupy and so a licensee cannot be in adverse possession while the licence is in force.

25–94 In one English case, a unilateral licence was held to have been created and to have had the effect of stopping time running against the owner of the paper title. In *BP Properties Ltd v Buckler*,[185] the Buckler family had been in possession of Great House Farm near Penarth from about 1916. For the purpose of the present case, it is only relevant to say that in 1955 Western Ground Rents Ltd had obtained judgment against Mr Buckler for non-payment of rent. No attempt was made to enforce it as Mrs Buckler had recently come out of hospital after a serious operation and objected strongly to leaving the premises. In 1962 possession proceedings were again brought and a new possession order was obtained in December 1962. Again, no attempt was made to enforce the order. Mr Buckler died and Mrs Buckler remained in possession of the land. In 1974 BP Pension Trust Ltd, which had acquired the freehold, began an action for possession. This was adjourned and in the same year BP Trust applied for leave to enforce the original order made in 1962. This was granted, subject to a stay of execution until October 1974. A press campaign was then launched on behalf of Mrs Buckler, claiming that she was an elderly widow being evicted from the house she and her family had occupied "for centuries". BP Properties, to whom the freehold had been transferred, offered to allow Mrs Buckler to remain in occupation of the house and garden rent-free for as long as she wished and "for the rest of your life if you so desire". Mrs Buckler did not reply. She was left in possession until her death in 1983. BP Properties then began an action for possession against Mrs Buckler's son. He claimed to be entitled under a possessory title derived from the possession of his parents and subsequently himself.

---

[183] An acknowledgment of title or payment of rent will cause time to run afresh.
[184] [1982] I.R. 447.
[185] (1988) 55 P. & C.R. 337.

25–95 Hollis J. in the English High Court held that Mr Buckler's possession was not adverse up to his death. Time did not begin to run against the land-owner until then. He also held that from 1974, Mrs Buckler possessed the land under a licence from BP and so there was no 12-year period of adverse possession.

25–96 The unanimous judgment of the Court of Appeal was delivered by Dillon L.J. He held that Mr and Mrs Buckler were in adverse possession from the end of the tenancy in 1955 and possibly from the last payment of rent two years earlier, although the point was not crucial to the judgment. The judge held that the possession order in 1962 had been obtained within 12 years of 1955 or 1953 and so was valid. He also held that as the enforcement order had been obtained within 12 years of the possession order, the enforcement order was also valid. Then there remained the significance of the offer contained in two letters from BP Pension and Properties on 31 October 1974 to Mrs Buckler. BP relied on s.10(2) of the Limitation Act 1939 which provided that when land ceased to be in adverse possession, no fresh right of action "shall accrue" until adverse possession was resumed. It argued that she then became a licensee for life and time had ceased to run in her favour. But she had made no response (on her solicitor's advice) to the offer of a licence and was relying on the fact that, as the possession warrant issued in 1962 had been withdrawn by BP, her 12 years of adverse possession were completed by December 1974. Dillon L.J. construed her silence as meaning "she was not asserting during the time from the receipt of the letters ... any claim to ownership of the farmhouse and garden, or any intention to exclude the owner of the paper title".

25–97 Dillon L.J. went on to say, with dubious reasoning, that the nature of Mrs Buckler's possession after receipt of the two letters could not be decided by looking at what was "locked up in her own mind". One must look at the position from the standpoint of the person with the paper title. What could that person have done? The rule that possession is not adverse if it can be referred to a lawful title applies even if the person in possession did not know of the lawful title. Dillon L.J. took the view that, even though Mrs Buckler did not "accept" the terms of the letters, BP Properties would have been bound to treat her, in the absence by her of any repudiation of the two letters, as in possession as a licensee on the terms of the letters. BP could not evict her (if it could have done so at all) without determining the licence. Even accepting that there was such a licence, however, one might point out that BP could easily have terminated it by another letter.

25–98 From the proposition that possession is not adverse if it is referable to a lawful title, and that a person may be in possession by virtue of a lawful title even if he or she is unaware of it, the judge leaps to the conclusion, which in no way follows from these propositions, that a person may be in possession by virtue of a licence when he or she had merely been offered a licence but had not accepted the offer. The judge has invented the concept of a "unilateral licence", for which there was no previous authority. This "unilateral licence" had the effect, he found, of stopping time running against the licensor. In contract law silence does not constitute consent and an offer by one side which elicits no response from the other party does not constitute a contract. Yet the judge believed it could constitute a licence. In his favour it can be pointed out that not all licences are contracts, that a bare licence is, in the words of Vaughan C.J. in *Thomas v Sorrell*[186] in 1674, merely permission to do something which otherwise is a trespass. Nevertheless, the company did not purport to grant the widow permission, but to offer her a licence and so phrased it in terms of a proposal. Furthermore, the judgment is tainted with the unjustifiable assumption that it was acceptable to put words into the widow's mouth. It is open to question whether a similar assumption would have been made about a person not tarnished by the illegality of trespass. Perhaps the underlying consideration was that the present action was not concerned with the widow's continued occupation, but that of the son, and the same sympathetic factors did not apply in his case, but in reaching the desired result the judge undermines the existing understanding of the law of adverse possession.

25–99 Attempts by dispossessed landowners to extend the principle of law contained in *BP Properties Ltd v Buckler*[187] to cases where they argue that an implied licence should be inferred, have proven largely unsuccessful.[188] The 1957 Act does not contain specific sections which deem licences to terminate after a specific period, as in the case of a tenancy at will. Nevertheless, once the licence is revoked[189] or terminates because it was only to last until a particular event occurred or purpose has been fulfilled,[190] the licensee's possession becomes adverse to that of the licensor. Despite the above criticisms of *BP Properties Ltd v Buckler*,[191] it has been referred to with approval in a number of English judgments and it would be open to the Irish High Court to follow it in this jurisdiction.[192]

---

[186] (1674) Vaugh. 330 at 351.

[187] [1987] 2 E.G.L.R. 168.

[188] *Pavledes v Ryesbridge Properties Ltd* (1989) 58 P. & C.R. 459; *Colin Dawson Windows Ltd v Howard* [2005] EWCA Civ 9; *Batsford Estates (1983) Co Ltd v Taylor* [2005] EWCA Civ 489; *J Alston & Sons v BOCM Pauls Ltd* [2008] EWHC 3310 (Ch).

[189] *Cullen v Cullen* [1962] I.R. 268.

[190] *Bellew v Bellew* [1982] I.R. 447.

[191] [1987] 2 E.G.L.R. 168.

[192] See *Agnew v Barry* [2009] IESC 45 per Geoghegan J. (obiter) at 27–28.

CHAPTER 26

Succession

Let's talk of graves ... Let's choose executors and talk of wills.

— Shakespeare, *Richard II*, Act 3, scene 2

TESTAMENTARY SUCCESSION

26–01 The law relating to wills is governed by the Succession Act 1965 (the "1965 Act"), as amended.

A Will Takes Effect on Death

26–02 A will has no effect until the testator's death. It is usually said to be "ambulatory", or subject to change, until death. In the meantime, it merely declares the testator's intention.[1] The testator retains the power to revoke it and substitute other provisions, notwithstanding a declaration in the will to the contrary.[2]

Will Speaks from Death

26–03 Section 89 of the 1965 Act provides as follows:

"Every will shall, with reference to all estate comprised in the will and every devise or bequest contained in it, be construed to speak and take effect as if it had been executed immediately before the death of the testator, unless a contrary intention appears from the will."

Although a will "speaks from death", in that it is construed according to its meaning at the time of the testator's death, there are some exceptions. The "armchair principle", discussed below, is one. Another instance is s.60(3) (a) which provides that a reference to the child or children of a person who has adopted shall be read as including the adopted person.[3]

---

[1] *Re Westminster's Deed of Appointment* [1959] Ch. 265 at 271.

[2] *Vynior's Case* (1610) 8 Co. Rep. 81b.

[3] But see *Re Stamp, deceased* [1993] I.L.R.M. 383.

Making a Will
Capacity
26–04 Section 77(1) of the 1965 Act requires that, to be valid, a will must be made by a person who has attained the age of 18 or is or has been married. He or she must also be "of sound disposing mind".[4] This means that the testator must understand that he or she is making a will, know the nature and extent of his or her estate, and "be able to call to mind the persons who might be expected to benefit from his or her estate".[5] The court has an inherent jurisdiction, derived from the courts of equity, to refuse to grant probate of a will if the court is not satisfied that the will was the free act of the testator, such as where a testator was subject to "undue influence".[6] A will made by a person suffering from a mental illness may still be valid if made during a "lucid interval" and it is not invalidated by a subsequent relapse.[7] A testator must be given the opportunity of reading his or her will, or to have it read over by another person, so that he or she may know and approve of its contents, before or at the date of execution of the will.[8]

Formalities
26–05 Section 78 of the 1965 Act sets out the formal requirements of a will. These are essentially the same provisions as those first contained in the Wills Act 1837 which have been the subject of considerable case law. The presumption of due execution or compliance with formalities[9] operates here, but it does not cure all defects. It is discussed below.

History
26–06 Section 1 of the Statute of Wills 1634[10] required wills of real property to be in writing. The Statute of Frauds 1695[11] added the requirement that the will should be signed by the testator and witnessed in his or her presence by at least three witnesses. "Nuncupative", i.e. oral wills could be made of personal property, but the 1695 statute required them to be witnessed if the value of the property was over £30 and so it became the practice for wills of personal property to be in writing. The Industrial Revolution of the late 18th century led to an increased concern for certainty in law. Capitalists and industrialists

---

[4] *Banks v Goodfellow* (1870) L.R. 5 Q.B. 549 at 567; *In bonis Farrell* (1954) 88 I.L.T.R. 57.

[5] B. Spierin, *Succession Act 1965 and Related Legislation: A Commentary*, 5th edn (Dublin: Bloomsbury Professional, 2017), para.539. See *Re Flannery* [2009] IEHC 317 and *Scally v Rhatigan* [2010] IEHC 475; but see also *Laaser v Earls* [2016] IECA 63.

[6] See *Re Kavanagh; Healy v MacGillicudy* [1978] I.L.R.M. 175; *Lambert v Lyons* [2010] IEHC 29.

[7] J.C.W. Wylie, *Irish Land Law*, 5th edn (Haywards Heath: Bloomsbury Professional, 2013), para.16.04; A. Keating, *Keating on Probate*, 5th edn (Dublin: Round Hall, 2015), para.4–31.

[8] *Re the Estate of Courtney* [2016] IEHC 318; A. Keating, "Principles of Knowledge and Approval of Contents of Wills by Testators" (2017) 22(4) C.P.L.J. 66.

[9] *Omnia praesumuntur rite esse acta*: "all things are presumed to be correctly done". Co. Litt 6.

[10] Wylie, *Irish Land Law* (2013), para.16.05.

[11] Short Titles Act 1962. Following the English Statute of Frauds 1677.

needed certainty of the titles to the land they bought, reduction in the risks of their investment decisions and calculation of profit with some accuracy. Some economic uncertainties were unavoidable, but the law could be rendered more certain by legislation. The Wills Act 1837 set out to give greater certainty to wills of both real and personal property.

Writing
26–07 For a will to be valid it must be in writing.[12] It may be comprised of several documents.[13] An apparently *inter vivos* gift, if made conditional on the donor's death, may be granted probate as a will, if it complies with the formalities.[14] A "holograph" will, i.e. one written in the testator's own handwriting, is not exempt on that ground from other formalities, as is the case in some jurisdictions.[15]

Relaxation of the Formality Requirements
26–08 In the past, the formality requirements for wills were relaxed with regard to certain categories of person. Section 11 of the Wills Act 1837 allowed for informal wills in the case of soldiers[16] "in actual military service".[17] Actual military service extended to where orders of mobilisation had actually been issued and a person, knowing of them, had made a will in contemplation of actual military service.[18] There was a similar relaxation of the normal formalities for "mariners or seamen being at sea".[19] "At sea" was interpreted consistently with the phrase actual military service[20] so that a sailor on shore leave but under orders to rejoin his or her ship was deemed to be at sea.[21] Although the Wills Act 1837 (unsurprisingly) made no provision

---

[12] Succession Act 1965 s.78. Similar to s.9 of the Wills Act 1837, as amended by the Wills Act Amendment Act 1852.

[13] *Douglas-Menzies v Umphelby* [1908] A.C. 224 at 233; *In bonis Wafer* [1960] Ir. Jur. Rep. 19.

[14] *In the Goods of Morgan* (1866) L.R. 1 P.D. 214.

[15] In jurisdictions based upon or derived from Roman law, e.g. Scotland, a holograph will is recognised as valid without further formalities: *McGinn v Delbeke* (1927) 61 I.L.T.R. 117; *In the goods of Keenan* (1946) 80 I.L.T.R. 1. They are not excluded from the formalities of the 1965 Act, nor were they excluded from the 1837 statute.

[16] Anon, "Soldiers' Wills" (1944) 10 Ir. Jur. 8 at 14. This included female military personnel: *Re Rowson* [1944] 2 All E.R. 36 and an army nurse: *In bonis Stanley* [1916] P. 192.

[17] The phrase was contained in s.19 of the Statute of Frauds 1695. P. Critchley, "Privileged Wills and Testamentary Formalities: A Time to Die?" (1999) 58(1) Camb. L.J. 49.

[18] *In bonis Schroeder* [1949] I.R. 89 (Haugh J. applying *In bonis Ryan* [1945] I.R. 174); *Doherty v Mangan* [1943] I.R. 78.

[19] The phrase is contained in s.19 of the Statute of Frauds 1695. In *In the Goods of Hayes* (1839) 2 Curt. 338, it was held that it included a purser and an admiral. It included a female typist employed by the Cunard line on the *Lusitania*: *In the goods of Sarah Hale, deceased* [1915] I.R. 362.

[20] Wills (Soldiers and Sailors) Act 1918 s.2.

[21] *Re Yates* [1919] P. 93 (navy); *Re Rapley* [1983] 1 W.L.R. 1069 (merchant navy).

for informal wills by airmen, on the formation of the Royal Air Force in 1918 the privilege was extended to military airmen and airwomen.[22]

26–09 All of these provisions were repealed by the 1965 Act.[23] *Donatio mortis causa* may partly fill the gap, even more so if the decision in *Sen v Headley*,[24] which holds that the doctrine applies to land, is followed. *Donatio mortis causa* only applies if the donor is actually contemplating death. Merely being in military service would not be enough. *Donatio mortis causa* also requires (a) the relinquishment of dominion by the donor over the property, and (b) either the transfer of the thing itself or the indicia of title, although requirement (b) may be dispensed with if the donee is already in possession of the property.[25] Mere expression of intention, however, would not be sufficient.

Succession Act 1965 s.78

26–10 As well as being "in writing", a valid will must be executed in accordance with the following rules[26]:

1. Signed "at the foot or end thereof" by the testator, or by some person in his or her presence and at his or her direction.
2. The signature shall be made or acknowledged by the testator in the presence of each of two witnesses and each witness shall attest by his or her signature the testator's signature in the presence of the testator but no form of attestation shall be necessary nor shall it be necessary for the witnesses to sign in the presence of each other.
3. It is sufficient if the testator's signature, or of the person signing for him or her under r.1, "is so placed at or after, or following, or under, or beside, or opposite to the end of the will that it is apparent on the face of the will that the testator intended to give effect by the signature to the writing signed as his [or her] will."

Rules 4 and 5 concern the signature itself and are dealt with below.

Signature of Testator
The Signature

26–11 Rule 1 of s.78 requires that the will must be signed by the testator or by some other person in the testator's presence and by his or her direction. "Signed" has been given a wide interpretation and includes a mark,[27] as by an

---

[22] Wills (Soldiers and Sailors) Act 1918 s.5; *Doherty v Mangan* [1943] I.R. 78.
[23] Succession Act 1965 Sch.2.
[24] [1991] 2 All E.R. 636. The case was settled before the appeal to the House of Lords was heard.
[25] *Woodard v Woodard* [1991] Fam. Law 470.
[26] Succession Act 1965 s.78.
[27] *In bonis Kieran* [1933] I.R. 222; *Re O'Dea* [1932] L.J. Ir. 148; *In bonis Finn* (1936) 53 T.L.R. 153 (thumb mark). See also *In the Goods of Kieran* [1933] I.R. 222.

illiterate person, initials,[28] a name rubber stamped[29] onto the will, a former or assumed name[30] or the signature of someone other than the testator but who signed the will at the testator's direction, as r.1 allows.[31] The test is whether the testator intended the signature to execute the will. A seal is not enough.[32] A holograph will satisfy the requirement of signing if it contains the testator's name at the end, in an attestation clause or otherwise.[33]

"At the Foot or End Thereof"

26–12 The signature must be at the "foot or end" of the will.[34] The phrase comes from the Wills Act 1837. After 1837 the courts struck down a number of wills on the ground that this requirement had not been satisfied, and this led to the passing of the Wills Act Amendment Act 1852 which contained specific rules as to the positioning of the signature.[35] These rules are re-enacted in s.78, rr.4 and 5 of the 1965 Act, as follows:

"4. No such will shall be affected by the circumstances—

(a) that the signature does not follow or is not immediately after the foot or end of the will; or

(b) that a blank space intervenes between the concluding word of the will and the signature[36]; or

(c) that the signature is placed among the words of the testimonium[37] clause or of the clause of attestation, or follows or is after or under the clause of attestation, either with or without a blank space intervening, or follows or is after, or under, or beside[38] the names or one of the names of the attesting witnesses; or

(d) that the signature is on a side or page or other portion of the paper or papers containing the will on which no clause or paragraph or disposing part of the will is written above the signature; or

(e) that there appears to be sufficient space on or at the bottom of the preceding side or page or other portion of the same paper on which the will is written to contain the signature;

---

[28] *In bonis Emerson* (1882) 9 L.R. Ir. 443.

[29] *Jenkins v Gaisford* (1863) 3 Sw. & Tr. 93; *Re Bullock* [1968] N.I. 96.

[30] *In bonis Glover* (1847) 11 Jur. 1022; *In bonis Redding* (1850) 2 Rob. Ecc. 339.

[31] *In bonis Clark* (1839) 2 Curt. 329.

[32] *In bonis Emerson* (1882) 9 L.R. Ir. 443; *In bonis Lemon* (1896) 30 I.L.T.R. 127.

[33] *Re Rochford* [1943] Ir. Jur. Rep. 71.

[34] This requirement has been abrogated in England as to wills coming into effect after 1982: Administration of Justice Act 1982 s.17, substituting a new s.9 of the Wills Act 1837 as it applies in England.

[35] The rules are contained in s.1.

[36] *In bonis Rice* (1870) I.R. 5 Eq. 176 (the text of the will was on the first page, the second and third pages were blank, and the signatures of testator and witnesses were on the fourth page. It was held valid).

[37] OED: 2. "That concluding part of a document, usually commencing with the words 'In witness whereof', which states the manner of its execution."

[38] *Derinzy v Turner* (1851) 1 Ir. Ch. R. 341.

and the enumeration of the above circumstances shall not restrict the generality of rule 1.

5. A signature shall not be operative to give effect to any disposition or direction inserted after the signature is made."

26–13 The words at the end of r.4 make it clear that the general rule that the signature must be at the "foot or end" still applies, although with a wider definition than before, so that, for example, r.4(a) does not permit a signature to be at the beginning of the document. Rule 5 contains an ambiguity in that "after" could refer to time or place, but the other rules are clearly concerned with place and not time and "after" in r.4(a) clearly refers to place. Rule 3 gives further clarity by providing that "it is sufficient if the signature is so placed at or after, or following, or under, or beside, or opposite to the end of the will" that it is apparent on the face of the will that the testator intended to give effect by the signature to the writing signed as his or her will. The rules would not therefore be satisfied by a holograph will which began "The Will of John Brennan ...", John Brennan being the testator's name.[39]

Witnesses
Presence
26–14 Rule 2 above requires that the testator's signature must be "made or acknowledged by the testator in the presence of each of two witnesses and each witness shall attest by his [or her] signature the signature of the testator in the presence of the testator". This means, in other words:

1. the witnesses must both be present at the same time when they witness the making of the signature or the testator's acknowledgment of the signature; but
2. they need not be present when the testator signs the will, provided they are both present together when the testator acknowledges the signature;
3. they need not both be present at the same time when they sign the will as witnesses (r.2),[40] although each must do so in the testator's presence.

26–15 The testator and witnesses need not be in the same room. It is enough if a "line of sight" exists, e.g. an open door, so that the witnesses could have seen the testator sign.[41] "Presence" does not, however, require that the testator see the witnesses,[42] so a blind person can make a will.[43]

---

[39] See *Wood v Smith* [1992] 3 All E.R. 556. In England after 1982 the signature need not be at the "foot or end".
[40] This seems to have been the case under the Wills Act 1837: *Re Devlin* [1939] Ir. Jur. Rep. 85; *In bonis Flynn* [1957] Ir. Jur. Rep. 95.
[41] *Shires v Glascock* (1685) 2 Salk. 688 (hole in the wall); *Winchilsea v Wauchope* (1827) 3 Russ. 441 (if line exists, presumption of good attestation).
[42] *Tod v Earl Winchelsea* [1826] 2 C. & P. 488.
[43] *Re Piercy's Goods* (1845) 1 Robb. Eccl. 278.

26–16 Under r.2 it is not necessary to have a particular form of attestation clause, although it is desirable to have one.

Signature of Witness

26–17 The witness's signature may be initials,[44] a mark[45] or stamped.[46] It is not sufficient for a witness to acknowledge his or her signature: the witness must actually sign in the testator's presence.[47]

Attestation

26–18 The witnesses' signatures attest the testator's signature and not the will itself. Indeed, the witnesses need not know that the document is a will, or be aware of its contents.[48]

26–19 It is usual, although not necessary under r.2, for witnesses to be present at the same time when they sign the will, as well as when they witness the testator's signature, and attestation clauses normally state this. Rule 2 does not prescribe any particular form of attestation clause or require one to be used, but it is desirable, because, as the next section shows, if one is lacking the benefit of an attestation clause, the presumption of due execution may be lost.

Presumption of Due Execution

26–20 When an issue as to compliance with the statutory formalities arises, the courts have invoked the presumption *omnia praesumuntur rite esse acta*,[49] which is not confined to wills of proper execution.[50] The effect of the presumption is to shift the burden of proof onto those who assert that the formalities have not been complied with. However, it may not save the day in every case. *Clery v Barry*[51] attempted to confine the presumption, in cases on attestation by witnesses, to where the witnesses were dead or incapacitated or where their evidence was unreliable.[52] The case was applied in *Rolleston v Sinclair*[53] in which there was no attestation clause in the will and the evidence of both living witnesses was to the effect that they were not present at the same time when the testator signed the will. O'Connor M.R. said:

---

[44] *In bonis Strealey* [1891] P. 172.
[45] *In bonis Amiss* (1849) 2 Rob. Ecc. 116.
[46] *Re Bullock* [1968] N.I. 96.
[47] *Wyatt v Berry* [1893] P. 5. In England acknowledgment by a witness is now permitted: Administration of Justice Act 1982 s.17, substituting a new s.9 of the Wills Act 1837.
[48] *Re Devlin* [1939] Ir. Jur. Rep. 85.
[49] "All things are presumed to be correctly done": Co Litt 6.
[50] *Clarke v Early* [1980] I.R. 223.
[51] (1889) 21 L.R. Ir. 152.
[52] (1889) 21 L.R. Ir. 152 at 167.
[53] [1924] 2 I.R. 157.

"In my opinion no such presumption arises in this case, because of two circumstances: 1, the will contains no attestation clause; and 2, the witnesses to the will are living and were available. Counsel for the executors were not able to produce a single authority in aid of the presumption in such a case."[54]

26–21 The judge considered *Clery v Barry*[55] as an authority "for the proposition that it is only when witnesses (or other persons who, though not official witnesses, were present) are dead, or cannot give evidence through incapacity, or their evidence cannot be accepted on account of unreliability, that the doctrine of *omnia rite esse acta praesumuntur* can be applied."[56]

26–22 The benefit of an attestation clause was shown in *Kavanagh v Fegan.*[57] The will contained an attestation clause but a surviving witness was unsure whether she had signed before or after the testator. Hanna J. held that the presumption was not rebutted since the evidence was unreliable.[58]

26–23 The absence of an attestation clause is not necessarily fatal[59] but reliance will then have to be placed on the evidence. In *Clarke v Early*,[60] there was no attestation clause. The will contained a signature, apparently the testator's. There were signatures of witnesses below. A witness was found who said he knew the name of the other witness and that he was the testator's friend. The will was held invalid: the judge held there was a purported signature but there was no evidence the testator had signed the will.

Incorporation by Reference

26–24 The doctrine of incorporation by reference is a means in relation to wills whereby documents not attested in accordance with the formalities required of wills are nevertheless incorporated into the will by a reference to them in the will. The document itself must be sufficiently identified, by parol evidence if necessary. It must also have existed in complete form at the time of execution of the will[61]: the doctrine does not allow for the incorporation of future documents.[62]

Secret Trusts

26–25 The doctrine of secret trusts is closely related to the doctrine of incorporation by reference. As applied in Ireland, the doctrine of half-secret trusts

---

[54] [1924] 2 I.R. 157 at 162.
[55] (1889) 21 L.R. Ir. 152.
[56] [1924] 2 I.R. 157 at 163.
[57] [1932] I.R. 566.
[58] See *Re Spain* (1915) T.L.R. 435.
[59] *Scarff v Scarff* [1927] I.R. 13 (no attestation clause, will upheld).
[60] [1980] I.R. 223.
[61] *In bonis Mitchell* (1966) 100 I.L.T.R. 185.
[62] *Blackwell v Blackwell* [1929] A.C. 318 at 339.

may, by contrast, allow unattested documents created after the will is made to be incorporated into it.

Fully Secret

26–26 A fully-secret trust arises where A makes a gift of property in her will to B absolutely but tells B that he is to hold it on trust for C. In such a case equity will enforce the trust even though it does not appear on the face of the will. This is an exception to the formalities required of wills by statute. The courts have taken the view that equity will not allow a statute to be used for fraud. If B accepts the gift he cannot later plead the lack of statutory formalities in order to escape from the trust and claim the property for his own benefit.[63]

26–27 The objects of the trust may be communicated by the testator to the donee under the will at any time during the testator's lifetime, or by a sealed envelope containing a statement of the terms of the trust, to be opened on the testator's death.[64]

Half Secret

26–28 A half-secret trust arises where A makes a disposition by will to B and the will itself indicates that B is to take the property as trustee, but the objects of the trust are not disclosed in the will. The English courts in this case have required that the objects of the trust be communicated *at or before* the execution of the will[65] on the ground that to allow the objects to be communicated later would be to permit testators to reserve to themselves the power of making unattested dispositions by will.[66] The English position has also been defended on the ground that the restriction in the doctrine of incorporation by reference to documents in existence at the date of the will would be made meaningless where trusts were concerned because the restriction could be avoided by half-secret trusts. However, the first objection also applies to the doctrine of fully-secret trusts and so the distinction seems anomalous.

26–29 In Ireland there is a line of authority in favour of the view that the communication of the terms of a half-secret trust, as in the case of a fully-secret trust, may be made after the execution of the will in the testator's lifetime.[67] This position was affirmed by Barron J. in *In the Estate of Prendiville*.[68]

---

[63] *Cullen v Attorney General* (1866) L.R. 1 H.L. 190; *O'Brien v Condon* [1905] 1 I.R. 51; *Re Browne* [1944] I.R. 90.

[64] *Re Boyes* (1884) 26 Ch. D. 531; *Morrison v McFerran* [1901] 1 I.R. 360; *Re Keen* [1937] Ch. 236.

[65] *Johnson v Ball* (1851) 5 De G. & Sm. 85; *Re Keen* [1937] Ch. 236.

[66] *Blackwell v Blackwell* [1929] A.C. 318 at 339.

[67] *Moss v Cooper* (1861) 1 J. & H. 352; *Riordan v Bannon* (1875) I.R. 10 Eq. 469 at 477; *Re King's Estate* (1888) 21 L.R. Ir. 273; *Re Brown* [1944] I.R. 90.

[68] *In the Estate of Prendiville* [1995] 2 I.L.R.M. 578, citing *Re King's Estate* (1888) 21 L.R. Ir. 273 and *Re Brown* [1944] I.R. 90.

Lost Wills
Presumption of Intentional Destruction

26–30 What is the position where it is known that a testator made a will but it cannot be found when the testator dies? The courts have held that there is a presumption that it was destroyed intentionally.[69] The presumption may nevertheless be rebutted by evidence of the surrounding circumstances, such as proof of accidental destruction by fire, or the possibility that a disappointed relative had purloined it,[70] or that the testator's custody of his will was "anything but a close custody".[71] Baker J. stated *In the Estate of McDermott*[72] that it is well-established "that the burden of rebutting the presumption lies on he who sets up the will." As to the evidence which should be adduced to rebut the presumption, Baker J. stated that "the courts will look at the combination of circumstances from which the probabilities may be assessed and weighed. ... I consider that the evidence on which the court must form an opinion can be, and perhaps almost always will be, circumstantial evidence." The character of the testator and the character of possession, as well as the contents of the will itself, will all be relevant factors for consideration.[73]

Evidence of Contents

26–31 If the presumption of intentional destruction is rebutted, the contents of the lost will may be proved by secondary evidence, such as a copy of it, but there may be other forms of such evidence. For example, when the writer DH Lawrence died his will could not be found, but the court held that the presumption was rebutted by proof that the testator had asked someone to look for it shortly before he died. Probate was granted of it on proof that its contents were identical to that of another author.[74]

26–32 The contents of a lost will may also be proved by evidence of statements made as to its contents before or after the will was made, whether the maker of the statement (such as the testator) is available as a witness or not, as an exception to the hearsay rule. This is the effect of the extraordinary case of *Sugden v Lord St Leonards*.[75] Edward Sugden, later Lord St Leonards, had been Lord Chancellor of Ireland and later of England.[76] He was the most noted property lawyer of his time and a prolific author on the law of property, but when he died his will could not be found. He had certainly made one and

---

[69] *Welch v Philips* (1836) 1 Moo. P.C. 299; *Re Webb (deceased)* [1964] 2 All E.R. 91; A. Keating, "Rebutting the Presumption of Lost Wills" (2010) 28 I.L.T. 128.

[70] *In bonis Coster*, unreported, Supreme Court, 19 January 1978.

[71] *Sugden v Lord St Leonards* [1879] 1 P.D. 154 at 217.

[72] *In the Estate of McDermott* [2015] 3 I.R. 255.

[73] See A. Keating, "The Presumption of Revocation in Cases of Lost Wills" (2016) 21(2) C.P.L.J. 26.

[74] *The Times*, London, 4 November 1932.

[75] [1879] 1 P.D. 154.

[76] Lord Chancellor of Ireland 1834, 1841–46; Lord Chancellor Great Britain and Baron St Leonards, 1852.

had altered it from time to time. In his old age he often asked his daughter to recite the contents of it to him. His daughter had memorised the will and was able at the trial to write it out from memory. The Court of Appeal held that the presumption of intentional destruction was rebutted. This was not the only hurdle the court had to get over to prove the will. The daughter's evidence was hearsay. The majority of the court announced a new exception to the hearsay rule, namely, statements as to the contents of a lost will.

26–33 The case is open to a number of criticisms. The court may have been influenced by the identity of the testator. The English Court of Appeal in *Sugden* had allowed in, under their new exception to hearsay, statements made by the testator *after* the execution of the will. In *Woodward v Goulstone*,[77] the House of Lords declined to express a view as to whether such statements were admissible to prove a lost will, thus throwing doubt on the decision in *Sugden*.[78] *Sugden* has nevertheless been approved in Ireland.[79] There seems little reason to make the distinction, once the concession is made to admit hearsay evidence, apart from the fact that a testator's statements made after, perhaps long after, the will was made, may not be accurate, but arguably that should affect the credibility of the evidence rather than its admissibility.

26–34 In *Re Curtin*,[80] the will was lost or mislaid, but a photocopy of it existed, and there was evidence available to confirm due execution of the will and the accuracy of the photocopy. However, on the facts, Baker J. considered it likely that the testator had destroyed the will with the intention to revoke it:

"There is no declaration consistent with the contents of the will; there would be no absurdity or irrationality in the deceased dying intestate, and the persons that she would wish to benefit would be identical or more or less identical with those persons who would succeed on intestacy."[81]

26–35 Baker J. held that the testator "regarded the making of a will as a matter of some importance and this is consistent with her personality and character." Furthermore, the testator was found to be "a meticulous person" who had kept a copy of the will in her bedroom for some years. On the facts, therefore, the presumption of revocation was not rebutted.

Alterations
26–36 Section 86 of the 1965 Act provides as follows:

---

[77] (1886) 11 App. Cas. 469.
[78] In England, s.9 of the Civil Evidence Act 1968 gave statutory force to certain specified exceptions to the hearsay rule at common law. The exception in *Sugden* is not mentioned.
[79] *In bonis Ball* (1890) 25 L.R. Ir. 556 per Warren J.; *In bonis Gilliland* [1940] N.I. 125.
[80] [2015] IEHC 623.
[81] [2015] IEHC 623 at para.52.

"An obliteration, interlineation, or other alteration made in a will after execution shall not be valid or have any effect, unless such alteration is executed as is required for the execution of the will; but the will, with such alteration as part thereof, shall be deemed to be duly executed if the signature of the testator and the signature of each witness is made in the margin or on some other part of the will opposite or near to such alteration, or at the foot or end of or opposite to a memorandum referring to such alteration, and written at the end of some other part of the will."[82]

26–37 This differs from s.21 of the Wills Act 1837 which contained the words "no obliteration ... shall be valid ... *except so far as the words of the will before such alteration shall not be apparent* ... unless such alteration shall be executed in a like manner ... [as a will]". Courts in England and Ireland had interpreted these words to mean that an alteration was ineffective if the original words were still "apparent" in that they could still be read with the naked eye, assisted by any natural means such as holding the will up to the light or a magnifying glass, but not if only by producing another document such as an infra-red photograph revealing the hidden words.[83] If the alteration was ineffective, then probate would be granted with the original words. If the original words were not apparent, then the alteration was valid if executed as a will.

26–38 It seems clear that s.86, by omitting the words in italics, was intended to alter the law. If so, then alterations made after the will is executed are now effective in any case if attested in the same way as the will itself. This interpretation was adopted by Lardner J. in *Re Myles, deceased*[84] in declining to grant probate of a holograph will which had been signed by the testator and witnessed but without a proper attestation clause. There were a number of deletions initialled by the testator but neither signed nor witnessed. It was also unclear whether the alterations had been made before or after the execution of the will and the judge held that the presumption that they had been made after execution, and so would be invalid on that ground also, had not been rebutted.

Revocation
26–39 A testator may revoke a will in a number of ways.

Will or Codicil
26–40 A will may be revoked by a later will.[85] A mere declaration in the later will that "this is my last will" is not necessarily enough.[86] It is usual to insert a clause at the beginning in which the testator states: "I hereby revoke all former wills ...". The court may, however, hold that a will has been revoked by

---

[82] Wills Act 1837 s.21.
[83] *Re Itter* [1950] 1 All E.R. 68.
[84] [1993] I.L.R.M. 34 at 36.
[85] Succession Act 1965 s.85(2).
[86] *In bonis Martin* [1968] I.R. 1.

implication, as where a later will is inconsistent with an earlier one.[87] A later will does not, therefore, automatically revoke earlier ones, and so the testator's "will" may consist of more than one document.[88]

Destruction

26–41 Section 85(2) of the 1965 Act provides that a will may be revoked by "burning, tearing, or destruction of it by the testator, or by some person in his presence and by his direction, with the intention of revoking it".[89] There must therefore be both a physical act of destruction and a mental intention to destroy the will.

26–42 It would seem that "destruction" in s.85(2) is *ejusdem generis* with burning and tearing and so it must be physical destruction, not merely symbolic. In *Cheese v Lovejoy*,[90] the testator drew a line with a pen through the will, wrote "revoked" on the back and threw it into a waste paper basket. The housekeeper, who was present while this was done, later retrieved the will and produced it on the testator's death. The will was admitted to probate. It has been suggested that the word "cancelling" should be added to the list in s.85(2) to allow for symbolic destruction, a course of action which was recommended by the Real Property Commissioners in their report preceding the Wills Act 1837 but was not implemented.

Marriage

26–43 Section 85(1) of the 1965 Act, as amended by the Civil Partnership and Certain Rights and Obligations of Cohabitants Act 2010 ("CPA 2010"), provides that a will is revoked by the subsequent marriage or entry into a civil partnership of the testator, except a will made in contemplation of that marriage or civil partnership "whether so expressed in the will or not".[91] The latter phrase is not found in s.18 of the Wills Act 1837, which s.85(1) replaces. This appears to abolish the need for the will to be made *expressly* in contemplation of marriage to avoid being revoked by the subsequent marriage.

26–44 Section 85(1A) of the 1965 Act was inserted by the Marriage Act 2015. It states that where the parties to a subsisting civil partnership with each other marry each other, "a will made in contemplation of entry into the civil partnership or during the civil partnership by a testator who is a party to the marriage

---

[87] *In bonis Martin* [1968] I.R. 1; *In bonis Jennings* [1930] I.R. 196; *Pakenham v Duggan* (1951) 85 I.L.T.R. 21; *O'Leary v Douglas* (1879) L.R. Ir. 323 (two identical wills; held: later one revoked earlier one).

[88] *In bonis McCarthy* [1965] Ir. Jur. Rep. 56.

[89] Wills Act 1837 s.20, which contains the words "or otherwise destroying" in place of "destruction" in Succession Act 1965 s.85(2).

[90] [1877] 2 P.D. 251, on Wills Act 1837 s.20.

[91] Previously Wills Act 1837 s.18.

shall not be revoked by that marriage." A reference in the will to the testator's civil partner shall be construed as a reference to the testator's spouse.

Conditional

26–45 A revocation may be made subject to a condition precedent.[92] This doctrine may be applied not only to revocation by another will or codicil but even to revocation by destruction if secondary evidence of the destroyed will exists.[93]

26–46 The doctrine of "dependent relative revocation" is invoked where a testator revokes an earlier will in the mistaken belief that other provisions will then take effect.[94] The situations are as follows:

1. A testator revokes an earlier will by a later will in the mistaken belief that the later will is valid.[95] If the second will is invalid, the doctrine invalidates the revocation of the earlier will. This is evidently on the ground that otherwise the purported testator will die intestate. It may be noticed that if the purported revocation is contained in the invalid later will so that it is also invalid, then no special doctrine is actually required to reach this result, other than that which invalidated the later will.

2. A testator revokes a will, which has itself revoked an earlier will, in the mistaken belief that the earlier will thereby automatically revives. This is apparently a common mistake for testators to make. Thus, in *In bonis Hogan*,[96] the deceased, Mrs Hogan, made a will in 1977 and a later one in 1979 which revoked the 1977 will. On Mrs Hogan's death, only the will of 1977 could be found. Mrs Hogan's daughter, the applicant and executor of the 1979 will, deposed that she believed that Mrs Hogan had destroyed the 1979 will by burning it, although she had not seen this done. The applicant sought to have admitted to probate a copy of the 1979 will which had been kept by the testator's solicitor. The applicant contended that Mrs Hogan had only revoked the 1979 will by burning it in the belief that the 1977 will would automatically be revived. Gannon J. accepted this argument and admitted the copy of the 1979 will to probate. He held that the attempted revocation of the 1979 will by burning was ineffective since it was dependent on a condition which had not been fulfilled, namely the revival of the 1977 will.

---

[92] *Re Plunkett* [1964] I.R. 259; *In bonis Coster*, unreported, Supreme Court, 19 January 1978.

[93] *In re Hogan, deceased* [1980] I.L.R.M. 24; Brady, "A Case of Dependant Relative Revocation" (1980) 75 Gaz. L. Soc. Ir. 5.

[94] For a critique of the doctrine, see F. Newark, "Dependent Relative Revocation" (1955) 71 L.Q.R. 374.

[95] *Onions v Tyrer* (1716) 2 Vern. 741; *Re McClintock* [1943] I.R. 83; *Re McMullen* [1964] Ir. Jur. Rep. 33.

[96] *In re Hogan, deceased* [1980] I.L.R.M. 24.

3. A testator revokes a will in the mistaken belief that the rules of intestacy will distribute his or her property in accordance with the testator's wishes.

26–47 The justification for applying the doctrine has often been to give effect to an underlying intention of the testator not to die intestate.[97] Nevertheless the real intention of the testator is often more specific and is not implemented by the doctrine. The intention of Mrs Hogan in *In bonis Hogan* was, on the evidence which the court accepted, to reinstate the provisions of the 1977 will. The decision failed to give effect to this intention. One solution would be to change the law so that it conforms more closely to what testators believe it to be: there could be a presumption against revival, but rebuttable by evidence of intention to revive the earlier will.

Revival

26–48 It has been observed that "the whole area of revival of wills is fraught with difficulty."[98] A will which has been destroyed with the intention of revoking it cannot be revived.[99] If it has not been destroyed, a will can be revived by re-executing it or by executing a codicil showing an intention to revive the will.[100] The requirement to show intention to revive is important. It was stated in the English case of *In the Goods of Davis*[101] that there should be "some expression conveying to the mind of the court with reasonable certainty the existence of an intention to revive the will."[102]

26–49 The effect of the codicil coupled with the intention to revive is the same as if a new will had been made on the date of revival. The importance of this is that the revived provisions can apply to people or property not in existence at the date of the original will. It has already been seen that if Will No.1 is revoked by Will No.2, then the revocation of Will No.2 does not revive Will No.1.[103] This is contrary to what most people expect or assume to be the case and there is some logic behind their assumption. A double negative is a positive, and so a revocation of a revocation would be expected to cancel the revocation. The law does not, in any case, treat all cases of revocation as final, since it recognises revival by re-execution.

---

[97] *In bonis Hogan* [1980] I.L.R.M. 24.
[98] A. Keating, "The Revival of Wills by Codicil" (2016) 21(1) C.P.L.J. 2 at 6.
[99] *Re Hall* [1943] Ir. Jur. Rep. 25.
[100] Succession Act 1965 s.87; Wills Act 1837 s.22.
[101] [1952] P. 279
[102] More recently, see *Brennan v O'Donnell* [2015] 1 I.R. 296.
[103] *In bonis Hodgkinson* [1893] P. 339.

Republication

26–50 A codicil republishes any previous will which has not been revoked.[104] The effect of republication is the same as revival: it is as if a new will has been made at the date of republication.[105] A recent case in this area is *Brennan v O'Donnell*,[106] which involved two wills. One was executed in Ireland and the other was executed in the United States. The High Court outlined the principles governing the revival of wills, and considered the testator's knowledge and intention.[107]

Undue Influence

26–51 When it comes to wills there is no presumption of undue influence, whatever the relationship between the testator and the beneficiary.[108] The burden is on the person alleging undue influence to prove it.[109] It must be shown not only that a person had power to overbear the will of the testator, but that it was actually exercised and that the will was a result of the exercise of the power.[110]

Construction of Wills
The Intention of the Testator

26–52 The general principle of the construction of wills is that the courts attempt to carry out the testator's intention as expressed in the will.[111] The will is read as a whole, so that a specific intention in one part of the will overrides a general one.[112] The court's duty is to give effect to the testator's intention, however peculiar or eccentric.[113] The court will not rewrite a will,[114] but it may need to omit words which are shown not to express or to run contrary to the testator's intent.[115]

26–53 The testator is presumed to intend that words used are to be understood in their natural meaning unless there is something in the context or circumstances revealed by admissible evidence to the contrary.[116] However, this

---

[104] *Re Swiney* (1858) 6 Ir. Ch. R. 455.

[105] *Grealey v Sampson* [1917] 1 I.R. 286 at 296; *Mountcashell (Earl) v Smyth* [1895] 1 I.R. 346.

[106] [2015] IEHC 460.

[107] See Spierin, *Succession Act 1965* (2017), [630]–[634].

[108] *Healy v Lyons*, unreported, High Court, Costello J., 24 October 1978.

[109] *Re Breen, dec'd; Breen and Kennedy v Breen*, unreported, High Court, Barr J., 5 May 1995.

[110] *Re Breen, dec'd; Breen and Kennedy v Breen*, unreported, High Court, Barr J., 5 May 1995; *Kelly v Thewles* (1854) 2 Ir. Ch. R. 510.

[111] *Oliver v Menton* [1945] I.R. 6; *Re Moore* [1947] I.R. 205; *Re McCready* [1962] N.I. 43; *Williams and O'Donnell v Shuel and Barham*, unreported, High Court, Morris J., 6 May 1997.

[112] *Re Macandrew's Will Trusts* [1963] 3 W.L.R. 822 at 834; *Fitzpatrick v Collins* [1978] I.L.R.M. 244.

[113] *Re Macandrew's Will Trusts* [1963] 3 W.L.R. 822 at 834; *Fitzpatrick v Collins* [1978] I.L.R.M. 244.

[114] *Re Hogg* [1944] I.R. 244 at 258.

[115] *Re Hogg* [1944] I.R. 244 at 251.

[116] *Perrin v Morgan* [1943] A.C. 399 at 406.

does not always require the court to apply the literal meaning of words where that would lead to a result which was clearly not the intention of the testator. As Porter M.R. put it in *Re Patterson*[117]:

"It is the duty of a court of construction to ascertain, if it be possible, what the testator really meant from the language he has used. That does not mean that the exact words he has used are in all cases to be followed in their literal meaning, even if it would be plain that to do so would frustrate the real intention. If, having considered the will and the whole will, it is plain that to place a literal meaning upon one clause would defeat the clear intent, it may be necessary to 'do violence' (as an eminent judge once expressed it), to the language used."[118]

26–54 The judge also quoted a passage from Hawkins' *Construction of Wills*[119]:

"[T]he intention of the testator, which can be collected with reasonable certainty for the entire will, with the aid of extrinsic evidence of a kind properly admissible, must have effect given to it, beyond, and even against, the literal sense of the particular words and expressions. The intention, when legitimately proved, is competent not only to *fix* the sense of *ambiguous* words, but to *control* the sense even of *clear* words, and to *supply* the place of *express* words, in cases of difficulty or ambiguity."

26–55 Both these passages were quoted in the Supreme Court in the peculiar circumstances of *Curtin v O'Mahony*.[120] A testator had left a dwelling house to a beneficiary absolutely. The will then provided that, in the event of the testator selling the house, his entire estate, both real and personal, was to be divided into shares for a number of charitable and other bequests. The house in fact remained unsold at the testator's death. It was argued that the testator did not actually intend the condition as to the sale of the house to apply to the division of the entire estate and therefore to the charitable and other legacies. It was argued that his true intention must have been that the legacies should take effect in any case, and that the proceeds of the house were to be included in the division if the house were to be sold by the testator in his lifetime. The Supreme Court held that the literal meaning of the words would lead to an absurd result clearly not intended by the testator. He clearly did not intend the residue of his estate to fall into intestacy. Furthermore, the court held that it was not necessary to resort to extrinsic evidence to reach that conclusion. The court held that a phrase limiting the operation of the condition could be supplied by construction. O'Flaherty J. noted that the facts raised a direct conflict between two principles: that the court will not rewrite a will and, on the

---

[117] [1899] 1 I.R. 324.
[118] [1899] 1 I.R. 324 at 331, cited in *Curtin v O'Mahony* [1992] I.L.R.M. 7 at 12.
[119] F.V. Hawkins, *Construction of Wills* (Dublin and London: William Maxwell, 1863).
[120] [1992] I.L.R.M. 7.

other hand, that a will must be read so as to give effect to the testator's intention. The judge commented further on Porter M.R.'s remarks cited above, specifically as to where the testator's intention can only be carried out by *inserting* words in a will by construction:

> "The Master of the Rolls went on to warn however that great care must be taken in applying this doctrine. It must be clear not alone that words have been omitted but also what the substance of the omitted clause is because otherwise the court would be not construing but making a will."[121]

26–56 *Curtin v O'Mahony* must certainly be an extreme example of the doctrine of construction, but few would criticise the result.

26–57 In *Crawford v Lawless*,[122] the deceased left pecuniary legacies in his will to both his marital child and the defendant, describing each of them as his "daughter". He then left the residue of his estate upon a discretionary trust for beneficiaries defined as "… my children, their spouses and my grandchildren …". The defendant was his wife's daughter and was not his issue, but had been treated by him as a daughter during his life. Smyth J. held that there was sufficient evidence in the will itself to conclude that the testator intended the word "children" to include the defendant. He had referred to her earlier in the will as his "daughter"; "children" clearly referred to more than one child and the ordinary meaning of the word had to be modified to make harmonious sense of the will as a whole.

Other Policies

26–58 The general principle of seeking the intention of the testator may on occasion give way to rules of construction which impose various policies on wills. The rule in *Shelley's Case* is an example. However, there has long been a judicial tendency towards the testator's intent as primary and old rules have been modified in this direction, *Shelley's Case* in wills also being an example. In other cases, policies of a public nature were and may still be applied where the intention expressed in the will is unclear. The class-closing rules favour the early vesting of property in the interests of the donee and the operation of a free market where the testator has not been specific as to the definition of the class. In the case of extrinsic evidence, discussed below, the reluctance of the courts in the past, and possibly still today, to admit such evidence where it would contradict or vary the terms of the will is partially attributable to a policy of discouraging litigation. Nevertheless, when the courts face the issue directly today, the general trend is to reassert the intention of the testator as the controlling principle.

---

[121] [1992] I.L.R.M. 7 at 12–13.
[122] [2002] 4 I.R. 416.

Section 99 and Favor Testamenti
26–59 Section 99 of the 1965 Act provides as follows:

> "99.—If the purport of a devise or bequest admits of more than one inter-
> pretation, then, in case of doubt, the interpretation according to which the
> devise or bequest will be operative shall be preferred."

It has been argued that this introduced a new principle into the construction
of wills, similar to *favor testamenti* in civil law systems,[123] although it is also
arguable that the principle already existed in the common law.[124]

Extrinsic Evidence: Before the Succession Act 1965
26–60 Before 1 January 1967, the general rule was that extrinsic evidence
was inadmissible if its effect would be to contradict the terms of the will.
The policy reason, when it was articulated, was usually said to be that if extrinsic evidence were admissible where the will itself was clear, disappointed relatives would frequently attempt to challenge wills and try to show by extrinsic
evidence that the testator had intended to benefit them rather than the person to
whom the will referred. This could give rise to protracted, expensive and probably inconclusive litigation. There were, however, a number of real or apparent
exceptions to the principle and the law was in a far from satisfactory state.

The Armchair Principle
26–61 First, the courts were prepared to put themselves in the position of the
testator at the time he or she wrote the will, to sit "in the testator's armchair".[125]
They would do this for a number of purposes. Extrinsic evidence was admissible as to the state of the property itself and other material facts relating to it
at the date of the will.[126] Extrinsic evidence was always admissible to explain
a special meaning attached to the words by the testator him or herself. This
did not contradict the meaning of the words, but rather established what the
meaning was. It was a special application of the construction of documents.
The meaning of the words in the will is not necessarily the ordinary meaning.
Thus, in *Thorn v Dickens*,[127] the will, said to be the shortest on record, consisted only of the words "All to mother". Evidence was admitted to show that
the gift was intended for the testator's wife, since the testator always referred

---

[123] See J.C. Brady, "The '*Favor* Testamenti' in Irish Law" (1980) 15(1) Ir. Jur. (ns) 1.

[124] *Winter v Perratt* (1843) 9 Cl. & Fin. 606 at 687, cited in *In the Estate of Bayley* [1945] I.R.
224.

[125] *Boyes v Cook* (1880) 14 Ch. D. 53 at 56 per James L.J.: "you may place yourself, so to speak,
in [the testator's] armchair, and consider the circumstances by which he was surrounded, when
he made his will to assist you in arriving at his intention."

[126] *Pierce v McNeale* [1894] 1 I.R. 118, citing *Innes v Sayer* (1851) 3 Mac. & G. 606 at 614 per
Lord Truro.

[127] [1906] W.N. 54.

to her as "mother".[128] Evidence was admitted in another case[129] to show that a testator, who had no children of whom he was the biological father, intended to benefit his stepchildren when he used the phrase "my children". Evidence could also be admitted to show that the testator had a closer relationship with one party or relative than to another.

26–62 Although it is sometimes said that the literal interpretation must first be applied before resorting to the "armchair" principle, this is not always followed in practice, as *Thorn v Dickens* demonstrates.

26–63 Evidence of the religious views of a testator could be admitted to explain a statement in a will which might bear a special meaning because of those views. In *Bunbury v Doran*,[130] a testator left the freehold of his house to beneficiaries "until I am able to live there and enjoy it myself". Extrinsic evidence showed that the testator held religious views, apparently peculiar to himself, to the effect that he would return to live on earth after his death for a period which he described as "the millennium", and had said that he would live in his house during that period. The court indicated that evidence of more orthodox beliefs, such as Judaism or Islam, would be admissible for this purpose,[131] although it did not find it necessary to admit the extrinsic evidence to resolve the case. The event specified was rejected as impossible and the gift declared absolute, even though it appeared to be a determinable interest. Today, the State is prohibited by Art.44.2.3° of the Constitution from imposing any disabilities or making any discrimination on the ground of religious belief, and a court could be bound to uphold the gift as a determinable interest.

26–64 Evidence was also admissible of the surrounding circumstances, habits and position of the testator's family. Thus, in *In the Goods of Twohill*,[132] the testator appointed as executor "my brother-in-law Edmund O'Kelly". He had no such brother-in-law. He did have a brother-in-law called Edward O'Kelly. Evidence was admitted showing that Edward was the only person to whom the name and description in the will could be applied.

True Equivocation (Latent Ambiguity)
26–65 Where the description in a will applied, and applied accurately, to more than one person or thing, there was said to be "true equivocation" or latent ambiguity. The ambiguity was latent because it only appeared when extrinsic facts were taken into account.

---

[128] It was a custom in some parts of England, and indeed in other parts of the world, for husbands to refer to their wives in this way after they had borne children.
[129] *Re Jeans* (1895) 72 L.T. 834.
[130] (1875) I.R. 9 C.L. 284.
[131] (1874) I.R .8 C.L. 516 at 523.
[132] (1879) 3 L.R. Ir. 21. See also *Charter v Charter* (1874) L.R. 7 H.L. 315.

26–66 In a case of latent ambiguity, it was said that the courts should first attempt to resolve the ambiguity by construction, using the armchair principle if required. In *Healy v Healy*,[133] the testator gave a farm to "my nephew Joseph Healy", then a legacy to "Joseph Healy, the son of my brother Joseph Healy", and the residue to "the said Joseph Healy". There were two nephews called Joseph Healy, one the son of the testator's deceased brother James, and the other the son of the testator's living brother Joseph. It was held, on construction of the will itself, that Joseph the son of James took the farm and the residue. One reason given for that conclusion was that when the testator used the name Joseph Healy without further qualification, he was thinking of Joseph the son of James. The court also concluded that this displaced the normal inference that the word 'said' referred to the immediately antecedent name.

26–67 If construction failed, extrinsic evidence was admissible to determine which of the persons or things were intended to be referred to.[134] In *Re Jackson*,[135] the phrase was "my nephew, Arthur Murphy". The testator had three nephews called Arthur Murphy. Evidence of intention was admitted, showing which one the testator had intended to benefit. The admission of extrinsic evidence did not infringe the main principle in such a case, since whichever person the evidence pointed to, it would not contradict the will. Thus, if a devise referred to "my son John" and the testator left two sons called John, evidence was admissible to show that the testator believed one of them to be dead and intended to benefit the other.[136] Both sons were accurately referred to as "my son John".

Patent Ambiguity

26–68 The courts took the view that true equivocation literally arose only if the ambiguity appeared when extrinsic facts were taken into account, such as the fact that there were two people of the same name. Hence it was also referred to as *latent* ambiguity. In the case of latent ambiguity, extrinsic evidence was admissible.

26–69 If, however, the description applied with equal accuracy to two or more persons or things and these were mentioned elsewhere in the will by descriptions which made their separate identity clear, the ambiguity was said to be *patent*. Extrinsic evidence was inadmissible since it would add something to the will. It would connect the ambiguous description with one of the two specific descriptions and this connection was not provided for by the will itself. This fine distinction was not universally adhered to and the cases on patent ambiguity were not consistent. Thus, evidence of intention was admitted in the case of a will in which the devise was to "George Gord, the son of Gord" even

---

[133] (1875) 9 I.R. 418, Rolls.
[134] *Phelan v Slattery* (1887) 19 L.R. Ir. 177.
[135] [1933] 1 Ch. 237.
[136] *Lord Cheyney's Case* (1591) 5 Co. Rep. 68a at 68b.

though it appeared from other parts of the will itself that there were two people called George whose fathers had the surname Gord.[137]

Inaccuracy

26–70 Another distinct possibility was that the description in the will did not apply accurately to any one thing or person. The position was complicated by the fact that courts did not always recognise this as a distinct category.

One Candidate

26–71 In some cases, there might only be one "candidate" to whom the description might, however inaccurately, be applied. In such a case, the court might admit evidence to show that fact, supposedly on the armchair principle. *In the Goods of Twohill*[138] is probably an example of this.

26–72 Sometimes the problem could be resolved by rejecting an inaccurate part of the description, so that what remained then referred accurately only to one person. In *Dooley v Mahon*,[139] the gift was to "Monimia Mahon, the daughter of my brother Walter". The only daughter of Walter was called Monimia, but had married a man called Smith. She had also died before the date of the will, as the testator had been aware. The testator had another niece, called Monimia Mahon, who survived her. It was held that the gift went to the latter person. The testator had given a name and relationship which fitted only one person living at the time she made the will. The surplus description, naming the brother as "Walter", was rejected.

More than One Candidate

26–73 A description in the will may not describe accurately any person or thing at all. Since this could only be known by taking account of facts extrinsic to the will, the situation could probably be accurately described as a type of latent ambiguity. These were generally the most difficult cases to reconcile. On the one hand, it was often said that extrinsic evidence was inadmissible because its effect would necessarily be to contradict the will. The courts would not allow evidence to show that the testator had made a mistake and had really meant to refer to some thing or somebody whose description differed from that in the will. Some cases, however, while excluding evidence of instructions given by the testator to legal advisers, and their impressions of what the testator intended, admitted evidence of the armchair type to discover the true intention of the testator.

---

[137] *Doe d Gord v Needs* (1836) 2 M. & W. 129.
[138] (1879) 3 L.R. Ir. 21. See also *Charter v Charter* (1874) L.R. 7 H.L. 315.
[139] (1877) I.R. 11 Eq. 299.

26–74 In *Re Noble's Trusts*,[140] the testator, an 80-year-old woman, left property to "the five children of the late Post Captain Horatio Nelson Noble, my husband's son". The husband had two sons. One was called Horatio Nelson Noble, who, despite his first names, had been a major in the Indian Army and had died many years before. The other, Jeffrey Noble, had been a Post Captain in the Navy and had died shortly before the testator. Each son had five children living at the time the will was made. The testator had made the understandable mistake of thinking that the stepson called Horatio Nelson had joined the Navy. Sullivan M.R. refused to allow evidence of what had passed between the testator and her solicitor, and of the impressions of her solicitor and doctor as to her intentions. He did, however, admit evidence that she had been on terms of intimacy with Jeffrey and his children and had little to do with the children of Horatio. He also admitted, more dubiously, evidence that the draft will had referred to the rank as "Captain" and she had instructed the solicitor to insert "Post" before it. The judge took this as evidence that she had clearly in mind the naval officer. The court held that the children of Jeffrey took under the will.

26–75 If the description applied with greater accuracy to one person rather than to another, the courts were sometimes prepared to reject additional mistaken phrases if the remaining part of the description would accurately describe one person. Sometimes they did so after admitting extrinsic evidence, and sometimes without doing so.

26–76 In *Re Plunkett's Estate*,[141] the testator left property "to FF and his sister MF, my granddaughter, share and share alike, said MF now living in France with her uncle M". MF was not then living with uncle M and had never done so. Her sister, CF, was living with uncle M and had done so for some time. The court held it to be a case of latent ambiguity so that extrinsic evidence was admissible, but the evidence was inconclusive and the case was decided in favour of MF on the ground that the name should control the description. The basic principle is to find the testator's dominant intention. In *Re Plunkett* the name came first and this may have pointed to the name being uppermost in the testator's mind.

26–77 In *Re Callaghan*,[142] the gift was to "my god-daughter, JW". JW was not his god-daughter, but JW's sister, AW, was. Gavan Duffy J. held that the legacy should go to AW.[143] *Dooley v Mahon*[144] might also be taken as an example of this situation.

---

[140] (1870) I.R. 5 Eq. 140.
[141] (1861) 11 I.R. Ch. R. 361.
[142] [1937] I.R. 84.
[143] *Re Blayney* (1875) I.R. 9 Eq. 413; *Re Blake's Trusts* [1904] 1 I.R. 98.
[144] (1877) I.R. 11 Eq. 299.

26–78 A case which is difficult to explain satisfactorily is *Re Julian*.[145] A Protestant woman by her will bequeathed a sum of money to "The Seamen's Institute, Sir John Rogerson's Quay, Dublin". The bequest was claimed by two bodies: the Catholic Seamen's Institute, Sir John Rogerson's Quay, Dublin, and the Dublin Seamen's Institute, Eden Quay, Dublin, which was a Protestant body. The executors issued a summons to determine questions arising on the construction of the will and it was sought to prove the intention of the testator by the introduction of parol evidence of her religion, of her association with the Dublin Seamen's Institute, Eden Quay, and of a mistake, on the part of the solicitor who engrossed the will, in regard to the address of the institute as it appeared in the will. The testator in giving instructions to her solicitor had expressed her doubt as to the correct address of the institute and the solicitor had consulted a book of reference in which the only seamen's institute mentioned was the one at Sir John Rogerson's Quay, Dublin. The High Court held that the parol extrinsic evidence could not be admitted to show the intention of the testator because the institute which was to benefit had been clearly identified in the will. The intention of the testator was therefore frustrated and the benefit of her gift went to the Catholic Seamen's Institute, Sir John Rogerson's Quay, and not to the Seamen's Institute, Eden Quay, with which she had been associated. Kingsmill Moore J. said:

> "This is by no means the first—and, equally certainly, will not be the last—case in which a judge has been forced by the rules of law to give a decision on the construction of a will which he believed to be contrary to the intentions of the testator. The law reports are loud with the comments of judges who found themselves in similar plight; but I consider the law to be well established and conclusive ...".[146]

26–79 It is nevertheless questionable, whatever the state of the law, whether the facts should have impelled the judge to a conclusion which was clearly not what the testator intended. The phrase in the will was "The Seamen's Institute, Sir John Rogerson's Quay, Dublin", while the institute at that address was in fact called the "Catholic Seamen's Institute". This should have been enough to take it out of the "clarity" category to which the judge treated the facts as belonging, and to put it instead into the "inaccuracy: more than one candidate" category to which it properly belonged. Extrinsic evidence could then have been introduced.

26–80 In cases of inaccuracy with more than one candidate, the extrinsic evidence might not resolve the issue, in which case the legacy would simply fail and the property would go to the residuary legatee if there was one, or on intestacy if there was none.

---

[145] [1950] I.R. 57.
[146] [1950] I.R. 57 at 66.

Clarity: No Doctrine of Mistake

26–81 If the description in the will described accurately only one person or thing, extrinsic evidence was not admissible to show that a mistake had been made and that the testator had intended instead to refer to another person or thing. The intention which the court looked to was the intention *as expressed in the will*, i.e. as expressed in the words actually used, and the court would only go beyond the words if the intention was unclear. The reason for excluding such extrinsic evidence was probably a policy against "opening the flood-gates of litigation", as it was thought that many disappointed relatives would bring actions based upon such evidence which would often be inconclusive. Nevertheless, armchair evidence was sometimes admitted to indicate, not that the testator had made a mistake, but to show that the person apparently referred to was not the one to which the testator intended the description to apply. A dubious case is *Henderson v Henderson*,[147] in which the will referred to "my grandson, Robert William Henderson". The testator had such a grandson, but also a grandson William Robert Henderson. Kenny J. admitted armchair evidence and held that the legacy went to William Robert. This seems to have gone too far, because admitting armchair evidence could only have had the purpose of showing that the testator had made a mistake.

Equitable Presumptions

26–82 Extrinsic evidence was sometimes admissible to rebut equitable presumptions, as where two gifts were made in separate testamentary instruments to the same person. Equity presumed the second gift to be a repetition of the first and that only one gift was intended.[148]

Extrinsic Evidence: Succession Act 1965 s.90

26–83 Section 90 of the 1965 Act provides as follows:

> "90.—Extrinsic evidence shall be admissible to show the intention of the testator and to assist in the construction of, or to explain any contradiction in a will."

This was intended to effect some change in the law, but it has been a matter of controversy as to how extensive the change is.[149]

26–84 The effect of s.90 was extensively considered in *Rowe v Law*.[150] By her 1967 will, the testator devised and bequeathed all her property, which she called her trust fund, to her trustees on trust (1) to discharge out of it her debts, funeral and testamentary expenses and subject to that, (2) to set aside out of the capital of the trust fund a sum of £1,000 for the purchase and furnishing

---

[147] [1905] 1 I.R. 353.
[148] *Hurst v Beach* (1819) 5 Madd. 351 at 360.
[149] Wylie, *Irish Land Law* (2013), paras 16.39–16.40.
[150] [1978] I.R. 55 at 62.

of a cottage for the use of the second and third defendants during their joint lives and the life of the survivor, and subject to that "as to any balance then remaining" to invest it and pay the income to the second and third defendants during their joint lives and to the survivor during his or her life, and subject to a further legacy to stand possessed of "the trust fund then remaining" and to pay and transfer it to the plaintiffs in equal shares. The testator died in 1972 and probate was granted to the first defendant. The second and third defendants contended that, by her bequest of "any balance then remaining" in clause 2 of her will, the testator had intended to bequeath to them her entire estate less the payments of her debts, funeral and testamentary expenses, and the £1,000. Extrinsic evidence was available to support, and to controvert, that contention.

26–85 It was held by Kenny J. in the High Court that the words used by the testator in the will were not ambiguous and did not raise any difficulty of construction. The testator had expressed clearly an intention to give the second and third defendants life interests in the balance of the £1,000 only, as distinct from the balance of the entire estate. The will being clear, the issue then was as to whether s.90 allowed extrinsic evidence to be admitted to prove a contrary intention expressed elsewhere. Kenny J. held that s.90 did not authorise the introduction of extrinsic evidence to establish an alleged intention on the part of the testator which conflicted with the intention expressed in the will.

26–86 The Supreme Court upheld Kenny J. The majority agreed that s.90, whatever changes it might have made, did not allow in extrinsic evidence if the will was clear. O'Higgins C.J., dissenting, thought that s.90 had changed the law in a more radical way, to allow extrinsic evidence "where there is a contradiction in the will itself and ... where there is a contradiction between the actual intention of the testator and what was said in the will".[151]

26–87 However, Henchy J. laid stress on the word "and" in the phrase "and to assist" in s.90:

> "I read Section 90 as allowing extrinsic evidence to be received if it meets the double requirement of (a) showing the intention of a testator and (b) assisting in the construction of, or explaining any contradiction in, a will. The alternative reading would treat the section as making extrinsic evidence admissible if it meets the requirement of either (a) or (b). That, however, would produce unreasonable and illogical consequences which the legislature could not have intended. If the section made extrinsic evidence admissible merely because it satisfies requirement (a), then in any case the court could go outside the will and receive and act on extrinsic evidence as to the intention of the testator."[152]

---

[151] [1978] I.R. 55 at 67.
[152] [1978] I.R. 55 at 72.

26–88 In O'Higgins C.J.'s view, one of the aims of the legislation was to alter the law to prevent a recurrence of a case such as *Re Julian*.[153] The judge evidently assumed that the result in *Re Julian* was produced by the state of the law at the time, but this is open to doubt: the will was not unambiguous and the phrase did not accurately identify the beneficiary. In Henchy J.'s view, *Re Julian* was a case of inaccuracy:

"To sum up: Section 90 allows extrinsic evidence of the testator's intention to be used by a court of construction only when there is a legitimate dispute as to the meaning or effect of the language used in the will. In such a case (*e.g.*, *In re Julian* [[1950] I.R. 57]) it allows the extrinsic evidence to be drawn on so as to give the unclear or contradictory words in the will a meaning which accords with the testator's intention as thus ascertained."[154]

26–89 *Rowe v Law*[155] means that, whatever change s.90 was intended to bring about, it does not allow the admission of extrinsic evidence where the will is clear. The change therefore appears to be that extrinsic evidence is now admissible in cases of patent ambiguity or inaccuracy.

26–90 The Supreme Court in *Rowe* upheld the earlier decision in *Bennett v Bennett*.[156] The testator in that case had left farms to "my nephew Denis Bennett". The testator never had a nephew called Denis Bennett. He had a brother Denis Bennett, who renounced any claim under the will, and several nephews whose surname was Bennett but whose Christian names were not Denis. He had a nephew William Bennett whose claim was supported by the testator's brother and all the other nephews. The judge found that the extrinsic evidence showed that William had lived with his uncle and had worked the lands for some time before his uncle's death without any payment. The testator had also told William's father that the land was to go to William after his, the testator's, death. The whole family believed that William was to have the land. There was no explanation as to how the wrong name came to be inserted in the will. Parke J. held that the testator's intention was that the land should go to William and so ordered. The judge held that s.90 had altered the common law so that extrinsic evidence could now be introduced where the will "cannot be construed literally having regard to the facts existing at the testator's death". The judge evidently believed that the section would produce a different result on the facts before him than would have been the case at common law, but this does not appear to be so, as *In the Goods of Twohill*[157] and *Re Noble's Trusts*[158]

[153] [1950] I.R. 57.
[154] [1978] I.R. 55 at 73.
[155] [1978] I.R. 55 at 62.
[156] Unreported, High Court, Parke J., 24 January 1977.
[157] (1879) 3 L.R. Ir. 21. See also *Charter v Charter* (1874) L.R. 7 H.L. 315.
[158] (1870) I.R. 5 Eq. 140.

illustrate, for closeness of relationship was armchair evidence, but the view may have been influenced by *Re Julian*.[159]

26–91 In *Fitzpatrick v Collins*,[160] the High Court took the view that s.90 does not admit extrinsic evidence where a situation had not been foreseen by the testator at all. A testator left a will in which he provided that in the event of his wife "surviving me for the space of two months", he left all his property to her. He further provided that "in the event of my wife surviving me for the space of not more than two months", he left her only £500, with a further bequest for masses. He thus made no provision for what was to happen in the event of his wife dying before he did, so that if that occurred there would be an intestacy and the property would go to the next-of-kin. As it turned out, his wife died eight years before he did. McWilliam J., applying *Rowe v Law*, held that s.90 only applied where there was an ambiguity or contradiction in the terms of the will and there was no such ambiguity or contradiction here. The testator clearly had not directed his mind to the situation that might arise if his wife were to die before he did. Had he done so, he might well have made similar provisions as to those he had made in the event of her surviving him by not more than two months, but he had not done so, and it was not for the court to make a will for the testator to cover situations which he had overlooked.

26–92 In *Curtin v O'Mahony and Attorney General*,[161] Finlay C.J. and O'Flaherty J. in the Supreme Court indicated obiter[162] that a full court might reconsider the majority judgment in *Rowe v Law*.[163] Counsel for the appellants in the appeal had disclaimed any request to the court to reconsider *Rowe v Law*. The court in *Curtin* felt able to reach the result intended by the testator by supplying a phrase by construction.

26–93 Despite the obiter statement in *Curtin*, the Supreme Court in *Re Collins*[164] approved *Rowe v Law*. In *Collins* the testator left the contents of her house to the plaintiffs. There was no specific devise of the house itself, but there was a residuary devise in favour of a charity. The plaintiffs sought to admit extrinsic evidence that the testator intended to leave the house as well as the contents to the plaintiffs. The evidence was conflicting, one plaintiff and another witness saying that the testator had said she would leave the house to the plaintiffs, another witness saying merely that the testator said she would leave "most of her estate" to the plaintiffs, and the testator's solicitor gave evidence that she had only given specific instructions as to the contents and had not mentioned the house. Barron J. in the High Court dismissed the claim. Despite the fact that he preferred the evidence of the plaintiffs, he held the will

---

[159] [1950] I.R. 57.
[160] [1978] I.L.R.M. 244.
[161] [1992] I.L.R.M. 7.
[162] No extrinsic evidence was proffered in the case as to the testator's intention.
[163] [1978] I.R. 55.
[164] *Re Collins; O'Connell v Bank of Ireland* [1998] 2 I.L.R.M. 465.

was clear and unambiguous and there was therefore no basis for the admission of the evidence. The Supreme Court dismissed the appeal and dismissed the submission of the plaintiffs that *Rowe v Law* was wrongly decided. Keane J. found that *Curtin* was distinguishable in that a partial intestacy would not be caused in the present case by an application of the literal meaning of the will. Keane J. concluded:

> "S. 90 of the 1965 Act was, at least, intended to alter the law by enabling extrinsic evidence to be adduced as to the intention of the testator where that would assist in the construction of, or explain contradictions in, the will. The submission on behalf of the plaintiff, however, is that it was intended to go radically further and enable such evidence to be adduced, not merely with the view to resolving ambiguities or uncertainty in the language used, but to supplement, and even to contradict, what the testator had actually said, however clear and unambiguously, in the will itself."[165]

26–94 The court therefore endorsed the view of Henchy J. in the majority in *Rowe*, that there must either be a contradiction in the will, or at least something which creates the need for "assistance", before s.90 comes into play. Keane J. went on to consider *Re Julian*[166] and concluded that it might have been differently decided after s.90, even taking into account the ratios of *Rowe v Law* and the present case on the interpretation of that section. As was pointed out in the first edition of this work, the will did not describe accurately and unambiguously the institution referred to.

26–95 The interpretation of s.90 which confines extrinsic evidence to a case of genuine ambiguity on the face of a will was repeated in Smyth J.'s decision in *Crawford v Lawless*.[167] The interpretation at issue was the word "children", the designated beneficiaries of a discretionary trust set up to dispose of the residue of the testator's estate. The testator had a marital daughter and two non-marital sons. The defendant was the daughter of the testator's wife and another man. She had been conceived during a period of separation between her mother and the testator. Following a reconciliation, the defendant lived with her mother and the testator and her half-sister, who was the testator's marital daughter. The defendant and the marital daughter were brought up as sisters, and the testator acted towards the defendant as though she were his daughter. Later, the defendant and his wife separated for a second time and a clause in their separation agreement stated that the testator had no responsibility towards the defendant. Despite this, following another reconciliation, the defendant moved back into the testator's home and was again treated by him as his daughter. In his will the testator bequeathed a specific cash legacy to the

---

[165] [1998] 2 I.L.R.M. 465 at 476.
[166] [1950] I.R. 57.
[167] [2002] 4 I.R. 416.

defendant, describing her as "my daughter". A similar cash legacy was left to the testator's marital daughter.

26–96 The plaintiff was the solicitor who had drafted the will and also an executor and trustee. She gave evidence that the testator's stated intention in his discretionary trust had been to benefit the marital daughter only, he believing that the defendant was being otherwise adequately provided for. The plaintiff had been unaware of the existence of the non-marital children. The use of the plural "children" was explained on the basis that the form of discretionary trust had been adapted from a precedent model and was designed to accommodate the possibility of the testator's begetting another child later.[168] Smyth J. found this explanation unconvincing, having regard to the then ages of the testator and his wife,[169] and the fact that, in the event of a subsequent divorce and marriage to a younger woman, the second marriage would revoke the testator's will.[170] The judge, following the decisions in *Rowe v Law*[171] and *Re Collins, deceased; O'Connell v Bank of Ireland*,[172] held that this was not a case for admittance of extrinsic evidence, but the application of principles of construction.

26–97 According to Smyth J., "[t]he primary duty of the court in the construction of the will is to consider the words used and to ascertain from them the testator's intentions."[173] In this consideration, it is "the nomenclature used by the testator, taking his will as the dictionary for which you are to find the meaning of the terms he has used …". On this basis, Smyth J. professed himself "at a loss to understand the meaning of language if you are not to impute to that same person who, when he speaks of 'my children' as including the defendant, the person to whom he earlier referred as 'my daughter'."[174] The use of the plural clearly envisaged benefaction for more than one child; the testator had consistently treated the defendant as his daughter during life and described her elsewhere in his will as his daughter. Accordingly, the case could be resolved by applying principles of construction, without reference to extrinsic evidence.

---

[168] It is not uncommon for the courts, applying the principle of *de bene esse*, to hear what the extrinsic evidence, if available, would have been, and then make a decision on the basis of the applicable legal principles as to whether it should be considered or not.

[169] The testator then being in his late 60s, his wife in her late 50s.

[170] Succession Act 1965 s.85(1).

[171] [1978] I.R. 55. Smyth J. cited with approval that part of the judgment of Griffin J. (at 76) which had quoted Langdale M.R. in *Martin v Drinkwater* (1839–40) 2 Beav. 215 at 218: "you are at liberty to prove the circumstances of the testator, so far as to enable the court to place itself in the situation of the testator at the time of making his will, but you may not prove either his motives or his intentions".

[172] [1998] 2 I.R. 596.

[173] [2002] 4 I.R. 416 at 425.

[174] [2002] 4 I.R. 416 at 422.

26–98 A similar approach was applied, albeit perhaps less satisfyingly, by the same judge in *Butler v Butler*.[175] The plaintiff and the three defendants were all children of Thomas Butler who died in his early 50s in 1966. The interpretation at issue was a clause in the will of Thomas Butler's father, Timothy Butler, who had died in 1963, having made his last will and testament in 1956:

> "As to all the rest, residue and remainder of my property ... I give devise and bequeath the same to my son Martin Butler for and during the term of his natural life and after his death to such of the children of my said son Thomas Butler as he shall by Deed or Will appoint and in default of appointment to all of the children of my said son Thomas Butler as tenants in common in equal shares."

26–99 The issue was whether "he", before "shall by Deed or Will appoint", referred to Thomas Butler, the father of the children intended to be benefited by the exercise of the power, or their uncle, Martin Butler. Thomas Butler died in 1966 without having exercised the power. If he had been the intended donee of the power, all his children, the plaintiff and the three defendants, took equally following Martin's death. Smyth J. found as a fact that this had been the basis on which the family proceeded from the time the will was made, 1956, up to 2002 when Martin died. By will dated 1996, Martin had purported to exercise the power of appointment, on the basis that he had been its donee, in favour of his nephew, the plaintiff.

26–100 Several difficulties arose here. One was that, as the testator of the will whose residue clause was the subject of contention had died before the coming into effect of the 1965 Act, s.90 could be of no relevance. Another was that, as the will had been made half a century prior to the action, there was no extrinsic evidence available anyway. In its absence, Smyth J. considered "contextual factual information ... about the state of the families and the members in the families". This made it abundantly clear that the principal aim of Timothy had been to benefit his two sons and their dependants. At the time of Timothy's death, his son Martin, though married, had no children. Thomas had four children, the parties to the action. Various property dealings entered into by the parties between 1963 and 2002 had proceeded on the basis that all four children of Thomas would take as tenants in common following the death of Martin, in one instance the three defendants entering into a deed of consent in order to facilitate a mortgage transaction that involved the plaintiff and a site hewn from the lands in question. Indeed, Smyth J. found that the behaviour by the plaintiff had encouraged a belief on the part of the defendants that the four of them would inherit as tenants in common after Martin's death, on the basis of which the defendants had acted to their detriment, so that "[t]he ingredients of an estoppel are present". Even so, the existence of an estoppel, the judge acknowledged, could have no bearing on the construction of the will.

---

[175] [2006] IEHC 104.

"While certain events occurred after the coming into effect of the will of the deceased ... the factual context in which the will was 'made' is where most if not all assistance in the construction of the will is to be obtained. In short, the will must be looked at and construed as at the date of its making and at the date of death."[176]

26–101 In terms of pertinent facts at the date of the testator's death, in 1963, the most relevant one was that "the base level intention of the testator was that the objects of the power were to take equally". Hence it was more likely that their father rather than their uncle would be in a better position to determine in favour of which child or children the power of appointment should be exercised. There was no risk of intestacy arising which would have to be avoided through careful or creative construction.[177] If the donee were found to be Thomas, in default of appointment the plaintiff and the defendants would all take as tenants in common; if the donee were found to be Martin, the power had been validly exercised by his will in favour of the plaintiff.

26–102 Smyth J. decided to apply a set of interpretative guidelines which had been elaborated by Lowry L.C.J., in the Northern Ireland Court of Appeal, in *Heron v Ulster Bank*,[178] and approved by the Irish High Court in *Howell v Howell*[179] and *Bank of Ireland v Gaynor*.[180] The following are the guidelines posited by Lowry L.C.J.[181]:

"1. Read the immediately relevant portion of the will as a piece of English and decide if possible what it means.

2. Look at the other material parts of the will and see whether they tend to confirm the apparently plain meaning of the immediately relevant portion or whether they suggest the need for modification in order to make harmonious sense of the whole or, alternatively, whether an ambiguity in the immediately relevant portion can be resolved.

3. If ambiguity persists, have regard to the scheme of the will and consider what the testator was trying to do.

4. One may at this stage have resort to rules of construction, where applicable, and aids such as the presumption of early vesting and the presumption against intestacy and in favour of equality.

5. Then see whether any rule of law prevents a particular interpretation from being adopted.

6. Finally, and I suggest not until the disputed passage has been exhaustively studied, one may get help from the opinions of other courts and judges on similar words, rarely as binding precedents, since it has been

---

[176] [2006] IEHC 104 at para.12.

[177] Such as had arisen, for example, in *Curtin v O'Mahony* [1992] I.L.R.M. 7.

[178] [1974] N.I. 44 at 52.

[179] [1992] I.R. 290 (Carroll J.).

[180] Unreported, High Court, Macken J., 29 June 1999.

[181] Also cited with approval by Smyth J. in *Crawford v Lawless* [2002] 4 I.R. 416 at 420–421.

well said that 'no will has a twin brother' (per Werner J. in *In the matter of King* (1910) 200 NY 189, 192), but more often as example (sometimes of the highest authority) of how judicial minds nurtured in the same discipline have interpreted words in similar contexts."

26–103 Evidence had been offered that, considered purely as a piece of English, the critical location of the word "he" in the contested residuary clause was consistent with either Thomas or Martin being the donee of the power. This, however, was to take the clause in isolation from "the factual context under [sic] which the deceased made his will." Smyth J. decided that, as had Carroll J. in *Howell v Howell*, Guideline 1 should be applied only to the specific part of the will which had given rise to the difficulty. In the instant case, the immediately relevant portion of the will was not the whole clause in which the power of appointment was contained but that portion of it alone which actually conferred the power: "such of the children of my said son Thomas Butler as he shall by Deed or Will appoint". If this construction were applied, Thomas was the clear donee of the power, and following the failure of appointment, the plaintiff and defendants took as tenants in common.[182]

26–104 Taking Guideline 2, it would certainly be "harmonious" with the sense of the whole will that the father of the objects of the power should be the party appointed to exercise that power.[183] Having regard to Guideline 3 and

> "the scheme of the will as a whole, to decide what the testator was trying to do, it seems to me that he was ultimately trying to benefit the children of Thomas Butler … [I]n seeking to resolve the apparent ambiguity, if such exists, in favour of Thomas Butler, being the person with the power, it seems to me that the parent of the objects of the power would be the person best placed to decide how the power was to be exercised. It fits in with what the testator in my judgement was trying to do and the testator would not have anticipated the untimely death of his son, Thomas".[184]

This construction would also accord with Guideline 4 and the presumption of equality there identified.

26–105 In *Thornton v Timlin*,[185] the will contained a number of specific bequests, one of which was to "Mayo County Council (Ballina area) workers". Mayo County Council used no such phrase to describe a group of workers, and the plaintiff sought to have extrinsic evidence introduced to assist with the

---

[182] It is interesting to observe that this approach is at variance with that adopted by Smyth J. in *Crawford v Lawless* [2002] 4 I.R. 416.

[183] In this connection, Smyth J. accepted as good logic the observation made by Kearns J. in *Re ABC, deceased* [2003] 2 I.R. 250 that "[p]arents must be presumed to know their children better than anyone else."

[184] [2006] IEHC 104 at para.54.

[185] [2012] IEHC 239.

construction of this bequest. There were two lists of Council staff available, one dating from the time of the testator's death in 2006, and a second dating from 2012. Both lists contained around 70 names. The value of the gift was £500, which would not have stretched very far between 70 beneficiaries, but there was a significant residue in the estate of over €200,000.

26–106 In *Black v Sullivan*,[186] the testator bequeathed her apartment to "Rosemary Black (daughter of my niece, Maureen Black)". Maureen Black had three daughters, none of whom were named Rosemary. However, extrinsic evidence in the form of affidavits from family members demonstrated that the testator had a close relationship with one of her grand-nieces, Barbara Black. They spent time together when the testator visited her niece's family home, and the other two grand-nieces lived elsewhere. The testator had expressed an intention to leave her apartment to Barbara. All of the family members (including the two other grand-nieces) agreed that the testator had presumably intended Barbara Black to be the beneficiary. White J. noted that the extrinsic evidence here helped to show the intention of the testator, and assisted in the construction of her will.

Meaning of "Children", "Issue", etc.

26–107 The Status of Children Act 1987[187] amended the 1965 Act so that the expression of a relationship in a will is now deduced irrespective of whether the relevant person's parents were married to each other,[188] unless a contrary intention is shown.[189] Thus, a gift to "the children of X" now includes the non-marital as well as the marital children of X, while a gift to "the legitimate children of X" would include only marital children.[190]

26–108 The Children and Family Relationships Act 2015 outlines who are the parents of a child born as a result of Donor-Assisted Human Reproduction (DAHR), although at the time of writing the relevant provisions have yet to be commenced. The parents are the child's mother,[191] and her spouse, civil partner or cohabitant, as the case may be.[192] The donor of a gamete or embryo is not the parent of a child born as a result of DAHR; nor have they any parental rights

---

[186] *Black v Anne Sullivan Centre Ltd, Our Lady's Hospice Ltd and Family Solidarity Ltd* [2016] IEHC 695.

[187] Enacted as a consequence of *Johnston v Ireland* (1987) 9 E.H.R.R. 203. See also the Law Reform Commission, *Report on Illegitimacy* (LRC 4-1982).

[188] Status of Children Act 1987 s.28, amending the Succession Act 1965 s.3, and adding s.4A.

[189] See also Status of Children Act 1987 s.28 adding to s.3 of the 1965 Act a definition of "issue" as including non-marital children (when read in conjunction with the new s.4A of the 1965 Act and s.3 of the Status of Children Act 1987).

[190] Status of Children Bill 1986, Explanatory Memorandum.

[191] The mother is defined in s.4 as "the woman who gives birth to the child". This affirms *MR v An tArd Chláraitheoir* [2014] IESC 6.

[192] Children and Family Relationships Act 2015 s.5(1), as amended by the Marriage Act 2015.

or duties in respect of the child.[193] It would therefore appear that such children would not be considered the "issue" of the donor.

Gifts on Attaining a Given Age with a Gift Over
26–109 The special rule which applied in this case, known as the rule in *Edwards v Hammond*,[194] is now said to be a rule of construction.

The Rule in Wild's Case
26–110 This rule, which used to apply where a testator left real property "to A and his [or her] children", has been abolished by the 1965 Act.

"Die without Issue"
26–111 At common law, if a testator left property "to A, but if he die without issue, to B ...", the gift was presumed, in the case of land, to give A a fee tail and in the case of personal property, an absolute interest. The failure of issue was construed, in the absence of an intention to the contrary, to mean an *ultimate failure of issue*. B would take the property not only if A died without issue living at his death, but also if A had issue at his death, but they died out later.

26–112 Section 29 of the Wills Act 1837 changed the law to give the phrase a more natural meaning. It provided that A would take a fee simple in the case of land and an absolute interest in the case of personalty, subject to a gift over to B if A had no issue living at his death.[195] This may have achieved greater fidelity to the intention of the testator, but was unsatisfactory in relation to A, since he could not be sure whether the gift would pass to B or not. Even if A had children or grandchildren, they might all die before he did. Section 10 of the Conveyancing Act 1882 altered this result in the case of *land* by providing that, as soon as any of A's issue reached 21, the gift over to B became void.

26–113 Section 29 of the Wills Act 1837 is repeated in s.96 of the 1965 Act but s.10 of the Conveyancing Act 1882 is extended by s.100 of the 1965 Act to include personalty and also in that the issue need only be living at A's death.

---

[193] Children and Family Relationships Act 2015 s.5(5) and (6).

[194] (1684) 3 Lev. 132.

[195] Section 29 of the Wills Act 1837 applied to "issue" and was limited to the use of that word, so that the section did not change the effect of the phrase "die without heirs of the body" which conferred an estate tail: *Re Sallery* (1861) 11 Ir. Ch. R. 236.

26–114 The statutory provisions do not cover all situations in which "die without issue" needs to be construed. In *Re O'Donoghue (deceased); Mulhern v Brennan*,[196] the testator left the residue of his property to sons, JA, JF, C, DG and PP, as tenants in common and "in the event of any of my children dying without issue ...", the surviving brothers or brother were to take the deceased brother's share but in the event of his leaving issue, the issue were to take the parent's share. All four sons survived the testator but died without issue. The judge found that there were two possible constructions: (a) the testator had not contemplated the possibility of all four sons dying without issue, and so there would be an intestacy, or (b) the last surviving brother took all. The judge applied the presumption that a testator does not intend an intestacy[197] and held that the surviving son took absolutely.

Legacies
26–115 In the past, a distinction was made between gifts of real property in wills, called *devises*, and gifts of personal property in wills, called *bequests* or *legacies*. The 1965 Act abolished some important distinctions between real and personal property under the old law, but still refers to "devises and bequests"[198] and a gift of "all my real estate" may still be termed a devise.

26–116 Although the word "legacy" was used to mean a bequest, it is now more frequently used as a general word including devises and bequests and is so used here.

Devises
26–117 A devise may be *general*, *specific* or *residuary*. A general devise would be a gift of "all my real estate" or "all my land". By s.92 of the 1965 Act, a "general devise" now carries with it not only freehold estates which the testator held at death but also leasehold estates. The section repeats s.26 of the Wills Act 1837.[199] Under s.26, a testator who had both land held in fee simple and leasehold estates and who devised "all my lands and tenements" to X would pass only the freehold land to X. However, if he had only leasehold land, the leasehold would pass. Section 26 reversed this artificial rule which depended upon the distinction insisted on at common law between real and personal property, leases being categorised as "chattels real", a type of hybrid. Nevertheless, a devise today of "all my real property" probably still raises a presumption that it carries with it only freehold land since that is apparently the intention of the testator.

26–118 A specific devise is a gift of a specific piece of real property, e.g. a gift of "my house called Dunromin" or "my land in County Meath". A residuary

[196] Unreported, High Court, McCracken J., 26 May 1998.
[197] *Re Harrison* (1885) 30 Ch. D. 390 at 393.
[198] For example, Succession Act 1965 s.93.
[199] That section was inserted because of the case of *Rose v Barlett* (1506) Cro. Car. 292.

devise is a gift of the residue of land after a specific devise, such as "the rest of my land I give to X". A residuary devise, or bequest, now constitutes a fund out of which the testator's funeral and testamentary expenses may be paid.[200]

Bequests
26–119 Bequests may also be general, specific or residuary. A *general* bequest is a gift of personal property by description, such as "one of my tables" when the testator has several, whereas a *specific* bequest refers to a particular piece of personal property, such as "the grandfather clock which my Aunt Betty gave me".[201] If a testator bequeaths a debt owed to the testator, that is a specific legacy.[202] If the testator bequeaths a sum of £50, or a sum of £50 to be paid out of a debt owed to him or her, then that is a general legacy. A gift of £50, without further qualification, is a gift to be paid out of the total amount of money in the testator's estate. The distinction between general and specific is significant in relation to ademption, discussed below.

Failure of Benefit
26–120 Gifts in wills may fail for a number of reasons, not all of which are dealt with here. The rules against remoteness have already been dealt with. The following are the main types of failure.

Ademption
26–121 Ademption is a term used to denote a failure of a gift in a will by some cause outside the will which affects the gift itself rather than the person who is intended to receive it. In the first case, the failure of property, the cause is that the property described in the will is no longer owned by the testator at his or her death. In the second case, that of ademption of legacies by portions, the failure is the existence of a gift outside the will and the application of the maxim of equity that "presumes an intention to fulfil an obligation".

26–122 Ademption may be contrasted with the doctrines of lapse and satisfaction. A gift is said to lapse when it fails because of the prior death of the intended beneficiary. Satisfaction is not easy to distinguish in all cases from ademption, and what word is used is not of great importance provided it is clear as to the effects in specific cases. Generally, the term "satisfaction" is used to refer to the failure of some disposition of property by a gift *within* the will under consideration. In the case of the satisfaction of legacies by legacies, the disposition of property may be within the will itself, i.e. the legacy is adeemed by another legacy within the same will.

---

[200] Succession Act 1965 Sch.1, Pt II; Administration of Estates Act (NI) 1955; Wylie, *Irish Land Law* (2013), para.16.24.

[201] Wylie, *Irish Land Law* (2013), para.16.24.

[202] *Duncan v Duncan* (1859) 27 Beav. 386; *McCoy v Jacob* [1919] 1 I.R. 134 at 138.

Failure of Property

26–123 Since a specific legacy refers to a unique item, the gift will become void if the item ceases to be part of the testator's estate by the time of his or her death.[203] It is said to be *adeemed*.[204] A general legacy, on the other hand, is said not to be adeemed. This is correct if, for example, the gift is of "one of my tables" and the testator still has some tables at the time of death, even though he or she may have sold one or more of them before death, or bought others. If, however, the testator is found to have no tables in his or her possession at the time of death, it is suggested that such a general legacy would be adeemed, since the entire class or category out of which the legacy is to be taken has ceased to exist. A general legacy depends upon the existence at the testator's death of a category of property to which the description in the will can refer.

26–124 A specific legacy is not adeemed if there is an item corresponding to the description in the will at the testator's death. Thus, a gift of "my grand-father clock" would not be adeemed if the testator had a grandfather clock at the time of making the will, then sold it later, but acquired another one which was the only one in his possession at the time of his death. This is really just an illustration of the rule that a will "speaks from death". In cases of doubt, judges tend to find that a legacy is general rather than specific when possible,[205] to avoid it being adeemed.[206]

Legacies by Portions

26–125 The doctrine of ademption in this situation was explained by Sullivan M.R. in *Curtin v Evans*[207]:

> "There is a presumption raised by the law against double portions; and accordingly, when a parent, or someone standing *in loco parentis*, gives by will a sum of money to a child, and afterwards a like or greater sum is secured by a settlement on the marriage of that child, the law presumes the legacy to be adeemed. But this is only a presumption, and therefore it may be rebutted by evidence of intention to the contrary. The burden of proof of intention to countervail the presumption rests on the person claiming the double portion. Parol evidence is admissible ... [but] the Court ought to view and examine it with scrupulous care and great discrimination."[208]

26–126 A legacy given to a child will be adeemed by a portion given by a marriage settlement even though the portion is settled on the husband and wife.[209]

---

[203] *Fitzgerald v Stirling* (1858) 6 Ir. Ch. R. 198 (testator left a life interest in chattel to J, later conveyed it by deed to J absolutely).

[204] Wylie, *Irish Land Law* (2013), paras 3.138–3.139.

[205] *Kelly v Frawley* (1944) 78 I.L.T.R. 46.

[206] *Re Gage* [1934] Ch. 536.

[207] (1872) I.R. 9 Eq. 553; Wylie, *Irish Land Law* (2013), para.3.139.

[208] (1872) I.R. 9 Eq. 553 at 557–558.

[209] *Barry v Harding* (1845) 7 Ir. Eq. R. 317.

If the portion is of less value than the legacy, then the legacy is adeemed *pro tanto*.[210] In the case of ademption of legacies by portions, the child must take the portion and cannot claim the adeemed legacy.[211] This may be contrasted with satisfaction of portions by legacies in which the child has an election, i.e. he or she may choose between the portion or the legacy.

26–127 Ademption in this sense is not confined to persons *in loco parentis* and the children for whom they are responsible. If a testator leaves a legacy to a stranger, either an individual or an organisation, and after making the will gives the stranger a gift for the same purpose, the legacy is presumed to be adeemed by the later gift.[212] The presumption only arises, in the case of a stranger, however, where the legacy was given for a particular purpose and the later gift was for the same purpose.[213] If the legacy was not for a clearly expressed purpose, then the stranger may take both gifts.[214]

26–128 English decisions deny that the rule against double portions can be applied if the effect is to confer a benefit on a stranger.[215] Thus, if the residue of the estate is given to children A and B and to S, a stranger, and the testator later gives a portion to A, the stranger could not benefit from the rule against double portions. If the residue was £15,000 and the portion given to A £3,000, S will only get the original £5,000 share. The residue is adeemed by the portion to the extent of £3,000, leaving £12,000 as residue which is divided between A and B.[216] English courts take the view that the principle behind the rule against double portions is to do justice between the children of the testator, or to preserve kinship solidarity.[217]

26–129 In *Re Bannon*,[218] a testator left a legacy of £300 to a nephew, J, and the residue of his estate to another nephew, X. J later became engaged to a niece of the testator's wife. The testator gave £225 towards the purchase price of business premises for the couple. The Supreme Court held that it had not been proved that the testator was *in loco parentis* to J, and so the presumption did not arise. Murnaghan J. took the view that, in a suitable case, the presumption would apply even if it benefited a stranger. The difficulty on the facts of the case was that, if the presumption were to apply, the stranger would inevitably benefit, which is not always so, as the case discussed in the previous paragraph illustrates. Authority must therefore be taken to be undecided on the point.

---

[210] *Edgeworth v Johnston* (1877) I.R. 11 Eq. 326.

[211] *Chichester v Coventry* (1867) L.R. 2 H.L. 71; *Rentoul v Fitzsimmons* (1900) 34 I.L.T.R. 194; *Hickey v O'Dwyer* [2006] 2 I.L.R.M. 81. See A. Keating, "The Defeasance of Testamentary Gifts by Ademption" (2009) 27 I.L.T. 209.

[212] *Griffith v Bourke* (1887) 21 L.R. Ir. 92 at 95.

[213] *Griffith v Bourke* (1887) 21 L.R. Ir. 92 at 95.

[214] *Griffith v Bourke* (1887) 21 L.R. Ir. 92 at 95.

[215] *Meinertzagen v Walters* (1872) L.R. 7 Ch. App. 670.

[216] *Re Vaux* [1938] Ch. 581 at 590.

[217] See the similar policy at work in class gifts.

[218] [1934] I.R. 701.

Satisfaction
Debts by Legacies

26–130 If a testator owes A a sum of money and dies without paying the debt, but leaves a legacy to B in her will equal to or greater than the debt, equity presumes "an intention to fulfil an obligation" and therefore presumes that the legacy was in satisfaction of the debt.[219] A legacy does not satisfy a debt *pro tanto*.[220] For the doctrine to operate the legacy must be equal or greater in value than the debt.

Portions by Legacies

26–131 This is the opposite case to that in the second type of ademption. It also depends on the equitable presumption against double portions. If a parent, or someone *in loco parentis*, undertakes to provide a portion, i.e. financial provision for a child such as on marriage or for education or establishment in a trade or profession, dies without providing it, but leaves a legacy to the child, the legacy will be presumed to be in satisfaction of the portion.[221]

26–132 In the past the rule was not applied to a mother[222] but this may no longer be the case in view of Art.40.1 of the Constitution. The formulation of the analogous rule in ademption of legacies by portions by Sullivan M.R. in *Curtin v Evans*[223] speaks of "parent".

26–133 It may be easier to rebut the presumption here than in the case of ademption of a legacy by a portion. The reason is that if the will comes before the settlement, then, since the will is not binding until the death of the testator, the settlement is more easily read as substituting provisions, whereas if the settlement comes before the will, the settlement already creates a binding obligation and the beneficiary may in any case insist on taking the benefit under the settlement.[224] It also explains why there is an election in the latter case, but not in the former.

Legacies by Legacies

26–134 Some writers[225] question whether this is a case of satisfaction. It may be more accurate to treat it as a special case of construction of wills. Where a will contains two legacies to the same person or institution, it is a matter of

---

[219] Wylie, *Irish Land Law* (2013), paras 3.136–3.137.

[220] *Coates v Coates* [1898] 1 I.R. 258; *Humphrey v Arabin* (1836) Ll. & G.t.P. 318.

[221] Wylie, *Irish Land Law* (2013), paras 3.136–3.137.

[222] *Warren v Warren* (1783) 1 Bro. C.C. 305; contrast *Re Eaderley's Will* [1920] 1 Ch. 397.

[223] (1872) I.R. 9 Eq. 553.

[224] *Chichester v Coventry* (1867) L.R. 2 H.L. 71 at 87.

[225] For example, Wylie, *Irish Land Law* (2013), paras 3.140–3.143.

construction whether the testator really intended to make two separate gifts to the same donee, or whether it was an oversight.[226]

Same Instrument

26-135 Where the legacies are contained in the same will or codicil and are of the same value, equity presumes that the testator did not intend both gifts to take effect, i.e. it was a mistake, and the legatee can take only one.[227] If they are of different value, the presumption is to the opposite effect, i.e. that they are both intended to take effect.

Different Instruments

26-136 Where the legacies are contained in different wills or codicils, equity presumes that both were intended to take effect.[228]

Election

26-137 Some cases of election in equity have already been dealt with. The more general principle known as "the doctrine of election" is, in effect, a means by which a testator may dispose of property which does not belong to him or her. If a testator purports to leave to A property in fact belonging to X, and also leaves a legacy to X, then if X wants to take the benefit of the legacy, X must dispose of her own property in accordance with the will or compensate A for its loss. The principle is that if X wishes to take the benefit under the will, she must also accept the burden.[229]

26-138 Early cases placed the doctrine on the basis of the implied intent of the testator, but it was held by the House of Lords in *Cooper v Cooper*[230] that election applies even where the testator makes a mistake as to the ownership of the property. Even so, Lord Hatherley was prepared to construct a theory of intent in such a case: he held that the testator can be taken to have the "ordinary intent" implied in making a will, that he or she intends that every part of it should be effective.[231] The theory seems to be an artificial one, designed to disguise the fact that the court of equity is acting on the conscience of the donee, an intervention which in earlier centuries the courts found no need to disguise. There are signs that today the courts may prefer to base the principle again on the conscience of the donee.[232]

---

[226] *Quinn v Armstrong* (1876) I.R. 11 Eq. 161.

[227] *Garth v Meyrick* (1779) 1 Bro. C.C. 30.

[228] *Walsh v Walsh* (1869) I.R. 4 Eq. 396; *Pakenham v Duggan* (1951) 85 I.L.T.R. 21.

[229] *Sweetman v Sweetman* (1868) I.R. 2 Eq. 141.

[230] (1874) L.R. 7 H.L. 53.

[231] (1874) L.R. 7 H.L. 53 at 70.

[232] *Re Mengel's Will Trust* [1962] Ch. 791.

26–139 Election is said to lead to compensation and not forfeiture. The person who may be called upon to elect has a choice of three courses of action. He or she may:

1. retain his or her own property and forgo the legacy, or
2. take under the will and dispose of his or her property as the will directs, or
3. retain his or her own property *and* take under the will, in which case he or she must *compensate* the other legatee for the loss of his or her property.

26–140 Not all of these options are rational in all cases. Thus, if X owns Gortbane which is worth €70,000 and the testator purports to leave it to A, and also leaves a legacy of €5,000 to X, X can keep Gortbane and forgo the legacy, or could take the €5,000 and hand over Gortbane to A, or keep Gortbane and the €5,000, but would then have to compensate A to the value of Gortbane. Most people in X's position in this case would prefer the first option. However, if the testator had merely purported to give A, his aged aunt, a right of residence in Gortbane, X might prefer to give the aunt a right of residence and take the €5,000.[233]

Lapse

26–141 The doctrine of lapse is in some respects the opposite of ademption. In ademption it is the non-existence of the property which causes the failure of the gift. In lapse it is the non-existence, i.e. death, of the intended recipient. Thus, if the testator leaves property to A and A dies before the testator, the general rule is that the gift does not take effect for the benefit of A's estate.

26–142 Co-ownership is a special case. If the testator leaves property to A, B and C jointly and A and B die before the testator, survivorship operates, rather than lapse, and C, if alive at the testator's death, may take the whole gift. If all three are dead, then the whole legacy lapses. If the gift is to A, B, and C with words of severance, then there is a tenancy in common. If A and B die before the testator, but C is still alive at the testator's death, the shares of A and B lapse, but not that of C. If all three are dead at the testator's death, then the whole gift lapses.

26–143 Where a legacy has lapsed, the destination of the property will depend on the wording of the residuary clause,[234] if there is one. Thus, in *Re Swiney*[235] the clause gave the residuary devisee "the residue of my estate … not herein specifically devised …". The will devised property X to C. C died before the testator. The lapsed property X was held to pass not to the residuary devisee but on a partial intestacy, and at that time it went to the heir at law. Property

---

[233] *Re Gordon's Will Trusts* [1978] Ch. 145.
[234] Succession Act 1965 s.91, reproducing Wills Act 1837 s.25.
[235] (1858) 6 Ir. Ch. R. 455.

X had been "specifically devised", even though the devise had failed. If there is no residuary clause, the property will pass on a partial intestacy.

(1) Charitable Gifts

26–144 A gift to charity may not lapse if the charity is dissolved provided the testator has shown a general charitable intention and the court is willing to apply it cy-pres.[236]

(2) Entails

26–145 Section 97 of the 1965 Act, reproducing s.32 of the Wills Act 1837, provides that the doctrine of lapse will not apply, unless there is a contrary intention, in the case of a gift of a fee tail or quasi-entail where the intended donee dies before the testator leaving issue capable of inheriting under the entail.[237]

(3) Gifts to Issue

26–146 Section 33 of the Wills Act 1837 provided that where the testator made a gift in favour of his or her child or remoter issue and the child or issue predeceased the testator, then subject to a contrary intention, the gift would not lapse if the child or issue left issue living at the death of the testator.

26–147 Section 98 of the 1965 Act repeats the provisions of s.33, but provides in addition that lapse will not apply (a) where the gift to the child or issue is made under a special power of appointment, and (b) where the gift is made to a class. Section 33 of the Wills Act 1837 applied, by its language, only to gifts made under general powers of appointment and so the 1965 Act abolishes the distinction in this respect. As to class gifts, the doctrine of lapse never applied. If a testator gave property "to my children", the class closed at the testator's death if there were children in existence at that point. Thus, under the normal class-closing rule, a child who died before the testator never became a member of the class, and so even if that child had children who were alive at the testator's death, they did not participate. The Wills Act 1837 did not remedy this situation. Although s.98 states that in all cases within its scope "the gift shall not lapse", the effect of the section in this instance appears to be to alter the class-closing rule where the class consists of children or remoter issue of the testator.

26–148 In *Elliott v Joicey*,[238] an English court held that, under s.33 of the 1837 Act, the requirement that the issue of a deceased child be living at the testator's death was not satisfied by a child in the womb. However, s.3(2) of the 1965 Act now excludes the effect of the case by providing that "descendants and

---

[236] Wylie, *Irish Land Law* (2013), paras 5.58–5.59.
[237] *Re Pearson* [1920] 1 Ch. 247.
[238] [1935] A.C. 209.

relatives of a deceased person begotten before his death but born alive there-after shall ... be regarded as having been born in the lifetime of the deceased and as having survived him".

26–149 "Child" or "issue" includes non-marital as well as marital children or issue in wills made after 14 December 1987.[239] However, in *Re Stamp, deceased*,[240] Lardner J. held that "issue" prima facie does not include adopted children even in a will made after the Adoption Act 1952. The will of John Stamp, who died in 1954, stated that should his son, Patrick Stamp, "die with-out leaving issue", the property bequeathed to him should be held in trust for the son of the testator's other son, Philip. Patrick was unmarried at the date of the will and at his father's death, and married two years later. There were no biological children of the marriage and in 1965 Patrick and his wife adopted a daughter and in 1967 a second daughter. Patrick applied to have it determined, on his own and his daughters' behalf, whether the word "issue" in the will included adopted children or not. The plaintiff submitted, inter alia, that the Supreme Court had held[241] that the effect of an adoption order under the Adop-tion Act 1952 was to take a child out of the family into which it was born and incorporate it into the adopting family and that the policy of the law and the Constitution is to regard adopted children for all purposes as equal to natural children of their parents. Lardner J., however, took the view that to hold that "issue" included adopted children would be to give the word a "specialist" meaning and not an "ordinary" meaning.

26–150 *Re Stamp* is wrongly decided. Adoption is a legal fiction. The fiction is that the adopted person is in law the child of the adopter, even though the child is not biologically the offspring of the adopter. The legal fiction also reflects the social fact that such children are treated and accepted as the children of their adoptive parents and this has been implemented by the Supreme Court decision upholding the Adoption Act 1952. The "ordinary" meaning of such words as "child" or "issue", etc. has therefore been changed by both social practice and constitutional principle. Section 27(4)(b) of the Status of Children Act 1987 now provides that an adopted person is entitled to take under a dis-position in the same manner as he or she would if he or she had been "born in lawful wedlock" to the adoptive parents.

---

[239] Status of Children Act 1987 s.28, amending the 1965 Act s.3 and adding s.4A. Section 4A pro-vides that "in deducing any relationship for the purposes of this Act, the relationship between every person and his father and mother, shall ... be determined in accordance with section 3 of the Act of 1987". This is subject to s.27A of the 1965 Act which deals with grants of probate and administration.

[240] [1993] I.L.R.M. 383.

[241] *Re the Adoption Act (No. 2) Bill 1987* [1989] I.R. 656.

Disclaimer

26–151 A beneficiary under a will cannot be forced to accept a gift under it and may disclaim it.[242] There is no formality for disclaimer which may be implied from conduct.[243]

Uncertainty

26–152 A gift in a will may fail for uncertainty if the property concerned or those who are to receive it are not identified with sufficient clarity to enable the court to carry out its terms. The rules as to admitting extrinsic evidence have already been dealt with.

26–153 Courts will attempt wherever possible to find the testator's meaning, even, sometimes, to the extent of giving specific content to a somewhat vague phrase.[244]

26–154 It has been suggested that a gift fails for uncertainty not because the property or the recipient cannot be ascertained but because of uncertainty of concept.[245] This is difficult to maintain if one takes into account the relevance of admissible extrinsic evidence. If, for example, the gift is to "my nephew Arthur Murphy" and the testator has two nephews called Arthur Murphy, then extrinsic evidence may show that the testator had in mind one of them rather than the other. On the other hand, extrinsic evidence may be inconclusive. The gift will then fail for uncertainty, although the "concept", in terms of its linguistic expression, is the same as before. A gift may fail for uncertainty not because the testator was unclear as to what he or she meant, but because the court is unable to discover what the testator's intention was.

Gifts to Witnesses

26–155 Section 82(1) of the 1965 Act provides as follows:

> "If a person attests the execution of a will, and any devise, bequest, estate, interest, gift or appointment, of or affecting any property (other than charges and directions for the payment of any debt or debts) is given or made by the will to that person or his spouse, that devise [etc.] shall, so far only as concerns the person attesting the execution of the will, or the spouse of that person, or any person claiming under that person or spouse, be utterly null and void."[246]

---

[242] *Townson v Tickell* (1819) 3 B. & Ald. 31; J. Brady, *Succession Law in Ireland,* 2nd edn (Dublin: Butterworths, 1995), para.6.02.

[243] *Re Birchall* (1889) 40 Q.B.D. 436.

[244] *Jackson v Hamilton* (1846) 3 Jo. & La T. 702; *Re Golay* [1965] 1 W.L.R. 969; R.E. Megarry, "Note" (1965) 81 L.Q.R. 481.

[245] *Re Gape* [1952] Ch. 418; R.E. Megarry, "Note" (1965) 81 L.Q.R. 481.

[246] Repeating s.15 of the Wills Act 1837. On "superfluous witnesses", see R. Grimes and K. Dowling, "The Cuckoo's Call and the Lesser-Spotted Superfluous Witness" (2014) 2(2) I.P.L.J. 9.

26–156 Subsection (2) makes it clear that the witness may nevertheless be admitted as a witness in court to prove the validity or invalidity of the will. The principle here is conflict of interest: the rule preserves the impartiality of witnesses and ensures that they have no improper motive in attesting the will. Since the main rule has this effect, there is no objection to their giving evidence as to attestation.

26–157 The general rule does not apply in the following cases.

(1) Signed Not as a Witness

26–158 If the beneficiary signs not as a witness but in some other capacity, such as where an executor signs above the attestation clause, believing that it is necessary for an executor to sign the will, the rule does not apply.[247]

(2) Fiduciary Gifts

26–159 If the witness is to take the gift not beneficially but as a trustee, the rule does not apply.[248]

(3) Secret Trusts

26–160 If the witness takes under a secret trust, the rule does not apply, presumably provided that the witness was unaware of the benefit at the time of attestation.[249]

(4) Subsequent Marriage

26–161 The rule does not apply to the spouse of an attesting witness who married the witness after the attestation of the will.[250]

(5) Confirmation

26–162 The rule does not apply if the gift to the witness is confirmed by a will or codicil which is not attested by the witness.[251]

(6) Sufficient Other Witnesses

26–163 The rule does not apply if the will would be validly attested even without the signature of the attesting beneficiary. In *In the Goods of Willis*,[252] the testator asked his sister, to whom he had left all his property, to sign the will after the attesting witnesses. She had done so only to please her brother

---

[247] *Re Parker* (1905) 39 I.L.T.R. 6.

[248] *Kelly v Walsh* [1946] I.R. 388; *Cresswell v Cresswell* (1868) L.R. 6 Eq. 69.

[249] *O'Brien v Condon* [1905] 1 I.R. 51; *Re Young* [1951] Ch. 344.

[250] *Tee v Bestwick* (1881) 6 Q.B.D. 311.

[251] *Re Marcus* (1887) 57 L.T. 399; *Gurney v Gurney* (1855) 3 Drew. 208; *In the Goods of Shaw* [1944] Ir. Jur. Rep. 77.

[252] (1927) 61 I.L.T.R. 48.

who was gravely ill. Sullivan P. granted probate omitting the sister's signature. The English case of *In the Estate of Bravda*[253] had come to a harsher decision the effect of which was only reversed in England in 1968.[254]

Unlawful Killing

26–164 In many legal systems, if someone entitled to benefit from the estate of a deceased person is convicted of a crime in which the unlawful killing of the deceased was an element, he or she is disqualified from obtaining the benefit, whether he or she is a beneficiary under a will[255] or on intestacy.[256] This is said to be based on the principle that a wrongdoer should not profit from his or her actions.[257]

26–165 Section 120 of the 1965 Act provides as follows:

"A sane[258] person who has been guilty of the murder or manslaughter of another shall be precluded from taking any share in the estate of that other, except a share arising under a will made after the act constituting the offence, and shall not be entitled to make an application under section 117."

26–166 Subsection (4) precludes a person who has been convicted of an offence against the deceased or a spouse or child of the deceased, punishable by imprisonment for four years, from taking the legal right share or making an application under s.117.

26–167 The basis of the rule has been considered in the chapter on co-ownership. The common law rule was not based simply upon a concern to frustrate an evil design, since it applied even where the killing was not intentional and even if the motive of the killing was not to obtain the benefit.

---

[253] [1968] 1 W.L.R. 492.

[254] Wills Act 1968 s.1.

[255] *Riggs v Palmer* 115 N.Y. 506 (1889) (note Gray J.'s dissenting judgment); *Van Alstyne v Tuffy* 169 N.Y.S. 173 (1918); *Cleaver v Mutual Reserve Fund Life Association* [1892] 1 Q.B. 147; *Borough Builders Ltd v Dublin Corporation* [1966] I.R. 285 (HC); *Re Nevin*, unreported, High Court, Shanley J., 13 March 1997.

[256] *Re Crippen's Estate* [1911] P. 108.

[257] For example, *Riggs v Palmer* 115 N.Y. 506 (1889); *Cleaver v Mutual Reserve Fund Life Association* [1892] 1 Q.B. 147 (CA (Eng)); *Re Crippen's Estate* [1911] P. 108; J.B. Ames, "Can a Murderer Acquire Title by his Crime and Keep It?" in J.B. Ames, *Lectures on Legal History and Miscellaneous Essays* (Cambridge: Harvard University Press, 1913); E.L. Ague, "Homicide—Effect on Wrongdoer's Inheritance, Intestate and Survivorship Rights" (1953) 7 Miami L.Q. 524; T.G. Youdan, "Acquisition of Property by Killing" (1973) 89 L.Q.R. 235.

[258] The Law Reform Commission has recommended that this provision should continue not to apply to persons who were insane at the time of committing the offence: Law Reform Commission, *Prevention of Benefit from Homicide* (LRC 115-2015). See *Nevin v Nevin* [2013] IEHC 80.

26–168 The notion that the rule is based upon the presumed intent of the testator is false since the principle has been applied in cases of intestacy.[259] What of a testator who was terminally ill and who had arranged with the legatee that she should kill him? Or, suppose a testator had given a number of people a good motive to kill him and had trusted that, given their character, they, or one of them, would do so? A court would surely not allow such legatees to take the property on the ground that it did not contradict the intention of the testator. Also, in other contexts, such as extrinsic evidence, courts have refused to give effect to the intent of the testator where it contradicts the express provisions of the will. One element in s.120 which points to its being based on intention is the exception of gifts made after the act constituting the offence, which suggests that the reason is that such a gift indicates forgiveness. If it is intended to incorporate a notion of forgiveness, then it should also have made it necessary to prove that the testator was *aware* at the time of making the later gift that the act was caused by the intended beneficiary.

26–169 Another suggested principle is that to allow a person to benefit from killing another would be to encourage crime,[260] but this again would seem to justify the rule only as to deliberate killing motivated by thought of gain.

26–170 A more likely explanation is that, if the killer were to benefit directly from the crime, it would outrage the feelings of ordinary law-abiding people.[261] Such a feeling of outrage, it could be argued, might tend to weaken adherence to the rule of law on the part of the otherwise law-abiding majority.

26–171 Section 120 does not provide expressly for exceptions to be made even in the case of manslaughter, which is an offence which can vary greatly in gravity from the deliberate to the unintentional.[262] Where, for example, a wife suffers years of domestic violence and finally "snaps" and kills her husband,[263] or from some other form of diminished responsibility,[264] arguably she should not automatically be deprived from benefiting from his estate or claiming her "legal right". Ordinary people would not necessarily be outraged by such a result. It also creates the anomaly that if X knocks down and kills A through negligence, not knowing the identity of his victim, he is debarred from inheriting from under A, but if he knocks down and kills B under identical circumstances, it has no effect on his entitlement under A's will, yet his degree of moral culpability is the same. It seems incongruous that a rule which

---

[259] *Re Crippen's Estate* [1911] P. 108.

[260] *Re H (deceased)*, unreported, Chancery Division, 19 June 1987.

[261] *Re Crippen's Estate* [1911] P. 108 at 112.

[262] Some English cases had refused to examine the degree of moral guilt in cases of manslaughter and applied the forfeiture rule: *In the Estate of Hall* [1914] P. 1 at 7; *Re Giles* [1972] Ch. 544 at 552.

[263] *Re K (deceased)* [1985] 1 Ch. 85.

[264] *Re Giles* [1972] Ch. 544.

is based purely upon ethical considerations should be applied without regard to the justice of the case at hand.

26–172 Some of these difficulties have been removed in England by the Forfeiture Act 1982, which expressly allows the forfeiture rule to be modified, except in the case of murder, to a range of benefits. Since the Act, the English courts have adopted the test in *Gray v Barr*[265] that the forfeiture rule will not be applied if the killing is unintentional.[266] The Supreme Court of New South Wales in *Public Trustee v Evans*[267] has declined to apply the rule in a case involving domestic violence. A wife, who had admittedly caused the death of her husband, had been acquitted of manslaughter, but the acquittal did not bar civil proceedings on the same facts and the Public Trustee had applied to the court to determine whether the rule of forfeiture should be applied. The court held that it should not, on the ground that the rule in the jurisdiction was judge-made and should not be applied where death results after unintentional killing in the context of domestic violence.

26–173 In view of these developments, it would seem right to amend s.120 to give a discretion to the court to set aside the general rule of forfeiture, either generally or in a number of specified circumstances.

26–174 Section 120 of the 1965 Act was considered by the High Court in *Cawley v Lillis*.[268] The defendant had been convicted of the manslaughter of his wife. They were joint tenants of their family home and of other assets. Because of the conviction, the defendant was precluded under s.120 of the 1965 Act from taking any share in his wife's estate and, in accordance with s.120(5) of the 1965 Act, that share was to be distributed as if he had pre-deceased her. Because the property held in a joint tenancy did not form part of the estate, the deceased's personal representatives and daughter (the plaintiffs) applied to the High Court to determine how the jointly-held assets were to be treated.

26–175 Laffoy J. considered three potential means of dealing with such a situation. The first was to treat the killer as having pre-deceased the other joint tenant. The second was to sever the joint tenancy. Ultimately, however, she opted for a third approach. Under common law principles, and in line with jurisprudence from Australia, Canada, New Zealand and the United States, Laffoy J. held that he held the joint assets on a constructive trust for himself and the deceased's estate in equal shares. Thus, the family home and other assets that had been held in a joint tenancy accrued to the defendant solely on the date of the deceased's death but the defendant held the deceased's share

---

[265] [1971] 2 Q.B. 554.
[266] *Re K (deceased)* [1985] 1 Ch. 85; *Re H (deceased)*, unreported, Chancery Division, 19 June 1987. But note *R. v Chief National Insurance Commissioner, Ex p. Connor* [1981] Q.B. 758, coming to a similar conclusion before the Act.
[267] [1985] 2 N.S.W.L.R. 188.
[268] [2011] IEHC 515.

on a constructive trust for the deceased's estate. The judge considered "that outcome, viewed objectively at that time, could not be regarded as conferring a benefit on the defendant as a result of the crime he committed" and was consistent with the principle that a person may not benefit from his wrongdoing.

26–176 The issue was the subject of scrutiny by the Law Reform Commission, which drafted a bill which has yet to be enacted.[269] The Succession (Amendment) Bill proposes to insert a new s.120A, which is in line with the second option proposed by Laffoy J. in *Cawley v Lillis*[270]:

> "[W]here there is only one surviving co-owner and that surviving co-owner has been found guilty of the murder, attempted murder, or manslaughter of the other co-owner ... (a) the joint tenancy, and (b) any rights in favour of the offender accruing therefrom, shall be deemed to have been terminated with effect from the date of the offence ... Where a joint tenancy has been terminated ... the entire interest in the property shall be deemed to have been vested in the estate of the deceased co-owner with effect from the date of the offence."

26–177 It also provides for a new s.120B to deal with situations involving more than two joint tenants. It remains to be seen whether legislative reform in this area will be forthcoming.

Simultaneous Death

26–178 The problem of *commorientes* (Latin: those dying together), has already been dealt with in the context of joint tenancy and survivorship. But it can also arise when parties own separate property.

26–179 We have seen that at common law there was no special rule and so if A and B died in the same accident, it was for the personal representatives of A, if they alleged that A had survived B and had inherited B's property, to prove their case, and it was often impossible to do so. The personal representatives of B, if they wished to allege that B survived A, were in the same position. Thus, there was, in effect, a presumption of simultaneous death.[271] Third parties could also be affected. Suppose that a husband left property in his will to his wife, but if she died in his lifetime, it was to go to X. The wife made a similar will leaving property to her husband, but to X if her husband died before she did. Both husband and wife were swept off a ship in a storm by the same wave. X could take nothing under either will because in neither case could she prove that the

---

[269] Law Reform Commission, *Issues Paper on Review of Section 120 of the Succession Act 1965 and Admissibility of Criminal Convictions in Civil Proceedings* (LRC IP 7-2014).
[270] [2011] IEHC 515.
[271] *Wing v Angrave* (1860) 8 H.L.C. 183.

condition had been fulfilled.[272] Section 5 of the 1965 Act[273] confirms that this is still the position, i.e. that they are all deemed to have died simultaneously.

Freedom of Testation

26–180 Historically, freedom of testation—the right of the individual to leave property by will—was asserted, in the case of real property, in opposition to the control of feudal lords. As such, it was progressive in the sense that its attainment was part of the historical process of replacing feudal forms of property with individual property. Individual freedom can, however, be exercised capriciously and irresponsibly. Many jurisdictions have limited freedom of testation in a new way, to ensure that testators do not entirely disinherit members of their own family. In *FM v TAM*,[274] Kenny J. contrasted the provisions of the 1965 Act with those in other jurisdictions:

> "The concept underlying the legislation in New Zealand, New South Wales and England is that the testator owes a duty to make reasonable provision for the maintenance of his widow and of his dependants. Our Succession Act, however, is based on the idea that a testator owes a duty to leave part of his estate to his widow (the legal right) and to make proper provision for his children in accordance with his means. It is not based on a duty to provide maintenance for his widow nor is it limited in its application to children who were dependant on him."[275]

26–181 The provisions may also be compared to those in Scotland where the widow is entitled to a half share if there are no children, and a third share if there are children, hence the expression "the widow's part, the bairn's part and the dead's part". There was a similar law in Ireland before the Statute of Distributions (Ireland) 1695, known as "the custom of Ireland".[276] Today, however, the children are not entitled to a specific share but are entitled to apply under s.117 for reasonable provision.

Legal Right of the Spouse or Civil Partner

26–182 Section 111 of the 1965 Act provides that if the testator leaves a spouse or civil partner and no children, the spouse or civil partner shall have a right to one-half of the estate.[277] If the testator leaves a spouse or civil partner and children, the spouse or civil partner shall have a right to one-third of the estate.[278] The right of the spouse or civil partner is known as the *legal right*

---

[272] *Underwood v Wing* (1855) 4 D.M. & G. 633; *Wing v Angrave* (1860) 8 H.L.C. 183; *In bonis Beynon* [1901] P. 141.

[273] As amended by Civil Law (Miscellaneous Provisions) Act 2008 s.67.

[274] (1972) 106 I.L.T.R. 82.

[275] (1972) 106 I.L.T.R. 82 at 86.

[276] Statute of Distributions (Ireland) 1695 s.10; *Re Urquhart* [1974] I.R. 197.

[277] Succession Act 1965 ss.111(1) and 111A (as inserted by the CPA 2010).

[278] Succession Act 1965 ss.111(2) and 111A.

and has priority over devises and bequests by will and shares on intestacy (i.e. where there is a partial intestacy).[279]

26–183 The legal right of the spouse or civil partner may be renounced by an ante-nuptial contract in writing between the parties to the intended marriage and also after marriage by a spouse or civil partner in writing and during the lifetime of the testator.[280] The main purpose was evidently to protect the interests of children of a previous marriage. A contract renouncing the legal right made after marriage need not be made between both parties to the marriage, but can be made between a spouse or civil partner and a person due to inherit from the other spouse or civil partner.[281] Such contracts may be invalid on the ground of undue influence, or some other form of unequal bargaining power.[282] A legacy to a spouse or civil partner is deemed, by s.114(2) of the 1965 Act, to have been intended to be in satisfaction of the legal right of the spouse or civil partner. A spouse or civil partner nevertheless has the right to elect between a legacy and the legal right.

Election of Spouse or Civil Partner
26–184 Where a person dies wholly testate, a spouse or civil partner has the right, under s.115 of the 1965 Act, to elect between a legacy in the will and his or her legal right. Section 115(4) provides that the personal representatives of the deceased have a duty to notify the surviving spouse or civil partner in writing of the right to elect under s.115. The election must be made either not later than six months from the receipt of notification, or within one year from the first taking out of representation of the deceased's estate, whichever is later.[283]

26–185 In default of election, the spouse or civil partner takes under the will and does not take his or her legal right under s.111.[284] This may reflect a policy that the 1965 Act only seeks to ensure that the testator leaves a part of his or her estate to his or her surviving spouse, without seeking to dictate how much or how little he or she shall leave, so that the legal right is more in the nature of a guideline.[285] However, it can lead to the result that the surviving spouse or civil partner takes nothing. In *Re Urquhart*,[286] a wife had left a legacy to her husband conditional on his surviving her for at least one month, the husband having made a similar provision for his wife. Both were involved in a car accident which caused their deaths. The husband survived the wife by only a day and did not recover consciousness. He therefore died without having made

---

[279] Succession Act 1965 s.112.
[280] Succession Act 1965 s.113.
[281] *JH v WJH*, unreported, High Court, Keane J., 20 December 1979.
[282] *JH v WJH*, unreported, High Court, Keane J., 20 December 1979.
[283] Succession Act 1965 ss.115(4) and 111A.
[284] Succession Act 1965 ss. 115(1)(b) and 111A. *JH v WJH*, unreported, High Court, Keane J., 20 December 1979.
[285] See *FM v TAM* (1972) 106 I.L.T.R. 82.
[286] [1974] I.R. 197.

an election under s.115. The Revenue Commissioners nevertheless claimed that the husband's half share in the wife's estate, being his legal right was, in terms of the Finance Act 1894, "property of which the deceased person was at the time of his death competent to dispose." A majority of the Supreme Court held that the husband was not "competent to dispose" of the legal right since he had not elected to take it in preference to the legacy. It was accepted that the reason for the husband's failure to elect was not relevant for this purpose. Henchy J., dissenting, did not accept that election was a condition precedent to being able to dispose of the interest, since, in his view, both election and disposition could take place simultaneously.[287] He conceded that the consequence of holding as he did—that the husband was competent to dispose of the interest at his death—was that the husband's estate would be liable to pay tax on a share which he had not elected to take, and had never received. The majority decision avoided this result. In the event, the husband's estate took neither the legal right, since in the view of the court he had failed to elect, nor the legacy, since the condition precedent had not been satisfied.

26–186 In *Re Cummins*,[288] the Supreme Court held that legal right does not depend upon the surviving spouse electing between it and a bequest in the will or a share on intestacy, so that, if the testator leaves a will which contains no provision for his or her spouse, the spouse still has the legal right share which vests on the death of the testator. The court distinguished *Urquhart* on the ground that in *Urquhart*, the need to elect arose, whereas in *Cummins* it did not. Barron J. quoted with approval a passage from Walsh J.'s judgment in *Urquhart*[289]:

> "In my opinion, the whole of this structure presupposes and is based on an assumption implicit in the statute, in addition to what is expressly stated in s 111, that a legal right arises on the moment of the death of the testator. Where there is no legacy or devise or where there is a legacy or a devise expressed to be in addition to the legal share, the legal share vests upon the death. But when a testator in his will makes a devise or bequest to a spouse and it is not expressed to be in addition to the share as a legal right, then the spouse has a statutory right to take the share as a legal right—but that share does not vest until he takes it."

26–187 Where a person dies partly intestate, the surviving spouse or civil partner may elect between (a) his or her legal right, and (b) his or her spouse or civil partner's share on intestacy and, *in addition*, the legacy under the will.[290]

---

[287] One objection to this is that property law, in its reifying way, would normally hold that election had preceded disposition by at least a nominal moment of time so that the interest could vest in the disponer.
[288] [1997] 2 I.L.R.M. 401.
[289] [1974] I.R. 197 at 211.
[290] Succession Act 1965 ss.115(2)(a) and 111A.

In default of election, the spouse or civil partner takes (b) and not the legal right.[291]

Spouse and Civil Partner's Right to Appropriate Dwelling

26–188 Section 56 of the 1965 Act provides that where the deceased's estate includes a dwelling in which, at the time of the deceased's death, the surviving spouse or civil partner was ordinarily resident, the surviving spouse or civil partner may require in writing the personal representatives of the deceased to appropriate the dwelling under s.55 wholly or partly in satisfaction of any share of the surviving spouse or civil partner.[292] The same right applies to household chattels.[293]

26–189 As with the right to elect, the deceased's personal representatives have a duty to notify the surviving spouse or civil partner of his or her right to appropriate. The right must be exercised not later than six months from the receipt of notification or one year from first taking out representation of the deceased's estate, whichever is later.[294] The right to appropriate applies whether the deceased dies testate or intestate.

Provision for Qualified Cohabitants

26–190 A qualified cohabitant for the purposes of the CPA 2010 is a person who has lived with another person of the same or opposite sex in a meaningful and committed relationship for at least five years, or for at least two years where they have dependent children.[295] A surviving qualified cohabitant may apply to the court for provision to be made for him or her out of a deceased cohabitant's estate within six months from the first taking out of a grant of representation to the estate.[296] Such provision can only be made out of the deceased cohabitant's "net estate", and "net estate" means the estate that remains after any other rights under the 1965 Act of a surviving spouse or civil partner have been satisfied.[297]

26–191 In *DC v DR*,[298] the plaintiff was the qualified cohabitant of a woman, JC, who died intestate. Baker J. in the High Court noted that the case law on s.117 of the 1965 Act (discussed below) could assist the court in making an order for proper provision. The High Court made provision for the plaintiff

---

[291] Succession Act 1965 ss.115(2)(b) and 111A.

[292] *Re Hamilton; Hamilton v Armstrong* [1984] I.L.R.M. 306 (application by spouse creates equity which can be enforced by spouse's personal representatives).

[293] Succession Act 1965 ss.56(2) and 111A.

[294] Succession Act 1965 ss.56(4) and 111A.

[295] CPA 2010 s.172. On "intimate and committed relationship", see *DC v DR* [2016] 1 I.L.R.M. 178.

[296] CPA 2010 s.194.

[297] CPA 2010 s.194(11).

[298] [2016] 1 I.L.R.M. 178.

valued at approximately 45 per cent of the €1.4 million estate. This was broadly in line with the deceased's wishes, as expressed during her lifetime.

Proper Provision for Children
General
26–192 Section 117 of the 1965 Act deals with a testator's child who feels that his or her parent has not made proper provision for him or her in the will. This has been the subject of close scrutiny by the Law Reform Commission, which published a report on s.117 in 2017.[299] The recommendations of the Commission are considered further below, after a discussion of s.117 as it currently stands.

26–193 Section 117 of the 1965 Act provides as follows:

"(1) Where, on application by or on behalf of a child of a testator, the court is of opinion that the testator has failed in his moral duty to make proper provision for the child in accordance with his means, whether by his will or otherwise, the court may order that such provision shall be made for the child out of the estate as the court thinks just.

(2) The court shall consider the application from the point of view of a prudent and just parent, taking into account the position of each of the children of the testator and any other circumstances which the court may consider of assistance in arriving at a decision that will be as fair as possible to the child to whom the application relates and to the other children.

(3) An order under this section shall not affect the legal right of a surviving spouse or, if the surviving spouse is the mother or father of the child, any devise or bequest to the spouse or any share to which the spouse is entitled on intestacy.

(3A) An order under this section shall not affect the legal right of a surviving civil partner unless the court, after consideration of all the circumstances, including the testator's financial circumstances and his or her obligations to the surviving civil partner, is of opinion that it would be unjust not to make the order.

...

(6) An order under this section shall not be made except on an application made within six months[300] from the first taking out of representation of the deceased's estate."

26–194 Subsection (3) debars any claim by a child where the testator left all his or her property to the surviving spouse and that surviving spouse is the other parent of the applicant. The policy behind the section is, presumably,

---

[299] Law Reform Commission, *Report on Section 117 of the Succession Act 1965: Aspects of Provision for Children* (LRC 118-2017).
[300] Previously 12 months; amended by Family Law (Divorce Act) 1996 s.46.

that the surviving spouse, being the mother or father of the relevant child or children, will provide for him, her or them out of the bequest, and that, accordingly, a bequest of all the testator's estate to the mother or father of a child discharges any moral duty to that child. This policy appears to be predicated on recognition of the reality in many cases that parents may cooperate with each other in discharging each other's statutory obligation to their children. In such event, the operation of the section is postponed until after the death of the surviving parent. In *W(C) v W(L)*,[301] O'Sullivan J. observed: "The subsection does appear to contemplate in certain circumstances the treatment of common parents as having what amounts to a shared obligation." In a situation to which subs.(3) applies, the court has no discretion in the matter: an order in favour of an applicant child under s.117 cannot be made.

26–195 In contrast, subs.(3A) gives the court a discretion whether to make or not to make an order in favour of an applicant child under s.117 where the testator is survived by a civil partner within the meaning of s.3 of the CPA 2010. The discretion is broadly cast ("after consideration of all the circumstances"), but, noticeably, identifies as relevant financial circumstances and the testator's obligations (which must be taken as not confined to legal obligations) to the surviving civil partner. Section 117(3) has no application in the case of opposite-sex cohabitant parents where the surviving parent is the mother or father of the applicant child: in such circumstances the court is not precluded from making an order in favour of an applicant child under s.117.

26–196 A new s.3A is prospectively inserted by s.69 of the Children and Family Relationships Act 2015, as follows:

"(3A) An order under this section—

(a) where the surviving civil partner is a parent of the child, shall not affect the legal right of that surviving civil partner or any devise or bequest to the civil partner or any share to which the civil partner is entitled on intestacy, or

(b) where the surviving civil partner is not a parent of the child, shall not affect the legal right of the surviving civil partner unless the court, after consideration of all the circumstances, including the testator's financial circumstances and his or her obligations to the surviving civil partner, is of the opinion that it would be unjust not to make the order."[302]

26–197 On the operation of s.117 generally, Kenny J. in *FM v TAM*[303] said:

---

[301] [2005] IEHC 325.

[302] This has yet to be commenced.

[303] (1972) 106 I.L.T.R. 82. See the similar statement by the same judge in *Re Moore, deceased*, unreported, High Court, Kenny J., 2 March 1970, cited in *MacNaghten v Walker* [1976–77] I.L.R.M. 106.

"The existence of a moral duty to make proper provision by will for a child must be judged by the facts existing at the date of death and must depend upon (a) the amount left to the surviving spouse or the value of the legal right if the survivor elects to take this, (b) the number of the testator's children, their ages and their positions in life at the date of the testator's death, (c) the means of the testator, (d) the age of the child whose case is being considered and his or her financial position and prospects in life, (e) whether the testator has already in his lifetime made proper provision for the child."[304]

26–198 In that case the testator had made no provision at all for his adopted son, who at the time of the testator's death was a married man "established in his own profession", had two children of his own and owned his own house. He had never been dependent on the testator. During the testator's life his wife had paid for the son's education, clothing and other incidental expenses. The testator had treated the boy with kindness but had told him he would not inherit the testator's farm in Co. Meath. He had evidently agreed to the boy's adoption to please his wife but had never treated him as his son in reality. The testator left the farm to his executors on trust for his wife for life and after her death to his two nephews. Kenny J. held that the moral duty posited by the section was not absolute and did not inevitably oblige the testator to leave his son anything by will. On the other hand, the fact that the testator honestly believed he had no moral duty to the applicant was not determinative of the matter. Neither was it absolutely necessary that the applicant child be dependent.[305]

26–199 In *Re IAC, deceased*,[306] Finlay C.J. approved of and added to the tests set out by Kenny J. in *FM v TAM*:

1. The phrase "failed in his moral duty to make proper provision for the child in accordance with his means" placed a "relatively high onus of proof [sic][307] on an applicant". It was not enough to show that the provision was "not as great as it might have been, or that compared with generous bequests to the other children or beneficiaries in the will, it appears ungenerous".
2. A court should not alter the terms of the will merely because on the facts as proved the court would most likely have made different provisions.

---

[304] (1972) 106 I.L.T.R. 82 at 87.

[305] More recent judicial pronouncements are consistent with the requirement that some actual need must be demonstrated on the part of the applicant child before the making of an order under s.117 will be contemplated: *Re W, decd.; W v D*, unreported, High Court, Parke J., 28 May 1975; *In the goods of JH, deceased* [1984] I.R. 599; *McC(M) v M(DH)* [2001] IEHC 152; *Re ABC, deceased* [2003] 2 I.L.R.M. 340.

[306] *Re IAC, deceased; CC v WC* [1990] 2 I.R. 143; [1989] I.L.R.M. 815 at 819; *Re PC, a Ward of Court; McGreevy v AC*, unreported, High Court, Carroll J., 10 October 1995.

[307] This should be "degree of proof".

3. Where the relationship between the testator and the children was one of care and kindness, the court should "entertain some significant reluctance" to vary the will.
4. Quite different considerations apply where there was a "marked hostility" between the testator and a particular child.
5. The extent of the moral duty can change between the executing of the will and the testator's death, as for example where an applicant child's marriage breaks down in the meantime and the testator is aware both of the fact of the matrimonial collapse and also that extra provision would be required to enable the child to cope with it.

26–200 In *Re LB, deceased; EB v SS*,[308] the Supreme Court again reviewed the applicable principles under s.117. Delivering the majority judgment, Keane J. observed:

1. An application cannot be defended simply by showing that the testator treated all his or her children equally: proper provision for the applicant child does not necessarily imply equal provision for all children.
2. A failure in moral duty can be found if the testator is shown to have disregarded the special needs (arising either from physical or mental disability) of any one child.
3. The understandable desire of parents to try to avoid friction among their children by treating them all as equally as possible needs to be recognised, although it cannot bind the court in its deliberations upon an application made under s.117.
4. In a situation where the testator seems to have discharged his or her moral duty to a child while alive, the fact that a parent can be expected to know the child better than anyone else can be taken into account in possibly explaining why the testator's earlier behaviour is not replicated in his or her will: a testator may reasonably have felt that further benefaction by will would not have done the child any good.

26–201 In *Re ABC, deceased*,[309] Kearns J. in the High Court set out, by way of summary of the applicable law, a list of principles underpinning the approach to be taken by the courts to an application made under s.117:

---

308 [1998] 2 I.L.R.M. 141.
309 [2003] 2 I.R. 250 at 262–264.

"(a) The social policy underlying s. 117 is primarily directed to protecting those children who are still of an age and situation in life where they might reasonably expect support from their parents, against the failure of parents who are unmindful of their duties in that area.

(b) What has to be determined is whether the testator, at the time of his death, owes any moral obligation to the children and if so, whether he has failed in that obligation.

(c) There is a high onus of proof placed on an applicant for relief under s. 117, which requires the establishment of a positive failure in moral duty.

(d) Before a court can interfere, there must be clear circumstances and a positive failure in moral duty must be established.

(e) The duty created by s. 117 is not absolute.

(f) The relationship of parent and child does not of itself, without regard to other circumstances, create a moral duty to leave anything by will to the child.

(g) Section 117 does not create an obligation to leave something to each child.

(h) The provision of an expensive education for a child may discharge the moral duty as may other gifts or settlements made during the testator's lifetime.

(i) Financing a good education to give a child the best start in life possible and providing money, which, if properly managed, should afford a degree of financial security for the rest of one's life, does amount to making 'proper provision'.

(j) The duty under s. 117 is not to make adequate provision but to make proper provision in accordance with the testator's means.

(k) A just parent must take into account not only his moral obligations to his children and his wife, but all his moral obligations, *e.g.* to aged and infirm parents.

(l) in dealing with a s. 117 application, the position of the applicant child is not to be taken in isolation. The court's duty is to consider the entirety of the testator's affairs and to decide upon the application in the overall context. In other words, while the moral claim of a child may require a testator to make a particular provision for him, the moral claims of others may require such provision to be reduced or omitted altogether.

(m) Special circumstances giving rise to a moral duty may arise if a child is induced to believe that by, for example, working on a farm he will ultimately become the owner of it, thereby causing him to shape his upbringing, training and life accordingly.

(n) Another example of special circumstances might be a child who had a long illness or an exceptional talent which it would be morally wrong not to foster.

(o) Special needs would also include physical or mental disability.

(p) Although the court has very wide powers both as to when to make provision for an applicant child, and as to the nature of such provision, such powers must not be construed as giving the court power to make a new will for the testator.

(q) The test to be applied is not which of the alternative courses open to the testator the court itself would have adopted if confronted with the same situation, but, rather, whether the testator's decision to opt for the course he did, of itself and without more, constituted a breach of moral duty to the plaintiff.

(r) The court must not disregard the fact that parents must be presumed to know their children better than anyone else."[310]

26–202 These tests represent an attempt to confine the jurisdiction of the court to where there is a marked difference between the provisions of the will and the provisions which a court would have substituted on the basis of the "prudent and just parent" test and so prevent a flood of applications under s.117.

The Time of Applying the Tests

26–203 Kenny J. in *FM v TAM*[311] took the view that the proper time to apply the tests of failure in moral duty was the date of the testator's death, not the date on which the will was made. He repeated this view in *Re NSM, deceased*,[312] adding that the testator could also be taken to have knowledge, immediately before the will took effect, of the incidence of taxation on his or her estate and, even more artificially, of the costs of litigation incurred in defending the estate against claims which would in reality be unknown at that time.[313] The notion that the tests under s.117 are applied at the testator's death is certainly consistent with s.89 of the 1965 Act which provides that wills "speak from death".[314] This raises the possibility that a provision which was adequate to discharge the moral duty at the date the testator made the will may cease to be so by the time of the testator's death, or vice versa. For example, a testator might have provided equally for a number of children whose circumstances and needs at the date of the will were approximately equal, but had changed significantly by the time of the testator's death so that one or more had needs greatly in excess of those of the other children, as where one child suffers a catastrophic injury requiring constant medical and nursing care for the remainder of his or her life.

---

[310] Although the list of applicable principles was represented by Kearns J. in *Re ABC, deceased* as having been agreed by counsel, and many of them have been lifted verbatim, or virtually verbatim, from earlier cases in which their relevance was first found applicable, nevertheless this list seems to have been accorded canonical status in subsequent decisions, in many of which either the entire list, or pertinent extracts from it, have been cited by the courts as representing the law to be applied: *H(E) v O'C(PE)*, unreported, High Court, Laffoy J., 28 March 2007; *C(A) (a minor) v F(J)* [2007] IEHC 399; *H (a minor) v H* [2008] IEHC 163.

[311] (1972) 106 I.L.T.R. 82.

[312] (1973) 107 I.L.T.R. 1 at 6.

[313] *Re NSM, deceased* was cited with approval and applied by O'Sullivan J. in *W(C) v W(L)* [2005] IEHC 325.

[314] In *McC(M) v M(DH)* [2001] IEHC 152, McCracken J. observed: "what I have to determine is not whether the testator failed in some way in his moral obligation to the applicants thirty years before his death, but whether, at the time of his death, he owed any moral obligation to the applicants, and if so whether he failed in that obligation. This is the extent of the court's powers under the [1965] Act."

26–204 Alternatively, a testator may make no provision at all for a child either during the testator's life or by will. At the time the will was made this was morally insupportable, but by the time the testator died the child concerned had become a millionaire and had no need of provision, nor would a just and prudent parent have thought it necessary to make any provision for that child.

26–205 In the first case the court would have jurisdiction to intervene. This may be justified on the ground that testators generally retain the power to alter the provisions of their wills up until their death and so the real failure of the testator was the failure to do so; but this is not entirely satisfactory as the testator may have ceased to have the capacity to make a new will by becoming senile, etc. Thus, it indicates that the test becomes somewhat artificial in such circumstances, since the testator has not subjectively failed to understand his or her moral duty. In effect, it gives power to the court to remake a will due to changed circumstances, whether or not the testator was responsible for the failure of the will to provide adequately or justly by the time of his or her death.

26–206 In the second case the court would lack jurisdiction to make provision for the child since at the time of the testator's death there could not be said to be a failure of moral duty, again on the basis of an objective test. In other words, the court would have to take into account, not the testator's actual state of mind or assessment of moral obligations, but what a "prudent and just parent" would have done if he or she had written the will immediately before death.

26–207 In certain circumstances a fluctuation in value, between the date of the will and the date of death, of assets which comprise, wholly or partially, the testator's estate can justify a court's finding that a testator has failed in his or her moral duty to make proper provision for a child in accordance with his or her means under s.117.[315] In *Re W, deceased; W v D*,[316] the testator had made his will in 1962 and died in 1973. Some children had been left farm lands and others not. In the 11 years between the testator's will and his death, the value of farm lands in Co. Meath had risen considerably. The result of this, according to Parke J., was that when the testator died, his will had become a "gross distortion" of his testamentary intentions. The testator was held to have failed in his moral duty to make proper provision for the applicants in accordance with his means.

26–208 It is open to question whether a testator would be held to owe a moral duty to children of whose existence the testator was unaware at his or her death, such as posthumous children or children of a brief liaison. It could be argued that the degree of knowledge attributed to a testator under Kenny J.'s tests in *Re NSM, deceased*[317] includes fictional knowledge of the existence of

---

[315] This principle does not apply to a fluctuation in value between the date of death and the date of the court hearing: *C(A) (a minor) v F(J)* [2007] IEHC 399.
[316] Unreported, High Court, Parke J., 28 May 1975.
[317] (1973) 107 I.L.T.R. 1 at 6.

children. The testator would in any case have been aware that there was a possibility of such children existing.

26–209 The approach generally taken is to regard the function of the court in dealing with an application under s.117 as falling into two stages: to decide whether "a positive failure in moral duty" has been established; and, only in the event that such failure has been established, the nature of the provision to be ordered by the court.[318] Accordingly, where the court decides to make provision for an applicant, having found the testator delinquent in his or her moral duty, it is entitled to have regard to changes in the value of the testator's assets between the time of his or her death and the date of the hearing.[319] There are therefore a number of pertinent matters which may have to be taken into account, as noted by Laffoy J. in *A v C and D*,[320] which include:

1. changed economic circumstances;
2. any variation in the value of assets that comprise the estate;
3. any variation in the capacity of assets forming all or part of an enterprise that has passed on death as a going concern to yield income;
4. relevant regulatory changes (e.g. by EU law in relation to subsidies) which may affect the profitability of any such enterprise between the date of the testator's death and the date of the hearing.

26–210 A variation between the value of the testator's estate as of the date of death and the date of the hearing can be most marked in a case where the national economy has undergone dramatic alteration in that period. This is a factor, as observed by Clarke J. in *C(A) (a minor) v F(J)*,[321] which must be taken into account in the event that a failure of moral duty is found to have occurred, but it cannot in any way justify "hindsight being used in relation to an assessment of the making of proper provision". In other words, regardless of the growth or depression of the value of assets in the estate through corresponding shifts in the national economy, the question of whether the testator's moral duty under s.117 has or has not been satisfied is solely referable to circumstances, including the value of the testator's estate, as of the date of death. Where the court is satisfied that there has been a failure of moral duty by the testator, then, according to Clarke J., the assets as of the date of the hearing "are the pool of resources which are available to make provision for any successful claimant and, indeed, for those who remain entitled to benefit under the will itself".[322]

---

[318] B. Spierin, *The Succession Act 1965 and Related Legislation: A Commentary*, 3rd edn (Dublin: Butterworths, 2003), [700], cited with approval by Laffoy J. in *A v C and D* [2007] IEHC 120.
[319] *MPD v MD* [1981] I.L.R.M. 179.
[320] [2007] IEHC 120.
[321] [2007] IEHC 399.
[322] A similarly dramatic devaluation of the property following the economic crash was seen in *Re MK, dec'd; MK v FD* [2011] IEHC 22.

Substantive Issues

General Considerations

26–211 In *MPD v MD*,[323] Carroll J. laid down a general test of the kind of provision which would be considered proper, which included "provision not only to house, clothe, maintain, feed and educate them and ensure that medical, dental and chemists' bills are provided for", as well as "some provision by way of advancement for them for life."[324] This would, of course, have to be considered in the light of the testator's means, which might not, for example, allow for an advancement for life.

26–212 A testator would not be justified in making a significantly greater provision for marital children as against non-marital children. The Status of Children Act 1987 was enacted in order to avoid discrimination against non-marital children, so it seems unlikely that such a disparity would be held proper. The courts regard marital and non-marital children alike in terms of the needs disclosed in a s.117 application. In *H (a minor) v H*,[325] Sheehan J. found that the testator clearly had not made proper provision for the applicant, a non-marital daughter, in accordance with his means; however, the judge also noted the moral duty owed by the testator to his wife and their two children, the younger of whom had a particular and enduring medical disability which required to be provided for on an ongoing basis. In accordance with s.117(2), the order made by the judge in favour of the applicant took due cognisance of the disclosed need of the younger marital child.

Equal Shares

26–213 A bequest giving equal shares to each child could be impugned by a child with significantly greater needs than the others, such as where he or she needed constant medical care.[326] On the other hand, if the deceased had died intestate, the rules of intestacy would give equal shares to each child and the court would have no jurisdiction to alter them. Section 117 contemplates that an equal division between children may be improper while there is no such possibility recognised on intestacy. The anomaly which exists between testate and intestate succession in this regard could arguably be solved by providing for a jurisdiction of the court to intervene in cases of intestacy where an equal division would not be equitable. Proposals have been made for reform to allow such a jurisdiction to be exercised.[327]

---

[323] [1981] I.L.R.M. 179.

[324] [1981] I.L.R.M. 179 at 189.

[325] [2008] IEHC 163.

[326] See *In the Estate of LB; EB v SS* [1998] 2 I.L.R.M. 141.

[327] See Dáil Debates, 28 October 1987, Col.1692. The Law Reform Commission has recommended such a change: *Report on Land Law and Conveyancing Law* (LRC 30-1989), p.23, and more recently, see Law Reform Commission, *Report on Section 117 of the Succession Act 1965: Aspects of Provision for Children* (LRC 118-2017).

26–214 In *RG v PSG*,[328] Carroll J. entertained an application under s.117 even though the total failure of the testator's will meant that his entire estate passed under the rules governing intestacy. The testator had three children, but left all his property to his wife who predeceased him. Accordingly, his property fell to be distributed on intestacy, which would have given each of the three children an equal share. The applicant son had been encouraged by his father to stay working on the family farm, which he had done for many years without reward. Against the argument that s.117 did not apply because the entire estate had devolved on intestacy, Carroll J. retorted that the state of testacy does not depend on the effectiveness of the terms of the will, but on the effectiveness of the execution of the will, and that once the will has been validly executed, testacy is established, so that the person is deemed to die wholly or partly testate as the case may be. The court awarded to the applicant the deceased's house, and part of his farm, livestock and machinery.

Where No Provision Is Made

26–215 If the testator makes no provision for a child, does this necessarily mean that the testator has failed in his or her moral duty? In *In the goods of JH, deceased*,[329] the testator left his home to his wife for life with remainder to a grandson. He left his farm to one son but made no provision for his other children. The High Court held that while a prudent parent might well decide not to divide the farm but to leave it to one child, it was a failure of his moral duty not to make any provision for his other children.[330] Nevertheless, there are certainly some cases where it seems clear that an application under s.117 will not succeed or may not succeed:

26–216

1. Under the discretion in s.117 itself, a testator may possibly be held to have acted as a just and prudent parent even though no provision was made for a child either by will or during the testator's life, taking into account the factors indicated by Kenny J. in *FM v TAM*. This might apply where one child is wealthy and requires no provision while the others are less so, and taking into account the means of the parent, etc., or where one child has an ongoing health problem which requires the testator to try to make provision into the indefinite future.

26–217 In *McC(M) v M(DH)*,[331] the testator had left money in trust to a daughter who had Down's Syndrome, with remainder after her death to three of his

---

[328] [1980] I.L.R.M. 225.

[329] *In the goods of JH, deceased; MFH v WBH* [1984] I.R. 599.

[330] But see Blayney J. obiter to the contrary in *In the Estate of JH de B* [1991] 2 I.R. 105 (HC), that if the plaintiff had been a farmer, which he was not, he might have had a justifiable complaint in not being given any land.

[331] [2001] IEHC 152.

remaining nine children. McCracken J. noted that only one of the testator's children had been given a third level education and that all of the rest, including the two applicants, had to make their own way in the world and had done so successfully. The two applicants were not among the three who had been bequeathed a remainder interest in the money left in trust for the daughter with Down's Syndrome. McCracken J. held that while the testator could be criticised for his failure to provide for his children during their childhood and early adult years, the question of whether the moral duty had been discharged fell to be decided as at the testator's death, and, in these circumstances, the judge felt that it had been. McCracken J. cited with approval and applied the following pronouncement of Barron J. in *In the goods of JH, deceased*:

> "[T]he court has no power to ensure that all or any particular part of the testator's disposable estate is divided between his children. The power of the court arises only to remedy a failure on the part of the testator to fulfil the moral duty owed towards the child. In general, this will arise where the child has a particular need which the means of the testator can satisfy in whole or in part. If no such need exists, even where no provision has been made by the testator by his will or otherwise, the court has no power to intervene."[332]

26–218

2. The phrase in s.117, "whether by his will or otherwise", indicates that the proper provision may be made in the testator's lifetime and this could justify an absence of provision in the will.

26–219 In *Re LB, deceased*,[333] the Supreme Court held that it was not entitled to take into account facts that had arisen after the testator's death. A posthumous circumstance could only become relevant if the court were to hold that the testator had failed in her moral duty and was then considering the extent of the provision that should be made for the applicant. The court also held that the fact that a testator has treated all of his or her children equally is not an answer to an application under s.117, since a testator was not free to disregard the special needs of one of his or her children, e.g. due to physical or mental disability. The desire of parents to avoid friction among their children by treating them equally must be recognised. In this case, generous financial provision was made for the plaintiff during the testator's life. She had to decide whether to make further provision for him in the hope that this time it would not be dissipated, or whether to give it to more deserving causes. Moreover, the testator might have taken the view that to make further provision for the plaintiff, even by way of trust, might not be in his best interests, given his drug and alcohol dependency issues. This was clearly a view which a responsible and concerned

[332] [1984] I.R. 599 at 608.
[333] *Re LB; EB v SS* [1998] 2 I.L.R.M. 141.

parent could take. The court held that in the circumstances there had been no breach of moral duty.

26–220 The court also held that while the plaintiff's mother might be regarded as being under a moral duty to make some provision for the plaintiff's children, that was not a matter which the court could take into account under s.117. Barron J., dissenting, while of the view that the plaintiff had been a "feckless character", expressed the opinion that his mother had a moral duty to make some provision in favour of the plaintiff so as to enable him to fulfil his obligations to his dependants. One might point out that even if the testator had made additional provision for the plaintiff with the notion of enabling him to provide for her grandchildren, there was no guarantee, given his history, that he would have applied the benefaction received in this intended way. Of course, the testator could have made specific provision for her grandchildren, in the form of a trust set up for their benefit, but her failure to do so could not be challenged by the grandchildren who have no claim under s.117. It is arguable that they should be able to claim.

26–221

3. It follows from s.117(3) that where the testator has bequeathed all his or her property to the surviving spouse and that spouse is the father or mother of the applicant child, the child is debarred from claiming. Similarly under s.117(3A) where the testator has bequeathed all of his or her property to a civil partner, except that the court has a discretion, having regard to all the circumstances, including the testator's financial circumstances and his or her obligations to the surviving civil partner, to make an order under the section in favour of an applicant child where it finds that there has been a failure in the testator's moral duty.

26–222

4. Under s.120, where the child has caused the death of the testator by murder or manslaughter, or had attempted to murder the testator, a claim is barred, unless the will was made subsequent to the act constituting the offence.

Behaviour towards Parent

26–223 Behaviour towards the parent by the applicant child can be relevant for determining whether there has been a failure of moral duty. In *McDonald v Norris*,[334] the relationship between the deceased and his son was very poor. The Supreme Court held that the extent to which bad feeling between parent and child affected the moral duty under s.117 to make proper provision for that child in accordance with the testator's means must depend upon the particular

---

[334] [1999] 4 I.R. 301.

circumstances of each individual case. Barron J. observed that the moral duty commenced at the child's birth and expired only with the life of the testator "unless in the meantime it has been satisfied or extinguished". In this case, even though the applicant's conduct towards his father was "very bad", it could be extenuated by the passing from father to son of genetic traits of "uncompromising stubbornness" which would not be likely to be replicated in dealings by either with a stranger. Furthermore, the father's behaviour to the son was less than exemplary. Barron J. ordered that the entirety of the testator's lands, bequeathed on trust to the defendant's daughter, be transferred to the applicant.

Other Moral Obligations

26–224 In determining whether the testator failed in his or her moral duty to an applicant child, the court should take into account *all* of the testator's moral duties. The testator may have moral duties to persons who could not themselves claim under s.117.

26–225 In *L v L*,[335] the testator was survived by his wife and children of his first marriage and by a woman and children of a union which the parties to it had apparently considered to be a second marriage. Costello J. held that the court should take into account all of the testator's moral obligations and that these included moral obligations to his non-marital children,[336] to parents,[337] and to persons with whom the testator had lived as husband and wife, whether or not the relationship constituted a marriage in law.[338] In relation to his own children, it might be right to make greater provision for some children than others based upon their needs, as where a child had a special talent which it would be morally wrong to ignore, or where one child had a disability and was in need of special medical care.[339]

26–226 In *Re ABC, deceased*,[340] in a s.117 claim by the children of the testator's first marriage, Kearns J. held that the moral duty owed by the testator to his aged mother and also to his second wife (even though she took by survivorship a "fine house" in which he had lived with her and also an income from property management) "must be taken into account when assessing the moral duty owed by the testator to his children". In *C(A) (a minor) v F(J)*,[341] Clarke J. held that the moral duty owed by a testator to the mother of his six-year-old non-marital daughter had to be taken into account to determine what order should be made in favour of that daughter where a failure of the testator's moral duty to his daughter (and also to an older non-marital daughter by a different mother) had been found to have occurred. According to

---

[335] [1978] I.R. 288.
[336] [1978] I.R. 288 at 293 and 294.
[337] [1978] I.R. 288 at 294.
[338] [1978] I.R. 288 at 296.
[339] [1978] I.R. 288 at 294.
[340] [2003] 2 I.R. 250.
[341] [2007] IEHC 399.

Clarke J., "the class of those to whom a moral duty may be owed can go beyond the class of those who might be entitled to make a legal claim on the estate if the deceased did not make provision, or proper provision, for them", and "may include, in an appropriate case, a joint parent of a child or children who remain in need of significant care". In this case, it was recognised that the care of the applicant daughter, then aged six, would devolve upon her mother for some considerable time to come. The mother of the elder daughter had since remarried and her daughter by the testator lived with her and her husband and the children of their marriage. Although Clarke J. also held that the testator had failed in his moral duty towards the elder non-marital daughter, he did not make a finding that a moral duty was owed by the testator to the elder daughter's mother.

26–227 In *In the Estate of JH de B, deceased*,[342] Blayney J. held that it was relevant to consider an obligation arising from the deceased's having created or encouraged an expectation in one child that some of the deceased's property would be given to that child. The testator's sole assets here consisted of his farm, machinery and stock. He also had debts. He bequeathed the farm to his wife for life with remainder to his eldest son, who at the testator's request had lived on the farm, together with his family, for a number of years prior to the testator's death. The testator had charged his funeral expenses and other legacies on the farm. In rejecting an application made by one of the three other children, Blayney J. held that the testator had already made proper provision for the applicant, and that it would be unfair, the testator having encouraged his eldest son to live with him, and having to that son's knowledge always intended to leave the farm to him, to deny to him the fruits of his expectation. Claims under s.117 brought by the two remaining children, which had been settled prior to hearing, had resulted in the settlement amounts being charged on the eldest son's remainder interest. Blayney J. expressed the view that it would be unfair for that remainder interest to be burdened with yet further sums and declined to make any order in favour of the applicant.

26–228 *In the Estate of JH de B, deceased* suggests that evidence which might fail if founding a claim based on proprietary estoppel might succeed as part of the evidence required under s.117. Sometimes a claim could be made under both heads, whereas in the past only a claim under s.117 would have been made, as for example in *MacNaughton v Walker*,[343] which involved allegations that the testator had induced a child to believe that he would be left a stud farm and that the child had shaped his life accordingly by training in stud management. On the other hand, the fact that a beneficiary had been promised the land

---

[342] [1991] 2 I.R. 105.
[343] [1976–77] I.L.R.M. 106.

by the testator and had relied on it by expending labour on the land or looking after the testator might be a reason for leaving the will intact.[344]

Provision for Child by Others

26–229 There are inconsistent judicial pronouncements as to whether provision made for an applicant child, either actually or potentially, by another party can be taken into account in determining failure by the testator to make proper provision for the child in accordance with his or her means. Much depends on the child's circumstances, and whether any current need is likely to be ongoing, and also the reasonableness or otherwise of the testator's being seen to rely upon bounty from another source. It is also possible that, where failure of moral duty has been found, the extent of relief to be ordered by the court for an applicant child will be tempered by awareness of the availability of assistance from elsewhere.

26–230 The courts tend to be critical of parents who fail to provide for children with physical or mental disabilities. _HL v Bank of Ireland_[345] involved an applicant child with serious mental illness. In considering whether a discretionary trust should be established in order to provide for the applicant's medical needs as they arose, Costello J. formed the view that private institutional care was more appropriate to the moral duty owed by the testator towards his child than the services of a regional health board which would have been far less costly. In deciding that a discretionary trust ought to be set up, Costello J. noted, in reducing a legacy to a grandchild so as to facilitate it, that that grandchild had a significant entitlement from the estate of her own parents.[346]

26–231 As against this, the courts can be more indulgent where the discharge of the testator's moral duty stands to be qualified by anticipated or actual benefaction of an applicant child by a legacy from another source. In _Re NSM, deceased_,[347] a testator had excluded his married daughters from his will on the basis that they had been well provided for by legacies from other relatives. According to Kenny J., while this was a factor that could be taken into account, it did not itself absolve the testator from his moral duty to make provision for them in accordance with his means. On the other hand, in _Re ABC, deceased_,[348] Kearns J. took judicial note of the fact that, by reason of the testator's predeceasing his own mother, who then died prior to the hearing, the testator's children had received moneys under a trust established by their grandfather, and also that money would accrue to them on foot of a further trust, set up by their father for their mother, whenever she died. Kearns J. held that the testator

---

[344] _Re PC, a Ward of Court; McGreevy v AC_, unreported, High Court, Carroll J., 10 October 1995.
[345] [1978] I.L.R.M. 160.
[346] In _Re Looney, deceased_, unreported, High Court, 2 November 1970, Kenny J. applied similar reasoning.
[347] (1973) 107 I.L.T.R. 1.
[348] [2003] 2 I.R. 250.

had not failed in his moral duty towards his children by setting up a discretionary trust from which they had the potential eventually to benefit. Applying a like logic, in *C(K) v F(C)*[349] the order made by Carroll J. took into account the fact that the sole beneficiary among 11 children had charged himself with trustee-type responsibilities towards the others.

26–232 In *C(A) (a minor) v F(J)*,[350] Clarke J. held that, to a limited extent, a bequest made by a testator to the mother of a non-marital daughter could be taken into account in terms of the order to be made in favour of the daughter, failure in the testator's moral duty to the child having been found. Although the bequest to her mother had not been attached by the testator with an obligation to apply any of it on behalf of their daughter, the judge's finding was based upon "the practical reality ... that the standard of living and care which [the plaintiff] will receive over the next significant number of years is largely dependent on the standard of living that will be available collectively to her and her mother and in those circumstances I am satisfied that it is appropriate to have regard to any bequest to the mother ... which is not abated as a result of these proceedings." Clarke J. emphasised that this observation was in no way to attenuate the extent of the moral duty by the testator towards his daughter.

26–233 In *W(C) v W(L)*,[351] O'Sullivan J. applied "prescient foreknowledge" to hold that a testator could reasonably have anticipated that a bequest to the applicant daughter by his wife, the daughter's mother, under a will made concurrently with the testator's own will, would be substantially supplemented by the circumstance that the mother would become non compos mentis and, following the testator's death, be made a ward of court, and that the Solicitor General, being appointed her committee, would seek on her behalf to elect to claim her legal right share against the testator's estate under the 1965 Act. The effect of this was that the applicant daughter, in due course inheriting one-third of her mother's estate, would stand to come into a far greater legacy than if her mother had remained compos mentis and had elected to take her inheritance under her late husband's will instead of the legal right share. The test to be applied, according to O'Sullivan J., was objective rather than subjective,[352] and fell to be satisfied with reference to the events that had actually taken place rather than what the testator might, from his own personal knowledge of his wife's character, have expected to happen. The result of this was that the

---

[349] [2003] IEHC 109.
[350] [2007] IEHC 399.
[351] [2005] IEHC 325.
[352] Following Keane J. in *JR v JR*, unreported, High Court, 13 November 1979. Applying this principle, O'Sullivan J. observed: "If the test were a subjective one it could well be said in the present case that the testator well knew that his wife would never claim her legal right share and would accept his will. Objectively, however, he must in my view of the authorities be credited with the foreknowledge that she would be taken into wardship and that her committee would, on her behalf, elect to take her legal right, one-third share of his estate."

testator was held to have failed rather less in the discharge of his moral duty than would otherwise have been the case, with a concomitant modification of the order made in favour of the applicant daughter by the court.

Who Are "the Other Children"?

26–234 Section 117(2) provides that in considering an application "from the point of view of a prudent and just parent", the court must arrive "at a decision that will be as fair as possible to the child to whom the application relates and to the other children." In *In the goods of JH, deceased*,[353] Barron J. interpreted "other children" to mean any other applicant child of the testator under s.117 whose claim was not being considered in the instant case or any child inheriting under the will, but not children who were neither claimants under s.117 nor beneficiaries. According to him, "the Court should not be required to take into account provision, or lack of provision, made for children not in either of these categories".

26–235 This is an unduly restrictive interpretation, since a child to whom a bequest has not been made and who is not an applicant under s.117 may be indirectly affected by a court order under s.117 in a way that would not be "fair" to that child.[354] This could arise, for example, where a child who was neither a s.117 claimant nor a beneficiary under the will was residing with or being maintained by a child who *was* a beneficiary whose ongoing capacity to provide for that other child might be diminished by the court's order. It is clear that such a concern was active in Carroll J.'s judgment in *C(K) v F(C)*.[355] The testator had 11 children and left all her property to one son. Two only of the remaining children instituted s.117 proceedings. One of these two, a daughter, had lived with and cared for their mother. The universal legatee and devisee indicated through his solicitor that he regarded himself as in effect a trustee for the rest of the children, although there was disagreement among the family as to the intended division of the property. At the time of the testator's death this son had been living in a caravan in the yard of her home. The applicant daughter who had lived with and cared for their mother had been obliged in the meantime to leave the house, and after a succession of indifferent accommodations, was living with another brother on a halting site. Carroll J. held that a secret trust had not been created, but that the self-declared fiduciary role assumed by the universal devisee and legatee had to be taken into account in any order made by the court. In the event that he took steps to honour his declared trust, the non-applicant brothers and sisters, despite not being beneficiaries under the will, would inevitably be affected by the exercise of the court's power. Citing Barron J.'s judgment in *In the goods of JH, deceased*, to the effect that the "other children" of whom the court is obliged to take account

---

[353] *In the goods of JH, deceased; MFH v WBH* [1984] I.R. 599.
[354] Spierin, *Succession Act 1965* (2017).
[355] [2003] IEHC 109.

are confined to applicants and beneficiaries, Carroll J. concluded that this did not apply to a case that involved "special circumstances". Accepting that the universal devisee was holding the money on a "solemn trust for his brothers and sisters", Carroll J. stated that she could *neither* limit her consideration to the two applicants and the universal devisee alone, *nor* regard an 11th share in the money as proper provision for the two applicants. Accordingly, the judge awarded €100,000 to the one daughter and €200,000 to the daughter who had lived with and looked after the testator. Interestingly, Carroll J. observed that she had considered awarding the daughter who had lived in the house a life interest in it, but concluded that this would not be an "ideal arrangement" if the daughter got to remain in the house while her brother had to bivouac in a caravan in the yard, and expressed the hope that the larger amount awarded to this daughter would enable her to "provide herself with reasonable accommodation".

Status of Children Act 1987

26–236 The Status of Children Act 1987 provides[356] that non-marital children may apply under s.117 irrespective of whether the testator executed the will before or after the Act came into force, but it confers no right to apply under s.117 in the case of the wills of testators who had died before the Act came into force.[357]

Time Limits

26–237 A s.117 application must be made within six months of first taking out representation to the deceased's estate.[358] This means that an application cannot be made under the section *prior* to extracting a grant of administration. Furthermore, the time limit applies to the first taking out of representation and so cannot be artificially extended by the later taking out of another grant of administration if the estate has been left wholly or partially unadministered under the first grant.

26–238 Since s.117 applications will normally be made by children, the question arises whether the minority of the applicant is a disability which has the effect of extending the time limit. Section 127 of the 1965 Act provides that s.49 of the Statute of Limitations 1957 "shall have effect in relation to an action in respect of a claim to the estate of a deceased person or to any share in such estate, whether under a will, on intestacy or as a legal right", as if three years were substituted for the six years mentioned in the section. If this applied to applications under s.117, then it would override the six months provision in the section itself and substitute for it the period of three years from the time

---

[356] Succession Act 1965 s.117(1A)(a), inserted by Status of Children Act 1987 s.31.

[357] Succession Act 1965 s.117(1A)(b).

[358] Succession Act 1965 s.117(6), amended by Family Law (Divorce) Act 1996 s.46. The limitation period runs from the time a grant of probate or a grant of letters of administration has issued. See *Re F, dec'd* [2013] IEHC 407.

the disability came to an end. The issue was whether a s.117 application could come within the phrase "a claim ... under a will, on intestacy or as a legal right". Carroll J. in *MPD v MD*[359] held that it could not. A s.117 application could not, in her view, be described as a claim to a legal right which the judge took to refer exclusively to the spouse's legal right.[360]

Imaginative Judicial Remedies

26–239 Section 117(1) provides that the court, if satisfied that the testator has failed in his or her moral duty to make proper provision for the applicant in accordance with his or her means, whether by will or otherwise, "may order that such provision shall be made for the child out of the estate as the court thinks just". This confers a large measure of discretion, which in many cases has been amply exercised. A classic instance is *HL v Bank of Ireland*.[361] In this case there had been an atrocious history of neglect and abuse by the testator of his family, and one of the children had a serious mental health affliction. Costello J. determined that the most effective way to produce a just outcome was to set up a discretionary trust in which all of the children were beneficiaries but the needs of the schizophrenic child were to be given paramount attention.

26–240 It seems, however, that a discretionary trust set up by the testator may incur the charge that, depending on the expression of wishes that accompanies it, it represents an evasion, rather than a discharge, of the testator's moral responsibility. In *Re ABC, deceased*,[362] a case in which the testator had set up a discretionary trust in consultation with his solicitor in order, inter alia, to deal with the possibility of claims under s.117, Kearns J. observed that "when a testator by his will creates a discretionary trust ... cases are bound to arise where the court may find it difficult, or even impossible, to determine if a testator who by so acting leaves it, in effect, to others to determine the apportionment of his assets, either between his children inter se, or between his children and others, has or has not discharged his moral duty under section 117." The judge observed that this was more likely to present a problem if the testator had not made provision for his children by way of advancement or other help during his lifetime. It can be particularly invidious if the children have to "sit back and

---

[359] [1981] I.L.R.M. 179.

[360] One wonders, in this case, why s.121(5), in dealing with an application under that section by a spouse, refers to a period of one year from taking out representation, but in the case of an application by a child, makes separate reference to an application under s.117. Until its amendment by s.46 of the Family Law (Divorce) Act 1996, the time limit under s.117 was also one year; why, therefore, does s.121(5) distinguish the two cases into two separate sub-clauses? Clarke J. stated in *LC (a minor) v HS* [2014] IEHC 32 that in an appropriate case, in order to ensure that proper provision has been made for the child of a testator in accordance with s.117, the court could grant an order under s.121 "as part of its inherent jurisdiction to provide just relief, even if no such claim was made".

[361] [1978] I.L.R.M. 160.

[362] [2003] 2 I.R. 250.

await the passage of time to see if the trust arrangements unfold in line with their hopes and expectations".

26–241 Perhaps the most versatile instance of the court's employing a veritable medley of mechanisms to come up with a just result is presented by *In the goods of JH, deceased.*[363] The testator had bequeathed a bungalow to his wife for life, with remainder to a grandson, and the residue of his estate, including a farm, to one of his nine children. Four of the remaining children also lived on the farm and took a claim under s.117. Finding that the testator had failed in his moral duty to the four applicant children, Barron J. ordered that:

- each applicant child be given a licence to reside on the farm for life or until marriage;
- in the event of marriage by any of the applicants, he or she was to be given a site on which to build a house;
- one of the applicants who had a disability was to have an exclusive licence to reside in part of the property along with such other of the applicants as might look after her, who was also to have an exclusive licence;
- the applicant with disability was to be paid maintenance by the son who was the testator's residuary devisee for as long as she remained unemployed and not in receipt of social welfare;
- each applicant and also the residuary devisee were to be paid one-fifth of the proceeds of sale if the property became development land and was sold;
- for as long as the residuary devisee used the lands for farming he was to pay a conacre rent to the applicants.

The Least Changes as Are Necessary

26–242 Despite the power granted to the court to make, in effect, any order it pleases, once a failure in moral duty on the part of a testator has occurred in a case to which s.117 applies, there has emerged a judicial tendency to make the least changes necessary to a will in order to achieve a result that is "as fair as possible to the child to whom the application relates and to the other children". In addition to the often-stated dictum that it is not the function of the court to seek to rewrite the testator's will, Herbert J. in *H(E) v O'C(PE)*[364] stated:

"[I]t is very important for the court, in determining the issues arising, consistent with its paramount duty of acting justly, fairly and impartially, to avoid to the greatest extent possible perpetuating or deepening any feelings of suspicion or hostility which this litigation has engendered amongst the family members."

---

[363] *In the goods of JH, deceased; MFH v WBH* [1984] I.R. 599.
[364] [2007] IEHC 68.

26–243 Sometimes, however, if the court finds the will to be flagrantly unfair, little will be left of it after the court has exercised its discretion. In *Re B, deceased; K v D*,[365] the testator, who had brutalised his children, bequeathed the greater part of his property to his niece and another woman. Kearns J. granted the entire estate to the applicant children, leaving only a modicum for the niece, stated to be on the basis of services rendered to the testator in his final years, and nothing to the other woman. A case more typical of the contemporary approach is *S(D) v M(K)*,[366] in which a testator, a farmer, who had two children, each with different disabilities, bequeathed different properties of varying values to each of them, and Carroll J. found it possible to rectify the inequity disclosed by making merely a minor adjustment to the will. Carroll J. found that the testator in his will had tried to balance his moral duty to each child, recognising that the greater duty was owed to the son on account of his more severe illness. Nevertheless, Carroll J. held that there had been a failure in the testator's moral duty towards his daughter, because the particular folio of land from which she was to take a building site was subject to a covenant that the land (which comprised about an acre) could not be used other than for the purpose of accommodating a single private dwelling house. Since the size of the site bequeathed to the daughter was not defined, and on account of the covenant the brother could not use what was left of the land for any purpose, Carroll J. held that justice would best be served by transferring the entire folio to the daughter and not making any other adjustments whatsoever.

26–244 In *H(E) v O'C(PE)*,[367] the applicant was a single mother who had long suffered from low self-esteem, compounded by consciousness that the second of her two children had not been accepted by the applicant's own mother, the testator. The applicant had a sister and two brothers. In finding that a failure in her moral duty by the testator to the applicant had occurred, Herbert J. expressed awareness, in anticipation of making any order, of the costs of administration of the estate, the amount of the deceased's debts and funeral expenses, the costs of the court action which would be borne by the estate, the cost of land sales and the sum likely to have to be paid for capital gains tax on a disposal of any land included in the estate.[368] The court then directed that the last will and testament of the testator be altered to the extent that a tract of land bequeathed to a son be instead transferred to the plaintiff, excepting a portion of it on which that son had built a house, and that this land be charged with payment of moneys to that son and the other son within a period of five years; that a piece of land bequeathed to the other son be appropriated for the payment of all debts, funeral, testamentary and administration expenses, including the costs of the instant proceedings; and in the event of this being insufficient, the shortfall to be made good out of the property bequeathed to the plaintiff and her sister.

---

[365] Unreported, High Court, Kearns J., 8 December 2000.
[366] [2003] IEHC 120.
[367] [2007] IEHC 68.
[368] In *H (a minor) v H* [2008] IEHC 163, Sheehan J. expressed similar sensitivity to the accrual of capital gains tax liability on the disposal of a farm which formed part of the estate.

26–245 A similar sensitivity to tampering with the testator's chosen benefaction was demonstrated by Laffoy J. in *A v C and D*.[369]

26–246 Sometimes, a court, in weighing up the testator's moral duties in the context of the specific provisions of his will and the differing circumstances of his various dependents, can produce an outcome that is fair both to the applicant child and any other children, with mathematical precision, as in Clarke J.'s decision in *C(A) (a minor) v F(J)*.[370]

The Policy Basis of Section 117

26–247 The decision in *FM v TAM*[371] prompts some conclusions as to the meaning and purpose of s.117. It is worthwhile considering some alternative policies on which it might be argued that the section is based:

1. There is a moral requirement on the testator to provide for dependants.[372] It is not necessary in order to succeed under the section for an applicant child to prove that he or she was dependent on the testator at the time of the testator's death, although some element of need, whether financial, medical or emotional, is likely to be required to be demonstrated before a "positive failure in moral duty" will be found to have occurred. The child in *FM v TAM* was not dependent and yet succeeded in an application under s.117.

2. There is a moral requirement on the testator to provide for blood relatives, i.e. a blood is thicker than water principle. The decision in *FM v TAM* is against such a policy. The child in that case was not a blood relative, but had been adopted, and yet succeeded under s.117. Moreover, in holding that the testator had not made proper provision in the circumstances of that case, Kenny J. necessarily accepted that the testator was not justified in preferring his nephews to his adopted son, evidently on the ground that the nephews were related by blood. On the other hand, the fact that "parents and children have the same genes and that an uncompromising stubbornness in the one is likely to be mirrored in the other" enabled Barron J. in the Supreme Court in *McDonald v Norris*[373] to hold that deplorable conduct exhibited by the applicant to the testator, which perhaps "would not have been the same had a stranger been involved", did not disentitle the applicant to relief under s.117, having regard to the history of hostility between them as disclosed by the facts of the case.

---

[369] [2007] IEHC 120.

[370] [2007] IEHC 399.

[371] (1972) 106 I.L.T.R. 82.

[372] This is, in essence, the policy basis for s.117 identified by Kearns J. in clause (a) of his summation titled "The Law" in *Re ABC, deceased* [2003] 2 I.R. 250 at 262–264.

[373] [1999] 4 I.R. 301, overruling McCracken J. in the High Court: [1999] I.L.R.M. 270. See also, O. Breen, "Children These Days – Section 117 of the Succession Act 1965 and the Moral Obligations of Parenthood" in O. Breen, J. Casey and A. Kerr (eds), *Liber Memorialis: Professor James C. Brady* (Dublin: Round Hall Sweet & Maxwell, 2001), p.72.

3. It is a public policy that the State should not have to provide for people who can be provided for by their own family. This policy seeks to protect the Welfare State against unnecessary claims. Although taxpayers may be under a moral duty to provide for members of society who cannot provide for themselves, where parents can provide they should do so. Again, this does not seem an adequate explanation of s.117, since the child does not have to establish that, but for the provision which he or she claims, that child would be a charge on State funds. Kenny J. perhaps suggests that this is an explanation for the New Zealand, Australian and English legislation, but it is doubtful whether it is any more satisfactory as an explanation in their case either.

4. To allow a testator to ignore completely members of his or her family would weaken the nuclear family as a social unit and would be unconstitutional. This, on the face of it, is more likely, given the importance which Art.41 of the Constitution attaches to the family as a social unit. One may note that the effect here of the Status of Children Act 1987 is that the right to apply under s.117 is no longer confined to the family based on marriage, which the Irish courts have traditionally held to be the constitutional family.[374]

5. The section aims to promote kinship solidarity by reducing feelings of resentment between children of the same parent.[375] We have argued that such policy in favour of kinship solidarity can be detected in other areas, such as the class-closing rules. It can be argued that in that context, the policy takes second place to a policy favouring the right to deal freely with property on the part of persons entitled to such interests, where the two policies conflict. There is no possibility of such a conflict in the context of s.117 and so the law may favour kinship solidarity. There may be a policy conflict of another kind: between the policy of kinship solidarity and the policy of carrying out the testator's intention. In this case the legislature decided in favour of reducing tensions between living persons in preference to giving effect to the wishes of the testator.

---

[374] *State (Nicolaou) v An Bord Uchtála* [1966] I.R. 567.

[375] Though not articulated in such terms in the course of his judgment, the painstaking care and explicitness with which Clarke J. in *C(A) (a minor) v F(J)* [2007] IEHC 399 apportioned the bulk of the available assets in the estate between the applicant, then aged six, and her sister, then aged 20, both being the testator's non-marital children by different mothers, is demonstrably consistent with a policy concern for kinship solidarity.

Proposed Reforms to Section 117

26–248 Given the changed demographics since the 1960s, s.117 of the 1965 Act has been the subject of scrutiny in recent years.[376] In its 2017 report on s.117,[377] the Law Reform Commission proposed some radical changes.[378] One of the core principles underlying the Commission's recommendations is a reaffirmation of testamentary freedom, and a move away from a presumption of entitlement to inherit. It recommended that the reference to "moral duty" be removed from the section, but that the court still continue to determine whether "proper provision" has been made for the child. The Commission recommended that a starting point in cases of this kind should be a presumption that a parent has properly provided for his or her child, if the child is aged over 18, or over 23 if in full-time education. This presumption could be rebutted on three grounds:

"(a) The applicant has a particular financial need, including such need by reason of the applicant's health or decision-making capacity;
(b) The estate contains an object of particular sentimental value to the applicant; or
(c) The applicant has relinquished or, as the case may be, had foregone the opportunity of remunerative activity in order to provide support or care for the testator or intestate during the testator's or the intestate's lifetime."[379]

26–249 These are intended to be narrowly drafted, reflecting a view that "it should only be in specific exceptional cases" that adult children "are awarded something out of the estate of their parents". The first and third grounds are in line with principles which have developed in other areas of property law and family law, for which there are well-developed tests, legal standards and precedents. Arguably the second ground, that of an item being of "sentimental value", is something of an outlier, in that it is rather vaguely defined and open to potential abuse.

---

[376] Law Reform Commission, *Issues Paper on Section 117 of the Succession Act 1965* (LRC IP 9-2016). Similar demographic trends have led to re-examinations of equivalent legal provisions by law reform bodies elsewhere over the past decade or so: England and Wales (Law Commission for England and Wales, *Intestacy and Family Provision Claims on Death* (Law Com. 31-2011)), Scotland (Scottish Law Commission, *Report on Succession* (Scottish Law Com. 215-2009)), New South Wales (New South Wales Law Reform Commission, *Uniform Succession Laws: Intestacy* (116-2007)) and British Columbia (British Columbia Law Institute, *Wills, Estates and Succession: A Modern Legal Framework* (45-2006)).

[377] Law Reform Commission, *Report on Section 117 of the Succession Act 1965: Aspects of Provision for Children* (LRC 118-2017).

[378] The possible implications, as outlined in the Issues Paper, for the rights of surviving spouses is considered by K. O'Sullivan, "Reform of Section 117 of the Succession Act 1965: Implications and Opportunities for the Protection of Surviving Spouses" (2017) 22(1) C.P.L.J. 9.

[379] Law Reform Commission, *Report on Section 117* (LRC 118-2017), para.2.208.

26–250 The Commission also recommended that, where a claim under s.117 is successful, the relief granted should be limited to that necessary to remedy the specific failure of duty identified in the proceedings.[380] It recommended the repeal of s.67A(3)–(7) and the extension of s.117 to include the children of intestates.[381] It recommended that a court should protect the legal right share of a surviving spouse who is not the parent of the child making the application.[382]

26–251 The Commission considered the issue of time limits under s.117, and recommended that it should continue to provide that an order shall not be made except on an application made within six months of the date of the first taking out of representation of the deceased's estate.[383] It recommended that no amendment should be made to impose a duty on personal representatives of a deceased person to notify potential claimants of their right to make an application under s.117.[384]

Disinheritance
26–252 Section 121 of the 1965 Act controls dispositions made within three years of death and intended to disinherit a spouse, civil partner or children.

Time Limits
26–253 The court may make an order (a) in the interest of the deceased's spouse or personal representative, within one year of the taking out of representation, or (b) in the interest of a child, on a s.117 application.[385]

Scope
26–254 Section 121 deals with attempts by a testator, or an intestate, to disinherit his or her spouse or civil partner or children. The section applies to "a disposition of property (other than a testamentary disposition or a disposition to a purchaser) under which the beneficial ownership of the property vests in possession in the donee within three years before the death of the person who made it or on his [or her] death or later".[386] The words seem apt to include a *donatio mortis causa*. In fact, the section would seem to catch all such gifts, no matter when the "subject matter" was transferred and the words of gift spoken, because a *donatio* only vests the beneficial ownership, in the sense of the equitable interest, in the donee at a moment immediately preceding the deceased's death.

---

[380] Law Reform Commission, *Report on Section 117* (LRC 118-2017), para.2.210.
[381] Law Reform Commission, *Report on Section 117* (LRC 118-2017), paras 3.52 and 3.54.
[382] Law Reform Commission, *Report on Section 117* (LRC 118-2017), para.3.67.
[383] Law Reform Commission, *Report on Section 117* (LRC 118-2017), para.4.65.
[384] Law Reform Commission, *Report on Section 117* (LRC 118-2017), para.4.116.
[385] Succession Act 1965 s.121(5).
[386] Succession Act 1965 ss.121(1) and 111A.

26–255 The section also contains an element of "overreaching" in that, if the donee has sold the property, the court order will be made against the consideration given by the purchaser in the hands of the donee.[387]

26–256 Where an application is made by a child, it seems that a combined application should be made under ss.117 and 121 together.[388] This does not, however, mean that a child can only challenge a disposition under s.121 if the donor died testate, because, as Carroll J. has pointed out, an application under s.121 has the effect, if successful, of deeming the disposition to have been made by will.[389] The applicant here gets the benefit of two fictions. The first is the statutory fiction that the disposition is made by will and the second is the declaratory theory of case law which in this instance maintains that a successful application was based upon grounds which were valid at the time the application was made.

Effect
26–257 If the court is satisfied that the disposition was made in order to defeat or substantially diminish the share of the spouse or civil partner, whether as a legal right or on intestacy, or the share of a child on intestacy, or to leave a child insufficiently provided for, the court may order that the disposition be deemed to be a disposition by will, whether the maker of the disposition died testate or intestate.[390] The court may also order that the disposition, or part of it, shall be deemed never to have had any effect and the donee of the property, or any person claiming through the donee, shall be a debtor of the estate for such an amount as the court may direct.[391] The court may also make such further orders as may seem "just and equitable having regard to the provisions and the spirit of this Act and to all the circumstances".[392]

Criticism
26–258 Section 121 is limited to dispositions which seek to disinherit the deceased's spouse or children, but since it applies where the deceased died intestate, the person entitled to the deceased's estate on his or her death may be neither a spouse nor a child, but remoter issue, such as a grandchild, or a collateral relation such as a cousin and this situation might have been foreseen by the deceased before he or she died. There is nothing in such a case to prevent a person disinheriting these remoter relations. This result may well have been intentional. It can be argued that while remoter issue may expect to inherit from a person who has neither spouse nor child, the deceased in such a case has no moral obligation to provide for them and so they correspondingly have

---

[387] Succession Act 1965 ss.121(8) and 111A.
[388] *MPD v MD* [1981] I.L.R.M. 179. Carroll J. concluded that this was the effect of s.121(5)(b).
[389] *MPD v MD* [1981] I.L.R.M. 179.
[390] Succession Act 1965 ss.121(2) and 111A.
[391] Succession Act 1965 ss.121(3) and 111A.
[392] Succession Act 1965 ss.121(4) and 111A.

no right to complain if the deceased chose to deprive them of their expectation. This result can also be seen as an example of how the law in this society concentrates moral obligations on the nuclear family at the expense of a wider "extended family" concept found in some other societies.

INFORMAL OR NON-TESTAMENTARY SUCCESSION

Contracts
Contract by Testator
26–259 A contract to make[393] or not to revoke a will may be enforced against a deceased person's personal representatives by an action for damages or for specific performance.[394] The revocation of a will even in breach of contract is still effective: the remedy is a contractual one imposed on the deceased's personal representatives.

Mutual Wills
26–260 Although this doctrine is usually referred to as "mutual wills", it actually refers to the effect of an *agreement* to make mutual wills. Like some other equitable doctrines, it can be traced to a single case, in this instance Lord Camden's decision in *Dufour v Pereira*[395] in 1769. As Lord Haldane expressed it in *Gray v Perpetual Trustee Co Ltd*,[396] if there is a "clear agreement", in the wills or elsewhere, that they are to be mutually binding (whether or not that is expressed in language of revocation), then there is a "floating trust", which becomes irrevocable on the death of the first testator and crystallises on the death of the second.

26–261 The doctrine applies when two people (usually, but not necessarily, spouses) make wills in which they each leave their property to the survivor of them with remainders over, usually to their children, or they each leave their property to a third party directly, such as their child,[397] in pursuance of an agreement[398] between them not to revoke their wills without the other party's consent.[399] If one party dies, the courts impose a trust on the survivor or his or her personal representatives in favour of the beneficiaries under the survivor's will. As with a contract not to revoke, the revocation by the survivor is not ineffective at law: the remedy is in equity by a constructive trust. Remarriage

---

[393] W.A. Lee, "Contracts to Make Wills" (1971) 87 L.Q.R. 358.

[394] W.A. Lee, "Contracts to Make Wills" (1971) 87 L.Q.R. 358.

[395] (1769) Dick. 419.

[396] [1928] A.C. 391.

[397] *Re Dale* [1994] Ch. 31.

[398] *Gray v Perpetual Trustee Co Ltd* [1928] A.C. 391; *Re Goodchild (deceased)* [1997] 3 All E.R. 63.

[399] *Dufour v Pereira* (1769) Dick. 419; *Re Green* [1951] Ch. 148.

revokes a will automatically, and although this also applies to mutual wills, it does not affect the trust.[400]

26–262 In a case in which mutual wills were made by parents in favour of their son, it was held that the consideration for the contract is the promise not to revoke the will before death. Consideration must move from promisor, but not necessarily towards the promisee. When the first to die does so without revoking the will, that is performance of the promise and renders the "floating trust" as to the other will irrevocable.[401]

26–263 In *Re Goodchild*[402] it was emphasised that for the doctrine to apply there must not only be an agreement but a binding contract. The emphasis may indicate that the doctrine is less favourably viewed than in the past and that judges may be astute in future to examine the evidence for an intention to create a binding contract. In *Goodchild*, H and W made simultaneous wills in similar form in favour of their son, S. After W's death, H remarried and died shortly after making a new will in favour of his second wife, D. D appealed against an award made to S (under a similar provision to s.117 of the 1965 Act). S cross-appealed against a decision that his parents' wills were not mutual wills. The English Court of Appeal held, dismissing the appeal and the cross-appeal, that on the evidence, the judge had been entitled to refuse to infer a legal contract between H and W. It was clear that W believed that her will had the effect of imposing a moral obligation on H to give to S the same proportion of her estate that would have been bequeathed to him had there been mutual wills. The judge's appraisal of the circumstances could not be faulted and the award to S was upheld.

Proprietary Estoppel
26–264 This has been dealt with in the chapter on licences, estoppel and constructive trusts.

The Rule in Strong v Bird
26–265 The rule in *Strong v Bird*[403] is that if A promises to make a gift of property to B but A fails to transfer title in his lifetime, then if B becomes the executor of A's estate, so that title vests in B in that capacity, the gift is perfected. B has common law title. Equity considers that no one has a better equity to the property than B and will not force B to hold it in a fiduciary capacity. It is sometimes said that the rule is an exception to the principle that equity will not perfect an imperfect gift, but equity really has no need to perfect the gift: the common law has done that and equity declines to intervene.

---

[400] *Re Goodchild (deceased)* [1997] 3 All E.R. 63.
[401] *Re Dale* [1994] Ch. 31.
[402] [1997] 3 All E.R. 63.
[403] (1874) L.R. 18 Eq. 315 (Jessel M.R.). The case itself is narrower than the principle for which it now stands.

26–266 The rule does not apply if the donor intended a future gift.[404] Also, the intent to make the gift must continue until death. The rule has been extended in England to administrators.[405] This has been criticised on the ground that the executor is appointed by the testator, whereas an administrator is appointed by the court[406] and also that it may be pure chance who, among a small class of potential administrators, is appointed. It is arguable that the criticism is not well founded, in that it matters not how the donee obtains the legal title, provided the grounds of equity are satisfied. There is nevertheless one problem: if a person would benefit from the rule if appointed, should that be taken into account by the court when appointing administrators?

Donatio Mortis Causa
The Doctrine
26–267 A *donatio mortis causa* is the relinquishment of "dominion" over property or the indicia of title to it by a donor who contemplates impending death, with the intention that it should be a gift,[407] the gift only taking effect in the event of the donor's death, being revocable until death occurs and revoked automatically if the immediate danger recedes. The gift must be made in contemplation of death "by which is meant not the possibility of death at some time or other, but death within the near future, what may be called death for some reason believed to be impending."[408]

26–268 *Donatio mortis causa* was introduced into the common law from Roman Law. It has often been regarded as something of an anomaly. The anomaly is threefold:

1. It avoids the formalities required of wills since the Wills Act 1837 and for many centuries required by the Statute of Frauds, or required by more recent statutes prescribing formalities for the transfer of property.
2. The doctrine is an exception to the rule that equity does not perfect an imperfect gift, although there are now an increasing number of exceptions to the rule, including proprietary estoppel.
3. The doctrine rests not upon the common law concepts of possession or the control of legal and equitable estates, but upon a modified version of the Roman concept of *dominium*, referred to in the cases as "dominion".

---

[404] *Re Freeland* [1952] Ch. 110.
[405] *Re James* [1935] Ch. 449.
[406] *Re Gonin* [1979] Ch. 16 at 34.
[407] Delivery for safekeeping is insufficient: *Bentham v Potterton*, unreported, High Court, Barr J., 28 May 1998 (appeal from Eastern Circuit, County Meath).
[408] *Re Craven's Estate* [1937] Ch. 423 at 426.

Application to Land

26–269 The English Court of Appeal in *Sen v Headley*[409] decided that the doctrine of *donatio mortis causa* applies to land. It had long been thought that the doctrine of *donatio mortis causa* had no application to land. The sole authority in England in favour of the alternative view was said to be *Duffield v Elwes*,[410] in which Lord Eldon decided that the doctrine applied to a gift by a mortgagee of money secured by mortgage, by the delivery of a mortgage deed, following Lord Hardwicke in *Richards v Syms*.[411] Lord Mansfield in *Martin v Mowlin*[412] had earlier held that a gift of money secured by mortgage carried with it the estate in the land held by the mortgagee as security. Lord Eldon nevertheless also maintained Lord Hardwicke's distinction between conditional mortgage estates and ordinary, absolute estates. Neither Lord Hardwicke nor Lord Eldon sought to justify the distinction in terms of deeper principle. They justified it on policy grounds, namely, the dangers of allowing informal transfers of property.

26–270 In *Sen v Headley*,[413] the plaintiff and the deceased had lived together as husband and wife for 10 years and although they later separated, they remained on good terms. Some years later the deceased became terminally ill with cancer. He was told that his condition was inoperable and that it would deteriorate. The plaintiff visited the deceased in hospital every day. They discussed what would happen to the house when, as seemed inevitable, the deceased died before the plaintiff. The deceased had said to the plaintiff when they were alone together: "The house is yours, Margaret. You have the keys. They are in your bag. The deeds are in the steel box." The deceased died three days later. The plaintiff had always had a set of keys to the house. After the deceased's death, the plaintiff found an additional and different set of keys in her bag. She believed the deceased must have put them in her bag on one of her visits to the hospital. She used one of the keys from this bunch to open a cupboard containing the steel box. She used another key from the bunch to open the box and took possession of the deeds. That key, as it turned out, was the only key to the box.

26–271 The plaintiff brought an action against the deceased's estate claiming that she was entitled to the house on the basis that it had been given to her by the deceased under a valid *donatio mortis causa*. The plaintiff made no claim to the contents of the house. The deceased's nephew, one of the next-of-kin, who were the beneficiaries of the estate, opposed the claim.

26–272 The Court of Appeal held that the doctrine did apply to land, (a) if made in contemplation of death, (b) if the gift was made on the condition that it was to be absolute only on the donor's death, (c) that there was delivery of

---

[409] [1991] Ch. 425.
[410] (1823) 1 Sim. & St. 239.
[411] (1740) Barn. Ch. 90.
[412] (1760) 2 Burr. 969.
[413] [1991] Ch. 425.

the essential indicia of title, such as the title deeds or land certificate, and (d) a parting with dominion over the land, by which the court appears to have meant the physical ability to deal with the land. The court further held that there had been a parting with dominion on the facts of the case.

26–273 Three factors seem to have influenced the decision. First, the judge indicated that while *donatio mortis causa* may be something of an anomaly, it would add to the anomaly to create an artificial distinction which was impossible to justify in terms of principle. Secondly, there had been developments in the law of choses in action which had established, in particular in *Re Dillon*[414] and *Birch v Treasury Solicitor*,[415] that parting with dominion could occur in the case of an intangible thing, such as a chose in action, by the transfer of the indicia of title[416] and that the documents transferred need not set out the terms on which the subject matter was held. Thirdly, the law of constructive trusts had developed since 1827 and such trusts were excluded from the formalities generally required for a transfer of land.[417]

Elements of the Doctrine
Dominion

26–274 The Court of Appeal in *Sen* held that there had been a parting with dominion and this was so notwithstanding that the deceased had retained keys of his own to the house. Nourse L.J. conceded that in common law terms, the deceased, by retaining his own keys to the house, had retained possession of the house, but held that he had not retained "dominion" because "the benefits which thereby accrued to him were wholly theoretical",[418] since the deceased at the time was confined in bed in hospital. "Dominion" is used in the sense of physical control. It neither implies nor requires legal control. Nourse L.J. rejected the view accepted by Mummery J. in the Chancery Division that *donatio mortis causa* could not apply to land because it would never be possible to say that a donor had relinquished *dominion* over the land, because, having parted with the title deeds or control over them, he or she could still create equitable interests, e.g. he or she could enter into a contract to sell the land, and so create a purchaser's equity, or by a declaration of trust or by proprietary estoppel, a constructive trust, and could create legal tenancies because an intending tenant is not entitled to inspect the title to the freehold.[419]

---

[414] (1890) 44 Ch. D. 76.
[415] [1951] Ch. 298.
[416] See the doctrine of constructive delivery in the United States: *Castle v Persons* 117 F 835 (1902).
[417] *Sen v Headley* [1991] Ch. 425.
[418] [1991] Ch. 425 at 438H.
[419] [1990] 1 All E.R. 898 at 907–908.

Relinquishment

26–275 Nourse L.J.'s statement that there had to be "a parting with dominion over the subject matter of the gift"[420] can be traced to Lord Kenyon C.J. in *Hawkins v Blewitt*[421]:

> "[P]ossession must be immediately given. That has been done here; a delivery has taken place; but it is also necessary that by parting with the possession, the deceased should also part with the dominion over it. That has not been done here."[422]

26–276 Lord Kenyon's words are more equivocal than those of Nourse L.J. Nourse L.J. reformulates the test of *donatio mortis causa* so that it relates (a) to *dominion* only, and (b) that "parting with", or relinquishment, is sufficient. The donor loses dominion but the donee does not have to acquire it.

Time of Relinquishment

26–277 In *Sen v Headley* the donor did not transfer the indicia of title nor relinquish dominion over the property at the time when he expressed the intention to make the gift. He had relinquished dominion in the subject matter of the gift sometime before, either when he entered hospital or when he put the keys to the cupboard and the steel box into the plaintiff's bag on one of her visits to the hospital. Yet this did not prevent the gift being a valid *donatio mortis causa*.

Indicia of Title

26–278 It appears from *Sen* that relinquishment of dominion, and not possession, is the test in relation to the indicia of title. Nourse L.J. remarked:

> "We do not suggest that there might never be a state of facts where there was a parting with dominion over the essential *indicia* of title to a chose in action but nevertheless a retention of dominion over the chose itself ... But nothing comparable happened here."[423]

26–279 In *Mills v Shields and Kelly (No.2)*,[424] Gavan Duffy P. held that certificates of shares in public companies in Ireland, certificates of public companies registered in England and post office savings certificates were not documents of such a nature that delivery of them could constitute a valid *donatio mortis causa* since they did not contain sufficient indicia of the terms of the contract under which they were held. This position is now in doubt following the English case of *Birch v Treasury Solicitor* disapproving of the dicta on which

---

[420] *Sen v Headley* [1991] Ch. 425 at 437.
[421] (1798) 2 Esp. 662 at 663.
[422] *Sen v Headley* [1991] Ch. 425 at 437.
[423] *Sen v Headley* [1991] Ch. 425 at 438F–G.
[424] [1950] I.R. 21.

Gavan Duffy P. relied.[425] A surer guide today is probably the "necessity of production" test adopted by the Australian courts.[426]

Keys

26–280 Where the deeds are contained in a box it may not be sufficient to hand over a key to the box, rather than the box itself, if the donor retains a duplicate key.[427] The same is probably true where the donor gives the donee the combination to a safe, since the donor retains the knowledge of the combination. Even though the donor may not have the practical prospect of using the key, or combination, he or she could give it to someone else.

26–281 In *Sen* the donor retained a key to the house itself, but this did not invalidate the *donatio* of the house. On the other hand, in the judge's view, it would have prevented a *donatio* of the contents of the house. At the beginning of his judgment, Nourse L.J. comments obiter that there could have been no claim to the contents of the house because there had been no delivery of them, apparently because the deceased had retained a key to the house.[428] Later, in dealing with the *donatio* of the house itself, the judge comments that the retention of a key to the house by the deceased was not fatal to the gift of the house because the deceased was in no position to use the key since he was in hospital.[429] In which case, why did the same fact negate a *donatio* of the contents? It can be argued that there is no reason why a claim to the contents of the house should not have succeeded, had it been made.

Donee in Possession

26–282 If the donee is already in possession of the land, would this necessarily preclude the owner making a *donatio* of it? It seems not. Again, possession in itself is not the test.

26–283 In *Woodard v Woodard*,[430] a case of a chattel, the deceased, on entering hospital where he subsequently died of leukaemia, said that he was giving his car to his son. The son, the defendant, was already in possession of the car, had a set of keys to it and was using it. Dillon L.J. in the English Court of Appeal held that the fact that the son was already in possession of the car did

---

[425] These are *Delgoffe v Fader* [1939] Ch. 922 and *Duckworth v Lee* [1899] 1 I.R. 405.

[426] See Brady, *Succession Law in Ireland* (1995), para.1.34.

[427] In *Sen v Headley* the key to the box was unique. In *Hawkins v Blewitt* (1798) 2 Esp. 662 at 663, *Reddel v Dobree* (1839) 10 Sim. 244 and *Re Johnson* (1905) 92 L.T. 357, the alleged donor delivered a locked box to the alleged donee and either retained or took back the key to it. In *Reddel v Dobree* he also reserved and exercised a right to take back the box. In each of them it was held that the alleged donor had retained dominion over the box and that there had been no *donatio mortis causa*. *Sen v Headley* [1991] Ch. 425 at 437–438; *Re Craven's Estate* [1937] Ch. 423 at 427.

[428] [1991] Ch. 425 at 431F.

[429] [1991] Ch. 425 at 438H.

[430] [1991] Fam. Law 470.

not prevent the words of gift acting as a *donatio mortis causa*. In arriving at this conclusion, the judge relied on earlier cases[431] on immediate gifts which had held that the fact that the donee was in possession as bailee did not prevent the gift being valid. On the face of it this seems dubious: in *donatio mortis causa* the test is not as to possession. Nevertheless, the elements of *donatio mortis causa* appear to be present. There was a relinquishment of dominion both over the car and over the keys. As in *Sen* they both occurred before the words of gift. Furthermore, neither appears to have been carried out with the intention of creating a gift. The intention then was to make a loan of the car to the son. The case reinforces the holding in *Sen* that *donatio mortis causa* can occur without the coincidence in time of the act of relinquishment with either (a) the words of gift, or (b) a specific intention to make the gift.

26–284 One further hypothetical suggests itself: suppose that A leaves his house to go into hospital, thereby relinquishing dominion over the land. The land is left in possession of X. A tells B that B is to have the land on A's death. B already has possession of the title deeds in some other capacity. Are words of gift alone sufficient in the case of land where the donee already has the title documents in his or her possession in some other capacity, the donor having previously relinquished dominion over the land?

Donor in Possession

26–285 Can a donor relinquish dominion if he or she is still physically present on the land, as where the donor is on his or her death bed in his or her own house on the land? The deceased could probably still make a valid *donatio* since, as in *Sen*, his or her ability to exercise physical control over the land would be merely theoretical. It is hard to accept that a landowner could only make a *donatio* of his or her own land if he or she died in hospital.

In Possession of a Third Party

26–286 What if the property is in a third party's possession at the time the words are spoken or instructions given? *Spratly v Wilson*[432] posed a hypothetical. A, who owns a watch which is in the possession of C, tells B to call at C's address and take away the watch, adding that it is to be a present. Is this a valid *donatio mortis causa*, there being no possession in A to begin with and no delivery by A to B? The key word here is "possession". A does not have possession of the watch, but she does have dominion. She has the ability to dispose of the watch, to cause, in this instance, possession to pass from C to B. Possession itself is not relevant: what is relevant is dominion and that is, arguably, relinquished.

---

[431] *Alderson v Peel* (1891) T.L.R. 8; *Re Stoneham* [1919] 1 Ch. 149.
[432] (1815) Holt N.P. 10.

Revocation
Express

26–287 The donor may expressly revoke the *donatio* during his or her life by recovering dominion or by notice. It has been held that it cannot be revoked by the donor by will since the *donatio* takes effect at death, whereas a beneficiary takes a beneficial interest later when the will is proved.[433] However, it is difficult to see why a will made *after* the *donatio*, if it contained an inconsistent gift, would not indicate an implied revocation by notice.

By Recovery

26–288 A *donatio mortis causa* is automatically revoked if the donor recovers from the condition which caused him or her to contemplate death.[434]

By Subsequent Dealing

26–289 In the case of choses in action it has been seen that the donor may retain the power to make declarations of trust or assign them for value. In the case of land the donor could also, while having parted with the title documents, create a valid lease, since the prospective tenant may not usually inspect the title to the freehold, create equitable interests such as rights by proprietary estoppel, constructive trust, etc. He or she may also exercise the legal power to revoke the *donatio mortis causa*. What would the position be if the donor, having made such a *donatio*, then made a declaration of trust, or created a valid tenancy or validly assigned the benefit of a mortgage? Mummery J. in the High Court in *Sen* was clearly of the view that such a subsequent dealing would take priority over the earlier *donatio*:

> "The beneficiary under such a declaration of trust and the purchaser under such a contract would be entitled to an equitable interest in the house, which would take priority over any claim that Mrs Sen would have by way of donatio mortis causa on Mr Hewett's death."[435]

26–290 However, a later disposition would not necessarily display an intention to revoke the earlier *donatio* entirely. The donor might intend only to revoke the gift in part in the sense that he or she intended from then on that the donee take the legal title, or a reversion, in the land. Whether a later transaction revokes an earlier *donatio* or merely "takes priority" over it in a more limited sense might depend on the evidence in each case.

---

[433] *Jones v Selby* (1710) Prec. Ch. 300.
[434] *Staniland v Willott* (1850) 3 Mac. & G. 664; *Castle v Persons* (1902) 117 F 835 (US Circuit Court of Appeals).
[435] [1990] Ch. 728 at 742H.

Death from a Different Cause

26–291 In *Mills v Shields and Kelly*,[436] it was held that if the donor contemplates death by one cause but dies from another, including suicide, that does not invalidate the gift. If the donor contemplated death by suicide, it was held in the past that the gift is invalid on the ground of a public policy against suicide or assisting suicide.[437] However, those cases were decided at a time when suicide (and hence attempted suicide) was still a crime. Attitudes in this area have changed and suicide is now regarded as more a matter for compassion than opprobrium. Suicide is no longer a crime.[438] Clearly, the cases on this point will have to be reviewed.

INTESTATE SUCCESSION

26–292 The law of intestate succession has been radically altered by the 1965 Act. Before these new rules are discussed, some account will be given of the old law.

Before 1967

26–293 Before the 1965 Act came into effect on 1 January 1967, the common law made a distinction between realty and personality.

Personalty

26–294 The feudal common law did not recognise that a person had more than a life interest in personal property because it passed on the death of a person to the bishop of the diocese where the deceased lived, to be used for charitable purposes. It may be that the property was regarded as *bona vacantia* on the death of the owner and vested in the Crown which at some time had granted the prerogative to the Church.

26–295 Later, members of the deceased's family established their claim. The wife and children became entitled to one-third of the estate each (*pars rationabilis*) and the deceased was able to dispose of the remaining third. This was confirmed by *Magna Carta* 1225.[439]

26–296 Section 10 of the Statute of Distributions (Ireland) 1695 abolished the previous law and gave property owners total freedom to dispose of personalty. Personal property left by will, by contrast with real property, did not pass directly to the donee, but vested in the executors.

---

[436] [1948] I.R. 367; *Wilkes v Allington* [1931] 2 Ch. 104.
[437] *Agnew v Belfast Banking Co* [1896] 2 I.R. 204; *Re Dudman* [1925] 1 Ch. 553.
[438] Criminal Law (Suicide) Act 1993.
[439] For Ireland and England.

26–297 If the deceased did not make a will, personal property was still liable to pass to the bishop—after the Reformation, this meant the bishop of the established Church of Ireland. The rule in Ireland was thus a denial not only of the rights which the family otherwise enjoyed, as it was in England, but a denial also of the religious freedom of the deceased and his or her family. A will deprived the bishop of the property, and apparently for this reason probate of a will was, until 1858, within the jurisdiction of the diocesan ecclesiastical court. This jurisdiction was open to the objection that it involved a conflict of interest: the Church had an interest in the outcome of the case. "Probate" is an order of the court certifying that a will is valid. Probate jurisdiction was vested in a Court of Probate in 1858[440] and transferred to the High Court by the Judicature (Ireland) Act 1877. The Circuit Court also has jurisdiction in some matters.[441]

26–298 On intestacy under the 1695 Act the widow took one-third and the remainder went to the children or those representing them, such as grandchildren.[442] If there were no children, the widow took half, the rest going to those most closely related by blood.

26–299 Apart from some minor changes in 1890[443] the law remained unchanged until the Intestates' Estates Act 1954, under which the widow became entitled to £4,000 or the whole estate if it were worth less than that figure, to be borne by both the real and personal property.

Realty

26–300 The feudal common law did not recognise that realty was devisable at all. The rules of descent, based on primogeniture, determined who would inherit the estate on the death of the present tenant. It has been seen that equity, through the means of uses, first permitted tenants to determine the destination of the estate after their death. Legal wills became possible after the Statute of Wills (Ireland) 1634. The old rules then only applied if a tenant died without making a will or if the will, or part of it, failed.

26–301 Under the old rules realty passed directly to the heir-at-law. It continued to do so after the 1634 statute and even as to realty devised by will. At common law realty was not chargeable with the deceased's debts, except for debts owed to the Crown and those which the deceased had specifically covenanted to bind the heirs as well as him- or herself. This position was changed by the Administration of Estates Acts 1833 and 1869 (Hinde Palmer's Act) which made realty generally available to pay debts.

---

[440] Probates and Letters of Administration Act (Ireland) 1857; Court of Probate Act (Ireland) 1859.

[441] Succession Act 1965 s.6.

[442] Wylie, *Irish Land Law* (2013), para.17.08.

[443] Intestates' Estates Act 1890.

When the Old Rules Still Apply
26–302 Although in general the old rules of descent ceased to have effect from 1 January 1967, there may still be some cases where they have to be applied, although these will be increasingly rare. These instances were dealt with in the second edition of this work and are not repeated here.

Succession Act 1965
26–303 Section 11 of the 1965 Act abolished "all existing rules, modes and canons of descent" including dower and curtesy, except in so far as they apply to a fee tail. The old rules were replaced with a new set of rules for determining inheritance of property. The new rules do not discriminate between real and personal property, nor between male and female nor, since the Status of Children Act 1987, between marital and non-marital children of the testator.[444] After payment of expenses, debts and liabilities and satisfying any legal right payable out of the estate, the deceased's property is to be distributed in accordance with Pt VI of the 1965 Act, the provisions of which are set out below.

Spouse, Civil Partner and Issue
26–304 Where the intestate leaves a spouse or civil partner but no issue surviving, the spouse or civil partner is entitled to the whole estate.[445] If both spouse or civil partner and issue survive the intestate, the spouse or civil partner takes two-thirds of the estate and the rest is distributed among the issue.[446] Distribution among the issue is in equal shares, i.e. *per capita*, where they are of equal degree of relationship, otherwise it is *per stirpes*.[447] If the intestate leaves issue but no surviving spouse, the issue take the whole estate, in equal shares if they are in equal degree of relationship, otherwise *per stirpes*.[448]

26–305 Where there is a surviving civil partner and issue, any one of the issue may apply to the court for additional provision to be made for him or her. The court may order such additional provision to be made where it is of the opinion that it would be unjust not to do so in the light of the circumstances of the case. Such circumstances include whether any provision was made for the issue during the deceased civil partner's lifetime, the age and financial requirements of the applicant issue, and the deceased's obligations to the surviving civil partner.[449] Under s.67A(4)(a), the court may not make an order reducing the share in the estate of any issue of the deceased civil partner, but, on the

---

[444] Succession Act 1965 Pt VI.
[445] Succession Act 1965 ss.67(1) and 67A (as inserted by the CPA 2010).
[446] Succession Act 1965 ss.67(2) and 67A.
[447] Succession Act 1965 ss.67(4) and 67A.
[448] Succession Act 1965 ss.67(3) and 67A.
[449] Succession Act 1965 s.67A(3), as inserted by the CPA 2010. The Children and Family Relationships Act 2015 proposes to insert three new subsections into s.67A(3). These are the facts which a court can take account of when deciding such cases: "(a) the extent to which the intestate has made provision for that child during the intestate's lifetime, (b) the age and reasonable financial requirements of that child, (c) the intestate's financial situation."

other hand, s.67A(4)(b) precludes the applicant issue from claiming a greater share of the estate than he or she would have been entitled to had the intestate died without leaving a civil partner.

Per Stirpes

26–306 Section 3(3) of the 1965 Act defines *per stirpes* distribution as where

> "any issue more remote than a child of the deceased shall take through all degrees, according to their stocks, in equal shares if more than one, the share which the parent of such issue would have taken if living at the death of the deceased, and no issue of the deceased shall take if the parent of such issue is living at the death of the deceased and so capable of taking."

26–307 In other words, the share of a child of the testator who predeceases the testator is shared equally among the children of that child, and similarly for later generations. *Per stirpes* is to be contrasted with *per capita* in which each member of a class takes an equal share. Thus, suppose an intestate, X, had three children, two sons, S1 and S2, and a daughter, D. X's spouse has predeceased him and so also have S1 and D. S1 leaves three children, GS1, GD1 and GD2. S2 is alive at X's death and has two children, GS2 and GD3. D leaves two children, GS3 and GD4. *Per stirpes* distribution is illustrated as follows:

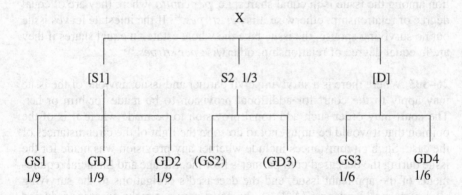

X's estate will be divided among his issue. The property is divided into three equal shares. These would have gone to S1, S2 and D if all three children had survived. However, S1 and D have both died before X and so their shares are further divided among their children in equal shares. S1 has three children and so S1's third share is divided again into three and the children each take one-ninth of the whole, while D has two children so D's one-third share is further divided by only two, leaving each of her children with one-sixth of the whole. S2 is still alive at X's death and takes his share. His own children take nothing. They are irrelevant. The same result would obtain if S2 had no children.

26–308 If *all* the intestate's children die before the intestate, so that those due to inherit are all grandchildren of the intestate, then it would seem that they take *per capita*, since they are all, in terms of s.67(3), in equal degree of relationship to the intestate. Thus, in the above example, if S1, S2 and D all died before the intestate, those due to take at the intestate's death are GS1, GD1, GD2, GS2, GD3, GS3 and GD4, all of whom are grandchildren. They are treated as a single class and distribution is made equally between them. This argument is reinforced by the consideration that this is what the 1965 Act itself prescribes in the situation, discussed below, namely where an intestate dies leaving neither spouse, issue nor parents, and brothers and sisters have all died leaving children. It seems that s.67(3) of the 1965 Act was intended to alter the position under the old law as to next-of-kin, in which distribution had been *per stirpes*, as decided in *Re Natt*.[450]

Non-marital Children

26–309 Another discrimination made by the common law rules of descent was the exclusion of children born out of wedlock, or "illegitimate" children as they were then called. It was also clear that the 1965 Act intended to continue to discriminate against "illegitimate" children and that the word "issue" in the statute excluded such children, who were given only a limited right to inherit on intestacy from their mother, but not from their father.[451]

26–310 The discrimination in the 1965 Act was challenged in *O'B v S*.[452] The plaintiff sister of the intestate applied for a grant of letters of administration of his estate. The application was opposed by the intestate's daughter, born out of wedlock, who claimed to be "issue" of the deceased within the 1965 Act and alternatively challenged the constitutionality of the 1965 Act if it were held to exclude non-marital children. The Supreme Court held that "issue", especially in ss.67 and 69 of the 1965 Act, was intended to include only "legitimate" issue, since the 1965 Act, in s.110, provided separate succession rights for non-marital children. This view would seem to be in accordance with the intention of the legislature at the time of passing the 1965 Act. The court, however, held further that the provisions were constitutionally justified by Art.41 which declares the constitutional object of protecting the family. The judges in earlier cases had held "family" in Art.41 to mean the "family based upon marriage",[453] although marriage is only referred to in Art.41.3. It is difficult to accept Brady's comment that the legal conclusions in *O'B v S* were "compelling and unavoidable".[454] The conclusions as to the intention of the legislature at the time of the passing of the 1965 Act are certainly compelling, but the constitutional conclusions were certainly not so. The judges themselves have

---

[450] (1888) 37 Ch. D. 517
[451] Succession Act 1965 s.110.
[452] [1984] I.R. 316.
[453] For example, *State (Nicolaou) v An Bord Uchtála* [1966] I.R. 567.
[454] Brady, *Succession Law in Ireland* (1995), para.8.19.

demonstrated the truth of this in holding that the constitutional protection of the family is now subject to "the exigencies of the common good", a phrase which does not occur in Art.41.[455] They have also held, when they felt called upon to do so, that Art.41 is an abstract statement of principle with few, if any, practical legal effects.[456] Moreover, it can be argued that the court in *O'B v S* failed to take into account, in their reading of the Irish Constitution, decisions of the European Court of Human Rights striking down similar discrimination against non-marital children. A more imaginative approach might have re-examined the "family based upon marriage" concept and examined the contradictions which it created. If the protection of Art.41 is confined to families based upon marriage, then families not based upon marriage will be left without protection and subject to the whim of an irresponsible parent. The "family based on marriage" concept arguably makes marriage the subject of protection of Art.41, not the family.

26–311 Whatever the rights and wrongs of *O'B v S*, the result in the case was felt to be out of line with modern opinion and with the European Court of Human Rights. The Status of Children Act 1987 inserted a new s.4A into the 1965 Act providing that in deducing any relationship for the purposes of the 1965 Act, the fact that a person's mother and father were or were not married to each other is not taken into account.[457] The constitutional issues raised in *O'B v S* may yet have to be resolved since the 1987 Act could be challenged constitutionally by marital children or those claiming through them as an infringement of Art.41.

Child in the Womb
26–312 Descendants and relatives of an intestate conceived before the intestate's death, but not born until after it, now inherit as if they had been born in the deceased's lifetime and had survived the deceased.[458]

Children Born as a Result of Donor-Assisted Human Reproduction
26–313 As noted above, the donor of an embryo or gamete is not the parent of a child subsequently born as a result of DAHR.[459] The Children and Family Relationships Act 2015 states that the parents of a child born as a result of DAHR are the mother[460] and the mother's spouse, civil partner or cohabitant.[461]

---

[455] *Fajujonu v Minister for Justice* [1990] 2 I.R. 151.

[456] *BL v ML* [1992] 2 I.R. 77.

[457] Status of Children Act 1987 s.28, amending the 1965 Act s.3 and adding s.4A. See also Children (Northern Ireland) Order 1995 (SI 755, NI 2), arts 155–157.

[458] Succession Act 1965 s.3(2); Administration of Estates Act (NI) 1955 s.13.

[459] Children and Family Relationships Act 2015 s.5(5) and (6). These provisions have yet to be commenced.

[460] Defined in s.4 as the woman who gives birth to the child.

[461] Children and Family Relationships Act 2015 s.5(1), as amended by the Marriage Act 2015. These provisions have yet to be commenced.

Such a child is not considered the "issue" of the donor and therefore would not inherit as such on intestacy.

Half-blood

26–314 Descendants and relatives of the half-blood are to be treated as, and inherit equally with, relatives of the whole blood of the same degree.[462]

Parents

26–315 Where the intestate dies leaving neither spouse nor issue, inheritance then passes to the parents, in equal shares if both are still alive.[463] If one survives the intestate, that parent takes the whole estate.[464]

Siblings and Their Issue

26–316 If the intestate dies leaving neither spouse, issue nor parents, inheritance now passes to the intestate's brothers and sisters in equal shares.[465] If a sibling has predeceased the intestate, while other siblings survive, the children of the deceased sibling take their parent's share under the principle of representation.[466]

26–317 Representation of siblings is confined to children and does not extend to other surviving issue of brothers and sisters, such as grandchildren.[467] The children take the share *per stirpes*.

26–318 If no sibling survives the intestate, the estate is distributed among the children of the brothers and sisters.[468] In this case, they take the estate in equal shares and not *per stirpes*.[469] The reason seems to be that where there are no surviving brothers or sisters, their children are all of the same degree of relationship and therefore take *per capita*.

26–319 Representation does not apply among collaterals, except in the case of siblings where some siblings survive the intestate and some do not.[470] Thus, if the intestate dies leaving only nephews and nieces, some of whom are alive

---

[462] Succession Act 1965 s.72; Administration of Estates Act (NI) 1955 s.14.

[463] Succession Act 1965 ss.68 and 67A.

[464] Succession Act 1965 ss.68 and 67A.

[465] Succession Act 1965 ss.69(1) and 67A.

[466] Succession Act 1965 ss.69(1) and 67A.

[467] Succession Act 1965 s.69(2); contrast Administration of Estates Act (NI) 1955 ss.10(1) and 67A.

[468] Succession Act 1965 s.69(2).

[469] Succession Act 1965 s.69(2).

[470] Succession Act 1965 ss.70(2) and 67A. It has been seen that where some brothers and sisters predecease the intestate while others survive, the children of those who predecease represent their parents, but brothers and sisters are not "next-of-kin" in the strict sense used in the 1965 Act. They take before resort is made to "next-of-kin" rules.

and some are dead, the surviving nephews and nieces take,[471] and the children of the deceased nephews and nieces do not represent their parents.

Next-of-kin

26–320 If the intestate dies leaving neither spouse, issue, parents, brothers, sisters nor children of brothers and sisters, then inheritance passes to "next-of-kin" in equal shares.[472] The 1965 Act replaces the common law definition of next-of-kin with a new one. "Next-of-kin" in s.71(1) is defined as "the person or persons who, at the date of the intestate's death, stand nearest in blood relationship to him" or her, and "nearest" is now defined by s.71(2) which provides as follows:

> "Degrees of blood relationship of a direct lineal ancestor shall be computed by counting upwards from the intestate to that ancestor, and degrees of blood relationship of any other relative shall be ascertained by counting upwards from the intestate to the nearest ancestor common to the intestate and that relative, and then downward from that ancestor to the relative; but, where a direct lineal ancestor and any other relative are so ascertained to be within the same degree of blood relationship to the intestate, the other relative shall be preferred to the exclusion of the direct lineal ancestor."

26–321 This method is derived from Roman law, via civil law, and was the old common law method. Representation does not apply among next-of-kin in its strict sense.[473]

26–322 The effect of the above rules would be as follows. If an intestate, N, dies leaving only an uncle and a grandfather, the grandfather will take to the exclusion of the uncle. Counting up to the grandfather gives two as the degree of relationship, whereas to reach the uncle one must count up from N to N's father, then the grandfather GF (as common ancestor) and down again to the uncle, making a degree of relationship of three. In this case the degree of relationship is *unequal* and the grandfather, as nearest relative, takes to the exclusion of the uncle, who is more remote. Where, on the other hand, the relationship is equal, the above rule prefers the younger generation, so that as between uncles and aunts and great-grandparents, who are all three degrees remote from N, the uncles and aunts are preferred. The following diagram may be useful in following these points:

---

[471] Succession Act 1965 ss.69(2) and 67A.

[472] Succession Act 1965 ss.70(1) and 67A.

[473] It has been seen that where some brothers and sisters predecease the intestate while others survive, the children of those who predecease represent their parents, but brothers and sisters are not "next-of-kin" in the strict sense used in the 1965 Act. They take before resort is made to "next-of-kin" rules.

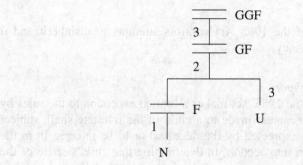

State as Ultimate Intestate Successor

26–323 In default of next-of-kin, the inheritance passes to the State as "ultimate intestate successor" under s.73(1) of the 1965 Act. This replaces the feudal law of escheat in the case of real property, and the principle of *bona vacantia* in the case of personal property when owned by natural persons. Where property is owned by corporations or limited companies, there is a survival of these doctrines, but the effect is similarly to vest the property in the State.[474]

The Application of Section 117 on Intestacy

26–324 An unsuccessful attempt was made during the passage of the Status of Children Bill to amend s.117 of the 1965 Act by including within the meaning of "testator" in that section any person dying intestate after the coming into effect of Pt V of the Status of Children Act 1987. Although it would have given a highly artificial meaning to the word, the idea was to give a discretion to the court in cases of intestacy to adjust the shares of children of the deceased in the same way that they now may do so in cases of testacy. The idea behind the proposal was that the rules of intestacy may be too rigid and may require adjustment in individual cases, bearing in mind the provision made by the intestate during his or her life for other children, etc. The Law Reform Commission recommended in 1989[475] and again in 2017 that s.117 should be amended to include the children of persons who die fully intestate.[476]

---

[474] See A. Keating, "The Recovery of Estates of Deceased Persons by a State Authority" (2013) 18(3) C.P.L.J. 54.

[475] Law Reform Commission, *Report on Land and Conveyancing Law: (1) General Proposals* (LRC 30-1989), para.45.

[476] Law Reform Commission, *Report on Section 117 of the Succession Act 1965: Aspects of Provision for Children* (LRC 118-2017), para.3.52. This would mirror the position in English law: the Intestates' Estates Act 1952 amended the Inheritance (Family Provision Act) 1938 to extend its application to intestacies.

Disinheritance

26–325 Section 121 of the 1965 Act controls attempts to disinherit and it applies in cases of intestacy.

Advancement and Hotchpot

26–326 Section 63 of the 1965 Act makes a limited exception to the rules by providing that an advancement made to a child of the intestate shall, subject to a contrary intention expressed by the deceased or to be inferred from the circumstances, be taken into account in determining that child's share of the estate. The section gives statutory form to the doctrine of "hotchpot" developed by courts of equity before the 1965 Act.[477] "Child" includes a person to whom the deceased was *in loco parentis*.[478] A child must bring advancements into account even in cases of partial intestacy,[479] but the principle does not apply to brothers or sisters or more remote descendants or relatives, unless the intestate stood *in loco parentis* to them. The principle was described by Lord Eldon as harsh for this reason.[480]

26–327 "Advancement" is given a statutory definition by s.63(6) of the 1965 Act as

> "a gift intended to make permanent provision for a child and includes advancement by way of portion or settlement, including any life or lesser interest and including property covenanted to be paid or settled. It also includes an advance or portion for the purpose of establishing a child in a profession, vocation, trade or business, a marriage portion and payments made for the education of a child to a standard higher than that provided by the deceased for any other or others of his children."

26–328 An advancement is deemed to be part of the deceased's estate and its value is that at the time of the advancement.[481] The value of the advancement is therefore added to the value of the estate at the deceased's death and the total divided into the number of shares. If the advancement is equal to or greater than the value of the share which the child is entitled to receive, the child takes nothing on distribution of the estate.[482] If it is less than the child's share on intestacy, the child is entitled only to the balance of the share left after deducting the amount of the advancement.[483] If the advancement is greater than the child's share on intestacy, the child is not a debtor to the estate of the balance in excess of the share, unless the advancement amounts, under s.121, to an attempt by the intestate to disinherit another potential beneficiary.

---

[477] *Noblett v Litchfield* (1858) 7 Ir. Ch. R. 575; *Re Tyrell* [1894] 1 I.R. 267.

[478] Succession Act 1965 ss.63(10) and 67A.

[479] Succession Act 1965 ss.74 and 67A.

[480] *Ex parte Pye* (1811) 18 Ves. Jun. 140 at 151.

[481] Succession Act 1965 s.63(2); Administration of Estates Act (NI) 1955 s.17.

[482] Succession Act 1965 s.63(3).

[483] Succession Act 1965 s.63(5).

Proprietary Estoppel

26–329 The courts are adept at finding their way around "unavoidable" results. An English court in *Re Basham*[484] found a way, via proprietary estoppel, of readjusting property interests in a deserving case where the deceased had died intestate and had not provided for his daughter in the way he had led her to expect.

Interest of Next-of-kin in Unadministered Estate

26–330 Pending the administration of the estate,[485] the legal title to the deceased's estate is vested in the President of the High Court.[486] Pending such appointment, the intestate successors have no right to possession and no title at law.[487] They have the right to assign[488] whatever interest they may turn out to have and they have the right to apply for the appointment of administrators and, when appointed, to force them to carry out the administration. Intestate successors have no title in equity, i.e. to a definite beneficial interest, since they cannot point to any particular piece of property and say "that is mine", since until administration is carried out and the amount of any debts has been established, it is unclear what, if any, property will remain for distribution.[489] As Keane J. held in *Gleeson v Feehan*,[490] it is

> "contrary to elementary legal principles to treat the persons entitled to the residuary estate of a deceased person as being the owners in equity of specific items forming part of that residue, until such time as the extent of the balance has been ascertained and the executor is in a position either to vest the proceeds of sale of the property comprised in the residue in the residuary legatees or, where appropriate, to vest individual property *in specie* in an individual residuary legatee."

Hence, if family members remain in possession of the land, their possession is adverse to that of the President of the High Court,[491] or a personal representative, if appointed, or the others entitled.[492] If they remain in possession for the requisite 12 years, they acquire title. If more than one intestate successor

---

[484] [1986] 1 W.L.R. 1498.

[485] *Gleeson v Feehan* [1997] 1 I.L.R.M. 522 at 537, citing *Commissioner of Stamp Duties (Queensland) v Livingston* [1965] A.C. 694 (Privy Council).

[486] Succession Act 1965 s.13, replacing s.3 of the Administration of Estates Act 1959.

[487] *Gleeson v Feehan* [1997] 1 I.L.R.M. 522 at 539–540.

[488] *Gleeson v Feehan* [1997] 1 I.L.R.M. 522 at 531.

[489] *Gleeson v Feehan* [1997] 1 I.L.R.M. 522 at 537.

[490] [1997] 1 I.L.R.M. 522 at 537.

[491] *Gleeson v Feehan* [1997] 1 I.L.R.M. 522.

[492] *Maher v Maher* [1987] I.L.R.M. 582.

remains in possession, they acquire title as joint tenants.[493] Again, as Keane J. observed in *Gleeson v Feehan*[494]:

> "Many people would instinctively think of a trespasser as a person who takes possession of land to which he has no right. It would seem inappropriate in everyday language to describe a member of a family who goes on living in the family home after the death of his parents as a 'trespasser'. If, however, a person has remained in what the law has come to call 'adverse possession' of land for the specified period prescribed by the relevant statute of limitations and thereby becomes the legal owner of the land, it may well be that, in strict legal theory, his possession throughout that period can also be described as that of 'a trespasser', however incongruous that description may appear to be when applied to a child who stays on in possession of the family home which everyone else has left."

Partial Intestacy

26–331 A partial intestacy occurs where a person leaves a will which disposes of only part of his or her estate. This may occur for various reasons. The testator may have forgotten that he or she owned some property, or, if the will was not professionally prepared, the testator may have omitted to appoint a residuary legatee. Section 74 of the 1965 Act provides that "the remainder shall be distributed as if he had died intestate and left no other estate".[495] It appears that s.67A(4) applies also where a civil partner dies partially intestate.

---

[493] *Gleeson v Feehan* [1997] 1 I.L.R.M. 522; *Maher v Maher* [1987] I.L.R.M. 582. *Coyle v McFadden* [1901] 1 I.R. 298 held that family members acquired title as joint tenants, but this was not followed by Palles C.B. in *Martin v Kearney* (1902) 36 I.L.T.R. 117, who held they acquired title as tenants in common in equity, but this was rejected by the High Court in *Maher v Maher* and the Supreme Court in *Gleeson v Feehan*. See also Keane J. at first instance in *Moloney v AIB* [1986] I.R. 67 and *Mohan v Roche* [1991] 1 I.R. 560.

[494] [1997] 1 I.L.R.M. 522 at 529.

[495] Repeating the provision in the Executors Act 1830.

Bibliography

Ackerman, B., *Private Property and the Constitution* (New Haven: Yale University Press, 1987)

Ague, E.L., "Homicide—Effect on Wrongdoer's Inheritance, Intestate and Survivorship Rights" (1953) 7 Miami L.Q. 524

Alexander, G.S., "The Dead Hand and the Law of Trusts in the Nineteenth Century" (1985) Stanford L.R. 1189

Ali, P.A.U., *Marshalling of Securities* (Oxford: Oxford University Press, 1999)

Ames, J.B., "Can a Murderer Acquire Title by his Crime and Keep It?" in J.B. Ames, *Lectures on Legal History and Miscellaneous Essays* (Cambridge: Harvard University Press, 1913)

Anderson, J.S., *Lawyers and the Making of English Land Law 1832–1940* (Oxford: Clarendon Press, 1992)

Anderson, P., *Lineages of the Absolutist State* (New York: Verso, 2013)

Andrews, M.E., *Law Versus Equity in The Merchant of Venice: a Legalization of Act IV, Scene I* (Boulder: University of Colorado Press, 1965)

Anon, "Soldiers' Wills" (1944) 10 Ir. Jur. 8

Archdall, M., *Monasticon Hibernicum* (Dublin: L White, 1786)

Atiyah, P.S., *The Rise and Fall of Freedom of Contract* (Oxford: Clarendon Press, 1979)

Atiyah, P.S., "When is an Enforceable Agreement not a Contract? Answer: When it is an Equity" (1976) 92 L.Q.R. 174

Baker, J.H. and Milsom, S.F.C., *Sources of English Legal History* (London: Butterworths, 1986); 2nd edn (Oxford: Oxford University Press, 2010)

Baker, J.H., *An Introduction to English Legal History*, 4th edn (Oxford: Oxford University Press, 2007; repr. 2011)

Baker, J.H., *Manual of Law French* 2nd edn (Aldershot: Scolar, 1979)

Baker, J.H., *Oxford History of the Laws of England* (Oxford: Oxford University Press, 2003)

Baker, J.H., "The Common Lawyers and the Chancery" (1969) Ir. Jur. (ns) 368

Baker, J.H., "The Use upon a Use in Equity 1558–1625" (1977) 93 L.Q.R. 33

Ball, F.E., *The Judges in Ireland, 1221–1921* (Dublin: Round Hall Press, 1993)

Bardon, J., *The Plantation of Ulster: British Colonisation in the North of Ireland in the Seventeenth Century* (Dublin: Gill & Macmillan, 2011)

Barton, J.L., "The Medieval Use" (1965) 81 L.Q.R. 562

Beale, H., Bridge, M., Gullifer, L. and Lomnicka, E., *The Law of Security and Title-Based Financing*, 2nd edn (Oxford: Oxford University Press, 2012)

Bean, J.M.W., *The Decline of English Feudalism, 1215–1540* (Manchester: Manchester University Press, 1968)

Bell, A.P., *Modern Law of Personal Property in England and Ireland* (Dublin: Butterworths, 1989)

Berger, C., *Land Ownership and Use*, 3rd edn (Boston: Little, Brown, 1983)

Bergin, T.F. and Haskell, P.G., *Preface to Estates in Land and Future Interests* (Brooklyn: Foundation Press, 1966)

Berry, H.F. (ed.), *Statutes, Ordinances and Acts of the Parliament of Ireland: King John to Henry V* (Dublin: HMSO, 1907)

Biehler, H., *Equity and the Law of Trusts in Ireland*, 6th edn (Dublin: Round Hall, 2015)

Biehler, H., "Remedies in Cases of Proprietary Estoppel: Towards a More Principled Approach?" (2015) 54(2) Ir. Jur. 79

Bilah, M.M., "The Prohibition of Riba and the Use of Hiyal by Islamic Banks to Overcome the Prohibition" (2014) 28 Ar. L.Q. 392

Binchy, D.A., *Críth Gablach* (Dublin: Stationery Office, 1941)

Blackstone, W., *Commentaries on the Laws of England*, 1st edn (London, 1765–69)

Bland, P., "A 'Hopeless Jumble': the Cursed Reform of Prescription" (2011) 16(3) C.P.L.J. 54

Bland, P., *Easements*, 3rd edn (Dublin: Round Hall, 2015)

Blom-Cooper, L. (ed.), *The Language of the Law* (London: Bodley Head, 1965)

Bodkin, E.H., "Rights of Support for Buildings and Flats" [1962] 26 Conv. (NS) 210

Bonfield, L., *Marriage Settlements, 1601–1740: the Adoption of the Strict Settlement* (Cambridge: Cambridge University Press, 1983)

Bork, R.H., *The Tempting of America: Political Seduction of the Law* (New York: Free Press, 1997)

Bork, R.H., "Neutral Principles and Some First Amendment Problems" (1971) 47 Ind. L.J. 1

Bracton (Henry de Bratton), *On the Laws and Customs of England* (Harvard: Belknap Press and Selden Society, 1968)

Bradley, K., Skehan, C. and Walsh, G. (eds), *Environmental Impact Assessment: A Technical Approach* (Dublin: DTPS Environmental Publications, 1991)

Brady, "A Case of Dependant Relative Revocation" (1980) 75 Gaz. L. Soc. Ir. 5

Brady, D., "Abolish Memorials and Bring Back the Lands Index in the Registry of Deeds" (1990) 8 I.L.T. 173

Brady, J.C., *Succession Law in Ireland*, 2nd edn (Dublin: Butterworths, 1995)

Brady, J.C., "The '*Favor Testamenti*' in Irish Law" (1980) 15(1) Ir. Jur. (ns) 1

Brand, P.A., "The Control of Mortmain Alienation in England, 1200–1300" in J.H. Baker (ed.), *Legal Records and the Historian* (London: Royal Historical Society, 1978)

Breen, O., "Children These Days – Section 117 of the Succession Act 1965 and the Moral Obligations of Parenthood" in O. Breen, J. Casey and A. Kerr (eds), *Liber Memorialis, Professor James C. Brady* (Dublin: Round Hall Sweet & Maxwell, 2001)

Brennan, G. and Casey, N. (eds), *Conveyancing* (Oxford: Oxford University Press, 2016)

Brennan, G., "Renewal Rights for Agricultural Tenants – Who Cares?" (2017) 22(2) C.P.L.J. 30

Brennan, G., "Vesting Certificates as Good Roots of Title: Fact or Fiction?" (1998) 3 C.P.L.J. 75

Breslin, J., *Banking Law in Ireland*, 3rd edn (Dublin: Round Hall, 2013)

British Columbia Law Institute, *Wills, Estates and Succession: A Modern Legal Framework* (45-2006)

Browder, O.L., Cunningham, R.A. and Smith, A.F., *Basic Property Law* (St Paul, Minn: West, 1984)

Browning, F., *Registration of Title in Ireland*, 2nd edn (Dublin: E. Ponsonby, 1912)

Bryson, W.H. (ed.), *Cases Concerning Equity and the Courts of Equity 1550–1660* (London: Selden Society, 2001)

Bryson, W.H., *The Equity Side of the Exchequer* (Cambridge: Cambridge University Press, 1975)

Bukowzyk, J.J., "The Decline and Fall of a Detroit Neighbourhood: Poletown vs GM and the City of Detroit" (1984) 41 Wash. & Lee L. Rev. 49

Burby, W.E., *Handbook of the Law of Real Property*, 3rd edn (St Paul, Minnesota: West, 1965)

Burke, B., *Burke's Irish Family Records* (London: Burke's Peerage, 1976)

Burn, E.H. and Cartwright, J., *Cheshire and Burn's Modern Law of Real Property*, 18th edn (Oxford: Oxford University Press, 2011)

Butt, P. and Eagleson, R., *Mabo: What the High Court Said and What the Government Did*, 2nd edn (Sydney: Federation Press, 1996)

Callis, R., *On the Statute of Sewers*, 4th edn (London: W Clarke, 1810)

Campbell, F. and Varley, T., *Land Questions in Modern Ireland* (Manchester: Manchester University Press, 2013)

Cannon, R., "Section 47 of the Civil Law (Miscellaneous Provisions) Act 2008 and ss.191 and 192 of the Residential Tenancies Act 2004: New Developments in Relation to Contracting Out under the Landlord and Tenant (Amendment) Act 1980" (2008) 13(3) C.P.L.J. 68

Cannon, R., "The Bigoted Landlord: A Re-Examination of *Schlegel v Corcoran and Gross*" (2005) 12 D.U.L.J. 248

Canny, M., "Fire Safety Legislation and Regulation of Overcrowding in Private Rented Dwellings: The Complexities Examined" (2018) 23(1) C.P.L.J. 17

Carson, T. H. and Bompas, H.B., *Carson's Real Property Statutes [based on Shelford's Real Property Statutes]*, 2nd edn (London: Sweet & Maxwell, 1910), reprint by Professional Books, 1981

Casner, A.J., "Class Gifts Other Than to 'Heirs' or 'Next of Kin': Increase in the Class Membership" (1937) 51 Harv. L.R. 254

Charleton, P., McDermott, P. and Bolger, M., *Criminal Law* (Dublin: Butterworths, 1999)

Cherry, B.L., Russell, A.E. and Rawlence, C.V. (eds), *Wolstenholme's Conveyancing and Settled Land Acts*, 10th edn (London: Stevens, 1913), reprint by Professional Books, 1981

Cherry, R., *The Irish Land Law and Land Purchase Acts 1860 to 1901*, 3rd edn (Dublin: J. Falconer, 1903)

Chesterman, M.R., "Family Settlements on Trust: Landowners and the Rising Bourgeoisie" in G.R. Rubin and D. Sugarman (eds), *Law, Economy and Society 1750–1914: Essays in the History of English Law* (Abingdon: Professional Books, 1974)

Clark, R., *Contract Law in Ireland*, 8th edn (Dublin: Round Hall, 2016)

Clark, S., *Social Origins of the Irish Land War* (Princeton, N.J.: Princeton University Press, 1979)

Clarke, A. and Kohler, P., *Property Law* (Cambridge: Cambridge University Press, 2004)

Coke, Sir Edward, *The First Part of the Institutes of the Laws of England: or a Commentary upon Littleton* (London: 1628; 11th edn, 1719)

Commission of Investigation into the Banking Sector in Ireland, *Misjudging Risk: Causes of the Systemic Banking Crisis in Ireland* (Dublin, 2011)

Connolly, S.J., *Religion, Law and Power: The Making of Protestant Ireland 1660–1760* (Oxford: Clarendon Press, 1992)

Connor, G. and Flavin, T., "Strategic Unaffordability and Dual-Trigger Mortgage Default in the Irish Mortgage Market" (2015) 28 J.H. Ec. 59

Conway, H., *Co-Ownership of Land: Partition Actions and Remedies*, 2nd edn (Haywards Heath: Bloomsbury Professional, 2012)

Conway, H., "When is a Severance Not Actually a Severance?" (2009) 16 Aust. Prop. L.J. 278

Coote, R.H., *A Treatise on the Law of Mortgages*, 7th edn by S.E. Williams (London: Stevens and Sons, 1904)

Cosgrove, A. (ed.), *A New History of Ireland. Vol.II, Medieval Ireland, 1169–1534* (Oxford: Oxford University Press, 2008)

Costello, J., "Wards of Court—A General Guideline of the Procedures Involved" (1993) 78 Gaz. L. Soc. Ir. 143

Costello, K., "Married Women's Property in Ireland 1800–1900" in N. Howlin and K. Costello (eds), *Land and the Family in Ireland, 1800–1950* (London: Palgrave, 2017)

Coughlan, P., "Enforcing Rights of Residence" (1993) 11 I.L.T. 168

Coughlan, P., "Restraint on the Alienation of Fee Simples – A Repugnant Policy?" (1990) 12 D.U.L.J. 147

Critchley, P., "Privileged Wills and Testamentary Formalities: A Time to Die?" (1999) 58(1) Camb. L.J. 49

Crooks, P. and Mohr, T., *Law and the Idea of Liberty in Ireland from Magna Carta to the Present* (Dublin: Four Courts Press, 2018)

Crowley, J., Smyth, J. and Murphy, M., *Atlas of the Great Irish Famine* (Cork: Cork University Press, 2012)

Cryan, A., "Changing Demographics: Legal Responses to Polygamy and the Challenges Ahead for Ireland" (2016) 19(4) I.J.F.L. 82

Cullen, L., "Catholics Under the Penal Laws" (1986) 1 Eighteenth-Century Ir. 23

Cunningham, R., Stoebuck, W. and Whitman, D., *The Law of Property* (St Paul, Minn.: West Pub. Co, 1984)

Dawson, N., "Covenants 'Against' Subletting" (1983) 34 N.I.L.Q. 56

Dawson, N., "The Giant's Causeway Case: Property Law in Northern Ireland 1845–1995" in N. Dawson, D. Greer and P. Ingram (eds), *One Hundred and Fifty Years of Irish Law* (Dublin: Round Hall Sweet & Maxwell, 1996)

de Blacam, M., *Private Rented Dwellings*, 2nd edn (Dublin: Round Hall Press, 1993) de Londras, F. and Kelly, C., *European Convention on Human Rights Act: Operation, Impact and Analysis* (Dublin: Round Hall, 2010)

de Londras, F., *Principles of Irish Property Law*, 2nd edn (Dublin: Clarus Press, 2011)

de Moleyns, T., *The Landowner's and Agent's Practical Guide*, 8th edn by A.W. Quill and F.P. Hamilton (Dublin: E. Ponsonby, 1899)

Deeney, J., *Registration of Deeds and Title in Ireland* (Haywards Heath: Bloomsbury Professional, 2014)

Delaney, V.K., "Equitable Interests and Mere Equities" [1957] 21 Conv. 195

Dewhurst, E., "The Power of Sale without a Court Order: A Deprivation of Possession or a Contractual Right?" (2009) 14(1) C.P.L.J. 13

Dictionary of Irish Biography; From the Earliest Times to the Year 2002, J. McGuire and J. Quinn (gen. eds), 9 vols (Royal Irish Academy and Cambridge University Press, 2009), online database version

Digby, K.E., *Introduction to the History of the Law of Real Property* (Oxford: Clarendon Press, 1875)

Dixon, M., "Invalid Contracts, Estoppel, and Constructive Trusts" [2005] Conv. 207

Dodd, S., "Development on the Foreshore" (2006) 13 I.P.E.L.J. 63

Donaldson, A.G., *The Application in Ireland of English and British Legislation made before 1801* (PhD, 2 vols (Queen's University, Belfast, 1952))

Donelan, E., *Energy and Mineral Resources Law in Ireland* (Dublin: Round Hall, 1985)

Donnelly, M., *The Law of Credit and Security*, 2nd edn (Dublin: Round Hall, 2015)

Dooley, T., *The Land for the People: The Land Question in Independent Ireland* (Dublin: UCD Press, 2004)

Douglas, S., "The Scope of Conversion: Property and Contract" (2011) 74 M.L.R. 329

Dowling, A., "Of Ships and Sealing Wax: The Introduction of Land Registration in Ireland" (1993) 44 N.I.L.Q. 360

Dowling, A., "The Baby and the Bathwater: The Administration of Justice (Ireland) Act 1707, s 23" (1996) 47 N.I.L.Q. 428

Doyle, C., "Judgment Mortgages - A False Dawn" (1993) 87 Gaz. L. Soc. Ir. 297

Dromgoole, S., "Protection of Historic Wreck: the UK Approach. Part 1: The Present Legal Framework" (1989) 4(1) I.J.E.C.L. 26; "Protection of Historic Wreck: the UK approach. Part 2: Towards Reform (1989) 4(2) I.J.E.C.L. 95

Dudley-Edwards, R., "Magna Carta Hiberniae" in J. Ryan (ed.), *Féil-Sgríbhinn Eóin Mhic Néill: Essays and Studies Presented to Professor Eóin MacNeill on the Occasion of his Seventieth Birthday* (Dublin: Three Candles, 1940)

Duffy, D. and O'Hanlon, N., "Negative Equity in Ireland: Estimates Using Loan-Level Data" (2014) 7(3) J. Eur. R.E.R. 327

Dunlop, R., "The Plantation of Leix and Offaly" (1891) 6 Eng. Hist. Rev. 61

Dunlop, R., "The Plantation of Munster 1584–1589" (1888) 3 Eng. Hist. Rev. 250

Dwyer, D., "A Pro-Tenant Shift in the Balance of Unreasonable Withholding of Consent to Assignment – _Perfect Pies v Chupn Ltd_" (2016) 21(1) C.P.L.J. 12

Edgeworth, B., Rossiter, C.J. and Stone, M.A., _Sackville and Neave, Property Law: Cases and Materials_, 7th edn (Chatswood, N.S.W.: LexisNexis Butterworths, 2004)

Edmonds, J., _International Timesharing_ (London: Services to Lawyers Ltd, 1984)

Elliott, D.W., "Non-Derogation from a Grant" (1964) 80 L.Q.R. 244

Emden, C.S., "The Law of Treasure Trove, Past and Present" (1926) 167 L.Q.R. 368

Falconbridge, J.D., Rayner, W.B. and McLaren, R.H., _Falconbridge on Mortgages_, 4th edn (Agincourt, Ontario: Canada Law Book Ltd, 1977)

Farrand, J.T., _Emmet on Title_, 18th edn (London: Oyez Longman, 1983)

Farwell, G., _A Concise Treatise on Powers_, 2nd edn (London: Stevens and Sons, 1893)

Fearne, C., _Essay on the Learning of Contingent Remainders and Executory Devises_, 1st edn (London, 1772); 10th edn by Charles Butler (London: Saunders & Benning, 1844; repr., Abingdon: Professional Books Ltd, 1982)

Ferguson, W.D., _Tenure and Improvement of Land in Ireland_ (Dublin: E.J. Milliken, 1851)

Filgate, W.H., _A Popular Treatise on the Law of Landlord and Tenant in Ireland_ (Dublin: Hodges and Smith, 1849)

Finlay, J.T., _A Treatise on the Law of Renewals_ (Dublin: J. Cumming, 1829)

Firth, C.H. and Rait, R.S., _Acts and Ordinances of the Interregnum 1642–1660_ (London: HMSO, 1911)

Fitzgerald, B., _Land Registry Practice_ (Dublin: Round Hall, 1989)

Flaherty, M.S., "The Empire Strikes Back: _Annesley v Sherlock_ and the Triumph of Imperial Parliamentary Supremacy" (1987) 87 Colum. L.R. 593

Forde, M., _Constitutional Law of Ireland_ (Dublin: Mercier Press, 1987)

Furlong, J.S., _The Law of Landlord and Tenant as Administered in Ireland_, 2nd edn (Dublin: E. Ponsonby, 1869)

Galligan, E. and McGrath, M., _Compulsory Purchase and Compensation in Ireland: Law and Practice_, 2nd edn (Haywards Heath: Bloomsbury Professional, 2013)

Gaunt, J. and Morgan, P., _Gale on Easements_, 16th edn (London: Sweet & Maxwell, 1997)

Getzler, J., _A History of Water Rights at Common Law_ (Oxford: Oxford University Press, 2006)

Gilbert, J., _The Law of Uses and Trusts_, 3rd edn by E.B. Sugden (London: W. Reed, 1811)

Gillespie, R., "A Manor Court in Seventeenth Century Ireland" (1998) 25 Ir. Ec. Soc. Hist. 81

Glanville, R. de, _The Treatise on the Laws and Customs of the Realm of England Commonly Called Glanvill_, G.D.G. Hall (ed.) (London: Nelson, 1965)

Glister, J., "Section 199 of the Equality Act 2010: How Not to Abolish the Presumption of Advancement" (2010) 73 M.L.R. 807

Goldstein, M.I., "Rights of Entry and Possibilities of Reverter as Devices to Restrict the Use of Land" (1940) 54 Harv. L.R. 248

Goode, W.J., "The Resistance of Family Forces to Industrialization" in J.M. Eekelaar and S.N. Katz (eds), *Marriage and Cohabitation in Contemporary Societies: Areas of Legal, Social and Ethical change* (Toronto: Butterworths, 1980)

Goodeve, L.A., *The Modern Law of Real Property*, 4th edn (London: Sweet & Maxwell, 1897)

Gordon, W.M., *Scottish Land Law* (Edinburgh: Green, 1989)

Goymour, A., "Cobbling Together Claims Where a Contract Fails to Materialise" (2009) 68(1) Camb. L.J. 37

Goymour, A., "Mistaken Registrations of Land: Exploding the Myth of 'Title by Registration'" (2013) 72 Camb. L.J. 617

Gray, K. and Gray, S., "Civil Rights, Civil Wrongs and Quasi-Public Space" [1999] E.H.R.L.R. 46

Gray, K.J. and Gray, S.F., *Elements of Land Law*, 5th edn (Oxford: Oxford University Press, 2009)

Gray, K.J. and Gray, S.F., *Land Law*, 7th edn (Oxford: Oxford University Press, 2011)

Gray, K.J. and Symes, P.D., *Real Property and Real People* (London: Butterworths, 1981)

Greer, S., "*Horsham Properties Group Ltd v Clark*: Possession – Mortgagee's Right or Discretionary Remedy?" [2009] Conv. 516

Griffith, M.C., *Calendar of Exchequer Inquisitions, Formerly in the Office of the Chief Remembrancer of the Exchequer Prepared from the MSS of the Irish Record Commission* (Dublin: Stationery Office for the Irish Manuscripts Commission, 1991)

Grimes, R. and Dowling, K., "The Cuckoo's Call and the Lesser-Spotted Superfluous Witness" (2014) 2(2) I.P.L.J. 9

Ground Rents Commission, *Report on Ground Rents* (Dublin: Stationery Office, 1964)

Hale, Sir Matthew, *De Jure Maris* (London, 1746)

Hall, E.G. and O'Connor, E.R., *The Supplement to O'Connor's The Irish Notary* (Dublin: Faculty of Notaries Public in Ireland, 2007)

Hand, G.J., *English Law in Ireland 1290–1324* (Cambridge: Cambridge University Press, 1967)

Hardiman, D., "Deposit of Title Deeds" (1999) 6(1) C.L.P. 3

Hargrave, F., *Jurisconsult Excercitations*, 3 vols (London, 1811–13)

Hargreaves, A.D., *An Introduction to the Principles of Land Law*, 2nd edn (London: Sweet & Maxwell, 1944)

Hargreaves, A.D., "Terminology and Title in Ejectment" (1940) 56 L.Q.R. 376

Harnedy, D., "Constitutionality of Planning and Development (Housing) and Residential Tenancies Act 2016" (2017) 22(4) C.P.L.J. 73

Harpum, C., "*Long v Gowlett*: A Strong Fortress" [1979] Conv. 113

Harpum, C., Bridge, S. and Dixon, M., *Megarry & Wade: The Law of Real Property*, 7th edn (London: Sweet & Maxwell, 2008); 8th edn (2012)

Harvey, B.W., "Irish Rights of Residence—The Anatomy of a Hermaphrodite" (1970) 21 N.I.L.Q. 389

Harvey, S., "The Knight and the Knight's Fee in England" (1970) 49 P. & P. 3

Hawkins, F.V. and Ryder, E.C., *The Construction of Wills* (London: Sweet & Maxwell, 1863)

Hayton, D., "Revolution in Restrictive Covenants Law?" (1980) 43 M.L.R. 445

Hayton, D.J., *Registered Land*, 3rd edn (London: Sweet & Maxwell, 1981)

Hegel, G.W.F., *Elements of the Philosophy of Right* (Berlin, 1820)

Hewitt, E.P., *A Treatise on the Statutes of Limitations* (London: Sweet & Maxwell, 1893)

Heydon, J.D., *The Restraint of Trade Doctrine* (London: Butterworths, 1971)

Hogan, D., "Arrows Too Sharply Pointed: the relations of Lord Justice Christian and Lord O'Hagan, 1868–1874" in J.F. McEldowney and P. O'Higgins (eds), *The Common Law Tradition: Essays in Irish Legal History* (Dublin: Irish Academic Press, 1990)

Hogan, G. and Whyte, G., *J.M. Kelly: The Irish Constitution*, 4th edn (Dublin: Butterworths, 2003)

Hogan, G., "The Constitution, Property Rights and Proportionality" (1997) 32(1) Ir. Jur. 373

Hogg, J.E., "The Effect of Tenure on Real Property Law" (1909) 98 L.Q.R. 178

Hohfeld, W.N., "Fundamental Legal Conceptions as Applied in Judicial Reasoning" (1917) 26 Yale L.J. 710

Holdsworth, W., *A History of English Law*, 17 vols (London: Methuen, 1925; repr. 1966)

Holdsworth, W., "Terminology and Title in Ejectment – A Reply" (1940) 56 L.Q.R. 479

Honohan, P., *The Irish Banking Crisis: Regulatory and Financial Stability Policy 2003–2008* (Dublin, 2010)

Honoré, A.M., "Ownership" in A.G. Guest (ed.), *Oxford Essays in Jurisprudence* (London: Oxford University Press, 1961)

Hood Phillips, O., *Shakespeare and the Lawyers* (London: Methuen, 1972)

Hopkins, N., "The *Pallant v Morgan* 'Equity' – Again" [2012] Conv. 327

Hourican, M., "The Introduction of 'New Model' Constructive Trusts in this Jurisdiction" (2001) 6(2) C.P.L.J. 49

Howarth, W. and Jackson, S., *Wisdom's Law of Watercourses*, 6th edn (London: Sweet & Maxwell, 2011)

Hurst, D.J., "The Transmission of Restrictive Covenants" (1982) 2(1) L.S. 53

James, R.W. and Fimbo, G.M., *Customary Land Law of Tanzania: A Source Book* (Nairobi: East African Literature Bureau, 1973)

James, R.W., *Land Tenure and Policy in Tanzania* (Nairobi: East African Literature Bureau, 1971)

Jarman, T., *A Treatise on Wills*, 8th edn by Raymond Jennings & John C. Harper (London: Sweet & Maxwell, 1951)

Jennings, R. and Harper, J.C., *A Treatise on Wills by Thomas Jarman*, 8th edn (London: Sweet & Maxwell, 1986)

Johnson, W.J., "The First Adventure of the Common Law" (1920) 36 L.Q.R. 9

Jones, N.G., "The Use upon a Use in Equity Revisited" (2002) 33 Cambrian L.R. 67

Jones, N.G., "Tyrrel's Case (1557) and the Use upon a Use" (1993) 14 J. Leg. Hist. 75

Jordan, M., "Illegality and the Law of Fast-Fish and Loose-Fish" (2017) 57 Ir. Jur. 14

Keane, R., *Equity and the Law of Trusts in the Republic of Ireland*, 1st edn (London: Butterworths, 1988); 2nd edn (Haywards Heath: Bloomsbury Professional, 2011)

Keating, A., "A Re-Formulated Proprietary Estoppel and Remedial Constructive Trusts" (2016) 31(1) I.L.T. 174.

Keating, A., *Keating on Probate*, 5th edn (Dublin: Round Hall, 2015)

Keating, A., "Principles of Knowledge and Approval of Contents of Wills by Testators" (2017) 22(4) C.P.L.J. 66

Keating, A., "Rebutting the Presumption of Lost Wills" (2010) 28 I.L.T. 128

Keating, A., "The Defeasance of Testamentary Gifts by Ademption" (2009) 27 I.L.T. 209

Keating, A., "The Presumption of Revocation in Cases of Lost Wills" (2016) 21(2) C.P.L.J. 26

Keating, A., "The Recovery of Estates of Deceased Persons by a State Authority" (2013) 18(3) C.P.L.J. 54

Keating, A., "The Revival of Wills by Codicil" (2016) 21(1) C.P.L.J. 2

Kelly, F., *A Guide to Early Irish Law* (Dublin: Dublin Institute for Advanced Studies, 1988)

Kelly, J., "Hidden Treasure and the Constitution" (1988) 10 D.U.L.J. 5 at 18

Kelly, J.M., *A Short History of Western Legal Theory* (Oxford: Clarendon Press, 1992)

Kenna, P., *Housing Law, Rights and Policy* (Dublin: Clarus Press, 2011)

Kenny, P.H. and Kenny, A., *The Trusts of Land and Appointment of Trustees Act 1996* (London: Sweet & Maxwell, 1997)

Killip, J., "Marshalling - Nothing and then Two Come Along at the Same Time" (2015) 28 Insolv. Int. 114

Kingston, J., "Rich People Have Rights Too? The Status of Property as a Fundamental Human Right" in L. Heffernan (ed.), *Human Rights: A European Perspective* (Dublin: Round Hall Press, 1994)

Knafla, L.A., *Law and Politics in Jacobean England: the Tracts of Lord Chancellor Ellesmere* (Cambridge: Cambridge University Press, 1977)

Kolbert, C.F. and O'Brien, T., *Land Reform in Ireland: A Legal History of the Irish Land Problem and Its Settlement* (Cambridge: University of Cambridge Department of Land Economy, 1975)

Land Law Working Group (NI), *Final Report* (London: HMSO, 1990)

Law Commission for England and Wales, *Intestacy and Family Provision Claims on Death* (Law Com. 31-2011)

Law Commission for England and Wales, *Land Registration for the Twenty-First Century: A Conveyancing Revolution* (Law Comm. 271-2001)

Law Commission for England and Wales, *Making Land Work: Easements, Covenants and Profits à Prendre* (327/2011)

Law Commission for England and Wales, *The Rules against Perpetuities and Excessive Accumulations* (Law Com No. 251) (London: Stationery Office, 1998)

Law Reform Commission, *Consultation Paper on Business Tenancies* (LRC CP 21-2000)

Law Reform Commission, *Consultation Paper on Judgment Mortgages* (LRC CP 30-2004)

Law Reform Commission, *Consultation Paper on Multi-Unit Developments* (LRC CP 42-2006); *Report on Multi-Unit Developments* (LRC 90-2008)

Law Reform Commission, *Consultation Paper on Reform and Modernisation of Land Law and Conveyancing Law* (LRC CP 34-2004)

Law Reform Commission, *Consultation Paper on the General Law of Landlord and Tenant* (LRC CP 28-2003)

Law Reform Commission, *Issues Paper on Compulsory Acquisition of Land* (LRC IP 13-2017)

Law Reform Commission, *Issues Paper on Review of Section 120 of the Succession Act 1965 and Admissibility of Criminal Convictions in Civil Proceedings* (LRC IP 7-2014)

Law Reform Commission, *Issues Paper on Section 117 of the Succession Act 1965* (LRC IP 9-2016)

Law Reform Commission, *Prevention of Benefit from Homicide* (LRC 115-2015)

Law Reform Commission, *Report on Gazumping* (LRC 59-1989)

Law Reform Commission, *Report on Illegitimacy* (LRC 4-1982)

Law Reform Commission, *Report on Interests of Vendor and Purchaser in Land during the Period between Contract and Conveyance* (LRC 49-1995)

Law Reform Commission, *Report on Land Law and Conveyancing Law: (1) General Proposals* (LRC 30-1989)

Law Reform Commission, *Report on Land Law and Conveyancing Law (6): Further General Proposals Including the Execution of Deeds* (LRC 56-1998)

Law Reform Commission, *Report on Land Law and Conveyancing Law (7): Positive Covenants over Freehold Land and Other Proposals* (LRC 70-2003)

Law Reform Commission, *Report on Reform and Modernisation of Land Law and Conveyancing Law* (LRC 74-2005)

Law Reform Commission, *Report on Section 117 of the Succession Act 1965: Aspects of Provision for Children* (LRC 118-2017)

Law Reform Commission, *Report on the Law of Landlord and Tenant Law* (LRC 85-2007)

Law Reform Commission, *Report on the Rule against Perpetuities and Cognate Rules* (LRC 62-2000)

Law Reform Commission, *Report on Title by Adverse Possession of Land* (LRC 67-2002)

Law Reform Commission, *Report on Trust Law: General Proposals* (LRC 92-2008)

Leach, W. Barton, "Perpetuities: Staying the Slaughter of the Innocents" (1952) 68 L.Q.R. 85

Leach, W. Barton, "The Rule Against Perpetuities and Gifts to Classes" (1938) 51 Harv. L.R. 1329

Lee, W.A., "Contracts to Make Wills" (1971) 87 L.Q.R. 358

Leyser, J., "Ownership of Flats: Comparative Study" (1958) 7 I.C.L.Q. 31

Longfield, R., *The Fishery Laws of Ireland* (Dublin: Ponsonby, 1863)

Loveland, I., "Twenty Years Later – Assessing the Significance of the Human Rights Act 1998 to Residential Possession Proceedings" [2017] 3 Conv. 174

Lyall, A. (ed.), *Irish Exchequer Reports: Reports of Cases in the Courts of Exchequer and Chancery in Ireland 1716–1734* (London: Selden Society, 2008)

Lyall, A., "Class-Closing Rules and Future Interests in Freeholds: Law and Political Economy" (1985) 20 Ir. Jur. 66

Lyall, A., "Freehold Covenants and What to Do with Them" (1991) 9 I.L.T. 157

Lyall, A., "Human Rights and Conditional and Determinable Interests in Freeholds" (1987) Ir. Jur. 250

Lyall, A., "Irish Heraldic Jurisdiction" (1993) 10 C.o.A. (ns) 134; (1994) 10 C.o.A. (ns) 179

Lyall, A., "Land Law and Reform in Ireland" in P. Jackson and D.C. Wilde (eds), *The Reform of Property Law* (Aldershot: Ashgate, 1997)

Lyall, A., "Leases, Time Certain and the 2006 Bill: A Comment" (2007) 12(1) C.P.L.J. 31

Lyall, A., "Life Tenants and Insurance" (2008) 13(2) C.P.L.J. 26

Lyall, A., "Non-Derogation from a Grant" (1988) 6 I.L.T. 143

Lyall, A., "Quia Emptores in Ireland" in O. Breen, J. Casey and A. Kerr (eds), *Liber Memorialis: Professor James C. Brady* (Dublin: Round Hall Sweet & Maxwell, 2001)

Lyall, A., "The Case of the Moveable Land" (1968) 1 E. Afr. L. Rev. 95

Lyall, A., "The Family Home Protection Act 1976 and Conveyances Other Than by Spouses" (1984) 6 D.U.L.J. (ns) 158

Lyall, A., *The Irish House of Lords as a Court of Law 1782–1800* (Dublin: Clarus Press, 2013)

Lyall, A., "The Purchaser's Equity: an Irish Controversy" (1989) 7 I.L.T. 270

Lynch-Robinson, C. and Lynch-Robinson, A., *Intelligible Heraldry* (London: Macdonald, 1953)

Lyne, J., *A Treatise on the Leases for Lives, Renewable for Ever* (Dublin: Hodges and Smith, 1837)

MacCurtain, M. and O'Dowd, M., *Women in Early Modern Ireland* (Edinburgh: Edinburgh University Press, 1991)

Macfarlane, A., *The Origins of English Individualism: The Family, Property and Social Transition* (Oxford: Blackwell, 1978)

Macfarlane, B. and Robertson, A., "The Death of Proprietary Estoppel" (2008) 4 L.M.C.L.Q. 449

Macnevin, R.C., *The Practice of the Landed Estates Court in Ireland* (Dublin: Hodges Smith & Co., 1859)

Madden, D.H., *A Practical Treatise on the Registration of Deeds, Conveyances, and Judgment-Mortgages*, 2nd edn (Dublin: W. McGee, 1901)

Maddox, N., *Mortgages: Law and Practice*, 2nd edn (Dublin: Round Hall, 2017)

Maddox, N., "The Law and Practice of Judgment Mortgages" (2006) 11 B. Rev. 189

Maginn, C., "'Surrender and Regrant' in the Historiography of Sixteenth-Century Ireland" (2007) 38(4) Sixteenth Cent. J. 955

Maguire, J.A., *A Compendium of the Law and Practice Relating to the Registration of Deeds, Wills, Judgment Mortgages, and Other Facts Affecting Title to Land in Ireland* (Dublin: Hodges, Figgis, 1900)

Maine, H., *Dissertations on Early Law and Custom* (London: John Murray, 1883)

Maitland, F.W. (ed.), *Bracton's Note Book* (London: C.J. Clay & Sons, 1887)

Maitland, F.W. (ed.), *Select Passages from the Works of Bracton and Azo* (London: B. Quaritch, 1895)

Maitland, F.W., *Equity: A Course of Lectures* (Cambridge: University Press, 1936)

Maitland, F.W., *Select Pleas in Manorial and Other Seignorial Courts* (London: B. Quaritch, 1889)

Maitland, F.W., *The Forms of Action at Common Law* (Cambridge: Cambridge University Press, 1910; repr. 1968)

Malcomson, A.P.W., *John Foster: The Politics of the Anglo-Irish Ascendancy* (Oxford: Oxford University Press, 1978)

Martin, J., "Recent Cases: Constructive Trusts and Licensees; Re Sharpe" [1980] Conv. 207

Maudsley, E. and Burn, H., *Maudsley and Burn's Land Law, Cases and Materials*, 5th edn (London: Butterworths, 1986)

Maudsley, R.H., "Note" (1965) 81 L.Q.R. 183

Maudsley, R.H., *The Modern Law of Perpetuities* (London: Butterworths, 1979)

Mautner, M., "'The Eternal Triangles of the Law': Toward a Theory of Priorities in Conflicts Involving Remote Parties" (1991) 90 Mich. L. Rev. 95

McAuslan, J.P.W., "Control of Land and Agricultural Development in Kenya and Tanzania" in G.F.A. Sawyerr (ed.), *East African Law and Social Change* (Nairobi: East African Publishing House, 1967)

McCarthy, J., "The Multi-Unit Developments Act 2011: Are We Still Stuck in the MUD?" (2011) 16 C.P.L.J. 8

McDermott, S. and Woulfe, R., *Compulsory Purchase and Compensation: Law and Practice in Ireland* (Dublin: Butterworth, 1992)

McEnery, M.J. and Refaussé, R., *Christ Church Deeds* (Dublin: Four Courts Press, 2001)

McFarlane, B., "Proprietary Estoppel and Failed Contractual Negotiations" [2005] Conv. 501

McGrath, C.I., "Securing the Protestant Interest: the Origins and Purpose of the Penal Laws of 1695" (1996) 30 (117) I.H.S. 25

McGrath, N., "Reforming the Company Charge Register in Ireland" in L. Gullifer and O. Akseli (eds), *Secured Transactions Law Reform: Principles, Policies and Practice* (Oxford: Hart, 2016)

McGuire, W.J., *The Succession Act 1965* (Dublin: Incorporated Law Society of Ireland, 1981)

McIvor, F.J. (ed.), *Elegantia Juris: Selected Writings of Francis Headon Newark* (Belfast: Northern Ireland Legal Quarterly, 1973)

McMahon, B. and Binchy, W., *Law of Torts*, 3rd edn (Dublin: Butterworths, 2000)

McMahon, R., "Manor Courts in the West of Ireland Before the Famine" in D.S. Greer and N.M. Dawson (eds), *Mysteries and Solutions in Irish Legal History* (Dublin: Four Courts Press, 2001)

McNeil, K., *Common Law Aboriginal Title* (Oxford: Clarendon, 1989)

Mee, J., "From Here to Eternity? Perpetuities Reform in Ireland" (2000) 7 D.U.L.J. 91

Mee, J., "Palm Trees in the Rain: New Model Constructive Trusts in Ireland" (1996) 1(1) C.P.L.J. 9

Mee, J., "Partition and Sale of the Family Home" (1993) 15 D.U.L.J. 78

Mee, J., "Return of Fertile Octogenarians" (1992) 14 D.U.L.J. 69

Mee, J., "The Fee Tail: Putting Us Out of its Misery" (2005) 10(1) C.P.L.J. 4

Mee, J., "The Land and Conveyancing Law Reform Bill 2006: Observations on the Law Reform and a Critique of Selected Provisions – Part II" (2006) 11(4) C.P.L.J. 91

Megarry, R.E. and Wade, H.W.R., *The Law of Real Property*, 3rd edn (London: Stevens, 1966); 4th edn (1975)

Megarry, R.E., "Note" (1965) 81 L.Q.R. 481

Megarry, R.E., *A Manual of the Law of Real Property*, 3rd edn (London: Stevens, 1962); 6th edn (1982); 7th edn (1993)

Meredith, A.C., "A Paradox of Sugden's" (1918) 34 L.Q.R. 253

Millet, P., "*Crabb v Arun District Council* - A Riposte!" (1976) 92 L.Q.R. 342

Milsom, S.F.C., *Historical Foundations of the Common Law*, 2nd edn (London: Butterworths, 1981)

Montrose, J.L., "Equitable Deposits of Title Deeds" (1940) 4 N.I.L.Q. 64

Moore, B., *Social Origins of Dictatorship and Democracy: Lord and Peasant in the Making of the Modern World* (Boston: Beacon Press, 1993)

Morgan, J., "Digging Deep: Property Rights in Subterranean Space and the Challenge of Carbon Capture and Storage" (2013) 62 I.C.L.Q. 587

Morris, J.H.C. and Leach, W. Barton., *The Rule against Perpetuities*, 2nd edn (London: Sweet & Maxwell, 1986)

Morris, J.H.C., "The Rule Against Perpetuities and the Rule in *Andrews v Partington*" (1954) 70 L.Q.R. 61

Moynihan, C.J. and Kurtz, S.F., *Introduction to the Law of Real Property* (St Paul: West, 2002)

Murray, J.B.C., *History of Usury* (Philadelphia: J.B. Lippincott & Co, 1866)

Neuberger, Lord, "The Stuffing of Minerva's Owl? Taxonomy and Taxidermy in Equity" (2009) 68 Camb. L.J. 537

New South Wales Law Reform Commission, *Uniform Succession Laws: Intestacy* (116-2007)

Newark, F., "Dependent Relative Revocation" (1955) 71 L.Q.R. 374

Newark, F.H., "Notes on Irish Legal History" (1946–48) 7 N.I.L.Q. 121

Newsom, G.H., "Universal Annexation?" (1981) 97 L.Q.R. 32

Newsom, G.H., "Universal Annexation? A Postscript" (1982) 98 L.Q.R. 202

Ní Chatháin, Ú., "Section 62 of the Housing Act 1966 and the Implications of the Decision in Donegan" (2012) 17(3) C.P.L.J. 54

NI Survey Working Party of Faculty of Law, *The Queen's University Belfast Survey of the Land Law of Northern Ireland* (Belfast: HMSO, 1971)

Nicholls, K.W., *Gaelic and Gaelicised Ireland in the Middle Ages* (Dublin: Gill and Macmillan, 1972)

Nicholls, K.W., "Irishwomen and Property in the Sixteenth Century" in M. MacCurtain and M. O'Dowd (eds), *Women in Early Modern Ireland* (Edinburgh: Edinburgh University Press, 1991)

Nicholls, K.W., *Land, Law and Society in Sixteenth Century Ireland* (O'Donnell Lecture, University College Cork, 1976)

Nicholls, K.W., "Some Documents on Irish Law and Custom in the Sixteenth Century" (1970) 26 An. Hib. 105

Nield, S. and Hopkins, N., "Human Rights and Mortgage Repossessions: Beyond Property Law Using Article 8" (2013) 33 L.S. 431

Nwabueze, B.O., *Nigerian Land Law* (Enugu: Dobbs Ferry, NY, 1972)

O'Connor, E.R., *The Irish Notary; A Treatise on the Law and Practice of Notaries in Ireland* (Abingdon: Professional Books Ltd, 1987)

O'Dell, E., "Unjust Enrichment and the Remedial Constructive Trust" (2001) 23 D.U.L.J. 71

O'Donnell, D., "Property Rights in the Irish Constitution: Rights for Rich People, or a Pillar of Free Society?" in E. Carolan and O. Doyle (eds), *The Irish Constitution: Governance and Values* (Dublin: Round Hall, 2008)

O'Laughlin, M.C., *The Irish Book of Arms: Genealogy and Heraldry from the Earliest Times to the 20th Century* (Kansas City: Irish Genealogical Foundation, 2000)

O'Sullivan, D., "Rent, Regulation and the Public Interest in Ireland" (2016) 21(4) C.P.L.J. 74

O'Sullivan, K., "'A Lot Done, More to Do?': Local Authority Housing Standards in Ireland" (2018) 23(1) C.P.L.J. 2

O'Sullivan, K., "Judgment Mortgages and the Family Home Protection Act 1976: A Renewed Call for Reform" (2014) 17(3) I.J.F.L. 77.

O'Sullivan, K., "Low Flying Drones and the Ownership of Airspace in Ireland" (2016) 21 C.P.L.J. 7

O'Sullivan, K., "Reform of Section 117 of the Succession Act 1965: Implications and Opportunities for the Protection of Surviving Spouses" (2017) 22(1) C.P.L.J. 9

Oireachtas Library & Research Service, *Ireland's Mineral Exploration and Mining Policy* (25 July 2015)

Osborough, W.N., "Discoveries from Armada Wrecks" (1970) 5 Ir. Jur. (ns) 88

Osborough, W.N., "The Failure to Enact an Irish Bill of Rights: A Gap in Irish Constitutional History" (1998) 33 Ir. Jur. 392

Otway-Ruthven, A.J., *A History of Medieval Ireland*, 2nd edn (London: Benn, 1980)

Otway-Ruthven, A.J., "Knight's Fees in Kildare, Leix and Offaly" (1965) 91 J.R.S.A.I. 163

Otway-Ruthven, A.J., "The Native Irish and English Law in Medieval Ireland" (1950) 7 I.H.S. 1

Palmer, N.E., "Treasure Trove and the Protection of Antiquities" (1981) 44 M.L.R. 178

Paton, G.W., "Bees and the Law" (1939–41) 2 Res Jud. 22

Pawlisch, H., *Sir John Davies and the Conquest of Ireland* (Cambridge: Cambridge University Press, 1985)

Penner, J.E., *The Idea of Property in Law* (Oxford: Oxford University Press, 1997)

Pine, L.G. (ed.), *Burke's Genealogical and Heraldic History of the Landed Gentry of Ireland*, 4th edn (London: Burke's Peerage Ltd, 1958)

Plucknett, T.F.T., *A Concise History of the Common Law*, 5th edn (Boston: Little Brown, 1956)

Plucknett, T.F.T., *Legislation of Edward I* (Oxford: Oxford University Press, 1949)

Pollock, F. and Maitland, F.W., *The History of English Law before the Time of Edward I*, 2nd edn (Cambridge: University Press, 1968)

Pollock, F. and Wright, R.S.W., *An Essay on Possession in the Common Law* (Oxford: Clarendon, 1888)

Pollock, F., *The Land Laws* (London: Macmillan, 1883)

Posner, R., *The Economic Analysis of Law*, 5th edn (New York: Aspen, 1998)

Potter, H., *Historical Introduction to English Law and its Institutions* (London: Sweet & Maxwell, 1958)

Powell, R., "Determinable Fees" (1923) 23 Colum. L.R. 207

Powell, R.R.B., *Law of Real Property* (New York: Matthew Bender, 1968)

Power, A., *Intangible Property Rights in Ireland*, 2nd edn (Haywards Heath: Tottel, 2009)

Pritchard, A., "Making Positive Covenants Run" [1973] 37 Conv. 194

Radcliffe, G., *Real Property* (Oxford: Oxford University Press, 1933)

Reeves, J. and Finlason, J.F., *Reeves' History of English Law, From the Time of the Romans, to the End of the Reign of Elizabeth* (London: Reeves & Turner, 1869)

Rheinstein, M. (ed.), *Max Weber on Law in Economy and Society*, translated by Shils and Rheinstein (Cambridge, Mass: Harvard University Press, 1954)

Richardson, H.G., "Magna Carta Hiberniae" (1942) 3 I.H.S. 31

Richey, A.G., *Irish Land Laws*, 2nd edn (London: Macmillan, 1881)

Roberts, N., "Access to Quasi-Public Spaces – Whose Visitor?" [2007] Conv. 235

Robinson, S., *Transfer of Land in Victoria* (Sydney: Law Book Co, 1979)

Roebuck, P., "The Irish Registry of Deeds: A Comparative Study" (1973) 18 I.H.S. 61

Rose, C.M., "Property as Storytelling: Perspectives from Game Theory, Narrative Theory, Feminist Theory" (1990) 2 Yale J.L. & Human. 37

Ryan, F., "The Rise and Fall of Civil Partnership" (2016) 19(3) I.J.F.L. 50

Ryan, F., *Civil Partnership and Certain Rights and Obligations of Cohabitants Act 2010* (An Annotation) (Dublin: Round Hall, 2011)

Ryan, F., *Civil Partnership: Your Questions Answered: A Comprehensive Analysis of the Civil Partnership Bill* (Dublin: GLEN, 2009)

Sanders, F.W., *An Essay on the Uses and Trusts, and on the Nature and Operation of Conveyances at Common Law and those Deriving their Effect from The Statute of Uses*, 2nd edn (London: Privately Printed, 1799)

Scamell, E.H., "Legal Aspects of Flat Schemes" (1961) 14 Curr. L.P. 161

Scamell, E.H., "Positive Covenants in Conveyances of the Fee Simple" [1954] 18 Conv. 546

Scottish Law Commission, *Report on Succession* (Scottish Law Com. 215-2009)

Secher, U., *Aboriginal Customary Law: A Source of Common Law Title to Land* (Oxford: Hart Publishing, 2014)

Sheppard, F. and Belcher, V., "The Deeds Registries of Yorkshire and Middlesex" (1980) 6 J. Soc. Arch. 275

Sheppard, W., *The Touchstone of Common Assurances*, 6th edn by Edward Hilliard (London: Strahan & Woodfall, 1791)

Sheridan, L.A., *Survey of the Land Law of Northern Ireland* (Belfast: HMSO, 1971)

Sheridan, L.A., "*Walsh v Lonsdale* in Ireland" (1952) 9 N.I.L.Q. 190

Sherrin, C.H., "The Application of the Class-Closing Rules to the Construction of Wills", PhD thesis (University of London (Ext), 1972)

Siegal, S.A., "John Chipman Gray, Legal Formalism and the Transformation of Perpetuities Law" (1982) 36 Miami L. Rev. 439

Simpson, A.W.B. (ed.), *A Biographical Dictionary of the Common Law* (London & St. Paul, Minn: Butterworths & Mason Pub. Co, 1984)

Simpson, A.W.B., *A History of the Land Law*, 2nd edn (Oxford: Clarendon, 1986)

Simpson, S.R., *Land Law and Registration* (Cambridge: Cambridge University Press, 1976)

Sinnott, M., "The Appellate Jurisdiction of the Houses of Lords of Great Britain and Ireland: Chief Barron Gilbert's Role in the *Annesley v Sherlock* Affair" (2016) 16 U.C.D.L.R. 90

Smith, D.A., "Was There a Rule in *Shelley's Case?*" (2009) 30 J. Leg. Hist. 53

Smythe, H., *The Law of Landlord and Tenant in Ireland* (Dublin: A. Milliken, 1842)

Snell, E.H.T., Baker P.V. and Langan, S.J.H., *Snell's Principles of Equity*, 28th edn (London: Sweet & Maxell, 1982)

Spierin, B., *Succession Act 1965 and Related Legislation: A Commentary*, 5th edn (Dublin: Bloomsbury Professional, 2017)

Squibb, G.D., *The High Court of Chivalry: A Study of the Civil Law in England* (Oxford: Clarendon Press, 1959)

Sufrin, B., "An Equity Richly Satisfied" (1979) 42 M.L.R. 574

Sugden, E.B., *A Practical Treatise of Powers*, 8th edn (London: H. Sweet, 1861)

Sugden, E.B., *A Treatise of the Law of Property as Administered by the House of Lords* (London: Sweet, 1849)

Sugden, E.B., *An Essay on the New Statutes: Relating to Limitations of Time, Estates Tail, Dower, Descent, Operation of Deeds, Merger of Attendant Terms, Defective Executions of Powers of Leasing, Wills, Trustees and Mortgages* (London: S. Sweet, 1852)

Sutherland, D.W., *The Assize of Novel Disseisin* (Oxford: Clarendon, 1973)

Swadling, W.J., "Taylor v Dickens" (1998) 6 Rest. L. Rev. 220

Sweet, C. (ed.), *Challis's Law of Real Property*, 3rd edn (London: Butterworth, 1911)

Sweet, C., "The Rule in *Whitby v Mitchell*" (1905) 25 L.Q.R. 385

Symes, L.M., *Handbook of the Law of Future Interests* (St Paul, Minnesota: West, 1966)

Tawney, R.H., *Religion and the Rise of Capitalism* (London: Murray, 1926)

Thomas, G., *Thomas on Powers*, 2nd edn (Oxford: Oxford University Press, 2012)

Thompson, M.P., "Paths and Pigs: Case Comment" [1995] Conv. 239

Todd, P.N., "Annexation after Federated Homes" [1985] 3 Conv. 177

Tolson, S.M., "Land Without Earth: Freehold Flats in English Law" [1950] 14 Conv. (NS) 350

Treitel, G.H., "Jane Austen and the Law" (1984) 100 L.Q.R. 549

Underhill, A. and Hayton, D.J., *Law Relating to Trusts and Trustees*, 14th edn (London: Butterworths, 1987)

Underhill, A., *Acquisition and Valuation of Land Committee, Fourth Report* (London: HMSO, 1919)

Veall, D., *The Popular Movement for Law Reform, 1640–1660* (Oxford: Clarendon Press, 1970)

Wade, H.W.R., "Restrictive Covenant—Benefit—Assignment—Building Scheme" (1957) 15(2) Camb. L.J. 146

Wagner, D.O., "Coke and the Rise of Economic Liberalism" (1935) 6 Ec. Hist. Rev. 30

Waite, A., "Disrepair and Set-off of Damages against Rent: the Implications of British Anzani" [1983] Conv. 373

Wallace, H., "Part Performance Re-examined" (1974) 24 N.I.L.Q. 453

Walsh, R., "'The Principles of Social Justice' and the Compulsory Acquisition of Private Property for Redevelopment in the United States and Ireland" (2010) 32 D.U.L.J. 1

Walshe, W., "From Riches to Rags: Expropriation by the Ground Rents Acts" (2014) 19(2) C.P.L.J. 40

Wambaugh, E. (ed.), *Littleton's Tenures in English* (Washington, DC: J. Byrne, 1903)

Waters, D.M., *The Constructive Trust: The Case for a New Approach in English Law* (London: Athlone Press, 1964)

Wigmore, J.H., *Evidence in Trials at Common Law*, 4th edn (Boston, Mass.: Little, Brown, 1988)

Williams, G., "The Concept of Legal Liberty" (1965) 56 Colum. L.R. 1129

Williams, J. and Williams, C.P., *Principles of the Law of Real Property*, 23rd edn (London: Sweet & Maxwell, 1920)

Williams, J., *The Seisin of the Freehold* (London: H. Sweet, 1878)

Williams, J., *The Settlement of Real Estates, being Twenty-four Lectures Delivered in Gray's Inn Hall in the Year 1876* (London: 1879)

Williams, N., *Armas: Sracfhéachaint ar Araltas na hÉireann* (Baile Átha Cliath: Coiscéim, 2001)

Wonnacott, M., *Possession of Land* (Cambridge: Cambridge University Press, 2006)

Woodman, G., "Note" (1980) 96 L.Q.R. 336

Woods, U., "Adverse Possession and Administered Estates: an Unfair Solution to a Redundant Irish Problem?" (2016) 67(2) N.I.L.Q. 137

Woods, U., "Adverse Possession of Unregistered Leasehold Land" (2001) 36 Ir. Jur. 304

Woods, U., "Commonhold: An Option for Ireland?" (2003) 38 Ir. Jur. 285

Woods, U., "Unilateral Severance of Joint Tenancies – the Case for Abolition" (2007) 12(2) C.P.L.J. 47

Wylie, J.C.W. and Woods, U., _Irish Conveyancing Law_, 3rd edn (Dublin: Butterworths, 2005)

Wylie, J.C.W., _A Casebook on Equity and Trusts in Ireland_ (Abingdon: Professional Books Ltd, 1984)

Wylie, J.C.W., _A Casebook on Irish Land Law_ (Abingdon: Professional Books Ltd, 1984)

Wylie, J.C.W., _Irish Land Law_, 2nd edn (Abingdon: Professional Books, 1986); 5th edn (Haywards Heath: Bloomsbury Professional, 2013)

Wylie, J.C.W., _Landlord and Tenant Law_, 2nd edn (Dublin: Bloomsbury, 1998); 3rd edn (London: Bloomsbury, 2014)

Wylie, J.C.W., _The Land and Conveyancing Law Reform Acts: Annotations and Commentary_, 2nd edn (London: Bloomsbury, 2017)

Yager, T., "What Was Rundale and Where Did It Come From?" (2002) 70 _Béaloideas_ 153

Yale, D.E.C. (ed.), _Lord Nottingham's Manual of Chancery Practice and Prolegomena of Chancery and Equity_ (Cambridge: Cambridge University Press, 1965)

Youdan, T.G., "Acquisition of Property by Killing" (1973) 89 L.Q.R. 235

Index